Human Resource Management

HOUGHTON MIFFLIN COMPANY

Boston Toronto

Dallas
Geneva, Illinois
Palo Alto
Princeton, New Jersey

SECOND EDITION

Human Resource Management

Cynthia D. Fisher
Bond University

Lyle F. Schoenfeldt
Texas A & M University

James B. Shaw
Bond University

This book is dedicated, with much love and appreciation, to our parents
Hazel, Eleanor, and Roland Fisher
Jeanette and (the late) Robert Schoenfeldt
James and Wanza Shaw

Sponsoring Editor: Diane L. McOscar
Development Editor: Susan M. Kahn
Project Editor: Margaret M. Kearney
Senior Production/Design Coordinator: Karen Rappaport
Senior Manufacturing Coordinator: Marie Barnes
Marketing Manager: Robert Wolcott

Printed in the U.S.A.

Library of Congress Catalog Number: 92-72373

ISBN: 0-395-52367-2

123456789-*DH*-96 95 94 93 92

Contents

PART TWO

Planning for Organizations, Jobs, and People

2

PART THREE

Acquiring Human Resources

5

PART FIVE

Rewarding Employees

11

13

PART SIX

Maintaining Human Resources

14

15

16

PART SEVEN

Multinational Human Resource Management

17

Preface

Human Resource Management, second edition, has been designed to provide a comprehensive, current, and research-based introduction to the human resource management function for students, practicing managers, and human resource professionals. The book is designed for a survey course in human resource management at the junior, senior, or graduate level. The authors have fifty years of combined experience in teaching human resource management, both domestically and abroad. Drawing from this experience, as well as from findings reported in the most recent literature, we have produced a text that we believe to be logically organized, clearly presented, fully substantive, and on the cutting edge of human resource management for today's world.

Three major themes guide our text. The first theme, which has been expanded in this edition, is the global and cultural dimension of human resource management. Human resource management in multinational organizations is introduced in Chapter 1, integrated throughout the text as appropriate, and discussed extensively in the last chapter, "Managing Human Resources in Multinational Organizations." Further, up-to-date "International Perspective" boxes provide comparative information on how other nations and cultures deal with human resource management issues.

The second theme focuses on the human resource manager's responsibilities for facilitating ethical behavior by employees and for dealing ethically with employees. This theme is introduced in the first chapter and reinforced throughout the book via new "Ethical Perspective" boxes. Topics include whistleblowing, civil liberties inside the organization, procedural and distributive justice in reward systems, computer monitoring of employee behavior, privacy, and other ethical dilemmas confronting HR practitioners. Also discussed are the role of inappropriate reward systems in producing unethical behavior, and ethical decision making in international situations when the moral standards and laws regarding human resources in the host country may differ from those of the home country.

The third theme, introduced in Chapter 1 and carefully integrated throughout the text, is utility or cost/benefit analysis. Human resource programs can produce quantifiable return for organizations, but the results of programs are seldom carefully evaluated in dollar terms. In order to document the benefits and justify the costs of human resource activities in organizations that are increasingly conscious of reducing expenditures, utility analysis is recommended. Utility is discussed in connection with recruiting, selection, training, performance appraisal, employee-assistance programs, and turnover-reduction efforts.

In addition to the above themes and thorough coverage of basic human resource management activities, this book contains more extensive treatment than other textbooks at this level of strategic human resource management, the role of human resource managers in improving productivity and quality, organizational exit, and human resource information systems.

NEW IN THE SECOND EDITION

- Greatly expanded coverage of international human resource management with the addition of a new chapter (Chapter 17) devoted entirely to this topic, plus new and updated "International Perspective" boxes.
- Extensive discussion of a variety of ethical issues in the employee-organization relationship, in the form of completely new "Ethical Perspective" boxes.
- Improved coverage of strategic human resources management. Chapter 2, "The Strategic Management of Human Resources," has been revised around a new case example, and moved to the front of the book from its placement near the end of the first edition. This placement allows instructors to easily raise strategic practice choice issues as each succeeding HR function is discussed.
- Extensive revision of Chapter 10 on the role of HR managers in productivity and quality improvement, with particular attention to recent thought on the importance of achieving a quality orientation throughout the organization.
- Two revised Computers in Human Resources inserts and a new computer exercise.
- A discussion of career planning and new types of career paths in Chapter 3, "Human Resource Planning."
- Thorough updates to all chapters with the most recent developments in law, practice, and research.

PEDAGOGICAL FEATURES

- A chapter outline introduces students to the text material and provides an overview of important concepts and topics.
- Numerous figures and tables highlight important points and expand upon text discussion to aid in the understanding of key concepts.
- A complete chapter summary reviews the major topics discussed.
- Questions for discussion stimulate recall of information as well as the application of concepts to real-world situations and problems.
- End-of-chapter cases and exercises help students develop skills and integrate human resource management concepts with their own knowledge and work experience.
- Extensive subject and author indexes facilitate many uses of the book.
- Full Instructor's Resource Manual provides test questions, and transparency masters and transparencies.

OVERVIEW OF CONTENTS

The book is organized into seven sections, logically following the progression of individuals into, through, and out of the organization.

Part One, "Overview and Introduction," defines human resource management; outlines the plan of the book; introduces the international, ethics, and utility themes; explores the differing expectations of the multiple constituencies of the human resource management function; introduces the idea of strategic human resource management; considers trends and challenges that are affecting the practice of human resource management; and explores career tracks and preparation for the human resource profession.

Part Two, "Planning for Organizations, Jobs, and People," is composed of three chapters. Chapter 2 focuses on strategic issues in human resource management. This chapter demonstrates that human resource management practices are critical for successful strategy implementation, and that the human resource manager is a vital part of any management team. Chapter 3 discusses forecasting the demand for and the supply of human resources, planning programs to deal with anticipated shortfalls or surpluses, and planning managerial succession. Numerous examples are used throughout this chapter, and a new section on career planning has been added. Chapter 4 contains a very thorough discussion of job analysis techniques and the practical and legal issues involved in planning and conducting job analysis projects. Job analysis requirements imposed by the recent Americans with Disabilities Act are discussed.

Part Three is entitled "Acquiring Human Resources." It begins with a detailed presentation in Chapter 5 of the latest Equal Employment Opportunity law and enforcement procedures. Chapter 6 describes internal and external recruitment techniques, how to plan and evaluate recruiting efforts, the use of the realistic job preview, and the latest research on how job applicants respond to recruiters and make decisions about job offers. Chapter 7 introduces correlation and regression, reliability, and validation methods. Decision making in selection and evaluating the utility of a selection system round out the chapter. Chapter 8 describes specific selection tools, including biodata and ability, work sample, trainability, personality, interest, and honesty tests. The interview is thoroughly discussed, including the particularly effective techniques of behavior description and situational interviewing. The use of physical exams and drug screening is discussed. The risk of suit for negligent hiring or defamation is also discussed in the context of effective reference checking. Finally, a number of methods for managerial selection are described.

Part Four, "Building Individual and Organizational Performance," includes two chapters. Chapter 9 provides a complete discussion of human resource development, from needs assessment through training design to evaluation. New employee orientation is also discussed. The most recent research on trainee motivation, transfer of training, and adult learning is included, computer-based and interactive-video-disk training are explored, and calculating the utility of training programs is discussed. New topics in this edition include facilitating managerial learning through job assignments, team building, and training for autonomous work groups. Chapter 10 focuses on the human resource manager's expanding role in productivity and quality improvement efforts within the organization. This chapter starts by defining productivity and quality, discussing how they can be measured, and describing the relationship between productivity and quality. Next, steps in implementing a quality/productivity improvement effort are described, followed by discussion of a number of types of interventions at the organizational, group, individual, and work environment level. The chapter closes with a clear delineation of how specific HR activities might be modified to facilitate quality improvement efforts.

Part Five covers performance appraisal and reward systems. Chapter 11 describes the attributes of a good appraisal system and discusses the relative merits of trait, behavior, and results-oriented appraisal instruments. Methods of providing performance feedback in the appraisal interview are discussed. Chapter 12 describes the basics of developing a compensation system, beginning with the concepts of internal and external equity and motivation. Job evaluation methods, wage surveys, and the laws that regulate compensation are described. The issue of comparable worth is discussed extensively. Chapter 13 explores individual and group pay-for-performance systems and includes expanded coverage of executive compensation. The second part of this chapter describes a variety of employee benefits. The laws covering benefits are discussed, and issues such as cost containment and flexible benefits are addressed.

Part Six discusses "Maintaining Human Resources." Chapter 14 addresses safety and health, including occupational safety and health laws, standards, and enforcement procedures. Current topics such as right-to-know laws, job-induced mental illness, second-hand smoke in the workplace, and cumulative trauma disorders, including carpal tunnel syndrome, are also discussed. The last part of this chapter covers stress management and employee assistance and fitness programs. Chapter 15 describes the history and legal environment of unions, the process of certification, preparation for and the conduct of collective bargaining, strikes and other dispute resolution procedures, and the grievance process. Chapter 16 addresses the often ignored final step in human resource management—organizational exit. Employment-at-will, discharge for cause, layoffs, and retirement are discussed. Causes of voluntary turnover and methods of strategically managing turnover are also described.

The last part of the book consists of a new chapter, "Managing Human Resources in Multinational Organizations." The chapter begins by describing how international HRM differs from purely domestic practice, and discussing the different approaches to international human resource management taken by various organizations. A good portion of the chapter focuses on the special problems of managing expatriate employees, such as their selection, training, compensation, and repatriation. The remainder of the chapter considers culture and related issues in selecting, appraising, and compensating host country nationals when doing business abroad.

In addition to these chapters, there are two special inserts addressing the use of computers in human resource management. The first of these, which appears after Chapter 8, describes human resource information systems and issues surrounding their capabilities, development, and implementation. The second computer insert follows Chapter 16. It provides examples of computer applications in most functional areas of HRM, and closes with a hands-on exercise in using a spreadsheet program to answer applied questions about compensation.

ACKNOWLEDGMENTS

We would like to thank everyone who adopted the first edition of this text, and hope that you will find this edition even more satisfying.

A number of individuals provided reviews and suggestions that helped in improving this text. We appreciate their time and effort.

Yohannan Abraham
Southwest Missouri State University

Alan Cabelly
Portland State University

Thomas Daymont
Temple University

Mildred Doering
Syracuse University

Walter O. Einstein
Southeastern Massachusetts University

David M. Hegedus
University of Wisconsin, Oshkosh

Bruce H. Johnson
Gustavus Adolphus College

Nancy McDaniel
Hocking College

Jeff Mello
Northeastern University

Marsha P. Miceli
Ohio State University

R. LaVelle Mills
Tarleton State University

Jonathan S. Monat
California State University, Long Beach

William M. Moore
Drake University

Earl C. Nance
Brewton Parker College

Gary C. Raffaele
The University of Texas at San Antonio

Hyman Sardy
Brooklyn College

Paul L. Wilkens
Florida State University

Arthur Yeung
University of Michigan

We would also like to thank the following individuals for special contributions.

Ricky Griffin of Texas A & M University for instigating this writing project in 1984. Without Ricky's initial guidance and persuasion, the first edition of this book would never have been written.

William Dunsmuir of Bond University for expert suggestions on the revised productivity and quality chapter.

Marick Masters of the University of Pittsburgh for writing much of the first edition chapter on labor relations and collective bargaining.

Raphael Gely of Texas A & M University for updating the labor relations and collective bargaining chapter.

Len Bierman of Texas A & M University for updating the equal employment opportunity chapter.

Jon Beard of the University of Richmond for writing the first edition Human Resource Information System inserts, portions of which survive into this edition, and for writing the first edition Instructor's Manual.

Kay McGlashan Perales of Texas A & M University for spending her summer updating the Instructor's Resource Manual with Test Questions.

Hewitt Associates of The Woodlands, Texas, for the generous access to their extensive library.

Mary Bosch of Texas A & M University for her valuable research efforts.

John Delery of Texas A & M University for his valuable feedback.

Ben and Cyn D. would like to thank Bond University for being a great place to work and bringing us to the lovely Gold Coast of Australia.

Lyle would like to thank his family, Wanda, Beth, Todd, and Sarah, for their special support during the writing of this book.

C. D. F.
L. F. S.
J. B. S.

PART ONE

Overview and Introduction

An Introduction to Human Resource Management

Some organizations are more successful than others. Simply from a consumer perspective it is possible to identify companies that produce better products or provide superior services compared to their competitors. This is true for products as diverse as automobiles, appliances, or audio equipment and for services that range from higher education to automobile repair. People notice these differences and develop clear preferences as a result.

Although people may not think about it as often, they have corresponding preferences with respect to organizations as places to work. Through job experience, campus activities, community involvement, and various opportunities to interact with others, people develop ideas about what to expect in the work environment. People exhibit pride and loyalty in working for successful organizations that treat them well. Of course, any discussion about characteristics of organizations that treat people well includes such matters as pay and benefits, but these are unlikely to be the only areas of expectation. Most employees want to feel that they are part of a team, that their opinions are valued, and that they will have an opportunity to grow and be promoted. For most people it is important to be treated equitably with respect to pay. In other words, people want rewards to be based on their contributions. In addition, people want to be treated fairly and with dignity in all their interactions with the organization and with their supervisors.

One way to gain insight into the process of managing human resources is by considering what differentiates organizations as places to work. As might be expected, no one or two things make some organizations great places to work and other organizations less desirable employers. Table 1.1 indicates some of the characteristics that earmark an organization as a great place to work. As seen in Table 1.1, the foundation of excellence in an employment relationship includes four dimensions, each with a set of policies or practices. The *basic-terms-of-employment* dimension includes fair pay and benefits, along with an organizational commit-

TABLE 1.1 Policies and Procedures Indicative of Great Places to Work

Basic Terms of Employment	*The Job*	*Workplace Rules*	*Stake in Success*
1. Fair pay and benefits: a. compare well with similar employers b. square with company's ability to pay 2. Commitment to job security 3. Commitment to safe and attractive working environment	1. Maximizes individual responsibility for how job is done 2. Flexibility about working hours 3. Opportunity for growth: a. promotes from within b. provides training c. recognizes mistakes as part of learning	1. Reduces social and economic distinctions between management and other employees 2. Right to due process 3. Right to information 4. Right to free speech 5. Right to confront those in authority 6. Right *not* to be part of the family/team	1. Shares rewards from productivity improvements 2. Shares profits 3. Shares ownership 4. Shares recognition

Source: From *A Great Place to Work* by Robert Levering. Copyright © 1988 by Robert Levering. Reprinted by permission of Random House, Inc.

ment to job security and a commitment to an appropriate working environment. The *job* dimension includes the opportunity for the individual to assume responsibility, organizational flexibility in policies and practices, and opportunities for individual growth. The *workplace-rules* dimension includes a commitment to reducing social and economic distinctions along with a set of employee rights. Finally, the *stake-in-success* dimension includes the willingness to share rewards, profits, ownership, and recognition.

It is easier for companies to be benevolent employers in the good times. Top companies to work for, however, tend to be good to their people in bad times as well as good times. The best companies will go to extraordinary lengths to soften the blow for affected employees. For example, International Business Machines Corp. (IBM) has done an exemplary job of first reducing numbers by offering those who qualify the opportunity to retire early and then providing those to be laid off with sufficient notice, generous severance arrangements, and abundant assistance in finding other employment.[1]

A look at a well-known company, Apple Computer, shows how product and human resource management innovation can be combined. Apple Computer launched the personal computer industry in the late 1970s. Having pioneered in product innovation, Apple employees at all levels believed, not surprisingly, that they were part of an important revolution—a revolution that permitted people to take advantage of an intelligent tool previously available only to large corporations, universities, and government. The result has been an unusual corporate culture, emphasizing customer service, individual achievement and performance, product excellence, informality, team spirit, individual reward, and good management.[2] As far as rewards are concerned, Apple Computer regularly distributed a percentage of quarterly profits to employees, which led to an estimated 300 Apple employees becoming millionaires, almost all while under forty years of age.

As noted earlier, few things in business stand still, and this is especially true in technology-based companies. In the mid-1980s, Apple Computer found itself struggling to maintain its initial success. New products were developed, such as the Macintosh and laptop models, and further technology, such as pen-sensitive screens, is being explored.[3] John Scully replaced Steven Jobs—who, along with Steven Wozniak, had founded Apple—as chairman. Joint ventures and other collaborations were sought, such as the much publicized collaboration with IBM to create a standard-setting system by which computers operate.[4] Yet through it all, Apple has continued to emphasize its customer orientation, product excellence, individual productivity, and team spirit.

Not all companies identified as excellent in terms of profits and growth, however, are known for innovations in human resource management.[5] For example, McDonald's, an extremely successful company by most standards, has built most of its success on hiring part-time, mostly teen-age, employees.[6] Profits by McDonald's and the franchisees who own most of the outlets depend on low wages and an assembly-line operation, which leaves the employees with little time to think.

It could be said that McDonald's has done it the old-fashioned way, and therein lies the challenge for human resource management in the coming decades.

It must reach beyond traditional employment practices to develop and manage the process whereby organizations can achieve success in multiple areas. Ultimately, organizations that are most successful over an extended period of time are those that are both innovative—as places to work and in the products and services they offer—and profitable.

The general purpose of this text is to explore the range of practices that define human resource management and its relationship to other organizational objectives, such as quality of the product or service and financial success. This chapter examines some of the general issues related to human resource management, including

- the scope of human resource management,
- themes and perspectives that define human resource management,
- challenges facing human resource management, and
- professional opportunities in human resource management.

A DEFINITION OF HUMAN RESOURCE MANAGEMENT

Human resource management (HRM) involves all management decisions and practices that directly affect or influence the people, or **human resources**, who work for the organization. In recent years, increased attention has been devoted to how organizations manage human resources. This increased attention comes from the realization that an organization's employees enable an organization to achieve its goals, and the management of these human resources is critical to an organization's success.[7] The following points are key to understanding human resource management:

- Organizations are subject to external forces such as the economy, labor markets, legal requirements, and actions by competitors.
- An organization's internal environment is characterized by such elements as goals and values of management, corporate culture, strategy, the technology on which the organization depends, the organizational structure (e.g., centralized versus decentralized), and size.
- Organizations are made up of employees who are characterized in terms of their motivation to perform and the personal qualities they bring to the organization, such as abilities, interests, personality, and attitudes.
- Employees perform jobs that result in job and organizational outcomes.
- Jobs can be described in terms of requirements and rewards.
- Job outcomes include performance, productivity, quality, satisfaction, and the retention of the employee as a contributing member of the organization.
- The "bottom line" for the organization is survival as a competitive and growing organization that continues to make a profit.

TABLE 1.2 Human Resource Management: Major Areas and Related Topics

Major Areas	*Related Topics*
Planning for Organizations, Jobs, and People	
The Strategic Management of Human Resources	Human Resource Management Practices for a Retrenchment Strategy
Human Resource Planning	Strategic Compensation
Job Analysis: Procedures and Choices	Forecasting the Demand for Labor
	Career and Succession Planning
	Methods of Job Analysis
	Purposes of Job Analysis
Acquiring Human Resources	
Equal Employment Opportunity: The Legal Environment	Title VII of the Civil Rights Act
Recruiting and Job Search	Affirmative Action
Measurement and Decision-making Issues in Selection	Evaluating Recruiting Sources
Assessing Job Candidates: Tools for Selection	Realistic Job Previews
	Reliability
	Determining the Validity of a Selection Device
	Interviews
	Selection Tests
Building Individual and Organizational Performance	
Human Resource Development	Principles of Learning
Human Resource Approaches to Productivity and Quality Enhancement	Training Methods
	Total Quality Management
	Employee Participation Schemes
Rewarding Employees	
Performance Appraisal	Methods of Appraisal
Compensation System Development	Providing Feedback to Employees
Performance-based Pay and Benefits	Evaluating the Worth of Jobs
	Gain Sharing Programs
	Controlling Benefit Costs
Maintaining Human Resources	
Safety and Health: A Proactive Approach	Occupational Safety and Health Act
Labor Relations and Collective Bargaining	Stress at Work
Organizational Exit	How Unions Are Formed
	Collective Bargaining
	Employment-at-Will
	Strategically Managing Turnover
Multinational Human Resource Management	
Managing Human Resources in Multinational Organizations	Staffing of Foreign Plants
	Selection and Training of Expatriates

The number of activities involved in human resource management is potentially large, depending on the size of the organization and its needs. For the purposes of the present discussion, human resource (HR) activities are organized into six general areas that constitute the sections of this text. The general areas, along with related topics that constitute the chapters of this text, are shown in Table 1.2.

Figure 1.1 is a human resource management model that illustrates how HRM activities come to bear on an organization's environment, employees, jobs, job outcomes, and organizational outcomes. All of these forces are in turn affected by the organization's external environment. Note that the HRM activities in the model represent the sections and chapters of the text as listed in Table 1.2. The model appears at the beginning of each major section of the text, with relevant topics highlighted.

FIGURE 1.1 Human Resource Management Model

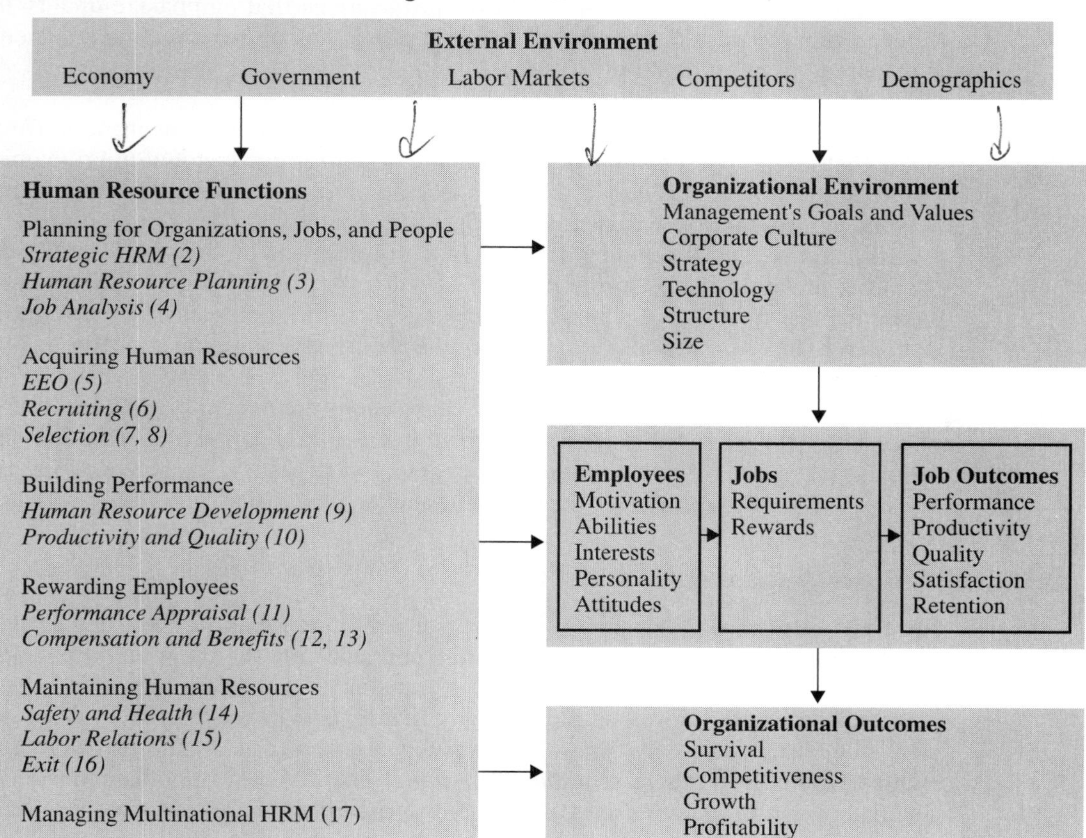

HUMAN RESOURCE MANAGEMENT FUNCTIONS

Within each functional area of human resource management, many activities must be accomplished so that the organization's human resources can make an optimal contribution to the organization's success.

Planning For Organizations, Jobs, and People

The Strategic Management of Human Resources A recent development has been the closer integration of the HR department with managerial planning and decision making. Increasingly, top management is realizing that the time to consider HR limitations or strengths is when strategic business decisions are being formulated, not after they are made. For instance, a decision to open a new facility should be made only after considering the availability of labor at the new location and the availability of experienced managers to run the facility. Furthermore, closer integration can result in HR practices that help to elicit and reward the types of behavior necessary for the organization's strategy. Suppose an organization is planning to become known for its high-quality products. Ideally, HR practitioners will design appraisal and reward systems that emphasize quality in order to support this competitive strategy. Strategic human resource management is discussed in more detail in Chapter 2.

Human Resource Planning The planning process is essential to meet the staffing needs that result when complex and changing organizations encounter a dynamic business environment. The planning process involves forecasting HR needs and developing programs to ensure that the right numbers and types of individuals are available at the right time and place. Organizations depend on "what if" scenarios that look at future needs in the context of work force demographics, economic projections, anticipated technological changes, recruitment success, retention goals, and shifts in organizational strategy. Specific HR planning procedures are discussed in Chapter 3.

Careful descriptions and analyses of current jobs are needed to plan for future selection systems and training programs and to ensure that appraisal and compensation systems are rationally based on job demands. The development and use of job analysis information is the topic of Chapter 4.

Acquiring Human Resources

Once HR needs are determined, the next step is filling positions. Staffing activities include recruiting applicants, screening and selecting the most qualified candidates, and filling some positions through transfer or promotion.

Staffing is a far more complex activity than in previous times when employment managers could rely on a "help wanted" sign in front of the plant or recommendations from current employees. Equal employment opportunity (EEO) laws, along with the increased complexity of positions to be filled, have required more sophisticated procedures to identify and select potential employees. The legal environment—specifically EEO laws—associated with organizational entry and progression is discussed in Chapter 5.

The selection process includes several important steps. The first is carefully defining the open position and determining what skills are needed to successfully hold the job. Having determined the specific skills and competencies, employment managers frequently go to great lengths to increase applicant flow, through a variety of recruitment strategies. These activities are the subject of Chapter 6.

The employment manager must then utilize carefully developed and validated procedures in screening and evaluating job candidates. These may include application blanks, interviews, ability tests, and reference checks, to name a few of the possibilities. Information from several of these procedures is then combined into a judgment of the potential of the applicant as an employee. These activities constitute the measurement and decision-making process in selection, the topics addressed in Chapters 7 and 8.

More recently, organizational restructuring has become an additional staffing activity. This activity may be conducted either in response to acquisitions and divestitures that are due to economic circumstances or as part of a productivity improvement strategy. Here the question is not one of recruitment, selection, and placement, but of reducing employment and optimally redeploying the remaining employees.[8] Employment managers have needed to design and implement review processes to determine which specific individuals are to be laid off or reassigned and to deal with severance benefits.

Building Individual and Organizational Performance

Human resources are unique in their potential to grow and develop to meet new challenges. As noted earlier, the chance to develop and move up is important in how employees regard organizations as places to work. At the same time, organizations choose to spend substantial sums to train and develop their employees.

Employees may be trained or developed by formal or informal procedures. Formal training is often associated with the introduction to a new job; it is also a means of keeping up with technological or procedural changes. Formal training can be coordinated and taught by HR or technical professionals at the organization, or employees may be sent to training programs offered by professional associations or universities.[9]

Informal training occurs on the job and is administered by superiors and peers. The HR department may provide train-the-trainer courses and coordinate on-the-job-training (OJT) opportunities with employee career plans and the organization's forecast of HR needs. Procedures for determining training needs and then constructing, delivering, and evaluating HR development programs to meet these needs are the topics of Chapter 9.

Some organizations undertake other interventions that operate through the human element and are aimed at enhancing productivity, quality, or service. The need to be competitive in a global economy, along with changing demographics and values of workers, has resulted in the realization that traditional ways of structuring work may need to be reconsidered. Recently, some of the most popular HR innovations have focused on improving motivation and involving employees in the decision-making process. For example, many U.S. corporations have implemented quality circles and their more involving successor, total quality management programs. Still other successful organizations are allowing autonomous teams of workers to manage themselves, taking responsibility for the planning, coordinating, and quality control activities traditionally reserved for supervisors.[10] A variety of productivity- and quality-enhancing innovations are discussed in Chapter 10.

Rewarding Employees

Performance appraisals are a crucial link in the HRM process: they are the means by which organizations assess how well employees are performing and determine appropriate rewards or remedial actions. The HRM role in appraisal is one of working with line managers to establish the appraisal process, the performance dimensions to be measured, the procedures to ensure accuracy, and requirements for discussion of appraisal results with employees.

Another important HR role in the appraisal of employees is to monitor the process and its results. Performance appraisal is not a favorite managerial activity, yet it is important that it be undertaken in a timely manner and be done as accurately as possible. Issues relating to performance appraisal are discussed in Chapter 11.

A logical result of the appraisal process is determining which employees most deserve rewards. Allocating rewards is a complex and specialized activity. Rewards include both direct compensation (salary or hourly wages) and indirect compensation (benefits) that organizations offer to employees in return for their effort.

Intuition would suggest that the higher the compensation an employee receives, the greater that employee's satisfaction. Indeed, this tends to be the case, although the relationship is not a strong one.[11] In addition to the level of pay, a successful compensation system is based on fairness: the perceived equity of pay differentials for different jobs within the organization, the perceived equality of pay for similar jobs either within the organization or in competitor companies, and the perceived fairness of the differences in pay between employees who are in the very same job. Employees bring a variety of perspectives to bear in deciding whether they are satisfied with the compensation they receive, thus making the management of compensation a particularly challenging HR activity.[12]

If this were not enough of a challenge, compensation practices are also affected by legal requirements of equal pay for equal work, minimum wage and overtime provisions, and required benefits, such as Social Security. Finally, compensation systems do not exist in a vacuum. They need to be designed to mesh with the strategic objectives of the organization. They also need to integrate the realities of prevailing pay levels in the labor market with an organization's profitability and ability to pay. The general issues related to developing reward systems are the subject of Chapter 12, while specific concerns associated with performance-based reward systems and benefits are covered in Chapter 13.

Maintaining Human Resources

The job of the HR manager does not stop once employees are hired, trained, and paid. Additional issues relate to retaining and maintaining a healthy, willing work force. The fifth major section of this book focuses on employee health and safety, industrial relations, and the management of organizational exit.

An important source of workplace change has been the desire to promote a safer and more healthful work environment. Part of the concern for health and safety is a result of the Occupational Safety and Health Act of 1970. A second source of such change has been societal concern about exposure to hazardous substances or stress in the workplace. Organizations are taking more responsibility for helping employees deal with problems caused by stress or substance abuse. Increasingly, too, they are providing preventive programs focusing on fitness and healthy lifestyles. These issues are discussed in Chapter 14.

A part of the HRM function is establishing and maintaining effective relationships with employees. The process of collective bargaining requires unionized companies to negotiate with employee representatives on wages (e.g., base pay, increases, overtime), benefits (e.g., vacations, holidays, pensions), hours (e.g., breaks, cleanup time), and other conditions of work, such as seniority, discipline, and discharge procedures. Companies with nonunionized employees have found it necessary to display equal concern for these issues in order to maintain a positive, nonunion relationship with their employees.

For organizations with unions certified to represent employees, the union contract is an important document. Those involved in human resource management must be intimately familiar with the contract and the issues it covers. This familiarity is important both for the contract negotiation process and for using the contract to guide day-to-day HR activities. The topics of labor relations and collective bargaining are covered in Chapter 15.

Another issue of great importance to HR managers is turnover, both voluntary and involuntary. Research over the years has demonstrated that voluntary turnover—that is, the departure of current employees for other opportunities—generally results from several factors, including the personal characteristics of the employee, economic conditions, and other job or career alternatives.[13] Voluntary turnover affects the organization directly in that employees with the best work qualifications are likely to find it easier to develop employment alternatives. HR managers are interested in reasons for voluntary turnover and in developing programs to keep valued employees.

A more recent concern has been involuntary turnover—that is, the decision by the organization to terminate employees. Whether in response to acquisitions and divestitures or as a result of economic circumstances, HR managers have had to consider reducing employment, optimally redeploying remaining employees, and helping those terminated with outplacement or assistance in finding a position with another organization.[14]

In recent years there has been greater emphasis on the right of individuals to due process, dignity, and self-expression in the workplace.[15] This trend is especially apparent in the case of employment-at-will, a legal theory that states that either the employee or the employer can terminate the employment relationship at any time for any reason. Recent state laws and court decisions have limited the employer's right to terminate an employee at will.[16] These changes indicate that an implied contract or promise of fair treatment may exist as part of an employment relationship. Both voluntary and involuntary turnover and the associated HR challenges are the topics of Chapter 16.

Multinational Human Resource Management

Chapter 17 extends the concerns of the previous chapters to an international arena. More than ever before, U.S. companies are drawing on and contributing to a global economy. Foreign firms are establishing operations in the United States, and increasing numbers of both large and small U.S. firms are establishing plants and operations outside the borders of the United States. In preparation for the 1992 integration of the European Community (EC), many U.S. firms entered joint ventures or built production facilities in Europe. Eastern Europe and the Commonwealth of Independent States (formerly the Soviet Union) are being dramatically reshaped and as such represent potential international opportunities for firms of other nations, including the United States. North America is fast becoming an open trade region, as evidenced by the proposed North American Free Trade Agreement. Other global expansions are also taking place, including new opportunities in the Pacific Rim and South America, to name a few.

Examples of internationalized corporate operations and their impact on human resource management abound. Many of the foreign automobiles on U.S. highways were manufactured in this country. The challenge to organizations such as Nissan Motor Co. is selecting and training a U.S. labor force to fit the standards and procedures preferred by the foreign parent company. To what extent can or should Japanese HR practices be imported and applied at plants in the United States?

On the other side of the coin, approximately 40 percent of all new McDonald's restaurants are being opened outside the United States.[17] From an HRM perspective, the objectives are to develop U.S. managers who are ready and willing to work effectively abroad, to select foreign nationals as employees for these overseas sites, and to develop and implement HR policies and practices that optimally merge the concerns of both the home and the host country.

RECURRING THEMES IN HUMAN RESOURCE MANAGEMENT

Four general concerns span all functions of human resource management in organizations: the increasing globalization of HR activities, the need to demonstrate the utility of HR endeavors, maintaining ethical policies and behavior within the organization, and the increasing use of computerized HR information systems.

International Human Resource Management

The impact of the dynamic international economy has become a major new force in business in general and in human resource management in particular. Much of this book describes state-of-the-art HR practice in North America; however, other nations have sometimes chosen different approaches to dealing with the human side of organizations. For instance, centralized government assignment of workers to employers largely replaces organizationally administered recruiting and selection in the People's Republic of China. Although interesting in their own right, these varied practices are also important realities faced by multinational firms doing business overseas. Thus, many chapters of this text include an International Perspective box comparing HRM practices in the United States with those of other countries. The specific issues of managing human resources in multinational organizations are the focus of Chapter 17.

A Utility Perspective

Another ever-present reality in today's organizations is the need to substantiate the cost-effectiveness of programs, approaches, and policies. Top management wants to know in "bottom-line" (i.e., dollar) terms the extent to which the benefits of a policy or program outweigh the costs. Although HR programs can have a significant impact on profits, little has been done thus far to evaluate HR programs in these terms. The utility perspective is basically a method that allows a manager to compare the costs associated with selecting, training, and rewarding employees against the dollar benefits resulting from these efforts. For example, many training programs are proposed and undertaken without examining the extent of increased productivity (benefit) as opposed to the costs of training material, time away from the job for those being trained, salary of the trainer, and so forth.

There is an ever-increasing need for HR managers to speak the language of business and, in so doing, justify the economic value of existing or proposed programs.[18] The key question decision makers must answer with respect to all programs is this: "How can we best allocate our limited resources in the most cost-effective way?" As with international considerations, the concept of utility spans all areas of human resource management and is thus considered in many chapters of this text.

Maintaining Ethical Policies and Behavior

It has long been recognized that managers have a duty to serve the interests of the business and its owners (shareholders). In the last two decades, however, there has been an increasing realization that profit cannot be the only goal—that managers and corporations have a duty to behave in a responsible fashion toward a set of stakeholders which goes well beyond owners. These stakeholders include customers, the community in which the business is located, employees, and even nonhuman entities, such as the environment.

The HR manager has a special role in ensuring that the organization deals fairly and ethically with its employees and that employees deal fairly with each other, the organization, and clients. Some theories of ethics list the duties that human beings owe to each other in general. Although organizations are not necessarily subject to all the ethical duties to which persons are,[19] at least some of these duties might be applied to businesses to guide their dealings with employees and applicants.[20] These duties include

- respecting persons and not using them solely as means to one's own ends.
- not doing any harm.
- telling the truth.
- keeping promises.
- treating people fairly and without discrimination.
- not depriving people of basic rights, such as the right to free speech and association.

In organizational terms, fulfilling these duties may translate into

- instituting careful health and safety practices, informing employees of potentially hazardous working conditions, and taking responsibility for occupational disease and stress-related illnesses traceable to working conditions (see Chapter 14).
- being truthful in recruiting (see Chapter 6).
- avoiding the use of invalid and discriminatory selection, appraisal, and advancement systems (see Chapters 7, 8, and 11).
- providing equal pay for work of comparable worth (see Chapter 12).
- providing ways for employees to voice their concerns and not illegally constraining employees from exercising their right to form a union (see Chapter 15).
- following fair policies in regard to discipline, termination for cause, and reductions in force (see Chapters 3, 15, and 16).

Clearly, as an intermediary between the organization and the employee, the HR professional has a large role to play in ensuring fair treatment. In fact, the Society for Human Resource Management (SHRM) has recognized this role by adopting a Code of Ethics to guide the activities of HR professionals. This code is reproduced in Figure 1.2.

The HR function is also charged with protecting the organization from potentially unethical employees. According to the "bad apple" perspective, some individuals are simply predisposed to behave unethically and should be weeded out by the selection process. Applicants who are likely to steal from their employer, take bribes, demand kickbacks, violate the law, or work under the influence of drugs may sometimes be identified by careful background investigation, reference checks, or paper-and-pencil honesty testing (see Chapter 8).

FIGURE 1.2 Code of Ethics of the Society for Human Resource Management

Code of Ethics

As a member of the Society for Human Resource Management, I pledge myself to:

- Maintain the highest standards of professional and personal conduct.
- Strive for personal growth in the field of human resource management.
- Support the Society's goals and objectives for developing the human resource management profession.
- Encourage my employer to make the fair and equitable treatment of all employees a primary concern.
- Strive to make my employer profitable both in monetary terms and through the support and encouragement of effective employment practices.
- Instill in the employees and the public a sense of confidence about the conduct and intentions of my employer.
- Maintain loyalty to my employer and pursue its objectives in ways that are consistent with the public interest.
- Uphold all laws and regulations relating to my employer's activities.
- Refrain from using my official positions, either regular or volunteer, to secure special privilege, gain or benefit for myself.
- Maintain the confidentiality of privileged information.
- Improve public understanding of the role of human resource management.

This Code of Ethics for members of the Society for Human Resource Management has been adopted to promote and maintain the highest standards of personal conduct and professional standards among its members. Adherence to this code is required for membership in the Society and serves to assure public confidence in the integrity and service of human resource management professionals.

Source: Reprinted with permission from *HRMagazine* published by the Society for Human Resource Management, Alexandria, VA.

ETHICAL PERSPECTIVE

Encouraging Ethical Behavior in Organizations

Ethical behavior in organizations can be encouraged in a number of ways, many of which require action by the HRM department. Ethical or unethical behavior is not entirely an individual matter; it is determined at least in part by factors in the organization. In other words, people are influenced by the forces surrounding them—their peers, superiors, the reward system, group norms, and organizational policies. Consequently, HR managers can influence behavior in organizations through orientation programs for new employees, employee training, codes of ethics, and the discipline system, among others.

New Employee Orientation One important aim of new employee orientation programs is to teach newcomers the norms, attitudes, and beliefs that prevail in the organization. The organization's values and guiding principles can be communicated explicitly through formal presentations and implicitly through organizational stories and myths. For example, telling a story about an organizational hero who defied authority to do what was "right" can send a powerful message. The goal is to convince new employees that the values they are being taught are not just window-dressing but represent the values and beliefs of the organization's leadership—the tone at the top of the organization.

Employee Training As jobs become more complex, it is difficult to provide specific guidelines to handle every situation. Therefore, an increasing number of companies have recently added ethics training to their list of management development programs. Allied Corporation's ethics seminars are intended to help employees "gain a broader perspective of their responsibilities," explained Edward Hennessy, chairman and CEO of the firm. "Our managers must be capable of recognizing the ethical dimensions of their business decisions" (Ethics Resource Center Report 1985).

Particular industries, organizations, and jobs within organizations present unique ethical dilemmas for many employees whose religious or moral upbringing does not necessarily equip them to handle the complex ethical problems they may face on the job. For instance, insider trading is not prohibited by the teachings of any major faith! Employees need help in recognizing the ethical component of work-related problems and in developing strategies for resolving the conflicting values inherent in ethical dilemmas. A thorough assessment of ethical problems characteristic of the particular industry or organization can provide the basis for developing an effective training program.

Citicorp provides a model for ethics training. The corporate HR group has developed a board game based on realistic business scenarios requiring decisions having an ethical component. Each scenario has four possible solutions. Employees play the game in teams and try to reach consensus on the best solution for each scenario. There are four levels of play, corresponding to the decisions faced by entry-level employees, supervisors, middle managers, and executives. Thus far, the game has been used by more than 30,000 Citicorp employees around the world. One of the game's developers says, "We think one of the reasons this approach is so effective is that it creates a dialog on ethics—it makes it OK to talk about ethics out loud with peers and management" (Ireland 1991). It is also very important for top management to model and reinforce ethical behavior and for organizational policies to state clearly that unethical behavior will not be tolerated. Citicorp embodies these ideas by distributing a sixty-page booklet on corporate ethics to all officers, and by having top managers sit in each time the ethics game is played by employees.

Codes of Ethics Many organizations have drawn up formal codes of ethical conduct, but their influence on behavior is uncertain. In some organizations, employees think of these codes as a facade. They are not backed up by informal organizational norms; nor are they assessed during performance appraisal or enforced in any other way. Such codes are ineffective. However, if codes of ethics are consistent with organizational norms, are distributed to employees, and are enforced, they are likely to be effective.

Discipline System Employees expect inappropriate behavior to be disciplined. Failure to respond to unethical behavior may lead to feelings of inequity on the part of ethical employees and threaten the entire social system that supports ethical behavior in the organization. Breaches of the code should be handled fairly and consistently, providing due process through the organization's discipline and grievance procedures.

Sources: D. R. Cressey and C. A. Moore, "Managerial Values and Corporate Codes of Ethics," *California Management Review,* 1983, pp. 53–57; Karin Ireland, "The Ethics Game," *Personnel Journal,* March 1991, pp. 72–75; Linda Trevino, "The Influence of Vicarious Learning and Individual Differences on Ethical Decision Making in the Organization: An Experiment," Ph.D. dissertation, Texas A&M University, 1987; "Allied Corporation: Ethics Education of Managers," *Ethics Resource Center Report,* Vol. 2, 1985, p. 1.

Although there is some merit to the "bad apple" perspective, it is far from the whole story. Employees do not make ethical choices in a vacuum or entirely on the basis of their preexisting values and ethical upbringing. Instead, they behave within a context that includes organizational training, role models, formal rules and policies, and appraisal and reward systems. It is the responsibility of the HR manager to ensure that these influences are positive and consistent with the ethical values desired by the top managers of the organization. The Ethical Perspective box on the facing page lists some ways in which HR staff can help to elicit and maintain ethical behavior among employees. Ethical Perspective boxes in subsequent chapters will raise additional issues of concern to the responsible HR practitioner.

Human Resource Information Systems

In the past decade, computers have become an increasingly important tool for managing human resources. **Human resource information systems (HRISs)** have replaced manual employee record-keeping and payroll systems and have also allowed more sophisticated reporting and forecasting with respect to HR issues. Computers are used in virtually all the HR activities discussed in this book. Rather than reiterating their role in each chapter, we have included two special sections on HRISs. The insert following Chapter 8 discusses the design and capabilities of HRISs. The second insert, following Chapter 16, gives examples of HRIS applications in a number of functional areas.

ALTERNATE VIEWS OF HUMAN RESOURCE MANAGEMENT

Multiple Constituencies

Although it has been traditional to organize HRM activities by function (such as staffing, compensation, and labor relations), another way to look at human resource management is in terms of the multiple constituencies served by the HRM department and what each values as important. The HRM department plays a support or service role in the organization and as such it interacts with a variety of constituencies. (A constituency is defined as any group of supporters, customers, or clientele.) A study examining such a perspective provides an interesting look at HR activities as viewed by distinct groups of organization members receiving the services.[21]

The initial phase of the research consisted of developing a list of activities that make up the HR mission. An exhaustive process resulted in a list of 101 activities that were considered the most important in human resource management. Through a statistical technique, these 101 activities were organized into the eight dimensions shown in Table 1.3.

Four internal organizational constituencies were defined as (1) top executives, (2) managers and supervisors, (3) professional employees (e.g., engineers, scientists, nurses, accountants), and (4) hourly workers. The researchers indicated that these four constituencies have the most frequent interactions with HR managers and are the major service users or resource providers. A total of 150 organizational units took part in the study. The sample from these organizations consisted of 148 executives, 847 managers, and 884 nonmanagement employees, including 484 professional and 400 hourly employees. Each participant completed a confidential mailed survey in which he or she rated the importance of the various activities.

The results appear in Table 1.4. Mean ratings and rankings of importance of each of the eight activities indicate different constituency perspectives. Top executives ranked legal compliance and administrative service as most important and organization/employee development and labor relations as least important. Managers regarded administrative service and policy adherence as the most important activities and staffing/human resource planning and labor relations as least important. Professionals thought that the most important activities were administrative service and compensation/employee relations, whereas staffing/human resource planning and labor relations were least critical. Finally, hourly employees regarded compensation/employee relations and administrative service as the most important activities and staffing/human resource planning and labor relations as least important.

There were both similarities and differences in the perceptions of the value of HR activities. Each of the four constituencies rated labor relations least important. Each group also rated the administrative service activity as either first or second in importance. There was agreement on other activities, such as all groups rated staffing/human resource planning and organization/employee development as sixth or seventh. The activity on which the constituencies most differed

TABLE 1.3 Important HR Activities

Activity	*Examples*
Staffing/Human Resource Planning	Developing staffing plans Developing succession plans Advising management on staffing policy
Organization/Employee Development	Organizational development activities Assessing training needs Advising on organizational design
Compensation/Employee Relations	Implementing policy on equal pay Resolving salary problems Establishing systems for performance appraisal
Employee Support	Operating health maintenance programs Operating employee assistance programs Counseling employees
Legal Requirements/Compliance	Operating Affirmative Action programs Auditing EEO compliance Ensuring compliance with employment regulations
Labor/Union Relations	Negotiating labor agreements Administering labor contracts Conducting labor/management meetings
Policy Adherence	Administering disciplinary procedures Ensuring uniform application of policies across units Administering attendance and leave policies
Administrative Services	Communicating compensation and benefit programs Orienting new hires Presenting human resource informational material at meetings

Source: Adapted from Anne S. Tsui and George T. Milkovich, "Personnel Department Activities: Constituency Perspectives and Preferences," *Personnel Psychology,* Autumn 1987, p. 535. Reprinted by permission.

was compensation/employee relations; hourly employees rated it first, professionals rated it second, managers rated it third, and top executives rated it fourth. Perhaps understandably, line executives rated legal compliance first, whereas all other constituencies rated it fourth or fifth.

This research provides an interesting perspective on HR activities and how they are viewed by various organizational constituencies. As such, the research offers a useful framework for understanding the conflicting demands HR professionals face. As Anne Tsui and George Milkovich suggest, "Personnel activities or priorities are not always logically derived from factors such as strategy, structure, or environmental contingencies but may result from the demands of the powerful or politically active constituencies."[22] The several HR constituencies are

TABLE 1.4 Importance Ratings of Eight HR Activities by Four Constituencies

	*Constituency Ratings and Rankings**			
Activity	*Executives*	*Managers*	*Professionals*	*Hourly*
Staffing/Human Resource Planning	3.16 (6)	3.52 (7)	3.49 (7)	3.74 (7)
Organization/Employee Development	3.13 (7)	3.53 (6)	3.61 (6)	3.91 (6)
Compensation/Employee Relations	3.77 (4)	4.01 (3)	3.97 (2)	4.28 (1)
Employee Support	3.22 (5)	3.68 (5)	3.68 (4)	4.11 (4)
Legal Compliance	4.01 (1)	3.81 (4)	3.63 (5)	3.97 (5)
Labor Relations	2.51 (8)	2.45 (8)	2.25 (8)	2.47 (8)
Policy Adherence	3.88 (3)	4.03 (2)	3.82 (3)	4.15 (3)
Administrative Services	3.90 (2)	4.08 (1)	4.04 (1)	4.25 (2)

*Ratings were on a 1 (not important) to 5 (extremely important) scale. Rank of the activities is based on the eight means within a constituency with 1 = most important and 8 = least important.

Source: Adapted from Anne S. Tsui and George T. Milkovich, "Personnel Department Activities: Constituency Perspectives and Preferences," *Personnel Psychology,* Autumn 1987, p. 531. Reprinted by permission.

seeking different services, and each needs to be appropriately served. Successful HR programs seek to accommodate multiple constituencies.

Strategic Impact of Human Resource Management

Traditionally, the major perspective on human resource management has been a functional one, with HR departments being organized into subunits for recruitment and selection, training, compensation, and labor relations. The multiple constituency perspective represents an alternate approach. One way of integrating the functional and multiple constituency approaches is by looking at human resource management as a vehicle for bringing to reality the organization's strategic objectives.

Many organizational decisions are not seen as affecting employees, but in fact they have critical impact on them. Examples of business decisions made by operating managers and their impact on human resources are shown in Figure 1.3. It is clear that various HR functions would be needed to fully implement the intended action. As an example, the top management decision of a major airline to purchase a small number of new jumbo jets will be discussed in detail. The airline decided to buy the new equipment after deciding to fly a new intercontinental route. The airline needed to acquire a class of airplane it had previously not

FIGURE 1.3 Strategic Decisions and Their Implications for Human Resource Management

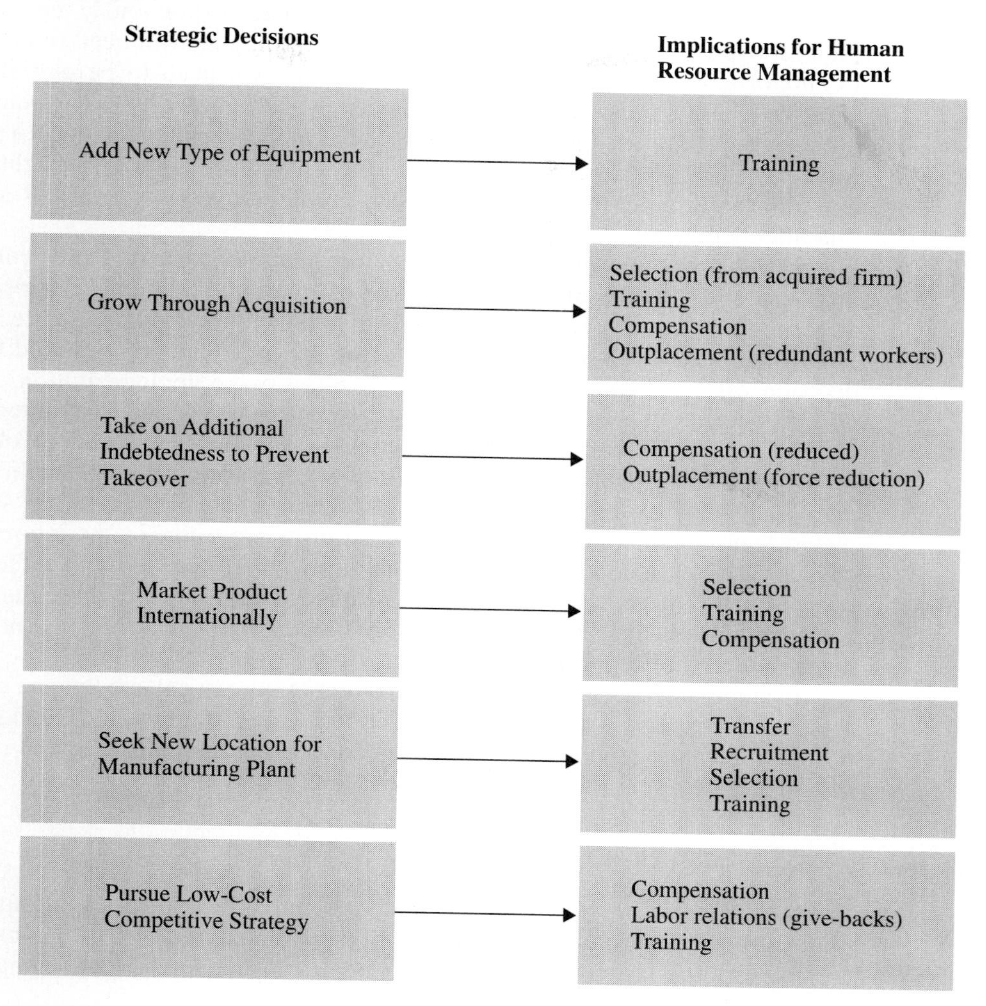

owned. Guiding the decision are factors of cost, financing, the suitability of the jet for the intended routes, and HR issues.

Such a decision has major HR implications, which will ripple throughout the organization. To begin with, pilots identified to fly the new class of equipment, generally the most experienced captains with the airline, will need extensive training on the new aircraft. Of course, this will create training needs throughout the cockpit ranks as other captains move up to more sophisticated equipment: first officers (copilots) qualify as captains, and flight engineers move up to first officers. Cabin attendants will need training in service and in the safety features of the airplane. Ground crews will need to be trained in any new procedures for loading and unloading the airplane. Maintenance mechanics will need training in routine and special servicing requirements of planes previously unfamiliar to them. For purchasing agents, different parts and supplies will need to be ordered to support the equipment. Perhaps construction will need to be undertaken to alter the airport gates from which passengers will enter and leave the plane. Marketing representatives will need to know the airplane's special features to promote travel on it. What is not realized is the fact that the seemingly straightforward decision to purchase the new jets has set in motion a vast series of HR activities that affects many parts of the organization.

The manner in which HR decisions are made and carried out will have a profound effect on the employees involved. At the same time, these decisions will affect the long-range evaluation of the decision to fly the routes, the decision on the purchase of aircraft, and the success of the organization. A sound business decision will not be successful if HR difficulties make implementation problematic. The airline has borrowed $120 million for each plane and has interest payments of approximately $700,000 each month, assuming a 7 percent rate of interest on the loan. If the plane remains idle as a result of failure in the HR chain outlined previously—for example, because maintenance mechanics have not yet completed their certification or too few cockpit crew are trained—the interest in excess of $23,000 for one day is a cost the airline must bear with no offsetting income. Furthermore, the passengers scheduled to fly that day must make other arrangements and may be reluctant to return to travel on an airline that previously disappointed them.

In summary, there is increased realization of the critical importance of human resource management in organizational effectiveness. Simply put, HRM is the set of functions and activities that are designed to bring the employee and organization together so that the goals of both are met.

Political Influence Perspective

Another perspective, which is frequently the topic of cynical discussion, is the political considerations that enter into organizational and HR decisions. In this context, **politics** refers to "the methods or tactics involved in managing" an organization.[23]

As Gerald Ferris has pointed out, organizations are generally thought of as efficient, machinelike entities.[24] Of course, such is not the case. Politics is the space between the perfect workings of a rational and efficient organization and the messiness of the interaction of people. The greater the gap, the more political tactics become a way of life in achieving job and organizational outcomes.

Such a realization is important for HR managers. Some HR activities tend inherently to be less rational and efficient than others and hence subject to tactics and potential manipulation.[25] For example, contrast HR planning and performance appraisal. HR planning involves gathering data in important areas and making assumptions about the future. It is data oriented and one of the more rational HR activities. Consequently, one would expect fewer political tactics to be involved. Performance appraisal involves every member of the organization. Although the intention is to be data oriented, the data generally consist of performance information on people and are subject to a wide range of potential perceptual distortions. Yet the impact of how individuals are evaluated has important implications for future rewards and career progression. Therefore, systems of performance appraisal, unless carefully structured and carried out, will be subject to political manipulation.[26]

FUTURE CHALLENGES TO HUMAN RESOURCE MANAGEMENT

As we move through the final decade of the twentieth century and on to the twenty-first, there can be little doubt that human resource management faces some of the greatest challenges since its definition as a separate staff function almost a century ago. This renewed vigor stems from numerous influences, such as the changing nature of the economy and government-legal influences, new organizational forms, global competition, and the increased feeling that organizations are vehicles for fulfilling societal goals. Some of the factors that have forced human resource management to be transformed from a narrowly defined specialty into a more strategic function are discussed in the sections that follow.

Corporate Reorganizations

The 1980s were characterized by corporate acquisitions and mergers. Hardly a week went by without one or more instances of one corporation purchasing another, of two corporations joining forces, or of companies undergoing massive reorganizations in an effort to fend off hostile takeover bids.[27] The reorganizations continue in the 1990s but for different reasons. A renewed emphasis on competitiveness is forcing corporations to cut layers of managers and restructure work forces.[28]

It is difficult to imagine circumstances that pose a greater challenge for human resource management than the reorganizations that have characterized the last decade.[29] Such reorganizations inevitably affect many organizational levels and employees. Furthermore, given the complexities of the situation, decisions may be slow in coming. In the meantime, employees are left wondering what, if any, role they will play in the "new organization."[30] As a result of reorganizations, employees may face these potential changes:

- Loss of job, pay, and benefits
- Job changes, including new roles and assignments
- Transfer to new geographic location
- Changes in compensation and benefits
- Changes in career possibilities

- Changes in organizational power, status, and prestige
- Staff changes, including new colleagues, bosses, and subordinates
- Change in corporate culture and loss of identity with the company

There is little indication that the pace of corporate reorganizations will slacken in the near future, and a recent survey of almost 600 organizations showed that between 60 and 70 percent of the respondents were evaluating downsizing and/or reorganization for their firms.[31] As shown in Table 1.5, thirteen of the top Fortune 25 industrial companies announced staff reductions in 1991, totaling almost 200,000 employees. To a greater extent than ever before, corporations consider reorganizations (acquisitions, mergers, divestitures, downsizing) as routine business transactions. Yet an important key to the success of almost any reorganization is the management of human resources.

Global Competition

A long-term trend with profound and far-reaching implications for HR professionals is that of a global economy. International competition in goods and services is forcing major economies into a global affiliation.[32] Rather than being the dominant economic force, the United States is one of a small (and changing) group of eco-

TABLE 1.5 Work Force Reductions Made or Announced in 1991 by Fortune 25 Industrial Companies

Rank	*Company*	*Reductions*
1	General Motors	104,000
3	Ford	2,000
4	IBM	43,000
6	General Electric	4,300
9	Du Pont	10,000
11	Chrysler	3,000
14	Shell Oil	4,650
17	United Technologies	500
20	Eastman Kodak	6,000
21	Arco	2,100
22	Xerox	2,500
23	PepsiCo	1,800
24	McDonnell Douglas	3,800
	Total Work Force Reductions	187,650

Source: Compiled from business publications by Aneil Mishra of the University of Michigan.

nomically strong countries. In addition, the United States is no longer an isolated national economy but part of a world economic community.

The transition has not been an easy one for U.S. industry. For example, even in recent times, the United States has had strong textile and apparel industries. U.S. companies supplied many parts of the world with finished cloth products. As competition with Third World countries increased, United States manufacturers insisted that their products were superior to the less expensive imports. Consumers soon realized, however, that imported textile and apparel products were as good as the domestic counterparts and also cheaper. The result can be seen by simply examining the labels of the apparel in your wardrobe or other finished textile products. There is virtually no U.S. textile industry at this time.

What has transpired in the textile industry is an example of a trend toward a global economy. From an HR perspective, this trend has represented a monumental challenge. Relationships between employees and employer have been shaken in industries that have been dramatically reduced in the United States, such as the shoe, automobile, steel, and electronics industries. The readjustment for workers in these industries usually has involved switching from the declining manufacturing sector of the economy to the service sector.

As a response to increasing international competition, many **international joint ventures (IJVs)** have been formed. IJVs are a means for U.S. corporations to have international presence without establishing a wholly owned subsidiary abroad. An IJV is achieved when a new organization or partnership is formed by two or more companies from different countries for the purpose of conducting a new business. As such, IJVs have become the most widespread form of U.S. multinational investment.

One study identified seventeen HR issues related to IJVs. These issues were categorized into the nine subject areas indicated in Table 1.6. In general, these issues arise from the somewhat different goals of the host and foreign partners or from the different organizational climates or procedures within the IJV and either the host or foreign parent.

More and more, HR professionals are becoming primarily responsible for helping to make the efforts at business globalization effective. The need to identify and place U.S. employees, mainly managerial and professional personnel, in foreign subsidiaries or joint ventures is one of the important challenges of the 1990s and beyond. The problems associated with the selection, training, and compensation of expatriate managers will be discussed in Chapter 17.

Slower Growth

Slower growth in markets and, in some cases, declining markets have reduced opportunities in many organizations. For example, in the mid-1980s, growth came to a stop for Southwestern Bell Telephone, the largest of the seven regional telephone companies and an organization that had seen steady growth for more than two decades. One result of the changed circumstance was the greatly diminished opportunity for talented employees. In the past, newly hired hourly employees

TABLE 1.6 HR Challenges Associated with International Joint Ventures (IJVs)

Human Resource Management Area	*Example of Human Resource Management Challenge*
Staffing	Management at the host country partner may perceive providing jobs for their citizens as a more important objective than increasing profits.
Promotion	Blocked promotion of host country nationals in the IJV may result from reserving top positions for expatriates from the foreign parent.
Loyalty	Because of the multiplicity of entities involved in the IJV, loyalty conflicts may occur.
Delegation	Parent companies limit the delegation of authority to IJV and/or disagree on the desired extent of autonomy.
Decision Making	Decision making is a particularly complicated process because of the conflicting expectations of the entities involved.
Unfamiliarity	Each employee group may experience feelings of strangeness and lack of familiarity with the employees of the other entities. Expatriates may be unfamiliar with the environment and culture of the host country.
Communication	Communication blockages can result because of interpersonal problems between geographically dispersed managers.
Information	Information flow from the host or foreign parent to the IJV may be restricted because of suspicion regarding the intentions of the other parent.
Compensation	Dissatisfaction with compensation gaps between host country nationals and expatriates can develop. Difficulties in assessing the performance of IJV staff stem from the different procedures and performance standards of the parent companies.

Source: Adapted from Oded Shenkar and Yoram Zeira, "Human Resources Management in International Joint Ventures: Directions for Research," *Academy of Management Review,* Fall 1987, pp. 546–557. Reprinted by permission.

started in a routine but important job and then moved into other areas, usually within one year. With growth at a standstill, employees with many years of seniority are still in entry-level positions.

Of course, many of those pushed out of organizations because of the massive layoffs that have dominated the news view others in situations of diminished opportunity to be the fortunate ones. Recall that the HR survey of almost 600 organizations, which was cited earlier, showed that between 60 and 70 percent of organizations were evaluating downsizing for their firms.[33] Economic downturn aside, the movement to slower growth is a long-term trend. It is driven by some of the following changes:

- The use of information technology in place of human resources
- Continued automation, requiring fewer workers

- Flatter organizations, with fewer layers between top and bottom, thus cutting out unneeded managers
- Plant closings to bring production capacity in line with business realities
- Redesigning of the work force to be more flexible, as by using temporary workers[34]

Clearly, managing human resources in times of slower or negative growth will be a significant challenge for the HR professional in the 1990s.

Increasing Diversity in the Work Force

Another major challenge for human resource management is the changing nature of the work force. Figure 1.4 illustrates the dimensions of diversity, with six pri-

FIGURE 1.4 Primary and Secondary Dimensions of Diversity

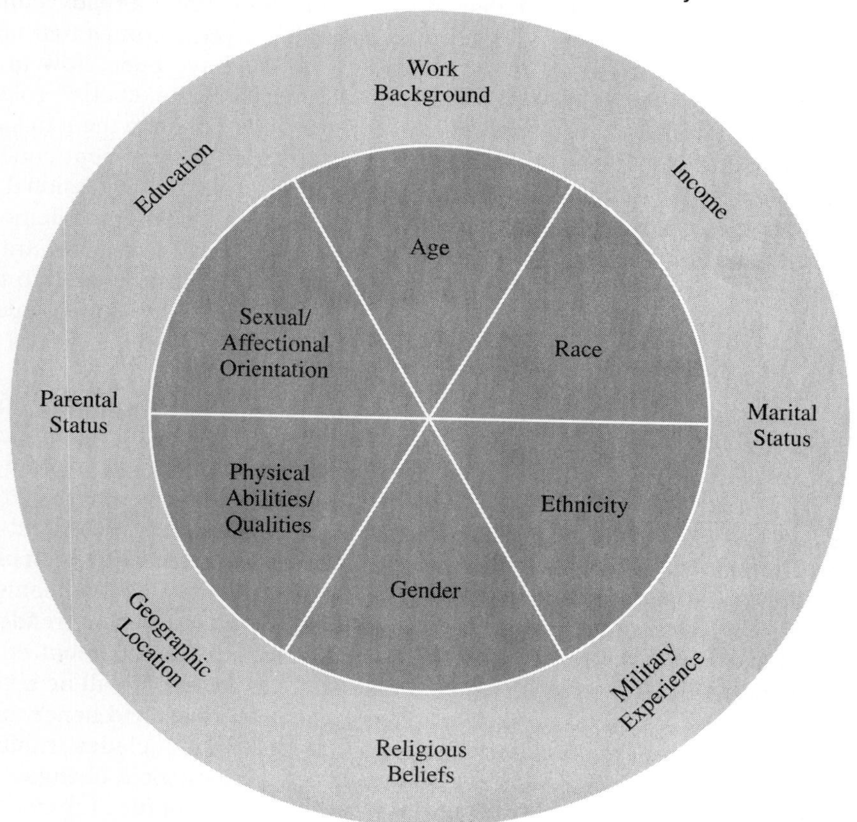

Source: Marilyn Loden and Judy B. Rosener, *Workforce America: Managing Employee Diversity as a Vital Resource*, p. 20. © 1991 by Business One Irwin. All rights reserved. Reprinted by permission.

mary elements at the core surrounded by secondary dimensions. Taken together, the increased diversity of the work force has caused organizations to re-examine policies, practices, and values. The important earmarks of the increased diversity are as follows:

- The number of women and minorities has increased dramatically.
- Hispanics are the fastest-growing segment of the minority population in the United States, numbering 22 million in the 1990 census—a 50 percent increase in the decade of the 1980s and a growth rate five times that of non-Hispanics.[35]
- Asian-Americans, though constituting only 2.6 percent of the U.S. population, tend to be affluent and well educated and are outperforming North American whites in the classroom and the workplace.
- The work force continues to age.

Progress in accommodating employee diversity has already been dramatic, and many readers will think that most organizations have already climbed the growth curve with respect to opportunities for the diverse groups that now make up the work force. However, lasting improvements have been slow in coming. How many organizations have women and minorities in executive roles? Even organizations with a substantial record of progress do not have them in significant numbers at higher levels. An example of this situation is the recent concern with the underrepresentation of minorities in managerial roles in professional sports.

Another challenge that has resulted from changing work force demographics concerns dual-career couples—that is, couples where both partners are actively pursuing professional careers. Organizations have been accustomed to using job moves and physical relocation as an important means of developing talent. Men or women moving through organizational ranks to upper-level positions need experience in a variety of roles in different organizational units. Frequently, physical relocation has been required. The increasing number of dual-career professionals limits individual flexibility in accepting such assignments and may hinder organizational flexibility in acquiring and developing needed talent.

Still another trend that is posing a challenge for human resource management relates to the increasing average age of the work force. The "graying of the work force" is a result of two trends. First, legislation pushed back and then eliminated the retirement age. The number of older persons is increasing, and some of them are electing to continue working. At the same time, demographic trends have resulted in a smaller percentage of young adults. By 2010, 25 percent of the U.S. population will be at least fifty-five years old, and 14 percent will be sixty-five or older.[36] There is a shrinking base of college-age individuals and hence an increasing average age of the work force. One HRM challenge includes training to upgrade the skills of older workers in the face of technological change. A second challenge is to ensure that younger workers have opportunities for career growth and promotion, despite the large number of more senior employees in the organization.

Each dimension and trend can be examined as an isolated aspect of the challenge to HR managers; however, it is the interconnectedness and the dynamic interaction of these forces that is reshaping organizations and how they relate to the work force.

Employee Expectations

As levels of education have increased within the population, values and expectations among employees have shifted. At present, fully one-quarter of the work force has a college degree. The result has been an emphasis on increased participation by employees at all levels. Previous notions about managerial authority are giving way to employee influence and involvement, along with mechanisms for upward communication and due process.[37]

Another expectation by employees is that the electronic and telecommunication revolutions will improve the quality of work life. Innovations in communications and computer technology will accelerate the pace of change and as a result lead to many innovations in human resource management.

Finally, employers are taking steps to support employees' family responsibilities.[38] Once able to assume that the demands of male employees' home lives were taken care of by their wives, employers are now being pushed to pay attention to family issues, such as day care, sick children, elder care, schooling, and so forth.[39] One result that is increasingly becoming reality is the opportunity to work at home. Alvin Toffler estimates that the information revolution will shift millions of jobs out of the factories and offices and into the home.[40]

Organizations as Vehicles for Reaching Societal Goals

During the past two decades, there has been an increasing trend toward viewing organizations as vehicles for achieving social and political objectives. The beginning of this trend was signaled by the adoption of the 1964 Civil Rights Act by the U.S. Congress. This legislation required organizations to deal fairly with minorities—including women and racial and religious minorities—in hiring, promotion, and other aspects of human resource management. Other legislation followed, including requirements that organizations provide affirmative opportunities for the disabled, employees with the HIV virus, and veterans. Another law prohibits discrimination against employees over the age of forty. More recently, there has been discussion in the U.S. Congress of legislation mandating such benefits as family leaves for the birth or adoption of a child and certain family emergencies. A further issue discussed as a legislative possibility is comparable worth—that is, mandating equal pay for women doing jobs equivalent in value but different in content from jobs typically held by men (see Chapter 12).

Such legislative requirements generally follow a realization that important issues need national attention. As entities within the larger society, organizations are influenced by the ideology and culture around them. As changes occur in the larger society, organizations also must adapt and change. The results of social and legislative changes are added pressures on organizations. HR practices are not formed in a vacuum but must represent the societal ideology in which they are embedded.

All of this adds up to extensive economic, social, political, and technological changes that affect what organizations do and the expectations of their employees. In addition, procedures used in the past to handle the human side of business are no longer effective. The net result is a tremendous challenge for HR managers.

JOBS AND CAREERS IN HUMAN RESOURCE MANAGEMENT

Jobs and careers in human resource management can be both challenging and rewarding. The purpose of this section is to examine HRM jobs, typical compensation, and future HRM career opportunities.

What competencies are required if one is to be effective as an HR professional? A recent study has suggested that HR professionals in the 1990s will be expected to contribute to the strategic direction of the organizations that employ them by helping to create and sustain the competitive advantage of the firm.[41] The following competencies are considered critical to this expanded role:

- *Business Capabilities.* Knowledge of financial, strategic, and technological aspects of analysis, marketing and sales, computer information systems, customer relations, and production capabilities.
- *Human Resource Practices.* Attracting and promoting appropriate people, designing development programs, developing effective appraisal programs and feedback processes, communicating organizational and HR policies, and providing a mechanism for integrating different business units.
- *Managing the Change Process.* Establishing trust, providing vision, putting problems in the context of larger systems, clarifying roles and responsibilities, encouraging creativity, and being proactive in bringing about change.

These competencies represent a mix of skills that can be acquired through education (e.g., general business knowledge, functional HR expertise) and experience. The HR professional of the 1990s is viewed as a strategic partner in running the business.[42]

Types of Jobs

Opportunities vary across organizations, and they vary within organizations depending on the level at which one is working. Professional positions can be divided into three categories: HR specialist, HR manager, and HR executive. In addition, there are numerous support positions (e.g., clerical personnel and computer programmers).

Human Resource Specialist HR specialist jobs are usually the entry-level positions for an HRM career. Included would be such roles as interviewer, compensation analyst, benefits coordinator, job analyst, and trainer. In larger organizations, there may be promotional opportunities within the specialized function. For example, a new specialist may begin as an interviewer, move up to coordinating college recruiting in a region, and progress to supervising all college recruiting.

Alternately, an entry-level specialist may work in a smaller company or plant as one of two or three professionals providing HR services. In this case, the specialist may do a little of everything. For example, in any given day, the specialist might run an orientation program for new employees, interview applicants, develop information for contract negotiations, or check with other companies in the area regarding hourly wages.

HR specialists typically have formal college training in human resource management or a related area, such as industrial-organizational psychology, adult education, or industrial relations. Some organizations hire business or liberal arts graduates with excellent interpersonal skills to start in a specialist role while continuing their education in an HR resource program at the master's degree level.

Human Resource Manager The HR manager is a generalist who administers and coordinates programs spanning several functional areas. The HR manager is usually a top-ranked person at a plant or facility and, as such, is expected to be knowledgeable about all areas of human resource management, to oversee the implementation of organizational human resource policies at the facility, and to advise line managers on human resource issues.

Another role for the HR manager would be to head a functional personnel activity at the corporate level. Many large organizations are organized into relatively autonomous divisions. Typically, such organizations have functional specialists at the corporate level to translate corporate strategy into HR policy and to coordinate this policy throughout all divisions. For example, the corporate headquarters may have a manager of affirmative action to develop a comprehensive plan based on corporate objectives and commitments. The manager would then coordinate with divisional HR managers to make sure that plans at the local level are consistent with corporate objectives.

The HR manager is an experienced professional, usually someone who has served in several specialist positions. The individual in such a position will have obtained knowledge and skills through experience but may or may not have a degree in human resource management.

Human Resource Executive The top-level HR executive, usually a vice president of the organization, has the responsibility of linking corporate policy and strategy with human resource management. The top HR executive would also be expected to have input into organizational goals, especially as these goals affect or are affected by personnel activities. It is important to consider HR opportunities and limitations in establishing overall organizational directions.

Compensation for HR Professionals

The Society for Human Resource Management conducts an annual survey of compensation for HR professionals. The 1991 survey included more than 22,000 HR professionals in almost 1,400 organizations. The 22,000 respondents represent many industries and both small and large employers. These results are presented in three ways: compensation for top HR executives (Table 1.7); pay for HR professionals (Table 1.8); and pay for HR professionals by company size (also Table 1.8).

In Table 1.7, pay for top HR executives is given for both large (greater than 10,000 employees) and small (less than 250 employees) organizations. On the average, top HR executives for large companies earn over $200,000 with bonus, while their counterparts in small companies average about half that amount. A recent *Wall Street Journal* report on the review of 1991 corporate reports found that at nine U.S. companies the HR executive was among the five highest-paid officers, with several earning over $600,000.[43] According to the *Wall Street Journal,* top HR executives in the largest businesses typically earn between $300,000 and $400,000.

Table 1.8 displays compensation information for several of the HR professional job titles, both overall and by size of employer. Average salaries vary from $37,600 for compensation administrators to just over $47,000 for labor relations generalists. The average for all HR professional positions is just over $40,000. As shown in Table 1.8, the connection between salary and employment size is straightforward. In general, larger companies pay from 11 percent to over 30 percent more than smaller organizations.

Career Opportunities

The career outlook for HR professionals is reasonably strong. The external factors discussed previously—events related to corporate reorganizations, global competition, and changes in work force demographics—represent long-term trends

TABLE 1.7 Pay for HR Top Executives, 1991

	Company Size	
	Large (>10,000 Employees)	*Small (<250 Employees)*
Base Salary	$158,000	$92,000
Total Cash Compensation	$203,000	$105,000
Percentage of Bonus Eligible	86%	77%
Bonus as Percentage of Base	41%	25%

Source: L. Kate Beatty, "Pay Goes Up as HR Jobs Broaden," *HRMagazine,* September 1991, p. 56. Reprinted with the permission from *HRMagazine* published by the Society for Human Resource Management, Alexandria, VA.

TABLE 1.8 Pay for HR Professionals, 1991

HR Professional	*Average Base Salary*	*Company Size*	
		Large (>10,000 Employees)	*Small (<250 Emp)*
Labor Relations Generalist	$47,100	$50,000	na
Managerial/Executive Recruitment Specialist	44,500	46,100	$40,600
Safety Specialist	42,700	41,800	36,000
HR Generalist	41,000	43,000	33,400
Benefits Planning Analyst	41,000	43,300	39,000
Senior Compensation Analyst	40,300	42,300	38,100
EEO Specialist	39,900	41,500	36,000
Senior Training Specialist	39,300	39,000	33,700
Professional/Technical Recruitment Specialist	37,700	39,000	31,500
Compensation/Benefits Administrator	37,600	42,100	30,900

Source: L. Kate Beatty, "Pay Goes Up as HR Jobs Broaden," *HRMagazine,* September 1991, pp. 56, 57. Reprinted with the permission from *HRMagazine* published by the Society for Human Resource Management, Alexandria, VA.

that have transformed the way organizations interact with employees. HR professionals are in a pivotal position in terms of these challenges.

An even more promising trend is the strategic role played by HR professionals. More and more, organizational effectiveness is being determined by the degree to which strategic objectives are formulated in light of HR considerations. This means that HR professionals must look ahead with respect to corporate objectives—whether they involve a new line of business, a possible acquisition, or a new corporate emphasis—and make sure that the HR policy is consistent with the overall objectives.

The increased status of human resource management can be illustrated by tracking HR reporting relationships over the past several years. Ten to fifteen years ago, senior HR executives typically reported to the third level of management—for example, to an administrative vice president. Now senior HR managers often report to first- or second-level managers—for example, to the president or executive vice president. Today many senior HR executives are officers of the corporation and represent the HR point of view as members of the board of directors.[44]

Career Progression

Entry The HR competencies discussed earlier in this section give an idea of how one can build a career in this area. Technical knowledge is essential. For most, the entry point with a college degree is the position of technical specialist. Many business schools have a specialization in human resource management, including courses in most of the major areas addressed as topics in this text. One can also major in liberal arts—for example, in psychology, sociology, or economics, perhaps with a minor in business—and then gain further learning on the job as a technical specialist. The Society for Human Resource Management (formerly called the American Society for Personnel Administration) has student chapters at many colleges and universities. Campus chapters of SHRM provide speakers, field trips, and internship opportunities for participating students.

Many institutions of higher education have graduate programs in human resource management. Such a program would normally lead to a master's degree in business, with a specialization in human resource management. A typical curriculum would include courses in business (accounting, finance, marketing, organizational sciences) and graduate-level study in major HRM areas. Frequently, students would be encouraged to hold an internship as an HR assistant for a semester.

A final entry route is as a line employee who transfers into human resource management. After gaining experience as a supervisor, for instance, it may be possible to switch areas and become an HR specialist.

The competition for entry-level HRM jobs is often quite stiff. These jobs attract new graduates, internal candidates, and would-be career changers from other human service areas, such as teaching and social work. The key to getting interviews and landing the first job is experience: students who have completed one or more personnel internships have much greater success in the HRM job market.

Advancement Career advancement is earned by gaining experience in the major areas of human resource management and at different levels within the organization. Table 1.9 illustrates how one might progress. Hypothetical organizational structures within typical HR departments are shown in Figure 1.5. These department structures show the different specialist, managerial, and executive roles that might exist in a large corporate environment.

It is not necessary to rotate through all major areas and levels of an organization when pursuing a career in human resource management, although it is important to gain experience in most of the areas. Progression is not always stepwise, from plant to division to corporate headquarters. It is possible to start at the plant, move to the division or headquarters, and then move back for further experience at the plant.

Certification as an HR Professional

The Human Resource Certification Institute, an affiliate of the Society for Human Resource Management, is a nonprofit corporation that recognizes and accredits individuals who have met experience requirements and have demonstrated a mas-

TABLE 1.9 Typical Job Activities in Conjunction with Human Resource Management

	Possible Job Activity		
Experience Area	*Plant*	*Division*	*Corporation*
Planning	Analyze jobs for compensation decisions.	Analyze human resource considerations associated with plant expansion.	Analyze human resource considerations associated with new line of business.
Organizational Entry	Visit technical schools to recruit hourly workers. Test applicants for hourly positions.	Visit colleges to recruit graduates. Develop affirmative action goals.	Develop company-wide EEO plan. Develop succession plan for key executives.
Developing Employees	Orient new employees. Monitor plantwide suggestion system for productivity improvement.	Establish quality circle program for productivity improvement.	Plan job rotation of experienced managers for further training.
Performance, Evaluation, and Reward Systems	Apply job evaluation procedure to new job titles. Supervise performance evaluation.	Develop policy for annual wage and salary increases.	Plan bonus system for corporate executives.
Maintaining Human Resources	Resolve employee grievances. Conduct exit interviews.	Negotiate contract with union.	Develop plans for organizational retrenchment.

tery of the HR body of knowledge.[45] The levels of certification offered by the institute, and the requirements for each level, are as follows:

- *Professional in Human Resources.* Four years of professional HRM experience or two years of HRM experience and a related bachelor's degree or one year of HRM experience and a related graduate degree.
- *Senior Professional in Human Resources.* Eight years of professional HRM experience or six years of HRM experience and a related bachelor's degree or five years of HRM experience and a related graduate degree; the most recent three years of experience must include policy-developing responsibility.

In addition to meeting the education and experience requirements, applicants must pass an intensive, four-hour examination to demonstrate mastery of the var-

FIGURE 1.5 Organization Charts for Typical Human Resource Departments

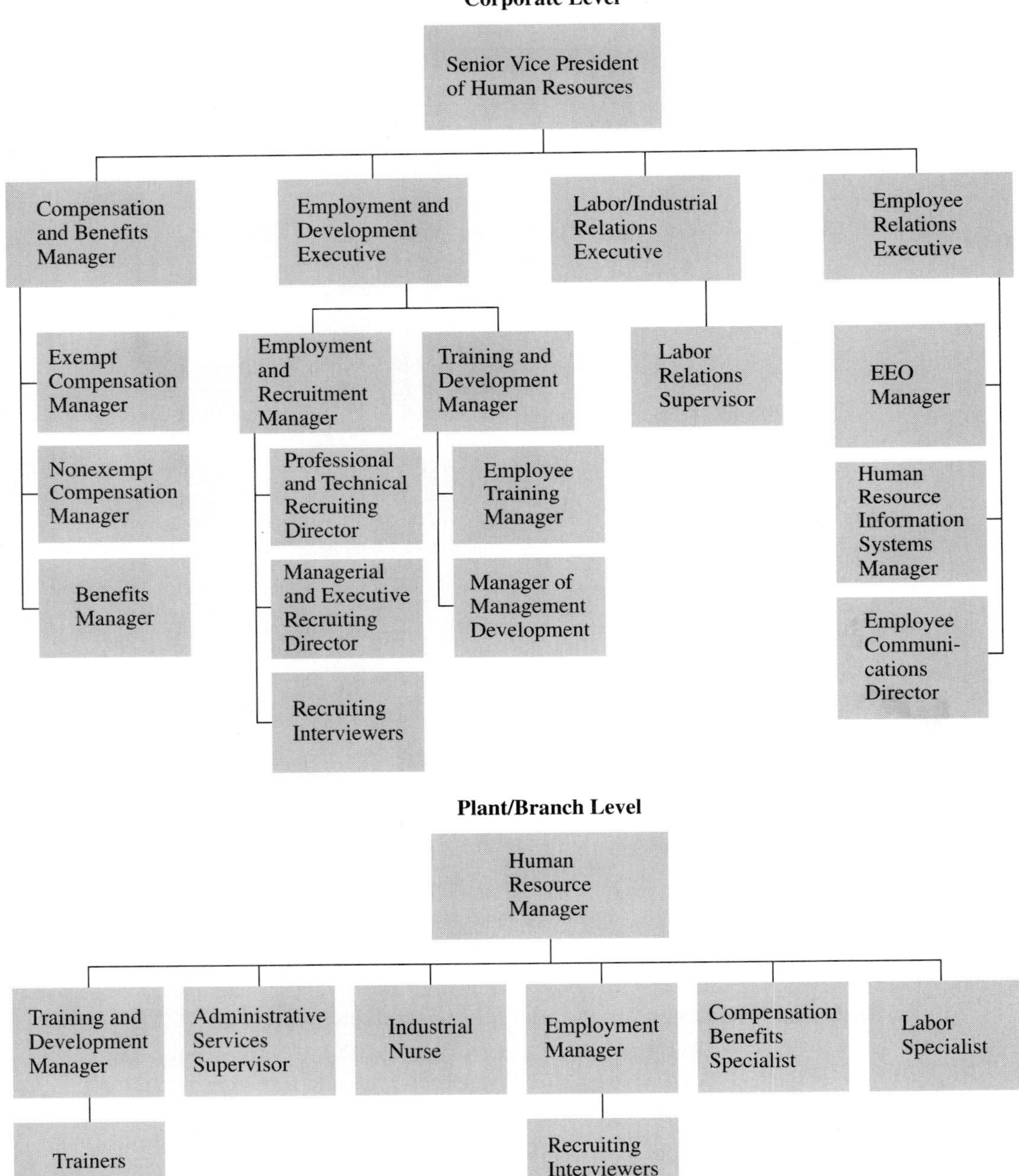

ious types of knowledge. The certifications serve largely to indicate the qualifications of the recipients and ensure the professionalization of the HR field.

SUMMARY OF KEY POINTS

Human resource managers perform an identifiable set of activities that affect and influence the people who work in an organization. These activities include HR planning, job analysis, recruitment, selection, placement, career management, training, designing performance appraisal and compensation systems, and labor relations.

The current challenge of human resource management is to integrate programs involving human resources with strategic organizational objectives. More and more, organizations are under tremendous competitive pressure worldwide. HR managers must find ways to develop effective international programs to meet this challenge. Another important aspect of human resource management is the need to ensure the cost-effectiveness of programs and policies through the optimal utilization of human resources.

Since the HR department plays a support role within the organization, it interacts with a variety of constituencies. It is important to note that the needs of these constituencies are likely to vary. Research offers a useful framework for understanding the conflicting demands on HR professionals.

The challenges to human resource management in the 1990s will involve setting directions and formulating policies to address current and future business trends. The challenges of corporate reorganizations, global competition, declining markets, increasing diversity in the work force, employee expectations, and legal and governmental requirements will allow HR managers to play a dynamic and pivotal role in meeting organizational goals.

Career opportunities are many and varied. The entry-level position is often that of technical specialist. In this role, one would assume responsibility for handling and coordinating well-defined HR programs in a single area. Progression would be to HR manager, a generalist responsible for administering programs across activity areas. The final step would be that of HR executive. In this role, one assumes responsibility for overseeing major areas of activity and for integrating organizational and HR objectives.

Questions for Discussion

1. Describe the major types of HRM activities.
2. Think of the jobs you have had in the past or expect to seek in the future. What two features of this employment did you (or will you) value most? How can HRM activities contribute to the presence and success of these employment features?
3. In what ways has increased international competitiveness influenced human resource management? What types of organizational changes have resulted from

increased international competition, and how has the field of human resource management helped achieve these changes?

4. What are some of the HR considerations in the success of international joint ventures?
5. A company is considering a major business decision to open a new plant. What are some of the HR considerations that need to be factored into the decision?
6. Describe the major constituencies served by the HR function. Why and to what extent do the constituencies differ in the activities they consider most important?
7. What are some of the factors that have increased the organizational status of the HR function?
8. What do you think are the two most important challenges to HR managers in the next five years? Why did you pick these two?
9. What type of careers are available in human resource management? What kinds of entry-level positions are available? What should an individual do to prepare for a career in HRM?
10. Based on your own part-time or full-time work experiences, how could the HR function be improved?
11. What problems does the need to justify activities on a cost/benefit perspective pose for HRM?
12. How does the HR function become involved with business ethics concerns in the organization?

EXERCISE 1.1

Human Resource Management in the News

Divide the class into groups of three or four students each. Assign one of the following nine sources to each group:

Business Magazines *Business Week* (last three months); *Fortune* (last three months); *Harvard Business Review* (last six issues)

Newspapers (last two weeks): *The Wall Street Journal, The New York Times* or other major daily, local newspaper

News Magazines (last three months): *Time, U.S. News & World Report, Newsweek*

Each group is to go to the library and search their assigned source for

1. articles directly relevant to HRM, such as layoffs, union activities, recruiting and selection practices, employment law developments, compensation practices, training and development programs, productivity improvement techniques, turnover, performance appraisal, discipline and discharge, and so forth.

2. articles about aspects of the environment which have indirect implications for HRM, such as changing social values, demographics, technological change, trends in the economy, and so on.

Each group of students should then organize its materials and prepare an oral summary of what it has found. (Flip chart pads and/or blank overhead transparencies and markers should be made available to students in each group as they prepare their presentation.)

International Option Additional groups may be assigned to search recent English language publications in a specific country or geographical region. Their task would be to look for articles related to human resource management that might be of interest to a multinational organization with operations in the target country or region. Examples of sources and regions are given below:

Europe *London Times, International Herald Tribune,* Major English language dailies in France, Germany, Spain, and other countries

Pacific Rim *Asian Wall Street Journal, Far Eastern Economic Review,* Major English language dailies in Tokyo, Hong Kong, Taiwan, Singapore, and Seoul

Australia *The Australian* (newspaper), *Business Review Weekly*

Presentation Option 1: Time permitting, each group will make a five- to seven-minute presentation of its findings to the entire class.

Presentation Option 2: Combine groups into triads (quartets if international groups were formed), each triad consisting of a newspaper group, a business magazine group, and a news magazine group (and an international group). Each triad (quartet) should move to a separate room (or a corner of the classroom). Then each group should present its summary to the other groups in the triad (quartet).

EXERCISE 1.2

Jobs in Human Resource Management

Form the class into groups of four to five students each. Read the brief descriptions of different human resource management jobs given below.[46] In groups, discuss the following questions:

1. Which job does each of you prefer, and why?
2. What do you see as the advantages and disadvantages of each job?
3. What skills, experience, and formal education would be needed to do each job well?
4. How do you suppose that each job has changed in the past thirty years? How might each change further between now and 2010?

5. How might each job be different (or would it even exist) in
   a. a medium sized company in a lesser developed country?
   b. a state-owned enterprise in a communist country with a centrally controlled economy?

MANAGER, PERSONNEL (alternate titles: MANAGER, HUMAN RESOURCES)
Plans and carries out policies relating to all phases of personnel activity: Recruits, interviews, and selects employees to fill vacant positions. Plans and conducts new employee orientation to foster positive attitude toward company goals. Keeps record of insurance coverage, pension plan, and personnel transactions, such as hires, promotions, transfers, and terminations. Investigates accidents and prepares reports for insurance carrier. Conducts wage survey within labor market to determine competitive wage rate. Prepares budget of personnel operations. Meets with shop stewards and supervisors to resolve grievances. Writes separation notices for employees separating with cause and conducts exit interviews to determine reasons behind separations. Prepares reports and recommends procedures to reduce absenteeism and turnover. Represents company at personnel-related hearings and investigations. Contracts with outside suppliers to provide employee services, such as canteen, transportation, or relocation service. May prepare budget of personnel operations, using computer terminal. May administer manual and dexterity tests to applicants. May supervise clerical workers. May keep records of hired employee characteristics for governmental reporting purposes. May negotiate collective bargaining agreement with BUSINESS REPRESENTATIVE, LABOR UNION.

MANAGER, COMPENSATION (alternate titles: WAGE AND SALARY ADMINISTRATOR)
Manages compensation program in establishment: Directs development and application of techniques of job analysis, job descriptions, evaluations, grading, and pricing in order to determine and record job factors and to determine and convert relative job worth into monetary values to be administered according to pay-scale guidelines and policy. Analyzes company compensation policies, government regulations concerning payment of minimum wages and overtime pay, prevailing rates in similar organizations and industries, and agreements with labor unions, in order to comply with legal requirements and to establish competitive rates designed to attract, retain, and motivate employees. Recommends compensation adjustments according to findings, utilizing knowledge of prevailing rates of straight-time pay, types of wage incentive systems, and special compensation programs for professional, technical, sales, supervisory, managerial, and executive personnel. Approves merit increases permitted within budgetary limits and according to pay policies. Duties may also include administration of employee benefits program.

MANAGER, EMPLOYMENT (alternate titles: EMPLOYMENT SUPERVISOR)
Manages employment activities of establishment: Plans and directs activities of staff workers concerned with such functions as developing sources of qualified applicants, conducting screening interviews, administering tests, checking references and background, evaluating applicants' qualifications, and arranging for preliminary indoctrination and training for newly hired employees. Keep records and compiles statistical reports concerning recruitments, interviews, hires, transfers, promotions, terminations, and performance appraisals, utilizing knowledge of job requirements, valid se-

lection processes, and legislation concerning equal employment practices. Coordinates employment activities, such as those concerned with preparing job requisitions; interviewing, selecting, and hiring candidates; on-the-job indoctrination and additional training; supervisory follow-up, development, and rating of employees; and conducting exit interviews. Analyzes statistical data and other reports concerning all aspects of employment function in order to identify and determine causes of personnel problems and to develop and present recommendations for improvement of establishment's employment policies, processes, and practices.

MANAGER, LABOR RELATIONS (alternate titles: LABOR RELATIONS REPRESENTATIVE)
Manages labor relations program of organization: Analyzes collective bargaining agreement to develop interpretation of intent, spirit, and terms of contract. Advises management and union officials in development, application, and interpretation of labor relations policies and practices, according to policy formulated by DIRECTOR, INDUSTRIAL RELATIONS. Arranges and schedules meetings between grieving workers, supervisory and managerial personnel, and BUSINESS REPRESENTATIVE, LABOR UNION, to investigate and resolve grievances. Prepares statistical reports, using records of actions taken concerning grievances, arbitration and mediation cases, and related labor relations activities, to identify problem areas. Monitors implementation of policies concerning wages, hours, and working conditions, to ensure compliance with terms of labor contract. Furnishes information, such as reference documents and statistical data concerning labor legislation, labor market conditions, prevailing union and management practices, wage and salary surveys, and employee benefits programs, for use in review of current contract provisions and proposed changes. May represent management in labor contract negotiations. May supervise employees and be known as Labor Relations Supervisor. May be employed by firm offering labor relations advisory services to either management or labor and be known as Labor Relations Consultant. May be employed by governmental agency to study, interpret, and report on relations between management and labor and be known as Industrial Relations Representative.

TRAINING REPRESENTATIVE (alternate titles: TRAINING INSTRUCTOR)
Develops and conducts training programs for employees of industrial, commercial, service, or government establishment: Confers with management to gain knowledge of work situation requiring training for employees to better understand changes in policies, procedures, regulations, and technologies. Formulates teaching outline and determines instructional methods, utilizing knowledge of specific training needs and effectiveness of such methods as individual training, group instruction, lectures, demonstrations, conferences, meetings, and workshops. Selects or develops teaching aids, such as training handbooks, demonstration models, multimedia visual aids, computer tutorials, and reference works. Conducts training sessions covering specified areas such as those concerned with new employee orientation, on-the-job training, use of computers and software, apprenticeship programs, sales techniques, health and safety practices, public relations, refresher training, promotional development, upgrading, retraining displaced workers, and leadership development. Tests trainees to measure progress and to evaluate effectiveness of training. May specialize in developing instructional software.

EMPLOYMENT INTERVIEWER (alternate titles: PERSONNEL INTERVIEWER; PLACEMENT INTERVIEWER)
Interviews job applicants to select people meeting employer qualifications: Reviews employment applications and evaluates work history, education and training, job skills, compensation needs, and other qualifications of applicants. Records additional knowledge, skills, abilities, interests, test results, and other data pertinent to selection and referral of applicants. Reviews job orders and matches applicants with job requirements, utilizing manual or computerized file search. Informs applicants of job duties and responsibilities, compensation and benefits, work schedules and working conditions, company and union policies, promotional opportunities, and other related information. Refers selected applicants to person placing job order, according to policy of organization. Keeps records of applicants not selected for employment. May perform reference and background checks on applicants. May refer applicants to vocational counseling services. May conduct or arrange for skills, intelligence, or psychological testing of applicants. May evaluate selection and placement techniques by conducting research or follow-up activities and conferring with management and supervisory personnel. May specialize in interviewing and referring certain types of personnel, such as professional, technical, managerial, clerical, and other types of skilled or unskilled workers. May search for and recruit applicants for open positions. May contact employers in writing, in person, or by telephone to solicit orders for job vacancies for clientele or for specified applicants and record information about job openings on job order forms to describe duties, hiring requirements, and related data.

JOB ANALYST (alternate titles: PERSONNEL ANALYST)
Collects, analyzes, and prepares occupational information to facilitate personnel, administration, and management functions of organization: Consults with management to determine type, scope, and purpose of study. Studies current organizational occupational data and compiles distribution reports, organization and flow charts, and other background information required for study. Observes jobs and interviews workers and supervisory personnel to determine job and worker requirements. Analyzes occupational data, such as physical, mental, and training requirements of jobs and workers and develops written summaries, such as job descriptions, job specifications, and lines of career movement. Utilizes developed occupational data to evaluate or improve methods and techniques for recruiting, selecting, promoting, evaluating, and training workers, and administration of related personnel programs. May specialize in classifying positions according to regulated guidelines to meet job classification requirements of civil service system and be known as Position Classifier.

Notes and References

1. "Can John Akers Save IBM?" *Fortune,* July 15, 1991, pp. 40–56; "The New IBM: Is It New Enough?" *Business Week,* December 16, 1991, pp. 112–118.
2. Robert Levering, Milton Moskowitz, and Michael Katz, *The 100 Best Companies to Work for in America* (Reading, Mass.: Addison-Wesley, 1985), pp. 11–14.
3. "But Can It Leap Tall Buildings?" *Business Week,* December 23, 1991, p. 94.
4. "What's Ailing Big Blue?" *Business Week,* June 17, 1991, pp. 24–32.
5. Thomas Peters and Robert Waterman, *In Search of Excellence* (New York: Harper & Row, 1982), pp. 3–26.

6. Levering, Moskowitz, and Katz, *The 100 Best Companies*, pp. 389–391; Robert Levering, *A Great Place to Work: What Makes Some Employers So Good (and Most So Bad)* (New York: Avon, 1988), pp. 128–129.
7. Randall S. Schuler, "Repositioning the Human Resource Function: Transformation or Demise?" *Academy of Management Executive*, 1990, pp. 49–60.
8. James W. Walker and Gregory Moorhead, "CEO's: What They Want from HRM," *Personnel Administrator*, December 1987, pp. 50–59.
9. "The Workers of the Future," *Fortune*, Spring/Summer 1991, pp. 68–72.
10. "Smart Moves by Quality Champs," *Fortune*, Spring/Summer 1991, pp. 24–28.
11. H. G. Heneman III, "Pay Satisfaction," in K. Rowland and J. Ferris (eds.), *Research in Personnel and Human Resources Management*, vol. 3 (Greenwich, Conn.: JAI Press, 1985).
12. R. W. Scholl, E. A. Cooper, and J. F. McKenna, "Referent Selection in Determining Equity Perceptions: Differential Effects on Behavioral and Attitudinal Outcomes," *Personnel Psychology*, vol. 40, 1987, pp. 113–124.
13. William H. Mobley, R. W. Griffith, H. H. Hand, and B. M. Meglino, "Review and Conceptual Analysis of Employee Turnover Process," *Psychological Bulletin*, Vol. 16, (1979) pp. 493–522.
14. M. L. Marks and P. Mirvis, "Merger Syndrome: Stress and Uncertainty," *Mergers and Acquisitions*, Summer 1985, pp. 50–55.
15. G. Odiorne, "HRM Policy and Program Management: A New Look at the 1980s," in *Human Resources Management in the 1980s*, ed. S. J. Carroll and R. S. Schuler (Washington, D.C.: Bureau of National Affairs, 1983).
16. Jean M. McEnery and Mark L. Lifter, "Demands for Change: Interfacing Environmental Pressures and the Personnel Process," *Public Personnel Management*, Spring 1987, pp. 61–87.
17. "McWorld?" *Business Week*, October 13, 1986, pp. 78–86.
18. L. M. Cheek, "Cost Effectiveness Comes to the Personnel Function," *Harvard Business Review*, May–June 1973, pp. 96–105.
19. John Ladd, "Morality and the Ideal of Rationality in Formal Organizations," in *Ethical Issues in Business*, ed. Thomas Donaldson and Patricia H. Werhane, 3rd ed. (Englewood Cliffs, N.J.: Prentice-Hall, 1988), pp. 110–122.
20. Kenneth Goodpaster and John B. Matthews, Sr., "Can a Corporation Have a Conscience?" *Harvard Business Review*, January–February 1982, pp. 132–141.
21. Anne S. Tsui and George T. Milkovich, "Personnel Department Activities: Constituency Perspectives and Preferences," *Personnel Psychology*, Autumn 1987, pp. 519–537.
22. Ibid., p. 535.
23. *The American Heritage Dictionary* (Boston, Mass.: Houghton Mifflin, 1985).
24. Gerald R. Ferris and Thomas R. King, "Politics in Human Resources Decisions: Walk on the Dark Side," *Organizational Dynamics*, Winter 1991, pp. 59–71.
25. Gerald R. Ferris and Timothy A. Judge, "Personnel/Human Resources Management: A Political Influence Perspective," *Journal of Management*, 1991, pp. 447–488.
26. Ferris and King, "Politics in Human Resources Decisions," pp. 59–71; C. O. Longenecker, H. P. Sims, and D. A. Gioia, "Behind the Mask: The Politics of Employee Appraisal," *Academy of Management Executive*, August 1987, pp. 183–193.
27. A New Strain of Merger Mania," *Business Week*, March 21, 1988, pp. 122–126.
28. Robert M. Tomasko, *Downsizing: Restructuring the Corporation for the Future* (New York: American Management Association, 1987); "The Age of Consolidation," *Business Week*, October 14, 1991, pp. 86–94.
29. David M. Schweiger, John M. Ivancevich, and Frank R. Power, "Executive Actions for Managing Human Resources Before and After Acquisition," *Academy of Management Executive*, May 1987, pp. 127–138; Cynthia D. Fisher, "Current and Recurrent Challenges in HRM," *Journal of Management*, 1989, pp. 157–180.

30. M. L. Marks, "Merging Human Resources: A Review of Current Research," *Mergers and Acquisitions,* Summer 1982, pp. 38–44; "Downsizing Affects Style, Not Just Size, WAI Hears," *Work in America,* 1987, No. 7, pp. 1–2.

31. *1991 Survey of Human Resources Trends* (Grosse Point, Mich.: HRStrategies, 1991), p. 18.

32. John Naisbitt, *Megatrends* (New York: Warner Books, 1982), pp. 55–77.

33. *1991 Survey of Human Resources Trends,* p. 18.

34. Joseph F. Coates, Jennifer Jarratt, and John B. Mahaffie, *Future Work: Seven Critical Forces Reshaping Work and the Work Force in North America* (San Francisco: Jossey-Bass, 1990), pp. 248–256; regarding plant closings, see also "GM Slices and GM Slashes, but the Flab Survives," *Business Week,* December 23, 1991, p. 27; and "Can GM Remodel Itself?" *Fortune,* January 13, 1992, pp. 26–34.

35. U.S. Department of Commerce, Bureau of the Census, *Statistical Abstract of the United States, 1989* (Washington, D.C.: U.S. Government Printing Office, 1989).

36. U.S. Senate Select Committee on Aging, *Aging America: Trends and Projections,* 1987–1988 (Washington, D.C.: U.S. Department of Health and Human Services, 1988).

37. Frank P. Doyle, "People-Power: The Global Human Resource Challenge for the '90s," *Columbia Journal of World Business,* Spring/Summer 1990, pp. 36–45.

38. Peter A. Morrison, "Families and the Workplace: Changing Demographic Realities," *Outlook,* February 1988, pp. 1–6.

39. Coates, Jarratt, and Mahaffie, *Future Work,* pp. 99–109.

40. Alvin Toffler, *The Third Wave* (New York: Bantam, 1981).

41. David Ulrich, Wayne Brockbank, and Arthur Yeung, "HR Competencies in the 1990s," *Personnel Administrator,* November 1989, pp. 91–93.

42. Audrey Freedman, *The Changing Human Resources Function* (New York: The Conference Board, 1990).

43. "They're Making it Big in Human Resources," *The Wall Street Journal,* December 20, 1991, p. B1.

44. Kirkland Ropp, "HR Management for All It's Worth," *Personnel Administrator,* September 1987, pp. 34–40, 120–121.

45. Raymond B. Weinbert, Robert L. Mathis, and David J. Cherrington, *Certification Study Guide* (Alexandria, Va.: Human Resource Certification Institute, 1991).

46. These descriptions are from the *Dictionary of Occupational Titles,* 4th ed., rev. (Washington, D.C.: U.S. Department of Labor, 1991), pp. 108–109, 110, 111.

occupational and industry trends are highlighted next, with emphasis given to how these factors affect organizations. The final section of the chapter describes how planners can take potential shortages and surpluses into account to plan human resource programs and address the career needs and goals of employees.

WHAT IS HUMAN RESOURCE PLANNING?

A Basic Definition

An organization would not build a new plant, conduct the ribbon-cutting ceremony, and then begin to worry about how to staff the facility. A firm cannot hire several hundred engineers and get them on board overnight; nor can it develop management talent in just a few weeks. Foresight is necessary to ensure that appropriate staffing will be available for an organization's future plans. Likewise, in a declining economy, planning ahead is critical to prevent overstaffing and the subsequent need for layoffs. In its broadest form, **human resource planning** is concerned with the flow of people into, through, and out of an organization. HR planning necessarily involves a focus on employees' changing skill levels and the way in which those skills match organizational needs. The following is a traditional definition of HR planning:

> Human resource planning is the process through which organizational goals, as put forth in mission statements and business plans, are translated into human resource objectives concerning staffing levels and flow rates and, from these, into an integrated set of personnel policies and programs. Human resource planning helps to assure that organizations are neither over- nor understaffed, that the right employees are placed in the right jobs at the right time, that organizational and environmental change is anticipated and adjusted to with a minimum of cost, and that there is direction and coherence to personnel activities.[1]

Strategic Human Resource Planning

The above definition takes organizational plans and goals as a given and concerns itself with providing the people needed to carry out those plans. In most organizations, HR planning (if it occurs at all) follows this traditional approach. However, more recent conceptualizations of **strategic human resource planning** emphasize a proactive role for the HR function, as a partner in formulating strategic organizational plans, as well as providing HR programs to best ensure effective implementation of those plans.[2]

HR planners at AT&T's Business Markets Group recently began a process of integrating HR planning with strategic planning. They identified four trend areas (technological innovations, legal and regulatory changes, demographic and social changes, and globalization) that are expected to influence staffing requirements and availability for their group in the coming decade. HR planners are working closely with AT&T management to develop the HR programs needed for this organization to achieve its strategic goals in a changing environment.[3]

Many organizations that engage in some human resource forecasting do not yet have a system for *strategic* human resource planning.[4] There is some evidence that a firm's environment may affect the degree to which HR planning activities are integrated with strategic planning. Organizations that exist in unstable environments, face stiff competition, and have experienced staffing difficulties are more likely to involve HR planners in the corporate strategic planning process. Involvement also seems to be greater when the top HR person reports directly to the CEO, has past line experience to provide credibility and a broad view of the business, and is backed up with an excellent human resource information system (HRIS) that produces the type of information needed in the strategic planning process.[5]

A Model for Human Resource Planning

The first step in any form of HR planning is to collect information. A forecast or plan cannot be any better than the data on which it is based. HR planning requires two types of information: data from the external environment and data from inside the organization[6] (see Figure 3.1). Data from the external environment include information on current conditions and predicted changes in the general economy, the economy of the specific industry, the relevant technology, and the competition. Any of these factors may affect the organization's business plans and thus the need for human resources. Furthermore, planners must be aware of labor market conditions such as unemployment rates, skill availabilities, and the age, race, and sex distributions of the labor force. Finally, planners need to be aware of federal and state regulations: those that directly affect staffing practices, such as affirmative action or retirement-age legislation, and those that indirectly affect requisite staffing levels. An example of the latter might be environmental protection rules that increase the need for in-house environmental specialists to monitor compliance with the rules.

Consider the case of a large, state-supported four-year university. What kind of information about the external environment should the university have for HR forecasting? Clearly, the need for faculty and support staff depends heavily on enrollment, so the university's HR planners must learn all they can about present enrollment, recent enrollment trends, and the projected sizes of high school graduating classes in the state. The planners will also want to know about environmental factors that may affect the number of graduates continuing on to college, such as economic conditions in the state and the availability of low-cost student loans. Furthermore, the planners will need information about their competitors. Will a new community college be opening? Will other four-year institutions in the state be attracting a larger- or smaller-than-usual share of college-bound students? Planners might also wish to look at the availability of new faculty and staff in the labor market. If the university needs more staff members, will it be able to find qualified applicants for the openings?

The second major type of necessary information comes from inside the organization. Internal information includes short- and long-term organizational

FIGURE 3.1 Human Resource Planning Model

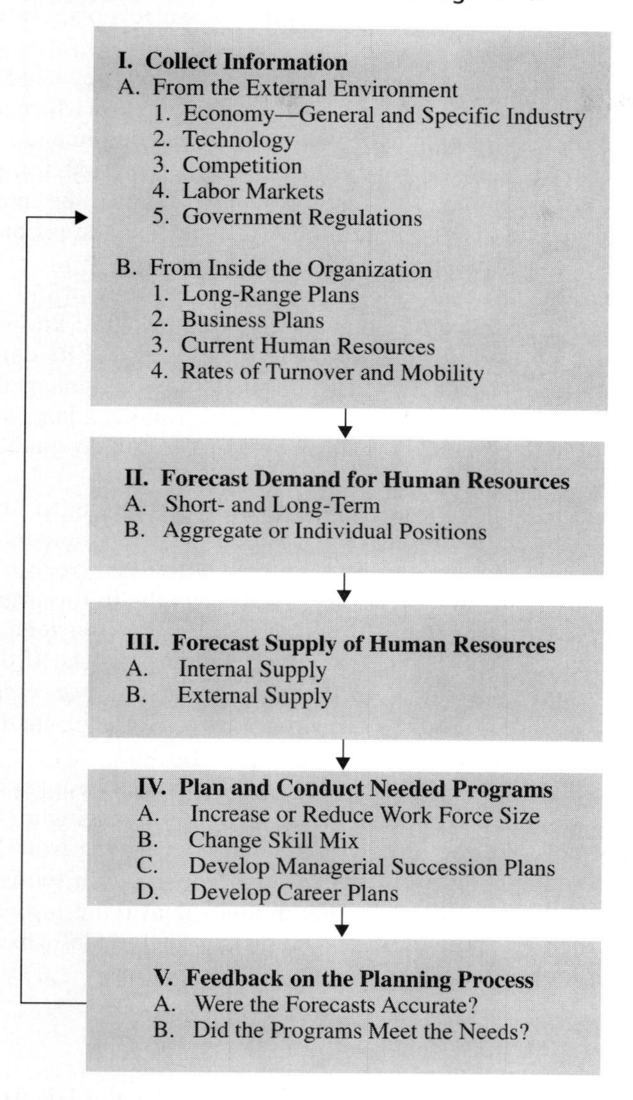

plans. Obviously, plans to build, close, or automate facilities will have HR implications, as will plans to modify the organization's structure, buy or sell businesses, and enter or withdraw from markets. Information is also needed on the current state of human resources in the organization, such as how many individuals are employed in each job and location and how many are expected to leave or retire during the forecast period.

The university's planners will need to know about internal plans to add or eliminate departments or degree programs, build new dorms, or change admission standards. They will also need to gather data on the current level of staffing in each job, as well as anticipated retirements and average turnover rates among different categories of employees.

Once planners have the external and internal information they need, they can forecast the future **demand** for employees. At a minimum, this forecasting includes estimating the number of employees who will be needed in each job in the coming year. Longer-term demand forecasts may also be made for particular points in the future. Next, planners forecast the **supply** of labor: the internal supply of employees and their skills and promotability, as well as the probable availability of various types of people in the external labor market.

HR planners can also forecast different scenarios for the various strategies they are considering. For instance, top management may wish to know the magnitude of the expected job loss if a plant were to be closed and its capacity, together with some employees, transferred to another facility. Management may also want to know the feasibility and cost of hiring and training a large number of new employees in order to expand operations or shift to a high-quality service strategy.

The final step in HR planning is to plan specific programs to ensure that supply will match demand in the future. These programs often include recruiting plans and may also include training and development activities, incentives or disincentives to early retirement, modifications of career paths in the organization, or a variety of other HR management programs. Note that the feedback loop shown in Figure 3.1 allows for learning from past planning efforts. If demand or supply forecasts were not as accurate as desired, forecasting processes can be improved in subsequent years. Similarly, if programs prove to be inadequate or inappropriate, they can be modified.

Recently, some scholars have criticized this systematic, linear model of HR planning as being too slow and cumbersome for a rapidly changing and less predictable world. They describe the ideal HR planner as a roving troubleshooter, identifying and even anticipating problems through consultation with line managers and then solving the problems. In this model, identifying issues that are causing a problem is the first step; additional steps may include information gathering, short- and long-term forecasting, and planning programs.[7]

Who Plans?

Traditional HR planning is usually initiated and managed by the HR department. However, since information is needed from all parts of the organization, line managers must be involved in the HR planning process, with some planning methods requiring more manager involvement than others. Strategic HR planning involves top management as well as HR experts and may rely on information from many levels of management.

Not all organizations engage in HR forecasting and planning, though more and more are doing so each year. One survey found that only 60 percent of the companies responding reported that they engaged in HR forecasting of any sort.[8]

As with many other HR activities, larger firms are more likely than smaller firms to have HR planning systems.[9] Because of the large number of individuals involved, the military leads in the development of sophisticated HR planning systems.

Who Is Planned For?

In designing a human resource planning system, there are several choices regarding whom to plan for. One choice is to plan at the aggregate level, for jobs or job families. This type of planning is typically used for jobs with multiple incumbents and for jobs at or below the middle-management level. An organization may forecast that 35 electrical engineers will be needed at the California development laboratory or that a total of 540 semiskilled assemblers will be needed in the whole organization. The focus is on the number of persons needed for a particular job, not on specific individuals who will fill the positions.

Many large organizations plan for each job, but this may not always be necessary. The alternative is to plan for only those jobs that logic or experience indicate are problematic. For instance, a large hospital may need to plan carefully for pharmacists and nurses if there is a chronic shortage of these professionals. But the hospital may find that it does not need to engage in long-range planning for janitors or food service personnel if they can be hired and trained quickly when demand increases.

In addition to aggregate planning—or instead of it—many organizations plan at the individual level. For important jobs, particularly upper-management positions, these organizations identify specific employees who are likely successors when a position becomes vacant due to promotion or retirement. A succession plan for a top managerial position might identify from one to three possible replacements and specify the additional training each needs to become fully qualified for that position at some point in the future.

When Is Planning Done?

Usually, an organization mounts a major planning effort once a year, but modifications can be made on the basis of new information throughout the year. For instance, an unexpected recession certainly would indicate that near-term recruiting plans should be reconsidered. The appearance of a problem or new issue in staffing may also trigger the need for further planning.

The planning process can focus on one of several time horizons. For example, organizations at the elementary stage of development of the HR planning function typically plan for the short term—just one year in advance and with particular emphasis on recruiting needs. Organizations with more experience in HR planning and more complex needs might also plan for the intermediate term—two to three years out. Some organizations engage in long-range HR planning—more than three years into the future. Plans for executive succession often incorporate these longer time horizons.[10]

FORECASTING THE DEMAND FOR LABOR

Once the HR planners have collected information from both internal and external sources, they next forecast the demand for labor. How many and what type of people will be needed to carry out the organization's plans in the future? These forecasts are grounded in information about the past and present and in assumptions about the future. Different methods of forecasting the demand for labor require different assumptions. Some of the more common assumptions are that past trends and relationships among variables will hold up in the future, that the productivity ratio is constant (or follows a specified curve) as the number of units produced increases, and that the business plans of the organization, sales forecasts, and so on are reasonably descriptive of what will actually happen. In a highly volatile business, these assumptions may not be valid. It is always wise to list explicitly one's assumptions in forecasting and to put no more faith in the forecast than in the assumptions on which it was based.

Demand forecasting methods can be divided into two categories: judgmental and mathematical. In practice, most organizations use some combination of the two methods. For example, expert judges might estimate the values of some variables and then use these values in prediction equations; or experts might integrate the results of mathematical methods with less quantifiable information into a final forecast.

Judgmental Methods

Judgmental methods make use of knowledgeable people to forecast the future. Judgmental methods do consider quantitative data but allow for intuition and expertise to be factored in as well. These methods may be used by small organizations or by those new to HR forecasting who do not yet have the database or expertise to use some of the more complex mathematical models. Judgmental methods may also be preferred when an organization or environment is in a state of transition or turmoil; at such times, past trends and correlations cannot be used to make accurate predictions about the future.

Perhaps the simplest judgmental method is **bottom-up,** or **unit, forecasting**: each unit, branch, or department estimates its own future need for employees. Ideally, managers receive some guidance and information, which they combine with their own perspectives to reach the estimates. The sum of the estimated unit needs is the demand forecast for the whole organization. HR planners may wish to review the unit forecasts carefully before summing, in order to control managers' natural tendencies to exaggerate the needed size and importance of their units.[11]

Houston Lighting and Power has developed a spread-sheet-based bottom-up planning system that provides line managers with information on present staffing levels in the job classes they supervise, asks for estimated changes in workload and productivity, and requests estimates of HR needs in each of the next five years. The estimates are approved by the next level of management and then forwarded to the HR planning group, which integrates them into an organization-wide forecast.[12]

Another judgmental method involves **"top-down" forecasting** by experienced top managers and executives. These experts meet to discuss how trends, business plans, the economy, and other factors will affect the need for human resources at various levels of the organization. Besides predicting the most likely future demand, these experts may also make separate forecasts based on best and worst case scenarios. For instance, they might forecast what the need for labor will be if almost everything that could go wrong does go wrong (a recession; the organization loses the product liability suit now being tried; the company does not land the government contract it has bid for). After completing such exercises, the experts can be fairly certain that the actual demand for labor will fall somewhere in between their best and worst case predictions. Many of the mathematical forecasting methods also lend themselves to this type of what-if assessment.

One highly structured judgmental method of expert forecasting utilizes the **Delphi technique** to achieve group consensus on a forecast.[13] In using this technique, the experts do not meet face to face. This is more economical if they are assigned to different locations; it can also improve the quality of decision making by minimizing disruptive personality conflicts and preventing the loudest group member from dominating the decision process. The first step in the Delphi process is to develop an anonymous questionnaire that asks the experts for an opinion and why they hold that opinion. The results of this questionnaire are compiled and returned to the experts, along with a second anonymous questionnaire. In this way, the experts can learn from each other and modify or elaborate their positions in the second questionnaire. The process continues through several more rounds until the experts agree on a judgment.

In one published test of the Delphi technique, a national retail company predicted the number of buyers needed in one year. The experts were seven managers, who responded to five rounds of questionnaires. In the first round, estimates ranged from thirty-two to fifty-five buyers. By the fifth round, estimates narrowed to between thirty-four and forty-five buyers, with a mean of thirty-eight. The Delphi predictions were not made public or used in recruitment planning that year so that the company could evaluate their accuracy compared with actual end-of-year staffing levels. At the end of the year, thirty-seven buyers were actually employed. The Delphi method proved to be much more accurate than three simple mathematical models also applied to the same buyer forecasting problem.[14]

A complete Delphi process utilizing several rounds of anonymous questionnaires may take months to complete, so this method is not appropriate if results are needed quickly. As with any expert forecasting method, participants should be knowledgeable about the topic. Their existing knowledge can be supplemented by providing information on past and current staffing, business performance, business plans, and the like.

Simple Mathematical Methods

The simplest mathematical methods of forecasting utilize only one factor to predict demand. For example, to predict the need for labor, one could examine staffing levels during the last few years, note the trend, and extend this trend to the upcoming year. A better method would be to use forecasts of the coming year's sales, production, or another business factor related to the need for labor. This information would then be combined with productivity ratios to predict the number of direct labor employees needed.[15]

The **productivity ratio** is the average number of units produced per direct labor employee per year. Suppose a company produces sofas and knows from past history that the productivity ratio is about fifty sofas per furniture assembler per year. If the marketing department expects to sell 10,000 sofas in the coming year, then the company needs 10,000 / 50 = 200 furniture assemblers.

Direct-to-indirect-labor **staffing ratios** are used to calculate the number of individuals required in other jobs. For instance, if the sofa firm generally has one supervisor for every twenty-five assemblers, then eight supervisors will be needed for two hundred assemblers. Past experience may also show that three shipping-and-receiving clerks are required for every fifty assemblers. This means that the company needs a total of twelve clerks.

Productivity and staffing ratios based on historical data may be modified judgmentally if the ratios are expected to change. For instance, if the union has negotiated a new contract requiring 30-minute-shorter workdays and more paid holidays, the expected productivity ratio should be adjusted downward. If labor-saving personal computers will be installed for the clerks, the staffing ratio may change, with fewer clerks needed to service the same number of direct workers.

Forecasting with productivity ratios is based on the assumption that the number of employees needed increases linearly with the amount of work to be done. This assumption is not always correct. Envision, for example, a company that has handled increasing demand for its product by having employees work overtime. However, at some point, the company will not be able to cope with increasing sales in this way and may decide to add a second shift or open a new plant. At that juncture, a big jump in staffing will occur, resulting in a discontinuous relationship between output and labor demand.

An elaboration of forecasting based on productivity ratio involves the use of **learning curves**. The assumption underlying learning curves is that the productivity ratio changes with experience. That is, it increases as more and more units are produced after an initial start-up period.[16] The increase occurs because workers are learning to do repetitive operations more efficiently, the whole organization is developing better procedures for scheduling and solving problems with the new product, and the manufacturing department is working the bugs out of the production process.

Historically, learning curve analysis has been used most when organizations build relatively few, large items. Common sense suggests, for instance, that building the second Boeing 767 jetliner probably took substantially less time than building the first one and that the third one could be produced in even less time. Studies of productivity in industries as diverse as automobiles, musical instruments, and apparel all show that following a start-up or model change, labor hours per unit continue to decline (at a decreasing rate) for months and months as efficiency increases.[17] A typical learning curve is displayed in Figure 3.2.

To apply learning curve analysis, planners must calculate the **progress index (PI)** for similar past start-ups. The PI is the percent of learning that occurs each time output is doubled.[18] PIs between 80 and 90 percent are often observed; such PIs indicate that each time the total output since start-up doubles, the number of labor hours for the second half of the production run declines to 80 to 90 percent of the amount needed for the first half of the run.

A different demand forecast method may be suitable for companies that do a great deal of contract work. For these firms, the amount of labor needed depends directly on how many contracts they land. If the firms can calculate the number of people or labor hours needed for each contract, these figures can be multiplied

FIGURE 3.2 Learning Curve with a Progress Index of .80

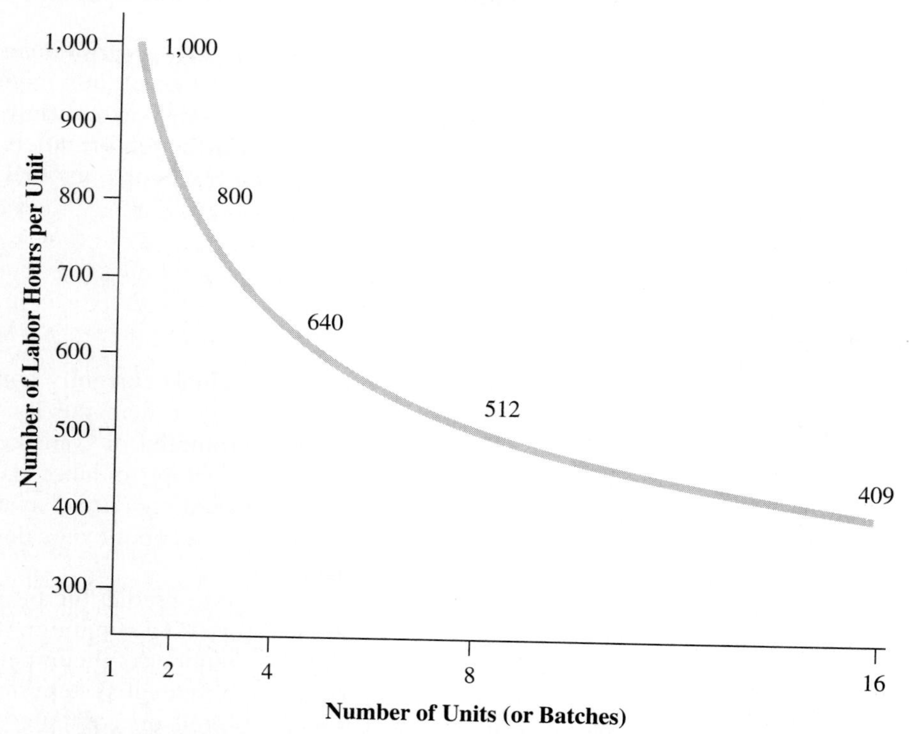

Source: Adaptation of Figure 3-5 from *Personnel Management: Managing Human Resources* by Paul S. Greenlaw and John P. Kohl. Copyright © 1986 by Harper & Row, Publishers, Inc. Reprinted by permission of HarperCollins Publishers.

by the estimated probability of receiving each contract and then summed to estimate the most likely aggregate labor demand figure. Forecasts of this type tend to be accurate only if there are many pending contracts to sum over and if one can correctly estimate the probabilities of receiving various contracts.[19]

Complex Mathematical Methods

Some forecasting methods utilize more complicated statistical techniques. Large organizations with a long history of HR planning are likely to employ these methods. One such method, called **multiple regression**, uses several factors that correlate with labor demand to forecast future demand. Examples of such factors include sales, profits, capital investments, and gross national product (GNP). Historical data are used to derive an equation describing the relationships of these factors to employment levels; then current or predicted values of the factors are inserted into the equation to predict future demand. This method can be applied only when sufficient historical data exist to allow for the derivation of stable regression equations, when fairly strong relationships exist between the factors and labor demand, and when no dramatic changes in productivity or product mix are anticipated.[20]

A second forecasting method employs **linear**, or **goal**, **programming** to determine optimal staffing levels given a set of constraints. Constraints might include compensation budgets, minimum and maximum ratios between various kinds of jobs, or minimum and maximum output figures. Further information on these techniques is available in most operations research textbooks, as well as in the sources listed in the endnote.[21]

THE INTERNAL SUPPLY OF LABOR

The **internal supply of labor** consists of all the individuals currently employed by an organization. These employees can help to fill future demands by remaining employed in their current positions or by being promoted or transferred to fill vacancies elsewhere in the organization. The internal supply of labor is constantly changing as new people enter and others resign, retire, die, or are discharged. The skill mix also changes as people move in and out and as employees develop new skills through training or on-the-job experience.

To keep track of the current internal supply and to predict the future supply, planners need some sort of supply information system. At a minimum, this system may consist of simple staffing tables that show the number of incumbents in each job within the organization. For small companies, a manual system may suffice, but increasingly, employee information is being stored on computers, some of which have very sophisticated retrieval and analysis capabilities. The next sections describe two such systems: skills inventories and human resource information systems.

Skills Inventories

A **skills inventory** is a manual or computerized system designed to keep track of employees' experience, education, and special abilities. The skills inventory information form in Figure 3.3 shows what might appear on a typical skills inventory. The key words describing the specific occupational area (general ledger bookkeeping) and activities performed (supervising) are drawn from a standardized manual developed for the organization. Planners need comparable information about employees, and using standard terminology is the surest way to achieve this goal.

The inventory can be used to assess the current supply of employees of various sorts. For instance, an employer might wish to know how many people are presently working as salespersons, how many people have current or past experience in firefighting, or how many certified professional engineers are employed. The inventory can also be used to identify candidates for promotion or transfer.

FIGURE 3.3 Skills Inventory Information Form

SKILLS INVENTORY

Employee Name: I. M. Nameless
Employee Number: 28036

Date Printed: 1-1-78
Department: 319

KEY WORDS

Word	*Description*	*Activity*
1. Accounting	Tax accounting	Supervising and analyzing
2. Bookkeeping	General ledger	Supervising
3. Auditing	Computer records	Analyzing

WORK EXPERIENCE

	From	*To*	*Description*
1.	1973	1978	Chief Tax Accountant at XYZ Stores
2.	1965	1973	Bookkeeper at XYZ Manufacturing
3.	1964	1965	Auditing Training at XY Bank

EDUCATION

Degree	*Major*	*Year*
1. MBA	Business Administration	1964
2. BS	Accounting	1962

SPECIAL COURSES

Course	*Date*
1. Management theory	1974
2. Business planning	1971
3. Computer audits	1965

MEMBERSHIPS

1. American Accounting Society
2. American Management Association

LICENSES

Name	*Date*
1. CPA	1965

LANGUAGES

Name	*Fluency*
1. Spanish	Fluent
2. French	Read

POSITION PREFERENCE

1. Accounting
2. Auditing

LOCATION PREFERENCE

1. San Francisco
2. San Diego

HOBBIES

1. Bridge
2. Amateur radio
3. Boating

Employee Signature: ____________________
Date: __________

Personnel Department: ____________________
Date: __________

Source: From Richard A. Kaumeyer, Jr., *Planning and Using Skills Inventory Systems* (New York: Van Nostrand Reinhold, 1979). Reprinted by permission.

Suppose a large company has an opening for an experienced petroleum geologist who is willing to relocate and who speaks fluent Arabic. A personnel requisition form that describes the opening will be generated using the same standard key words that are used in the skills inventory. The inventory system will then be able to generate a list of all qualified employees in the organization. The inventory can also help to identify individuals who are ready for particular training or development courses. In addition, through the items on location and position preference, the inventory can ensure that employees' own career plans and wishes are considered when the organization makes transfer or promotion decisions.

Clearly, skills inventories can be very useful tools for assessing the internal supply of labor. Any such system, however, must be accurate and current to be maximally useful. Gathering and updating employee information is a large and critical job. Often initial information is collected by questionnaire. Every year thereafter, employees receive a printout of their information, which they update as needed.[22] In addition, some updates may be made automatically. For instance, a list of attendees at a company-sponsored training program could be merged with a computerized skills inventory to update the records of those who were trained.

The skills inventory systems described in this chapter are somewhat limited in that they do not contain all the information that organizations have on employees.[23] There is an increasing movement toward full-blown, highly integrated human resource information systems that can do much more than simple skills inventory systems.[24]

Human Resource Information Systems

A true **human resource information system (HRIS)** combines in one system all the information that organizations typically keep on employees and on positions. Ordinarily, an HRIS evolves gradually from previously separate and somewhat redundant systems.[25] For instance, an organization may have a computerized skills inventory, a computerized compensation and benefits system, a computerized job/position database used for recruiting, and perhaps manual files of performance appraisal information. These independent systems probably use the computer as a high-speed clerk and nothing more.[26] An HRIS can be formed by combining all these types of employee data into a single database. All job and position information may go into a second, interacting database. The software can then produce regular reports on equal employment opportunity (EEO) and affirmative action (AA), staffing levels and turnover statistics, monthly compensation cost predictions, and the like. HR staff can also make specific inquiries—for instance, how many employees would qualify for an enhanced retirement program? More information about HRISs appears in the inserts following Chapters 8 and 16.

Predicting the Internal Supply of Labor

Given the necessary data in staffing tables, a skills inventory, or a more complex HRIS, HR professionals can predict the internal supply and distribution of labor in the future.

Markov analysis is a fairly simple method of predicting the internal supply of labor at some future time. The heart of Markov analysis is the **transition probability matrix**, which describes the probabilities of an incumbent staying in his or her present job for the forecast time period (usually one year), moving to another job in the organization, or leaving the organization. When this matrix is multiplied by the number of people beginning the year in each job, the results show how many people are expected to be in each job by the end of the year.

To develop the transition probability matrix, planners take the following steps:

1. Specify a mutually exclusive and exhaustive set of states that include every job between which people can move and an exit state for those who quit, die, retire, or are fired.

2. Gather data from each of the last several years on what transition rates actually occurred between each state. Such data could show, for instance, that during the past year 15 percent of the people who began the year in job A left the organization, 10 percent were transferred to job B, and 5 percent were promoted to job C.

3. Attempt to develop stable, reliable estimates of expected future transition rates. Some judgment is required at this step. Many organizations use the previous year's transition rates. However, if the previous year was atypical (with an unusually high or low rate of movement), planners may find it better to average the rates over the last several years. This third step is very important because the accuracy of prediction depends on using correct transition rates. If movement rates vary widely from year to year, planners may not be able to use Markov analysis to forecast internal supply.[27]

Once the transition probability matrix is developed, applying it is a simple matter (see Table 3.1). To produce predictions, the matrix is multiplied by the vector of the number of incumbents in each state. For instance, job A began the year with sixty-two incumbents. Fifteen percent of those incumbents ($0.15 \times 62 = 9$) left the organization; 10 percent ($0.10 \times 62 = 6$) moved to job B; and 5 percent ($0.05 \times 62 = 3$) moved to job C. That leaves forty-four of the original incumbents in job A. However, 15 percent of the seventy-five people ($0.15 \times 75 = 11$) in job B transferred to job A; so the total number of employees in job A at the end of the year is fifty-five ($44 + 11$). (These numbers have been rounded to whole digits because fractions of employees are not meaningful.)

Markov analysis describes what is expected to happen if existing transition rates remain the same. This type of analysis can also be used speculatively to assess the impact of possible modifications in transition rates. For instance, suppose that job D is going to be understaffed because of an unusually large number of retirements. In the past, this job has been filled largely by promotions from job B. Planners might use the Markov model to determine what would happen if the rate of lateral transfers from job C to job D were increased or if the rate of promotion from job B were increased. Planners could experiment with different probabilities until they found a workable solution.

TABLE 3.1 Markov Analysis

	Transition Probability Matrix				
	(Time 2)				
(Time 1)	*Job A*	*Job B*	*Job C*	*Job D*	*Exit*
Job A	0.70	0.10	0.05	0	0.15
Job B	0.15	0.60	0.05	0.10	0.10
Job C	0	0	0.80	0.05	0.15
Job D	0	0	0.05	0.85	0.10

	Matrix Applied to Incumbents*					
	Initial Staffing Level	*Job A*	*Job B*	*Job C*	*Job D*	*Exit*
Job A	62	44	6	3	0	9
Job B	75	11	45	4	8	7
Job C	50	0	0	40	2	8
Job D	45	0	0	2	38	5
Predicted end-of-year staffing level		55	51	49	48	29

*Numbers have been rounded to whole digits because fractions of employees are not meaningful.

The state of New York has recently developed a work force planning process that uses Markov models to predict employee flows between jobs and agencies. The model is useful in predicting staffing changes due to retirement and turnover. In combination with external data on occupational trends and employee availability, the model output also allows planners to identify jobs that will present staffing problems and to experiment with different methods of filling expected demand. For instance, rather than trying to hire a type of professional expected to be needed in three years time but hard to find, the state might try to hire new employees at a subprofessional level now and develop them in time to meet anticipated needs. The model is being further developed to improve its accuracy. Because the probability of movement out of a job (due to promotion, quitting, or retirement) has been found to depend not just on the job currently held, but also on age and/or tenure in the job, the model will be elaborated by the addition of new states representing tenure breakdowns within each job category.[28]

Markov analysis is widely used and easy to apply. However, it has been criticized for certain weaknesses and limitations.[29] Transition probabilities must be relatively stable or estimable for Markov analysis to be accurate. Also, the probabilities will not be reliable if there are only a few incumbents in each job. Generally, Markov analysis works best if there are at least fifty people in each job or state.[30]

A second weakness is conceptual rather than statistical. Markov analysis assumes that the probability of movement is determined solely by the employee's initial job state. The probability of moving to job B depends entirely on where the employee began the year, in job A, C, or D. In actual practice, however, people move within organizations because of the pull of vacancies rather than the push of their current assignments. Thus, the true probability of moving to job B also depends on the number of vacancies in job B.

A newer approach to predicting internal movement and supply that takes this dynamic into account is called **renewal**, or **replacement**, **analysis.** Basically, this method is driven by destination demand—the number of vacancies anticipated in higher-level jobs. Transition matrices help identify how the demand can be filled by internal movements from lower-level positions. These movements create additional vacancies and in turn drive further movement at even lower job levels.[31]

More complex methods of forecasting internal supply are available in goal programming, network analysis, and computer simulation. Simulations may use both replacement and Markov analyses, utilize the age and promotability information stored on each of thousands of employees, and allow a variety of different HR policies and assumptions to be applied and evaluated.[32]

The U.S. Navy has developed a very sophisticated HR forecasting model to help reduce employment levels in shipyards. Markov analysis showed that allowing natural attrition and typical transition rates to take their course would reduce overall employment levels, but in a way that was unbalanced across critical shipyard occupations. To keep each of eighteen different occupations staffed at the desired level, attrition needed to be combined with modified transfer rates and carefully planned hiring in some areas. Adding goals to the model and predicting two years into the future on a quarterly basis allowed the reductions to be thoroughly planned and accomplished with minimal disruption of work efficiency.[33]

Implications of Internal Supply and Distribution

Careful study of internal supply and distribution reports may allow HR planners to anticipate and head off a variety of problems. For instance, planners might notice that a particular unit or job family contains a high proportion of employees nearing retirement age. This may signal the need to establish a high-volume training program to prepare replacements for these positions.

The Union Oil Company of California developed an internal flow model that produces statistics on the replacement ratio, or the number of employees in a given five-year age bracket who are waiting to fill each job currently held by someone in the next-older age bracket. Ratios that are too high are a concern because they mean that upward progress is blocked and younger employees are likely to become frustrated in their careers.[34] Ratios that are too low indicate a possible future shortage of experienced employees for higher-level jobs.

Recent research in **organizational demography** indicates that the age and tenure distributions within an organization may have a number of interesting effects. The idea underlying studies of organizational demography is that members who joined an organization at the same time (cohorts) share memories of the same organizational history and probably feel some solidarity with and loyalty toward others who joined at the same time.

Consider the two hypothetical tenure distributions shown in Table 3.2. Theory suggests that larger cohort groups typically have more power, and their views of the world tend to dominate organizations. Thus, the large number of relative newcomers in organization B probably would exert much more control than people of similar tenure in organization A. Also, organization B would probably be more innovative and open to change because of the large number of newcomers. When it is time to replace a top executive, organization B would be more likely to hire an outsider, and organization A would be likely to promote an insider, because the latter organization has more senior candidates available. Furthermore, theorists would predict that organization B would tend to be fairly bureaucratic because it would need formal rules to guide and control the activities of its large population of unsocialized newcomers. Organization A, on the other hand, might function more like a clan because its employees would have had ample time to develop a common value system that makes explicit rules unnecessary.

There is also evidence that turnover tends to be greatest within smaller (and hence less powerful) cohorts. Thus, long-service members would be more likely to leave organization B, and new members would be most likely to leave organization A. Finally, cooperation and integration across tenure cohorts is predicted to be facilitated by a fairly even distribution of tenure. Sparsely populated spans,

TABLE 3.2 Hypothetical Tenure Distributions of Two Organizations

	Percent of Employees	
Years of Service	*Organization A*	*Organization B*
35–40	20%	5%
30–34	15	5
25–29	15	10
20–24	15	15
15–19	15	5
10–14	10	5
5–9	5	30
0–4	5	25

such as the one between the 5–9-year and 20–24-year groups in organization B, are expected to increase the difficulty of communication and coordination.[35]

Research in organizational demography is fairly new and not yet conclusive. If further study supports some of these novel ideas, organizations may find that they need to strategically manage the distribution of tenure, as well as the absolute number of employees and their distribution across jobs.

THE EXTERNAL SUPPLY OF LABOR

As they hire new workers, lay off or discharge others, and lose current employees to other firms, organizations continuously interact with external labor markets. Therefore, to plan effectively, HR planners must understand how to assess and adjust to the **external supply of labor**.

Some Definitions

A great deal of data are collected and published monthly about the labor supply, but making sense of these data requires an understanding of a few basic concepts and definitions.[36]

The **civilian labor force** comprises all people sixteen years or older who are not in the military and who are employed or seeking work. The civilian labor force does not include "discouraged workers" who have given up looking for work or people who are institutionalized in prisons and mental hospitals.

The **labor reserve** is made up of people aged sixteen and over who choose not to work; they include students, full-time homemakers, and retired persons. These people are considered a *reserve* in the sense that they could conceivably become workers in an emergency or for the right incentive.

The **labor force participation rate** is the percentage of the total working-age population that is currently in the labor force. The participation rate is often calculated separately for various subgroups. For instance, at the end of 1991, the participation rate of males twenty years or older stood at about 78 percent, indicating that most males were either working or seeking work. In contrast, the participation rate of females in the same age range was about 58 percent.[37]

The **unemployment rate** is the percentage of the labor force that is seeking work rather than working. When the unemployment rate is high and many people are out of work, the labor market is described as "loose," meaning that employers can find new employees easily. Conversely, a "tight" labor market occurs when unemployment is very low and employers have great difficulty in finding new workers.

The Bureau of Labor Statistics conducts a monthly Current Population Survey, using a representative sample of households nationwide. Each month the bureau reports these labor force statistics in its journal, *Monthly Labor Review.* This journal also contains analyses of new developments and trends in the labor supply.

Labor Markets

The concept of labor markets is an important one. A **labor market** is the area from which an employer typically recruits to fill a position; this area varies according to the type of job being filled. For instance, the labor market for secretaries, plumbers, cashiers, and so on is usually the immediate, surrounding geographical area. This is so because workers are seldom willing to move for these jobs, and employers find it unnecessary to mount a nationwide search to fill them. For these jobs, the labor market is defined by how far potential employees are willing to commute to work. For other jobs—such as college professor, top manager, or research chemist—the labor market may well be nationwide or even international. Finally, there may be intermediate labor markets for skilled jobs for which incumbents are willing to move but for which employers need not search too widely. For example, hospitals in Texas may recruit at Texas and Oklahoma nursing schools but probably feel no need to recruit in Minnesota.

Before making decisions, employers must be sure that information is collected on the right labor markets. Knowing that the unemployment rate is very high for the country does not guarantee that a firm will be able to find sufficient new employees at any specific location. Labor markets are based on skills as well as geography. For instance, the nationwide labor market for entry-level electrical engineers may be quite a bit tighter or looser than the local labor market for secretaries or refrigeration mechanics. Data on local and regional labor market conditions are available from state employment service offices.

In summary, there is a great deal of available data on current labor markets. This information might be quite helpful to the recruiter who is attempting to fill positions right now, but for most HR planning purposes, data projecting the future status of various labor markets will be more useful. Fortunately, the Bureau of Labor Statistics publishes such projections, and every two years it issues a revised outlook for the next fifteen-year period.

Trends in Demographics and the Labor Supply

The rate of population growth, and thus the number of people potentially available as employees, has not followed a smooth pattern over the last fifty years. The peaks and valleys in the age distribution of the population have created some interesting problems for employers.

The term *baby boom* has been used to describe the large group of children born between 1945 and 1962 to people who had postponed marriage and childbearing during World War II. The coming of age of this group, plus a huge increase in female participation in the labor force, accounted for the labor force's rapid growth of 3 percent per year in the 1970s. However, following the baby boom was a baby bust, in which relatively few children were born between 1963 and the mid-1970s. It is the latter generation that has reached working age and entered the labor force in the late 1980s and in the 1990s. By the end of the 1980s, the labor force growth rate had slowed to 1.6 percent per year, and it is expected to drop to 1.3 percent for the period from 1990 to 2005.[38]

Another trend, called the *baby boom echo,* is the increasing number of babies being born as baby boomers have their own families. These children will not have a direct impact on the labor force until the late 1990s and onward, but they will have an indirect effect much sooner. Specifically, they will stimulate a great demand for trustworthy child care workers, and the demand for schoolteachers, which dropped off dramatically in the early 1970s, is expected to rebound in the 1990s.[39]

What implications do these demographics have for organizations? One effect is that some organizations that depend primarily on young, part-time workers have been facing a labor shortage as the baby bust generation enters the work force. HR planners at fast-food chains and grocery stores have had to worry about where their cooks, counter help, checkers, shelf stockers, and baggers will come from. Wages for these positions have risen to attract the available young people, and some organizations have successfully turned to retirees to fill the gap.[40] The *Times-Mirror* newspapers have hired off-duty mail carriers to deliver papers because they were unable to recruit enough school-age boys and girls for the task.[41] In the last few years, many states have clamped down on the employment hours of teen-agers in an effort to boost school performance, making this source of labor even scarcer.[42] Still, in most labor markets, the shortage of young workers has not been as severe as originally predicted, for the baby bust generation began work in a time of corporate downsizing and slower economic growth. The number of young workers will start to increase again by 1996, easing the shortages that did occur.[43]

A second effect involves the aging of the labor force (see Figure 3.4). The large baby boom generation is now well into middle age. The median age of employees in 1990 was 36.6, and it is expected to reach 40.6 by 2005.[44] Middle-aged workers want job security, advancement, status, challenge, and interesting work. Organizations are finding it hard to provide these conditions to such a large number of employees, especially in the difficult economic climate of the late 1980s and early 1990s. (See the discussion beginning on page 124 for more on how organizations are coping with this situation.) After 2005, as the baby boomers grow old and retire, a brand new set of social and employment problems may emerge.

Besides changes in the raw numbers of workers available, shifts are also occurring in the race and sex composition of the labor force.[45] The report *Workforce 2000,* published in 1987, received widespread coverage and discussion in the media and by HR professionals.[46] One of the most interesting predictions in this report concerns the increasing diversity in the work force of the future.[47] The latest predictions from the Bureau of Labor Statistics verify this trend. Table 3.3 shows the expected race and sex distribution of the total labor force and new labor force entrants predicted to the year 2005. White males will drop from 43.1 percent of the labor force in 1990 to 38.2 percent in 2005. Furthermore, less than one-third of new entrants will be the young white males historically preferred by recruiters. Two-thirds of new workers will be female, Hispanic, black, or Asian.

HR planners need to consider the qualifications, not just the numbers, of persons in the labor force and how these may or may not match the jobs available.

FIGURE 3.4 The Middle-Aging of the Work Force

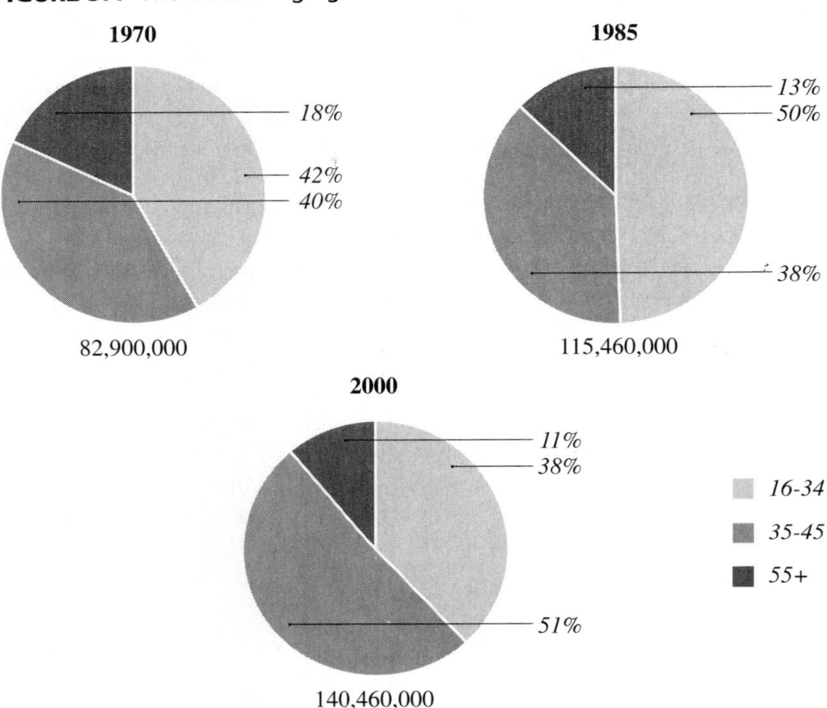

Source: Reproduced with permission from Coates, Joseph F., Jarratt, Jennifer and Mahaffie, John B. *Future Work: Seven Critical Forces Reshaping Work and the Work Force in North America*, p. 9 (Figure 1–1.1, "The Middle-Aging of the Work Force"). Copyright 1990 by Jossey-Bass Inc., Publishers. For use by the Houghton Mifflin Company. All rights reserved.

As can be seen in Table 3.4, many of the fastest-growing occupations require relatively high levels of education, but the fastest-growing groups of new labor force entrants are those with traditionally low levels of educational attainment. Futurologist Joseph Coates states that there has been "a catastrophic cognitive collapse in education of grades K through 16," so that even graduates are often not qualified for jobs requiring math, writing, and technical reading.[48] Innovative HR strategies may be needed to attract or create qualified workers in the next decade. Alternatively, firms are sending work offshore to the increasingly well qualified, low labor cost work forces of Asia and Latin America.[49]

Industry and Occupational Trends

In addition to projecting the size of various groups in the labor force, the Bureau of Labor Statistics also predicts which occupations and industries will be growing or declining in the near future. Nearly all of the net job growth between now and

TABLE 3.3 Increasing Diversity in the Labor Force

Percent	*Labor Force, 1990*	*Entrants, 1990–2005*	*Leavers, 1990–2005*	*Labor Force, 2005*
Total	100.0	100.0	100.0	100.0
Men	54.7	50.5	57.3	52.6
Women	45.3	49.5	42.7	47.4
White, non-Hispanic	78.5	65.3	81.8	73.0
Men	43.1	32.2	47.6	38.2
Women	35.4	33.1	34.2	34.8
Black	10.7	13.0	10.5	11.6
Men	5.3	6.2	5.2	5.7
Women	5.4	6.8	5.3	5.9
Hispanic	7.7	15.7	5.2	11.1
Men	4.6	9.1	3.1	6.6
Women	3.1	6.6	2.1	4.6
Asian and other	3.1	6.0	2.4	4.3
Men	1.7	3.0	1.3	2.2
Women	1.4	3.0	1.1	2.1

Source: Adapted from Howard N. Fullerton, Jr., "Labor Force Projections: The Baby Boom Moves On," *Monthly Labor Review,* November 1991, p. 41.

TABLE 3.4 Projections for the Twenty Fastest Growing Occupations by Percent

Occupation	*Employment (in thousands)*		*Numerical Change*	*Percent Change*
	1990	*2005*		
Home health aides	287	550	263	91.7
Paralegals	90	167	77	85.2
Systems analysts and computer scientists	463	829	366	78.9
Personal and home care aides	103	183	79	76.7
Physical therapists	88	155	67	76.0
Medical assistants	165	287	122	73.9
Operations research analysts	57	100	42	73.2
Human services workers	145	249	103	71.2
Radiologic technologists and technicians	149	252	103	69.5
Medical secretaries	232	390	158	68.3
Physical and corrective therapy assistants and aides	45	74	29	64.0
Psychologists	125	204	79	63.6

TABLE 3.4 Projections for the Twenty Fastest Growing Occupations by Percent (*cont.*)

Occupation	*Employment (in thousands)* 1990	2005	*Numerical Change*	*Percent Change*
Travel agents	132	214	82	62.3
Correction officers	230	372	142	61.4
Data processing equipment repairers	84	134	50	60.0
Flight attendants	101	159	59	58.5
Computer programmers	565	882	317	56.1
Occupational therapists	36	56	20	55.2
Surgical technologists	38	59	21	55.2
Medical records technicians	52	80	28	54.3

Source: George Silvestri and John Lukasiewicz, "Occupational Employment Projections," *Monthly Labor Review*, November 1991, p. 81.

2005 is expected to occur in the service-producing sector, including areas such as transport, retail trade, health care, and business, social, and legal services.[50] Table 3.4 shows the occupations predicted to have the fastest growth rates in the next decade. Note that the growth rates do not represent the largest occupations or the most new jobs but rather the highest percentages of increase. For instance, the number of home health aides will nearly double. On the other hand, Table 3.5 shows the twenty occupations with the fastest expected growth in absolute numbers of jobs. The largest growth in absolute numbers is predicted for retail salespersons, nurses, cashiers, and general office clerks.

PLANNING HUMAN RESOURCE PROGRAMS

Having made demand and internal supply forecasts and considered the state of the external labor market, the HR planner can anticipate future problems with employee supply and plan programs for offsetting them. The following sections deal with planning for labor shortages and surpluses, planning for a new start-up, and managerial succession planning. The final two sections consider career planning and changes in career paths for individual employees.

Planning for Shortages

When demand exceeds internal supply, employers usually go to the external labor market to recruit new employees. However, employers are finding that recruiting is not as easy as it was in the past because of a shortage of qualified employees.[51]

TABLE 3.5 Twenty Occupations with the Largest Projected Growth in Absolute Numbers

Occupation	*Employment (in thousands)*		*Numerical Change*	*Percent Change*
	1990	*2005*		
Salespersons, retail	3,619	4,506	887	24.5
Registered nurses	1,727	2,494	767	44.4
Cashiers	2,633	3,318	685	26.0
General office clerks	2,737	3,407	670	24.5
Truckdrivers, light and heavy	2,362	2,979	617	26.1
General managers and top executives	3,086	3,684	598	19.4
Janitors and cleaners, including maids and housekeeping cleaners	3,007	3,562	555	18.5
Nursing aides, orderlies, and attendants	1,274	1,826	552	43.4
Food counter, fountain, and related workers	1,607	2,158	550	34.2
Waiters and waitresses	1,747	2,196	449	25.7
Teachers, secondary school	1,280	1,717	437	34.2
Receptionists and information clerks	900	1,322	422	46.9
Systems analysts and computer scientists	463	829	366	78.9
Food preparation workers	1,156	1,521	365	31.6
Child care workers	725	1,078	353	48.8
Gardeners and groundskeepers, except farm	874	1,222	348	39.8
Accountants and auditors	985	1,325	340	34.5
Computer programmers	565	882	317	56.1
Teachers, elementary	1,362	1,675	313	23.0
Guards	883	1,181	298	33.7

Source: George Silvestri and John Lukasiewicz, "Occupational Employment Projections," *Monthly Labor Review,* November 1991, p. 82.

Innovations in recruiting may be necessary (they are discussed further in Chapter 6), and in some cases, employers may have to create qualified workers where none existed before.

For instance, Barden, a ball-bearing manufacturer in Connecticut, experienced great difficulty in filling its labor needs in an area with a low, 2.5 percent unemployment rate. Then it discovered the answer to its labor shortage in immigrants whose English was too poor to make them attractive to other employers. The organization retained the Berlitz language training company to provide four hours of English instruction each day for three weeks. The result was competent, committed, and self-confident employees.[52]

When faced with a shortage, employers should consider other alternatives to hiring additional full-time employees. For instance, employers might encourage employees who are nearing retirement age to continue working by increasing the pension formula to reward extra years of service more heavily, or they might rehire retired employees on a part-time basis. If a shortfall is caused or worsened by high turnover, employers should attempt to identify the causes of turnover and act to remedy them. If successful, this course of action would save recruiting and training costs and might substantially improve employees' attitudes.

If the long-range plan suggests that demand will peak quickly and then return to a lower level, hiring new permanent employees would be unwise. For relatively short periods of increased demand, employers could pay for overtime rather than hire additional employees. Overtime work must be compensated at one and one-half times the regular hourly rate, but it may still be more economical than hiring, training, and providing benefits to new employees who are not needed over the long term. Alternatively, employers may choose to subcontract some work to another company during the demand peak or to acquire temporary workers from firms specializing in such services.[53] These options are summarized in Figure 3.5.

Planning for Surpluses

When forecasts show that internal supply will exceed demand, employers must make plans to reduce supply. If the problem is recognized far enough in advance, attrition may take care of the overage if employees who leave are not replaced. This alternative is the least costly, both in terms of money and company reputation. If attrition is insufficient, employers can offer incentives for early retirement.

FIGURE 3.5 Program Planning Options

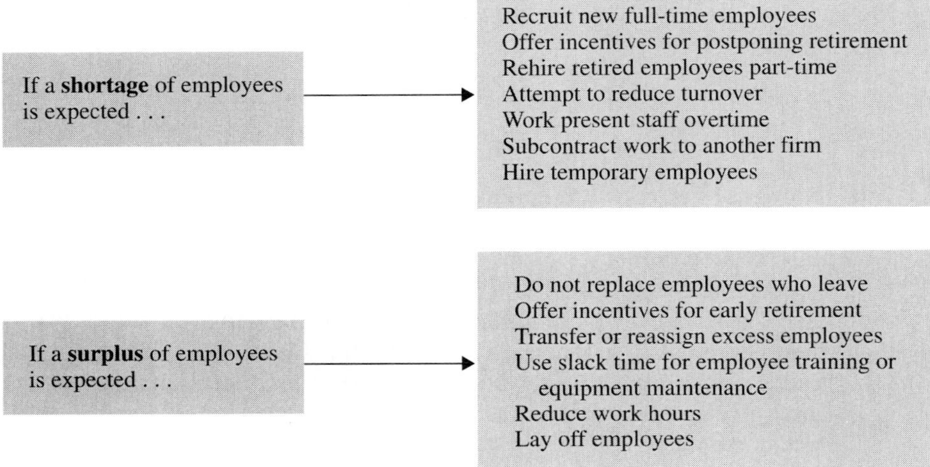

(Under the Age Discrimination in Employment Act of 1967, employees cannot be forced to retire, except in individual cases where there is a documented medical or job performance problem.) A major oil company offered such an incentive program to managers, expecting about 2,000 employees to accept it. To the company's surprise and dismay, nearly 6,000 managers accepted the early retirement package. Needless to say, HR planners and trainers had to scramble to deal with the sudden shortfall of experienced managers.

Depending on the nature of the surplus, a firm may be able to transfer or reassign employees to jobs in parts of the organization that are still experiencing demand. Or, if the firm expects the surplus to be short-lived and can afford to keep excess workers on the payroll, the company can use the slack time to provide cross-training in related jobs to increase work force skills and flexibility. Alternatively, excess workers can perform equipment maintenance and overhaul or other activities that were postponed when demand was high.[54]

An option that allows retention of all or most employees but still realizes payroll savings is to reduce work hours, perhaps to a four-day, 32-hour workweek. In this way, a company can spread a 20 percent decrease in demand (and in pay) equitably across the whole work force, rather than keep 80 percent of employees full-time and lay off 20 percent. This alternative has become especially popular in states that permit workers on partial layoff to collect unemployment compensation for the days they do not work.

An oil-field equipment company in Houston successfully implemented a three-week-on, one-week-off partial layoff schedule for skilled machinists during the oil bust in the mid-1980s. The aim was to retain a complete, skilled work force for the time when the oil business rebounded. The plan was discussed in advance with the union and approved overwhelmingly by the employees. The coordination costs of having employees in and out offset some of the potential wage savings of partial layoffs, however. The Houston firm found that rotating layoffs did not work very well for office and clerical employees, so it let go 20 percent of these employees and retained the rest on a full schedule.

As indicated in Figure 3.5, the last resort is to lay off excess employees. This action obviously is bad for the employees, but it is also bad for the employer. Laying off workers damages a company's reputation as a good place to work and can be costly. Laid-off workers are entitled to collect unemployment compensation from a state-managed fund. The fund is supported by employer contributions, and the rate at which a firm is required to contribute depends on its past history of employee claims against the fund. Thus, layoffs now will convert into higher premiums in the future.

Unfortunately, studies show that layoff is often the option chosen because HR managers usually have less than two months between the time a surplus of employees is first noticed and the time that staff reductions must be completed.[55] Better planning might lengthen this interval and allow the use of other methods to reduce staff. Note that a federal law (the Worker Adjustment and Retraining Notification Act) passed in 1988 requires that employers give employees sixty days' notice before closing an entire plant or laying off fifty or more people.[56]

Many responsible companies provide outplacement services to employees who must be let go. At a minimum, such services may include sessions on how to prepare a résumé and conduct a job search. When Ford Motor Co. closed an assembly plant in California in 1983, it provided a very thorough program for dislocated employees. Working with the union and several state agencies, it offered counseling, assessment of skills, basic education, vocational retraining, prepaid tuition assistance, on-the-job training, help with job searches, and preferential hiring at other Ford plants. As a result of this program, more than 80 percent of the dislocated employees found new jobs rapidly—with a less-than-usual occurrence of the adjustment problems associated with widespread job loss (drug and alcohol abuse, and child and spouse abuse, mental illness, and suicide).[57] Chapter 16 discusses outplacement in more detail.

When a company must lay off some but not all employees, it should have a fair procedure for deciding who must go. For unionized employees, layoff procedures are usually specified in the contract, with seniority often being an important factor. All employers should have a **reduction in force (RIF)** policy prepared well in advance of the need to reduce employment levels (see Figure 3.6). While such a policy might reward longer-service employees for their loyalty, it should also reflect what is best for the company. This means that marginal performers or unskilled, easily replaceable employees should be released first. A firm should make every effort to retain good performers and skilled employees; although some of the latter may have to move down to less skilled jobs for a while, at least they will receive paychecks and will be available to move back up when business improves. Several recent studies have shown that fair and generous treatment of laid-off employees can sustain morale and performance of the employees who are not laid off. Unfair treatment may cause layoff survivors to suffer from stress, fear, and guilt.[58]

Planning for a New Establishment: Opening the Mirage

A demanding and successful exercise in HR planning was recently reported in the *Cornell Hotel and Restaurant Administration Quarterly*: the preparation for opening the new Mirage hotel and casino in Las Vegas.[59] This property cost $635 million and has 3,049 rooms, a 105,000-square-foot casino, and 12 food and beverage outlets. All these facilities were opened virtually simultaneously in what is called in the business a "hard" opening. Obviously, a great deal of HR planning was necessary to carry out this feat.

Planning began two years in advance of the opening with the hiring of a vice president for human resources. His first task was to gather data on labor market demographics, wage trends, competitors' expansion plans, and the opening experiences of other luxury hotels. Then he calculated the number of employees needed to run the facility (initially estimated at 5,000) and adjusted this figure for the expected number of no-shows (those hired before opening who did not turn up), early turnovers, and the expected lower-than-usual productivity of individuals just learning their jobs. These projections produced a target number of hires and allowed the estimation of the number of applications needed to produce that number of qualified staff (estimated at 47,000). Later, estimates of the likely volume of business were increased, so employee projections increased as well. Ultimately, 6,200 people were hired out of 57,000 applicants.

The next task of the HR vice president was to consider sources for these applicants. He decided that some experienced employees would come from the company's other Las Vegas casino and that the local labor market would be sufficient to supply the rest. He directed special attention to jobs known to be problematic in the area, such as housekeeper. In this case, he offered a cash bonus to employees who referred a friend to the job of housekeeper.

In addition to planning for numbers of employees in each job category, the HR vice president had to plan their training and schedule their starting dates. He hired forty-two middle managers early and put them through a half-year training program; he hired and trained supervisors; finally, he had each supervisor conduct training for his or her work group. The hotel and casino opened successfully in early December 1989, six weeks ahead of the original schedule.

Managerial Succession Planning

Regardless of expansion or contraction of the total work force in an organization, the need for good managers is critical and continuous. More and more organizations are planning for managerial succession and development because they have found that it takes years of systematic grooming to produce a successful top manager. The benefits of a formal succession planning system are outlined in Table 3.6. How companies practice succession planning varies.[60] Most successful programs, however, seem to include top management's involvement and commitment, high-level review of succession plans, formal assessment of the performance and potential of candidates, and written development plans for individual candidates.[61]

Plans should center on especially important jobs and should identify correctly the skill requirements of those jobs. For instance, IBM's Executive Resources Planning System focuses on the job of director and identifies candidates with the potential to move up to this level.[62] At Union Oil Company, planners identify an apex job within each functional area and focus on candidates for future openings in this job. In the marketing function, for instance, the apex job is field division sales manager.[63] At Crocker National Bank, the goal is to develop general bankers able to move into senior positions.[64]

Most managerial succession planning systems rely on committees of higher-level managers to identify high-potential candidates and plan developmental activities for them.[65] Development plans include formal training programs and a series of job assignments leading to the apex job. The plans are usually formally presented to yet higher-level managers for review. At Crocker National Bank, interdivisional meetings are also part of the process because general banker candidates

FIGURE 3.6 A University Reduction in Force Policy

For Employees Other Than Faculty

I. Policy Statement

The Southeastern State University System endeavors to provide stable employment. Situations including, but not limited to, a lack of funds, lack of work, reorganization, or changes in research needs or technologies, however, may require a reduction in the work force to assure the continued quality and efficiency of the System.

A reduction in force (RIF) may take the form of elimination of jobs, reduction in percent of effort, or reduction in salary. The provisions of this policy are not to be used to dismiss an employee if the sole cause for dismissal is either misconduct or lack of satisfactory performance. RIF decisions will be made without regard for the employee's race, color, sex, religion, national origin, age, non-job-related physical or mental handicap, or Vietnam-era veteran's status.

II. Procedures

The Chief Executive Officer of the System Part will determine when a need exists for a formal reduction in force. When such a determination has been made, the following steps will be taken to implement the decision.

A. Careful analysis will be performed to determine in which areas, activities, programs, or organizations, reductions must be effected. If an entire activity is to be eliminated, steps B and C below are not applicable.
B. Within the affected area, the jobs that will need to be performed after the reduction must be identified.
C. Present employees will be carefully evaluated as to their qualifications and ability to perform the jobs as determined in step B (above). Additionally, evaluations may take the following into consideration:
   1. Ability to adjust to the necessary changes in the organization's operation and to contribute to ongoing programs
   2. Effectiveness on the job, including performance and past achievement
   3. Versatility (whether the individual has the ability to move into another area of operations)

FIGURE 3.6 A University Reduction in Force Policy (*cont.*)

4. Special skills that are necessary to a particular function
5. Motivation and initiative
6. Potential
7. Length of time in service with the Southeastern State University System

D. After the job functions and the individual employees have been evaluated, the determination as to which employees will be subject to the RIF will be made. The documentation used in the evaluation process, along with the explanation, will be sent through appropriate administrative channels to the Chief Executive Officer. If the CEO concurs with the recommendation, the department head will notify the affected employee(s) of the RIF decision.

E. An employee who is designated for RIF must be given written notice as soon as practicable, but not less than 30 calendar days prior to layoff. An employee with ten or more years of service within the Southeastern State University System, however, will be notified not less than 60 days prior to layoff.

III. Placement Efforts

Employees designated for RIF will be given reasonable time off to interview for other jobs prior to the date of dismissal. Every reasonable effort shall be made by personnel offices to place dismissed employees in comparable positions for which they are qualified.

IV. Recall

An employee who has been dismissed under the provisions of this policy will be offered the same position if it is reestablished within six months of the dismissal, provided the employee has retained the ability to perform the work. An employee on layoff status who does not respond within 7 calendar days of receipt of a notice regarding either a recall to work or an opportunity to interview for an open position forfeits all further recall rights.

V. Appeal Rights

(This lengthy section specifies appeal procedures for RIFed employees who believe that the RIF policy has not been properly applied.)

TABLE 3.6 Benefits of Formal Succession Planning

- Provides a logical and specific connection to business and strategic planning.
- Provides more systematic bases to judge the risks of making particular succession and development moves.
- Assists developing systematized succession plans which fit with the distinct trend to codify, wherever possible, more general and comprehensive corporate planning actions.
- Reduces randomness of managerial development movements.
- Helps to anticipate problems before they get started—and thereby avoids awkward or dysfunctional situations.
- Increases awareness of state-of-the-art advances.
- Increases managerial depth, which can be called upon as needed.
- Provides a logical approach for locking succession planning into the process of human resource planning—connecting formats (data, timing) with process (judgments, discussions, analyses).
- Facilitates integration of the many components of human resource planning after having done many of these separately in the past.
- Improves the identification of high potentials and/or future leaders.
- Exploits the use of computer power or capabilities to improve succession planning formats and processes further.
- Broadens the use of "cross-functional development" techniques to improve competencies and quality of decision making.
- Stimulates inquiry into the fit of succession planning with the philosophy of the organization.
- Improves internal promotion opportunities.
- Overcomes the limitations of "reactive management" approaches and goes to planned management of managerial positions.
- Establishes a logical basis for widening choice among qualified candidates.
- Improves fulfillment of "equal employment opportunity" objectives.
- Makes informal but critical criteria such as "fit" of the person more explicit.

Source: Elmer H. Burack, *Creative Human Resource Planning and Applications: A Strategic Approach* (Englewood Cliffs, NJ: Prentice-Hall, 1988), p. 167. Reprinted with permission of the author.

need to be transferred across divisions to acquire a sufficiently broad base of experience.

In addition to planning for the development of individuals, these systems also result in the identification of viable near-term replacements for important positions. The traditional format for displaying such information is the **replacement chart**. The chart in Figure 3.7 shows how long an incumbent is expected to remain in his or her present position and lists one to three individuals who are now or soon will be ready to assume the position. In a thorough system, the chart is

FIGURE 3.7 Replacement Chart

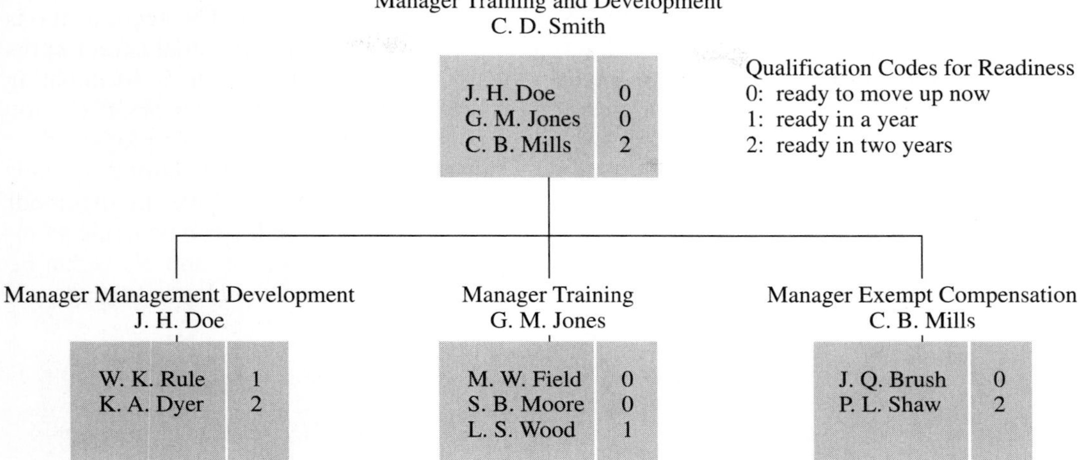

backed up by formal evaluations of performance and potential as well as comprehensive development plans for each possible replacement.

Some organizations have extremely detailed and long-range succession plans. For instance, a 1988 article reported that Exxon Corporation had already hired and was busy grooming the individual it expected to be chief executive officer in the year 2010.[66] On the other hand, one succession consultant has strongly criticized today's succession planning systems. He suggests that "thousands of managerial hours are expended to prepare flashy presentations and lengthy tomes identifying candidates for jobs that probably will not exist in three years. . . . Predicting succession in an era of constant change is fast becoming an impossibility."[67] He also feels that present succession systems attempt to plan for too many people and rely too heavily on formal management courses rather than on constant challenge through job assignments.

Career Planning

Top management candidates are not the only employees in need of career planning attention from the organization. Lower-level managers, professionals, and nonexempt employees also desire satisfying careers and may leave organizations that are not seen as offering appropriate opportunities. Having defined career goals and being aware of other job opportunities within the firm may also motivate employees to work harder at developing their skills because they understand how effort now will pay off later. Realizing this, more and more organizations are becoming involved in formal career planning activities with their employees.[68]

Career planning involves several steps. The first is self-assessment—that is, coming to understand who one is, what one values, what one is good at and enjoys, and what one wants to accomplish over the longer term. The second step is gathering information about different job opportunities and potential career paths either inside or outside the present organization. The third step is formulating career goals and a plan for achieving them. Plans may include on or off the job training, special assignments, and changes in job, occupation, or employer.

Individuals can, and traditionally have, engaged in career planning on their own, with little assistance from their employer. However, employer involvement is desirable because better information on internal career paths can be made available, a larger percentage of employees can be induced to plan, and plans can be more realistic in view of future organizational needs and development opportu-

TABLE 3.7 Organizational Career Planning and Development Tools

A. Self-assessment tools
   1. Career-planning workshops
   2. Career workbooks
   3. Preretirement workshops
B. Individual counseling
   1. Personnel staff
   2. Professional counselor
      a. Internal
      b. External
   3. Outplacement
   4. Supervisor or line manager
C. Internal labor market information/placement exchanges
   1. Job posting
   2. Skills inventories
   3. Career ladders/career path planning
   4. Career resource center
   5. Other career communication formats
D. Organizational potential assessment processes
   1. Assessment centers
   2. Promotability forecasts
   3. Replacement/succession planning
   4. Psychological testing
E. Developmental programs
   1. Job rotation
   2. In-house human resource development programs
   3. External seminars/workshops
   4. Tuition reimbursement/educational assistance
   5. Supervisor training in career counseling
   6. Dual-career programs
   7. Mentoring systems

Source: Reproduced with permission from Hall, Douglas T. *Career Development in Organizations,* p. 61 (Table 1, "Organizational Career Development Tools").

nities. Table 3.7 lists the many tools that organizations may utilize to facilitate employee career planning.

Figure 3.8 gives an example of how one organization, Corning Glass Works, assists nonexempt employees with career planning. The system starts with an introductory videotape and then offers three computer-aided modules on assessing one's current satisfaction, values, interests, and skills. This is followed by a discussion with one's manager to ensure that the self-assessment of skills and

FIGURE 3.8 Career Planning at Corning Glass Works

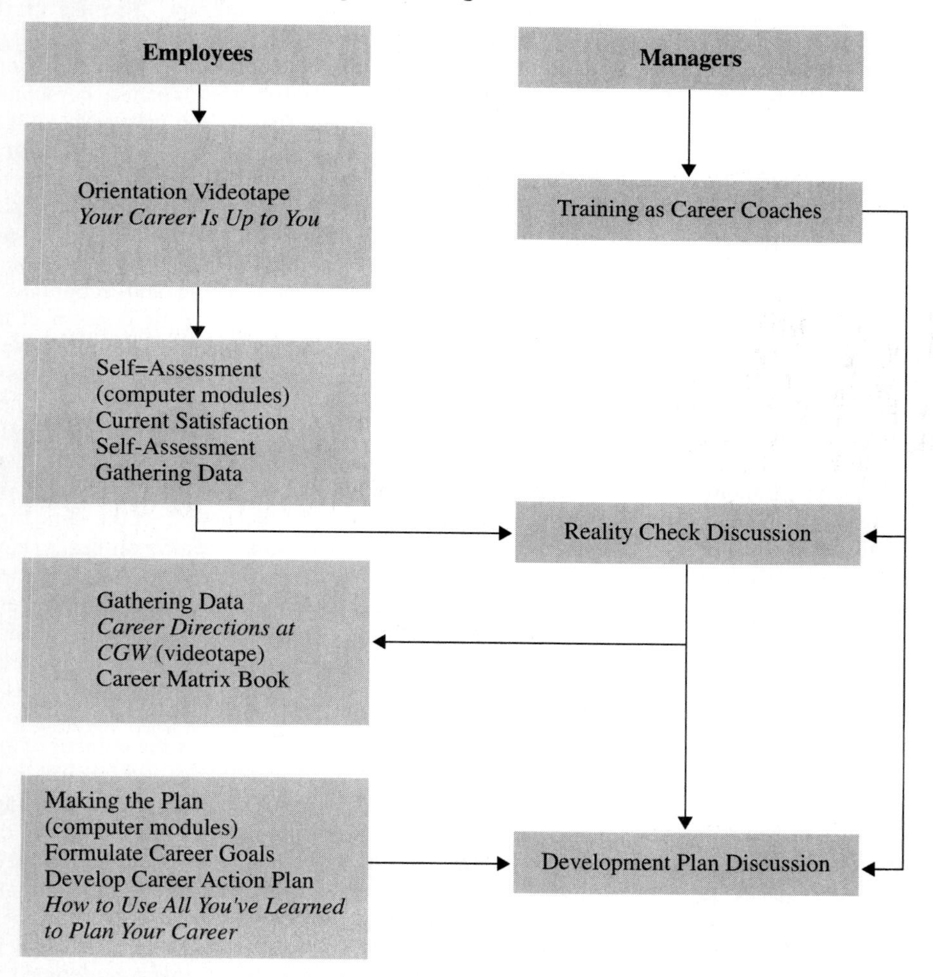

Source: Reproduced with permission from Leibowitz, Zandy B., Farren, Caela and Kaye, Beverly L. *Designing Career Development Systems*, p. 170 (Figure 17, "Corning Glass Works Career Planning and Information System"). Copyright 1986 by Leibowitz, Farren, Kaye and Jossey-Bass Inc. For use by the Houghton Mifflin Company. All rights reserved.

INTERNATIONAL PERSPECTIVE

Balancing the Supply and Demand of Human Resources in Japan

To manage the flow of human resources within their organizations, some large and prestigious Japanese firms adopted the policy of "lifetime employment" after World War II. The employees covered by this policy comprise 22 to 30 percent of the full-time work force. Many are white-collar and some are blue-collar workers. They are guaranteed job security from the time they are hired—upon graduation—until they reach the retirement age of fifty-five.

One of the reasons underlying the lifetime employment system and its related norms is the desire of Japanese employers to inhibit the mobility of highly trained workers. Until recently, if an employee resigned from a major firm, no other big firm would hire the person. The employee had to seek a lower-paying position at a smaller company or join a foreign-owned enterprise doing business in Japan. Because either alternative represented a substantial loss of status, turnover was almost nonexistent. In addition, the majority of workers retired at the same age, so predicting the future supply of this rather static work force was quite simple for HR planners.

The demand for workers, however, is still tied to the market's demand for firms' products and/or services. If Japanese firms had to retain all employees on the payroll at all times, they could not survive economic downturns. Therefore, many employees do not receive lifetime employment. Prominent among these are female workers. Firms expect women to retire upon marriage or the birth of their first child. Most firms also rely on large numbers of temporary, seasonal and part-time employees. In fact, blue-collar workers often sign six-month labor contracts, and farmers take short-term labor contracts during the winter season. In addition, lifetime employees who want to continue working after the age of fifty-five do so at a lower salary and with no job security.

Finally, major firms contract out a great deal of work to smaller firms when business is good. When times are hard, this work is done in-house by the small core of lifetime blue-collar employees. Individuals unfortunate enough to be working for subcontractors during those times lose their jobs; many small companies go bankrupt. Because of the unrestricted ease with which firms can acquire and jettison temporary and subcontracted workers, it seems that Japanese personnel planners should find it relatively easy to deal with short-term shortages and overages of labor. But Japanese HR planners may have to contend with substantial changes in the size and nature of company work forces in the not-too-distant future.

Recent demographic and economic trends seem to be weakening the concept of lifetime employment in Japan. The Japanese work force is aging, there is heightening pressure to extend the retirement age, and economic growth is slowing. These factors together are saturating the upper levels of organizations, thereby reducing the opportunities for younger workers to be promoted. At the same time, foreign-owned firms opening offices in Japan are offering attractive jobs with competitive wages, faster promotion, and more responsibility to experienced employees. These new opportunities are stimulating more midcareer job changes than in the past, as well as reducing the stigma attached to changing jobs. An indicator of this trend is the number of employment agencies in Tokyo—up from 50 in 1985 to over 250 in 1990. More and more Japanese firms are finding that they need to hire at the middle and upper management levels to acquire the skills needed for major strategy changes such as overseas expansion.

Some scholars predict that these social and business forces will transform lifetime employment practices over the next decade. And top firms will not be entirely sorry to see the system change. Labor costs have skyrocketed because salaries are tied to seniority, and the young lifetime employees hired when business was booming in the 1960s and 1970s are an increasingly expensive commitment.

Sources: Thomas E. Maher, "Lifetime Employment in Japan: Exploding the Myth," *Business Horizons,* November-December 1985, pp. 23–26; Satoshi Kamata, *Japan in the Passing Lane: An Insider's Account of Life in a Japanese Auto Factory* (New York: Pantheon Books, 1982); Thomas J. Billesbach and Janet M. Rivea, "Lifetime Employment: Future Prospects for Japan and the U.S.," *SAM Advanced Management Journal*, Autumn 1985, pp. 26–30, 46; and Carla Rapoport, "The Switch is On in Japan," *Fortune*, May 21, 1990, p. 144.

potential is reasonably accurate from the point of view of the organization. Employees then view a videotape about career paths and options and read a workbook that provides information on job duties and skill requirements, pay, typical career paths, and historical career movement data within the organization. Two more computer modules, another videotape, and a second meeting with the manager help in formulating career goals and detailing action plans.

Adapting to a Changing World: New Organizational Structures and Career Patterns

Sluggish economic growth, stronger global competition, and the glut of middle-aged baby boom workers have sparked a set of changes in organizational structures and employee career patterns that have challenged the ingenuity of HR planners. A strong trend since the mid-1980s has been called **restructuring, downsizing,** or more euphemistically, **rightsizing**. Organizations are cutting their labor costs by reducing the size of their permanent full-time staff. These cuts have affected middle managers as well as blue-collar workers. Organizations have abolished entire levels of management to become "flatter," quicker to respond, and closer to the customer.

Many major companies, such as Polaroid Corp., Eastman Kodak Company, AT&T and IBM, which used to offer de facto employment security, have abandoned these policies and no longer think in terms of providing a guaranteed "thirty-year-long career" to all employees.[69] To meet varying labor needs, the new rightsized firms hire temporary workers or contract out work to smaller firms and consultants. When business volume declines, the temporaries, subcontractors, and consultants face unemployment, but the organization is able to maintain its small staff of regular employees.[70] Note that this approach has something in common with the Japanese practice of lifetime employment for a subset of employees (See the International Perspective box.) There has also been a substantial rise in part-time employment, both because part-timers are less expensive and

FIGURE 3.9 Career Patterns

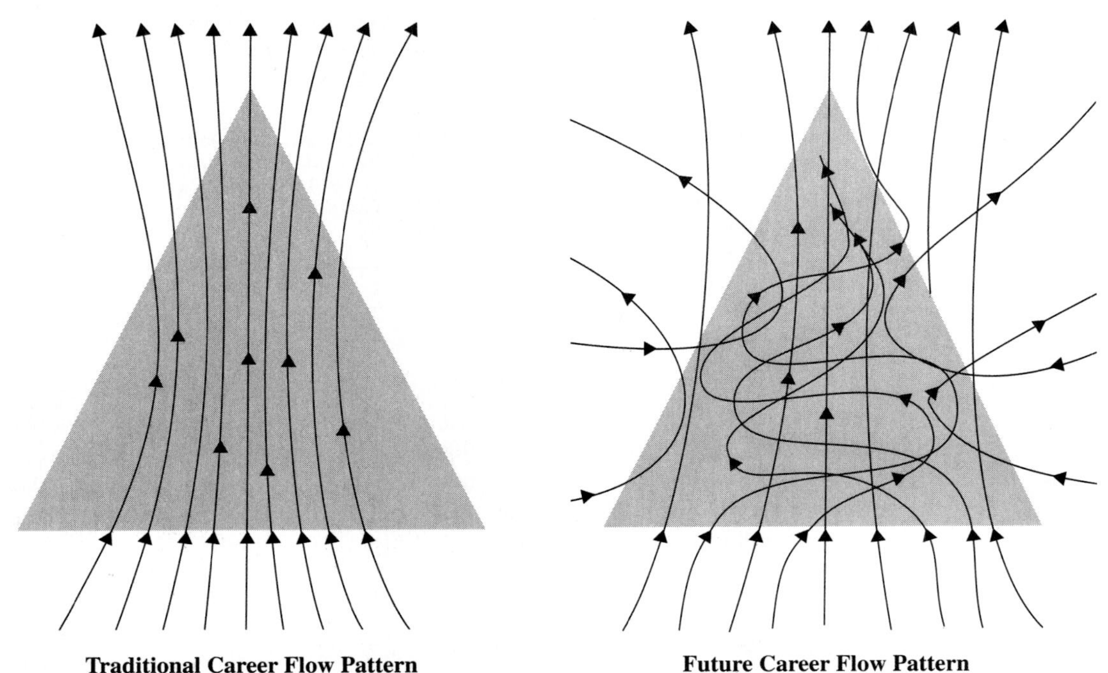

Source: Joel R. DeLuca, "Strategic Career Management in Non-Growing Volatile Business Environments," *Human Resource Planning*, Vol. 11, No. 1, 1988, pp. 51 and 53. Reprinted with permission from the Human Resource Planning Society.

receive fewer fringe benefits and because they provide greater flexibility in scheduling employees for peak demand periods.[71]

Career patterns for individual employees are also changing. The top of Figure 3.9 shows a traditional career pattern, in which one enters an organization near the bottom, works there for many years, and gradually and predictably moves up, retiring from a fairly high-level position. The bulge of baby boomers has made climbing the hierarchy much more competitive, and the flattening of organizational structures has reduced the number of management positions just as the number of candidates has increased. This has caused a great deal of frustration as today's middle-aged employees see themselves failing to advance as rapidly as they had expected.[72] Some of these individuals are leaving big companies to start their own businesses or free-lance as consultants. Others have adopted a career pattern that involves moving between employers more frequently than their predecessors might have.

Organizations are trying to maintain the motivation and creativity of the remaining career-plateaued employees by developing alternatives to the traditional hierarchical career path. Some of these alternatives are depicted in the bottom portion of Figure 3.9. Note that some arrows enter the organization then leave fairly soon, representing temporary employees who move from organization to organization. Others follow a "spiral" career path involving a number of lateral moves between functional areas. This combines broadening experience and the continuous challenge of new tasks with slower hierarchical progress.[73] Salary progress is still possible, as variety of skills is rewarded and pay is not based merely on hierarchical level. Professional career ladders, which reward growing expertise in a single technical speciality without the need to move into management, are also becoming more common.

TABLE 3.8 Baby Boomer Characteristics and Possible Organizational Responses

Profile of Baby Boom Characteristics	*Recommended Organizational Action*
1. Concern for basic values	1. a. Replace promotion culture with psychological success culture b. Examine, change corporate career criteria c. Focus on corporate ethics
2. Freedom to act on values	2. a. Support spiral career paths b. More lateral mobility c. De-couple rewards and the linear career path
3. Focus on self	3. Build on-going development into the job through self-development and life-long learning
4. Need for autonomy	4. More flexible careers
5. Less concern with advancement	5. More diversity in career paths. More change within present job, within present function, within present location, and across function and locations
6. Crafting	6. Reward quality performance, not potential
7. Entrepreneurship	7. a. Create internal entrepreneurial assignments b. Encourage employee career exploration (internally and externally)
8. Concern for work/home balance	8. a. More organizational sensitivity to home life b. Training for managing the work-home interface c. Inclusion of spouse in career discussions d. Career assistance for employed spouse e. Flexible benefits to help meet family needs (e.g., child care, elder care, care for sick children) f. More flexible work arrangements

Source: Douglas T. Hall and Judith Richter, "Career Gridlock: Baby Boomers Hit the Wall," *The Executive*, August 1990, Copyright © 1990 by *The Executive*, p. 19. Used with permission.

Broadening the responsibilities of previously entry-level jobs is another possible solution to the dual problems of slowed progress up the hierarchy and a scarcity of entry-level workers. Baby boomers may have to stay in "low" level jobs longer, but the jobs can be enriched to include more challenging work, as well as the tasks usually performed by inexperienced new hires.[74]

Spiral or cross-organizational career paths may offer another attraction to today's employees: the possibility of staying in one location much longer. With the increasing number of dual career couples, transferring employees is more difficult than in the past. Thus, an individual may prefer to remain in the same community for a long period, moving between different types of jobs within the same site or moving within the same specialty across local employers.

Unfortunately, HR specialists are finding that it is difficult to change the prevailing "up-or-out" culture of most organizations, which defines lack of upward progress as abject failure.[75] Traditional linear career planning is less feasible than before, but employer-initiated creative career planning is even more important to effectively utilize talent and provide satisfying careers for today's employees. The situation is further complicated by the unique values and needs that characterize baby boomers as employees. Table 3.8 identifies some of these characteristics and suggests how human resource experts might modify organizational practices to satisfy them better.

SUMMARY OF KEY POINTS

Organizations must plan for human resources. Otherwise, they run the risk of having (1) employees of insufficient skill or number to meet the organization's needs or (2) an excess of costly employees whose pay and benefits eat into profits. HR planning is based on information about the organization's internal and external environments and on assumptions about what will happen in these environments in the future. Planning may be at the aggregate level of jobs or job families or at the individual level, as in the planning of managerial succession and development. Strategic human resource planning involves HR experts in formulating and implementing the organization's strategy in the light of HR opportunities and constraints.

HR planners may use judgmental methods, such as unit forecasting or the Delphi technique, to predict a firm's need for labor at a particular point in the future. Mathematical techniques may be used for this same purpose. HR planners predict the future internal supply of labor, drawing on skills inventories, human resource information systems, and Markov analyses to make their forecasts. Planners also gather information on relevant external labor markets to determine the availability of potential new employees.

After both demand and supply forecasts are made, planners reconcile the two to determine areas in which more or fewer employees will be needed. Then they design programs to increase or reduce the size of the work force or to change employees' skills to match the forecasted needs. A number of alternatives for dealing with employee shortages and overages are available. Through careful planning, an organization can anticipate needs and implement programs to meet them before the needs actually materialize and cause problems for the organization. Succession planning ensures the supply of qualified and experienced top managers for the future, and creative career planning is needed to develop and motivate employees whose progress up the hierarchy is slowed by restructuring and the aging of the work force.

Questions For Discussion

1. Why should organizations engage in HR planning? Why do some organizations need relatively more complex and comprehensive HR planning systems than do others?
2. What are the benefits of strategic HR planning?
3. When are judgmental methods of demand forecasting preferred over mathematical methods? When is the reverse true?
4. Describe the idea behind the learning curve approach to demand forecasting.
5. Why is the internal supply of labor not static? How can organizations keep track of their internal supply of labor?
6. Describe the advantages and disadvantages of Markov analysis for predicting the future internal supply of labor.
7. What is organizational demography, and what implications might it have for HR planning?
8. What kinds of information might an HR planner want to gather about the external labor market?
9. How are changing demographics likely to affect organizations in the next decade?
10. What can an organization do when a shortage of employees is anticipated?
11. What can an organization do when it expects the internal supply of labor to exceed the demand for labor?
12. What purposes are served by managerial succession planning? What are some characteristics of an effective managerial succession planning system?
13. Describe how you would like your future employer to assist you in planning your career. What should your role and responsibilities be in planning your own career?
14. How are traditional career paths changing, and why? Do your career aspirations fit in with the changes that are occurring?

EXERCISE 3.1

Human Resource Planning at a University

Suppose you are the dean of a college of business administration at a well-funded private university, and you are interested in forecasting the needed size and composition of your faculty for the next three academic years. Your college consists of four departments (management, marketing, finance, and accounting).

1. What information would you want to gather about the current faculty? What information would you want about past trends in the behavior of faculty members at your institution?
2. What is the key determinant of the total number of faculty needed in each department? What information would you want to gather, both inside and outside the university, to predict and use information about this key determinant? Be thorough.
3. How would you go about predicting the internal supply of faculty in each department?
4. How would you go about predicting the number of faculty members needed in each department?
5. Suppose your college is part of a state system of public universities rather than a private institution. Does this situation suggest any additional types of data that you should gather before making your forecast? In what ways might being publicly funded affect your ability to follow through on your HR forecast?

EXERCISE 3.2

Predicting Supply and Demand

It is now January 1994. Your task is to predict supply and demand for each job category as of January 1995 and to plan what to do to meet the demand.

Supply

Present Number of Employees (Beginning of 1994)	*Transition Probability Matrix*				
	Operatives	*Clerical*	*Sales*	*Management/ Staff*	*Exit*
700 Op.	*.80*	*0*	*0*	*0*	*.2*
150 Cl.	*.10*	*.80*			*.10*
50 Sa.			*.80*	*.10*	*.10*
100 M/S				*.90*	*.10*

January 1995 predicted supply

575		40	95
Operatives	Clerical	Sales	Management/ Staff

Demand

1. Your 700 operatives this year will produce 100,000 products. Improvements to the plant scheduled for completion in December 1994 will enable production of

120,000 products. You plan to hire more operatives in order to utilize this new capacity to the fullest in 1995. The improvements to the plant will also result in an increase in productivity so that each worker will be able to produce 5 percent more next year than this year.

2. The use of a new computerized billing system will increase the productivity ratio of clerks to 135 percent of the current ratio. The workload for the clerks will not change from what it is this year.
3. Because of a large standing order, fewer salespersons will be needed. It is estimated that a sales force of forty people will be sufficient to handle business at the beginning of 1995.
4. The ratio of management and staff to operative should be the same as it is at present.

January 1995 predicted demand

______	______	40	______
Operatives	Clerical	Sales	Management/ Staff

Human Resource Plan What discrepancies will exist and how will you deal with them for each group (operatives, clerical, sales, management/staff)? Be innovative and suggest several solutions.

Notes and References

1. Lee Dyer, "Human Resource Planning," in *Personnel Management,* ed. Kendrith Rowland and Gerald Ferris (Boston: Allyn and Bacon, 1982), p. 53.
2. Randall S. Schuler and James W. Walker, "Human Resources Strategy: Focusing on Issues and Actions," *Organizational Dynamics,* Summer 1990, pp. 4–19.
3. Miriam M. Graddick and Pamela C. Jones, "Human Resource Planning and Business Planning: A Case Analysis and Framework for Full Integration," in *Human Resource Forecasting and Strategy Development,* ed. Manuel London, Emily S. Bassman, and John P. Fernandez (New York: Quorum, 1990), pp. 155–166.
4. Karen A. Golden and Vasudevan Ramanujan, "Between a Dream and a Nightmare: On the Integration of the Human Resource Management and Strategic Business Planning Processes," *Human Resource Management,* Winter 1985, pp. 429–452.
5. Paul F. Buller, "Successful Partnerships: HR and Strategic Planning at Eight Top Firms," *Organizational Dynamics,* 1988, Vol. 17, No. 2, pp. 27–43.
6. Emily S. Bassman, "Strategic Use of Environmental Scanning Data," in *Human Resource Forecasting and Strategy Development,* ed. Manuel London, Emily S. Bassman, and John P. Fernandez (New York: Quorum, 1990), pp. 29–37.
7. Schuler and Walker, "Human Resources Strategy: Focusing on Issues and Actions," pp. 4–19; James W. Walker, "Human Resource Planning, 1990s Style," *Human Resource Planning,* 1990, Vol. 13, No. 4, pp. 229–240.
8. Michael J. Feuer, Richard J. Niehaus, and James A. Sheridan, "Human Resource Forecasting: A Survey of Practice and Potential," *Human Resource Planning,* Vol. 7, 1984, pp. 85–93.

9. Harvey Kahalas, Harold L. Pazer, John S. Hoagland, and Amy Levitt, "Human Resource Planning Activities in U.S. Firms," *Human Resource Planning,* Vol. 3, 1980, pp. 53–66.

10. Susan E. Jackson and Randall S. Schuler, "Human Resource Planning: Challenges for Industrial/Organizational Psychologists," *American Psychologist,* February 1990, pp. 223–239.

11. A. M. Bowey, "Corporate Manpower Planning," *Management Decision,* Vol. 15, 1977, pp. 421–469.

12. Daniel N. Bulla and Peter M. Scott, "Manpower Requirements Forecasting: A Case Example," in *Strategic Human Resource Planning Applications,* ed. Richard J. Niehaus (New York: Plenum, 1987), pp. 145–155.

13. Andre L. Delbecq, Andrew H. Van de Ven, and David H. Gustafson, *Group Techniques for Program Planning* (Glenview, Ill.: Scott, Foresman, 1975), pp. 83–107.

14. George T. Milkovich, Anthony J. Annoni, and Thomas A. Mahoney, "The Use of the Delphi Procedures in Manpower Forecasting," *Management Science,* December 1972, pp. 381–388.

15. Elmer H. Burack and Nicholas J. Mathys, *Human Resource Planning: A Pragmatic Approach to Manpower Staffing and Development* (Lake Forest, Ill.: Brace-Park Press, 1989).

16. W. Bert Bowers, "Who's Afraid of the Learning Curve?" *Purchasing,* March 1966, pp. 77–79, 134.

17. Nicholas Baloff, "Extension of the Learning Curve—Some Empirical Results," *Operations Research Quarterly,* December 1971, pp. 329–340.

18. Ibid., p. 330.

19. Don R. Bryant, Michael J. Maggard, and Robert P. Taylor, "Manpower Planning Models and Techniques," *Business Horizons,* April 1973, pp. 69–78.

20. Lee Dyer, "Human Resource Planning," p. 53. See Robert H. Meehan and S. Basheer Ahmed, "Forecasting Human Resources Requirements: A Demand Model," *Human Resource Planning,* 1990, Vol. 13, No. 3, pp. 297–308, for an example of using regression to predict demand in a public utility company.

21. Bowey, "Corporate Manpower Planning," pp. 421–469; Bryant, Maggard, and Taylor, "Manpower Planning Models and Techniques," pp. 69–78. For further information on linear or goal programming, see C. J. Verhoeven, *Techniques in Corporate Manpower Planning* (Boston: Kluwer, 1982); Richard C. Grinold and Kneale T. Marshall, *Manpower Planning Models* (New York: North-Holland, 1977); Richard J. Niehaus, *Computer-Assisted Human Resources Planning* (New York: Wiley, 1979).

22. William E. Bright, "How One Company Manages Its Human Resources," *Harvard Business Review,* January–February 1976, pp. 81–93.

23. Bob D. Hilton, "A Human Resource System That Lives Up to Its Name," *Personnel Journal,* July 1979, pp. 460–465.

24. Wayne F. Cascio and Elias M. Awad, *Human Resource Management: An Information Systems Approach* (Reston, Va.: Reston, 1981), pp. 40–93; Albert Walker, *Human Resource Information Systems: Design and Application.* (New York: Wiley, 1984).

25. H. W. Hennessey, Jr., "Computer Applications in Human Resource Information Systems," *Human Resource Planning,* Vol. 2, 1979, pp. 205–213.

26. Vincent R. Ceriello, "A Guide for Building a Human Resource Data System," *Personnel Journal,* September 1978, pp. 496–503.

27. John A. Hooper and R. F. Catalanello, "Markov Analysis Applied to Forecasting Technical Personnel," *Human Resource Planning,* Vol. 4, 1981, pp. 41–47.

28. Christie Teigland and Lori Hewig, "Projecting Workforce Needs in Government: The Case of New York State," in *Human Resource Forecasting and Strategy Development,* ed. Manuel London, Emily S. Bassman, and John P. Fernandez (New York: Quorum, 1990), pp. 41–51.

29. Herbert G. Heneman III and Marcus B. Sandver, "Markov Analysis in Human Resource Administration: Applications and

Limitations," *Academy of Management Review,* October 1977, pp. 535–542.

30. Richard J. Niehaus, "Human Resource Planning Flow Models," *Human Resource Planning,* Vol. 3, 1980, pp. 177–187.

31. For more information, see Guy E. Miller, "A Method for Forecasting Human Resource Needs Against Internal and External Labor Markets," *Human Resource Planning,* Vol. 3, 1980, pp. 189–200.

32. Niehaus, "Human Resource Planning Flow Models," pp. 177–187; Bryant, Maggard, and Taylor, "Manpower Planning Models and Techniques," pp. 69–78.

33. E. S. Bres III, R. J. Niehaus, F. J. Sharkey, and C. L. Weber, "Use of Personnel Flow Models for Analysis of Large Scale Work Force Changes," in *Strategic Human Resource Planning Applications,* ed. Richard J. Niehaus (New York: Plenum, 1987) pp. 157–167.

34. Bright, "How One Company Manages," pp. 81–93.

35. Jeffrey Pfeffer, "Organizational Demography," in *Research in Organizational Behavior,* Vol. 5, ed. L. L. Cummings and B. M. Staw (Greenwich, Conn.: JAI Press, 1983), pp. 299–357.

36. *Handbook of Methods,* Bulletin 2285, Washington, D.C.: Bureau of Labor Statistics, 1988.

37. Current Labor Statistics, *Monthly Labor Review,* December 1991, p. 79.

38. Ronald E, Kutscher, "New BLS Projections: Findings and Implications," *Monthly Labor Review,* November 1991, pp. 3–12.

39. George Silvestri and John Lukasiewicz, "Occupational Employment Projections," *Monthly Labor Review,* November 1991, pp. 64–94.

40. Paul Magnusson and Susan B. Garland, "Jobs, Jobs, Jobs Galore," *Business Week,* April 18, 1988, pp. 26–28.

41. Martin M. Greller and David M. Nee, *From Baby Boom to Baby Bust: How Business Can Meet the Demographic Challenge* (Reading, Mass.: Addison-Wesley, 1989).

42. Richard R. Nelson, "State Labor Legislation Enacted in 1990," *Monthly Labor Review,* January 1991, pp. 41–56.

43. Kutscher, "New BLS Projections," pp. 3–12.

44. Howard N. Fullerton, Jr., "Labor Force Projections: The Baby Boom Moves On," *Monthly Labor Review,* November 1991, pp. 31–44.

45. Joseph F. Coates, Jennifer Jarratt, and John B. Mahaffie, *Future Work: Seven Critical Forces Reshaping Work and the Work Force in North America* (San Francisco: Jossey-Bass, 1990).

46. Linda Thornburg, "What's Wrong with WorkForce 2000?" *HRMagazine,* August 1991, pp. 38–41.

47. William B. Johnston and Arnold H. Packer, *Workforce 2000* (Indianapolis: Hudson Institute, 1987).

48. Cited in Thornburg, "What's Wrong with WorkForce 2000?" p. 39; see Horst Brand, "Setting New Standards for Skills in the Workplace," *Monthly Labor Review,* November 1990, pp. 48–50, for a review of several major reports on worker qualifications and future job demands.

49. Robert O. Metzger and Mary Ann Von Glinow, "Off-site Workers: At Home and Abroad," *California Management Review,* Spring 1988, pp. 101–111.

50. Max L. Carey and James C. Franklin, "Industry Output and Job Growth Continues Slow into Next Century," *Monthly Labor Review,* November 1991, pp. 45–63.

51. Martha J. Finney, "The ASPA Labor Shortage Survey," *Personnel Administrator,* February 1989, pp. 35–42.

52. Schuler and Walker, "Human Resources Strategy: Focusing on Issues and Actions," pp. 4–19.

53. Marc J. Wallace, Jr., and M. Lynn Spruill, "How to Minimize Labor Costs During Peak Demand Periods," *Personnel,* July–August 1975, pp. 61–67; Leonard Greenhalgh, Anne T. Lawrence, and Robert I. Sutton, "Determinants of Work Force Reduction Strategies in Declining Organizations," *Academy of Management Review,* April 1988, pp. 241–254; A. Halcrow, "Tem-

porary Services Warm to the Business Climate," *Personnel Journal,* October 1988, pp. 84–89.

54. Rene J. Schoysman, "Planning Manpower in a Downturn Economy," *Journal of Systems Management,* May 1980, pp. 31–33.
55. J. T. McCune, R. W. Beatty, and R. V. Montagno, "Downsizing: Practices in Manufacturing Firms," *Human Resource Management,* Vol. 27, 1988, pp. 145–161.
56. "President Lets Plant Closing Become Law Without His Signature," *Ideas and Trends in Personnel,* August 9, 1988.
57. Gary B. Hansen, "Innovative Approach to Plant Closings: The UAW-Ford Experience at San Jose," *Monthly Labor Review,* June 1985, pp. 34–37.
58. Joel Brockner, "The Effects of Work Layoffs on Survivors: Research, Theory, and Practice," in *Research in Organizational Behavior,* Vol. 10, ed. Barry M. Staw and L.L. Cummings (Greenwich, Conn.: JAI Press, 1988), pp. 213–255.
59. Information in this section comes from Robert W. Eder, "Opening the Mirage: The Human-Resources Challenge," *Cornell Hotel and Restaurant Administration Quarterly,* August 1990, pp. 25–31; quote: 26–27.
60. David W. Rhodes, and James W. Walker, "Management Succession and Development Planning," *Human Resource Planning,* Vol. 7, 1984, pp. 157–173; S. D. Friedman, "Succession Systems in Large Corporations: Characteristics and Correlates of Performance," *Human Resource Management,* Vol. 25, 1986, pp. 191–213.
61. James K. Wellington, "Management Succession at Arizona Public Service," *Human Resource Planning,* Vol. 4, 1981, pp. 157–167.
62. Lee Dyer and Nelson O. Heyer, "Human Resource Planning at IBM," *Human Resource Planning,* Vol. 7, 1984, pp. 111–125.
63. Bright, "How One Company Manages Its Human Resources," pp. 81–93.
64. Jofannie Houk, "Human Resource Planning at Crocker National Bank," *Human Resource Planning,* Vol. 4, 1981, pp. 37–46.
65. See Diana Kramer, "Executive Succession and Development Systems: A Practical Approach," in *Human Resource Forecasting and Strategy Development*, ed. Manuel London, Emily S. Bassman, and John P. Fernandez (New York: Quorum, 1990), pp. 99–112, for detailed advice on setting up a succession planning system.
66. G. L. McManis and M. S. Leibman, "Succession Planners," *Personnel Administrator,* August 1988, pp. 24–30.
67. David W. Rhodes, "Succession Planning—Overweight and Underperforming," *Journal of Business Strategy,* November/December 1988, pp. 62–64; quote is from p. 62.
68. Zandy B. Leibowitz, Caela Farren, and Beverly L. Kaye, *Designing Career Development Systems* (San Francisco: Jossey-Bass, 1988).
69. Thomas A. Kochan, John P. MacDuffie, and Paul Osterman, "Employment Security at DEC: Sustaining Values Amid Environmental Change," *Human Resource Management,* Summer 1988, pp. 121–143.
70. Joel R. DeLuca, "Strategic Career Management in Non-Growing Volatile Business Environments," *Human Resource Planning,* Vol. 11, No. 1, 1988, pp. 49–61; Amanda Bennett, "Growing Small: As Big Firms Continue to Trim Their Staffs, 2-Tier Setup Emerges," *The Wall Street Journal,* May 4, 1987, pp. 1, 20.
71. Chris Tilly, "Reasons for the Continuing Growth of Part-Time Employment," *Monthly Labor Review,* March 1991, pp. 10–18.
72. Douglas T. Hall and Judith Richter, "Career Gridlock: Baby Boomers Hit the Wall," *The Executive,* August 1990, pp. 7–22.
73. DeLuca, "Strategic Career Management in Non-Growing Volatile Business Environments," pp. 49–61.
74. Greller and Nee, *From Baby Boom to Baby Bust.*
75. Hall and Richter, "Career Gridlock," pp. 7–22; Greller and Nee, *From Baby Boom to Baby Bust.*

4

Job Analysis: Procedures and Choices

Without adequate knowledge of what employees do on their jobs, organizations cannot develop effective human resource procedures for selecting, promoting, training, appraising, and compensating employees. How, for example, can an organization hire an employee without first knowing what behaviors, abilities, knowledge, and equipment are required to perform the job? How can an organization train an employee without first knowing exactly what he or she must do on the job? Job analysis provides organizations with this essential information.

In this chapter we examine job analysis and the job analysis process. We discuss the four phases of job analysis: determining the scope of the job analysis, choosing the method to be used, collecting and analyzing data, and assessing the job analysis procedure for effectiveness and reliability.

JOB ANALYSIS DEFINED

Job analysis can be defined as "obtaining information about jobs."[1] Generally, job analysis involves the following steps:

1. Collecting and recording job information.
2. Checking the job information for accuracy.
3. Writing job descriptions based on the information.
4. Using the information to determine what skills, abilities, and knowledge are required on the job.
5. Updating the information from time to time.[2]

Job analysis data serve as the foundation for most of the HRM practices discussed in this book. Chapter 4 is organized around the four major phases of job analysis. Before outlining these four phases, we will define some basic terms with which all job analysts should be familiar.

The activities that employees perform can be organized into a hierarchy based on their relative complexity and breadth:

- A **task** is one of the smallest units of work activity. It is "a meaningful unit of work activity generally performed on the job by one worker within some limited time period. . . . It is a discrete unit of activity and represents a composite of methods, procedures and techniques."[3]
- A **duty** is a loosely defined area of work that contains several distinct tasks that are performed by an individual.
- A **position** is the set of tasks and duties performed by a single individual in an organization. Each person in an organization has a position.
- A **job** is "a group of positions that are identical with respect to their major or significant tasks and sufficiently alike to justify their being covered by a single analysis."[4]
- An **occupation** refers to a general class of jobs that may be found in many organizations.
- A **career** is the sequence of jobs that an individual has held throughout his or her working life.

For example, during the course of a *career,* a person may have held several *jobs* in the *occupation* of nursing. One job may have been that of a surgical nurse. Each surgical nurse in a hospital holds a particular *position* that consists of several related *duties*. These duties might include preparing the operating room for surgery and monitoring the patient's vital signs during surgery. The duty of preparing the operating room for surgery could include several *tasks,* such as sterilizing surgical instruments, checking monitoring instruments to ensure that they are working properly, and obtaining supplies of blood.

Two other job analysis terms are important:

- A **job description** is a written narrative describing the activities performed on a job; usually it also includes information about the equipment used and the working conditions under which the job is performed.
- A **job specification** outlines the specific skills, knowledge, abilities, and other physical and personal characteristics that are necessary to perform a job.

THE JOB ANALYSIS PROCESS

The basic job analysis process consists of ten steps, which can be grouped into the four major phases shown in Figure 4.1. In phase 1, the job analyst determines

FIGURE 4.1 Job Analysis Process

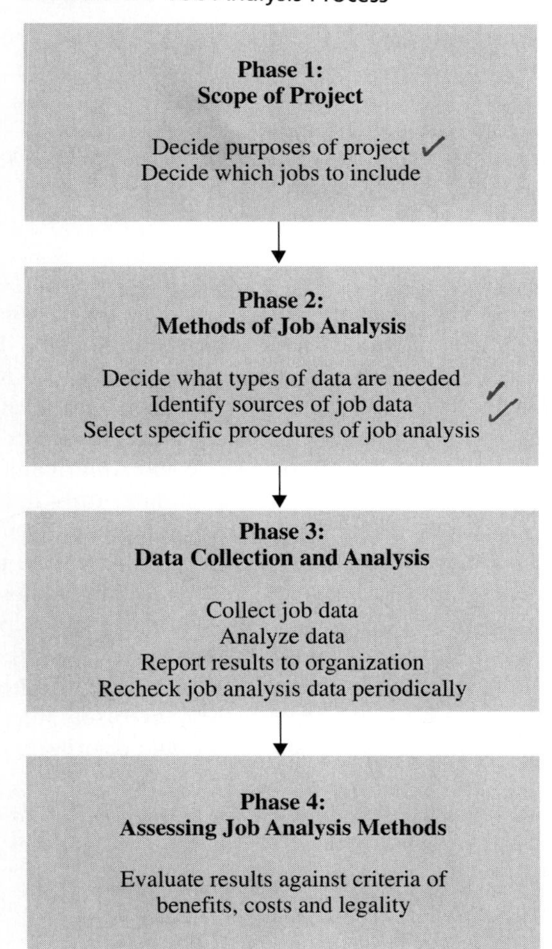

the scope of the job analysis project—specifically, the purposes of the job analysis and the jobs for which information needs to be collected. In phase 2, the job analyst decides what method or methods of job analysis to use—what types of job data are needed, what sources for that data are available, and what specific job analysis procedures should be used to collect these data. Phase 3 of the process is the collection and analysis of the job information. In this phase, the job analyst collects the job information, analyzes the data using appropriate techniques, reports these data in an understandable and useful way, and rechecks the job analysis information periodically to ensure its continuing validity. In phase 4, the job analyst assesses the overall value of the job analysis project in terms of its costs, benefits, and legality.

PHASE 1: THE SCOPE OF THE JOB ANALYSIS

To determine the scope of any job analysis effort, an organization must resolve two issues. First, the organization must decide what it hopes to accomplish with the job analysis data; second, it must identify the jobs that it wants to include in the analysis program. Top management throughout the organization, and particularly within the HR function of the company, must be involved in these decisions.

Uses of Job Analysis

Perhaps the most common uses of job analysis are in setting up personnel selection procedures (test development and validation), training employees, developing performance appraisal instruments, and establishing pay systems. Knowing what duties a job requires and what skills are needed to perform these duties is obviously critical in setting up an appropriate selection system. However, job analysis has become even more important in selection since the Americans with Disabilities Act went into effect in 1992. This act (discussed more fully in Chapter 5) outlaws discrimination against mentally and physically handicapped individuals who are able to perform the *essential functions* of a job, either in the usual way or with *reasonable accommodation* to their needs, such as workbenches designed to accommodate wheelchairs. To assure that truly qualified disabled people are not misjudged but that those not able to do the job are properly rejected, organizations must be sure that their job descriptions very clearly identify the essential functions or fundamental duties of jobs and convert these precisely into minimum physical and mental requirements.[5] Table 4.1 shows a range of other uses for job analysis.

For prospective employees, job analysis data can provide realistic information about what jobs will be like. Studies have found that such realistic "job previews" reduce applicants' unrealistically high expectations about jobs and thus reduce early employee dissatisfaction and turnover.[6] For new hires, job analysis data can help orient them to their positions.

TABLE 4.1 Uses of Job Analysis

Recruiting and Selecting Employees	*Developing and Appraising Employees*	*Compensation*	*Job and Organizational Design*
Human resource planning	Job training and skill development	Determining pay rates for jobs	Job design/redesign to improve efficiency or motivation
Identifying internal labor markets	Role clarification	Ensuring equal pay for equal work	Determining lines of authority and responsibility
Recruitment	Employee career planning	Ensuring equal pay for jobs of comparable worth	Determining necessary relationships among work groups
Selection	Performance appraisal		
Placement			
Equal employment opportunity			
Realistic job previews			

Job analysis data can provide the information needed to develop job-relevant training programs and performance appraisal systems. In addition, such data can help supervisors and employees clarify conflicts and ambiguities in employees' roles.

Job analysis data can be used to determine the similarity of jobs and thus the feasibility of transfers between jobs. In the U.S. Air Force, job analysis data have been used to identify jobs that individuals can transfer to with minimal retraining. In planning their own careers, employees can use job analysis information to plot career paths and make maximum use of their past experience in moving to different, more challenging jobs.

A traditional use of job analysis has been in the area of job evaluation, to determine the relative worth of jobs and thereby develop equitable compensation structures. The Equal Pay Act of 1963 mandates that employees who are in jobs that require the same skill, effort, and responsibility and that are performed under the same working conditions be paid similarly unless certain exceptions apply.[7] Job analysis provides a way for organizations to determine the relative similarity of two jobs.

Job analysis procedures have been used to design jobs for maximum efficiency. The effectiveness of the Japanese automobile and electronics industries has often been attributed to group management techniques.[8] Some of their successes, however, stem from the use of very detailed job analysis methods to determine the nature of jobs and to design work environments that allow workers to perform those jobs efficiently. In many cases, careful analysis of the actions required to perform a particular task or job has enabled Japanese firms to replace human workers with robots.

One use of jobs analysis data not included in Table 4.1 is job classification. The reason for this omission is that, in many of the uses listed, job classification is an intermediate step between the collection and use of the data. In job classification, the job analyst uses information to categorize similar jobs into a job family. The analyst can then develop selection, appraisal, pay, or other procedures for an entire job family, rather than for a single job. For example, in the area of personnel selection, research has shown that cognitive ability tests may be extremely useful in selecting among job applicants across a wide variety of jobs. Job analysis data help to identify groups of jobs for which a single cognitive ability test might serve as predictor of future job performance among job applicants.[9] This concept, known as "validity generalization," will be discussed in greater detail in Chapter 7.

Determining Which Jobs to Analyze

The following three factors determine which jobs should be included in a job analysis program:[10]

- **Diversity** (the range of jobs being analyzed): a single job (college professors); jobs within an occupation (educators, including college professors and elementary school teachers); or jobs in several occupations (state employees, including teachers and police officers).
- **Distribution** (the geographic site(s) of the jobs being analyzed): a single location (New York City); a region (the Northeast); an entire country (all U.S. locations); or a worldwide spread (all U.S. and foreign locations).
- **Employment setting** (the firms or facilities that will be covered by the job analysis): a single plant (the Borger, Texas, refinery of Philips Petroleum Company); a single organization (all plants and offices of Philips Petroleum); a single industry (all oil companies); or several industries (the oil, gas, nuclear, mining, and solar energy industries).

The number of jobs included in the job analysis program influences the specific job analysis procedures used. Some procedures are extremely difficult and expensive to conduct if the scope of the analysis is very large. Other analysis procedures have been designed specifically for large-scope projects. For example, one way of collecting job information is to observe employees actually performing the jobs. If International Business Machines Corp. (IBM) were to use this procedure for collecting information about all the jobs in IBM worldwide, this job analysis project would cost millions of dollars and take years to complete. If, on the other hand, IBM were interested only in the job of keyboard assemblers at a single plant, this observation method of collecting job information might prove quite useful.

PHASE 2: THE METHODS OF JOB ANALYSIS

To determine the method or methods of job analysis to use, the job analyst must decide on (1) the types of data to collect, (2) the sources of information from which to get the data, and (3) the specific procedure of job analysis to implement.

Types of Job Data

Several types of data can be collected in a job analysis project. These data include behavioral descriptions, ability requirements, job characteristics, and information about the equipment used on the job.[11]

Behavioral descriptors specify job- and worker-oriented activities. Job-oriented activities are the accomplishments of the job—what actually gets done. These activities are described in job-specific terms, such as "paints houses," "repairs carburetors," or "arrests burglars." Worker-oriented activities are the human behaviors (e.g., hand and arm movements); mental processes (e.g., decision making); or personal job demands (e.g., amount of physical energy expended) that occur on the job. Worker-oriented activities do not indicate what work gets done, but rather the processes used to get it done.

Ability requirements represent human abilities that are necessary to perform a job. E. A. Fleishman has developed a list of psychomotor and physical proficiency abilities that may be required in the performance of work.[12] For example, a secretarial or assembly job might require psychomotor abilities such as manual dexterity, finger dexterity, and arm-hand steadiness. In contrast, the job of a football team's offensive lineman would necessitate physical proficiency abilities such as explosive strength, gross body coordination, and stamina.

E. J. McCormick and his associates have developed a list of seventy-six human attributes that may be required on a job.[13] These attributes include physical abilities such as static strength or manual dexterity, cognitive abilities like intelligence and verbal comprehension, and situational attributes such as being able to work under time pressure or being able to work alone.

Environmental or intrinsic **job characteristics** are other factors that job analysts may need to identify.[14] For example, a questionnaire called the **Job Diagnostic Survey (JDS)** was developed to measure the following five motivational characteristics present in jobs:

- *Skill variety*—the degree to which a job requires a diversity of activities that utilize different skills and talents of an employee
- *Job identity*—the degree to which a job requires completion of a "whole," identifiable piece of work
- *Job significance*—the degree to which a job has substantial importance to other people and society as a whole
- *Autonomy*—the degree to which a job provides an employee with substantial freedom in order to determine exactly how the job will be performed
- *Feedback*—the degree to which an employee is able to learn from the job or other people how well he or she is performing[15]

Including this type of information in a job analysis provides a broader view of the job and the job's environment. Other job characteristics that might be assessed include the working conditions of the job (Is the job performed indoors or outdoors?); the "social environment" of the job (Does the employee work in a very crowded area with many others or in a private office?); and the work schedule of the job (Is it a regular day or night shift?).

When machines, tools, equipment, or other work aids are involved in the performance of a job, data about them should be included in the job analysis. An employer looking for a secretary obviously needs to know if he or she can operate the office equipment—be it a manual typewriter, dedicated word processor, or personal computer.

Another decision that the job analyst must make about the type of data to collect is whether to collect data in a qualitative or quantitative format. Qualitative data are verbal, narrative descriptions of the behaviors, abilities, characteristics, and equipment associated with the job. Quantitative data are numerical values that indicate the extent to which the behaviors, abilities, characteristics, and equipment are involved in the performance of the job. For example, a job analyst who collects qualitative data about a job might learn that typing letters is really important on the job. By collecting data in a quantitative format, the analyst might instead find that 70 percent of an employee's time is spent typing letters.

A big advantage of quantitative data is that they allow the job analyst to compare different jobs. Using qualitative data, the job analyst might find that for one job "typing letters is very important" and for another job "typing letters is critical." How then can the job analyst compare these two jobs? Is "very important" the same as "critical"? If, instead, the job analyst were to collect quantitative data, he or she might find that typing letters is 50 percent of one employee's job but 80 percent of another's.

Sources of Job Data

Although the most direct source of information about a job is the job incumbent, a number of other—human and nonhuman—sources are available (see Table 4.2). These sources may provide information that the average job incumbent cannot, thereby enabling the job analyst to question the incumbent more effectively.

The first place a job analyst should look for information about a job is in job analysis data that already exist. However, the job analyst should view these data with caution. They may have been developed using inadequate procedures, or they may no longer be valid descriptions of present-day jobs.

Although people such as job analysts, trainers, supervisors, and other experts may never have performed a certain job, they may be knowledgeable about the content and context of the work. For instance, an engineer who designed a nuclear reactor probably could offer considerable insight into the job of a nuclear reactor operator.

In deciding which sources to use in a given job analysis, the job analyst should follow these guidelines:

- For nonhuman sources, use those sources that are most recent.
- Use several sources of information whenever possible.

The job analyst who is using job incumbents and supervisors as a source of information should make sure that these individuals have had an adequate oppor-

TABLE 4.2 Sources of Information About Jobs

Nonhuman Sources	*Human Sources*
Existing job descriptions and specifications	Job analysts
Equipment maintenance records	Job incumbents
Equipment design blueprints	Supervisors
Architectural blueprints of work area	Job experts
Films of employees working	
Training manuals and other job training materials	
Popular literature, such as magazines or newspapers	

tunity to perform the job or observe the job being performed. According to several studies, the amount of job knowledge that sources have influences the accuracy and reliability of the information they provide.[16] Job incumbents who are interviewed should also be representative of the types of people who do the job. The job analyst should collect information from both males and females if both sexes perform the job. In a 1989 study, Neal Schmitt and Scott Cohen found significant differences in the job analysis ratings made by male and female police officers, indicating that, even though their job titles were identical, the duties performed by the two sexes were somewhat different.[17] A more recent study has supported these results, although the impact of the job incumbent's sex on job analysis ratings may be partially due to different levels of job experience between the two sexes—that is, women tended to have less job experience than men.[18] Probably it is best to collect information from both high and low performers, although some studies have found no difference in the type of information provided by these two groups.[19] It is particularly important to collect information from individuals with varying levels of experience on the job since the duties performed by individuals with greater or lesser amounts of job experience have been shown to vary substantially.[20]

Paying careful attention to who provides job analysis data is important for at least two reasons. First, since job data are the foundation for many other HR practices, to have a good foundation, data must be collected from accurate, reliable sources. Second, when organizations find themselves defending their personnel practices in court (as in the case of a sex, race, or age discrimination suit), judges are increasingly interested in the adequacy of the sources of job analysis information.[21]

Individuals who provide job analysis information are commonly called **subject matter experts**, or **SMEs**.[22] There are two basic approaches to selecting SMEs. One method, the stratification approach, involves collecting data (background, performance, tenure, and so on) about potential SMEs and using this information to select those who will provide job information.[23] Another approach is to collect information from all employees on the job and then use only that information that appears most reliable. One way of screening information is to compare an individual's responses about the job with the average responses of everyone providing job data. Individuals whose responses are highly deviant would not be used. Another method involves the use of a "carelessness index" to screen job data.[24] The job analyst examines individual responses to see if there is any tendency to mention job duties that obviously do not exist on the job. The data from such careless individuals would be rejected.

Job Analysis Procedures

The simplest job analysis procedures are **narrative job descriptions.** Data collected from various sources are transformed into written descriptions of job activities. Another category of analysis procedures is called **engineering approaches.** These procedures evolved from work in industrial engineering and engineering psychology. Typically, they identify the individual motions of hands, arms, and other body parts that are used to perform a job. **Structured job analysis procedures** use very definite physical structures (e.g., questionnaires consisting of specific items) and/or distinctive sets of routines to collect job information. **Managerial job analysis procedures** are specifically designed for analyzing managerial jobs. The nature of supervisory and executive jobs makes them particularly difficult to analyze. Thus, relatively few successful procedures for managerial job analysis have been developed.

Narrative Job Descriptions Narrative job descriptions and specifications are the simplest form of job analysis. The job analyst collects qualitative data from various sources of job data. Most frequently, the analyst interviews employees and supervisors or observes workers performing the job. The narrative job descriptions resulting from these processes typically include job title; job identification number; name of the department or division where the job is performed; name of the job analyst; brief written summary of the job; list of the job's major duties; description of the skills, knowledge (including education), and abilities needed to perform the job; list of the machines, tools, and equipment used on the job; and an explanation of how the job relates to other jobs in the organization. An example of a narrative job description is presented in Figure 4.2.

In writing these descriptions, job analysts try to describe the job in a terse, direct style with concrete, simple language. They avoid technical terms (unless they are widely used on the job) and make minimal use of adjectives, gerunds, and participles. The following are some guidelines for writing job descriptions:

- Use present-tense, active verbs (e.g., *drives* a truck, *replaces* brake shoes, *inspects* circuits).
- Make each sentence reflect an objective that is achieved by the actions described.
- Use words that provide necessary information; omit all other words.
- Use words that have only one meaning and that describe specifically how the job is performed.[25]

FIGURE 4.2 Narrative Job Description

Job title: Receptionist
ID number: 071-582-911A
Division: Customer Credit

Organization: Bonwit-Maxwell Department Stores
Job analyst: Edward Bourgois
Date analyzed: November 7, 1985

Job Summary

Answers inquiries and gives directions to customers, authorizes cashing of customers' checks, records and returns lost charge cards, and sorts and reviews new credit applications.

Job Duties

1. Answers inquiries and gives directions to customers. Greets customers at information desk and ascertains reasons for visits to credit office. Sends customers to Credit Interviewer to open credit accounts, to Cashier to pay bills, to Adjustment Department to obtain correction of errors in billing. Directs customers to other store departments on request, referring to store directory.
2. Authorizes cashing of checks. Authorizes cashing of personal or payroll checks (up to a specified amount) by customers desiring to make payment on credit account. Requests identification such as driver's license or credit card from customers, and examines check to verify date, amount, signature, and endorsement. Initials check and sends to Cashier.
3. Answers telephone calls from customers reporting lost or stolen charge cards and arranges details of cancellation of former cards and replacements. Obtains all possible details from customers regarding lost or stolen cards and submits data to Head Authorizer for processing. Notifies Head Authorizer immediately to prevent fraudulent use of missing cards. Orders replacement cards for customers when confirming letters are received.
4. Records charge cards that have inadvertently been left in sales departments and returns them to customers. Stamps imprint of cards on sheets of paper, using imprinting device. Dates sheets and retains for own records. Fills out forms, posting data such as customer's names, addresses, and dates cards were returned. Submits sheets to Head Authorizer.
5. Sorts and records new credit applications daily. Separates regular Charge Account applications from Budget Accounts. Breaks down charge account applications into local and out-of-town applications, and arranges them alphabetically within each group. Counts number of applications in each group and records in Daily Record Book. Binds each group of applications with rubber band and transmits to Tabulation Room.

Skills, Knowledge, Abilities

Education Needed: 6th grade
On-the-job Training: 3-5 weeks

Machines, Tools, Equipment, Work Aids

Impressing device-small, hand-operated device similar to stapler; used to make credit-card impressions on paper.

Relationships to Other Jobs

Promotion from: This is an entry-level job.
Promotion to: Credit Interviewer
Supervision received: Credit manager
Supervision given: No subordinates of this job

Transfers: None

Source: Adapted from U.S. Department of Labor, Manpower Administration, *Handbook for Analyzing Jobs* (Washington, D.C.; United States Government Printing Office, 1972), pp. 37–40.

The uses of narrative job descriptions are relatively limited. The information provided is so general that its use in developing specific performance appraisal or training content is difficult. The same problems exist for use of narrative descriptions in pay determination or job design. However, narrative descriptions are useful for recruiting and orientation, for creating realistic job previews, and for career planning.

Engineering Approaches This category of job analysis procedures involves an examination of the specific body movements and/or procedural steps that are used to perform a particular task. The job analyst collects data by observing actual employees on the job, films of employees working, or both films and live employees. The analyst develops an operation chart to show the actions of an employee performing a task. The chart uses symbols to represent the worker's specific actions and the sequence in which they occur; through the use of symbols and brief phrases, a detailed description of the task emerges. A typical operation chart is shown in Figure 4.3.

Micromotion studies are very similar to operation charts. They are most appropriate for the analysis of jobs that contain very short-cycle, repetitive tasks (e.g., soldering the electrical circuits on the chassis of a television set). The job analyst develops a list of basic body motions and uses it to analyze all the tasks included in the study. Several standard lists of basic body motions have been developed.[26] These lists include such motions as search, select, grasp, hold, position, inspect, assemble, and disassemble. The analyst films workers performing a task and then analyzes the film to identify the separate motions and the time required to complete each motion. The term **time and motion study,** which derives from this analysis of time and motions, is often used to describe this category of job analysis procedures.

The engineering approaches to job analysis provide detailed information about jobs. These methods concentrate on tasks and/or basic body movements, are relatively objective in their manner of collecting information, and usually result in some form of quantitative data. The data are particularly useful for the design of equipment to be used on the job. However, these procedures provide little of the broader context in which the job is performed. They present little direct information about the environment in which the work takes place or the abilities that are necessary to perform the job.

Structured Job Analysis Procedures Although there are many different structured job analysis procedures, we will discuss six that are representative. Each procedure provides a different view of jobs and is suitable for different uses.

Critical Incidents Technique (CIT) J. C. Flanagan developed the **critical incidents technique (CIT)** for assembling lists of behaviors that are critical to job performance. The procedure consists of four steps.[27]

1. A panel of experts provides written examples of behaviors that represent effective or ineffective performance on the job. These examples describe a given

INTERNATIONAL PERSPECTIVE

Job Analysis: Not Needed In Japan

In the United States, careful job analysis underlies many aspects of good personnel practice, particularly recruitment and selection, training, and compensation. Definite jobs are advertised, and applicants are hired on the basis of their job-specific qualifications. Successful candidates may then enter training programs designed for those particular jobs. Compensation is closely tied to job content, via a procedure known as job evaluation.

In Japan, large companies have little need for job descriptions and specifications (except where they apply to the design of work environments) because of the different philosophy that guides their employment practices. In recruiting white-collar employees, traditional Japanese companies do not advertise specific jobs but instead look for new graduates who "fit" with the organization and can contribute in a variety of roles. Employers assume that these individuals will pursue long careers within their organizations and that they will work in many different areas. In evaluating candidates, employers place much more emphasis on personality, attitudes, formal education, and family background than on specific job-related skills or knowledge.

Because Japanese employees are hired without regard to specific skills, employers invest in extensive in-house training of new hires. Organizations expect such investments to pay off because trainees normally continue to work for them for the duration of their careers. Initial training is comprised of orientation to the entire organization, including its style and culture. More specific training is provided on the job, by job rotation, or by assigned "seniors" who mentor new employees. This combination reduces the need for job analysis as a source of formal training-program content.

Another area where job descriptions are not needed is salary determination. Japanese salaries are based largely on seniority and education, with allowances for housing, transportation, and family size. Individuals who are performing the same job may receive very different salaries for their equal contributions—a practice that is perceived as unfair in the United States.

In sum, Japanese managers see job descriptions as unnecessary at best and harmful at worst. In their eyes, job descriptions stifle flexibility and initiative. But loosely defined job responsibilities, they believe, allow employees to assume responsibility for and become involved in many different kinds of tasks, thus facilitating the lifelong on-the-job learning that Japanese organizations so prize. Finally, because of the emphasis placed on achieving results through cooperative groups and work teams, Japanese management views job descriptions at the level of the individual job as irrelevant.

Sources: Ryokichi Hirono, "Personnel Management in Foreign Corporations," in *The Japanese Employee*, ed. Robert J. Ballon (Rutland Vt.: The Charles E. Tuttle Company, 1969), pp. 251–271; J. Ballon, *The Japanese Employee*, pp. 123–165; Malcolm Trevor, *Japan's Reluctant Multinationals* (New York: St. Martin's Press), pp. 59–68; Malcolm Trevor, Fochen Schendel, and Bernhard Wilpert, *The Japanese Management Development System* (London: Frances Pinter, 1986), pp. 8, 9, 254; and David E. Bowen, Gerald E. Ledford, Jr., and Barry Nathan, "Hiring for the Organization, Not the Job," *The Executive*, November 1991, pp. 35–51.

FIGURE 4.3 Operation Chart

OPERATION CHART

SUMMARY PER 1 PIECES

	PRESENT		PROPOSED		DIFFERENCE	
	LH	RH	LH	RH	LH	RH
OPERATIONS	2	6				
TRANSPORTS	3	6				
HOLDS	9	0				
DELAYS	0	2				
TOTAL	14	14				

COMPANY A. C. Wright Corp.
DEPARTMENT Assembly
OPERATION Assemble ball point pen No. RT 45
OPERATOR R. O. Jenkins
CHARTED BY S. O. J. DATE
PRESENT ~~PROPOSED~~ METHOD
SHEET 1 OF 1

LEFT HAND		RIGHT HAND
To barrel	1	To ink cartridge
Grasp barrel	2	Grasp ink cartridge
To assemble area	3	To assembly area
Hold barrel	4	Insert cartridge in barrel
" "	5	To spring
" "	6	Grasp spring
" "	7	To assembly area
" "	8	Assemble spring on cartridge
" "	9	To cap
" "	10	Grasp cap
" "	11	To assembly area
" "	12	Assemble cap to barrel
To rack	13	Wait for left hand
Place in rack	14	" " " "
	15	
	16	
	17	
	18	
	19	
	20	

Action	Symbol	Definition
Operation	○	Change object in physical or chemical nature, assemble or disassemble, or arrange for another operation.
Transport	⇨	Move object from one place to another.
Inspect	□	Examine object for quality/quantity.
Delay	D	Retain object in a location to await another action with no authorization needed to perform the next action.
Storage	▽	Retain object in a location to prevent unauthorized removal.

Source: From Amrine, Ritchey, and Moodie, *Manufacturing Organization & Management,* 5th edition, © 1987, p. 117. Reprinted by permission of Prentice-Hall, Inc. Englewood Cliffs, New Jersey.

incident: what led up to it, exactly what the employee did, the consequences of the behavior, and to what extent the consequences of the behavior were under the control of the employee.[28] The following example of a critical incident shows good performance on the job by a night security guard.

The security guard heard a strange hissing sound coming from the basement. He investigated the noise and found a gas leak in the building's furnace. He immediately cut off the gas to the furnace, preventing an explosion, and called the utility company to arrange for the repair of the leak.

2. All the examples generated in step 1 are put on index cards and then sorted into groups of similar behaviors (e.g., handling emergency situations). This sorting may be done by either the job analyst or a group of experts on the job.
3. The categories identified in step 2 are defined and named by either the job analyst or job experts.
4. The job behavior categories are rated according to how critical or important they are for job performance. This rating is done by a group of job experts.

Using the CIT, job analysts can identify major types of behaviors that correlate with effective or ineffective performance. The CIT is well suited for developing performance appraisal systems and also for determining the training needs of employees. However, it supplies limited information about "whole" jobs, since it does not identify the common, routine behaviors performed on jobs. This limitation in Flanagan's approach can be eliminated easily by extending the CIT procedure. In the extended critical incidents technique, statements concerning average performance are also collected to allow a better overall view of job behaviors.[29]

Department of Labor (DOL) Method The **Department of Labor (DOL) method**, described in the Department of Labor's *Revised Handbook for Analyzing Jobs*, uses data concerning the work performed and worker traits.[30] Trained job analysts obtain data from reviews of written materials, observation of job incumbents, and interviews with job incumbents and supervisors. The analysts then record these data, organize them into subcategories, and rate the various worker functions and traits (see Table 4.3).

The "worker functions" subcategory of the DOL method is particularly important. The three worker-function scales are based on the assumption that all job activities involve *data, people,* or *things*. Additional assumptions are that a relatively limited number of different types of activities can occur with respect to data, people, and things, and that these activities can be reliably rated. The structured job analysis procedure described next, functional job analysis, provides a description of the rating scales. Any job can be rated using these scales, and any job can be compared with any other job based on these ratings. In the DOL procedure, information is recorded on a standardized job analysis schedule. A completed schedule for the job of a dough mixer is presented in Figure 4.4.

Although its developers suggest that the DOL procedure may be used for a variety of purposes, its actual utility is somewhat restricted. The DOL method

TABLE 4.3 Categories of Work Performed and Worker Traits

Work Performed	*Worker functions.* What workers do in the performance of a job with respect to data (information and ideas); people (interpersonal communication); and things (equipment, materials, products).
	Work fields. Characteristics of the machines, tools, equipment, and work aids used; techniques used in performing the job (e.g., painting, secretarial skills, computing).
	Machines, tools, equipment, work aids. Actual devices used in performing the job.
	Materials, products, subject matter, services. Basic materials used (e.g., steel or petroleum); final product made (e.g., cars or gas); subject matter applied (metallurgy or chemistry); service rendered (e.g., educational or medical) in terms of 55 groups with 580 categories listed by the Department of Labor.
	Tasks. Specific work activities performed on the job.
Worker Traits	*General educational development.* Those aspects of education that relate to a person's ability to reason and use mathematics or language skills on the job.
	Specific vocational preparation. Preparation needed to acquire specific techniques or information used in performing the job.
	Aptitudes. Specific capacities or aptitudes needed to learn and perform the job.
	Temperaments. "Adaptability" characteristics needed by the worker to perform the job.
	Interests. Worker's preference for certain kinds of job experiences and situations.
	Physical demands. Physical capacities required of the worker on the job.
	Environmental conditions. Physical surroundings of the job that place demands on the worker.

Source: Adapted from *Job Analysis: An Effective Managerial Tool* by S. E. Bemis, A. H. Belenky, and D. A. Soder. Reprinted by permission of BNA Books, Washington, D.C.

identifies specific tasks performed on the job but does not tie the ratings of worker traits directly to these tasks. In other words, it uses a "whole job" perspective—it assesses the level of a particular ability by considering all the tasks that make up a job, not just the task requiring that ability. According to recent court rulings, when job data are used for personnel selection purposes, ratings should be made relative to *each* task rather than to the job as a whole. Nevertheless, the DOL procedure is important because it is the cornerstone of other job analysis procedures.

Data on thousands of jobs have been collected using this method and published in the *Dictionary of Occupational Titles* (*DOT*), which provides valuable information to job analysts and HR managers.[31] Each job in the *DOT* has a nine-digit code number, and the jobs are arranged according to these numbers. The

FIGURE 4.4 DOL Job Analysis Schedule

JOB ANALYSIS SCHEDULE

1. Estab. Job Title DOUGH MIXER
2. Ind. Assign. (bake. prod.)
3. SIC Code(s) and Title(s) 2051 Bread and other bakery products

DOT Title ______ Code 520.762

Ind. Desig. ______ WTA Group Oper. Control p.436

4. JOB SUMMARY:

Operates mixing machine to mix ingredients for straight and sponge (yeast) doughs according to established formulas, directs other workers in fermentation of dough, and cuts dough into pieces with hand cutter.

5. WORK PERFORMED RATINGS:

	D	P	(T)
	Data	People	Things
Worker Functions	5	6	2

Work Field 146 - Cooking, Food Preparing

M.P.S.M.S. 364 - Bakery Products

6. WORKER TRAITS RATINGS:

GED	1 (2) 3 4 5 6
SVP	1 2 3 (4) 5 6 7 8 9
Aptitudes	G 3 V 3 N 3 S 3 P 3 Q 4 K 3 F 3 M 3 E 4 C 4
Temperaments	D F I J (M) P R S (T) V
Interests	(1a) 1b 2a 2b 3a 3b 4a (4b) 5a (5b)
Phys. Demands	S L M (H) V 2 (3) (4) 5 (6)
Environ. Cond.	(I) O B 2 3 4 (5) 6 7

7. a. Elementary 6 High School None Courses ______
   b. College ______ Courses ______
8. Vocational Preparation
   a. College None Courses ______
   b. Vocational Education None Courses ______
   c. Apprenticeship None
   d. Inplant Training None
   e. On-the-Job Training six months
   f. Performance on Other Jobs DOUGH-MIXER HELPER - one year
9. Experience One year as DOUGH-MIXER HELPER
10. Orientation Four hours
11. Licenses, etc. Food Handlers Certificate issued by the Health Dept

Source: U.S. Department of Labor, Employment and Training Administration, *The Revised Handbook for Analyzing Jobs* (Washington, D.C.: United States Government Printing Office, 1991).

FIGURE 4.4 DOL Job Analysis Schedule (*cont.*)

12. Relation to Other Jobs and Workers
    Promotion: From DOUGH-MIXER HELPER To Baker
    Transfers: From None To None
    Supervision Received by Baker
    Supervision Given DOUGH-MIXER HELPER

13. Machines, Tools, Equipment, and Work Aids
    Dough mixing machine; balance scales; hand scoops; measuring vessels; portable dough troughs.

14. Materials and Products
    Bread dough

15. Description of Tasks:
    1. Dumps ingredients into mixing machine: Examines production schedule to determine type of bread to be produced, such as rye, whole wheat, or white. Refers to formula card for quantities and types of ingredients required, such as flour, water, milk, vitamin solutions, and shortening. Weighs out, measures, and dumps ingredients into mixing machine. (20%)
    2. Operates mixing machine: Turns valves and other hand controls to set mixing time according to type of dough being mixed. Presses button to start agitator blades in machine. Observes gauges and dials on equipment continuously to verify temperature of dough and mixing time. Feels dough for desired consistency. Adds water or flour to mix measuring vessels and adjusts mixing time and controls to obtain desired elasticity in mix. (55%)
    3. Directs other workers in fermentation of dough: Prepares fermentation schedule according to type of dough being raised. Sprays portable dough *Trough* with lubricant to prevent adherence of mixed dough to trough. Directs DOUGH-MIXER HELPER in positioning trough beneath door of mixer to catch dough when mixing cycle is complete. Pushes or directs other workers to push troughs of dough into fermentation room. (10%)
    4. Cuts dough: Dumps fermentated dough onto worktable. Manually kneads dough to eliminate gases formed by yeast. Cuts dough into pieces with hand cutter. Places cut dough on proofing rack and covers with cloth. (10%)
    5. Performs miscellaneous duties: Records on work sheet number of batches mixed during work shift. Informs BAKE SHOP FOREMAN when repairs or major adjustments are required for machines and equipment. (5%)

16. Definition of Terms
    Trough - A long narrow, opened vessel used for kneading or washing ingredients.

17. General Comments
    None

18. Analyst Jane Smith Date 3/21/70 Editor John Riley Date 3/30/70
    Reviewed By Alexandra Purcey Title, Org. Foreman, Bake Shop
    National Office Reviewer Mary Moore

first three digits indicate the major occupational category into which the job falls. The second three digits are the worker-function ratings. The final three digits are used to provide each job with a unique DOT code number.

Functional Job Analysis (FJA) In **functional job analysis (FJA)**, a modification of the DOL method, trained job analysts review written materials, observe workers performing the job, and interview job incumbents and supervisors for information.[32] Others familiar with the job then review all this information to ensure its validity and reliability. There are five steps in the FJA procedure.[33]

1. The job analyst and top management decide on the goals, purposes, and objectives of the FJA project.

2. Job analysts identify and describe the tasks performed on the job in a standardized written format, outlining what action occurs, to what purpose, and under what specific conditions.

3. Job analysts analyze each task using seven scales: three worker-function scales (see Table 4.4), a worker-instruction scale, and three scales concerning general educational development in reasoning, mathematics, and language. The worker-function scales indicate the type of behavior engaged in toward data,

TABLE 4.4 Worker-Function Scales in Functional Job Analysis

Data	*People*	*Things*
1. Comparing	1a. Taking instructions 1b. Serving	1a. Handling 1b. Feeding/off-bearing 1c. Tending
2. Copying	2. Exchanging information	2a. Manipulating 2b. Operating/controlling 2c. Driving/controlling
3a. Computing 3b. Compiling	3a. Coaching 3b. Persuading 3c. Diverting	3a. Precision working 3b. Setting up
4. Analyzing	4a. Consulting 4b. Instructing 4c. Treating	
5a. Innovating 5b. Coordinating	5. Supervising	
6. Synthesizing	6. Negotiating 7. Mentoring	

Note: The higher the scale number, the more complex the function is. Precise definitions of the worker functions can be found in the source of this table.

Source: A. S. Fine, *Functional Job Analysis Scales: A Desk Aid* (Kalamazoo, Mich: W. E. Upjohn Institute for Employment Research, 1973). Reprinted by permission of the author.

people, and things; these scales also indicate the percentage of time spent on each task involved with data, people, and things. For example, in performing one task, an employee might spend 70 percent of the time working with people, 10 percent working with data, and the remaining 20 percent working with things.

4. Job analysts write performance standards to describe how to assess the performance of workers. For example, for the task of typing letters, the performance standard might read: "Letters are typed with no typographical, grammatical, or spelling errors." A numerical performance standard for the same job might read: "No more than one spelling error per page of typing." Job analysts might establish either of these performance standards.

5. Job analysts identify the training needed by the employee to perform the job. This analysis of training content identifies the functional, specific content, and adaptive skills needed to perform the task. For the job of typist, a worker might need to be trained in how to type (functional skill) and in the proper format of business letters (specific content skill). The training analysis might also indicate that a good typist must be able to "pace his or her work"—an adaptive skill that enables the worker to perform the task properly over time.

The FJA method has been used to analyze many different jobs. It has a wide range of applications but is not particularly useful for job classification or evaluation unless combined with other techniques. Although the FJA method has many similarities to the DOL procedure, its one advantage is that it analyzes each task separately. This characteristic provides a much more detailed picture of the job and makes the FJA method more widely applicable for organizational purposes.

Position Analysis Questionnaire (PAQ) Designed by E. J. McCormick to analyze a wide variety of jobs,[33] the **Position Analysis Questionnaire (PAQ)** consists of 194 items: 187 items characterize the worker-oriented activities involved in performing a job, and seven items deal with pay issues.[34] The items of the PAQ are grouped into six divisions. The first division includes items on the sources of information that workers use in performing a job; the second division concerns the mental processes used on the job; and the third division identifies the actual output of the job. The final three divisions of the PAQ deal with relationships with other persons, the job context, and other job characteristics. Sample items within each of the six divisions are shown in Table 4.5.

To complete the PAQ, a job analyst, supervisor, or job incumbent uses one of six rating scales. (The job analyst usually rates the PAQ items during an interview with a job incumbent or supervisor.) The six scales used to rate PAQ items are (1) extent of use, (2) importance to the job, (3) amount of time, (4) possibility of occurrence, (5) applicability, and (6) special code. The special code scales are constructed for specific items and vary in their exact format. Depending on the nature of the item, each is rated using only one of the scales. Typically, a PAQ analysis is completed for several individual positions with the same job title. The results of these analyses are then averaged to get a better, more reliable picture of the job.

TABLE 4.5 Six Divisions of the PAQ

	Description	*Sample Items*
1. Information Input	How and from where does the worker get information used in performing the job?	Use of written materials Near visual differentiation
2. Mental Processes	What reasoning, decision-making, planning, and information-processing activities are used in performing the job?	Level of decision making Coding/decoding
3. Work Output	What physical activities are performed, and what machines, tools, or devices are used?	Use of keyboard devices Assembling/disassembling
4. Relationships with Other Persons	What interactions with other people are involved in performing the job?	Instructing; Contacts with public, customers
5. Job Context	In what physical or social environment is the job performed?	High temperature Interpersonal-contact situations
6. Other Job Characteristics	What other activities, conditions, or characteristics are relevant to job performance?	Specified work pace Amount of job structure

Source: Reprinted, by permission of the publisher, from *Job Analysis: Methods and Applications,* by E. J. McCormick, pp. 144–145, © 1979 AMACOM, a division of the American Management Association. All rights reserved.

The items of the PAQ can be grouped into thirty-two divisional and thirteen overall job dimensions (see Table 4.6). Each job dimension represents a category of worker-oriented activities that may occur on the job. The job-dimension scores represent the actual levels of these activities that occur on a particular job. In addition to job-dimension scores, L. D. Marquardt and McCormick have developed procedures using the PAQ to provide scores on seventy-six human attributes.[35] These attribute scores indicate the levels at which various physical, cognitive, and situational abilities are involved in job performance.

The PAQ has been used extensively for personnel selection, job classification, and job evaluation. However, its use in performance appraisal and training systems is limited. The worker-oriented PAQ items make analyzing a wide variety of jobs easier, but they also make it difficult to translate PAQ scores directly into specific performance standards or training content.

Task Inventory Procedure R. E. Christal has conducted extensive research in the U.S. Air Force and has developed what is commonly known as the **task inventory procedure** of job analysis.[36] A task inventory is "a form of structured job analysis questionnaire that consists of a listing of tasks within some occupational

TABLE 4.6 PAQ Job Dimensions

Divisional Dimensions*	
Division 1: Information Input	1. Interpreting what is sensed 2. Using various sources of information 3. Watching devices/materials for information 4. Evaluating/judging what is sensed 5. Being aware of environmental conditions 6. Using various senses
Division 2: Mental Processes	7. Making decisions 8. Processing information
Division 3: Work Output	9. Using machines/tools/equipment 10. Performing activities requiring general body movements 11. Controlling machines/processes 12. Performing skilled, technical activities 13. Performing controlled manual/related activities 14. Using miscellaneous equipment/devices 15. Performing handling/related manual activities 16. General physical coordination
Division 4: Relationships with Other Persons	17. Communicating judgments/related information 18. Engaging in general personal contacts 19. Performing supervisory/coordination/related activities 20. Exchanging job-related information 21. Public/related personal contacts
Division 5: Job Context	22. Being in a stressful/unpleasant environment 23. Engaging in personally demanding situations 24. Being in hazardous job situations
Division 6: Other Job Characteristics	25. Working nontypical versus day schedule 26. Working in businesslike situations 27. Wearing optional versus specified apparel 28. Being paid on a variable versus salary basis 29. Working on a regular versus irregular schedule 30. Working under job-demanding circumstances 31. Performing structured versus unstructured work 32. Being alert to changing conditions
Overall Dimensions†	1. Having decision-making, communicating, and general responsibilities 2. Operating machines/equipment 3. Performing clerical/related activities 4. Performing technical/related activities 5. Performing service/related activities 6. Working regular day versus other work schedule

TABLE 4.6 PAQ Job Dimensions (*cont.*)

Overall Dimensions (cont.)	7. Performing routine/repetitive activities 8. Being aware of work environment 9. Engaging in physical activities 10. Supervising/coordinating other personnel 11. Public/customer/related contacts 12. Working in an unpleasant/hazardous/demanding environment 13. Having a nontypical schedule/optional apparel style

*Divisional PAQ job dimensions were formed by factor analyzing the items within each division separately.

†Overall PAQ job dimensions were formed by factor analyzing all items at the same time.

Source: E. J. McCormick, R. C. Mecham, and P. R. Jeanneret, *Position Analysis Questionnaire (PAQ) Technical Manual (System II)* (Logan, Utah: PAQ Services, Inc., 1977). Reprinted by permission.

field . . . and [a] provision for some type of response scale for each task."[37] A task inventory is job oriented: items in the inventory deal with what gets done on the job. Because it is job oriented, a task inventory must be developed for each category of jobs that is to be analyzed. In contrast to the PAQ, there is no single version of the task inventory. Developing a task inventory involves six major steps:[38]

1. Determine the jobs to include in the inventory. Most task inventories are developed for use in analyzing an occupation rather than a single job. The job analyst must select the geographical distribution and employment setting to cover.

TABLE 4.7 Anatomy of a Task Statement

	Three basic elements		
	1. A specific, *present-tense action verb* describing what is done 2. A brief description of the *object of the verb* 3. When necessary, a *qualifying phrase* to distinguish the task from other similar tasks on the job		
	Action Verb	*Object*	*Qualifying Phrase*
Sample Task Statements	Type	grade reports	on word processor.
	Interview	job applicants	for managerial jobs.
	Adjust	coolant flow	on nuclear reactor.
	Replace	brake shoes.	

Source: Adapted from H. L. Ammerman, *Performance Content for Job Training*, Vol. 2 (Columbus, Ohio: Center on Education and Training for Employment (formerly CVE), Ohio State University). Copyright 1977. Used with permission.

2. *Construct a list of tasks.* Using written materials, as well as interviews with job incumbents and supervisors, the job analyst produces an initial list of tasks performed. The analyst describes the tasks using statements written in a standardized format. The format used in writing task statements is described in Table 4.7. A group of individuals familiar with the occupation reviews the list of task statements. A pilot study using job incumbents may be conducted with this list to ensure that all relevant tasks are included and that the wording of the task statements is appropriate.

3. *Plan the survey and analyses.* The job analyst must decide what information about tasks is needed. The analyst may collect several different types of data, such as whether the task is performed on a specific job, the importance of the task to the job, the criticality of the task, the relative time spent performing the task, the complexity of the task, and the difficulty of learning the task.

Recent studies have indicated that asking incumbents to rate a task using several different rating scales may not be necessary. Lee Friedman, in a 1990 study, found that relative-time-spent and task importance scales yielded highly redundant information.[39] Ratings of task frequency, on the other hand, did seem to provide unique information. Another study found that task importance could be strongly predicted from ratings of task criticality and difficulty of learning the task.[40] Thus, asking job incumbents to rate their job using all three scales seems unnecessary.

A portion of a typical task inventory is shown in Figure 4.5. Usually the analyst runs a pilot study to ensure that the instructions are clear and that the format of the inventory is appropriate and easy to use. Once the inventory is ready, the job analyst plans how it will be administered, which job incumbents will be selected to complete the inventory, and what analyses will be conducted on the data that are collected.

4. *Administer the task inventory.* The job analyst administers the inventory by handing it out to select employees during work hours or mailing it to employees. Once the inventories have been distributed, the analyst uses some form of follow-up to ensure that they are completed and returned.

5. *Process the survey data.* As the inventories are returned, they are checked to make sure that they have been filled out properly. The data are then coded and analyzed using a variety of statistical procedures. These procedures usually include identifying tasks that are most important to the job and clustering similar jobs into job families. Once important tasks have been identified, additional data on these tasks may be collected to determine the skills, knowledge, or abilities that are required to perform the tasks.

6. *Report the data.* Once all analyses are complete, the job analyst must write reports that summarize the findings of the project. These reports may include suggestions on how the task inventory data may best be used to improve selection, training, performance appraisal, or other HR practices in the organization.

FIGURE 4.5 Sample Task Inventory

Data Processing Task Inventory	Page 14 of 26 Pages	
Listed below are a duty and the tasks which it includes. Check all tasks which you perform. Add any tasks you do which are not listed, then rate the tasks you have checked.	Check	Time Spent
H. Operating Automatic Data Processing Equipment	✓ If Done	1. Very Much Below Average 2. Below Average 3. Slightly Below Average 4. About Average 5. Slightly Above Average 6. Above Average 7. Very Much Above Average
1. Analyze job steps to determine data recovery points.		
2. Analyze machine operation through use of messages received from the equipment.		
3. Analyze machine operation through use of conditions displayed.		
4. Determine cause of machine stops and malfunctions.		
5. Interrogate memory locations on the console.		
6. Load programs and data cards.		
7. Locate tapes in storage media or tape library.		
8. Maintain card files (source object, etc.).		
9. Maintain current run tapes.		
10. Maintain levels of data processing supplies.		
11. Maintain technical files on equipment operation and procedural changes.		
12. Make switch settings.		
13. Operate card reader.		
14. Operate collator.		
15. Operate console.		
16. Operate decollator.		
17. Operate document writer.		
18. Operate forms bursting equipment.		
19. Operate interpreter.		
20. Operate key punch machines or verifiers.		

Source: H. L. Ammerman, *Performance Content for Job Training,* Vol. 3 (Columbus, Ohio: Center on Education and Training for Employment (formerly CVE), Ohio State University). Copyright © 1977. Used with permission.

Task inventories provide a wealth of information about the jobs within a specific occupational field. They are useful when the job analyst needs to collect data from several job incumbents who are spread over a large geographical region. Once they are designed, the inventories are relatively easy to complete and may be mailed to employees. When only a few employees are involved, however, task inventories are not cost-effective, since they are expensive to develop. The information obtained from task inventories is very useful in the design of training programs.

Conversely, task-inventory data cannot be used to compare jobs in very different occupational fields. No two task inventories are exactly the same, and comparing across inventories that have been developed for two different occupations is practically impossible. Likewise, task inventories are not suited for organization-wide evaluation purposes. Comparing very different jobs for the purpose of determining equitable compensation requires the use of a common set of job characteristics.

Ability Requirements Scales Both the PAQ and task inventory methods focus on behavioral requirements of jobs. The **Ability Requirement Scales,** developed by E. A. Fleishman and his associates, measure abilities needed to perform jobs.[41] Job experts are asked to rate the extent to which fifty-two abilities are required to perform the job. These include abilities such as oral comprehension, number facility, night vision, dynamic flexibility, and selective attention. To rate these abilities, job experts receive rating scales in which the ability is carefully defined and distinguished from other abilities; the rater uses a seven-point rating scale, in which each point on the scale is "anchored" with a behavioral example. For example, for rating the ability of static strength, the "1" level on the rating scale is anchored with the statement "Lift one package of bond paper," and "7" point on the scale is anchored with "Reach over and lift a 70 lb. box onto a table." Once important abilities have been identified, individual tasks on the job that require those abilities can be identified. The Ability Requirement Scales are particularly appropriate for use in job classification and the development of personnel selection systems.

Managerial Job Analysis Procedures The final group of job analysis procedures are those used specifically for the analysis of managerial and professional jobs. Since most of these techniques have not been widely used in organizational settings, it is impossible to make an accurate assessment of their utility as job analysis procedures.

Management Position Description Questionnaire (MPDQ) Walter W. Tornow and Patrick R. Pinto developed the **Management Position Description Questionnaire (MPDQ)**, a 208-item questionnaire that is used to describe managers' jobs.[42] Based on earlier work by J. K. Hemphill, the MPDQ is completed by incumbent managers, who use a six-point scale to rate each item.[43] Statistical analyses have shown that the 208 items can be grouped into 13 major categories (see Table 4.8).

TABLE 4.8 Thirteen Categories of the MPDQ

Number	*Category*	*Definition*
1	Product, Marketing, and Financial Strategy Planning	Thinking and planning to insure the long-range business growth and stability of the company
2	Coordination of Other Organizational Units and Personnel	Coordinating the activities of individuals and groups over which the manager has no direct control
3	Internal Business Control	Reviewing and controlling the financial, human, and other resources of the company
4	Products and Services Responsibility	Controlling the technical aspects of products and services to insure proper production timing and quality
5	Public and Customer Relations	Maintaining the company's reputation with customers and the public in general through direct contact with these individuals
6	Advanced Consulting	Applying technical competencies to deal with special problems that arise in the organization
7	Autonomy of Action	Handling job activities with little direct supervision
8	Approval of Financial Commitments	Approving large financial commitments by the organization
9	Staff Service	Providing staff services such as fact-finding and record keeping for superiors
10	Supervision	Planning, controlling, and organizing the work of others through face-to-face contact with subordinates
11	Complexity and Stress	Operating under high stress to meet deadlines and perform required job activities
12	Advanced Financial Responsibility	Making large-scale financial investments and other financial decisions that will directly influence the company's performance
13	Broad Personnel Responsibility	Engaging in activities that have very broad responsibility for the management of human resources and the policies affecting employees in the company

Source: Adapted from W. W. Tornow and P. R. Pinto, "The Development of a Managerial Job Taxonomy: A System for Describing, Classifying, and Evaluating Executive Positions," *Journal of Applied Psychology,* Vol. 61 (1976), pp. 410–418. Copyright 1976 by the American Psychological Association. Adapted by permission of the author.

Supervisory Task Description Questionnaire (STDQ) The **Supervisory Task Description Questionnaire (STDQ)**, a 100-item questionnaire used to analyze the jobs of first-line supervisors, is completed by job incumbents, who rate each item using a six-point "amount of time spent" scale and a five-point "importance" scale.[44]

The items of the STDQ can be grouped into seven major categories: (1) working with subordinates, (2) organizing work, (3) work planning and scheduling, (4) maintaining efficient/quality production, (5) maintaining safe/clean work areas, (6) maintaining equipment and machinery, and (7) compiling records and reports.

Professional and Managerial Position Questionnaire (PMPQ) The **Professional and Managerial Position Questionnaire (PMPQ)** consists of ninety-three items, divided into three major sections: job activities, personal requirements, and other information.[45] The first section, job activities, includes items on six major types of activities: (1) planning and scheduling activities, (2) processing information and ideas, (3) exercising judgment, (4) communicating, (5) interpersonal activities and relationships, and (6) technical activities.

The second section of the PMPQ concerns the personal requirements needed for job performance. This section contains personal-development items dealing with the educational, training, and experience requirements of the job. The section also includes personal-characteristics items used to indicate whether traits such as adaptability are needed on the job. The final section of the PMPQ, other information, includes items on the number of personnel supervised by the employee, whether or not the employee is a member of professional organizations or has a professional license or certification, and the salary of the employee.

PHASE 3: DATA COLLECTION AND ANALYSIS

The job analyst must deal with several issues related to collecting and analyzing job data. The job analyst may have made all the right decisions up to this point about the scope and method of the job analysis project. However, if the procedures used in collecting the job data and analyzing those data are incomplete or incorrect, the job analysis project will be a failure.

Collecting Job Data

The first important aspect of collecting job data is to get the organization ready. Second, the job analyst must be aware of the sources of bias that may influence the accuracy of the data collected. Finally, the job analyst must be sure that interviews, if used, are conducted in a skillful manner.

Getting the Organization Ready Before data collection can begin, the job analyst must make sure that members of the organization understand and are committed to the project. To do this, the analyst can use the following guidelines:

1. Involve top management from the very start of the project. Have top management indicate to employees its support of the project, the purpose of the project, and how the project will benefit the organization.

2. Coordinate all activities associated with the project through the organization's HRM function.

3. Before talking to any employee, notify the immediate supervisor about the reason for the talk and get his or her approval.

4. Provide all persons involved in the data collection phase with information about the objectives and nature of the project. Provide this information *before* data collection and reinforce it throughout the project.

Sources of Bias The primary concern in collecting data about a job is that these data provide an accurate, up-to-date, and representative picture of work activities. One major source of bias that can occur during data collection results from the sampling procedures used to select data sources. Sampling bias occurs because jobs are dynamic.

Job dynamics result from three major processes.[46] One such process is **time-determined changes.** Differences in the same job may correspond to the different times at which it is performed (e.g., during a day shift or a night shift, during the winter or summer). Therefore, the job analyst must collect samples of job data that represent the different times at which a job is performed. Jobs are also dynamic because of **employee-determined changes.** Different people perform the same job in slightly different ways. Characteristics such as the employee's experience with the job or the employee's sex may influence job data.[47] The best way to take into account the influence of these personal differences on job data is to collect job data from many individuals.[48] Finally, jobs are dynamic because of **situation-determined changes.** The job of an insurance salesperson in Tampa, Florida, may change dramatically if a hurricane roars through the city. Thus, the job data obtained must reflect these situation-determined changes so that they are recognized and incorporated into the overall picture of the job. By sampling across time, situations, and people, job analysts can reduce the bias in data and provide more accurate pictures of jobs.

Job Analysis Interviews E. J. McCormick provides a useful set of guidelines for conducting job analysis interviews (see Figure 4.6). Although such guidelines are helpful, there are no simple methods for conducting good interviews. Interviewing is a skill that must be developed through practice.

Analyzing Job Data

Once quantitative job data are collected, numerous methods are available for analyzing them. A good job analyst should have a thorough knowledge of statistics or, at least, sufficient knowledge to be able to work closely with experts in statistical methods. Before collecting data, the analyst should decide what analysis procedures to use. Unless these decisions are made in advance, the job analyst may find that the data collected are not amenable to the analysis procedure(s) that he or she wants to use.

Once data have been collected, the analyst should always carry out a reliability check. Reliability in this case refers to *inter-rater reliability*. If job data are collected from several sources (e.g., several job incumbents), the job analyst

FIGURE 4.6 Guidelines for Job Analysis Interviewing

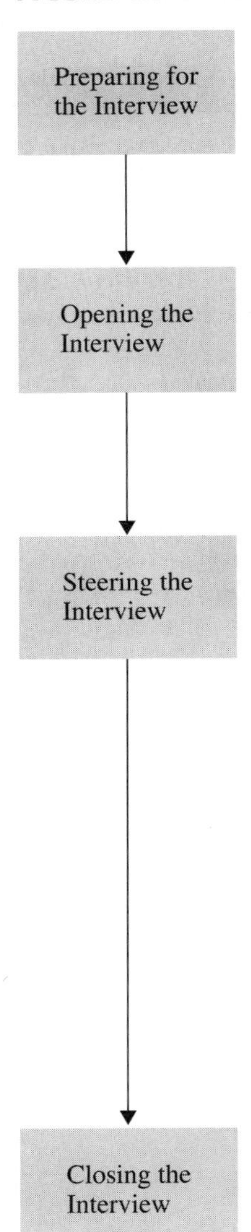

Build the interviewee's interest in advance through well-prepared announcements; be sure that the interviewee is notified in advance about the exact time and place of the interview.

Select a place for the interview that insures privacy and comfort.

Avoid or minimize obvious status symbols that would indicate that the interviewer is of higher status than the interviewee.

Put the worker at ease. Learn his or her name in advance. Introduce yourself and talk about pleasant topics until the worker is at ease.

Clearly describe the purpose of the interview, making sure that the worker understands what is to be accomplished and how the information he or she provides will benefit the organization and its workers.

Encourage the worker to talk. Be courteous and show a sincere interest in what is being said.

Help the worker talk about job duties in an orderly and logical sequence, according to the time sequence in which the duties occur or in order of their importance to the job.

Keep the interview alive by probing for more information, using "expectant pauses," asking unobtrusive and neutral questions, or summarizing what the worker has recently said.

Allow the worker sufficient time to think about and construct a response to a question. Ask only one question at a time and do not rush.

Avoid questions which can be answered with only a yes or no.

Avoid leading questions.

Use simple, easily understood language.

Do not be aloof or condescending. Show a personal interest in the worker.

Try to establish a steady, comfortable pace for the interview. Do not let the worker stray from the subject.

Try to get all the information you need about the job that the worker can provide.

Indicate that the interview is nearing an end by the kinds of questions you ask and the inflection in your voice.

Summarize the major information that the worker has provided. Ask the worker if your summary adequately represents what was discussed in the interview.

Explain to the worker how valuable the information provided will be.

End the interview on a friendly note.

Source: Reprinted, by permission of the publisher, from *Job Analysis: Methods and Applications,* by E. J. McCormick, pp. 38–39, © 1979 AMACOM, a division of the American Management Association. All rights reserved.

should check to determine how well these sources agree on the characteristics of the job. A low level of agreement among data sources would indicate that either some sort of bias is present or major differences in the jobs of the data sources exist.

Reporting and Rechecking Job Data

Once all the analyses have been completed the job analyst must prepare a report of the results. This report should include the purpose and scope of the project, a summary of the specific methods used and why they were used, an explanation of the analyses conducted and what information they provided, and a strategy as to how the information gained from the project can be used in the future. The report should be written in a form that is easy for the average manager (with no technical expertise in job analysis methods) to understand. The very best job analysis project is worthless unless managers can understand what was done and what were the results of the project.

The final part of the job analysis process is to recheck the results of the project periodically. Since jobs are dynamic, the information collected about a job today may not accurately represent the job five years from now. Thus, data must be updated periodically to incorporate job changes. Otherwise, the organization may find itself selecting, training, or appraising the performance of employees for jobs that no longer exist.

PHASE 4: ASSESSING JOB ANALYSIS METHODS

There are several factors that may be used to assess job analysis methods. Some criteria that serve as the basis for assessments are presented in Table 4.9. A study utilizing these criteria compared several structured job analysis procedures (see Table 4.10). Although these criteria can be helpful in comparing different methods, which method is best depends on the particular objectives of the organization, as well as on cost limitations and other factors governing the project.

Legality is a final criterion that might be used to assess a job analysis method. Legality is the extent to which the job analysis procedure would be acceptable to the courts if it were used as evidence to support the personnel selection, training, performance appraisal, or pay practices of the organization. Several issues relating to job analysis appear to be of particular concern to the courts: (1) the accuracy of the job analysis information, (2) the extent to which individuals who provide job information agree with one another about job characteristics and tasks, (3) the extent to which, if different methods of job analysis are used, the different methods yield similar results, and (4) whether or not the job analysis method chosen is appropriate to the particular purpose for which it is being used.[49] Court decisions indicate that certain types of analysis methods are preferred over others. Reviews of court decisions involving job analysis procedures have provided

TABLE 4.9 Ten Criteria for Assessing Job Analysis Methods

Number	*Criterion*	*Definition*
1	Purposes Served	Can the data collected be used for a variety of purposes?
2	Versatility	Can a method be used to analyze many different jobs?
3	Standardization	Does a method provide data that can be easily compared to data collected by other methods?
4	User Acceptability	Do users of the method accept it as a reasonable way to collect job data?
5	Training Required	How much training is needed before individuals can use it to collect data in the organization?
6	Sample Size	How large a sampling of information sources is needed before an adequate picture of the job can be obtained?
7	Off-the-Shelf	Can the method be used directly off-the-shelf, or must considerable development work be done to tailor it for use in a particular organization?
8	Reliability	Does the method produce reliable data?
9	Time to Complete	How long does it take to analyze a job using the method?
10	Cost	How much does the method cost to implement and use?

Source: From E. L. Levine, R. A. Ash, M. Hall, and F. Sistrunk, "Evaluation of Job Analysis Methods by Experienced Job Analysts," *Academy of Management Journal,* Vol. 26 (1983), pp. 339–348. Reprinted by permission.

job analysts with guidelines for collecting job data in a manner that will be upheld in court.[50] These guidelines include the following:

- State clearly the purposes and intended uses of the job analysis data.
- Use a job analysis method that has proven relevant for those purposes.
- Summarize the results of the job analysis in a clear, readable, written document.
- Collect job data from several sources (i.e., incumbents and supervisors) and from a representative sampling of each source.
- Use human sources that are well acquainted with the job.
- Make quantitative checks of the reliability and accuracy of the job data.
- Produce some form of task statements (like those produced in the functional job analysis or task inventory procedures). This need not be the only type of data collected, but task statements must be included at some point in the process.
- List all tasks that are part of the job in the job analysis results, but use only the most important tasks in the development of selection, appraisal or other systems.

TABLE 4.10 Comparision of Four Structured Job Analysis Procedures

	Methods[a]			
Purposes	*CIT*	*FJA*	*PAQ*	*TI*
Job Description	L	H	M	H
Job Specification	L	H	M	L
Job Classification	L	H	M	H
Job Design	L	H	M	H
Job Evaluation	L	H	H	M
Performance Appraisal	H	H	L	M
Legal Requirements	L	H	M	H
Practicality				
Versatility	M	H	L	H
Standardization	L	M	H	H
Acceptability	M	H	L	H
Training Required[b]	H	L	H	L
Sample Size[c]	L	H	H	L
Off-the-Shelf	L	H	H	L
Reliability	L	H	H	H
Time to Complete[d]	L	M	H	L
Cost[e]	L	M	H	L

Note: Originally in this study, six methods of job analysis were investigated. These six procedures were categorized into those which received the two highest ratings (H), two lowest ratings (L), and the middle rating (M). Only the four methods we have discussed in this text are listed here.

[a]CIT = Critical Incidents Technique; FJA = Functional Job Analysis; PAQ = Position Analysis Questionnaire; and TI = Task Inventory Technique.
[b]Higher ratings indicate lower amounts of training time required.
[c]Higher ratings indicate smaller samplings needed.
[d]Higher ratings indicate less time required to complete.
[e]Higher ratings indicate lower costs to perform.

Source: Adapted from E. L. Levine, R. A. Ash, H. Hall, and F. Sistrunk, "Evaluation of Job Analysis Methods by Experienced Job Analysts," *Academy of Management Journal,* Vol. 26 (1983), pp. 339–348. Reprinted by permission of the author.

- Document and explain carefully all steps, procedures, results, and analyses involved in the job analysis project. Use the results of the job analysis for the purposes for which the job analysis project was originally intended.

By following these guidelines, the job analyst can greatly increase the likelihood that job analysis procedures will be acceptable from a legal perspective.

SUMMARY OF KEY POINTS

Conducting a good job analysis is far more complex and difficult than it might seem. It requires that the job analyst make many important decisions. The analyst, in conjunction with management, must decide on the purpose and desired uses of the job analysis data. Job analysis may be used for human resource planning and recruitment. It may also be used to develop sound employee selection and placement procedures. Job analysis serves as the basis for developing training and performance appraisal programs and can be used to set wage rates across different jobs.

Once the organization decides how it plans to use the job analysis data, the job analyst must determine what jobs will be analyzed, what type of information is needed, and the sources of that information. Information about behavioral descriptors, ability requirements, and other job characteristics, such as the motivational nature of the job, can be collected. The job analyst may also want information concerning the machines, tools, and equipment that are used on the job and the working conditions in which the job takes place. The analyst can choose among a variety of human and nonhuman sources to provide these data.

Based on these decisions, the job analyst chooses from a myriad of job analysis procedures, ranging from simple narrative descriptions to highly complex micromotion or structured procedures. The functional job analysis method provides data that are useful in identifying worker traits needed to perform the job, as well as information useful in developing standards for employee performance. The task inventory is excellent for collecting data from large numbers of job incumbents and is particularly helpful in developing personnel selection tests and training programs. The Position Analysis Questionnaire is an excellent method for comparing a wide variety of very different jobs.

Once job data are collected, they must be analyzed for reliability and accuracy and then summarized and used within the organization. The job analyst must recheck these data periodically and assess their overall value—their costs and benefits—to the organization, as well as their versatility.

Job analysis methods should be designed so they can be performed reliably and in a standardized way throughout the organization. Methods should be assessed in terms of the time needed to teach individuals how to do the analysis, the time needed to complete the analysis, and the costs of collecting data. Any method used by an organization should also conform to standards set down in recent legal decisions that have specified what the courts consider a "good" job analysis procedure.

Questions For Discussion

1. What is job analysis, and why is it important to an organization?
2. What is the difference between a job description and a job specification?
3. Suppose that your company wants to develop a method for selecting job applicants with the highest potential for doing well on the job. What type of job analysis data (behavioral descriptors, ability requirements, or job characteristics) would be most useful in setting up this selection system?
4. How do the advantages of quantitative job data compare with those of qualitative job data?
5. What general guidelines should the HR specialist use when deciding how many and what sources of job information to use in a job analysis project?
6. Compare and contrast the Position Analysis Questionnaire and task inventory methods of job analysis. What are the relative advantages and disadvantages of each?
7. What does the phrase "jobs are dynamic" mean? Why is the dynamic nature of jobs important to the specialist conducting a job analysis project?
8. Table 4.9 lists ten criteria for assessing job analysis methods. Suppose you are the HR manager of a small company employing 150 people. Which of the ten criteria would you find most important in assessing a job analysis project? Suppose your company had 5,000 employees rather than 150. Would the list of most important criteria change for you? Why?

EXERCISE 4.1

Conducting a Job Analysis

This exercise will give you some hands-on experience in conducting a job analysis. You will interview a job incumbent and then use the information you collect in that interview to describe the job performed by the incumbent. It is important that the job incumbent has held the position long enough to really know what it involves. In conducting the job interview, you should first review the job analysis form and instructions provided here. In your interview, you must collect enough information about the job to complete this form. Before starting the interview, spend some time planning how you will proceed and writing down some of the questions you will ask. Refer to Figure 4.6 for guidance on conducting the interview.

Instructions for Filling Out the Job Analysis Form

1. *Job Identification*

   Organization: name of organization

DOT code: number of job description in the *Dictionary of Occupational Titles* most similar to this job — look this up in the library.
Incumbent: name of job incumbent interviewed
Analyst: name of person analyzing job
Date: date of interview

2. *Job Summary*. Provide an overview (one to three sentences) of the job being analyzed. Do not write this job summary until you have completed the remaining parts of this job analysis form.
3. *Duties Performed*. Identify the major duties that are performed on the job. Arrange these duties in either chronological order (i.e., in the time sequence in which the tasks are usually performed) or the order of importance to the job. Indicate the percentage of time spent on each duty during a typical workday. You will probably need more space than allowed on this sample form.
4. *Supervision Given*. How many subordinates does the job incumbent supervise? What are the titles of those subordinates?
5. *Supervision Received*. What is the job title of the job incumbent's supervisor? How closely is the incumbent supervised?
6. *Relationship to Other Jobs*.
   Promoted from: What position would the incumbent usually hold prior to this job?
   Promoted to: What is the most likely position to which the incumbent would be promoted?
7. *Machines, Tools, and Equipment Used*. List these devices and define any that are not commonly known.
8. *Working Conditions*. Indicate the physical environment of the job (e.g., indoors or outdoors, physically hazardous surroundings).
9. Job Specifications
   Physical requirements: List any special physical skills or abilities needed to perform the job (e.g., being able to lift 50 pounds).
   Educational requirements: Indicate the minimum level of education necessary *to perform the job*. Do not list what the organization specifies as the necessary educational level because organizations often require a higher level of education than is actually needed to perform the job. Also list any certificates or licenses required.
   Special skills: List any special skills needed (e.g., the artistic skills of a musician).
   job. Do not include "experience" that is easily acquired on the job.
   Training required after hire: Indicate any specific job training that is necessary after the employee enters the job.
10. *Unusual Terms*. Define any terms used in the preceding analysis that would not be commonly understood.

Jobs: P. 341

P. 516

JOB ANALYSIS FORM

1. *Job Identification*

   Organization ______________________________

   Job title ______________________________

   DOT code ______________________________

   Incumbent ______________________________

   Analyst ______________________________

   Date ______________________________

2. *Job Summary*

____

____

____

____

____

3. *Duties Performed*

____

____

____

____

____

____

____

____

____

____

4. *Supervision Given*

____

____

____

____

5. *Supervision Received*

____

____

____

____

6. *Relationship to Other Jobs*

Promoted from ______________________________

Promoted to ______________________________

7. *Machines, Tools, and Equipment Used*

____

____

____

____

8. *Working Conditions*

____

____

____

____

9. *Job Specifications*

Physical requirements: ______________________________

____

____

____

Educational requirements: ______________________________

____

____

____

Special skills: ______________________________

____

____

____

Experience required: ______________________________

____

____

____

Training required after hire: ______________________________

____

____

____

10. Unusual Terms

____

____

____

____

EXERCISE 4.2

Job Dynamics

As explained in this chapter, jobs are, by nature, dynamic. That is, they change over time, people, and situations. In the past twenty to twenty-five years, a technological revolution has occurred in many job situations. The use of computers and computerized equipment, such as robots, has become widespread. At the same time, a revolution has occurred in the labor market; many more women and minorities have entered the work force. This exercise focuses on some of the dramatic effects that changes in technology and the labor market have had on the nature of jobs.

1. The class should divide into groups of three or four students.

2. Each group should identify one or two jobs that group members feel have been particularly dynamic over the past ten to twenty years (i.e., jobs in which the basic nature of the activities performed has changed substantially). What specific factors have caused the jobs to change?

3. For each job identified, the group should compare the past activities performed on the job (ten to twenty years ago) with those performed at present. The group should prepare a job specification for the past job and the present job. What sorts of skills, abilities, knowledge, and experience were needed to perform the past job? What sorts are needed to perform the present job?
4. *Optional:* Each group should select one of the jobs it has discussed and present its analysis to the class.

Notes and References

1. E. J. McCormick, *Job Analysis: Methods and Applications* (New York: AMACOM, 1979), p. 20.
2. C. H. Stone and D. Yoder, *Job Analysis 1970* (report prepared for Department of Human Resources Development, State of California, Contract UI–7–7158, California State College, Los Angeles, 1970), pp. 6–7.
3. H. L. Ammerman, *Performance Content for Job Training,* Vol. 2 (Columbus, Ohio: Center for Vocational Education, Ohio State University, 1977), p. 21.
4. McCormick, *Job Analysis,* p. 19.
5. Matt Chalker, "Tooling Up for ADA," *HRMagazine,* December 1991, pp. 61–65.
6. J. P. Wanous, *Organizational Entry* (Reading, Mass.: Addison-Wesley, 1980).
7. Equal Pay Act of 1963 (401 FEP Manual 451).
8. W. Ouchi, *Theory Z: How American Business Can Meet the Japanese Challenge* (Reading, Mass.: Addison-Wesley, 1981).
9. Jen A. Algera and Martin A. Greuter, "Job Analysis for Personnel Selection," in *Advances in Selection and Assessment,* ed. Mike Smith and Ivan Robertson (New York: Wiley, 1989), pp. 7–30.
10. Ammerman, *Performance Content for Job Training,* pp. 15–16.
11. E. A. Fleishman and M. K. Quaintance, *Taxonomies of Human Performance: The Description of Human Tasks* (Orlando, Fla.: Academic Press, 1984); McCormick, *Job Analysis;* G. R. Wheaton, *Development of a Taxonomy of Human Performance: A Review of Classificatory Systems Relating to Tasks and Performance* (report prepared for Department of Defense, Advanced Research Projects Agency, Contract F–44620–67–C—0116, December 1976).
12. Fleishman and Quaintance, *Taxonomies of Human Performance,* pp. 162–167; E. A. Fleishman, "Toward a Taxonomy of Human Performance," *American Psychologist,* Vol. 30, 1975, pp. 1127–1149; E. A. Fleishman, "Relating Individual Differences to the Dimensions of Human Tasks," *Ergonomics,* Vol. 21, 1978, pp. 1007–1019.
13. L. D. Marquardt and E. J. McCormick, *Attribute Ratings and Profiles of the Job Elements of the Position Analysis Questionnaire (PAQ)* (West Lafayette, Ind.: Department of Psychological Sciences, Purdue University, 1972).
14. A. J. Farina, Jr., and G. R. Wheaton, "Development of a Taxonomy of Human Performance: A Task Characteristics Approach to Performance Prediction," *JSAS Catalogue of Selected Documents in Psychology,* Vol. 3, 1973, pp. 26–27.
15. J. R. Hackman and G. R. Oldham, "Development of the Job Diagnostic Survey," *Journal of Applied Psychology,* Vol. 60, 1975, pp. 159–170.
16. A. S. DeNisi, E. T. Cornelius III, and A. G. Blencoe, "Further Investigation of Common Knowledge Effects on Job Analysis Ratings," *Journal of Applied Psychology,* Vol. 72, No. 2, 1987, pp. 262–268; L. Friedman and R. J. Harvey, "Can Raters with Reduced Job Descriptive Information Provide Accurate Position Analysis Questionnaire (PAQ) Ratings?" *Personnel Psychology,* Vol. 39, No. 4, 1986, pp. 779–790; R. J. Harvey and T. L. Hayes, "Monte Carlo Baselines for Interrater Reliability Correla-

tions Using the Position Analysis Questionnaire," *Personnel Psychology,* Vol. 39, No. 2, 1986, pp. 345–358; R. J. Harvey and S. R. Lozada-Larsen, "Influence of Amount of Job Descriptive Information on Job Analysis Rating Accuracy," *Journal of Applied Psychology,* Vol. 73, No. 3, 1988, pp. 457–461.

17. Neal Schmitt and Scott A. Cohen. "Internal Analysis of Task Ratings by Job Incumbents," *Journal of Applied Psychology,* Vol. 74, No. 1, 1989, pp. 96–104.

18. Frank J. Landy and Joseph Vasey. "Job Analysis: The Composition of SME Samples," *Personnel Psychology,* Vol. 44, No. 1, 1991, pp. 27–50.

19. P. R. Conley and P. R. Sackett, "Effects of High- Versus Low-Performing Job Incumbents as Sources of Job-Analysis Information," *Journal of Applied Psychology,* Vol. 72, No. 3, 1987, pp. 434–437.

20. Landy and Vasey, "Job Analysis," pp. 27–50.

21. J. Hogan and A. M. Quigley, "Physical Standards for Employment and the Courts," *American Psychologist,* Vol. 41, No. 11, 1986, pp. 1193–1217.

22. S. B. Green and T. Stutzman, "An Evaluation of Methods to Select Respondents to Structured Job-Analysis Questionnaires," *Personnel Psychology,* Vol. 39, 1986, pp. 543–564.

23. Landy and Vasey, "Job Analysis," pp. 27–50.

24. Ibid.

25. McCormick, *Job Analysis,* p. 64.

26. Ibid., pp. 76–77.

27. J. C. Flanagan, "The Critical Incidents Technique," *Psychological Bulletin,* Vol. 51, 1954, pp. 327–358.

28. M. D. Dunnette, *Personnel Selection and Placement* (Belmont, Calif.: Wadsworth, 1966).

29. S. Zedeck, S. J. Jackson, and A. Adelman, *Selection Procedures Reference Manual* (Berkeley, Calif.: University of California, 1980).

30. U.S. Department of Labor, Employment and Training Administration, *The Revised Handbook for Analyzing Jobs* (Washington, D.C.: United States Government Printing Office, 1991).

31. U.S. Dept. of Labor, *Dictionary of Occupational Titles,* 4th ed., revised (Washington, D.C.: U.S. Dept. of Labor, 1991).

32. S. A. Fine, *Functional Job Analysis Scales: A Desk Aid* (Kalamazoo, Mich.: W. E. Upjohn Institute for Employment Research, 1973); "Functional Job Analysis: An Approach to a Technology for Manpower Planning," *Personnel Journal,* Vol. 53, 1974, pp. 813–818; S. A. Fine, A. M. Holt, and M. F. Hutchinson, *Functional Job Analysis: How to Standardize Task Statements* (Kalamazoo, Mich.: W. E. Upjohn Institute for Employment Research, 1974).

33. S. E. Bemis, A. H. Belenky, and D. A. Soder, *Job Analysis: An Effective Managerial Tool* (Washington, D.C.: Bureau of National Affairs, 1983), pp. 21–23.

34. E. J. McCormick, P. R. Jeanneret, and R. C. Mecham, "A Study of Job Characteristics and Job Dimensions as Based on the Position Analysis Questionnaire (PAQ)" *Journal of Applied Psychology,* Vol. 56, 1972, pp. 347–368.

35. Marquardt and McCormick, *Attribute Ratings.*

36. R. E. Christal, *The United States Air Force Occupational Research Project* (Air Force Human Resources Laboratory, Lackland Air Force Base, Tex. AFHRL–TR–73–75, 1974).

37. McCormick, *Job Analysis,* pp. 117, 119.

38. Ammerman, *Performance Content for Job Training.*

39. Lee Friedman, "Degree of Redundancy Between Time, Importance, and Frequency Task Ratings," *Journal of Applied Psychology,* Vol. 75, No. 6, 1990, pp. 748–752.

40. Juan I. Sanchez and Edward L. Levine, "Determining Important Tasks Within Jobs: A Policy Capturing Approach, *Journal of Applied Psychology,* Vol. 74, No. 2, 1989, pp. 336–342.

41. E. A. Fleishman, *Manual for the Ability Requirements Scale (MARS, revised)* (Palo Alto, Calif.: Consulting Psychologists Press, 1991); and E. A. Fleishman and M. E.

Reilly, *Human Abilities: Their Definition, Measurement, and Job Task Requirements* (Palo Alto, Calif.: Consulting Psychologists Press, 1991).

42. W. W. Tornow and P. R. Pinto, "The Development of a Managerial Job Taxonomy: A System for Describing, Classifying, and Evaluating Executive Positions," *Journal of Applied Psychology,* Vol. 61, 1976, pp. 410–418.

43. J. K. Hemphill, *Dimensions of Executive Positions* (Columbus, Ohio: Bureau of Business Research, Ohio State University, 1960).

44. B. E. Dowell and K. N. Wexley, "Development of a Work Behavior Taxonomy for First-Line Supervisors," *Journal of Applied Psychology,* Vol. 63, 1978, pp. 563–572.

45. J. L. Mitchell and E. J. McCormick, *Development of the PMPQ: A Structured Job Analysis Questionnaire for the Study of Professional and Managerial Positions* (West Lafayette, Ind.: Research Foundation, Purdue University, 1979).

46. D. T. Campbell, M. D. Dunnette, E. E. Lawler III, and K. E. Weick, Jr., *Managerial Behavior, Performance, and Effectiveness* (New York: McGraw-Hill, 1970).

47. E. T. Cornelius III, A. S. DeNisi, and A. G. Blencoe, "Expert and Naive Raters Using the PAQ: Does It Matter?" *Personnel Psychology,* Vol. 37, 1984, pp. 453–464; R. D. Arvey, E. M. Passino, and J. W. Lounsbury, "Job Analysis Results as Influenced by Sex of Incumbent and Sex of Analyst, *Journal of Applied Psychology,* Vol. 62, 1977, pp. 411–416.

48. Dunnette, *Personnel Selection and Placement.*

49. Hogan and Quigley, "Physical Standards for Employment and the Courts," pp. 1193–1217.

50. D. E. Thompson and T. A. Thompson, "Court Standards for Job Analysis in Test Validation," *Personnel Psychology,* Vol. 35, 1982, pp. 865–874.

P A R T
T H R E E

Acquiring Human Resources

External Environment
Economy Government Labor Markets Competitors Demographics

Human Resource Functions

Planning for Organizations, Jobs, and People
Strategic HRM (2)
Human Resource Planning (3)
Job Analysis (4)

Acquiring Human Resources
EEO (5)
Recruiting (6)
Selection (7, 8)

Building Performance
Human Resource Development (9)
Productivity and Quality (10)

Rewarding Employees
Performance Appraisal (11)
Compensation and Benefits (12, 13)

Maintaining Human Resources
Safety and Health (14)
Labor Relations (15)
Exit (16)

Managing Multinational HRM (17)

Organizational Environment
Management's Goals and Values
Corporate Culture
Strategy
Technology
Structure
Size

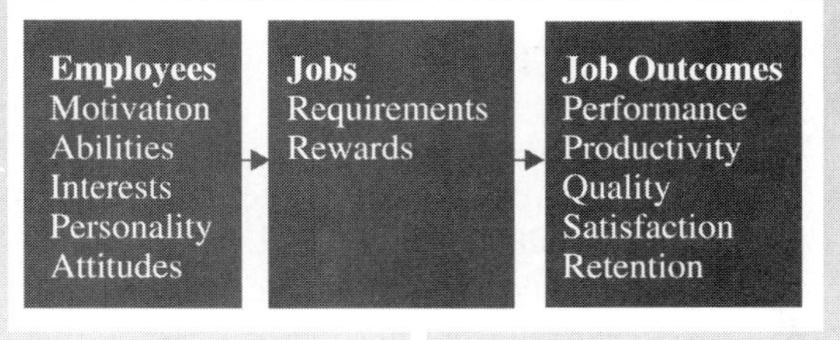

Organizational Outcomes
Survival
Competitiveness
Growth
Profitability

5

Equal Employment Opportunity: The Legal Environment

In this chapter, the term **equal employment opportunity (EEO)** is used to represent a collection of legal and social policies that state that members of U.S. society should have equal access to, and treatment in, employment. Since the mid-1960s, EEO laws and regulations have influenced almost every aspect of human resource management. All managers and supervisors must be familiar with EEO policies.

An organization should develop HR practices consistent with EEO laws and regulations for two reasons. First, equal employment opportunity is the law of the land. Companies that intentionally or unintentionally violate EEO laws are subject to a variety of penalties. These penalties include making back pay settlements of thousands (and sometimes millions) of dollars, paying for the legal defense of the organization in court, paying the legal costs of the person or persons filing the charges of discrimination if the company is found guilty, and losing federal contracts that the company might have. In a recent discrimination case, a female American Airlines executive who was passed over for promotion was awarded $7.1 million.[1]

The second reason for conforming to EEO laws and regulations is that it makes good sense from an HR perspective. The goal of human resource management is to make maximum use of all human resources available to an organization. By discriminating against individuals because of their race, sex, national origin, or other characteristics, an organization is turning away potential employees who could make valuable contributions to the company. Obviously, the costs to an organization of such potential human resource losses are more difficult to measure than the direct monetary losses associated with court settlements. However, from the perspective of good human resource management, these human resource losses should be considered equally as significant as direct monetary losses.

This chapter describes the important components of the EEO environment with which all HRM specialists should be familiar. A familiarity with the EEO environment can help organizations avoid both the financial and the human costs inherent in violating EEO laws and regulations.

THE EEO ENVIRONMENT

Several major components make up the EEO environment; they are shown in Table 5.1. Discrimination in our society can take many forms, but this text focuses only on discrimination in employment situations. Legal and regulatory documents include amendments to the U.S. Constitution; laws passed by the federal, state, and local governments; presidential executive orders; and guidelines prepared by government agencies. These documents define employment discrimination. Agents of enforcement include the Equal Employment Opportunity Commission (EEOC), the Office of Federal Contract Compliance Programs (OFCCP), the Department of Justice, and the court systems. These agents can take a variety of administrative and judicial enforcement actions against organizations that discriminate illegally. The final component in the EEO environment is management and its preventive and corrective responses to EEO legislation and regulations.

DISCRIMINATION DEFINED

Many people assume that discrimination implies some form of illegal act. In fact, *to discriminate* means simply to distinguish clearly or differentiate. One example of desirable discrimination is discrimination between good and poor workers in a company's performance appraisal system.

Illegal discrimination occurs when unfair actions are taken toward members of a protected class. A **protected class** consists of individuals who share some

TABLE 5.1 Components of the EEO Environment

	Specific Elements
Employment Discrimination	Overt discrimination Disparate treatment Disparate impact
Legal and Regulatory Documents	U.S. Constitution and amendments State and local laws Laws passed by Congress Presidential executive orders Guidelines of U.S. government agencies
Agents of EEO Enforcement	Equal Employment Opportunity Commission Office of Federal Contract Compliance Programs U.S. Department of Justice Federal and state court systems
Management's Responses	Preventive actions Corrective actions

Source: Adapted from James Ledvinka and Vida G. Scarpello, *Federal Regulation of Personnel and Human Resource Management*, 2/e (Boston: PWS-Kent Publishing Company, 1991), 29, 211.

characteristic in common, such as their race, color, religion, sex, national origin, age, handicap status, or status as military veterans. These individuals are protected in that laws prevent discrimination against them because of the characteristic they have in common. Suppose, for instance, that a white employee was given a reprimand for fighting with another employee, whereas a black employee was fired for an identical violation of company policy. Such discrimination is illegal.

Laws preventing discrimination have been passed when Congress or a state legislature has had evidence that individuals with some particular characteristic in common have been treated unfairly in our society. For example, during the civil rights movement of the 1960s, several laws were passed to protect citizens from racial discrimination in housing, employment, and voting rights because strong evidence existed that racial discrimination (left over from pre–Civil War days) still existed.

LEGAL AND REGULATORY DOCUMENTS

Four major types of documents define illegal discrimination in employment: the Constitution, laws passed by Congress and other legislative bodies, executive orders issued by the president, and guidelines issued by government agencies. The important EEO laws and regulatory documents are summarized in Table 5.2.

TABLE 5.2 Major EEO Laws and Regulatory Documents

Law or Document	*Type of Discrimination Prohibited*	*Employers Covered*
Fifth Amendment—U.S. Constitution	Deprivation of employment rights without due process	Federal government
Fourteenth Amendment—U.S. Constitution	Deprivation of employment rights without due process	State governments
Civil Rights Act of 1866	Racial discrimination in employment	Private employers, unions, employment agencies
Civil Rights Act of 1871	Deprivation of employment rights	State/local governments
Equal Pay Act of 1963	Sex discrimination in pay	All employers, unions
Title VII—Civil Rights Act of 1964 (amended 1972)	Employment discrimination based on race, color, religion, sex, national origin	Private employers, government, unions, employment agencies
Age Discrimination in Employment Act of 1967 (amended 1978)	Employment discrimination based on age (ages 40–70)	Private employers, unions, employment agencies
Vocational Rehabilitation Act of 1973	Employment discrimination based on mental or physical handicaps	Federal contractors, government
Immigration Reform and Control Act of 1986	Discrimination based on citizenship or national origin	Employers generally
Older Workers Benefit Protection Act of 1990	Expands protections of Age Discrimination in Employment Act	Private employers, unions, employment agencies
Americans with Disabilities Act of 1991	Discrimination based on physical or mental handicap	Employers generally
Civil Rights Act of 1991	Discrimination based on race, color, religion, sex or national origin	Employers generally
Executive Order 11246 (amended by Executive Order 11365)	Same as Title VII with affirmative action required	Federal contractors
Uniform Guidelines (interpretive document for EEO laws)		

Source: Adapted in part from James Ledvinka and Vida G. Scarpello, *Federal Regulation of Personnel and Human Resource Management,* 2/e (Boston: PWS-Kent Publishing Company, 1991), 30–32.

The Constitution

The Fifth Amendment to the U.S. Constitution states that "no person shall . . . be deprived of life, liberty, or property, without due process of law." This amendment relates to the actions of the federal government toward federal employees. The Fourteenth Amendment applies due process to actions taken by state governments and provides state employees "equal protection of the laws." If a government worker is fired without a due process hearing, that worker can possibly file suit in court, (1) using either the Fifth or the Fourteenth Amendment as the basis for the case and (2) arguing that he or she is being deprived of property, without due process of law.

Federal Legislation

Although many EEO laws have been passed by state and local governments, we will limit our discussion to those passed by the U.S. Congress. Managers should, however, be aware of state EEO laws, since these laws are sometimes more stringent than federal laws. For example, a Texas state law prohibiting age discrimination covers individuals between the ages of twenty-one and seventy. The federal age discrimination law applies only to persons who are over forty.

Civil Rights Acts of 1866 and 1871 The Civil Rights Act of 1866 provides all citizens the same right to make and enforce contracts as "white citizens" have.[2] This law has been interpreted by the courts as prohibiting racial discrimination by employers, unions, and employment agencies in the making of employment contracts.[3] It is often combined with the Civil Rights Act of 1871, which gives all people in the United States the right to sue if deprived of constitutional rights as a result of state action, custom, or conspiracy.[4]

Equal Pay Act of 1963 The Equal Pay Act prohibits wage discrimination among employees on the basis of sex, when the work requires equal skill, effort, and responsibility and is performed under similar working conditions.[5]

- *Skill* is defined as the experience, training, education, or other abilities needed to perform the job.
- *Effort* can be mental and/or physical in nature (for example, lifting 100-pound sacks of grain or working in a job that requires constant attention to detail). It is the degree or amount, not the nature, of the effort that is considered.
- *Responsibility* is the degree of accountability for people, equipment, money, or other things that the job entails.
- *Working conditions* include the physical surroundings and hazards under which the job is performed.

Court cases indicate that jobs need not be identical to be considered substantially equal to one another.[6] These rulings prevent organizations from giving men and women different job titles and paying them different wages, even though they do essentially the same work. In other words, if a female executive secretary has essentially the same job duties as a male office manager, she must be paid the same wage. However, in jobs that are substantially equal, pay differentials between some male and female employees may be allowed as long as the differences are based on one of the following factors:

- Bona fide seniority systems
- Differences in the quality of performance
- Piece-rate pay systems, where pay is tied directly to the number and quality of units produced
- Factors other than sex (such as night shifts paying more than day shifts)

Civil Rights Act of 1964 The most important legislation concerning equal employment opportunity is the Civil Rights Act of 1964, amended by the Equal Employment Opportunity Act of 1972, the Pregnancy Discrimination Act of 1978, and the Civil Rights Act of 1991.[7]

Title VII of the Civil Rights Act Title VII is the portion of the 1964 Civil Rights Act that is most relevant to employment discrimination. It prohibits employment discrimination based on race, color, religion, sex, or national origin. It protects employees from discrimination in such terms and conditions of employment as selection, placement, promotion, discharge, training, and pay and benefits. The Equal Employment Opportunity Commission (EEOC) was created by the 1964 law to enforce the provisions of Title VII.

As amended, Title VII applies to private employers that have fifteen or more employees on each working day of twenty or more calendar weeks in the current or preceding year. Title VII also applies to labor unions, employment agencies, state and local governments and their agencies, colleges, and universities. It protects all employees and applicants for employment in these organizations. There are some exceptions to this coverage, however. Religious organizations are not covered by certain religious discrimination aspects of Title VII. Elected public officials and their staffs and members of the Communist party are not protected. Employees who apply for jobs that require national security clearance are subject to special policies.

Pregnancy Discrimination Act of 1978 This act, which amended Title VII, was passed to protect pregnant women from employment discrimination.[8] The Pregnancy Discrimination Act of 1978 (PDA) requires employers to be nondiscriminatory in providing employee benefits such as health insurance, sick leave, pensions, and vacation time. If an employer provides sick leave and health or disability insurance to employees generally, it cannot specifically exclude childbirth and related medical conditions. Other important aspects of the PDA include the following:

- Elective abortions may be excluded from health insurance plans but not from other benefits, such as sick leave. Medical problems resulting from abortions may not be excluded from medical insurance.
- Employers must provide medical benefits to the husbands of female employees if they provide benefits to the wives of male employees.
- Employers must provide leave of absence or sick leave for childbirth on the same basis as for any other medical disability.
- Employers must allow women to work until their pregnancy results in physical disability that (1) interferes with their job performance and (2) is the same level of disability that would cause workers with other medical problems to have to stop working.
- Employers must allow women to return to work after childbirth on the same basis as for other disabilities.

In 1987, the U.S. Supreme Court faced the issue of whether a state statute that required employers to provide leave and reinstatement to employees disabled by pregnancy was pre-empted, or overridden, by the nondiscrimination mandates of the PDA. At issue in *California Federal Savings & Loan* v. *Guerra* was a California statute providing such pregnancy leave.[9] The employer in the case argued that under the law pregnant employees are treated differently from other employees and that the California law was thus not consistent with the PDA. Justice Thurgood Marshall, writing the opinion for the Court, disagreed with this assertion and held that the PDA did *not* pre-empt this California statute. Justice Marshall wrote that the favorable treatment given to pregnant workers under the California statute was not of the kind that was meant to be outlawed by the PDA. The PDA was meant essentially to prevent *harmful* discriminatory action being taken against pregnant employees.

Title VII and Fetal Protection Policies In the 1991 case of *United Auto Workers* v. *Johnson Controls,* the U.S. Supreme Court examined the validity under Title VII of a company's fetal protection policy that said that all women of childbearing age were excluded from certain jobs involving lead exposure.[10] Opponents of the policy argued that the policy constituted sex discrimination, in that fertile men were given a choice of whether or not they wanted to risk lead exposure but fertile women were not given this choice. The Supreme Court upheld this point of view, ruling that the company's fetal protection policy did constitute unlawful sex discrimination and that no valid bona fide occupational qualification (discussed later in the chapter) was advanced. The court rejected arguments that the policy was necessary for safety reasons.

Sexual Harassment Another type of sex-related discrimination that is covered by Title VII is **sexual harassment.** Because Congress did not discuss on-the-job sexual behavior in its passage of Title VII, the courts originally interpreted this omission to mean that sexual behavior was not a form of sex discrimination. However, in *Barnes* v. *Costle* (1977), sexual harassment was recognized for the first time as a form of sex discrimination under Title VII.[11] The Equal Employment Opportunity Commission has defined illegal sexual harassment in the following way:

> Unwelcome sexual advances, requests for sexual favors, or other verbal or physical conduct of a sexual nature constitute sexual harassment when
>
> - submitting to or rejecting such conduct is an explicit or implicit term or condition of employment;
> - submitting to or rejecting the conduct is a basis for employment decisions affecting the individual; or
> - the conduct unreasonably interferes with an individual's work performance or creates an intimidating, hostile, or offensive working environment.[12]

These EEOC guidelines were upheld by the U.S. Supreme Court in the significant 1986 case of *Meritor Savings Bank* v. *Vinson.*[13] In that case, the employer bank argued that Title VII's prohibition of discrimination with respect to "compensation, terms, conditions, or privileges" of employment involved only "tangible losses" of "an economic character." Essentially, the employer was arguing that only "quid pro quo" sexual harassment—that is, a situation in which continued employment or an employment benefit is conditioned on sexual conduct—should be unlawful under Title VII. Thus, the case of an employee's being fired for not having sex with a boss would constitute clearly unlawful quid pro quo harassment. On the other hand, if no clear quid pro quo situation is involved, there is no legal violation.

In the *Meritor* case, the Supreme Court rejected this narrow interpretation of Title VII and held that "environmental" sexual harassment, as defined in the EEOC's guidelines, was also unlawful. In the Supreme Court's opinion, any workplace conduct that is sufficiently severe or pervasive so as to alter the conditions of an individual's employment and create an "abusive" working environment can be unlawful. Thus, under the *Meritor* case, sexual jokes, pornographic pictures, and so forth can, under certain circumstances, constitute unlawful sexual harassment under Title VII.

The Supreme Court also ruled in *Meritor* that the fact that the sexual relationship between parties at the workplace is "voluntary" may be irrelevant. The critical issue in such cases is whether the sexual advances at issue were "unwelcome" and whether they were sufficiently severe to be "abusive." If so, they may be held unlawful under Title VII.

In the *Meritor* case, the Supreme Court did somewhat duck the critical issue of when is an employer responsible for the harassing actions of its employees. A lower court hearing the case had held that employers are strictly liable for the hostile work environment that is created by a supervisor's sexual advances to an employee, even if the employer neither knew nor could have reasonably known of the alleged misconduct. The Supreme Court rejected this notion and held that the lower court had erred in concluding that employers are always automatically liable for acts of sexual harassment committed by their supervisors. On the other hand, the Supreme Court also rejected the notion that absence of notice to an employer necessarily insulates the employer from liability. Instead, the Supreme Court avoided issuing a definitive ruling on employer liability, holding only that the general rules regarding employer responsibility for the actions of employees should apply.

Finally, the Supreme Court in *Meritor* rejected the bank petitioner's argument that the failure of the complainant to report the harassment by way of the bank's existing grievance procedure insulated the bank from liability. The Supreme Court held that the complainant may have failed to report the violation for a variety of reasons and that such a failure to report does not necessarily alter the bank's liability.

The issue of sexual harassment in the workplace was brought starkly to the nation's attention during the fall 1991 confirmation hearings for U.S. Supreme Court Justice Clarence Thomas. Thomas was charged by Anita Hill, a former employee, with sexually harassing her when he was her boss. Hill, however, just as in the case of the complainant in the *Meritor* case, had failed to use existing grievance procedures to report the harassment at the time it purportedly happened. There was also no evidence that Thomas had taken any quid pro quo actions against her because of her failure to submit to his alleged advances. Indeed, there was evidence that Thomas had gone out of his way to help her with her future career advancement. Nevertheless, it should be clear that under the standards of the *Meritor* case, Anita Hill's failure to report and the absence of any quid pro quo activity would not legally insulate Thomas from liability if her allegation were true.

The Hill-Thomas controversy clearly illustrates the sometimes difficult issues of proof in sexual harassment cases. In some cases—for instance, when pornographic material is displayed at the workplace—harassment may be clearly out in the open, but often the events that transpire are just between the parties involved. Thus, unless tape-recording or other devices had been used and such documentation is available, it may never be possible to know which party is actually telling the truth.

Age Discrimination in Employment Act of 1967 The Age Discrimination in Employment Act (ADEA), amended in 1986, prohibits employment discrimination against job applicants and employees aged forty or over.[14] The legislation applies to private firms that employ twenty or more people on each working day of twenty or more calendar weeks in the current or preceding year. Employment agencies, labor unions, and federal, state, and local government employees are covered by the law.[15] This law has effectively banished any mandatory retirement age. It also prohibits discrimination based on age in recruiting, hiring, promoting, firing, and laying off employees and in most other terms and conditions of employment. The federal law applies only to persons aged forty and above. A twenty-five-year-old worker is not protected by the act.

Older Workers Protection Act of 1990 The Older Workers Protection Act amended the ADEA to make clear that certain previously permitted age-based distinctions in employee benefits plans are unlawful. More specifically, the new law overturned the U.S. Supreme Court's 1989 decision in *Public Employees Retirement System of Ohio* v. *Betts,* which held that employer decisions concerning employee benefits were generally not subject to challenge under the ADEA.[16] The 1990 law also sets very strict standards regarding employee waivers and releases of age discrimination claims—that is, situations in which employees, as a condition for receiving a severance or other payment from their employer, sign a waiver, or release, giving up any future age discrimination claim. Under the new law, employees must be given at least three weeks to consider any waiver or release agreement and even then have a week after signing the agreement to revoke it.

Vocational Rehabilitation Act of 1973 The Vocational Rehabilitation Act requires employers who have federal contracts of $2,500 or more to take affirmative action toward qualified handicapped individuals.[17] The laws that have been discussed thus far require only that employers do not discriminate against certain types of persons. The affirmative action components of the Vocational Rehabilitation Act and the executive orders (discussed later in the chapter) require employers to develop more active procedures for seeking out and accommodating the needs of workers protected by the laws.

Americans with Disabilities Act of 1990 The enactment of the Americans with Disabilities Act (ADA), which went into effect on July 26, 1992, fulfilled a campaign pledge made by President George Bush in 1988. The scope of the new law is vast, and extends far beyond the employment context. For example, all new apartment and business buildings must be made accessible to the disabled. With respect to employment, the new law affects *all* employers with more than twenty-five employees. This requirement will be lowered to fifteen employees in 1994. Thus, the ADA is significantly broader in application than the Vocational Rehabilitation Act of 1973, which applies only to federal contractors, although the new law does not mandate any affirmative action. Simply put, the ADA prohibits discrimination on the basis of disability—in hiring and in all terms, conditions, and privileges of employment. Unlike the Vocational Rehabilitation Act, which is administered by the Department of Labor, the ADA is administered by the EEOC. The EEOC has estimated that its caseload will increase by 15 to 20 percent as a result of passage of the new law. The EEOC has issued comprehensive regulations dealing with the ADA.

Defining "Disability" At the heart of the ADA is the definition of disability. The act defines **disability** as (1) a physical or mental impairment that substantially limits one or more of the major life activities of an individual, (2) a record of such an impairment, or (3) being regarded as having such an impairment. The term *physical or mental impairment* is defined broadly. It includes any physiological disorder or condition, cosmetic disfigurement, or anatomical loss affecting one or more of several body systems, as well as any mental, physical, or psychological disorder.

The definition of mental or psychological disorder includes emotional and mental illness, mental retardation, and learning disabilities. This definition is so broad that it includes virtually the entire spectrum of psychological disorders; as such, it prompted considerable debate in Congress during legislative consideration of the bill. At the urging of Senator Jesse Helms of North Carolina, various conditions—including kleptomania, compulsive gambling, sexual behavior disorders, and pyromania—were specifically excluded from the definition of *disability* under the ADA. Homosexuality and bisexuality were also excluded from the definition of disability on the grounds that they are not impairments. Nevertheless, the ADA covers hundreds of psychological disorders. The act also specifically states that persons with the acquired immune deficiency syndrome (AIDS) and those who are HIV positive (infected with the human immunodeficiency virus) are protected under the ADA.

Interestingly, the ADA only protects disabilities that "substantially limit one or more major life activities." A common cold, for example, although a disability, does not "substantially limit" any "major life activities." The EEOC in its regulations has stated that it will examine the nature, severity, duration, and impact of the given impairment on a case-by-case basis to determine whether the impairment does substantially limit a major life activity and thus constitute a disability under the new law. It should be noted, however, that the ADA covers people who are viewed by employers as having a substantially limiting impairment, even if the impairment does not necessarily have this effect. For example, an executive whose high blood pressure has clearly been controlled by medication probably cannot be denied a promotion for that reason.

Reasonable Accommodation Although the ADA, unlike the Rehabilitation Act, does not require affirmative action, it does impose an affirmative obligation on employers to make "reasonable accommodations" to the known disabilities of an applicant or an employee unless the employer demonstrates that this would constitute an "undue hardship." The concept of **reasonable accommodation** is not unique to the ADA. Title VII of the Civil Rights Act, for example, requires employers to reasonably accommodate the religious practices of their employees so long as such accommodations do not constitute an "undue hardship." Such accommodations may include job transfers, work schedule changes, or other actions that allow workers to meet both their religious and their job responsibilities.

With respect to the disabled, employers are required to make reasonable accommodations of a kind that will allow individuals to perform the essential functions of the job. Reasonable accommodations often involve changes in the workplace, the job itself, and the equipment used to perform the job. For example, employers may modify elevators to include Braille floor indicators, alter bathrooms to meet the special needs of disabled workers, and build ramps to allow wheelchair access to buildings.

Employers are not required to accommodate the needs of handicapped workers in every case. Employers may argue that changes necessary to accommodate a worker would cause undue hardship—that is, the accommodation would be extremely costly to the company and/or would disrupt the efficient, safe operation of the company. Whether or not an accommodation is reasonable or results in undue hardship for the employer depends on several factors:

- The nature of the job itself (whether it can be changed to accommodate a certain type of handicap).
- The size of the company.
- Union agreements that might preclude certain types of work-schedule or work-rule changes.
- The cost of the accommodation for the employer.

AIDS-related Cases As noted earlier, AIDS is clearly a disability under the ADA, and employers cannot require a test for AIDS or any other medical examination as a condition of making an offer of employment. Once an offer of employment has been made, however, employers can make the offer conditional on the taking of such an examination. An employer cannot generally discriminate against a job applicant who is HIV positive, although such a person may be lawfully excluded from coverage under the employer's health insurance plan if the plan excludes other preexisting conditions. The following are some general guidelines for dealing with the AIDS issue:

- Treat AIDS like any other disease that is covered by state or federal laws against discrimination.
- Educate coworkers about AIDS.
- Maintain confidentiality of all medical records.
- Do not in any way discriminate against a person with AIDS.
- Do not exclude AIDS victims from training or consideration for promotion.
- Accommodate or make a good effort to accommodate the AIDS victim.[18]

Immigration Reform and Control Act of 1986 The Immigration Reform and Control Act (IRCA) provides sanctions for companies and individuals within the companies who knowingly hire illegal aliens.[19] The IRCA covers companies with three or more employees. For first offenses, fines of $250 to $2,000 per illegal alien may be imposed. A pattern of violation by a company may result in fines of up to $10,000 and six-month jail sentences. Employers must collect sufficient information from job applicants to confirm their legal status within the United

States, and both the applicant and the company must fill out an I-9 form. Companies must retain their employment records for three years after hire or for one year following termination, whichever comes first.

Civil Rights Act of 1991 One of the fundamental purposes of this legislation was to reverse the U.S. Supreme Court's 1989 decision in *Wards Cove Packing Co.* v. *Antonio*.[20] In *Wards Cove*, the Court made it more difficult for employees to prove discrimination in "disparate impact" cases (to be discussed later in the chapter). The new legislation overturns *Wards Cove* and essentially puts into law the Supreme Court's 1971 decision in *Griggs* v. *Duke Power Company*, which obliges employers to prove that a practice causing a "disparate impact" was required by a "business necessity."[21] The new act also overturns another 1989 U.S. Supreme Court decision which held that the Civil Rights Act of 1866 did not apply to cases in which an employee was discharged but only to those cases relating to the formation of a contract such as hiring. The new legislation makes it clear that the Civil Rights Act of 1866 does indeed apply to discharge cases.

The Civil Rights Act of 1991 also amends Title VII to provide that an unlawful employment practice may be established by demonstrating that race, color, religion, sex, or national origin was a *motivating factor* for an adverse employment decision, even though other legitimate factors also motivated the decision. The act further expands the scope of Title VII and the ADA to apply to U.S. citizens employed in foreign countries by American-owned or American-controlled employers. There is an exemption, however, in instances in which compliance would cause the employer to violate the law of the country in which the employer is located. This provision in the new law overturns a 1991 Supreme Court decision, which held that Title VII did not apply outside the United States to protect U.S. citizens working for American-owned or American-controlled companies.

Traditionally, damage awards under Title VII have been limited to back pay, lost benefits, and attorney's fees and costs. The new law, however, provides monetary awards of compensatory and punitive damages in cases of *intentional discrimination*. (The law specifically excludes the application of these damages in "disparate impact" cases.) Under the new law, compensatory damages can cover emotional pain and suffering and enjoyment of life, but the amount of punitive damages that can be awarded is limited by the size of the given employer. When compensatory or punitive damages are sought, either party may demand a jury trial.

The Civil Rights Act of 1991 has other significant provisions. For example, it amended section 703 of Title VII to explicitly prohibit "race norming" of employee or job candidate test scores—that is, altering test scores on the basis of race, sex, national origin, or other criteria. The new law also established a formal commission to study the artificial barriers to advancement that women and other minorities face in the workplace—the so-called "glass ceiling" problem (to be discussed in more detail later in the chapter).

Executive Orders

Presidential **executive orders** are another type of document that addresses employment discrimination. Executive Order 11246, issued by President Lyndon Johnson in 1965, prohibits discrimination based on race, color, religion, or national origin. Executive Order 11375, issued in 1967, prohibits discrimination based on sex. Both of these executive orders apply to federal agencies and companies with federal contracts of $10,000 or more. The Office of Federal Contract Compliance Programs (OFCCP) within the Department of Labor ensures that federal contractors comply with the provisions of these executive orders.

Whereas Title VII prohibits discrimination, Executive Orders 11246 and 11375 establish the concept of **affirmative action** for organizations. These executive orders require employers to take the following affirmative actions:

- Treat job applicants and employees without regard to race, color, religion, or national origin.
- State in advertisements that all applicants will be treated equally.
- Tell all labor unions and subcontractors associated with the company about the company's commitments under the orders.
- Include the equal opportunity obligation in all subcontracts and purchase orders.
- Comply with all provisions of the orders and provide information to federal agencies when requested.
- File regular compliance reports describing hiring and other employment practices.

"Glass Ceiling" Initiative On August 9, 1991, the Labor Department issued its "Report on the Glass Ceiling Initiative." This report, the result of an intensive study by the OFCCP of nine corporate work forces, focused on the general paucity of women and minorities in top managerial positions in the nation's largest corporations. This lack of minorities and women in top positions has been termed a "glass ceiling," which women and minorities can see through but not get through. The report made recommendations regarding development, training, and other approaches designed to facilitate the movement of women and minorities into the executive suite. As noted earlier, the Civil Rights Act of 1991, which became effective on November 21, 1991, established a special "Glass Ceiling" Commission to study these issues further.

Affirmative Action Plans Companies with large federal contracts (of $100,000 or more) must formulate detailed **affirmative action plans (AAPs)** to ensure their compliance. These AAPs consist of four parts:

1. A utilization analysis that shows the percentage of men, women, and minorities employed in the company.

2. An availability analysis that indicates the availability of men, women, and minorities in the relevant labor market.
3. An identification of problem areas (using utilization and availability data) that identifies any inequities between the availability and actual representation of men, women, and minorities in the company.
4. Corrective actions, with goals and timetables, that outline the employer's plans to achieve employment parity.

Utilization Analysis The employer identifies the number of men, women, and minorities who are employed in each job group (utilized) within the company. The employer may also collect data on the nature of recent hiring decisions (e.g., out of twenty recent applicants hired for the job of carpenter, ten were women) and on the number of offers made to minority applicants (e.g., ten blacks were offered the job of first-line production supervisor, but only one accepted). Other data might include a work force comparison of the employer and similar companies in the same geographic region or a statistical report on the increase in the company's minority or female employees over a designated time period.

Availability Analysis In its AAP, the employer must indicate the availability of men, women, and minorities in the labor market. There is considerable disagreement over what geographic area constitutes the appropriate labor market from which to collect data. Factors that affect the appropriateness of the geographic region are (1) the area in which the employer presently recruits employees, (2) the area in which current employees and job applicants typically live, (3) the availability of public transportation, and (4) the type of job involved. Even when the appropriate geographic region can be determined, there remains the problem of identifying exactly how many qualified, potentially employable individuals live in that region. As a result, the availability analysis can become a fairly subjective process.

Identification of Problem Areas The employer examines utilization and availability data for instances of underutilization, in which utilization is less than availability, or for instances of concentration, in which certain jobs are filled almost exclusively by members of a particular sex or minority.

Table 5.3 presents hypothetical utilization and availability analyses. A comparison of row 2 (percent of utilization) and rows 8 and 10 shows that black women are both seeking work and qualified at a considerably higher rate than their current utilization for the job group of technicians. White men and women are somewhat overutilized. Black male utilization and availability are relatively equal—that is, parity exists for black men. This table also reflects an instance of concentration. Since 70 percent of the technicians are men, men are concentrated in this job group.

Corrective Actions, with Goals and Timetables If utilization problems exist, the company must develop a set of specific actions that will achieve parity. At Acme Electronics Corporation, these actions might include increasing recruitment efforts at predominantly black universities, advertising in women's magazines, or developing special training programs to help current (particularly black) female employees acquire skills that would allow them to become technicians. The employer must specify the goals it hopes to achieve by these actions and the targeted deadlines for their achievement. Acme Electronics, for example, might set the goal of increasing the number of black female technicians by 100 percent (from ten to twenty) within two years.

The Problem of Reverse Discrimination One problem that organizations often face when specifying goals and timetables for affirmative action programs is **reverse discrimination.** Title VII prohibits discrimination in employment based on race, color, sex, national origin, or religion. Because previous hiring practices have often been discriminatory, many companies have implemented selection procedures designed not only to prevent discrimination but also to make up for and correct the effects of past discrimination. For example, an organization might have established a hiring quota to increase the number of women in managerial positions; this quota might require that one female manager be hired for every male hired. Inevitably, the question before the courts has become, Do such voluntary quota systems constitute a form of illegal reverse discrimination against nonminority males?

Steelworkers* v. *Weber In *Steelworkers* v. *Weber* (1979), the Supreme Court ruled that a quota system used by Kaiser Aluminum & Chemical Corporation to admit persons into a training program did not constitute illegal reverse discrimination because the quota system was designed to correct the effects of the company's past discriminatory practices against blacks.[22] The *Weber* decision has been supported in several later court rulings, which have strongly backed the use of voluntary procedures to correct past discrimination.[23]

Firefighters Local Union 1784* v. *Stotts One important case indicates that actions taken as part of bona fide seniority systems may take precedence over voluntary quota systems. The city of Memphis, Tennessee, had instituted procedures to increase the number of minority firefighters in the city. During a period of layoffs, however, a "last hired, first fired" policy was implemented, and it had an adverse impact on recently hired black firefighters. In *Firefighters Local Union 1784* v. *Stotts* (1984), the Supreme Court supported the seniority-based layoff policy and ruled that black firefighters could claim protection from the policy only if they had personally and directly been the object of hiring discrimination by the city of Memphis.[24] (Later in this chapter, we outline some steps that management

TABLE 5.3 Hypothetical Utilization and Availability Analyses: Acme Electronics Corporation

Job Group: Technicians
Relevant Labor Area: Standard Metropolitan Statistical Area
Prepared by: J. B. Shaw, EEO Coordinator
Date: 2/6/92

		Total	*Male*	*Female*	*White Male*	*White Female*	*Black Male*	*Black Female*
Utilization	1. Size of Utilized Population	500	350	150	200	140	150	10
	2. Percent of Utilization	100%	70%	30%	40%	28%	30%	2%
Availability	3. Size of Available Population	100,000	49,000	51,000	20,000	21,000	29,000	30,000
	4. Percent of Availability	100%	49%	51%	20%	21%	29%	30%
	5. Size of Work Force	60,000	36,000	24,000	16,200	14,400	19,800	9,600
	6. Percent of Work Force	100%	60%	40%	27%	24%	33%	16%
	7. Individuals Seeking Work	3,500	1,925	1,575	578	709	1,347	866
	8. Percent Seeking Work	100%	55%	45%	17%	20%	29%	24%
	9. Individuals with Requisite Skills in Reasonable Recruiting Area	42,000	25,200	16,800	13,104	9,240	12,096	7,560
	10. Percent of Individuals with Requisite Skills	100%	60%	40%	31%	22%	29%	18%

Note: In actual utilization and availability data, information would be presented for Total, Male, Female, White Male and Female, Black Male and Female, Hispanic Male and Female, Asian Male and Female, and American Indian Male and Female.

Source: Adapted from *EEO Compliance Manual,* 1979. Reprinted by permission of Prentice-Hall, Inc., Englewood Cliffs, New Jersey.

can take to minimize the possibility that a quota system set up as part of an AAP results instead in reverse discrimination.)

City of Richmond* v. *J. A. Croson The city of Richmond had enacted an ordinance requiring prime contractors on city projects to subcontract at least 30 percent of the dollar amount to minority-owned businesses. The ordinance was passed in response to the fact that virtually none of the city's contracts had been awarded to minority businesses, even though 50 percent of the city's population was black. No direct evidence, however, was ever uncovered to prove that the city or its prime contractors actually discriminated against minorities. In *City of Richmond* v. *J. A. Croson* (1989), the U.S. Supreme Court ruled that the city of Richmond's program violated the equal protection clause of the U.S. Constitution because no evidence had been presented to demonstrate *specific instances* of minority discrimination.[25] Set-aside programs of this kind would thus be permissible only if designed to correct demonstrable acts of past discrimination. The Supreme Court's *Croson* decision put into question minority business set-aside programs in nearly forty states and two hundred cities and counties throughout the United States.

Uniform Guidelines

In 1978, the EEOC, along with several other government agencies, issued a set of guidelines for hiring employees. These guidelines, officially called the *Uniform Guidelines on Employee Selection Procedures* (also called the *Uniform Guidelines*), outline what organizations should do to avoid illegal discrimination in selecting employees.[26] The EEOC has also issued special guidelines on sex, national origin, age, and religious discrimination. Although organizations are not required to follow the practices detailed in the *Uniform Guidelines,* the EEOC uses them to determine which charges of discrimination brought to it are legitimate and should be taken to court. In November 1991, a major controversy erupted when the White House "floated" a proposed executive directive dismantling the *Uniform Guidelines*. This proposed directive was quickly rescinded on the personal order of President George Bush.

ENFORCEMENT OF EEO LAWS AND REGULATIONS

In the majority of EEO cases, individuals who believe that they have been discriminated against bring complaints to the EEOC or to the OFCCP (although the OFCCP usually turns individual discrimination complaints over to the EEOC). These agencies examine the facts of each case, decide whether or not illegal discrimination has occurred, and attempt to arrange a settlement between the individual and the organization. If no settlement is reached, the agencies cannot force a settlement on an employer but may take the issue to federal court. The courts can force an organization to make changes in its selection or other HR practices.

The individual who files a complaint with the EEOC or OFCCP is called the *complainant* or the *charging party.* In court, this individual may be called the *plaintiff.* The organization against which the complaint is filed may be referred to as the *respondent* or, in court, as the *defendant.*

Equal Employment Opportunity Commission

Besides Title VII problems, the EEOC handles issues related to the Equal Pay Act, the Pregnancy Discrimination Act, the Age Discrimination in Employment Act, and the Vocational Rehabilitation Act. The major activity of the agency is to process complaints of discrimination related to these laws. A schematic of the complaint processing procedure is presented in Figure 5.1. Procedural steps must occur within certain time limits after the discriminatory act has occurred; these time limits are included in the figure.

The Charge A charge is filed against an organization, usually by a private individual. This charge must be made to the federal EEOC or to a state or local EEO agency within 180 days of the occurrence of the discriminatory act. If the charge is first processed by a state or local agency, and if that agency's actions are not satisfactory to the individual, the individual has up to 300 days from the occurrence, or 30 days after the state or local agency has concluded its investigation and rulings, to file with the federal EEOC.[27]

The Investigation The EEOC must investigate the charge to see if discrimination has occurred. The EEOC may interview the complainant and personnel in the organization (e.g., supervisors or coworkers) to determine the facts; the EEOC may also ask the organization to provide data (from personnel files) relevant to the charge. Once the investigation is complete, the EEOC makes a ruling. An example of an EEOC ruling is presented in Figure 5.2. The EEOC may rule that there is reasonable cause to believe that discrimination has occurred. If reasonable cause is found, the EEOC attempts to conciliate the dispute. If no reasonable cause is found, the EEOC dismisses the case. Complainants may then, on their own, file suit against the company in federal court.

The Conciliation Meeting An EEOC mediator (conciliator) meets first with the complainant to work out an acceptable settlement and then tries to get the employer to agree to it. This process of trying to reach an out-of-court settlement is called **conciliation.** The conciliator then draws up a conciliation agreement, which is signed by the complainant, the employer, and the EEOC. The conciliation agreement is a written document that lists the violations that occurred and the agreed-upon corrective actions that will be taken by the employer. The agreement might include actions such as granting the employee a promotion that had been denied because of discrimination, giving back pay, or instituting new company policies to prevent discrimination in the future. If a conciliation agreement is not achieved, the EEOC may then file suit against the company in federal court or

FIGURE 5.1 EEOC Complaint Processing Procedure

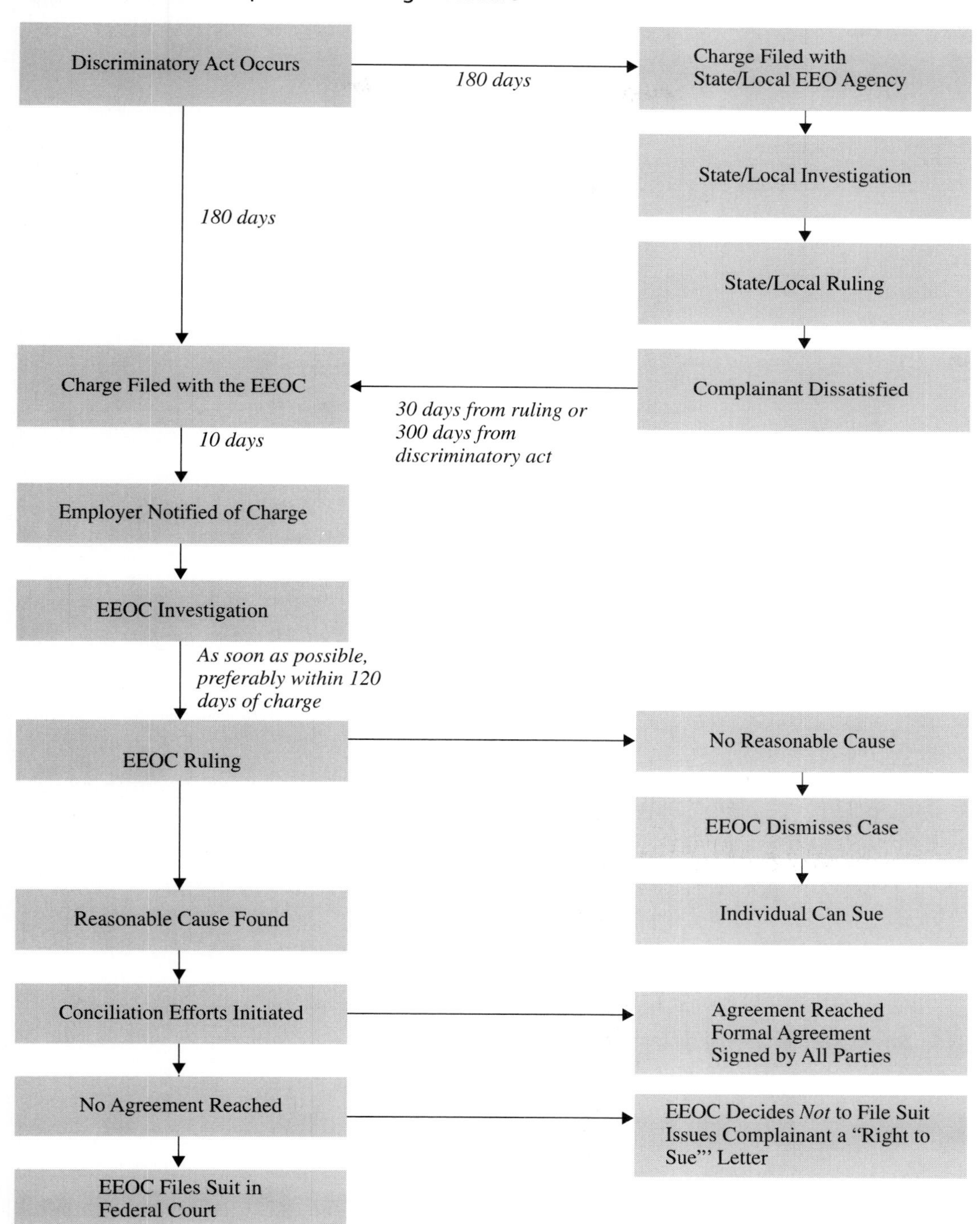

FIGURE 5.2 EEOC Ruling

Summary of Charge

Charging Party, a male, alleges that Respondent unfairly compensated him because of the sex of the students that he coaches in violation of Title VII of the Civil Rights Act of 1964, as amended (the Act), 42 U.S.C. §2000e *et seq.* (1982).

Summary of Investigation

The Charging Party is a male coaching girls' junior varsity softball who alleges that coaches of boys' sports in comparable positions receive higher compensation for similar work. Charging Party does not allege that he was paid less because of his sex; instead, he claims that he is "being unfairly compensated by the respondent because of the sex of the students that [he] coach[es]."[1] The issue to be resolved is whether Charging Party's allegation that he was unfairly compensated because of the sex of the students he coaches states a claim of discrimination under the Act.

The Charging Party was hired by Respondent school district in 1967 as a school teacher. In the spring of 1980, Charging Party agreed to coach girls' junior varsity softball as a paid extra activity under Respondent's collective bargaining agreement. The agreement provided that persons coaching school sports would be paid $6.93 per hour. Respondent establishes its salary for these positions by estimating the number of hours required to coach each sport for that season and multiplying that estimate by the hourly rate. It bases these estimates upon such factors as number of tournament games, number of pre-season and weekly practice sessions, and additional on-call obligations to serve as assistant or substitute coaches for the school's other varsity teams. Using this formula, girls' junior varsity softball, the sport which Charging Party had agreed to coach, was credited with seventy five hours and he was paid $519.75 for the season. Boys' reserve baseball was credited with one hundred and fifty hours and its coach was paid $1,039.50 for the season, while boys' freshman baseball was credited with one hundred and twenty five hours and its coach was paid $866.25 for the season.

Charging Party and Respondent agree that all coaches, regardless of their sex, the sport they coach, or the sex of the persons they coach, receive the same $6.93 per hour for their coaching duties according to the requirements of Respondent's collective bargaining agreement. There is no dispute between the parties concerning the facts and circumstances which gave rise to this charge.

Section 703(a)(1) of the Act makes it unlawful for an employer "to discriminate against any individual with respect to his compensation, terms, conditions, or privileges of employment, because of such individual's . . . sex[.]"

The issue of whether, under the Act, a claim of disparate treatment in the payment of salaries can be based upon the sex of the students being coached was addressed in *Jackson v. Armstrong School District,* 430 F. Supp. 1050 (W.D. Penn. 1977). *Accord, Kenneweg v. Hampton Township School District,* 438 F. Supp. 575 (W.D. Penn. 1977). In *Jackson,* female coaches claimed that their employer had violated the Act by denying them higher wages because they coached women's sports. They did not allege that they had been denied positions coaching men's sports because of their sex. The court dismissed the female coaches claim for failure to state a claim of discrimination on the basis of their sex, as Section 703(a)(1) of the Act requires. The court pointed out that "[i]t is clear from the statute that the sex of the claimants must be the basis of the discriminatory conduct. Here plaintiffs are not discriminated against because of *their* sex." *Jackson,* 430 F. Supp. at 1052 (emphasis in original).[2] In reaching its decision that the female coaches had not stated a claim under the Act, the court in *Jackson* relied on the Fifth Circuit Court of Appeals decision in *Stroud v. Delta Airlines, Inc.,* 554 F.2d 892 (5th Cir.), *cert. denied,* 434 U.S. 844 (1977), where the court stated:

> The Supreme Court has noted that the objective of Congress in passing the Civil Rights Act of 1964, of which the sex discrimination provision was a part, was to achieve equality of employment opportunity and to remove certain barriers. These barriers are those which operate to favor one group of employees *identifiable* by race, color, religion, sex, or national origin. *Alexander v. Gardner Denver Co.,* 415 U.S. 36 . . . [1974] . . .

Stroud at 893 (emphasis in original).

It is the Commission's view, based upon the plain language of the statute and the courts' interpretation of it, that a charge which alleges discrimination on the basis of the sex of the persons that the charging party is coaching does not state a claim of discrimination under the Act. It is necessary that the claim of discrimination be based upon the sex, race, religion, color or national origin of the charging party as required by Section 703(a)(1)[3] or on the basis of retaliation as required by Section 704(a) of the Act.

FIGURE 5.2 EEOC Ruling (*cont.*)

Conclusion

The Commission is without authority to process this charge because Charging Party has failed to state a claim under the Act. This charge is returned to the District Office for dismissal pursuant to Section 1601.19 of the Commission's Procedural Regulations, 29 C.F.R. §1601.19 (1984) and Section 4.4 of Volume I of the Commission's Compliance Manual.

[1]The Charging Party does not allege, and the evidence does not show, that the coaches of girls' sports are predominantly women and that, because of that fact, the coaches of girls' sports, including the Charging Party, are being discriminatorily compensated. Therefore, that issue is not addressed in this decision.

[2]The court in *Jackson* recognized that if it were to allow the claim of the female coaches, it would also have to allow the claim of male coaches who might allege that their employers discriminated against them on the basis of the sex of the persons that they were coaching. The court stated:

> Following [the female coaches'] argument further [,] the male coaches of women's basketball would be free to lodge the same charge. In turn we envision the anomalous situation of the school district, which shows no sexual preference towards women's basketball coaches, being sued for discriminatory practices. This is not what Title VII says nor contemplates. It was designed to curb discriminatory practices committed against certain classes—e.g., sex, race, or ethnic derivation—of employees with the idealistic goal of engendering parity for all.

Jackson v. Armstrong School District, 430 F. Supp. 1050, 1052 (W.D. Penn. 1977).

[3]Claims of persons holding coaching positions alleging discrimination on the basis of their sex have uniformly been recognized by the courts. *Harrington v. Vandalia-Butler Board of Education,* 418 F. Supp. 603, 606 (S.D. Ohio), *rev'd on other grounds,* 585 F.2d 192 (6th cir. 1978), *cert. denied,* 441 U.S. 932 (1979) (female physical education teacher stated claim when she alleged discrimination on basis of her sex because of her employer's failure to provide her with adequate instruction area, adequate office space, and private shower and toilet facilities, similar to those provided to male physical education teachers); *Strong v. Demopolis City Board of Education et al.* 515 F. Supp. 730, (S.D. Ala. 1981) (female coach who alleged she was paid less than a male coach because of her sex stated claim under the Act; and *Burkey v. Marshall County Board of Education,* 513 F. Supp. 1084 (N.D. W.Va. 1981) (refusal to hire female coach for male sports and paying equally qualified female coach less than male coaches with comparable duties discriminated against the female coach on the basis of her sex).

provide a **right-to-sue letter** to the complainant, who can then file suit on his or her own behalf.

EEOC and Judicial Enforcement The EEOC enforces the laws through conciliation agreements or the federal courts. The courts may order a company to take the following actions:

- Remedy the effects of past discrimination by granting back pay, promotions, or retroactive seniority to specific individuals who have been discriminated against.[28]
- Cease discrimination by modifying discriminatory policies and practices or by the use of temporary quotas to achieve racial balance.[29]
- Pay the attorney's fees of the complainant.

Office of Federal Contract Compliance Programs

The Office of Federal Contract Compliance Programs enforces the provisions of executive orders relating to employment discrimination. A primary function of the OFCCP is to conduct reviews to ensure that affirmative action programs required by the executive orders are carried out. The review process used by the OFCCP is outlined in Figure 5.3.

Types of Reviews The OFCCP may conduct a complaint investigation when an individual files a complaint of discrimination against a company. The OFCCP often turns the complaint over to the EEOC but can choose to investigate the complaint itself. A pre-award review of an organization may be conducted before it receives a federal contract. A regular compliance review may be conducted of an organization covered by executive orders, even if no complaint of discrimination has been filed.

The Review Procedure In the first phase of a review—the **desk audit**—the OFCCP requests the contractor to provide relevant information about its recruitment activities, hiring practices, and the make-up of its present work force. The OFCCP reviews this material to see if there is evidence of discrimination or if practices dictated by the executive orders are being followed. If there is no evidence of violations, the review may end. If possible violations are found, the OFCCP conducts an on-site review and seeks other information to confirm or refute the violations. The OFCCP may request additional personnel data and conduct interviews with company employees. When the on-site review is completed, the OFCCP may take additional information from the company and conduct an off-site analysis.

OFCCP Decisions The OFCCP may take one of three actions:

- Notify the contractor that it is in compliance.
- Find that the contractor is not in compliance and turn the case over to the Justice Department for prosecution in the federal courts.
- Find the contractor not in compliance, issue a show cause statement, and attempt to remedy the violations through additional OFCCP involvement.

A **show cause statement** includes a list of the violations that the OFCCP has identified, a list of actions that the contractor must take to correct these violations, and a request that the contractor reply in writing as to how it will correct the violations and/or present further evidence to prove that no violations have actually occurred. If a satisfactory agreement is not reached, the OFCCP may enforce its decision using administrative procedures or turn the case over to the Justice Department.

Administrative and Judicial Enforcement The OFCCP may enforce its rulings by taking the case to an administrative law judge within the Department of Labor. This judge can rule against the company and (1) cancel the company's federal contract, (2) suspend the company from receiving contracts for a specified time period, (3) permanently prevent the company from receiving federal contracts, or (4) take other appropriate actions.

FIGURE 5.3 OFCCP Review Procedure

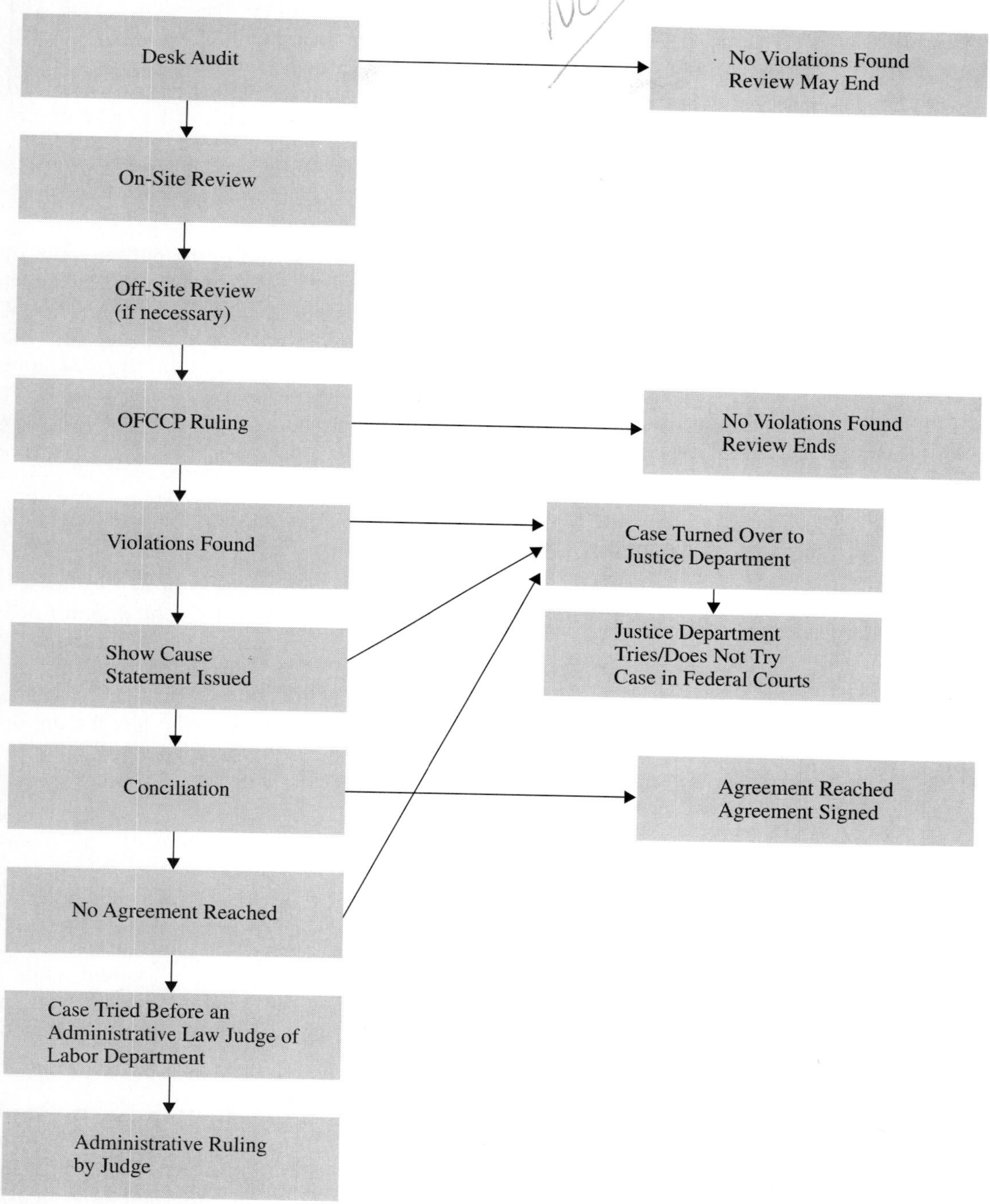

Desk Audit

No Violations Found
Review May End

On-Site Review

Off-Site Review
(if necessary)

OFCCP Ruling

No Violations Found
Review Ends

Violations Found

Case Turned Over to
Justice Department

Justice Department
Tries/Does Not Try
Case in Federal Courts

Show Cause
Statement Issued

Conciliation

Agreement Reached
Agreement Signed

No Agreement Reached

Case Tried Before an
Administrative Law Judge of
Labor Department

Administrative Ruling
by Judge

Alternatively, the OFCCP can turn the case over to the Justice Department at several junctures before or after a show cause statement has been issued. The Justice Department decides whether the case is strong enough to take to court. The court can provide "injunctive relief"—that is, make the company stop acting in ways that violate the executive orders, suspend or cancel the company's federal contracts, and/or institute other actions similar to the methods of EEOC enforcement discussed earlier.

The Federal Courts

Typically, the federal court system serves as the final step in the enforcement of EEO laws. A discrimination suit may pass through three levels in the federal court system. First, the suit is filed in a federal district court. The Civil Rights Act of 1991 allows discrimination cases to be brought to a jury. Prior to this act, all Title VII cases were decided by judges. If the decision is appealed, then the case goes to the federal district circuit court of appeals, which usually has three or more judges who hear the case as a panel. Finally, from the circuit courts, the case may be appealed to the U.S. Supreme Court.

PROVING ILLEGAL DISCRIMINATION

The court system has a very formal process for establishing guilt in EEO cases. This process is associated with the concept of burden of proof. The plaintiff provides evidence to indicate a **prima facie case** of discrimination. *Prima facie* simply means "on the face of it" or "at first sight." The evidence presented must suggest, at first sight, that the employer has discriminated. Once a prima facie case has been established, the burden of proof shifts to the employer, who has the opportunity to show that its actions were not illegal and are justified by sound business reasons.

The Prima Facie Case

The most direct way to establish a prima facie case is to show that the employer overtly discriminated against a member of a protected class. Statements by the employer such as "We do not hire blacks as managers" or job advertisements such as "Management trainee position: women need not apply" would make a convincing prima facie case. But rarely do such blatant examples of discrimination exist. A prima facie case is usually established by proving disparate treatment or disparate impact.

Disparate Treatment (*McDonnell Douglas Corp. v. Green*) **Disparate treatment** occurs when one employee is treated differently from other workers because of his or her race, sex, national origin, or the like. In such a situation, different standards are applied to different types of people. The court case that most clearly describes how illegal discrimination can be proved in a case of disparate treatment is *McDonnell Douglas Corp.* v. *Green* (1973).[30] In this case, Green, a black mechanic/technician at McDonnell Douglas Corp., was laid off as part of a company-wide work force reduction. Green protested that his layoff was racially motivated and joined protests against McDonnell Douglas that included blocking highway accesses to the McDonnell Douglas plant. Green was arrested for these protest activities. In 1965, McDonnell Douglas placed job advertisements for qualified mechanics/technicians. Green applied for the job but was rejected. He filed a case of racial discrimination against McDonnell Douglas. In deciding this case, the Supreme Court said that, first, Green had to prove a prima facie case of discrimination by showing the following:

- He was a member of a protected class.
- He applied for a job for which he was qualified.
- He was rejected.
- The employer continued to seek applicants for the job.

These criteria for showing a prima facie case of discrimination have become known as the ***McDonnell Douglas* v. *Green Rule*.** Green's situation met the requirements of this rule and indicated a prima facie case of racial discrimination. The Supreme Court stated, however, that simply showing a prima facie case of discrimination did not end the process: the employer had to be given the chance to defend its actions. In this case, McDonnell Douglas defended itself by stating that Green had been rejected because he participated in illegal actions against the company (the blocking of highways to the plant). The Supreme Court accepted this defense as reasonable. The Court then stated that Green should have the opportunity to prove that the organization's rationale for his rejection was, in fact, a cover-up for a racially discriminatory decision. The Court suggested that data showing that McDonnell Douglas had rehired white workers, but not black workers, who had committed acts of similar seriousness against the company would be useful in invalidating the company's defense. Data showing that McDonnell Douglas had a general pattern of discriminatory practices against blacks (e.g., that McDonnell Douglas hired very few minority workers for any jobs) would also be useful. The Court indicated that Green had not provided sufficient evidence to refute the company's rationale for rejecting his application.

Disparate Impact (*Griggs* v. *Duke Power Co.*) In *Griggs* v. *Duke Power Co.* (1971), the Supreme Court established the concept of disparate impact as a type of discrimination.[31] The *Griggs* approach was specifically upheld by Congress in the Civil Rights Act of 1991. **Disparate impact,** also called **adverse impact,** occurs when the same standards are applied to all employees but have very different consequences for particular groups. In the *Griggs* case, Willie Griggs, a black man, applied for the job of coal handler at the Duke Power Company. The company, which required that all coal handlers have high school diplomas, rejected Griggs because he did not. Griggs filed a suit against the company claiming that

Anti-Nepotism Rules—Fair or Unfair?

Nepotism is showing favoritism to relatives and close friends. Examples include hiring or promoting a relative largely because of the relationship, and at the expense of more qualified candidates who are not related to the decision maker. The authors of a text on business ethics point out that nepotism raises a number of moral concerns, among them "disregard both of managerial responsibilities to the organization and of fairness to all other applicants" (Shaw and Barry, 1989, p. 240).

To prevent this potential conflict of interest and the unfairness that may arise when relatives are hired, a number of organizations have adopted anti-nepotism rules of some sort. The most extreme rule prohibits the employment of a relative of an employee anywhere in the organization, even at another site. Less extreme rules prohibit the employment of related people at the same site or in the same department. The most limited type of anti-nepotism rule is a no-supervision rule, which states that one may not have decision-making authority (regarding job assignment, appraisal, hiring, or compensation) over a relative.

Anti-nepotism rules were formulated to prevent abuses of the power to hire and served this role reasonably well until the explosion of dual-career couples in the 1970s. Suddenly, rules that were intended to prevent the hiring of unqualified (usually male) relatives of (usually male) employees were having quite a different effect: prohibiting the employment of highly qualified individuals who just happened to be married to a current employee or job applicant, or prohibiting the continued employment of coworkers who meet and marry after hire. If the spouse is qualified on his or her own merits, a rule intended to guarantee fairness in employment now causes unfairness.

The most difficult situation arises when coworkers marry. Presumably, both were originally employed on their own merits, but a no-spouse rule may now decree that one must transfer to another department or leave the organization altogether. This situation seems quite unfair, as a private off-the-job matter (one's marriage partner) is presumed to have an immediate and deleterious effect on ability to perform the job properly.

Most no-spouse rules are written in sex-neutral language (no "spouses" versus "no wives of male employees"), but some have been challenged in court. Title VII-based challenges focus on the fact that anti-nepotism rules often have adverse impact on women (tending to prohibit the employment of wives when the husband is employed first, which is often the situation). In one case where a no-spouse rule produced severe adverse impact on women, the employer was able to convince the court that the rule was a business necessity. In the case of coworkers who marry, the Fifth and Fourteenth Amendments, which protect the right to marry, have been invoked. With very rare exceptions (under some state laws prohibiting marital status discrimination), the courts have upheld no-spouse rules. Thus, the rules are legal, though the consequences may not always be fair.

Some organizations are accommodating dual-career couples by relaxing stringent anti-nepotism rules that were adopted before large numbers of married women entered the labor force. Many firms find that these antiquated rules can deny them the services of potentially excellent employees and complicate the recruiting of professionals, who are often married to other professionals. A sensible policy for many organizations seems to be to emphasize ability and merit rather than relationship or nonrelationship and to adopt a no-supervision-of-spouses rule. The latter seems useful for preventing any suspicion of favoritism and reassuring employees not related to the boss that even-handed treatment will prevail.

Sources: Len Bierman and Cynthia D. Fisher, "Anti-Nepotism Rules Applied to Spouses: Business and Legal Viewpoints," *Labor Law Journal*, 1984, pp. 634–642; Christine M. Reed and Linda J. Cohen, "Anti-Nepotism Rules: The Legal Rights of Married Co-workers," *Public Personnel Management*, Spring 1989, pp. 37–43; William Shaw and Vincent Barry, *Moral Issues in Business* (Belmont, Calif.: Wadsworth), 1989.

the diploma requirement had nothing to do with a person's ability to do the job and that it discriminated against blacks, since fewer blacks had high school diplomas than did whites. In this case of adverse impact, the Supreme Court ruled that in proving a prima facie case of discrimination Griggs did not have to show that Duke Power Company intended to discriminate against blacks, but simply that the policies of the company had an adverse impact on them. The *Griggs* ruling and other court decisions have held that at least three types of data can be used to show a prima facie case of disparate impact.[32] These types of data are presented in Table 5.4.

A comparison of the actual impact of selection procedures may be used to determine if disparate impact exists. In comparison 1 of Table 5.4, the minority-members-hired–minority-applicants ratio is compared with the majority-members-hired–majority-applicants ratio. If these ratios are radically different from one another, the difference would indicate that discrimination might have occurred somewhere in the selection process. Alternatively, if an organization had some specific qualification that it required of employees—a high school diploma in the case of Duke Power Company—disparate impact could be shown by looking at the potential effect the requirement would have on minority and majority applicants.

In comparison 2 of Table 5.4, only 50 percent of the minorities in the labor market have a high school education, as opposed to 80 percent of the majorities. A significant adverse impact could occur if an organization used a high school education as a selection requirement. The third type of disparate impact data involves comparing the proportion of minorities in the company's work force to the proportion of minorities in the local population. If minorities comprise 41.7 percent of the local population but only 6 percent of the company's work force, this inequity might constitute a prima facie case of discrimination.

In *Griggs* v. *Duke Power Co.,* the prima facie case of discrimination was established using data that showed the potential impact of the hiring requirement on black applicants (see comparison 2 of Table 5.4). In rebutting the prima facie case, the company argued (1) that the hiring requirement was fair because it was applied to all applicants and (2) that there was no intention to discriminate. The good intent of the company was demonstrated by its practice of helping to fund the education of workers who attempted to complete their high school education. The Court rejected this defense, saying that impact, not intent, was the key issue in determining discrimination. Moreover, the company had no proof that having a high school diploma was in any predictable way related to on-the-job performance of employees.

Four-Fifths Rule A major question related to proving disparate impact is, How do we decide when the impact is adverse enough to be considered discriminatory? The EEOC has developed a rule of thumb for determining adverse impact. It is called the **Four-Fifths Rule.** The EEOC applies this rule to actual impact data to determine whether or not a prima facie case of discrimination exists.[33] The rule states that if the minorities-hired–minority-applicants ratio is less than four-fifths (80 percent) of the majority-members-hired–majority-applicants ratio, then a

TABLE 5.4 Types of Data Used to Show Disparate Impact

Comparison/ Type of Data	*Ratio 1*				*Ratio 2*				*Ratio 1/Ratio 2*
1. Comparison of Actual Impact	*Minorities* Hired*	*Minority Applicants*	*Ratio Hired*	*Percent Hired*	*Majorities Hired*	*Majority Applicants*	*Ratio Hired*	*Percent Hired*	*60% Minorities Hired*
Hiring Data	60	100	60/100	60%	75	110	75/110	68.2%	68.2% Majorities Hired
2. Comparison of Potential Impact	*All Minorities in Labor Market*	*Qualified† Minorities in Labor Market*	*Ratio of Potentially Hireable Minorities*	*Percent of Potentially Hireable Minorities*	*All Majorities in Labor Market*	*Qualified Majorities in Labor Market*	*Ratio of Potentially Hireable Majorities*	*Percent of Potentially Hireable Majorities*	*50% Potentially Hireable Minorities*
Labor Market Data	10,000	5,000	5,000/ 10,000	50%	25,000	20,000	20,000/ 25,000	80%	80% Potentially Hireable Majorities
3. Comparison of Work Force to Population	*Minorities in Company Work Force*	*Total Company Work Force*	*Minority Ratio to Total Work Force*	*Minority Percent of Total Work Force*	*Minorities in Local Population*	*Total Local Population*	*Minority Ratio to Population*	*Minority Percent of Population*	*6% Minorities in Work Force*
Population and Company Data	30	500	30/500	6%	25,000	60,000	25,000/ 60,000	41.7%	41.7% Minorities in Population

**Minorities* means protected classes such as blacks, Hispanics, or women.

†In this context, the term *qualified* means that the person has some specific qualification that the employer seeks in hiring workers (for example, a high school diploma).

prima facie case of discrimination exists. For example, in comparison 1 of Table 5.4, the minority ratio is 60/100 (60 percent, or .60), and the majority ratio is 75/110 (68.2 percent, or .682). To compare the two selection rates, .60 is divided by .682, to equal .879 (or 87.9 percent). Thus, the minority ratio is greater than four-fifths (or 80 percent) of the majority ratio, and no prima facie case exists.

Retaliation A special form of disparate treatment is **retaliation.** Employers cannot retaliate—by firing, demoting, harassing, or otherwise treating employees unfairly—because employees have filed discrimination charges. In *EEOC* v. *Union Bank of Arizona* (1976), the court ruled that protection against retaliation should be extended even to employees who suffered retaliation because their employer mistakenly believed that they had filed a charge.[34] In *United States* v. *City of Socorro* (1976), a federal district court ruled that it was illegal discrimination to retaliate against an employee whose spouse had filed a charge of discrimination.[35] Employees who are retaliated against can get injunctive relief from the retaliation.[36] Section 706 of Title VII of the Civil Rights Act of 1964 allows the EEOC to seek immediate relief from retaliation for an individual filing a charge of discrimination, even though the EEOC has not completed its processing of the charge.

Rebutting a Prima Facie Case

A company can defend itself against a prima facie case by using the defenses of job relatedness, bona fide seniority system, or business necessity.

Job Relatedness Showing **job relatedness** is a defense that is appropriate in situations in which an apparently neutral practice of the organization has a disparate impact on some protected class.[37] The company must show that its procedures are related to employee performance. For example, an employer may be able to justify the adverse impact on women caused by a 6-foot, 2-inch requirement by showing that individuals who are less than 6 feet, 2 inches have difficulty performing the job. The height requirement would not constitute illegal discrimination because it relates directly to the ability of workers to perform their job.

If an employer can show that individuals who score below 70 on an ability test have difficulty performing the job, then hiring only applicants with scores of 70 or above may be justified, even if this selection requirement adversely affects black applicants. However, proving that a particular hiring requirement is job-related is not easy. In *Albermarle Paper Company* v. *Moody* (1975), Albermarle had used test scores of verbal and nonverbal intelligence in selecting job applicants.[38] The company had hired an industrial psychologist to determine the job relatedness of these tests, and the psychologist had found a significant correlation between test scores and supervisor ratings of employee performance. Moody, a black employee of Albermarle, filed a charge of racial discrimination against the company and successfully proved that the tests had an adverse impact on black job applicants. In ruling on the case, the Supreme Court stated that to show job relatedness, a company must first analyze and document the tasks and responsibilities of the job. The Court also stated that performance standards must be clear and unambiguous so as to allow the employer to accurately determine which employees are high (or low) performers. Albermarle had met neither of these requirements. No systematic job analysis had been conducted, and the performance ratings used were highly subjective and ambiguous in nature. The Court ruled in favor of Moody. A very detailed description of the processes by which an organization can show job relatedness of hiring requirements is provided in the *Uniform Guidelines*.

Bona Fide Occupational Qualification Another defense against a prima facie case is the **bona fide occupational qualification (BFOQ).** The BFOQ defense relates to situations in which the employer has used criteria such as sex, race, or religion in making decisions about employees or job applicants. Thus, requiring that only male actors be considered for the role of Julius Caesar would be justifiable since "maleness" is an inherent part of the character of Julius Caesar. In *Dothard* v. *Rawlinson* (1977), the Supreme Court held that refusing to hire females as prison guards in an all-male prison was justifiable as a BFOQ.[39] Since the BFOQ defense involves the direct use of race, sex, religion, or the like in making selection decisions, organizations hoping to use this defense must have very convincing evidence to support their cases. In *Diaz* v. *Pan American World Airways* (1971), the company had used sex (only women were hired) as a BFOQ for hiring flight attendants.[40] Pan Am did not have any strong evidence to prove that only women were capable of performing the flight attendants' essential duties of serving food and drinks and providing for the safety of the passengers. A federal court ruled that sex was not a BFOQ for the job of flight attendant.

Bona Fide Seniority System A third possible defense is the **bona fide seniority system.** Organizational actions that result in disparate treatment or disparate impact may be justified if the actions are part of a bona fide seniority system. In *Teamsters* v. *United States* (1977), the Supreme Court decided that seniority systems that had the effect of locking minorities into lower-level jobs were valid, as long as the intent of the seniority systems was not to discriminate.[41] The definition of a bona fide seniority system as one that does not intend to discriminate has been supported in other court decisions.[42] In *Firefighters Local Union 1784* v. *Stotts,* discussed earlier, the "last hired, first fired" policy used by the city of Memphis in laying off firefighters had an adverse impact on black employees. Nevertheless, the Supreme Court ruled that the policy was justified because it was part of a bona fide seniority system.

Business Necessity A final defense is **business necessity.** Employers may justify practices that result in disparate treatment or disparate impact if the actions are essential to efficient and safe operation of the company. In *Furnco Construction Corporation* v. *Waters* (1978), the Supreme Court accepted the company's practice of requiring job applicants to possess certain experience, skills, and training, since improper performance of the job could result in serious physical harm to employees.[43] These requirements had an adverse impact on black job applicants but were justified by business necessity. Employers using the business necessity defense have generally been required to prove that there existed an overriding necessity, not simply a purpose for their actions.[44]

MANAGEMENT'S RESPONSE

The final factor in the EEO environment is management and the responses it makes to EEO laws and regulations. In this section, we examine the actions that management should take in order to deal effectively with equal employment opportunity.

Take Control

The most important step in dealing effectively with EEO activities is for management to take control of them in the organization.[45] The key elements of control are information, policy, and communication. An organization should regularly conduct a self-analysis to examine the status of minority, female, and handicapped workers. The company may wish to develop and regularly update special logs on a variety of personnel decisions. A sample data log of employee discipline/discharge decisions is presented in Figure 5.4. This information allows the company to identify areas in which disparate impact or disparate treatment may be occurring and provides the basis for a defense of company policies in discrimination suits.

An organization should collect information concerning the potential impact that new HR policies may have on its work force. For example, organizations forced to make layoffs should evaluate the likely impact of these layoffs on minorities, women, and older workers.[46] If need be, the companies could take steps to lessen the adverse effect of the layoffs on these protected groups and to prevent discrimination complaints.

All organizations should develop formal, written policies concerning equal employment opportunity. An example of such a policy against sexual harassment is presented in Figure 5.5. However, policies are effectively only to the extent that they are understood by employees.

The last element of control is communication. The organization should make sure that EEO policies are displayed widely and prominently throughout the company. The organization should develop special training programs to transmit knowledge of EEO issues and the company's EEO policies to managers, first-line supervisors, and other key employees.

Make Procedures Objective and Job Related

Employers' decisions about hiring, firing, promoting, or providing benefits to employees must be objective and job-related. Testing procedures used to hire

FIGURE 5.4 Discipline/Discharge Log

Location: ______ *From:* ______ *To:* ______

Name	Race / Sex	Handicap / Age	A. Type of Discipline	B. Job-Related Reason for Discipline	C. Job-Related Reason for Discharge	D. Type of Separation	Reason for Other Type of Separation	Date Recalled or Returned if Laid Off or on Leave of Absence

Race: M—Minority
NM—Non-minority

Sex: F—Female
MA—Male

Handicapped—H

Age—Put age if employee is 40 years of age or older.

A. Type of Discipline
1—Verbal warning
2—First written warning
3—Second written warning
4—Demotion
5—Suspension (specify number of days)
6—Discharge

B. Job-Related Reason for Discipline
1—Unsafe work performance
2—Ineffective work performance
3—Failure to obey a supervisor
4—Failure to obey the employer's policy
5—Interfering with the work performance of other employees
6—Unexcused lateness or tardiness
7—Unexcused absences
8—Other (specify)

C. Job-Related Reason for Discharge
1—Did not receive written recommendation from drug or alcoholism counselor or physician to work
2—Did not receive written recommendation from physician or counselor to work because of mental, physical, or emotional condition
3—Unsafe work performance
4—Ineffective work performance
5—Failure to obey a supervisor
6—Failure to obey the employer's policy
7—Interfering with the work performance of other employees
8—Unexcused tardiness
9—Unexcused absences

D. Type of Separation
1—Resignation
2—Layoff
3—Sick leave
4—Other leave of absence
5—Death
6—Retirement
7—Disability
8—Discharge

Put proper symbols, numbers, or answers in each column

Source: Adopted from *Employing Handicapped Persons: Meeting EEO Obligations* by V. Grossman. Reprinted by permission of BNA Books, Washington, D.C.

employees should be validated using techniques consistent with the EEOC's *Uniform Guidelines*. (These techniques are discussed in more detail in Chapter 8.) When decisions are based on performance evaluations of employees, the procedures used to assess performance should be as objective and directly related to the job as possible. Job analysis should be used to determine the important aspects of job performance. Performance should be assessed by persons who have been trained in performance-rating techniques and have had adequate time to observe the performance of the individual(s) being rated. (The details of how to set up a good performance appraisal system are discussed in Chapter 11.)

FIGURE 5.5 A Corporate Policy Against Sexual Harassment of Employees

Policy of Acme Electronics Corporation

Corporate policy is that all employees have the right to work in an environment free of discrimination. One form of discrimination is **sexual harassment.** Corporate policy concerning sexual harassment is as follows:

Any employee found engaging in sexual harassment will be subject to:

- Official reprimands that will be placed in the employee's permanent personnel file
- Suspension from work without pay
- Demotion to a lower-paying job assignment
- Discharge from the company
- Other appropriate action

No supervisor shall explicitly or implicitly threaten that a subordinate's refusal to submit to sexual advances will result in adverse effects on the worker's employment, pay, promotions, assigned duties, or any other condition of employment. Acme employees are prohibited from engaging in behavior of a sexual nature that would create an offensive, unpleasant, or otherwise hostile work environment, e.g., telling jokes of a sexual nature, offensive flirtations, sexual advances or propositions, comments concerning the bodies of members of the opposite sex, or using sexually explicit words that might be considered offensive.

Acme Corporation encourages any employee who feels he/she has been the victim of sexual harassment to report the incident to his/her supervisor or to Bob Farrow, Chair of the EEO Compliance Committee (456-2534, Room 423 in the Personnel Office). The incident will be investigated, and corrective action will be taken if appropriate. Acme management is committed to eliminating this type of behavior from our company and will take every step necessary to protect individuals from it.

Develop Grievance Procedures

In cases of discharges, promotions, or sexual, racial, ethnic, or religious harassment, the availability of formal grievance procedures often aids in resolving complaints of discrimination so that the EEOC's involvement is not necessary. Every employer should have a formal grievance procedure that employees can use to deal with possible cases of discrimination. Such a procedure is usually available in unionized companies. Nonunionized organizations should also develop a formal grievance procedure. Figure 5.6 shows how such a procedure might work.

Act Affirmatively

If evidence of discrimination exists in the organization, management should develop policies to correct the situation. These plans should be consistent with guidelines set forth by the OFCCP and the EEOC. In developing these plans, organizations should make use of the minority, female, and handicapped workers already in the company.[47] These employees, formally brought into the process,

FIGURE 5.6 EEO Grievance Procedure for Sexual Harassment Complaint

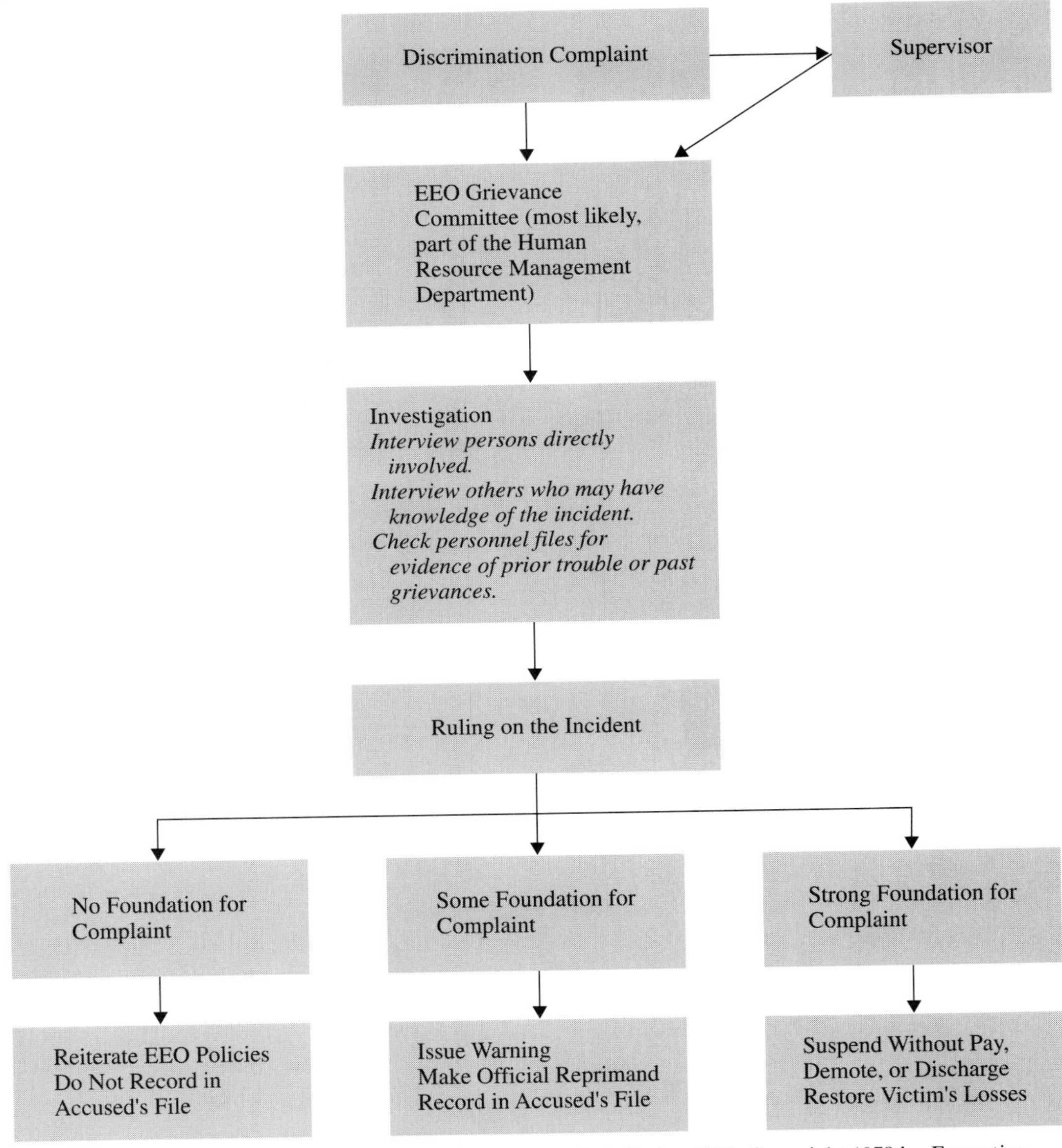

Source: Reprinted with permission from EEO TODAY, Vol. 5, Spring 1978. Copyright 1978 by Executive Enterprises, Inc., 22 West 21st Street, New York, N.Y. 10010–6904. All Rights Reserved.

can provide useful insights and information about how best to recruit and retain minority, female, and handicapped workers. Employers should take into account the Supreme Court decision in *Steelworkers* v. *Weber,* discussed earlier in this chapter. In that case, the Court ruled that voluntary quota systems are acceptable to the extent that employers do the following:

- Avoid quota systems when no evidence of past discrimination exists.
- Develop plans that do not require the discharge of, or have other significant ill effects on, majority workers.
- Avoid setting minority quotas of greater than 50 percent.
- Develop plans that are temporary in nature and will end once the negative effects of past discrimination are corrected.[48]

If a Complaint Is Filed

If, despite the best efforts of the organization, an employee files a discrimination complaint with the Equal Employment Opportunity Commission, the actions of management remain critical. Management might make some of the following suggested responses:

1. When notified by the EEOC that a charge has been filed, ask for a copy of the charge to find out precisely what the company has allegedly done.

2. Conduct an internal investigation to see if the charge is valid. During the investigation, take great care not to pressure or harass the individuals who made the charge. Such harassment might result in the company's being charged with retaliation.

3. Respond to the charge in writing. The response should be absolutely accurate and clearly state the organization's position. If the internal investigation shows that discrimination actually occurred, management should attempt to reach an equitable settlement with the employee.

4. Cooperate within reasonable limits with the EEOC or the OFCCP. During the EEOC's fact-finding investigation or the OFCCP's compliance review, the agency may ask for a large number and great variety of personnel documents. Management should take the position that it will gladly cooperate but will only provide documents that are relevant to the case at hand. Management need not turn over every available personnel document. Which data are turned over should result from a negotiation between management and the investigators. By providing unrestricted access to personnel data, the saying "Give me enough time and documents, and I'll find something illegal" will surely apply.

SUMMARY OF KEY POINTS

There are many different aspects of discrimination under EEO law. These range from broad concepts, like disparate treatment and disparate impact, to more specific instances, such as sexual harassment, pregnancy discrimination, discrimination against the handicapped, and reverse discrimination. The U.S. Constitution, the laws passed by Congress and state legislatures, presidential executive orders, and guidelines of U.S. government agencies all provide protection against these various types of discrimination. The process by which an individual can prove discrimination by an employer has been clearly set out in the courts. This process requires the plaintiff to initially prove a prima facie case of discrimination, using data that show (1) that he or she has been treated differently from other employees because of his or her race, sex, religion, color, national origin, or handicapped status or (2) that company policies have an adverse impact on some protected class. The organization then has an opportunity to defend its actions, on the basis of a BFOQ, seniority system, job relatedness, or business necessity.

Along with state and federal court systems, the Equal Employment Opportunity Commission, the Office of Federal Contract Compliance Programs, and the Justice Department all serve to help enforce the laws and executive orders that prohibit discrimination. These agents of enforcement have a wide array of potential sanctions that can be used against organizations that discriminate.

The final element in the EEO environment is management. By taking control, making HRM procedures objective and job-related, setting up procedures to handle discrimination complaints when they arise, and acting affirmatively, management can prevent itself from becoming the object of discrimination lawsuits. At the same time, management can make maximum use of all the human resources available to it.

Questions for Discussion

1. Why should an organization be interested in complying with EEO regulations?

2. What sort of practices are prohibited by the Pregnancy Discrimination Act of 1978?

3. Do you agree with the U.S. Supreme Court's decision in the *Meritor* case? What is "environmental" sexual harassment? How do you prove this?

4. Suppose that a friend of yours has been exposed to the AIDS virus. Your friend's employer learns about this and fires your friend. Is this illegal employment discrimination?

5. Title VII of the Civil Rights Act of 1964 prohibits discrimination in employment based on race, color, sex, religion, or national origin.

Executive Orders 11246 and 11375 require employers with federal contracts to act affirmatively in hiring employees. What is the difference between not discriminating and acting affirmatively?

6. What are the roles of the Equal Employment Opportunity Commission and the Office of Federal Contract Compliance Programs?
7. To prove that an organization has illegally discriminated against a person, the individual(s) must first show evidence of a prima facie case of discrimination. How is this done in a situation where disparate treatment has occurred? Where adverse impact has occurred?
8. Why are the Supreme Court cases *Griggs* v. *Duke Power Co.* (1971) and *Albermarle Paper Co.* v. *Moody* (1975) important for understanding discrimination in employment?
9. What arguments can an organization use to defend itself against a prima facie case of employment discrimination?
10. Why are control, information, and communication so important for management in dealing with EEO opportunity issues in the organization?

CASE 5.1

Affirmative Action at Amalgamated Steel Corporation

You have just been hired as the new EEO coordinator for Amalgamated Steel Corporation, headquartered in Iron Ore, Pennsylvania. Your predecessor, George Kiley, had recently prepared utilization and availability analyses in anticipation of developing a new affirmative action program for Amalgamated Steel. The data from those analyses are presented on the following data sheet. The director of human resource management, Alice Rice, has indicated that development of the new affirmative action program is a top priority project and has asked you to complete the process that was begun by your predecessor.

Your first task is to use the data provided to identify problem areas of underutilization and concentration. Your second task is to prepare a report for Rice outlining steps that Amalgamated Steel could take to help alleviate these problems.

Amalgamated Steel Corporation Employee Utilization and Availability Data

Job Group: Production Operators
Relevant Labor Area: Standard Metropolitan Statistical Area
Prepared by: George Kiley, EEO Coordinator
Date: 5/16/88

		Total	*Male*	*Female*	*White Male*	*White Female*	*Black Male*	*Black Female*
Utilization	1. Size of Utilized Population	1,500	1,440	60	960	45	480	15
	2. Percent of Utilization	100%	96%	4%	64%	3%	32%	1%
Availability	3. Size of Available Population	100,000	49,000	51,000	25,000	23,000	24,000	38,000
	4. Percent of Availability	100%	49%	51%	25%	23%	24%	28%
	5. Size of Work Force	60,000	36,000	24,000	16,200	14,400	19,800	9,600
	6. Percent of Work Force	100%	60%	40%	27%	24%	33%	16%
	7. Individuals Seeking Work	3,500	1,925	1,575	578	709	1,347	866
	8. Percent Seeking Work	100%	55%	45%	17%	20%	29%	24%
	9. Individuals with Requisite Skills in Reasonable Recruiting Area	42,000	25,200	16,800	13,104	9,240	12,096	7,560
	10. Percent of Individuals with Requisite Skills	100%	60%	40%	31%	22%	29%	18%

Note: In actual utilization and availability data, information would be presented for Total, Male, Female, White Male and Female, Black Male and Female, Hispanic Male and Female, Asian Male and Female, and American Indian Male and Female.

Source: Adapted from *EEO Compliance Manual,* 1979. Reprinted by permission of Prentice-Hall, Inc., Englewood Cliffs, New Jersey.

EXERCISE 5.1

EEO Exercise: An International Comparison

The purpose of this exercise is to give you an appreciation of the impact that EEO legislation has had on employment practices in the United States. In this exercise, you will look at a very common employment recruiting practice in the United States and compare it with the same practice in other countries. Specifically, you are going to focus on the practice of recruiting employees through the use of newspaper advertisements and the extent to which the wording of the ads may discriminate in a way that would be illegal in the United States.

1. The class should be divided into an even number of groups of two or three students.
2. Half of the groups should choose a country from a different geographical region (e.g., France, Germany, South Africa, Mexico, Singapore, Australia, New Zealand, Japan, Korea, Taiwan). For each group representing a foreign country, assign a partner group to represent the United States.
3. Using the university library, group members should identify English-language newspapers from the country they represent and collect from these papers examples of employment ads. Make copies of the ads to bring to class. The ads should represent a wide variety of jobs, including low-skilled, blue-collar, professional, and executive positions. Groups representing the United States should look for employment ads for the same job categories in major newspapers around the country.
4. Title VII of the Civil Rights Act of 1964 says that employers should not discriminate in their employment practices on the basis of race, color, religion, national origin, or sex. Other legislation and federal regulations prohibit discrimination based on age and handicapped status. In this step, each group representing a foreign country should meet with its U.S. partner to discuss the extent to which employment ads in the foreign country are more (or less) discriminatory than those found in the United States. What types of discrimination are found in the ads? Are discriminatory ads more prevalent for certain types of jobs?
5. *Optional:* Each pair of groups should then present their findings to the class.

Notes and References

1. "Former American Airlines Executive Awarded over $7 Million in Bias Case," *BNA Daily Labor Report,* January 28, 1992, p. A5.
2. Civil Rights Act of 1866, Section 1981 (401 FEP Manual 81).
3. *Johnson* v. *Railway Express Agency,* U.S. Supreme Court, 10 FEP 831 839 847 (1975).
4. Civil Rights Act of 1871, Section 1983 (401 FEP Manual 81).
5. Equal Pay Act of 1963 (401 FEP Manual 451).
6. *Schultz* v. *Wheaton Glass Co.,* 421 F.2d 259 (3rd Cir. 1970).
7. Civil Rights Act of 1964 (401 FEP Manual 1); 401 FEP Manual 11.

8. *General Electric Co.* v. *Gilbert,* 423 U.S. 822 (1976).
9. *California Federal Savings & Loan* v. *Guerra,* 479 U.S. 272 (1987).
10. *United Auto Workers* v. *Johnson Controls,* 111 S. Ct. 1196 (1991).
11. *Barnes* v. *Costle,* 561 F.2d 983 (D.C. Cir. 1977); *Fisher* v. *Flynn,* 598 F.2d 663 (1st Cir. 1979); and *Williams* v. *Civiletti,* 487 F. Supp. 1389, 22 FEP 1311 (1980).
12. Discrimination Because of Sex, Title VII of the Civil Rights Act of 1964, as amended; Adoption of Final Interpretive Guidelines, 29 CFR Part 1604, Section 1604.11(a), 1980.
13. *Meritor Savings Bank* v. *Vinson,* 477 U.S. 57 (1986).
14. Age Discrimination in Employment Act of 1967 (401 FEP Manual 351).
15. *EEOC* v. *Wyoming,* U.S. Supreme Court, 31 FEP 73, 406 (1983).
16. *Public Employees Retirement System of Ohio* v. *Betts,* 109 S. Ct. 2854 (1989).
17. Vocational Rehabilitation Act of 1973 (401 FEP Manual 501).
18. K. L. Sovereign, *Personnel Law,* 2d ed. (Englewood Cliffs, N.J.: Prentice-Hall, 1989), p. 79.
19. Immigration Reform and Control Act of 1986, 8 USC 1324 (a).
20. *Wards Cove Packing Co.* v. *Antonio,* 109 S. Ct. 2115 (1989).
21. *Griggs* v. *Duke Power Co.,* 401 U.S. 424, 3 FEP 175 (1971).
22. *Steelworkers* v. *Weber,* 443 U.S. 193, 20 FEP 1 (1979).
23. *Edmonson* v. *U.S. Steel Corp.,* District Ct. Alabama, 20 FEP 1745 (1979); *Moseley* v. *The Goodyear Tire & Rubber Co.,* 612 F.2d 187, 22 FEP 121 (1980); and *Wright* v. *National Archives and Records Service,* 4th District California, 21 FEP 8 (1979).
24. *Firefighters Local Union 1784* v. *Stotts,* U.S. Supreme Court, 34 FEP 1702 (1984).
25. *City of Richmond* v. *J. A. Croson,* 109 S. Ct. 707 (1989).
26. *Uniform Guidelines on Employee Selection Procedures,* 29 Code of Federal Regulations, Part 1607 (1978).
27. On November 20, 1990, the EEOC announced that it would consider charges by "testers" in the investigation and prosecution of job discrimination claims. Testers are individuals who seek employment in an attempt to prove discrimination but without the intention of actually accepting employment if it is offered. Although the use of testers to prove discrimination has become a fairly well accepted practice in the housing discrimination context, the use of such "testers" in the employment context is quite controversial. The U.S. Chamber of Commerce, for example, has expressed concern over the EEOC policy, noting that it will cause employers to expend needless time, effort, and money interviewing individuals who are not really interested in employment.
28. *Albermarle Paper Co.,* v. *Moody,* 422 U.S. 405, 10 FEP 1181 (1975).
29. *Clark* v. *American Marine Corp.,* 437 F.2d 959, 3 FEP 155 (1971).
30. *McDonnell Douglas Corp.* v. *Green,* 411 U.S. 792 5 FEP 965 (1973).
31. *Griggs* v. *Duke Power Co.,* 401 U.S. 424, 3 FEP 175 (1971).
32. The other court decisions include *Hazelwood School District* v. *United States,* 433 U.S. 299, 15 FEP 1 (1977); and *Teamsters* v. *United States,* 431 U.S. 324, 14 FEP 1514 (1977).
33. Although the concept of a prima facie case was developed in the court system, the type of evidence that indicates a prima facie case is also the type that the EEOC and OFCCP look for in their own investigations of organizations. The agencies look for evidence of disparate treatment and disparate impact. Of course, the OFCCP also examines the extent to which organizations are following the actions set forth in their affirmative action programs.
34. *EEOC* v. *Union Bank of Arizona,* 12 FEP 527 (D. Arizona), 1976.
35. *United States* v. *City of Socorro,* 25 FEP 815 (D. New Mexico), 1976.
36. *Drew* v. *Liberty Mutual Insurance Co.,* 480 F.2d 69, 5 FEP 1077 (1973).
37. Ibid.
38. *Albermarle Paper Co.,* v. *Moody,* 422 U.S. 405, 10 FEP 1181 (1975).
39. *Dothard* v. *Rawlinson,* 433 U.S. 321, 15 FEP 10 (1977).

40. *Diaz* v. *Pan American World Airways,* 442 F.2d 385, 3 FEP 337 (1971).
41. *Teamsters* v. *United States,* 431 U.S. 324, 14 FEP 1514 (1977).
42. *Pullman-Standard* v. *Swint,* 456 U.S. 273, 28 FEP 1073 (1982); and *American Tobacco Co.* v. *Patterson,* 456 U.S. 63, 28 FEP 713 (1982).
43. *Furnco Construction Corp.* v. *Waters,* 438 U.S. 537, 17 FEP 1062 (1978).
44. *Robinson* v. *P. Lorillard Co.,* 444 F.2d 829, 3 FEP 653 (1971); and *Bethlehem Steel Co.* v. *United States,* 446 F.2d 652, 3 FEP 589 (1971).
45. R. Peres, *Dealing with Employment Discrimination* (New York: McGraw-Hill, 1978). p. 133.
46. V. Grossman, *Employing Handicapped Persons: Meeting EEO Obligations* (Washington, D.C.: BNA, 1980).
47. Ibid.
48. L. S. Kleiman and R. H. Faley, "Voluntary Affirmative Action and Preferential Treatment: Legal and Research Implications," *Personnel Psychology,* Vol. 41, 1988, pp. 481–496.

6

Recruiting and Job Search

Recruiting is the process by which organizations locate and attract individuals to fill job vacancies. Except in times of economic retrenchment, most organizations have a continuing need to recruit new employees to replace those who leave or are promoted, and to permit organizational growth. Recruiting can be quite expensive. A survey by the Employment Management Association in 1990 reported that the cost per hire to recruit an exempt employee was between $4,000 and $4,500, not including relocation costs.[1] (**Exempt employees** are those not subject to the minimum wage and overtime pay provisions of the Fair Labor Standards Act. Exempt workers include salaried managerial, administrative, and professional employees.) U.S. recruiting costs are modest compared with the average cost of recruiting white-collar workers in Japan. Japanese companies are spending

$40,000 and more to recruit *each* new graduate from a top university.[2] They are willing to spend that much because 95 percent of the time the graduate will stay with the initial employer for his entire career.

Recruitment follows HR planning and goes hand in hand with the selection process by which organizations evaluate the suitability of candidates for various jobs. Without accurate planning, organizations may recruit the wrong number or type of employees. Without successful recruiting to create a sizable pool of candidates, even the most accurate selection system is of little use. Chapter 6 concentrates on how to plan and conduct a successful and cost-effective recruiting effort. It highlights methods that can be used to locate candidates from within the organization, and from the outside labor pool. It also focuses on the job applicant and the ways in which a candidate looks for and chooses a job. The chapter closes with a discussion of the measures that can be used to evaluate the effectiveness of the recruitment process.

OVERVIEW OF THE RECRUITMENT PROCESS

Figure 6.1 presents an overview of the recruitment process from the perspective of the organization and the candidate. This flow chart displays the recruiting process as it unfolds over time. When a vacancy occurs and the recruiter receives permission to fill it, the next step is a careful examination of the job and an enumeration of the skills, abilities, and experience needed to perform the job successfully. Existing job analysis documents can be very helpful in this regard. In addition, the recruitment planner must consider other aspects of the job environment—for example, the supervisor's management style, the opportunities for advancement, pay, and geographical location—in deciding what type of candidate to search for and what search methods to use. After carefully planning the recruiting effort, the recruiter utilizes one or more methods to produce a pool of potentially qualified candidates.

A firm can generate candidates *internally,* from among its present employees who desire promotion or transfer, or *externally,* from the labor market. The organization then screens the candidates, evaluates some more thoroughly, and offers the best ones the position. Throughout the recruiting process, the organization attempts to "sell" itself to the more promising candidates—that is, to convince them that the organization is a good place to work and that it offers what they want in the way of both tangible and intangible rewards.

Candidates searching for an employer go through a parallel set of activities—first acquiring occupational skills and experience, next searching for job openings through a variety of methods, and then applying for jobs that appear to be a suitable match for their qualifications. As the process continues, applicants attempt to "sell" organizations on their abilities, while at the same time collecting information that allows them to evaluate the companies and the jobs.

In the recruiting and selection process, the organization's and individual's goals may conflict. The organization is trying to evaluate the candidate's strengths

FIGURE 6.1 The Recruitment Process

Organization

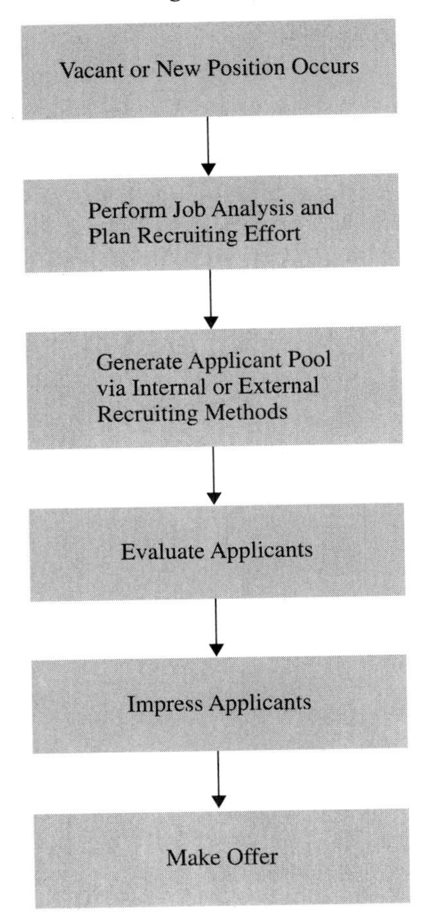

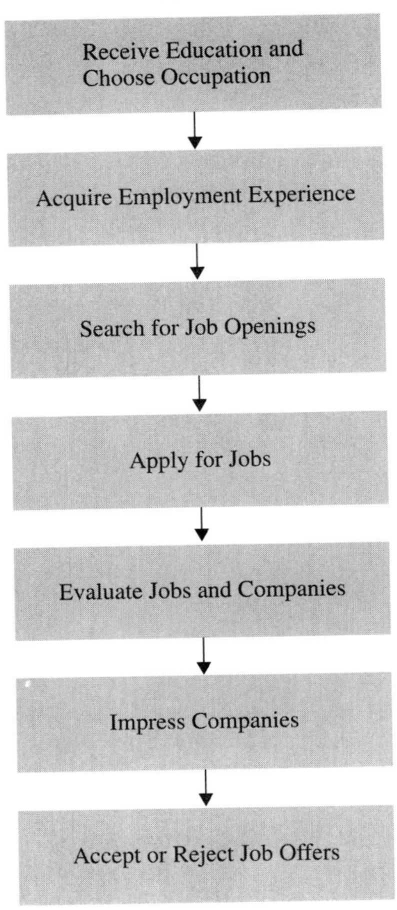

and weaknesses but the candidate is trying to present only strengths. Conversely, although the candidate is trying to ferret out both the good and the bad aspects of the prospective job and employer, the organization may prefer to reveal only positive aspects. In addition, each party's own goals may conflict. The organization wants to treat the candidate well to increase the probability of job-offer acceptance, yet the need to evaluate the candidate may dictate the use of methods that alienate the prospect, such as background investigations or stress interviews. Analogously, the applicant wants to appear polite and enthusiastic about the organization to improve the probability of receiving an offer, but he or she may also want to ask penetrating questions about compensation, advancement, and the company's financial health and future.[3]

PREPARING FOR RECRUITING

A successful recruiting effort requires careful planning and coordination. In most medium and large organizations, HRM professionals do most of the recruiting. These people may be personnel generalists who spend some of their time performing recruitment activities or full-time recruiters who specialize in seeking and screening potential new employees. A separate recruiting function with at least one full-time recruiter tends to exist in organizations that have a continuing need to recruit a minimum of fifty to one hundred exempt employees each year.[4] Recruiters may make hiring decisions for some lower-level jobs, but ordinarily they locate, evaluate, and then refer the most qualified candidates to the manager in whose unit the vacancy has occurred. This manager, called the **hiring manager,** makes the final hiring decision, often in consultation with other managers. In order to find the right kind of candidates, recruiters must work closely with hiring managers throughout the recruitment process.

The recruiter's first step after receiving an assignment is to meet with the hiring manager to find out more about the position to be filled. The two of them must work out specifications in terms of what types of education, skills, and experience are needed and desired.[5] Besides obtaining the needed information about the job's requirements, the recruiter must also identify what might attract candidates to the job. With this information, the recruiter can begin to plan where to look for applicants, how many to look for, and how to screen them.

Throughout the recruiting process, the hiring manager should stay in close touch with the recruiter. The hiring manager should examine résumés or applications that have passed initial screening by the recruiter and also review some of the applications that the recruiter rejected during the first step. Such involvement on the part of the hiring manager allows feedback as to whether or not the recruiter's decisions are consistent with the hiring manager's preferences.

Internal or External Sources?

Often an early task in recruitment planning is to decide whether a position is to be filled internally or externally. In some cases, there is no decision to be made. For instance, entry-level jobs must be filled externally, and for other positions, the company's policy or union contract may require that internal sources be utilized first. Most organizations use a mixture of internal and external sources—promoting from within when qualified employees are available and recruiting from external sources when new skills are needed or growth is rapid. Each type of source has its advantages and disadvantages.

Advantages of Internal Recruiting When an internal source is used, the vacancy is filled by a person of known ability. Since the employer has observed the employee in one position, there is less guesswork involved in assessing his or her suitability for a second position. In contrast, assessments of external recruits are based on less reliable sources, such as references, and relatively brief encounters, such as interviews. Another advantage of promoting from within is that doing so motivates current employees. Skilled and ambitious employees are less likely to quit and more likely to become involved in developmental activities if they believe that promotion is likely.[6] Also, training and socialization time is reduced when openings are filled internally because a current employee has less to learn about the organization and its idiosyncratic procedures than a newcomer. Recruiting may also be faster and less expensive if an internal candidate can be found. Finally, in times of impending retrenchment, filling as many jobs as possible internally maximizes job security for present employees.

Disadvantages of Internal Recruiting If the organization is expanding rapidly, there may be an insufficient internal supply of qualified individuals above the entry level. This situation may result in people being promoted before they are ready or not being allowed to stay in a position long enough to learn how to do a job well. Also, when one vacancy is filled internally, a second vacancy is created—the position of the individual who was promoted or transferred to fill the first vacancy. If this slot is also filled internally, then another vacancy occurs. This movement of personnel is called the **ripple effect.** In one organization, 195 initial vacancies eventually resulted in 545 job movements.[7] Another disadvantage of internal recruiting is that some organizations' internal recruiting procedures are extremely cumbersome. They may involve a "bureaucratic nightmare" of forms, waiting times, eligibility lists, and requirements of permission to interview from the candidate's current superior.[8] Figure 6.2 is an example of the many steps in an internal recruitment process in one organization. Still another disadvantage of internal recruiting is that an organization can become inbred and lose flexibility if all its managers are homegrown. Finally, meeting affirmative action goals can usually be accomplished only by aggressive external recruiting.

Advantages of External Recruiting Recruiting from external sources can bring in new ideas and viewpoints, avoid the confusion that accompanies the ripple effect, meet affirmative action goals, and cope with the demands of rapid growth without overusing inexperienced personnel. Another advantage may be savings in training costs. Hiring experienced workers away from other companies may cut down on the need for a comprehensive training and development program in-house. Finally, there may be instances that require a severe shakeup or turnaround. Particularly at the upper management level, an outsider with no prior commitment to present employees or ongoing projects may be the only individual with enough objectivity (and even ruthlessness) to bring about needed changes and enunciate a new vision for the organization.[9]

Disadvantages of External Recruiting One disadvantage of external recruiting is the cost. Because the external labor market is much larger and harder to reach than the internal one, recruiting externally usually takes longer and costs more. With external recruiting, there is also the risk of hiring a candidate who does not live up to the apparent high potential displayed during the selection process. Finally, too much external recruitment is discouraging to current employees because it reduces their chances to move up in the organization.

FIGURE 6.2 Internal Recruitment Process

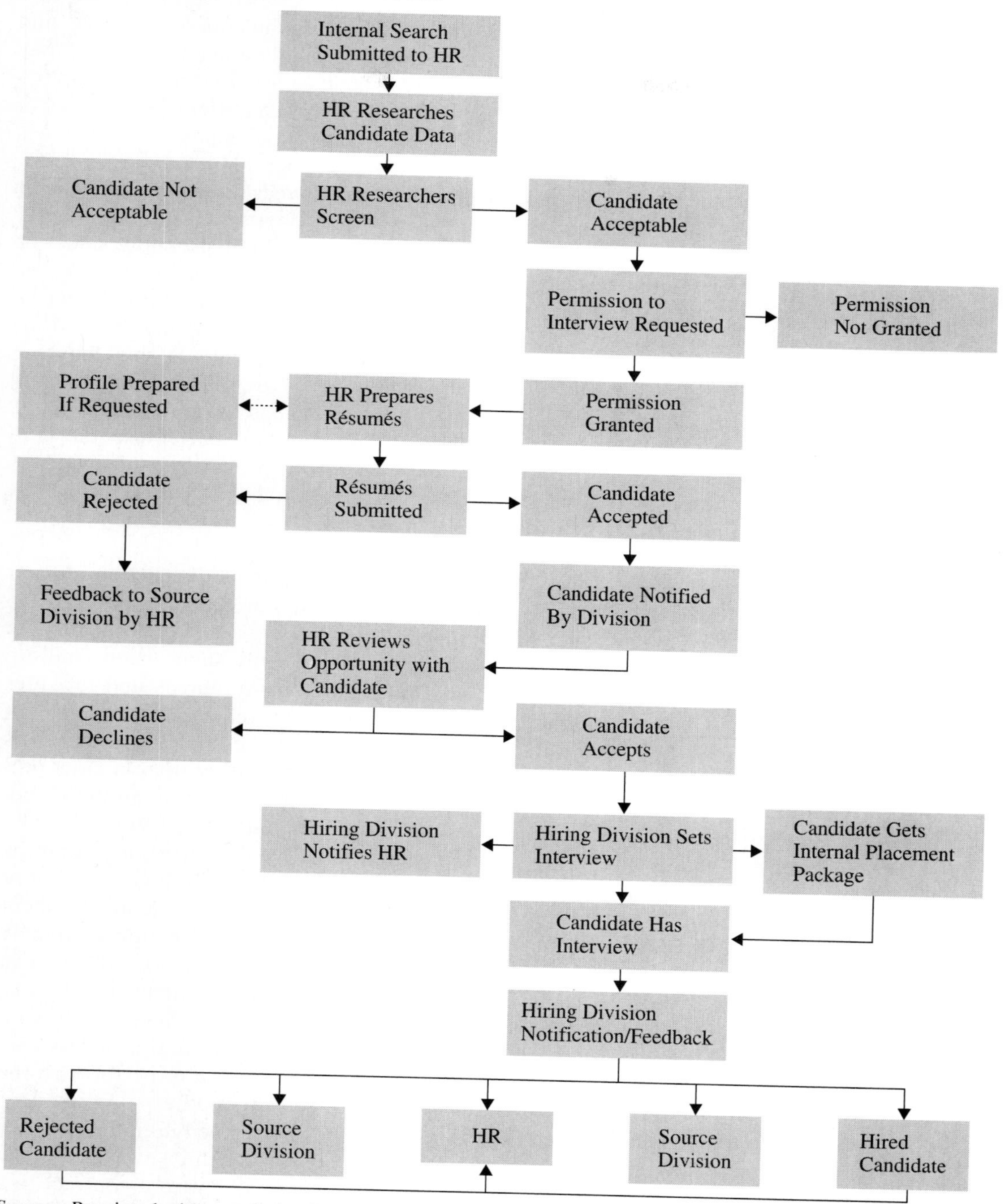

Source: Reprinted with permission from Bernhard Welle, Vice President, Human Resources, Dial Corp., Phoenix, AZ.

Alternatives to Recruiting

Many firms have no desire to repeat the painful retrenchments of the 1980s and are reluctant to recruit enough full-time staff to meet all their needs. Instead, they have adopted the staffing strategy of keeping a small cadre of permanent employees (who are relatively insulated from layoff), along with a buffer of temporary or contract workers. This strategy is also employed in large Japanese companies. (See the International Perspective box in Chapter 3, page 124.)

Several alternatives to recruiting and hiring employees directly are increasing in popularity. The first is to use temporary workers obtained from a temporary help agency. The temporary help industry has been expanding rapidly since the 1970s.[10] **Temporaries** are especially helpful for covering peak demand periods, especially in an uncertain economic climate when demand could drop precipitously. Temporaries may cost more per hour worked, but they are paid only for the time they actually work. Another advantage of using temporaries is that they are quickly and easily available; therefore, recruiting costs are minimal. In addition, the temporary help agency has already selected and trained the temporaries; thus, training costs are low because the temporaries require only a brief orientation to the company. Historically, temporaries have been used primarily in jobs such as assembler, laborer, secretary, clerk, or truck driver. In today's work environment, however, they are available for a variety of other professions, including nursing, computer programming, engineering, and accounting.[11]

Employee leasing is a way to obtain the services of individuals over a longer time period than would normally be the case with temporaries. An employee leasing firm recruits, hires, trains, and compensates employees, and the organization that leases them provides their work facilities, direct daily supervision, and duties. For example, a nursing services firm employs many nurses and provides them to hospitals on a contract basis. This arrangement relieves the hospitals of a great deal of HRM responsibility. In the future, a number of HR professionals may find themselves working in employee leasing firms rather than in large production-oriented companies. Employee leasing provides the organization flexibility to change the number of employees easily and without actual layoffs.[12]

Yet another alternative to recruiting and hiring to staff a function within the organization is to hire an outside firm to perform the entire function, either on or off the organization's premises. New thought in the area of strategic management suggests that unless an organization can perform a support function extremely well, it should consider subcontracting that function, so that the organization can concentrate all available resources on building unique core competencies. By hiring out such functions as maintenance, security, and office services, the organization can achieve greater efficiency by having these activities performed by specialists. Also, the organization can place competitive pressure to perform on the supplier, in that the supplier can always be replaced by another supplier. This type of incentive is not present when the function is performed in-house.

A similar solution is for the organization to contract with a single individual or consultant on a project basis. For instance, a firm may award a contract to a freelance computer consultant to do a piece of programming rather than hire an

Recruiting and Job Search in China: Revolutionary Concepts

Recruitment by organizations and job search by individuals have been virtually nonexistent in the People's Republic of China until fairly recently. A policy popularly called "The Iron Rice Bowl" guaranteed everyone a job for life, and an "equal, though equally poor, standard of living" (*The Economist*, Sept. 27, 1986, p. 43). Unskilled workers were assigned jobs by a municipal labor bureau, and skilled technicians and new college graduates were assigned jobs centrally by a national labor bureau. The assigned employer provided lifetime employment, housing, medical care, and a pension; the firm was forbidden to discharge employees for any reason but criminal acts. Changing employers was equally difficult. An employee had to get the approval of the present employer, the new employer, and at least one labor bureau.

When Chinese industry began to modernize and participate in joint ventures with companies from abroad, the weaknesses of this system became apparent. Foreign firms attempting to open manufacturing facilities in China had great difficulty in obtaining skilled labor. Often, the only technical people available to them were new graduates, because experienced scientists and technicians were already assigned to employers who would not release them.

Another weakness was inappropriate assignments made by labor boards with insufficient knowledge of the technical requirements of new scientific and skilled jobs. In fact, a major student complaint during the Tienamen Square demonstrations in 1989 concerned the perceived high likelihood of being assigned to an unimportant rural post which did not relate to one's university training. Overseas Chinese students still voice this complaint, often when applying for permanent residence in the country in which they are attending university!

In response to some of these problems, the government began limited experiments with a labor contracting system in 1980. New entrants into the labor force in selected cities and some college graduates were allowed to find jobs on their own. Employment agencies to help in the matching process began to open, and labor bureaus and employers were instructed to become more cooperative in permitting the transfer of skilled employees. For the first time, discharge of redundant or poor-performing employees was allowed. These employees were added to the pool of labor allowed to find their own jobs.

Despite these change attempts, reform has been slow and painful. The urban unemployment rate reached 3 percent in 1990, up from near zero when all labor was centrally assigned. In addition, the government has found that allowing university graduates freedom to find their own jobs does not always meet the needs of the state. Very few are willing to accept assignments in remote areas where living standards are poor, so central assignment had to be reimposed in 1985. Graduates can refuse a state-assigned position, but they are required to reimburse the government for the entire cost of their education before seeking jobs on the open market.

China's best technical institution, Qinghua University, has recently pioneered a modified job assignment system that gives employers and employees a bit more choice. The University invited work units with approved vacancies to campus for a career fair/interviewing day, in which students met with prospective employers. If both parties felt that the match was good, a contract was signed. Students who were not selected were centrally assigned to a work unit as per the usual practice. The University is proud that "70 percent of its 1991 graduates had talked with employing units before signing their contracts" (*China Today*, November 1991, p. 17).

Sources: "Smashing the Bowl," *The Economist*, September 27, 1986, pp. 43–44; Robert Delfs, "Iron Rice Bowl in Shards," *Far Eastern Economic Review*, October 16, 1986, pp. 69–70; "How University Graduates Find Work," *China Today*, November, 1991, pp. 16–19; Solving China's Employment Problems, *China Today*, June 1991, pp. 14–17.

additional full-time programmer. In many cases, the individuals providing these services are former employees whom the firm has laid off or who have quit the firm to begin their own consulting business.[13]

All of these options—temporaries, employee leasing, subcontracting—greatly reduce an organization's employment levels and thus its recruiting needs.

Planning for Recruiting

Assume that after weighing the above considerations a firm decides to recruit externally. Before beginning the recruiting effort, the firm must plan which methods it will use, how intensively it will use them, and when it will begin recruiting to produce the required number of candidates at the time they are needed.

As a rule, higher-level positions take longer to fill. Table 6.1 shows the average time that it took a sample of Fortune 1000 companies to fill positions in each of four salary ranges. Note that nearly all positions paying less than $25,000 per year could be filled in two months or less, whereas almost all positions paying more than $100,000 took substantially longer to fill.

Several other factors, including the following, may make recruiting more difficult or time consuming:

- The need for a confidential search and/or the requirement that no advertising be done.
- A technically complex position for which qualified individuals are hard to find.

TABLE 6.1 Average Time to Fill Positions in Four Salary Ranges

	Percent of Companies Filling Positions in Each Salary Range			
Average Time	*Less than $25,000*	*$25,000 to $49,000*	*$50,000 to $100,000*	*Greater than $100,000*
Less than 2 weeks	6%	—	—	—
2–4 weeks	52%	18%	4%	3%
1–2 months	28%	53%	25%	3%
2–4 months	6%	22%	38%	33%
4–6 months	1%	4%	17%	20%
More than 6 months	—	1%	7%	13%
Do not know	7%	2%	9%	28%

Note: These data are the results of a survey of Fortune 1000 personnel managers. Each percent represents the total percent of positions in that salary range.

Source: From *Robert Half on Hiring* by Robert Half. Copyright © 1985 by Robert Half. Reprinted by permission of Crown Publishers, Inc. and John Boswell Associates.

- Competition in the marketplace for the type of candidates needed.
- A poor industry, company, or division reputation.
- Low pay relative to what other firms are offering to similarly qualified individuals.
- An unclear job description or confusing reporting relationships.
- No housing assistance or relocation costs paid by the company.
- An undesirable location.

These factors either make it difficult to locate candidates or make candidates less willing to entertain offers.[14] Under any of these conditions, recruiters should begin the search early.

If data from past recruiting efforts are available, recruiters should calculate, for different types of positions, the average time between the first contact with an applicant and the first day on the job. Such data can help in determining how far in advance to begin the recruiting process.[15]

An article by Robert Armacost and Rohne Jauernig contains a sophisticated example of recruitment planning in a large city. The municipality authorized a single position, that of pension financial manager, in early November and requested that it be filled by the first or second week of January. This was a high-level position that involved managing a $14-billion pension fund. The city's civil service rules specified a complex set of recruiting and selection steps. The recruiter assigned to the project first estimated the time required to complete each step, determined which steps could occur concurrently, and identified steps that were critical in that they could slow down the entire project. The recruiter applied the Critical Path Method (CPM) and the Program Evaluation Review Technique (PERT) to identify the quickest way to move through the set of activities to the final step of producing a ranked eligibility list of candidates. The recruiter also identified activities that could be speeded up over their expected duration by overtime work ("crashed"). Ultimately, the recruiter forwarded the eligibility list to decision makers just forty-one days after the project began. Table 6.2 shows the activities involved, the estimated and actual time in days to complete each one, and the activities that were "crashed" through overtime to keep the recruitment plan on schedule when other activities took longer than expected.[16]

More commonly, recruitment planning uses somewhat less sophisticated methods. Recruiting goals are usually expressed in terms of the number of positions to be filled. However, knowing that the firm needs to hire fifteen engineers does not immediately tell a recruiter how extensively to search. What the recruiter really needs to know is how many applications or initial interviews will be needed to locate fifteen engineers who are not only able to pass all the selection hurdles but also willing to accept a job offer. Based on past experience in similar situations, the recruiter may be able to calculate yield ratios for different jobs or recruiting methods. A **yield ratio** is the number of candidates who pass each stage of the selection process and enter the next stage compared to the number who entered each stage to begin with. For instance, suppose that (1) 25 percent of the applicants who submitted résumés in response to a newspaper advertisement

TABLE 6.2 Finding a Pension Financial Manager: Time in Days for Recruitment and Selection Activities

Activities	*Expected Time*	*Actual Time*	*Crash Time*	*Crash Cost*
Job analysis and Announcement Sheet	2.33	2.0		
Education and Experience Questionnaires	1.0	0.5		
Advertisement/legal notice	1.0	3.5		
Recruitment/accepting applications	20.17	23.0		
Application review	2.33		1.0	$124
Oral Board list development	1.92	3.0		
Lining up raters	1.25		0.5	$69
Questionnaire rating form	1.08	0.5		
Oral examination and rating form	4.83		1.0	$263
Ranking questionnaires	7.17	6.0		$155
Scheduling oral examinations	1.92	0.5		$132
Oral examination	2.0	2.0		
Eligibility list development	2.0		1.0	$94

Adapted from Robert L. Armacost and Rohne L. Jauernig, "Planning and Managing a Major Recruiting Project," *Public Personnel Management*, Summer 1991, p. 123. Reprinted with permission of *Public Personnel Management*, International Personnel Management Association, Alexandria, VA.

meet the criteria for being invited to a screening interview; (2) about 50 percent of those who are screened are invited back for further interviews; (3) about 20 percent of those invited back decline to pursue their applications; (4) 33 percent of the remaining candidates receive job offers, and (5) 75 percent of the candidates who are offered jobs accept (see Figure 6.3). Based on yield ratios for past recruiting, the HR professional could calculate that the firm has to attract 600 candidates to apply to produce 15 eventual hires. Previous experience data also could help the recruiter plan how many campuses to visit or how many ads to place to produce 600 applicants. Of course, dramatic changes in the unemployment rate may make projections based on previous recruitment data inaccurate.

Most organizations recruit each year to meet that year's needs. They may recruit many people in a boom year and very few during years when the industry, economy, or company is on a down cycle. HR planners at Union Oil Company of California realized that such short-range recruitment planning was not very efficient. In boom years, the company was attempting to hire many people at the same time that its competitors were also recruiting heavily. This concurrent recruiting drove up starting salaries and resulted in lower-quality hires. During the leaner years of the cycle, top graduates were willing to work at lower pay rates

FIGURE 6.3 Recruiting Yield Pyramid

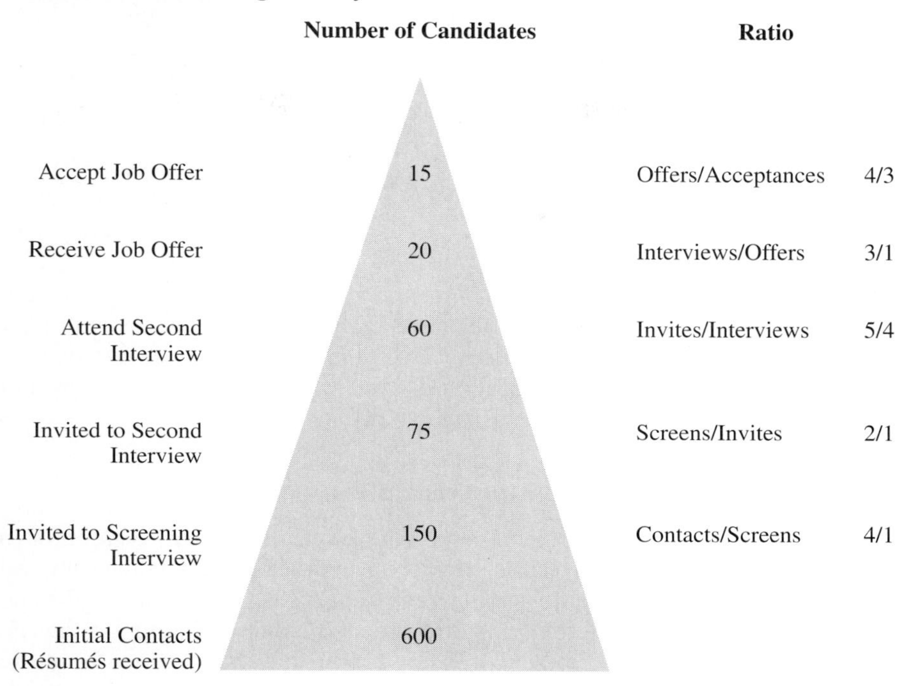

and were readily available since competitors were not hiring. Consequently, Union Oil began to plan campus recruiting on a five-year schedule, spreading its hiring evenly over the period and thus maximizing applicant quality while controlling salary costs.[17]

Recruitment Information Systems

Before beginning to recruit candidates, the HR professional must have a system for tracking applicants as they move through the recruitment and selection process. The system may be manual or computerized, depending on the number of applicants handled. (See the inserts on pages 348 and 767 for more on human resource information systems in general.)

An efficient recruitment information system must ensure that candidates do not get lost but instead move through the process and stay informed of their status. An applicant who is deemed unsuitable should receive a polite letter to that effect as soon as possible after the decision. Good candidates who are pending should receive encouraging letters to keep them interested in the organization. Such conscientious communication enhances an organization's image, even among candidates who are eventually rejected.

The recruitment information system must be able to generate reports on applicant characteristics to determine whether adverse impact is occurring or affirmative action efforts have broadened the applicant pool as intended. The statistics generated must cover the percentages of black, other minority, and female applicants to various job categories. The recruitment information system should also be able to provide data necessary to calculate yield ratios, average time from first contact to first day on the job, and other indexes helpful in planning and evaluating recruiting.[18]

INTERNAL RECRUITING

Most companies fill vacancies internally whenever possible. A variety of internal recruiting methods are used for nonexempt positions and exempt positions. **Nonexempt employees** are not exempt from the minimum wage and overtime pay provisions of the Fair Labor Standards Act. They are usually paid by hourly wages, whereas exempt employees are salaried.

Internal Recruiting for Nonexempt Positions

Some small or nonunionized companies have an informal system for locating promotable employees. When openings occur, the hiring manager may rely on memory to suggest candidates or may ask supervisors to recommend employees who appear qualified. The obvious drawbacks of such a system are that (1) good candidates may be overlooked, (2) favoritism may be displayed, and (3) qualified candidates may be hoarded by a supervisor who prefers to keep them in the department rather than recommend them to deserved promotions elsewhere. A more systematic method would involve the use of a skills inventory system to locate all viable candidates.

The most commonly used system for internal recruitment is **job posting and bidding,** in which employees nominate themselves if they are interested in being considered for an opening. Many large and/or unionized companies use this method, and all but the very top civil service jobs are filled internally by this method. The HR manager posts openings on bulletin boards or publishes them in an in-house newspaper. These postings describe the jobs, locations, pay rates, and qualifications, and encourage all interested employees to apply. The hiring manager and a personnel representative evaluate the candidates and make the selection decision. Employees who applied but were not selected often receive feedback. This feedback loop demonstrates that the system operates in an open and fair manner and helps rejected candidates understand how to improve their qualifications for future openings.[19]

In unionized companies, the basis of selection and other details of the post and bid process are spelled out in the union contract. Two types of clauses are common. The first type says that the hiring manager will select the applicant with the most seniority if he or she is at least minimally qualified. The second type of clause says that the hiring manager will select the most qualified person, but if there are two equally qualified candidates, the hiring manager will choose the one with the most seniority. In nonunionized organizations, policies may state that the selection decision will be based primarily on the applicant's ability to do the vacant job and secondarily on the applicant's performance, attendance, and seniority in the present job.[20]

Internal Recruiting for Exempt Positions

Posting and bidding is quite rare as a method of internal recruiting for professional and managerial positions in the private sector, although a few organizations have used it successfully. For instance, a Fortune 30 energy company had success with a system that posted all exempt jobs paying less than $50,000.[21] The company, however would never use this method to fill top management positions. Organizations trying to fill vacant managerial slots might identify candidates by consulting replacement charts or by forming a nominating committee of higher managers who pool their information to generate a slate of candidates. Larger organizations, however, have found that they need a more systematic method of identifying candidates, particularly if they wish to encourage transfers across divisional lines. These firms are developing managerial succession plans and computerized information systems on managers' education, skills, performance, experience, and job and location preferences. When vacancies occur, the information system can quickly search and produce a list of potential candidates.[22]

EXTERNAL RECRUITING

External recruiting methods are often grouped into two classes: informal and formal. **Informal recruiting methods** tap a narrower labor market than formal methods. Informal methods include rehiring former employees or former cooperative education students and hiring from among those who apply without being solicited (such applicants are called "walk-ins" or "gate hires"). Another informal method is having present employees refer others or encourage their friends to apply ("word-of-mouth" recruiting). **Formal recruiting methods** search the labor market more widely for candidates with no previous connection to the company.

Informal Methods

Informal methods, because they can be implemented quickly, are by far the most commonly used methods for hiring clerical and blue-collar personnel. Most organizations maintain a file of recent unsolicited applications that can be searched when a vacancy occurs. Also, employees can easily spread the word when a firm is hiring. Informal methods tend to be inexpensive, with rare exceptions (e.g., some high technology firms in California's Silicon Valley have offered bounties of up to several thousand dollars to employees who successfully refer a computer programmer or engineer). One drawback of rehiring former employees and word-of-mouth advertising is that these methods may reduce the likelihood of a firm's

TABLE 6.3 Methods Used for Recruitment

	Office/ Clerical	*Production/ Service*	*Professional/ Technical*	*Commissioned Sales*	*Managers/ Supervisors*	*All*
Internal Sources						
a. Promotion from within	94%	86%	88%	75%	95%	99%
b. Employee referrals	87	83	78	76	64	91
c. Walk-in applicants	86	87	64	52	46	91
Advertising						
d. Newspapers	84	77	94	84	85	97
e. Journals/ magazines	6	7	54	33	50	64
f. Radio/television	3	6	3	3	2	9
g. Direct-mail	4	3	16	6	8	17
Employment Services						
h. U.S. Employment Service (USES)	19	20	11	7	7	22
i. State employment service	66	68	38	30	23	72
j. Private employment agencies	28	11	58	44	60	72
k. Search firms	1	<1	36	26	63	67
l. Employee leasing firm	16	10	6	2	<1	20
m. Computerized resume service	0	0	4	0	2	4
n. Video interviewing service	0	<1	1	0	1	2
Outside Referral Sources						
o. Local high schools/trade schools	60	54	16	5	2	68
p. Technical/ vocational institutes	48	51	47	5	8	77
q. Colleges/ universities	24	15	81	38	45	86
r. Professional societies	4	1	5	19	37	55

TABLE 6.3 Methods Used for Recruitment (*cont.*)

	Office/ Clerical	*Production/ Service*	*Professional/ Technical*	*Commissioned Sales*	*Managers/ Supervisors*	*All*
s. Unions	1	10	1	0	1	10
t. Community agencies	33	32	20	16	10	39
Special Events						
u. Career conferences/ job fairs	20	16	44	19	19	52
v. Open house at your organization	10	8	17	8	7	22
Other	5	5	7	6	7	9
Number of respondents	245	221	237	96	243	245

Source: Reprinted with permission: *Table 1, Sources Which Respondents Use to Locate Candidates,* pp. 2-104–2-104, from *Human Resources Planning Employment and Placement*, ASPA/BNA Series No. 3, edited by Wayne Cascio. Copyright © 1989 by the Bureau of National Affairs, Inc., Washington, D.C. 20037.

meeting its affirmative action goals. If a firm's work force is primarily nonminority, then the friends referred by present employees are likely to be nonminority as well. Thus, companies should supplement informal methods with formal methods that reach a wider audience.

University cooperative education programs or internships are excellent informal methods of recruiting that provide companies with the opportunity to assess the ability of new professionals and get an inside track on hiring the best ones. Young professionals can be very impressed by a properly structured internship experience and may strongly desire to return to the same company full time after graduation. Kraft General Foods hires 300 interns each summer. The company has concluded that the program gives it a competitive edge in attracting scarce food science and engineering graduates.[23] A side benefit of cooperative and internship programs is that they keep the company well publicized on campuses at no additional cost.[24]

Formal Methods

Formal methods of external recruiting entail searching the labor market for candidates who have no previous connection to the firm. These methods traditionally have included newspaper advertising, use of employment agencies and executive search firms, and campus recruiting. Table 6.3 shows the percentage of firms using various recruiting methods for five types of jobs. Newspaper advertising is very popular, with 97 percent of the respondents using this method for at least some jobs.[25]

As employers have had to contend with labor shortages in some regions and occupations, they have used additional recruitment methods. Table 6.4 shows some new methods of attracting employees that complement traditional recruiting activities. Other innovative methods include working with community-based organizations such as counseling and job-training centers for the disadvantaged, and educational institutions. As an example of the former, United Parcel Service (UPS) installations in northern New Jersey successfully hired 1,500 employees through the Main Street Counseling Center, a community-based organization in Essex, New Jersey. Recruitment personnel from UPS worked closely with the center to specify job requirements and set up screening processes that led to referral of qualified candidates to UPS for a final hiring decision.[26]

If suitable employees simply are not available, recruiters may have to work with educational institutions to increase the number of qualified individuals. For

TABLE 6.4 Innovative External Recruiting Methods

Telerecruiting Phone calls to potential candidates, with names obtained from mailing lists of professional associations, schools, and mailing list companies.

Direct Mail Using lists from above sources.

Point-of-Sale Recruiting Messages (posters, literature, messages on the back of cash register tapes) Useful if customers are potentially qualified applicants.

Talent Scout Cards One organization in need of customer-oriented service staff gave its managers "talent scout" cards inviting prospective candidates to apply for jobs. Managers were asked to distribute the cards to exceptionally friendly, helpful customer service personnel they encountered while doing their own shopping.

Posters Displayed on community bulletin boards, parks, laundromats, banks, etc.

Door Hangers Useful for recruiting in a specified geographical area

Radio Alone or to refer candidates to open houses or large newspaper ads.

Billboards Fixed highway displays or electronic billboards with varying messages.

Hotlines and 800 Numbers Telephone lines with either recorded job vacancy messages or live interviewers. Live lines are increasingly being made available on Sundays, when most newspaper ads appear and candidates have the time to follow up on openings.

Information Seminars On job hunting skills, or on topics specific to one's industry, such as new developments in artificial intelligence. The latter may attract qualified professionals who would be reluctant to attend an open house or job fair, where the recruiting purpose was more explicit.

Welcome Wagon, Relocation Consultants, Realtors These organizations are aware of newcomers to the community. Increasingly, spouses of individuals transferred into the community are seeking work, and can be located through these sources.

Referral Programs Employee referral systems are common, but now some firms are encouraging their customers and suppliers to refer candidates as well.

Outplacement Firms and Local Layoffs Skilled employees who have lost their jobs through no fault of their own may be found by contacting outplacement firms and by monitoring the local paper for layoffs at other establishments in the community.

Source: Compiled from Catherine D. Fyock, "Expanding the Talent Search: 19 Ways to Recruit Top Talent," *HRMagazine*, July 1991, pp. 32–35. Reprinted with the permission from *HRMagazine* published by the Society for Human Resource Management, Alexandria, VA.

instance, banks in Dade Country, Florida, asked the local school board to add a teller training program to its vocational preparation offerings. Employers assisted in developing program content, recruiting instructors, and monitoring results. Nearly all of the graduates have been placed, and the banks have alleviated their shortage of candidates.[27]

Recruitment Advertising The most common formal recruiting method is advertising. Recruitment advertising has an obvious target—people who are seeking work—and an obvious goal—attracting these job seekers to apply for a job at a particular company. Recruitment ads, however, reach a much wider audience. Estimates are that only 10 to 20 percent of the readers of help-wanted ads are currently seeking work. About 70 to 75 percent of readers are happily employed but skim the ads regularly to see what is available. These readers are unlikely to apply immediately but are developing images of the employers whose ads they see. A well-designed, informative advertisement may help convince these people to consider the company at some later date when they are interested in a new job. Another audience for ads is a company's own employees. When one company discontinued its regular recruitment advertising, it found that its employees were suddenly nervous and that rumors of layoffs were circulating. A final audience is made up of clients, stockholders, brokers, activists, and regulators, all of whom may have some interest in an organization's activities.[28]

The main purpose of a recruitment ad is to generate a **qualified response**—that is, to produce applications from candidates who are at least minimally qualified for the job. To elicit a qualified response, the ad must contain enough information about the job, necessary qualifications, location, and pay rate to allow uninterested or unqualified people to make the decision *not* to apply. At the same time, the ad must attract qualified candidates by conveying a good impression of the company or division and by emphasizing the advantages of the particular job. To achieve its objectives, an ad must not misrepresent the job and raise unrealistic expectations in candidates. Rather, it should clearly describe the legitimate attractions of the job.[29]

One form of advertisement is a **blind ad,** in which the company does not identify itself but rather asks candidates to reply to an anonymous post office box. A company may use *blind ads* when it does not want competitors to know that it is planning an expansion, when it does not want its own employees to know that one of them may be replaced, or when the company has a poor reputation as an employer. Blind ads typically yield a significantly lower response rate than non-blind ads and should not be used unless there is a very good reason. A survey conducted in Europe in the late 1980s discovered that 75 percent of job ad readers said that the organization's name was a crucial piece of information and should always be included in a job advertisement.[30]

Figure 6.4 contains a selection of hypothetical recruitment ads. The two at the top are better designed than those at the bottom. Note that the top ads specifically mention that the organization is an equal opportunity employer (EOE). Ads placed by companies with government contracts must contain such a line to

FIGURE 6.4 Effective, Ineffective, and Possibly Illegal Ads

CPAs

FINANCIAL SERVICES, INC.
is seeking two CPAs to join
our new Baltimore office

—Three to five years of experience required
—Expertise in corporate taxation preferred
—Travel an average of two days per week

Excellent opportunities for management development and advancement with our rapidly expanding firm. Competitive salary plus liberal benefits and vacations.

Send resume to 301 North 16th Street, Baltimore, MD 21201

EEO/AA

ClockWatchers, Inc.

Needs Assemblers Now

We have immediate openings for assembler trainees on the evening shift at our St. George timepiece assembly facility. No experience necessary, all training provided. Preference given to candidates with a stable work and personal history. Manual dexterity test will be administered to all candidates. $4.50 per hour plus incentive pay, medical and dental benefits, paid holidays, and a smoke free work environment.

Call 931-4674 for an appointment with our recruiter.

EEO M/F

MKT REP

Major nat'l. co. seeks reps w/ col. degree. Comp. sal., tng. prog., adv. opp. 329-601-4388.

GIRL FRIDAY to provide a variety of services in small office. Must type from dictaphone, use word processor, file, answer phone. Some bookkeeping experience desired. Four-day work week and good benefits. Hall's Auto Glass, 701-3241

Older married couple wanted to manage apartment complex. Duties include maintenance and book keeping. Housing provided. 623-7171.

WANT A GOOD JOB????

Ten people needed immediately. Must be self-motivated and have own car. Earn up to $1500/mo.
P.O. Box 2720, Chicago, IL 60601

SUMMER JOBS

Male college students wanted as life guards. Must have Red Cross certification. Apply in person from 2-5 pm daily, Palmdale Parks and Recreation Department, 2700 Rosemont Rd.

encourage qualified individuals of all races and both sexes to apply. Three of the ads in the lower section of Figure 6.4 do not meet EEOC requirements because they specify a preference for younger people, males, or females when neither age nor sex is a bona fide occupational qualification. The other two ads in the lower portion suffer from excessive abbreviation and insufficient information about the company, nature of work, and skills required.

The greatest concentration of ads usually appears in Sunday newspapers in larger cities. For a firm seeking a person whose skills are relatively common in the general population (such as a clerk, nurse, typist, laborer, or salesperson), the newspaper is a good place to advertise. If, however, a company is seeking a person with a specialized skill or knowledge (such as a nuclear physicist), it should choose advertising sources that specifically target the population of qualified persons, such as publications and conventions of professional organizations.[31] For example, universities looking for new faculty for the management department could advertise in the semiannual Academy of Management Placement Roster and conduct screening interviews at the Academy's annual professional meeting.

Employment Agencies Another formal method of recruiting is to use an employment agency. An agency finds and prescreens applicants, referring those who seem qualified to the organization for further assessment and final selection. An agency can screen effectively only if it has a clear understanding of the position it is trying to fill. Thus, it is very important that an employer be as specific and accurate as possible when describing a position and its requirements to an employment agency.

Employment agencies are covered by Title VII of the Civil Rights Act and thus are forbidden to discriminate in screening and referring candidates on the basis of race, color, sex, religion, and national origin. Sometimes, however, agencies have been known to discriminate at the request of firms. For instance, in a survey of recruiters for executive search firms, 14 percent reported having been asked not to refer Jewish candidates for certain positions.[32]

Alternatively, an employment agency may discriminate without the client organization's knowledge if the agency's recruiters mistakenly believe that a certain race or sex of candidate is more likely to be welcomed or if the agency uses an invalid selection device with adverse impact in screening. In this case, both the agency and the client organization could face discrimination charges.[33]

Agencies that provide employment services can be publicly funded or for-profit agencies. On occasion, unions provide employment services as well.

Public Job Service Agencies Every state has a publicly funded **job service agency** that is affiliated with the U.S. Employment Service (USES). These public agencies have a number of offices throughout each state. In addition to administering unemployment compensation, public job service agencies attempt to find jobs for those seeking work. In most cases, able-bodied persons who are collecting unemployment compensation must register with the job service agency; however, anyone who is seeking work may register as well.

State job service agencies interview job seekers to find out about their skills, experience, and preferences. Employers call in their vacant jobs and describe the job specifications. The agency then matches applicants, by hand or by computer, and refers qualified persons to the employer for interviews. State job service agencies may also test applicants when requested to do so by employers.

Public job service agencies primarily fill blue-collar and clerical positions (see Table 6.3). Sometimes however, the agencies are able to fill higher-level openings. If an opening cannot be filled locally, an employer may request that the position be placed in the USES job bank, so that state job service agencies all over the country hear of the opening. State and USES employment agencies offer all services with no direct charge to either the job seeker or the employer.

Job Training Partnership Act Programs A federally funded employment program was established by the **Job Training Partnership Act (JTPA).** This act, which was passed in 1983, replaced the Comprehensive Employment and Training Act (CETA). The purpose of JTPA is to find permanent private sector jobs for displaced and hard-to-employ individuals. The focus is on training or retraining—either on or off the job—that will enhance long-term employability. CETA, in contrast, often provided job training for which there was no real demand in the local area or placed individuals in federally funded "make-work" jobs.[34]

The JTPA is administered through local Private Industry Councils (PICs) of volunteer businesspeople and community leaders. Each PIC decides what type of program will be most useful in its particular labor market. Sometimes PICs fund classroom training in skills that are in demand locally. The heart of the JTPA, however, is the employer reimbursement plan. An employer that hires an eligible individual signs a contract with the PIC stating that the firm will train the person in a designated skill and then retain that person on a permanent basis if his or her performance is acceptable. In return, the PIC reimburses the employer for one-half of the employee's pay during the training period. Reimbursable periods vary according to the complexity of the skill being taught but average about sixty days. At the end of the contract, the employee has both a skill and a job, and the employer has been compensated for taking the time and risk to train the individual.

An example of a successful JTPA project is one sponsored by the San Gabriel, California, PIC. California State University at Los Angeles and the international engineering firm Santa Fe Braun established a joint program to retrain displaced engineers and drafters and place them in computer-aided drafting jobs.[35] On the other hand, there are reports of employers, consultants, and training companies billing the government for ineffective or nonexistent training, or for on-the-job training that would have been provided in any case. One organization received a subsidy for training an oil-burner technician who was already qualified and experienced; another received a subsidy for up to six months for each employee trained to work in a car wash![36]

Private, For-Profit Agencies Organizations use private, for-profit employment agencies to produce a set of prescreened candidates; job seekers use them to locate a suitable position. For each successful placement, agencies charge a fee that can range from 10 to 30 percent of the employee's first year pay. The fee may be paid by either the applicant or the employer. Employment agencies usually consider job seekers rather than organizations to be their clients. Accordingly, their primary goal is to find positions for job seekers rather than to find just the right applicants for companies. Employment agencies typically handle jobs paying under $30,000 or $40,000 per year.

Unions Unions sometimes provide employment services for their members. For construction workers and longshoremen, labor contracts may specify that employers first seek candidates at the union hiring hall before recruiting elsewhere. The union hall refers union members seeking jobs to companies for evaluation and selection.

Executive Search Firms **Executive search firms** recruit managerial talent for positions paying $50,000 to $150,000 or more per year. They view the organization rather than the candidate as their client. In fact, most executive search firms are not interested in receiving unsolicited applications or résumés. Instead, they conduct a separate nationwide, or even international, search for each position that they contract to fill.

Most of the Fortune 1000 companies make some use of executive search firms, or "head-hunters." These firms charge substantial fees, usually equal to one-third of the estimated first-year cash compensation (salary and bonus) for the position, plus search expenses. Many head-hunters charge this fee whether or not the search results in a candidate being hired. They see themselves as a group of professionals who are paid to use their skills to make the search rather than to guarantee its outcome. Other search firms, usually operating at the low end of the managerial salary range, work on a contingency-fee basis and receive the full fee only if there is a successful placement. In either case, the employer pays the fees, not the candidate.

One survey showed that about 40 percent of all executive searches were successfully complete within the time specified by the contract. An additional 15 to 20 percent were eventually completed, and 40 percent failed.[37] Among the many reasons why a search might fail to produce an acceptable candidate are the following:

- Unclear or unrealistically high job specifications
- Poor company or industry reputation
- Internal politics in the hiring organization
- Insufficient research staff at the search firm
- Use of an overly specialized search firm[38]

Most of these reasons need no further explanation, but it might be helpful to understand a little more about overly specialized search firms. Typically, a firm that is hired to conduct a search agrees not to raid the client organization for a period of two years. Thus, the agency is barred from calling on that organization's employees as prospects in subsequent searches for other organizations. Executive search firms that have been very successful in writing a lot of contracts or that are highly specialized in a discipline (e.g., data processing management) or in an industry (e.g., the petroleum industry) may eventually find themselves forbidden to recruit from the most likely sources of candidates, compromising their ability to conduct effective searches. The largest executive search firm in the United States, Korn/Ferry International, was barred from approaching the employees of 2,150 corporations in 1989 because of searches the firm had done for these corporations in the preceding two years.[39]

Given the high cost and relatively low success rate, why do so many companies use executive search firms? There are several reasons. First, search firms are better at finding candidates who are already employed and who may not be actively considering a job change. Second, using search firms tends to be faster for a company than if it were to do its own recruiting. The search firm may already have extensive files of possible candidates and is experienced in locating additional names. Search firms claim they can fill a position in about half the time that a company would need to do its own recruiting. Third, the search firm can keep the hiring company's name a secret until the final referral stage if the company does not want others to know that staffing changes are contemplated in important positions. A final reason is that directly seducing a competitor's employees is considered bad form, but hiring a third party to do it is more acceptable.

The search process consists of several steps. Most search firms begin by drawing on the files accumulated in previous searches. Some firms claim to have extensive data bases. Executive recruiters also search published sources, such as business periodicals and alumni directories of prestigious schools.[40] In addition, they phone organizations, trying to acquire information about managers who may fit the profile they are looking for. They may attempt to extract names, titles, and responsibilities of executives from secretaries, sometimes by misrepresenting themselves as writers for a business publication or as compilers of an industry directory.[41] Finally, recruiters phone prospects and try to interest them in the job. Recruiters proceed to interview the better prospects and check references before referring the top candidates to the hiring company for final selection. Occasionally, the search firm may continue its involvement in the process by serving as a mediator while the chosen candidate and the employer negotiate the details of the employment contract.[42]

Campus Recruiting Campus recruiting is widely used by large and medium-sized firms that need highly educated entry-level employees. Campus recruiting can be very productive for an organization, as many good candidates can be interviewed in a short period of time and at a single location. Furthermore, it is convenient because the college recruitment center provides both space and administrative support.[43] Campus recruiting is moderate in cost. It is more expensive than word-of-mouth recruiting, gate hiring, or limited advertising, but it is less expensive than using employment agencies (when the company pays the fee).

One disadvantage of college recruiting is that candidates are available to start work only at certain times of the year. Other disadvantages include the lack of experience and the inflated expectations often held by new graduates, the high cost of hiring graduates for positions that may not really require a college degree, and the difficulty of evaluating candidates who do not possess much relevant work history.

In planning a firm's college recruiting program, the recruiter must first decide how many schools to visit. Experts advise that more intensive recruiting at a smaller number of appropriately selected schools tends to be more effective than brief visits to a larger number of schools. Recruiters usually choose universities on the basis of the company's past experience with their graduates, the degrees offered, the reputation of the school, the demography of the student body (sex, age, and minority composition), the geographic location, and the quality of the college placement office.[44]

After targeting a subset of schools, the recruiter makes an effort to build up the company's reputation with students and disseminates detailed information on the types of careers available before making the interview visit. By visiting the same schools year after year, the firm can develop visibility and maintain an ongoing relationship with placement center officials. Making company literature widely available on campus, awarding scholarships and prizes, employing students in internship and work study programs, and sending executives into the classroom as guest speakers are all ways to increase a company's visibility on campus. Some organizations are dropping the term "campus recruiting," which implies a one-dimensional activity conducted a few weeks a year, in favor of the concept of a "university relations program." The latter brings home the importance of maintaining year-round visibility on selected campuses using a variety of methods.[45]

Although campus interviewers may be full-time HR professionals, they often are people who work in some other capacity during most of the year. For instance, engineering managers may be pressed into service to conduct campus interviews with engineering students for a few weeks each year. Candidates usually value the opportunity to be interviewed by someone in their own specialty, but this practice can backfire if the interviewer is not well trained for the role.[46] Before embarking on recruiting tours, managers should receive in-depth training on how to conduct interviews and should be made aware of EEO issues.

Campus interviews are usually followed by site-visit or plant-trip invitations to the best candidates. The firm should plan these visits carefully to make a good impression. For instance, the firm should pay all travel expenses in advance. The trip itself should be well organized, with interviews, meals, and tours carefully scheduled so that candidates are not left at loose ends. Candidates particularly enjoy having a sponsor to shepherd them through the entire trip. They also like talking to employees in positions similar to the one for which they are being considered.

Affirmative Action Recruiting Organizations with government contracts of over $100,000 must have a written affirmative action plan (AAP). This document includes goals for increasing the number of women and minorities in job classes in which they are currently underutilized by the organization. Thus, many organizations are attempting to increase their hiring of women for upper-level or nontraditional jobs and their hiring of minorities for a wide range of jobs.

In order to hire minorities, firms must first find and attract applicants. Advertising is one way to do this. Firms should design ads carefully so that they do not convey stereotypes or preferences for male or nonminority applicants; the ads should also carry a line about the employer's commitment to equal employment opportunity. When seeking candidates for jobs not usually performed by one sex, companies should run ads that are sexually neutral or, from time to time, ads that are specially worded for affirmative action.

Figure 6.5 shows three ads for the job of a telephone operator: a sexually biased ad, a neutral ad, and an affirmative action ad. Research using these ads has shown that a sexually biased ad deters opposite-sex readers from applying for jobs, whereas neutral and affirmative action ads generate significantly more interest among the underutilized sex.[47] The Maryland State Police Department found that using a picture of a black officer on a recruiting billboard produced more minority applicants in two months than all other methods combined had produced during the preceding two years.[48]

In addition to advertising content, location is very important. Firms should place ads in minority and foreign language newspapers, as well as in major dailies in cities with large minority populations. Firms should also consider advertising in military publications because the armed forces are disproportionately nonwhite and individuals finishing a tour of duty often make excellent employees. Other effective locations for ads are on minority or foreign language radio stations, as well as in newsletters of professional organizations (e.g., the Association of Black Psychologists or the Society of Women Engineers) that reach a desired audience.

Other affirmative action recruiting methods include recruiting on predominantly black or female campuses, using the public job service office, and using private employment agencies that specialize in minority placement. Participation in summer job programs for disadvantaged youth may help identify candidates for later permanent hiring, as well as improve the company's reputation in the minority community. Recruiting teams should include minority group members, and interviewers should be trained to talk to all kinds of people, to focus on job-relevant abilities, and to differentiate between distracting mannerisms and actual ability to do the job.

THE APPLICANT'S POINT OF VIEW

This section discusses the methods candidates use to search for jobs, the ways applicants evaluate job offers and make decisions about accepting jobs, and a technique that helps applicants make better decisions and produces more suitable employees for organizations.

FIGURE 6.5 Three Ads for a Telephone Operator

Sexually Biased

WHO SAYS IT'S A MAN'S WORLD?
Behind every man's telephone call, there is a woman. She's a smart woman. She's efficient. She has to be. She places the complex long-distance calls people cannot place themselves or helps them locate telephone numbers. Hers is a demanding job. But we make it worth her while. We can make it worth your while, too. Not only do we pay a good salary to start but we also offer group life insurance, group medical coverage, good vacations with pay, and free pensions. A stepping stone to management positions.

Neutral

We need calm, cool-headed men and women with clear, friendly voices to do that important job of helping our customers. They must be capable of handling emergency calls quickly and competently. They also place the complex long-distance calls people cannot place themselves or help them locate hard-to-find telephone numbers. Theirs is a demanding job. But we make it worth their while. We can make it worth your while, too. Not only do we pay a good salary to start but we also offer group life insurance, group medical coverage, good vacations with pay, and free pensions. A stepping stone to management positions.

Affirmative Action

Rick Wehmhoefer of Denver, Colorado, is one of several hundred male telephone operators in the Bell system. Currently, Rick is a directory assistance operator. "So far, my job has been pleasant and worthwhile," he says. "I enjoy assisting people." We have men like Rick in a lot of different telephone jobs. Both men and women work as Bell System mechanics, truck drivers, installers, and engineers. We want the men and women of the telephone company to do what they want to do and do best. Today, when openings exist, local Bell Companies are offering applicants and present employees some jobs they may never have thought about before. We want to help all advance to the best of their abilities.

Source: By Sandra & Daryl Bem from *Contemporary Problems in Personnel*, Hamner & Schmidt, eds. Copyright © 1977 by St. Clair Press. Reprinted with permission from John Wiley & Sons.

TABLE 6.5 Search Methods Used by Job Seekers and Job Finders

Search Method	*Job Finders Who Used Method (%)*	*Job Seekers Who Used Method (%)*
Contact employers directly	66%	72%
Friends and relatives	60%	14%
State employment service	34%	28%
Private employment agencies	21%	9%
Want ads	46%	26%
Union	6%	0%

Source: From Bradley R. Schiller, "Job Search Media: Utilization and Effectiveness," *The Quarterly Review of Economics and Business,* Winter 1975, p. 57. Reprinted by permission.

Job Search

Research on the methods job seekers use to find work indicates that the majority of jobs are obtained through informal sources. One survey determined that 60 to 90 percent of blue-collar employees found their jobs informally, as did 60 to 84 percent of managers, professionals, and technicians. Contacting employers directly (in person, by phone, or by letter) and seeking help from friends and relatives seem to be the most effective methods of job search for many types of candidates.[49]

Table 6.5 shows the results of a Census Bureau survey of job seekers who either found jobs or were still seeking jobs during the year preceding the survey. Clearly, most respondents used more than one method to search for a job. Furthermore, job finders used more methods than unsuccessful job seekers. Other research confirms that using multiple search methods, using them frequently, beginning to search for work as early as possible, making many contacts, and not interrupting one's search for a vacation or other reason all help to reduce the duration of unemployment.[50] Being financially insecure and/or having a family to support are also correlated with speed of job finding, probably because individuals in such situations are more likely to take the first offer they receive.[51] Drawing unemployment compensation has the unfortunate and unintended effect of lengthening the period of unemployment by removing the incentive to search intensively and allowing job seekers the luxury of refusing lower-paying jobs.[52]

Job Choice

How do people decide which of several job offers to accept? There has been a fair amount of theorizing on this topic over the years. Early work in this field assumed that job offers were simultaneous and so candidates simply picked the best job. In real life, however, candidates seldom have more than one or two offers at the same time. Thus, their decision process is more complicated; it is sequential rather than simultaneous. As a result, it seems likely that job seekers **satisfice,** or take the first offer that is at least minimally acceptable on all important dimensions, rather than **optimize,** or make a very long and costly search to find the best possible job.[53]

Which factors do job seekers look at when evaluating a job offer? The research literature offers three views:

1. Individuals make rational choices based on *objective factors* such as pay, location, and opportunity for advancement.

2. People form gut-level preferences for one job over another based on *subjective factors* that they may not even be aware of.

3. Job seekers do not have enough information to differentiate on the basis of either objective or subjective factors about the company or job; consequently, they tend to be unduly influenced by certain *recruiting factors,* such as the interviewer's skill or politeness.[54]

Objective Factors Approach According to the **objective factors approach,** candidates evaluate job offers on their merits. Thus, it is necessary to find out which aspects of jobs are desirable to candidates. Table 6.6 shows how men and women

TABLE 6.6 Median Ranks of Importance of Ten Job Factors to Men and to Women and to Others

Factor	*Men*	*Ascribed to Other Men*	*Women*	*Ascribed to Other Women*
Advancement	3.3	3.8	5.3	4.3
Benefits	6.8	5.2	8.0	5.9
Company Reputation	4.5	6.8	4.6	7.1
Co-workers	6.0	7.7	5.2	7.3
Hours	7.6	5.4	6.9	5.0
Pay	5.6	2.1	6.0	2.1
Security	2.5	3.6	4.9	5.4
Supervisor	6.3	7.4	5.3	7.0
Type of Work	3.3	4.9	1.5	3.5
Working Conditions	7.9	6.9	6.5	6.8

Note: Self rating data were collected from 39,788 men and 16,833 women between 1945 and 1975. Preferences ascribed to others were collected from the same respondents between 1949 and 1975.

Source: Data from Clifford E. Jurgenson, "Job Preferences (What Makes a Job Good or Bad?)," *Journal of Applied Psychology*, June 1978, pp. 267–276. Reprinted by permission of the author.

in one large study ranked the importance of ten job factors. These same respondents also ranked the factors according to how they thought others felt about them. Note that both men and women claimed that pay is the most important attribute to others but is only fifth or seventh in importance to themselves. Researchers agree that pay is probably quite important to most people but that it is socially undesirable to admit this publicly. Further analyses of this survey indicate that young people and single men are less attracted to benefits and that more educated respondents are quite interested in the type of work and less concerned with job security.[55]

Table 6.7 shows how college seniors ranked the importance of compensation/benefits features of jobs. Every benefit listed has the same cost to the organization, but college seniors did not find them all equally attractive. Guaranteed cost-of-living increases and company-paid insurance were the students' top choices, whereas 30-minute-shorter workdays and early retirement were least preferred. Campus recruiters were also polled concerning their beliefs about college students' preferences. In several important areas, the recruiters did not perceive

TABLE 6.7 College Seniors' Ranking of Compensation/Benefits Features of Jobs

Students' Ranking	*Recruiters' Ranking**	*Salary or Benefits Feature*
1	1	Annual cost-of-living increase of $1,080
2	5	Medical and life insurance premiums worth $90/month paid by company
3†	6	Yearly option to buy 216 shares of company stock at 80% of market value
4†	2	Three more weeks of paid vacation each year
5	10	50% increase in yearly pension payments after retirement
6	7	Paid 15-week leave of absence every five years
7	3	15 Fridays off with pay every year
8	4	Four-day workweek (9.5 hours per day) at same salary
9	8	Flextime (arrive between 6 a.m. and 9 a.m., leave between 3 p.m. and 6 p.m.)
10	11	Retire at age 62.5 with same benefits as for age 65
11	9	Workday reduced from 8 hours to 7.5 hours for the same salary

*This ranking represents the order of preferences that recruiters ascribed to college seniors.

†Students gave these items an equal ranking.

Source: Data from Kermit R. Davis, Jr., William F. Giles, and Hubert S. Feild, Jr., "Compensation and Fringe Benefits: How Recruiters View New College Graduates' Preferences." Reprinted with the permission from *HRMagazine*, published by the Society for Human Resource Management, Alexandria, VA.

these preferences accurately. The students were much more interested than recruiters had expected in insurance, stock options, and increased pensions but less interested in flextime, shorter workdays, four-day weeks, and some Fridays off.

The recruiting implications of the objective job factors approach are straightforward. Organizations and recruiters need to find out which job factors are important to most candidates and then attempt to make these factors available. The most important and influential factors should receive the most emphasis in recruiting literature and in other communications with candidates. In other words, recruiters need to apply market research techniques to the task of selling the organization's merits to job candidates.[56]

Subjective Factors Approach Those favoring the **subjective factors approach** say that applicants evaluate the "perceived ability of a firm to provide satisfaction for [their] deep-seated and often unrecognized emotional needs."[57] There is some support for the idea that individuals are attracted to organizations whose images or climates match their personality.[58] For instance, security-minded individuals might gravitate toward paternalistic organizations. From a recruiting standpoint, this approach suggests that applicants must have enough contact with the organization to assess whether or not the subjective aspects of the organization fit their own needs. Recruiting literature might also discuss the organization's culture and prevailing values to help applicants assess the fit with their own preferences.

Recruiting Factors Approach Those who take the **recruiting factors approach** hold that candidates do not usually acquire enough knowledge of either organizations or jobs to make a rational decision between job offers. This lack of discriminating information causes job seekers, particularly inexperienced ones, to be unduly influenced by recruiting factors such as the interest and concern the recruiter shows or the smoothness with which the recruiter handles paperwork.

A great deal of research verifies that recruiting factors do have some impact on job-choice decisions. For instance, students are more impressed when the recruiter has the title *Director of Recruiting* than when the same person uses no title. Students are unfavorably impressed by interviewers who are lacking in verbal fluency (who pause, repeat themselves, or stumble when asking questions).[59] Another study found that interviewers who are pleasant, conduct interviews in an organized fashion, are knowledgeable about the job, and have read the applicant's résumé before the interview make a better impression and increase the probability of job-offer acceptance.[60] Interviewers who present a balanced (positive and negative) picture of the job are perceived as being more credible and trustworthy than those who present only positive information.[61] Long time lags between selection steps (for instance, a wait of two months after a screening interview before the applicant is invited on a plant trip), poorly organized site visits, and stress interviews tend to sour applicants on a company. Finally, a recruiter who stays in touch with a candidate after an offer is extended helps increase job-offer acceptances and increases the rate at which candidates who have accepted actually show up to begin work.[62]

FIGURE 6.6 Factors Affecting Job Choice

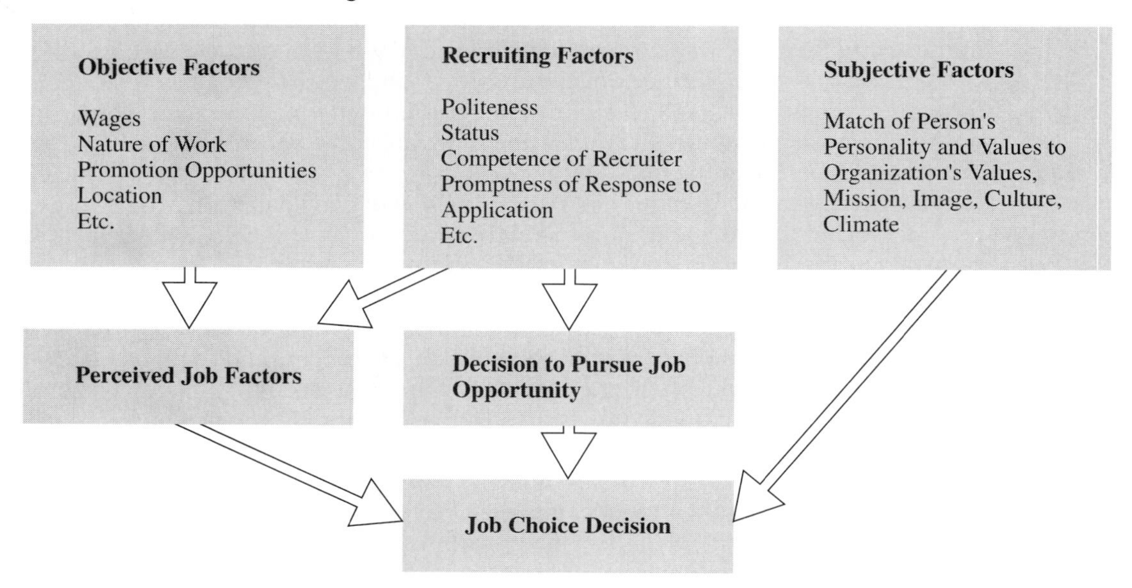

The recruiting factors approach to job choice clearly points to the importance of a highly professional recruiting function. Interviewers need to be trained or selected for both style and substance. More specifically, it has been suggested that effective recruiters "must possess an image and appearance that reflects favorably on the organization; an outgoing nature; flexibility, willingness to take necessary risks, ability to think on one's feet, skill in setting priorities; self-motivation, and salesmanship," as well as communication, interpersonal abilities, and familiarity with the organization.[63] In addition to these personal traits and skills, which aid in making a good impression, recruiters must be sure that contacts with candidates are timely and informative and that site visits are well choreographed.

Recent research has begun to integrate these three views of the applicant decision process, as shown in Figure 6.6. It appears that recruiting factors have their greatest impact on applicant reactions early in the recruiting process, at the initial enquiry and first interview stage. Good treatment here means that candidates are more likely to decide to pursue their application with the organization. Also, a competent recruiter can influence candidate perceptions of the objective factors in the job by providing greater amounts of relevant information. Objective factors are not always accurately perceived by applicants, but these factors and the candidate's perceptions of them become much more important as candidates learn more and move closer to their final decision about which job to accept.[64] Although recruiting factors may not always directly affect final job choice decisions, a professional approach to recruiting is necessary to attract and sustain the interest of desirable job candidates.

Realistic Job Preview

Once a new employee has been recruited and selected, he or she must adjust to the new job and organization. There may be problems at this step, as evidenced by the high rate of turnover among new hires in their first few months. One reason for the turnover may be that the job did not match the newcomer's expectations or desires.[65] The recruitment process may be partly responsible for this mismatch, as recruiters tend to present jobs in very favorable terms in order to increase candidates' offer acceptance rate.

One way to prevent these problems is to use a **Realistic Job Preview (RJP),** a down-to-earth presentation of both the favorable and unfavorable aspects of the job. Ideally, each stage of recruiting is honest and realistic. An RJP may take the form of a booklet or film about the job, realistic information delivered by an interviewer, or a work sample test that exposes the candidate to actual job conditions and activities. Table 6.8 contrasts the contents of an RJP recruiting film with the contents of an unrealistically positive film that was shown to telephone-operator applicants.

Many studies have compared the attitudes and behaviors of realistically recruited employees with those of unrealistically recruited persons. Overall, these studies show that RJPs reduce turnover, lower recruits' expectations about the job, slightly reduce the job-offer acceptance rate, and slightly increase job satisfaction and commitment to the organization among new hires.[66] Several reasons for these effects have been suggested and have received varying degrees of support by researchers.[67]

1. Self-selection. If the RJP helps the applicant realize that the job will not be personally satisfying, the applicant may choose not to take the job, or select

TABLE 6.8 A Comparison of a Realistic Job Preview Film and a Traditional Recruiting Film

Material in Both Films	*Material in Traditional Film*	*Material in RJP Film*
Customers can be quite unfriendly at times; work is fast-paced; helping customers can be satisfying; dealing with others is a large part of the job. Action shots of operators handling an emergency call, a "wise guy" call, a credit-card call, an overseas call, a "nasty" customer, and a directory-assistance request	Everyone seems happy at work; the work is exciting, important, and challenging.	The job is routine, lacks variety, and may become boring. Supervision is close so that there is little freedom and limited opportunity to make friends with coworkers. Employees are criticized for poor performance but seldom praised for good performance. The job is challenging at first, but once it is learned, it is easy.

Source: Reprinted, by permission of the publisher, from "Tell It Like It Is at Realistic Job Previews" by John P. Wanous, *Personnel*, July–August 1975, pp. 50–60, © 1975 American Management Association, New York. All rights reserved.

himself or herself out of the organization's selection process. Without this realistic information, the applicant might have accepted the offer and could have become an early turnover statistic.

2. *Commitment to the decision.* When the RJP is presented before the candidate accepts or rejects the job offer, the candidate feels that she or he has made an informed decision about the job. Having accepted a job known to include difficult moments or distasteful duties, a newcomer feels less justified in reversing the decision and quitting when an unpleasant event actually occurs.

3. *Lowered expectations.* The aim of an RJP is to lower, or make more realistic, the expectations that the newcomer holds about the job. One theory of job satisfaction states that dissatisfaction is a function of the discrepancy between what one expects and desires on a job and what one actually gets. Lowering expectations reduces the gap between expectations and reality; consequently, dissatisfaction decreases. Since dissatisfaction is one cause of turnover, this mechanism can explain both attitudinal and behavioral differences between RJP and no-RJP groups.

4. *Coping.* Research has shown that unpleasant events are less stressful and more effectively dealt with if they are expected rather than if they are surprises. It is possible that the RJP operates by improving the ability of new hires to cope with negative aspects of the job. The RJP may stimulate newcomers to mentally rehearse their reactions to anticipated job problems and so increase their ability to deal with problems when they occur.

RJPs are most useful when recruiters present them early in the recruiting process (so that the self-selection and commitment processes can occur). RJPs are particularly effective for jobs in which there tends to be early high turnover and for entry-level jobs in which applicants are unlikely to have an accurate picture of the job or occupational field prior to applying.[68] RJPs make the most sense when there are plenty of applicants for the available openings; if some decide to decline offers, the jobs can still be filled. Finally, RJPs are most effective in reducing turnover when unemployment is low. In this situation, applicants will be most likely to turn down a job offer that does not suit them because other jobs are readily available.[69]

EVALUATION OF RECRUITMENT

A firm should evaluate its recruitment process along with all of its other personnel activities. Collecting appropriate evaluation measures on past recruiting efforts can help an organization to predict the time and budget needed to fill future openings, identify the recruiting methods that yield the greatest number or the best quality of candidates, and evaluate the job performance of individual recruiters.

Measures Used to Evaluate Recruiters

In appraising the performance of individual recruiters, the HR manager must keep in mind the difficulty of the search assignments, as well as the number of positions the recruiter filled. A recruiter will be able to locate ten qualified laborers more quickly than ten engineers, and ten engineers more quickly than ten executives.[70] After allowing for differences in assignment difficulty, the appraiser might count the number of applications the recruiter processed, the hires the applications produced, and the eventual job successes of those the recruiter recommended for hire. Finally, the appraiser might survey applicants who both accepted and rejected offers to see if their treatment by various recruiters could have been improved.[71]

Measures Used to Evaluate Recruiting Sources

When a variety of sources or methods of recruiting have been used, it makes sense for the HR manager to evaluate each to see if some are consistently superior to others. Inefficient sources can be dropped from future recruiting efforts. Some of the criteria that are used to evaluate sources and methods are total cost, cost per hire, number of applicants generated, yield ratios, and eventual job tenure and performance of hires. Table 6.9 shows some hypothetical evaluation results. As a rule, gate hires and employee referrals tend to be quick and low in cost. Advertising and campus recruiting take the longest and cost more. Recruiting through agencies is intermediate in terms of the time it takes to fill positions, but it is often the most costly method (with the exception of public job service agencies, for which there is no fee).[72]

Differences in the Quality of Recruiting Sources

Research on the quality of different recruiting sources offers some interesting viewpoints. Stephen Mangum asserts that the best jobs are filled internally or through informal recruiting methods, such as word of mouth, and that the best candidates also find new jobs informally, through a network of contacts who are aware of their abilities. He suggests that only the least desirable jobs and least employable people are left to be matched through formal methods, such as newspaper ads and employment agencies.[73] Although this argument may be overstated, there is a body of research to support the idea that informal sources do produce the best candidates. A series of studies of employee tenure indicate that candidates who are referred by a current employee, who are rehired, or who turn in an unsolicited application stay on their new jobs significantly longer than those hired through agencies or newspaper ads.[74] The research on the job performance of hires from different sources is less extensive and less conclusive than that on turnover, but some evidence for similar differences does exist.[75]

Two rationales for differences in the applicant quality of recruiting sources have been advanced. One, based on RJP research, suggests that informal sources,

TABLE 6.9 Example of Recruiting Source Evaluation Data

	Source Characteristics						
Recruiting Source	*Cost per Hire*	*Contacts per Hire*	*Offers per Hire*	*Days from First Contact to First Day on Job*	*Mean Years Since College Graduation*	*Turnover in First Year*	*Mean First-Year Performance (5-point scale)*
Unsolicited applications	$ 200	6	1.5	30	8.2	10%	3.4
Employee referrals	$ 300	3	1.2	35	7.1	6%	3.8
Campus recruiting	$2,500	6	3	100	0.2	20%	3.2
Employment agencies	$6,000	5	2	40	5.9	12%	2.8
Advertising	$ 500	12	2	50	8.6	30%	2.6

such as rehires and employee referrals, yield candidates who have been told about both the good and bad aspects of the job and thus have a lower turnover rate. The second explanation is that sources may simply tap into different kinds of people in terms of ability level, motivation, or experience. Anyone can read a newspaper, but perhaps it takes a candidate with a bit more initiative to research a company enough to make an unsolicited application or to find out about an opening from contacts. In addition, more experienced employees may be more likely to have and use a network of informal sources, whereas new labor force entrants may tend to use newspapers and agencies to find positions; we know that younger people also have higher turnover rates.[76] There is some support in the research literature for all of these propositions.[77]

Ideally, each firm should conduct its own analysis of source quality for each type of job. Recruiting sources that are of low quality can be utilized less intensively or eliminated altogether in future recruiting. In one study of recruiting sources for bank tellers, the researcher estimated that by discontinuing use of the three worst sources the bank could save $180,000 (in 1970 dollars) over four years in reduced turnover, recruiting, and training costs.[78]

SUMMARY OF KEY POINTS

Perhaps the first decision a company must make in recruiting an employee to fill a vacancy is whether the position will be filled by a current employee through internal recruiting or by a new hire from the external labor market. Internal and external recruiting have their own advantages and disadvantages. A firm that chooses internal recruiting has several methods available, including the job posting and bidding (self-nomination) process, nomination by superiors, and searches of the human resource information system.

If a firm chooses external recruiting, it must plan carefully and may consider a wide variety of methods. Informal methods, such as gate hires and employee referrals, are inexpensive and often produce very good candidates. Formal methods include recruitment advertising, using employment agencies, and campus recruiting. Advertising makes vacancies known to a large number of potential applicants. Properly written ads can produce qualified applicants, help a firm meet its affirmative action goals, and enhance a company's public image. Employment agencies and executive search firms may be used to locate and prescreen applicants. Using private agencies and search firms is costly but may bring a company results significantly faster than if the company did its own recruiting. Campus recruiting is used by many organizations to hire entry-level professional and technical employees. A carefully planned university relations program can make campus recruiting very effective.

From the job seeker's point of view, organizations and jobs may be evaluated on the basis of objective factors, subjective factors, or recruiting factors. Ideally, job seekers should be given realistic job previews that help them to select jobs that they will like and to reduce turnover and dissatisfaction due to unmet expectations.

After a company completes a recruiting effort, it should evaluate both its recruiters and the methods they used. In this way, the firm can exclude from future recruiting efforts costly methods or those that produced few or low-quality applicants.

Questions for Discussion

1. Explain how the organization's and candidate's goals in the recruiting process may conflict. How might these conflicts affect the eventual success of the recruiting and job search process?
2. What are the pros and cons of using some form of temporary or leased employees rather than hiring permanent employees?
3. Suppose that a regional sales manager who needs to hire four salespeople delegates recruiting and initial screening to the regional HR office. What types of information must be exchanged between the sales manager and the recruiter in order to maximize the likelihood of a successful recruiting effort?
4. How are yield ratios used in recruitment planning?
5. How does internal recruiting for a nonexempt position typically differ from internal recruiting for an exempt position?
6. Think of a job that seems hard to fill in your local labor market. Utilizing a wide variety of methods, design a recruitment campaign to attract candidates to this job.
7. Describe the services provided by various types of employment agencies and search firms. Why might a company use these organizations rather than doing its own recruiting?
8. Suppose that an organization plans to recruit on your campus on a regular basis. What sorts of activities might it pursue to maximize recruiting success?
9. Suppose that you have a friend who is unemployed. What advice can you give your friend about how to search for a job effectively?
10. Describe three views of how candidates evaluate organizations when choosing among job offers. What are the recruiting implications of each view?
11. What is a realistic job preview? Describe the effects it has and the four possible explanations for these effects.
12. How and why should recruiting methods and sources be evaluated?

EXERCISE 6.1

Creating Effective Recruitment Ads

1. Bring the help-wanted section of a newspaper to class.
2. Read through and circle ads that strike you as being especially effective and well-designed.
3. Put a box around ads that strike you as unusually poor or ineffective.
4. In small groups, compare your findings and attempt to derive a set of guidelines for creating an effective ad.
5. Pick one or two of the poorer ads and rewrite them following these guidelines. You may make up additional information to the extent that it is needed to complete the ad.

EXERCISE 6.2

Developing Recruiting Plans

Design a recruiting campaign for each of the six situations described below. Include an explicit definition of the labor market you intend to reach; then select the method(s) you will use to reach this target audience. How will you attract *qualified* candidates to apply? Justify why your recruiting plan is appropriate and cost-effective for the particular job you are trying to fill. Explain why your six recruiting plans differ from each other.

1. A small (twenty-five employees), family-owned, air conditioning business in Houston needs to hire two refrigeration mechanics to service domestic and commercial air conditioning units.
2. An international computer manufacturer needs to hire 200 graduates in computer science for entry-level positions.
3. A moderate-sized publishing company based in New York needs a new vice president of finance.
4. A prestigious medical school wishes to fill the post of chief of ophthalmic surgery.
5. A large insurance company's regional office needs to hire twenty word processor operators.
6. A seventy-outlet retail clothing store chain needs to fill two middle management positions in its headquarters. The HR director realizes that all the current middle managers are white males.

Notes and References

1. "Survey Report: Hiring Costs Decreased in 1990," *HR Focus,* November 1991, p. 6.
2. "For Your Information," *Personnel Journal,* May 1991, p. 16.
3. Lyman W. Porter, Edward E. Lawler III, and J. Richard Hackman, *Behavior in Organizations* (New York: McGraw-Hill, 1975).
4. J. Scott Lord "Internal and External Recruitment," in *Human Resource Planning, Employment, and Placement,* ed. Wayne F. Cascio (Washington, D.C.: Bureau of National Affairs, 1989) pp. 73–102.
5. Robert Half, *Robert Half on Hiring,* (New York: Crow, 1985).
6. Dave R. Dahl and Patrick R. Pinto, "Job Posting: An Industry Survey," *Personnel Journal,* January 1977, pp. 40–42.
7. Elmer H. Burack and Nicholas J. Mathys, *Human Resource Planning: A Pragmatic Approach to Manpower Staffing and Development* (Lake Forest, Ill.: Brace-Park Press, 1980); and D. Geoffrey John, "Staffing with Temporary Help," *Personnel Administrator,* January 1987, pp. 96–99.
8. Lord "Internal and External Recruitment," pp. 73–102.
9. K. H. Chung, M. Labatkin, R. C. Rogers, and J. E. Owers, "Do Insiders Make Better CEOs than Outsiders?" *Academy of Management Executive,* November 1987, pp. 325–331; A. Gupta, "Contingency Perspectives on Strategic Leadership: Current Knowledge and Future Research Directions." In D. C. Hambrick, ed. *The Executive Effect: Concepts and Methods for Studying Top Managers* (Greenwich, Conn.: JAI Press, 1988).
10. Gladys Fazio Garlitz, "Temporary Workers: A Changing Industry," *Personnel Administrator,* March 1983, pp. 47–48; J. L. Simonetti, N. Nykudym, and L. M. Sell, "Temporary Employees: A Permanent Boom?" *Personnel,* August 1988, pp. 50–56.
11. Garth Mangum, Donald Mayall, and Kristin Nelson, "The Temporary Help Industry: A Response to the Dual Internal Labor Market," *Industrial and Labor Relations Review,* July 1985, pp. 599–611; Max Messmer, "Right-Sizing Reshapes Staffing Strategies," *HRMagazine,* October 1991, pp. 60–62.
12. John Ross, "Effective Ways to Hire Contingent Personnel," *HRMagazine,* February 1991, pp. 52–54.
13. Martin M. Greller and David M. Nee, *From Baby Boom to Baby Bust* (Reading, Mass.: Addison-Wesley, 1989), ch. 4.
14. Donn L. Dennis, "Evaluating Corporate Recruiting Efforts," *Personnel Administrator,* January 1985, pp. 21–26.
15. Roger H. Hawk, *The Recruitment Function* (New York: American Management Association, 1967).
16. Robert L. Armacost and Rohne L. Jauernig, "Planning and Managing a Major Recruiting Project," *Public Personnel Management,* Summer 1991, pp. 115–126.
17. William E. Bright, "How One Company Manages Its Human Resources," *Harvard Business Review,* January–February 1976, pp. 81–93.
18. This section draws on Christine White and Abbie W. Thorner, *Managing the Recruitment Process* (New York: Law and Business, 1982).
19. Dave R. Dahl and Patrick R. Pinto, "Job Posting: An Industry Survey."
20. Garry G. Wallrapp, "Job Posting for Non-Exempt Employees: A Sample Program," *Personnel Journal,* October 1981, pp. 796–798.
21. James T. Gunn, "An Open Job-Bidding System for Professionals and Managers: Fact or Fiction," *Human Resource Planning,* Vol. 2 (1979), pp. 187–195.
22. James K. Wellington, "Management Succession at Arizona Public Service," *Human Resource Planning,* Vol. 4, 1981, pp. 157–167; and Donald F. Parker, John A. Fossum, Jan H. Blakslee, and Anthony J. Rucci, "Human Resources Planning at American Hospital Supply," *Human Resource Planning,* Vol. 6, 1983, pp. 207–217.
23. Harriet Edleson, "Innovative Internships," *HRMagazine,* July 1991, pp. 39–41.
24. Robert E. Hite, "How to Hire Using College Internship Programs," *Personnel Journal,* February 1986, pp. 110–112.
25. Bureau of National Affairs, "Recruiting and Selection Procedures" in Personnel Policies Forum Survey, No. 146 (May) 1988, p. 7.

26. Andrew S. Bargerstock and Gerald Swanson, "Four Ways to Build Cooperative Recruitment Alliances," *HRMagazine,* March 1991, pp. 49–51, 79.
27. Ibid.
28. Van M. Evans, "Recruitment Advertising in the 80's," *Personnel Administrator,* December 1978, pp. 21–25, 30.
29. Margaret Magnus, "Recruitment Ads That Work," *Personnel Journal,* August 1985, pp. 42–63; Nancy A. Mason and John A. Belt, "Effectiveness of Specificity in Recruitment Advertising," *Journal of Management,* Vol. 12, 1986, pp. 429–432; Karel De Witte, "Recruitment Advertising," in *Assessment and Selection in Organizations,* ed. Peter Herriot (Chichester: Wiley, 1989), pp. 205–217.
30. De Witte, "Recruitment Advertising," pp. 205–217.
31. Robert A. Martin, "Employment Advertising—Hard Sell, Soft Sell, or What?" *Personnel,* May–June 1971, pp. 33–40.
32. S. L. Slavin and M. A. Pradt, *The Einstein Syndrome: Corporate Anti-Semitism in America Today* (Lanham, Md.: University Press of America, 1982).
33. Stephen Rubenfeld and Michael Crino, "Are Employment Agencies Jeopardizing Your Selection Process?" *Personnel,* September–October 1981, pp. 70–77.
34. James W. Hunt, *The Law of the Workplace* (Washington, D.C.: BNA Books, 1984).
35. Philip Farish, "Recruitment Sources," in *Human Resource Planning, Employment, and Placement,* ed. Wayne F. Cascio (Washington, D.C.: Bureau of National Affairs, 1989) pp. 103–134.
36. "90 Days to Learn to Scrub? Sure, If Uncle Sam's Paying," *Business Week,* January 20, 1992, pp. 70–71.
37. William Dee, "Evaluating a Search Firm," *Personnel Administrator,* March 1983, pp. 41–43, 99–100.
38. Loretta D. Foxman and Walter L. Polsky, "Career Counselor," *Personnel Journal,* February 1985, pp. 21–22, and March 1985, pp. 14–16; see also John Wareham, "The Search," *Across the Board,* September 1979, pp. 28–31.
39. Dyan Machan, "The Clients are Restless," *Forbes,* July 10, 1989, pp. 114–118.
40. Florence Berger, "Executive Search: The Headhunter as Matchmaker," *The Cornell Hotel and Restaurant Administration Quarterly,* May 1983, pp. 55–61.
41. John C. Perham, "How Recruiters Get the Lowdown," *Dun's Business Month,* May 1985, pp. 60–61.
42. Larry Reibstein, "Offers and Counteroffers: Attitudes Change in Executive Search Game," *The Wall Street Journal,* May 5, 1986, p. 21.
43. This section draws on Stephen D. Bruce, *College Recruiting* (Stamford, Conn.: Bureau of Law and Business, 1983).
44. Maury Hanigan, "Key Campus Strategies," *HRMagazine,* July 1991, pp. 42–44.
45. Lord, "Internal and External Recruitment," p. 73–102.
46. John W. Boudreau and Sara Rynes, "Giving It the Old College Try," *Personnel Administrator,* March 1987, pp. 78–83; Sara L. Rynes and John W. Boudreau, "College Recruiting in Large Organizations: Practice, Evaluation, and Research Implications," *Personnel Psychology,* Vol. 39, 1986, pp. 729–757.
47. Sandra L. Bem and Daryl J. Bem, "Does Sex-Biased Job Advertising Aid and Abet Sex Discrimination?" in *Contemporary Problems in Personnel,* ed. W. Clay Hamner and Frank L. Schmidt (Chicago: St. Clair Press, 1977), pp. 445–455.
48. The remainder of this section is based on Robert Calvert, Jr., *Affirmative Action: A Comprehensive Recruitment Manual* (Garrett Park, Md.: Garrett Park Press, 1979).
49. Michael C. Keeley and Philip K. Robins, "Government Programs, Job Search Requirements, and the Duration of Unemployment," *Journal of Labor Economics,* July 1985, pp. 337–362; Bradley R. Schiller, "Job Search Media: Utilization and Effectiveness," *The Quarterly Review of Economics and Business,* Winter 1975, pp. 55–63; and Samuel J. Yeager and Thomas Vocino, "Sources of Information used by Professionals in Government to Find Jobs: Effectiveness and Impact," *Review of Public Personnel Administration,* Fall 1983, pp. 100–113.
50. Lee D. Dyer, "Job Search Success of Middle-Aged Managers and Engineers," *Industrial and Labor Relations Review,* April 1973, pp. 969–979; and Graham L. Reid, "Job Search and the Effectiveness of Job

Finding Methods," *Industrial and Labor Relations Review,* July 1972, pp. 479–495.

51. Dyer, "Job Search Success of Middle-Aged Managers and Engineers," pp. 479–495.
52. John M. Barron and Otis W. Gilley, "The Effect of Unemployment Insurance on the Search Process," *Industrial and Labor Relations Review,* April 1979, pp. 363–366; and Harry C. Benham, "UI Effects on Unemployment: Some Data on Competing Theories," *Industrial Relations,* Fall 1983, pp. 403–409.
53. Donald P. Schwab, "Recruiting and Organizational Participation," in *Personnel Management,* ed. Kendrith M. Rowland and Gerald R. Ferris (Boston: Allyn and Bacon, 1982), pp. 103–127; Donald P. Schwab, Sara L. Rynes, and Ramon J. Aldag, "Theories and Research on Job Search and Choice," in *Research in Personnel and Human Resources Management,* ed. Kendrith M. Rowland and Gerald R. Ferris (Greenwich, Conn.: JAI Press 1987), pp. 129–166.
54. Orlando Behling, George Labovitz, and Marion Gainer, "College Recruiting: A Theoretical Base," *Personnel Journal,* January 1968, pp. 13–19.
55. Clifford E. Jurgenson, "Job Preferences (What Makes a Job Good or Bad?)," *Journal of Applied Psychology,* June 1978, pp. 267–276.
56. Hanigan, "Key Campus Strategies," pp. 42–44.
57. Behling, Labovitz, and Gainer, "College Recruiting: A Theoretical Base," pp. 15-16.
58. Victor R. Tom, "The Role of Personality and Organizational Images in the Recruiting Process," *Organizational Behavior and Human Performance,* September 1971, pp. 573–592.
59. Donald P. Rogers and Michael Z. Sincoff, "Favorable Impression Characteristics of the Recruitment Interviewer," *Personnel Psychology,* Autumn 1978, pp. 495–504.
60. Neal Schmitt and Brian W. Coyle, "Applicant Decisions in the Employment Interview," *Journal of Applied Psychology,* April 1976, pp. 184–192.
61. Cynthia D. Fisher, Daniel R. Ilgen, and Wayne D. Hoyer, "Source Credibility, Information Favorability, and Job Offer Acceptance," *Academy of Management Journal,* March 1979, pp. 94–103.
62. Thomas Bergmann and M. Susan Taylor, "College Recruitment: What Attracts Students to Organizations," *Personnel,* May-June 1984, pp. 34–46; Sara L. Rynes, Herbert G. Heneman III, and Donald P. Schwab, "Individual Reactions to Organizational Recruiting: A Review," *Personnel Psychology,* Autumn 1980, pp. 529–542.
63. Lord, "Internal and External Recruitment," p. 82.
64. Michael M. Harris and Laurence S. Fink, "A Field Study of Applicant Reactions to Employment Opportunities: Does the Recruiter Make a Difference?" *Personnel Psychology,* Vol. 40, 1987, pp. 765–784; M. Susan Taylor and Thomas J. Bergmann, "Organizational Recruitment Activities and Applicants' Reactions at Different Stages of the Recruitment Process," *Personnel Psychology,* Vol. 40, 1987, pp. 261–286; Gary N. Powell, "Applicant Reactions to the Initial Employment Interview: Exploring Theoretical and Methodological Issues," *Personnel Psychology,* Spring 1991, pp. 67–83.
65. Robert J. Vandenberg and Vida Scarpello, "The Matching Model: An Examination of the Processes Underlying Realistic Job Previews," *Journal of Applied Psychology,* February 1990, pp. 60–67.
66. Steven L. Premack and John P. Wanous, "A Meta-analysis of Realistic Job Preview Experiments," *Journal of Applied Psychology,* November 1985, pp. 706–719.
67. James A. Breaugh, "RJPs: A Critical Appraisal and Future Research Directions," *Academy of Management Review,* October 1983, pp. 612–619.
68. Richard R. Reilly, Barbara Brown, Milton R. Blood, and Carol Z. Malatesta, "The Effects of Realistic Previews: A Study and Discussion of the Literature," *Personnel Psychology,* Winter 1981, pp. 823–834.
69. John P. Wanous, *Organizational Entry* (Reading, Mass.: Addison-Wesley, 1980).
70. See Donn L. Dennis, "Evaluating Corporate Recruiting Efforts," pp. 21–26, for guidance on the relative difficulty of searches and how to take this difficulty into account in evaluation.

71. Roger H. Hawk, *The Recruitment Function.* (New York: American Management Association, 1967).

72. Roger H. Hawk, *The Recruitment Function.*

73. Stephen L. Mangum, "Recruitment and Job Search: The Recruitment Tactics of Employers," *Personnel Administrator,* June 1982, pp. 96–104.

74. James A. Breaugh, "Relationships Between Recruiting Sources and Employee Performance, Absenteeism, and Work Attitudes," *Academy of Management Journal,* March 1981, pp. 142–147; Martin J. Gannon, "Source of Referral and Employee Turnover," *Journal of Applied Psychology,* June 1971, pp. 226–228; and Phillip J. Decker and Edwin Cornelius III, "A Note on Recruiting Sources and Job Survival Rates," *Journal of Applied Psychology,* August 1979, pp. 463–464.

75. Breaugh, "Relationships Between Recruiting Sources and Employee Performance, Absenteeism, and Work Attitudes," pp. 142–147; and David F. Caldwell and Austin Spivey, "The Relationship Between Recruiting Source and Employee Success: An Analysis by Race," *Personnel Psychology,* Spring 1983, pp. 67–72.

76. De Witte, "Recruitment Advertising," pp. 205–217.

77. James A. Breaugh and R. B. Mann, "Recruiting Source Effects: A Test of Two Alternative Explanations," *Journal of Occupational Psychology,* Vol. 57, 1984, pp. 261–267; Maureen A. Conard and Steven D. Ashworth, "Recruiting Source Effectiveness: A Meta-analysis and Re-examination of Two Rival Hypotheses," paper presented at the First Annual Conference of the Society for Industrial and Organizational Psychology, Chicago, April 1986; and Philip G. Swaroff, Lizabeth A. Barclay, and Alan R. Bass, "Recruiting Sources: Another Look," *Journal of Applied Psychology,* November 1985, pp. 720–728.

78. Gannon, "Source of Referral and Employee Turnover," pp. 226–228.

Measurement and Decision-Making Issues in Selection

Personnel selection is a process of measurement, decision making, and evaluation (see Figure 7.1). The goal of a personnel selection system is to bring into an organization individuals who will perform well on the job. As noted in Chapter 5, a good selection system must also be fair to minorities and other protected classes.

To have an accurate and fair selection system, an organization must use reliable and valid measures of job applicant characteristics. In addition, a good selection system must include a means of combining information about applicant characteristics in a rational way and producing correct hire and no-hire decisions.

FIGURE 7.1 The Selection Process

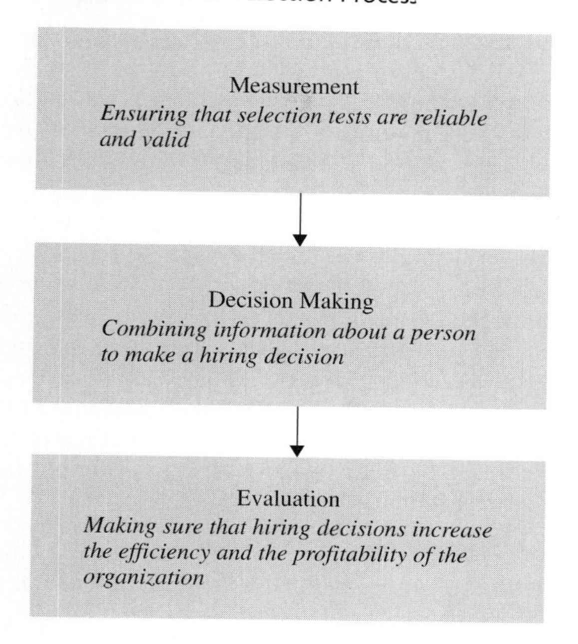

A good personnel selection system should add to the overall effectiveness of the organization.[1]

This chapter addresses each of these areas in turn. First, it introduces the statistical methods needed to understand reliability and validity. Next, it considers why reliability of selection instruments is important and offers examples of several common methods of assessing reliability. Then the discussion moves to the several ways in which selection tests can be validated so the results can be used to make hiring decisions. The chapter describes four different methods of using test scores to make these decisions. The final sections examine the factors that affect the costs of selection systems and describe the many benefits that can be realized from a properly designed selection process.

STATISTICAL METHODS IN SELECTION

In order to understand how reliability and validity are assessed, one must first understand two statistical methods—correlation and regression. Correlation is used to assess the strength and direction of a relationship between variables, whereas regression makes use of the relationship to predict scores on one variable from scores on one or more other variables. Only a brief discussion of these methods is offered here; those desiring more detail on these statistical procedures should refer to a basic textbook on statistics.

Correlation Analysis

Correlation analysis is used to determine the *degree of relationship* between two variables. For example, an HR specialist may wish to know whether the mechanical ability of employees is related to their job performance. If a relationship exists, then a mechanical ability test given to job applicants might be useful in deciding who should be hired. One method of examining relationships between two variables is to use a **scattergram**.

Figure 7.2 shows a scattergram in which mechanical ability test scores and job performance scores of several employees have been plotted. It is obvious from the scattergram that some degree of relationship exists. Individuals who have high mechanical ability also tend to be better performers. However, using only a scattergram, the HR specialist has no easy way to describe this relationship or to determine exactly how strong the relationship is.

The **Pearson product moment correlation coefficient** (represented by the symbol r) is a numerical index that indicates the direction and degree of linear relationship between two variables. The Pearson correlation coefficient has several important characteristics, among them the following:

- The numerical value of r ranges from -1.0 to $+1.0$.
- The sign of the correlation ($-$ or $+$) indicates the direction of the relationship.

FIGURE 7.2 Scattergram Showing Relationship Between Mechanical Ability Test Scores and Job Performance

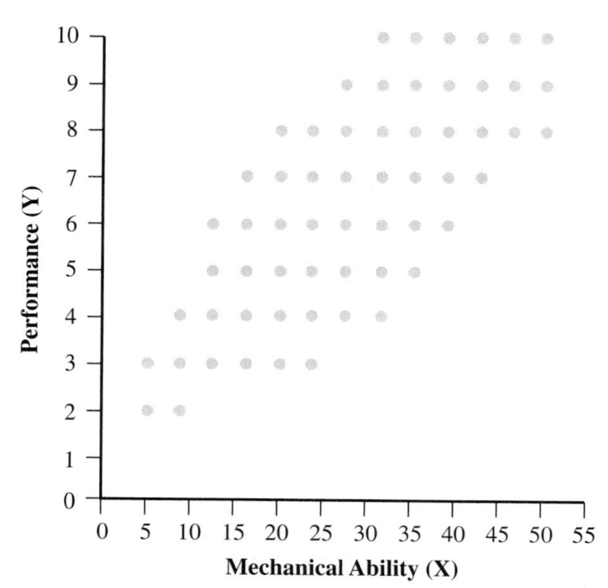

- The magnitude of r indicates the strength of the relationship.
- This numerical index is appropriate only for describing linear (straight-line) relationships.

Several different strengths and directions of correlations are presented in Figure 7.3. When $r = +1.0$, a perfect positive linear relationship exists between two variables (Figure 7.3a). A perfect positive linear relationship exists when, as variable X increases, variable Y increases in some exactly proportional manner. When $r = -1.0$, a perfect negative relationship exists, but in this case, as variable X increases, variable Y decreases (Figure 7.3b). When $r = +.70$ or $-.70$ (Figures 7.3c and d), a relationship between X and Y exists, but it is not as strong (not as exactly proportional) as when $r = +1.0$ or -1.0. Figure 7.3e depicts a zero relationship between X and Y. In the right corner (Figure 7.3f), r also equals 0.0, but for another reason. In this case, X and Y are related, but the relationship cannot be represented by a straight line (the Pearson correlation coefficient is only appropriate for describing linear relationships).

Regression Analysis

Regression analysis allows HR specialists to use a known relationship between variables to predict an individual's future behavior. If a correlation exists between mechanical ability and job performance, HR specialists can use regression analysis to predict the future performance of an individual whose mechanical ability is known.

The Pearson correlation coefficient indicates how close to a straight line the relationship between two variables is. Regression analysis answers the question, to *which* straight line is the relationship closest? Regression analysis does this by identifying the equation for the line that best fits a set of data (data for several individuals on two variables, X and Y).

The job performance and mechanical ability levels of ten individuals are represented in Figure 7.4. In Figure 7.4a, the line that best fits this data has been drawn. In Figure 7.4b, a non-best-fitting line has been drawn. A complex mathematical formula is used to compute the equation for the best-fitting line. By means of this formula, the HR specialist would find that the equation for the best-fitting line (shown in Figure 7.4a) is

$$Yp = .128X + 1.9$$

where Yp = predicted performance
X = mechanical ability
.128 = the slope of the line
(i.e., for every unit that X increases, Y increases .128 units)
1.9 = the Y-intercept
(i.e., the point where the line crosses the Y-axis).

The HR specialist can use the regression equation to predict performance of a job applicant by inserting the measured mechanical ability of the applicant into

FIGURE 7.3 Examples of Strengths and Directions of Correlations

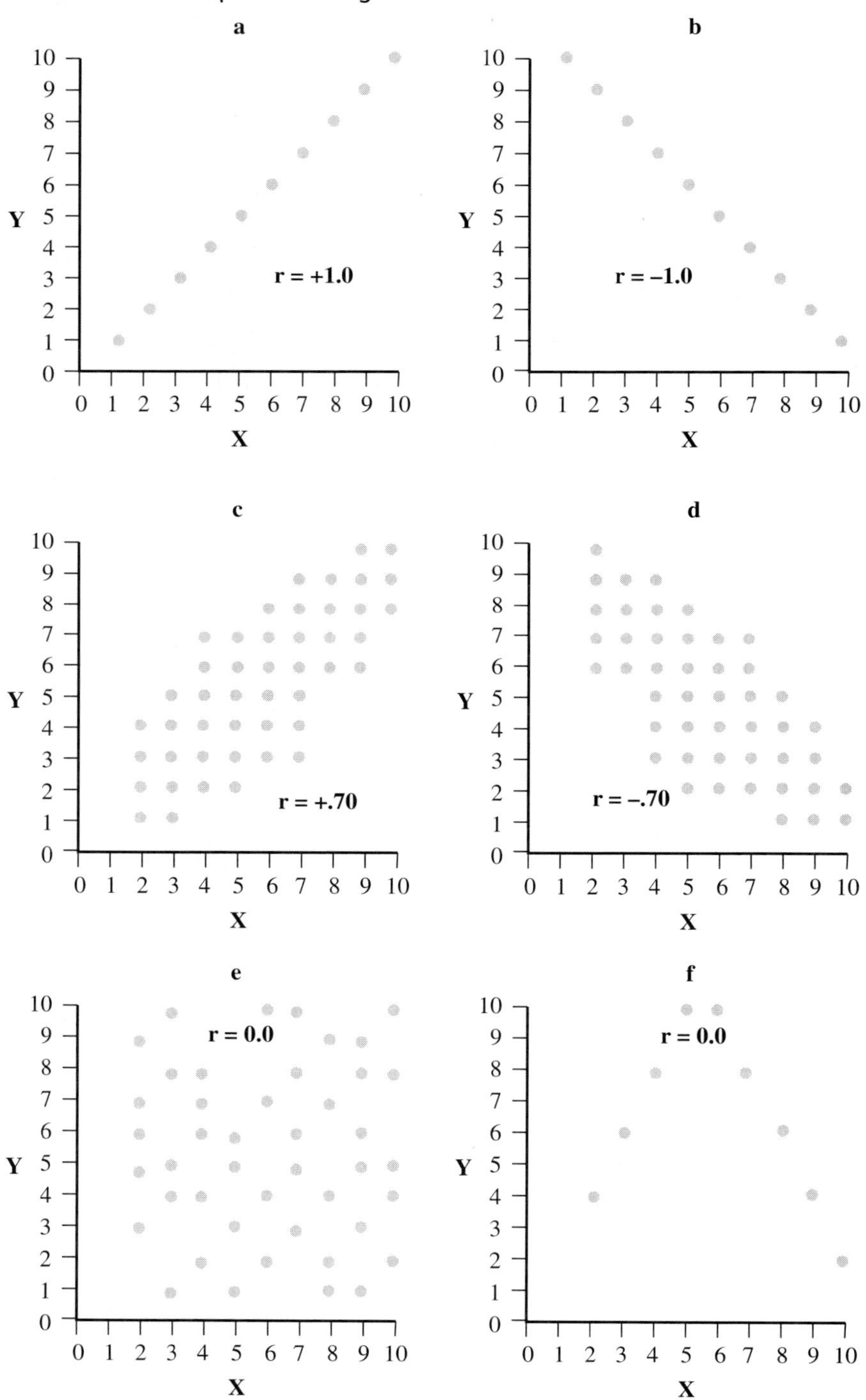

FIGURE 7.4 Best-Fitting and Non-Best-Fitting Regression Lines

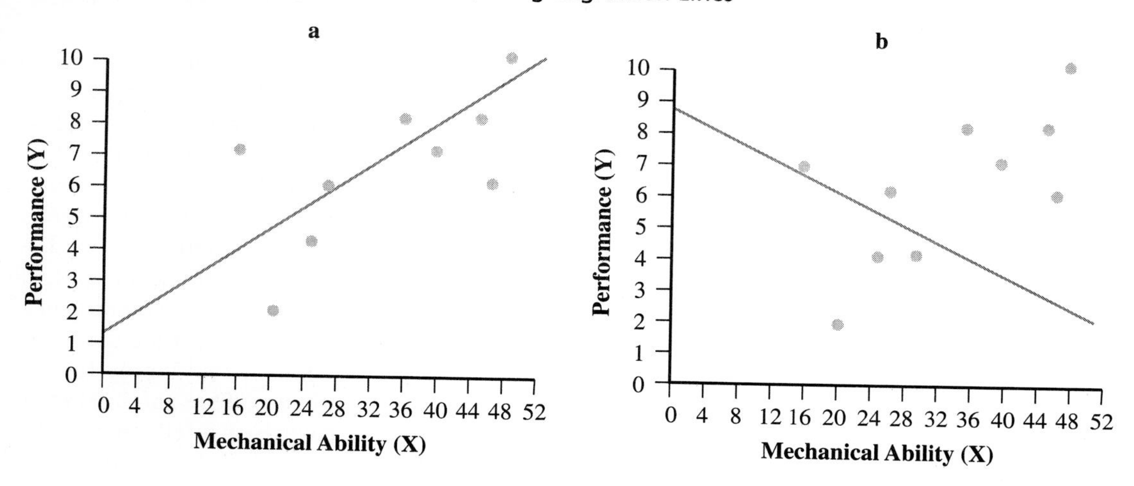

the formula. If Joe scored 35 on the mechanical ability test, then Joe's predicted performance would be $Yp = .128(35) + 1.9 = 6.38$. The use of the regression equation in this manner is called **point prediction**. How accurately the regression equation actually predicts Joe's performance depends on the strength of the relationship between mechanical ability and performance. As the strength of the relationship increases (r approaches $+1.0$ or -1.0), the accuracy of prediction increases. If $r = 0.0$, then predictions based on a regression equation would be no better than random guesses.

Multiple Correlation and Regression Analysis

Rarely in personnel selection do HR specialists predict the performance of job applicants using information about only one ability or characteristic. Information used in selecting employees usually includes data from multiple sources, such as interviews, application blanks, references, and ability tests. **Multiple correlation analysis** indicates the degree of relationship between one variable (e.g., job performance) and a *set* of other variables. **Multiple regression analysis** allows the HR specialist to identify a prediction equation, in the form of

$$Yp = b_1X_1 + b_2X_2 + \ldots b_nX_n + a$$

where Yp = predicted performance
$b_1 \ldots b_n$ = the slope coefficients
$X_1 \ldots X_n$ = the various types of scores collected on individuals
a = the Y-intercept.[2]

RELIABILITY

An organization's personnel selection system should use reliable and valid measures of a job applicant's characteristics in order to make correct hiring decisions. **Reliability**, discussed in this section, refers to consistency of measurement.[3] For instance, an intelligence test would be reliable if all of its items consistently measured the same thing (presumably intelligence), and if scores for a single individual were reasonably consistent over time. An individual should get about the same score if his or her intelligence is measured with the same test twice, a few weeks apart. Validity, discussed in the next section, has to do with whether or not the test measures what it is supposed to measure (intelligence), and whether test scores are significantly correlated with job performance (e.g., does intelligence correlate with success in the job of college professor? shoe maker? truck driver?).

In our discussion, the term *test, measure,* or *instrument* may apply to any form of measurement that takes place in the selection process. Thus, an interview is considered as much a test as a paper-and-pencil measure of intelligence. The concept of reliability applies equally to both.

Systematic Error Versus Random Error

Anytime a measure is taken of an individual, there will be some error in that measurement. For example, if a thermometer were used to take the temperature of a patient, the observed temperature could consist of several major components:

$$X = T + S + E$$

where X = the *measured* body temperature of the patient in degrees Fahrenheit
T = the *true* body temperature of the patient
S = systematic error or bias in the temperature reading
E = random error affecting the reading.[4]

Ideally, X should equal T. In personnel selection, however, this rarely (if ever) occurs. **Systematic error**, or **bias**, occurs when a test is inaccurate by a constant amount. For example, the thermometer may be faulty and thus always measures the temperatures of patients one degree higher than their true temperatures. **Random error** affects a test by causing the score to be sometimes higher and sometimes lower than the true score, in an unpredictable way. Random error could occur if a patient does not hold the thermometer in the right place in the mouth for the appropriate length of time or if a patient has taken a hot or cold drink. At different times, a patient could get a temperature reading that is lower or higher than his or her true internal body temperature.

The key difference between systematic error and random error is that systematic error affects measurement in a consistent, predictable fashion, whereas random error, by definition, is inconsistent or variable in its effect. A test score is reliable if random error is low, so that there are minimal fluctuations in observed scores. Note that consistency in measurement includes both true score, which is stable and systematic error, which is also stable. A test can be consistent even if systematic error is present. Ideally, the HR specialist wants tests that have neither systematic nor random error.

Sources of Error

Several specific types of errors may affect the consistency of tests. The sources of these errors are:

1. *Temporary, internal personal factors*—fatigue, boredom, motivational level, and anxiety.
2. *Changes in situational factors*—room temperature, lighting, and noise level during testing.
3. *Item content*—changes in the items on a test over different forms of the test. A test may have several versions, with the assumption made that items selected for one form are equivalent (i.e., comparable in content and difficulty) to items in another form. If the forms are not truly equivalent, differences in item content would reduce the reliability of test scores.
4. *Pure chance*—totally random events that affect a person's score (e.g., accidentally marking the wrong answer on the computerized answer sheet or forgetting to answer some questions).

Methods of Measuring Reliability

The three common methods of assessing reliability are test-retest, parallel forms, and internal consistency.[5] In each of these methods, the correlation coefficient is used as the index of reliability. Typically, a correlation of about .80 or higher is considered good reliability. Not all of these methods must be used in every situation, and in some instances a particular method may be totally inappropriate.

Test-Retest The **test-retest method** examines the consistency of a test over time. A single group of people take a test (time 1). Later, the same people take the same test again (time 2). The correlation is computed between the time 1 scores and the time 2 scores. This correlation is called the **coefficient of stability.** It is important that time 1 and time 2 be far enough apart so that individuals cannot remember their responses from the first testing.

Parallel Forms The **parallel forms method** of assessing reliability is appropriate when two versions of the same test are used. This method has two variations. In the first, a sample group is given both forms (A and B) of the test at the same time. The two different forms are then scored separately for each person, and a correlation is computed between the form A and form B scores. This correlation is called the **coefficient of equivalence**. In the second variation, a sample group is given form A of the test at time 1. Later, at time 2, the same group is given form B. A correlation is computed between the form A/time 1 score and the form B/

time 2 score for each person. This is called the **coefficient of stability and equivalence**.

Sometimes *people* can be viewed as parallel forms of a test. Suppose a job applicant is interviewed by several different interviewers. The interviewers rate the applicant separately on several dimensions. In this case, the interviewers can be viewed as parallel forms of the same interview test. It is therefore important to know how one interviewer's rating of the candidate correlate with the other interviewers' ratings of the same candidate. This correlation among evaluators who are sizing up the same set of applicants is referred to as **interrater reliability**. One caution should be noted about interrater reliability: sometimes interrater reliability is low, and that is all right. Suppose that an applicant is being interviewed for a first-line supervisory position by three different people—a midlevel manager, a technical specialist, and a person who would be a subordinate of the applicant if the applicant were hired. It might well be that the interrater agreement among these three interviewers would be quite low since each of them would bring to the interview situation very different perspectives of the job for which the applicant is being considered. In this case, our interviewers cannot really be viewed as "parallel forms" of the same interview "test." A low level of agreement among the interviewers would not necessarily mean that our interview procedure is faulty. On the other hand, if all three interviewers were technical specialists, a lack of agreement would probably indicate that our interview procedure has some definite reliability problems.

Internal Consistency The third method of assessing reliability is **internal consistency**. It is similar to the parallel forms method except that individual items on a test, rather than whole tests, are assessed for their equivalence to one another. This type of reliability helps to assess whether all the items on a test are measuring the same trait or ability; that is, whether the test's content is internally consistent. In this method, a group of people are given a test. A coefficient is computed that represents the average correlation of each item on the test with each other item. This is called **coefficient alpha** and is the preferred measure of internal consistency in most situations.[6] Coefficient alpha will be high (.80 or above) if most of the items on the test measure the same thing.

Another way of measuring internal consistency is the **split-half procedure**. A test is given to a group of individuals; then the test is arbitrarily split into two halves—for example, odd-numbered and even-numbered items. Each person receives two scores—one for each half of the test. A correlation is computed between the two sets of scores. Unfortunately, the split-half method is susceptible to some problems. Suppose that on a ten-item test of mechanical ability items 1 through 8 measure mechanical ability but items 9 and 10 erroneously measure verbal ability rather than mechanical ability. If the test items were split odd-even, the scores on each half of the test would appear equal, even though two inappropriate items were actually on the test.

Each method of assessing reliability provides different information about the types of errors that may affect a particular test. Table 7.1 summarizes the reli-

TABLE 7.1 Errors Tapped by Reliability-Measuring Methods

	Reliability Method			
Type of Error	*T-RT*	*PF* (T_1)	*PF* ($T_1 - T_2$)	*IC*
Person over Time	Yes	No	Yes	No
Situation over Time	Yes	No	Yes	No
Item Content	No	Yes	Yes	Yes
Pure Chance	Yes	Yes	Yes	Yes

Symbol	*Method of Correlation*	*Coefficient*
T-RT	Test-Retest	coefficient of stability
PF(T_1)	Parallel Forms (with both forms given at same time)	coefficient of equivalence
PF($T_1 - T_2$)	Parallel Forms (with form A given at time 1 and form B given at time 2)	coefficient of stability and equivalence
IC	Internal Consistency	coefficient alpha

ability-measuring methods and the types of errors tapped by each. Clearly, to cover all possible sources of error, the use of multiple methods may be necessary. For example, the internal consistency method reveals nothing about errors resulting from personal or situational factors over time. Similarly, the test-retest method says nothing about whether or not the items on a test are equivalent.

Having reliable measures is critical to establishing a personnel selection system. Reliability information can be obtained from several sources: (1) reliability studies conducted by the organization that will use the tests, (2) reliability information provided by commercial test publishers that sell the tests, (3) data from other companies that have used the same tests in their selection systems, or (4) data from individuals who have used the tests in research studies.

Reliability serves as the foundation on which the validity of a test can be established. If a test cannot measure people consistently, it cannot possibly be valid. The next section discusses the concept of test validity.

VALIDITY

One definition of **validity** is an "integrated evaluative judgment of the degree to which empirical evidence and theoretical rationales support the adequacy and appropriateness of inferences and actions based on test scores or other modes of assessment."[7] What this definition implies is that when we "validate" a test we are not validating the *test* itself but rather the *inferences and actions* we take as a result of test scores. In personnel selection, tests are used to measure some characteristic—for instance, mechanical ability—that is believed to relate to how well the person will be able to perform the job. In this situation, we are assuming that the test actually measures mechanical ability and that, based on how an applicant scores on the test, we can infer whether the individual will be able to perform the job. We then take action based on an applicant's test scores (we hire or do not hire the person). Validity deals with the issues of (1) whether the test is an adequate measure of the characteristic it supposedly measures and (2) whether inferences and actions based on test scores are appropriate.

Note that nothing in the law *requires* organizations to validate all selection tests. The organization would only need validity evidence *if* an applicant were to file a complaint and was able to establish a prima facia case of adverse impact. Then the employer might use validity data to show that the test was a good selection device that was necessary to improve the quality of hiring. However, techniques for validation were developed long before the passage of EEO laws. It makes sense to validate, even if a test has no adverse impact and the validity data will never be needed in court. This is because no organization should want to spend time and money using a selection device that may not be useful. Validation shows the usefulness of a test in identifying applicants who will make good employees.

The EEOC's *Uniform Guidelines on Employee Selection Procedures* and the Society for Industrial and Organizational Psychology's *Principles for the Validation and Use of Personnel Selection Procedures* identify three types of validity: construct validity, content validity, and criterion-related validity.[8] Although traditionally these types of validity have been treated as separate concepts, each really deals with a different aspect of the more general definition of validity just given.[9] Taking a somewhat traditional approach, we examine each of the three aspects of validity in turn.

Construct Validity

Although it is an essential aspect of validity, construct validity has received less attention in personnel selection than criterion-related or content validity. **Construct validity** deals with two issues: what the test measures and how well the test measures it.[10] Construct validity is particularly important when the human resource specialist attempts to measure abstract characteristics that are not readily observable. Some examples include creativity, intelligence, and various personality traits. Construct validity is determined through a very complicated process. No single study is sufficient to prove construct validity because there is no perfect criterion variable against which to validate the test. Thus, the researcher must use several different techniques to demonstrate that the test appears to behave the

INTERNATIONAL PERSPECTIVE

The Validity of Educational Level for Selection: Some Different Perspectives

In *Griggs* v. *Duke Power Company* (1971), the Supreme Court ruled that requiring a high school diploma in selection was illegal because the company could provide no evidence that a high school education was a valid predictor of job performance. Elsewhere, however, the use of educational level as an important or even sole factor in selection is widespread. Japan, Taiwan, Korea, and Singapore see selection based on education level as a means of achieving broader organizational and national goals, and show much less concern about whether educational level is a valid predictor of performance on specific jobs.

In Japan, the "best" organizations recruit only students who have graduated from the top universities. Singapore provides another example in which the concern for job-specific validity often takes a back seat to the concern for broader (in this case, national) issues. In a study conducted by Morgan Guaranty Trust Company of New York, the economic success of Singapore, Korea, Taiwan, and Hong Kong was attributed partly to their success in increasing the education level of their populations. In line with government policy, organizations in Singapore place very high importance on educational level in their selection decisions. The importance of education continues beyond the selection stage; both the earnings and promotions of Singaporeans are substantially dependent on their education levels. Thus, substantial incentives exist for obtaining and then furthering educational credententials.

For both Japan and Singapore, the use of education level as a primary selection tool has resulted in considerable national benefits. However, because the link between education and performance on specific jobs is often tenuous, there are dangers associated with this practice. These dangers lie primarily in the underutilization of available human resources. Individuals who, for whatever reason, do not achieve high levels of education, may through experience and/or natural ability have skills of great value to organizations. In Japan and Singapore, these individuals often find it impossible to gain access to positions commensurate with their true abilities. Thus, both the individuals and organizations lose.

K. F. Taylor (1987) cites other dangers of "credentialism":

- Performance appraisal, promotions, and compensation may be based on continued educational attainment rather than on actual contributions to the organization.
- When less-educated employees see that their opportunities for advancement and increased pay are restricted, they may exhibit lower motivation and productivity.

Tony Buon and Bob Compton (1990) point out that credentialism also tends to perpetuate social inequality, if access to more prestigious education is based partly on social class.

Source: K. F. Taylor, "Interactions Between Human Resource Management and Governmental Education and Training Policies in Newly Industrialized Countries" (discussion paper presented at the International Conference on Human Resource Management, National University of Singapore, December 1987); S. S. Tan, "Asian NICs' Lessons for Debt-Ridden Countries," *The Straits Times*, March 18–19, 1987 (cited in K. F. Taylor, p. 4); Tony Buon and Bob Compton, "Credentials, Credentialism, and Employee Selection," *Asia Pacific Human Resource Management*, November 1990, pp. 126–132.

way a test of the construct is expected to behave. For instance, a researcher who is trying to develop a new test to measure anxiety might, as a first study, give the new test along with several existing tests to a sample of individuals. The individuals' scores on the new test should correlate strongly with their scores on other accepted measures of anxiety, but their scores should not correlate with tests of other constructs such as intelligence. As a second study, the researcher might administer the new test to two sets of people: for example, a group of soldiers going into battle and a group of individuals given moderate doses of relaxation drugs. If the test actually measures anxiety, it should show differences between the two groups. When choosing tests to use in personnel selection, the human resource specialist should try to use tests that have evidence of construct validity—that is, tests that developers have proved measure the characteristics they are purported to measure.

Content Validity

Content validity is very closely related to the concept of construct validity, and evidence of content validity can be used to support the construct validity of a particular test. Content validity deals with whether or not a test is *representative* of some construct's "domain." Unlike construct validity, however, content validation is most appropriately done when the construct being measured consists of readily observable behaviors. Suppose, for instance, than an organization develops a technical math test for use in selecting engineering technicians. The test includes math problems in addition, subtraction, division, and multiplication. However, the job of an engineering technician in the organization requires an individual to work on advanced trigonometry, geometry, and calculus problems. Is the math test a representative sample of the types of math problems that are performed on the job? Content validity deals with this issue. In the example above, the math test is not content-valid. Although it does measure some aspects of technical math, it does not adequately sample all aspects of the domain of technical math problems confronted on the job.

Determining the content validity of a test is primarily a judgmental process, which usually begins with a very thorough job analysis, often through the task inventory method. Test items are then evaluated as to the degree to which they correspond to the skills and knowledge needed to perform critical job tasks. For instance, a typing test may be purchased or constructed for the job of secretary, and a test for knowledge of construction and electrical standards may be written for the job of building inspector. The content validity of the tests can then be verified by a panel of experts familiar with the jobs. One quantitative approach to judging content validity is described in Figure 7.5. This approach uses a panel of experts to rate the items on a test as to whether or not each represents essential aspects of the same domain. These ratings yield a content validity ratio for each item. This allows the HR specialist to compare the content validity of one test

FIGURE 7.5 Content Validity Procedure

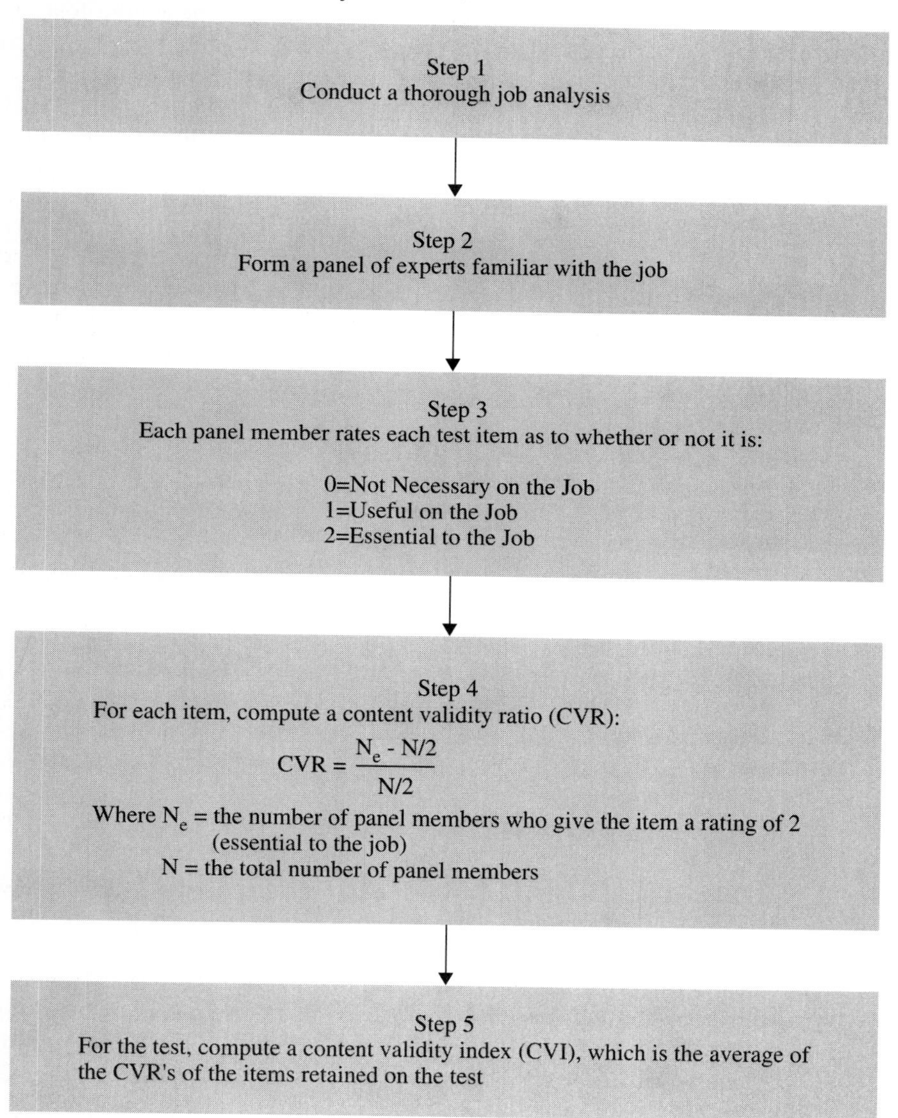

Source: Adapted from C. H. Lawshe, "A Quantitative Approach to Content Validity," *Personnel Psychology,* Vol. 28 (1975), pp. 563–575. Reprinted by permission.

item with that of another and to delete poor items. Averaging the content validity ratios of all items yields a content validity index for the whole test. This index can be used to compare several proposed tests to identify the test that most closely corresponds to the performance domain of a given job.

It is important to remember that job analysis is the key to content validity. Without a good, thorough description of the job, any subsequent content validation of tests for that job will not be accepted by the courts. In addition, the content validity of test items must be determined by experts who are knowledgeable about the job.[11] Both construct and content validity deal with whether a test is an adequate measure of the characteristic that it is supposed to measure. Furthermore, content validity, because it examines the extent to which test items reflect critical aspects of job performance, also helps the HR professional determine whether inferences based on test scores about the likely future performance of job applicants are warranted, as are the actions (hire/not hire) that might be taken as a result of those inferences.

Criterion-related Validity

In examining the **criterion-related validity** of a test, the HR specialist determines whether or not individuals' test scores are related to some important criterion variable. The criterion variable is simply whatever aspect of an individual's behavior the HR specialist is trying to predict, such as job performance, absenteeism, or turnover. Most frequently, the criterion variable is some measure of job performance (for the remainder of the discussion on validity, we will assume that that is the case). In using a test in personnel selection we are making an inference that applicants who score in a particular manner on the test will be better performers than those who score in some other way. Criterion-related validation procedures directly test the appropriateness of that inference.

In conducting any kind of criterion-related study, the first step always is to analyze the job. Information about the nature of the job helps the HR specialist choose one or more tests that seem likely to predict job performance. For instance, after analyzing the job of sewing machine operator, the HR specialist may choose tests of manual dexterity and hand-eye coordination as predictors. Information from the job analysis is also used to develop a criterion measure of job performance. The criterion measure might be job performance rating scales filled out by the supervisor or objective measures of the quality and quantity of output produced by individuals. A validity study is then conducted to determine whether or not the tests actually correlate with the job performance criterion as expected.

Criterion-related validity is generally regarded as the preferred way of showing that a selection test is job related (see the section "Make Procedures Objective and Job Related" in Chapter 5).[12] The two major procedures for determining the criterion-related validity of a test are concurrent validation and predictive validation.

Concurrent Validation **Concurrent validation** is a procedure that involves three steps:

1. Select a sample of current employees.
2. Give each employee the proposed selection test and simultaneously collect information on the criterion variable.
3. Compute the correlation between test scores and criterion scores.

In the case of eighty currently employed sewing machine operators, for instance, this procedure might indicate a statistically significant correlation of .35 between manual dexterity test scores and the number of shirts sewed in the past month. This finding suggests to the HR specialist that perhaps the manual dexterity test can be used to select new sewing machine operators who will tend to be high performers.

Although concurrent validation seems relatively simple, it has two major problems. The first problem concerns the representativeness of the sample of employees. The purpose of the validation procedure is to determine whether or not the relationship between the test scores and job-performance scores is strong enough to support use of the test in selecting job applicants. The question that arises is this: Does the relationship between test and performance scores for present employees apply equally well to job applicants?

The second major problem with concurrent validation is called **restriction of range**. Since present employees are used, it is unlikely that the sample will include individuals who are extremely poor performers (they would already have quit or been fired). The absence of very low performers results in a restriction of range on the performance scores found in the validation sample. If, in addition, the test is related to job performance, a restriction of range in the test scores can also occur because low performers, who would probably do poorly on the test, are absent from the sample. The effect of this double-edged restriction of range is to cause the correlation between the test scores and performance scores in the validation sample to appear lower than it should be.

This problem is presented graphically in Figure 7.6. In the hypothetical unrestricted sample (Figure 7.6a), it is clear that the correlation between *X* (test) and *Y* (performance) scores is quite high. Figure 7.6b shows a restricted sample in which no very low performers are represented. The correlation between *X* and *Y* in this figure appears considerably lower than in Figure 7.6a.

Restriction of range is a problem because it may cause the HR specialist to conclude that a test is not related to job performance when it really is. By selecting a representative sample to participate in the validation study, the HR specialist can reduce restriction of range, although not eliminate it entirely. Also, the HR specialist can use statistical methods developed specifically to estimate what the correlation between variables would be if no restriction of range were present.[13]

Predictive Validation Another method of determining criterion-related validity is through **predictive validation**, a procedure that uses the scores of actual job

FIGURE 7.6 Effects of Restriction of Range

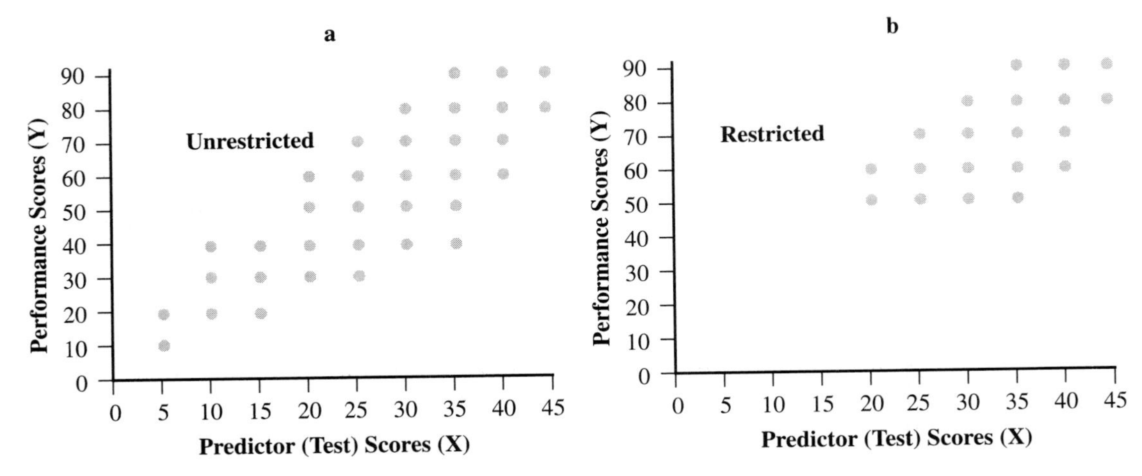

applicants who are tested (time 1) and then hired. Their test scores are *not* used by HR specialists in deciding whom to hire, since the test has not yet been proved valid. Instead, the HR specialist measures their job performances after a period of time (time 2) and then computes the correlation between time-1 test scores and time-2 performance scores.[14]

Problems associated with predictive validation are the sample size and time required to perform a typical predictive study. At one time, researchers thought that a predictive study could be conducted if 30 applicants were tested and hired for the same job. More recent analyses have indicated that sample sizes of over 200 are actually needed to produce accurate information about test validity.[15] Obtaining sample sizes this large may be impossible for all but very large companies. If, for instance, a small shoe factory hires about 20 new shoemakers a year, it would take the factory years to acquire data from the necessary number of individuals. On the other hand, a concurrent validation study might be feasible since all presently employed shoemakers could be used. A comparison of the concurrent and predictive validation procedures is presented in Figure 7.7.

In practice, there can be several variations of the basic concurrent and predictive procedures outlined in Figure 7.7.[16] For example, in a predictive validation study, applicants who have taken the predictor test could be hired using existing procedures or a random selection process. Using existing selection procedures would introduce a degree of restriction of range into the predictive study. It would also make it somewhat more difficult to generalize the results of the predictive study to *any population of job applicants,* since the individuals in the study are a *select* group of applicants. However, it may be impossible, in a practical sense, to hire applicants on a purely random basis. Variations on the basic concurrent validation procedure can also occur. In selecting present employees to participate

FIGURE 7.7 Concurrent and Predictive Validation Procedures

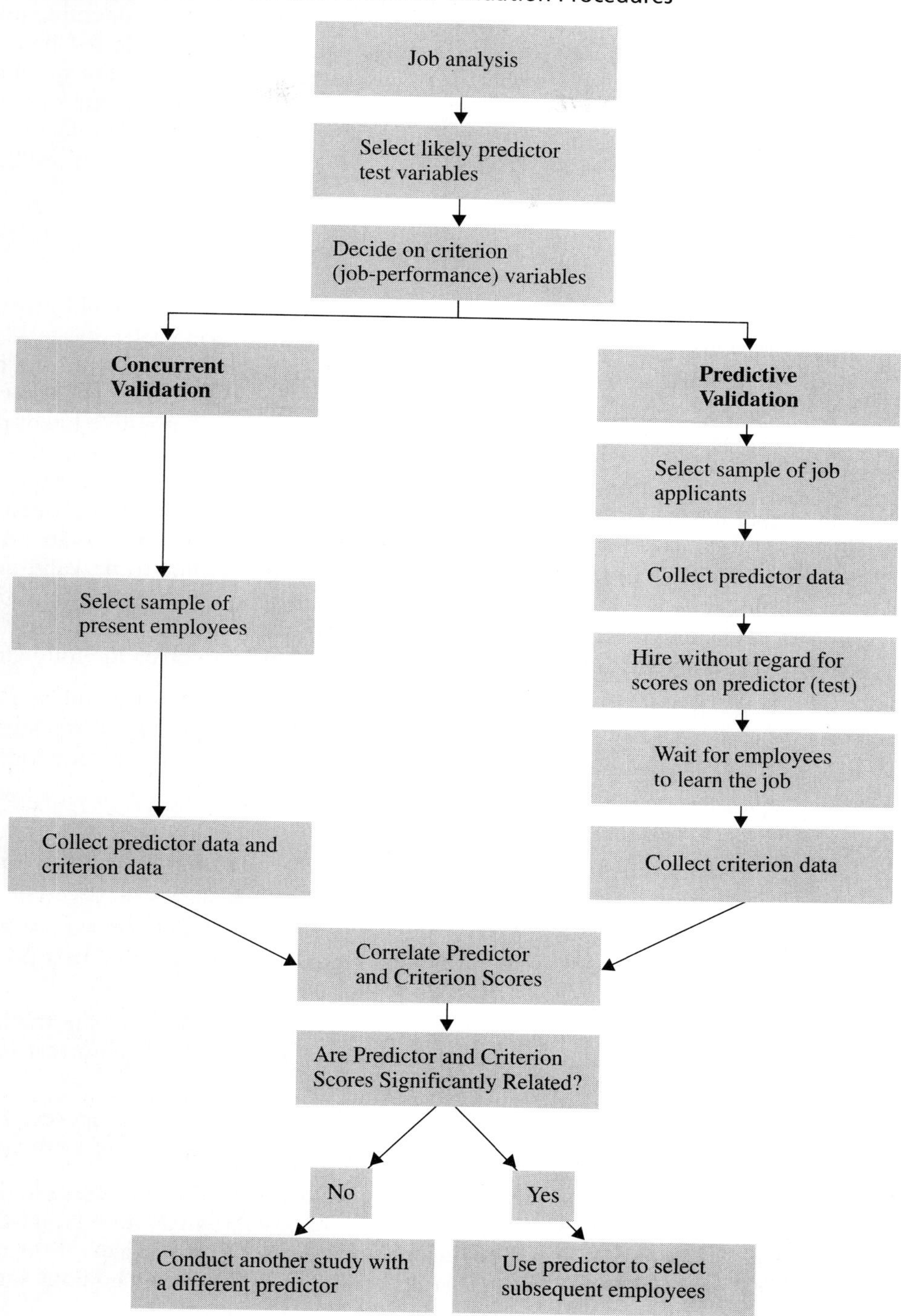

in the study, the HR specialist may choose employees who have been in their jobs only a short amount of time or may select workers with considerable job experience. Better measures of job performance may be available for more tenured workers, but employees with relatively little job experience are probably more like job applicants. There is no single best method for conducting predictive or concurrent validation studies; therefore, the HR specialist must select the specific procedures that best fit the jobs, employees, applicant pool, and predictor tests being investigated.

Cross-Validation

In the case of criterion-related validity, the HR specialist should cross-validate the results of any validation studies before actually using selection tests on a permanent basis. To **cross-validate** simply means to recheck the results of a particular validity procedure on another sampling of individuals. Cross-validation is necessary because, although regression equations do the best possible job of predicting the criterion in the sample in which they were developed, some of this predictability may result from unique or chance factors in that particular sample. The hope is that much of the predictability stems from a true relationship between variables that will occur in all samples. The purpose of cross-validation is to verify that a test that is valid (predictive) in one sample will continue to be valid in another, similar sample. If it is, then the HR specialist can confidently apply the test to select from among future samples of job applicants.

Cross-validating a concurrent validation study involves the following steps:

1. Randomly divide the sample of employees into two subsamples: a "development" subsample on which to develop the regression equation, and a "holdout" subsample on which to cross-validate the equation.
2. Collect predictor test and criterion (job-performance) data on all persons in both subsamples.
3. Using correlation analysis, examine the relationship between predictor and criterion scores in the development subsample.
4. If there is a strong correlation between predictor and criterion scores in the development subsample, derive a regression equation that best predicts the criterion scores of employees in the subsample.
5. Use this regression equation to predict the criterion scores in the holdout subsample. To do so, insert the holdout members' predictor test scores into the equation.
6. Calculate the correlation between the predicted criterion scores (Yp) of the holdout subsample and the *actual* criterion scores (Y) that were collected.

If the correlation between predicted and actual criterion scores in the holdout group is high, then the predictor test has *cross-validated*—that is, it has shown a strong relationship with the criterion scores in both subsamples. If the correlation between predicted and actual criterion scores is low in the holdout sample, then the test did not cross-validate. The test should not be used to select employees since its relationship to the criterion (job performance) is unstable across different samples of the same type of people.

In addition to cross-validating before using a test to select employees, the HR specialist should recheck the validity of tests after the selection system has been implemented. The need to recheck validity is due to a phenomenon referred to as the "dynamic criterion."[17] Over time, there may be systematic changes in the critical behaviors needed on a job. Likewise, the performance appraisal system used in the organization may change.[18] As a result, tests that adequately predicted job performance in 1980 may not predict performance in 1990. Therefore, the HR specialist should periodically recheck selection tests to ensure that validity remains high over time.

Special Concerns in Validation

In addition to being interested in the construct, content, and criterion-related validity of selection tests, the HR specialist is also concerned with some other issues. The first of these relates to the *fairness* of tests used in selecting both majority and minority employees. Test fairness refers to whether or not a test makes equally accurate predictions of future performance for majority and minority group members.

Differential Validity and Differential Prediction The EEOC's *Uniform Guidelines* state that an organization must examine any selection system that has an adverse impact on minority employees to determine whether or not the selection test is fair.[19] Until recently, there were considered to be two basic aspects of test fairness—differential validity and differential prediction.[20] However, in *Golden Rule Insurance Company et al.* v. *Washburn et al.* and *Allen* v. *Alabama State Board of Education,* a new issue in test fairness has evolved; it is referred to as measurement bias.[21]

Differential Validity Differential validity is presented graphically in Figure 7.8. In Figure 7.8a, it is clear that for majority employees a strong relationship exists between performance and mechanical ability. This is not the case for minority employees. **Differential validity** exists when the correlation between test scores and performance for one group is significantly lower than the correlation for another group.[22] In Figure 7.8b, no differential validity exists. The relationship between mechanical ability and performance for both groups is essentially equal, although minority members tend to score lower on the test. Also, if a regression equation were developed using all the employees, the predictions based on that equation would not systematically over- or underpredict for either group.

Differential Prediction In Figure 7.8c, no differential validity exists. However, if a regression line equation were developed using the total sample (line *T*), this equation would tend to systematically underpredict minority-group perfor-

FIGURE 7.8 Differential Validity and Differential Prediction

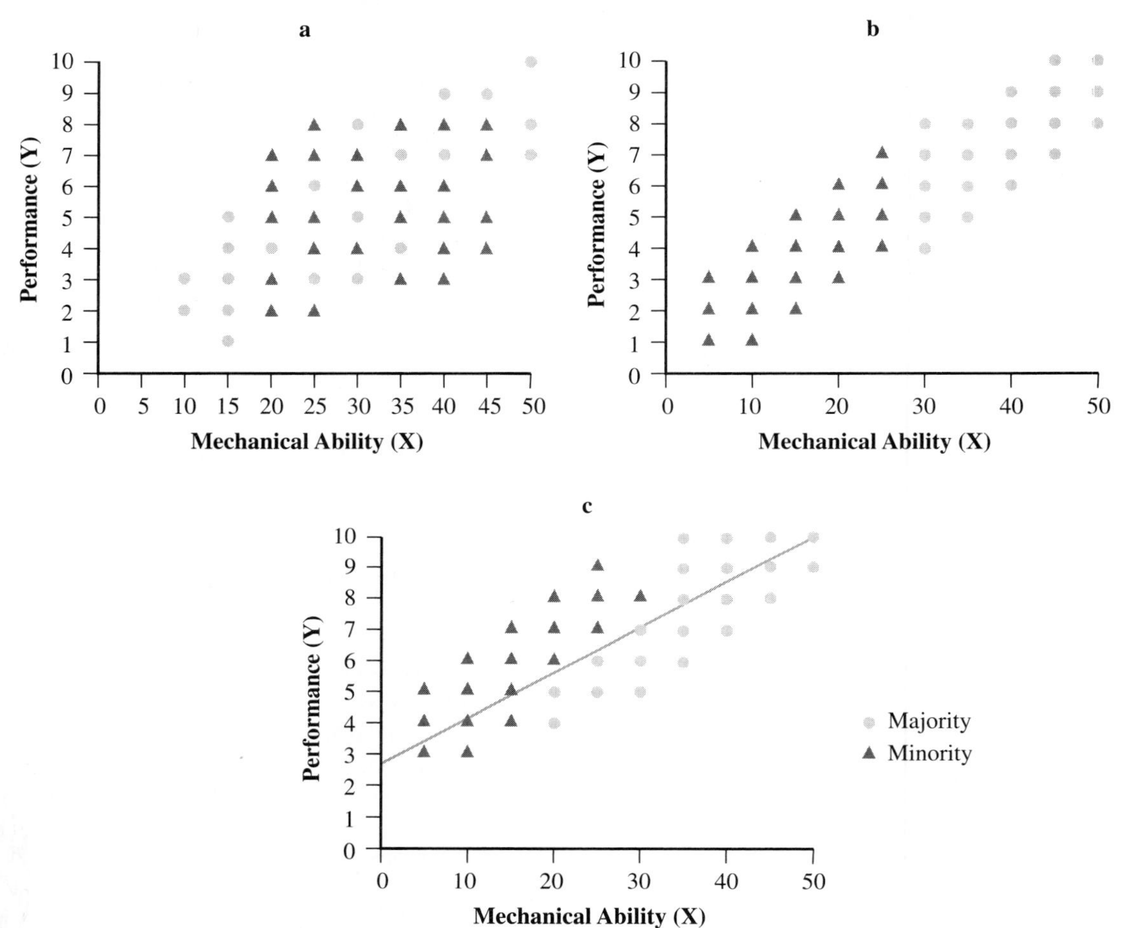

mance but overpredict majority-group performance. This is referred to as **differential prediction**. Although differential validity and differential prediction are issues that should be investigated in every criterion-related validation study, in reality these problems rarely occur.[23] In most cases, selection tests predict performance for minority employees about as well as for majority employees.

Measurement Bias In differential validity and differential prediction, the focus of concern is on whether overall test scores correlate with job performance at different levels (or result in different regression equations) for minority and majority groups. In both the *Golden Rule* and *Allen* cases, the courts focused their attention on whether or not minority and majority group members scored differently on *individual test items*. In both court cases, the defendants agreed to modify their method of developing predictor tests. For example, in the *Golden Rule* case, the defendant agreed to include in the predictor test only those items for which the proportion of correct responses by majority members and minority members differed by no more than 15 percent. This focus on individual item measurement bias could make the development of valid selection tests very difficult. In a 1987 study, however, the measurement bias of two English and mathematics tests was analyzed.[24] The study indicated that when minority and majority member responses were compared, many items on the two tests showed some degree of measurement bias. These differences, however, were generally quite small and tended to cancel each other out across items. Thus, they had no cumulative biasing effect on the overall test scores of minority and majority members.

Validity Generalization Along with the largely erroneous assumption that validity of selection tests may change depending on the types of people being tested, there has also been a long-standing assumption that validity varies from one job to another and from one organization to another. This assumption is based on many studies that have found that a test that validly predicts performance in one job does not correlate significantly with performance in a similar job in the same organization or in a different organization. In recent years, strong arguments have been made against this assumption of *situational specificity*.[25] The argument against situational specificity is for **validity generalization**—that is, that test validity is readily applicable across a variety of organizations and similar jobs. This approach suggests that most differences in the observed validity of tests across situations result from methodological and statistical problems, rather than from true differences in the strength of relationships between predictor and criterion. Proponents of validity generalization submit that if these problems are controlled, tests found to be valid predictors of performance for a job family will be useful for selecting for that job family in all organizations.[26]

Proponents of validity generalization argue that tests of general cognitive ability are good predictors of job performance across a wide variety of jobs. They argue that general cognitive ability predicts whether or not an individual will be able to adequately learn a job. The degree of learning then influences job performance.[27] The validity generalization approach to selection is becoming more widespread, with even government agencies such as the U.S. Job Service employing validity generalization techniques.[28] Although some researchers question the statistical procedures used in validity generalization studies, more recent studies have shown support for the generalization approach.[29] One such study, conducted in the U.S. Army, showed that selection tests could be generalized across nine jobs for four of five performance criteria.[30] Another study, using biographical data collected from over 20,000 individuals in more than 50 organizations, indicated that the same biographical data could be used to predict performance of supervisors of different race, sex, experience, or tenure across all of the organizations included in the sample.[31] HR specialists may draw on published validity generalization studies to find out which tests appear to have predictive validity for a given class of jobs, then proceed to use those tests in selection for that type of job.

There are problems in using this approach. For example, it drastically contradicts EEOC guidelines for selection test development since no job analysis is required and situational specificity is ignored. Recent studies have also shown that test validities may vary depending on the type of job performance measures used.[32] Validities resulting from studies in which subjective performance ratings were used were higher than those in which objective production quantity measures of performance were used. Studies using measures of performance quality showed very low test-performance validities.[33] In addition to these problems, there are certain advantages of doing one's own validation studies. These studies allow the organization to look at the predictive power of unique combinations of tests and of tests predicting unique local measures of job performance. They also allow the organization to develop local norms and cut-off scores for the tests to use in hiring decisions.[34]

A concept that is similar but not identical to validity generalization is **job component validity.**[35] This approach to validity, also known as **synthetic validity,** may be useful when predictive or concurrent validation procedures are not feasible.[36] The basic idea of job component validity is presented in Table 7.2.

Job component validity requires that all jobs be broken down into some finite number of components (such as the job dimensions of the Position Analysis Questionnaire in Table 4.6). In Table 7.2, ten such components can be used to describe

TABLE 7.2 Job Component Validity

		Component Required/Not Required		
Job Component	*Predictor (Test)*	*Job A*	*Job B*	*Job C*
1	T1	Y*	N*	Y*
2	T2	N	Y	N
3	T3	Y	N	N
4	T4	Y	Y	N
5	T5	N	N	Y
6	T6	Y	N	N
7	T7	Y	N	N
8	T8	N	N	N
9	T9	N	Y	N
10	T10	Y	N	Y

*Y (yes) means that the job component is required to perform the job; N (no) means that it is not.

any job. It is assumed that each test—T1 through T10—is related to the ability of a person to perform each corresponding job component. (Thus, T1 is predictive of a person's performance of job component 1.) The validity of these tests is established through traditional criterion-related validity studies conducted in other organizations.

In Table 7.2, job analysis procedures were used to determine which job components are required to perform each of three jobs—jobs A, B, and C. Job A involves components 1, 3, 4, 6, 7, and 10. Since tests that measure a person's ability to perform each of these components have been identified, the proponents of job component validity argue that they can use tests 1, 3, 4, 6, 7, and 10 to select employees for this job. For job B, they can use tests 2, 4, and 9; and for job C, tests 1, 5, and 10.

Several different approaches to job component validity have been developed,[37] including one that results in an actual criterion-related validity coefficient between predictor test scores and rated performance.[38] This method uses the Position Analysis Questionnaire to identify the behavioral elements that make up the job. Tests that measure the ability to perform each of the elements have been identified. Employees are given these tests, and an overall "suitability for the job" score is computed. Although the job component approach has a logical and intuitive appeal, it has not been reviewed extensively in the courts. Therefore, organizations hesitate to use it because of uncertainty over whether this procedure would be upheld as an acceptable method for justifying selection procedures that have an adverse impact on minority groups.

DECISION MAKING IN SELECTION

Generally, the HR specialist collects several types of information about job applicants before making a selection decision. In the process, the specialist uses reliable and valid selection procedures to collect this information. But managing the selection program does not end there. The HR specialist still has the problem of how to use these sources of information to make the best final hire/no-hire decision. At least four different methods exist for combining information and making a selection decision: multiple regression, multiple cutoff, multiple hurdle, and profile matching.

Multiple Regression

Multiple regression is a purely statistical approach to selection decision making.[39] Earlier, we stated the equation for a multiple regression: $Yp = b_1X_1 + b_2X_2 + b_3X_3 + \ldots + b_nX_n + a$. This is the equation that best represents the linear relationship between some criterion variable and a set of predictor variables that have been weighted (b_1, b_2, and so on) so as to maximize their relationship with the criterion.

Suppose that the multiple regression equation is

$$Yp = 2X_1 + 3.5X_2 + .5X_3 + 20$$

where Yp = predicted job performance
X_1 = score on a mechanical-ability test
X_2 = number of years' experience in a similar job
X_3 = rating of job applicant in an interview

Three individuals apply for the job. They are given the mechanical-ability test, asked about their previous experience, and interviewed by the HR manager, who rates each applicant on a ten-point scale. Their scores are as follows:

	Mechanical Ability	*Experience*	*Interview Rating*
Joe	20	5 years	9
Al	5	15 years	7
Sally	25	4 years	5

Joe's predicted performance score is 2(20) + 3.5(5) + .5(9) = 62. Al and Sally's predicted scores are 66 and 66.5, respectively. If one job opening exists, Sally would be hired.

Multiple regression assumes that applicant characteristics are compensatory in nature. *Compensatory* means that a high score on one characteristic can make up for a low score on another characteristic. In the above example, Sally's high level of mechanical ability compensated for her low levels of experience and interview performance. The HR specialist must be certain that this assumption of compensatory characteristics is appropriate for the position being filled. Furthermore, when the regression equation is developed from relatively small criterion-related validation samples, researchers have found that the weights generated by multiple regression (b_1,b_2, and so on) are not very stable from one sample to another.[40] Consequently, the HR specialist must develop regression equations using large samples and periodically revalidate the equations to make sure that they still result in the best possible prediction of performance.

Multiple Cutoff

If the assumption of a compensatory relationship among predictor variables is inappropriate, other decision-making methods may be needed. In the multiple cutoff method, job applicants are required to have some minimum level of each predictor variable. Multiple cutoff is a noncompensatory model of selection. In the previous example with Joe, Al, and Sally, suppose that a multiple cutoff procedure is used. Cutoffs for each of the three predictor variables are set so that the minimum level of mechanical ability needed is 10, five years of experience are required, and an interview rating of 5 is necessary. Using this approach, Joe, not Sally, would be hired, since Sally does not meet the minimum standard for experience. An advantage of the multiple cutoff method is that it is conceptually simple and easy to explain to managers. In operation, however, it is more difficult than it seems.[41]

If only a single predictor test is used, the cutoff score can be set using data on (1) how many job openings are likely to occur over a set time period, (2) how many job applicants are likely to apply during that period, and (3) the likely distribution of scores for applicants on that predictor test. The number of job openings and applicants can be obtained from company files on past openings and applicant flow. The likely distribution of test scores can be obtained from situations in which the test was given to other groups of job applicants. If 20 job openings will occur in the next year and 200 people are likely to apply for them, then the appropriate cutoff would be the 90th percentile score on the predictor—that is, the score that passes the top 10 percent of job applicants. Although this procedure is relatively easy when dealing with a single predictor test, it becomes dramatically more difficult as the number of tests increases. When several tests are used, the setting of cutoffs tends to become a trial-and-error procedure. Different cutoffs are tried for each predictor until a set of cutoffs is found that selects the best applicants but allows enough applicants to be hired to fill the job openings. A more systematic method requires job experts to rate the probability that a barely or minimally competent person would answer each item or perform each part of the test correctly. The cutoff score is then calculated as the average rated probability for each item, averaged across all items on the test, multiplied by the total number of test items.[42] One problem with this method is that the cutoff set may be too high, and so not enough applicants would qualify for the positions that must be filled. The cutoffs set may need further trial-and-error adjustment to ensure that applicants are available to fill empty positions.

An analysis of court cases involving the use of cutoff scores in selection has yielded some guidelines as to what the courts consider a "good" cutoff score.[43] Cutoff scores should enable the organization to select qualified candidates who are capable of learning the job and performing it in a safe, efficient manner; at the same time, these scores should allow the organization to meet any affirmative action goals it might have set. Cutoff scores should be based on factors such as the validity and reliability of the predictor tests used, as well as on the opinion of "experts." Luckily for HR specialists, the courts have accepted the fact that cutoff scores are somewhat imprecise. Thus, the courts do not require evidence that a person who scores one point below the cutoff would be a poor performer whereas an individual one point above the cutoff would perform well.

Multiple Hurdle

In both the multiple regression and multiple cutoff procedures, the decision making is *nonsequential*. Each applicant takes all the predictor tests, and the organization then makes the decision to hire or not hire. More often, however, selection is a *sequential* process, in which applicants pass through several selection stages (with individuals being rejected at each stage) before some are hired.[44] The multiple hurdle method can be described as a sequential multiple cutoff approach.

Using the previous example with Joe, Al, and Sally, a multiple hurdle procedure could be described as follows. All three applicants fill out an application blank that asks them to indicate their years of previous experience in similar jobs. This would be the first hurdle in the selection process. Sally would not pass this hurdle and would be excluded from further testing. Joe and Al both clear this first hurdle and move on to the second stage of selection. In this stage, Joe and Al take the mechanical-ability test. Joe successfully meets the minimum level of mechanical ability required; Al does not. Al would be excluded from further testing. The HR specialist then interviews Joe and eventually hires him.

One advantage of the multiple hurdle approach is that it can be more cost-effective than either the multiple regression or multiple cutoff method. To illustrate, suppose that (for each applicant) the application blank costs $.50, the mechanical-ability test costs $5, and the interview costs $20. Using multiple regression or multiple cutoff, the total cost of processing 100 applicants would be $25.50 × 100 = $2,550. But suppose, instead, that a multiple hurdle approach is used. Of the 100 applicants, only 50 pass the first hurdle (years of experience) to go on to the second, the mechanical-ability test. Of these 50, only 10 go on to the interview. The cost to the organization of this selection system would be $.50(100) + $5(50) + $20(10) = $500. This method represents a considerable saving over multiple regression and multiple cutoff.

One problem with the multiple hurdle approach is restriction of range. In the first step of the process, the sample of job applicants is relatively unrestricted. As the applicants move through the process, more and more are rejected. By the time the final group of applicants reaches the last hurdle, they represent a very select sample of people, making validation of the final hurdles very difficult. Selection procedures that are sufficiently sensitive to differentiate among the individuals in this final group are difficult to design.

Profile Matching

The three previous methods of decision making assume that *more is better.* Given two people who meet the minimum cutoff on some predictor, the individual with the higher level of that predictor will be selected. In multiple regression, the person with the highest predicted score will be hired. **Profile matching** assumes that there is some *ideal* level of predictor variables that an applicant should have, rather than some minimum level that must be met or exceeded. In profile matching, groups of good and of poor employees are identified. Individuals in these groups are measured on several likely predictor variables. If good performers score differently from poor performers on a characteristic, then the variable is useful in selecting good performers. Once several variables that differentiate between good and poor performers have been identified, an ideal profile of the successful employee is developed. For example, the ideal employee might have av-

TABLE 7.3 Hiring Decisions Based on Three Decision-Making Methods

	Test 1	*Test 2*	*Test 3*
Regression Weights	.6	.3	.1
Average Score of Successful Job Incumbents	20	50	5
Minimum Cutoff Score Set by Job Experts	15	45	5
George's Scores	70	44	65
Maria's Scores	50	47	45
Bill's Scores	16	43	6

If only one job opening is available,

- *multiple regression* would select George because his *Yp* of 61.7 is greater than Maria's 48.6 or Bill's 23.1.
- *multiple cutoff* would select Maria because George and Bill do not meet the minimum cutoff for test 2.
- *profile matching* would select Bill because his pattern of scores most closely matches that of successful job incumbents.

erage intelligence, good social skills, a low need for dominance over others, and a high level of planning ability. In profile matching, the job applicants hired are those who most closely match the profile of a successful employee.

A comparison of the decisions made by profile matching, multiple regression, and multiple cutoff is presented in Table 7.3. One common procedure for determining the degree of profile match is to sum the squared differences between an applicant's score on each predictor variable and the profile score for that variable. Thus, the tally of Bill's profile-match score would be: $(16 - 20)^2 + (43 - 50)^2 + (6 - 5)^2 = 66$. If you calculate the match scores for George and Maria, you find that their match scores are larger than Bill's. The smaller the score, the closer the match; thus, Bill would be hired if the profile matching procedure is used.

The results reached by these decision-making procedures are quite different. In deciding which procedure to use, the HR specialist must take into account whether a compensatory or noncompensatory model is more appropriate. The number of applicants and the cost of testing are also important considerations. It may be possible to combine several of the methods within a single selection system. For example, applicants could be given several tests early in the hiring process. These test scores could be combined using multiple regression to decide which applicants go on to the second phase of selection. In the second phase, several more tests could be given and a multiple cutoff procedure used. In the third phase, a profile-matching procedure could be employed to make the hire/no-hire decisions. All three steps of this process, taken together, form a multiple hurdle approach to selection.

UTILITY OF A SELECTION SYSTEM

In evaluating a selection system, the HR specialist needs to know if the system has utility for the organization. **Utility** concerns the overall value of the selection system to the organization; it is analogous to cost/benefit analysis. The economic benefit of a properly developed selection system can be impressive. For example, one analysis of white-collar jobs in the U.S. government indicated that selection of workers based on valid measures of cognitive ability (instead of nontest measures, such as education level) would produce an increase in output worth $600 million in a one-year period.[45] The HR specialist should evaluate the potential utility of a selection system not only after it is ready to be implemented, but also throughout its development. Asking the right questions at the right time can save time, effort, and money.

The utility of a selection system is composed of three major factors: the efficiency of selection, the standard deviation of performance in dollars, and the costs associated with selection.

Efficiency of Selection

Whenever an organization makes hiring decisions, some of those decisions are correct and some are not. The results of a selection process are presented graphically in Figure 7.9a. This scattergram represents the relationship between X, some predictor variable, and Y, the known *future* performance of a group of job applicants. All applicants above the horizontal line are successful performers, whereas those below the line are unsuccessful. The vertical line represents a cutoff score on the predictor variable set by the organization. Individuals who score to the right of the cutoff would be hired; those to the left would not. Four types of selection decisions are represented in Figure 7.9a.

Quadrant A: true positive decisions, in which the individuals who are hired turn out to be good performers

Quadrant B: false negative decisions, in which individuals are *not* hired but would have turned out to be good performers (e.g., a National Football League team does not draft a particular college player, and later this player becomes a star running back for another team)

Quadrant C: true negative decisions, in which individuals who would have been unable to perform the job are not selected

Quadrant D: false positive decisions, in which individuals who are hired turn out to be poor performers

If no selection system is used (ignore the cutoff line) and the organization simply hires people on a random basis, the proportion of successful performers hired to unsuccessful performers hired would equal (A + B)/(A + B + C + D). If scores on the predictor variable are used to select employees, the proportion of successful to unsuccessful persons selected would equal A/(A + D). The efficiency of the selection system can thus be defined as

FIGURE 7.9 Efficiency in Selection Decision Making

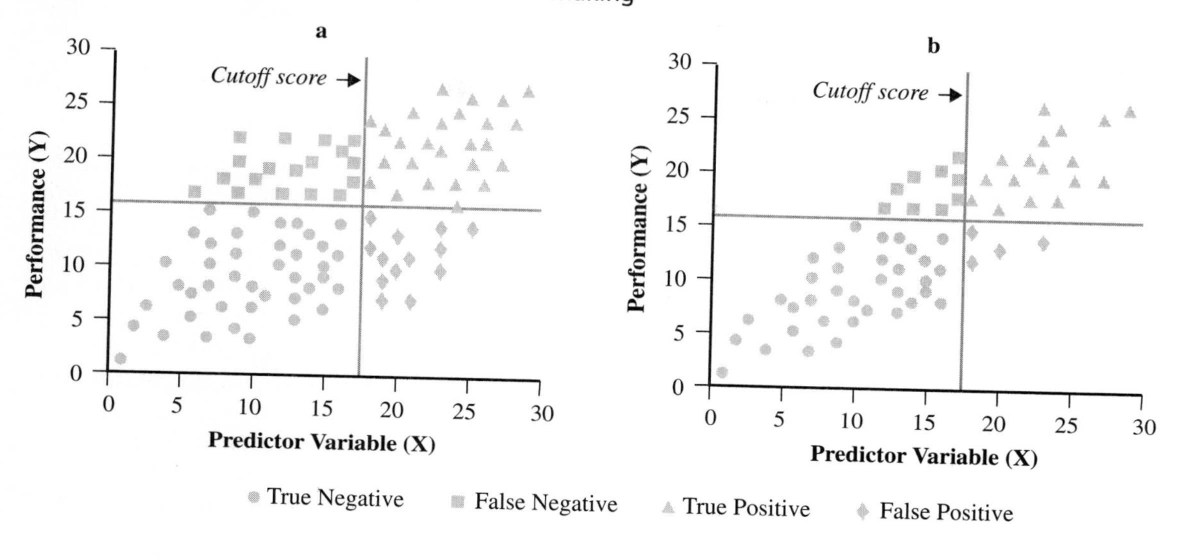

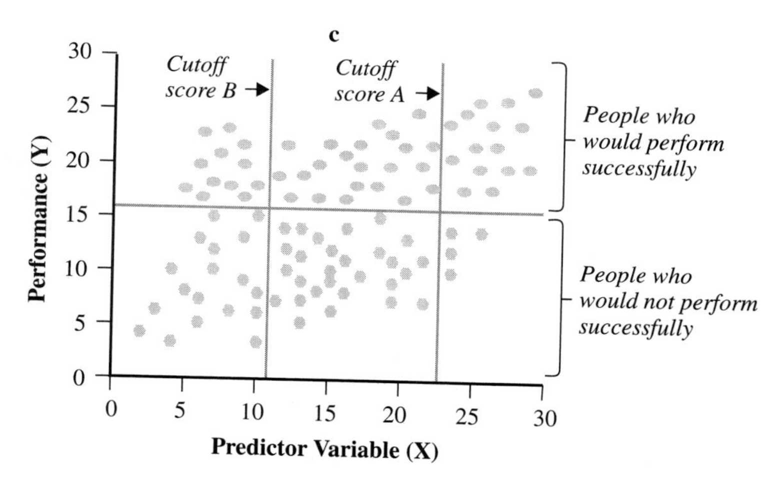

$$\text{Efficiency} = A/(A + D) - (A + B)/(A + B + C + D)$$

Efficiency is the extent to which the system increases the proportion of successful selections. This definition assumes that no selection procedures are presently being used by the organization. If the organization is using some existing system, then the efficiency of the new system can be defined as

$$E = [A/(A + D)]_n - [A/(A + D)]_o$$

where n = new selection system
o = old selection system

In this equation, the only goal of the organization is to maximize the number of true positive decisions and minimize false positives. There is no concern for false negative decisions.

Three factors affect the efficiency of a selection system: validity, selection ratio, and base rate of success.

Validity The validity, or degree of relationship between the predictor variable and job-performance (criterion) variable, affects the efficiency of the selection system.[46] The stronger the relationship, the more "valid" the predictor and the greater the accuracy of the selection decisions based on that predictor. Figure 7.9b presents the relationship of validity to efficiency graphically. (Figures 7.9a, b, and c use the same predictor cutoff and success points.) In Figure 7.9a, the correlation between *X* and *Y* is approximately .50; the efficiency of the predictor is about .17. That is, with random selection, 50 percent of the persons hired are successful, but with a predictor test as the basis for selection, 67 percent of the persons selected are successful ($E = .67 - .50 = .17$). In Figure 7.9b, the validity of the predictor is .75, and the efficiency increases to .27. In other words, random selection yields 50 percent successful employees, but using the predictor test increases the percentage of successful employees hired to 77 percent. Thus, as validity increases, so does efficiency.

Selection Ratio A second factor that affects efficiency is the selection ratio.[47] The **selection ratio (SR)** is defined as the number of job openings divided by the number of job applicants. If the organization has to fill 20 job openings and 100 people apply for them, $SR = 20/100 = .20$. Figure 7.9c illustrates the relationship between the selection ratio and efficiency. Assume that the correlation between *X* and *Y* is .50. If 100 applicants apply for 20 jobs, then the cutoff score (A) on the predictor test is set so that the top 20 applicants are selected. Of those selected, nearly 80 percent will turn out to be successful employees, whereas if no selection test is used, only 50 percent of those hired will be good performers. If 70 job openings have to be filled from 100 applicants, the cutoff score (B) is set to hire the top 70 applicants. In this case, only 55 percent of those selected will be successful performers. When $SR = .20$, $E = .80 - .50 = .30$. When $SR = .70$, $E = .55 - .50 = .05$. Thus, generally, as the selection ratio decreases, efficiency increases, if the validity of the test is constant. However, if *SR* is very small (e.g., one job and 1,000 applicants), the sheer cost of testing the applicants may outweigh any gain due to selecting the one right person for the available job.

Base Rate of Success The **base rate of success (BRS)**, the third factor that affects efficiency, is the proportion of applicants who successfully perform a job when they are hired randomly, without the use of a selection system.[48] Suppose that Acme Paper Company decides to set up a selection system for the job of packer/stacker. The job requires an employee to place 5-pound stacks of paper into boxes, seal the boxes with tape, and stack the boxes on top of other boxes. If Acme Paper hires people randomly, what proportion will be able to perform the job of packer/stacker? Nearly everyone. In this situation, Acme Paper Company will gain very little from the use of a selection test. Suppose, instead, that Acme Paper Company is interested in developing a selection system for a job that only one of 10,000 people performs successfully—that is, a job with a very low BRS. Although the efficiency of the system that could select this one person would be very great, Acme Paper faces a problem. It will probably be impossible to devise such a sensitive system. Generally, midlevel BRSs (.40 to .60) have the highest potential for increased selection efficiency.

The **Taylor-Russell tables** have been developed to show how efficiency varies as a function of validity, selection ratio, and base rate of success.[49] Table 7.4 contains a portion of these tables. The entries in the table represent the proportion of applicants selected who will be successful. Three different base rates of success are represented, along with four different levels of validity, and selection ratios

TABLE 7.4 Examples from the Taylor-Russell Tables

Base Rate of Success (BRS)	*Level of Validity*	*Selection Ratio (SR)*										
.30	*r*	*.05*	*.10*	*.20*	*.30*	*.40*	*.50*	*.60*	*.70*	*.80*	*.90*	*.95*
	.00	.30	.30	.30	.30	.30	.30	.30	.30	.30	.30	.30
	.25	.50	.47	.43	.41	.39	.37	.36	.34	.33	.32	.31
	.50	.72	.65	.58	.52	.48	.44	.41	.38	.35	.33	.31
	.75	.93	.86	.76	.67	.59	.52	.47	.42	.37	.33	.32
.50	*r*	.05	.10	.20	.30	.40	.50	.60	.70	.80	.90	.95
	.00	.50	.50	.50	.50	.50	.50	.50	.50	.50	.50	.50
	.25	.70	.67	.64	.62	.60	.58	.56	.55	.54	.52	.51
	.50	.88	.84	.78	.74	.70	.67	.63	.60	.57	.54	.52
	.75	.99	.97	.92	.87	.82	.77	.72	.66	.61	.55	.53
.70	*r*	*.05*	*.10*	*.20*	*.30*	*.40*	*.50*	*.60*	*.70*	*.80*	*.90*	*.95*
	.00	.70	.70	.70	.70	.70	.70	.70	.70	.70	.70	.70
	.25	.86	.84	.81	.80	.78	.77	.76	.75	.73	.72	.71
	.50	.96	.94	.91	.89	.87	.84	.82	.80	.77	.74	.72
	.75	1.00	1.00	.98	.97	.95	.92	.89	.86	.81	.76	.73

Source: Adapted from H. C. Taylor and J. T. Russell, "The Relationship of Validity Coefficients to the Practical Effectiveness of Tests in Selection," *Journal of Applied Psychology,* Vol. 23, 1939, pp. 565–578.

ranging from .05 to .95. The Taylor-Russell tables can be used to determine the efficiency of a selection system compared with no selection system, or they can be used to compare one selection system with another. For each base rate of success, the row corresponding to $r = 0.00$ represents the use of no selection system, and each entry in this row equals the base rate. Suppose that Acme Paper Company has no present selection procedures and that $BRS = .50$. If the company develops a selection test (test A) where $SR = .40$ and where validity = .25, the proportion of successful employees selected will rise to .60, and the efficiency will be .10 ($E = .60 - .50$). If an alternative predictor test (test B) is available—where validity = .75, $BRS = .50$, and $SR = .40$—the proportion of successful employees selected will be .82. The increased efficiency of using test B instead of test A would be $E = .82 - .60 = .22$. Whether Acme Paper Company decides to use test A or test B might then depend on the cost of test A versus the cost of test B. If test A costs $.50 per applicant to administer, and test B costs $50 per applicant, the gain in efficiency might not be worth the additional cost of test B. Obviously, efficiency is not the only factor that determines the utility of a selection system.

Standard Deviation of Performance in Dollars

Utility models require another concept before utility can be calculated: the **standard deviation of performance in dollars (SDP)**. This variable is much more difficult to measure than the selection ratio or base rate. It is predicated on the assumption that an employer can put a dollar value on the performance of an employee. Many researchers have attempted to measure performance in terms of this dollar criterion.[50]

Proponents of the dollar criterion suggest that an organization should be able to measure the output of an employee and place a dollar value on that output (e.g., an employee produces 600 widgets that are each sold for a profit of $.50). The organization should also be able to compute the cost of the employee to the company (e.g., salary, fringe benefits, and so on). The dollar value of the employee would be equal to the profits attributable to that employee minus the costs to the company of employing the person.

Unfortunately, few jobs allow for such an easy computation of costs versus profits. For example, how can an organization calculate the dollar value of a mid-level manager, or of an assembly-line worker whose performance is directly affected by the actions of employees farther up the line? Sometimes cost accounting procedures have been used to estimate the dollar value of employee performance.[51] Other researchers have suggested that cost accounting procedures are simply not applicable when trying to determine the value of an employee's performance and the utility of selection procedures used to hire that employee.[52] These researchers have developed more subjective procedures that assess SDP using ratings made by job experts.[53] One procedure has shown that the difference in dollar value of an employee representing the 85th percentile level of performance and an employee performing at the 50th percentile level is equal to about 40 percent of the salary of the job.[54]

The greater the standard deviation of performance in dollars, the greater the utility. A **standard deviation** is a statistic that measures the variability of a distribution of scores. Thus, a large standard deviation of performance in dollars means that the dollar value of a high performer is much greater than that of a low performer. A low standard deviation of performance in dollars indicates that there is little difference in the value of high and low performers. Selection systems developed for jobs in which there is little difference in the dollar value of high and low performers will be of less overall utility. Selection systems used for jobs in which performance differences reflect very different levels of employee dollar value will have greater potential utility.

For instance, a valid test for selecting mail clerks may produce less payoff *per hire* than another test of equal validity used to select vice presidents. This is because the value to the organization of hiring a good versus a poor mail clerk is probably substantially less than the value of hiring a good versus a poor vice president. However, the *total* payoff to the organization also depends on the number of persons hired. If fifty good mail clerks are hired using a valid test, their combined contribution to the organization may exceed the utility gained by hiring one good vice president.

To summarize the preceding discussion on factors affecting the benefits to be gained from a selection system, a test is more likely to have utility if the following conditions are present:

- Validity is high.
- The selection ratio is reasonably low.
- The base rate of success is moderate.
- The job has a large standard deviation of performance in dollars.
- Many positions are to be filled.

Costs Associated with Selection

Several different costs are associated with any selection system. One of the most obvious is the cost of testing. Given two selection procedures of equal validity, the test that costs less will provide the organization with the greater value for its investment in selection. Furthermore, if either the selection ratio or base rate of success is extremely low, the organization is faced with the cost of testing many applicants when only a few of them will actually be hired. Another cost issue relevant to selection utility is the differential costs associated with making specific types of selection errors.[55] Consider the costs of making a *false positive* hiring decision—that is, hiring someone who is not a successful performer. These costs are (1) recruiting and testing costs, (2) induction and orientation costs, (3) training costs, (4) employee relations costs when the employee is fired, and (5) costs associated with firing the employee (e.g., severance pay).[56]

Analogously, *false negative* hiring decisions also entail certain costs. These include (1) competitive-advantage costs (e.g., the NFL team that fails to draft a particular player later loses in the Super Bowl because that player scores the winning touchdown against them), and (2) legal costs. False negative applicants often are minority members and/or women. If these individuals file suit against the company and are able to prove that they really were qualified for the job, both actual and reputation costs to the company can be high. These types of costs associated with false negative decisions are often referred to as the *social consequences* of selection decisions.[57]

Traditionally, HR specialists have tried to avoid false positive errors but have paid little attention to false negative errors. Thus, HR specialists have set selection test cutoffs to minimize the number of false positive errors. If the costs associated with both types of selection errors are taken into account, however, employers can achieve the greatest utility by setting cutoff scores that reduce the overall number of both false positive and false negative hiring decisions.[58]

SUMMARY OF KEY POINTS

A personnel selection system requires effective measurement, decision-making, and evaluation methods. The first requirement of a selection instrument is that it be a reliable measure. Reliability can be assessed over time, between forms, or within the context of a single test. If an instrument does not measure something consistently (reliably), it cannot possibly predict a criterion—so it cannot be valid.

Validity is usually established by using one of the criterion-related methods (predictive or concurrent) or by proving that the content of the selection device matches critical job content. When HR specialists try to validate purchased tests for use in their own organizations, they check to be sure that test developers have shown evidence for the construct validity of the test; that is, whether the test correctly measures the trait or ability supposed to be measured. Additional concerns about validation include whether the results of the validation study are stable and useful in subsequent samples of applicants (whether the test cross-validates) and whether the test predicts the job performance of minority and majority group members with equal accuracy and fairness.

Given valid measures, HR specialists must choose a decision-making strategy that takes into account the nature of the job, the number of applicants and job openings, and the costs of testing. Strategies include multiple regression, multiple cutoff, multiple hurdle, and profile matching.

For any selection system, the organization must make an attempt to evaluate the utility of the system. The organization should not wait until after the selection system has been developed and implemented to judge its likely utility. The company should evaluate data on probable validities, selection ratios, previous base rates of success, the standard deviation of performance in dollars, and the cost of tests before the development procedure begins. By analyzing these factors before spending the time, effort, and money to develop a selection system, HR specialists can more wisely develop and use selection procedures in their organizations.

Questions for Discussion

1. Why are the Pearson correlation coefficient and regression analysis important statistical devices in personnel selection?
2. The reliability of a test indicates that the extent to which random error influences test scores. Why is this factor of concern to the HR specialist who is setting up a selection system?
3. What are the different ways of assessing reliability, and what sources of error are captured by each method?
4. How are the predictive and concurrent methods for determining criterion-related validity similar to or different from one another?
5. What is content validity? How does it differ from construct validity?
6. Why should a personnel selection test always be cross-validated?
7. If the proponents of validity generalization are correct, what implications does this assumption have in developing selection systems in organizations?
8. HR specialists can take either a compensatory or a noncompensatory approach to combining information about a job applicant when making a final hire/no-hire decision. How do these two approaches to decision making differ from one another?
9. What is the utility of a personnel selection system? What factors influence the utility of a selection system?

CASE 7.1

The Validation Study

For the past ten years, Eastern Amalgamated Paper Company (EAPCO) has used the Delta Intelligence Test (DIT) to select employees for its unskilled production jobs. There are approximately 1,000 employees in these jobs, and the average turnover rate is high—35 percent per year. Job applicants have not been considered unless they score above the national average score of all employees taking the DIT. This national average score is published yearly by Selection Systems Inc., the developer of the DIT, and is based on the test scores of more than 100,000 job applicants.

In analyzing the hiring patterns of the company, John Williamson, the new manager of human resources at EAPCO, noticed that a large number of black applicants failed the test. For every 100 white applicants, 85 passed the DIT, and approximately 50 were actually hired by the company. In contrast, for every 100 black applicants, 30 passed the DIT, and 20 were subsequently hired. Williamson was concerned about the potential legal implications of this hiring system. He could find no evidence that systematic job analyses had been conducted on the production jobs or that EAPCO had validated the DIT against any measure of job performance. Validity data on the DIT were available from Selection Systems. These data typically consisted of the results of concurrent validation studies conducted by organizations using the DIT. Williamson decided that it was time for a local validation study to be done.

Williamson contacted Validation Consulting Inc. (VCI), a local consulting firm, and hired it to conduct the study. One week later, Steven Pinoche, a partner at VCI, arrived at Williamson's office. Pinoche spent the morning discussing the present selection system with various managers and first-line supervisors at the plant. He returned one week later and presented Williamson with a plan for validating the DIT.

The study was designed as a concurrent validation procedure. Pinoche recommended using just one department in the study in order to save money. This unit included 110 employees, 104 white and 6 black. Because many of these employees had been with the company for several years and had not taken the DIT since their initial hiring, each employee was given the DIT again. At the same time, the supervisor was asked to rate the overall performance of each employee on a 3-point scale of good, average, or poor.

Test scores and performance data for each employee in the study were returned to Pinoche. Statistical analyses were conducted on this data, and a significant correlation was found between DIT scores and rated job performance. In his report to Williamson, Pinoche concluded that the Delta Intelligence Test was related to job performance and was therefore a valid test for use in selecting employees to fill unskilled production jobs.

Six months after the study was completed, James Wilson, a black applicant, took and failed the DIT and, as a result, filed a charge of racial discrimination against EAPCO. The EEOC attempted to conciliate between Wilson and EAPCO, but the company refused to offer an agreement that Wilson would accept. The EEOC decided to file suit against EAPCO in federal court.

Hiring data from EAPCO's personnel records clearly indicate a prima facie case of discrimination, but the company argues that this adverse impact is justifiable because DIT scores are related to performance on the job.

1. Suppose that you are the judge hearing this case. You must evaluate the adequacy of EAPCO's validation study. What would your analysis be?
2. What did EAPCO do right/wrong in the validation project?
3. How confident/skeptical would you be that the DIT is really a good predictor of a job applicant's ability to perform an unskilled production job, as it is being used by EAPCO?

EXERCISE 7.1

Content Validation: An Experiential Exercise

This chapter presented the concept of content validation. Given the difficulties associated with establishing the criterion-related validity of selection tests, content validity is often an acceptable (and sometimes the only) alternative. A procedure for determining content validity is described in Figure 7.5. In this exercise, you will use that procedure to content-validate an actual test of a professor's teaching performance.

Teaching evaluation forms are widely used in universities and colleges to appraise the classroom performance of instructors. Although these evaluations are more often used within a college or university to determine faculty promotions and pay increases, the evaluations can also play an important role in the selection of new instructors for positions in the institution. A job applicant's previous teaching evaluations (from another school) may be used in deciding whether or not the applicant should be hired.

1. Divide into groups of five to ten students.
2. The instructor should give a copy of a teaching evaluation form to the members of each group. Each group can get either the same form or a different form. The form can be the one used in their institution or one from another school.
3. The students in each group serve as the "content validation experts" who make judgments about the validity of the items in the form. Using the procedure described in Figure 7.5, each student rates each item in the teaching evaluation form. Then, based on the ratings of all group members, the group computes the content validity ratio for each item and the content validity index of the form.
4. The groups should report their findings to the class as a whole. If the groups validated the same teaching evaluation form, the class can discuss any differences among the groups in the content validity indexes they computed. If the groups rated different forms, the form with the highest content validity index can be discussed. One of the questions to focus on is, what items were included in the other forms that caused their content validity indexes to be lower?

Notes and References

1. R. M. Guion, "Recruiting, Selection, and Job Placement," in *Handbook of Industrial and Organizational Psychology,* ed. M. D. Dunnette (Chicago: Rand-McNally, 1976), pp. 778–828.
2. For a more detailed description of multiple correlation and regression analysis, see J. Cohen and P. Cohen, *Applied Multiple Regression/Correlation Analysis for the Behavioral Sciences* (Hillsdale, N.J.: Erlbaum and Associates, 1975), pp. 73–122.
3. R. M. Guion, *Personnel Testing* (New York: McGraw-Hill, 1965), Chapter 2.
4. J. C. Nunnally, *Psychometric Theory* (New York: McGraw-Hill, 1967), p. 172.
5. American Psychological Association, *Standards for Educational and Psychological Tests* (Washington, D.C.: APA, 1985).
6. L. J. Cronbach, "Coefficient Alpha and the Internal Structure of Tests," *Psychometrika,* Vol. 16, (1951), pp. 297–334.
7. S. Messick, "Validity," in *Educational Measurement,* ed. R. L. Lim (New York: American Council on Education, Macmillan, 1989) pp. 13–103.
8. *Uniform Guidelines on Employee Selection Procedures* (Washington, D.C.: Bureau of National Affairs, 1979), Society for Industrial and Organizational Psychology, *Principles for the Validation and Use of Personnel Selection Procedures,* 3rd ed., 1987.
9. J. F. Binning and G. V. Barrett, "Validity of Personnel Decisions: A Conceptual Analysis of the Inferential and Evidential Bases," *Journal of Applied Psychology,* Vol. 74, 1989, pp. 478–494; M. R. Carrier, A. T. Dalessio, and S. H. Brown, "Correspondence Between Estimates of Content and Criterion-Related Validity Values," *Personnel Psychology,* Vol. 43, 1990, pp. 85–100; M. D. Dunnette and W. C. Borman, "Personnel Selection and Classification Systems," in *Annual Review of Psychology,* ed. J. Rosenzweig and L. Porter (Palo Alto, Calif.: Annual Reviews, Inc., 1979); Messick, "Validity," pp. 13–103.
10. F. B. Brown, *Principles of Educational and Psychological Testing* (New York: Holt, Rinehart and Winston, 1976).
11. *United States* v. *State of South Carolina,* 445 F. Supp. 1094, 15 FEP 1196 (1977).

12. For an example of the legal importance of this concept, see also *Griggs* v. *Duke Power Co.*, 401 U.S. 424, 3 FEP 175 (1971).

13. R. L. Thorndike, *Personnel Selection: Test and Measurement Techniques* (New York: Wiley, 1949).

14. For a description of several other versions of the basic predictive validity procedure, see R. M. Guion and C. J. Cranny, "A Note on Concurrent and Predictive Validity Designs: A Critical Reanalysis," *Journal of Applied Psychology,* Vol. 67, 1982, pp. 239–244.

15. F. L. Schmidt, J. E. Hunter, and V. W. Urry, "Statistical Power in Criterion-Related Validity Studies," *Journal of Applied Psychology,* Vol. 61, 1976, pp. 473–485.

16. M. Sussman and D. U. Robertson, "The Validity of Validity: An Analysis of Validation Study Design," *Journal of Applied Psychology,* Vol. 71, 1986, pp. 461–468.

17. G. V. Barrett, M. S. Caldwell, and R. A. Alexander, "The Concept of Dynamic Criteria: A Critical Reanalysis," *Personnel Psychology,* Vol. 38, 1985, pp. 41–56.

18. D. L. Deadrick and R. M. Madigan, "Dynamic Criteria Revisited: A Longitudinal Study of Performance Stability and Predictive Validity," *Personnel Psychology,* Vol. 43, 1990, pp. 717–744.

19. *Uniform Guidelines,* p. 30.

20. T. A. Cleary, "Test Bias: Prediction of Grades of Negro and White Students in Integrated Colleges," *Journal of Educational Measurement,* Vol. 5, 1968, pp. 115–124; R. M. Guion, "Employment Tests and Discriminatory Hiring," *Industrial Relations,* Vol. 5, 1966, pp. 20–37.

21. *Golden Rule Insurance Company et al.* v. *Washburn et al.* No. 419–76 (stipulation for dismissal and order dismissing the case), Circuit Court of the 7th Judicial District, Sangamon County, Illinois, 1984; *Allen* v. *Alabama State Board of Education,* No. 81-697-N (consent decree filed with the U.S. District Court, Middle District of Alabama, Northern Division), 1985; F. Drasgow, "Study of the Measurement Bias of Two Standardized Psychological Tests," *Journal of Applied Psychology,* Vol. 72, 1987, pp. 19–29.

22. L. G. Humphreys, "Statistical Definitions of Test Validity for Minority Groups," *Journal of Applied Psychology,* Vol. 58, 1973, pp. 1–4.

23. V. R. Boehm, "Negro-White Differences in Validity of Employment and Training Selection Procedures: Summary of Recent Evidence," *Journal of Applied Psychology,* Vol. 56, 1972, pp. 33–39; J. E. Hunter and F. L. Schmidt, "Differential and Single Group Validity of Employment Tests by Race," *Journal of Applied Psychology,* Vol. 63, 1978, pp. 1–11; F. L. Schmidt and J. E. Hunter, "Employment Testing: Old Theories and New Research Findings," *American Psychologist,* Vol. 36, 1981, pp. 1128–1137.

24. F. Drasgow, "Study of the Measurement Bias of Two Standardized Psychological Tests," *Journal of Applied Psychology,* Vol. 72, 1987, pp. 19–29.

25. F. L. Schmidt and J. E. Hunter, "Development of a General Solution to the Problem of Validity Generalization," *Journal of Applied Psychology,* Vol. 62, 1977, pp. 529–540.

26. F. L. Schmidt, J. E. Hunter, and K. Pearlman, "Task Differences as Moderators of Aptitude Test Validity in Selection: A Red Herring," *Journal of Applied Psychology,* Vol. 66, 1981, pp. 166–185.

27. J. E. Hunter, "Cognitive Ability, Cognitive Aptitudes, Job Knowledge, and Job Performance," *Journal of Vocational Behavior,* Vol. 29, 1986, pp. 340–362.

28. R. M. Madigan, D. Scott, D. L. Deadrick, and J. A. Stoddard, "Employment Testing: The U.S. Job Service Is Spearheading a Revolution," *Personnel Administrator,* September 1986, pp. 102–112.

29. H. G. Osburn and J. C. Callender, "Bias in Validity Generalization Variance Estimates: A Reply to Hoben Thomas," *Journal of Applied Psychology,* Vol. 75, 1990, pp. 328–333.

30. L. L. Wise, J. McHenry, and J. P. Campbell, "Identifying Optimal Predictor Composites and Testing for Generalizability Across Jobs and Performance Factors," *Personnel Psychology,* Vol. 43, 1990, pp. 355–366.

31. H. R. Rothstein, F. L. Schmidt, F. W. Er-

win, W. A. Owens, and C. P. Sparks, "Biographical Data in Employment Selection: Can Validities Be Made Generalizable?" *Journal of Applied Psychology,* Vol. 75, 1990, pp. 175–184.

32. H. H. Meyer, "Predicting Supervisory Ratings Versus Promotional Progress in Test Validation Studies," *Journal of Applied Psychology,* Vol. 72, 1987, pp. 696–697.

33. B. R. Nathan and R. A. Alexander, "A Comparison of Criteria for Test Validation: A Meta-Analytic Investigation," *Personnel Psychology,* Vol. 41, 1988, pp. 517–535.

34. Messick, "Validity."

35. E. J. McCormick, *Job Analysis* (New York: Prentice-Hall, 1979).

36. C. H. Lawshe, "Employee Selection," *Personnel Psychology,* Vol. 5, 1952, pp. 31–34.

37. Nathan and Alexander, "A Comparison of Criteria," pp. 517–535; E. S. Primoff, *Test Selection by Job Analysis: The J-Coefficient, What It Is, How It Works,* Technical Series No. 20 (Washington, D.C.: U.S. Civil Service Commission, Standards Division, 1955).

38. J. R. Hollenbeck and E. M. Whitener, "Criterion-Related Validation for Small Sample Contexts: An Integrated Approach to Synthetic Validity," *Journal of Applied Psychology,* Vol. 73, 1988, pp. 536–544.

39. Cohen and Cohen, *Applied Multiple Regression/Correlation Analysis for the Behavioral Sciences,* pp. 73–122.

40. W. F. Cascio, E. R. Valenzi, and V. Silbey, "Validation and Statistical Power: Implications for Applied Research," *Journal of Applied Psychology,* Vol. 63, 1978, pp. 589–595; W. F. Cascio, E. R. Valenzi, and V. Silbey, "More on Validation and Statistical Power," *Journal of Applied Psychology,* Vol. 65, 1980, pp. 135–138.

41. L. S. Buck, "Guide for Setting of Appropriate Cutting Scores for Written Tests," in *Manpower Planning and Programming,* ed. E. H. Burack and J. W. Walker (Boston: Allyn and Bacon, 1972).

42. T. J. Mauer, R. A. Alexander, C. M. Callahan, J. J. Bailey, and F. H. Dambrot, "Methodological and Psychometric Issues in Setting Cutting Scores Using the Angoff Method," *Personnel Psychology,* Vol. 44, 1991, pp. 235–262.

43. W. F. Cascio, R. A. Alexander, and G. V. Barrett, "Setting Cutoff Scores: Legal, Psychometric, and Professional Issues and Guidelines," *Personnel Psychology,* Vol. 41, 1988, pp. 1–24.

44. L. J. Cronbach and G. C. Gleser, *Psychological Tests and Personnel Decisions* (Champaign, Ill.: University of Illinois Press, 1965).

45. F. L. Schmidt, J. E. Hunter, A. N. Outerbridge, and M. H. Trattner, "The Economic Impact of Job Selection Methods on Size, Productivity, and Payroll Costs of the Federal Work Force: An Empirically Based Demonstration," *Personnel Psychology,* Vol. 39, 1986, pp. 1–30.

46. H. E. Brogden, "On the Interpretation of the Correlation Coefficient as a Measure of Predictive Efficiency," *Journal of Educational Psychology,* Vol. 37, 1946, pp. 64–76.

47. Cronbach and Gleser, *Psychological Tests.*

48. P. E. Meehl and A. Rosen, "Antecedent Probability and the Efficiency of Psychometric Signs, Patterns, or Cutting Scores," *Psychological Bulletin,* Vol. 52, 1955, pp. 194–216.

49. H. C. Taylor and J. T. Russell, "The Relationship of Validity Coefficients to the Practical Effectiveness of Tests in Selection," *Journal of Applied Psychology,* Vol. 23, 1939, pp. 565–578.

50. H. E. Brogden and E. K. Taylor, "The Dollar Criterion—Applying the Cost Accounting Concept to Criterion Construction," *Personnel Psychology,* Vol. 3, 1950, pp. 133–154.

51. W. F. Cascio and J. R. Morris, "A critical reanalysis of Hunter, Schmidt and Coggin's 'Problems and Pitfalls in Using Capital Budgeting and Financial Accounting Techniques in Assessing the Utility of Personnel Programs,'" *Journal of Applied Psychology,* Vol. 75, 1990, pp. 410–417; and S. F. Cronshaw and R. A. Alexander, "Why Capital Budgeting Techniques Are Suited for Assessing the Utility of Personnel Programs: A Reply to Hunter, Schmidt and Coggin," *Journal of Applied Psychology,* Vol. 76, 1991, pp. 454–457.

52. J. E. Hunter, F. L. Schmidt, and T. D. Coggin, "Problems and Pitfalls in Using Capital Budgeting and Financial Accounting Techniques in Assessing the Utility of Personnel Programs," *Journal of Applied Psychology,* Vol. 73, 1988, pp. 522–528.
53. W. F. Cascio and V. Silbey, "Utility of the Assessment Center as a Selection Device," *Journal of Applied Psychology,* Vol. 64, 1979, pp. 107–118.
54. F. L. Schmidt, J. E. Hunter, R. C. McKenzie, and T. W. Muldrow, "Impact of Valid Selection Procedures on Work Force Productivity," *Journal of Applied Psychology,* Vol. 64, 1979, pp. 609–626.
55. L. Siegel and I. M. Lane, *Personnel and Organizational Psychology* (Homewood, Ill.: Irwin, 1982).
56. M. D. Dunnette, *Personnel Selection and Placement* (Monterey, Calif.: Brooks/Cole, 1966), pp. 174–175.
57. Messick, "Validity," pp. 13–103.
58. E. E. Cureton, "A Recipe for a Cookbook," *Psychological Bulletin,* Vol. 54, 1957, pp. 494–497.

8

Assessing Job Candidates: Tools for Selection

The selection process for assessing job applicants follows human resource planning and recruiting. The purpose of selection is to identify from a pool of applicants those individuals who will be hired. Ideally, the people who are hired will be better employees, on average, than those who are rejected. If the selection devices used to assess candidates have been properly chosen and validated, this goal should be realized. Chapter 8 discusses the benefits of proper selection, the selection process itself, and the range of selection devices available to human resource professionals.[1]

OVERVIEW OF THE SELECTION PROCESS

Benefits of Proper Selection

Organizations vary in the complexity of their selection systems. Some merely skim application blanks and conduct brief, informal interviews, whereas others engage in testing, repeated interviewing, background checks, and so on. Although the latter system is more costly per applicant, many benefits are realized from careful, thorough selection. A prominent sociologist has pointed out that organizations need to have members who are both skilled and motivated to perform their organizational roles. Such members can be identified by careful selection or developed after selection by extensive training and socialization. Thus, cursory selection may greatly increase training and monitoring costs, whereas spending more on the selection process will reduce these posthire expenses.[2]

The dollar savings (utility) of appropriate selection procedures can be very large. For instance, researchers estimated that using cognitive ability tests for selection could yield the 5,000-member Philadelphia Police Department $18 million in savings from increased performance for each year's hires. Similarly, the U.S. government, by improving selection strategies for its work force of 3 million people, could save $15.6 billion annually.[3]

The Process of Selection

Most organizations use more than one selection device to gather information about applicants. Often these devices are used sequentially, in a multiple-hurdle decision-making scheme: candidates must do well on an earlier selection device to remain in the running and be assessed by later devices. Figure 8.1 shows a fairly typical order in which selection devices might be used.

Often the HR department takes responsibility for the first few hurdles of assessing application blanks, conducting brief screening interviews, and administering ability tests. Then, one or more managers or supervisors interview the survivors of these hurdles. Finally, pending acceptable reference, offers are made, medical checks are completed, and hiring is finalized. In one survey, the immediate supervisor made the actual decision to hire in 52 percent of the companies; the department/division head made the decision in 32 percent of the firms; and the personnel officer either made or influenced the final decision in 19 percent of the firms.[4] In a more recent survey, companies reported which selection devices they used to hire employees in five job groups, from production workers to managers.[5] The percentage of organizations using each device for each job group is shown in Table 8.1.

ETHICAL PERSPECTIVE

Dilemmas for HR Practitioners

As a staff function, human resource management provides services upon request to other units of the organization, each with its own agenda. One purpose of the HR unit is to develop and enforce practices that comply with the law and provide fair and even-handed treatment for all employees. It is not uncommon for HR managers to be pressured to violate either laws or organizational procedures to achieve an end desired by the requesting unit. The requestor may not be aware of the laws or procedures, in which case the answer is education. In many other situations, however, the requestor simply believes that his or her needs are more important than adherence to a consistent policy, and thus the requestor may attempt to circumvent or subvert the formal system to meet his or her personal desires.

A very common example is the manager who comes to the HRM unit and says, "I have an opening and I already know who I want to hire: Bill Jones. How do I do it?" The HR manager, particularly in a public sector organization, must immediately try to explain the necessity for internal job posting, external advertising, and a truly open search for the best qualified candidate, with affirmative action goals in mind.

Other frequent problems are managers who exaggerate staffing needs in an effort to build an empire or secure a larger budget or who "pad" job descriptions in an effort to get their subordinates' jobs upgraded to a higher pay rate. Though one may sympathize with the managers in these scenarios, fairness, consistency, and internal equity require that the HR professional insist that proper procedures be followed in each case. Unfortunately, such insistence may reduce the HR manager's popularity with the clientele he or she is supposed to serve; it may even impede career progress, depending on whose requests are denied.

A number of other problematic scenarios are described by some practitioners. For instance, one individual tells of cases in which "deals" were habitually cut with employees who were about to be fired for cause. To save face, management would agree to allow the employees to resign and to give them neutral rather than negative references. The HR manager experienced ethical problems with the requirement to give neutral references because the offenses leading to the resignations were often of the type likely to be repeated when these people were hired by unsuspecting new employers.

Another ethical dilemma mentioned by one practitioner involves deciding when to act on hearsay about an employee. Suppose an HR manager hears informally from a friend in the organization that an employee is sexually harassing a subordinate, even though there is no formal complaint from the subordinate; yet the harassment, if it is happening, is entirely unacceptable, and the organization has a duty to remedy the situation. A similar problem might occur when drug or alcohol abuse is suspected, but the employee's accident or absenteeism record is not yet bad enough to trigger official action. Waiting for the problem to intensify to the point at which HR managers are formally notified may expose other employees to continued hazards and increase the employer's liability; yet beginning an investigation on the basis of hearsay may be difficult to justify.

FIGURE 8.1 Typical Order in Which Selection Devices Are Used

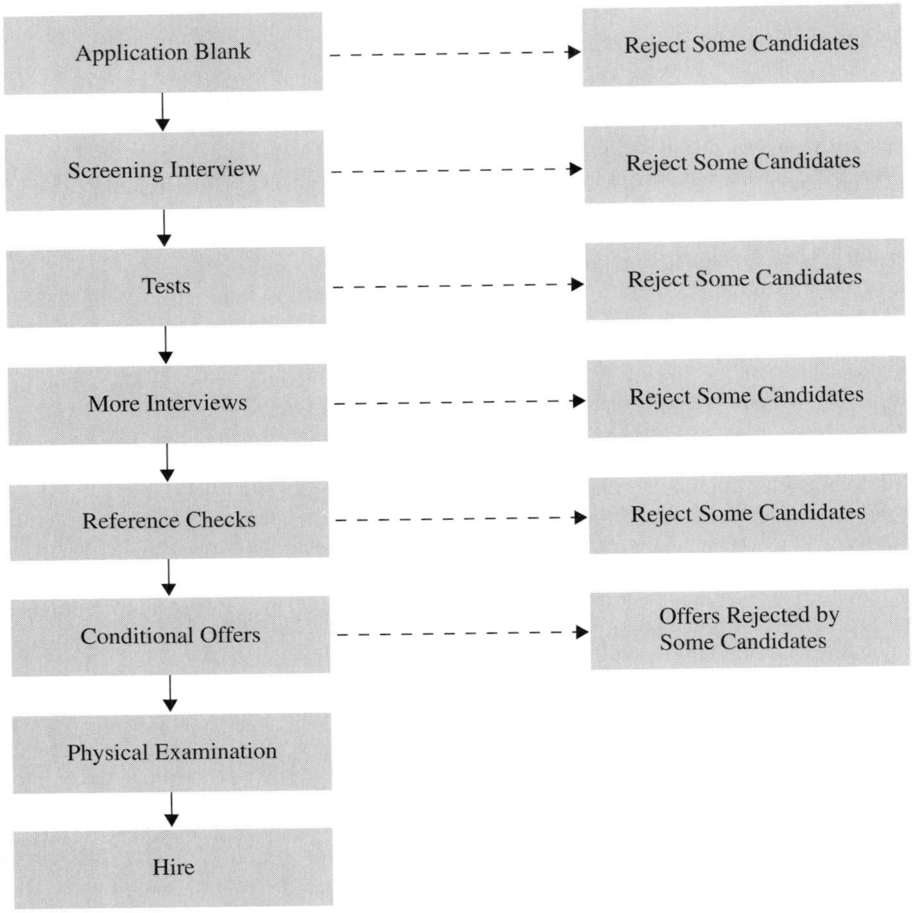

Application Blank	Reject Some Candidates
Screening Interview	Reject Some Candidates
Tests	Reject Some Candidates
More Interviews	Reject Some Candidates
Reference Checks	Reject Some Candidates
Conditional Offers	Offers Rejected by Some Candidates
Physical Examination	
Hire	

APPLICATION BLANKS AND BIODATA

Uses of Application Blanks

The application blank and/or the résumé represents the first selection hurdle for most jobs. Application blanks typically request information about education, work history, and skills, as well as the names and addresses of the applicant and several references. Most of the information requested is factual and can be verified, such as degrees earned or dates of employment. Application blank or résumé fraud is not uncommon. Some studies have found that 20 to 50 percent of candidates falsify or slightly inflate some of their credentials.[6] Thus, seeking outside confirmation of important credentials is a wise practice.

TABLE 8.1 Popularity of Selection Devices for Different Job Classes

	Percent of Companies					
	*Any Job Category**	*Office/ Clerical*	*Production/ Service*	*Professional/ Technical*	*Commissioned Sales*	*Managers/ Supervisors*
(Number of companies)	*(245)*	*(245)*	*(221)*	*(237)*	*(96)*	*(243)*
Skill performance test/or work sample	63%	55%	19%	10%	4%	3%
Medical examination	57	43	57	47	46	45
Mental ability test	31	23	10	8	9	9
Job knowledge test	27	14	14	14	3	5
Drug test	26	21	26	22	23	21
Personality test	17	1	2	6	23	13
Assessment center test	12	**	1	3	4	10
Physical abilities test	11	1	12	2	1	1
Written honesty test	7	4	6	2	4	3
Polygraph test	5	2	4	2	5	2
Genetic screening	3	2	2	2	—	1
AIDS test	1	**	**	1	—	**
Other	2	**	1	1	1	1

Note: Percentages for each job category group are based on the number of organizations that provided data for that category, as shown by the numbers in parentheses.

*Percentages in this column show the proportion of all responding organizations that administer a pre-employment test to applicants in any job category.

**Less than 0.5%

Source: Reprinted with permission from *Recruiting and Selection Procedures*, Personnel Policies Forum Survey No. 146, p. 17 (May 1988). Copyright 1988 by The Bureau of National Affairs, Inc. (800-372-1033).

Most organizations use application blanks or résumés to screen out candidates who do not meet the minimum job specifications on education or experience. Beyond these basics, a manager or HR officer may informally evaluate the application to find the candidates who look most promising. The criteria applied in making this judgment may not be explicit, job related, or consistent from one screener to the next, and so may pose a potential legal problem.

A second way that organizations can use application blank data is to apply a validated weighting scheme, in which only items known to relate to later job success are scored and utilized in decision making. **Weighted application blank (WAB)** procedures have been shown to produce scores that predict performance, tenure, and employee theft. Because the weights are valid and are applied consistently to all applicants, this method of using application blank data is more defensible than the above-mentioned informal evaluation.

Biodata is a term used to refer to any type of personal history, experience, or education information. Some organizations use a biographical-information questionnaire instead of or in addition to the usual application blank. These biodata questionnaires may be much more detailed than application blanks. Sample questions might include: "Do you repair mechanical things in your home, such as appliances?" "As a child, did you collect stamps?" or "How many times did your family move while you were growing up?" One such biodata question—"Did you ever build a model airplane that flew?"—was almost as powerful a predictor of success in flight training during World War II as the entire U.S. Air Force battery of selection tests.[7] Biodata characteristics that have been found helpful in selecting life insurance agents include educational attainment, financial success and stability, and "natural market"—that is, whether the candidate's friends and acquaintances are the sort of people who tend to buy life insurance.[8]

Questions to Avoid on an Application Blank

To comply with federal employment laws, a firm must not discriminate in hiring on the basis of age, race, color, sex, religion, national origin, or non-job related handicap. This does not mean that it is illegal for a recruiter to ask about age, religion, and so on in the selection process; it is just illegal for the recruiter or interviewer to act on this information in a discriminatory fashion. In the interests of playing it safe, however, interviewers should avoid questions about any of these subjects unless they are clearly job related. Such questions are sometimes illegal under state and city human rights laws.

In addition, interviewers should avoid questions that appear neutral but cause disparate impact if used as selection standards—for example, questions about height and weight. Examples of inquiries that tend to exclude a disproportionate share of minorities are those concerning arrest record, type of military discharge, credit rating, and home ownership. Table 8.2 lists some permissible and inadvisable questions. Employers should bear in mind that they can and should ask any truly job-related questions. Accordingly, when interviewing candidates for the job of a bank guard, the recruiter for the bank should ask about armed robbery convictions; when hiring for a job that involves control of money, the recruiter should ask about embezzlement convictions; and when selecting truck drivers, the recruiter should ask about traffic violations.

Validation and Biodata

Overall Level of Validity In most studies that compare the validity of different types of predictors, empirically scored biodata are one of the strongest predictors of subsequent job behavior.[9] Biodata have predicted success in occupations as

TABLE 8.2 Questions Not to Ask Job Candidates*

Topic	*Question*
Name	Mrs., Mr., Miss, Ms.? Maiden name?
Address	Own or rent home?
Birthplace	Birthplace of applicant, spouse, parents? (Inadvisable question because it indicates national origin.)
Age	Age, date of birth, year of high school graduation?
Religion	Religion, religious holidays celebrated, pastor/rabbi's name as a reference?
Race or Color	Race, color of hair or eyes, photo with application?
Citizenship	Of what country are you a citizen? (Ask only, Do you have permission to live and work in the United States?)
Language	Mother tongue?
Clubs and Organizations	What organizations do you belong to? (Inadvisable question because it may indicate sex, nationality, or race.)
Sex	Male or female? Sexual preference? Are you pregnant?
Family	Marital status, number of dependents, plans for more children and child care?
Height and Weight	What is your height and weight? (Ask only if height and weight are bona fide occupational qualifications.)
Handicaps	Do you have any handicaps?
Arrests	Have you ever been arrested?
Convictions	Have you ever been convicted of a crime? (Ask only about recent or job-related convictions.)
Military Record	Type of discharge?

*For more information, see Clifford M. Koen, Jr., "The Pre-employment Inquiry Guide," *Personnel Journal,* October 1980, pp. 825–829; and Richard S. Lowell and Jay DeLoach, "EEO: Are You Overlooking the Application Form?" *Personnel,* July–August 1982, pp. 49–55.

diverse as U.S. Navy underwater demolitions expert, naval midshipman, pilot, office worker, engineer, research scientist, salesperson, supervisor, and manager.[10] James Asher offers the following theories for the high predictive power of biodata.

1. Nonfiction theory. Reporting on the verifiable aspects of one's past history reveals the truth about one's entire relevant past. A person's past history probably provides a sounder basis for predicting future behavior than does a short experience such as the interview, in which candidates are on their best behavior and can present an artificially positive picture of themselves.

2. Relevant item theory. Weighted application blanks are valid because the only items that receive weights are those that are individually valid. Thus, every item is related to the criterion. In contrast, in most tests only the total score is validated against the criterion. If some individual items do not predict job success, they are still part of the total score and may depress the overall validity of the test.

3. Point-to-point theory. Biodata use past behavior to directly predict future behavior of the same type. There is no need to hypothesize or measure intervening constructs that may be imperfectly related to behavior, either past or future. For instance, high school grade point average (GPA) is the best predictor of college GPA. There is no need to measure an abstract trait such as verbal ability or intelligence to predict college GPA.[11]

Constructing a Weighted Application Blank (WAB) There are several procedures for deriving valid application blank weighting schemes. In all of them, the first step is deciding what criterion to predict and defining high and low levels of this criterion. For instance, if tenure is the criterion of interest, *high* could be defined as staying at least one year after hire and *low,* as leaving before the end of one year. The steps involved in deriving weights are described in Figure 8.2 and Table 8.3. Before they are used to screen new applicants, the weights must be cross-validated to ensure that they are stable and generalizable to a different sample rather than merely the result of chance relationships in the development sample.

Unfortunately, relatively few organizations use WABs, even though WABs tend to be quite helpful in predicting performance. They are also quick and inexpensive to apply, as well as easy to develop and validate, given a suitable sample size. In the absence of large sample sizes, it may be possible to construct a content-valid version of the application blank—specifically, an experience or accomplishment record.

Experience and Accomplishment Records

Rather than relying on informal methods of evaluating candidate training, job experience, and accomplishments, some organizations are beginning to use content-valid **job-experience questionnaires** to screen candidates for technical and professional jobs. The usual procedure is to conduct a job analysis by the task inventory method, in order to identify the most important or time-consuming tasks. The results of this job analysis are turned into questions about past work experience with each task or with each type of equipment used. Usually a content-evaluation panel of job experts verifies the job relatedness of each question.

Applicants answer each task question by selecting one of the following responses: "I have never done this task"; "I have done it under supervision"; "I have done it on my own"; or "I have supervised and/or taught this task." To discourage inflated self-ratings, the questionnaire may ask applicants to list the names and addresses of people who can verify their experience with each task. In addition, some job-experience questionnaires contain a few plausible-sounding but nonexistent task statements (such as typing from audio-FORTRAN reports, operating matriculation machines, monitoring fiscal binaries, or cleaning chartels). Applicants who claim to have performed these nonexistent tasks may be exaggerating their experience with real tasks.[12]

FIGURE 8.2 Steps in Constructing a Weighted Application Blank

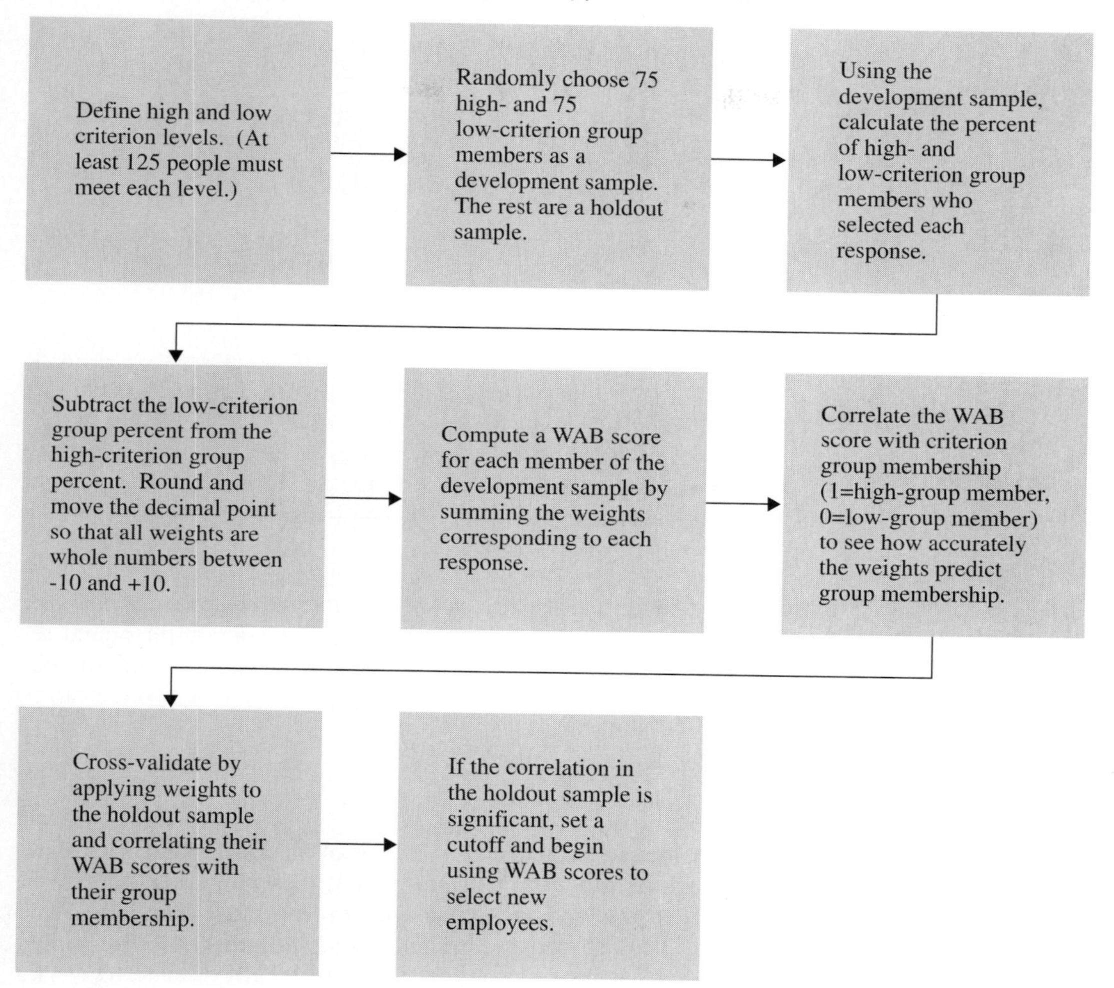

When selecting experienced professionals to hire or promote, a firm may find it helpful to use a specially structured, content-valid **accomplishment record**. To develop such a form for promoting attorneys, a federal regulatory agency used the following procedure. First, it performed a job analysis using the critical incident method. Incidents were sorted into eight job dimensions, including research, oral communication and assertive advocacy, independent work, and use of legal knowledge. Three hundred attorneys then provided examples of their accomplishments on each dimension. Next, a group of job experts applied a complicated sorting and rating procedure to generate keys and guidelines for scoring applicant accomplishments. The agency trained evaluators to use the keys reliably. Finally,

TABLE 8.3 Application Blank Responses and Corresponding Weights

	Percent of Responses			
Criterion	*Low*	*High*	*Difference*	*Weight*
1. Number of jobs held in last five years:				
1	10%	50%	40%	4
2	30	30	0	0
3 or more	60	20	−40	−4
2. Reason for leaving last job:				
Better opportunity	10	40	30	3
Dissatisfied	20	10	−10	−1
Laid off	40	40	0	0
Fired	30	10	−20	−2
3. Number of languages spoken:				
1	70	60	−10	−1
2	30	30	0	0
3	0	10	10	1

the agency applied the system to assess the accomplishments of attorneys seeking promotion. Figure 8.3 shows one of the dimensions from the accomplishment record, guidelines for scoring that dimension, and a specific accomplishment submitted by a candidate for promotion.[13]

TESTS

A **test** is a means of obtaining a standardized sample of behavior. Tests are **standardized** in content, scoring, and administration. That is, every time the test is given, its questions are identical or, in the case of tests with more than one form, equivalent. The scoring rules are constant. The administration is also the same: all test takers get the same instructions, have the same length of time to work, and take the test under similar conditions of lighting, noise, and temperature. Because tests are standardized, they provide information about job candidates that is comparable for all applicants. Other aspects of competing candidates cannot be compared so readily. For instance, grade point averages could be compared, but if candidates went to different schools or took somewhat different courses, this measure would not mean exactly the same thing for all applicants.

Testing and EEO

Before Title VII of the Civil Rights Act became law, quite a number of firms tested applicants for blue-collar jobs. General intelligence and mechanical comprehension tests were especially popular, although they were seldom empirically vali-

FIGURE 8.3 Sample Dimension of an Accomplishment Record

Using Knowledge

General Definition

Interpreting and synthesizing information to form legal strategies, approaches, lines of argument, etc.; developing new configurations of knowledge, innovative approaches, solutions, strategies, etc.; selecting the proper legal theory; using appropriate lines of argument, weighing alternatives and drawing sound conclusions.

Guidelines for Rating

In Using Knowledge, accomplishments at the lower levels are characterized by the resolution of legal issues which lack impact and importance or issues easily resolved by existing case law or precedent. At progressively higher levels, the accomplishments describe the formulation of increasingly complex legal strategies or the resolution of difficult legal issues which may be included in a case or procedures of substantial import. At the highest levels, accomplishments may refer to the assumption of significant personal responsibility in drafting major rules, regulations, proposed statutes, or like materials. Awards or commendations are likely.

Time period:

General statement of what you accomplished:

I was given the task of transferring our antitrust investigation of into a coherent set of pleadings presentable to and the Commission for review and approval within the context of the Commission's involvement in shopping centers nationwide.

Description of exactly what you did:

I drafted the complaint and proposed order and wrote the underlying legal memo justifying all charges and proposed remedies. I wrote the memo to the Commission recommending approval of the consent agreement. For the first time, we applied antitrust principles to this novel factual situation.

Awards or formal recognition:
none

The information verified by: *John* *Compliance*

Source: From Leaetta M. Hough, "Development and Evaluation of the 'Accomplishment Record' Method of Selecting and Promoting Professionals," *Journal of Applied Psychology,* February 1984, pp. 135–146. Copyright 1984 by the American Psychological Association. Reprinted by permission of the author.

dated for the jobs in question. As Title VII was interpreted by the courts over the years, the doctrine of disparate impact developed, along with the requirement to demonstrate the job relatedness (validity) of tests that excluded a disproportionate share of minority applicants. When the courts rejected some reasonably well conducted validity studies as inadequate, many firms simply gave up testing in order to avoid the possibility of litigation and the cost of further validation.[14] Instead, they used unscored and subjective procedures for hiring and promoting decisions.

In the late 1960s and early 1970s, there were many allegations that tests were culturally biased and thus unfair to minority applicants. Extensive research and a report by a blue-ribbon committee of the National Research Council (NRC), however, indicates that properly constructed ability tests do measure people of different races with equal accuracy.[15] Any differences in test performance that may occur seem to mirror true differences in ability and in likely job performance. The NRC study committee therefore recommended that tests cease being the scapegoat for blocking minority achievement and instead be used, together with other measures of capability, to help identify and select qualified individuals.[16]

In 1988, the U.S. Supreme Court ruled that informal and subjective methods of making employment and advancement decisions were not immune from legal challenge if they created adverse impact.[17] This ruling opened the door for a return to testing, on the basis that a properly validated test would be more effective and stand up to legal challenge better than an informal decision-making procedure. As shown in Table 8.1, 31 percent of the firms in a national survey used cognitive ability tests, whereas 27 percent relied on job knowledge tests. Less than half of the respondents, however, said that their tests had been validated according to the *Uniform Guidelines on Employee Selection Procedures*.[18]

Paper-and-Pencil Tests of Ability

Properly chosen paper-and-pencil tests of cognitive ability have been found to have high validity and utility in the selection process.[19] Such ability tests are usually developed by psychologists and are purchased by organizations from test publishers. Tests that are readily available cover such abilities as general intelligence, numerical ability, verbal ability, clerical ability, abstract reasoning, and mechanical aptitude.[20] Some large organizations or industry associations employ psychologists to develop and validate tests suited to their particular needs, such as computer programming aptitude or stockbroker aptitude. The U.S. Army has recently completed a massive, seven-year project to develop additional selection and placement tests for new recruits.[21]

In the past, industrial psychologists have recommended the use of tests that measure very specific and visibly job-related abilities, such as mechanical aptitude for mechanical jobs and verbal aptitude for clerical jobs. There is increasing evidence, however, that the single construct of general cognitive ability, or intelligence, underlies scores on a number of different specific ability tests and that general cognitive ability predicts success on virtually all jobs.[22] Thus, we may see a return to testing of general cognitive ability, at least for preliminary applicant screening, and the use of more specific ability tests for placement or further selection within groups of similar general ability.[23]

As discussed in Chapter 7, the procedure for empirical validation begins with job analysis, followed by selection of potential predictors, development of criteria, and collection and analysis of validity data. The selection of potential predictors is very important. Because so many published tests are available, a firm must collect information and consider it carefully before selecting several tests for a validation effort. The choice process should involve reading test reviews written by knowledgeable people and carefully reading the **test manual**, which details test content, purpose, administration, scoring, and developmental procedures. Among the several characteristics to look for in a published test are the following:[24]

- *Specific ability assessed*. The test should measure aptitudes or abilities that make sense for the job in question. For instance, for the job of proofreader, a firm might try a test of spelling ability.
- *Reliability*. The test should have high internal consistency reliability and reliability over time. Tests that are used to make important decisions about individuals, as in the selection process, must have high reliability (at least .80 but preferably higher).
- *Proper test development procedures*. Developing a test entails much more than writing questions on a piece of paper. HR managers should check to be sure that thorough test development procedures have been followed. These procedures include item and factor analysis, trying out successive versions of the test on large samples of people, developing evidence for the construct validity of the test, and compiling normative data on large samples of people.
- *Administrative ease*. HR professionals must consider whether the test can be given to a group of people at the same time or whether it must be administered individually; how much time and expertise are required to administer, score, and interpret the test; and how much the test materials will cost.
- *Past success*. HR specialists should find out whether past empirical validation studies on similar jobs have been successful, the extent to which the test is being used in the industry, and the record (if any) of the test in EEO proceedings.

We have been referring to these tests as paper-and-pencil tests to distinguish them from performance tests (work samples and trainability tests), which are discussed in the next section. Nevertheless, some standard written tests are now administered and scored by computer rather than on paper. An additional advance is to program the computer to create a customized test for each candidate by selecting items on the basis of the correctness of past answers. For instance, if a moderately difficult item is answered correctly, the computer will next present a more difficult item. If the test taker fails this item, the computer will next choose an item between the first and second in difficulty. Called **adaptive testing**, this method quickly zeroes in on the person's true ability level by selecting the most diagnostic items for the person being tested.[25]

Work Sample and Trainability Tests

Work sample and trainability tests ask applicants to do a portion of the job to demonstrate that they have the skill to perform or to learn the job. Because these tests are developed directly from a thorough job analysis and are double-checked by one or more panels of job experts, they are said to have a *point-to-point correspondence* with the job and are considered content-valid. Properly developed tests of this sort need not be empirically validated. Work sample and trainability tests are the most popular type of testing presently being conducted for employment purposes, with 63 percent of firms using "skill performance" or work sample tests.

Work Sample Tests **Work sample tests** are used when the applicant is expected to possess one or more crucial job skills—skills that the organization does not intend to teach to new hires. After conducting a thorough job analysis to verify the level and need for these kinds of skills, the HR specialist can construct a carefully standardized work sample test. For example, if 80 percent of the job of secretary requires typing manuscripts from handwritten copy, then the work sample test should include typing from handwritten copy. The tester should give all candidates the same copy, equipment, instructions, and length of time to complete the test. Scoring standards that have been developed in advance should be applied consistently for all applicants.

In a recent application of work sample testing, one company developed a set of four role plays for selecting telemarketing representatives. Candidates for telephone sales jobs made two simulated "cold calls" and returned two calls to hypothetical clients who had already indicated interest in the product. The supervisor playing the role of the client was trained to follow each of the four scripts fairly closely. This supervisor and another trained supervisor who also listened to the calls rated the candidate on communication, social sensitivity, sales ability, and overall performance. In a concurrent validation design, a composite of these ratings significantly predicted telephone sales performance.[26] See Table 8.4 for further examples of work sample tests.

Work sample tests may also be paper-and-pencil tests of job knowledge. For instance, the HR specialist might develop a written test assessing knowledge of electrical standards to help select building inspectors. Some firms have used technical reading comprehension tests to assess candidates applying for jobs in which employees need to obtain critical information from manuals or other written sources.[27]

There are two other important points to remember about work sample tests. First, the work sample test does not need to represent the entire job. Some skills may be better assessed by an interview or an ability test, and certain aspects of

TABLE 8.4 Work Sample Tests

	Test of Skill	*Definition*
Construction Superintendent	Blueprint reading	Locate errors in blueprints.
	Scrambled subcontractors test	Correctly order the desired sequence of 30 building subcontractors needed to construct a building from start to finish.
	Construction-error recognition test	Locate errors (25 in all) built into a small test building.
	Planning and scheduling exercise	Matching employee skills to job and schedule demands in a written exercise.
	Structured interview	Questions focusing on security of tools and materials, site safety, relationships to building inspector and other regulators, and ethical issues in dealing with subcontractors.
Police Emergency Operator/Dispatcher	Listening, recording, and spelling test	Listen to tape-recorded emergency calls and correctly record important information on forms provided.
	Memory test	Recall information on locations and activities of several patrol units after information has been presented orally.
	Phone-call simulation	Role-play the handling of calls from distraught callers in simulated emergency situations. Callers are role-played with experienced operators trained to behave consistently with all applicants. Scores are based on skill and judgment in calming the caller and eliciting the most important information.

Sources: For first example (construction superintendent), David D. Robinson, "Content-Oriented Personnel Selection in a Small Business," *Personnel Psychology,* Spring 1981, pp. 77–87. For second example (police emergency operator/dispatcher), Neal Schmitt and Cheri Ostroff, "Operationalizing the 'Behavioral Consistency' Approach: Selection Test Development Based on a Content-Oriented Strategy," *Personnel Psychology,* Spring 1986, pp. 91–108.

the job that can be readily taught to new hires should not be included. Second, the skills that are tested should be *important* skills, whether or not they take up a large portion of time on the job.[28]

Trainability Tests **Trainability tests** are used for semiskilled jobs in which the candidate is not expected to know the skill when applying for the job. The first part of the process consists of a carefully standardized period of instruction during which the trainer introduces a task, explains and demonstrates each step, and has the candidate perform the task once or twice while being coached. The second portion is the test, during which the candidate performs the task several times without coaching. The trainer observes and uses a checklist to record errors. At the conclusion of the performance period, the instructor rates the overall trainability of the candidate.

Figure 8.4 is an instructor's evaluation form used in trainability tests for overlock sewing machine operators who have been taught to sew a simple bag. Trainability tests have been used successfully for sewing-machine operators, electronic assemblers, bricklayers, carpenters, lathe operators, milling-machine operators, and a variety of simple U.S. Navy jobs. In addition, they have been used to select current employees for advanced training on new digital equipment in the telephone industry.[29]

Advantages of Work Sample and Trainability Tests Work sample and trainability tests have many advantages. First, when empirical validation studies have been conducted, the predictive power of work sample tests has been found to be quite high.[30] Trainability tests have shown moderate validities with job success, though the strength of the correlations sometimes diminishes over time, indicating that eventually even less trainable employees are able to learn the job. Second, work sample and trainability tests can be developed and used even for very small samples, unlike tests requiring empirical validation. Third, these tests tend to have less adverse impact then cognitive ability tests. In addition, they possess excellent face validity; thus, applicants who do poorly can readily understand why they are being rejected and probably will not file complaints of unfair treatment. Finally, since work sample and trainability tests embody important aspects of the job, they can serve as realistic job previews. Candidates who do not enjoy the work sample may choose to turn down a job offer, thus sparing the organization the expense of hiring, training, and then losing an employee to early turnover.[31]

Interest and Personality Inventories, Honesty Tests

Unlike the tests already described, interest inventories and personality tests do not have *correct* answers. The intent of these tests is to elicit *self-descriptive* answers. Measures of interest, personality, and honesty must be developed as carefully as measures of cognitive ability. In evaluating such measures, one would expect to see a complete test manual detailing extensive development work utilizing large samples. In other words, the types of tests described here are *not* the same as the seven- or eight-item "personality test," one might find in the magazine section of a Sunday newspaper.

Interest Inventories In an **interest inventory**, the applicant answers questions that are meant to pinpoint his or her likes, dislikes, preferences, and so on. Two widely used inventories are the **Kuder Preference Record** and the **Strong-Campbell Interest Inventory**. Figure 8.5 shows questions from the Strong-Campbell Interest Inventory. On the basis of many such questions, interest-profile scores are generated for each test taker. These profiles are then matched with the average profiles of successful incumbents in different occupations. If the test taker's interests

FIGURE 8.4 Instructor's Scoring Sheet for a Trainability Test

Overlock Trainability Assessment Form

Factory ______________________ *Assessor* ______________________

Name ______________________ *Date* ______________________

	Bag 1	Bag 2	Bag 3
Aligns wrong seam first			
Presents incorrect corner			
Forgets to position cloth correctly			
Forgets to align seam			
Puts thumb on top			
Does not use fingers of left hand correctly			
Does not use fingers of right hand correctly			
Seam not completed in one sew			
Does not remember cutting method *on last seam*			

Other errors (please describe)

Total errors

Overall ratings

Positioning of hands good	Always	generally	sometimes	rarely
Positioning of feet good	Always	generally	sometimes	rarely
Notices errors and subsequently corrects	Always	generally	sometimes	rarely

Please circle appropriate letter.

A Extremely good. The assessor would expect him [/her] to become a very good machinist in a short time.

B Fairly good without being outstanding. The assessor would expect him [/her] to reach 100 performances in a reasonable time.

C Good enough for simple work. The assessor would expect him [/her] to become a steady worker on a simple machine or task.

D Would have difficulty in training. The assessor would expect him [/her] to take longer training and to perform a simple task.

E Would not be trainable. Even with a great deal of attention, he [/she] would not make the grade, even on an easy operation.

Source: From I. T. Robertson and R. M. Mindel, "A Study of Trainability Testing," *Journal of Occupational Psychology,* June 1980, pp. 131–138. Reprinted by permission.

FIGURE 8.5 Selected Items from the Strong-Campbell Interest Inventory

I. Choose whether you like, dislike, or are indifferent to the following:

A. Occupations:
- Advertising executive
- Judge
- Professional gambler
- YWCA staff director

B. School Subjects:
- Algebra
- Dramatics
- Mechanical drawing
- Physics

C. Activities
- Adjusting a carburetor
- Taking responsibility
- Arguments
- Pursuing bandits in a sheriff's posse

D. Amusements:
- Golf
- Looking at things in a hardware store
- Formal dress affairs
- Playing chess

II. Indicate your preference in each of these pairs of activities:
- Selling things house to house/Gardening
- Drawing a definite salary/ Receiving a commission
- Working in a large corporation with little chance of being president before age 55/ Working for yourself in a small business

III. Indicate whether or not these statements describe you:
- Have more than my share of novel ideas
- Win friends easily
- Stimulate the ambitions of my associates

Source: From Lesly Berger, "Starting Over: Would You Be Happier Doing Something Else?" *Working Woman*, June 1985, pp. 124–127. Reprinted by permission from *Working Woman* magazine. Copyright 1985 by Working Woman Inc.

match those of a physician, for instance, then the assumption is made that the test taker may be suited for this occupation.

Interest inventories are often used for vocational guidance but seldom for selection. One reason is that they are quite transparent. Applicants can easily tailor their responses to make themselves appear more suitable for a particular job. In any case, the match of interests to job requirements seems to be a better predictor of job satisfaction than of job performance. Interest inventories may be used after hire for placement purposes, to help a firm assign the most suitable person to each open position. When the inventory is used for this purpose rather than selection, it is more reasonable to assume that the test taker will be motivated to respond honestly.

Personality Inventories **Personality inventories** are sets of objectively scored questions or statements to which the test taker responds *yes* if the item is self-descriptive and *no* if it is not. Some personality inventories are long—up to 400 questions or even more—and some ask extremely personal questions about religious beliefs, sexual fantasies, and other non-work-related issues that an interviewer would never even consider asking. Applicants may justifiably feel that their privacy has been invaded when asked to take some personality tests.

There are many well-developed personality inventories available for purchase. Most give scores on a number of traits, such as dominance, tolerance, extroversion, aggression, self-esteem, authoritarianism, neuroticism, and independence. Even though these inventories are scored objectively, their proper interpretation may require special training.

Historically, predictive validities have tended to be lower for personality measures than for other types of tests.[32] These low validities have been attributed to (1) the transparency of some personality inventories, (2) the "shotgun" approach of attempting to find relationships between many personality dimensions and job performance without giving much thought to the actual demands of the job, and (3) the fact that very few jobs require one and only one type of personality for success. There may be several ways to do the same job well, perhaps by being diligent or creative or persuasive. Thus, for many years industrial psychologists have recommended that personality tests not be used in selection. Recently, however, a number of studies have shown that appropriately chosen personality measures (with a logical connection to job demands) often do help predict interpersonal aspects of job success, although cognitive ability measures remain the best predictors of job performance.[33]

Recent advances in understanding the dimensions of personality seem likely to bear fruit in the selection arena. Until the last few years, there was no clear consensus on the structure of personality, and various personality inventories assessed a differing number of traits, from one or two to sixteen or more. Factor analyses of large numbers of these inventories have now revealed that much of the variance is accounted for by the "big five" personality dimensions defined in Table 8.5. When past selection research is categorized into these five factors, there is evidence that some personality dimensions are consistently related to job success. For instance, conscientiousness is related to success in job training, to

TABLE 8.5 The "Big Five" Personality Dimensions

1. Extraversion ⟷ Introversion
2. Friendliness, agreeableness ⟷ Hostility, noncompliance
3. Neuroticism ⟷ Emotional stability
4. High Conscientiousness, dependability, and self-control ⟷ Low Conscientiousness, dependability, and self-control
5. High Intellect, High Openness to Experience and New Ideas ⟷ Low Intellect, Low Openness to Experience and New Ideas

Source: Table designed from material appearing in Figure 1, page 421 of the *Annual Review of Psychology*, volume 41, 1990.

job performance, and to personnel data such as absenteeism and disciplinary actions on virtually all jobs. Openness to experience predicts success in training, while extraversion is positively related to success in management and sales.[34] None of these correlations are large, but they do exist and may be of use when combined with appropriate ability measures.

An example of a particularly appropriate use of personality tests in selection is provided by a nuclear utility company. To meet a Nuclear Regulatory Commission requirement that reactor operators be emotionally stable, the company retained a psychological consulting firm to assess this personality trait in applicants. The psychologists first performed a job analysis and collected critical incidents of unreliability or emotional instability among nuclear plant operators. Then the consultants clearly defined the construct of *behavioral unreliability* and selected subscales from several existing personality inventories to assess the various aspects of unreliability. They also developed an interview procedure to assess these aspects. The company uses the test and interview procedures to screen candidates for high-risk jobs. It rejects the least stable ones, then bases further selections from the stable group on job-related ability rather than personality.[35]

Honesty Tests Many employers today are interested in screening out job candidates who may be likely to steal from them. Estimates of the cost to American business of employee theft, pilferage, or unexplained inventory shrinkage range from $5 billion to $40 billion per year.[36] Employers who subscribe to the "bad apple" theory believe that rejecting potential thieves and hiring only honest employees will greatly reduce losses. This view is only partly correct, since research has shown that posthire factors such as pay equity, job satisfaction, and opportunity to steal also play a role in determining actual theft.[37]

Traditionally two methods have been used to identify potentially dishonest employees: polygraph examinations and paper-and-pencil tests. The polygraph, or lie detector, measures and graphs respiration, blood pressure, and perspiration while the person being tested answers questions. Doubts about the validity of the polygraph and horror stories of honest individuals who were discharged or denied employment because of erroneous polygraph results have led to legal restrictions on the use of polygraphs.

The Employee Polygraph Protection Act of 1988 prohibits private sector employers from using polygraph tests on applicants or employees, with a few exceptions. Companies that provide security services or manufacture and distribute controlled drugs may continue to use polygraphs; polygraph tests may also be used for investigating specific crimes against the employer, such as theft or embezzlement. In no case, however, may a company discharge or discipline an employee solely on the basis of polygraph results.[38] Polygraphs are still legal for use in the public sector.[39]

Since polygraph testing has been restricted, paper-and-pencil honesty tests have increased in popularity. Commercially available honesty tests assess attitudes toward theft and ask about past dishonest behavior. Sample questions might include "Should a person be fired if caught stealing $10?" "What percentage of people take more than $1 per week from their employers?" "Compared with other people, how honest are you?" "Have you ever stolen anything from an employer?" Most available tests have satisfactory reliability and, surprisingly, do seem to have some validity in identifying individuals who have been caught stealing in the past or who will be caught stealing in the future.[40]

In recent years, another type of test related to honesty has appeared. This newer version focuses more on general personality traits like unreliability rather than on specific attitudes toward theft. These measures not only predict theft but also composite measures of other types of counterproductive behavior, such as abuse of sick leave, excessive grievance filing, drug use at work, aggression, and rule breaking.[41] These behaviors are more common than outright theft and can cost organizations a great deal of money and aggravation.

THE INTERVIEW

Virtually all organizations use interviews as a selection device for most jobs. Most commonly, candidates are interviewed by at least two people before being offered a job. Typically, an HR specialist and the individual who will be the candidate's immediate supervisor conduct these interviews. For managerial and professional jobs, it is common for the candidate to have a third interview with a higher level manager, such as a division head.[42] Because the interview is so popular, one might expect that it is a highly useful selection device. Unfortunately, this is often not the case. This section considers the reliability and validity of the interview.

Reliability of the Interview

In the interview context, reliability is consensus, or agreement, between two interviewers on their assessments of the same candidates. This is called **interrater reliability**. Research shows that it is usually quite poor. Interviewers might agree fairly well on the overall assessment of a candidate (one is outstanding, another is a dismal prospect) and on factual issues (the candidate has or has not worked on a similar job in the past), but interviewers seem unable to agree on more subjective or future-oriented characteristics (whether the candidate is creative or will be able to work without close supervision).[43]

Validity of the Interview

Historically, the predictive validity of the interview has been quite low. One estimate is that the average validity of a selection interview is .14, and many studies have failed to find significant correlations when interviews are used as predictors of job performance.[44] On the other hand, recent research has suggested that some individual interviewers may be valid, whereas many others are not. Past validation studies have lumped interviewers together, so the predictive validity of the best interviewers may have been obscured.[45] What can go wrong in the typical interview to cause the interviewer to make inaccurate predictions? It seems that interviewers often commit judgmental and perceptual errors that compromise the validity of their assessments.[46]

Similarity Error Interviewers are positively predisposed toward candidates who are similar to them (in hobbies, interests, or personal background). They are negatively disposed toward candidates who are unlike them. When the dissimilarity or similarity is not job related, it may still color the interviewer's judgment and introduce invalid variance into the interviewer's ratings.

Contrast Error When several candidates are interviewed in succession, raters tend to compare each candidate with the preceding candidates rather than with an absolute standard. Thus, an average candidate might be rated as higher than average if he or she comes after one or two poor candidates and lower than average if he or she follows an excellent interviewee.

Overweighting of Negative Information Interviewers tend to see their job as a search for negative or disqualifying information about candidates. Thus, they may overreact to a single minor piece of negative information; also, they are more likely to change their initial opinion of a candidate from positive to negative than from negative to positive.[47]

Race, Sex, and Age Bias Interviewers may be more or less positive about a candidate on the basis of the candidate's race, sex, or age. In general, interviewers rate blacks more favorably than similarly qualified whites, and females lower than comparable males. There is some evidence that sex interacts with the nature of the job. For example, interviewers assess men and women who are applying for jobs traditionally held by their sex positively, but less positively when these same individuals are applying for jobs held predominantly by the opposite sex.[48] Finally, there is evidence of a "beautyism" bias—that is, attractive males receive a positive rating, whereas attractive females get less credit for their own success and are rated somewhat more negatively, especially when they are applying for responsible positions.[49]

First Impression Error Some interviewers tend to form a first impression of candidates rather quickly, based on a review of the application blank or on the first few moments of the interview. Thus, this impression is based on relatively little information about the candidate. Nevertheless, the initial judgment may be resistant to change as more information or contradictory information is acquired. In addition, the interviewer may choose subsequent questions based on the first impression, in an attempt to confirm the positive or negative impression.[50]

Traits Rated and Halo Error **Halo error** occurs when either the interviewer's overall impression or strong impression of a single dimension spreads to influence his or her rating of other characteristics. For instance, if a candidate impresses the interviewer as being very enthusiastic, the interviewer might tend to rate the candidate high on other characteristics, such as job knowledge, loyalty and dependability. This is especially likely to happen when the interviewer is asked to rate many traits or to rate traits that are difficult to observe in a short interview. Research has shown that only a few traits, such as intelligence and sociability, can be accurately assessed in the typical interview.

Role of Nonverbal Factors Many studies have demonstrated that interviewers are influenced by nonverbal factors in the interview. Candidates who wear appropriate clothing, make eye contact, smile, show animation, speak fluently, and modulate their voices make more positive impressions on interviewers.[51] For jobs involving technical skill and low contact with others, this interviewer tendency probably weakens validity. On the other hand, it may contribute valid variance to the prediction of success in jobs involving a great deal of public contact.

Faulty Listening and Memory An interviewer may miss a substantial portion of what the interviewee says because of poor listening habits or preoccupation with what to ask next. Immediately after the interview, an interviewer who has not taken notes may have forgotten up to 75 percent of the information given by the candidate.

Despite these problems, interviewers tend to believe that they are "good judges of character" and "can spot a winner at fifty paces." In part, this self-perception may stem from the fact that professional interviewers and recruiters seldom get feedback on the eventual performance of people they have recommended for hire. In the absence of evidence to the contrary, they believe that their procedures and decisions are correct.

Types of Interviews

Interviews can be classified by their degree of structure, or the extent to which interviewers plan the questions in advance and ask the same questions of all the candidates for the job. Three types of interviews, based on three degrees of structure, can be defined: unstructured, semistructured, and structured interviews.

Unstructured Interviews In the **unstructured interview**, questions are not planned in advance, and interviews with different candidates may cover quite different areas of past history, attitudes, or future plans. Unstructured interviews have low interrater reliability and are seldom valid. Because questions are not planned, important job-related areas may remain unexplored, and illegal questions may be asked on the spur of the moment. Thus, unstructured interviews should not be used for evaluating job candidates.

Semistructured Interviews The **semistructured interview** involves some planning on the part of the interviewer but also allows flexibility in precisely what the interviewer asks candidates. In an excellent book on semistructured interviewing techniques, Thomas Moffatt suggests that interviewers plan their objectives in terms of what they hope to learn about the candidate and then use a "cone" approach to elicit this information.[52] A *cone* is a mini-interview on a particular topic, such as the candidate's last job, feelings about working in groups, or military experience. Each cone is introduced by a very broad question, which is followed by more specific questions on aspects of the topic. These questions may vary from interviewee to interviewee, but all pertain to the topic of the cone. The interviewer might plan to include four to eight cones in an hour-long interview.

In the cone approach, most questions are designed to elicit a reasonably lengthy response. As in all types of interviews, leading questions are avoided. Leading questions are those that imply a correct answer, such as "You don't plan to remain a secretary for your whole life, do you?" Finally, yes-no and short-answer questions are used sparingly because they tend to turn the interview into an interrogation and do not provide as much useful information as longer answers. Figure 8.6 is a partial example of a cone on the candidate's last job.

Structured Interviews In general, the more structured the interview, the greater the interrater reliability. Thus, the highest reliability is realized in the structured interview. In a **structured interview**, all questions are planned in advance and are asked of each candidate in exactly the same order. The only difference between interviews with different candidates might be in the probes, or follow-up questions, if a given candidate has not answered a question fully. Three types of structured interviews have been discussed in the research literature: the patterned interview, the situational interview, and the behavior description interview.

In the traditional **patterned interview**, questions tend to focus on past work activities, education, career goals, and so on. The questions may be job related, or they may be simply questions that interviewers typically ask, such as, "What are your strengths and weaknesses," "What do you plan to be doing five years from now?". This type of structure does increase interrater reliability and may prevent the interviewer from talking too much, but it does not necessarily result in high validity.

High predictive validity depends on eliciting from the candidate relevant information on the skills, abilities, and attitudes needed for job success. The **situational interview** and the **behavioral description interview** attempt to collect and properly evaluate job-relevant information. Both of these structured approaches begin with a thorough job analysis. Interview questions are based directly on the job analysis and are double-checked by job experts so that the interview is demonstrably content-valid.

The situational interview, which was developed by Gary P. Latham and his colleagues, involves three types of interview questions.[53] The first type of question is situational, or hypothetical. The interviewer asks the candidate what he or she would do in a particular job situation. For instance, the interviewer might ask a candidate for camp counselor how he or she would respond to a child who was

FIGURE 8.6 Cone Method of Semistructured Interviewing

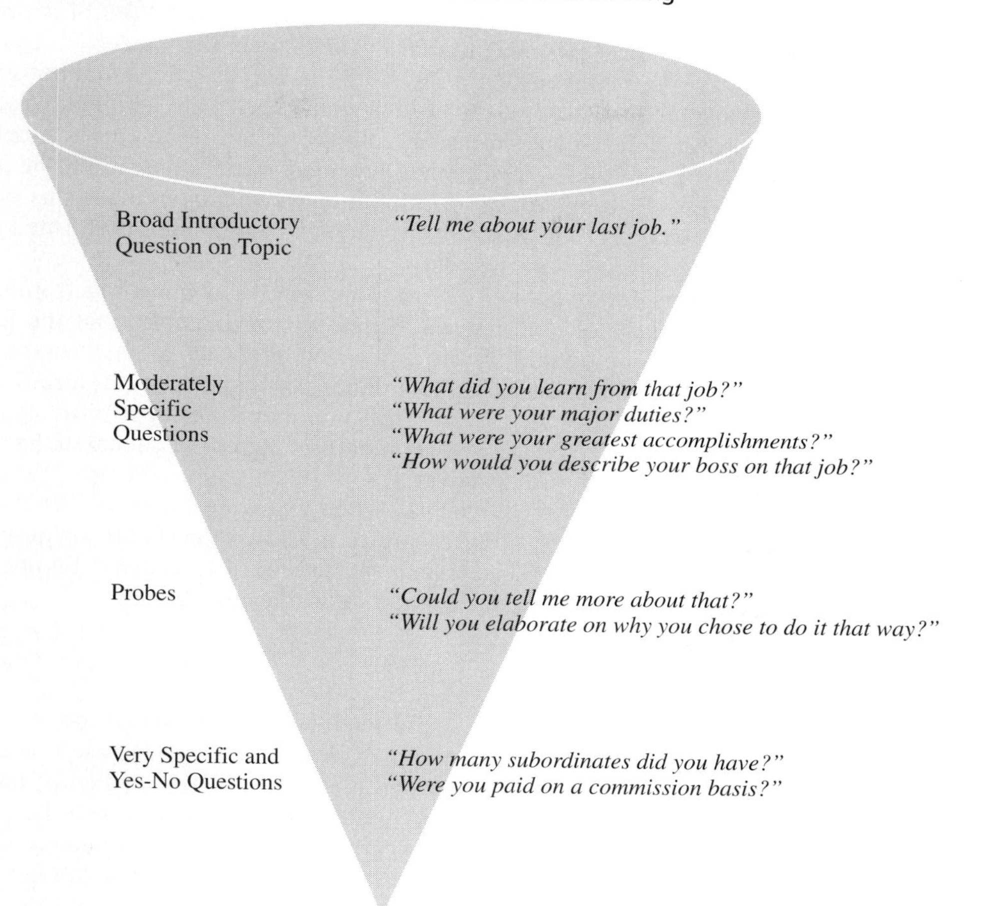

very homesick or who was disruptive. The second type of question involves job knowledge, such as defining a term, explaining a procedure, or demonstrating a skill. Job-knowledge questions may be written rather than oral, depending on their number. The last type of interview question focuses on the employee's willingness to comply with job requirements such as different shifts, travel, or physically demanding work.

As the job experts develop the questions, they also write sample good, average, and poor responses. This answer key helps interviewers give more reliable ratings of candidates' answers. In the situational interview, a panel of three or more interviewers conducts all the interviews. The interviewers do not attempt to reach a consensus on each candidate. Instead, their independent ratings are averaged to produce an overall score for each candidate.

Tom Janz developed the behavior description interview. This approach to structured interviewing is based on the assumption that "the best predictor of future performance is past performance in similar circumstances."[54] Traditionally, interviewers often applied this principle by asking candidates about experience with tasks similar to those of the job for which they were applying. According to Janz, however, interviewers often fall into the "experience equals excellence fallacy" by assuming that if a candidate has performed a task at all, he or she has performed it well. Behavior description interviewing overcomes this problem by requiring candidates to give specific examples of how they performed job duties or handled job problems in the past.

Job experts derive behavior description interview questions from the critical incidents technique of job analysis. Suppose, for example, that the job expert, using this technique, identifies one dimension of a sales job as "establishing new client contacts." Then, based on this dimension, a behavior description item for experienced candidates might be: "Tell me about the most difficult new client contact you have made in the last six months." After the candidate has described a specific incident, the interviewer's next questions might be, "What was the obstacle you faced? What did you say when you were stumped? What did you do to overcome the difficulty?"[55] Research has shown that behavior description interviews are much more valid than unstructured interviews.[56] Figure 8.7 offers other examples of behavior description interview questions.

Improving the Interview

Clearly, the interview can be a useful selection device, though often its potential is not properly utilized. Ideally, the interview should be (1) based on a thorough job analysis, (2) highly structured, and (3) conducted by a panel of interviewers who have been trained to avoid common errors. Validity seems to be enhanced if interviewers act more as information gatherers than as decision makers. Also, the statistical combination of interviewer item or dimension ratings often yields more valid predictions than overall subjective judgments of individual interviewers or panels.[57] To be effective, the interview should have the well-planned and reasonable objective of assessing important applicant characteristics that cannot be better evaluated by other selection methods.

PHYSICAL TESTING

One of the final steps in the selection process may be a physical examination or test.

The Physical Exam

The physical exam has traditionally been part of the selection process. As shown in Table 8.1, it is the second most commonly used selection test, with 57 percent of organizations using the physical exam for at least some job categories as of

FIGURE 8.7 Sample Questions from a Behavior Description Interview for the Job of Probation Officer

Job Dimension:
Practical Knowledge of Rules

In any position related to government agencies, there are many rules, regulations, and policies that need to be understood. Tell me about a time when your knowledge and understanding helped you work through a difficult case.

- What were the particular circumstances of the case?
- What rules, regulations, or policies did you find helpful in dealing with the case?
- How were they helpful?
- What was the outcome of the situation?
- What feedback did you receive from your client regarding the way you handled the case?
- What comments did your supervisor make?

Now I would like you to tell me about a time when you didn't adhere to the proper rules, regulations, or policies, and the results were a bit sticky.

- What led to the situation?
- What steps did you take in working through the situation?
- What reasons did you have for handling the situation the way you did?
- What was the outcome?
- How were those involved in the situation affected?
- How would you handle this kind of situation if it came up again?
- What were your supervisor's comments?
- How often does this type of situation occur over a 6-month period?

Can you tell me about a time when a colleague recognized that you had done the appropriate thing in an ambiguous situation?

- What was the situation?
- What was it about the situation that made it ambiguous?
- How did you handle the situation?
- What was the outcome?
- How did your coworker bring his or her feelings to your attention?
- How would you handle the situation differently if it came up again?

Source: From Tom Janz, Lowell Hellervik, and David C. Gilmore, *Behavior Description Interviewing: New, Accurate, Cost Effective*. Copyright © 1986 by Allyn and Bacon, Inc. Reprinted with permission.

1988. The exam is required by law for some jobs, such as pilot, interstate truck driver, and any position that involves handling of food. Even if they are not required, physical exams are still useful for the following purposes:

1. To reject persons who are physically unable to do the job.
2. To place individuals in jobs that they are fit enough to handle—for instance, to place individuals with chronic bronchitis in jobs in which they will not be exposed to high concentrations of dust or irritating fumes.
3. To prevent the spread of contagious diseases to current employees.
4. To document preexisting injuries and illnesses in order to prevent fraudulent group insurance or workers' compensation claims.

As with all selection devices, reliability, validity, and utility are relevant in the evaluation of physical exams. Reliability may not be extremely high. Physicians who are not knowledgeable about job demands may not be able to agree on whether a candidate is suitably fit. Moreover, some physiological measures, such as blood pressure, are not highly reliable over time. The validity of the physical exam is also questionable. When jobs require unusual strength or stamina, actual physical tests are likely to be more valid than a physician's opinion. In terms of utility, physical exams are expensive, since they must be individually administered by a costly tester. Thus, physical exams should be used only for good and sound reasons, rather than as a routine procedure for all jobs. In many cases, a health history questionnaire can be a satisfactory and cost-effective substitute for the physical exam.[58]

Additional limitations are placed on the physical exam as a selection device by the Americans with Disabilities Act, which went into effect in 1992. This act states that individuals may not be rejected due to physical inability to perform a "marginal" job function. *Marginal* means infrequent and nonessential. Thus, determinations of physical ability to do the job must be based on a clear understanding of which job duties are essential and which are marginal. Furthermore, an employer may not require physical exams (or other health-related information) until after the candidate receives a conditional offer of employment. An employer that uses a physical exam must give the exam to all candidates who have been offered jobs, not just to those who appear to have disabilities.[59] Because of these changes in the law, the physical exam seems likely to become less popular as a selection technique.

Strength and Fitness Testing

For physically demanding jobs, employers may be wise to directly measure applicant strength or fitness as part of the selection process. Research has shown that strength and fitness are positively related to the successful completion of training and negatively related to the incidence of lower-back injuries for steelworkers, underwater demolition divers, and telephone and outdoor-craft workers. It has also been found that a person's maximum oxygen uptake (aerobic power) should be at least 2.5 times the level required on a continuing basis during an 8-hour shift.[60] Thus, ability to perform a demanding job during a brief work sample does not necessarily mean that a person is fit enough to do the same job all day.

It is possible to put together a battery of physical tests that will be content-valid. The procedure involves a special job analysis and a rating of the physical requirements of each task on scales developed by Edwin Fleishman; the process may also involve objective measures of the heart rates or oxygen uptakes of current employees.[61] Based on this information, appropriate tests of strength, endurance, or flexibility can be selected and cutoff points can be established. Employers should be aware that physical testing frequently has an adverse impact on female candidates. Consequently, the job relatedness of the tests must be carefully established.

Other Health-related Indicators

Drug Testing Recently, more and more employers have adopted drug- and alcohol-screening programs for both applicants and current employees. There are good reasons to avoid hiring substance abusers. Drug and alcohol abusers have much higher rates of absenteeism and accidents. Furthermore, employers may be liable for negligent hiring if a drug-using employee causes an accident that harms others. There are no federal right-to-privacy statutes that prevent employers from conducting drug testing, even when tests tap off-the-job rather than on-the-job drug use. Court rulings, however, have sometimes upheld and sometimes struck down employer drug-testing programs. In 1988, the Supreme Court upheld a drug-testing program for federal drug enforcement agents and also approved mandatory tests for train crews after accidents.

A number of researchers have recently evaluated job candidates' attitudes toward drug testing. They have found that drug users are more negative than nonusers to the idea of drug testing, but that most job candidates say they are less likely to apply to an organization that requires drug testing than to one that does not. As might be expected, candidates give less approval to alcohol testing than to testing for illegal drugs. Attitudes toward testing also vary with the job involved. Testing is much more strongly approved for jobs involving danger to the incumbent or risk to others, such as airline pilot, surgeon, police officer or firefighter, air traffic controller, nuclear engineer, and truck driver, than for less risky jobs, such as janitor, salesperson, or secretary. Finally, testing for candidates and incumbents is more acceptable when the system is seen as providing "procedural justice." This means that the system is perceived as fair and open, retesting is available, the reasons for testing are clearly explained, and testing is announced and scheduled in advance rather than being random and unannounced.[62]

The U.S. Postal Service recently ran an experimental drug-testing program in selected sites. More than 5,000 job candidates were tested, and 9 percent were found to be drug users. Second tests on some specimens showed virtually no errors—no nonusers were mistakenly declared users, suggesting that properly conducted testing is highly reliable and hence fair to applicants. Because this was a predictive validation study, results of the drug tests were kept confidential and not used in selection. When criterion data were collected fifteen months after hiring, drug users were found to have experienced 60 percent more absenteeism and were 47 percent more likely to have been involuntarily discharged. Utility analysis was applied to determine the net gain to the Postal Service if drug screening were to be widely implemented as a selection procedure. The cost of testing ($11 per applicant) was minimal compared to the cost of increased absenteeism and terminations for cause that occurred when drug users were hired. The researchers estimated that if all 180,000 applicants were tested in a given year, the return to the Postal Service over an average career of ten years for the 61,588 people hired in that year would be $52,750,000.[63]

Smoking An increasing number of companies show preference for nonsmokers in the hiring process. As long ago as 1981, research suggested that each smoker cost the organization up to an additional $4,500 per year. This figure was based on the higher rates of illness, absenteeism, and death among smokers; the increased costs of health and property insurance for a smoking work force; increased maintenance costs and quicker depreciation of carpet and furnishings; and time lost while employees' hands and attention were taken up by smoking.[64]

More recently, the effect of second-hand smoke on nonsmoking colleagues has attracted much attention. Immediate effects range from slight aggravation to debilitating allergy attacks, and the U.S. surgeon general has estimated that each year from 2,400 to 5,000 people die of lung cancer induced by exposure to the smoke of others.[65] Some states and cities have laws regulating smoking in the workplace to protect nonsmokers from secondhand smoke. Although decisions have been mixed, some plaintiffs have won workers' compensation when disabled by the smoking of coworkers. In one case, an organization was found guilty of negligence when it failed to act on complaints about a smoky environment and a nonsmoking employee subsequently developed lung disease.[66] Such cases suggest that employers would be wise to limit smoking at work, although a complete ban on the hiring of smokers might be an extreme response. Approximately one-third of the adult population smokes, and excluding these individuals from consideration would substantially restrict the applicant pool.

REFERENCE AND BACKGROUND CHECKS

Most organizations check candidates' references as part of the selection process. The goal in reference checking may be merely to verify information that the candidate has already given the organization, such as academic degrees, dates of employment, job responsibilities, and salary; or it may be to discover new information on the characteristics and past performance of the candidate. In some cases, more extensive background investigations may be undertaken, either by the organization or by an investigative services firm hired by the employer.

Obtaining Reference Information

Employers usually collect reference information from a candidate's former employers, teachers, or other knowledgeable persons the candidate lists. Ideally, an organization should seek additional reference information from people other than those the candidate gives. To get additional references, an employer should ask the listed references for the names of other people who might know the candidate well enough to comment on his or her qualifications. Background information may be solicited from neighbors, credit agencies, and court or police records.

Information from references may be solicited in writing, in a phone interview, or in a face-to-face interview. Generally, letters are the least useful. Because writers have time to carefully censor what they say, their letters are nearly always positive and relatively unrevealing. Interviewing the references can be more helpful, as an interview allows the interviewer to establish a rapport with the reference, note voice tones that may convey doubts about the candidate, and probe more deeply into important issues.[67] Phone interviews are more common and more economical than face-to-face interviews with references. As with any interview, the reference interview should be carefully planned in advance and focus on job-related issues.

Validity and Legality of Reference Information

Studies of the validity of reference information agree that predictive validity tends to be low but is sometimes significant.[68] The most informative references are former or current superiors who know the candidate's work well and who have observed the candidate perform in a similar job. In addition, reference information may be accurate if (1) the reference knows that the candidate is being thoroughly assessed and (2) if the reference has no hidden motivations, such as to keep the candidate from leaving the present job or to unload a problem employee on an unsuspecting new employer. References may be of more use to screen out candidates who have falsified their credentials or who have had behavioral problems on several past jobs than to predict the job performance of reasonably qualified candidates.

There may be two kinds of legal problems associated with references. The first involves possible lawsuits for defamation when an employer or former employer gives a negative reference. Thus, many companies are discouraging candidates' superiors from giving any reference information at all. Instead, these firms are handling all requests for reference information centrally, from the personnel office, and they are limiting the information to facts such as dates of employment and job title.[69] Although this policy may be wise for an employer or former employer, it certainly complicates the task of the potential future employer who would like a frank assessment of a candidate.

The second legal problem involves the new employer. If an employer hires someone who subsequently causes injury to another—and the employer should have known about the employee's propensity to commit injurious acts through reference and background checks—then the employer is liable for **negligent hiring**. For instance, a company was found guilty of negligent hiring when its apartment manager used his pass key to enter the apartment of a resident and rape her. The organization should have discovered the manager's past conviction for rape and not hired him in a capacity that allowed this kind of access.[70]

SELECTING MANAGERS

The selection of managers for hire or promotion is a particularly important and difficult task, and is approached in different ways around the world (see the International Perspective box). There are many different ways to be a successful manager, but one thing is certain: managing requires a wide range of skills. Thus, single-factor ability tests are seldom very useful in selecting managers. Nevertheless, some studies have found significant correlations between mental-ability tests and managerial performance, and occasionally a personality characteristic like extroversion, need for power, need for achievement, or general activity can have some predictive success.[71] As a rule, the best predictors of managerial success tend to be broader measures, such as supervisor ratings of promotion potential or assessment center ratings.

Assessment Centers

An **assessment center** is a content-valid work sample of the managerial job, most often used to select nonmanagerial employees for promotion to low-level management positions. As these individuals are not currently performing managerial duties, an appraisal of their work performance is not likely to predict success in the job of manager or supervisor. Hence, there is a need for a work sample test for the managerial job. Assessment centers have also been used to select salespersons and higher-level managers. Assessment centers can last from one day to one week and have three characteristics: multiple means of assessment, multiple assessees, and multiple assessors.

Characteristics of Assessment Centers *Multiple means of assessment,* or different situational exercises and tests, cover a wide range of activities and skills that are performed by a manager. Assessment centers virtually always include an **in-basket test**, in which the candidate is given a stack of letters and messages to deal with. He or she must prioritize the problems and act on each, by making a decision or an appointment, referring, delegating, or asking for more information.

Assessment centers also include some sort of **leaderless group discussion** exercise, because so much of a manager's time is spent in meetings or groups of some sort. Assessment centers may also include two-person role-playing (salesperson with customer, supervisor with problem subordinate); management games;

INTERNATIONAL PERSPECTIVE

Selecting Managers in Britain and France: The Case Against Graphology

A survey conducted in 1989 revealed some interesting differences in approaches to managerial selection between large companies in France versus Great Britain. Both were heavy users of applications forms and interviews, but the French were more likely than the British to use multiple interviews before making a decision. Reference checks were widely used in Britain, with 74 percent of firms saying that they "always" checked references on managerial job applicants. French firms used references much less, with only 11 percent always checking references. French firms were relatively more fond of personality tests and less fond of cognitive ability tests compared to British firms. Both biodata and assessment centers were more likely to be used in Britain than in France.

One of the most striking differences between countries involved the use of graphology, or handwriting analysis. Ninety-seven percent of British firms "never" used the technique, whereas 73 percent of French firms made some use of it, and 17 percent "always" used it in managerial selection. These findings seem consistent with a general tendency for the French to use more qualitative methods, whereas British (and American) HR managers seem to prefer quantitative selection tools for which validity evidence is available.

Graphology, although rare, is not unheard of in selection situations in the United States. As typically used, a job candidate is asked to write a biographical paragraph about himself or herself. The graphologist then interprets the pattern of tilts and loops in the letters, the size and neatness of the handwriting, and other characteristics believed to indicate something about the author's personality.

Does the method have any validity for diagnosing personality or predicting job success? Recall that reliability is a prerequisite to validity. However, the interrater reliability of graphologists is quite low. There are several schools of thought on how to interpret different handwriting characteristics, and individuals trained in different approaches tend not to agree with each other. This suggests that validity cannot be high.

Research has shown that very modest validities may be obtained from handwriting analysis. However, virtually identical validities are obtained when either psychologists or laypersons not trained in graphology read the same handwriting passages! It appears that any validity at all comes from the biographical information in the passage, not from the diagnostic value of the handwriting per se. When applicants are asked to copy a standard paragraph in their own handwriting, graphologists have zero validity for predicting job success.

Thus, it would seem that there is no empirical support for the use of graphology, whether in the United States, in Britain, or in France. The authors of the survey suggested that French preferences for multiple interviews and graphology may both be due to the high uncertainty avoidance trait in their culture (see Chapter 17). Multiple interviews probably reduce the risk of making a mistake, and at the very least diffuse responsibility for a bad decision among several people. The mystique of graphology also helps remove uncertainty for believers.

Sources: Viv Shackleton and Sue Newell, "Management Selection: A Comparative Survey of Methods Used in Top British and French Companies," *Journal of Occupational Psychology,* 1991, pp. 23–36; Gershon Ben-Shakhar, Maya Bar-Hillel, Yoram Bilu, Edor Ben-Abba, and Anat Flug, "Can Graphology Predict Occupational Success? Two Empirical Studies and Some Methodological Ruminations," *Journal of Applied Psychology,* November 1986, pp. 645–653; Gershon Ben-Shakhar, "Non-conventional Methods in Personnel Selection," in Peter Herriot (ed.), *Assessment and Selection in Organizations* (Chichester: John Wiley & Sons, 1989), pp. 469–485.

interviews with assessors; written tests of intelligence or personality; and possibly preparing and delivering a speech. Throughout all these exercises, assessees are observed and evaluated on dimensions such as decision making, planning, leadership, persuasiveness, energy, interpersonal sensitivity, and communication. The choice of assessment dimensions and exercises is based on a careful job analysis of the type and level of managerial job for which candidates are being evaluated.

If group exercises are to be used, more than one candidate must be assessed at the same time. Typically, six to twelve candidates will form an assessment center class. Three to six assessors will be used to observe and evaluate the performance of the candidates. Assessors are usually managers two to three levels higher than the job for which they are assessing candidates. Assessors undergo training on the exercises and assessment dimensions, observe candidates during the exercises, and then meet for one or two days after the candidates leave in order to make ratings and to hammer out an assessment report on each candidate's managerial potential and development needs. There is some evidence that serving as an assessor has the side benefit of improving a manager's interviewing and communication skills.[72]

Validity and Utility of Assessment Centers Studies have shown that assessment center data do predict both short- and long-term success and advancement in management positions. Validities are often quite high. Furthermore, assessment centers are equally valid for all sexes and races and do not seem to produce adverse impact.[73] There are some questions about the construct validity of assessor ratings;[74] but despite these issues, well-designed centers do seem to be effective in identifying management potential. Assessment centers are probably the most expensive selection device in common use. However, the high validity and the potential losses from hiring an incompetent manager seem more than enough to offset the cost, leading to the conclusion that assessment centers are likely to offer high utility.[75]

Other Selection Methods for Managers

When the use of an assessment center is not feasible, careful reference checking and behavior description interviewing by a panel probably hold the most promise as selection methods for managers. Following a careful job analysis, behavior description interview formats should be developed for both candidates and their references. A thorough investigation of candidates' past behavior in situations similar to those of the new job should provide the most useful information.

Stephan Motowidlo and his colleagues have recently developed a paper-and-pencil judgment test for selecting entry-level managers in the telecommunications industry. They collected more than 1,200 critical incidents of interpersonal and problem-solving tasks encountered by entry-level managers; then they distilled these into 55 scenarios. Each scenario presents a supervisory problem with five to seven possible solutions, and the candidate has to pick the solution that he or she is most likely to use and the one that seems least appealing. A scoring key was developed by consulting higher-level managers. In a concurrent validation design, scores on this test were found to be significantly correlated with ratings of supervisory performance.[76]

Some organizations hire a consulting clinical or organizational psychologist to provide **individual assessment** of candidates for middle- and upper-level management positions. The assessment process normally includes gathering information about the job and organization, and then gathering information from the candidates by means of a personal history questionnaire, cognitive and personality tests, and a clinical interview. Finally, all this information is combined judgmentally, and the assessor writes a report detailing the candidate's strengths, weaknesses, and suitability for the job. There is no empirical data available on the validity of these judgments because sample sizes are very small. Unfortunately, however, there is evidence that interrater reliability is low when more than one expert assesses the same candidate.[77]

Finally, in selecting higher-level managers, an organization or subunit may find that its business strategy and environment are important in determining the type of managerial skills needed.[78] Table 8.6 lists some recommendations for candidate skills and attitudes that best match various business situations and strategies. Behavior description and situational interview questions might be used to assess these characteristics.

SUMMARY OF KEY POINTS

A wide variety of selection devices may be used to assess job applicants. One of the most common is the application blank. This device may be used informally for screening or systematically through the weighted application blank procedure. Biodata—whether obtained through application blanks, biodata questionnaires, or experience and accomplishment records—are often impressively valid predictors of job success. Properly chosen tests of cognitive ability are also excellent predictors, as are work sample and trainability tests.

Interest inventories are not especially useful in selection, but personality tests seem to be making a comeback and can have modest but consistent validity for some aspects of job success. Honesty tests are being used increasingly to screen out employees who may steal from their employers or otherwise present behavioral problems. The use of pre-employment polygraphs for this purpose is now illegal in the private sector.

Interviews are a widely used selection device. The traditional interview is seldom valid, but current techniques, such as situational and behavior description interviewing, show promise when interviewers are properly trained and prepared.

The physical examination is often the final step in the hiring process. The Americans with Disabilities Act requires that a conditional job offer be made before a physical exam is given. A few companies use strength or fitness tests as

TABLE 8.6 Suggestions for Selecting Executives Who Match Business Strategy

Situation	*Major Job Thrusts*	*Specific Characteristics of Ideal Candidates*
Start-up	Creating vision of business	Vision of finished business
	Establishing core technical and marketing expertise	Hands-on orientation: a "doer"
	Building management team	In-depth knowledge in critical technical areas
		Organizing ability
		Staffing skills
		Team-building capabilities
		High energy level and stamina
		Personal magnetism and charisma
		Broad knowledge of all key functions
Turnaround	Rapid, accurate problem diagnosis	"Take charge" orientation: strong leader
	Fixing short-term and, ultimately, long-term problems	Strong analytical and diagnostic skills, especially financial
		Excellent business strategist
		High energy level
		Risk taker
		Handles pressure well
		Good crisis-management skills
		Good negotiator
Liquidation/Divestiture of Poorly Performing Business	Cutting losses	"Callousness": tough-minded, determined—willing to be the "bad guy"
	Making tough decisions	Highly analytical regarding costs/benefits—does not easily accept current ways of doing things
	Making best deal	Risk taker
		Low glory seeking: willing to do dirty jobs—does not want glamour
		Wants to be respected, not necessarily liked

Source: Reprinted from "Strategic Selection: Matching Executives to Business Conditions" by Marc Gertstein and Heather Reisman, *Sloan Management Review,* Winter 1983, pp. 33–49, by permission of the publisher. This material is an adaptation of a full table.

predictors of success on physically demanding jobs. Many more use drug tests as screening devices.

Because résumé fraud is not uncommon, organizations find it a wise practice to verify important credentials before making job offers. In addition to verifying credentials, reference checks may be used to discover additional information about job candidates.

Selecting managers is an especially difficult task because managerial jobs are highly complex and require many different skills. The assessment center, though expensive, can be a content-valid way to identify management talent.

Questions for Discussion

1. Describe how to construct a weighted application blank (WAB). Why do WABs tend to have high validity?
2. What are some questions that should not be included in an application blank? Why?
3. What is an experience record? How would you establish the validity of an experience record?
4. What qualities would you look for in a test if you were picking one for a validation effort in your organization?
5. How would you go about designing a work sample test for the job of college student?
6. How does a trainability test differ from a work sample test? What are the advantages of each type of test? Can you think of any disadvantages?
7. Debate this statement: for most jobs, personality tests should be used in selection.
8. What types of honesty tests are available and when might they be most useful?
9. Why is the typical interview such an unreliable and invalid predictor of job success?
10. What is meant by the degree of *structure* in an interview? How does structure affect reliability and validity?
11. Describe several techniques for improving the interview.
12. Why would an organization choose to use a physical exam as the last step in the selection process? In what ways must the organization be cautious in using the exam?
13. Discuss drug and alcohol screening of job candidates. How do you feel about a company gathering information on off-the-job, recreational activities of candidates? How do job candidates tend to feel about this practice?
14. How and why should reference information be collected about job candidates? What legal problems can arise with giving and collecting references?

15. How would you go about selecting first-line supervisors in a manufacturing plant? A top executive to head the North American division of the company?
16. How were you selected for the last job you held? How effective was this selection system? How could it be improved?
17. Consider the type of job you wish to obtain after graduation from your current course of study. How should incumbents for this type of job be selected in order to maximize their chances of being successful performers?

EXERCISE 8.1

Developing Interview Questions

The dean of admissions at Ivy League Private University has always selected candidates for admission on the basis of high school grade point averages and SAT scores. However, the dean is finding that this method is only partially successful. A fair percentage of students who appeared to have adequate ability quit or fail early in their course of study. The dean has read about recent advances in interviewing techniques and has decided to add a personal interview to the admission process in the hope of improving retention and pass rates. The dean has asked your group to develop a set of behavior description interview questions for use in admission interviews.

You should consider yourselves to be both personnel selection experts and subject matter experts with regard to the job of "student."

1. In the latter capacity, develop as many true critical incidents as you can involving success or failure in university studies. Remember that the interview will be used in conjunction with grade point averages and SAT scores, so you need not focus heavily on academic ability or intelligence in your questions. Instead, focus on other attributes that your incidents suggest might be important to success in business studies.
2. Make a list of the attributes, attitudes, traits, or types of behavior that your incidents lead you to believe are important.
3. Write behavior description questions to assess the past, verifiable existence of these attributes and behaviors in high school seniors and develop scoring guidelines for interviewers.
4. Conduct one or more interviews with a student or students from another group.
5. Fine-tune your questions and scoring key based on the test interview.
6. Make recommendations for the use of your interview questions. At what point in the admission process should the interview be conducted? How much weight should it carry relative to the other admission criteria? Should the interview be conducted by a single person or by a panel? Who should serve as interviewers? What are the utility considerations in adding this interviewing procedure to the selection process?

EXERCISE 8.2

Developing a Selection System

Choose one of the jobs below and recommend a complete selection system for the job. First list job specifications—what exactly are you looking for in a good candidate? Then decide how you will assess these qualities in a candidate. Discuss what types of measures and procedures you will use and the order in which you will use them.

Airplane Pilot, Commercial Pilots airplane to transport passengers, mail, or freight. Reviews ship's papers to ascertain factors, such as load weight, fuel supply, weather conditions, and flight route and schedule. Orders changes in fuel supply, load, route, or schedule to ensure safety of flight. Reads gauges to verify that oil, hydraulic fluid, fuel quantities, and cabin pressure are at prescribed levels prior to starting engines. Contacts control tower by radio to obtain takeoff and landing clearances and instructions. Pilots airplane to destination, adhering to flight plan and to regulations and procedures of aviation authorities, company, and airports. Logs information such as time in flight and fuel consumed. Must hold commercial pilot certificate.

Television News Reader Prepares and reads news on regular news program. Reads emergency news flashes and may read advertising copy. Interviews guests on film and live. Describes and comments on events such as parades, speeches, and emergencies, speaking extemporaneously. Consults with news director and newswriters regarding time allocation and coverage of stories. May operate control board, recording equipment, and videotape splicer.

Building Construction Supervisor Arranges for subcontracts with building subcontractors specializing in grading, foundations, carpentry, roofing, painting, landscaping, and so forth. Schedules subcontractors in the correct order at the correct times. Supervises subcontractors to ensure that blueprints and specifications are met. Inspects work daily and orders changes when deviations are found. Oversees workplace safety and arranges site security to prevent theft of materials or equipment. Works with building inspectors to ensure that construction standards are met.

Post Office Clerk Receives letters and parcels and sells postage stamps and money orders. Weighs packages to determine charges. Computes cost of insuring and registering mail. Answers questions concerning postal regulations or procedures. Places mail into slots or sacks after sorting by mail code or destination. Takes complaints regarding lost mail or mail theft, fills out forms, and submits them for investigation.

Zoo Keeper Cleans animal enclosures by hosing, sweeping, raking, scrubbing, and removing manure, soiled bedding, and unused food. Maintains enclosure materials such as nest boxes, plants, decorative materials, and bedding. Feeds and waters animals, preparing diet as instructed by animal manager. Inspects and monitors animals and reports injuries, illnesses, or unusual behavior. Assists veterinarian in capturing and immobilizing animals when necessary.

Notes and References

1. See Neal Schmitt and Ivan Robertson, "Personnel Selection," *Annual Review of Psychology,* Vol. 41, 1990, pp. 289–319, for a review of recent research on selection devices.
2. A. Etzioni, *A Comparative Analysis of Complex Organizations.* (New York: Free Press, 1975); C. L. Mulford, G. E. Klonglon, G. M. Beal, and J. M. Bohlen, "Selectivity, Socialization, and Role Performance," *Sociology and Social Research,* Vol. 53, 1968, pp. 68–77.
3. John E. Hunter and Frank L. Schmidt, "Ability Tests: Economic Benefits Versus the Issue of Fairness," *Industrial Relations,* Fall 1982, pp. 293–308.
4. "Selection," *Bureau of National Affairs Fair Employment Practices Manual,* 1983, pp. 201–229.
5. "Recruiting and Selection Procedures," *Personnel Policies Forum Survey No. 146,* May 1988, Washington, D.C.: Bureau of National Affairs.
6. John Andrew, "Resume Liars Are Abundant, Experts Assert," *The Wall Street Journal,* April 24, 1981, p. 25; Irwin L. Goldstein, "The Application Blank: How Honest Are the Responses?" *Journal of Applied Psychology,* October 1971, pp. 491–492.
7. James J. Asher, "The Biographical Item: Can It Be Improved?" *Personnel Psychology,* Summer 1972, pp. 251–269.
8. "Spotting a Winner in Insurance," *Business Week,* February 12, 1979, pp. 122, 127.
9. R. R. Reilly and G. T. Chao, "Validity and Fairness of Some Alternative Employee Selection Procedures," *Personnel Psychology,* Spring 1982, pp. 1–62; J. E. Hunter and R. F. Hunter, "Validity and Utility of Alternative Predictors of Job Performance," *Psychological Bulletin,* Spring 1984, pp. 72–98.
10. Robert Helmreich, Roger Bakeman, and Roland Radloff, "The Life History Questionnaire as a Predictor of Performance in Navy Diver Training," *Journal of Applied Psychology,* April 1973, pp. 148–153; William A. Owens, "Background Data," in *Handbook of Industrial and Organizational Psychology,* ed. Marvin D. Dunnette (Chicago: Rand McNally, 1976); Russell J. Drakely and Peter Herriot, "Biographical Data, Training Success, and Turnover," *Journal of Occupational Psychology,* Vol. 61, 1988, pp. 145–152, Hannah R. Rothstein, Frank L. Schmidt, Frank W. Erwin, William A. Owens, and C. Paul Sparks, "Biographical Data in Employment Selection: Can Validities Be Made Generalizable?" *Journal of Applied Psychology,* April 1990, pp. 175–184; Craig J. Russell, Joyce Mattson, Steven E. Devlin, and David Atwater, "Predictive Validity of Biodata Items Generated from Retrospective Life Experience Essays," *Journal of Applied Psychology,* October 1990, pp. 569–580.
11. James J. Asher, "The Biographical Item," pp. 251–269.
12. Cathy D. Anderson, Jack Warner, and Cassie C. Spenser, "Inflation Bias in Self-Assessment Examinations: Implications for Valid Employee Selection," *Journal of Applied Psychology.* November 1984, pp. 574–580; David C. Myers and Sidney A. Fine, "Development of a Methodology to Obtain and Assess Applicant Experiences for Employment," *Public Personnel Management Journal,* Spring 1985, pp. 51–64; Ronald D. Pannone, "Predicting Test Performance: A Content Valid Approach to Screening Applicants," *Personnel Psychology,* Autumn 1984, pp. 507–514. See also Michael A. McDaniel, Frank L. Schmidt, and John E. Hunter, "A Meta-analysis of the Validity of Methods for Rating Training and Experience in Personnel Selection," *Personnel Psychology,* Vol. 41, 1988, pp. 283–309.
13. Leaetta M. Hough, "Development and Evaluation of the 'Accomplishment Record' Method of Selecting and Promoting Professionals," *Journal of Applied Psychology,* February 1984, pp. 135–146.
14. Judy D. Olian and John C. Wilcox, "The Controversy Over PACE: An Examination of the Evidence and Implications of the Luevano Consent Decrees for Employment Testing," *Personnel Psychology,* Autumn 1982, pp. 659–676.
15. J. E. Hunter, F. L. Schmidt, and R. Hunter, "Differential Validity of Employment Tests by Race: A Comprehensive Review and

Analysis," *Psychological Bulletin,* July 1979, pp. 721–735.

16. Alexandra K. Wigdor and Wendell Garner, eds., *Ability Testing: Uses, Consequences, and Controversies: Part I* (Washington, D.C.: Committee on Ability Testing, National Research Council, National Academy Press, 1982), pp. 145–147.
17. *Watson* v. *Fort Worth Bank and Trust,* (1988), 47 FEP Cases 102, US SupCt, No. 86–6139, June 29.
18. "Recruiting and Selection Procedures."
19. See Keith Hattrup and Neal Schmitt, "Prediction of Trades Apprentices' Performance on Job Sample Criteria," *Personnel Psychology,* Autumn 1990, pp. 453–466; Hunter and Hunter, "Validity and Utility of Alternative Predictors," pp. 72–98; Scott L. Martin and Karen B. Slora, "Employee Selection by Testing," *HRMagazine,* June 1991, pp. 68–70.
20. Joyce Hogan and Robert Hogan, eds., *Business and Industry Testing: Current Practices and Test Reviews* (Austin, Texas: Pro.ed, 1990).
21. This effort is called "Project A" and is detailed in a special issue of *Personnel Psychology,* Summer 1990.
22. John Hawk, "Real World Implications of g," *Journal of Vocational Behavior,* Vol. 29, 1986, pp. 411–414; John E. Hunter, "Cognitive Ability, Cognitive Aptitudes, Job Knowledge, and Job Performance," *Journal of Vocational Behavior,* Vol. 29, 1986, pp. 340–362; Arthur R. Jensen, "g: Artifact or Reality?" *Journal of Vocational Behavior,* Vol. 29, 1986, pp. 301–331.
23. R. L. Thorndike, "The Role of General Ability in Prediction," *Journal of Vocational Behavior,* Vol. 29, 1986, pp. 332–339.
24. C. Paul Sparks, "How to Read a Test Manual," in *Business and Industry Testing,* ed. Hogan and Hogan, pp. 36–47.
25. David Bartram, "Computer-based Assessment," in *Assessment and Selection in Organizations,* ed. Peter Herriot (Chichester, England: Wiley, 1989), pp. 369–390.
26. Paul Squires, Steven J. Torkel, James W. Smither, and Margaret R. Ingate, "Validity and Generalizability of a Role-play Test to Select Telemarketing Representatives," *Journal of Occupational Psychology,* Vol. 64, 1991, pp. 37–47.
27. Rosemarie J. Park, Rene V. Davis, Elizabeth K. Rengel, and Rebecca L. Storlie, "The Selection and Validation of a Reading Test to be Used with Civil Service Employees," *Public Personnel Management.* Fall 1985, pp. 275–284; Lyle F. Schoenfeldt, Barbara B. Schoenfeldt, Stanley R. Acker, and Michael R. Perlson, "Content Validation Revisited: The Development of a Content-Oriented Test of Industrial Reading," *Journal of Applied Psychology,* October 1976, pp. 581–588.
28. C. H. Lawshe, "A Quantitative Approach to Content Validity," *Personnel Psychology,* Winter 1975, pp. 563–565.
29. I. T. Robertson and R. M. Mindel, "A Study of Trainability Testing," *Journal of Occupational Psychology,* June 1980, pp. 131–138; and Arthur I. Siegel, "The Miniature Job Training and Evaluation Approach: Additional Findings," *Personnel Psychology,* Spring 1983, pp. 41–56; Richard R. Reilly and Edmund W. Israelski, "Development and Validation of Minicourses in the Telecommunication Industry," *Journal of Applied Psychology,* Vol. 73, 1988, pp. 721–726.
30. James J. Asher and James A. Sciarrino, "Realistic Work Sample Tests: A Review," *Personnel Psychology,* Winter 1974, pp. 519–533; and Ivan Robertson and R. S. Kandola, "Work Sample Tests: Validity, Adverse Impact, and Applicant Reaction," *Journal of Occupational Psychology,* September 1982, pp. 171–183.
31. Wayne F. Cascio and Neil F. Phillips, "Performance Testing: A Rose Among Thorns?" *Personnel Psychology,* Winter 1979, pp. 751–766; and J. L. Farr, B. S. O'Leary, and C. J. Bartlett, "Effect of a Work Sample Test upon Self-Selection and Turnover of Job Applicants," *Journal of Applied Psychology,* October 1973, pp. 283–285; Sylvia Downs, "Job Sample and Trainability Tests," in *Assessment and Selection in Organizations,* pp. 391–399.
32. Neal Schmitt, Richard Z. Gooding, Raymond A. Noe, and Michael Kirsch, "Meta-analysis of Validity Studies Published Between 1964 and 1982 and the Investigation of

Study Characteristics," *Personnel Psychology,* Autumn 1984, pp. 407–422.

33. Seymour Adler and Howard M. Weiss, "Recent Developments in the Study of Personality and Organizational Behavior," in *International Review of Industrial and Organizational Psychology,* ed. C. L. Cooper and I. Robertson (Chichester, England: Wiley, 1988), pp. 307–330; David V. Day and Stanley B. Silverman, "Personality and Job Performance: Evidence of Incremental Validity," *Personnel Psychology,* Spring 1989, pp. 25–36; John R. Hollenbeck and Ellen M. Whitener, "Reclaiming Personality Traits for Personnel Selection: Self-esteem as an Illustrative Case," *Journal of Management,* Vol. 14, 1988, pp. 81–91; Robert L. Helmreich, Linda L. Sawin, and Alan L. Carsrud, "The Honeymoon Effect in Job Performance: Temporal Increases in the Predictive Power of Achievement Motivation," *Journal of Applied Psychology,* Vol. 71, 1986, pp. 185–188; Leaetta M. Hough, Newell K. Eaton, Marvin D. Dunnette, John D. Kamp, and Rodney A. McCloy, "Criterion-Related Validities of Personality Constructs and the Effect of Response Distortion on Those Validities," *Journal of Applied Psychology,* October 1990, pp. 581–595.
34. Murray R. Barrick and Michael K. Mount, "The Big Five Personality Dimensions and Job Performance: A Meta-Analysis," *Personnel Psychology,* Spring 1991, pp. 1–26.
35. Sandra O. Davis, "The Design and Conduct of Individual Psychological Assessments in Industry," paper presented at the First Annual Conference of the Society for Industrial and Organizational Psychology, Chicago, April 10–11, 1986.
36. Thomas L. Bright and Charles J. Hollon, "State Regulation of Polygraph Tests at the Workplace," *Personnel,* February 1985, pp. 50–56; "Companies Pay a Big Price for Employee Theft," *HR Focus,* January 1992, p. 14.
37. Richard C. Hollinger and John P. Clark, *Theft by Employees* (Lexington, Mass.: Lexington Books, 1983).
38. "Congress Clears Lie-Detector Ban," *Congressional Quarterly Weekly Reports,* June 11, 1988, p. 1630.
39. Lawrence S. Kleiman, Robert H. Faley, and David W. Denton, "Legal Issues Concerning Polygraph Testing in the Public Sector," *Public Personnel Management,* Winter 1990, pp. 365–379.
40. Paul R. Sackett, Laura R. Burris, and Christine Callahan, "Integrity Testing for Personnel Selection: An Update," *Personnel Psychology,* Autumn 1989, pp. 491–529.
41. Joyce Hogan and Robert Hogan, "How to Measure Employee Reliability," *Journal of Applied Psychology,* April 1989, pp. 273–279.
42. "Recruiting and Selection Procedures," *Personnel Policies Forum Survey No. 146,* May 1988.
43. Eugene C. Mayfield, "The Selection Interview: A Reevaluation of Published Research," *Personnel Psychology,* Autumn 1964, pp. 239–260; Eugene C. Mayfield, Steven H. Brown, and Bruce W. Hamstra, "Selection Interviewing in the Life Insurance Industry: An Update of Research and Practice," *Personnel Psychology,* Winter 1980, pp. 725–740.
44. Tom Janz, Lowell Hellervik, and David C. Gilmore, *Behavior Description Interviewing* (Boston: Allyn and Bacon, 1986); Hunter and Hunter, "Validity and Utility of Alternative Predictors," pp. 72–98.
45. Thomas W. Dougherty, Ronald J. Ebert, and John C. Callender, "Policy Capturing in the Employment Interview," *Journal of Applied Psychology,* Vol. 71, 1986, pp. 9–15; George F. Dreher, Ronald A. Ash, and Priscilla Hancock, "The Role of Traditional Research Design in Underestimating the Validity of the Employment Interview," *Personnel Psychology,* Vol. 41, 1988, pp. 315–327; Angelo J. Kinicki, Chris A. Lockwood, Peter W. Hom, Rodger W. Griffeth, "Interviewer Predictions of Applicant Qualifications and Interviewer Validity: Aggregate and Individual Analyses," *Journal of Applied Psychology,* October 1990, pp. 477–486.
46. Richard Arvey and James Campion, "The Employment Interview: A Summary and Review of Recent Research," *Personnel Psychology,* Summer 1982, pp. 281–322; Neal Schmitt, "Social and Situational Determinants of Interview Decisions: Implications for the Employment Interview," *Personnel Psychology,* Spring 1976, pp. 79–101.

47. M. M. Okanes and H. Tschirgi, "Impact of the Face-to-Face Interview on Prior Judgments of a Candidate," *Perceptual and Motor Skills,* February 1978, pp. 46, 322.
48. Richard D. Arvey, "Unfair Discrimination in the Employment Interview: Legal and Psychological Aspects," *Psychological Bulletin,* July 1979, pp. 736–765.
49. Madeline E. Heilman and Melanie Stopeck, "Attractiveness and Corporate Success: Different Causal Attributions for Males and Females," *Journal of Applied Psychology,* May 1985, pp. 379–388.
50. John F. Binning, Mel A. Goldstein, Mario F. Garcia, and Julie H. Scattaregia, "Effects of Pre-Interview Impressions on Questioning Strategies in Same- and Opposite-Sex Employment," *Journal of Applied Psychology,* Vol. 73, (1988), pp. 30–37; Therese Hoff Macan and Robert L. Dipboye, "The Relationship of Interviewers' Preinterview Impressions to Selection and Recruiting Outcomes," *Personnel Psychology,* Winter 1990, pp. 745–768.
51. See Sandra Forsythe, Mary Frances Drake, and Charles E. Cox, "Influence of Applicant's Dress on Interviewers' Selection Decisions," *Journal of Applied Psychology,* May 1985, pp. 374–378; Robert Gifford, Cheuk Fan Ng, and Margaret Wilkinson, "Nonverbal Cues in the Employment Interview: Links Between Applicant Qualities and Interviewer Judgments," *Journal of Applied Psychology,* November 1985, pp. 729–736; Thomas V. McGovern and Howard E. A. Tinsley, "Interviewer Evaluation of Interviewee Nonverbal Behavior," *Journal of Vocational Behavior,* October 1978, pp. 163–171.
52. Thomas L. Moffatt, *Selection Interviewing for Managers* (New York: Harper and Row, 1979).
53. Gary P. Latham, Lise M. Saari, Elliot D. Pursell, and Michael A. Campion, "The Situational Interview," *Journal of Applied Psychology,* August 1980, pp. 442–427; Elliott D. Pursell, Michael A. Campion and Sarah R. Gaylord, "Structured Interviewing: Avoiding Selection Problems," *Personnel Journal,* November 1980, pp. 907–912; Michael A. Campion, Elliott D. Pursell, and Barbara K. Brown, "Structured Interviewing: Raising the Psychometric Properties of the Employment Interview," *Personnel Psychology,* Vol. 41, 1988, pp. 25–42; Jeff A. Weekley and Joseph A. Gier, "Reliability and Validity of the Situational Interview for a Sales Position," *Journal of Applied Psychology,* Vol. 72, 1989, pp. 484–487.
54. Janz, Hellervik, and Gilmore, *Behavior Description Interviewing.*
55. Ibid., pp. 64–65.
56. Tom Janz, "Initial Comparisons of Patterned Behavior Description Interviews Versus Unstructured Interviews," *Journal of Applied Psychology,* October 1982, pp. 577–580; Janz, Hellervik, and Gilmore, *Behavior Description Interviewing;* Christopher Orpen, "Patterned Behavior Description Interviews Versus Unstructured Interviews: A Comparative Validity Study," *Journal of Applied Psychology,* November 1985, pp. 774–776.
57. Frank Landy, "The Validity of the Interview in Police Officer Selection," *Journal of Applied Psychology,* April 1976, pp. 193–198; Dougherty, Ebert, and Callender, "Policy Capturing in the Employment Interview," pp. 9–15.
58. Dennis Malcolm, "Physical Testing," in *Recruitment Handbook,* ed. Bernard Ungerson, (Aldershot, Hants, England: Gower, 1983), pp. 83–95.
59. David Israel and Debra Scott, "Hiring Under the ADA," *HRMagazine,* November 1991, pp. 87–88.
60. Michael A. Campion, "Personnel Selection for Physically Demanding Jobs: Review and Recommendations," *Personnel Psychology,* Autumn 1983, pp. 527–550.
61. Edwin A. Fleishman, "Evaluating Physical Abilities Required by Jobs," *Personnel Administration,* June 1979, pp. 82–90; Barton N. Daniel, "Strength and Endurance Testing," *Personnel Journal,* June 1987, pp. 112–122.
62. Michael Crant and Thomas S. Bateman, "An Experimental Test of the Impact of Drug-Testing Programs on Potential Job Applicants' Attitudes and Intentions," *Journal of Applied Psychology,* April 1990, pp. 127–131; Mary A. Konovsky and Russell Cropanzano, "Perceived Fairness of Employee

Drug Testing as a Predictor of Employee Attitudes and Job Performance," *Journal of Applied Psychology,* October 1991, pp. 698–707; Kevin R. Murphy, George C. Thornton III, and Kristin Prue, "Influence of Job Characteristics on the Acceptability of Employee Drug Testing," *Journal of Applied Psychology,* June 1991, pp. 447–453; Kevin R. Murphy, George C. Thornton III, and Douglas H. Reynolds, "College Students' Attitudes Toward Employee Drug Testing Programs," *Personnel Psychology,* Autumn 1990, pp. 615–631.

63. Jacques Normand, Stephen D. Salyards, and John J. Mahoney, "An Evaluation of Preemployment Drug Testing," *Journal of Applied Psychology,* December 1990, pp. 629–639.

64. William L. Weis, "Can You Afford to Hire Smokers?" *Personnel Administrator,* May 1981, pp. 71–78.

65. Philip R. Voluck, "Burning Legal Issues of Smoking in the Workplace," *Personnel Journal,* June 1987, pp. 140–143; Paul G. Engel, "No Smoking! More Companies Are Imposing Bans," *Industry Week,* November 11, 1985, pp. 20–21. Liz Batten "Stubbing Out Passive Smoking." *Personnel Management*, August 1992, pp. 24–27.

66. *McCarthy* v. *State of Washington Department of Social and Health Services,* No. 7667–5–11 Ct. App. December 8, 1986.

67. Paul Dobson, "Reference Reports," in *Assessment and Selection in Organizations,* pp. 455–468.

68. James C. Baxter, Barbara Brock, Peter C. Hill, and Richard M. Rozelle, "Letters of Recommendation: A Question of Value," *Journal of Applied Psychology,* June 1981, pp. 296–301; Alan Jones and Elizabeth Harrison, "Prediction of Performance in Initial Officer Training Using Reference Reports," *Journal of Occupational Psychology,* March 1982, pp. 35–42.

69. Charles S. White and Lawrence S. Kleiman, "The Cost of Candid Comments," *HRMagazine,* August 1991, pp. 54–56; Betty Southard Murphy, Wayne E. Barlow, and D. Diane Hatch, "Job Reference Liability of Employers," *Personnel Journal,* September 1991, pp. 22, 26.

70. Ann Marie Ryan and Marja Kasek, Negligent Hiring and Defamation: Areas of Liability Related to Pre-Employment Inquiries," *Personnel Psychology,* Summer 1991, pp. 293–319.

71. I. T. Robertson and P. A. Iles, "Approaches to Managerial Selection," in *International Review of Industrial and Organizational Psychology,* ed. C. L. Cooper and I. Robertson (Chichester, England: Wiley, 1988), pp. 159–211; Glen Grimsley and Hilton F. Jarrett, "The Relationship of Past Managerial Achievement to Test Measures Obtained in the Employment Situation: Methodology and Results," *Personnel Psychology,* Spring 1973, pp. 31–48; Michael J. Stahl, "Achievement, Power, and Managerial Motivation: Selecting Managerial Talent with the Job Choice Exercise," *Personnel Psychology,* Winter 1983, pp. 775–789.

72. Robert V. Lorenzo, "Effects of Assessorship on Managers' Proficiency in Acquiring, Evaluating, and Communicating Information About People," *Personnel Psychology,* Winter 1984, pp. 617–634.

73. Barbara B. Gaugler, Douglas B. Rosenthal, George C. Thornton III, and Cynthia Bentson, "Meta-analyses of Assessment Center Validity," *Journal of Applied Psychology,* August 1987, pp. 493–511; Joel L. Moses and Virginia R. Boehm, "Relationship of Assessment Center Performance to Management Progress of Women," *Journal of Applied Psychology,* August 1975, pp. 527–529; J. R. Huck and D. W. Bray, "Management Assessment Center Evaluations and Subsequent Job Performance of White and Black Females," *Personnel Psychology,* Spring 1976, pp. 13–30; Neal Schmitt, Jeffrey R. Schneider, and Scott A. Cohen, "Factors Affecting Validity of a Regionally Administered Assessment Center," *Personnel Psychology,* Spring 1990, p. 1–12.

74. Michael T. Brannick, Charles E. Michaels, and David P. Baker, "Construct Validity of In-Basket Scores," *Journal of Applied Psychology,* December 1989, pp. 957–963; Ted H. Shore, George C. Thornton III, and Lynn McFarlane Shore, "Construct Validity of Two Categories of Assessment Center Dimension Ratings," *Personnel Psychology,* Spring 1990, pp. 101–116; Richard Klimoski

and Mary Brickner, "Why Do Assessment Centers Work? The Puzzle of Assessment Center Validity," *Personnel Psychology,* Vol. 40, 1987, pp. 243–260.

75. Wayne F. Cascio and V. Sibley, "Utility of the Assessment Center as a Selection Device," *Journal of Applied Psychology,* April 1979, pp. 107–118.

76. Stephan J. Motowidlo, Marvin D. Dunnette, and Gary W. Carter, "An Alternative Selection Procedure: The Low-Fidelity Simulation," *Journal of Applied Psychology,* December 1990, pp. 640–647.

77. Ann Marie Ryan and Paul R. Sackett, "A Survey of Individual Assessment Practices by I/O Psychologists," *Personnel Psychology,* Autumn 1987, pp. 455–488; Ann Marie Ryan and Paul R. Sackett, "Exploratory Study of Individual Assessment Practices: Interrater Reliability and Judgments of Assessor Effectiveness," *Journal of Applied Psychology,* August 1989, pp. 568–579.

78. James P. Guthrie and Judy D. Olian, "Does Context Affect Staffing Decisions? The Case of General Managers," *Personnel Psychology,* Summer 1991, pp. 263–292.

Computers in Human Resource Management

Human Resource Information Systems: Definition and Design

In 1980, the New York City Department of Personnel provided services such as employment testing and training to more than sixty operating agencies consisting of over 200,000 employees. The department also audited and confirmed the legality of thousands of personnel appointments, transfers, and promotions each year. To accomplish this audit function, the department compared payroll changes with various government documents and manually kept and updated official employee history cards for each employee. The problems encountered with the manual system included the following:

- An enormous amount of staff time was required to satisfy inquiries about the history and current status of an employee.
- The payroll audit process, a comparison of payroll changes with promotion reports and employee history cards, was very time consuming, with serious backlogs and delays in attempting to catch errors and unauthorized transactions.
- The payroll audit was often out of date.
- There were no backup copies of the employee history cards in the event that one was lost or destroyed.
- Because the manual records were often out of date and far behind in processing, it was impossible to verify employee eligibility for promotion before a civil service advancement test was given.

This section is modified and updated from a similar section written by Dr. Jon Beard of the University of Richmond (Virginia) for the first edition of this book.

A survey of the needs of the Department of Personnel identified the payroll audit and employee history activities as the areas needing the most urgent attention. The department made plans to develop an on-line computerized **human resource information system (HRIS)** and hired an outside organization to design, develop, and implement the new system.

During the fifteen months of design and development, a number of things happened. The people who were initially assigned to act as part-time liaisons between the development group and the personnel department soon found themselves working on the project full time. There were constant disagreements and battles over what the new system should and should not include. One problem area during the system design was the approval process for the system. People in the personnel department who were going to be using the system were not very knowledgeable about software system design; however, they had to approve the designs. Other users were worried that their jobs were in danger of being eliminated or that their expert knowledge would no longer be valuable to the organization. Many of these people resisted the proposed benefits of the new system. It was also discovered that the manual systems allowed many deviations from and exceptions to normal operating procedures. A computerized system would require more consistency and fewer exceptions in processing personnel data. Therefore, uniform methods of handling the audit process had to be reintroduced.

The original plans had projected an HRIS that would generate information for thirty regular reports. This entire set of report programs was to be implemented simultaneously. Later in the planning stage, the planners chose a phased implementation whereby smaller sections, consisting of only a few report programs, were to be implemented at one time. This allowed the users time to learn the smaller sections for each type of report and to identify missing pieces or problem areas. An all-at-once implementation approach would have meant a longer wait for the system to be ready and might have overwhelmed those trying to test and use the system.

Once implementation was completed, several unexpected benefits surfaced. Because the new system would automatically audit payroll changes, personnel department employees could concentrate on other tasks. A number of employees were transferred to an investigative unit to enter, track, and verify documents that would be used later by the audit system. As personnel department employees learned to use the new system, they found that they had more control over the flow of inquiries. The personnel department could now manage the work, not just process it. In addition, the new HRIS allowed them to track the workload, including monitoring the number and type of inquiry transactions, personnel department productivity, and turnaround times on various types of inquiries. The system has been evaluated as highly successful.[1]

This example presents many of the major factors in the design and development of a human resource information system. Important issues include deciding whether a system is needed, choosing what to include in the system, purchasing or designing the system, and implementing and maintaining the system. These issues are discussed in the following sections.

INTRODUCTION TO HRIS

The concept of a human resource information system was introduced in Chapter 3, in connection with HR planning. An HRIS is "the system used to acquire, store, manipulate, analyze, retrieve, and distribute pertinent information regarding an organization's human resources."[2] Often HRISs evolve from previously separate computer systems such as payroll, employee skills inventories, and Equal Employment Opportunity (EEO) files. HRISs are also being used for tracking employee training and development activities and needs, performance appraisal, employee benefits, labor relations, and almost every other area of human resource management. An HRIS will allow top management and HR managers to be more than just administrators of HR data. The HRIS provides management with the opportunity to use HR information to support and guide decision making and long-range planning. This section begins with a general explanation and description of an HRIS.

What Is a Human Resource Information System?

A full-blown human resource information system for a larger organization is comprised of the components and capabilities listed below and shown in Figure 1.

- A computerized data-based management system.
- Screens for inputting data.
- Programs for cross-checking data and transaction accuracy.
- Modules for performing specific functions, such as tracking applicant flows, and for generating regular reports, such as monthly compensation costs or positions filled versus vacant.
- Query programs for requesting special information combinations or "what if" analyses.

Databases State-of-the-art systems today feature **relational databases**. These systems reduce the need to keep and maintain duplicate data. For instance, in earlier, nonrelational systems, information on employee name, age, home address, job title, and pay rate would be repeated in the payroll file, the benefits file, and probably several other places as well. Any change, such as a new home address, would require information to be updated separately in each file. The possibility of errors and inconsistent information was very great, as was the time involved in updating.

With a relational database, information appears only once, in an appropriate table—for instance, a table on payroll, on demographics, on benefits, or on employee skills. The computer knows how to link the tables together and can locate and combine information from many tables to produce the needed report or analysis.

FIGURE 1 A General HRIS Model

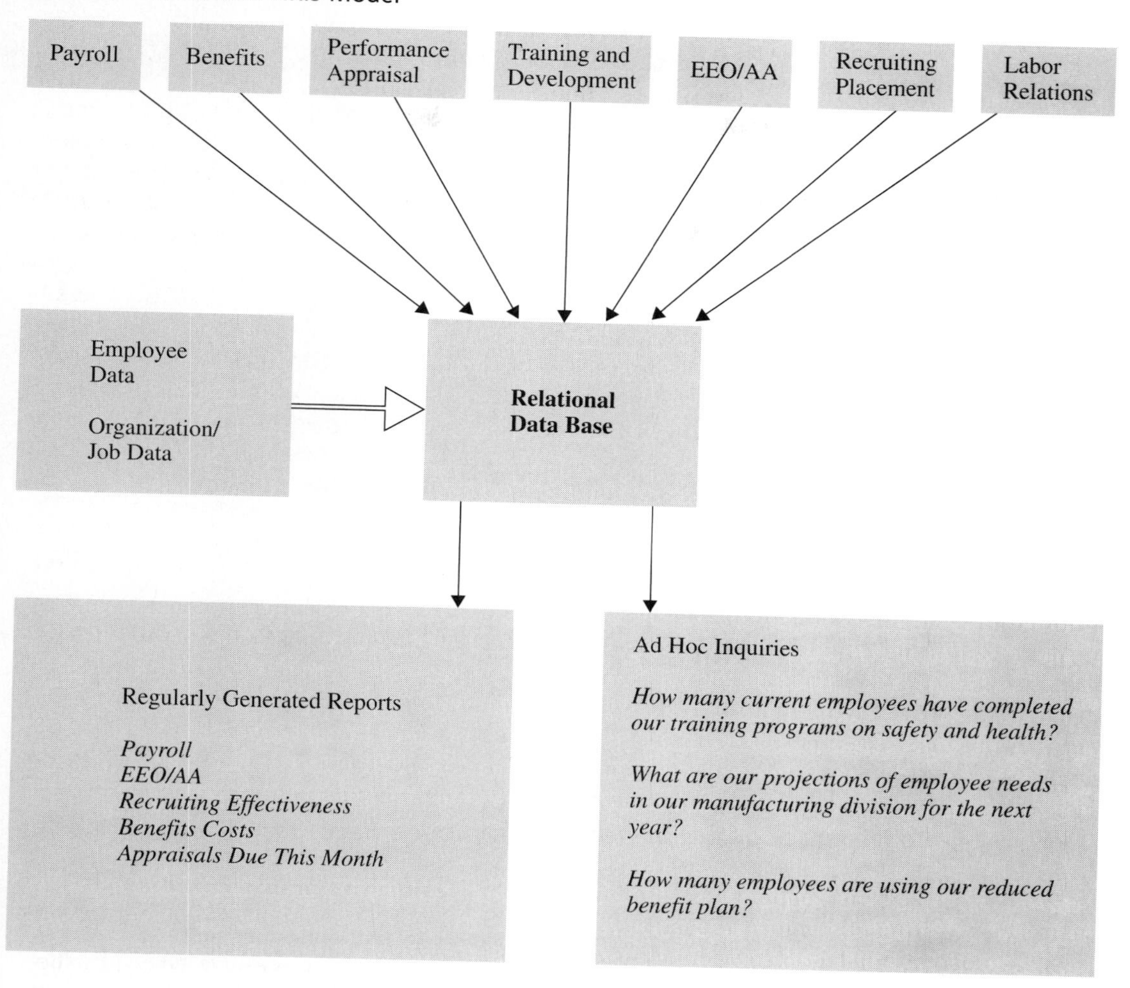

Screens Each module in the HRIS will have its own screens for data entry and retrieval. Figure 2 is an example of a screen for basic personnel data. Screens are often organized by employee. So, for Susan B. Day, it will be possible to call up and modify one or more screens containing Susan's information on each of the following topics: basic personnel data, compensation history, benefits, recent appraisal results and review dates, training received, and so on.

Cross-checking Some relational databases have built-in systems to catch inconsistencies or prevent errors. This feature, called *referential integrity,* can opera-

FIGURE 2 Sample of Data Input Screen

Employee Data System

Name	Susan B. Day	Date of Birth	11-7-57
Social Security	03-453-6917	Sex	F
Address		Race	C
Street	36 Main Street		
City	Anytown	Handicap	N/A
State	LA		
Zip Code	71031	Marital Status	M
Home Telephone	391-452-9101	Dependents	
		Number	2
Emergency Contact		Dates of Birth	
Name	Mark R. Day		12-3-90
Relationship	Husband		6-21-87
Daytime Phone	319-331-4792		

Screen 1 of 3 Last Updated 5-20-93 Press F1 to advance to next screen

ETHICAL PERSPECTIVE

Privacy and Accuracy of Computerized Employee Records

Privacy is an area of growing concern to employees and to human resource managers. Although there is no explicit constitutional right to privacy, certain amendments and federal laws have some relevance to this issue, and some states have enacted privacy laws. Privacy considerations, whether derived from legal requirements or from basic respect for individuals, may constrain the type and amount of information that employers gather about applicants and employees and also the way that the information is stored, used, and disseminated by organizations.

With more and more employee records stored in computers, there is some concern that unauthorized persons could gain access to employee information of a confidential nature, such as performance appraisals, salary data, or drug test results. There are many technical approaches to restricting computer users' access to successively more sensitive types of information, and employers with a computerized HRIS should be sure that such security systems are in place. HRIS security systems include limiting physical access to terminals by unauthorized persons, such as locking offices after hours, or key card access to the human resource information center. More important is probably multilevel password protection to limit access to data files. Some individuals will have passwords that allow them to view only selected types of information. Others may be authorized to view a wider range of information, and still others will be allowed to both view and edit information. As HRISs become more user friendly and more available to managers outside the HR specialty, security becomes a more pressing concern.

Another employee records issue is accuracy. Ideally, employees should be permitted to view their personnel records from time to time to make sure that they are timely and accurate. Some HRISs automatically produce "turnaround documents" when employees' files are modified. These are paper copies sent to employees showing the changes made and requesting correction if needed. For instance, if an employee fills out a change in his or her flexible benefits scheme, the HRIS will return a copy of the inputted changes to the employee for verification.

HR professionals should purge employee records regularly to remove dated or irrelevant information. The following are some suggestions for proper handling of employee records:*

- Establish and circulate to employees clearly written guidelines that describe company information-handling practices and restrictions.
- Tell applicants and employees the type of third parties outside the organization that will be contacted and how the information will be used. Obtain written consent prior to gathering the information.
- Collect and retain only the employee information needed for business or legal reasons, and establish controls for internal use and external release of this information.
- Maintain sensitive information—security and medical reports, investigative and grievance files, insurance and benefit records, comparative evaluations, etc.—apart from other employee information and restrict its use to a tightly controlled need-to-know basis.
- Have employees review their personnel file on a scheduled basis. Allow them to copy, request corrections and dispute their records. State clearly which records may and may not be inspected and for what reasons.
- Purge personnel files and other records of all irrelevant information.
- Require information requestors to justify the relevance of all employee data solicited to the needs and purposes of their units.

*Robert W. Goddard, "Shedding Light on Employee Privacy." Reprinted from *Management World,* January, 1987, with permission from AMS, Trevose, PA 19047. Copyright 1987 AMS.

Sources: Richard Stouffer, "Computerized Personnel Records Require Confidential Treatment," *Data Management,* December 1985, pp. 32–33; Robert W. Goddard, "Shedding Light on Employee Privacy," *Management World,* January 1987, pp. 18–20; Michael J. Kavanagh, Hal G. Gueutal, and Scott I. Tannenbaum, *Human Resource Information Systems: Development and Application* (Boston: PWS-Kent, 1990); Lynn E. Adams, "Securing Your HRIS in a Microcomputer Environment," *HRMagazine,* February 1992, 56–61.

tionalize an organization's policies within the information system. For instance, the system may not allow a new employee to be hired unless a vacancy has been approved; nor will it allow a position to be deleted as long as it has an incumbent on record.[3] This helps ensure that all transactions in the database are consistent with each other, with policy, and with what is actually happening in the organization. At the data input end, the system may catch keyboarding errors by rejecting out-of-range values such as an age of 124 or an annual salary of $3,500. (See the Ethical Perspective box for more information on privacy and accuracy issues in HRISs.)

Modules Most systems will have a number of modules that perform specific functions and produce regular reports. The most basic module, which virtually all systems have, contains employee information such as age, sex, date of hire, and the like, which can be accessed by other modules as needed. Additional modules perform applicant tracking, EEO/AA reporting, recruitment source evaluation and costing, performance appraisal recording and scheduling, skills inventory, position control, benefits management, compensation and payroll, training record keeping, and human resource planning.[4]

Query Programs More sophisticated HRISs do not just produce regular reports; they can also produce special reports, answer questions interactively, and play an important role in decision support. For instance, suppose an organization is considering offering an enhanced retirement package. Appropriate queries to the HRIS may generate predictions of how many people will qualify for and probably accept each type of enhanced package, and how their departure will impact total compensation costs, staffing levels, promotion rates and patterns, and training needs.

Why Is an HRIS Needed?

Early examples of HRISs existed primarily in the aerospace and defense-related industries in the 1960s and early 1970s. Access to large computer systems and the wide variety of specialized projects undertaken by these organizations created the environment for the early human resource information systems. These systems often contained employee skills inventories to assist managers in identifying employees who possessed specific skills for large, technical projects. Many organizations outside these industries had computerized payroll systems, but few developed consolidated HRISs until the late 1970s or early 1980s.

HRISs have been increasing in importance and popularity during the past fifteen years for several reasons. As organizations grow in size, the maintenance and use of employee information becomes more and more difficult. Large organizations, especially those with multiple sites in several distant locations, may have trouble maintaining accurate and timely information on their employees. HRISs, with their rapid processing speed and their ability to store large amounts of data, can help alleviate some of these problems. Table 1 shows one example of an employee database, indicating close to 140 items of data that may be routinely kept and updated.

A second reason for the increase in HRISs is the rapid reduction in the cost of computing. A typical microcomputer today costs only a few thousand dollars (including software and printing facilities) and can process information similar to the midrange mainframe computers of the mid-1970s, which often cost over $1 million and required a full complement of maintenance programmers and operating staff.

TABLE 1. Typical Data Elements in a Human Resource Information System

Address (work)
Address (home)
Birthdate
Child support deductions
Citizenship
Claim pending (description)
Claim pending (outcome)
Claim pending (court)
Claim pending (date)
Date on current job
Department
Dependent (sex)
Dependent (number of)
Dependent (relationship)
Dependent (birthdate)
Dependent (name)
Discipline (appeal date)
Discipline (appeal outcome)
Discipline (date of charge)
Discipline (hearing date)
Discipline (outcome)
Discipline (type of charge)
Division
Driver's license (number)
Driver's license (state)
Driver's license (exp. date)
Education in progress (date)
Education in progress (type)
Educational degree (date)
Educational degree (type)
Educational major
Educational minor
Educational level attained
EEO-1 code
Emergency contact (phone)
Emergency contact (name)
Emergency contact (relation)
Emergency contact (address)
Employee weight
Employee number
Employee code
Employee status
Employee height
Employee date of birth
Federal job code
Full-time/part-time
Garnishments
Grievance (type)
Grievance (outcome)
Grievance (filing date)
Handicap status
Health plan coverage
Health plan (# dependents)
Injury (date)
Injury (type)
Job location
Job preference
Job position number
Job title
Leave of absence (start date)
Leave of absence (end date)
Leave of absence (type)
Life insurance coverage
Marital status
Marriage date
Medical exam (date)
Medical exam (restrictions)
Medical exam (blood type)
Medical exam (outcome)
Miscellaneous deductions
Name
Organizational property
Pay status
Pension plan
Performance rating
Performance increase ($)
Performance increase (%)
Phone number (work)
Phone number (home)
Prior service (hire date)
Prior service (termination date)
Professional license (type)
Professional license (date)
Race
Rehire code
Religious preference
Salary
Salary compa ratio
Salary (previous)
Salary (change date)
Salary (change reason)
Salary (change type)
Salary (points)
Salary (range)
Schools attended
Service date
Service branch
Service discharge type
Service ending rank
Service discharge date
Sex
Sick leave (used)
Sick leave (available)
Skill function (type)
Skill subfunction (type)
Skill (number of years)
Skill (proficiency level)
Skill (date last used)
Skill (location)
Skill (supervisory)

(continues)

TABLE 1. Typical Data Elements in a Human Resource Information System (*cont.*)

Social security number	Supervisor's name	Training schools (completed)
Spouse's employment	Supervisor's work address	Transfer date
Spouse's date of death	Supervisor's work phone	Transfer reason
Spouse's name	Supervisor's title	Union code
Spouse's birthdate	Termination (date)	Union deductions
Spouse's sex	Termination (reason)	United Way deductions
Spouse's social security number	Training schools (attended)	Vacation leave (available)
Start date	Training schools (date)	Vacation leave (used)
Stock plan membership	Training schools (held)	Veteran status

Source: D. Harris, "A Matter of Privacy: Managing Personnel Data in Company Computers." Reprinted, by permission of publisher, from *Personnel,* February/1987 © 1987. American Management Association, New York. All rights reserved.

The large computer systems of the 1970s were often batch-processing systems. This means that requests for information were gathered together and run as a batch at a certain time or at the end of the day. A microcomputer—small in size and low in price—can be located on someone's desk and provide almost immediate access to HR data. Several microcomputers can be linked together or linked to a larger computer in a network. Before microcomputers, management requests for data and information contained in the large computer systems often would require the creation of new programs in specialized programming languages by the programming staff. Depending on the complexity of the request, this process might take weeks or months to complete.

Microcomputers, with their database and spreadsheet programs, allow managers and HR specialists to create their own ad hoc programs quickly. If the microcomputers are linked to a larger computer, the needed data can often be downloaded to the microcomputer for individual use. In one survey, 75.5 percent of the respondents reported the use of a mainframe computer for some HR applications, whereas 68.3 percent of the respondents reported the use of microcomputers. Microcomputers allow managers to do some of their own programming and HR data processing without major assistance from the programmers for the mainframe system.[5]

Another reason for the growth in HRISs is the need to produce reports and monitor information on employees in order to comply with legal requirements. Legislation has increased the need to keep accurate and timely information on race, sex, age, and veteran and handicap status of job applicants and current employees. The Consolidated Omnibus Budget Reconciliation Act (COBRA) of 1985 is an example of a law that has greatly increased recordkeeping demands on HR departments. (See Chapter 13 for more information on COBRA.)

The purpose of COBRA is to extend group health care coverage to eligible terminated employees, at the employees' own expense, for a prescribed period of time after departure. COBRA modules for HRISs flag eligible employees, produce a standard letter informing employees of their rights, record acceptances and rejections of the benefit, invoice and record premium payments, and provide notice when eligibility runs out.[6] Figure 3 shows some information on one such commercially available module.

Finally, as competition has increased, organizations have come to realize that managing their human resources is as important as managing their financial and raw material resources. To manage human resources properly requires detailed information for making complex decisions. How many people will we need next year? Who needs specific types of training? What kind of employee turnover do we have at each plant? The HRIS can assist HR managers and top-level management in moving beyond simple, administrative human resource management to thoughtful and planned human resource management.

Many organizations are now planning and acquiring their second or even third HRIS since they first began to use computers to track employee information. As

FIGURE 3 A COBRA Module for HRIS

Benefit Continuation Management System, Version 3.1

Benefits Concepts Systems Inc.
396 Wampanoag Trail
East Providence, RI 02915
(401) 438-7100

bcsi
Benefit Concepts Systems, Inc.

Introduced: 1986
Installed Base: 250
Language: dBase, Clipper compiled
Program Size: 300K, 5 MB for 400 records
List Price: $1,995. Maintenance $395.
Hardware Requirements: IBM PC (or 100-percent compatible) with DOS 2.1 or higher, a hard drive and a minimum of 512K usable RAM.
Product Use: Automatically performs all the functions necessary to meet COBRA compliance.

Source: Gina Williams, "Managing COBRA with BCMS," *HRMagazine*, February 1990, p. 25. Reprinted with the permission from *HRMagazine* published by the Society for Human Resource Management, Alexandria, VA.

old systems become overburdened with excessive modifications, new hardware and software capabilities emerge, and legal and managerial information demands increase, the market for both first-time and upgraded HRISs continues to grow.

ACQUIRING AND IMPLEMENTING AN HRIS

A human resource information system can be as large or as small as is necessary and may contain only one or two modules or up to twenty or so. Hundreds of HRIS software packages are being marketed for both mainframe and microcomputers. Some of these packages are complete human resource information systems, whereas others are small components of individual applications. A great many decisions need to be made in the course of adopting and implementing an HRIS. Figure 4 provides an overview of this process. Some of the major decision points are discussed below.

HRIS Needs Assessment

The specific needs of the organization should dictate the type of human resource information system chosen. Any project as potentially expensive, complex, and time consuming as the addition or upgrading of an HRIS requires careful analysis and planning. Thus, the first step must be a careful needs assessment, involving interviews with users and an audit of current practices, functions, and desired new capabilities. The organization must decide what its goals are for the HRIS. Is the HRIS intended to assist in managing HR data? In other words, is management looking for a better way to make strategic use of HR data or is it just trying to computerize a manual process? Will management need quick and easy access to HR information on an ad hoc basis, or will information be available mainly in regular and formal report form? Who will have access to the HRIS data? Will the system have to interface with other systems? How might the organization's future needs be met by the system or its available add-ons? What are the projected short- and long-term costs of the HRIS? What are the short- and long-term benefits? These are the kinds of questions that an organization must address when deciding on the type and size of an HRIS. This needs assessment phase is time consuming but critical to getting a system that will suit the organization and its users.[7]

Microcomputer or Mainframe? Based on the particular needs of the organization, a decision must be made on the type and size of the HRIS. Will the HRIS reside on a microcomputer, several microcomputers, a mainframe computer, or some combination of microcomputers and mainframe computers? The answer to this question will have a major impact on the initial expense of the HRIS. Microcomputers can perform much of the processing required for many HR applications. If the organization is not too large, the entire system could be maintained on one microcomputer or several networked microcomputers. There is no specific definition of what is too large. The limiting factors will be the amount of data to

FIGURE 4 Phases of HRIS Acquisition

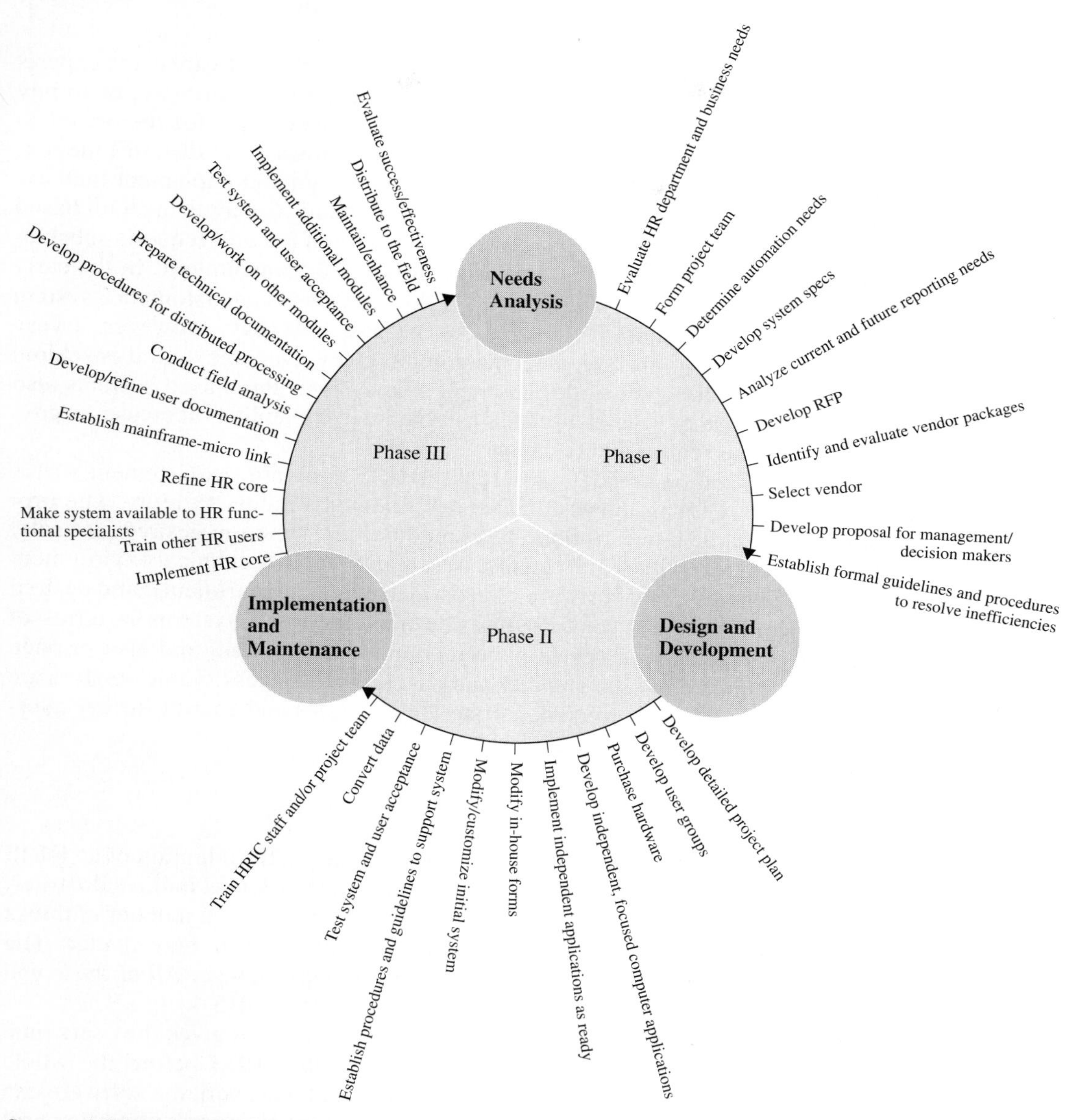

Source: Michael J. Kavanagh, Hal G. Gueutal, and Scott I. Tannenbaum, *Human Resource Information Systems: Development and Application* (Boston: PWS-Kent Publishing Company, 1990), p. 98.

be kept, how long it will take to do processing for a typical application, and how many people need access to the information simultaneously.

Build or Buy? Another decision is whether to develop the software using experts already within the organization, to buy and use off-the-shelf software, or to buy software but then have it extensively modified and customized for the organization. Building an HRIS within the organization requires a great deal of time, expertise, and money. Systems often take longer to design and implement than expected, so there is a potential for conflict and delay. Customizing purchased software is quicker than building a system from scratch but still requires substantial development time, as well as extensive in-house documentation. In the early days of HRISs, it was often necessary to build or extensively customize a system in order to get the capabilities needed. In the past few years, however, a very great number of programs have become commercially available, and it is seldom necessary or cost-effective to design one's own system. Purchased systems also have the advantage of regular updates as computer capabilities increase or government reporting requirements change.[8]

If the organization decides to purchase HRIS software, management writes a detailed request for proposals and invites selected vendors to reply. The proposal should include a description of the modules and function desired; security, access, and data integrity requirements; information on the technical environment (hardware, languages, and software already in use in the department); and desired vendor support services. Vendors describe their proposed systems in terms of these requirements, give a cost for the recommended system, and also provide information on their financial stability and past project success. Some vendors are invited to the organization to demonstrate their systems and answer further questions before a purchase decision is made.[9]

Implementation

After the organization selects a vendor, the final stages in the adoption of an HRIS take place: testing, implementation, and maintenance. As was indicated earlier, in the account of the New York City Department of Personnel, a number of things can alter the implementation process. For example, the design may change. The project may run behind schedule. Project members may change. All of these will have an impact on the design and implementation of the HRIS.

A phased implementation is often the best process, for it gives the users time to explore and learn about smaller subsections of the HRIS before the whole system is installed. During this learning time, any problems with the software can be identified and corrected before major damage is done to current operating procedures. Repair of problems at this stage is much easier than when the system has already been fully implemented and people are waiting on the system for their work. During phased implementation, data from older computer systems and manual records are fed into the new system, users are trained, and any needed local documentation is developed.

Finally, the system is maintained on an ongoing basis. Vendor updates are installed, tested, and trained for, modifications are well documented, and new modules are added as needed. After the system is in place, periodic audits will ensure that it is still meeting users' needs effectively.[10] Many large organizations now have a **human resource information center (HRIC)**, staffed by one or more dedicated professionals who are experts on both computer systems and human resource management, and who oversee the acquisition, implementation, and maintenance of the HRIS.[11] For most HR practitioners, the HRIC represents a substantial improvement over the early days, when all HRIS issues had to be negotiated with the electronic data processing/information systems department.

Clearly, many issues remain to be addressed in the development and utilization of an HRIS. This discussion has only briefly introduced some of the most critical issues in HRIS design and implementation. Most HR practitioners will have to acquire skills in HRIS use, and some can expect to become deeply involved in system development and acquisition decisions. More specific applications of the HRIS to various HR functions are described in the second insert on computers in human resources, which follows Chapter 16.

Notes and References

1. S. Rosenberg, "Flexibility in Installing a Large-Scale HRIS: New York City's Experience," *Personnel Administrator,* December 1985, pp. 39–46.
2. Michael J. Kavanagh, Hal G. Gueutal, and Scott I. Tannenbaum, *Human Resource Information Systems: Development and Application* (Boston: PWS-Kent, 1990), p. 29.
3. Row Henson, "Computer Databases Built for HR," *HRMagazine,* April 1991, pp. 59–61.
4. Kavanagh, Gueutal, and Tannenbaum, *Human Resource Information Systems.*
5. M. Magnus and M. Grossman, "Computers and the Personnel Department," *Personnel Journal,* April 1985, pp. 42–48.
6. Gina Williams, "Managing COBRA with BCMS," *HRMagazine,* February 1990, pp. 25–26.
7. Timothy R. Adams, "Buying Software Without the Glitches," *HRMagazine,* January 1990, pp. 40–42.
8. William A. Minneman, "A Home Buyer's Guide to HRIS," *HRMagazine,* June 1990, pp. 79–84.
9. Minneman, "A Home Buyer's Guide to HRIS."
10. Joanne Wisneiwski, "The Needs-Based HRIS Audit," *HRMagazine,* September 1991, pp. 61–82.
11. Kavanagh, Gueutal, and Tannenbaum, *Human Resource Information Systems.*

PART FOUR

Building Individual and Organizational Performance

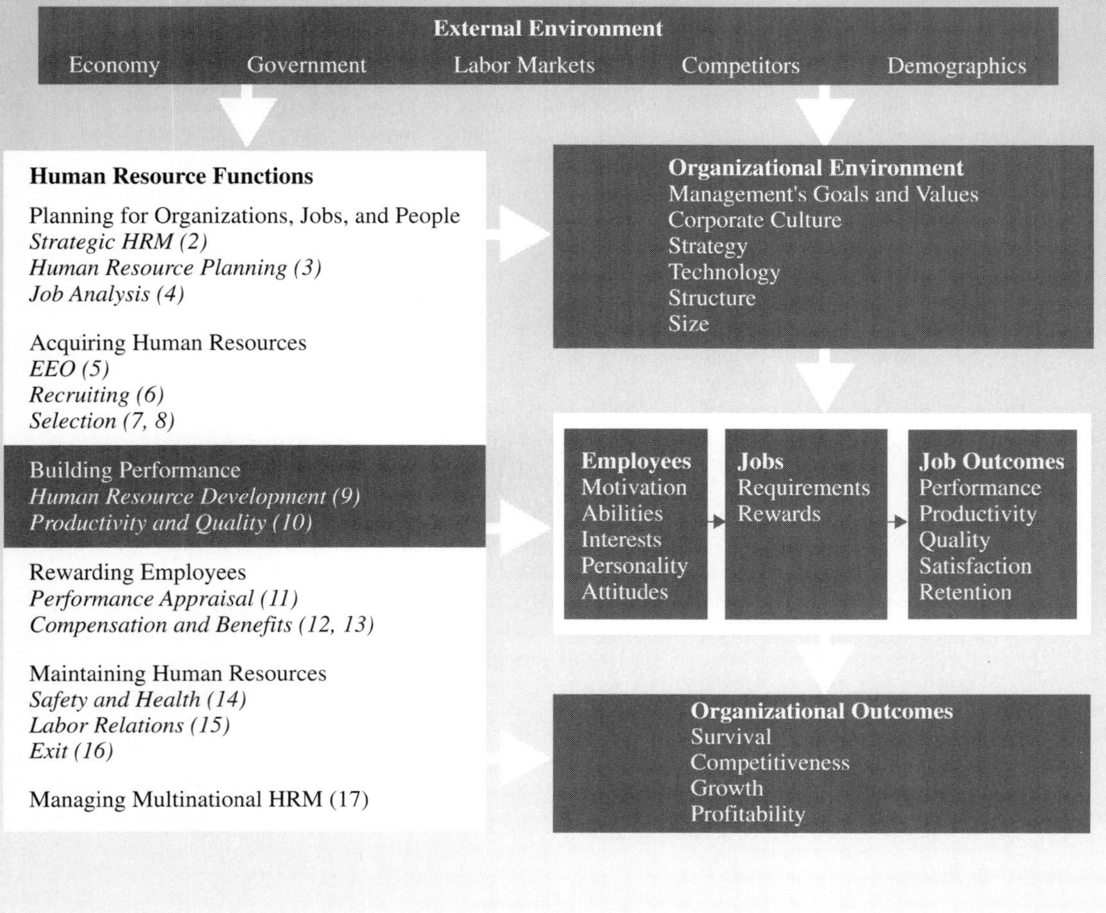

External Environment
Economy Government Labor Markets Competitors Demographics

Human Resource Functions

Planning for Organizations, Jobs, and People
Strategic HRM (2)
Human Resource Planning (3)
Job Analysis (4)

Acquiring Human Resources
EEO (5)
Recruiting (6)
Selection (7, 8)

Building Performance
Human Resource Development (9)
Productivity and Quality (10)

Rewarding Employees
Performance Appraisal (11)
Compensation and Benefits (12, 13)

Maintaining Human Resources
Safety and Health (14)
Labor Relations (15)
Exit (16)

Managing Multinational HRM (17)

Organizational Environment
Management's Goals and Values
Corporate Culture
Strategy
Technology
Structure
Size

Employees
Motivation
Abilities
Interests
Personality
Attitudes

Jobs
Requirements
Rewards

Job Outcomes
Performance
Productivity
Quality
Satisfaction
Retention

Organizational Outcomes
Survival
Competitiveness
Growth
Profitability

9

Human Resource Development

All organizations, whether public or private, are attempting to achieve goals and objectives. It does not matter whether the objectives are return on investment, market share, social well-being, or defense of the country; organizations must have competent employees who can perform the necessary tasks to accomplish those objectives. HR planning and careful selection initially provide an organization with its employees, but additional training and development are usually required to convey job-specific knowledge to employees and to build increasing skills over the course of a career. The training function, now popularly called **human resource development (HRD)**, coordinates the provision of training and development experiences in organizations.

This chapter examines the training process, which begins with the diagnosis of training needs and the establishment of clear objectives for training programs. The next step is to design and deliver training programs that use appropriate methods and procedures to maximize the learning and subsequent job performance of trainees. Finally, training programs are evaluated to see whether they met their objectives and were cost-effective.

HUMAN RESOURCE DEVELOPMENT: AN INTRODUCTION

Organizations provide training for many reasons: to orient new hires to the organization or teach them how to perform in their initial assignment, to improve the current performance of employees who may not be working as effectively as desired, or to prepare employees for future promotions or for upcoming changes in design, processes, or technology in their present jobs. Recent changes in the environment of business have made the HRD function even more important in helping organizations maintain competitiveness and prepare for the future.[1] Technological innovations such as robots, desktop publishing, and computer-aided design require training for affected employees. Competitive pressures are also changing the way organizations operate and the skills that their employees need. For instance, more and more organizations are providing quality management and customer service training in an attempt to keep up with rising consumer expectations.[2] Restructuring and downsizing mean that many employees need to be trained to take on expanded responsibilities.

The declining level of new-hire literacy and numeracy, coupled with greater diversity in the labor force, has stimulated a number of employers to furnish basic education in reading, mathematics, writing, and English as a second language.[3] This same diversity has prompted many organizations to offer training on dealing with diversity and multiculturalism in the work force. The aging of the work force means that more retraining is necessary and that some training methods must be adapted to better fit the needs of older learners.[4]

The long arm of the federal government is also reaching into the organizational training room with a growing list of mandated training topics. Industries such as air transport and nuclear power generation are especially closely regulated with regard to extent, content, and methods of employee training. The Occupational Safety and Health Administration (OSHA) requires that all employees working around hazardous chemicals be trained in how to detect dangerous situations, protect themselves from exposure, and understand the potential adverse effects of exposure. Health care workers must be trained in how to avoid AIDS exposure, and under the Drug-Free Workplace Act, government contractors must educate employees about the dangers of drug and alcohol dependency.[5] Training must be tailored to fit the organization's strategy and structure. For instance, an organization whose strategy involves providing exceptional service through a committed, long-service cadre of extremely well qualified employees will need more complex training and career development systems than an organization that competes on the basis of simple, low-cost services provided by transient, unskilled employees. An organization using a decentralized structure will need to

TABLE 9.1 Types of Training Provided to Employees in 1991

Types of Training	*% Providing*[a]	*In-House Only (%)*[b]	*Outside Only (%)*[c]	*Both (%)*[d]
New-Employee Orientation	82	76	.3	7
Performance Appraisals	76	53	3.3	20
Leadership	69	16	13	40
Hiring/Selection Process	65	31	7	27
Interpersonal Skills	64	19	8	37
Word Processing	63	24	12	28
New Equipment Operation	62	34	4	25
Team Building	61	16	10	34
Delegation Skills	60	18	12	29
Listening Skills	59	22	8	30
Time Management	59	15	14	30
Train-the-Trainer	59	18	15	26
Product Knowledge	58	40	2	16
Goal Setting	58	21	8	30
Personal Computer Applications	57	17	7	33
Motivation	57	15	9	33
Decision Making	56	16	11	29
Safety	56	25	2	29
Stress Management	54	14	15	26
Computer Programming	54	10	15	29
Problem Solving	53	16	7	30
Quality Improvement	50	17	3	30
Managing Change	49	14	10	25
Conducting Meetings	48	23	7	18
Writing Skills	47	13	15	20
Public Speaking/Presentation	47	14	11	22
Planning	46	18	3	25
Data Processing	45	13	9	22
Negotiating Skills	43	11	12	21
Management Information Systems	43	8	10	25
Substance Abuse	42	11	11	20
Finance	41	13	11	18
Smoking Cessation	39	9	18	12
Strategic Planning	38	11	8	12
Ethics	37	18	4	19
Marketing	37	10	8	19

TABLE 9.1 Types of Training Provided to Employees in 1991 (*cont.*)

Types of Training	*% Providing*[a]	*In-House Only (%)*[b]	*Outside Only (%)*[c]	*Both (%)*[d]
Outplacement/Retirement Planning	36	19	8	9
Purchasing	29	11	7	11
Creativity	27	8	5	14
Reading Skills	20	6	7	8
Foreign Language	16	5	8	4
Other (Topics Not Listed)	6	3	.5	2

Source: Chris Lee, "Who Gets Trained in What." Reprinted with permission from the October 1991 issue of *Training* magazine. Lakewood Publications, Minneapolis, MN.

Of All Organizations with 100 or More Employees. . .

[a]Percent that provide each type of training.

[b]Percent that say all training of this type is designed and delivered by in-house staff.

[c]Percent that say all training of this type is designed and delivered by outside consultants or suppliers.

[d]Percent that say training of this type is designed and delivered by a combination of in-house staff and outside suppliers.

teach middle managers somewhat different skills than an organization using a highly centralized structure.

Table 9.1 summarizes the specific types of training that U.S. organizations provided to their employees in 1991. New employee orientation was the most widely provided training. Looking at training types in more general terms, 87 percent of organizations provided management development courses, 86 percent offered technical knowledge and skills training, and 83 percent taught supervisory skills. Most organizational training aims at enhancing work-related behavior, although some organizations offer training programs that help employees satisfy their own personal goals. For example, large corporations like General Motors and General Electric offer personal finance programs, dual-career marriage seminars, and retirement planning courses.

Costs of Human Resource Development

Besides being one of the most important HRM functions, HRD is also one of the most expensive. A survey of American organizations conducted by *Training* magazine revealed that in 1991 these organizations spent $43.2 billion on formal training for their employees.[6] This amount does not include the cost of employee salaries during training or the hard-to-quantify costs of informal on-the-job training and coaching. Organizations with fewer than 100 employees were not included in the survey, so the actual amount spent on training was probably considerably

FIGURE 9.1 1991 Dollars Budgeted for Formal Training (by U.S. organizations with 100 or more employees)

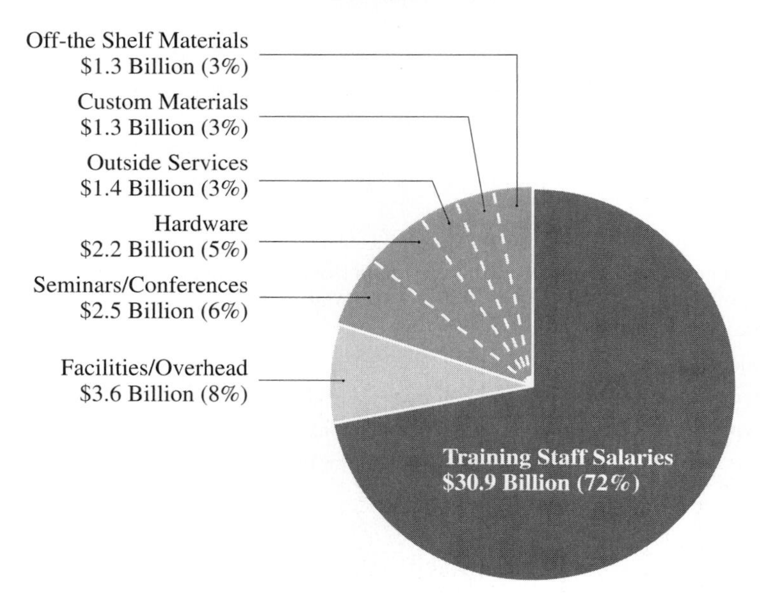

Definitions

Facilities/Overhead—*charges to the training department for buildings, classrooms or other space to be used, remodeled or built during 1991, and for utilities, administrative support from other departments, etc.*

Outside Expenditures—*dollars budgeted for the following five categories:*

- Seminars/Conferences—*training by outside providers conducted either at the respondent's location or off-site, including public seminars but not trainee travel and per diem costs.*
- Hardware—*audiovisual and video equipment, computers, teleconferencing equipment, etc.*
- Outside Services—*consultants (not acting as seminar leaders), printing, material production costs, etc.*
- Custom Materials—*audiovisual, video, printed material, computer courseware, etc., tailored to meet respondent's needs or designed specifically for respondent's organization.*
- Off-the Shelf Materials—*prepackaged in any format: books, films, computer courseware, structured classroom packages, etc.*

Source: Jack Gordon "Training Budgets: Recession Takes a Bite." Reprinted with permission from the October 1991 issue of *Training* magazine. Lakewood Publications, Minneapolis, MN.

higher than $43.2 billion. Figure 9.1 gives a breakdown of how this money was spent. Seventy-two percent was spent on training department salaries, and $8.7 billion went to outside vendors of training programs, equipment, and services.

Relationship of HRD to Other HRM Functions

HRD is linked to many of the other HRM functions. For example, the HR planning function identifies the skills and number of employees needed by the organization. The recruiting and selection function attempts to locate individuals with these skills in the labor force. Information on projected HR needs and the probable qualifications of new hires helps the HRD staff determine the amount and level of training that must be provided for new employees. High selection standards for education and experience can reduce the need for formal training programs, and excellent in-house training may reduce the demand for applicants who are already highly skilled.

Performance evaluations are another link between HRD and other HR functions. Performance evaluations specify whether employees are performing to desired standards and help the employer identify performance discrepancies that may signal the need for additional training. Performance evaluations may also be used as criteria for evaluating training effectiveness, in that trainees should receive better evaluations after training than before. Training is also closely linked to the career planning function and serves as one source of input into succession planning systems.

Training is seen as pivotal in implementing organization-wide culture change efforts, such as developing a commitment to customer service, adopting total quality management, or making a transition to self-directed work teams.[7] Finally, in organizations that use a pay-for-skills system (see Chapter 12), training may be directly related to compensation. As employees complete cross-training programs and demonstrate mastery of an additional job or skill, their base pay is increased.

A Systems Model of the Training Cycle

Because the objective of HRD is to contribute to the organization's overall goals, training programs should be developed systematically and with the organization's true needs in mind. However, often they are not. Instead, training objectives may be undetermined or hazy, and the programs themselves may not be evaluated rigorously or at all. In fact, it sometimes seems that what is important is that the training program is "attention getting, dramatic, contemporary, or fun. Whether or not [the program] changes behavior becomes secondary."[8]

One solution for this haphazardness is to develop training programs following the systematic approach presented in Figure 9.2. The model shows three phases: (1) the assessment phase, (2) the training phase, and (3) the evaluation phase.[9] The rest of this chapter focuses on these three phases of the training cycle. Figure

FIGURE 9.2 Training Systems Model

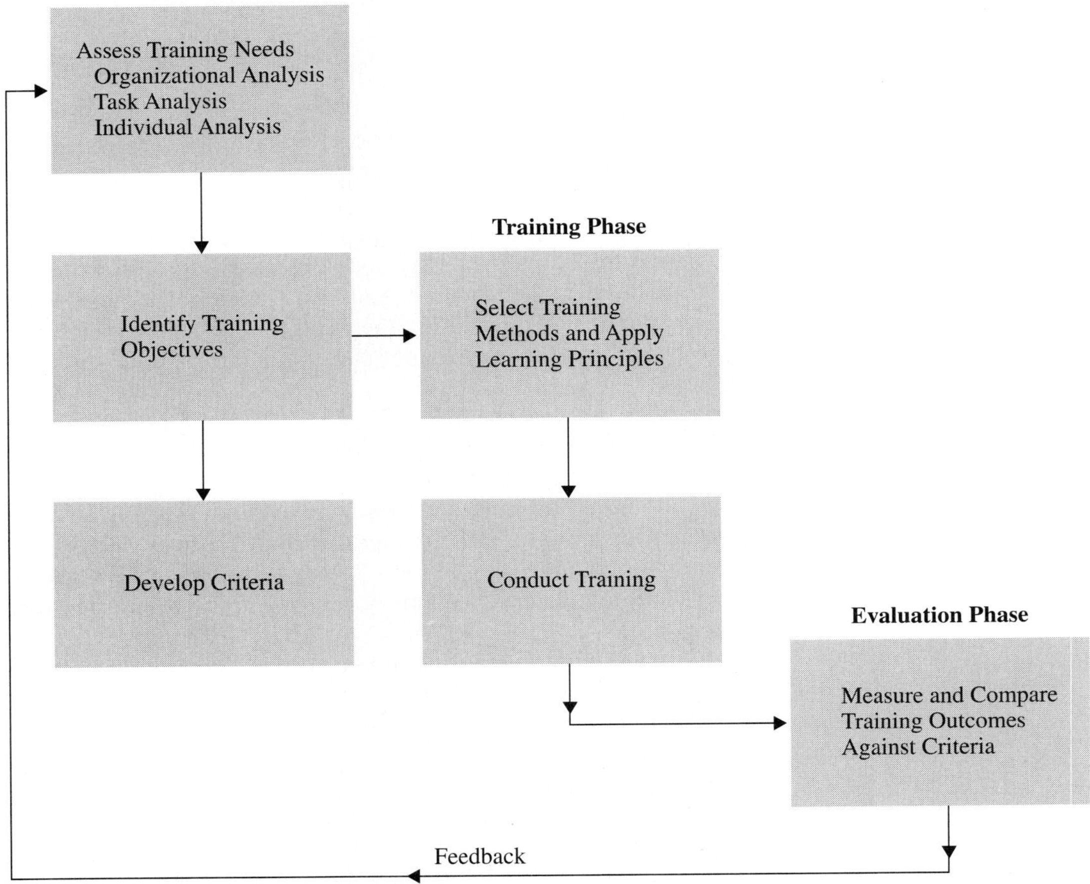

Source: Adapted from I. L. Goldstein, *Training in Organizations: Needs Assessment, Development, and Evaluation* (Monterey, Calif.: Brooks/Cole, 1986), p. 16. Reprinted by permission.

9.3 gives an example of a breakdown of management and HRD department activities as an organization moved through the training cycle from beginning to end.

THE NEEDS ASSESSMENT PHASE

Successful training begins with a thorough **needs assessment** to determine *which employees* need to be trained and *what* they need to be trained to do. Allison Rossett and Joseph W. Arwady state: "The question is not *whether* you will solicit

FIGURE 9.3 A Summary of the Training Cycle

Steps	Management Actions	Training Department Actions
Management Goals	Management decides that it wants to reach certain target markets using telemarketing techniques.	No decision making. Should actively pursue up-to-date knowledge of management direction and key goals.
Training Needs Identified	Makes a decision that a segment of the new agent orientation program should cover target markets and how to use telemarketing techniques to reach those markets.	Suggests and recommends ways that training might best be used. May identify areas that could best be learned on the job, recommend ways for line managers to support desired performance, etc.
Audience and Training Content Determined	Hires new agents. Determines training schedule. Provides key people for training departments to interview to determine training content.	Conducts a content analysis using interview and observation data. Recommends training content. Makes suggestions on prerequisite skills.
Training Designed and Delivered	Communicates expectations to trainees prior to program, including on-the-job application of skills to be learned.	Provides advice on how to conduct pre-course discussions with trainees. Designs and delivers a program that enables students to use telemarketing techniques to reach certain target markets.
Skills Applied On-the-Job	Gives specific assignments for new agents to use telemarketing techniques to reach certain target markets. Gives rewards for effort and results in this area.	Provides suggestions on how to follow through on and support the skills learned in the program.
Training Outcomes Evaluated	Determines if new agents are using the telemarketing techniques and if their performance shows that the techniques are helping them reach target markets.	Gathers specific data on the application of new skills. Provides feedback to management on revisions to training content, audience, pre-course preparation and/or supervision for application on the job.

Source: Adapted with permission from the January 1987 issue of *Training,* The Magazine of Human Resources Development.

this kind of information through needs assessment. It's *how much* of it you will do and using which tools."[10] The culmination of the assessment phase is a set of objectives specifying the purpose of the training and the competencies desired in trainees after they complete the program.

Needs assessment takes time and money. Unfortunately, a great many organizations undertake training without this necessary preliminary investment. In one survey, 81 percent of organizations said that they identified training needs only by reacting to problems that cropped up and to requests by superiors.[11] A survey of management training practices found that only 27 percent of organizations systematically assessed the training needs of their managers.[12] Often there is no systematic effort to predict future training needs or to determine if perceived needs and problems really exist and can be properly addressed by training. Not infrequently, an organization undertakes training as a knee-jerk reaction to a perceived problem or as a response to a popular fad in training programs. An example of a fad in the mid-1980s was the widespread adoption of a management training package based on Thomas J. Peters and Robert H. Waterman's best-selling book *In Search of Excellence*.[13] Training that is undertaken without a careful analysis of whether or not it is needed is likely to be ineffective and a waste of money. Inappropriate training can also sour the attitudes of trainees toward all organizationally sponsored training and reduce their motivation to attend future and perhaps more useful programs.

Purposes and Methods of Needs Assessment

An organization can use many methods of gathering information and several sources of information for needs assessment, as shown in Table 9.2. The choice of methods and sources depends partly on the purpose of the training. If the purpose is to improve employees' performance in the present job, then clearly the trainer must begin by looking at present performance and identifying performance deficiencies or areas where there seems to be room for improvement. Sources of information on performance deficiencies include supervisors' and clients' complaints, performance appraisal data, objective measures of output or quality, and even special performance tests given to determine the current knowledge and skill level of employees. In addition, HRD specialists might collect critical incidents of poor job performance and look at accident reports to locate possible skill or knowledge problems.

Individual or group interviews with superiors, target individuals, or even clients are another means of gathering information on performance discrepancies and perceived training needs. Group techniques are especially helpful for anticipating future training needs, for prioritizing training demands, or for ambiguous situations. A group of executives, for instance, might work together to predict and prioritize the new skills that will be needed by top managers in the organization over the next decade.

When a large number of potential trainees are involved or when they are geographically dispersed, a subsample may be selected for needs assessment in-

TABLE 9.2 Methods and Sources of Information for Needs Assessment

Methods of Gathering Data for Needs Assessment
Search of Existing Records
Individual Interviews
Group Interviews
Delphi Technique
Nominal Group Technique
Questionnaires
Performance Tests
Written Tests
Assessment Centers
Observation
Collection of Critical Incidents
Job Analysis
Task Analysis
Sources of Information
Existing Records (e.g., output, quality, waste, downtime, complaints, accident reports, requests for training, exit interviews, performance appraisals, equipment operation manuals, procedures manuals, job descriptions, hiring criteria, personnel files)
Incumbents
Superiors
Subordinates
Subject Matter Experts
Clients

terviews, or a questionnaire on needs assessment may be developed for wider distribution. Typically, existing data will be scrutinized and some interviews will be held prior to designing the questionnaire. An important advantage of methods that involve large numbers of superiors and potential trainees in the assessment phase is that such early participation may enhance acceptance and commitment to the eventual training product.[14]

Once the organization has identified a performance deficiency, the next step is to determine whether the deficiency should be addressed by training. In some cases, motivation, constraints, or poor task design cause the deficiency. In such situations, training in job skills would not solve the performance problem.

Robert F. Mager and Peter Pipe have developed a useful flow chart to determine if training can correct a performance deficiency.[15] The flow chart is reproduced in Figure 9.4. A number of decision points are identified in the flow chart. By answering questions at each of these decision points, the training specialist can determine whether training is the answer to the performance deficiency. For

FIGURE 9.4 Performance Discrepancy Diagnosis Flow Diagram

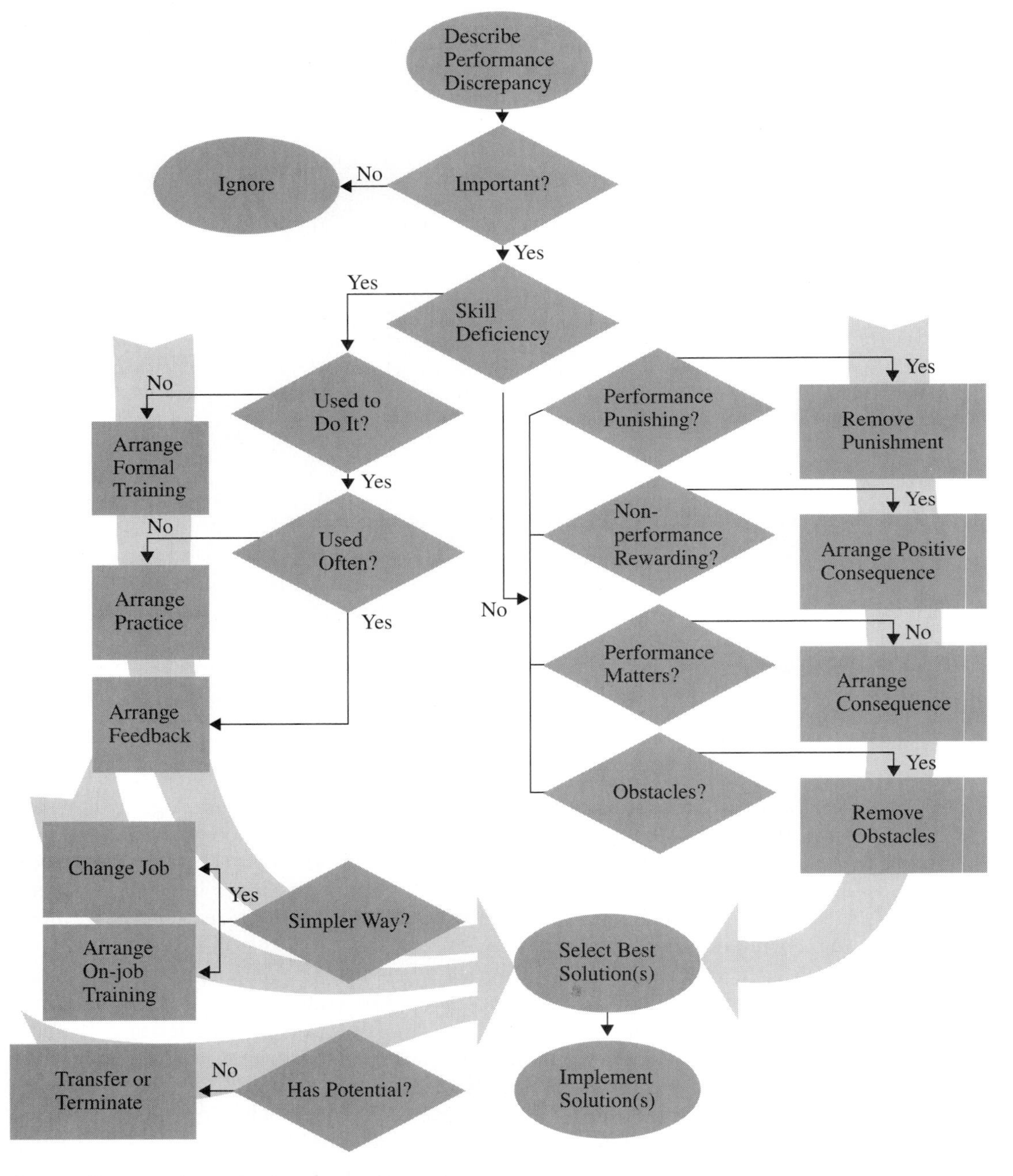

Source: From *Analyzing Performance Problems* by R. F. Mager and Peter Pipe. Copyright © 1984 by David S. Lake Publishers, Belmont, CA 94002.

instance, if the employee used to be able to perform as desired, he or she may simply need practice, performance feedback to facilitate self-correction, or a job aid (such as a checklist of steps) rather than full-blown training. If the employee could do the job correctly if his or her life depended on it, then motivation may be the problem. Perhaps good performance is being ignored or even punished, while poor performance is accepted without criticism. In these cases, the solution is to act on the environment and reward system rather than to train the employee.

If training is being planned for current employees destined for promotion or transfer, needs assessment is more complex. The training specialist must measure the demands of the future job and then attempt to assess the ability of the employees to meet those demands. Because the employees being assessed do not yet hold the future job, their current level of performance may or may not indicate their ability to do the future job. Therefore, the training specialist may have to use special techniques to assess the employees' level of skill and knowledge relative to the demands of the future job. Such techniques include assessment centers (for candidates under consideration for management jobs) and tests or supervisory ratings of relevant abilities.

When training is being designed for new hires, the methods used must be slightly different.[16] Training is designed based on a careful analysis of job content and the assumed characteristics of the trainees. If the trainees are not yet hired, it is difficult to assess their current level of knowledge. Thus, the training specialist must coordinate closely with the staffing manager as the latter sets hiring criteria and evaluates candidates. For instance, the training specialist can design a more advanced training program for entry-level drafters if the staffing manager includes completion of a high school mechanical-drawing course as a requisite job qualification. Similarly, the training specialist could consider scores on a job-knowledge selection test given to applicants for the job of welder when designing posthire training for this group.

Three Levels of Needs Assessment

Regardless of the specific methods used to evaluate needs, any thorough assessment effort must address three key areas: the organization, the job and task, and the individual.

Organizational Analysis **Organizational analysis** looks at the proposed training within the context of the rest of the organization. Table 9.3 provides a list of issues that may be explored in the organizational analysis portion of the needs assessment. A prime consideration is whether or not the proposed training will be compatible with the organization's strategy, goals, and culture. Corporate culture compatibility is especially important for management training and executive development. Efforts to train managers to lead, make decisions, or communicate in ways that are not valued or expected by powerful others in the work environment are doomed to failure.

TABLE 9.3 Issues in Organizational Analysis

- What are the training implications of the organization's strategy?
- How does this training program fit in with the organization's future plans and goals?
- Where in the organization is training needed?
- How are various units performing compared with expectations or goals?
- In which units is training most likely to succeed?
- Which units should be trained first?
- Can the organization afford this training?
- Which training programs should have priority?
- Will this training adversely affect untrained people or units?
- Is this training consistent with the organization's culture?
- Will this training be accepted and reinforced by others in the organization, such as the trainees' superiors and subordinates?

The impact that the training of one unit has on other related units must also be considered in an organizational analysis. For instance, if the accounting group is trained to use new procedures, then the other groups that either provide input to the accounting group or utilize the reports produced by this group may also need some orientation. Or, imagine the chaos that could result if workers near the start of an assembly line were trained to do their jobs 20 percent more quickly, while other workers down the line were not prepared for the upsurge in product flow.

If training is to be provided to a large number of employees throughout the organization, the organizational analysis may ask which units should receive the training first. The answer may be the units that need it most. Alternatively, one may decide to begin with units known to be especially receptive to training in order to develop a record of success and a positive image for the training program among others in the organization.

The organization's future plans must also be considered. For instance, a training specialist would not want to plan a massive training effort for a product or process that top management plans to discontinue in a year or two. Finally, the availability of trainers, facilities, financial resources, and the priorities of competing training programs must be considered as part of the organizational analysis.

Task Analysis The duties and responsibilities of the job are the focus of the second stage of needs analysis, called **task analysis**. Several approaches for analyzing jobs are available (see Chapter 4). Although any of these methods could be used as inputs into training needs assessment, the task inventory and critical incident methods are especially helpful. Task inventories can pinpoint specific tasks performed on the job, and the critical incidents method helps identify tasks that are not being performed correctly.

Once the above methods have identified the duties or tasks for which training may be needed, the next step is to develop a detailed analysis of each task. The purpose of this step is to verify that the task is important and should be trained, and to develop in-depth information about the task knowledge and procedures that should be taught. The trainer will need to call on **subject-matter experts** such as superiors and high-performing employees to generate this information. Some of the questions to ask the experts are shown in Table 9.4. Written documents such as equipment instruction manuals and procedure manuals are another source of detailed task information.

Individual Analysis The final level of analysis looks at the individuals to be trained. The **individual analysis** attempts to determine which employees should receive training and what their current levels of skill and knowledge are. The trainer may single out individuals on the basis of their past performance or select an entire work group or all incumbents with a specific job title. Then the trainer assesses, or at least estimates, the skill and knowledge levels of the chosen trainees, so that the training is neither too simple nor too complex.

Attention must focus on prerequisite basic skills, as well as on existing job-related skills and knowledge. For instance, Hewlett-Packard Co. conducted a training program on statistical quality control for a number of its employees. Later the company found that the employees were unable to use the techniques they had been taught. Careful investigation revealed that many of the employees were unable to do basic mathematics but had been too embarrassed to make this known during the training. To resolve this problem the company offered a remedial program in basic math to 500 employees.[17] If a better individual analysis had been conducted before the quality control program was initiated, the trainer could have included basic math at the start of the course, and the employees would have been better prepared to benefit from the training.

If individual analysis indicates a wide range of trainee skills and knowledge, trainers may wish to group employees into remedial and advanced groups. Alternatively, trainers could choose a training method that allows for self-paced learn-

TABLE 9.4 Some Task Analysis Questions

- How hard is this task?
- Can it be learned on the job, or should it be taught in training?
- How important is it that incumbents be able to do this task from the very first day on the job?
- What are the consequences of performing this task incorrectly?
- What knowledge, skills, information, equipment, materials, and work aids are needed to do this task?
- What signals the need to perform this task?
- Exactly what are the steps in performing this task?
- How can the incumbent tell if the task has been performed correctly?

ing or individualized instruction. Whenever possible, this kind of variance should be recognized and planned for before the training begins, so that all trainees can have an appropriate and satisfying learning experience.

Identifying Training Objectives

The final step in the assessment phase is to translate the needs identified by the organizational, task, and individual analyses into measurable objectives that can guide the training effort. Training can be evaluated at four levels: reaction, end-of-training learning, on-the-job behavior, and results.[18] Analogously, objectives can be written for each of these levels.[19] For instance, *reaction* refers to how the trainees feel about the training—whether or not it is interesting and satisfying. A reaction objective might be to have an average rating of four on a five-point scale of trainee satisfaction. The opposite end of the evaluation continuum is *results*—that is, measurable outcomes at the group or organizational level. A results objective might be to reduce by 20 percent the total number of products that fail inspection.

Reaction and results objectives are not very useful for specifying exactly what must go on in the training program or what individual trainees must master. *Behavioral objectives* specify these critical requirements—that is, what will the trainee learn and how will that learning be demonstrated after training. A behavioral objective states *what* the person will be able to do, *under what conditions,* and *how well* the person will be able to do it.[20]

The following examples are *inadequate* behavioral objectives:

- Be able to perform as a project supervisor after training.
- Develop an appreciation of statistical quality control techniques.

These objectives fail to specify what behaviors the trainee will display at the end of the training or when the individual is back on the job. They also do not specify how well or under what conditions the trainee will be able to perform, and so are not helpful in designing the training program. On the other hand, the following examples meet all the requirements for *good* behavioral objectives:

- Within one minute, be able to point to the seven emergency exits on a Boeing 747 airliner.
- Within fifteen minutes, given an automotive manual, be able to locate and adjust all spark plugs to the gap width specified in the manual.

With these behavioral objectives in hand, the training specialist can begin to plan both the training and evaluation phases of the training cycle.

THE TRAINING PHASE

Once the training specialist has identified training needs and prepared behavioral objectives, the next step is to develop a training program that will achieve those objectives. This is accomplished by selecting training methods and developing training materials that convey the knowledge and skills identified in the behavioral objectives. It is important to understand how people learn—that is, to understand learning principles—in order to design an effective training program.

Learning Principles

Years of research have identified a number of principles that facilitate the learning process. This section briefly examines these principles.

Preconditions for Learning For training to be most successful, two preconditions for learning—readiness and motivation—should exist. **Trainee readiness** means that trainees possess the background skills and knowledge necessary to learn the material that will be presented to them. For instance, knowing basic math is a prerequisite for learning statistical quality control techniques. Some top U.S. business schools feel that several years of work experience is a prerequisite that enhances readiness to learn in M.B.A. programs. The other precondition for learning is **trainee motivation**. Ideally, trainees should see a need for the new skills and understand how successful training will benefit them. Although some learning can occur without motivation, learning is much more efficient if trainees want to learn. There are several ways to increase trainee motivation.

Research has shown that the attitudes and expectations of trainees as they begin a training program can affect their reactions to the program and the amount they learn.[21] Individuals who freely choose to attend a training program learn more than those who are required to attend.[22] Moreover, individuals who are committed to their careers and have engaged in career planning seem to respond better to training.[23] Organizations can influence the attitudes of potential trainees by involving them in the needs assessment phase and/or by giving them a realistic training preview—a synopsis of what benefits they can expect from the training program and how it fits into their career plans.

Two additional ways to increase motivation are goal setting and self-efficacy enhancement. A number of studies have shown that when individuals set specific goals for themselves, they perform better than when they have no goals or vague goals.[24] For a long training program, trainees should have a clear picture of their final desired goal but should also set intermediate goals, allowing them to get a feeling of success and progress as they increase their mastery of different components of the training program.

Self-efficacy expectations are simply one's beliefs that one will be able to perform a task successfully. These beliefs are a strong determinant of persistence and eventual success with difficult tasks.[25] Thus, it has been suggested that trainers attempt to increase the efficacy expectations of trainees by (1) *persuasion*—telling the trainees that they can do it, that there is a high rate of success in the program; (2) *modeling*—showing the trainees (in person or on videotape) others like themselves who have succeeded in training; or (3) *enactive mastery*—causing the trainees to experience success in the early stages of training.[26] Since mastery is usually the most potent method of increasing efficacy expectations, trainers should structure early success opportunities into the training program and provide positive feedback on initial performance improvements.

In addition to the two preconditions for learning—trainee readiness and motivation—several other important learning principles must be considered in the design of a training program. These learning principles involve

- conditions of practice.
- knowledge of results.
- overcoming interference
- transfer of training.
- adult learning principles.

Conditions of Practice Actively practicing the skill or task being learned can increase learning. Therefore, a key factor in designing training is whether to have the *whole* task learned and practiced as one unit or to break down the task into separately learned and practiced *parts*. If the task is simple, it can be learned and practiced as a whole. If the task is complex, it probably should be broken down into component parts that can be practiced as separate elements. Note, however, that some extremely complex tasks with very interdependent steps cannot be broken down into meaningful parts and must be learned and practiced as a whole. In any case, at the end of the training program, the entire task must be performed by the trainee as one complete unit.

Because at some point the trainee must be able to integrate the parts into a whole task, Irwin L. Goldstein recommends that trainers use a progression method.[27] With the progression method, the trainee practices one part of the task during the first training session. During the next training session, the trainee learns a new part of the task, practices the new part, and then practices parts one and two together. This progression continues until the trainee learns all parts of the task and demonstrates successful performance of the total task.

Another condition of practice that the trainer must consider is whether the practice should be *distributed* (divided into spaced segments) or *massed* (scheduled in one long session). Cramming the night before an exam is an example of massed practice. Research has shown that when a task is difficult, complex, or meaningless, and must be remembered over a long period of time, distributed practice is better than massed practice.[28] Massed practice seems to be better for simple tasks. Massed practice is also superior if the correct response is difficult to perform and is easily forgotten. For instance, a person who is trying to learn a precise physical skill, such as serving a tennis ball or bowling a strike, should practice until he or she "gets the feel" and then continue drilling for a while longer. The person who stops practicing for the day after getting the movement right only once will probably forget the correct feel and find it slow to return in the subsequent practice session.

A final condition of practice that the trainer must consider is, How much practice is enough? **Overlearning** is practicing far beyond the point at which the trainee has mastered and performed the task correctly several times. Overlearning is particularly useful for critical tasks that are performed infrequently or under stress, such as cardiopulmonary resuscitation (CPR) or an airline crew's activities during a flight emergency. Overlearning should be used in training when the trainee is learning a task in which the first reactions must be absolutely correct. Overlearning is important for several reasons:

1. It increases retention over time.
2. It makes the behavior more automatic.
3. It increases the quality of performance under stress.
4. It helps trainees transfer what they have learned to the job setting.[29]

Knowledge of Results For effective learning to take place, trainees need to receive **feedback**, or **knowledge of results**, on how they are performing. Feedback is critical for both learning and motivation.[30] If feedback is not provided, trainees may learn the technique incorrectly or lose the motivation to learn. Feedback, because it makes the learning process more interesting for trainees, maximizes trainees' willingness to learn. Feedback is also necessary if goals for maintaining or improving performance have been set.

The trainer should plan to give plenty of feedback and encouragement early in the training program. At first, the trainer should praise any improvement at all. Gradually, as trainees' skills increase, the trainer should raise the performance level required to receive positive feedback. Later in the program, the trainer should teach trainees how to evaluate their own performance, and trainees should move toward reliance on self-generated feedback rather than feedback from others. This increases the likelihood that trainees will be able to continue to perform correctly when back on the job.

Overcoming Interference **Interference** occurs when habits and/or learning acquired prior to training make it difficult for the trainee to absorb new material. Interference is most severe when the trainee has learned a strong stimulus-response connection in the past and now has to learn a totally different response to the same or similar stimulus. One of the authors of this book experienced a great deal of interference when attempting to learn to sail a boat. Many years of daily horseback riding had established a strong connection between the stimulus "sensation of excessive speed" and the response "pull back on the reins." When the sailboat picked up too much speed, she automatically pulled back on the rope attached to the boom. Unfortunately, this action can be counted on to make sailboats increase speed and tip over. Despite understanding the principles of sailing and knowing that the correct response was to slacken the rope, the old habit of pulling back was almost irresistible.

Interference can be a special problem when the new correct response must be performed reliably under stress. Under stress, individuals have a tendency to revert to their old habitual responses. Suppose, for example, that an individual who learned to drive in the United States visited England and began to drive on the left-hand side of the road. In an emergency situation, the driver's old habit of keeping to the right would probably take over.

The trainer should try to anticipate any inappropriate habits that trainees might bring with them to the learning situation and explicitly address them in the training program. To overcome interference, the trainer should clearly teach the principles underlying the new correct response and provide a great deal of practice to increase the strength of the new stimulus-response connection.

Transfer of Training If learning that has occurred in the training session is not transferred to the job, the training program has been a waste of company resources. Many training programs have been criticized for their lack of impact on trainees' actual behavior on the job.

Table 9.5 lists traditional ways that learning theorists recommend to maximize transfer of training. Besides these guidelines, organizations can follow a number of other procedures to enhance transfer. During the training, the trainer should emphasize the usefulness of the new material, drawing on illustrations from the work environment. In addition, as trainees learn skills, the trainer should ask them to set specific and measurable goals for performing the new behaviors back on the job. After the training, trainees should be encouraged to assess themselves against these personal goals on a regular basis.[31]

If new managerial behaviors or leadership styles are being taught throughout the organization, top management should be trained first and then successively lower levels of management. This sequence ensures that when individual managers return from training, their supervisors are already familiar with the new behaviors and should be willing to encourage their use. If superiors are not going to receive the training, they should be briefed on what their subordinates are learning and how they can support the use of the new skills.

If a training program is held in several sessions over the course of weeks or months, trainees can be given homework assignments that require them to apply what they are learning to an actual work problem and report back at the next

TABLE 9.5 Ways Organizations Can Maximize Transfer of Training

1. Maximize the similarity between the training situation and the job situation.
2. Provide as much experience as possible with the task being taught.
3. Provide a variety of examples when teaching concepts or skills.
4. Label or identify important features of the task.
5. Make sure that general principles are understood before expecting much transfer.
6. Make certain that the training behaviors and ideas are rewarded in the job situation.
7. Design the training content so that the trainees can see its applicability.

Source: From *Developing and Training Human Resources in Organizations* by Kenneth N. Wexley and Gary P. Latham. Copyright © 1982 by Scott, Foresman and Company. Reprinted by permission of HarperCollins Publishers.

session. Some training programs are structured to include an initial classroom component, followed by an on-the-job application project and then a presentation of project results to the rest of the class and higher management. This sequence ensures serious efforts to learn and apply the new skills to solving real-world problems.

Whenever possible, groups or teams that will be working together should be trained together, so that they can learn both the training content and how to apply it in the unique mix of personalities and abilities found in their own team. Intact group training should also facilitate the development of group norms that support the new behaviors.

When employees at the same level from across the organization have been trained but are relatively isolated from other trainees in daily interaction, peer support groups may be useful in facilitating transfer. Trained managers should make an effort to meet every few weeks to reinforce each other and share their experiences in applying the new ideas they have learned. Periodic formal refresher training is also helpful.

Finally, a model borrowed from addiction research has been adapted to facilitate transfer of training back to the job. Called the **relapse prevention model**, its goal is to help trainees avoid relapsing into their old behavior patterns. This model suggests that training time should be devoted both to anticipating situations that could cause relapse and to planning strategies for dealing with these situations in advance.[32] For instance, if managers who have just been taught to use a participative leadership style expect a relapse to the old autocratic style when working under a tight deadline, they can plan how to avoid the relapse.

Trainers should plan as carefully for transfer of training as they do for the classroom portion of the training. The more of the above suggestions a training program implements, the more likely it will be to produce positive transfer to the job.

Adult Learning Principles Most instructional techniques are based on the science of teaching children, which is called **pedagogy**. Some educators believe that different techniques are more effective with adult learners. The science of teaching adults has been labeled **andragogy**. Andragogy is based on assumptions about key differences between adult and child learners. Malcolm Knowles has enunciated several differences that adult educators consider important. First, adults already have a great deal of knowledge and experience that they can learn from and share with others. Second, adults want to take responsibility for themselves and their learning. Third, adults are problem centered; they want to learn things that have immediate usefulness in solving current problems.[33] These characteristics mean that adults may resent being treated like children in a learning situation. That is, when a trainer assumes that adults know very little, that their experience is irrelevant, and that they should learn exactly and only what the trainer tells them to learn, adults do not learn effectively. One author suggests that the best and brightest employees often avoid organizational training programs because these pedagogically oriented programs insult their intelligence.[34]

Andragogy suggests that learning should be active and student-centered rather than passive and instructor-centered. Instructor-centered teaching occurs when teachers decide what students should learn, present that content as they think best, and then test the learners' mastery of it. A student-centered approach allows learners to be involved in diagnosing their own training needs, picking their own learning goals and objectives, and even structuring their own evaluation, thus ensuring that trainees consider the program relevant.[35] Andragogy also recommends that training focus on real-world problems, perhaps through techniques such as case studies and role-playing (discussed later in this chapter). Finally, andragogy acknowledges and uses the experience and knowledge that adults bring with them. Group discussions can be very effective in getting learners to share relevant experiences and to explicitly discover principles that they already know on an intuitive level. According to one adult trainer, "Never teach an adult something he or she already knows, and never tell a group anything you can get from the group itself."[36] The trainer should take the role of facilitator rather than teacher, providing input and guidance only when the group falters in its self-directed learning.

In recent years, the principles of andragogy have been challenged.[37] There is no concrete evidence that the learning process is truly different for adults as compared with children; some children respond well to student-centered learning, and sometimes adults prefer direction and instructor-imposed structure to self-diagnosis and personal responsibility for learning. Thus, a pure andragogical approach is not always appropriate just because the learners are adults. For instance, it does not apply when the program teaches completely unfamiliar technical or physical skills, or when the trainees have chosen to attend in order to learn from an acknowledged expert in the field. However, andragogical principles can contribute much to the design of management development programs and can be used in varying degrees to increase the motivation and personal responsibility of trainees in many kinds of programs. Switching between instructor-centered methods such as lectures and student-centered methods such as group discussion can help ensure relevance and maintain learner interest over the course of a long training day.

John W. Newstrom and Mark L. Lengnick-Hall suggest that two learning models, pedagogy and andragogy, are too few to cover the diversity of training situations encountered in organizations. They propose a number of characteristics of learners aside from chronological age that may influence which learning approach is most successful (see Table 9.6). For instance, they suggest that learners with short attention spans should receive a wide range of different teaching methods, whereas those with low self-confidence should be exposed to new material more slowly and with a chance for early success in an easy application. Highly instrumental trainees should receive minimal theory and plenty of opportunity to practice clearly job-related skills; low-interest trainees should be started off with graphic examples of how the training content can help them.[38]

In conclusion, all of the above-mentioned learning principles must be considered in the design of training programs. If these principles are ignored, an effective training program is much less likely to result.

TABLE 9.6 Characteristics That May Affect Optimal Teaching Style

1. **Instrumentality.** Degree to which the trainee is concerned with the immediate applicability of the concepts and skills being taught.
2. **Skepticism.** Degree to which the trainee exhibits a questioning attitude and demands logic, evidence, and examples.
3. **Resistance to Change.** Degree to which the trainee fears the process of moving to the unknown, or the personal effects of that process.
4. **Attention span.** Length of time the trainee can focus attention before substantial attentiveness is diminished.
5. **Expectation Level.** Level of quality (process) and quantity (content) that the trainee requires from the trainer or the training.
6. **Dominant Needs.** Range of intrinsic and extrinsic individual needs that currently drive the trainee.
7. **Absorption Level.** Pace at which the trainee expects and can accept new information.
8. **Topical Interest.** Degree to which the trainee can be expected to have personal (job-relevant) interest in the topic.
9. **Self-Confidence.** Degree to which the trainee independently and positively views him- or herself and thus requires high or low levels of feedback, reinforcement, and success experiences.
10. **Locus of Control.** Degree to which the trainee perceives that she or he can implement the training successfully back on the job with or without organizational support.

Source: John W. Newstrom and Mark Lengnick-Hall, "One Size Does Not Fit All." Reprinted from *Training and Development*.

Technical Training

Historically, the term *training* has been used to refer to job-skill or technical training for nonmanagement employees, and the term *development* has been reserved for the education of managers. In some cases, different teaching methods have been used, and much of the learning content has been different. Today, the distinction between training for managerial and nonmanagerial employees is blurring as responsibility is delegated downward to self-managed work teams in some organizations. More and more nonmanagers are being trained in managerial skills such as problem solving, decision making, and planning. This section discusses the training methods more commonly used for technical training, whereas the next section focuses on methods used for developing management skills.

With the training objectives defined and the learning principles in mind, the trainer must choose an appropriate training method. Perhaps the first decision to be made is whether to conduct the training on the job or away from the job.

On-the-Job Training **On-the-job training (OJT)** is conducted at the work site and in the context of the actual job. Approximately 90 percent of all industrial training is conducted on the job.[39] On-the-job training has several advantages:

1. Because the training setting is also the performance setting, the transfer of training to the job is maximized.
2. The costs of a separate training facility and full-time trainer are avoided.
3. Trainee motivation remains high because it is obvious to the trainees that what they are learning is relevant to the job.

A good OJT program should be constructed as carefully as a formal classroom training program. Ideally, the supervisor or peer who acts as the trainer will be taught how to introduce and explain each new task. The trainer should consider carefully the order in which to introduce new tasks and should prepare a written list of objectives for each stage of the training process.[40] Periodically, the trainer should give the trainee performance tests to ensure that the material is being mastered and to maintain trainee motivation through feedback.[41] **Job Instruction Training**, a procedure developed to train new defense-plant workers during World War II, is outlined in Table 9.7. This is a proven and systematic way to teach a new task. On the negative side, OJT may suffer from frequent interruptions as the trainer or trainee is called away to perform other organizational duties. Moreover, what many organizations call OJT is really no training at all. Employees are abandoned on the job and expected to pick up necessary skills as best they can. Often these employees are not informed about important but infrequent events (such as emergency procedures or annual maintenance) and may learn bad habits and unsafe procedures from coworkers.

Apprenticeship Training **Apprenticeship training** is a combination of on- and off-the-job training. The Department of Labor regulates apprenticeship programs, and often management and a union jointly sponsor apprenticeship training. Apprenticeship programs require a minimum of 144 hours of classroom instruction each year, together with on-the-job experience working with a skilled worker. These programs can last from two to five years, depending on the complexity of the skill being taught. Skilled trades that are usually learned through apprenticeship training include the bricklaying, sheet-metal, carpentry, plumbing, and electrical trades.[42] The International Perspective box describes a very effective apprenticeship training system in Germany.

Off-the-Job Training **Off-the-job training** is conducted in a location specifically designated for training. It may be near the workplace or away from work, at a special training center or a resort. Conducting the training away from the workplace minimizes distractions and allows trainees to devote their full attention to the material being taught. However, off-the-job training programs often do not provide as much transfer of training to the actual job as do on-the-job programs.

Some of the methods and materials used for off-the-job training are lectures, group discussions, role-playing, assigned reading, case studies, and videotapes. Another method is **vestibule training**. Much like on-the-job training, vestibule training requires trainees to do the whole job, using the same tools and machines that are used on the job. However, the training takes place in a vestibule, or sep-

TABLE 9.7 Job Instruction Training Procedure

How to Get Ready to Instruct	
1. Have a timetable. —How much skill you expect and when. 2. Break down the job. —List the important steps. —Pick out the key points. 3. Have everything ready. —The right equipment, material, and supplies. 4. Have the workplace properly arranged. —As you would expect the worker to maintain it.	
How to Instruct	
Step 1: Prepare the Worker	*Step 3: Try Out Performance*
a. Put the worker at ease. b. Find out what he or she knows. c. Arouse interest. d. Place the worker correctly.	a. Have the worker perform the operation. b. Have the worker explain the key points. c. Correct errors. d. Reinstruct as needed.
Step 2: Present the Operation	*Step 4: Follow-up*
a. Tell. b. Show. c. Explain. d. Demonstrate.	a. Put the worker on his own. b. Encourage questioning. c. Check frequently. d. Taper off assistance.

Source: From *Developing and Training Human Resources in Organizations* by Kenneth N. Wexley and Gary P. Latham. Copyright © 1982 by Scott, Foresman and Company. Reprinted by permission of HarperCollins Publishers.

arate workshop used just for training. A trainer is present at all times, and the trainees are protected from the hustle and pressure that occur on the job itself. Vestibule training provides a very high rate of transfer of training.

Increasingly, off-the-job training is utilizing high-tech methods for training delivery, among them the following:

Computer-Assisted Instruction **Computer-assisted instruction (CAI)** is an outgrowth of the programmed learning methods offered by mechanical teaching machines and programmed learning texts in the 1960s. In these applications, the computer simply presents a block of information and then asks the trainee questions to assess his or her mastery. If the trainee's answer is correct, the computer proceeds to the next block of information. If the trainee's answer is wrong, the

INTERNATIONAL PERSPECTIVE

Apprenticeship Training in Germany: A Model for the U.S.?

The German (formerly West German) system for helping young people enter the work force and prepare for a meaningful career is widely acknowledged to be extremely effective. About 1.8 million young people are apprentices in Germany each year, and 65 to 70 percent of those finishing middle school each year make the transition directly into an approved apprenticeship program. Over a three-year apprenticeship, individuals work on the job up to four days per week and spend at least one day a week in a specialized vocational school. The Federal Vocational Training Institute, which includes representatives of employers, unions, and the government, has developed apprenticeship standards and curricula for nearly 400 occupations.

This level of training is expensive, with German employers spending seventeen times as much for training an apprentice as do U.S. employers for training the average employee per year. The system is funded in Germany partly by employers and employer associations, and partly by the government.

Apprenticeship programs do exist in the United States, but they are much less popular, with about 300,000 participants per year. Also, apprentices tend to be in their middle twenties rather than 16 to 18 as in Germany. However, the U.S. government and American employers are becoming more and more concerned about the "forgotten youth" who drop out of high school or college and never acquire marketable skills. With an impending labor shortage, it becomes a practical as well as humanitarian exercise to help these individuals find a productive place in the work force. It is thought that properly structured apprenticeship programs would give young students an incentive to stay in school and improve their academic performance, as well as a chance to learn a useful skill.

The Department of Labor's Work Based Learning Commission is drafting a plan to expand private sector apprenticeship programs, and the Apprenticeship 2000 Project has been funding pilot programs for easing the school-to-work transition since 1990. The focus is not just on traditional trades like plumbing and carpentry, but also on areas such as healthcare, hospitality, and food services. In the wake of the 1992 Los Angeles riots and amid strident promises from both political parties to "do something" about the poverty and unemployment in inner cities, it seems likely that more extensive apprenticeship programs will be one of the remedies adopted.

Sources: Margaret Hilton, "Shared Training: Learning from Germany," *Monthly Labor Review,* March 1991, pp. 33–37; Karen Matthes, "Apprenticeships Can Support the 'Forgotten Youth,'" *HRFocus,* December 1991, p. 19; U.S. Congress, Office of Technology Assessment, *Worker Training: Competing in the New International Economy.* Report No. OTA-ITE-457, Washington, U.S. Government Printing Office, 1990.

program may repeat the same material or may branch to a different remedial exercise, depending on which wrong answer the trainee gave.

Computer-Managed Instruction **Computer-managed instruction (CMI)** is much more complex. In this type of program, the computer assesses the trainee's initial level of competence and then provides a customized set of learning modules and exercises. The trainee's performance is assessed frequently, and the training content is modified continuously to best suit the learner.[43]

Computer-Based Training **Computer-based training (CBT)** includes both CAI and CMI. According to a *Training* magazine survey, 43 percent of firms are currently using CBT.[44] CBT is most commonly used to deliver training *about* computers, but a wide range of other topics can also be addressed. There are many advantages to CBT, both in terms of the logistics of delivering training to trainees and in terms of effective learning. These advantages are listed in Table 9.8. Of course, there are also disadvantages to CBT. The start-up costs are very high, as each trainee needs access to a computer. Also, there is no opportunity for trainees to interact with each other. Steelcase, a large office furniture manufacturer, decided that CBT did not meet its need for training salespeople because the skills needed were largely interpersonal and trainees seemed to learn a lot from each other when interacting in training groups.[45]

Interactive Video Training The latest high-tech training method is called **Interactive video training (IVT)**. This is CBT with the addition of a videodisc or videocassette player and a color monitor. It has the advantages of CBT plus the ability to use sound and high-quality moving pictures to demonstrate learning con-

TABLE 9.8 Advantages of Computer-Based Training

Logistical Advantages

- Training can be conducted at remote sites and on all shifts.
- Training can be fit into lulls in the work schedule that would otherwise be unproductive.
- Managers and supervisors can be trained in their offices so they are available to handle job problems if needed.
- Trainer costs are very low once the program is established.
- Trainee transportation and lodging costs are non-existent.
- There is consistent quality of instruction over time and from group to group, unlike programs relying on several in-person trainers.
- Programs are not susceptible to disruptions due to unexpected trainer turnover or illness.
- Changes and updates can be distributed to all sites very quickly.

Learning Advantages

- CBT is self-paced, and the average time to complete a learning unit is up to 30% faster than when the same material is presented using traditional group instruction methods.
- Retention is at least as good as with other methods and is sometimes superior.
- CBT provides immediate feedback.
- Low achievers have a greater chance of success with CBT than with classroom training.
- Interactive programs can provide remedial and customized instruction according to each learner's needs.

Based on Stephen Schwade, "Is It Time to Consider Computer-based Training?" *Personnel Administrator,* February 1985, pp. 25–35. Reprinted by permission of the author.

tent and provide problems for trainees to solve. An IVT system has been developed for use in medical schools to teach diagnostic skills. Besides producing laboratory test results, the system can generate sound (as would be heard through a stethoscope) and real-time moving pictures (like those created by an ultrasound machine).[46] As with other forms of CBT, IVT requires active participation by learners and provides immediate feedback on the correctness of responses. IVT is most often used for individual training in a self-paced format, although a third of organizations using the technology sometimes apply it in a group or classroom setting.[47]

IVT was used by 16 percent of organizations with more than 100 employees and by 24 percent of organizations with more than 2,500 employees according to a 1991 survey.[48] Shell Oil Company has implemented IVT in twelve manufacturing plants and three retail training centers and is very happy with the results. Shell's task was to furnish up-to-date training on new products, plant operation, and safety to thousands of employees spread all over the country and working three different shifts. IVT supplied the answer. Employees can receive training "on-site, on demand, and on shift" when there is a temporary lull in the workload. Employees have adapted to the system quickly and enjoy the self-paced nature of the learning experience. The average completion time of a module is about 60 percent of the time taken to cover the same material in a traditional classroom. Shell has more than 200 IVT units, each made up of an IBM PS/2 computer, a videodisc player, monitor, and a printer. Ninety training modules have been developed or modified for Shell's use, and more are in the works. Programs plus equipment costs came to about $3 million in the first three years, but Shell training executives believe that IVT will be less expensive in the long run than fielding a huge team of trainers or paying employees to attend training outside their regular shift times.[49]

The Future of the Traditional Training Room The demise of the traditional training room has been predicted (wrongly) since the first primitive teaching machine was developed. Experts, however, are once again confident that more and more training will be delivered by computer or IVT systems and that face-to-face training jobs will decline while instructional systems design jobs increase. By the year 2000, IBM expects to deliver 60 percent of all training outside the classroom using some form of advanced technology. Ford currently uses IVT for mechanic training at 1,500 dealerships nationwide. Even content that has always required face-to-face interaction, such as sales training, may soon be offered by IVT utilizing complex role-playing videos with stop-action.[50]

In some ways, computer-based training in its advanced forms is consistent with the ideas of andragogy in that it is self-paced and tailored to the individual learner; in addition, employees can choose to view a training module when they feel the need for it in solving a current job problem. As more and more employees work on computers on a daily basis, days-long off-the-job training programs may be replaced by a large menu of short, on-demand tutorials or access to expert systems to help employees solve current problems or refresh skills needed at the moment. Training can be "just in time," rather than "just in case," and thus be seen as much more relevant. It has also been suggested that CBT methods are ideal for work forces with high diversity in age, learning speed, and skill, which could cause difficulty in a traditional classroom setting.[51]

Selecting a Training Method Figure 9.5 shows the most commonly used instructional methods, based on a 1991 survey of companies with more than 100 employees. The vast majority of organizations use videotapes and lectures in at least some of their training programs. Given a wide range of possible training methods,

FIGURE 9.5 Percent of Organizations Using Different Instructional Methods for Employee Training

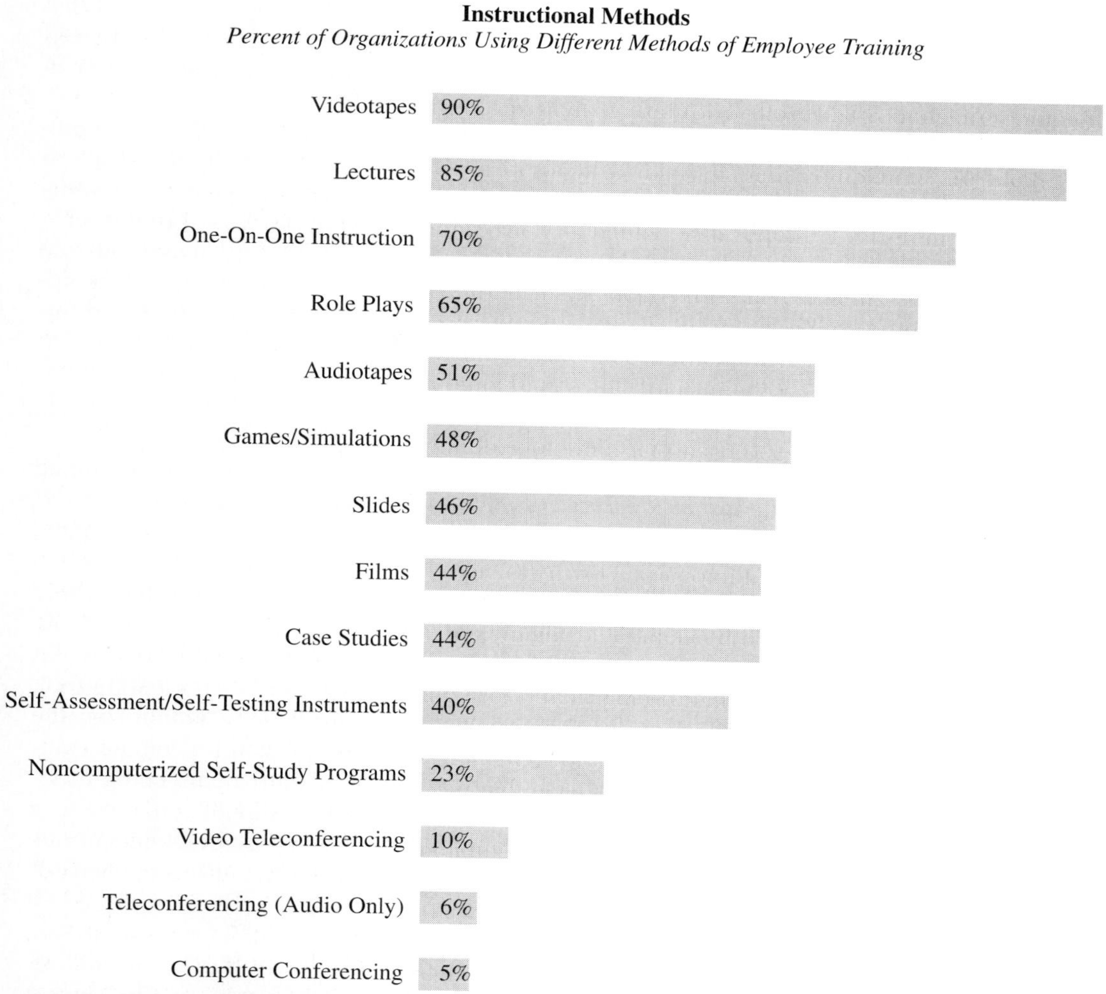

Instructional Methods

Percent of Organizations Using Different Methods of Employee Training

Method	Percent
Videotapes	90%
Lectures	85%
One-On-One Instruction	70%
Role Plays	65%
Audiotapes	51%
Games/Simulations	48%
Slides	46%
Films	44%
Case Studies	44%
Self-Assessment/Self-Testing Instruments	40%
Noncomputerized Self-Study Programs	23%
Video Teleconferencing	10%
Teleconferencing (Audio Only)	6%
Computer Conferencing	5%

Source: Chris Lee, "Who Gets Trained in What." Reprinted with permission from the October 1991 issue of *Training* magazine. Lakewood Publications, Minneapolis, MN. All rights reserved.

how does an organization go about selecting the best method? Clearly, the firm must consider the cost of the method, the number of individuals to be trained, their location, and the availability of skilled trainers. The most important criterion in selecting a training method, however, is that it be consistent with the training content. The method must convey needed information and prompt trainees to engage in the appropriate type and amount of practice for the skills they are trying to learn. For example, lectures, CBT, or assigned readings can be used to convey factual content, but they are inadequate for teaching physical or interpersonal skills. A group interaction method would be better suited for teaching interpersonal skills, whereas vestibule or on-the-job training should be used to teach a physical skill.

Often it will be necessary to use different training methods at different points during the training process. For instance, the first step may require a method that is good for conveying information or an overview (lectures, videotape), whereas later steps may require hands-on practice alternating with additional study of principles.

A final decision is whether the training should be conducted by the company's in-house training staff, local subject matter experts, company managers or supervisors, or by an outside firm. Outside firms offer a variety of canned training programs that may fit an organization's needs to varying degrees. Limited customization of these existing packages may be possible. Alternatively, an outside firm can develop a training program specifically for an organization.[52] This approach is costly but may prove worthwhile if in-house training resources are inadequate and good training is crucial for proper job performance.

Management Development

This section focuses on management education and development. As mentioned earlier, training cannot be designed effectively without knowledge of job demands. Thus, we first consider the nature of managerial work. An award-winning study published in the *Academy of Management Executive* identified seven clusters of managerial tasks and assessed the relative importance of each to three levels of management. The findings are shown in Table 9.9 and Figure 9.6. Note that acting as a spokesperson for one's group to others in the organization was a role that was equally important for all levels of management. Other clusters took on differential importance according to management level, with monitoring the external environment being more important for executives than for middle managers or supervisors, and managing the performance of individuals being especially important for first-line supervisors. These findings should not replace a needs assessment in one's own organization, but they have obvious implications for designing a management training curriculum that meets the differing needs of each level of management.[53]

Because managerial work is important, complex, and challenging, many organizations provide regular management training. In 1991, almost 280 million hours of supervisory and management training were delivered in the United

TABLE 9.9 Clusters of Managerial Tasks and Task Examples

1. **Managing Individual Performance**
   Motivate subordinates.
   Provide performance feedback.
   Resolve performance problems.
   Blend subordinates' goals with work requirements.
   Improve communication among subordinates.
2. **Instructing Subordinates**
   Inform subordinates about procedures and assignments.
   Explain work assignments.
   Provide technical advice to subordinates.
   Train subordinates.
3. **Planning and Allocating Resources**
   Establish target dates for work products.
   Estimate group resource requirements.
   Decide on resource distribution.
   Translate general directives into specific plans.
4. **Coordinating Independent Groups**
   Stay informed of goals and actions of top management.
   Persuade other groups to provide resources needed by your group.
   Monitor events outside your group that may affect its performance.
   Persuade other managers to support your initiatives.
5. **Managing Group Performance**
   Define areas of responsibility for subordinate managers.
   Inform managers when their groups' performance fails to meet goals.
   Monitor own group's performance.
6. **Monitoring the Business Environment**
   Develop/maintain relationships with management-level clients.
   Participate in task forces to identify new business opportunities.
   Monitor sales performance.
   Gather information about outside business trends.
7. **Representing Your Staff**
   Develop relationships with other managers that can help your group.
   Communicate your group's needs to others.
   Provide information about your group's activities to others.

Source: Data from Allen I. Kraut, Patricia R. Pedigo, D. Douglas McKenna, and Marvin D. Dunnette, "The Role of the Manager: What's Really Important in Different Management Jobs," *Academy of Management Executive,* November 1989, pp. 286–292.

States.[54] The results of all this attendance, however, are not always clear because management development programs are seldom rigorously evaluated. A comprehensive review of the evaluations that have been done concluded that many types of management development programs do have a beneficial impact on job behavior.[55] Among these programs, those that provide carefully designed training linked to a thorough needs assessment should be more effective than faddish programs purchased from vendors of canned, one-size-fits-all management development packages.

FIGURE 9.6 Importance of Management Tasks for Three Levels of Management

Numbers Refer to the Percentage of Managers Who Said the Task Was of "The Utmost" or "Considerable" Importance

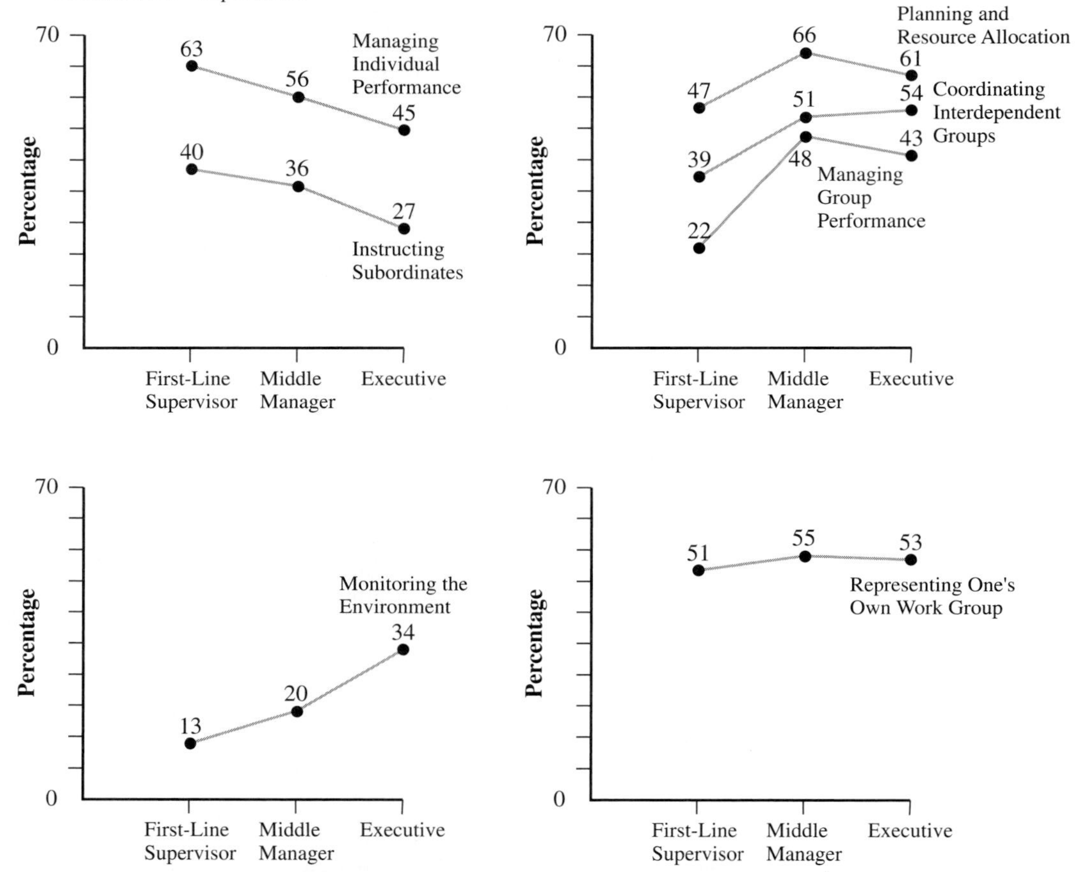

Source: Adapted from "The Role of the Manager: What's Really Important in Different Management Jobs," by Allen I. Kraut et al. from *Academy of Management Executive,* November 1989, vol. 3, no. 4, pp. 287–289.

On-the-Job Methods Although most formal managerial development takes place off the job, a great deal of learning occurs on the job. There have been several recent studies of managerial learning and skill development as a result of on-the-job experience. This research suggests that managers learn the most from assignments that are very difficult and challenging, such as building a new start-up operation or turning around a failing operation; from assignments that represent a major change or increase in responsibility, such as moving from a staff to a line position, moving to a different functional area, or moving to a job with greatly increased responsibilities for people, dollars, or units; and from hardships, such as a personal or business failure or dealing with very difficult individuals. Thus, a complete program of management development should include a job assignment and succession system that stretches people to their limits.[56] In addition to major full-time assignments, organizations use four common on-the-job management development techniques: coaching, committee assignments, job rotation, and understudy assignments.

Coaching One of the most popular on-the-job methods is **coaching**, in which experienced managers guide the actions of less experienced managers. Very much like a pitching coach, managerial coaches help inexperienced managers develop their delivery. For example, the coach may help the inexperienced manager work through a decision that has to be made, give advice on how to develop a cohesive team of loyal subordinates, or help negotiate a contract with a key supplier or customer. Often the experienced manager is the model for correct behavior or skills. The key advantage of this method is that it provides rapid feedback on performance and learning by doing. A potential disadvantage is that it perpetuates the status quo, since the less experienced manager may adopt the same values and perspectives as the coach.

Committee Assignments Often, organizations assign junior executives to committees where they can observe more experienced managers in action. Much organizational work takes place in committees. Therefore, the intent of this management development technique is to use normal committees as training vehicles. One new inexperienced manager may be assigned to each committee. Although the inexperienced manager may actively participate and contribute, the major reason for his or her presence is to observe others in action. In particular, the inexperienced manager can observe the interpersonal processes, agreements and disagreements, decision-making processes, negotiations, and successes and failures of the committee.

Job Rotation **Job rotation** means moving from one job assignment to another within the same organization. Each assignment usually lasts four to six months. Job rotation provides the inexperienced manager with a broad understanding of the organization—its purpose and its goals. Another effect of job rotation is to turn specialists into generalists. A person whose entire career is spent in one functional area becomes a specialist but may not develop a general, overall perspective on the organization. Upper-level managers, in particular, need such a general outlook as they spend more and more of their time managing the total organization and less and less time managing a specialized functional area. Job rotation is a management development technique that provides this outlook.

Understudy Assignments An **understudy** is a person who acts as an assistant to someone else. Similar in concept to coaching, this management development method is a full-time mentor-understudy arrangement, whereas coaching is only periodic. The understudy works with the mentor on a daily basis to learn how the job is done. During the manager's absence, the understudy performs the role of the manager on noncritical activities. From this experience, the understudy develops valuable managerial skills. One problem with this technique is that some managers feel threatened by understudies and may not do a conscientious job of developing them.

Off-the-Job Methods Most formal managerial development programs occur off the job and away from the normal place of work. One reason for this is that a program is considered more of a perk if it is conducted in an exotic off-site location, rather than in-house, at the everyday workplace. Another reason for the off-site locale is to remove the manager from the daily environment of the organization and thereby minimize interruptions and distractions. Organizations can conduct their own management development programs or send managers to generic management-skills programs offered by consulting firms or universities. A number of training methods are used in off-the-job management development programs. However, caution must be exercised in planning and selecting these methods, as a few may be offensive or threatening to participants (see the Ethical Perspective box).

Sensitivity Training **Sensitivity training** is also called **laboratory**, or **T-group, training**. The aim of sensitivity training is to make the participants more aware of their own behavior and how their behavior is perceived by others, as well as to increase their awareness and acceptance of others' differences. Sessions are usually conducted in small groups of eight to fourteen individuals who are strangers to each other at the outset. Aided by a professional trainer, the individuals discuss themselves, their feelings, and the group process.

Research conducted on sensitivity training programs concludes that they can effectively change individuals' behavior. The most frequent changes include a more favorable self-concept, reduced prejudice, modified scores on tests of interpersonal relations, and changed interpersonal behavior as perceived by others. However, although sensitivity training can provide a powerful personal growth experience, it does not seem to help trainees become better managers.[57] Thus, the technique has lost favor in the last decade.

Team Building Many organizations have turned to **team building** in place of sensitivity training. With sensitivity training, stranger groups are used to develop generic group and self-perception skills. The results, however, indicate minimal transfer to the work setting. Team building, on the other hand, focuses on intact work groups and strives to develop their ability to work together effectively on the types of tasks they face each day. Figure 9.7 shows a questionnaire that helps indicate when team building may be needed.

Team building often starts with a data collection phase, utilizing individual interviews with team members or questionnaires. The trainer seeks information about how the group works together, what problems exist, and what norms are followed. This information is summarized and fed back to the group so that they

ETHICAL PERSPECTIVE

Ethical Issues in Training

A recent issue in human resource development concerns the possibility that some organizationally sponsored training may violate employee rights to privacy, self-determination, and religious freedom. There have been allegations that some forms of training are nothing more than brainwashing, particularly those that draw on "New Age" philosophies. One HR trend spotter cites four examples: (1) a management training program developed by the founder of Est; (2) corporate training offered by and based on the teachings of the Church of Scientology; (3) Krone training, based on mind control techniques and the teachings of a controversial mystic; and (4) the Japanese-originated "hell camp" management training method, designed to destroy self-esteem and then rebuild it in the corporate image. These types of training sometimes require the disclosure of very personal information that is not related to work and that participants may feel invades their privacy. In addition, some New Age training programs contain a quasi-religious or spiritual component that some employees find contrary to their own religious preferences.

Employers who choose to offer this type of training should take care that employees' religious freedom and privacy rights are not violated. It has been recommended that employers make any questionable training entirely voluntary and provide an alternate means of learning the same job skills for those who find the New Age approach offensive. Vendors of this training should be carefully selected, training content and practices should be investigated in advance, and employees should be allowed to leave during the training if they find it distasteful.

Another form of training that may pose a problem is adventure-based outdoor leadership programs. These programs usually last from two or three days to several weeks and require the participants to engage in vigorous and often frightening outdoor activities, such as rock climbing, rappelling, and white-water rafting. The aim is to challenge the artificial limitations people put on themselves ("Oh, I can't do THAT!"), to build confidence, and to have people learn to work as a team. These programs have become increasingly popular in the last fifteen years, and many are offered by reputable organizations such as Outward Bound. Because the programs are very intense, powerful personal learning can occur, though transfer back to the work setting is not assured.

Adventure training may pose a problem because of the potentially hazardous activities and the mental stress and fear that these activities arouse. Once on the course, social pressure to participate in terrifying exercises can be extremely strong, and embarrassment at failing or refusing to try acute. As with New Age training, only reputable vendors with excellent safety records should be used, and participation in the program as a whole and in any single activity should be voluntary.

Sources: Mary F. Cook, "What's Ahead in Human Resources?" *Management Review,* April 1988, pp. 41–44; Patricia S. Eyres, "Keeping the Training Department Out of Court," *Training,* September 1990, pp. 59–67; J. W. Long, "The Wilderness Lab," *Training and Development Journal,* May 1984, pp. 59–69.

FIGURE 9.7 Does Your Team Need Team Building?

To what extent is there evidence of the following problems in your work unit? Circle the number that coincides with the level of evidence.

	Low Evidence		Some Evidence		High Evidence
1. Loss of production or work-unit output.	1	2	3	4	5
2. Grievances or complaints within the work unit.	1	2	3	4	5
3. Conflicts or hostility between unit members.	1	2	3	4	5
4. Confusion about assignments or unclear relationships between people.	1	2	3	4	5
5. Lack of clear goals, or low commitment to goals.	1	2	3	4	5
6. Apathy or general lack of interest or involvement by unit members.	1	2	3	4	5
7. Lack of innovation, risk taking, imagination, or initiative.	1	2	3	4	5
8. Ineffective staff meetings.	1	2	3	4	5
9. Problems in working with supervisor.	1	2	3	4	5
10. Poor communications: fear of speaking up; not listening to one another; not talking together.	1	2	3	4	5
11. Lack of trust between unit members or between member and supervisor.	1	2	3	4	5
12. Decisions that unit members do not understand or agree with.	1	2	3	4	5
13. The feeling that good work is not recognized or rewarded.	1	2	3	4	5
14. Lack of encouragement for unit members to work together in a better team effort.	1	2	3	4	5

Scoring Add the circled numbers of the fourteen items. If the total is between 14 and 28, there is little evidence that the unit needs team building. If the score is between 29 and 42, there is some evidence but no immediate pressure unless several items are very high. If the score is between 43 and 56, a team building program should be given serious consideration. If the score is over 56, team building should be a top priority for the work unit.

Source: William G. Dyer, *Team Building,* © 1987 by Addison-Wesley Publishing Co., Inc. Reprinted with permission of the publisher.

can take an objective look at their functioning and decide how they wish to change it. The facilitator helps the team understand the feedback and develop action plans for improving group processes. These plans may include training in specific skills, such as active listening, problem analysis and group decision making, consensus seeking, conflict resolution, and so on.[58]

Team building without the feedback but with a heavy emphasis on group problem-solving skills is also commonly provided to new teams when self-directed work groups are started.[59] For instance, teams of autoworkers were trained together before the opening of the new Saturn plant. Table 9.10 lists the topics that are often covered in training for self-managed work teams.

Behavioral Modeling Training **Behavioral modeling training** is based on social learning theory, which holds that most human behavior is learned by observing others and then modeling their behavior when appropriate.[60] Learning from others reduces the need for trial-and-error learning.

A. P. Goldstein and M. Sorcher have adapted social learning theory to supervisory training.[61] They argue that rather than telling supervisors how to administer discipline or handle a complaining employee, training programs should

TABLE 9.10 Types of Training Offered to Self-directed Work Teams

Type of Training	*Percentage of Responding Companies That Offer Each*
Problem solving	83
Meeting skills	65
Communication skills	62
Handling conflict	61
SDT roles and responsibilities	58
Quality tools and concepts	56
Evaluating team performance	39
Work flow and process analysis	36
Selecting team members	35
Presentation skills	35
Influencing others	29
Budgeting	14

The results are from a 1990 survey by DDI, AQP, and Industry Week.

Source: Richard Wellins and Jill George, "The Key to Self-directed Teams." Reprinted from the *Training and Development Journal*. Copyright © April 1991, the American Society for Training and Development. Reprinted with permission. All rights reserved.

show managers—through videotaped dramatizations using actor-models—and then allow them to practice the new skills.

Behavior modeling training typically follows a fixed sequence of steps. First, the trainer introduces a single interpersonal skill, perhaps in a short lecture that conveys some of the principles underlying the skill. Second, trainees view a videotape of a supervisor performing the skill correctly. Then the trainer plays the tape again, calling attention to key principles, or steps, called *learning points*. Table 9.11 lists learning points that might be dramatized in a videotape module on how to handle a complaining employee. Research suggests that retention is improved when trainees generate their own learning points after watching the videotape, rather than passively receiving these points from the trainer.[62] Third, trainees practice the skill by **role-playing** with other trainees. For instance, trainees may take turns playing the roles of supervisor and subordinate so that each trainee has an opportunity to practice the supervisory skill being taught. Fourth, trainees get feedback on the effectiveness of their role-playing behavior. Practice continues until the trainees feel confident with their new skill.

Research has shown that behavior modeling training is an effective way to teach the interpersonal skills required of supervisors.[63] Organizations do not need to develop their own videotapes, as several vendors offer behavior modeling programs that feature the generic skills needed by most supervisors.

Case Study The **case study** method was developed at the Harvard Business School in the 1920s.[64] This method presents the trainee with a written description of an actual or hypothetical problem in an organizational setting. The trainee is required to read the case, identify the problem, and recommend solutions.

The case study method has several intended purposes. First, it shows trainees that there is usually no easy solution to complex organizational problems. Second, it helps trainees realize that different perspectives and solutions to the same case may be equally valid. Third, case studies help managerial trainees develop their problem-solving skills.

TABLE 9.11 Learning Points from a Behavior Modeling Module on Handling a Complaining Employee

1. Avoid responding with hostility or defensiveness.
2. Ask for and listen openly to the employee's complaint.
3. Restate the complaint for thorough understanding.
4. Recognize and acknowledge his or her viewpoint.
5. If necessary, state your position non-defensively.
6. Set a specific date for a follow-up meeting.

Source: Reprinted with permission from A. P. Goldstein and M. Sorcher, *Changing Supervisory Behavior,* Copyright 1974, Pergamon Books Ltd.

Some management scholars claim that the case method does not teach general management principles. These critics cite the lack of guided instruction, which puts trainees at risk of drawing the wrong inference from the case material.[65] One study has determined that another problem can occur if the trainer is too dominant in the case study discussion.[66] Trainer dominance makes the trainees dependent on the trainer for the "right" answer when there is not supposed to be a single right answer. Nevertheless, the case study method is considered to be one of the best for developing problem-solving skills among managers and executives.[67] Because the cases mimic real-life problems, trainees generally see them as quite relevant.

Simulation Techniques **Simulation techniques** try to replicate the work setting in which the trainee will have to perform. Using a facsimile of the real situation, the trainee tries out different behaviors or strategies. The objective is to have trainees learn from their own actions, as well as from the group discussion that follows the simulation in a debriefing session.[68] Different forms of simulation include

- in-basket exercises.
- two-person role-playing exercises.
- leaderless group discussions.
- large-scale behavioral simulations.
- computerized business decision-making games.

In-basket exercises have been used since the 1950s to assess and develop managerial skills. In-basket tests are described in Chapter 8 as a managerial selection device, but this individual-level simulation can also be used to teach managers how to prioritize work and make decisions. Some recently developed in-basket exercises are run on microcomputers. The electronic in-basket exercise asks the trainee to make a decision; then the program responds with the next decision point, based on the previous one. In this way, the trainee is able to experience the consequences of past decisions and to make future decisions based on past decisions.

The **role-playing technique** was developed in the 1930s.[69] In two-person role-playing, trainees and sometimes trainers assume the roles of characters and act out a simulated situation. The primary purposes of role-playing are to analyze interpersonal problems and to develop human relations skills. The technique can also be used to place an individual in another person's role, such as a manager in a subordinate's situation. Such role reversal allows the manager to experience firsthand what the subordinate experiences. The success of this method depends on the participants' willingness to adopt the roles and to react as if they are really in the work environment. If the participants do not become thoroughly involved, very little learning takes place.

One advantage of this technique is the dynamics of the role-playing as it unfolds. Decisions must be made on the spot. Participants must respond immediately to the other players. This spontaneous action moves the role-playing closer to reality for the trainee. For example, interpersonal interaction in a role-play is often characterized by real emotion and feeling. Thus, the trainee must deal not only with the factual content of the communications but also with the emotional and interpersonal parts of it.

The **leaderless group discussion**, another technique used in assessment centers, has equal applicability for training. It is a larger-group simulation, featuring four to eight trainees working together to solve a hypothetical problem. Often, group members are assigned different roles to play in the simulation and given information unique to that role. For instance, a common scenario involves a city council trying to make a decision about the allocation of funds. Different trainees take on the roles of the police commissioner, head librarian, sanitation engineer, director of recreation and parks, and so on. In analyzing their behavior after the simulation, individuals learn more about their interpersonal and decision-making skills and styles.

An increased level of complexity is represented by **large-scale behavioral simulations**. These involve simulated organizations of up to twenty people in different roles, lasting from six hours to several days. Simulations at this level of complexity are typically used with executives rather than lower-level supervisors because sophisticated interpersonal and decision-making skills are prerequisites for learning from an extremely complex simulation.[70]

Another simulation technique is the **computerized business decision-making game**. Since 1957, when the first business game appeared, more than 1,000 business simulations have become commercially available.[71] A business simulation or game may be defined as a sequential decision-making exercise structured on a model of a business operation, in which the trainee assumes the role of managing the simulated operation.[72] In the game, the trainee or group of trainees is asked to make decisions about organizational matters such as investment in research and development, pricing, and entering new markets. Based on these decisions, the program provides computer-generated feedback on how the organization performed. With this new information in hand, the trainee is asked to make another series of decisions, which are used in the next run of the simulation.

The primary objectives of these business games are to teach general management skills such as decision making, setting priorities, long-range planning, and effective use of time, personnel, and equipment. In addition, trainees develop an appreciation of the complexity of organizations and the many factors that must be considered before making a decision. The games can also teach individuals the concepts of teamwork and risk taking, and the importance of functional skills.

Business simulation games provide two advantages in training managers. First, they allow managers to experience real-world problems without having to suffer the consequences of poor decisions. Second, they allow time to be compressed. With one of these games, trainees can experience several years of organizational performance in just a few hours. The major disadvantage of these games is that sometimes trainees focus on beating the system rather than on learning the management principles being presented by the simulation.

New Employee Orientation

A very common type of training is new employee orientation. All employees, whether managerial or nonmanagerial, should be provided with a systematic orientation when they first join an organization. Newcomers have much to learn about their supervisors and coworkers, the demands of their job, company rules and procedures, and the organization's culture and assumptions. Until employees learn enough to feel comfortable in these areas, they experience uncertainty and stress.[73]

Employees usually say that their best source of information about the organization is coworkers. Thus, if at all possible, newcomers should be assigned a "buddy" or be given a position in which they have plenty of access to friendly coworkers.[74] In addition, the organization should provide one or more orientation sessions. Some organizations simply give a presentation on employee benefits. Such material is often confusing, however, and it is seldom of immediate value to the employee. Newcomers are much more interested in learning the formal and informal rules that govern daily behavior on the job than in learning how to fill out insurance claim forms. Thus, organizations would do better to save benefits presentations until after new employees feel comfortable in their jobs and have attention to spare.

A more relevant new employee orientation might feature two parts: (1) an introduction to the specific job and department, provided by the supervisor, and (2) several sessions of general orientation to the company, provided by the HRM department. Supervisors should be trained to orient new employees and should use a checklist to be sure that they cover all important points. Table 9.12 lists sample contents for both parts of the orientation process.

A good orientation program can help employees feel comfortable and become competent in their jobs quickly. It may also help to reduce turnover among newcomers, who sometimes become frustrated and feel overwhelmed as they struggle to learn new jobs.[75] Another important aim of an orientation program is to teach newcomers the ethical norms, beliefs, and attitudes that prevail in the organization. The organization's values and guiding principles can be communicated explicitly through formal presentations and implicitly through organizational stories and myths. For example, telling a story about an organizational hero who defied authority to do what was "right" can send a powerful message. The goal is to convince new employees that the values they are being taught are not just window-dressing but represent the values and beliefs of the organization's leadership—the tone at the top of the organization.

THE EVALUATION PHASE

The final phase in the training cycle is the evaluation phase. **Evaluation** is the determination of the extent to which the training activities have met their goals. Unfortunately, the evaluation is often done poorly or ignored altogether. One

TABLE 9.12 Content of a Two-Phase New-Employee Orientation System

Administered by the Supervisor

About the Department:
- Relationships to other units
- Mission and goals
- Procedures
- Work flow
- Facilities
- Schedule
- Introductions to coworkers

About the Job:
- Work station
- Duties
- Goals/performance standards
- Tools and equipment
- Where to go, who to ask for help
- On-the-job training

Human Resource Issues:
- Performance appraisal schedule and content
- Promotion criteria
- Salary increase schedule and criteria
- Training plans

Administered by a Trainer, with Guest Appearances by Company Leaders

About the Organization:
- History
- Products
- Goals
- Organization structure
- Who's who in the organization
- Culture, ethical principles

Rules and Procedures:
- Employee handbook
- Work hours
- Vacation and leave
- Provision of pay and benefits
- Discipline system
- Complaint/suggestion systems

Source: Based on G. Dessler, *Personnel Management* (Reston Va.: Reston Publishing Company, 1984), pp. 223–227.

reason for this is that managers simply tend to assume that training will work. Another is that a manager who champions a training program may feel threatened by the prospect of an objective evaluation of the program's effectiveness.

The basic approach to evaluation should be to determine the extent to which the training program has met the objectives identified prior to the training. Planning for the evaluation should start at the same time that planning for the training program begins. If the goals of the program are clearly stated as specific objectives, the appropriate evaluation method can be implemented at the same time as the program.

Evaluation Levels and Measures

Donald L. Kirkpatrick developed the best-known and most widely used framework for the evaluation of training programs.[76] Kirkpatrick identified the four levels of evaluation shown in Figure 9.8. Each level answers a very important but different question about the effectiveness of the program. If possible, a good evaluation should include measurements at all four of these levels.

Reaction The first level is called *reaction,* or the participants' feelings about the program. That trainees enjoyed a program does not mean that the program was useful to the organization. However, unpopular programs attract few trainees and are likely to be canceled; therefore, trainers must be concerned with reaction.[77] Reaction information is usually gathered by questionnaire during or immediately after the program. Experienced trainers refer to reaction questionnaires as "smile sheets" because the results are nearly always positive. It seems that nearly everyone enjoys getting out of the office for a day and being pampered at the conference center.

Learning The second level of evaluation has to do with *learning*. Learning measures assess to what degree trainees have mastered the concepts, information, and skills that the training tried to impart. Learning is assessed during and/or at the end of the training program with paper-and-pencil tests, performance tests, and graded simulation exercises.

Behavior On-the-job *behavior* is the third level of evaluation in Kirkpatrick's approach. On-the-job behavior can be assessed by any of the performance evaluation techniques discussed in Chapter 11. Behavior ratings can be collected from the superior, peers, subordinates, or clients of the trained employees.

Results The final level of evaluation is *results*. At this level, the impact of the training program on the work group or organization as a whole is assessed objectively. The appropriate objective measures to use depend on the content and objectives of the training. Sample measures of results include cost savings, profit, productivity, quality, accidents, turnover, and employee attitudes.

FIGURE 9.8 Four Levels of Training Evaluation

Level	Questions Being Asked	Measures
Results	Is the organization or unit better because of the training?	Accidents Quality Productivity Turnover Morale Costs Profits
Behavior	Are trainees behaving differently on the job after training? Are they using the skills and knowledge they learned in training?	Performance appraisal by superior, peer, client, subordinate
Learning	To what extent do trainees have greater knowledge or skill after the training program than they did before?	Written Tests Performance Tests Graded Simulations
Reaction	Did the trainees like the program, the trainers, the facilities? Do they think the course was useful? What improvements can they suggest?	Questionnaires

Source: Reprinted with permission from the November 1983 issue of *Personnel Administrator,* copyright, 1983, the Society for Human Resource Management, Alexandria, VA.

Kirkpatrick suggests that these four levels of evaluation may form a hierarchy. Accordingly, change farther up the hierarchy of outcomes is unlikely unless change has occurred lower in the hierarchy. That is, if no learning has occurred, it is unlikely that on-the-job behavior will change. If behavior does not change, it is unlikely that measurable improvements in results will be observed.

Evaluation Designs

Designing a good evaluation effort involves knowing when to collect evaluation measures and which groups to collect them from.[78] Together, these factors define the experimental design used to assess the impact of the training.

Because reaction measures simply assess whether or not participants like the training and think it will be useful, these measures are collected during or immediately after the training. Ideally, an additional reaction questionnaire should be sent to participants several months after the training, to see if they still believe that the training has been of use in their jobs.

The purpose of learning, behavior, and results measures is quite different from that of reaction measures, in that the trainer is to discover whether or not a change has occurred in the variable being measured—that is, are trained employees behaving differently now than they were before the training? If there has been a change, the trainer will want to know whether or not it can be attributed to the training program—that is, did the training program bring about the change?

There are two basic strategies for determining whether a change has occurred. The first is to compare the trainees after the training to the way they were before the training. At the very least, this comparison involves the collection of evaluation measures at two points in time. The second strategy is to compare the learning, behavior, or results of the trained group to the learning, behavior, or results of a group that has not been trained but is otherwise identical to the trained group. The strongest evaluation designs draw on both of these strategies.

There are many complex and highly effective designs for evaluating training. This section covers only a few of the more straightforward ones (see Figure 9.9). The first two designs are too simple to be useful, but they demonstrate some of the pitfalls that trainers encounter in performing evaluations.

One-Shot Posttest-Only Design Suppose that an evaluation is not planned prior to the training. Partway through the training, the trainer decides to evaluate the program and proceeds to collect learning, behavior, or results data from the trained group after the training. This is called a **one-shot posttest-only design**. It is completely worthless and should not be used to evaluate training. Because there is no pretraining measure and no untrained group for purposes of comparison, there is no way to determine whether or not a change has occurred, much less whether any change has been caused by the training.

One-Group Pretest-Posttest Design Another simplistic design is the **one-group pretest-posttest design**, in which the training group is assessed both before and

FIGURE 9.9 Designs for Evaluating Training

Poor (But Commonly Used) Designs

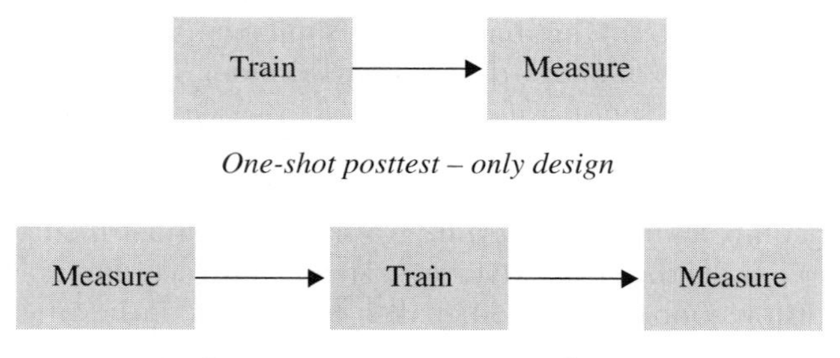

One-group pretest – posttest design

Stronger Designs for Training Evaluation

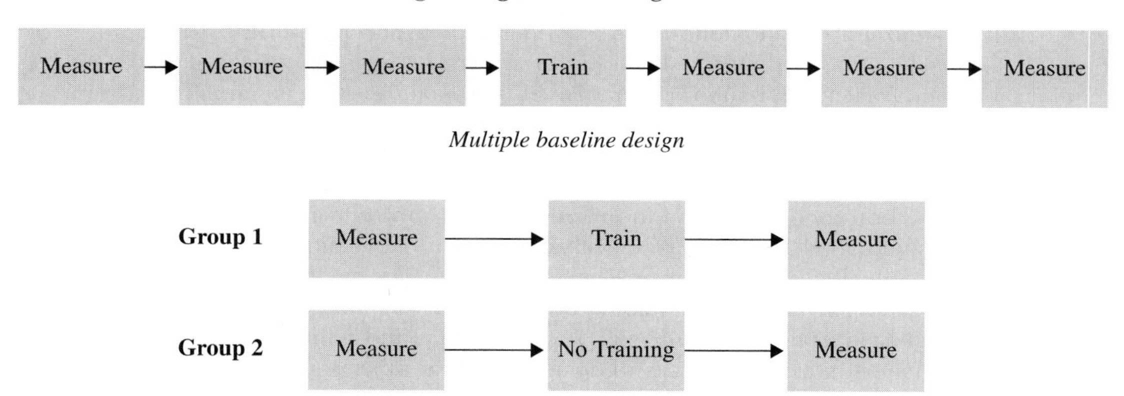

Pretest – posttest control – group design

after the training. Although this design does allow a trainer to determine if there has been a change in learning, behavior, or results, it does not enable the trainer to conclude that the training brought about the change. A change from one time period to another can be caused by anything that occurs between measurements, not just by the training. For instance, there can be a change in the work environment, such as a new supervisor, revised work methods, employee turnover, a change in the pay system, or union activity. Or, an event outside of work that coincides with the training program can be the actual cause of the change.

Suppose a firm is teaching a course on business ethics one hour a week for two months. The trainer measures knowledge and attitudes about business ethics before and after the training and finds both have improved. Possibly, this change occurred because of the training. But, suppose that at the same time the training was taking place a major insider trading scandal was revealed and several public figures were indicted for ethical violations. The trainees' changes in knowledge and attitudes could have been caused by the publicity attached to these events rather than by the training. The evaluators, however, would not know this from a one-group pretest-posttest design; they might mistakenly conclude that the training caused the changes and therefore would be equally effective if repeated for other groups of managers in the firm.

Alternatively, a natural process of maturation or development could have caused the employees to be different than they were several months earlier. Simple experience on the job could make people better performers at the time of the posttest than they were at the time of the pretest, and this improvement might occur regardless of any formal training program. Thus, it is clear that a one-group design with just one pre- and posttest is not very helpful in evaluating training.

Multiple-Baseline Design An improved evaluation design that avoids some of the above-mentioned problems is the **multiple-baseline design**. In this design, the trainer measures the group several times both before and after the training. The trainer probably should not use an obtrusive measure, such as a questionnaire or learning test. Trainees could improve over time just because they are gaining practice with the measure. Objective measures of behavior or results are less obtrusive, and they are easy to collect repeatedly.

The multiple-baseline design allows the trainer to observe trends in performance and to see if there is a change in the trend immediately after the training. For instance, a trainer may find that employees are slowly improving with experience over time but that a big jump in performance occurs after the training. The average results of a training group on a series of evaluations might be 10, 11, and 12 on pretests and then 15, 17, and 18 after the training. This design enables the trainer to detect training effects over and above maturation effects and also helps to rule out coincidental factors as explanations for any changes occurring immediately after the training. It would be an extreme coincidence if either work-environment or off-the-job events occurred exactly and only at the same time as the training. Thus, if this design is used, the trainer can be more certain that the training caused the observed change. This design is the best one to use if all employees are to be trained simultaneously, leaving none to serve as a control group.

Pretest-Posttest Control-Group Design An even better design uses a control group of employees who are very similar to the training group except that they do not receive the training (at least not yet). In the **pretest-posttest control-group design**, both the group to receive the training and the control group are measured at least once before and once after the training. This design allows the trainer to draw quite firm conclusions about (1) whether any change has occurred and (2) if it has, whether the change has resulted from the training.

The trainer might normally expect to find that the trained group improves from pretest to posttest, whereas the control group stays the same. However, other patterns of results can also be interpreted under this design. For instance, if the training group is the same after the training as before, but the control group is worse on the posttest than on the pretest, then the training was probably effective in preventing a decline in performance that would otherwise have occurred.

Using the Evaluation to Improve Training

Information from the training evaluation can be used in making decisions about whether to continue the training program or how to improve it. Modifying the training based on reaction measures is fairly straightforward. A boring speaker can be replaced, a film rated as irrelevant dropped, or a caterer changed, depending on the feedback received. If a sound evaluation design was used, additional modifications of the training might be suggested by scores on the learning, behavior, or results measures.

If insufficient learning occurred, the training presentation itself may have been at fault. Information may have been presented unclearly, or inadequate time and practice may have been allowed for trainees to absorb the material. Alternatively, trainee readiness or motivation may have been deficient, so that an otherwise well-designed training experience had no real impact on the trainees.

If behavior on the job did not improve, despite gains in learning, the fault could lie in the needs assessment, the training program itself, or in the work environment. If the initial needs assessment was not performed correctly, trainees might have been taught material that was not relevant to the demands of their jobs. Thus, while they might have learned something from the training, what they learned is not something that they can use. Another possibility is that the training content might have been appropriate, but there was insufficient emphasis either on transfer of training to the job or on relapse prevention. Finally, the fault could lie in the work environment if supervisors and others have not accepted and reinforced the new behaviors.

When learning and behavior change but results do not improve, the appropriateness of the training or validity of the results measures should be scrutinized. If people are behaving differently but the behavior has no impact on the bottom line, then the training may be teaching the wrong things. This problem could stem from a poor needs assessment procedure. If, on the other hand, the trained behaviors are better and more effective than the behaviors used previously, then the problem may be simply that the results measures are too coarse or contaminated to register their beneficial effect. Results measures like profit and turnover are affected by many factors outside the organization, such as general economic and labor market conditions. Perhaps a training program does have a beneficial impact, but the impact is simply not visible against larger trends in global results measures.

Utility of Training

In Chapter 7, the concept of utility was applied to selection systems. **Utility** is the net dollar gain realized by an organization as a result of adopting a given HRM practice. Several authors have developed methods of quantifying the benefits of training programs.[79] For instance, one study estimated that the net return to a bank (over a five-year period) of a four-day training program for sixty-five supervisors would be $148,400.[80]

Calculating utility requires both assessing the costs of the training and putting a dollar value on the benefits of the training. Some cost categories associated with training are shown in Table 9.13. They include one-time costs incurred in developing the program initially, costs that are incurred each time the program is repeated, and costs incurred for each person trained.[81]

It is harder to put a dollar value on the benefits of training than it is to assess the costs. First, one must estimate how much better a trained employee will perform than an untrained employee. The dollar payback of a certain percentage of improvement in performance depends on the importance of the job. It is probably worth more to an organization to increase an executive's performance by 10 percent than to increase a secretary's performance by 10 percent. The amount gained per trainee per year is multiplied by the number of persons trained.

Next, the duration of the training's impact must be estimated. Because the benefit of training an employee is lost when that employee quits, turnover rates are often built into utility calculations. But even if an employee stays with the organization, the effects of some kinds of training gradually wear off, as trainees forget what they have learned or the knowledge becomes obsolete. Thus, an estimate of the "half life" of the training intervention must also be factored in.[82]

The final step in calculating utility is to subtract the total costs from the total benefits of a particular training program given to a specified number of people. Estimating the necessary parameters and calculating utility can be extremely

TABLE 9.13 Costs of Training

One-Time Costs

- Needs Assessment Costs
- Salaries of Training Designers or Consultants
- Purchase of Reusable Training Equipment and Materials
- Full-Scale Evaluation of the Program When First Offered

Per-Session Costs

- Trainer Salaries, Travel, and Lodging
- Facilities Rental

Per-Trainee Costs

- Trainee Wages or Salary During Training
- Transportation, Food, and Lodging for Trainees During Training
- Nonreusable Training Materials, Handouts, etc.

complex, but by doing so, an employer can build a solid justification for a training program on purely economic grounds. Properly conceived and implemented training programs can have definite effects on organizational performance and profits.[83]

SUMMARY OF KEY POINTS

Training is a planned effort by an organization to facilitate employees' learning of job-related knowledge and skills for the purpose of improving performance. A systematic approach to training involves three phases: assessment, training, and evaluation. The assessment phase determines who needs to be trained and what they need to be trained to do. Assessment involves organizational analysis, task analysis, individual analysis, and the identification of clear and measurable training objectives.

The training phase includes developing training materials and procedures, and actually conducting the training. The design of a training program must consider issues such as conditions of practice, knowledge of results, interference, transfer of training, and adult learning principles. The selection of training techniques involves choosing among a variety of on-the-job and off-the-job methods. Apprenticeship and vestibule training programs combine elements of on- and off-the-job training.

Management development is intended to improve the present and future performance of managers. On-the-job methods for management development are coaching, committee assignments, job rotation, and understudy assignments. Off-the-job methods include team building, behavior modeling, and various simulation techniques.

In the evaluation phase, the training is evaluated (1) to determine whether it has achieved its objectives and (2) to make improvements in the training program. Four levels of evaluation measures should be collected: reaction, learning, behavior, and results. A sound experimental design should be used to assess the impact of the training. Finally, the utility of a training program can be calculated by assessing its costs and putting a dollar value on its benefits to the organization.

Questions for Discussion

1. In what ways does the HRD function relate to other HRM functions?
2. How does needs assessment for current employees differ from needs assessment for the development of a training program for new hires?
3. What are some possible causes of performance deficiencies other than a need for training?
4. What concerns are addressed at the organizational analysis phase of training needs assessment?

5. How would you conduct the task analysis phase of training needs assessment for the job of fast-food chef?
6. What are the purposes of the individual analysis phase of training needs assessment?
7. Write a good and a poor behavioral objective for your learning from this chapter. Explain why the first is good and the second is poor.
8. Describe two preconditions for learning, and tell how trainers can influence each.
9. Explain how conditions of practice should be manipulated to facilitate the learning of different types of material.
10. What is overlearning? When and why should it be used?
11. Explain how interference may inhibit trainee learning. Think of an example in which earlier learning or habits made it harder for you to learn a new task.
12. How can a trainer facilitate transfer of training?
13. Explain why adult learners may need to be treated differently than child learners.
14. What are the advantages and disadvantages of on-the-job training?
15. Think up three specific training situations in which CBT would be suitable and three in which it would be inappropriate.
16. Describe common methods of on-the-job training for managers.
17. What is team building and when is it appropriate?
18. What is behavior modeling training? For what type of content is it most useful?
19. What simulation techniques can be used in management training?
20. Describe how you were oriented as a new employee on your last job. How could this orientation have been improved?
21. Explain the four levels at which training can be evaluated. How could your learning in this course be evaluated at each of the four levels?
22. Describe the two most useful designs for evaluating training, and tell why these designs are superior to the one-shot posttest-only and one-group pretest-posttest designs.
23. Explain how utility concepts can be used to estimate the net dollar value of a training program.

EXERCISE 9.1

Training Exercise

You are to develop a training program to teach adults to drive. The adult trainees have never had driver's licenses, but they have high school educations. The objective of the training program is to teach the trainees both the rules of the road and actual driving skills (steering, accelerating and braking, signaling, shifting, parking, and so on). The trainees must learn the driving rules and skills well enough to be able to pass the written and driving parts of the state driver's license exam in a standard transmission car.

1. How will your training program incorporate or deal with each of the following learning principles or conditions? Are there any that will not concern you?
   a. Readiness
   b. Motivation
   c. Interference
   d. Feedback
   e. Overlearning
   f. Distributed versus massed practice
   g. Whole versus part learning
   h. Transfer of training
2. What training methods will you use? In what order?
3. How will the success of your program be evaluated?

EXERCISE 9.2

Planning a Needs Assessment

You have just been hired for a newly created position, director of management development, at Acme Pharmaceuticals. This organization has grown rapidly in the last five years and now employs 2,500 people. At the moment, all in-house training is aimed at hourly, technical, and first-line supervisory personnel. Middle-level managers are occasionally sent to university-sponsored development programs, but only on a haphazard basis. Your boss, the vice president of human resources, has suggested that your first project be to develop a curriculum, or set of courses (both in and out of house), that would meet the needs of middle-level managers. Middle-level managers are defined as individuals who oversee a functional department, a group of professionals, or several production groups, each headed by a first-line supervisor. There are about 100 people in this category. Because of rapid growth, many of these individuals have been in their middle-level managerial positions for less than eighteen months.

The vice president of human resources understands the necessity of a thorough needs assessment but would like your preliminary report on what needs have been identified within two and a half months. As far as resources, you have adequate funds, a secretary, and a ten-hour-per-week college intern to help with this project.

A constraint is that the middle-level managers, though all located at one convenient facility, are very busy and not likely to gladly give up much time for your project. You have also noted that there is an "ethic of personal excellence" in the organization's culture. Advancement is based on proven performance and is very competitive among people at the same level. You have noticed a strong reluctance among middle-level managers to admit any errors or weaknesses.

You and your new management training office have no track record or credibility to draw on at this time, but your boss is committed to a prompt follow-through, based on your training recommendations.

How will you conduct your needs assessment project?

1. What sources of information will you use? What sources did you consider and then reject? Why?

2. What methods of data collection will you use? What methods did you consider and then reject? Why?

3. What is your time frame? That is, in what order will you accomplish things, and how much time will you allot for each?
4. What problems might you encounter? What could you do to offset them?

Notes and References

1. Irwin L. Goldstein and Patrice Gilliam, "Training System Issues in the Year 2000," *American Psychologist,* February 1990, pp. 134–143.
2. Catherine Bellizzi and Mona Piontkowski, "Semitrends: Changing Times in the Seminar Game," *Training,* June 1990, pp. 35–40; Chris Lee, "Who Gets Trained in What," *Training,* October 1991, pp. 47–59.
3. William Wiggenhorn, "Motorola U: When Training Becomes an Education," *Harvard Business Review,* July–August 1990, pp. 71–83; Joseph F. Coates, Jennifer Jarratt, and John B. Mahaffie, *Future Work: Seven Critical Forces Reshaping Work and the Workforce in North America* (San Francisco: Jossey-Bass, 1990).
4. Harvey L. Sterns and Dennis Doverspike, "Aging and the Training and Learning Process," in *Training and Development in Organizations,* ed. Irwin L. Goldstein and Associates (San Francisco: Jossey-Bass, 1989) pp. 299–332; Manuel London and Emily Bassman, "Retraining Midcareer Workers for the Future Workplace," in *Training and Development in Organizations,* pp. 333–375.
5. Patricia S. Eyres, "Keeping the Training Department out of Court," *Training,* September 1990, pp. 59–67; Beverly Geber, "When the Government Makes you Train," *Training,* June 1990, pp. 49–54.
6. Jack Gordon, "Training Budgets: Recession Takes a Bite," *Training,* October 1991, pp. 37–45.
7. John K. Berry, "Linking Management Development to Business Strategies," *Training and Development Journal,* August 1990, pp. 20–22; Richard Wellins and Jill George, "The Key to Self-Directed Teams," *Training and Development Journal,* April 1991, pp. 26–31.
8. J. R. Hinrichs, "Personnel Training," in *Handbook of Industrial and Organizational Psychology,* ed. M. D. Dunnette (Chicago: Rand-McNally, 1976), p. 830.
9. Irwin L. Goldstein, *Training in Organizations: Needs Assessment, Development, and Evaluation,* 2nd ed. (Pacific Grove, Calif.: Brooks/Cole, 1986), pp. 17–25.
10. Allison Rossett and Joseph W. Arwady, *Training Needs Assessment* (Englewood Cliffs, N.J.: Educational Technology Publications, 1987), p. 68.
11. L. A. Digman, "Determining Management Development Needs," *Human Resource Management,* Winter 1980, pp. 12–17.
12. Lise M. Saari, Terry R. Johnson, Steven D. McLaughlin, and Denise M. Zimmerle, "A Survey of Management Training and Education Practices in U.S. Companies," *Personnel Psychology,* Winter 1988, pp. 731–743.
13. Thomas J. Peters and Robert H. Waterman, *In Search of Excellence: Lessons from America's Best Run Companies* (New York: Harper & Row, 1982).
14. Rossett and Arwady, *Training Needs Assessment,* p. 76.
15. Robert F. Mager and Peter Pipe, *Analyzing Performance Problems,* 2nd ed. (Belmont, Calif.: Pitman Learning, 1984), p. 3.
16. Goldstein, *Training in Organizations,* p. 11.
17. V. S. Kaman and J. P. Mohr, "Training Needs Assessment in the 80's: Five Guideposts," *Personnel Administrator,* October 1984, pp. 47–53.
18. Donald L. Kirkpatrick, "Four Steps to Measuring Training Effectiveness," *Personnel Administrator,* November 1983, pp. 19–25.
19. F. O. Hoffman, "The Hierarchy of Training Objectives," *Personnel,* August 1985, pp. 12–16.
20. Robert F. Mager, *Preparing Instructional Objectives* (Belmont, Calif.: Lake Publishing, 1975).
21. R. A. Noe, "Trainees' Attributes and Attitudes: Neglected Influences on Training Effectiveness," *Academy of Management Review,* October 1986, pp. 736–749.
22. W. D. Hicks and R. J. Klimoski, "Entry

into Training Programs and Its Effects on Training Outcomes: A Field Experiment," *Academy of Management Journal,* September 1987, pp. 542–552; Timothy T. Baldwin, Richard J. Magjuka, and Brian T. Loher, "The Perils of Participation: Effects of Choice of Training on Trainee Motivation and Learning," *Personnel Psychology,* Spring 1991, Vol. 44, No. 1, pp. 51–65.

23. R. A Noe and N. Schmitt, "The Influence of Trainee Attitudes on Training Effectiveness: Test of a Model," *Personnel Psychology,* Autumn 1986, pp. 497–523.

24. Edwin A. Locke and Gary P. Latham, *A Theory of Goal Setting and Task Performance* (Englewood Cliffs, N.J.: Prentice-Hall, 1990).

25. A. Bandura, "Self-Efficacy: Toward a Unifying Theory of Behavioral Change," *Psychological Review,* 1977, pp. 191–215.

26. Marilyn E. Gist, Catherine Schwoerer, and Benson Rosen, "Effects of Alternative Training Methods on Self-Efficacy and Performance in Computer Software Training," *Journal of Applied Psychology,* December 1989, pp. 884–891; Marilyn E. Gist, "The Effects of Self-Efficacy Training on Training Task Performance," *Proceedings of the 46th Annual Meeting of the Academy of Management,* August 1986, pp. 250–254, and "Self-Efficacy: Implications for Organizational Behavior and Human Resource Management," *Academy of Management Review* July 1987, pp. 472–485.

27. Goldstein, *Training in Organizations,* p. 81.

28. Frank N. Dempster, "The Spacing Effect: A Case Study in the Failure to Apply the Results of Psychological Research," *American Psychologist,* August 1988, pp. 627–634.

29. K. N. Wexley and G. P. Latham, *Developing and Training Human Resources in Organizations* (Glenview, Ill.: Scott, Foresman, 1981), p. 58; Joel D. Schendel and Joseph D. Hagman, "On Sustaining Procedural Skills over a Prolonged Retention Interval," *Journal of Applied Psychology,* October 1982, pp. 605–610.

30. D. R. Ilgen, C. D. Fisher, and M. S. Taylor, "Motivational Consequences of Individual Feedback on Behavior in Organizations," *Journal of Applied Psychology,* August 1979, pp. 349–371.

31. K. N. Wexley and T. T. Baldwin, "Post-training Strategies for Facilitating Positive Transfer: An Empirical Exploration," *Academy of Management Journal,* September 1986, pp. 503–520; Timothy T. Baldwin and J. Kevin Ford, "Transfer of Training: A Review and Directions for Future Research," *Personnel Psychology,* Spring 1988, pp. 63–105.

32. R. D. Marx, "Relapse Prevention for Managerial Training: A Model for Maintenance of Behavior Changes," *Academy of Management Review,* 1982, pp. 433–441; Marilyn E. Gist, Anna G. Bavetta, and Cynthia Kay Stevens, "Transfer Training Method: Its Influence on Skill Generalization, Skill Repetition, and Performance Level," *Personnel Psychology,* Autumn 1990, pp. 501–523.

33. Malcolm Knowles, *The Adult Learner: A Neglected Species* (Houston: Gulf Publishing, 1978).

34. R. F. Crapo, "It's Time to Stop Training . . . And Start Facilitating," *Public Personnel Management,* Winter 1986, pp. 443–449.

35. For more on managing student-centered learning experiences, see Jill Baldwin and Hank Williams, *Active Learning: A Trainer's Guide* (Oxford, England: Blackwell, 1988).

36. Crapo, "It's Time to Stop Training," p. 446.

37. D. Feuer and B. Geber, "Uh-oh . . . Second Thoughts About Adult Learning Theory," *Training* December 1988, pp. 31–39; Sharon B. Merriam, "Adult Learning and Theory Building: A Review," *Adult Education Quarterly,* Summer 1987, pp. 187–198.

38. John W. Newstrom and Mark L. Lengnick-Hall, "One Size Does Not Fit All," *Training and Development Journal,* June 1991, pp. 43–48.

39. Bureau of National Affairs, "Planning the Training Program," *Personnel Management,* (Washington, D.C.: BNA Books, 1975), p. 102.

40. Alice Bird McCord, "Job Training" in *Training and Development Handbook,* ed. Robert L. Craig, 3rd ed. (New York: McGraw-Hill, 1987), pp. 363–382.

41. J. J. Connor, *On-the-Job-Training* (Boston: International Human Resource Development, 1983).

42. Wexley and Latham, *Developing and Training Human Resources,* pp. 111–114.

43. S. Schwade, "Is It Time to Consider Computer-Based Training?" *Personnel Administrator,* February 1985, pp. 25–35.
44. Chris Lee, "Who Gets Trained in What," *Training,* October 1991, pp. 47–59.
45. Schwade, "Is It Time to Consider Computer-Based Training?" pp. 25–35.
46. M. J. Ruhl and K. Atkinson, "Interactive Video Training: One Step Beyond," *Personnel Administrator,* October 1986, pp. 66–70.
47. Lee, "Who Gets Trained in What."
48. Ibid.
49. Ron Zemke, "Shell Scores with Interactive Video," *Training,* September 1991, pp. 33–38, quote from p. 34.
50. Beverly Geber, "Goodbye Classrooms (Redux)," *Training,* January 1990, pp. 27–35.
51. Ibid.
52. J. N. Gee, "Training Program Haute Couture," *Personnel Administrator,* May 1987, pp. 69–72.
53. Allen I. Kraut, Patricia R. Pedigo, D. Douglas McKenna, and Marvin D. Dunnette, "The Role of the Manager: What's Really Important in Different Management Jobs," *Academy of Management Executive,* November 1989, pp. 286–292.
54. Lee, "Who Gets Trained," pp. 47–59.
55. M. J. Burke and R. R. Day, "A Cumulative Study of the Effectiveness of Managerial Training," *Journal of Applied Psychology,* May 1986, pp. 232–245.
56. Morgan W. McCall, Jr., "Developing Executives Through Work Experience," *Human Resource Planning,* Vol. 11, No. 1, 1988, pp. 1–11; Jean M. Bartunek and Meryl Reis Louis, "The Design of Work Environments to Stretch Managers' Capacities for Complex Thinking" *Human Resource Planning,* Vol. 11, No. 1, 1988, pp. 13–22.
57. Peter Smith, "Controlled Studies of the Outcomes of Sensitivity Training, *Psychological Bulletin,* July 1976, pp. 597–622; John P. Campbell and Marvin D. Dunnette, "Effectiveness of T-Group Experiences in Managerial Training and Development," *Psychological Bulletin,* August 1968, pp. 73–104.
58. Steven L. Phillips and Robin L. Elledge, *The Team Building Source Book* (San Diego: University Associates, 1989).
59. Richard Wellins and Jill George, "The Key to Self-Directed Teams," *Training & Development Journal,* April 1991, pp. 26–31.
60. A. Bandura, *Social Learning Theory* (Englewood Cliffs, N.J.: Prentice-Hall, 1973).
61. A. P. Goldstein and M. Sorcher, *Changing Supervisor Behavior* (New York: Pergamon Press, 1974).
62. P. M. Hogan, M. D. Hakel, and P. J. Decker, "Effects of Trainee-Generated Versus Trainer-Provided Rule Codes on Generalization in Behavior-Modeling Training," *Journal of Applied Psychology,* August 1986, pp. 469–473.
63. G. P. Latham and L. M. Saari, "The Application of Social Learning Theory to Training Supervisors Through Behavioral Modeling," *Journal of Applied Psychology,* Vol. 60, 1979, pp. 550–555; Steven J. Mayer and James S. Russell, "Behavior Modeling Training in Organizations: Concerns and Conclusions," *Journal of Management,* Spring 1987, pp. 21–40.
64. M. P. McNair, ed., *The Case Method at the Harvard Business School* (New York: McGraw-Hill, 1954).
65. J. P. Campbell, M. M. Dunnette, E. E. Lawler III, and K. E. Weick, Jr., *Managerial Behavior, Performance and Effectiveness* (New York: McGraw-Hill, 1970).
66. C. Argyris, "Some Limitations of the Case Method: Experiences in a Management Development Program," *Academy of Management Review,* Vol. 5, 1980, pp. 291–298.
67. S. J. Carrol, Jr., F. T. Paine, and J. J. Ivancevich, "The Relative Effectiveness of Training Methods—Expert Opinion and Research," *Personnel Psychology,* Vol. 25, 1972, pp. 495–510.
68. Peter F. McAteer, "Simulations: Learning Tools for the 1990s," *Training and Development,* October 1991, pp. 19–22; George C. Thornton III and Jeanette N. Cleveland, "Developing Managerial Talent Through Simulations," *American Psychologist,* February 1990, pp. 190–199.
69. W. Wohlking and H. Weiner, "Structured and Spontaneous Role Playing: Contrast and Comparison," *Training and Development Journal,* January 1971, pp. 8–14.
70. Thornton and Cleveland, "Developing Managerial Talent," pp. 190–199.

71. S. Carey, "These Days More Managers Play Games, Some Made in Japan as a Part of Training," *The Wall Street Journal,* October 7, 1982, p. 29.
72. P. S. Greenlaw, L. W. Herron, and R. H. Rawdon, *Business Simulation in Industrial and University Education* (Englewood Cliffs, N.J.: Prentice-Hall, 1962), p. 5.
73. C. D. Fisher, "Organizational Socialization: An Integrative Review," in *Research in Personnel and Human Resources Management,* ed. Kendrith M. Rowland and Gerald R. Ferris, Vol. 4, 1986, pp. 101–145.
74. M. R. Louis, B. Z. Posner, and G. N. Powell, "The Availability and Helpfulness of Socialization Practices," *Personnel Psychology,* Winter 1983, pp. 857–866.
75. Daniel C. Feldman and Jeanne M. Brett, "Coping with New Jobs: A Comparative Study of New Hires and Job Changers," *Academy of Management Journal,* June 1983, pp. 258–272.
76. Kirkpatrick, "Four Steps To Measuring Training Effectiveness," pp. 19–25.
77. J. J. Phillips, *Handbook of Training Evaluation and Measurement Methods* (San Diego: University Associates, 1983).
78. This section is based on C. D. Fisher, "Laboratory Research" in *Method and Analysis in Organizational Research,* ed. T. S. Bateman and J. R. Ferris (Reston, Va.: Reston Publishing Co., 1984), pp. 169–185; T. D. Cook and D. T. Campbell, "The Design and Conduct of Quasi-Experiments and True Experiments in Field Setting," in *Handbook of Industrial and Organizational Psychology,* ed. M. D. Dunnette (Chicago: Rand McNally, 1976), pp. 223–326.
79. Richard A. Swanson and Deane B. Gradous, *Forecasting Financial Benefits of Human Resource Development* (San Francisco: Jossey-Bass, 1988); Wayne F. Cascio "Using Utility Analysis to Assess Training Outcomes" in *Training and Development in Organizations,* pp. 63–117.
80. J. E. Mathieu, and R. L. Leonard, Jr., "Applying Utility Concepts to a Training Program in Supervisory Skills: A Time-Based Approach," *Academy of Management Journal,* June 1987, pp. 316–335.
81. W. J. McKeon, "How to Determine Off-Site Meeting Costs," *Training and Development Journal,* May 1981, pp. 116–122.
82. F. L. Schmidt, J. E. Hunter, and K. Pearlman, "Assessing the Economic Impact of Personnel Programs on Work Force Productivity," *Personnel Psychology,* Summer 1982, pp. 333–347.
83. J. S. Russell, J. R. Terborg, and M. L. Powers, "Organizational Performance and Organizational Level Training and Support," *Personnel Psychology,* Winter 1985, pp. 849–863.

10

Human Resource Approaches to Productivity and Quality Enhancement

The job of any manager ultimately entails contributing to the organization's survival and success. Increasingly, this means being conversant with approaches to improving productivity and quality and being able to play an effective role in organizational efforts to become more competitive on these dimensions. As will be clear by the end of this chapter, the role of the human resource manager is critical in these efforts.

Some aspects of an organization's productivity and quality depend directly on the skills and abilities, training, and motivation of employees. Appropriate HR planning, selection, job design, training and development, appraisal, and compensation should help in providing the human inputs needed for effective organizational performance. But a 1990s view of quality goes beyond these basics. As experts on people, attitudes, and effective communication, HR managers have a role in facilitating the acceptance of quality- and productivity-oriented changes. They can help in building an organizational culture that supports outstanding performance and in gaining employee commitment to making it all work.

THE PRODUCTIVITY AND QUALITY IMPERATIVES

Throughout the 1980s, there was much talk of a productivity crisis in the United States.[1] In the early 1980s, high labor costs reduced the competitiveness of U.S. goods in the international marketplace compared with products made in lower-wage countries, such as Korea or Taiwan. Furthermore, the rate of increase in output-per-worker-hour slowed dramatically in the 1970s and early 1980s. In fact, only the United Kingdom experienced slower growth.[2] Japan, Italy, France, and Germany had substantially higher rates of productivity growth through the 1970s (see Figure 10.1).

Concern about productivity has prompted a great deal of research and innovation in recent years. Productivity rose in more than 75 percent of the industries surveyed by the Bureau of Labor Statistics in 1986, and it rose again in more than two-thirds of the industries in 1987.[3] For the period from 1970 to 1990, the average rate of productivity growth was 3.1 percent.[4]

In the early 1980s, another major concern came to light—that of quality. Japanese and German goods were widely acknowledged to be superior in quality to many domestically produced goods, customers were becoming increasingly sensitive to quality, and U.S. organizations were at a loss as to how to respond. There was a frantic and often unsuccessful rush to copy Japanese management practices, in the naive hope that these practices would automatically raise quality. Quality expert Philip B. Crosby called this period a search for "fairy dust solutions such as quality circles."[5] In the time since then, a great deal of research, consultant, and management attention has been given to achieving high quality, and a number of approaches have been developed, refined, and widely adopted.

It is fair to say that there has been a revolution in thinking about quality among American managers in the past ten years. No longer regarded as "nice to have, but optional," quality improvement is now recognized as absolutely essen-

FIGURE 10.1 Average Annual Percent Changes in Manufacturing Productivity in Seven Countries and Europe, Selected Periods, 1960–1990

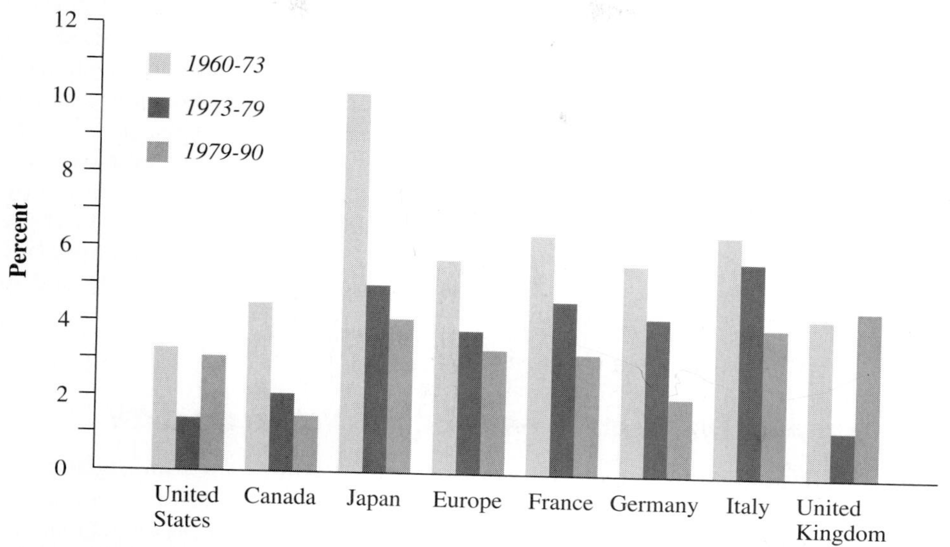

Source: Arthur Neef and Christopher Kask, "Manufacturing Productivity and Labor Costs in 14 Economies," *Monthly Labor Review*, December 1991, p. 31.

tial, because standing still on quality is tantamount to falling behind one's competitors at home and abroad. The Malcolm Baldrige National Quality Awards program has gained a tremendous amount of visibility and publicity since its inception in 1987, and many companies are using the award criteria as guidelines for their own quality assessment and improvement efforts.[6] A listing of these criteria can be found in Table 2.1.

Quality demands are being imposed not just by end consumers of manufactured goods but by intermediate consumers as well. Many large organizations now demand that their suppliers have a sound *quality process* for ensuring that quality is a high priority, that it is built into products, and that it is continuously improved. For instance, General Motors Corp. required that Velcro USA not just meet quality standards for binding tape used in automobile manufacture but also implement a total quality management process and philosophy.[7] Such vendor certification requirements for quality are increasingly common.

The new concern for quality is not restricted to manufacturing industries but has taken root in the service sector as well.[8] It can be argued that quality is even more important in services, as services are rendered to clients in real time. There is no chance to inspect and correct errors before the product reaches the client; the service produced is either good or not good, and it is consumed the moment it is produced. Furthermore, many quality improvement efforts in all sectors are directed toward providing better service to customers, whether those customers are internal or external to the organization and whether the product they require is tangible or intangible.

Some of the new approaches to improving organizational performance rely heavily on computer-controlled manufacturing, statistical methods, and new arrangements with suppliers, such as just-in-time delivery systems. Many approaches, however, emphasize the human role in improving organizational effectiveness, either alone or in conjunction with some of the above methods. Any major change targeted at productivity or quality impacts employees' jobs and is critically dependent on employees for success. This chapter shows how HR managers can assist in productivity and quality improvement efforts at the organizational, group, and individual levels. But first it considers the importance of effectively measuring productivity and quality, defines productivity and quality, and discusses the relationship between these two concepts.

DEFINING AND MEASURING PRODUCTIVITY AND QUALITY

Before taking steps to improve productivity or quality, an organization must devise accurate, understandable, and usable measures of these concepts. Measures are used to determine where, when, and what kind of problems exist and whether various changes have improved the situation. Measures are critical for the scientific and statistical mindset advocated by most scholars on productivity and quality improvement. Because off-the-cuff opinions of how a unit is doing or whether things are getting better are not acceptable, good measures are crucial. In addition, the feedback provided by such measures can strongly motivate employees and help maintain interest in a productivity or quality improvement program. These measures can also provide an objective basis for reward systems.

Each organization, work group, and even individual may need to develop productivity and quality measures that are most suited to their needs in order to best capture the essence of the work they are expected to accomplish. Before measures can be developed, however, the concepts of productivity and quality have to be understood.

Productivity Defined

Most simply, **productivity** is the ratio of output to input. Thus, productivity refers to the *efficiency* of production. A *complete* or *total* measure of productivity consists of all of an organization's outputs divided by all of its inputs. Inputs include things such as raw materials, electric power, labor, equipment, facilities and capital.[9] Total measures are relatively rare and probably not as useful to the HR manager as are partial measures, which focus on a more limited set of inputs or outputs. Partial measures of productivity might include finished wheel barrows per ton of steel or hamburgers cooked per kilowatt hour of electricity. Of particular interest might be labor productivity, such as refrigerators produced per labor hour or number of claims processed per clerk per day. It is important to remember, however, that labor productivity is not solely a function of how hard employees work. It also very largely depends on the work environment and processes, such as quality and supply of materials, design of the workstation, machine maintenance and modernity, design of the product, and the prescribed production process.

Measuring Productivity

The basic idea of output over input is more easily applied to manufacturing organizations with tangible products. However, it is both necessary and possible to assess productivity in other types of organizations. For example, how would the productivity of a service firm, such as a hospital, or one of its employees be measured? A hospital is in the business of making an unhealthy person healthy. Productivity could reflect the number of patients who recover or the efficiency of resource usage, such as the number of occupied beds. A nurse's productivity could reflect the number of patients cared for or how fast rounds are completed; both evaluations use a quantity perspective. If the evaluation takes into account the number of mistakes made or how many patient complaints are filed, then a quality dimension has been added.

Financial institutions, such as banks, also require a different perspective on productivity. A bank has no tangible output; its success is measured by how much money the bank can acquire using its depositors' investments. Therefore, a bank's productivity can be assessed with a financial ratio, such as return on investment or return on assets. If quality is a concern, then other financial ratios (such as the number of bad loans compared to the total number of loans) can be used. The productivity of an individual bank employee, such as a teller, could be assessed quantitatively by the number of transactions processed. The quality dimension could be assessed by the number of customer complaints, mistakes, and cash drawer imbalances.

Finally, how can the productivity of managers and professionals be measured? A manager's job typically involves accomplishing goals through supervising others. Top-level executives are often evaluated by the performance of the organization. That performance might be evidenced by the price of the stock, profitability, or successful accomplishment of organizational goals. First-line supervisors might be evaluated by their subordinates' performance, turnover, and grievances. Middle managers' productivity is often difficult to measure or assess directly. Organizations that try to evaluate the productivity of these managers often do so indirectly, through performance appraisal systems (see Chapter 11).

Different types of organizations have different definitions and ways of measuring productivity, depending on the processes involved in their respective industries. The strategic goals of an organization provide its most important dimensions of productivity. Does the company stress low-cost production, innovation, or superb service? Each goal calls for different objectives, and therefore each implies different criteria for defining organizational performance. However, there are some common elements in any effective productivity measure. Measures should

- assess quality as well as quantity.
- be consistent with the organization's mission and strategy.
- be integrated with reward systems to create motivation.
- involve employees in their design and construction.
- cover elements over which employees have some control.[10]

Quality Defined

There are as many definitions of **quality** as there are authors on the subject, but two basic approaches can be discerned. The first and most traditional approach defines quality as "conformance to specifications." That is, the product or component is not defective if it is within the tolerances specified in advance. An example might be that a filled 500-gram box of cereal is acceptable if it contains between 497 and 503 grams of cereal. Note that this measure has no reference to customer wishes. All boxes may be perfectly filled, but if customers prefer to buy much smaller or much larger boxes of cereal, the perfectly filled 500-gram boxes will not sell.

The second major approach to measuring quality remedies this problem. It defines quality as "meeting customer requirements" and looks to measures such as customer satisfaction with the product's features and value.[11] It may seem that this approach is not workable for employees who do not directly interact with external customers or produce the product sold to them. For instance, HR managers and plant maintenance engineers probably do not have a direct effect on the satisfaction of external customers. However, this approach points out that *every* employee provides products or services to someone, and that it is these "customers," whether they are inside or outside the organization, who must be satisfied. HR managers provide services to management, employees, applicants, and external constituencies such as Occupational Safety and Health Administration (OSHA) inspectors. Maintenance engineers provide service to internal customers with equipment repair needs. In order to provide high-quality work, the organization must determine the needs of these various customers and continuously encourage efforts to meet them.

Measuring Quality

Any number of quality measures are possible, and the most suitable ones depend on the particular situation. Some typical measures appear in Table 10.1. Experts on quality emphasize a statistical approach to interpreting variance in quality measures such as on-time delivery or reject rate. They point out that variability in results can be due to two classes of sources: common causes and special causes.

Common causes represent the normal variation around an average for a given process. It is impossible to produce exactly the same result time after time be-

TABLE 10.1 Some Possible Quality Measures

- Number of work improvement suggestions submitted per worker per year
- Number of suggestions implemented per year
- Defect rate
- Scrap rate
- Rework percentage
- Mean time between failures
- Machine availability or machine downtime
- Customer satisfaction
- Repeat sales
- Variation around target specifications
- Hours of training per employee per year
- Customer demanded lead time to manufactured lead time

cause of small variations in materials, human behavior, machine capability, and so on. These minor variations can compound when combined into a finished product. For instance, if each link in a chain saw is just slightly off the ideal size (but still within specifications), the chain may be substantially too long or too short when all the links are combined. *Special causes* are unusual situations that create a result which is extreme compared to the average. Examples would be a worn bearing that starts to cause excessive vibration in a machine and significantly degrades its normal performance, or a new operator who makes an error in following a standard procedure.

Ongoing efforts should be made to improve process design so that common-cause variation is reduced and outputs are as consistent as possible over time. In our chain saw example, this would mean making all of the saw links as close to the same size as possible, perhaps by improving the sensitivity of the measuring device used, so that all completed chains were in the required size range. Variation due to special causes should raise a red flag, as on-the-spot diagnosis and corrective action are necessary. However, reacting to a common cause as if it were a special cause may result in unnecessary corrections or overcorrections aimed at a single event when there was really nothing unusual in the process needing attention.[12] Thus, improving quality depends on having good measures and understanding what variation in those measures really means.

Productivity Versus Quality: The End of a Myth

Thus far we have considered productivity and quality as more or less separate ideas. Historically, there has been a tendency to assume that productivity and quality were inversely related—that is, if one made products faster, quality would necessarily be lower, and that high quality could only come at the cost of less output per unit of input. In fact, these assumptions are very often false. Evidence has been mounting that quality pays off in a number of ways, so that the total productivity of the organization can be magnified by a concerted effort to improve quality. Some 1990s quality experts have rejected Michael Porter's view that organizations should pursue either a low-cost or a high differentiation strategy,[13] suggesting instead that low cost and differentiation based on quality often go hand-in-hand.[14]

Consider the costs imposed by poor quality in the manufacturing sector. First there is the cost of identifying poor-quality products—usually with armies of inspectors poring over finished products and rejecting many of them. Then there is the cost of reworking defective products that are repairable, and the cost of scrapping those that are not repairable. If defects are not caught and an item fails when it is already in the customer's hands, there is both the cost of field repair and the substantial loss of good will that accompanies such a failure. There are further costs in loss of reputation and future business, which are harder to quantify. Conventional wisdom holds that a satisfied customer will tell a few people about a good product, but a dissatisfied customer will tell everyone he or she knows. All these costs increase inputs and/or reduce acceptable outputs and thus lower productivity. Most managers underestimate the costs of poor quality, assuming that it is 5 percent of sales or less. In fact, a more typical figure for U.S. businesses is 20 to 30 percent of sales.[15]

Improving quality throughout the organization can result in substantial savings. Fewer inspectors are needed if quality is designed into the product and employees are taught to deal with quality problems at each step of the production process. Fixing an error after two or three parts have been assembled is much easier than disassembling an entire device to fix the same problem if it is not caught until the final inspection. Fewer employees will be needed for rework and for field repairs, less material will be wasted, and fewer customers will be alienated. By doing things right the first time, it is possible to produce more output from the same input, thus simultaneously improving quality, customer satisfaction, and productivity.

In the service sector, one indicator of quality is repeat business. If good service is provided, customers should keep coming back. But what if providing good service costs more or takes longer per transaction? This may cause some traditional measures of productivity, such as clients served per hour, to fall. When viewed in a broader perspective, however, high-quality customer service usually pays off for the organization, mainly because it costs much more to find a new customer than to provide repeat service to an existing customer. Besides, repeat customers tend to increase their level of spending on the service being provided as their trust in the provider grows. In sum, it is much more profitable to keep an existing customer than to replace one who has departed because of poor-quality service.[16] Clearly, then, quality, productivity, and profitability can and do go hand in hand in virtually all kinds of businesses.

PLANNING PRODUCTIVITY AND QUALITY INTERVENTIONS

Each organization needs to tailor its own productivity/quality improvement approach. The literature offers a number of approaches, associated with such scholars as Philip Crosby, Joseph Juran, W. Edwards Deming, Armand J. Feigenbaum, and Genichi Taguchi.[17] However, any plan for improving performance first requires careful diagnosis of the problem and then attention to the issue of getting the solution accepted and fully implemented in the organization.

Diagnosis and Benchmarking

Prior to undertaking any approach to improving productivity and quality, the organization must develop a thorough understanding of the current state of affairs, so that it can choose appropriately targeted methods and monitor progress empirically. Frequently, when managers are faced with poor productivity or quality, they attribute the difficulty to low employee effort or carelessness. The fact that partial productivity measures are often based on labor cost also tends to mislead management into focusing too much blame on employees. However, programs to improve employee motivation will have minimal impact if productivity problems are due to defective raw materials or poorly conceived manufacturing processes.

The left side of Figure 10.2 shows where one fabrication and assembly plant's production costs come from. In this case, only 10 percent of costs are direct labor costs. The pie chart on the right shows the way that the company had been spending its $2 million annual productivity improvement budget. A full 39 percent was devoted to the direct labor component, even though substantial gains in this area would have only a limited impact on total production costs. Once the plant manager collected the information shown in Figure 10.2, he was better able to diagnose the cause of poor productivity. He has now shifted a larger portion of the productivity improvement budget to trying to reduce the overhead, which contributes 30 percent to production costs.[18]

Clearly, careful diagnosis must precede any efforts to improve productivity and quality. A typical process for thoroughly assessing the organization's situation might include the following activities:[19]

- Development and application of empirical measures of performance, including customer satisfaction, waste, rejects, productivity, and so forth.
- Construction and administration of a quality values survey. Employees are asked their perceptions of the importance of quality in the organization's culture, the extent to which risk taking to enhance quality is approved or punished, the extent to which quality is recognized and rewarded, the extent to which effective training for quality has been provided, and so on.
- **Benchmarking**, or studying the performance and practices of the world leaders in the industry or function being assessed.[20]

- Analysis and feedback of the above information to top management.
- Planning and setting goals for the effort to improve performance.

Obtaining Commitment

No improvement plan, no matter how well it is suited to the situation, will succeed without the understanding and commitment of employees. All stages of planning and implementation should include getting more people on board and overcoming or minimizing resistance to change. The assessment and benchmarking process just described is often very powerful in gaining top management commitment to a change. Others who have been involved in the survey or the benchmarking study are also likely to see a need for change and increase their level of commitment. In general, wider employee involvement at early stages will pave the way for wider acceptance in later stages. HR managers can provide a valuable service to other managers by emphasizing this point and developing mechanisms for employee input.

It seems to be critical that top management commit to and lead major organizational change efforts. Turning all responsibility for the program over to the HR department or hired consultants is a sure recipe for failure. Given ongoing and visible commitment at the top, a number of steps are needed to convert the rest of the organization. These almost always include extensive educational efforts, and may also include pilot projects that demonstrate the utility of the change being proposed. The training starts with basic quality awareness and an explanation of why changes are needed. It then moves on to specific tools for measuring and controlling quality, and finally tackles interpersonal skills for working more effectively to solve problems that cut across individuals or departments.[21] Table 10.2 contains recommendations concerning which employees should get what kinds of education about quality in an organization that has adopted **total quality management (TQM)**.

A rule of thumb for organizations attempting major changes is that such changes will be at least three times as difficult and take twice as long to implement as expected; miracles do not happen overnight. Nevertheless, more and more organizations are managing to make the transition to a high-quality mentality. Table 10.3 shows a model of the steps involved in moving an organization from first awareness that quality matters all the way to a world-class competitor in the quality race.

Types of Interventions

Organizations can choose from a large number of possible methods to deal with perceived productivity and/or quality problems. Some of these methods focus on the entire organization and entail changes in the organization's culture, values, and relationships between work units. Total quality management exemplifies this type of intervention. Other interventions focus primarily at the group level, through such means as autonomous work groups and quality circles. Still other

FIGURE 10.2 How One Company Didn't Match Productivity Improvement Spending to Production Costs

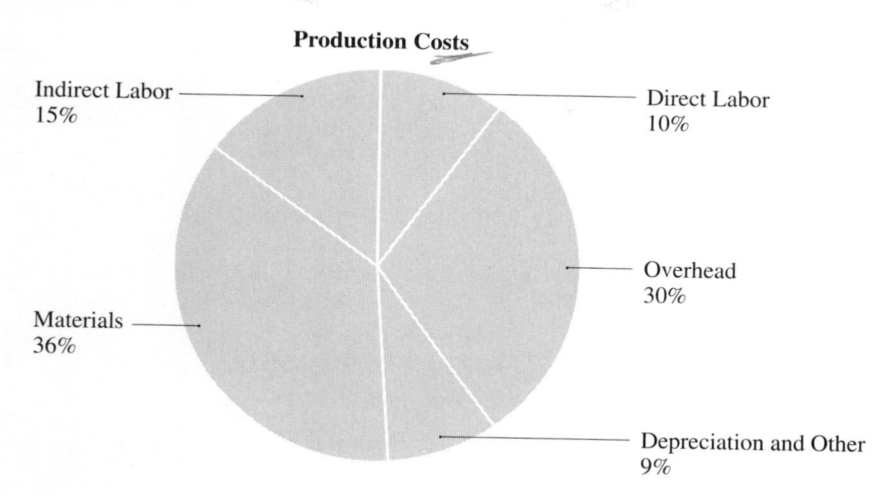

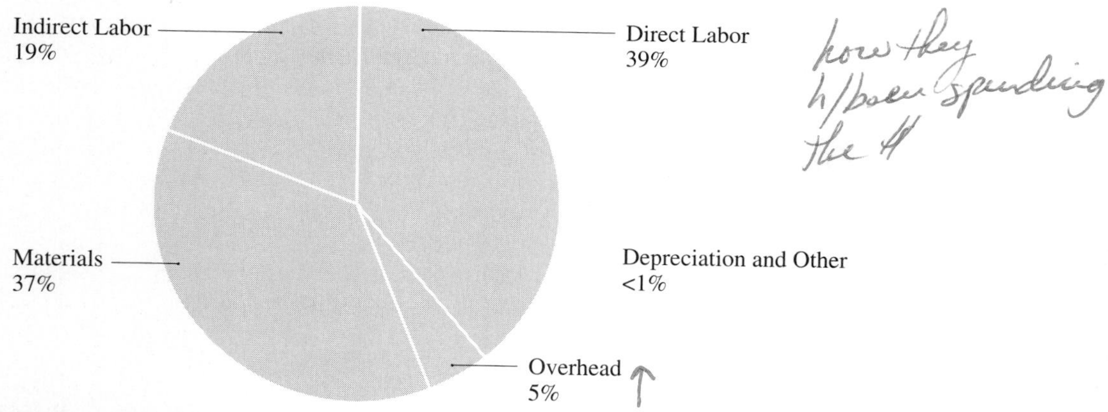

Source: Reprinted by permission of Harvard Business Review. An exhibit from "No-Nonsense Guide to Measuring Productivity" by W. Bruce Chew, January/February 1988. Copyright © 1988 by the President and Fellows of Harvard College; all rights reserved.

interventions mainly target individuals and their motivation; they range from individual goal setting and financial incentives to job redesign and enrichment. Finally, some interventions concentrate on the environment and equipment in an attempt to improve performance. Examples would be automation and ergonomic work environment design.

These methods are not as distinct as they may at first appear. TQM often includes quality improvement groups; it also redefines the job responsibilities of every employee. Job enrichment efforts may involve a switch from individual job

TABLE 10.2 The Quality Education Matrix

	Executives	*Middle Managers*	*Engineers*	*Supervisors*	*Workers*
Quality improvement overview	X	X	X	X	X
Employee involvement	X	X	X	X	X
Leadership/facilitator workshop	X	X	X	X	
Team building	X	X	X	X	X
Creative thinking	X	X	X	X	X
Supplier management	X	X	X		
Setup reduction and cellular processes		X	X	X	X
Problem solving—basic	X	X	X	X	X
Problem solving—advanced statistical process control	X	X	X	X	X
Problem solving—train the trainer		X		X	X
Design of experiments		X	X	X	X
Total quality control audit	X	X			
Competitive benchmarking	X	X	X		
Statistical thinking (how to understand variability and the correct approach to reducing it)	X	X	X	X	X
Quality function deployment	X	X	X	X	
Total productive maintenance	X	X	X	X	X
General business perspective				X	X
Parameter design using Taguchi methods			X		
Policy deployment	X	X	X	X	

Source: David L. Muthler and Lucy L. Lytle, "Quality Education Requirements," as it appears in *Total Quality: An Executive's Guide for the 1990s*, edited by Ernst & Young Improvement Consulting Group, Homewood, IL, Dow Jones-Irwin, 1990.

TABLE 10.3 Conceptual Model Showing Major Steps to World-Class Status

I *Top Management Awareness and Education*	*II* *Building a Critical Mass*	*III* *Achieving Total Quality Control*	*IV* *World-Class Quality/ World-Class Competitor*
Understand need and benefits Learn and apply: Quality improvement process Problem-solving tools Statistical thinking Develop vision, change strategy, plans Form steering committee	25–50% of management committed to quality Pilot projects (limited scope) Education in quality concepts/philosophy (20–30%) Training in basic tools (10–20%) Facilitation training (EI, team process) Education in advanced tools (1–2%)	All employees in all departments introduced to basic tools/ philosophy of total quality control (TQC) Organizationwide commitment Many cross-functional improvement efforts Suppliers heavily involved TQC promotion organization/ upper management audits Ways of life: Customer orientation Continuous improvement Elimination of waste Prevention, not detection Reduction of variation Statistical thinking/use of data Adherence to best known methods Respect for people and their knowledge Use of best available tools	Design quality dominates efforts Reorganization around key products/services Process institutionalized and self-sustaining Totally consistent management practices 50% + trained in advanced tools

Source: From "The Quality Imperative," by Ronald M. Fortuna from *Total Quality: An Executive's Guide for the 1990s*, edited by Ernst & Young Improvement Consulting Group. Copyright © 1990 by Richard D. Irwin, Homewood, IL.

activities to work teams, whereas quality circles often recommend improvements in the physical work environment or equipment. Nevertheless, it is useful to examine these four types of interventions separately.

ORGANIZATIONALLY FOCUSED INTERVENTIONS

Although it is beyond the scope of this book to explore organizational level quality-enhancing interventions in great depth, we will discuss several major thrusts in this area.

Common Principles

Each "quality guru" has his or her own specific prescriptions for success, but there is a large amount of overlap in the philosophies and principles of the more popular approaches. These similarities are listed in Table 10.4. One of the underlying themes is **kaizen**, a Japanese word meaning "continuous improvement involving everybody."[22] The idea is that quality improvement is not a one-time affair but a constant search for better ways to do things. Substantial gains in productiv-

TABLE 10.4 Common Principles Underlying Most Modern Approaches to Quality

- Customer-first orientation.
- Top management leadership of the quality improvement process.
- Focus on continuous improvement.
- Respect for employees and their knowledge; employees are actively involved in the improvement process.
- Reduction of product and process variation.
- Provision of ongoing education and training to employees.
- Familiarity with a statistical way of thinking and the use of statistical methods throughout the organization.
- Emphasis on prevention rather than detection.
- View of vendors as long-term partners.
- Performance measures that are consistent with the goals of the organization.
- Standardization—the development of and adherence to the best known ways to perform a given task.
- Product or service quality begins with its definition and design.
- Cooperation and involvement of all functions within an organization.
- Awareness of the needs of internal customers.
- Substantial cultural change.

Source: Ronald M. Fortuna "The Quality Imperative," as it appears in *Total Quality: An Executive's Guide for the 1990s,* edited by Ernst & Young Improvement Consulting Group, Homewood, IL, Dow-Jones Irwin, 1990. p. 110.

ity and quality are achieved by the cumulative impact of many small, incremental changes to which everyone can contribute, rather than solely by dramatic, expensive, and centrally planned innovations.

Total Quality Management

Total quality management (TQM) is an extremely popular set of methods for improving quality and productivity.[23] It has been adopted by thousands of companies, including Corning Glass Works, General Motors, McCormick Spice, and Westinghouse Electric Corp. TQM replaces traditional beliefs about quality with a new set of principles. Dated principles that it debunks include the following:

- High quality costs more.
- Quality can be improved by inspection.
- Defects cannot be eliminated completely.
- Quality control is the job of the quality control department.[24]

William H. Wagel identifies four new principles of total quality management:

1. *Meet the customer's requirements on time, the first time, and 100 percent of the time.* In total quality management, every employee is considered both a customer and a vendor: each person uses products or services provided by other people either inside or outside the organization, and each supplies products or services to internal or external customers. Each employee identifies his or her customers and meets with them to clarify requirements—what the customer needs from the employee—then strives to satisfy customer expectations at all times. Quality is the job of each employee, not of the quality control department.

2. *Strive to do error-free work.* Total quality management rejects the notion of an "acceptable quality level," such as 95 percent correct. This dated view suggests that defects are inevitable and can be tolerated, whereas total quality management strives to reduce defects to zero.

3. *Manage by prevention.* Quality cannot be inspected into a completed product; it has to be designed and built into the product from the very beginning and at all stages of production. W. Edwards Deming says that 85 percent of quality defects are caused by management, meaning that opportunities for errors were designed into the product or production process. To correct these errors, every incident of poor quality is investigated and traced to its source; then changes are made to assure that the defect will not happen again.

4. *Measure the cost of quality.* Some authors assert that quality is free; that is, the costs of preventing a defect from the beginning will be lower than the costs of detecting and then correcting defects in finished products. Total quality management interventions usually include a system for assessing the costs of quality, in order to demonstrate that prevention is the least costly way to achieve high quality.[25]

The basis of TQM systems is employees' awareness of quality as an organizational priority. Thus, the first step in total quality management is training for all employees, as described earlier. After basic quality awareness training, additional training on statistical process control would also be common. Most TQM programs also include suggestion systems and quality improvement teams or quality circles (discussed below). They also encourage, formally or informally, cross-functional management—a collaboration between the different units that interact to produce a product. For instance, purchasing, engineering, and production groups must cooperate to locate causes of defects and to redesign systems to eliminate these causes.

Some companies require their suppliers to have TQM systems in place, and some have even offered TQM training to their suppliers. Following Japanese precedents, it is becoming more common for U.S. firms to reduce their number of suppliers and build long-term relationships with a smaller number of firms rather than seeking the lowest bid and changing suppliers frequently. These sustained relationships allow the supplier to better understand and respond to the buyer's needs, in terms of both quality of the product and delivery requirements.

Business Process Improvement

Generally attributed to IBM, **business process improvement** is a set of practices for regularly examining and improving the processes that go on in an organization. A process is a repeated set of activities, often carried out in sequence by several departments, that adds value and produces measurable outputs. Examples include billing, distribution, materials management, and procurement.[26] In a traditional approach to quality, each department involved in a process would try to do its portion of the activity more quickly and accurately, but the entire process from start to finish was unlikely to be critically evaluated or redesigned. Thus, very dated, inefficient systems might be tweaked into becoming faster, but still dated and inefficient, systems.

In business process improvement, someone is assigned responsibility for the whole process. This manager works with a cross-functional team to assess the state of the process and develop new ways to perform it better. Statistical quality measurement and analysis techniques may be used, and small-scale experiments with new processes may be tried. The process is then redesigned, and further improvements made with experience. The steps in business process improvement used at IBM are shown in Table 10.5.

One example of a successful implementation of this approach involved accounts payable at Ford Motor Co. After benchmarking its accounts payable function against Mazda Motor Corporation, Ford realized that its employee head count in this function was probably five times what it needed to be. By helping employees do the same tasks faster, only a 20 percent reduction in staff would be possible. But by redesigning the entire system for keeping track of orders, deliveries, and invoices, the company dramatically simplified the process. Before the changes, clerks had to check and match fourteen items on three forms before paying an invoice; they spent much of their time trying to unravel mismatches.

TABLE 10.5 Business Process Analysis Methodology Steps

1. Assign ownership.
   —Charge key managers to improve process.
2. Perform activity analysis at task level.
   —Establish measurements, true cost of quality.
3. Document current procedures.
   —Iterate with key employees until accuracy is achieved.
4. Document the process.
   —Functional/cross-functional relationships.
5. Determine process requirements and secure customer concurrence.
6. Assess impact of any mismatch.
   —Prioritize problems based on requirements vs. existing process.
7. Analyze potential solutions to bring process into conformance.
   —Eliminate failure cost and improve control through:
   a) Process simplification by elimination of redundant tasks, combining like tasks, adding missing tasks.
   b) Restructure and automate where appropriate.
   —Review additional resources, retraining requirement, new capital equipment, etc.
   —Pilot test process changes with specific pass/fail criteria to ensure fix is permanent and complete.
8. Select and implement best alternatives.
9. Update target and measurement criteria for new process.
10. Establish regular next level management review plan vs. actual.
11. Feedback new management control activity requirements.
12. Update managers' performance plan to be quality specific for the new process.

Source: H. James Harrington, *The Quality/Profit Connection* (Milwaukee, Wis.: ASQC Quality Press, 1989). Reprinted with the permission of ASQC Quality Press.

Now only three items have to be matched, and a computer system does the matching automatically and prepares the check. The function requires 75 percent fewer people, and errors have been substantially reduced.[27]

GROUP-FOCUSED INTERVENTIONS

A number of productivity and quality improvement interventions fall under the heading of **group-focused interventions**; these programs may also be referred to as examples of **participative management** or **employee involvement**. Group-focused interventions are based on the belief that employees at all levels in the organization desire to contribute to the effective functioning of the organization, that everyone has useful insights to contribute, and that groups are a good forum for generating and refining ideas. Thus, the objective of group participative programs is to empower groups of employees to identify and solve performance problems in their own area of expertise.[28]

Group programs include part-time **work improvement teams**, also known as **quality circles (QCs)**, in which members get together a few hours a week to solve

INTERNATIONAL PERSPECTIVE

Productivity Issues in Russia

During the 1980s, labor productivity in the Soviet Union was low and stagnant. In 1990 and 1991, productivity actually declined. There are many possible reasons for this history of low productivity, including antiquated facilities, inefficient centralized planning, and problems of labor supply and employee motivation. The latter two deserve further discussion in the context of this chapter.

Prior to Gorbachev's reforms, unemployment did not exist in the Soviet Union—every citizen was guaranteed a job. As a result, very few individuals were seeking employment at any point in time. Because locating additional employees was difficult, managers tended to overstaff and hoard employees.

Western observers in the 1980s reported that employee motivation was just as problematic as the supply of labor. Workers were often absent, drunk, or asleep on the job. Many took time off from their regular jobs to work a second job or to stand in lines for scarce goods. Since discharge was rarely allowed and workers were in short supply, employers did not impose discipline for absenteeism or poor work. The Soviet Union had also long pursued a low wage policy in an effort to "decommoditize" labor. That is, on the socialist principle that one individual employing another for wages necessarily exploits the one being employed, wages were deemphasized and the employer supplied many nonwage benefits such as housing, medical care, vacation trips, and household goods. This situation made it very hard to use monetary incentives as a motivator, and led to the common expression by Soviet workers, "We pretend to work and they pretend to pay us."

Over the years, Soviet leaders tried several methods of enhancing productivity through motivation. One method—*socialist competitions* between work groups, plants, or cities—invoked workers' socialist values in an attempt to increase production, but the workers usually ignored the competitions. A second method—incentive pay for exceeding an output norm—was actually defeated by the government itself. By raising the production norms nearly every year, the government in effect cut the rate paid per piece. In self-defense, workers began restricting their output. In recent years, wage increases over 3%, even when justified by productivity increases, attracted a very high tax, so there was no incentive to work hard for an increase.

A third method—the *work brigade*—occasionally proved successful and has long been a feature of Soviet employment. A brigade, or group of 8 to 200 workers at the same site, was responsible for an identifiable component of a company's production process. A brigade received a group incentive payment for exceeding the performance standard assigned to it. Often, the group bonus was divided among brigade members based on the brigade leader's perceptions of individual performance or attendance during the bonus period. In some cases, the brigade system resulted in job enrichment, because brigade members had autonomy in structuring their work, could rotate jobs within the group, and could cross-train in other skills required in the brigade. It would seem that this system would be effective in motivating increased output; in fact, some brigades showed productivity gains of 10 to 15 percent. However, the average gain in productivity following the implementation of the brigade concept was usually only 1 to 2 percent. This may have been due to the formation of brigades that were too large for group incentives to be motivational, a lack of receptiveness to job enrichment in older and less-educated workers, lack of necessary skills training, or to the low-incentive value of pay increases in an economy that offered very few consumer goods on which to spend additional income.

Recent modifications of the brigade system

allowed brigade members more autonomy. In some cases, the brigades were encouraged to become economically accountable units with their own production quotas and budget. Even more autonomous versions of the brigade are the "lease-contract brigade" and the "production cooperative." These versions more nearly resemble Western style employee-buyouts, with brigade members taking full responsibility for the success of their venture.

Russia and several other former Soviet republics are moving toward a more market-driven system, in terms of both the labor market and the goods and services market. Progress is slow, however, and unemployment is becoming a problem for the first time. Throwing off entrenched bureaucratic habits and the legacy of seventy years of central planning is extremely difficult for managers in the newly independent republics. The task for human resource managers in the former Soviet republics is to learn to acquire, retain, and motivate a work force with very little work ethic, and to train employees in the skills needed for improved productivity. Unfortunately, Russia and the other republics lack skilled HR managers, because under the old system these individuals performed few and very routine functions.

Sources: Trevor Buck and John Cole, *Modern Soviet Economic Performance* (Oxford, Eng.: Basil Blackwell Ltd., 1987), pp. 95–105, 147; Leonard J. Kirsch, *Soviet Wages: Changes in Structure and Administration since 1956* (Cambridge, Mass.: MIT Press, 1972), pp. 41–42, 64–65; Don Van Atta, "A Critical Examination of Brigades in the USSR," *Economics and Industrial Democracy,* 1989, Vol. 10, pp. 329–340; Guy Standing, "Wages and Work Motivation in the Soviet Labour Market," *International Labour Review,* 1991, Vol. 130, pp. 237–253; V. I. Shcherbakov, "Remuneration of Labour in the USSR: Problems and Prospects," *International Labour Review,* 1991, Vol. 130, pp. 227–236; Stephenie Overman, "Help Wanted: HR Pros to Transform Soviet Work Force," *HRMagazine,* January 1991, pp. 44–45, 78.

problems, and full-time **autonomous work groups** in which most of the responsibility for ongoing production is delegated to the work group itself.[29] Note that group participative programs are also intended to motivate individuals. Inviting employees to use their creative abilities and become responsible for their performance would clearly constitute a type of job enrichment. The main point of the programs described in this section, however, is to give some problem-solving responsibilities to the people who have the best information on how to deal with daily productivity or quality issues.

Work Improvement Teams (Quality Circles)

Work improvement teams, or quality circles as they were commonly called in the 1980s, have been termed "the most popular form of participative management in American history." It was estimated that several hundred thousand employees belonged to QCs by 1988, and the number is surely much larger now. Quality circles have proven especially popular in the aerospace, automobile, steel, and consumer goods industries.[30]

A quality circle consists of a small number of volunteers, typically eight to ten employees from the same department, who meet a few hours each week to examine productivity and quality problems. Initially, these circles may be led by a supervisor, but they usually evolve to nonmanagement leadership. QC members identify a problem, study it, and present their recommendations for change and improvement to a committee of higher management.[31]

Quality circles are not limited to manufacturing work. At Velcro USA, half of the teams are in administrative units.[32] Potentially large gains can result when quality circles made up of managers analyze their process of holding meetings and figure out how to make that activity more efficient.[33] Furthermore, it is not always true that QC members come from the same department. Cross-functional QCs are sometimes assembled to work on larger problems that transcend departmental boundaries.

Effectiveness of Work Improvement Teams Quality circles can be effective. Some organizations have reported a return on investment ranging from 200 to 800 percent. Experts have also suggested that, since the technique is a participative one, improved employee morale should be an additional result. However, this is not always the case.[34] In one review of research, about half of the studies of QC implementations reported uniformly positive results—that is, improvement in all variables measured in the study (such as productivity, quality, absenteeism, or job attitudes). One-quarter of the studies found that QCs had some beneficial effects, and the other quarter reported no beneficial changes.[35] Other reviews are less positive, particularly about the effects of quality circles on productivity and quality.[36]

Work improvement teams are often part of organizational-level changes toward a total quality management culture. In this context, they seem likely to succeed, as they will be embedded in a supportive environment and be consistent with other changes taking place at the same time. If QCs are adopted as a standalone program that is inconsistent with other systems in the organization, the prospects for success diminish. However, quality circles have been suggested as a bridge between a nonparticipative approach to management and more far-reaching changes in the work structure, such as autonomous work groups.[37]

Problems in Implementing Work Improvement Teams When implementing work improvement teams, companies must address several possible problems. Often managers and workers are skeptical of the program because they view it as simply another fad that is being imposed on them. Supervisors may also tend to be nervous about such a program, viewing it as a threat to their authority. Moreover, employees who volunteer for QCs may wish to air complaints against management or discuss issues such as wages and benefits. These issues are usually explicitly off limits for quality circles, but when employees find that they must comply with this ban, they may become disillusioned about the depth of management's commitment to participation.

Another typical problem with QCs, especially early in the program, is that they stretch the volunteerism concept. When circles are just being formed, they require much time and effort, something workers might be unprepared for.[38] Most quality circles begin with a great deal of training in identifying work problems,

TABLE 10.6 Phases of a Quality Circle Program's Life

Phase	*Activity*	*Destructive Forces*
1. Start-up	Publicize Obtain funds and volunteers Train	Low volunteer rate Inadequate funding Inability to learn group process and problem-solving skills
2. Initial problem solving	Identify and solve problems	Disagreement on problems Lack of knowledge of operations
3. Presentation and approval of initial suggestions	Present and have accepted initial suggestions	Resistance by staff groups and middle management Poor presentation and suggestions because of limited knowledge
4. Implementation of solutions	Relevant groups act on suggestions	Prohibitive costs Resistance by groups that must implement
5. Expansion and continued problem solving	Form new groups Old groups continue	Member-nonmember conflict Raised aspirations Lack of problems Expense of parallel organization Savings not realized Rewards wanted
6. Decline	Fewer groups meet	Cynicism about program Burnout

Source: Reprinted by permission of Harvard Business Review: An exhibit from "Quality Circles After the Fad" by Edward E. Lawler, III, and Susan A. Mohrman, January/February 1985.

applying statistics to track and evaluate quality, and working together in a group. This stage can be frustrating for employees who want to get right to work on a problem. For circles to succeed over the longer term, management needs to show its commitment by implementing some of the groups' suggestions and providing prompt feedback on the disposition of all suggestions.

Table 10.6 shows the phases in the life of a quality circle program and the problems encountered in each phase. It seems that QCs have a definite life cycle of from one to three years. Few circles continue to operate beyond this period of time because they run out of either interest or easily solved problems.

Autonomous Work Groups

Another group-based method for improving performance is the autonomous work group, which is given near-total responsibility for producing a product or service.

The group makes most of the production decisions, such as scheduling, assigning work, deciding on methods, and even selecting new members and allocating pay raises. Management is responsible for providing information to the group on costs, quality, output requirements, and any technical assistance that is requested.[39] When this concept is used throughout much of the organization, the result is called a "high-involvement organization."

Companies that have been integrating autonomous work groups into their plants include Procter & Gamble, Cummins Engine Company, General Motors, Westinghouse Electric, TRW Inc., Sherwin-Williams Company, and IBM. These companies claim that the teams can increase productivity by 30 to 50 percent. However, the firms also caution that the concept does not fit all situations. For autonomous work teams to function, the company must develop very loose control systems, remove bureaucratic procedures, guarantee job security, and permit radical changes in the typical manager-subordinate relationship. Where unions exist, the company must convince the union to loosen its restrictive demands, especially concerning narrow job classifications.[40]

Controlled research on the effects of autonomous work groups is difficult to perform. Existing studies, however, verify claims that sometimes, but not always, autonomous work groups result in increased productivity.[41] The concept is gaining in popularity and is being extended to the service sector, so there seems to be informal evidence that it can work. As a rule, autonomous work groups are easier to implement at a new facility when a new work force is hired. Converting existing plants and work forces is more difficult but has been done successfully.[42]

An example of the autonomous group method is provided by a confectionery factory in England, where a new plant was designed specifically for autonomous groups. Each group of eight to twelve employees was responsible for a single product line; all group members were expected to learn to perform the eight different jobs involved in making their product. There were no supervisors. Groups made their own decisions about job allocation and scheduling at weekly meetings. The groups had some input in selecting new group members, and they had full responsibility for meeting production, hygiene, and quality standards; recording output; ordering raw materials; calling for engineering support when needed; and even delivering finished goods to stores. This innovation raised the intrinsic job satisfaction of employees and saved the company money by eliminating supervisory positions.[43]

An Example of a Successful Group-Focused Intervention

Robert D. Pritchard and his colleagues have reported a highly successful group-focused productivity intervention conducted in five support units at a U.S. Air Force base.[44] This intervention utilized group participation in designing productivity and quality measures, then group-focused feedback, goal setting, and rewards to motivate improvement. The most unique aspect of this intervention was probably the development of the unit effectiveness measure. Supervisors and employees worked together, with guidance from the researchers, to define and construct indices of performance in their units. A multi-step procedure was followed.

First, unit members agreed on what their primary products or services were. For instance, a communication and navigation equipment repair unit decided that two of its "products" were meeting repair demand and producing high-quality repairs. In the second step, measures of each product were devised. Meeting repair demand was operationalized as the number of units repaired divided by the number brought in for repair in a given month. Quality of repairs was assessed by the percentage of units that failed again immediately after being reinstalled in planes. The third step was to agree on how effective the maximum, minimum, and intervening levels of performance were on each indicator. For instance, the group decided that a 2 percent failure rate after reinstallation was the best that could possibly be attained, given the unreliable nature of electronic components. It decided that a 20 percent failure rate was the worst that could realistically occur. A midpoint, representing neither good nor poor unit performance, was pegged at a 10 percent failure rate. Levels in between these were also rated for effectiveness, with the results shown in Figure 10.3.

Note that the same-size improvement in performance has a different meaning at different points in Figure 10.3. Improving from a 12 to an 8 percent failure rate represents a bigger gain in effectiveness (from below expectations to above expectations) than jumping from 6 to 2 percent (from very good to excellent). This reflects the fact that all productivity gains do not have the same value to an or-

FIGURE 10.3 Relationship of One Quality Indicator to Effectiveness

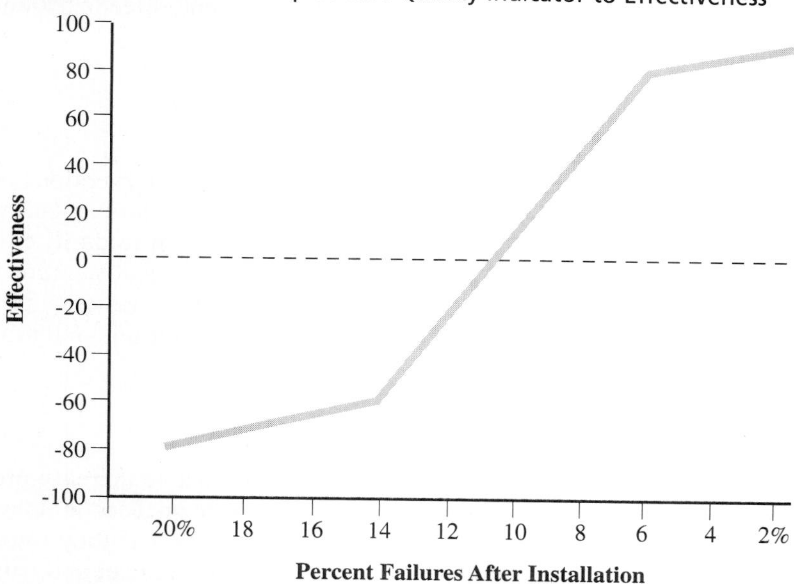

Source: Robert D. Pritchard, Steven D. Jones, Philip L. Roth, Karla K. Stuebing, and Steven E. Ekeberg, "Effects of Group Feedback, Goal Setting, and Incentives on Organizational Productivity," *Journal of Applied Psychology,* 1988, Vol. 73. No. 2, p. 342. Copyright 1988 by the American Psychological Association. Reprinted by permission.

ganization. The slopes of the curve for an indicator also suggest when energy might be more profitably spent elsewhere. Once the failure rate is reduced to 6 percent, a greater payoff in total effectiveness may be realized by concentrating on improving a different indicator (such as percentage of repairs completed on time) than on becoming perfect on the first indicator.

After indicators were developed, baseline data on effectiveness were gathered in all units for eight months. Starting with the ninth month, the feedback intervention began. Each unit received a monthly report of its effectiveness on each indicator; the report was posted in the work area and discussed in a monthly meeting. Feedback was given for five months, and then units were trained to set their own goals. Goal setting plus feedback continued for an additional five months. Then the tangible reward of time off with pay for meeting various effectiveness levels was added for the final five months of the study.

Gains in effectiveness were calculated as a percentage of the maximum possible gain. The maximum possible gain was defined as moving from the baseline level on an indicator to the maximum possible level (that is, 2 percent failures for the quality-of-repair indicator). Summing across indicators, the units in the study achieved 50 percent of the maximum possible gain during the months when only feedback was given. When goal setting was added, performance increased to 75 percent of the maximum possible gain. The time-off incentive caused only a 1 percent additional rise, to 76 percent. However, this does not mean necessarily that the incentive was ineffective. Perhaps the units had already improved as much as was humanly possible. One might also expect that a tangible reward would help maintain long-term interest in the effectiveness feedback and goals.

INDIVIDUAL-LEVEL INTERVENTIONS

A third focus for productivity and quality improvement interventions is the individual. Interventions aimed at individuals generally try to clarify exactly what the individual is expected to do and then motivate the person to do it, either by rewards of some kind or by making the work more intrinsically interesting. This section examines several individual-level interventions, including financial rewards, suggestion systems, behavior modification, goal setting, and job redesign.

Financial Rewards

One of the most common methods that organizations use to increase productivity is performance-based pay systems. For such systems to succeed, employees must desire more pay, believe that they will receive more pay if they improve their performance, be physically able to improve their performance, and trust that the organization will administer the pay for performance system fairly. There are many systems available for linking pay to individual, group, or organizational productivity.

Incentive Systems Individual incentive systems and commission plans directly tie the size of each individual's paycheck to output. A great deal of research has shown that individual incentives are effective in increasing output. One study tracked changes in productivity at an iron foundry for 114 months. At the 45th month, the company introduced an incentive system to replace the previous hourly rate pay system. As shown in Figure 10.4, productivity jumped sharply. This jump is attributed to the fact that the workers quickly learned that greater output would result in greater rewards. Note, however, that productivity continued on an upward trend for years after the incentive system was first introduced. The researchers believe that this trend was caused by employees gradually devising and implementing more and more efficient ways to do their jobs. Without the incentives, employees would probably not have been motivated to come up with these strategies for improving performance. Note that labor cost per ton and grievances did not increase as a result of the incentive system.[45]

FIGURE 10.4 Trend in Monthly Productivity Before and After Incentive Intervention

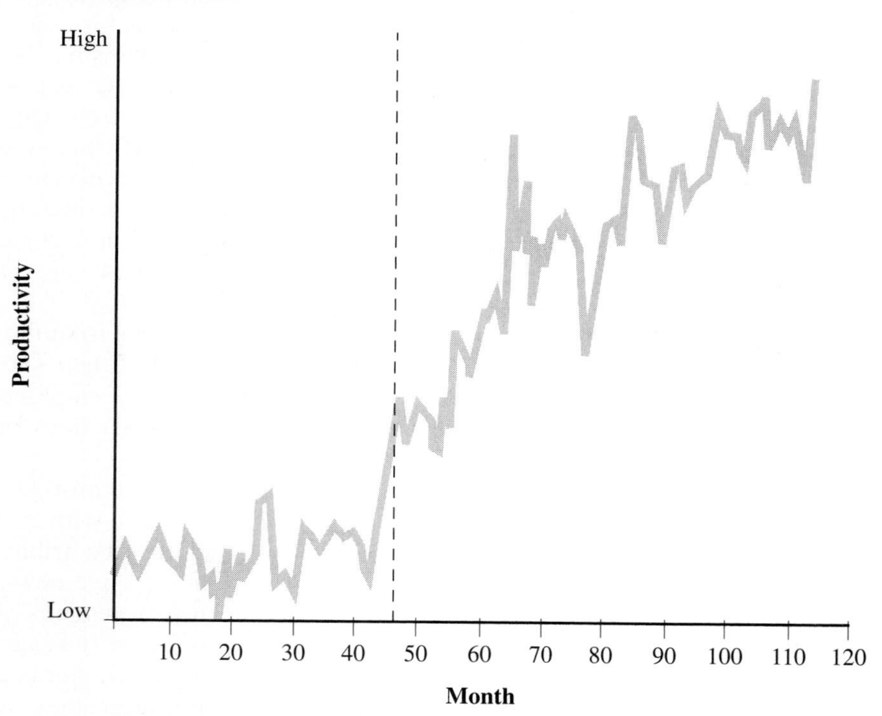

Source: John A. Wagner III, Paul A. Rubin, and Thomas J. Callahan, "Incentive Payment and Nonmanagerial Productivity: An Interrupted Time Series Analysis of Magnitude and Trend," *Organizational Behavior and Human Decision Processes,* August 1988, Vol. 42, p. 59. Reprinted by permission.

Alternatives to individual incentives include various plans for rewarding employees on the basis of group or company performance. For instance, plantwide gain sharing plans return to employees 50 to 75 percent of the dollars saved when productivity increases beyond an agreed-upon standard. These plans, discussed in detail in Chapter 13, can be quite effective in motivating employees to work both smarter and harder.

Pay for Skills A new pay system, often used in autonomous work groups, is **pay for skills** (see Chapter 13). New employees start at a base wage and earn increases by mastering additional skills needed for the tasks performed by their group. This method not only encourages employees to learn all the jobs in their group but also provides greater variety and more interesting work. Problem solving regarding quality should also improve when employees understand the entire process and all the jobs involved. Management realizes additional benefits in greater flexibility in covering jobs when employees are absent.

Suggestion Systems

Suggestion systems have long been in place in American organizations, but they have seldom been especially effective at generating new ideas for improved quality or productivity. The failure of traditional suggestion systems has been attributed to a difficult and time-consuming procedure for submitting suggestions, the need to demonstrate the cost-effectiveness of any proposed change, slow response to suggestions by management, general lack of a participative ethic, and an overemphasis on monetary benefits. The disadvantage of paying monetary suggestion bonuses that are a percentage of the dollar savings generated by the suggestion is that minor changes or hard-to-quantify changes are not suggested. Yet according to the kaizen philosophy, it is precisely these minor suggestions that multiply over time to produce big improvements.[46]

Japan originally borrowed the idea of suggestion systems from the U.S. Air Force, but the Japanese have made it a much bigger part of their success than most U.S. organizations. Matsushita had the largest number of employee suggestions in Japan in 1985—more than 6 million. The most suggestions made by a single individual in a year was a mind-boggling 16,821.[47]

Recently, some U.S. firms have designed suggestions systems that overcome the problems identified above. These systems go hand-in-hand with an employee involvement philosophy that everyone has valuable ideas to contribute. United Electric Controls Company provides an example of an effective new-style suggestion system. The company places emphasis on making suggestions rather than on determining their exact value, and pays a $100 bonus for every suggestion that is implemented. Everyone who submits a suggestion in a given month receives a chance in a monthly prize drawing, and people whose suggestions are implemented receive two chances. The process of submitting a suggestion has been streamlined to a one-page form. The employee submits the form to the immediate superior, who can implement the suggestion at once if it is straightforward. More complex ideas go to a volunteer committee of workers for evaluation. Feedback is provided on the percentage of the work force involved in suggestions in a given year (65 percent in 1990), and the company has set a goal of 100 percent participation. Although tangible rewards are part of the system, participants say that recognition and the fact that management is listening to them are at least as satisfying as the prizes.[48]

Behavior Modification

Behavior modification is a popular technique for improving employee productivity, especially for nonmanagement workers. Behavior modification does not focus on the underlying motivation of the employee; it simply attempts to change behaviors by manipulating the consequences of the behaviors.[49] Behavior modification has been very successful in a wide variety of situations. Michigan Bell Telephone used behavior modification to increase the service promptness, productivity, and attendance of its operators by 50 percent.[50]

Consequences of Behaviors Consequences can be used to modify employee behaviors through positive reinforcement, punishment, or extinction.

Positive Reinforcement The first and most common way to modify behavior is by positive reinforcement. **Positive reinforcement** is giving rewards to employees immediately after they have performed in a desirable way. The purpose is to increase the probability of occurrence of desired behaviors by associating them with rewards. Rewards need not be tangible. In fact, the most commonly used reward in organizational behavior-modification programs is feedback. Table 10.7 identifies several other types of positive reinforcers.

Punishment Another consequence, **punishment**, is the administration of an aversive stimulus to reduce the frequency of undesirable behaviors. Punishment can be effective if employees clearly understand which behaviors are unacceptable and are warned in advance that punishment may be administered. It is very important that punishment be administered fairly and impartially and that it occur as soon as possible after the undesired behavior.

Punishment has some potential drawbacks. It may tend to alienate employees and/or lead to the filing of grievances alleging unfair discipline. However, punishment can be a reasonable way to deal with persistent undesired behaviors. For example, suppose that an employee continually makes long-distance personal calls from work, and all the manager's attempts to change this behavior have failed. Finally, the manager decides to dock the employee's pay for the cost of past calls and suggests that suspension or termination will follow continued abuse of the phone system. Although this punishment may solve the problem, it is not conducive to positive supervisor-subordinate relationships.

TABLE 10.7 Possible On-the-Job Reinforcers

Social	*Special Privileges*
Verbal praise	Own parking space
Special job title	No-punch lunch
Recognition in front of coworkers	Birthday off
Notes of thanks	Longer coffee breaks
Picture in company paper	Flexible work schedule
Pats on the back	Training for better job
Greetings from boss	Earned time off
Material	*Tokens*
Awards/plaques	Telephone credit cards
Fringe benefits	Points backed by prizes
Special badges or insignias	Coupons redeemable at local stores
Raises/bonuses	Chances to win a prize (lottery)
Large office	
Performance appraisal ratings	
Free tickets to sporting events	

Source: Rodney R. Nordstrom and R. Vance Hall, "The Platinum Rule," Copyright 1986, *Training and Development Journal,* American Society for Training and Development. Reprinted with permission.

Extinction **Extinction**, sometimes the preferred alternative to punishment, is simply ignoring an undesirable behavior that the manager wishes to stop. If the behavior brings no positive consequences, not even attention from the superior, supposedly it should disappear eventually and be replaced with a behavior that is rewarded. Unfortunately, since many undesirable organizational behaviors are inherently rewarding, ignoring them is an ineffective way to extinguish them. For instance, suppose that workers violate safety rules by not wearing their hard hats because the hats are uncomfortable. The manager's ignoring the violation certainly does not solve the problem in this case because employees' violation of the rule is positively reinforced by the natural consequence of comfort.

The ideas of reinforcement, punishment, and extinction can also be used to diagnose productivity problems. If reward systems are not carefully designed, they may be rewarding the wrong behaviors or unintentionally punishing desired behaviors. Managers will get the behaviors they reward, whether or not these are the behaviors they actually intend to elicit from their employees. For instance, a supervisor might accidentally reward poor performance by lightening the workload of an employee who cannot be trusted to do anything correctly, and that same supervisor might inadvertently punish top performers by loading extra work on them because they do it well.[51]

The Behavior Modification Process Applying behavior modification to improve productivity is fairly simple, as illustrated in Figure 10.5. The process begins when

FIGURE 10.5 Behavior Modification Process

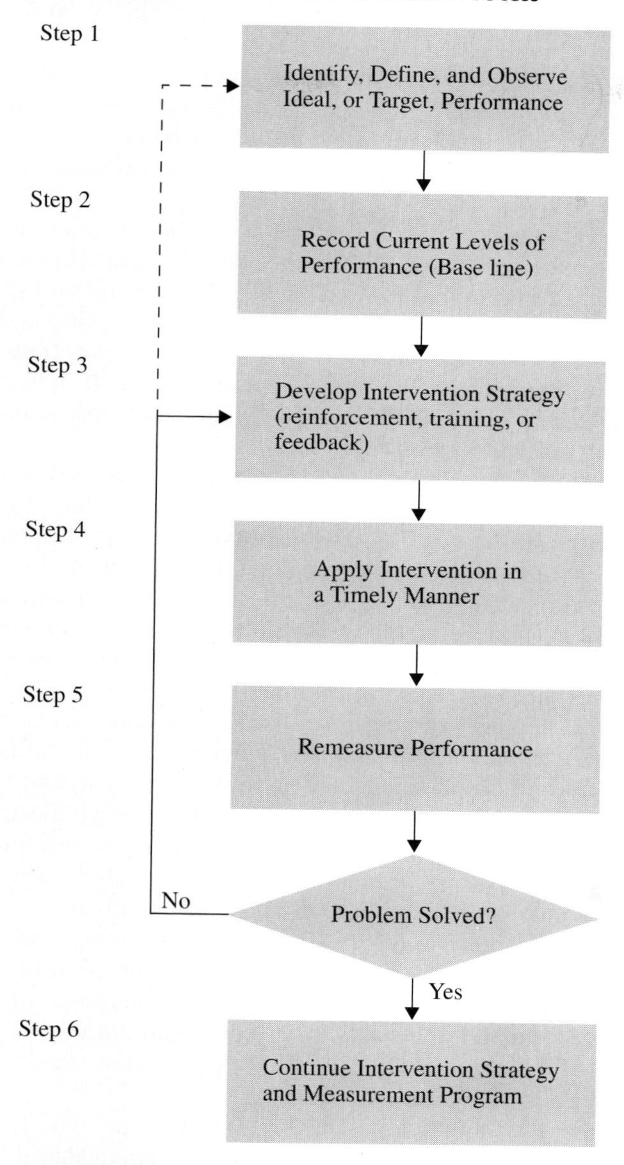

Source: Rodney R. Nordstrom and Vance Hall, "The Platinum Rule," Copyright 1986, *Training and Development Journal,* American Society for Training and Development. Reprinted with permission.

the manager determines which behaviors are desired and which are not. In the second step, the manager measures current levels of performance on the selected behaviors.

In the third step of the behavior modification process, the intervention strategy is developed. This third step is a three-part process: (1) powerful and durable reinforcers are selected, (2) employees are told which behaviors are to be rewarded, and (3) the work situation is designed so that subordinates are able to perform the desired behavior and receive the reward.

The fourth step is the critical one in a successful behavior modification program. In this step, the manager must faithfully measure the desired behaviors and administer the appropriate rewards in a timely fashion. In the fifth and sixth steps, current performance is compared with that at preintervention levels to determine whether or not behaviors have changed as intended. If they have, then the manager simply keeps reinforcing the behaviors to maintain them. If behaviors have not improved, the organization should reevaluate what it is using as reinforcers. Perhaps a different reward will work better.

Often the most effective way to change behavior is to use several types of consequences at the same time to reduce an undesired behavior and to replace it with a desired behavior. In the case of a widespread tardiness problem, a firm might institute a system of increasingly severe penalties for repeated instances of tardiness, use feedback charts to display graphically changes in tardiness behavior over time for the work group as a whole, praise individuals for each week of on-time attendance, and offer complimentary doughnuts and coffee to employees who arrive ten minutes before the start of their shift.

Preston Trucking Company provides an example of a very successful behavior modification (or *performance management*) intervention. In the late 1970s, satisfaction was low and labor-management relations were tense and confrontational. Management knew that it would not be competitive enough to survive after the deregulation of the trucking industry unless major changes were made. With the help of an experienced performance management consultant, Preston management developed "a data-oriented approach to management, relying on measurements, feedback, and the use of positive reinforcement." Management consulted the union, and the membership voted to adopt the performance management system. Critical behaviors were identified and measured on a regular basis. Large charts were posted in every work area so that employees could see how they were doing. Praise, recognition, and merit pay were used to reinforce employees and work groups that met their goals.

Productivity increased dramatically, and Preston won the 1986 U.S. Senate Productivity Award. The maintenance shop became so efficient that it began taking in outside work, bringing in more than $3 million per year by working on trucks owned by other companies. This nonpunitive, positive-reinforcement program paid off in other ways as well. Grievances declined sharply, and the company developed an excellent relationship with the Teamsters Union. Supplementing the performance management system were very active suggestion and work improvement team systems. Because of the excellent work climate, Preston

Trucking was selected in 1987 as one of the top ten companies to work for in America.[52]

Behavior modification techniques were developed decades ago and used in organizations quite successfully starting in the early 1970s. In today's more open and participative organizational cultures, behavior modification may sound too manipulative and unilateral to be attractive; it is often presented as something managers *do to* workers in order to control them. However, this need not be the case. Individuals and groups can certainly be involved in designing their own performance management system, from identifying critical behaviors and developing feedback measures to selecting desirable rewards and devising a system for dispensing them when performance warrants.

Behavioral Self-Regulation A new twist to behavior modification is **behavioral self-regulation**. In using this technique, people identify behaviors that they wish to perform and then promise themselves rewards for performing the desired behaviors. This technique can be used by anyone who wishes to work more effectively, though it is most often recommended for managers and professionals who are assumed to be well motivated at the outset. For instance, a lawyer might promise himself the reward of a cup of coffee as soon as he finishes the next two pages of the brief he is working on. Or a manager could promise herself that she will work on a task she enjoys if she finishes a disliked activity first.

Another part of this technique is (1) to analyze the environmental cues that lead to the performance of desired and undesired behaviors and (2) to modify the environment so that it triggers desired behaviors rather than undesired ones. For instance, if making a priority list of tasks to accomplish each day is desired behavior, a manager could hang a sign in front of her desk reminding her of this time-management principle. Or, if a supervisor feels that he is too easily and frequently distracted from productive activity by the delivery of mail and messages, he could ask his assistant to hold all nonurgent mail and messages until late in the day.[53]

Goal Setting

Goal setting is a proven technique that is often quite successful in improving motivation and job performance. Goal setting is effective with employees as diverse as managers and professionals, salespeople, and hourly workers like tree planters and truck drivers.

Four Characteristics of Effective Goals Two decades of research have shown that, to be effective, goals must have four characteristics.

1. The goals must be *difficult but not impossible* to accomplish. Consequently, employees can feel challenged and also experience a sense of achievement when they successfully meet their goals.

2. The goals must be *specific and measurable*. Vague goals, such as "do your best" or "try to improve" are not nearly as effective as specific goals, such as "try to sell $100,000 of product."
3. The goals must be *accepted* by the employee, who then must strive to meet them. One way to ensure acceptance is to allow participation in goal setting. Either the subordinate can set the goal, or the subordinate and superior can decide jointly on what the goal will be. However, reasonable goals assigned by the superior without the subordinate's participation are often accepted just as well.
4. *Feedback* is necessary for goal setting to be effective over time. Feedback can be intrinsic to the task, so that the employees themselves can tell how close they are to meeting their goal; it can be delivered impersonally by production reports or progress graphs; or it can be delivered face to face by a superior.[54]

Why Goal Setting Works There are several possible reasons for the success of goal-setting programs. First, setting a specific goal clarifies what behaviors are desired. Many people suffer from role ambiguity (see Chapter 14)—that is, they are not really sure what they are supposed to be doing and expend effort on unnecessary tasks. As a result, their productivity may be low. Specific goals should remedy this problem. Second, specific and difficult goals with feedback allow people to receive motivational rewards for meeting their goals. The rewards may be praise or more tangible rewards from a superior, or just the good feeling of having succeeded in a challenging endeavor. Finally, having a goal may motivate people to think more strategically about their job duties. Someone with a challenging goal may devise a more efficient way to get the job done when otherwise he or she would not have given it any thought.[55]

In practice, goal setting has much in common with behavior modification. In both cases, desired behaviors are clarified and feedback is provided. However, goal setting is a cognitively based approach, which assumes that people's beliefs and intentions are important, whereas behavior modification assumes that conditioning the behavior of people is as straightforward and mindless as training a laboratory animal. Nevertheless, both types of programs have proved to be highly effective in increasing productivity in organizations.

Job Redesign

A popular technique that is sometimes applied to productivity and quality problems is redesigning a job in order to increase its motivating potential. This technique is known as **job redesign** or **job enrichment**. It is based on the premise that altering certain aspects of the job to satisfy employees' psychological needs will motivate workers to try harder to do a good job.

Job redesign attempts to correct the mistakes of previous job-design methods. In the past, jobs were designed with the principles of simplification, standardiza-

FIGURE 10.6 Job Characteristics Theory

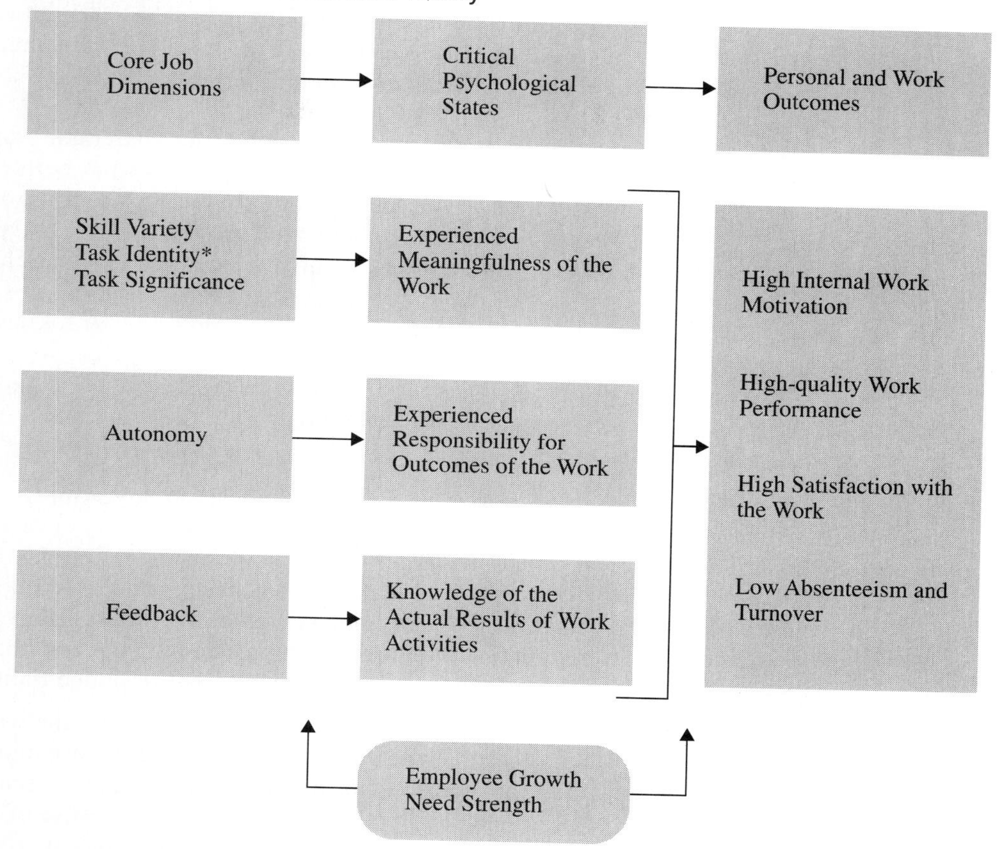

* *Task identity means doing a whole identifiable piece of work, such as assembling an entire television set.*

Source: From J. R. Hackman and G. R. Oldham, "Motivation Through the Design of Work: Test of a Theory," *Organizational Behavior and Human Performance*, Vol. 16, 1976, pp. 250–279. Reprinted by permission of Academic Press and the authors.

tion, and specialization. This led to the removal of many sources of satisfaction and motivation from the job.[56] Contemporary theory, illustrated in Figure 10.6, attempts to expand the scope of the job to increase its *variety, significance, identity, autonomy, and feedback*. These dimensions satisfy the individual's psychological needs for personal control, knowledge of results, and meaningfulness of work. Because the job satisfies the individual's psychological needs, the employee enjoys the job more and may strive to do higher-quality work of which he or she can be proud. Redesigning a job to be more interesting and satisfying, however, does not guarantee that productivity will improve. The interesting way to do the job may not be the most streamlined and efficient way. The research results are mixed, with some job redesign efforts resulting in increased performance and others not having this effect.[57] Nevertheless, under the right conditions, job enrichment can pay off.[58]

One of these conditions is the level of "growth need strength" among employees. It seems that some employees respond to enriched work better than others. Individuals who are high on the personality characteristic of "growth need strength" are most likely to enjoy the challenges provided by an expanded job. Individuals low on this trait are not particularly attuned to receiving this kind of satisfaction from their work. They may agree that the redesigned jobs are more interesting but also tend to feel that they should be paid more for taking on added responsibilities.

A number of specific changes may be made in the way a job is performed in order to increase the job's motivating potential. The following kinds of changes are typical:

1. *Combining tasks.* This involves giving to a single employee a set of interrelated tasks that might previously have been performed by several workers in an assembly-line fashion. This larger unit of work results in an identifiable product for which the employee can feel personally responsible. In one early job-enrichment experiment, the twenty-one separate tasks involved in compiling a phone directory were combined and given to a single employee so that each employee became responsible for putting together an entire phone book.

2. *Establishing client relationships.* This involves empowering the employee to go directly to his or her "client," whether inside or outside the organization, to clarify questions regarding the work. Prior to enrichment, typically only the supervisor would contact clients; so employees had no direct sense of who they were working for, why the work was important to the client, or exactly what the client needed or wanted. Modifying a "typing pool" system so that each typist is permanently assigned to a few specific managers would be an example of establishing client relationships.

3. *Opening feedback channels.* This can be accomplished by direct client contact, increased feedback from the superior, or increased self-monitoring. Some job-enrichment programs make employees their own quality control inspectors, thus allowing them to generate instant feedback on performance.

4. *Forming natural work units.* Work teams are established to be responsible for a meaningful unit of work. For instance, a team of ten autoworkers may assemble an entire engine.

5. *Vertical loading.* This approach involves increasing the amount of responsibility and decision-making authority granted to employees. It may include decisions about how to make the product, when to stop machines for repair, whether or not a given part is acceptable, and so on.[59]

TABLE 10.8 Summary of Studies Comparing Four Motivational Techniques

Technique	*Number of Studies*	*Median Improvement*	*Percentage Showing Some Improvement*	*Percentage Showing 10% or More Improvement*	*Range*
Money	10[a]	+30%	100%	90%	+3% to +49%
Goal setting	17	+16%	100%	94%	+2% to +57.5%
Participation	16	+0.5%	50%	25%	−24% to +47%
Job enrichment	13 (10)[b]	+17% (8.75%)[b]	92% (90%)[b]	61% (50%)[b]	−1% to +63% (−1% to +61%)[b]

Source: Edwin A. Locke, "Employee Motivation: A Discussion," *Journal of Contemporary Business,* 1982, Vol. 11, p. 75. Reprinted by permission of the author.

[a]Individual piece rate studies only.
[b]Excluding three questionable studies.

Relative Effectiveness of Individual-Level Interventions

Even when programs are chosen and implemented appropriately, not all programs are equally powerful. Two reviews have compared the effectiveness of different interventions. The results of the earlier review by Edwin A. Locke appear in Table 10.8. Locke concluded that financial incentives are the most effective way to increase productivity. Goal setting is also quite effective, whereas participative decision-making systems and job redesign are relatively less certain to produce significant improvements.

A review by Richard A. Guzzo and his colleagues at New York University suggests that employee training and goal setting are most likely to improve productivity, followed closely by sociotechnical system innovations (including autonomous work groups) and carefully designed financial incentives. On the whole, job redesign is less powerful but still has a significant impact on productivity.[60] The review by Guzzo and his associates also suggests that combined interventions are more effective than single-method programs. Almost any method can work by being carefully implemented and by involving all parties effectively.

WORK ENVIRONMENT INTERVENTIONS

Productivity and quality are a combination of many different variables—organizational culture, employee skills and abilities, and employee motivation. These topics have been discussed earlier in this book or in this chapter. This section focuses on some additional contributors to productivity and quality: the physical environment and equipment.

No matter how skilled or motivated employees are, if they are not provided with the correct materials and equipment or if there are flaws in the plant layout, productivity and quality will suffer. Three environmental methods for improving performance include enhancing the design of the work site and tools, introducing computers, robots, and automation, and fail-safing the work process.

Ergonomic Work Site and Equipment Design

For years scientists have been examining physical features of the workplace for their effects on productivity.[61] For instance, one study determined that darkness, little opportunity for privacy, and densely packed work areas are related to employee dissatisfaction.[62] Office designers are recognizing that rapid changes in technology have placed new demands on workers and their environments. Employees' psychological needs, as well as organizations' need for flexibility, must be considered.

Flexibility can be enhanced by such structural features as floors with cavities for rapid changes in wiring, cables, and plumbing. Modular furniture, full-height movable walls, and prewired systems furniture are other similar means for enhancing flexibility without disrupting the work processes.[63] Employees' requirements can be satisfied through proper lighting, pleasant color schemes, and the ability to personalize the work area.[64] Even simple variations in ceiling heights can create the illusion of open spaces and private areas.[65] Aetna Life has redesigned its home office and purchased special "team" furniture to facilitate the operation of self-managed work groups. The new furniture keeps team members close together and features both private work stations and a central meeting area with a large table.[66]

There are many other ways that organizations can make changes in the design of the workplace to improve performance. One option for detecting problems resulting from poor workplace design is to train supervisors in ergonomics and scientific management.[67] **Ergonomics** is an applied science concerned with the purposeful design of equipment and arrangement of things to fit the requirements of the human body, including movement patterns, senses, and physical limitations. The benefit of this training is that it moves the responsibility for a productive work site design from uninvolved engineers to people who are involved daily. A furniture factory that used this method discovered and corrected several workplace design problems (see Table 10.9). In an organization with a participative culture and work improvement teams, such training might be provided to the employees themselves rather than just to the supervisors.

Modern engineers are applying the principles of ergonomics in designing workplace equipment. One example is adjustable office furniture. Traditionally, chairs, tables, desks, and other furniture have been designed to fit average-sized people. Consequently, people who did not have a standard body size were often uncomfortable, suffering from such problems as muscle cramps, headaches, and backaches. New designs remove these troubles because they are adjustable

TABLE 10.9 Solutions to Workplace Design Problems in a Furniture Factory's Chair Assembly Line

Problem	*Suggestion*
Excessive travel and backtracking on front press	Rearrange area to eliminate backtracking.
Not enough room in knock-up area (fronts); completed work placed in inconvenient place	Use a longer table or create more working space on current table.
Excessive travel and backtracking required to pick up parts for chair knock-up	Rearrange area so parts are closer to work area.
Area cluttered with stacked chairs, hoses, and cords	Clean up area. Organize chair knock-up so that work-in-process inventory doesn't stack up.
Stand for installing arms seems to cause awkward positions for the worker	Use better stand.
Work accumulating at assembly end of line faster than packers can handle it	Shift people when inventory starts to build.
Excessive transportation for packing materials; excessive backtracking	Reorganize line so that flow can be straight. Standardize and specialize packing jobs and insure that someone is responsible for keeping each component available.
Chairs accumulating at end of line because they are the wrong kind for current packing needs	Organize chairs at beginning of line so they will be in proper order for packing.

Source: T. C. Padgett, "Getting Supervisory Help in Improving Productivity," Copyright 1987, *Training and Development Journal,* American Society for Training and Development. Reprinted with permission.

enough to accommodate most human body types. Other recent changes in work site design have come about because of the increasing incidence of repetitive strain injuries such as carpal tunnel syndrome (see Chapter 14).

Computers and Automation

New technology is also influencing productivity through the use of computers, automated equipment, and robots. One way that computers are being used is to monitor employee behavior (see the Ethical Perspective box for a discussion of this practice). Computers have already made a huge difference in office productivity, and another giant leap forward seems set to occur in the next decade: **electronic data interchange** between firms. When buyers and suppliers have computers that can communicate with each other through one of several commercial networks now in existence, a truly paperless workplace may be attained. Immense saving in time should occur, and errors should be less frequent, as data

ETHICAL PERSPECTIVES

Computer Monitoring of Employee Behavior

One controversial way in which high technology is being used to measure and enhance productivity is computer monitoring of employee performance. If an employee is already working on a computer and/or a telephone (as a secretary, insurance or banking clerk, telephone operator, or airline reservation agent, for example), it is possible to design a program to record lines of text inputted, length of breaks from work, average duration of phone calls, or number of transactions conducted in a given period of time. Estimates made in 1987 were that 6 million workers in the United States were being electronically monitored at work, and as the pace of technological change accelerates, this number seems certain to grow quickly.

Some people believe that electronic monitoring constitutes an invasion of privacy, strips workers of their autonomy and dignity, and will result in a return to the exploitative sweatshop mentality of the last century. It can be construed as treating employees like machines rather than human beings. Ethicists might suggest that monitoring systems use employees entirely as means to the organization's ends and thus fail to show the respect for persons that is at the heart of many theories of ethics.

Others suggest that employers have the right, and even the duty (to shareholders and clients), to monitor employee behavior to improve productivity and ensure quality. They further contend that monitoring can provide much more accurate performance information than traditional appraisal systems, which rely on subjective ratings and may be biased in a number of ways (see Chapter 11). Reward systems based on electronic monitoring should be more likely to meet the duty of fairness than those relying on supervisor ratings of performance. Monitoring can also provide more regular and timely feedback to employees, helping them learn and develop more quickly and giving them additional control over their fate.

Once ethical issues are resolved, there are other problems that must be considered in electronic performance monitoring. One is that such monitoring may have negative consequences for aspects of performance that are not monitored. Employees tend to focus on the behaviors being monitored, to the exclusion of other job duties. One insurance company found that computer-monitored claim processors became reluctant to deal with customer questions over the phone because that activity was no longer assessed. Eighty percent of the monitored claim processors stated that the most important factor in their appraisal was the number of claim checks produced, whereas 86 percent of unmonitored workers in similar jobs in the same company said that the main factor in their appraisal was quality and accuracy of customer service. Thus, there is some danger that, as quantity measures of productivity increase with computer monitoring, the quality of service provided to clients may decline. However, this is not an inherent problem of electronic monitoring but a problem of faulty performance measurement design. Some electronic systems are able to assess quality, or a combination of electronic and other methods may be necessary to provide a well-rounded picture of performance.

Another issue concerns the way the system is used by management and perceived by employees. If supervisors use the system mainly to produce "gotcha's" rather than to provide timely positive feedback and if employees feel that they are being spied on or harassed by management, the system may contribute to absenteeism, turnover, and other stress symptoms. On the other hand, some employees enjoy receiving frequent feedback from a computerized monitoring system and engage in informal competitions with coworkers or other work groups based on computer results.

It has been suggested that a fair and effective monitoring system should include regular feedback to employees, appropriate measures, an appeal process, and clear notification to the workers that they are being monitored. Furthermore, supervisors should be trained to use the system in a sympathetic and developmental fashion.

Sources: John Chalykoff and Thomas Kochan, "Computer-Aided Monitoring: Its Influence on Employee Job Satisfaction and Turnover," *Personnel Psychology,* Winter 1989, pp. 807–834; Rebecca A. Grant, Christopher A. Higgins, and Richard H. Irving, "Computerized Performance Monitors: Are They Costing You Customers?" *Sloan Management Review,* Spring 1988, pp. 39–45; Janet L. Turnage, "The Challenge of New Workplace Technology for Psychology," *American Psychologist,* February 1990, pp. 171–178; Richard Lacayo, "Nowhere to Hide," *Time,* November 11, 1991, pp. 34–40.

will only have to be keyed in once, instead of separately by both buyer and seller.[68]

One article suggests that if U.S. businesses are to survive foreign competition, they must "automate, emigrate, or evaporate."[69] Certainly some have "evaporated" (gone out of business), and others are emigrating (moving manufacturing facilities to low-wage, developing nations); but a large number are automating their manufacturing process in some way. The Robot Institute of America defines a robot as "a programmable, multifunctional manipulator designed to move material, parts, tools, or other specialized devices through variable, programmed motions for the performance of tasks."[70] Some second-generation robots are "smart"—they can "see" or otherwise sense the location and configuration of parts and adjust themselves accordingly.

Robots are currently performing tasks in many industries, from automotive factories, where they cut and weld, to novelty companies, where they stretch and print designs on balloons. Robots are becoming lighter, faster, and stronger, and they are being integrated into advanced manufacturing systems consisting of several computer-controlled robots that can complete whole jobs. The use of robots in the United States is increasing at a rate of 8 to 10 percent annually.[71] At a McDonnell Douglas Corp. plant, an unattended system of two robots replaced twenty-one conventional machines for making missile casings. This new system reduced the processing time from 100 days to just 30 days. General Motors utilizes robots with lasers to detect minute flaws. The textile industry is developing robots with sight so that the very precise job of sewing sleeves into men's suits can be done by robots.

Robots can greatly increase productivity and quality for a number of reasons. First, they do not call in sick, go on strike, take vacations, or require lunch breaks. Further, robots can work three shifts and require no pension benefits. It has been estimated that the average blue-collar worker actually works only about 75 percent of his or her scheduled time. Robots' average "up time" is 95 percent. Robots may be used to replace employees in hazardous jobs and thus reduce worker injuries, occupational diseases, and their associated social and economic costs. Robots can also improve quality: they can be programmed to repeat the same operation in exactly the same way; and they may be able to detect small flaws that would escape a bored or fatigued employee.[72]

Robots, however, at least in the introductory stages, may be a mixed blessing. At this point, they are expensive and only larger firms are able to afford them. Because of the advantages listed above, robots are usually cost-effective, but only over the longer term.[73]

Another problem with integrating robot technology into the work process is that employees may show some resistance.[74] These new tools create many changes in how a job is performed, and many employees feel uncomfortable and stressed in the presence of such change. Two of the changes likely to be brought about by robots are decreased social interaction, because plants will use fewer and more widely spaced employees, and slowed promotion, as fewer supervisors and middle managers are required. However, the major reason many employees resist robots is fear of job loss.

Estimates of the number of employees who will be replaced by robots vary widely. One rule of thumb is that each robot replaces two workers. Some believe that a ratio of one robot to five or six workers may be more accurate. Others predict that robots may replace up to 3 million manufacturing employees by the year 2000.[75] In one survey, low-skilled employees were found to react most negatively to the introduction of robots because they feared losing their jobs. Highly skilled employees, on the other hand, saw robots as providing an opportunity to expand their skills.[76] The general rule that participation reduces resistance seems to apply to high-technology innovations as well. For instance, one federal agency reduced resistance to office automation by allowing employees to decide where to locate the equipment and how to make use of it.[77]

Fail-safing the Work Process

Another method of improving quality is to design the work process or equipment in such a way that doing things incorrectly is either not possible or else triggers immediate feedback. The Japanese call this approach **poka-yoke**, or fail-safing. Examples include designing parts so that they can be put together only in the correct way or creating a parts dispenser that releases exactly the number of items (screws, for instance) needed for a particular assembly. After finishing the piece, the worker can immediately tell if anything has been left out because there will still be a screw left in the tray. Another example would be a counter and jig clamp system to hold a part while spot welds are made on it. The counter counts the number of welds made and will not release the clamps until the correct number of welds has been made. Systems like this catch errors before they can be passed along in the production process.

Another method of discovering and correcting errors immediately after they are made is called **autonomation**. This is some kind of automatic checking system that shuts down the process when an error is detected. An example would be a scale that automatically weighs each box as soon as it is filled and stops the filling operation if the weight is not correct.[78]

THE ROLE OF HR MANAGERS IN PRODUCTIVITY AND QUALITY IMPROVEMENT EFFORTS

HR managers have several roles in quality and productivity improvement efforts. The first may be to apply quality principles to improve their own operations and better satisfy their clients. Administrative work is often a fertile site for quality circle improvement ideas. HRM systems may also be prime candidates for process improvement efforts. For instance, it may be possible to substantially streamline an internal job posting and promotion system, such as that shown in Figure 6.2, or to improve or simplify forms and record-keeping practices to save time and reduce errors. Some HRM departments are already practicing benchmarking by comparing their operations in selected areas with recognized "best practice" HRM departments in other organizations.

A second role for the HR professional is to facilitate the implementation of quality or productivity interventions in the rest of the organization through HR activities such as staffing, training, appraisal and compensation, and labor relations. Each of these may require attention so that it optimally fits the organization's new goals, work methods, and culture.[79] Examples of fitting each activity to current quality interventions are discussed below.

Staffing

Major changes in job responsibilities, such as those occasioned by a shift to total quality management or autonomous work groups, require substantial changes in the type of people recruited and selected. In addition to looking for core job skills, one would also like to see basic mathematical skills (to learn statistical process control techniques) and interpersonal skills (to work effectively in groups). Japanese firms building plants in the United States are using a great deal of cognitive testing to ensure that employees have the mental capability to participate fully in a high-quality work environment. Interpersonal skills and the motivation to take responsibility may be assessed in interviews and by group exercises or mini-assessment centers. In sum, organizations with a high-quality philosophy need to be more selective than usual. Fortunately, modern new plants featuring autonomous work groups tend to attract a large number of applicants, so a favorable selection ratio permits more careful selection. In preparing to open its plant in Georgetown, Kentucky, Toyota screened 50,000 applicants for 3,000 factory jobs. Finalists underwent eighteen hours of assessment, including knowledge and attitude tests, an assessment center focusing on interpersonal skills, a long interview, and a manufacturing exercise that provided a realistic job preview.[80]

An additional staffing issue in implementing autonomous work groups and other highly participative systems is that some old-style supervisors have a hard time changing their management approach in the required way. If training and coaching are ineffective in helping them to make the transition to a more participative workplace, enhanced retirement or outplacement and replacement may become the only alternatives.

Training

As mentioned above, most quality interventions rely heavily on training (see Tables 10.2 and 9.10), as do autonomous work groups and pay-for-skills systems, which require a high level of cross-training. The HR role may be to purchase training services, develop in-house training packages, conduct employee training, and/or train large numbers of supervisors to become trainers in their own units.

Appraisal and Reward Systems

It is very important that appraisal and reward systems support the types of behaviors the organization desires from employees. Often, reward systems developed before TQM will be inconsistent with the new culture and behaviors. For instance, appraisal systems that penalize risk taking and mistakes, demand individual results at all costs, and provide for individual incentives or merit pay may be a hindrance in implementing group-based systems intended to foster innovative experimentation. For the latter, appraisal systems that assess cooperation, team skills, and creativity would be better. Group-based incentives, gain sharing, or pay for skills would be more suitable reward systems than individual incentives or merit pay.

Changing the appraisal and reward system can be a crucial part of successful culture change in an organization. The HR manager's role is to assess the fit of existing systems to the intervention, and consider recommending a change. In truly participative systems, groups of employees might become involved in designing any changes to these systems.

Labor Relations

Systems involving widespread employee involvement require close cooperation with the employees' union. This is because job duties may change, expanding across traditional craft boundaries, and employees may take on decision-making responsibilities formerly reserved for supervisory staff. A cooperative labor relations climate makes implementing these changes much easier. Cooperation removes overt organized resistance and provides another credible channel of communication to employees about the need for changes and the likely benefits of improved performance for all concerned. In some participative interventions, the most time-consuming activity has been to get traditionally adversarial managers and union leaders to jointly design the program prior to its implementation. But once cooperation is forthcoming, the rest of the process is fairly smooth.[81]

The new Saturn plant provides a graphic example of union/management cooperation in implementing autonomous work groups in a new facility. The United Auto Workers Union has been involved with General Motors managers from the first stages of plant design. Union/management teams traveled more than 2 million miles to visit the world's best small-car manufacturing plants and devise a cooperative work system that would work for GM. The UAW signed a pathbreaking labor agreement designed to increase cooperation and the spreading of responsibility from management to line workers. Each manager is "paired" with a similarly ranked union official, with whom he or she consults daily on virtually all decisions. Supporting this system is a massive amount of training to enable employees to take on the new responsibilities being urged on them by both management and union leaders.[82]

SUMMARY OF KEY POINTS

Pressures on American businesses to improve productivity and quality have been mounting over the past decade. Productivity, defined as the ratio of outputs to inputs, and quality, defined as conformance to specifications or meeting customer requirements, have both increased in importance. The good news is that these two goals can be achieved concurrently. Research shows that producing high-quality products and services can actually be less expensive than producing low-quality products and services.

A number of methods for improving productivity and quality are available, from organizationally based culture changes and group-oriented approaches to individual motivational methods. In addition, work-environment and equipment changes are also possible. It is not uncommon to see a single quality improvement program that draws on all four of these approaches to some degree. For any type of program to be effective, it must be preceded by an appropriate diagnosis, and careful thought must be given to building commitment to the new system.

Effective organization-wide quality improvement methods typically involve all employees and focus on both continuous small improvements (kaizen) and major innovations of business processes. Most approaches emphasize careful quality measurement, appropriate use of statistics for understanding variation in quality, and an experimenting mindset to find the most effective way to make things better.

Total quality management is a philosophy and culture change that uses a variety of techniques to make everyone in the organization responsible for supplying products and services that must meet customers' needs 100 percent of the time. Business process improvement uses cross-functional teams to improve entire systems of work so that they are more efficient.

Group-oriented participative methods increase the amount of responsibility and decision-making power that line employees have in productivity and quality issues. Work improvement teams (quality circles) allow groups of employees to spend company time preparing suggestions on how to improve the work process. Autonomous work groups are a more radical innovation, usually replacing the supervisor role with group decision making about work practices.

Increasing employee effort is a common approach for improving productivity. One way to do this is by performance-based pay systems. Another technique is behavior modification, in which the consequences of behavior are manipulated to get results. Positive reinforcement increases desired behaviors, whereas punishment and extinction are used to eliminate undesired behaviors.

Goal setting can be a very effective way to improve performance. Specific and challenging goals, with feedback on goal attainment, can both motivate high performance and clarify the organization's expectations of employees. Job redesign attempts to improve motivation by restructuring the work so that it provides more feedback and intrinsic rewards for the employees. Tasks are rearranged so that employees use a variety of skills to complete meaningful units of work for an identifiable client.

Management can improve environmental support by using proper plant or office design and giving employees well-designed tools and equipment. Integrating high-technology equipment, such as robots and computers, is also an environmental method for increasing productivity and quality. Systems that automatically fail-safe the work process are another alternative.

In sum, increased demands for quality and productivity are challenging many organizations in the 1990s. In response, major changes are occurring in organizational culture and practices. The success of these changes depends on enthusiastic and educated participation by all employees. HR managers have a large role to play in supplying and cultivating these employees.

Questions for Discussion

1. Productivity and quality can be defined in many ways, depending on an organization's goals and production processes. How might productivity be defined and measured at a McDonald's restaurant? At an automobile transmission repair shop? At an oil refinery? How might these same organizations assess quality?
2. Why is measurement important in productivity and quality improvement efforts?
3. How are productivity and quality related to each other?
4. What are some of the costs of poor quality?
5. In what way might you diagnose quality and productivity problems in a system at your university, such as the registration system?
6. Suppose you decided to try to improve the registration process by additional automation and computers. What issues might arise in selling this change to the employees who handle registration?
7. What common principles underlie a great many currently popular approaches to improving quality?
8. What is kaizen?
9. Describe an organization that has successfully implemented TQM. What kinds of ideas are central to this organization? What kinds of systems might you see in place for monitoring and improving quality? Pick an organization you are familiar with and brainstorm about how it would be changed by a true commitment to TQM.
10. What is business-process improvement? Nominate a process with which you are familiar that could benefit from the application of this approach.

11. Describe quality circles. What are some of the positive results of quality circles? Some potential problems?
12. If you were a blue-collar worker, would you rather be part of an autonomous work group or part of a traditionally managed work unit? Why?
13. Explain how behavior modification can be used to change employee behavior.
14. Develop a behavioral self-management program to help you meet your performance goals in this class.
15. Explain how and why goal setting works.
16. What is job redesign? Why would it be used by an organization? Pick a job you are familiar with and redesign it following Hackman and Oldham's model of which job characteristics are important (Figure 10.6).
17. What potential advantages and disadvantages would you point out to a manager who is considering adding robots to the plant?
18. What are autonomation and poka-yoke?
19. What are the range of ways in which human resource managers may be called on to participate in quality and productivity improving interventions?

CASE 10.1

An Individual-Level Productivity Case

You are a consultant who has been called in to deal with a productivity and quality problem in the secretarial pool of the Whole World Encyclopedia Company. The pool consists of eight word processor operators who serve a staff of about forty full-time professional writers. The writers turn in their work in roughly typed, handwritten, or on audiocassettes. The writers have been complaining about poor word processing service for some time, and the company has finally decided to look into the problem.

The pool's productivity has not been carefully measured before. Typically, the only measure has been the number of manuscript pages completed each day. Because this number is quite high, the office manager maintains that there is no productivity problem. However, when this figure is broken down into new pages versus reworked pages (previously word-processed pages to which corrections have been made), the latter account for much of the volume. This fact is consistent with the writers' complaints that new work is turned around slowly and is so full of errors that invariably it must be sent back for corrections. The word processing operators do not seem to use their spelling checkers on a regular basis; nor do they proofread all their work. Furthermore, writers complain that, because corrections are not made properly, a second round of reworking is often required.

Your investigation of the word processing pool reveals the following facts:

1. Word processor operators are hired on the basis of a typing test given on an electric typewriter. Proofreading skills are not assessed. After being hired, operators are given half a day of training on the word processor; then they begin to work in the pool. You occasionally see an operator ask another operator how to use various features of the word processing package.

2. Work is passed out by the office manager in the order in which it is received from the writers. As each operator finishes a piece, he or she goes to the manager to get the next piece. Some operators say that they particularly enjoy and are good at typing from cassettes, doing tables and figures, or processing straight text from paper copy. These different skills and preferences are not considered when the office manager assigns work.
3. Operators do not label their work with their names or initials. When work comes back for correction, it is corrected by whoever is free, not by the person who originally did the work.
4. The work environment is clean, well lit, and quiet. There is a sufficient supply of computers, software, and printers.
5. Turnover is high, about 50 percent per year. Absenteeism is also high. The manager is lenient about verifying illness when sick leave is claimed. Therefore, most employees use their sick leave as soon as it is accrued to take a day off from work. On the other hand, the manager is a stickler about punctuality. Pay is docked one half-hour if employees arrive more than two minutes late for work. Thus, when employees come, they come on time. However, after clocking in, they often socialize with doughnuts and coffee for up to forty-five minutes before they actually begin to work.
6. Operators are paid an hourly wage that is average for the area. Annual increments are based on seniority; there is no performance appraisal system in place for the operators.
7. Operators complain that their jobs are boring. They say that they feel like cattle in a corral; they have never even met the writers they serve. If they have a question about a part of a manuscript they are working on, they have to resolve it as well as they can because they are not permitted to call the writer to ask for clarification.

With this information, you feel ready to make a diagnosis and suggest some changes to improve the situation. Prepare your diagnosis: tell what is going wrong here and why. Prepare your suggestions for changing any aspects of this job situation that you think need improvement. Be as thorough as possible.

EXERCISE 10.1

A Productivity and Quality Intervention Exercise

Working in small groups, discuss how you might define, measure, and improve productivity and quality in one of the following three settings. Prepare an oral report of your conclusions.

1. Discuss how the productivity and quality of a university academic department and its faculty members might be defined. The three categories usually included are teaching, research, and service. (Time permitting, you might wish to interview some faculty members about their views on productivity and quality measurement in an academic setting.) List a number of ways in which

you might measure the performance in each different category. Is it typical to consider client satisfaction an important indicator of quality in this setting? Should it be?

Now go through the chapter and discuss whether—and how—each approach to enhancing productivity and quality might be applied to an academic department.

2. Consider how the productivity and quality of a human resource management department might be defined. Which clients must be satisfied? Suggest a number of possible measures of HR department performance. Go through the chapter and discuss whether—and how—each method of enhancing performance might be applied to a human resource management department.
3. Choose an organization with which the whole class is familiar, such as a grocery store or fast-food outlet. Discuss how productivity and quality might be measured in this setting. Go through the chapter and discuss whether—and how—each method of enhancing performance might be applied to this organization.

Notes and References

1. Norman Jonas, "Can America Compete?" *Business Week,* April 20, 1987, pp. 45–47.
2. Joan Berger, "Productivity: Why It's the No. 1 Underachiever," *Business Week,* April 20, 1987, pp. 54–55.
3. Arthur S. Herman, "Productivity Continued to Rise in Many Industries During 1987," *Monthly Labor Review,* March 1989, pp. 13–20.
4. Arthur Neef and Christopher Kask, "Manufacturing Productivity and Labor Costs in 14 Economies," *Monthly Labor Review,* December 1991, pp. 24–37.
5. Philip B. Crosby and Curt Reimann, "Criticism and Support for the Baldrige Award," *Quality Progress,* May 1991, p. 42.
6. Shari Caudron, "How Xerox Won the Baldrige," *Personnel Journal,* April 1991, pp. 98–102; Robert C. Hill and Sara M. Freedman, "Managing the Quality Process: Lessons from a Baldrige Award Winner," *The Executive,* February 1992, pp. 76–88.
7. K. Theodor Krantz, "How Velcro Got Hooked on Quality," *Harvard Business Review,* September–October 1989, pp. 34–40.
8. Ron Zemke and Dick Schaaf, *The Service Edge* (New York: New American Library, 1989).
9. W. Bruce Chew, "No-Nonsense Guide to Measuring Productivity," *Harvard Business Review,* January–February 1988, pp. 110–118; Daniel J. B. Mitchell, *Human Resource Management: An Economic Approach* (Boston: PWS-Kent, 1989), pp. 50–51; Robert H. Hayes, Stephen C. Wheelwright, and Kim B. Clark, *Dynamic Manufacturing* (New York: The Free Press, 1988), pp. 130–160.
10. Robert O. Brinkerhoff and Dennis E. Dressler, *Productivity Measurement: A Guide for Managers and Evaluators* (Newbury Park, Calif.: Sage Publications, 1990).
11. Ronald M. Fortuna, "The Quality Imperative," in *Total Quality: An Executive's Guide for the 1990s,* Ernst & Young Quality Improvement Consulting Group, (Homewood, Ill.: Dow Jones-Irwin, 1990), pp. 3–25; D. Garvin, *Managing Quality: The Strategic and Competitive Edge* (New York: Free Press, 1988), pp. 41–46.
12. Ernest C. Huge, "Measuring and Rewarding Performance," in *Total Quality: An Executive's Guide for the 1990s,* pp. 70–88; Genichi Taguchi and Don Clausing, "Robust Quality," *Harvard Business Review,* January–February 1990, pp. 65–75.
13. Michael E. Porter, *Competitive Advantage* (New York: Free Press, 1985).
14. Paul A. L. Evans, "Human Resource Management and Globalization," Invited speech, Third Conference on International Personnel

and Human Resource Management, July 3, 1992, Berkhampstead, England.

15. Fortuna, "The Quality Imperative."
16. Frederick F. Reichheld and W. Earl Sasser, Jr., "Zero Defections: Quality Comes to Services," *Harvard Business Review,* September–October 1990, pp. 105–111.
17. Arthur R. Tenner and Irving J. DeToro, *Total Quality Management: Three Steps to Continuous Improvement* (Reading, Mass.: Addison-Wesley, 1992).
18. Chew, "No-Nonsense Guide to Measuring Productivity," pp. 110–118.
19. Stephen L. Yearout and Lucy N. Lytle, "Assessing Quality," in *Total Quality: An Executive's Guide for the 1990s,* pp. 89–99.
20. Robert Camp, *Benchmarking: The Search for Industry Best Practices that Lead to Superior Performance* (Milwaukee, Wis.: ASQC Quality Press, 1989) Karen Bemowski, "The Benchmarking Bandwagon," *Quality Progress,* January 1991, pp. 19–24; Michael J. Spendolini, *The Benchmarking Book* (New York: AMACOM, 1992).
21. Ernest C. Huge, "Helping Managers Get Religion: Developing Leadership Commitment to Quality Improvement," in *Total Quality: An Executive's Guide for the 1990s,* pp. 26–38.
22. Masaaki Imai, *Kaizen: The Key to Japan's Competitive Success* (New York: McGraw-Hill, 1986).
23. Masao Nemoto, *Total Quality Control for Management* (Englewood Cliffs, N.J.: Prentice-Hall, 1987).
24. Chao-Hsien Chu, "The Pervasive Elements of Total Quality Control," *Industrial Management,* September–October 1988, pp. 30–32.
25. William H. Wagel, "Corning Zeroes in on Total Quality," *Personnel,* July 1987, pp. 4–9.
26. Edward J. Kane, "IBM's Quality Focus on the Business Process," *Quality Progress,* April 1986, pp. 24–33.
27. Michael Hammer, "Reengineering Work: Don't Automate, Obliterate," *Harvard Business Review,* July–August 1990, pp. 104–112.
28. Joseph J. Gufreda, Larry A. Maynard, and Lucy N. Lytle, "Employee Involvement in the Quality Process," in *Total Quality: An Executive's Guide for the 1990s,* pp. 162–176.
29. Eric Sundstrom, Kenneth P. De Meuse, and David Futrell, "Work Teams: Applications and Effectiveness," *Psychological Bulletin,* February 1990, pp. 120–133.
30. Gerald E. Ledford, Jr., Edward E. Lawler III, and Susan A. Mohrman, "The Quality Circle and Its Variations," in *Productivity in Organizations: New Perspectives from Industrial and Organizational Psychology,* ed. John P. Campbell, Richard J. Campbell, and Associates (San Francisco: Jossey-Bass, 1988), pp. 255–294.
31. Edward E. Lawler and Susan A. Mohrman, "Quality Circles: After the Honeymoon," *Organizational Dynamics,* Spring 1987, pp. 42–55.
32. Krantz, "How Velcro Got Hooked on Quality."
33. Gufreda, Maynard, and Lytle, "Employee Involvement in the Quality Process."
34. Thomas C. Head, Julie L. Molleston, Peter F. Sorensen, and Joseph Cargano, "The Impact of Implementing a Quality Circles Intervention on Employee Task Perceptions," *Group and Organizational Studies,* December 1986, pp. 360–373.
35. Murray R. Barrick and Ralph A. Alexander, "A Review of Quality Circle Efficacy and the Existence of a Positive-Finding Bias," *Personnel Psychology,* Autumn 1987, pp. 579–592.
36. Ledford, Lawler, and Mohrman, "The Quality Circle and Its Variations," *Perspectives from Industrial and Organizational Psychology,* pp. 255–294.
37. Ricky W. Griffin, "Consequences of Quality Circles in an Industrial Setting: A Longitudinal Assessment," *Academy of Management Journal,* June 1988, pp. 338–358.
38. Gordon W. Meyer and Randall G. Stott, "Quality Circles: Panacea or Pandora's Box?" *Organizational Dynamics,* Spring 1985, pp. 35–50.
39. Thomas M. Rohman, "Bosses—Who Needs 'Em?" *Industry Week,* February 23, 1987, pp. 15–16.
40. John Hoerr, "Getting Man and Machine to Live Happily Ever After," *Business Week,* April 20, 1987, pp. 61–62.

41. Paul S. Goodman, Rukmini Devadas, and Terri L. Griffith Hughson, "Groups and Productivity: Analyzing the Effectiveness of Self-Managing Teams," in *Productivity in Organizations,* pp. 295–327.
42. Edward E. Lawler III, "The New Plant Revolution Revisited," *Organizational Dynamics,* Autumn 1990, pp. 5–14; Brian Dumaine, "Who Needs a Boss?" *Fortune,* May 7, 1990, pp. 52–60.
43. Toby D. Wall, Nigel J. Kemp, Paul R. Jackson, and Chris W. Clegg, "Outcomes of Autonomous Work Groups: A Long-Term Field Experiment," *Academy of Management Journal,* June 1986, pp. 280–304.
44. Robert D. Pritchard, Steven D. Jones, Philip L. Roth, Karla K. Stuebing, and Steven E. Ekeberg, "Effects of Group Feedback, Goal-Setting, and Incentives on Organizational Productivity," *Journal of Applied Psychology,* Vol. 73, 1988, pp. 337–358.
45. John A. Wagner III, Paul A. Rubin, and Thomas J. Callahan, "Incentive Payment and Nonmanagerial Productivity: An Interrupted Time Series Analysis of Magnitude and Trend," *Organizational Behavior and Human Decision Processes,* August 1988, pp. 47–74.
46. Imai, *Kaizen.*
47. Ibid., p. 112.
48. Dawn Gunsch, "Award Programs at Work," *Personnel Journal,* September 1991, pp. 85–89.
49. W. Clay Hamner and Ellen P. Hamner, "Behavior Modification and the Bottom Line," *Organizational Dynamics,* Spring 1975, pp. 2–21.
50. Aubrey C. Daniels, "Performance Management: The Behavior Approach to Productivity Improvement," *National Productivity Review,* Summer 1985, pp. 225–236.
51. Steven Kerr, "On the Folly of Rewarding *A* While Hoping for *B,*" *Academy of Management Journal,* December 1975, pp. 766–783.
52. Patti Watts, "Preston and the Teamsters Keep on Trucking," *Management Review,* March 1988, pp. 22–24.
53. Charles C. Manz, *The Art of Self-Leadership* (Englewood Cliffs, N.J.: Prentice-Hall, 1983).
54. Edwin A. Locke and Gary P. Latham, *A Theory of Goals Setting and Task Performance* (Englewood Cliffs, N.J.: Prentice-Hall, 1990).
55. Gary P. Latham and Thomas W. Lee, "Goal Setting," in *Generalizing from Laboratory to Field Settings,* ed. E. A. Locke (Lexington, Mass.: Lexington Books, 1986), pp. 101–117.
56. J. Richard Hackman and Greg R. Oldham, *Working Redesign* (Reading, Mass.: Addison-Wesley, 1980).
57. Lisa R. Berlinger, William H. Glick, and Robert C. Rodgers, "Job Enrichment and Performance Improvement," in *Productivity in Organizations,* pp. 219–254.
58. Richard A. Guzzo, Richard D. Jette, and Raymond A. Katzell, "The Effects of Psychologically Based Intervention Programs on Worker Productivity: A Meta-Analysis," *Personnel Psychology,* Summer 1985, pp. 275–291.
59. Richard E. Kopelman, *Managing Productivity in Organizations* (New York: McGraw-Hill, 1986), pp. 211–243.
60. Guzzo, Jette, and Katzell, "The Effects of Psychologically Based Intervention Programs on Worker Productivity."
61. Elton Mayo, *The Human Problems of an Industrial Civilization* (New York: Macmillan, 1933).
62. Greg R. Oldham and Yitzhak Fried, "Employee Reactions to Work Space," *Journal of Applied Psychology,* January 1987, pp. 75–80.
63. Joseph S. Hicinbothem, "Choosing a Work Station: What Research Indicates," *Office,* March 1987, pp. 38–42.
64. Robert Crawmer, "Flexibility for Interiors," *Nation's Business,* March 1987, pp. 38–42.
65. Designing Flexibility into an Office Layout," *Office,* March 1987, pp. 15–18.
66. Brian Dumaine, "Who Needs a Boss?" pp. 52–60.
67. Thomas C. Padgett, "Getting Supervisory Help in Improving Productivity," *Training and Development Journal,* January 1987, pp. 48–50.
68. "Sun Rises Slowly on the New Era," *Business Review Weekly,* April 10, 1992, pp. 81–82; Stewart Cater, "Networks Learn to Talk

to Each Other," *Business Review Weekly,* April 10, 1992, p. 87.

69. Olga L. Crocker and Richard Gueller, "The Effects of Robotics on the Workplace," *Personnel,* September 1988, p. 26.
70. Ibid.
71. Russel Mitchell, Richard Brandtt, Zachary Schiller, and James Ellis, "Boldly Going Where No Robot Has Gone Before," *Business Week,* December 22, 1986, p. 45.
72. Crocker and Gueller, "The Effects of Robotics" pp. 26–36.
73. Thomas M. Rohan, "Putting Exotic Technology to Work," *Industry Week,* January 20, 1986, pp. 37–42.
74. Zane Quible and Jane N. Hammer, "Office Automation's Impact on Personnel," *Personnel Administrator,* September 1984, pp. 25–32.
75. Oded Shenkar, "Robotics: A Challenge for Occupational Psychology," *Journal of Occupational Psychology,* March 1988, pp. 103–112.
76. Georgia T. Chao and Steve W. J. Kozlowski, "Employee Perceptions on the Implementation of Robotic Manufacturing Technology," *Journal of Applied Psychology,* February 1986, pp. 70–76.
77. Linda K. Carlisle, "Working with Employees to Develop an Automated Personnel System," *Personnel Administration,* September 1984, pp. 75–85.
78. Examples in this section come from Ernest C. Huge, "Quality of Conformance to Design," in *Total Quality: An Executive's Guide for the 1990s,* pp. 132–151; and Genichi Taguchi and Don Clausing, "Robust Quality."
79. For more detail on how HR can support the shift to a quality mentality, see Randall S. Schuler and Drew L. Harris, "Deming Quality Improvement: Implications for Human Resource Management as Illustrated in a Small Company," *Human-Resource Planning,* Vol. 14, 1991, pp. 191–207.
80. "Japan's Gung-Ho U.S. Car Plants," *Fortune,* January 30, 1989, pp. 78–85.
81. Mitch Fields, Quality of Work Life consultant, personal communication, April 1992.
82. Charlene Marmer Solomon, "Behind the Wheel at Saturn," *Personnel Journal,* June 1991, pp. 72–74.

PART FIVE

Rewarding Employees

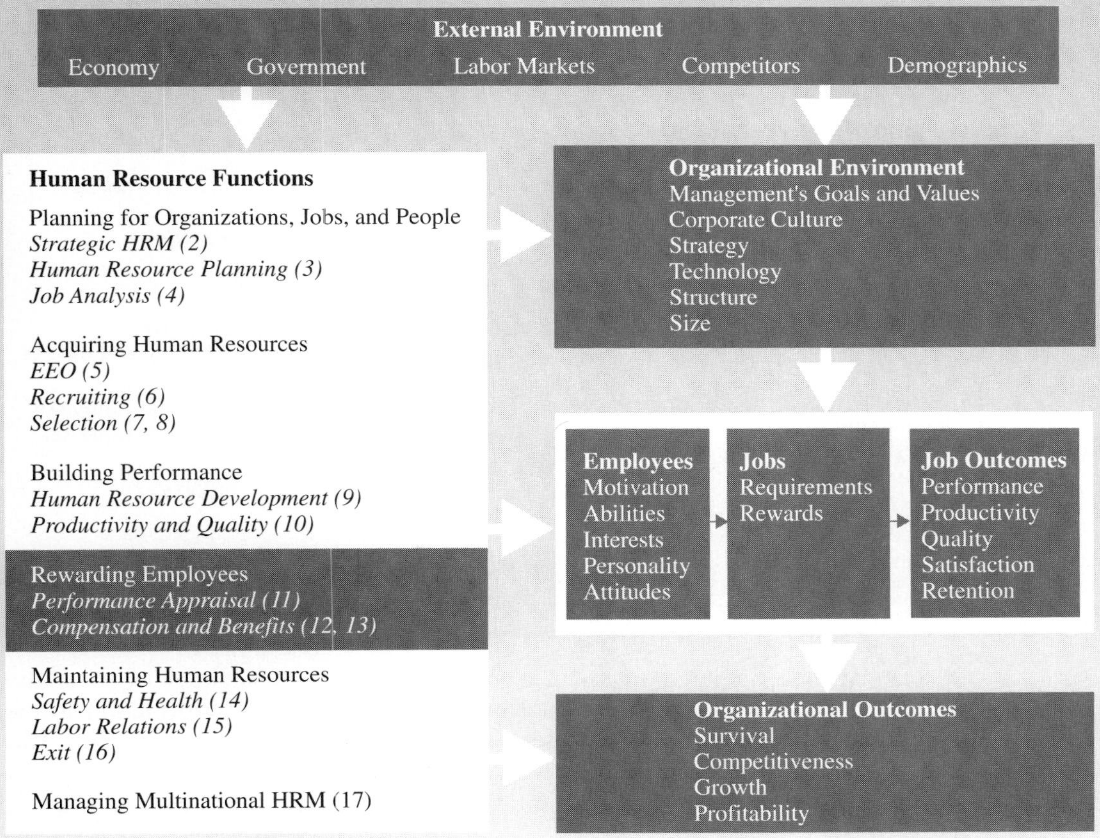

External Environment
Economy Government Labor Markets Competitors Demographics

Human Resource Functions

Planning for Organizations, Jobs, and People
Strategic HRM (2)
Human Resource Planning (3)
Job Analysis (4)

Acquiring Human Resources
EEO (5)
Recruiting (6)
Selection (7, 8)

Building Performance
Human Resource Development (9)
Productivity and Quality (10)

Rewarding Employees
Performance Appraisal (11)
Compensation and Benefits (12, 13)

Maintaining Human Resources
Safety and Health (14)
Labor Relations (15)
Exit (16)

Managing Multinational HRM (17)

Organizational Environment
Management's Goals and Values
Corporate Culture
Strategy
Technology
Structure
Size

Employees
Motivation
Abilities
Interests
Personality
Attitudes

Jobs
Requirements
Rewards

Job Outcomes
Performance
Productivity
Quality
Satisfaction
Retention

Organizational Outcomes
Survival
Competitiveness
Growth
Profitability

11

Performance Appraisal

A critical factor related to an organization's long-term success is its ability to measure how well employees perform and then use that information to ensure that performance meets present standards and improves over time. This process is referred to as performance appraisal or performance evaluation. It is a complex task that is difficult to do, and as we will see, it is not done well by most organizations.

This chapter explains some of the ways that performance appraisal information can be used; it also explores the difficulties of developing a performance appraisal system. Several different methods of assessing performance are examined. The final part of the chapter focuses on one particularly important part of an appraisal system: the process by which performance feedback is provided to employees.

THE PERFORMANCE APPRAISAL PROCESS

Performance appraisal is the process by which an employee's contribution to the organization during a specified period of time is assessed. **Performance feedback** then lets employees know how well they have performed in comparison with the standards of the organization. Performance appraisal and feedback can be an emotionally laden process that dramatically affects employees' attitudes toward the organization and themselves. If used effectively, performance appraisal can improve employee motivation and performance. If used inappropriately, it can have disastrous effects.

Appraisal and feedback can occur informally, as when a supervisor notices and comments on a good or poor performance incident. A more formal method is the structured annual performance review, in which a supervisor assesses each employee's performance using some official appraisal procedure. Larger organizations tend to use both formal and informal methods, whereas many smaller organizations use only informal supervisory feedback.

Over the years, a great deal of research has been devoted to performance appraisal systems. This research has looked at who should do the appraisal, what methods of appraising are best, when and how often appraisals should be done, and for what purposes appraisal information should be used. The conclusions from this vast body of research are not always straightforward.

STRATEGIC IMPORTANCE OF PERFORMANCE APPRAISAL

Strategically, it is hard to imagine a more important HR system than performance appraisal. As shown in Chapter 1 (Figure 1.1) and clarified in subsequent chapters, organizations strive to do the following at all levels:

- Design jobs and work systems to accomplish organizational goals.
- Hire individuals with the abilities and desire to perform effectively.
- Train, motivate, and reward employees for performance and productivity.

It is this sequence that allows organizations to diffuse their strategic goals throughout the organization. Within this context, the evaluation of performance is the control mechanism that provides not only feedback to individuals, but also an organizational assessment of how things are progressing. Without performance information, managers of an organization can only guess as to whether employees are working toward the right goals, in the correct way, and to the desired standard.

Performance appraisal plays another important role in organizational strategy, that of assuring **strategy-consistent behavior.** A truism of organization life is that people engage in the behaviors that they perceive will be rewarded. Employees want to be rewarded and will do those things the organization is emphasizing. For example, if the focus is on service, employees will behave in ways that gain the rewards associated with service delivery. If the focus is on cost control, employees will seek ways to control cost and thus be recognized and rewarded. If the focus is on rewarding productivity, employees will strive for productivity. In this context, performance appraisal becomes a means of knowing if employee behavior is consistent with the overall strategic focus and a way for bringing to the fore any negative consequences of the strategy-behavior link. For example, a single-minded productivity focus may include potential negative consequences, such as decreased quality and cooperation. Performance appraisal is an important organizational mechanism to elicit feedback as to the consistency of the strategy-behavior link.

Performance appraisal is also a mechanism to reinforce the values of the organization. For example, how is an organization that articulates the value of developing its people to know if this value is shared by managers throughout the organization? A history of developing people or communication from the highest executives are not enough. Managers typically have more to do than time to get it done and will let slide what is not reinforced. If managers are held accountable for developing their people by being judged on this task in their own performance appraisal, they will be likely to spend more time developing subordinates.

FUNCTIONS OF PERFORMANCE APPRAISAL

A recent survey delineated twenty purposes, divided into four major categories, for which formal performance appraisals can be used; these multiple uses are illustrated in Table 11.1. Developmental uses of appraisal focus on improving employees' future performance and career advancement, whereas administrative uses include decision making about merit raises and promotions. Appraisal information is also used to contribute to organizational well-being (for instance, to anticipate HR needs) and for documentation (for instance, to provide criteria for validation research).[1] Each of these applications of performance appraisal information is explored in this section.

Performance Appraisal as an Employee Development Tool

Performance appraisal can be used in several ways to encourage employee development. It plays a role in reinforcing and improving performance and in determining career goals and training needs.

TABLE 11.1 Multiple Organizational Uses for Performance Appraisal Information

General Applications	*Specific Uses*
Developmental Uses	Identification of Individual Training Needs
	Performance Feedback
	Determining Transfers and Job Assignments
	Identification of Individual Strengths and Weaknesses
Administrative Uses/ Decisions	Salary
	Promotion
	Retention or Termination
	Recognition of Individual Performance
	Layoffs
	Identification of Poor Performers
Organizational Maintenance/ Objectives	Human Resource Planning
	Determining Organization Training Needs
	Evaluation of Organizational Goal Achievement
	Information for Goal Identification
	Evaluation of Human Resource Systems
	Reinforcement of Organizational Development Needs
Documentation	Criteria for Validation Research
	Documentation of Human Resource Decisions
	Helping to Meet Legal Requirements

Source: J. N. Cleveland, K. R. Murphy, and R. E. Williams, "Multiple Uses of Performance Appraisal: Prevalence and Correlates," *Journal of Applied Psychology,* Vol. 74, 1989, pp. 130–135. Copyright © 1989 by the American Psychological Association. Adapted by permission.

Reinforcing and Sustaining Performance Using performance appraisal as an employee development tool can place the supervisor in a supportive, reinforcing role. By providing feedback on past performance, a supervisor can encourage employees to sustain good behavior. Praise can augment any financial rewards that the employee may receive. In our Western culture, virtually all employees like to be told when they are doing a good job.

Improving Performance The supervisor can use performance appraisal data to suggest ways in which employees might perform better in the future. The supervisor can point out strengths and weaknesses and help employees identify more effective ways to accomplish important tasks. Additionally, the supervisor can discuss work goals with the employee and agree upon a timetable for achieving these goals. A more detailed discussion of how to use performance feedback to improve employee performance is provided later in this chapter.

Determining Career Progression Goals The performance appraisal session gives the supervisor and employee an opportunity to discuss the employee's long-term career goals and plans. The supervisor can advise the employee on the steps to take to reach these goals. On the basis of past performance, the supervisor can give the employee short-term, specific suggestions on how to improve performance in ways that will help the employee achieve longer-term career goals. As a result, the employee may become more highly motivated to perform well in his or her present position since it is seen as a necessary step toward an ultimate goal.

Determining Training Needs Performance appraisal can determine the training needs of individual employees. If particular employees are not performing up to expectations, a training program may enable them to correct any skill or knowledge deficiencies. Employees who are performing well above the requirements of the position can be placed in a development program that will prepare them for promotion to a higher-level job. Performance appraisal also supplies information useful in developing training programs that will fit the needs of most employees. For example, if employees' communication skills are rated uniformly low, the company can develop a program to address this need.

Performance Appraisal as an Administrative Tool

Besides their use in employee development, performance appraisals also play a role in administrative decision making. Performance appraisals are used to link rewards to performance and to evaluate the effectiveness of HR policies and practices.

Linking Rewards to Performance Performance appraisals are part of the reward and punishment system of an organization. Employees who receive favorable evaluations tend to receive organizational rewards, such as merit pay increases and bonuses, whereas those with unfavorable evaluations receive organizational sanctions, including demotions or discharge. Other personnel decisions commonly linked to performance appraisals include promotions, layoffs, transfers, and discipline decisions.

The goal in linking pay and other personnel decisions to performance level is to motivate employees to perform better. Unfortunately, matching performance and reward is much easier said than done. The performance of individuals must be accurately assessed, the rewards provided must truly be of value to employees, and the organization must develop a performance-based reward system that employees perceive as being fairly administered. The system will fail if employees believe managers and supervisors distribute rewards on the basis of favoritism or political considerations.

Evaluation of HRM Policies and Programs Performance appraisal data can also be used to evaluate the effectiveness of HRM programs. Appraisals can be performed before and after an intervention to measure the amount of change that has occurred. Interventions that might be evaluated with performance appraisal data include training programs, job enrichment or redesign, quality circles, and the like. Research designs for evaluating interventions were discussed in Chapter 10. Recall from Chapter 8 that the empirical validation of selection devices requires scores on a job performance criterion. This information is usually collected by some method of performance appraisal.

Self-managed Teams as a Performance Appraisal Challenge

More and more companies are looking to **self-managed teams** (also called autonomous work groups) as the productivity and quality of work life breakthrough of the 1990s.[2] Self-managed teams create several challenges for performance appraisal. When teams perform highly interdependent activities, evaluating them using an appraisal system that focuses only on individual results may be inaccurate as well as discouraging to necessary team work. In addition, when teams are working effectively, they manage themselves. There is no supervisor, yet historically it is the supervisor who has made performance appraisal judgments about employees. The team has the responsibility for hiring, firing, and evaluating its own team members.[3] Consequently, teams are responsible either for developing a performance appraisal system for their members or for adapting an existing system to suit the purposes of the team. The important point is that the team assumes responsibility for its composition, its progress, and its results. Therefore, it must have in place a mechanism to gather the information needed to do its job, including information related to the administrative and development decisions indicated in Table 11.1. It also assumes responsibility for acting on the information: feeding it back to members, addressing performance issues, and so forth. Self-managed teams may require the development of an entirely new approach to performance appraisal.

CRITERIA FOR A GOOD APPRAISAL SYSTEM

Surveys find that the overwhelming majority of both private and public sector organizations use some type of performance appraisal.[4] Between 30 and 50 percent of employees believe that formal performance appraisals are ineffective and that less than 20 percent of performance appraisal systems accomplish the goals the organization has established.[5] A nationwide survey of 3,500 companies showed that the most frequently mentioned HR concern was the organization's appraisal system.[6] Sadly, many appraisal systems are poorly designed.[7] The Ethical Perspective box gives some advice for designing appraisal systems that employees perceive as fair and just.

Developing a Procedurally Just Performance Appraisal Process

When organizations make decisions about people, such as whom to hire or promote, what appraisal ratings or merit raise to give, or how to discipline a particular infraction, it is very important that the decisions are seen as fair and just. Research has shown that at least two aspects of justice influence employees' job satisfaction and organizational commitment, and both must be considered in organizational decisions.

The first type is *distributive justice,* or the perceived fairness of particular outcomes. It has to do with the distribution of rewards and punishments across people. Distributive justice would exist if employees agreed that the best person had been chosen for a promotion, that the punishment fit the crime in a discipline case, or that the size of merit raises accurately reflected true differences in performance across the people involved. Distributive justice is specific to a particular decision—we might agree that one promotion decision was fair, but that is no guarantee that we will think the next one is fair. This is because distributive justice doesn't include evaluation of the fairness of the method or process by which the decision was made. The latter is called *procedural justice*. Presumably, a just policy or procedure should help assure equitable outcomes every time, whereas a single instance of distributive justice could occur by chance, favoritism, or some other unfair process.

What makes an allocation procedure just? Following are six rules for procedural justice (Folger and Greenberg 1985, p. 146):

- Consistency Rule: allocation procedures should be consistent across persons and over time;
- Bias Suppression Rule: personal self-interest in the allocation process should be prevented;
- Accuracy Rule: decisions must be based on accurate information;
- Correctability Rule: opportunities must exist to enable decisions to be modified;
- Representativeness Rule: the allocation process must represent the concerns of all recipients; and
- Ethicality Rule: allocations must be based on prevailing moral and ethical standards.

Performance appraisal represents a situation in which decisions are made about individuals (allocation of ratings or rankings and associated rewards) and the potential for misunderstandings and feelings of injustice are great. This means that a very fair and clear process should be adopted.

Research has shown that appraisals are seen as more fair when consistent standards are applied to all ratees, there is a system by which the ratee can appeal or rebut the evaluation, and when raters are familiar with ratee's work, solicit employee input before assigning ratings, provide prompt feedback, and allow two way communication in the appraisal interview. In addition, procedures should be more likely to be perceived as fair if employees understand the rating dimensions and superior's expectations well before the rating takes place. Ideally, ratees would also have input into determining the rating criteria.

These appraisal procedures meet most of the six rules given above, and should help to assure that the emotionally-laden process of performance appraisal is seen as fair, in so far as is humanly possible.

Sources: Robert Folger and Jerald Greenberg, "Procedural Justice: An Interpretive Analysis of Personnel Systems," *Research in Personnel and Human Resource Management,* 1985 Vol. 3, pp. 141–183; Robert Folger, Mary A. Konovsky, and Russell Cropanzano, "A Due Process Metaphor for Performance Appraisal," *Research in Organizational Behavior,* 1992, Vol. 14, pp. 129–177; Robert Folger and Mary A. Konovsky, "Effects of Procedural and Distributive Justice on Reactions to Pay Raise Decisions," *Academy of Management Journal,* March 1989, pp. 115–130; Jerald Greenberg, "Determinants of Perceived Fairness of Performance Evaluations," *Journal of Applied Psychology,* May 1986, pp. 340–342.

The fundamental decisions about what type of performance to assess and how to measure that performance should be shaped by four desirable criteria: validity, reliability, freedom from bias, and practicality.

Validity

A good measure of performance should measure important job characteristics (relevancy) and be free from extraneous or contaminating influences; it should also encompass the whole job (not be deficient).[8] As discussed in Chapter 7, a measure is construct-valid if it accurately measures what it claims to measure. A measure has content validity if it measures all important parts of a construct and does so in a representative way. The relationship between these two types of validity and the concepts of relevance, contamination, and deficiency is quite clear. A relevant measure assesses aspects of performance that are truly important in determining job effectiveness. For example, a relevant measure for assessing the performance of a college professor would include teaching performance. A measure is not deficient if it measures *all* important aspects of performance. In the case of the college professor, the measure of performance would be deficient unless it assessed such factors as research and publications, as well as teaching performance. A measure is free of contamination if it avoids assessing other constructs besides performance. If the professor's performance rating included an assessment of how well the professor's shoes were shined, the measure would be contaminated by this irrelevant content. The relationships between relevance, deficiency, and contamination are presented graphically in Figure 11.1.

A performance appraisal system must be valid. It is essential that a good job analysis be conducted before developing the performance measure so that all relevant aspects of performance are covered and irrelevant factors do not contaminate the appraisal measure.

Reliability

Interrater reliability is the most relevant type of reliability for performance appraisal. It is high when two or more raters agree on the performance of an employee, and low when they do not. Interrater reliability is usually quite good when performance raters come from the same level of the organization, such as two superiors or two peers of the person being rated. However, there is often legitimate disagreement between raters at different levels, such as a peer and a superior or a superior and a subordinate. Thus, high interrater reliability is expected only among raters at the same organizational level. In a study of almost 10,000 employees from 79 organizations, Hannah R. Rothstein found that interrater reliabilities—that is, the correlation (see Chapter 7) between two raters observing the same employee—typically ranged from 0.65 to 0.73, a high enough level to lend confidence to the stability of the rating process.[9]

Internal consistency reliability and reliability over time are not especially important in performance appraisal because performance itself may not be internally

FIGURE 11.1 The Relationships Between Relevance, Deficiency, and Contamination

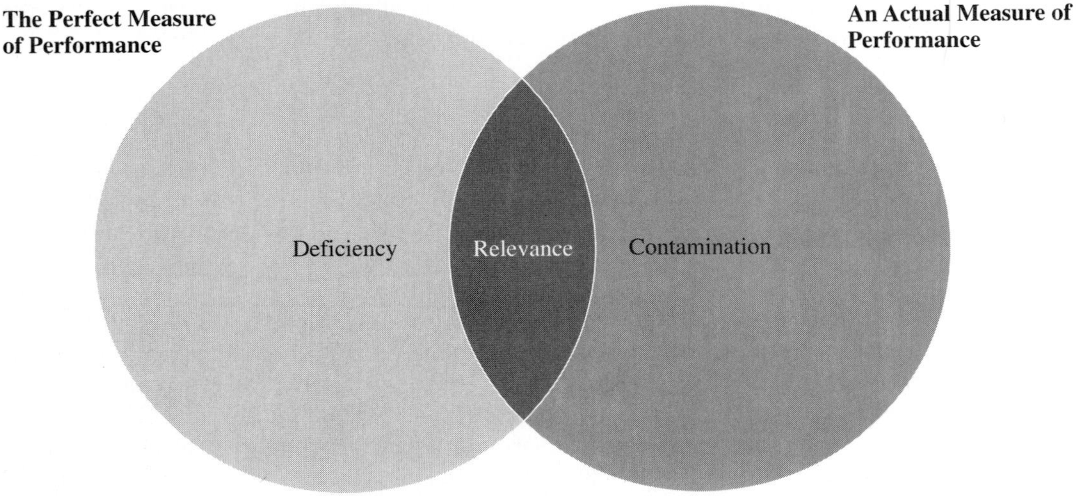

Relevance: *The overlap between the perfect measure of performance and an actual measure*

Deficiency: *Important aspects of a perfect measure of performance that are not included in the actual measure the organization is using*

Contamination: *Aspects unrelated to performance that are somehow included within the actual measure*

consistent or stable over time. A person may be very good at certain aspects of a job but quite weak at others, so a measure that accurately gauged these different aspects of performance would not show high internal consistency. Similarly, because performance may improve with experience or training and fluctuate with effort or luck, strong stability over time is not necessarily expected.

For more objective measures of performance, another aspect of reliability is important. Suppose absenteeism from work is used as one measure of an employee's performance. If the supervisor sometimes records when the employee is absent and sometimes does not, then this measure of performance is unreliable. Thus, when evaluating the reliability of performance appraisals, it is very important to know exactly what type of measure is used, and, in the case of subjective ratings of performance, who is making the ratings.

Freedom from Bias

In performance appraisal, the criterion of freedom from bias has two components. The first concerns legal issues of fairness to employees; the second has to do with the subjectivity of one person's judgments about the performance of others.

Legal Issues of Fairness In one sense, an appraisal is free from bias if it is fair to all employees regardless of their race, sex, national origin, handicap status, and so on. Employment legislation permits employers to use a bona fide appraisal system, but not one that has an unjustifiable adverse impact on minorities, women, older employees, or other protected groups of people.[10] In *Brito* v. *Zia Co.* (1973), the court ruled that the *Uniform Guidelines* (see Chapter 5) were applicable and must be followed in evaluating the adequacy of a performance appraisal instrument.[11] Spanish-surnamed workers were reinstated with back pay because the company had used a performance appraisal instrument of questionable validity to make layoff decisions. In addition, Spanish-surnamed employees were promoted significantly less frequently than were other employees. The court was critical of Zia's subjective appraisal process, noting that some supervisors making ratings had never directly observed the employees' performance. Zia Company failed to present evidence of the validity of its appraisal procedure.

In June 1989, the Supreme Court reaffirmed the importance of objective standards in performance appraisal in the case of *Price Waterhouse* v. *Hopkins*.[12] Ann B. Hopkins filed charges of sex discrimination against the accounting firm of Price Waterhouse after being turned down for promotion to partner despite high performance. Hopkins charged that sex stereotyping was involved in the decision: she had been told she would have "to walk more femininely, talk more femininely, dress more femininely, wear makeup, have her hair styled, and wear jewelry" to be considered for promotion.[13] The court ruled in Hopkins's favor, stating that her obligation to show that gender was a factor in the employment decision had been satisfied, whereas Price Waterhouse failed to show that the same decision would have been made in the absence of gender as a factor. The court's decision dealt with the effect of sex stereotyping in the workplace and the need for objectivity in performance evaluation.[14]

Although there is no legal mandate for an organization to have and use an appraisal system that meets some state-of-the-art requirement for soundness, the methods of appraisal that an organization employs should not adversely impact groups protected by the law (see Chapter 5)—for example groups based on race, sex, national origin, handicap status, or age. If challenged, the organization will seek to defend itself on the basis of the soundness, objectivity, and validity of its appraisal system. Most performance appraisal systems currently in use would probably not fare too well if they were subjected to legal challenge. A system can be discriminatory for any of the following reasons.

1. The rating content is not job related or valid.
2. The content of the ratings is not developed from a thorough job analysis.
3. The raters do not observe ratees performing their work.
4. Ratings are based on raters' evaluations of subjective or vague factors.
5. Ratings are not collected and scored under standardized conditions.[15]

An employer can reduce the probability of a legal challenge in several ways. A primary rule is to use only appraisal systems that are based on a thorough job analysis. The appraisal process should incorporate only those duties or characteristics that are important for job performance. Supervisors must be trained to use the rating instrument properly, and the results and rationale for all evaluations must be carefully documented. If possible, formal appeal mechanisms should be established, and ratings should be reviewed by upper-level or human resource managers. Finally, some form of counseling should be offered to help poor performers improve.

It is worth noting that cases brought under the federal Age Discrimination in Employment Act (ADEA, see Chapter 5) have not scrutinized the defendant organization's appraisal system. The intent of the ADEA is to protect those aged forty or over from discriminatory employment decisions. A recent study of more than fifty-three age discrimination cases found that, in contrast to Title VII cases, the outcome of ADEA cases was not influenced by the soundness of the performance appraisal system.[16] Formal performance evaluation procedures were not required by the courts for an employer to mount a successful defense; instead, less reliable sources of employee performance information have been accepted as conclusive evidence substantiating an employer claim of nondiscrimination in employment decisions. However, employers would be wise to have a sound, objective, and valid appraisal system to defend ADEA charges should they arise. It should be added, too, that research has generally shown that there is no relationship between age and performance, despite the prevalence of a stereotype of older workers being less effective.[17]

Freedom from Rating Errors When an appraisal system requires individuals to make subjective judgments about the performance of others, the second component of freedom from bias becomes important. Ratings may be biased, either intentionally or unintentionally. The common rating errors are described below and shown graphically in Figure 11.2. Some of these errors also occur in interviewing—another situation in which one person judges and evaluates another.

Leniency Errors Sometimes raters give employees more positive performance ratings than they deserve. For example, an analysis of U.S. Marine Corps officer fitness reports showed that, on a 9-point scale, with 9 representing "outstanding performance," the average performance ratings for a sample of more than 2,000 officers was 8.2.[18] Although officers are well trained and devoted to their service, it is difficult to believe that almost all of them are truly outstanding. For a large number of employees, one would expect the true distribution of performance ratings to approximate a bell-shaped curve (see the curve indicating true distribution of performance in Figure 11.2a). When **leniency error** occurs, most employees receive very high performance ratings (see the curve indicating leniency error). Leniency is a very common type of rating bias.

FIGURE 11.2 Leniency, Severity, Central Tendency, and Halo Errors

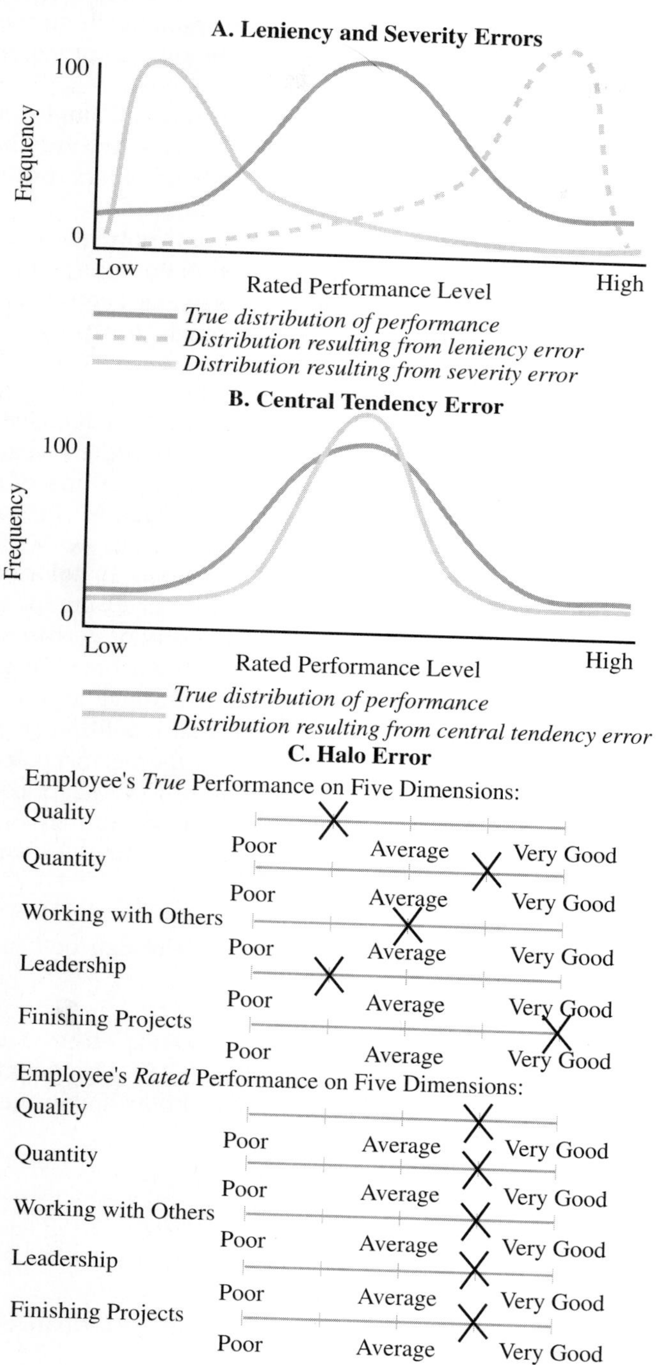

Severity Errors Sometimes raters evaluate employees more unfavorably than their performance warrants. When such **severity errors** occur, as shown in Figure 11.2a, the distribution of performance ratings shifts dramatically to the left of the true distribution of performance. Severity error is the reverse of leniency error.

Central Tendency Errors Sometimes a supervisor rates all employees near the midpoint of a performance scale. Few if any employees receive very high or very low ratings. As Figure 11.2b shows, such **central tendency errors** result in a rating distribution that is highly compressed around the middle.

When central tendency, leniency, or severity errors are frequent, an appraisal system cannot accomplish its purpose of differentiating among good and poor workers. When one of these errors (leniency, severity, or central tendency) occurs, nearly everyone receives the same rating—a high, low, or average score, depending on the type of error.

Halo Errors Whereas leniency, severity, and central tendency errors occur when several employees are appraised, **halo error** involves the rating of a single individual on several aspects of performance. This pervasive form of rating error has been long recognized, yet is not well understood.[19] Jack M. Feldman defines halo error in terms of a very high correlation among ratings across several performance areas or, more simply put, the tendency of raters to color performance judgments by general feelings toward the individual.[20] For example, a supervisor may be asked to rate an employee on quality and quantity of performance, working with coworkers, leadership, and finishing projects on time. In general, one would expect an employee to be good at some tasks, average at others, and perhaps weak in some performance areas. The individual would receive some high ratings, some low, and some average, depending on the performance area. The correlation among those ratings would be moderate to low. When halo error occurs, an employee receives nearly identical performance ratings on all performance areas, and the resulting correlation among the ratings is very high. An example of halo error is given in Figure 11.2c.

Why Do Rating Errors Occur? Rating errors occur through both unintentional and intentional processes.

Unintentional Errors One way to examine why rating errors occur is to use the approach called **cognitive information processing (CIP).** Proponents of CIP argue that performance appraisal is best viewed as a complex memory task in which the assessors must

- acquire performance information about an employee.
- encode and store that information in their memory.
- retrieve that information at a later date when asked to assess the employee's performance.
- weigh and combine the information into an overall performance judgment.[21]

The amount of performance information available about an employee is enormous. Raters can notice and recall only a limited amount of information on each employee, and research has shown that they use a variety of methods to condense the information they do receive.[22] This can result in a variety of memory and judgment errors in appraisal. One cognitive short cut that people use in processing information about others is the schema. **Schemas** are simply mental categories that an individual uses to organize information and classify people.[23] For example, a supervisor might use two schemas in classifying employees: the good worker schema and the bad worker schema. Associated with each schema is a set of attributes, called a **prototype,** that represents the essential characteristics needed to be classified into that schema.[24] Thus, the prototype for the supervisor's good worker schema might include the following: never absent, writes well, always gets projects done on time, and gets along well with coworkers. A ratee need not exhibit all the prototype characteristics in order to be classified into the schema. For instance, noticing that an employee is never absent from work, the supervisor might categorize that person as a good worker, even without direct evidence that the employee writes well, hands in projects on time, or gets along well with coworkers.

When asked to assess the performance of an employee, a supervisor searches his or her memory to determine into which schema the employee has been placed. The supervisor recalls information about the employee, *including the schema prototype*. The supervisor's judgment of the employee is based not only on the precise behaviors observed, but also on the prototype associated with the schema. This recollection of behavior that never actually occurred (but that fits a particular schema) is the source of halo error. Often an employee rated high on work attendance will also receive positive ratings on all other aspects of performance *even though he or she may not have actually performed well in these areas*. Similarly, an employee originally categorized as a poor worker may be rated low on all criteria even though the supervisor may not really have observed poor performance in some areas. This process is shown in Figure 11.3.

Leniency and severity errors may also be influenced by the nature of schema prototypes. If a supervisor's prototype characteristics for the good worker are so extreme that few employees will ever exhibit behavior that allows them to be classified as good workers, severity error may occur. If some of the prototype characteristics of a good worker are very easy for most employees to exhibit, leniency error may occur.

Intentional Errors Sometimes supervisors intentionally rate employees inaccurately. A company vice president summarized one common view of the politics of appraisal:

> As a manager, I will use the review process to do what is best for my people and the division. . . . I've got a lot of leeway—call it discretion—to use this process in that manner. . . . I've used it to get my people better raises in lean years, to kick a guy in the pants if he really needed it, to pick up a guy when he was down or even to tell him that he was no longer welcome here. It is a tool that the manager should

FIGURE 11.3 How Information Processing Causes Rating Errors

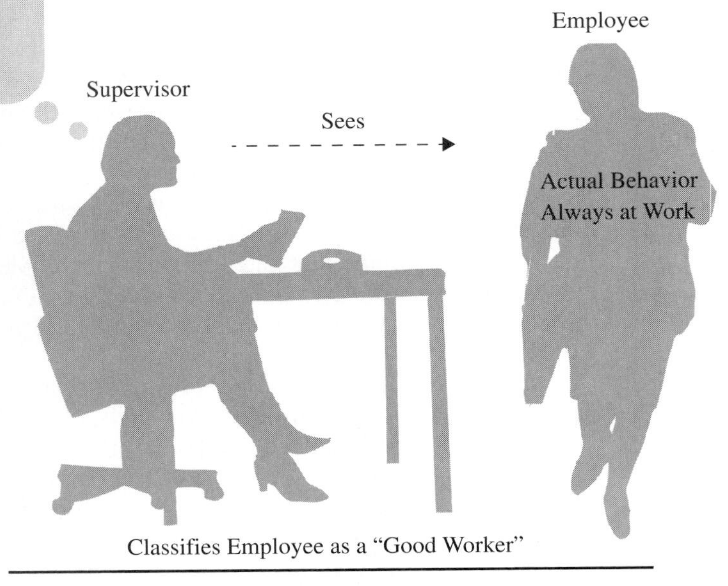

Time Passes

Performance Appraisal Time:
Supervisor Remembers Employee as "Good Worker"
Supervisor Recalls Prototype
- Never Absent
- Writes Well
- Always Finishes Projects on Time
- Gets Along Well with Coworkers

Supervisor Rates Employee Using Prototype, not Actual Behavior

> use to help him do what it takes to get the job done. I believe most of us here operate this way regarding appraisals. . . . Accurately describing an employee's performance is really not as important as generating ratings that keep things cooking.[25]

Recent work has begun to shed some light on how political factors affect performance appraisals.[26] For example, intentional leniency error can occur for several reasons. Supervisors may feel that having subordinates with high performance ratings will make them look good to their own superiors, or they may fear that their working relationship with employees will be ruined by an unfavorable

TABLE 11.2 Why Supervisors Inflate and Deflate Ratings

Reasons for Inflating
To maximize the merit raise an employee is eligible to receive, particularly when the merit raise ceiling is low.
To protect or encourage an employee whose performance has suffered because of personal problems. The supervisor feels sorry for the employee.
To avoid "hanging out dirty laundry" that would reflect badly on the supervisor or unit.
To avoid creating a written record of an employee's poor performance that becomes part of the employee's permanent record.
To avoid a confrontation with an employee.
To reward an employee who has shown improvement in performance, even though performance is still not high.
To increase the likelihood that an employee whom the supervisor does not like will be promoted out of the supervisor's work unit.
Reasons for Deflating
To shock an employee back onto a higher performance track.
To teach a rebellious employee a lesson about who is in charge.
To send a message to an employee that he or she should consider leaving the organization.
To build a strongly documented, written record of poor performance so that an employee can be fired.

Source: Based on C. O. Longenecker, H. P. Sims, and D. A. Gioia, "Behind the Mask: The Politics of Employee Appraisal," *The Academy of Management Executive,* Vol. 1, 1987, pp. 183–193.

appraisal. Also, supervisors simply find it difficult to give negative feedback to their employees and may inflate ratings to avoid this unpleasant task.[27] For these reasons, intentional leniency error is far more prevalent than severity error, although some intentional severity error can occur. The common reasons that supervisors give for inflating or deflating performance ratings are summarized in Table 11.2.

Halo error may also flow from intentional distortions in the rating process. For instance, it is not unusual for supervisors to determine an employee's overall rating first, then assign ratings on separate areas of performance to be consistent with the overall evaluation. Thus, a supervisor who wants to rate an employee moderately high overall, for any of the reasons cited above, will rate the person moderately high on each area of performance. The result is halo error.

Practicality

It takes time, effort, and money to develop, implement, and use a performance appraisal system. The benefits to the organization of using the system must outweigh its costs. The appraisal system should also be relatively easy to use and should have a high degree of employee and managerial acceptance. Even the best developed appraisal system is futile if it is not used.

The development and use of an appraisal system can be an expensive undertaking. Table 11.3 shows the estimated costs of developing a performance appraisal system that were reported in a study by M. A. Jones. The costs required to develop the system were distinguished from those needed to implement and run it within the organization. In all, the appraisal system that Jones analyzed cost more than $300,000 to develop and implement.

Since dollar costs are high, an important practical criterion against which to judge an appraisal system is the savings it might bring to the organization.[28] The process of measuring dollar return to an organization, called utility analysis, was discussed earlier in connection with both selection and training. Feedback, like training and careful selection, can improve employee performance. Estimates of performance improvement following feedback range from 8 percent to as much as 26 percent. The dollar value of improvements can be calculated using an estimate of the standard deviation of performance in dollars.[29] In one study, the cost of developing and implementing an appraisal system was estimated at $700 per

TABLE 11.3 Costs of Developing and Implementing an Appraisal System

Cost Item	*Development*	*Implementation*
Operating Costs		
Production and Development	$ 53,900	$ 18,100
Data Entry Hardware	N/A	400
Paper	1,700	800
Mailing/Distribution	500	6,600
Training	N/A	23,500
Human Resource Costs		
Job Analysts/Experts	37,000	N/A
Clerical	11,200	11,100
Professional Coordinator	N/A	7,200
Consultant	25,500	1,500
Rater Time	N/A	80,700
Ratee Time	N/A	29,800
Total	129,800	179,500
Grand Total		$309,300

Source: Adapted from M. A. Jones, "Estimating Costs in the Development and Implementation of a Performance Appraisal System" (paper presented at the First Annual Scientist-Practitioner Conference in Industrial-Organizational Psychology, Old Dominion University, Norfolk, Virginia, 1980). Reprinted by permission. Dollar figures have been rounded to nearest $100.

employee. Subtracting the costs of conducting appraisals and giving feedback from the estimated dollar value of performance improvements, analysts estimated that an organization in which 500 managers were appraised and provided feedback could realize benefits of $5.3 million in the first year.[30] Thus, even though appraisal systems are expensive to develop and implement, they offer great potential benefits.

DECIDING WHAT TYPES OF PERFORMANCE TO MEASURE

The criteria for evaluating performance appraisal systems described above provide the basis for making important decisions when developing an appraisal system. One crucial choice is simply what type of performance to assess. There are three basic categories of performance information. A *trait-based* appraisal system assesses the abilities or other personal characteristics of an employee. A *behavior-based* system measures the extent to which an employee engages in specific, relatively well-defined behaviors while on the job. Finally, a *results-based* system measures the "bottom line" associated with an employee's work: did the job get done, was a profit made?[31] Each type of appraisal system has some advantages and disadvantages. Figure 11.4 illustrates the three types of systems.

Trait-based Appraisals

Trait-based appraisals are used to assess the personality or personal characteristics of employees, such as their ability to make decisions, loyalty to the company, communication skills, or level of initiative. This type of appraisal asks a lot about what a person *is*, but relatively little about what he or she actually *does*. While trait-based appraisals are easy to construct, the disadvantages of focusing on traits are significant.

Trait-based approaches have questionable validity. Traits assessed in this type of appraisal often do not relate well to how employees really behave on the job because job behavior is strongly influenced by situational and environmental factors. An employee who is usually boisterous and aggressive with coworkers may act in a restrained, considerate manner when dealing with clients. Since the link between personal traits and actual job behavior is weak, trait-based systems are potentially more susceptible to charges of unfairness by minorities, women, and other protected groups. Trait-based systems are not likely to be accepted by the courts. As noted earlier, court decisions such as *Price Waterhouse* v. *Hopkins* have made it very clear that what is assessed in a performance appraisal system should have a clear link to effectiveness on the job.[32]

A further problem is that the interrater reliability of trait-based ratings is often low. The traits are difficult to define accurately, and the different frames of reference used by different raters make agreement among raters unlikely. A final disadvantage is that trait-based appraisals are not helpful for providing feedback to employees. For example, telling an employee that he or she is too shy is not

FIGURE 11.4 Examples of Trait-, Behavior-, and Results-based Performance Appraisal Systems

A. Trait-based Appraisal

Rate the employee on each of the following traits:

Trait					
1. Loyalty to Company	very low	low	average	high	very high
2. Communication Ability	very low	low	average	high	very high
3. Cooperativeness	very low	low	average	high	very high

B. Behavior-based Appraisal

Using the scale below, rate the frequency with which the employee exhibits the following behaviors:

1 = never 3 = sometimes 5 = almost always
2 = rarely 4 = frequently

_____ 1. Greets customers in a pleasant and friendly manner.

_____ 2. Is unable to explain technical aspects of a product to a customer.

_____ 3. Fills out charge card slips correctly, getting approval from supervisor for all charges above $300.00.

C. Results-based Appraisal

From your production and employee files, please provide the following information for this employee:

1. Number of units produced this month: _____
2. Number of units produced that were rejected and scrapped by quality control: _____
3. Number of units produced that were rejected and returned for repair by quality control: _____
4. Days this month the employee was absent without certified medical excuse: _____

very useful. The information does not indicate how the employee can be less shy. Also, the basic personality traits of individuals are relatively well fixed by the time they are hired by an organization and are very difficult to alter.

Behavior-based Appraisals

Appraisal can consider the behavior of employees rather than their personal traits. Behavior measures are appropriate when it is very important *how* a job is done. For example, a salesperson should greet customers as they enter the store, help them find what they are looking for, take their money promptly, and thank them for their business. In **behavior-based appraisals,** employees are assessed on what they *do* on their job. Such assessments are more acceptable to the courts than trait-based appraisals. Behavior measures can be very useful for feedback purposes because they indicate exactly what an employee should do differently. For instance, although a shy employee may always be shy, a behavior-based appraisal might point out particular things that the person could do differently, such as contributing ideas at regularly scheduled staff meetings.

Deficiency may be a problem with some behavior-based appraisals since they often will not include all behaviors that could lead to job effectiveness. For some jobs, effective performance can be achieved using a variety of different behaviors. For example, one salesperson may sell twenty cars a month using an aggressive, "pushy" style. Another salesperson may sell just as many cars using a reserved, considerate, fact-oriented approach. An appraisal system that assumes that an aggressive sales style is best would unfairly assess the performance of the second salesperson.

Results-based Appraisals

To avoid the problems inherent in a behavior-based approach, appraisals may measure the results of work behavior. This approach deals with bottom-line issues such as how many cars an employee sold or how much profit the employee brought into the organization during the month. When it is not important how results are achieved and when there are many different ways to succeed, a **results-based approach** would be appropriate. Under this approach, both of the car salespeople described above would receive the same evaluation, even though they achieved their results using very different means.

Despite their intuitive appeal, results-based appraisals pose questions of practicality, contamination, and deficiency. Results-based measures may be difficult to obtain for some jobs. What are the performance results of a high school teacher's behavior? Furthermore, results are not always under the control of an individual employee. Equipment breakdowns, a change in the economy, bad luck, inadequate budgetary or staff support, or other factors not directly controlled by an employee may greatly affect the job results.[33] Results measures are therefore contaminated by these external factors. Another problem is that results-based appraisals may foster a "results at all cost" mentality among employees.[34] For example, in an organization that evaluated its telephone order takers on the basis of sales, employees on the telephone bank learned to hang up on customers calling to cancel orders or arrange returns since these would count against sales. Obviously, such a practice was not what the organization intended and would hurt customer satisfaction and repeat sales.

Teamwork among employees may suffer if individuals are preoccupied with their own *personal* results and will not take the time to help coworkers. Results-based measures are deficient in that they may not tap such aspects of performance as cooperation, which may have important benefits for the organization. A final disadvantage is that results-based appraisals are less helpful for employee development. Although they may indicate that results are below acceptable levels, they do not always provide clear information on how to improve work performance.

Care must be taken in deciding what type of performance is appropriate to assess for a specific job. Unless a clear link between traits and job effectiveness can be shown, trait-based appraisals should be avoided; in general, fewer problems are associated with behavior- and results-based systems. A carefully constructed combination of behavior-based and results-based approaches may be most appropriate for many jobs. The next section of this chapter describes some specific methods of assessing performance. Some of these techniques are, by their nature, suited to assessing only one type of performance information. Others, particularly those involving subjective ratings, may be used to assess more than one performance type.

METHODS OF APPRAISING PERFORMANCE

Performance can be measured in many different ways. Most of the performance measures currently in use can be characterized as either objective or subjective. Objective measures are typically results-based measures of physical output, whereas subjective measures can be used to assess traits, behaviors, or results.

Objective Measures

Objective measures assess performance in terms of numbers, such as the amount of a product an employee produces or sells, the number of defective products produced, the number of times an employee is absent or late to work, or some other direct numerical index of how well or quickly an employee can perform certain tasks. There are five major types of objective measures: production measures, dollar sales, personnel data, performance tests, and business unit measures.

Production Measures The manufacturing industry has used production measures for at least the last 100 years. These measures simply involve counting the number of items produced by an employee or the number of defective units made, or obtaining some other quantitative index of production. Production measures can be appropriately used when an employee produces a measurable, physical product. As with any results-based assessment, production measures may not be available for many of the jobs in an organization, or they may be influenced by factors beyond an employee's control. For example, if a coworker is habitually late in getting raw materials to an employee, that employee's production rate could be slowed down. Or a worker may be assigned to an older piece of equipment or a machine that is prone to break down. For a production measure to be a valid measure of performance, three conditions must be met: (1) production should be on a repetitive basis, (2) the amount of product should be measurable, and (3) the employee should be primarily responsible for the amount produced.

Dollar Sales Sales performance is usually measured by the dollar amount of sales made in a given period of time. Typically, some minimum acceptable level of sales is defined, and performance beyond that quota is rewarded more highly. Sales measures are also results based and suffer from many of the same shortcomings as production measures. For example, a salesperson assigned to a rural territory may have to spend many hours traveling from town to town, whereas a salesperson assigned to a large city can devote more time to actual client contact. The salesperson in the city will probably sell more than the salesperson in the rural area, even if both work equally hard and are equally skilled. The sales measure is contaminated by this difference in sales territory, which creates a so-called **opportunity bias.**[35] Thus, it is appropriate to use dollar sales as an index of performance only when individuals have substantial control over their sales performance or when it is possible to adjust for contaminants, such as differences in sales territory.

Personnel Data Information from an employee's personnel file is sometimes used in performance assessment. Personnel measures would include such particulars as the number of times an employee has been absent or late to work and the number of reprimands or disciplinary actions taken against the individual.

Serious problems arise in the use of personnel data. One is contamination. If an employee is absent from work because of illness or is late to work because of a flat tire, does this mean that this employee is a poor performer? Personnel data are of questionable relevance. If an employee is habitually late to work but consistently produces more and better-quality products than coworkers, is the employee a poor performer? Personnel measures may also be unreliable, since some supervisors record absenteeism or tardiness more carefully than others. Personnel data should be used as a measure of performance only when a clear link can be made between the measure (for example, tardiness) and actual job effectiveness, such as the delay of the start of business as a result of an employee's tardiness.

Performance Tests Performance tests are work samples or simulations under standardized conditions. For example, telephone operators may all receive the same set of scripted calls and be evaluated on speed, accuracy, and courtesy of service. Pilots fly periodic "check rides" in flight simulators to assess their ability to handle both routine and emergency procedures. Performance tests are useful when it is difficult to collect comparable or uncontaminated performance data in any other way, but they suffer from three major problems. First, they tend to be deficient, since only some aspects of a job can be realistically simulated. Second, if employees know that they are being tested on their job effectiveness, they are likely to work very hard to perform the test well. Performance tests then become a measure not of typical performance but of maximum employee capability. The final problem is that of practicality. Many jobs simply do not lend themselves to this kind of assessment, and for those that do, performance tests are generally expensive and time consuming to develop and implement.

Business Unit Performance Measures The above objective measures are seldom useful for managers. However, the performance of upper-level managers and executives is sometimes assessed by objective measures of the performance of the business unit that they head. Measures might include stock price, return on equity, profit, or market share. Clearly, these measures can be contaminated by economic factors beyond the manager's control.

Each type of objective measure has its own strengths and weaknesses. For instance, objective measures have the advantages of being free from the types of errors and biases that plague subjective measures. However, objective measures seldom capture the individual's total contribution to the organization. Measures of quantity, quality, attendance, and even profit may represent important dimensions of performance but ignore dimensions such as cooperation or willingness to contribute in ways that go beyond the job description. Most organizations use subjective measures of performance either to supplement or to replace objective measures in the appraisal system.

Subjective Measures

Because they rely on human judgment, subjective measures are prone to the rating errors discussed earlier. Most performance appraisal systems place heavy emphasis on subjective ratings of performance. One study reported that among ninety-six police departments in major cities, nearly 90 percent used supervisory ratings as their primary performance appraisal tool.[36] Anyone who has the opportunity to observe an employee's performance, including superiors, peers, subordinates, and the employees themselves, can make subjective ratings. For the vast majority of organizations, however, it is the immediate supervisor who judges performance. Some of the advantages and disadvantages of using other sources of performance judgments are considered later in this section.

Unlike objective measures, subjective judgments can be used even when the employee does not produce a measurable physical product. Subjective ratings can be used to measure the behavior or personal traits of employees, as well as results. The major problem with subjective measures of performance is that the raters have to observe and evaluate job-related behavior. Raters may not have the chance to observe relevant behavior, and even if they do, their ratings may be biased. Several different types of subjective measures can be used. Generally, they can be classified as either comparative procedures (ranking) or assessments against absolute standards (rating).

Comparative Procedures Subjective comparison of the overall work performance of individual employees can yield a rank ordering of employees from best to worst. Three kinds of comparative procedures are used in performance appraisals: ranking, paired comparisons, and forced distributions.

Ranking When ranking is used, employees are compared directly against one another. Ranking is easy to explain, understand, and use. It is generally not time consuming and is less expensive than other evaluation techniques. The simplest ranking procedure is **straight ranking,** in which the evaluator arranges employees in order from best to worst, on the basis of their overall performance. First, the best employee is identified, then the second best, and so on until the worst employee is assigned the lowest rank.

In **paired comparison ranking,** all possible pairs of employees are formed. The evaluator indicates which individual in each pair is the better performer. An employee's rank is determined by the number of times that he or she is chosen as the better performer in a pair. The person chosen most often is ranked first. Use of this method requires the comparison of many pairs even when the total number of employees is not large. The formula for the number of possible pairs of employees is $[n(n-1)]/2$, where n = the number of employees. For example, if there are ten employees in a work group, $10(9)/2 = 45$ judgments must be made. In the case of twenty employees, 190 pairs must be compared. Paired comparison ranking is more complicated than straight ranking, but the process is believed to result in more consistent, reliable ranks than the straight ranking approach.

Forced Distribution When using a **forced distribution method,** the evaluator has to place a certain percentage of employees into each of several performance categories. For example, the categories might be set up so that 5 percent of the employees must be evaluated as unsatisfactory, 15 percent as fair, 50 percent as satisfactory, 20 percent as good, and 10 percent as outstanding. These judgments are usually based on an overall assessment of the employees' performance. Examples of performance levels and distribution targets in a forced distribution procedure are presented in Table 11.4.

Advantages and Disadvantages of Comparative Procedures Comparative procedures are easy to explain and use, help in making promotion and merit raise decisions, and serve as controls for leniency, severity, and central tendency errors. They have a number of disadvantages, however. Employees are evaluated according to their overall performance. The comparisons are highly subjective opinions, which the evaluator might have difficulty supporting with evidence. Comparative procedures provide no clue as to the absolute difference in perfor-

TABLE 11.4 Forced Distribution Appraisal Method

Performance Level	*Distribution Target*
Level 1. Employee is below acceptable performance standards.	5% of unit
Level 2. Employee meets acceptable performance standard but has room for improvement.	15% of unit
Level 3. Employee shows a uniformly good level of performance.	50% of unit
Level 4. Employee shows a very high level of performance.	20% of unit
Level 5. Employee consistently shows outstanding performance.	10% of unit

Each of the employees in a work unit is allocated to one of the performance levels shown in the table. Associated with each performance level is a "distribution target" that should be used in allocating employees to the various levels.

mance among employees. With comparative methods, the ordering of employees depends on the size and character of the particular work group. One group may consist of thirty employees whereas a second group may have only five members. It is impossible to determine whether the best employee in the first group is equal to the best individual in the second. Comparative methods also require that one evaluator know the performance of every employee in a unit. In large groups, this may not be possible.

Because comparative procedures generally do not focus on specific job-related behaviors, they risk legal challenge. The courts have ruled against companies when comparative methods have had an adverse impact on minorities or women. Another problem is that comparative methods are not useful for employee development. An employee learns how he or she compares with other employees, but this feedback does not indicate how to improve performance. Comparative procedures may foster competition and resentment among employees. After all, only one person can receive the top ranking.

A major problem with forced distributions is that a group of employees may not conform to the predefined distribution used in the procedure; in highly selected groups, a majority of employees may truly be outstanding. Employees are often unhappy with forced distribution systems because most employees believe they are above average.[37] A forced distribution system allows only a few to receive the ratings that most think they deserve. Supervisors generally dislike forced distribution systems because they limit the rater's discretion. Of course, in most cases, it was the inappropriate use of this rater "discretion" that caused the organization to institute the forced distribution system in the first place.

Despite their drawbacks, comparative methods can be a useful component of an overall performance appraisal system. They are useful in forcing evaluators to make distinctions between employees when differential rewards are to be distributed. In most situations, it may be best to combine comparative methods with other forms of performance assessment, such as the absolute standard approaches discussed below.

Absolute Standards Instead of comparing an employee's performance with that of fellow employees, an appraisal system can be based on absolute performance standards for the job. Each employee is evaluated against the standards. **Absolute standards** facilitate comparison of employees from different departments. Performance is measured on a number of specific dimensions so that employees can be given more helpful feedback than is generated by comparative procedures. Variations of the absolute standards technique include graphic rating scales, weighted checklists, the critical incidents technique, behaviorally anchored rating scales, and behavioral observation scales.

Graphic Rating Scales **Graphic rating scales** are the most widely used evaluation technique. The rater evaluates an employee on each of several performance dimensions using a continuum made up of clearly defined scale points. Figure 11.5

FIGURE 11.5 Examples of Typical Graphic Rating Scales

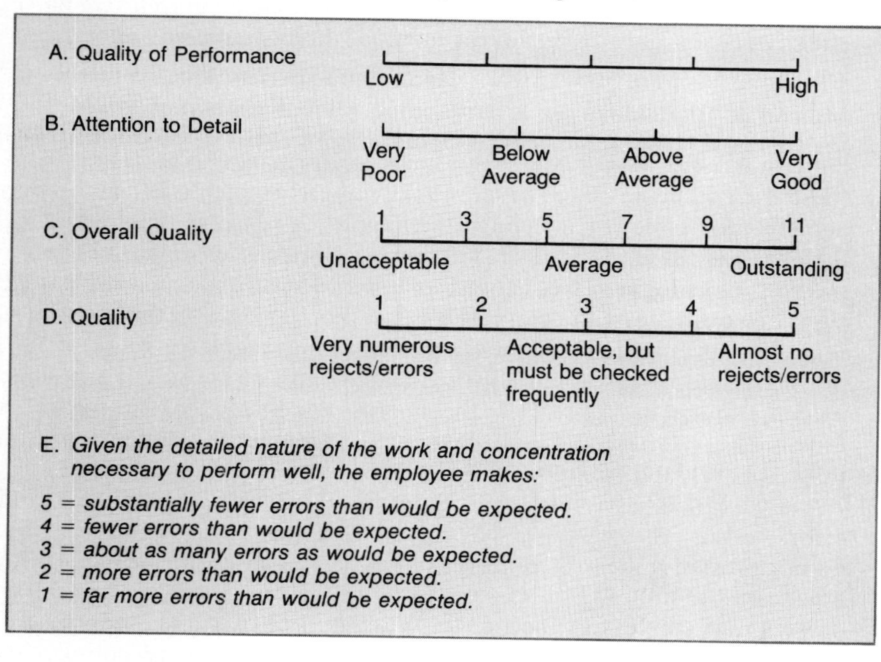

gives some examples of graphic rating scales for measuring performance along the dimension of quality. The rating dimensions should be based on a careful job analysis.

In the graphic rating scale method, the rater describes an employee as falling at some point on a performance continuum, such as unsatisfactory, average, or outstanding on each dimension. The scale points can be assigned scores (e.g., ranging from 5 points for outstanding to 0 points for unsatisfactory), and a total score for an employee can be computed by summing the ratings across all dimensions rated. If some characteristics are more important than others, the rating on these dimensions can be multiplied by an appropriate weight before the total is calculated.

Graphic rating scales have several advantages. They are relatively easy to develop and use, more than one performance dimension can be included, employees' scores can be compared, and the method is well accepted by raters. If properly developed for relevance and clarity, graphic rating scales can be just as reliable and valid as more complicated techniques. On the other hand, this method offers little protection from rating errors, such as leniency, severity, central tendency, and halo errors. Graphic rating scales are often criticized because the performance dimensions on which the employee is rated and the scale anchors used in making the rating may be ill defined and vague. In Figure 11.5, scale A does not define the dimension being rated, and the scale anchors are ambiguous and uninformative. Scales D and E provide more definition of the dimension and levels of performance assessed.

Mixed standard scales represent an effort to make graphic rating scales more effective (see Figure 11.6). In this method, three statements are written to define low, medium, and high levels of performance along each dimension.[38] In Figure 11.6, for example, item 7 represents good performance on a dimension that might be called "efficiency of work." Item 5 represents average performance on this dimension, and item 2 represents poor performance. The rating form presents these three items in mixed order, along with items from other dimensions. Raters complete the scales by deciding if the employee is worse than, equal to, or better than each of the performance statements. A special scoring procedure, shown at the bottom of Figure 11.6, is used to assign a performance score for each dimension. For example, if the employee is rated better than all three of the statements representing a particular dimension, he or she receives a score of 7. If the employee is rated worse than all three statements, a score of 1 is assigned. In the example shown in Figure 11.6, the employee is better than the "poor" statement for dimension 2, equal to the "average" statement for dimension 2, and worse than on the "good" statement, for a score of 4.

Mixed standard scales are supposed to reduce halo, leniency, and severity errors because the scale items are mixed randomly throughout the rating form and do not present a clear hierarchy from good to bad performance. Unfortunately, however, it is still easy to bias one's ratings. Mixed standard scales also allow the detection of careless or inconsistent ratings. For example, suppose a rater indicated than an employee was worse than the statement representing a low level of

FIGURE 11.6 A Mixed Standard Scale and Scoring Key with Example Ratings for One Employee

Dimension Represented[a]		Item	Employee Rating[b]
2(A)	1.	Has normal self-confidence, with only occasional uncertainty. Usually open and self-assured.	0
1(P)	2.	Some lack of efficiency. May take too much time to complete assignments and sometimes does not really finish them.	+
3(G)	3.	Written and oral reports are well formulated and thorough. They rarely need additional explanation.	+
2(P)	4.	He/she is shy and uncertain. Avoids situations that require the taking of a strong position.	+
1(A)	5.	He/she is efficient enough, usually gets through assignments in reasonable time.	+
3(P)	6.	Sometimes reports are so incomplete and poorly organized they are of little value and must be done over.	+
1(G)	7.	He/she is quick and efficient, able to keep work on-schedule. Really gets going on a new task.	0
2(G)	8.	Behaves confidently. Reacts in all situations without hesitation.	−
3(A)	9.	Reports are useful and meaningful, but often require additional explanation.	+

Scoring Key:

	Statements			Score
	Good	Average	Poor	
Ratings	+	+	+	7
	0	+	+	6
	−	+	+	5
	−	0	+	4
	−	−	+	3
	−	−	0	2
	−	−	−	1

Ratings by Dimension for Employee:

	G	A	P	Score
Dimension 1	0	+	+	6
Dimension 2	−	0	+	4
Dimension 3	+	+	+	7

[a]Numbers 1-3 indicate dimension that the statement represents. Letters in parentheses characterize statement: G = good performance, A = average performance, and P = poor performance. This information would not be provided on the actual rating form.

[b]Ratings are such that "+" = employee better than the statement, "0" = employee same as the statement, and "−" = employee worse than the statement.

Source: Adapted from F. Blanz and E. E. Ghiselli, "The Mixed Standard Scale: A New Rating System," *Personnel Psychology,* Vol. 25, 1972, pp. 185–199. Reprinted by permission.

work efficiency but also rated the employee equal to the statement representing average efficiency. Under the mixed standard procedure, this inconsistent evaluation of the employee could be identified and verified with the rater.

Weighted Checklists In another approach to appraisal, a rater is given a list of job-related characteristics or behaviors and is asked to check the items that are typical of a particular employee. When such a **weighted checklist** is developed, job experts indicate how good or poor each behavior is. These goodness weights are then used in summing ratings to determine the overall performance of an employee. The rater, however, is not made aware of the weights associated with each item. An example of a weighted checklist is given in Figure 11.7.

A variant of this technique is the **forced-choice system,** a procedure developed specifically to reduce leniency error. It is often easy for a rater using a standard weighted checklist to identify the most favorable items. Raters who wish to be lenient can check the items that make an employee look good, whether or not they represent the behavior of the employee. In the forced-choice procedure, items are assembled in pairs, and in each pair, the rater must choose the item that is more characteristic of the employee. The pairs are designed so that both items *appear* equally good or bad to the rater, but only one is actually related to actual job performance. Here is a forced-choice item pair for the job of college professor:

1. Lectures with confidence

2. Keeps the interest and attention of the class[39]

Only items that are important for job performance are scored in determining the performance level of the employee. In the example above, item 1 is socially desirable but has little to do with how effectively a professor actually teaches, whereas item 2 is truly diagnostic of good teaching.

Forced-choice items help control intentional leniency because the rater does not know which item to check to make the employee look good. Drawbacks are that the items are difficult to develop, and raters dislike the approach. Frustrated that they are not free to describe the employee as they want to, they may feel that they have been "tricked" into doing a proper evaluation. Finally, the results of the forced-choice approach allow only overall ("excellent," "average," "below average") feedback to employees. Because the rater is unaware of the key he or she cannot tell employees what behavior led to the overall rating or how they might change their behavior to improve performance.

Critical Incident Technique When performance appraisal is to be based on critical incidents, the evaluator keeps a log for each employee, recording behaviors and performance incidents that are particularly effective or ineffective. Incidents are recorded for each employee as soon as possible after they occur. At the end of the evaluation period, this log is used to evaluate the performance of the employee. The **critical incident technique** is time consuming for the evaluators, and it may be hard to quantify or structure the incidents into a final evaluation. However, since most evaluators have trouble remembering the full range of employee behavior over the rating period, a critical incident log can be very useful

FIGURE 11.7 Weighted Checklist for Supervisory Job, with Example Evaluation of One Supervisor

Instructions:
Check those statements that represent the typical actions of the employee.

	Statement	Value[a]
____	Acts decisively when encountering problems	4.9
____	Is fair to all subordinates in his/her promotion decisions	5.0
____	Provides temporary solutions to problems that keep on appearing	3.0
____	Assesses the mood of subordinates before pursuing a subject that would damage relationships	3.9
____	Evaluates performance once or twice a year	4.1
____	Is unwilling to point out subordinates' poor work performance	2.2
____	Conducts detailed discussions with workers to solve problems	4.6
____	Checks subordinates' work thoroughly and is sharp at finding errors	4.2
____	Gives merit increment to a poor performer	2.0
____	Carries out the policies of the company without regard to individual welfare or circumstances	2.3
____	Signs subordinates' work without carefully checking it	2.0
____	Is unable to provide guidelines for making decisions when faced with a problem	2.3
____	Maintains very good relations with other supervisors in the division	5.0
____	Shows concern for employee welfare but does not act on it	2.7

Performance Score for Employee = (4.9 + 3.9 + 4.1 + 2.2 + 2.0 + 2.0 + 5.0) = 24.1

[a]High values indicate that the statement represents good performance. These values would not be included on the actual rating form.

Source: James B. Shaw, Abdul Jalil bin Ismail, and Cynthia D. Fisher, "A Cognitive Categorization Approach to Managerial Performance Appraisal: Analysis of the Singapore Manager" (paper presented at the First International Conference on Personnel/Human Resource Management, National University of Singapore, December 1987). Reprinted by permission.

in supporting any of the more structured subjective methods described in this chapter. The log also helps the supervisor provide specific examples when explaining ratings to subordinates.

Behaviorally Anchored Rating Scales Some appraisal systems use graphic rating scales on which anchor points are defined in considerable detail, using examples of behavior that represent particular levels of performance. Such a **behaviorally anchored rating scale (BARS)** is developed for each of several important

FIGURE 11.8 Example of Behaviorally Anchored Rating Scale for the Performance Dimension of Problem Solving/Decision Making

Scale point	Behavioral anchor
7	Could be expected to conduct detailed talks with workers to solve technical problems
6	Could be expected to take problem to a higher level when problem is beyond his/her own powers to handle
5	Could be expected to solve problems as they arise
4	Could be expected to provide temporary solutions to problems that keep appearing
3	Could be expected to make decisions without considering reactions from subordinates
2	Could be expected to give personal feelings priority when making decisions
1	Could be expected to refuse to make decisions when needed

Source: Adapted from James B. Shaw, Abdul Jalil bin Ismail, and Cynthia D. Fisher, "A Cognitive Categorization Approach to Managerial Performance Appraisal: Analysis of the Singapore Manager" (paper presented at the First International Conference on Personnel/Human Resource Management, National University of Singapore, December 1987). Reprinted by permission.

performance dimensions. Raters are asked to mark the scale point that best represents the performance of an employee. Figure 11.8 illustrates a BARS developed for the performance dimension "problem solving/decision making" for the job of midlevel manager.

The development of BARS is a time-consuming and costly process that involves the efforts of many people. The steps are as follows:

1. A group of knowledgeable employees (perhaps including both workers and supervisors) identifies the important dimensions that make up effective performance. This group writes a clear definition for each dimension.
2. A second group comes up with as many critical incidents as it can to illustrate effective, average, and ineffective performance for each dimension.

3. A third group is given the list of dimensions and a stack of cards, each containing one of the critical incidents. The task of each member of this group is to assign each critical incident to the dimension it seems to characterize. This is called retranslation. Critical incidents that are not placed in the same dimension by a majority of the retranslation group are discarded as unclear.
4. A fourth group rates the level of performance each remaining incident represents. For example, suppose that the incident "smiles and greets customers" has been reliably sorted into the "customer service" dimension of performance. Members of the fourth group then rate this incident as to whether it represents outstanding, above-average, average, or below-average performance. The mean and standard deviation of these ratings are computed for each critical incident. Items are discarded if group members are unable to agree on the performance level represented. From the remaining items, incidents are chosen to anchor each point along the BARS. Each anchor is worded "Could be expected to . . ." so that it can be selected by a rater who has observed similar, but not precisely identical, behavior in an employee.
5. As a final step, the rating scale is pilot-tested in the organization.

Note that BARS can be developed with only two groups rather than four. In this case, the first group carries out steps 1 and 2, and the second group completes steps 3 and 4.

BARS are time consuming to develop because the development process involves so many people. Interestingly, this potential weakness is also the method's major advantage. The employees who are to be rated with the scales may have helped develop them. Their involvement increases the chance that the BARS will be a valid measure of performance and that the employees will accept its use. Since BARS are necessarily job related, they are less vulnerable to legal challenges than many other appraisal methods. Use of this method may not be practical, however. Each job category requires its own BARS, which may not be possible in many organizations, either for economic reasons or because there are too few employees in a particular job to make the development technique feasible.

It would seem that BARS should be superior to other appraisal techniques. However, some research has concluded that the use of BARS does not always reduce rating errors and in some cases introduces a new form of bias not found in other forms of rating.[40] Even so, BARS still have the advantage of increasing employee involvement in the appraisal development process. In constructing BARS, employees and supervisors may learn a great deal about the nature of the job and how it should be performed.

Behavioral Observation Scales Raters who use BARS may find it difficult to select a *single* scale point to represent the performance of an employee who sometimes engages in some very positive behaviors but at other times performs poorly.

FIGURE 11.9 Example of Behavior Observation Scale for the Performance Dimension Communicating with Subordinates

	Almost Never				Almost Always
Puts up notices on bulletin board when new policies or procedures are implemented	1	2	3	4	5
Maintains eye contact when talking to employees	1	2	3	4	5
Uses both written memos and verbal discussion when giving instructions	1	2	3	4	5
Discusses changes in policies or procedures with employees before implementing them	1	2	3	4	5
Writes memos that are clear, concise, and easy to understand	1	2	3	4	5

Total Performance Level	
Below adequate	*5 – 9*
Adequate	*10 – 14*
Good	*15 – 19*
Excellent	*20 +*

Source: Adapted from James B. Shaw, Abdul Jalil bin Ismail, and Cynthia D. Fisher, "A Cognitive Categorization Approach to Managerial Performance Appraisal: Analysis of the Singapore Manager" (paper presented at the First International Conference on Personnel/Human Resource Management, National University of Singapore, December 1987). Reprinted by permission.

Behavioral observation scales (BOS) were developed partly in response to this problem (see Figure 11.9).

To develop BOS, job experts first identify groups of similar behavioral incidents and form them into performance dimensions. In Figure 11.9, several behavioral incidents have been grouped to form a performance dimension called "communicating with subordinates." Job experts evaluate the behavioral incidents to make sure that they are relevant to the dimension and important for distinguishing between successful and unsuccessful employees. If experts cannot agree about an incident's relevance, it is discarded. A five-point frequency of occurrence scale is attached to each incident, which raters use to indicate how frequently each employee engages in the behavior.[41]

Behavioral observation scales have many advantages. They are based on a careful analysis of the job. The content validity of BOS incidents is directly evaluated, and they are likely to be found acceptable to the courts. BOS can also be helpful in providing performance feedback to employees. Because they use frequency scales rather than simply indicating the one behavior that best represents an employee's performance, BOS may provide a greater depth of performance information than BARS. Research, however, has not shown BOS to be clearly superior.[42]

Other Raters of Employee Performance In most organizations, subjective ratings of employee performance are provided by supervisors. However, there are several other potential sources for performance ratings, including employees themselves, peers, and subordinates. Each of these sources has its own advantages and disadvantages.

Self-Evaluation Employees are sometimes asked to evaluate themselves. It seems logical that individuals would be the best judges of their own performance, particularly if supervisors cannot observe them on a regular basis. If employees are asked to evaluate themselves, they may respond by becoming more motivated and involved in the evaluation process.

Self-ratings tend to show more leniency error than supervisor ratings, although halo errors are lower.[43] Self-evaluations have become popular as a part of the management by objectives process, in which the supervisor and the subordinate together set goals for future performance. (This process is considered later in this chapter.) Self-evaluation seems most appropriate when it is used as an employee development tool rather than to support administrative decisions.[44] It may also serve as an important input into a supervisory appraisal. An employee's self-appraisal may provide important information of which the supervisor was not aware. The supervisor can then factor this information into his or her performance ratings of the employee.

Peer Evaluation Compared with supervisory ratings, peer evaluations are more stable over time, can tap more dimensions of performance, are better able to distinguish effort from performance, and focus more on task-relevant abilities. One study has concluded that peer ratings may be the most accurate evaluations of employee performance.[45] Peer evaluations can be particularly useful when supervisors do not have the opportunity to observe an individual's performance, but fellow employees do.

Peers sometimes resist evaluating one another. An individual may not want to give a fellow employee a favorable evaluation for fear of looking inferior in comparison. On the other hand, an individual may not want to jeopardize a good working relationship by giving an unfavorable rating to a colleague. Friendship bias may lead an employee to rate his or her friends higher than other employees.

A survey of 218 industrial employees who had used a peer evaluation system for more than a year found a high degree of user acceptance.[46] It seems, however, that peer evaluations, like self-evaluations, are best used for employee development rather than for administrative decisions. The same survey found that users were more favorable in their attitudes toward peer appraisals that were used for developmental rather than evaluative purposes.

When teamwork, participation, and cohesiveness are part of the organization's culture, peer evaluations can work well. In organizations that are competitive and have a low level of trust among employees, peer evaluations may be little more than a way for employees to enhance themselves by belittling their fellow employees.

Subordinate Evaluation Evaluation by subordinates may provide valuable information. They know how well a supervisor performs with respect to leading, organizing, planning, delegating, and communicating. Subordinates, however, may inflate their rating of a supervisor, especially if they think that the supervisor will be able to discern who has given a particular rating. Complete anonymity is essential if this technique is to provide valid ratings. Open channels of communication and an abundance of trust between supervisors and subordinates are also needed if this type of evaluation is to be worthwhile. Like self- and peer evaluations, subordinate evaluation is useful for development but is not recommended as a tool for making administrative decisions.

Which Source to Use Supervisors, peers, subordinates, and employees themselves typically differ in their ability to appraise various dimensions of performance. These raters observe different behaviors and may interpret them with divergent standards. Consider the efforts of a ratee to influence another person. In the case of a superior, persuasive behaviors may be displayed. With peers, negotiation may occur, and with subordinates, orders may be given. Thus, each source has access to unique information about performance.[47] No one source has been found to be most effective. Perhaps the best approach is to use as many different sources as possible to maximize the breadth of information and cancel out biases unique to a particular source. Multiple sources can be used regardless of which specific subjective method of measuring performance is adopted.

Management by Objectives (MBO)

Management by objectives (MBO) is a very popular individualized method of evaluating the performance of managers and professionals. In several surveys of performance appraisal techniques, more than half of the organizations responding used some kind of MBO procedure to evaluate managers' performance.[48] The MBO process involves three steps:

1. The employee meets with his or her superior and agrees on a set of goals to achieve during a specified period of time. Goals should be quantifiable and should include an agreed-on target. Thus, instead of a vague goal of improving customer satisfaction, the goal might be to reduce customer returns to no more than 3 percent of the dollar amount of sales, that is, no more than $300 in returns for every $10,000 in sales.
2. Throughout this period, progress toward the goals is monitored, though the employee is left generally free to determine how to go about meeting goals.

3. A the end of the period, the employee and superior again meet to evaluate whether the goals were achieved and together decide on a new set of goals.

MBO has several advantages. Observable, results-oriented goals replace the difficult-to-observe, subjective traits that are sometimes used in other measures of performance. MBO can encourage innovation and creativity, since employees are free to determine how they will meet their goals. This approach can also lead to performance improvement, particularly if goals are specific, moderately difficult, and accepted by the employees. A "coordination advantage" can also result: top managers set goals with those immediately below them in the hierarchy, who in turn help set the goals of those below them. This cascading effect may help coordinate the activities of the entire organization, with all employees engaged in activities related to the overall objectives and strategy of the organization.

Not all MBO programs are successful. Some major reasons for failure are presented in Table 11.5. MBO is a difficult activity, requiring training and a large commitment of time and effort by top management and all other parts of the organization. Even when the method is used successfully, it is difficult to compare the performance of employees, since each has different goals and levels of goal accomplishment. Employees who have easy goals may seem to be better employees than those who have more difficult goals, since the first group is more likely to achieve its goals. Another problem can occur when managers, in an attempt to please *their* superiors, persuade employees to take on goals that are virtually impossible to achieve. Similarly, top management may set unrealistically high goals for a particular department. Management must set goals that are consistent with a unit's particular abilities and its importance to overall organizational success. Managers also need to guard against viewing agreed-upon goals as "set in stone." Circumstances in any organization can change, and a certain amount of adaptability and flexibility in MBO is both legitimate and necessary.

TABLE 11.5 Factors Contributing to MBO Program Failure

Lack of management support
Inadequate training of managers in how to use MBO
Easy goals
Setting unrealistically difficult goals
Lack of flexibility in setting goals for different units
Not altering goals to meet changes in circumstances
Pseudo-participation
Overemphasizing goal attainment
Excessive paperwork

Source: From *Performance Appraisal and Review* by Stephen J. Carroll and Craig E. Schneier, 1982, p. 150. Copyright 1982 by Scott, Foresman and Company. Reprinted by permission of the author.

Employees' participation in the goal-setting process is generally seen as an advantage of MBO. Sometimes, however, employees are accepting the goals desired by their supervisor, who simply goes through the motions of letting employees help set goals.[49] This problem is especially likely to occur when an organization has traditionally had an authoritarian managerial culture, and supervisors have not been adequately trained to adopt a more participative management style. Problems also arise when MBO goal attainment becomes the sole criterion on which merit pay and other reward decisions are made. Finally, many managers resent the extra paperwork generated by MBO programs, which may reduce their commitment to ensuring the success of the effort.

ENHANCING THE MEASUREMENT OF EMPLOYEE PERFORMANCE

In developing a performance appraisal system, particularly one that involves subjective evaluations of performance, a number of serious problems must be overcome. Training evaluators and giving them feedback are ways to improve raters' ability to make accurate appraisals.

Training Evaluators

Several rater training programs have been developed that aim to help evaluators produce reliable and accurate performance ratings. Programs can generally be classified into three types: rater error training, frame-of-reference training, and information processing training.

Rater Error Training People can be taught how to reduce rating errors, such as leniency, severity, central tendency, and halo errors.[50] In **rater error training (RET),** evaluators view examples of the common errors and receive suggestions on how to avoid them. RET has been found effective in reducing common rating errors. Several critics, however, have argued that error reduction often comes at the expense of rating accuracy.[51] For example, if a supervisor has many high-performing employees, all of them should be rated high. If the supervisor decides to avoid the appearance of leniency error by lowering the ratings of some employees, the evaluations become less accurate.

Frame-of-Reference Training Attempts have been made to reduce errors by developing a common frame of reference among raters for evaluating performance.[52] Examples of actual employee behavior in the organization are used to develop norms for good and poor performance. Raters are then trained to observe these behaviors and use them as the standard against which to judge the performance of employees.

In a review of the effectiveness of rater training programs, four of seven studies using **frame-of-reference training (FOR)** were reported to have reduced leniency error. Only three of ten studies using FOR training to reduce halo error reported positive results.[53] A more recent study focused on implementation problems associated with FOR training, including procedures to identify incidents and then understand differences between supervisors and subordinates with respect to appropriate frames of reference.[54] It appears that many of the implementation issues associated with that FOR training can be overcome, but that FOR training is most useful in improving rating accuracy when combined with other methods.

Information Processing Approaches Some training efforts focus on how performance raters observe, store, recall, and use information. In a 1980 study, raters were trained to avoid eight different "errors of observation."[55] Their accuracy in observing and remembering behavior improved, but no measures of rating error or rating accuracy were taken. A more recent study introduced two information processing methods of rater training that did increase rater accuracy.[56] **Observation training** (similar to the approach used in the 1980 study) focused on helping raters to improve the way they observed the behavior of employees and to identify important performance activities. **Decision-making training** introduced raters to good strategies for use in decision making and helped them identify mistakes in inference that supervisors often make when appraising performance. (Given several accurate pieces of information, a supervisor may make inappropriate inferences about them and their relation to one another and end up making a bad decision.)

Which Training Method Is Best? Since rater error training and frame-of-reference training have had limited success, information processing approaches may be the most promising methods for improving rating accuracy. However, regardless of which training method is used, raters who are actively involved in their training programs are more likely to learn to reduce rating errors. Involvement may be in the form of group discussions or of practice-rating an employee whose performance has been videotaped. Practice rating is followed by feedback on what the most accurate rating would have been. Both practice and feedback seem to be essential for effective training. Neither discussion nor lecture without practice and feedback has been shown to reduce rating errors.[57]

Feedback to Evaluators

Since feedback is an important component of successful training programs, rating the raters may be a good way to reduce systematic bias.[58] One approach is to structure an evaluator's own performance appraisal so that it pays attention to how well and accurately he or she rates the performance of others. That is, supervisors should be assessed on how well they appraise their subordinates. This approach should enhance motivation for the rating process and let raters know what others think of their evaluations. Another possibility is to require that supervisors' appraisal ratings be endorsed by their own superiors. This is a common practice. The superiors provide quality control by helping prevent extreme leniency, severity, or central tendency errors in the ratings.

FEEDBACK OF RESULTS: THE PERFORMANCE APPRAISAL INTERVIEW

One of the potentially most important uses of appraisals is providing performance feedback to employees. Most theories of work motivation point out that before employees can improve their performance they must know how well they are currently doing.

In the usual situation, neither the supervisor nor the employee looks forward to the appraisal interview. It can be an uncomfortable and anxiety-provoking experience for both parties. One would expect a supervisor to be apprehensive about discussing a negative evaluation with an employee, but most managers see little or no practical value in conducting performance appraisal interviews, no matter what the evaluation.[59] Conducting a good interview requires a great deal of effort and skill on the part of the supervisor. This section considers several types of feedback interviews, problems that can occur in giving feedback, and ways to improve the process.

Types of Feedback Interviews

The feedback interview is a discussion between the supervisor and the employee concerning the employee's past performance and how that performance can be improved in the future. The three main approaches to feedback discussion are often referred to as tell and sell, tell and listen, and problem solving.

Tell and Sell In a **tell-and-sell feedback interview,** the supervisor tells the employee how good or bad the employee's performance has been and then attempts to persuade the employee to accept this judgment. The employee has no input into the evaluation. Because it is very direct and one-sided, the tell-and-sell interview can lead to defensiveness, resentment, and frustration on the part of the subordinate. It fails to recognize the possibility that the employee may have information pertinent to the evaluation—information of which the supervisor is unaware. The employee may not accept the results of the interview and may not be committed to achieving the goals that are set. This may lead to poor performance in the future.

For new employees or those who have little desire for participation, the tell-and-sell interview can be effective in providing feedback and improving performance. New employees often feel unqualified to judge their own performance and prefer to be told how they are doing and what is expected of them.[60]

Tell and Listen In the **tell-and-listen approach** to the feedback interview, the supervisor tells the employee what has been right and wrong with the employee's past performance but then gives the employee a chance to react. The extent of the subordinate's participation in the interview can vary widely. The subordinate may simply be given an opportunity to react to the supervisor's statements or may be permitted to offer a full self-appraisal, challenging the supervisor's assessment. There is evidence that subordinates prefer even very limited participation to none at all.[61]

Problem Solving The employee has much more control over the **problem-solving interview.** Employees evaluate their own performance and set their own goals for future performance. The supervisor is primarily a helper and colleague rather than a judge, and proffers observations and advice in a noncritical manner. An active and open dialogue ensues, in which goals for improvement are established mutually. The problem-solving interview is more difficult for the supervisor than the other types of interviews, but it is more likely to result in employee acceptance and commitment to the established goals. Training can help supervisors learn to conduct such interviews effectively. A drawback of problem-solving interviews is that some employees may prefer a more direct approach. Some may be hesitant to discuss poor performance with their supervisor, particularly if personnel decisions such as salary increases will be based on the interview.

To by-pass some of the difficulties associated with the tell-and-sell and problem-solving interviews, a mixed approach has been recommended. The mixed interview uses the tell-and-sell approach to communicate administrative decisions, whereas the problem-solving approach is reserved for discussing employee development issues and planning for future performance.

Problems with the Appraisal Interview

Two major problems complicate the process of giving feedback to subordinates. The first has to do with disagreement about the rated level of performance and the second with the use of the appraisal interview for multiple purposes.

Disagreement and Defensiveness Supervisors and subordinates often disagree about how well the subordinate has performed. One recent review of studies found that the average correlation between subordinate and supervisor ratings was only 0.22.[62] Subordinates in the United States usually rate their performance higher than do supervisors. In only one of the eighteen studies reviewed were supervisors' ratings of subordinate performance higher than the subordinates' ratings of their own performance.

Even when supervisor and subordinate agree on the level of performance, they often disagree about its *causes*. Supervisors tend to feel that subordinates are personally responsible for their performance, especially poor performance. On the other hand, subordinates often (sometimes legitimately) blame poor performance on situational factors such as bad luck, lack of resources, or insufficient cooperation from others.[63]

Disagreement on either level of performance or cause sets the stage for subordinate defensiveness. The subordinate makes excuses for past performance and argues with the supervisor's rating. The subordinate becomes unable to listen and learn from any legitimate points the supervisor may have. Note that defensiveness is not restricted to employees who receive a low performance rating. One study found that subordinates who were judged "satisfactory" also became upset because they had expected higher ratings.[64]

Multiple Purposes Appraisal interviews are often used to review past performance, convey administrative decisions, plan for future work goals, and discuss the employee's career goals and development needs.[65] This is a great deal to accomplish in a single meeting. In addition, supervisors must play two incompatible roles in a multipurpose interview. For merit raise decisions to have credibility, they must be clearly linked to past performance. Thus, it is wise to couple these two purposes in the appraisal interview. However, conventional wisdom holds that it is counterproductive to discuss future goals and development in that same interview. Criticism of past work or announcement of a smaller-than-expected raise may make the subordinate defensive and unwilling to address performance improvement issues seriously. Thus, a separate interview a few weeks later has been recommended for developmental issues. This recommendation, however, which is accepted as gospel by many HR practitioners, is based on only a single study conducted in 1965.[66]

More recent research has challenged this view.[67] Two studies in field settings found that discussing salary issues did not hurt the developmental aspects of a feedback interview and, in fact, had some positive effects. Including salary discussion in the appraisal interview may force the supervisor to give more specific feedback in order to back up the decision. Salary discussion can also energize the interview and elicit more subordinate participation. Perhaps, with sufficient skill and tact on the part of the supervisor, both administrative and developmental purposes can be served in the same appraisal interview. A compromise position may be wisest: the supervisor can plan to talk about past performance, merit pay decisions, future performance goals, and development in a single interview; if the subordinate becomes defensive or upset after discussing past performance and salary, the supervisor can postpone any discussion of the future.

Impression Management in the Feedback Process Recent research has emphasized the role of impression management in the feedback process.[68] **Impression management** refers to behaviors by an employee designed to control how he or she appears to the supervisor. For example, impression management tactics could include (1) taking sole credit for positive events even when credit should be shared, (2) making the supervisor aware of your accomplishments, (3) arriving early or staying late to give the impression of being a hard worker, or (4) taking an interest in the supervisor's personal life and perhaps doing personal favors.[69]

Poorly performing employees use impression management strategies to minimize the amount of negative feedback they receive. For the employee, the goal is one of maintaining positive self-esteem. At the same time, such strategies on the part of the employee meet the needs of the supervisor, who generally has an underlying reluctance to give negative performance feedback. In any case, impression management tends to skew the appraisal and feedback interaction.[70]

Improving the Performance Appraisal Interview

Feedback is most effective in improving performance when it is specific, when it is accepted by the employee, and when it helps define clear goals for future performance.[71]

Feedback Specificity Feedback is particularly helpful if it comes from a behaviorally based appraisal instrument and if the performance rating is backed up with specific examples of good or poor performance. A critical incident log can be useful in providing this type of specific feedback. Specific feedback helps employees determine exactly what they should do differently to improve performance. Research has shown that subordinates prefer specific feedback in the appraisal interview, even if it concerns poor performance, to appraisals that contain only vague performance information.[72]

Subordinate Acceptance For feedback to be accepted by a subordinate, it must come from a credible, trustworthy source. Credibility is enhanced when the evaluator is seen as being knowledgeable about the subordinate's job, has had adequate opportunity to observe the behavior of the subordinate, and has clearly taken the time to prepare carefully for the appraisal interview. Research has shown that feedback is more likely to affect subsequent performance when it comes from a believable source.[73] In addition, feedback should be given often, and as soon as possible after both good and bad performance events, so that employees always know where they stand and can quickly take any necessary corrective action. The formal interview should be the culmination of the ongoing, continual process of informal performance feedback. Nothing in the annual appraisal interview should come as a surprise to the subordinate.

It may be particularly difficult for the subordinate to accept negative feedback. Destructive criticism and threats to the subordinate are ineffective and may cause subsequent performance to deteriorate.[74] Thus, the supervisor should discuss specific incidents of poor performance in a considerate, constructive way. Two studies have shown that when the supervisor attributes poor performance to situational causes, the subordinate is better able to accept negative feedback.[75] For example, a supervisor may note that a salesperson fell far below sales goals but also acknowledge that the economy was in a downturn (a possible external cause of poor performance). The supervisor can then proceed to discuss what the subordinate might do differently to improve performance even when economic conditions are poor. This approach will help minimize defensiveness on the part of the salesperson.

A number of studies support the notion that satisfaction with and acceptance of appraisal feedback are a function of the subordinate's contribution and participation in the discussion, for example, a problem-solving feedback interview.[76] Anything that moves the interview from an authoritarian boss-subordinate interaction to a discussion among two knowledgeable and committed individuals will enhance the acceptance of the results.

Setting Clear Goals The process of goal setting has already been discussed in the context of MBO and as a productivity-enhancing technique. Whatever appraisal system has been used, appraisal discussions should culminate in specific goals that focus the subordinate's attention on performance improvement. Later the supervisor should follow up on goal progress and give additional feedback when necessary to help the subordinate achieve the desired level of performance.

SUMMARY OF KEY POINTS

Performance appraisals can serve a strategic function by focusing employee efforts on the types of behaviors required for successful strategy implementation. Appraisals are also used (1) to make administrative decisions about employees, (2) to provide feedback for employee development, and (3) to evaluate HR policies and programs.

A good appraisal system should measure important job characteristics (relevancy), be free from extraneous or contaminating influences, and encompass all important aspects of the job (not be deficient). It should be reliable and avoid rating errors. Appraisal systems must be fair to minorities, women, and other protected groups. Appraisals must also be practical. Meeting all these criteria in one appraisal system is a challenge.

Performance measures can be characterized as objective or subjective. Objective and subjective measures can be used in combination. Subjective measures can compare employees with each other (ranking), or they can judge performance against absolute standards for the job (rating). A number of types of rating procedures can be used, including graphic rating scales, mixed standard rating scales, BARS, and BOS. Ratings may be obtained from subordinates, peers, or the employee being assessed, although most commonly the only rater is the employee's supervisor. An additional appraisal system, MBO, features joint superior and subordinate goal setting and performance appraisal against these individualized standards.

Performance appraisal is an important tool for motivating and improving employee performance. Unfortunately, its potential is seldom fully realized. Appraisals can be improved by careful development of an appropriate appraisal instrument, by training raters to use the system properly, and by providing feedback to raters as to how well they are performing their appraisal and development functions with their own subordinates. The annual performance appraisal interview is a valuable opportunity for the supervisor and subordinate to communicate about past performance, current concerns, and goals for the future. This meeting does not have to be an unpleasant confrontation and can enhance the relationship between the supervisor and the subordinate. When giving performance feedback to subordinates, supervisors must ensure that the feedback is credible, offers specific, constructive feedback accompanied by concrete examples of poor or good performance, allows an appropriate degree of participation, and results in performance goals for the future.

Questions for Discussion

1. What purposes can be served by performance appraisal?
2. What are the benefits to an organization of having a sound appraisal system?
3. How can an organization design a performance appraisal system or change one already in use to make it more resistant to legal challenge?
4. What types of errors characterize the performance appraisal process?
5. If you were an employee, which appraisal method would you want to be evaluated by?
6. What are some reasons why a supervisor would not want to give an accurate evaluation of a subordinate?
7. What are some of the advantages and disadvantages of using trait-based, behavior-based, and results-based types of appraisals?
8. Compare and contrast ranking versus rating systems of appraisal in terms of their advantages and disadvantages.
9. What are mixed standard scales, how do they work, and what special purposes do they serve?
10. What is the difference between the BARS and the BOS? Which do you think is better and why?
11. If you were developing an MBO program in your organization, what sort of problems with MBO would you try to avoid? How?
12. What does the cognitive information processing approach to performance appraisal say about how to improve appraisals?
13. Who should rate the performance of employees? Justify your answer.
14. What is the range of styles in which a performance appraisal interview might be conducted? For which situations might each style be best?
15. Is it possible for a supervisor to include discussions of past performance, merit raise, and future performance goals in the same appraisal interview?
16. How can superiors increase the effectiveness of the feedback they give to subordinates?

CASE 11.1

Management by Objectives in a State Agency

In her mail for May 15, Julia Sanchez, the director of teacher accreditation, found a memo from the director of human resources of the Texas Education Agency. The memo invited Julia to a June 10 meeting, one of a series of meetings being held to brief directors and department heads about the agency's new system for performance evaluation. The announcement mentioned the amount of time and effort that had gone into the planning of the new system, the commitment of the agency's top executives to the program, and the importance of the meeting. Julia noted the date on her calendar and looked forward to learning about what she hoped would be much-needed improvements in employee appraisal within one of the largest agencies in Texas.

On June 10, at 9:00 A.M., Sarah Amelio, the assistant director of human resources, welcomed the twenty-five managers invited to this meeting. She began by handing out literature on performance appraisal and then introduced the plan for the morning. Sarah intended to play a ten-minute video illustrating a typical appraisal feedback session between a supervisor and a subordinate at the Texas Education Agency. After the video, the interaction was to be critiqued; then the agency's new performance appraisal system was to be discussed.

The video showed a supervisor, Jerry Kelm, asking his subordinate, Mara Winic, to stop by at 4:45 P.M.; before she left for the day at 5:00 P.M., so that they could review Mara's performance for the past year. When Mara arrived, Jerry was busy attending to some last-minute arrangements for events of the following day. Jerry welcomed Mara, pulled the evaluation out of a folder, and asked her to look it over. He then left, and Mara reviewed the ratings that Jerry had given her. Jerry returned several minutes later and, while looking for some notes he needed, indicated to Mara that she was doing a fine job and that he hoped she would keep up the good work. Finally, finding the material he needed, Jerry asked Mara if she had any questions. Mara had none, and the meeting ended.

After the video, the workshop participants concluded that Jerry (a) was not prepared, (b) was preoccupied with other matters, (c) seemed annoyed by having to have the meeting, (d) was not specific, and (e) did not effectively communicate with Mara. One of the workshop participants jokingly mentioned that the feedback session looked all too familiar. Another participant, in defense of Jerry, brought out the fact that the current appraisal forms were based on vague traits and did not provide much useful material for a discussion of performance.

Sarah then gave an overview of the agency's new appraisal system and presented the new appraisal steps:

1. Meet with subordinates to discuss and agree on the expected results to be achieved—the goals for the year. Subordinates have a right to know what you expect of them.
2. Agree on the measurement standards that will indicate that goals have been achieved.
3. Provide help in the form of direction and training throughout the appraisal period to give subordinates a chance to show their ability and achieve their goals.
4. Offer formal and informal feedback to subordinates to let them know how they are doing.
5. Reward according to results. The rewards can include merit increases, recognition, training opportunities, and recommendations for promotion.

After Sarah's presentation, one of the managers asked, "Doesn't joint goal setting raise high expectation on the part of the employee, expectations that we cannot reward within the constraints of our state pay system?" Another manager noted, "We don't control anything and can't really reward subordinates." A third participant added, "What we are looking at is a system designed around the salary increases and bonuses available in the private sector, and the only rewards we control, in the state system, are intrinsic rewards." Sarah, rather surprised at the comments, responded, "This is what I like—all the reasons why the system can't work."

The remainder of the workshop had a negative tone that left Julia and others wondering if the system would work.

1. Were the participants resisting change or were they raising legitimate questions?

2. Is the management by objectives program workable in a state agency?

3. What are the differences between the private and public sectors with respect to appraisal systems?

4. If you were Sarah, how would you have answered the workshop participants' questions and comments?

EXERCISE 11.1

Assessing a Performance Appraisal Measure

This exercise is designed to give you hands-on experience in evaluating measures of performance that are actually being used by organizations.

Step 1. Two or three weeks before doing the exercise, obtain from an organization in your local area a copy of the appraisal instrument that is used in assessing employee performance. If possible, find out something about how the instrument was developed. Also find out for which jobs the appraisal instrument is used. Be sure that the name of the company is removed from all materials to ensure confidentiality. At least one week before the exercise bring to class the appraisal instrument, a description of how it was developed (if possible), and a list of jobs for which it is used.

Step 2. In class, break into groups of three or four. The instructor will have reviewed the appraisal instruments and made an overhead transparency of each instrument. Each group will be given one instrument, the description of the development process, and the list of jobs for which it is used.

Step 3. Each group will assess its appraisal instrument and prepare a brief analysis of it for the class. Among the issues that should be addressed in the analysis are the following:

- What type of performance information is being obtained—traits, behaviors, results, a combination?
- To what extent did supervisors, subordinates, and other job experts participate in the development process?
- Are the performance dimensions measured reasonable for the jobs involved?
- Are there any apparent deficiencies, irrelevant dimensions, or possible contaminants?

- Are the performance dimensions and rating anchors defined clearly enough so that raters will understand exactly what they are rating?
- Who should make the ratings—supervisor, peers, subordinates?
- Do any of the performance dimensions lend themselves to a more accurate rating by a particular type of rater or to more objective assessment?
- How would your group members feel if their performance was assessed using the instrument?
- How can the instrument be improved?

EXERCISE 11.2

Developing a Measure of Performance

In this exercise, you are given brief descriptions of three jobs. In doing the exercise you may wish to fill in information about a job from your own knowledge or experience. Keep a record of any information you add to the description provided.

Step 1. Divide into groups of three to five. Your instructor will assign one of the jobs to your group. Read the description of the job assigned to you.

Step 2. Your group's task is to develop a system for appraising the performance of employees on this job. Prepare a brief presentation to give to your fellow students. In this presentation you must specify

- the types of performance information you will collect—traits, behaviors, results.
- the exact method by which you will collect the information, and in the case of subjective ratings, who will make those ratings.
- the steps you will take to ensure that the information collected is reliable and valid.
- how often the measure(s) of performance will be obtained.

Job Descriptions *Post Office Clerk.* Receives letters and parcels and sells postage stamps and money orders. Weighs packages to determine charges. Computes cost of insuring and registering mail. Answers questions concerning postal regulations and procedures. Places mail into slots after sorting by mail code or destination. Takes complaints regarding lost mail or mail theft, fills out forms and submits for investigation.

Emergency Dispatcher/Operator. Answers telephone calls from the public regarding emergency situations that require police, fire, or medical assistance. Gathers pertinent information from callers using oral questionnaire and records data on a computer. Communicates with police, fire, or medical units in the field, dispatching them to appropriate locations. Monitors location and activities of all field units continuously. Upon request from field units, checks warrants for arrest, stolen vehicle reports, runaway reports, and so forth, using computer.

Animal Keeper (Zoological Garden). Cleans animal enclosures by hosing, sweeping, raking, scrubbing, and removing manure, soiled bedding, and unused food. Maintains enclosure materials such as nest boxes, plants, decorative materials, and bedding. Feeds and waters animals, preparing diet as instructed by the animal manager. Inspects and monitors animals and reports injuries, illnesses, or unusual behavior. Assists veterinarian in capturing and immobilizing animals when necessary.

Notes and References

1. P. W. Dorfman, W. G. Stephan, and J. Loveland, "Performance Appraisal Behaviors: Supervisor Perceptions and Subordinate Reactions," *Personnel Psychology,* Vol. 39, 1986, pp. 579–597.
2. "Who Needs a Boss?" *Fortune,* May 7, 1990, pp. 52–60.
3. F. Kanfer, "Self-Management Methods," in *Helping People Change: A Textbook of Methods,* ed. P. Karoly and A. Goldstein (New York: Pergamon, 1980), pp. 334–389.
4. Alan H. Locher and Kenneth S. Teel, "Appraisal Trends," *Personnel Journal,* Vol. 67, No. 9, 1988, p. 139.
5. Clinton O. Longenecker and Stephen J. Goff, "Why Performance Appraisals Still Fail," *Journal of Compensation and Benefits,* November-December 1990, pp. 36–41.
6. Berkeley Rice, "Performance Review: Examining the Eye of the Beholder," *Across the Board,* December 1985.
7. John H. Bernardin and L. A. Klatt, "Managerial Appraisal Systems: Has Practice Caught Up to the State of the Art?" *Personnel Administrator,* November 1985, pp. 79–86.
8. See H. E. Brogden and E. K. Taylor, "A Theory and Classification of Criterion Bias," *Educational and Psychological Measurement,* Vol. 10, 1950, pp. 159–186; also, Jeffrey S. Kane and Edward E. Lawler III, "Performance Appraisal Effectiveness: Its Assessment and Determinants," in *Research in Organizational Behavior,* Barry M. Staw, Ed. (Greenwich, Conn.: JAI Press, 1979), pp. 425–478.
9. Hannah R. Rothstein, "Interrater Reliability of Job Performance Ratings: Growth to Asymptote Level with Increasing Opportunity to Observe," *Journal of Applied Psychology,* Vol. 75, 1990, pp. 322–327.
10. Hubert S. Feild and William H. Holley, "The Relationship of Performance Appraisal System Characteristics to Verdicts in Selected Employment Discrimination Cases," *Academy of Management Journal,* Vol. 25, 1982, pp. 392–406.
11. *Brito* v. *Zia Company,* 478 F.2d 1200 (10th Cir. 1973); Gerald V. Barrett and Mary C. Kernan, "Performance Appraisal and Terminations: A Review of Court Decisions since *Brito* v. *Zia* with Implications for Personnel Practices," *Personnel Psychology,* Vol. 40, 1987, pp. 489–503.
12. *Price Waterhouse* v. *Hopkins,* 109 S.Ct 1775 (1989); Bill Shaw, "Employee Appraisals, Discrimination Cases, and Objective Evidence," *Business Horizons,* September/October 1990, pp. 61–65.
13. *Price Waterhouse* v. *Hopkins,* 109 S.Ct 1775 (1989).
14. Paul R. Sackett, Cathy L. Z. DuBois, and Ann Wiggins Noe, "Tokenism in Performance Evaluation: The Effects of Work Group Representation on Male-Female and White-Black Differences in Performance Ratings," *Journal of Applied Psychology,* Vol. 76, 1991, pp. 263–267.
15. W. H. Holley and H. S. Feild, "Performance Appraisal and the Law," *Labor Law Journal,* Vol. 26, 1975, pp. 423–430.
16. Christopher S. Miller, Joan A. Kaspin, and Michael H. Schuster, "The Impact of Performance Appraisal Methods on Age Discrimination in Employment Act Cases," *Personnel Psychology,* Vol. 43, 1990, pp. 555–578.
17. Glenn M. McEvoy and Wayne F. Cascio, "Cumulative Evidence of the Relationship Between Employee Age and Job Performance," *Journal of Applied Psychology,* Vol. 74, 1989, pp. 11–17; Bruce J. Avolio, David A. Waldman, and Michael A. McDaniel, "Age and Work Performance in Nonmanagerial Jobs: The Effects of Experience and Occupational Type," *Academy of Management Journal,* Vol. 33, 1990, pp. 407–422.

18. Cynthia D. Fisher and James B. Shaw, "Analysis of Officer Fitness Reports" (prepared for U.S. Marine Corps as part of an Office of Naval Research research grant, unpublished).
19. Brian E. Becker and Robert L. Cardy, "Influence of Halo Error on Appraisal Effectiveness: A Conceptual and Empirical Reconsideration," *Journal of Applied Psychology,* Vol. 71, 1986, pp. 662–671; R. Jacobs and S. Kozlowski, "A Closer Look at Halo Error in Performance Ratings," *Academy of Management Journal,* Vol. 28, 1985, pp. 201–212; Barry R. Nathan and Nancy Tippins, "The Consequences of Halo 'Error' in Performance Ratings: A Field Study of the Moderating Effect of Halo on Test Validation Results," *Journal of Applied Psychology,* Vol. 75, 1990, pp. 290–296.
20. Jack M. Feldman, "A Note on the Statistical Correction of Halo Error," *Journal of Applied Psychology,* Vol. 71, 1986, pp. 173–176.
21. For examples, see Kevin J. Williams, Angelo S. DeNisi, Bruce M. Meglino, and Thomas P. Cafferty, "Initial Decisions and Subsequent Performance Ratings," *Journal of Applied Psychology,* Vol. 71, 1986, pp. 189–195, and Cynthia Lee, "Increasing Performance Appraisal Effectiveness: Matching Task Types, Appraisal Process, and Rater Training," *Academy of Management Review,* Vol. 10, 1985, pp. 322–331.
22. Charles E. Lance and David J. Woehr, "Statistical Control of Halo: Clarification of Two Cognitive Models of the Performance Appraisal Process," *Journal of Applied Psychology,* Vol. 71, 1986, pp. 679–685.
23. S. T. Fiske and S. E. Taylor, *Social Cognition* (New York: Random House, 1984).
24. J. Crocker, S. T. Fiske, and S. E. Taylor, "Schematic Bases of Belief Change," in *Attitudinal Judgment,* ed. R. Eiser (New York: Springer-Verlag, 1984) pp. 197–226.
25. C. O. Longenecker, H. P. Sims, and D. A. Gioia, "Behind the Mask: The Politics of Employee Appraisal," *The Academy of Management Executive,* Vol. 1, 1987, pp. 183–193.
26. Beverly Geber, "The Hidden Agenda of Performance Appraisals," *Training,* June 1988, pp. 142–146.
27. Cynthia D. Fisher, "Transmission of Positive and Negative Feedback to Subordinates: A Laboratory Investigation," *Journal of Applied Psychology,* Vol. 64, 1979, pp. 533–540.
28. Frank J. Landy, James L. Farr, and Rick R. Jacobs, "Utility Concepts in Performance Measurement," *Organizational Behavior and Human Performance,* Vol. 30, 1982, pp. 15–40.
29. Ibid.
30. Ibid.
31. Gary P. Latham and Kenneth N. Wexley, *Increasing Productivity Through Performance Appraisal* (Reading, Mass.: Addison-Wesley, 1982).
32. *Brito* v. *Zia Company,* 478 F. 2d 1200 (10th Cir. 1973).
33. Larry H. Peters and Edward J. O'Connor, "Situational Constraints and Work Outcomes: The Influence of a Frequently Overlooked Construct," *Academy of Management Review,* Vol. 5, 1980, pp. 391–397.
34. Latham and Wexley, *Increasing Productivity.*
35. H. John Bernardin and Richard W. Beatty, *Performance Appraisal: Assessing Human Behavior at Work* (Boston: Kent Publishing, 1984).
36. Frank J. Landy and James L. Farr, "Police Performance Appraisal," *JSAS Catalog of Selected Documents in Psychology,* Vol. 6, 1976, p. 83.
37. Herbert H. Meyer, "Self-Appraisal of Job Performance," *Personnel Psychology,* Vol. 33, 1980, pp. 291–296.
38. Garry L. Hughes and Erich P. Prien, "An Evaluation of Alternate Scoring Methods for the Mixed Standard Scale," *Personnel Psychology,* Vol. 39, 1986, pp. 839–847.
39. H. John Bernardin and Richard W. Beatty, *Performance Appraisal: Assessing Human Behavior at Work* (Boston: Kent, 1984), p. 98.
40. T. A. DeCotiis, "An Analysis of the External Validity and Applied Relevance of Three Rating Formats," *Organizational Behavior and Human Performance,* Vol. 19, 1977, pp. 247–266; Kevin R. Murphy and J. I. Constans, "Behavioral Anchors as a Source of Bias in Rating," *Journal of Applied Psychology,* Vol. 72, 1987, pp. 573–577; Michael J.

Piotrowski, Janet L. Barnes-Farrell, and Francine H. Esrig, "Behaviorally Anchored Bias: A Replication and Extension of Murphy and Constans," *Journal of Applied Psychology,* Vol. 74, 1989, pp. 823–826.

41. Latham and Wexley, *Increasing Productivity.*

42. Ibid.

43. George C. Thornton III, "Psychometric Properties of Self-Appraisals of Performance," *Personnel Psychology,* Vol. 33, 1980, pp. 263–271.

44. Donald J. Campbell and Cynthia Lee, "Self-Appraisal in Performance Evaluation: Development versus Education," *Academy of Management Review,* Vol. 13, 1988, pp. 302–314.

45. Kenneth N. Wexley and Richard Klimoski, "Performance Appraisal: An Update," in *Research in Personnel and Human Resources Management,* ed. Kendrith M. Rowland and Gerald R. Ferris (Greenwich, Conn.: JAI Press, 1984), II, 35–80.

46. Glen M. McEvoy and Paul F. Buller, "User Acceptance of Peer Appraisals in an Industrial Setting," *Personnel Psychology,* Vol. 40, 1987, pp. 785–797.

47. Kane and Lawler, "Performance Appraisal Effectiveness," pp. 425–478 (endnote 8).

48. George S. Odiorne, *Management by Objectives II* (Belmont, Calif.: David S. Lake, 1979).

49. J. S. Kane and K. A. Freeman, "MBO and Performance Appraisal: A Mixture That's Not a Solution, Part Two," *Personnel,* February 1987, pp. 26–32.

50. H. John Bernardin, "Effects of Rater Training on Halo Errors in Student Ratings of Instructors," *Journal of Applied Psychology,* Vol. 63, 1978, pp. 301–308.

51. H. John Bernardin and M. R. Buckley, "Strategies in Rater Training," *Academy of Management Review,* Vol. 6, 1984, pp. 205–212; Jerry W. Hedge and Michael J. Kavanagh, "Improving the Accuracy of Performance Evaluations: Comparison of Three Methods of Performance Appraiser Training," *Journal of Applied Psychology,* Vol. 73, 1988, pp. 68–73; Kevin R. Murphy and William K. Balzer, "Rater Errors and Rating Accuracy," *Journal of Applied Psychology,* Vol. 74, 1989, pp. 619–624.

52. H. John Bernardin, "Rater Training: A Critique and Reconceptualization," *Proceedings of the Academy of Management,* 1979, pp. 131–135; Bernardin and Buckley, "Strategies in Rater Training."

53. David E. Smith, "Training Programs for Performance Appraisal: A Review," *Academy of Management Review,* Vol. 11, 1986, pp. 22–40.

54. Neil M. A. Hauenstein and Roseanne J. Foti, "From Laboratory to Practice: Neglected Issues in Implementing Frame-of-Reference Rater Training," *Personnel Psychology,* Vol. 42, 1989, pp. 359–378.

55. George C. Thornton and S. Zorich, "Training to Improve Observer Accuracy," *Personnel Psychology,* Vol. 29, 1980, pp. 351–354.

56. Hedge and Kavanagh, "Improving the Accuracy of Performance Evolutions," pp. 68–73 (endnote 51).

57. Bernardin, "Effects of Rater Training," pp. 301–308.

58. R. R. Sims, J. G. Veres, and S. M. Heninger, "Training Appraisers: An Orientation Program for Improving Supervisory Performance Ratings," *Public Personnel Management,* Vol. 16, 1987, pp. 37–46.

59. N. K. Napier and G. P. Latham, "Outcome Expectancies of People Who Conduct Performance Appraisals," *Personnel Psychology,* Vol. 39, 1986, pp. 827–837.

60. J. M. Hillery and K. N. Wexley, "Participation in Appraisal Interviews Conducted in a Training Situation," *Journal of Applied Psychology,* Vol. 59, 1974, pp. 168–171.

61. MaryBeth DeGregorio and Cynthia D. Fisher, "Providing Performance Feedback: Reactions to Alternate Methods," *Journal of Management,* Vol. 14, 1988, pp. 605–616.

62. Michael M. Harris and John Schaubroeck, "A Meta-analysis of Self-Supervisor, Self-Peer, and Peer-Supervisor Ratings," *Personnel Psychology,* Vol. 41, 1988, pp. 43–62.

63. T. R. Mitchell and L. S. Kalb, "Effects of Job Experience on Supervisor Attributions for Subordinate's Poor Performance," *Journal of Applied Psychology,* Vol. 67, 1982, pp. 81–188.

64. Jone L. Pearce and Lyman W. Porter, "Employee Responses to Formal Performance

Appraisal Feedback," *Journal of Applied Psychology,* Vol. 71, 1986, pp. 211–218.

65. M. W. McCall, Jr. and D. L. DeVries, "Appraisal in Context: Clashing with Organizational Realities" (technical report prepared for the Center for Creative Leadership, 1977).

66. Herbert H. Meyer, E. Kay, and J. French, "Split Roles in Performance Appraisal," *Harvard Business Review,* Vol. 43, 1965, pp. 123–129.

67. Dorfman, Stephan, and Loveland, "Performance Appraisal Behaviors," pp. 579–597; J. B. Prince and Edward E. Lawler III, "Does Salary Discussion Hurt the Developmental Performance Appraisal?" *Organizational Behavior and Human Decision Processes,* Vol. 37, 1986, pp. 357–375.

68. James R. Larson, Jr., "The Dynamic Interplay Between Employees' Feedback-Seeking Strategies and Supervisors' Delivery of Performance Feedback," *Academy of Management Review,* Vol. 14, 1989, pp. 408–422; Gerald R. Ferris, Timothy A. Judge, Kendrith M. Rowland, and Dale E. Fitzgibbons, "Subordinate Influence and the Performance Evaluation Process: Test of a Model," *Organizational Behavior and Human Decision Process,* in press.

69. S. J. Wayne and K. M. Kacmar, "The Effects of Impression Management on the Performance Appraisal Process," *Organizational Behavior and Human Decision Processes,* Vol. 48, 1991, pp. 70–88.

70. Elizabeth Wolfe Morrison and Robert J. Bies, "Impression Management in the Feedback-Seeking Process: A Literature Review and Research Agenda," *Academy of Management Review,* Vol. 16, 1991, pp. 522–541.

71. Barry R. Nathan, Allan M. Mohrman, Jr., and John Milliman, "Interpersonal Relations as a Context for the Effects of Appraisal Interviews on Performance and Satisfaction: A Longitudinal Study," *Academy of Management Journal,* Vol. 34, 1991, pp. 352–369; Daniel R. Ilgen, Cynthia D. Fisher, and M. Susan Taylor, "Consequences of Individual Feedback on Behavior in Organizations," *Journal of Applied Psychology,* Vol. 64, 1979, pp. 349–371.

72. Herbert H. Meyer, "A Solution to the Performance Appraisal Feedback Enigma," *Academy of Management Executive,* Vol. 5, 1991, pp. 68–76; Daniel R. Ilgen, Terence R. Mitchell, and J. W. Frederickson, "Poor Performers: Supervisors and Subordinates' Response," *Organizational Behavior and Human Performance,* Vol. 27, 1981, pp. 386–410.

73. P. Christopher Earley, "Trust, Perceived Importance of Praise and Criticism, and Work Performance: An Examination of Feedback in the United States and England," *Journal of Management,* Vol. 12, 1986, pp. 457–473.

74. Robert A. Baron, "Negative Effects of Destructive Criticism: Impact on Conflict, Self-Efficacy, and Task Performance," *Journal of Applied Psychology,* Vol. 73, 1988, pp. 199–207.

75. Brendan D. Bannister, "Performance Outcome Feedback and Attributional Feedback: Interactive Effects on Recipient Responses," *Journal of Applied Psychology,* Vol. 71, 1986, pp. 203–210.

76. Campbell and Lee, "Self-Appraisal in Performance Evaluation: Development Versus Evaluation," pp. 302–304.

12

Compensation System Development

An organization exists to accomplish specific goals and objectives. The individuals hired by the organization have their own needs. One is for money, which enables them to purchase a wide variety of goods and services available in the marketplace. Hence, there is a basis for an exchange: the employee offers specific behaviors desired by the organization to meet its goals and objectives in return for money, goods, and/or services. Taken together, the money, goods, and/or services the employer provides employees constitute the employer's compensation system.

The system that an organization uses to reward employees can play an important role in the organization's efforts to gain a competitive advantage and to achieve its major objectives. Compensation systems should attract and retain the talent an organization needs, encourage employees to develop the skills and abilities they need, motivate employees, and create the type of team culture in which employees care about the organization's success. Ideally, a reward system should align individual objectives with important strategic goals of the organization, but for most organizations the reality falls far short of this ideal.

The design and implementation of a compensation system is one of the most complex activities for which human resource managers are responsible. The following are some of the factors that contribute to this complexity:

- While other aspects of human resource systems (training, career management, appraisal systems, quality of work life programs) are important to some employees, compensation is considered crucial by virtually everyone.
- One goal of a compensation system is to motivate employees, yet there is tremendous variation in the value different individuals attach to a specific reward or package of rewards. A single individual's values may also change over time.
- The jobs in most organizations involve an almost endless variety of knowledge, skills, and abilities, and are performed in situations with a wide range of demands.
- Compensation systems consist of many elements in addition to pay for work; these components must be coordinated to work together.
- Employee compensation is a major cost of doing business—up to 80 percent for service firms—and can determine the competitiveness of a firm's products or services.
- A wide variety of federal and state regulations affect compensation systems.
- Employees, either directly or through collective bargaining arrangements, may desire to participate in the determination of compensation.
- The cost of living varies tremendously in different geographic areas, an important consideration for firms with multiple locations.

In most organizations the compensation system involves a multifaceted package, not just pay for work and performance. The components of the compensation

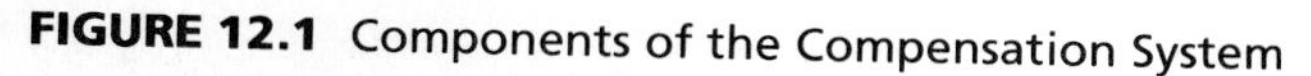

FIGURE 12.1 Components of the Compensation System

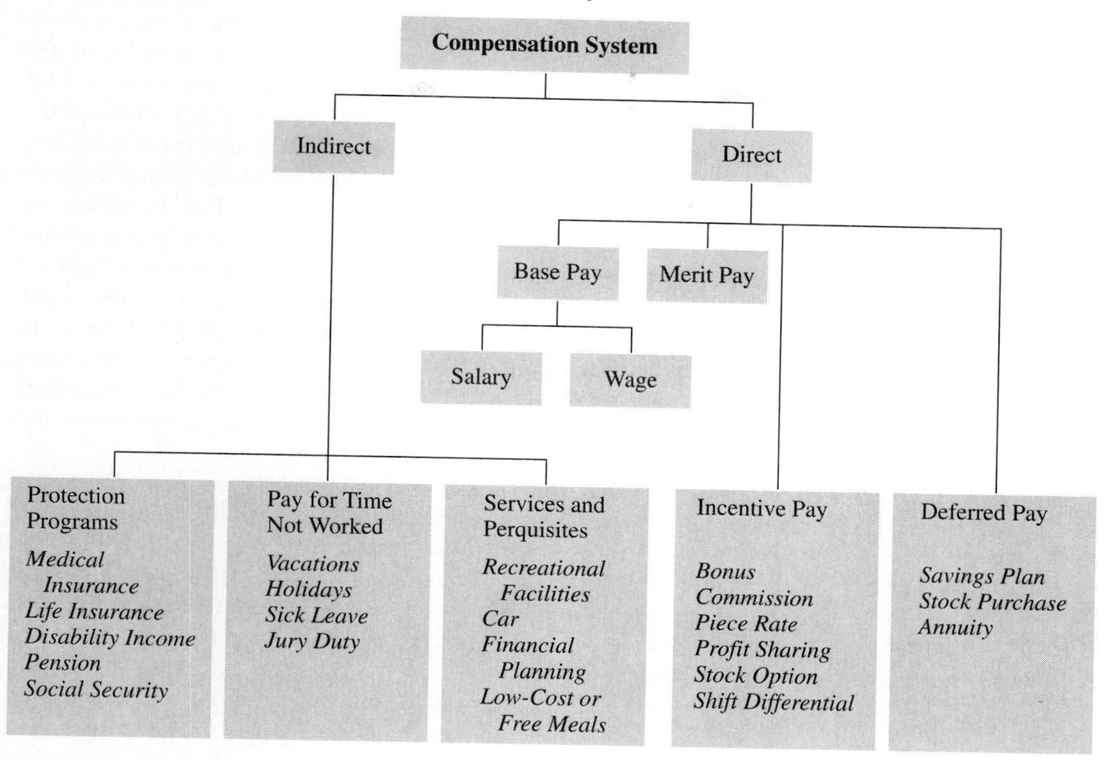

system can be roughly divided into direct (wages) and indirect (benefits) forms of compensation (see Figure 12.1). Chapter 12 discusses procedures for designing and administering a compensation system. Chapter 13 examines the special aspects of pay-for-performance systems, as well as indirect compensation.

EMPLOYEE SATISFACTION AND MOTIVATION ISSUES IN COMPENSATION DESIGN

People have no basic or instinctive need for money, a commodity that is important only if it can satisfy other needs. Organizations frequently overestimate the value workers place on monetary rewards.[1] For example, if money were the primary motivation for working, why would hourly employees object to overtime, given the premium rate of pay associated with it?[2] Many supervisors become frustrated and disillusioned when pay increases do not produce a corresponding rise in productivity. Still more troublesome is that the rewards that effectively motivate some workers do not succeed with others. The equity and expectancy theories (see Chapter 13) can help explain employees' reactions to compensation systems.

Equity Theory

Employees want to be treated fairly. **Equity** is the balance between the *inputs* an individual brings to a job and the *outcomes* he or she receives from it. Employee inputs include experience, education, special skills, effort, and time worked. Outcomes include pay, benefits, achievement, recognition, and any other rewards.

Individuals use a complex process to determine what is fair. Inputs are continually compared with outcomes—the individual's special skills and efforts are weighed against the pay and recognition given by the organization. However, inputs and outcomes are in different units, and are hard to compare to each other directly. Thus, **equity theory** suggests that individuals determine whether they are being fairly treated by comparing their own input/outcome ratio to the input/outcome ratio of someone else. This other person (or group of people) may be in the same job or in other jobs, in the company or outside the company, in the same industry or outside the industry. A sense of inequity arises when the comparison process uncovers an imbalance between inputs and outcomes of the employee compared with others.

Equity theory suggests that individuals will usually make some attempt to relieve the tension created by any perceived inequity.[3] An employee may perceive the ratio of his or her rewards and contributions to be less favorable than the ratio prevailing for others (see Figure 12.2). For example, a police officer may believe that he or she expends more effort at greater risk than is required of firefighters in the same community who receive the same pay. The police officer may seek to redress the inequity in several ways, perhaps by (1) reducing effort, (e.g., writing fewer citations); (2) working with colleagues to lobby the city council for higher pay for police officers; or (3) seeking employment in a community where police are paid more than firefighters. The desire to achieve equity even extends to the point of employee theft as a reaction to underpayment. In a recent study, employee theft rates were measured before, during, and after a period in which pay was temporarily reduced by 15 percent. Theft increased markedly in plants where pay was reduced and returned to prior levels when normal pay was resumed.[4]

People also notice when they are overrewarded in relation to others. In such a case, the individual might work harder than they did previously or volunteer for an extra assignment to eliminate the perceived inequity. Research has also shown that motivation from being overcompensated is relatively short-lived. Most individuals quickly decide that they deserve whatever pay rate they receive and do not try to sustain a higher level of performance.[5]

Satisfaction with Pay

Survey data regularly show compensation to be one of the areas of employment with which employees are least satisfied.[6] It is not unusual to find that individuals, otherwise satisfied with their career and the organization for which they work, believe that their compensation leaves something to be desired. Sometimes it seems that employees are never satisfied with their compensation.

FIGURE 12.2 Equity Theory

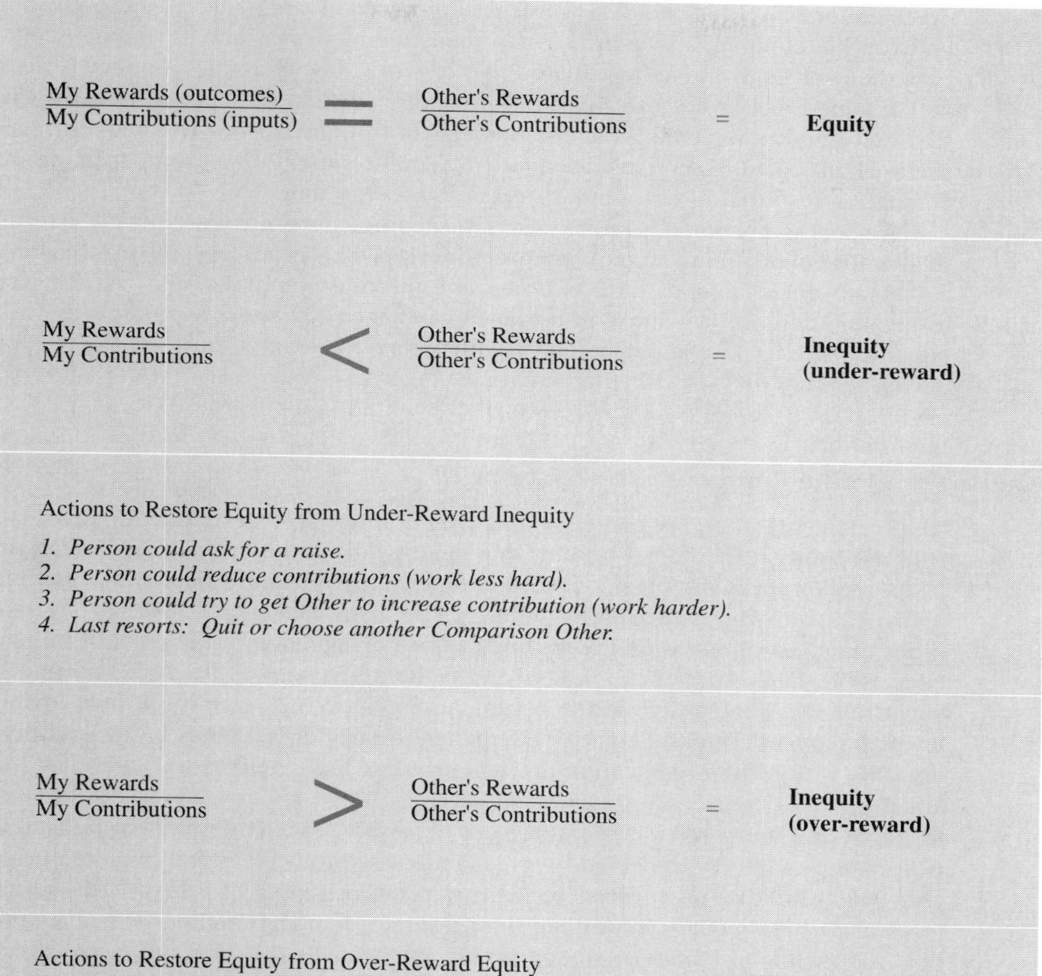

One reason for the reduced degree of satisfaction with compensation has to do with the number of possible comparisons.[7] Individuals seem to seek comparison information from a wide variety of sources, both internal and external to the organization, and then hold to the least favorable comparison. If there are not unfavorable comparisons with those in their line of work, individuals may compare themselves to those in a related line of work. For example, a police officer may compare his or her pay favorably with other police officers working for the same city and other cities, but feel underpaid in comparison with federal marshals. Highly paid executives frequently attempt to justify their compensation by comparing it to that of entertainers, who earn even more.

A successful compensation system needs to incorporate the equity concerns of all participants in the employment relationship. This is achieved by establishing a system which includes both external and internal comparisons in setting pay levels. In addition, it is more important to focus on the specific employees who are dissatisfied with compensation than on the overall level of satisfaction. If poor performers are dissatisfied, that may be as desired.

Designing Equitable Compensation Systems

Three elements of equity can be distinguished: internal, external, and individual. **Internal equity** refers to the relationship among jobs within a single organization. Employees expect the president of a company to earn more than the executive vice president, who in turn earns more than the plant manager, and so on. Among other things, compensation is presumed to be correlated with the level of knowledge, skill, and experience required to do the job successfully. Thus, no one is surprised that people high in the organizational structure earn more than lower-level employees. Internal equity exists when the pay differentials between different jobs within the organization are perceived as fair—neither too large nor too small.

External equity refers to comparisons of similar jobs in different organizations (for example, the pay received by presidents of various electrical manufacturing firms). It would be no surprise to learn that the president of a firm with annual sales of $1 billion earns more than the president of a $500-million firm. Presumably a doubling of company size requires more knowledge, skill, and experience on the part of its leader. Locality matters as well as industry and company size. When the secretary of an electrical manufacturer's plant manager worries about external equity, the comparison is likely to be to secretaries at the automobile plant across town rather than to electrical companies nationwide.

The final element, **individual equity,** refers to comparisons among individuals in the same job with the same organization. In many ways, this is the most critical question. If it is not answered satisfactorily, attention to internal and external equity will have been wasted. For example, suppose the human resource manager establishes, through internal and external comparisons, that all secretaries in the organization should receive between $1,500 and $2,000 per month. The problem now is to determine the pay rate of *each* secretary. Should long-service secretaries be paid more than those who have just been hired? If yes, what is the value of each additional year of service? Should pay differences be based on job performance? If so, how will performance be measured? How will the differences in performance be translated into pay differences? Employees must perceive that these questions are answered fairly in order for individual equity to exist (see the Ethical Perspective box).

There are accepted procedures for establishing internal, external, and individual equity with an organization. These procedures will be reviewed in the following sections.

ESTABLISHING INTERNAL EQUITY: JOB EVALUATION METHODS

The major purpose of job evaluation is to determine the relative worth of the jobs within an organization. A systematic comparison can define an internal job hierarchy that ranks jobs in terms of their relative contribution to the organizational objectives.

Fulfillment of a company's objectives depends more on the job done by its president than by its plant manager. But how much is the differential worth? Since there is no direct way to measure the value of jobs in relation to organizational objectives, rewards are usually based on important components generally agreed to make one job worth more than another. These aspects, called **compensable factors,** may include skills, effort, and education required; amount of responsibility involved; and working conditions.

Many companies employ some form of job evaluation. To be most effective, the process needs to involve the employees whose jobs are affected. The following questions need to be considered:

- Which of several possible evaluation procedures is to be used?
- Will one evaluation procedure be used throughout the organization, or will different procedures be used for broad classes of jobs (e.g., exempt versus nonexempt)?
- If the procedure that is selected takes into account several compensable factors, which of these factors are to be included, and how they are to be weighted?

The five most frequently used job evaluation methods are (1) job ranking, (2) job grading or classification, (3) the point method, (4) the Hay Plan, and (5) factor comparison. As shown in Figure 12.3, these methods can be classified on the basis of the approach taken. Along one dimension are job ranking and factor comparison, which compare one job with another, versus the other methods that compare the job with one or more rating scales. The other dimension considers the quantitative sophistication of the procedures.

ETHICAL PERSPECTIVE

Achieving Distributive Justice: Alternate Bases for Reward Allocation

The Ethical Perspective box in the previous chapter distinguishes between procedural and distributive justice and emphasizes the importance of clear, fair, and open decision-making processes for attaining procedural justice. Although procedural and distributive justice are intertwined, this discussion focuses primarily on distributive justice.

Recall that distributive justice involves a fair result in the distribution of any type of outcome across people. Here we concentrate on the outcomes of base salary and pay increases and how they are allocated across individuals in the organization.

Whether or not a given pay decision (and the rules and procedures generating it) is seen as just depends very much on the value basis chosen to underlie the decision. There are a number of bases on which pay allocation decisions can be made:

- *Equality*. Because all humans have equal value and dignity, all should be rewarded equally, regardless of ability, effort, performance, or any other factor.
- *Need*. Each individual should be rewarded according to his or her needs, with greater rewards flowing to those with greater needs, regardless of contribution.
- *Equity*. Each person should be rewarded in direct proportion to his or her individual contribution.

Socialist countries tend to emphasize the equality and need bases for reward distribution, and this is reflected in quite low pay differentials across levels. For instance, before China's recent reforms allowing small-scale entrepreneurship, the highest-paid person in the country made only six times what the lowest-paid person did.

Reward allocation partly on the basis of need does occur in some situations in the United States such as the housing allowances received by military personnel, which are keyed to the number of dependents as well as rank. Labor organizations often lean toward equality as the basis of compensation, at least within a single job category. However, Western work organizations and managers generally favor equity as the basis for reward distribution, with those who make greater contributions seen as deserving compensation. Note that there is still ample room for disagreement on which contributions should carry the most weight in pay allocation decisions. The choices include education, experience, effort, quality of output, amount of output, job importance, length of service, and so on.

Research has shown that individuals will choose different bases for reward allocation depending on the situation. When the primary goal is to preserve group harmony, avoid conflict, facilitate cooperation, or prevent turnover, decision makers favor an equality basis for compensation decisions. This is what Japanese organizations tend to do within tenure levels. When the decision is cast in terms of friendship rather than formal organizational roles, decision makers tend to distribute rewards on the basis of need, as one would do in a family situation. When the purpose is to weed out low performers, equity is chosen so that large pay differentials between performers send an unmistakable message.

Thus, there is no single basis for compensation decisions that will always be seen as fair. Justice seems most likely to be attained when the parties agree on the most appropriate basis for reward distribution, but such agreement cannot be assumed to occur without discussion.

Sources: Jerald Greenberg, "A Taxonomy of Organizational Justice Theories," *Academy of Management Review,* January 1987, pp. 9–22; Sara M. Freedman and John R. Montanari, "An Integrative Model of Managerial Reward Allocation," *Academy of Management Review,* July 1980, pp. 381–390; Rogene A. Buchholz, *Fundamental Concepts and Problems in Business Ethics* (Englewood Cliffs, N.J.: Prentice-Hall, 1989), pp. 35–42.

FIGURE 12.3 Job Evaluation Procedures

Basis for Job Hierarchy	Nonquantitative Comparison Involving Job as a Whole	Quantitative Comparison Involving Job Components
Job Versus Job Comparison	Job Ranking	Factor Comparison
Job Versus Scale Comparison	Job Grading or Classification	Point Method Hay Plan

Source: John M. Ivancevich, "Job Evaluation Procedures," from *Foundations of Personnel*. Copyright © 1992 by Richard D. Irwin.

Job Ranking

Job ranking, the simplest way to evaluate jobs, is primarily used in small organizations. Normally, a committee of managers reviews all the job descriptions and ranks them in order of their relative worth or importance to the organization. The ranking method is simple, inexpensive, fast, and easy to understand. However, it is nonquantitative and rather subjective, for although jobs are compared with each other, there is no explicit set of compensable factors used in this comparison. Additionally, simple ranking gives no information about the distances between jobs, making it difficult to assign salary levels. Even though there may be agreement that job A is more valuable than job B, the magnitude of the difference is not known. A final difficulty is purely practical. Except in a very small organization, there may be no one who is knowledgeable about every single job in the organization, as would be necessary for meaningful ranking.

A special method of ranking is the paired comparison technique. This method was discussed in Chapter 11 as a means of comparing employees to each other on the basis of overall performance. In the job evaluation context, the content and importance of different jobs, not on the performance of incumbents, is the object of comparison. In this approach, each job is compared directly against every other job, using a matrix of the type shown in Table 12.1. Reading across each row, an x is marked each time the job is rated more highly than the job in that column. (For example, the executive secretary job is ranked higher than computer operator but not higher than systems analyst.) The totals column records the number of comparisons in which the job is ranked higher. This total determines the job's rank. Though this technique is somewhat more systematic than simple ranking, the number of comparisons increases quite rapidly as the number of jobs increases. Some evidence suggests that the paired comparison approach is more reliable than simple ranking.[8]

TABLE 12.1 Paired Comparison Ranking Table

	Messenger	*Data Processing Manager*	*Data Entry Operator*	*Executive Secretary*	*Computer Operator*	*Systems Analyst*	*Control Clerk*	*Programmer*	*File Clerk*	*Assistant Director*	*Total*
Messenger	—										0
Data Processing Manager	X	—	X	X	X	X	X	X	X	X	9
Data Entry Operator	X		—						X		2
Executive Secretary	X		X	—	X		X	X	X		6
Computer Operator	X		X		—		X		X		4
Systems Analyst	X		X	X	X	—	X	X	X		7
Control Clerk	X		X				—		X		3
Programmer	X		X		X		X	—	X		5
File Clerk	X								—		1
Assistant Director	X		X	X	X	X	X	X	X	—	8

Instructions: Place X in box where job in row is more important than job in column.

Source: Richard Henderson, *Compensation Management: Rewarding Performance*, 5th ed., © 1989, p. 199. Adapted by permission of Prentice-Hall, Inc. Englewood Cliffs, New Jersey.

Job Grading or Classification

The **job grading** or **job classification method** is a nonquantitative job evaluation technique that compares the whole job with a predetermined standard. In this approach, jobs are assigned to predefined grades or classes. Job grading is common in the public sector. The federal government's General Schedule (GS) has eighteen grades: fifteen grades into which most jobs are classified, and three top "super grades" which cover senior executives. GS 11 through GS 15 include general management and highly specialized jobs; GS 5 through GS 10 are for management trainees and lower-level managers; and GS 1 through GS 4 are for clerical and nonsupervisory personnel. Table 12.2 contains representative examples of the type of grade descriptions used by the federal government. In the private sector, job classification is commonly used in managerial and scientific or engineering jobs.[9]

It is usually fairly easy for organizations to group jobs and for employees to accept the classifications. Flexibility is another advantage of the job classification method. It can be applied to a large number and wide variety of jobs. As the number of jobs in the organization grows, these new jobs can easily be assigned to the grades that already exist.

The job classification method has been criticized because subjective judgments are used to place jobs into the grades (for example, when a job seems to fall between two grades). A related disadvantage is that the job classification method relies heavily on the use of job titles rather than a more detailed examination of job content.

Point Method

As seen in Figure 12.3, unlike job ranking or classification, the **point method** breaks the job into components and evaluates each of these job elements against specially constructed scales. A quantitative approach, the point method is rather complex to design but relatively simple to understand and administer once it is in place. It is the most widely used method of job evaluation.

Four steps are followed in applying the point method: selection of compensable factors; establishment of factor scales; assignment of points to degrees; and application to organizational jobs.

Compensable Factors Compensable factors are those job dimensions or job requirements that will be the basis for paying employees. Organizations select three to twenty-five compensable factors, with the typical point method using about ten factors. The plan developed by the National Electrical Manufacturers Association (NEMA) involves eleven factors that are grouped into the following four dimensions: (1) skill (education, experience, knowledge); (2) effort (physical demand, mental or visual demand); (3) responsibility (equipment or process, material or product, safety of others, work of others); and (4) job conditions (working conditions, hazards).

TABLE 12.2 Grade Descriptions and Representative Job Titles from the Classification System Used by the Federal Government

Grade Level	*Grade Description*	*Jobs Included in Grade*
GS 1	Includes those classes of positions the duties of which are to perform, under immediate supervision, with little or no latitude for the exercise of independent judgment: —the simplest routine work in office, business, or fiscal operations; or —elementary work of a subordinate technical character in a professional, scientific, or technical field.	Typist, Messenger
GS 2	Includes those classes of positions the duties of which are: —to perform, under immediate supervision, with limited latitude for the exercise of independent judgment, routine work in office, business, or fiscal operations, or comparable subordinate technical work of limited scope in a professional, scientific, or technical field, requiring some training or experience; or —to perform other work of equal importance, difficulty, and responsibility, and requiring comparable qualifications.	Engineering aide
GS 5	Includes those classes of positions the duties of which are: —to perform, under general supervision, difficult and responsible work in office, business, or fiscal administration, or comparable subordinate technical work in a professional, scientific, or technical field, requiring in either case— —considerable training and supervisory or other experience; —broad working knowledge of a special subject matter or of office, laboratory, engineering, scientific, or other procedure and practice; and —the exercise of independent judgment in a limited field; —to perform other work of equal importance, difficulty, and responsibility, and requiring comparable qualifications.	Chemist, Accountant, Engineer (civil), Statistical clerk

Source: From *The Management of Compensation* by Alan N. Nash and Stephen J. Carroll (Copyright © 1976 by Wadsworth, Inc.) Reprinted by permission of the author.

Factor Scales Once the compensable factors have been chosen, scales reflecting different degrees within each factor are constructed. An example of the factor scales for the knowledge factor are defined in some detail in Table 12.3. As much as possible, each degree is defined to be equidistant from the adjacent degrees.

Assigning Points to Degrees The next step is to assign points to degrees. First, however, the job evaluation committee decides on the relative importance of the different factors. For instance, in the system in Table 12.4, the committee has decided that experience is the most important factor and has awarded it the largest number of points (110 for the highest degree). Education and knowledge are next in importance, followed by physical demand and working conditions, then the remaining factors. Once the highest degree of each factor is given a point allocation reflecting its importance, the lower degrees are assigned proportionately lesser point values in accord with factor importance.

TABLE 12.3 Defining a Compensable Factor and Associated Degrees: An Illustration

Knowledge
This factor measures the knowledge or equivalent training required to perform the job duties.
1st Degree
Use of reading and writing, adding and subtracting of whole numbers; following of instructions; use of fixed gauges, direct reading of instruments, and similar devices; where interpretation is not required.
2nd Degree
Use of addition, subtraction, multiplication, and division of numbers including decimals and fractions; simple use of formulas, charts, tables, drawings, specifications, schedules, wiring diagrams; use of adjustable measuring instruments; checking of reports, forms, records, and comparable data; where interpretation is required.
3rd Degree
Use of mathematics with the use of complicated drawings, specifications, charts, tables; various types of precision measuring instruments. Equivalent to one to three years' applied trades training in a particular or specialized occupation.
4th Degree
Use of advanced trades mathematics, together with the use of complicated drawings, specifications, charts, tables, handbook formulas; all varieties of precision measuring instruments. Equivalent to complete accredited apprenticeship in a recognized trade, craft, or occupation; or equivalent to a two-year technical college education.
5th Degree
Use of higher mathematics involved in the application of engineering principles and the performance of related practical operations, together with a comprehensive knowledge of the theories and practices of mechanical, electrical, chemical, civil, or like engineering field. Equivalent to complete four years of technical college or university education.

Source: Adapted from *Compensation* 3/e by George T. Milkovich and Jerry M. Newman. Copyright © 1990 by Richard D. Irwin.

TABLE 12.4 A Typical Point Plan

	Points				
Factors	*1st*	*2nd*	*3rd*	*4th*	*5th*
Skill					
1. Education	14	28	42	56	70
2. Experience	22	44	66	88	110
3. Knowledge	14	28	42	56	70
Effort					
4. Physical Demand	10	20	30	40	50
5. Mental Demand	5	10	15	20	25
Responsibility					
6. Equipment/Process	5	10	15	20	25
7. Material/Product	5	10	15	20	25
8. Safety of Others	5	10	15	20	25
9. Work of Others	5	10	15	20	25
Job Conditions					
10. Working Conditions	10	20	30	40	50
11. Hazards	5	10	15	20	25

Source: Richard Henderson, *Compensation Management: Rewarding Performance*, 5th ed., © 1989, p. 204. Adapted by permission of Prentice-Hall, Inc., Englewood Cliffs, New Jersey.

Application to Jobs Once the compensable factors have been identified, defined, and assigned points, jobs can be evaluated and "scored." In this process, the job evaluation committee will thoroughly review job analysis data and perhaps observe the job or speak with incumbents. Then it will determine which degree of each factor best describes that job. The points associated with these degrees are summed for each job. An example of this procedure is given in Table 12.5.

Note that the points assigned a job do not need to match exactly those of the plan (see knowledge factor in Table 12.5). In this example, the level of knowledge required by loading dock workers is between the first and second degrees (see Table 12.3), resulting in 21 points. Often jobs with similar point totals are grouped together for administrative convenience. For instance, all jobs with 150–180 points may form a single pay grade.

In principle, the point method could be used to develop a single set of factors and weights for all the jobs in the organization. In practice, however, organizations tend to use several different point plans. There may be one plan for office and clerical employees, another for production workers, and a third for managerial staff. Rarely do the same compensable factors apply to jobs at widely different levels. For example, the job condition factors shown in Table 12.4 are not equally applicable to office/clerical, production, and managerial workers. In such a case,

TABLE 12.5 Application of a Point System to Two Jobs

	Loading Dock Workers		*Forklift Repair Mechanics*	
Compensable Factors	*Degree*	*Points*	*Degree*	*Points*
Education	1	14	2	28
Experience	1	22	3	66
Knowledge	1–2	21	3	42
Physical Demand	4	40	2	20
Mental Demand	1	5	3	15
Responsibility for Equipment/Process	2	10	3	15
Responsibility for Material/Product	2	10	1	5
Responsibility for Safety of Others	1	5	1	5
Responsibility for Work of Others	1	5	1	5
Working Conditions	3	30	2	20
Hazards	4	20	3	15
Total Points		182		236

it may make sense to replace factors that do not apply with those more meaningful to the jobs involved. Physical demands and hazards, for instance, seldom appear in point systems for managerial jobs.

The Hay Plan

A well-known version of the point method was developed by Hay Associates, one of the largest compensation consulting firms in the world. The Hay Plan is used for evaluating managerial and executive positions by a large number of organizations worldwide.[10]

The universal factors used by the Hay Plan are know-how, problem solving, and accountability. These factors, along with the associated subfactors, are described in Table 12.6. **Know-how** is the total of all the knowledge and skills required to do the job; it includes the subfactors of technical knowledge, management responsibility, and responsibility for motivating others. **Problem solving** is the amount of original thinking required by the job for arriving at decisions; it includes the subfactors of degree of freedom and type of mental activity. **Accountability** is defined as being answerable for actions taken on the job; its three subfac-

TABLE 12.6 The Factors of the Hay Plan

Know-How	*Problem Solving (Mental Activity)*	*Accountability*
The sum total of all knowledge and skills, however acquired, needed for satisfactory job performance (evaluates the job, not the person). Know-How has three dimensions: • The amount of practical, specialized, or technical knowledge required • Breadth of management, or the ability to make many activities and functions work well together; the job of company president, for example, has greater breadth than that of a department supervisor • Requirement for skill in motivating people Using a chart, a number can be assigned to the level of Know-How needed in a job. This number—or point value—indicates the relative importance of Know-How in the job being evaluated.	The amount of original, self-starting thought required by the job for analysis, evaluation, creation, reasoning, and arriving at conclusions: Problem Solving has two dimensions: • The degree of freedom with which the thinking process is used to achieve job objectives without the guidance of standards, precedents, or direction from others • The type of mental activity involved; the complexity, abstractness, or originality of thought required Problem Solving is expressed as a percentage of Know-How for the obvious reason that people think with what they know. The percentage judged to be correct for a job is applied to the Know-How point value; the result is the point value given to Problem Solving.	The measured effect of the job on company goals. Accountability has three dimensions: • Freedom to act, or relative presence of personal or procedural control and guidance; determined by answering the question, "How much freedom has the job holder to act independently?"; for example, a plant manager has more freedom than a supervisor under his or her control. • Dollar magnitude, a measure of the sales, budget, dollar value of purchases, value added, or any other significant annual dollar figure related to the job. • Impact of the job on dollar magnitude, a determination of whether the job has a primary effect on end results or has instead a sharing, contributory, or remote effect. Accountability is given a point value independent of the other two factors.

The total evaluation of any job is arrived at by adding the points for Know-How, Problem Solving, and Accountability. The points are not shown here.

Source: Reprinted by permission from p. 301 of *Effective Personnel Management*, 3/e by R. S. Schuler, N. J. Buetell, and S. Youngblood.

tors are freedom to act, dollar magnitude, and impact. The Hay guide chart allows the evaluator to assign a point value for each factor. The total of the points across all factors is the value of the job.[11]

Factor Comparison

The **factor comparison method** is a method of quantifying the job versus job comparison (see Figure 12.3). It is the least commonly used method of job evaluation.[12] The first step is to select key jobs to help anchor the system. Key jobs are those that are found in many organizations and have relatively stable job content; they also have to be jobs for which the prevailing wage rates are known.[13] The second step is to rank the key jobs on a few compensable factors, such as skill, effort, responsibility, and job conditions. In Table 12.7 job 1 has lower skill requirements than all other jobs but is ranked highest on working conditions. The third step is to determine for each key job the amount of the present pay rate that is attributable to each of the factors. Of job 1's total rate of $4.75, $1.00 is allocated for its level of skill, $1.00 for effort, 50¢ for responsibility, and $2.25 for working conditions.

TABLE 12.7 A Factor Comparison Scale

Rate	*Skill*	*Effort*	*Responsibility*	*Working Conditions*
$ .25				Job 3
.50			Job 1	Job 4
.75				
1.00	Job 1	Job 1		Job 2
1.25	Job 2	Job 3		(Job X)
1.50		Job 2	Job 3	
1.75		Job 4		
2.00				
2.25		(Job X)		Job 1
2.50			Job 2	
2.75				
3.00				
3.25	Job 4		Job 4 (Job X)	
3.50				
3.75				
4.00	Job 3 (Job X)			
4.25				
4.50				
4.75				

	Hourly Rates
Job 1	$4.75
Job 2	$6.25
Job 3	$7.00
Job 4	$8.75

The factor comparison method can be applied to other jobs by comparing their standings on each factor with that of the key jobs and summing the associated dollar values to arrive at an hourly rate. For example, suppose that a new job, job X, is being evaluated. Job X is determined to have the same level of skill requirements as job 3 ($4.00); the same level of responsibility as job 4 ($3.25); somewhat more hazardous working conditions than job 2 ($1.25); and somewhat greater effort requirements than job 4 ($2.25). Thus, the appropriate hourly pay for job X would be $10.75.

The procedure is rather cumbersome; hence the relative infrequency of its use. Organizations interested in a quantitative approach to job evaluation are more likely to rely on a point system, which tends to be more straightforward and to result in a flexible approach.

Computerized Job Evaluation

The most popular job evaluation procedures were developed at a time when greater value was placed on having accurate narrative job descriptions. The most frequent means of collecting job data was by having analysts interview incumbents and/or observe work performed and then write job descriptions. This process is labor intensive, generates a tremendous amount of qualitative data, and must be updated frequently.

A recent trend is the computerizing of job evaluation.[14] Typically, after some training, incumbents complete structured questionnaires, such as the Position Analysis Questionnaire (see Chapter 4) or a task-oriented questionnaire (see Figure 12.4), which are then checked by supervisors. The questionnaires may also be completed by those who supervise the jobs being evaluated. Responses about time spent and importance of various tasks are then incorporated into a statistical (regression) technique to calculate job points and at the appropriate location of a job in the salary structure. Services that score the Position Analysis Questionnaire also provide job evaluation information.

Results of Job Evaluation

To some, job evaluation illustrates what is wrong with a traditional approach to human resources; they see it as an overly bureaucratic procedure that allows jobs to be placed in convenient, hierarchical boxes.[15] Many ask, why not simply establish the going rate through wage surveys (see next section) and use this information to guide salary decisions? In other words, why not by-pass the process of evaluating jobs?

In fact, this is frequently done and is termed **ranking to market.**[16] Salaries are based on a survey of salaries paid by competitors. Although expedient—and useful for many jobs, especially managerial and professional jobs—the method has disadvantages. First, such an approach allows competitors to dictate salaries, not strategic decisions within the organization. Second, not all jobs can be compared across firms. Comparisons can be made for key jobs and then pay established for

FIGURE 12.4 Sample Segment of Structured Job Evaluation Questionnaire

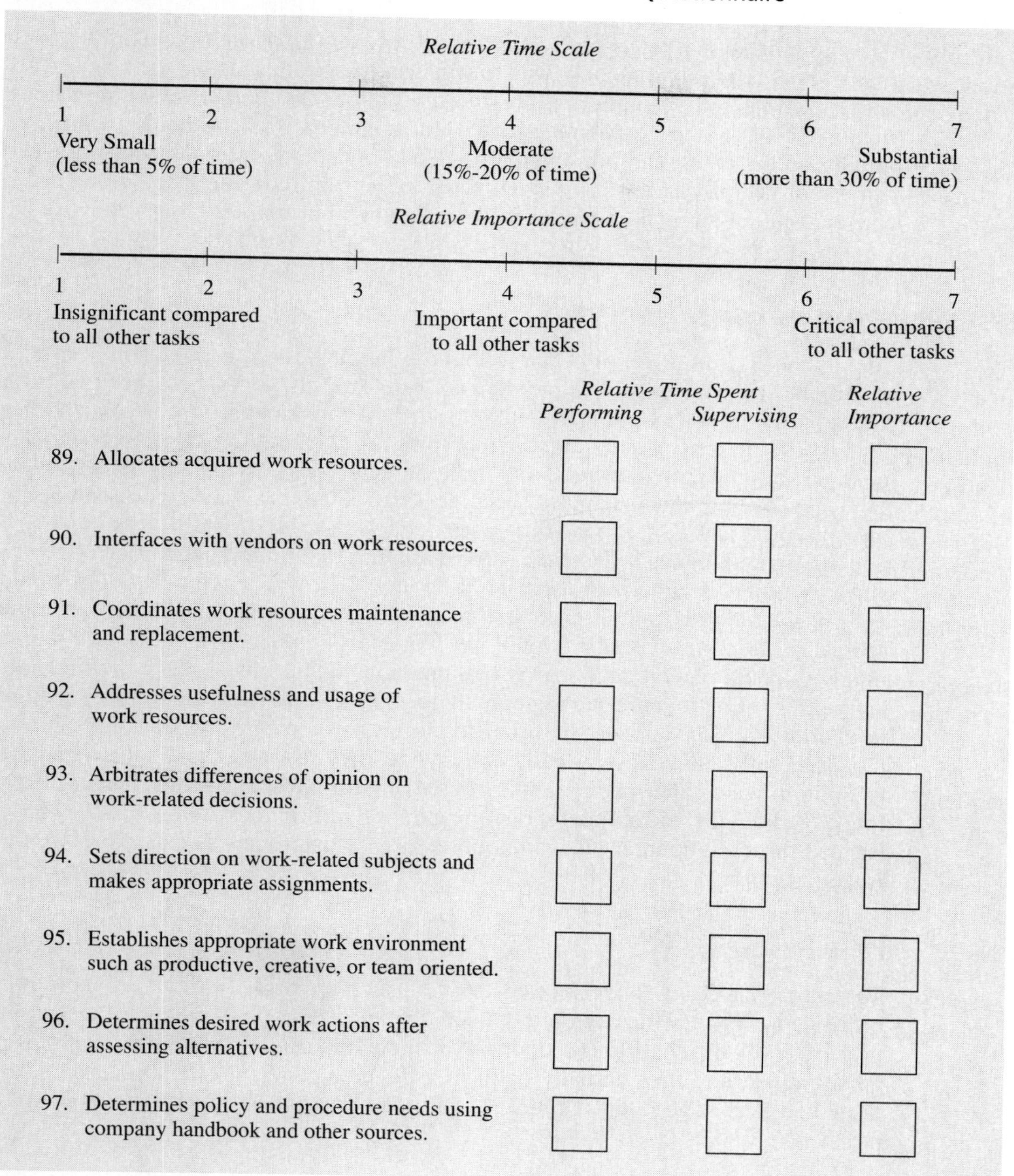

Relative Time Scale

1	2	3	4	5	6	7
Very Small (less than 5% of time)			Moderate (15%-20% of time)			Substantial (more than 30% of time)

Relative Importance Scale

1	2	3	4	5	6	7
Insignificant compared to all other tasks			Important compared to all other tasks			Critical compared to all other tasks

	Relative Time Spent Performing	Relative Time Spent Supervising	Relative Importance
89. Allocates acquired work resources.	☐	☐	☐
90. Interfaces with vendors on work resources.	☐	☐	☐
91. Coordinates work resources maintenance and replacement.	☐	☐	☐
92. Addresses usefulness and usage of work resources.	☐	☐	☐
93. Arbitrates differences of opinion on work-related decisions.	☐	☐	☐
94. Sets direction on work-related subjects and makes appropriate assignments.	☐	☐	☐
95. Establishes appropriate work environment such as productive, creative, or team oriented.	☐	☐	☐
96. Determines desired work actions after assessing alternatives.	☐	☐	☐
97. Determines policy and procedure needs using company handbook and other sources.	☐	☐	☐

Source: Reprinted with permission of Panel Publishers, Inc., 36 West 44th St., N.Y., N.Y. 10036, from *Topics in Total Compensation*, vol. 3, "Computerizing Job Evaluation for Greater Efficiency and Effectiveness," p. 248, Copyright 1989.

similar jobs, but this slotting of similar jobs is best accomplished by means of job evaluation.

Ranking to market is useful for some jobs, but for large organizations with many and varied jobs, the only way to construct a sound basis for the wage structure is through job evaluation. Once decisions about the *relative* value of jobs are made, the next step is assigning actual dollar amounts to the points, ranks, or grades produced by the job evaluation. The concept of external equity is very important in this process; pay levels must be set that consider the "going rate" for that type of job and employee in the relevant labor market.

ESTABLISHING EXTERNAL EQUITY

Just as there is no given price for a pound of apples, there is no absolute rate of pay for a job. You expect to pay less for apples at a farmers' market than at a supermarket, and less at a supermarket than at a convenience store. Small apples tend to cost less per pound than large apples. You expect to pay more for apples in some seasons than in others, and more in New York City than in Albany, New York. And if the price for apples seems too high, there is always the possibility of buying other, less expensive, fruit.

Pay to employees reflects the same dynamics that underlie the price of apples and consumers' reaction to these price differences. Just as you probably would not consistently shop at a store that charges higher prices, unless there is some special reason, you probably would not work for a company that offers less pay than you could receive at a nearby organization (again, unless there is some special reason). Employers need to compete for the skills and knowledge they require to operate their businesses—in order to attract workers with needed skills and to motivate and retain those already employed. They use wage and salary surveys to find out what other organizations are paying for particular skills. Then, in setting pay rates, they seek to integrate the external information with what they have learned through the internal evaluation of jobs. This process is called *pricing* the wage structure.

Wage and Salary Surveys

To establish a competitively priced wage structure, organizations typically rely on wage and salary survey data collected from other organizations. The survey process involves identifying the jobs to be included, selecting the organizations to be surveyed, and then actually collecting the data. The data then must be interpreted so that wage rates can be set within the context of the organization's pay policy.

Identifying Key Jobs In practice, employers do not seek market data on all jobs. Instead, they gather survey information only for key jobs, which generally have the following characteristics:

1. The job content is relatively stable over time.
2. The jobs occur frequently, both in the organization and in the surveyed organizations.
3. The jobs can be defined quite precisely.
4. The jobs are performed in a similar manner in most organizations.

Key jobs should span the range of positions to be included in the wage structure. For example, it would not be desirable to identify only entry-level positions as key jobs. Jobs at the middle and upper levels also need to be included. Moreover, jobs need to be carefully defined. For example, the job of secretary would seem to meet all the characteristics of a key job. However, in today's computer age, the secretarial job has been transformed. It is necessary to be specific as to the skills and responsibilities involved. Data may be collected on several clearly defined types or levels of secretaries.

Selecting Organizations to Survey Identifying organizations to survey can be important. In considering how to price its apples, a supermarket in New York City is not particularly concerned about supermarket prices in Albany since it will not lose any business to an Albany competitor. In the same way, organizations are interested only in rewards offered by their competitors in the same labor market.

Organizations to be covered in a wage survey typically include those that (1) employ workers with the same skills; (2) are within geographic distances that would make employees willing to commute or relocate; and (3) are in the same or similar industry. However, the considerations that go into selecting a set of organizations to be surveyed vary for different jobs. For example, it is far less important that these organizations be in the same industry when the survey focuses on wages of common jobs like secretary or truck driver. However, industry is crucial in establishing competitive pay for industry-specific jobs, for instance, petroleum engineers. The geographic area to be surveyed also depends on the job. For secretaries, all the relevant organizations competing for the skills are likely to be in the local area. For more complex jobs requiring sophisticated qualifications, however, the geographic area increases. Competition for managerial, professional, and technical jobs tends to be carried out at the regional or national level.

Other special considerations may also arise in selecting a sample of organizations to survey. For instance, suppose an organization makes wheel covers for General Motors Corp. at a plant in rural West Virginia. A local wage survey may show that wages for blue-collar workers of the type employed by the plant are quite low. However, because of intermittent activism by employees interested in being organized by the United Auto Workers, the management of this plant also needs to collect information on the pay and benefits of UAW members in plants elsewhere in the country. The wage level actually chosen may reflect both area and industry considerations.

Collecting Data Many organizations obtain the results of surveys undertaken by industry associations (e.g., the American Assembly of Collegiate Schools of Business), professional associations (e.g., the American Chemical Society, American Management Association), government agencies (e.g., the Bureau of Labor Statistics), or consulting firms (e.g., the Hay Group; Hewitt Associates; Towers, Perrin, Foster and Crosby). Numerous annual surveys cover a wide choice of job families and industries. At local levels, chapters of the Society for Human Resource Management or Chambers of Commerce often undertake surveys for their membership.

For a company that wants to collect and analyze its own data, it is important to obtain information on the characteristics of the responding organization, as well as on both direct and indirect compensation. The organizational information (e.g., total number of employees, sales, return on investment, product lines) is needed to judge the comparability of the competitor in terms of size, products, and financial condition. It is also crucial to know the types and amounts of benefits offered (e.g., fully covered medical plan versus plan supported in part by employee contributions), as well as incentives and hourly pay. Hourly pay rates or salaries may be misleading if bonuses for which employees are likely to qualify are not taken into account.

A salary survey report can take several forms. Table 12.8 illustrates a report published by the U.S. Bureau of Labor Statistics as part of its ongoing program of wage surveys in ninety geographical areas. The table gives information on a sample of jobs in Daytona Beach, Florida. (See the International Perspectives box for a comparison of compensation costs around the world.)

The report shows a detailed frequency distribution of hourly wage rates for each job, along with three summary measures: the mean, median, and middle (interquartile) range. The *mean* is computed by adding up the earnings of all workers and dividing the total by the number of workers. If the workers were ordered from highest earnings to lowest earnings, the *median* would be represented by the earnings of the person in the middle. The *middle range* refers to the middle 50 percent of the workers on the ordered list.

Of the three summary measures, the median is the most useful in setting wage ranges. The mean can easily become distorted if a few workers are paid at extreme rates. The median is not subject to such distortion.

Pay Level Policy

Once an organization has completed an internal job evaluation and obtained wage survey data, it needs to translate this information into pay rates for each class of jobs. This process involves appropriate interpretation of survey results, the merging of the job evaluation with the survey data, and consideration of the organization's pay level policy.

The first step in merging the internal and external data is a strategic decision on the organization's positioning vis-à-vis the competition. The three fundamental options are to match, lead, or lag behind the market.

By setting its pay levels at the market rate, or **matching the competition,** an organization tries to keep its labor costs comparable with those of competitors. Such an approach tends to neutralize pay as a factor in attracting, retaining, and motivating employees, while ensuring that labor costs are competitive.[17]

In adapting a **lead policy**—that is paying a higher wage rate than its competitors— a firm hopes to attract and retain higher-quality employees while maximizing satisfaction of its current employees. Firms with a lead policy want to be the preferred employer, so that they can select the best applicants while making it costly for competitors to persuade current employees to leave.[18] Frequently, such organizations have labor costs that represent a small proportion of the cost of production, or have higher levels of productivity, so that such a policy is affordable.

Some organizations follow a **lag approach,** setting their pay rates below those of their competitors. On the surface, it might seem that such a policy would inevitably lead to difficulties in attracting and retaining qualified employees. Some companies, however, have other ways to attract applicants, such as employment security (as with government jobs), superior benefits (e.g., holidays, vacation time), or an enjoyable environment. Some organizations, because of the nature of the business (e.g., entertainment, airlines) or excellent reputation, will attract well-qualified applicants even at below-market wages. Still other organizations may adopt a lag approach because they simply cannot afford to pay competitive salaries.[19]

Figure 12.5 diagrams how the three policies might be put into practice. The diagonal market line illustrates the gradual increase of market wage rates as different organizations implement changes at various times. At the beginning of the planning cycle (a year in this case), a firm with a lead policy sets its wage rates at the level that the market will reach only at the end of the year. A typical lag policy, by contrast, begins the year at a level equal to the market and is well behind by the end of the year. An organization with a match policy is actually paying wages equivalent to competition only at midyear. As can be seen, the match rate is above the market level at the start of the year and behind at the end.

Finally, an organization need not have one policy for all jobs. For example, an organization that can count on a steady supply of clerical and trade employees might adopt a policy of lagging behind the competition for these groups. But to attract the top professional talent, the same firm might adopt a lead policy in compensation for these groups.

Survey results are inevitably out of date when they reach the organization. For example, a survey initiated in mid-1992 might be compiled and ready for distribution by the end of the year. For most organizations, 1993 pay plans are already in place (based on 1991 survey results), and planning for 1994 is about to begin. If the 1992 survey information is to be used, it must be adjusted to reflect changes between the time of data collection and the plan period (mid-1992 through 1994 in the example discussed). The adjustment is based on historical trends from previous years, economic forecasts (e.g., productivity trends, cost of living changes), and judgment as to any special circumstances. In the example, figures

TABLE 12.8 Wage Survey for Daytona Beach, Florida, August 1991

Occupation	Number of workers	*Hourly earnings (in dollars)* Mean	Median	Middle Range	*Number of workers receiving straight-time hourly earnings (in dollars) of —* 4.25 and under 4.50	4.50 – 5.00	5.00 – 5.50	5.50 – 6.00	6.00 – 6.50	6.50 – 7.00	7.00 – 7.50
Accounting clerks	113	9.53	8.22	6.95– 9.88	—	—	—	—	15	15	10
Accounting clerks II	69	9.98	7.67	6.55–12.20	—	—	—	—	13	12	7
Accounting clerks III	35	8.65	8.22	7.50– 9.38	—	—	—	—	2	3	3
Key entry operators	40	7.19	6.50	5.75– 8.27	—	—	3	10	5	5	—
Key entry operators I	26	6.70	5.99	5.75– 7.50	—	—	3	10	5	1	—
Order clerks	24	8.05	7.69	6.50– 9.35	—	—	—	—	—	9	1
Payroll clerks	20	7.71	7.50	7.31– 8.00	—	—	—	—	—	3	2
Receptionists	11	7.69	7.88	— —	—	—	1	—	1	1	2
Secretaries	124	10.13	10.59	8.33–10.96	—	—	—	—	—	—	4
Secretaries I	14	7.69	7.63	— —	—	—	—	—	—	—	3
Secretaries II	47	9.61	10.32	8.17–10.59	—	—	—	—	—	—	1
Secretaries III	50	11.05	10.82	10.62–10.96	—	—	—	—	—	—	—
Switchboard operators	37	5.88	5.68	4.99– 6.32	—	10	6	3	11	4	—
Switchboard operator-receptionists	23	6.68	6.27	5.51– 7.75	—	—	5	2	7	2	1
Word processors	14	9.00	9.28	— —	—	—	—	—	2	—	—
Word processors II	12	9.46	10.31	— —	—	—	—	—	—	—	—
Computer operators	10	10.21	10.40	— —	—	—	—	—	1	—	1
Computer programmers	19	18.26	21.64	14.41–21.64	—	—	—	—	—	—	—
Drafters	81	12.72	12.75	10.63–14.57	—	—	—	—	—	—	—
Drafters III	51	11.70	12.74	9.50–12.93	—	—	—	—	—	—	—
Drafters IV	24	14.78	14.57	14.57–16.14	—	—	—	—	—	—	—
Electronics technicians	100	14.25	14.60	13.39–16.34	—	—	—	—	—	1	1
Electronics technicians II	68	14.68	14.29	13.40–16.34	—	—	—	—	—	—	—
General maintenance workers	139	6.01	5.82	5.25– 6.25	—	—	37	38	32	8	13
Maintenance carpenters	11	10.67	10.00	— —	—	—	—	—	—	—	—
Maintenance electricians	26	14.03	15.17	11.97–16.21	—	—	—	—	—	—	—
Maintenance mechanics (machinery)	50	9.96	9.00	7.90–10.20	—	—	—	—	—	—	10
Motor vehicle mechanics	55	9.92	8.68	7.28–11.90	—	—	—	—	4	8	2
Tool and die makers	92	12.82	12.60	12.60–14.05	—	—	—	—	—	—	—
Guards	227	4.71	4.35	4.25– 5.00	136	25	28	20	18	—	—
Guards I	227	4.71	4.35	4.25– 5.00	136	25	28	20	18	—	—
Janitors, porters, and cleaners	142	5.88	5.35	4.99– 6.50	6	30	36	17	17	11	5
Power-truck operators: Forklift operators	62	8.05	8.15	7.00–8.95	—	—	—	—	2	4	18
Receivers	15	9.69	10.34	9.00–10.34	—	—	—	—	—	1	—
Truckdrivers	234	10.31	8.42	6.50–17.06	—	—	3	54	1	2	18
Truckdrivers, heavy truck	105	6.90	6.25	5.50– 8.45	—	—	—	52	1	2	14
Warehousemen	36	6.70	6.00	5.00– 7.88	—	3	12	2	6	—	3

Source: U.S. Bureau of Labor Statistics Bulletin, August 1991.

from mid-1992 will need to be projected eighteen months to obtain the market level at the start of the 1994 plan year, and thirty months to estimate the market rate at the end of the plan year. Assuming that inflation and other factors will increase the market wage level at an annual rate of 4.5 percent, survey data should be multiplied by 1.0675 to represent the 6.75 percent increase (4.5% × 1.5 years) and 1.1125 to represent the 11.25 percent increase (4.5% × 2.5 years) to obtain the market rates for the beginning and end of 1994.

Number of workers receiving straight-time hourly earnings (in dollars) of—															
7.50 – 8.00	8.00 – 8.50	8.50 – 9.00	9.00 – 9.50	9.50 – 10.00	10.00 – 10.50	10.50 – 11.00	11.00 – 11.50	11.50 – 12.00	12.00 – 13.00	13.00 – 14.00	14.00 – 15.00	15.00 – 16.00	16.00 – 17.00	17.00 – 18.00	18.00 and over
8	23	5	5	4	5	1	—	—	4	1	—	—	1	8	8
3	12	1	—	—	2	1	—	—	2	—	—	—	—	8	8
4	9	4	2	3	2	—	—	—	2	—	—	—	1	—	—
5	3	5	—	1	—	2	—	—	1	—	—	—	—	—	—
3	1	—	—	1	—	2	—	—	—	—	—	—	—	—	—
4	1	2	2	2	—	1	2	—	—	—	—	—	—	—	—
9	4	—	—	1	1	—	—	—	—	—	—	—	—	—	—
2	—	3	—	—	1	—	—	—	—	—	—	—	—	—	—
9	20	4	—	3	15	44	11	4	3	4	2	1	—	—	—
8	2	1	—	—	—	—	—	—	—	—	—	—	—	—	—
1	16	2	—	1	8	12	2	3	1	—	—	—	—	—	—
—	1	1	—	2	6	31	1	1	1	3	2	1	—	—	—
1	—	1	1	—	—	—	—	—	—	—	—	—	—	—	—
2	—	2	2	—	—	—	—	—	—	—	—	—	—	—	—
1	4	—	—	—	4	3	—	—	—	—	—	—	—	—	—
1	4	—	—	—	4	3	—	—	—	—	—	—	—	—	—
—	—	—	1	1	2	—	—	3	—	1	—	—	—	—	—
—	—	1	—	—	1	—	—	—	1	1	2	1	—	—	12
1	2	2	4	10	1	2	2	2	27	4	13	3	4	1	3
—	1	1	2	10	1	1	2	2	27	2	2	—	—	—	—
—	—	—	2	—	—	—	—	—	—	2	11	3	4	1	1
—	2	—	4	—	—	3	2	3	7	9	24	10	24	10	—
—	—	—	2	—	—	3	—	3	7	6	14	—	24	9	—
5	3	2	—	—	—	—	—	1	—	—	—	—	—	—	—
2	1	1	1	—	1	—	2	—	1	1	—	—	1	—	—
—	—	—	—	1	1	1	2	3	2	—	1	6	9	—	—
10	1	1	9	5	3	—	1	—	—	1	—	—	9	—	—
—	—	14	—	2	2	8	1	1	5	—	3	3	—	2	—
—	1	—	—	1	3	3	3	1	51	6	17	6	—	—	—
—	—	—	—	—	—	—	—	—	—	—	—	—	—	—	—
—	—	—	—	—	—	—	—	—	—	—	—	—	—	—	—
—	5	9	2	3	1	—	—	—	—	—	—	—	—	—	—
2	7	23	6	—	—	—	—	—	—	—	—	—	—	—	—
—	2	—	1	1	9	1	—	—	—	—	—	—	—	—	—
16	29	5	27	4	2	1	—	—	—	2	—	—	—	70	—
8	4	—	24	—	—	—	—	—	—	—	—	—	—	—	—
1	3	—	1	—	1	—	2	—	2	—	—	—	—	—	—

ESTABLISHING INDIVIDUAL EQUITY

As mentioned earlier, jobs evaluated as having nearly the same value are usually combined into a single wage grade. It would be cumbersome to have fifty different wage rates for fifty different job titles, or a slightly higher rate for a job evaluated at 205 points versus one at 200 points. Thus, wage grades are established (for instance, all jobs with between 200 and 225 points would be a grade), and all jobs

A Comparison of Compensation Costs

Compensation rates vary substantially around the world: rates are lower or much lower in less developed countries compared with more developed ones, and rates in Europe tend to be higher than in the United States. The Bureau of Labor Statistics periodically compiles a report of compensation costs around the world. Although this survey focuses only on production workers in the manufacturing sector, it gives some idea of the general wage level in the country as a whole. In reporting the results, the present average U.S. hourly compensation cost is defined as 100, and other nations' costs are reported relative to this standard. The table below shows how other nations compared with the United States in terms of total hourly compensation costs (direct wages, pay for time not worked, and benefits) for production workers in the years 1985 and 1990.

Average Hourly Compensation Costs for Production Workers in Manufacturing Sector

Country	*1985*	*1990*
United States	100	100
Australia	63	88
Austria	56	114
Belgium	69	127
Brazil	9	19
Canada	83	107
Denmark	63	126
Finland	62	139
France	58	103
Hong Kong	13	22
Italy	56	110
Japan	50	87
Korea	10	28
Mexico	12	12
Norway	82	147
Portugal	12	24
Singapore	19	25
Spain	37	78
Sweden	75	141
Switzerland	75	139
Taiwan	12	27
United Kingdom	48	84
West Germany	74	144

Workers in Norway, the former West Germany, Sweden, Switzerland, and Finland had the highest pay in the world in 1990. Despite the very high rate of pay in Germany, public employees there went on an eleven-day strike for higher wages in the spring of 1992. They wanted a 9.5 percent increase rather than the 4.5 percent being offered by the government. Note that German workers also enjoy six weeks of paid vacation each year, fifteen paid public holidays, and the shortest regular workweek in the world. The public employees eventually settled for about 5.2 percent after the "most disruptive strike in German history" (Murray, 1992).

In terms of U.S. dollars, the average hourly compensation cost for Europe as a whole is just under $18 per hour, compared with the U.S. average of about $15 and the Japanese average of $13. The lowest wage countries in the report are Mexico and Brazil.

Differences in compensation and benefit costs are one major reason that many U.S. manufacturing jobs have gone abroad. Very few shoes, clothes, and televisions are produced in the U.S. anymore. Many are imported from Korea, Taiwan, Japan, and Singapore. As China's door opens wider, it is also seen as a low-wage haven for manufacturers willing to risk a joint venture. A number of U.S. companies have set up factories just across the border in Mexico, under the Maquiladora Program. Wage rates in these plants ranged from $0.95 to $1.70 per hour in 1990, including benefit costs. Compensation costs are so low that Japanese and Korean firms are even opening plants in Mexico. It was estimated that more than 487,000 Mexicans were employed in maquiladora plants in 1990.

Sources: Patricia Capdevielle, "International Comparison of Compensation Costs," *Monthly Labor Review,* August 1991, pp. 34–38; Ian Murray, "Deal Ends Record Strike in Germany," *The Weekend Australian,* May 9–10, 1992, p. 10; Mary B. Teagarden, Mark C. Butler, and Mary Ann Von Glinow, "Mexico's Maquiladora Industry: Where Strategic Human Resource Management Makes a Difference," *Organizational Dynamics,* Winter 1992, pp. 34–47; "Adios, $20-an-hour Laborers," *Financial Executive,* November/December 1990, pp. 7–8.

FIGURE 12.5 Pay Policies over Time: Lag, Match, and Lead Pay Structures

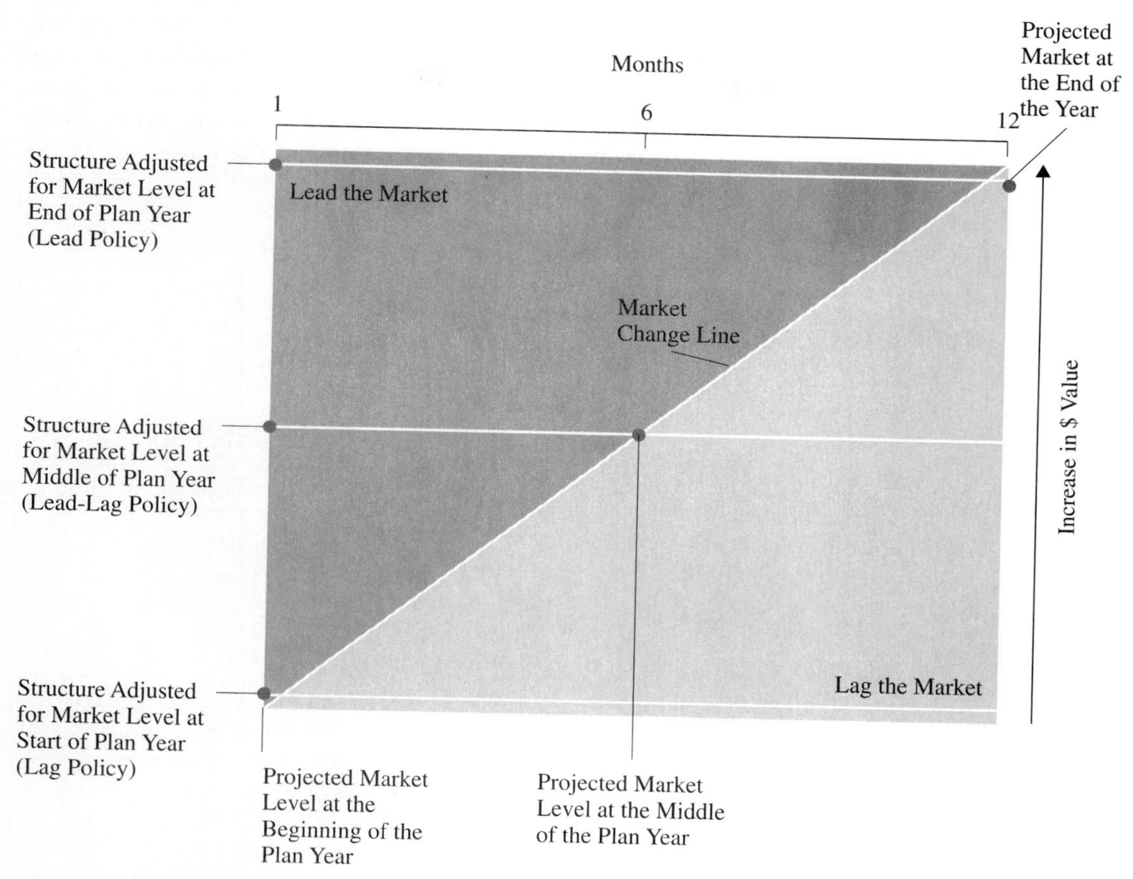

Source: Richard Henderson, *Compensation Management: Rewarding Performance,* 5th ed., © 1989, p. 477. Reprinted by permission of Prentice-Hall, Inc., Englewood Cliffs, N.J.

within the grade are paid identically. A single wage may be selected for each grade and paid to every person whose job falls in the grade. More commonly, however, a range of pay rates is set for each grade. When a range is set, the issue of individual equity becomes salient, and the organization must have a system for determining where in the range the compensation of each employee should be.

Designing Pay Ranges

The range associated with a pay grade sets the upper and lower bounds of possible compensation for individuals whose jobs fall in the grade. There is no optimum number of pay grades for a wage structure, although most organizations define ten to sixteen pay grades. The typical arrangement is ten grades for nonsupervisory jobs and thirteen for clerical jobs.[20]

The first step is to define the pay policy line linking pay to job evaluation points. Think of a graph with wage grades along the horizontal axis and pay (dollars) along the vertical axis. (See Figure 12.6) The policy line is based on salary survey data, appropriately adjusted and taking into consideration the firm's policy (lead, match, or lag). The points on the line will represent the midpoints of the ranges, which are calculated next.

FIGURE 12.6 Pay Ranges

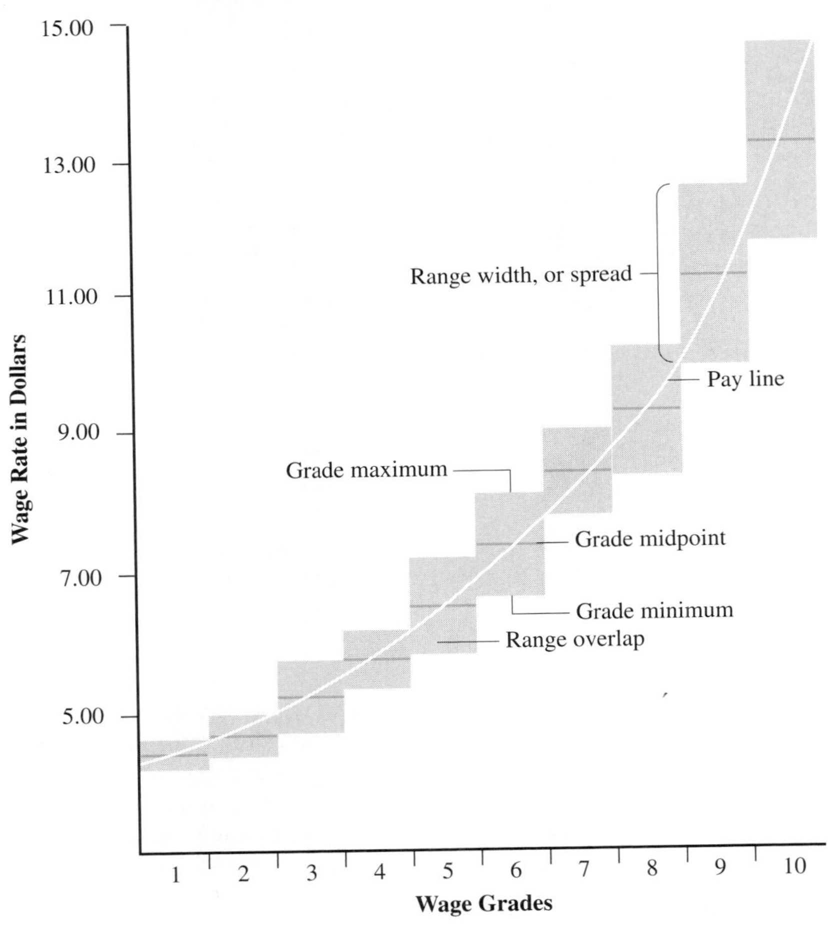

Source: Adapted from Marc J. Wallace, Jr., and Charles H. Fay, *Compensation Theory and Practice*, 2nd ed. (Boston, Mass.: PWS-KENT Publishing Company, 1988), p. 221.

Each grade has a minimum, a maximum, and midpoint. The spread around the midpoint may vary, with 10 to 20 percent on either side being typical, as shown in Figure 12.6. The percentage spread is frequently greater for higher-level positions, on the assumption that there is more leeway to make an outstanding or very poor contribution in these more important jobs.

It is important that adjacent grades overlap, as shown in Figure 12.6, since an experienced employee in a lower grade may make a greater contribution than a relatively new employee in the next higher grade. Well over half of a given pay range may overlap the adjacent pay grade.

Although each range has a maximum, the structure is dynamic. Ordinarily, the pay policy line and all the ranges are adjusted upward each year as inflationary and competitive pressures push wages upward. At some point, the top-performing employees will eventually reach the maximum within a range. They should then be considered for promotion to a higher grade. If the overlap between grades is too large, even a promotion may not bring a large enough salary increase to have incentive value.

When the wage structure is initially formed, it is not unusual to find employees who are currently being paid above the maximum for a range or below the minimum. Those below the minimum are usually increased to be within the range. If employees earning more than the maximum qualify for promotion, they can be moved to a job in a higher range commensurate with their existing pay. If promotion is not possible, the employee is "red circled": his or her pay is frozen at its present level until the range moves up, through annual increases, to include the individual. Thus, no one's pay is ever cut as a result of job evaluation.

Setting Individual Pay

Individual equity requires that rewards to employees be applied fairly across individuals performing the same job. The two commonly used approaches to determine how workers are placed and progress through the pay ranges are seniority and merit. A newer method bases increments on the number of skills mastered.

Seniority When based on seniority, pay increases depend solely on the employee's experience or length of service on the job. Individuals all start out with equal pay, and then progress through steps with each year of service. In addition to the step increases, the entire range (that is, the entry rate and each of the steps) is adjusted to reflect the results of salary surveys and economic trends.

The seniority system rewards a stable, experienced work force. Seniority systems are often used when employees are unionized, when employees do not accept or trust the concept of merit pay, when differences in performance are difficult to measure accurately, or when jobs call for very similar work performance or output. Assembly-line jobs, for example, typically require similar work performance and output from all workers.

Merit Pay Many organizations try to link compensation to actual job performance.[21] Merit increases are given, usually on an annual basis, with better performing employees receiving larger raises. In theory, merit increases allow management to use pay to motivate employees to higher levels of performance. However, considerable data suggest that merit pay may not be as desirable, as easy to implement, or as widely used as is commonly believed. The next chapter discusses in more detail the theory and practice of using incentives, including merit pay.

Many workers distrust merit reward systems because they do not feel their pay is related to their performance level. After comparing notes with their peers, employees may feel that they have not been treated fairly, usually because they perceive their own performance as being relatively high. In one study across all occupational groups, more than 95 percent of employees rated themselves as above average.[22]

One prescription for a successful merit system defines the following requirements:

1. A high level of trust and belief in management.
2. A correct and current job evaluation system and wage structure (alleviating the tendency to use supposed merit money to correct distortions caused by a wage structure that is incorrect or out of touch with the market).
3. Performance criteria agreed to by all levels of employees.
4. Job-specific, results-based criteria to reduce subjective bias.
5. Accurate performance appraisals. Since no single performance appraisal format is appropriate in all situations, alternate formats should be adopted for different situations.
6. Appropriate administrative practices, such as minimizing the time between the performance appraisal and pay increase, to maximize the reinforcement principle.
7. Skillfully administered feedback during the performance appraisal session, to ensure that employees are aware of expected performance.
8. Managers trained in the correct use of the compensation system.[23]

A typical system for relating performance to merit increases is shown in Table 12.9. In this example, salary increases range from zero to 15 percent and depend on both performance and current position in the range. The more meritorious the performance, the greater the increase. Within a given level of performance, those lower in the range receive larger percentage increases for several reasons. First, because those higher in the range already earn more, a smaller percentage increase can mean a larger absolute dollar amount. Second, if those higher in the range received increases of an equivalent percentage, they would capture most of the merit increase budget. Third, those toward the top of the range are candidates for rewards made through other mechanisms, such as promotion. Fourth, using smaller increases toward the top of the range helps keep people from hitting the maximum rate and thus becoming ineligible for further increases.

TABLE 12.9 Merit Pay Increase Matrix

Range Position	*Performance*				
	Outstanding	*Excellent*	*Good*	*Fair*	*Unsatisfactory*
Top Fifth	6%	6%	0%	0%	0%
Next Fifth	9%	6%	5%	0%	0%
Middle Fifth	11%	9%	6%	5%	0%
Next Fifth	13%	11%	8%	5%	0%
Bottom Fifth	15%	13%	10%	6%	0%

Skill-based Pay Still another basis for establishing individual pay rates has to do with the knowledge one has mastered on the job.[24] Skill-based pay plans analyze the job knowledge an employee will need to progress. All employees begin at an entry-level rate. As they learn additional skills and as the learning is verified through demonstration or tests, they qualify for increments in pay. Skill-based pay, along with the incentives it engenders for employees, is described further in the next chapter.

LEGAL REGULATION OF COMPENSATION SYSTEMS

The major factors influencing an organization's reward system include job content (assessed by job evaluation), market forces (supply of labor, competition for labor, and employer's ability to pay), and the pay policy of the organization. Certain legal constraints also influence all compensation systems. In fact, the recent increase in government regulations has made legal constraints a major factor in planning and administering a compensation system.

Legal issues related to direct compensation (pay rates, hours, and so forth) are considered in this chapter. Legislation that affects indirect compensation (pensions, Social Security, and so on) is discussed in the next chapter.

The Fair Labor Standards Act

The Fair Labor Standards Act (FLSA) of 1938 is the major law affecting direct compensation. Its provisions on the minimum wage, hours of work, and equal pay directly affect the design of compensation systems. Sections of the FLSA dealing with child labor and record-keeping requirements are also important but have less direct consequence and are not considered in this chapter.

The terms *exempt* and *nonexempt* are crucial for understanding and complying with the FLSA. **Exempt employees** include executive, administrative, and professional employees who are exempt from the minimum wage and work hours provisions of the FLSA. **Nonexempt employees** are subject to the provisions of the FLSA.

To be exempt as an executive, an employee must supervise two or more employees, have the authority to hire and fire, and otherwise exercise independent judgment. Administrators need not supervise other employees but do need to exercise independent judgment in carrying out top-management policies. Professionals are exempt under the definition of the FLSA if they perform unstandardized artistic or intellectual work of a varied nature that requires independent judgment.

Correctly determining the exempt or nonexempt status of a job is important, although not always easy. For instance, we tend to think of accountants and engineers as professionals, but in some cases they are not professionals under the FLSA guidelines. A lower-level accountant who applies accounting principles with little independent judgment or a newly hired engineer who does drafting work for other engineers would not be exempt. Under the law, their employer is liable for overtime pay for these individuals.

A final class of individuals who are exempt from the FLSA is outside salespeople. An outside salesperson must spend 80 percent or more of the workweek away from the employer's place of business, making visits to customers. Outside salespeople need not be paid overtime, and they are often paid only by commission.[25]

Because the Constitution empowers Congress and the federal government to regulate interstate commerce, almost all employers are covered by the FLSA. The act applies to all employers producing goods for interstate commerce or having employees who handle, sell, or otherwise work on such goods or materials. This means that any organization that uses a product produced in another state (e.g., day-care facility using disposable diapers made in another state) is covered.

Minimum Wage The minimum wage provision of the FLSA establish the lowest pay an employer can offer an employee. After many years at $3.35 per hour, the minimum wage became a campaign issue in 1988. George Bush supported a rate of no more than $4.25 per hour, with the stipulation of a lower "training rate" for inexperienced employees during their first six months' employment. However, Congress feared that a training wage would create a permanent class of subminimum employees as companies replaced workers every six months in order to keep labor costs low. The bill, which finally passed in November 1989, allowed a training wage only for sixteen-to-nineteen-year-olds and an increase in the minimum wage to $3.80 on April 1, 1990, followed by an increase to $4.25 on April 1, 1991.

Despite the wide coverage of the minimum wage provisions, it does not apply to all nonexempt workers. Employers need not pay the minimum wage to apprentices or agricultural workers. If employees receive more than $30 per month in tips, employers may reduce the hourly wage below the minimum by a specified amount.

Hours of Work The overtime provisions of the FLSA require payment of one and one-half the regular hourly rate for work over forty hours per week. Union contracts may specify greater amounts (e.g., twice the regular hourly rate) or lower thresholds (e.g., overtime after thirty-five hours per week), which supersede the FLSA provisions.

Employers may pay overtime to exempt employees (executives and professionals) but are not obligated to do so. Salaried nonexempt employees are covered; to calculate appropriate overtime pay, their salary is converted into an hourly rate. Employers of nonexempt employees are required to keep thorough records of the hours worked, to be sure that employees receive overtime payment when it is due.

The Wage and Hour Division of the Department of Labor has responsibility for enforcing the FLSA. Most inspections are triggered by an employee complaint; but once the inspection begins, all records for all employees may be scrutinized. Back pay for all affected workers can be ordered. In 1987, the Department of Labor conducted 72,000 investigations and found $126 million in violations, mostly for unpaid overtime, involving over a half-million employees.[26] Therefore, it is wise for employers to know the provisions of the FLSA and to follow them carefully.

Equal Pay Act

Passed as an amendment to the FLSA, the Equal Pay Act (EPA) of 1963 requires an organization to offer equal pay for equal work, regardless of the sex of the employee. The EPA defines equal work as (1) requiring equal skill, (2) requiring equal effort, (3) requiring equal responsibility, and (4) being performed under similar working conditions. Thus, men and women performing the same job in the same location for the same employer must be offered the same pay, all other things being equal. The use of two job titles for what is essentially the same job as a pretext for paying one group less than the other is not permitted (for example, calling men "office managers" and women "senior secretaries" when their duties are identical).

Equal pay is not required if differences in the average pay of men and women arise because of a seniority system, a merit system, or a system that measures earnings by quantity or quality of production. In other words, the customary approaches used to establish individual pay are acceptable even if they create unequal pay between men and women. Such discrepancies would arise, for example, if an organization based individual pay on seniority, and most of its female employees were more recently hired.

The Equal Pay Act would seem to be a natural basis for pursuing the issue of comparable worth, a topic discussed later in this chapter. In fact, the rather strict requirements of identical skill, effort, responsibility, and working conditions have made it difficult to use this legislation as the basis for insisting on equal pay for work of comparable worth.

Other Laws Affecting Compensation

Other legal regulations that affect reward systems have to do with discrimination, wages paid by contractors who work for the United States government, and wage garnishment. In addition, some states have their own wage and hour laws.

Title VII of the Civil Rights Act prohibits discrimination on the basis of race, color, sex, national origin, and religion in all aspects of employment, including compensation. Thus, it would be illegal to pay minority employees less than similarly qualified nonminority employees for doing the same job in the same location.

A series of laws (Davis-Bacon Act of 1931, Walsh-Healy Public Contracts Act of 1936, and McNamara-O'Hara Service Contract Act of 1965) requires that suppliers of goods or services to the federal government pay at least the "prevailing wage" to their employees. In practice, the prevailing wage has usually been set by the Department of Labor as the average wage of unionized workers in an area or industry. Some argue that this causes wages to be artificially raised and costs the government more than it would have to pay without this law.[27] The intent, however, was to prevent the government from buying "sweatshop" goods, and thus indirectly exploiting workers.

A final law, the Consumer Credit Protection Act of 1968, covers wage garnishment, the procedure by which a creditor can get a court order compelling the employer to pay over a portion of an indebted employee's earnings. The act limits the amount that can be ordered withheld from each paycheck, and prohibits an employer from firing an employee for the first incident of garnishment.[28]

The regulatory context has a powerful influence on organizational reward systems. The human resource manager must carefully obey the law in many aspects of establishing and administering a compensation system. Regulatory constraints are equally significant with respect to benefits, a topic covered in the next chapter.

ADMINISTERING COMPENSATION SYSTEMS

Even the best designed compensation system will be ineffective if it does not gain employee acceptance, and this acceptance is often determined by the way the reward system is administered. This section discusses several of the major issues associated with the administration of compensation systems.

Pay Secrecy

The process by which a compensation system is formulated and administered is critical to the organization. One important administrative issue concerns the availability of compensation information to employees. Unfortunately, in most organizations the tendency is toward secrecy. Studies by Edward E. Lawler have shown that employees regularly misperceive the pay of others, including subordinates, peers, and superiors.[29] For example, superiors were perceived as receiving less than their actual salary, while subordinates and peers were thought to receive more than they actually did. Another study showed that managers make different pay allocation decisions when pay is secret than when it is open.[30] Secrecy makes it easier for allocators to use whatever criteria they wish, since their decisions are less likely to be known by others.

Just how much and what types of information about pay should be provided to employees is a question that is troubling to compensation professionals. This is not a simple question to answer. Much has been written about the effects of secrecy on the behavior and attitudes of employees.

On one end of the spectrum is a policy of full, or open, disclosure: information regarding individual salaries is available on request. When the government is the employer, full disclosure is the norm, because pay policies and even individual salaries are a matter of public record. Similarly, most union contracts spell out wages on the basis of job title and time in grade.

Most other employees are provided very little information about pay. In a survey conducted by the Bureau of National Affairs, only 18 percent of responding companies said that managers had knowledge of the salaries of their superiors or peers.[31] Open systems with regard to pay are the exception, not the rule.

The goals of achieving equity and, to the extent possible, participant satisfaction would seem to call for telling employees about pay policies and levels. For merit systems to have a motivating effect, employees need to know how effort translates into rewards. Information about the maximum and the average rise should be made available each year. Each employee should be told what the midpoint is for his or her job, as well as the pay range. In addition the organization should explain how it arrived at the pay structure. Allowing employees to see where their jobs are located in the wage structure should not create significant problems for an employer that has a well-designed job evaluation plan.

Employee Participation

People tend to be more committed to programs they had a hand in developing. When employees help create compensation plans, there is generally less resistance, and the plan is much more likely to be a successful motivator than would a plan imposed by management.[32]

It is appropriate to involve employees in many phases of a reward system. For example, a wide variety of employees should serve on job evaluation committees. If a point plan is adopted, it is reasonable to involve employees in identifying the compensable factors to be used and the weight to be assigned to each factor. Employees are also likely to have good insight into which competitor firms should be included in a wage survey.

There are several mechanisms for employee involvement. At the broadest level, employees can be surveyed to learn their preferences. Employee task forces can help integrate these preferences into a system. Such groups are usually an excellent way to involve employees in the decisions associated with a reward system.

The decision to involve employees in designing or administering a compensation system should not be made without deliberation, however. This approach is unlikely to work well unless the organization has already established an overall philosophy of participative management, as well as a reasonable climate of organizational trust. Participation takes considerable time, so if time and trust are limited, a more traditional, top-down approach might be more appropriate.

Wage Compression

Wage compression results when wages for new hires are increasing faster than the wages of people already on the payroll.[33] As a result, the pay differentials between jobs become very small. A study by Luis Gomez-Mejia and David B. Balkin of the compression in the salary differentials among professors in a business school provides a good example.[34] Salaries for newly hired assistant professors were increasing rapidly. For instance, inexperienced assistant professors were hired at $40,000 per year while other assistant professors with two or three years' experience were earning between $37,000 and $38,000, and several associate professors with as much as ten years' experience were earning only $45,000. Constrained by a limited budget, the dean chose to use the limited available funds primarily to recruit new faculty, who were getting attractive offers from other schools. This meant that the traditional wage differentials between ranks could not be maintained. The dean elected to create internal inequities in the interest of external competitiveness for new faculty.

Although wage compression must often be accepted in the short run, it can be extremely counterproductive if allowed to continue. In the business school example, senior faculty will become dissatisfied and search for new jobs at other universities. Since the best-qualified will most easily secure new positions, the average quality of the school's remaining faculty may decline.

Much of employers' resistance to increases in the minimum wage is not directly related to additional costs for entry-level jobs but to the threat of wage compression and the cost of preventing it. Similarly, managers frequently experience wage increases as a result of union negotiations. As wages of union members increase, the company raises salaries of lower- and middle-level managers to prevent wage compression.[35]

Impact of Inflation

Even well-designed compensation systems can have major problems in inflationary or deflationary times. In the late 1970s, many firms were limited to giving 10 percent merit raises to their best people even though the inflation rate was 13 to 14 percent. Employees felt that they were losing purchasing power. At a minimum, they hoped to keep even with inflation.

In the early 1980s, firms began catching up, giving raises in the 12 and 13 percent range. Then, when inflation had been checked, salary increases soon fell back to 7 percent. Thus far in the 1990s, merit budgets have averaged 4 percent or less. Under these circumstances, it has been difficult to convince employees that current salary increase levels are sufficient when expectations had adjusted to higher levels.[36] In order to maximize perception of fairness, it is essential to have good communication with employees about their compensation package and salary increases.

All-salaried Work Force

As part of the move to increase employee participation at all organizational levels, many firms have moved to an all-salaried work force. All employees, even the blue-collar workers, receive the agreed salary each pay period, and the size of their checks does not depend primarily on the number of hours worked. That is, employees are not docked for lateness or other absences. This policy is meant to eliminate the feeling of hourly employees that they are second-class citizens.

The employer remains responsible for enforcing the Fair Labor Standards Act, however, and from this perspective, nonexempt salaried employees are still paid by the hour. Employers must keep a record of hours worked (presumably by less obtrusive means than a time clock) and pay overtime to all nonexempt employees who work more than forty hours in any one week, whether or not they are otherwise treated as salaried employees by the employer.

Wage Concessions

It is not unusual to read about a strike resulting from an impasse in collective bargaining. Typically, the contract has expired, and the union and management cannot agree on wages. Perhaps the union is asking for a 21 percent increase over the three years of the contract period while the top management offer is 15 percent. The last several years have brought a new twist to this scenario. In one strike, management was asking the workers to take a 20 percent wage reduction. The employees, cabin attendants for TWA, were willing to accept a cut of only 15 percent, the result being a strike over the magnitude of the concession.[37]

Until the 1980s it was almost inconceivable that a well-entrenched union would agree to concessions (or reductions) in wages and benefits. Yet this is exactly what has been happening throughout the last decade, for several reasons. In the automobile, steel, and other manufacturing industries, less expensive foreign labor has forced American manufacturers to bring their costs in line. Wage concessions were one part of the strategy. In other industries, such as transportation, deregulation opened routes and activities to new competition. Low-cost, nonunionized airlines were flying many of the same routes, forcing the established unionized carriers to slash labor costs.

One solution adopted by some companies and unions was the two-tier wage contract. In this type of agreement, current employees continue to receive their existing wage rates, but any new hires after a specified date are paid at a much lower rate. This has proven to be a shortsighted solution, as it creates substantial internal inequity, and individuals hired at the lower rate do not feel fairly treated by either the union or the company. The problems intensify the longer the system is in effect, as the lower paid workers increase in number and in seniority.

THE ISSUE OF COMPARABLE WORTH

A policy of equal pay for equal work was mandated by the Equal Pay Act of 1963. The notion of **comparable worth** goes further, calling for jobs of equal pay for comparable work. Comparable worth is based on the idea that traditionally female-dominated jobs are underpaid relative to traditionally male-dominated jobs that require the same level of (although perhaps a different) skill and make an equally valuable contribution to the employer. The ideological and political debate surrounding comparable worth has been fierce. On one hand, Clarence Pendleton, chairman of the Civil Rights Commission during the Reagan administration, termed comparable worth "the looniest idea since Looney Tunes."[38] Others say comparable worth is the issue of the 1990s. This section examines the elements of this controversy.

The Earnings Gap

The comparable worth debate centers on what has come to be known as the **earnings gap.** Each year, the Bureau of the Census reports on the difference between women's and men's median incomes. As shown in Figure 12.7, full-time female employees earn about 71 cents for each dollar men earn. The greatest difference is for sales, where women earn 57 cents for each dollar men earn. Women in technical occupations are closest to men, earning 78 cents for every dollar men earn.

Part of the reason for this difference is that women tend to hold different jobs than men, even within an occupational category. For instance, women are more likely to be nurses than physicians, both professional occupations. Half of all working women are employed in only 20 of 427 census-defined occupations.[39] About 60 percent of men (or women) would have to change their occupations in order for men and women to be distributed equally across the occupations. Within each occupation, moreover, women and minorities tend to hold the lower-status jobs, rather than being paid less for doing the same job.[40] Women also tend to hold nonunion jobs, which are often paid less than the unionized jobs held more commonly by men.

In addition, there are differences in the salaries paid to men and women in the same type of job. As Figure 12.8 shows, women earn considerably less than men in science careers. Many factors other than gender may influence these pay differences. For example, differences in employee characteristics could be significant. It may be that men, as a whole, are entering the science professions with more education and more experience. A second explanation of the difference may be seniority. Males may have longer tenure (seniority) in the professions than women and may earn more for that reason. A third explanation could be related

FIGURE 12.7 A Comparison of Median Income of Male and Female Year-Round, Full-Time Workers for 1990

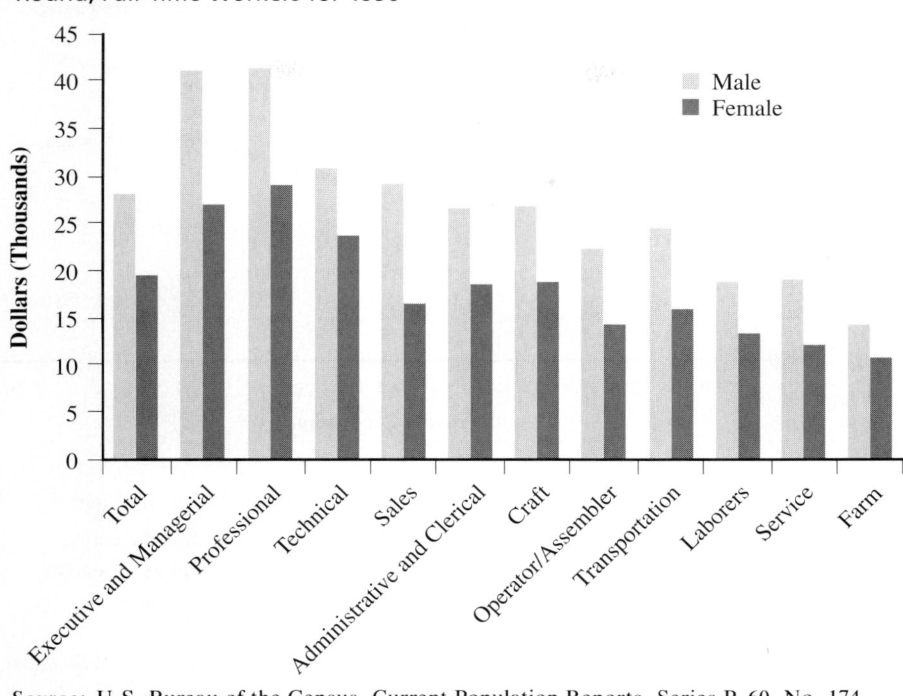

Source: U.S. Bureau of the Census, Current Population Reports, Series P–60, No. 174, *Money Income of Households, Families, and Persons in the United States: 1990*, U.S. Government Printing Office, Washington, D.C., 1991.

to work performance—for example, discoveries, publications, and conference presentations. Men, on the average, may be more productive than women. Still another explanation could have to do with types of employers preferred by men and women. It could be that men are employed by organizations with greater ability to pay than are women. For instance, female lawyers may more often seek jobs in public or legal aid organizations rather than private law firms.

Two examples illustrate why the comparable worth debate has aroused such passion. In San Jose, California, the positions of senior legal secretary (predominantly female) and senior carpenter (predominantly male) both were assigned 226 job evaluation points, yet the secretaries earned $665 per month whereas the carpenters earned $1,040 per month. In other words, the senior secretaries' earnings were only 64 percent of the senior carpenters'—despite equivalent job evaluation points.[41] The same San Jose study found that librarians (a predominantly female job) and street sweeper operators (predominantly male) received equivalent pay of $750 per month, even though librarians were assigned many more job evaluation points than sweeper operators.

FIGURE 12.8 Salaries of Men and Women in Science Careers, 1987

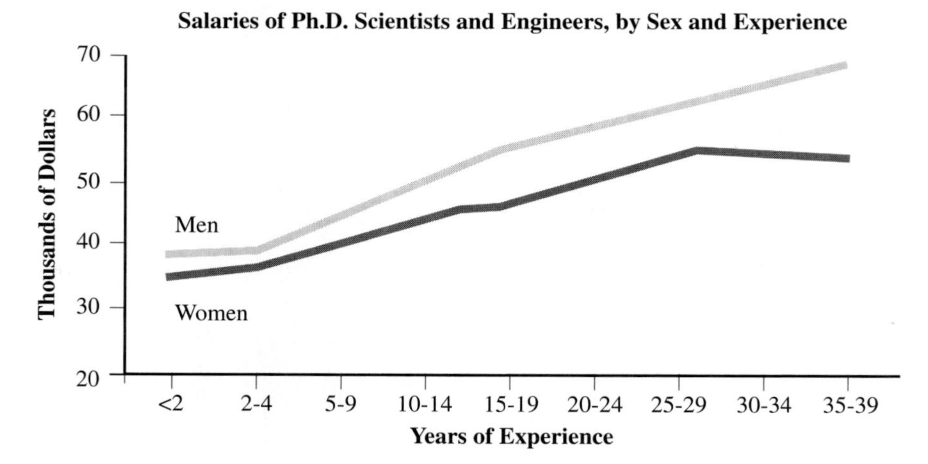

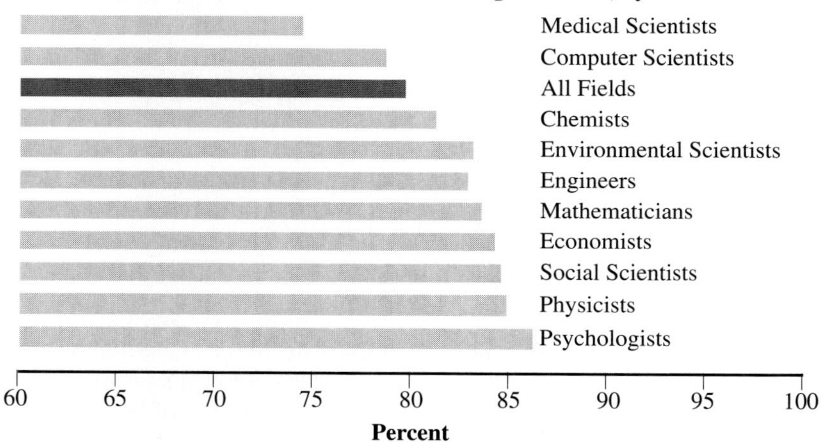

Source: Betty M. Vetter, "Bad News for Women Scientists—and the Country," *The AAAS Observer,* May 5, 1989, p. 9. Based on National Research Council Biennial Survey of Science, Engineering and Humanities Doctorates. Data for salaries by sex and experience are unpublished special tabulations. Data for women's salaries as a percentage of men's published by the National Science Foundation (1988) in *Characteristics of Doctoral Scientists and Engineers in the United States 1987* (NSF 88–331).

Legal and Judicial Developments

The Equal Pay Act has not been conducive to redressing issues of comparable worth. Instead, most court cases have relied on Title VII of the Civil Rights Act. Court have generally held that Title VII incorporates the equal pay for equal work standard (skill, effort, responsibility), along with the four affirmative defenses for pay differentials (seniority, merit, quality or quantity of work, or any condition other than sex), and allows a broader inquiry into compensation practices of defendants. The argument has been that workers in predominantly female jobs are paid less than workers in predominantly male jobs, and that this is discriminatory since the jobs, although different in content, are of comparable worth to the employer.

The early pay discrimination cases showed clearly that employers had to pay workers at the same rate in predominantly female jobs if those jobs required substantially the same work performed, knowledge, and skill as jobs filled predominantly by men. In *Schultz* v. *Wheaton Glass,*[42] men and women inspected and boxed empty bottles, yet men received 10 percent more for occasionally stacking boxes and performing other duties. The difference was ruled to be sex biased. In *Hodgson* v. *Brookhaven General Hospital,*[43] female aides claimed that their jobs were equal to those performed by more highly paid male orderlies. However, the hospital presented evidence that the duties performed by men were different, and the pay discrepancy was found to be legal.

Christensen v. *State of Iowa* was a major comparable worth case. Clerical workers (predominantly female) at the University of Northern Iowa argued that their jobs were equivalent to those of physical plant workers (predominantly male) in terms of job evaluation points, yet physical plant workers were paid at a higher rate. The university's defense was that conditions in the local labor market required it to pay physical plant workers more, to be competitive. The court sided with the university, noting that

> The value of the job to the employer [job evaluation] represents but one factor affecting wages. Other factors may include the supply of workers willing to do the job. . . . We find nothing in the text and history of Title VII suggesting that Congress intended to abrogate the law of supply and demand or other economic principles that determine wages for various kinds of work. We do not interpret Title VII as requiring an employer to ignore the market in setting wage rates for genuinely different work classifications.[44]

Comparable worth claims have consistently been rejected by the courts. The specific reasons for final rulings have varied but seem to reflect a sense that comparable worth is not a viable legal theory under Title VII.

Even though the courts have not been sympathetic to comparable worth, twenty states have specifically enacted legislation or adopted policies implementing comparable worth standards in the state civil service.[45] Minnesota's law is the most stringent, requiring all public employers (state, county, school district, and so on) to establish equitable compensation relationships between female- and male-dominated jobs.[46]

Comparable Worth and Job Evaluation

Job evaluation provides one possible means of equating jobs that are different in content but equal in value. However, even the values assigned to different compensable factors may tend to discriminate against traditionally female jobs. For instance, the level of skill required to operate a word processor or teach children may be underestimated, or the value of physical work performed in non-office settings may be overweighted.

To clarify the role of job evaluation in pay decisions, the Equal Employment Opportunity Commission (EEOC) initiated a study of pay-related job measurement by the National Academy of Science (NAS), an independent research institute. The NAS report acknowledged the difficulty of determining comparable worth and suggested that each employer equally compensate jobs of comparable value to the organization, whether or not the work content is substantially equal.[47]

However, there are legitimate criticisms of the use of job evaluation as a vehicle to establish comparable worth.[48] Clearly, the skill, effort, and responsibility framework of job evaluation does not cover all job factors important to working individuals. For example, the positions of senior legal secretary and senior carpenter in San Jose may have been equal in job evaluation points, but few would consider them equivalent alternatives in terms of the type of work done, types of colleagues, potential for flexibility in schedule, variety, work locations, and so forth.[49]

Alternatives

One argument against comparable worth is that it would be a threat to the labor market process of establishing wages based on supply and demand. Many contend that market rates accurately reflect job worth. The 1981 National Academy of Science report mentioned earlier noted that the market-wage disparity between positions filled primarily by women and those filled primarily by men tends to reflect past practices. The report adds, "one of the features of wage differentials between jobs held by men and by women is that they become customarily accepted as the standard rates for the jobs."[50] Thus, market forces do not always operate efficiently.

Market forces create many kinds of pay differences, not just between men and women. For example, college teachers in the liberal arts are paid less than engineering faculty, even though both jobs require similar skill, effort, and responsibility. The market forces that affect the two groups are quite different. Universities are locked in fairly high-level competition with private sector firms to attract doctoral engineers to join their faculties, whereas competition for doctoral philosophers is far less acute, primarily because there are fewer nonacademic opportunities.

Further, it would be financially and motivationally ineffective for a university to equalize salaries of the engineering and liberal arts faculty. Running counter to market trends would create its own set of perceived inequities. For example, chemical engineering faculty would see that liberal arts faculty were being given an above-market premium while they were not. As a result, the engineers would become more likely to seek higher-paying industry positions, whereas liberal arts faculty may not have such opportunities. In turn, academic institutions would need to raise salaries of chemical engineers to attract faculty, and the cycle would continue.

Ultimately, no job or group of jobs has an intrinsic economic worth. In the early 1980s, with the price of oil skyrocketing, the energy companies were outbidding each other to employ geologists and petroleum engineers. Salary offers were out of sight. Then the price of oil fell dramatically, and along with it job possibilities for geologists and engineers. New college graduates could not obtain job offers at any salary, and those in the work force were forced to switch to less lucrative careers in other industries.

Prospects for the Future

We still have not explained why jobs held predominantly by women, almost without exception, are paid less than those held predominantly by men. Are women's jobs fairly valued using existing procedures? Even though the courts and the federal legislation process have not sought to implement the notion of comparable worth, a number of states have proceeded in that direction.

The most aggressive approach has been in the province of Ontario, Canada. The Pay Equity Act of 1987 by the Ontario Legislative Assembly was designed to redress systemic gender discrimination in compensation for female jobs.[51] The law covers every company with more than ten employees. Most organizations, especially larger organizations, are re-evaluating jobs, using the point method or a computer-based evaluation procedure, to bring salaries of those in predominantly female jobs to the level of those of males in equivalent jobs. One organization with 15,000 employees in 580 jobs expects the cost to be a few million dollars annually in equity adjustments.[52]

The experience of the U.S. public sector in twenty states, along with the results in Ontario, Canada, suggest that comparable worth may yet become the issue of the 1990s. As a result, many major organizations are quietly working to reduce the gap between the pay of men and women.[53]

SUMMARY OF KEY POINTS

Compensation is an important human resource function. Pay issues are of concern to managers because of the high cost of labor to the company. Managers are also concerned about developing pay policies and methods that will help them attract, retain, and motivate employees.

The main problems in designing a direct compensation system revolve around internal, external and individual equity. Internal equity is based on paying jobs of equal value the same amount and paying jobs of different value an acceptable set of differentials. Internal equity is established through job evaluation.

Four general approaches to job evaluation have been discussed. The two non-quantitative methods that evaluate jobs as a whole are job ranking and job classification. The other two job evaluation methods break jobs down into compensable factors to evaluate their worth. These methods are the point and factor comparison methods. The Hay plan and computerized job evaluation procedures are variations of the point method. Job evaluation results in a wage structure or hierarchy of jobs.

The next step is to price the wage structure, being aware of external equity, or how the organization's wage rates compare with those of other employers in the labor market. Wage surveys are used to find out what other employers are paying for various jobs and to set equitable midpoints and ranges for each wage grade.

The final equity concern centers on setting the pay of individuals within a wage grade. Typical bases for this decision include seniority, merit, and skill. Merit pay systems have the potential to motivate high performance, but they are difficult to administer in a way that employees perceive as fair.

There are numerous legal constraints on compensation practices. The most important of these concern minimum wage and overtime pay and are found in the Fair Labor Standards Act and its many amendments. Additional issues in compensation include the secrecy or openness of pay systems, employee involvement in compensation decisions, and the concept of comparable worth.

Questions for Discussion

1. Identify at least four reasons that designing and implementing reward systems is one of the most complex HRM activities.
2. Distinguish between direct and indirect compensation.
3. What does equity theory say about the way individuals evaluate and respond to their pay level?
4. What are the major methods of job evaluation? Explain how each works.
5. Recommend a job evaluation system for a small family-owned business with six job titles and thirty incumbents. Recommend a system for an oil refinery with 800 employees in managerial, technical and blue-collar jobs. Why do your recommendations differ?
6. How would you go about designing a survey for setting the pay of trade employees (plumbers, electricians, welders, etc.) on your campus?
7. How would you go about designing a survey for setting the pay of faculty on your campus? In what ways would the survey for faculty differ from that for trade employees?
8. Which pay policy would you recommend to your university for trade employees? Which circumstances faced by your university influenced your recommendation?

9. Identify three major reasons that employees doing the same job in an organization might receive different compensation.
10. Discuss the evolution and current status of the minimum wage.
11. What is the major purpose of the Equal Pay Act? What does it require of employers?
12. What are the advantages and disadvantages of a policy of pay openness versus pay secrecy?
13. What are some of the factors that have led to employee wage concessions?
14. Why might two people disagree about whether or not a given pay system is fair? What are three factors on which distributive justice can be based?
15. What is meant by comparable worth and how does this issue affect the design of a compensation system?

CASE 12.1

A Dilemma for Magnolia State Bank

Magnolia State Bank, serving a small community, has successfully bid to take over the insolvent City Bank and Trust in the large city fifty miles away. The president of Magnolia State is anxious to examine the comparability of the wage plan of the newly acquired branch with that of the Magnolia headquarters location.

Tellers and clerks, the majority of the work force at Magnolia State Bank, receive a starting wage of $230 a week ($11,960 per year), which can increase to $280 ($14,560 per year) with experience. The cost of living in Magnolia is low, and Magnolia State Bank stands virtually alone as a prestigious employer with good working conditions. In fact, the low wage structure at Magnolia State Bank is part of the competitive strategy that has allowed the bank to maintain its position as the sole bank in the community.

City Bank and Trust is one of many banks in the large, nearby city. The cost of living is higher, and there are numerous reputable employers competing for available talent. As a result, City Bank and Trust has found that it must start clerks and tellers at $300 ($15,600), with ranges up to $385 ($20,000), to attract and retain employees with needed skills.

1. Could Magnolia State Bank justify continuing the 30 percent wage differences that exist between Magnolia and the newly acquired branch?
2. If yes, how would you, as president of Magnolia State Bank, explain the differences to employees in Magnolia? Given what you know about equity theory, how would employees be likely to respond? How would you address employee concerns?
3. If no, how would you proceed to merge the systems? What effect would wage reductions have on attracting and retaining employees at the city branch? What effect would wage increases have on the competitive position of the bank in Magnolia?

CASE 12.2

The Case of Frontier Steel*

Marvin Smith took pride in the company he founded, Frontier Steel, a small steel fabricator in the St. Louis area. He developed the company to its current 125 employees and considered each employee as a friend. In the early 1980s, he decided that having some employee paid by the hour and others as salaried employees created an unnecessary division within his "family." As a result, he sought help from a consultant and followed the recommendation to create an all-salaried work force at Frontier Steel. The time clock used by hourly employees was removed, and all employees were paid a fixed monthly salary.

Recently, Mary Jones, a long-time employee, was dismissed as a result of differences with her supervisor. Smith was surprised to learn that Jones had filed a federal wage-and-hour claim seeking back pay for the overtime she had worked over a five-year period. More specifically, approximately five years before Jones was dismissed, she asked and was granted permission to arrive at work 30 minutes early every day so she could ride to the plant with her husband. Jones was now claiming that these approximately 600 extra hours worked over the five years were overtime, a potential cost of $7,200. More troubling to Smith was the fact that many employees had been given permission to vary their schedules in the same way that Jones had done.

1. What are the rules governing an all-salaried work force?
2. Would Frontier Steel be liable for back time pay for all employees who worked extra? If yes, why? If no, what would determine liability?
3. What should Frontier Steel have done to avoid the type of claim Mary Jones filed?

EXERCISE 12.1

Developing a Compensation System

Imagine that there is currently no systematic plan for compensating the clerical staff of your college or university. You are asked to develop a compensation system for these employees. The objective is a system that is perceived as fair and equitable by the clerical personnel. Since the university needs financial resources for many other projects, it is extremely important that the plan minimize personnel costs. Explain how you will deal with each of the following:

1. Determining which jobs should be included as part of the clerical ranks

*Adapted from Kent Banning, "Know the Rules on Pay and Hours," *Nation's Business*, Vol. 79, April 1991, pp. 50–51.

2. The participation, if any, of clerical personnel in the development of their compensation system
3. Factors to be compensated, including factor scales and factor weights
4. The collection of job evaluation data
5. Selecting organizations to survey (how many, geographic location, types of organizations)
6. The recommended pay policy (lead, match, or lag)
7. Design of pay ranges (number and overlap)
8. The basis of individual pay (seniority, merit, skill, or other)

Notes and References

1. F. A. Heller and L. Porter, "Perceptions of Managerial Needs and Skills in Two National Samples," *Occupational Psychology,* Vol. 40, 1966, pp. 1–13.
2. "The High Price of Overtime," *The Los Angeles Times,* January 16, 1990, pp. A1, A20–A21.
3. J. Stacy Adams, "Toward an Understanding of Inequity," *Journal of Abnormal and Social Psychology,* October 1963, pp. 422–436.
4. Jerald Greenberg, "Employee Theft as a Reaction to Underpayment Inequity: The Hidden Cost of Pay Cuts," *Journal of Applied Psychology,* Vol. 75, 1990, pp. 561–568.
5. Edward E. Lawler, *Motivation in Work Organizations* (Pacific Grove, Calif.: Brooks/Cole, 1973).
6. Edward E. Lawler, *Strategic Pay* (San Francisco: Jossey-Bass, 1990).
7. Robert W. Rice, Suzanne M. Phillips, and Dean B. McFarlin, "Multiple Discrepancies and Pay Satisfaction," *Journal of Applied Psychology,* Vol. 75, 1990, pp. 386–393.
8. L. Dyer, D. P. Schwab, and R. D. Theriault, "Managerial Perceptions Regarding Salary Increase Criteria," *Personnel Psychology,* Vol. 29, 1976, pp. 233–242.
9. Robert B. Pursell, "R&D Job Evaluation and Compensation," *Compensation Review,* No. 2, 1972, pp. 21–31; T. Atchinson and W. French, "Pay Systems for Scientists and Engineers," *Industrial Relations,* Vol. 7, 1967, pp. 44–56.
10. Pursell, ibid.
11. Edward N. Hay and Dale Purves, "The Profile Method of High Level Job Evaluation," *Personnel,* September 1951, pp. 162–170.
12. Hewitt Associates, *Total Compensation DataBase CompBook 1989–1990* (Lincolnshire, Ill.: Hewitt Associates, 1990).
13. Donald P. Schwab, "Job Evaluation and Pay Setting: Concepts and Practices," in *Comparable Worth: Issues and Alternatives,* ed. E. Robert Livemash (Washington, D.C.: Equal Employment Advisory Council, 1980).
14. N. Fredric Crandall, "Computerizing Job Evaluation for Greater Efficiency and Effectiveness," *Topics in Total Compensation,* Vol. 3, 1989, pp. 241–250.
15. Lawler, *Strategic Pay.*
16. Hewitt Associates, *Total Compensation.*
17. Lester C. Thurow, *Generating Inequity: Mechanisms of Distribution in the U.S. Economy* (New York: Basic Books, 1975).
18. Daniel J. B. Mitchell, "How to Find Wage Spillovers (Where None Exist)," *Industrial Relations,* Fall 1982, pp. 392–398; H. Gregg Lewis, "Union Relative Wage Effects: A Survey of Macro Estimates," *Journal of Labor Economics,* January 1983, pp. 1–27.
19. Thomas A. Mahoney, *Compensation and Reward Perspectives* (Homewood, Ill.: Irwin, 1979).
20. R. M. Story, "Trends in Wage Administration," *Business Studies,* Fall 1967, p. 114.
21. W. A. Evans, "Pay for Performance: Fact

or Fable," *Personnel Journal,* September 1970, pp. 726–729.

22. Herbert H. Meyer, "The Pay-for-Performance Dilemma," *Organizational Dynamics,* Winter 1975, pp. 71–78.
23. Nathan B. Winstanley, "Are Merit Increases Really Effective?" *Personnel Administrator,* Vol. 4, 1982, pp. 23–31; regarding requirement 5, see also Michael Keeley, "A Contingency Framework for Performance Evaluation," *Academy of Management Review,* July 1978, pp. 428–438.
24. H. Tosi and L. Tosi, "What Managers Need to Know About Knowledge-Based Pay," *Organizational Dynamics,* Vol. 14, No. 3, 1986, pp. 52–64.
25. Larry M. Wolf and Kevin C. McCormick, "Highlights of Wage and Hour Law," presented at the Whiteford, Taylor, and Preston 1989 Employment Law Update, Baltimore, May 24.
26. Kent Banning, "Know the Rules on Pay and Hours," *Nation's Business,* Vol. 79, 1991, pp. 50–51.
27. Marc J. Wallace, Jr., and Charles H. Fay, *Compensation Theory and Practice* (Boston, PWS-Kent, 1988), pp. 136–138.
28. Ibid., pp. 138–139.
29. Edward E. Lawler, "Managers' Perception of Their Subordinates' Pay and of Their Superior's Pay," *Personnel Psychology,* Vol. 18, 1965, pp. 413–422.
30. L. H. Kidder, G. Bellettirie, and E. S. Cohn, "Secret ambitions and public performances," *Journal of Experimental Social Psychology,* Vol. 13, 1977, pp. 70–80; Kathryn M. Bartol and David C. Martin, "Effects of Dependence, Dependency Threats, and Pay Secrecy on Managerial Pay Allocations," *Journal of Applied Psychology,* Vol. 74, 1989, pp. 105–113.
31. Bureau of National Affairs, *Wage Administration,* 21.
32. E. E. Lawler III and J. R. Hackman, "The Impact of Employee Participation in the Development of Pay Incentive Plans: A Field Experiment," *Journal of Applied Psychology,* Vol. 53, 1969, pp. 467–471.
33. Thomas J. Bergmann, Frederick S. Hills, and Laurel Priefert, "Pay Compression: Causes, Results, and Possible Solutions," *Compensation Review,* Vol. 15, 2nd Qtr., 1983, pp. 17–26.
34. R. Gomez-Mejia and David B. Balkin, "Causes and Consequences of Pay Compression: The Case of Business Schools," working paper, Management Department, University of Florida, November 1984.
35. R. Kemp, Salary Compression Workshop, Regional Conference Proceedings, American Compensation Association, 1978.
36. Labor Letter, "A Special Report on People and Their Jobs in Offices, Fields, and Factories: Top Officers' Pay Slowed in 1982, but Fringes Abound," *The Wall Street Journal,* April 26, 1983, p. 1.
37. Carol J. Loomis, "The Comeuppance of Carl Icahn," *Fortune,* February 17, 1986, pp. 18–25.
38. Cathy Trost, "U.S. Aide Opposes Equal Pay for Jobs with Similar Value," *The Wall Street Journal,* November 19, 1984, p. 10.
39. U.S. Department of Labor Statistics, *Employment and Earnings,* January 1985.
40. G. Johnson and G. Solon, *Pay Differences between Women's and Men's Jobs* (Cambridge, Mass.: National Bureau of Economic Research, 1984).
41. Ronnie J. Steinberg, "Identifying Wage Discrimination and Implementing Pay Equity Adjustments," in *Comparable Worth: Issue for the 80's* (Washington, D.C.: U.S. Commission on Civil Rights, 1985), Vol. I.
42. *Schultz* v. *Wheaton Glass Co.,* 421 F2d 259 (1970).
43. *Hodgson* v. *Brookhaven General Hospital,* 436 F.2d 719 (5th Cir. 1970).
44. *Christensen* v. *State of Iowa,* 16 FEP Cases 232 (1977).
45. Thomas J. Patten, *Fair Pay* (San Francisco: Jossey-Bass, 1988).
46. Richard D. Arvey and Katherine Holt, "The Cost of Alternative Comparable Worth Strategies," *Compensation and Benefits,* Vol. 20, 1988, pp. 37–46.
47. Donald J. Treiman and Heidi I. Hartman, eds., *Women, Work, and Wages: Equal Pay for Jobs of Equal Value* (Washington, D.C.: National Academy Press, 1981).
48. Thurow, *Generating Inequity*. Peter B. Olney, Jr., "Meeting the Challenge of Compa-

rable Worth: Part 1," *Compensation and Benefits* Vol. 19, 1987, pp. 34–44.

49. *American Nurses Association* v. *State of Illinois,* 37 FEP Cases 495 (1985).

50. Treiman and Hartman, *Women, Work, and Wages.*

51. Kenneth A. Kovach and Peter E. Millspaugh, "Comparable Worth: Canada Legislates Pay Equity," *Academy of Management Executive,* Vol. 4, 1990, pp. 92-101; Lynne Kilpatrick, "In Ontario, 'Equal Pay for Equal Work' Becomes a Reality, but Not Very Easily," *The Wall Street Journal,* March 9, 1990, p. B1.

52. Kovach and Missapaugh, "Comparable Worth."

53. Aaron Bernstein, "Comparable Worth: It's Already Happening," *Business Week,* April 28, 1986, pp. 52, 56.

13

Performanced-Based Pay and Benefits

The facts of stagnant productivity and claims of declining competitiveness in American business have posed a difficult challenge for organizations in general, and for human resource specialists in particular.[1] HR managers must try to develop human resource programs that improve productivity and enhance effectiveness. Attaining these goals will help ensure that American businesses will be competitive in national and world arenas.[2]

One popular approach to enhancing productivity has been the linking of rewards to performance through various forms of incentive pay.[3] A recent survey of more than 300 manufacturing, service, and financial organizations by Hewitt Associates indicated that 97 percent of the organizations attempted to link pay with performance for top managers, 98 percent tried to make this linkage with salaried exempt employees, and 51 percent are linking pay to performance elsewhere in the organization.[4] The 51 percent in 1991 was up from 44 percent in 1989.[5] Most managers and many workers believe that performance should be the most important factor in determining salary increases.[6] Besides, studies indicate that linking pay to performance can lead to better employee performance.[7]

The goal of performance-based reward systems is to reward participants in direct relation to their individual performance and contribution to organizational success. In the past, compensation practice was dominated by traditional (fixed) pay plans, in which pay increases were given across the board or based on the cost of living or seniority. However, a survey by the American Productivity and Quality Center found a strong trend toward performance-based reward systems.[8] As Table 13.1 shows, incentive compensation plans are enjoying a wave of popularity.

The previous chapter defined organizational rewards as the money, goods, and/or services provided by an employer to its employees. Thus, the reward system includes more than just direct compensation, and direct compensation may include more than just base pay (salary or wage). This chapter covers some of the additional components that, taken together, make up the reward system. The first part of the chapter explores the elements of direct compensation that go beyond fixed salary and wages—specifically, various types of individual and group incentive systems. (The Ethical Perspective box provides a cautionary note for managers attempting to use reward systems to motivate appropriate employee behavior.) In the second part of the chapter, the discussion focuses on indirect compensation, particularly legislatively mandated benefits (such as Social Security and workers' compensation) and optional benefits (such as insurance, pension, vacation, and sick leave). The implementation and administration challenges associated with both incentives and benefits are examined.

LINKING PAY TO PERFORMANCE

Employers believe that reward systems in general, and incentive systems in particular, influence performance. Among respondents to an American Productivity and Quality Center survey of employers, for example, the vast majority believed

TABLE 13.1 Increasing Popularity of Incentive Systems

	Percent of Current Users Adapting in Each Time Period				
Years in Use	*Gain-ssharing*	*Small Group Incentives*	*Profit Sharing*	*Individual Incentives*	*Lump Sum Bonus*
Over 25	2.8%	6.2%	16.9%	13.3%	6.1%
16–25	0.7	8.4	17.4	12.2	7.6
11–15	4.9	6.2	14.5	10.2	3.0
6–10	18.7	17.4	21.5	22.1	12.9
1–5	72.9	61.8	29.5	42.3	70.5

Source: Adapted from *People, Performance, and Pay,* American Productivity & Quality Center, 1987. Reprinted by permission.

ETHICAL PERSPECTIVE

Reward Systems and Unethical Behavior

When individuals are caught in organizational wrongdoing, there is a tendency to blame the individual for some sort of character weakness and to suggest that the appropriate remedy is to hire more ethical employees. However, in many cases the organizational reward system is at least partly at fault. Some reward systems "lead employees into temptation" (Jansen and Glinow, 1985, p. 821) in subtle ways while others actively threaten employees with severe punishment if they fail to go along with organizational wrongdoing. Steven Kerr, in a classic article entitled "On the Folly of Rewarding A While Hoping for B" points out that employees are very good at figuring out what really gets rewarded, and doing (or appearing to do) those things, regardless of what the organization officially says it wants employees to do.

Erik Jansen and Mary Ann Von Glinow describe a common situation faced by employees called "ethical ambivalence." This occurs when the openly espoused norms or desires of the organization or some of its constituents (clients, regulatory agencies) are in conflict with the workings of the reward system and the norms generated by that system. Examples include the following contradictory pairs of norms (Jansen and Glinow, 1985; slightly modified):

Follow the rules	Get the job done any way you can
Take responsibility	Avoid committing yourself, pass the buck
Teamwork	Individual visibility, grandstanding
Develop and mentor subordinates	Look out for number one
Cooperate and help others	Look good compared to others

If the reward system pays off for cutthroat behavior, this is what the organization will get, despite upper management protestations that teamwork and cooperation should be the order of the day. If the organization wants high-quality work but only measures attendance and tardiness, it will get prompt attendance but probably not high-quality work. If the organization says that it wants good customer service but pays only for net sales, it will have salespeople who push unneeded merchandise onto customers and are very reluctant to take returns. There are cases on record in which sales employees make large purchases on their own credit cards to get their department over its quota for the month, then return the merchandise to another branch of the store. Clearly, this is not what the organization wants, but the reward system allows and even pays off for such behavior. And once any single person figures out how to outsmart the system, there is pressure on others to do likewise or fall behind.

Another point (from expectancy theory) is that people act on the basis of what they *think* will be rewarded or punished. A subordinate who is uncomfortable with an order received from a superior or some other company action may envision all kinds of negative consequences for speaking up and may feel pressure to comply whether or not the consequences would actually follow. This subtle or imagined pressure is probably behind a lot of the ethical conflicts experienced by employees in organizations.

Finally, there certainly are cases in which organizations intentionally threaten and pressure individuals to do the wrong thing—to falsify data to get a government contract, to cover up a problem with product safety, or to assure NASA that the space shuttle Challenger's O-rings really are safe for a cold weather launch.

The HR practitioner must remember that the appraisal and reward system is very potent. It can be harnessed to assess and encourage responsible and ethical behavior. However, it can also (either intentionally or unintentionally) motivate behavior that is interpersonally, organizationally, or socially dysfunctional. Careful attention to the design of appraisal and reward systems is necessary to ensure that they do in fact elicit the type of behavior the organization wants from its employees.

Sources: Erik Jansen and Mary Ann Von Glinow, "Ethical Ambivalence and Organizational Reward Systems," *Academy of Management Review,* October 1985, pp. 814–822; Steven Kerr, "On the Folly of Rewarding A While Hoping for B," *Academy of Management Journal,* December 1975, pp. 769–783; James A Waters, "Catch 20.5: Corporate Morality as an Organizational Phenomenon," *Organizational Dynamics,* Spring 1978; Saul W. Gellerman, "Why 'Good' Managers Make Bad Ethical Choices," in *Ethics in Practice: Managing the Moral Corporation,* ed. Kenneth R. Andrews and Donald K. David, Boston, Mass: Harvard Business School Press, 1989) pp. 18–25.

that various incentive pay systems have a very positive or positive effect on performance (Table 13.2). In addition, many workers prefer that pay be linked to performance, reinforcing the motivation to use such reward systems. There are both advantages and disadvantages in linking pay to performance.

Reasons to Link Pay to Performance

Motivation Several studies have indicated that when pay is contingent upon performance, individual and group performance is consistently higher than when this contingency is not present.[9] Vroom's **expectancy theory** suggests that a pay-performance link is essential for motivating performance.[10] Among approaches to understanding work motivation, the expectancy theory is widely accepted and has

TABLE 13.2 Ratings of the Overall Performance Impact of Reward Systems

Reward System	*(N)*	*Percent*[a]
Pay for Knowledge[b]	70	89%
Earned Time Off	99	85
Gained Sharing	170	81
Small Group Incentives	185	75
Profit Sharing	507	74
Individual Incentives[c]	192	73
All Salaried[b]	169	67
Lump Sum Bonus[b]	163	66
Recognition[c]	487	30

[a]Percent Reporting "Positive" or "Very Positive" on a scale of 1 to 5:
1 = very negative impact on performance
2 = negative
3 = no impact
4 = positive
5 = very positive impact on performance
[b]Only includes firms using plans with production and/or service workers.
[c]Percent reporting "effective" or "very effective" on scale of 1 to 5 from (1) not effective at all to (5) very effective.

Source: People, Performance, and Pay, American Productivity & Quality Center, 1987. Reprinted by permission.

fairly strong empirical support in applied and theoretical settings.[11] As shown in Figure 13.1, the expectancy model has three major components.

1. **Expectancy:** the individual's perceptions of the probability that effort will lead to task accomplishment or performance
2. **Instrumentality:** perceptions of the probability that performance will result in receiving rewards (such as pay or recognition)
3. **Valence:** the subjective value or desirability that the employee places on the attainment of a certain reward

The expectancy model can be summarized as

$$M = E\Sigma(IV)$$

where M = motivation, E = expectancy, I = instrumentality, and V = valence.

As an example of how expectancy theory works, consider the case of an organization sponsoring a contest to motivate its salespeople. A trip around the world will be awarded to the salesperson with the greatest dollar volume of sales for the calendar year. According to expectancy theory, the motivational impact of this contest would depend on individual salespeople's expectancy (perceived chance of being the top salesperson), instrumentality (belief that the company will actually award the prize), and valence (desirability of the round-the-world trip).

FIGURE 13.1 Major Elements of Expectancy Theory

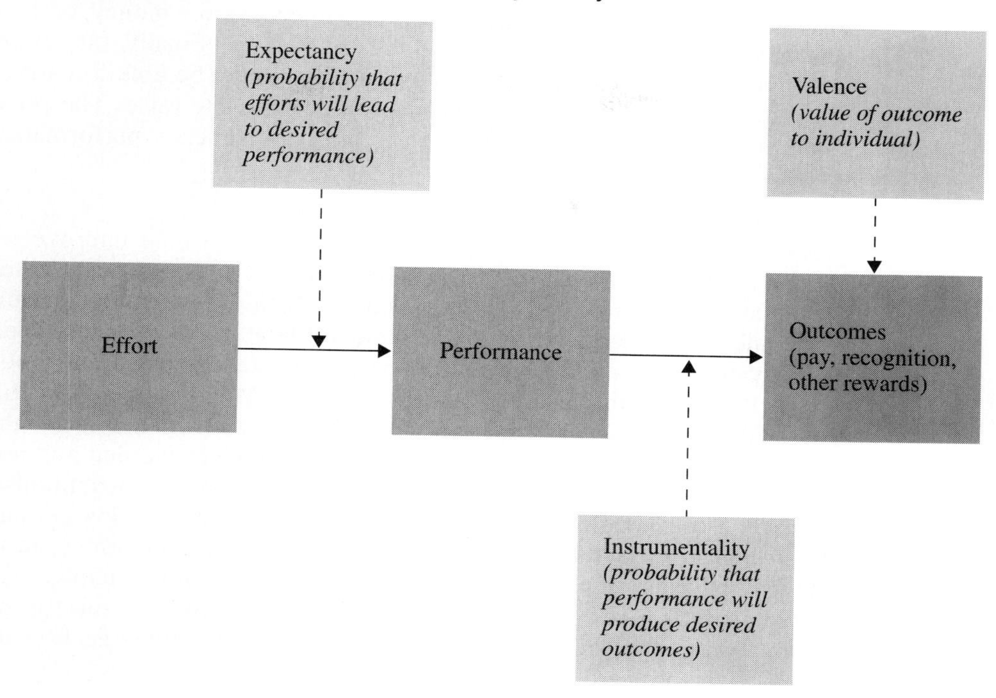

A salesperson who thinks she has a decent chance to win, believes the trip will be awarded, and has a strong desire to travel should be highly motivated by this contest. A second salesperson who believes that she has absolutely no chance of being the top seller (zero expectancy) will probably make little effort to win, even if she would greatly enjoy the trip. A third salesperson may have a very low instrumentality, believing that the company will not really award such an expensive prize. Mistrustful of the offered bargain, he will not be motivated by the contest. Also unresponsive will be a salesperson who feels that the reward is not positively valent (e.g., if he hates to travel and is terrified of airplanes).

To produce maximum motivation, all three components of the expectancy model must be high. Incentive compensation systems are designed to raise two of the three components. Instrumentality beliefs should be strengthened by making rewards contingent on good performance, and valence should be high because more money is a reward that most people find highly attractive.[12]

Expectancy theory offers useful guidelines to diagnose possible problems in incentive systems. First, one must ask whether employees believe that they can be good performers if they try. Are they properly selected, trained, and equipped to do the job? Do they get feedback so that they know where they stand and can take corrective action as necessary? Second, one must be sure that employees perceive a link between their performance and their rewards (instrumentality). Do they truly believe that better performance will make more money, or does a higher salary seem to be more a function of luck or politics? Finally, the offered reward must be of value (valence) to employees. They must be able to earn something they strongly desire, such as a promotion or a sizable raise. The prospect of a small merit raise may not be enough to motivate superior performance over an extended period of time.

Retention Linking pay to performance is likely to help improve work force composition. High performers will tend to gain a larger share of compensation resources and thus be motivated to stay with the organization. Below-average performers will become discouraged and will tend to leave the organization. Reward systems that are not linked to performance tend to have the opposite effect and thus result in the worst of both possibilities. Well-paid poor performers may stay with the organization; they are well rewarded and will not be sought by other organizations. By contrast, top performers feel underrewarded and are likely to be sought by organizations that appropriately value their contributions.

Some organizations link rewards to performance by using commissions as the primary or exclusive basis for compensation. Top performers in real estate and insurance agencies and in stock brokerage houses, for example, may earn ten times more than poor performers. It is not surprising that the top performers desire to continue earning several hundred thousand dollars each year, whereas the poor performers leave the profession quickly.

Productivity When performance is linked to rewards, those capable of doing what will lead to top productivity are motivated to do so. In the organizations mentioned above, nobody becomes productive by waiting for business to come along. The top performers make the extra effort that will result in productivity when they know they will share in the rewards of their productivity. In the financial services business, the "extras" that result in productivity frequently involve working evenings, entertaining clients, soliciting business, and volunteering in community activities, to name a few. Technical competence is important, but as one top performer was heard to say, "Not one in 500 makes it to the top ranks on technical skills alone."

Cost Savings An obvious benefit of pay for performance is the capability to link compensation costs with productivity results. By basing pay on performance, employers can ensure that compensation costs, typically a major cost of doing business, will be tied to organizational results. When the results are poor and the organization is less able to pay, compensation costs are lower. With a salaried and/or hourly work force, compensation costs are not related to business results and, even worse, continue to grow each year as cost-of-living and merit increases are added.

Organizational Objectives It is always a challenge to make sure that all employees understand organizational objectives. By linking pay to organizationally defined performance, it is also possible to ensure that individual objectives are in line with organizational objectives. Employees whose efforts are not synchronized with organizational objectives will not enjoy an equal share of the rewards.

Reasons Not to Link Pay to Performance

Linking pay to performance is not always possible or successful. The administration of the plan is critically important. If employees do not trust management's ability to make accurate performance distinctions, then the benefits of this type of system will be severely undermined. Pay-for-performance systems also take more time to administer successfully than do traditional reward systems. With fixed compensation (salary or wage), it is often a case of "set it and forget it." With pay for performance, one needs to re-evaluate the motivation, retention, productivity, and organizational objectives continually, with the idea of fine-tuning the system to make sure that rewards are aligned with desired performance.

A union's position on this type of reward system may also influence the feasibility of instituting a pay-for-performance system in a particular organization. Historically, unions have opposed performance-based pay systems. Although some unions are willing to back this type of compensation, most see no need to differentiate the pay of union workers who are doing the same job. Unions believe that pay differences based on subjective supervisor assessments of employee performance may foster discrimination or favoritism. Unions favor objective methods of determining pay increases, such as across-the-board increases or seniority increases. Unions also believe that merit pay plans may weaken solidarity, as employees compete against their fellow union members to receive the highest rewards. Unions may be more receptive to group incentive plans because they tend to result in cooperation rather than competition.

Factors Affecting the Design of Incentive Systems

There are numerous ways of linking pay to performance, each with its own advantages and drawbacks. One consideration is the level of aggregation of the incentive pay: will the incentive be based on the performance of the individual employee, the work group, the division, or the entire organization? Another consideration is degree of objectivity involved in measuring performance. Qualifying to receive the incentive may be based on a subjective supervisory rating of performance or on purely objective measures of productivity such as sales, production, or profit.

Other considerations in the design of an incentive system relate to the strength of the performance-pay linkage, the potential for negative side effects, whether the system encourages cooperation, and employee acceptance. The

TABLE 13.3 Ratings of Pay Incentive Plans*

	Basis for Reward	*Tie Pay to Performance*	*Produce Negative Side Effects*	*Encourage Cooperation*	*Employee Acceptance*
Salary Reward					
Individual Plan	Productivity	4	1	1	4
	Cost effectiveness	3	1	1	4
	Superiors' rating	3	1	1	3
Group Plan	Productivity	3	1	2	4
	Cost effectiveness	3	1	2	4
	Superiors' rating	2	1	2	3
Organizational Plan	Productivity	2	1	3	4
	Cost effectiveness	2	1	2	4
Bonus					
Individual Plan	Productivity	5	3	1	2
	Cost effectiveness	4	2	1	2
	Superiors' rating	4	2	1	2
Group Plan	Productivity	4	1	3	3
	Cost effectiveness	3	1	3	3
	Superiors' rating	3	1	3	3
Organizational Plan	Productivity	3	1	3	4
	Cost effectiveness	3	1	3	4
	Profit	2	1	3	3

*On a scale of 1 to 5, 1 = low and 5 = high.

Source: E. Lawler, *Pay and Organization Development*, © 1981 by Addison-Wesley Publishing Company, Inc. Reprinted with permission of the publisher.

results of Edward E. Lawler's analysis of incentive plans with respect to these criteria are shown in Table 13.3. Objective measures of performance (productivity and cost savings) tend to have greater employee acceptance and credibility. Individual incentive programs are often reported to yield higher productivity than group incentives. One explanation is that linking individuals' pay to the group's performance diffuses the connection between pay and each person's effort. Some individuals may have a tendency to "free-ride" (let others in the group do the work for them).[13] Research has shown that group members are especially likely to free-ride if their contribution to group performance is not readily identifiable and their loafing is unlikely to be noticed.[14]

On the other hand, group plans have some advantages not generally attainable with an individual incentive system. Group systems often result in more cooperation and coordination. They are better suited for organizations in which performance is difficult to measure at the individual level and success depends on effective teamwork.

INDIVIDUAL INCENTIVES

When individual productivity is measurable, individual incentives are most successful in boosting performance through a fairly direct link between performance and rewards. As Table 13.1 shows, the adoption of individual incentives has accelerated in recent years. Popular individual incentive plans in this section include piecework payment, commissions, and bonuses. Skill-based pay—a highly acclaimed recent innovation in individual incentives—and merit raises are also discussed.

Piecework Payment

Piecework payment is the most common form of individual incentive for production workers. Employees are paid a fixed rate for each unit of output produced. The amount to pay per unit of output is determined as follows. First, the typical pay rate for the job is determined, probably by a wage survey. Then, the typical output per day is measured. A time and motion study by industrial engineers may also provide information on the number of units that an employee should be able to make per day. The average daily wage is divided by average units per day to produce the price paid per piece. For example, if the average daily rate is $48 and each employee ought to be able to produce 96 units per day, the rate paid for each piece will be 50 cents.

Some piece-rate systems pay only on the basis of units produced, so an employee who made only 70 units would receive $35 for that day. Many piece-rate systems, however, guarantee a base wage equal to the standard output level, so that all employees making 96 or fewer units receive $48. The incentive is paid for all units in excess of the standard. Thus, an employee who made 110 units would receive $48 plus $7 (14 extra units × $0.50), or $55.

One drawback of this type of incentive is that workers may restrict output because of the possible adverse consequences associated with high productivity.[15] For example, workers may fear layoffs if all employees dramatically increase their output. Other workers may fear being ostracized by colleagues if they try to produce at a higher-than-normal level. Finally, workers may fear that if they consistently produce at a high rate, say 150 units per day, the time-and-motion study will be redone, thereby increasing the production standards and reducing the rate paid per piece. They would then have to work harder to earn the same pay.

An incentive system can sometimes lead to overemphasis on one dimension of a job and a neglect of other important job elements. For instance, a piece-rate system may increase output but also increase the number of units that fail to pass inspection. Other aspects of the job that do not directly convert into units of output, such as machine maintenance, housekeeping activities, or training of new employees, may be ignored under a piece-rate system.

The Taylor Plan A variation of the piece-rate system was developed by Frederick W. Taylor around the turn of the century. Unlike the straight piece-rate plan, the **Taylor Plan** offers differential piecework rates. In the example above, the Taylor

Plan might specify 50 cents per unit up to 96 units per day but reward workers producing 125 percent of standard or more (120 units) with the higher rate of 65 cents for each unit over 96.

Standard Hour Plan The **standard hour plan** is similar to the straight piecework plan except that the standard is set in time units. Automobile repair shops often use such systems. If the customer wants to know the cost of replacing an engine component, he or she will be given an estimate based on the mechanic's hourly rate multiplied by the average time needed to replace the component on cars of that type. If the charge is $30 per hour and the replacement of the component requires four hours on average, the expected labor cost would be $120. This is the labor cost quoted to the customer before work begins. An experienced mechanic may complete the job in three hours. The customer is still charged $120, and the mechanic is paid for four hours' work (the standard time allotted for the job). If the job takes longer than estimated, charges to the customer and payment to the mechanic are still based on four hours work. Standard hour plans are generally used with longer-cycle operations that are nonrepetitive.

Commissions

Commission reward systems, which are usually found in sales jobs, allow the salesperson to receive a percentage of his or her gross receipts (e.g., 5 percent of all sales). About two-thirds of all salespeople are paid on **commission** basis—either straight commission or a base salary plus commission.

Commission payments offer a very clear link between pay and worker performance and therefore are an effective financial incentive. Commission plans are easy to administer and justify because there is no subjective element, and rewards are purely a function of performance. Because of this clear link, department stores are converting thousands of hourly sales employees to straight commission.[16] The retailers hope that the potential for higher rewards to those with strong sales skills will motivate current staff and attract better salespeople in the future.

However, commission payment may reduce cooperative teamwork. Employees may compete with one another for sales and the most lucrative sales territory. In the case of department stores shifting to straight commission, sales staff may give customers a hard time on refunds or exchanges. If an employee's pay is based strictly on sales, all other coworker and company-related considerations may be secondary. For example, the salesperson who works hard to sell the customer a computer may not want to take the time to instruct him or her in its use. After the sale, service may not be what is expected or needed.

From the employee's point of view, a disadvantage of commission-based compensation is the unpredictable amount of take-home pay from week to week. Any number of things outside the employee's control, such as weather or economic conditions, may influence the number of sales and therefore the amount of reward. However, assuming that the salesperson can tolerate this kind of risk, commission plans offer considerable advantage to the organization by directly linking performance to rewards and keeping labor costs in line. Furthermore, for the employees who are effective, the rewards are far greater than they would otherwise be—perhaps even several times the amount that the employees could have expected if compensated by salary or wages.

Bonuses

One of the most popular trends in compensation is the use of **bonuses:** one-time lump-sum payments given for meeting a performance goal. Bonuses can be based on objective goal attainment or a subjective rating. In some organizations, all employees share in the bonus awards if organizational goals are met, while in others the size of the bonus is tied to each individual's performance. An example of the former approach is Ford Motor Co.'s award of an average bonus of $2,800 and $1,025 to each employee in 1988 and 1989, respectively, based on the company's performance in these years. (Bonuses were not awarded to Ford employees in 1990 and 1991 as a result of decreased organizational performance.) An example of a bonus based on individual performance is the clause in some baseball players' contracts that specifies that they will receive a bonus (usually several thousand dollars) if voted onto the all-star team or if they reach some other performance standard.

Table 13.4 shows a sample award distribution chart for lump-sum bonuses based on both organizational and employee performance. Plans such as this might also assign different bonus ceilings to levels within the organization. For instance,

TABLE 13.4 Lump-Sum Award Determination Matrix

	The Organization's Performance (Weight = .50)				
The Employee's Performance (Weight = .50)	*Outstanding (1.00)*	*Excellent (.80)*	*Commendable (.60)*	*Acceptable (.40)*	*Marginal or Unacceptable (0)*
Outstanding (1.00)	1.00	.90	.80	.70	.50
Excellent (.80)	.90	.80	.70	.60	.40
Commendable (.60)	.80	.70	.60	.50	.30
Acceptable (.00)	–0–	–0–	–0–	–0–	–0–
Unacceptable (.00)	–0–	–0–	–0–	–0–	–0–

Instructions. To determine the dollar value of each employee's incentive award, (a) multiply the employee's annual, straight time wage or salary times his or her maximum incentive award and (b) multiply the resultant product times the appropriate percentage figure from this table. For example, if an employee had an annual salary of $20,000 and a maximum incentive award of 10% and if her performance and the organization's performance were both "excellent," the employee's award would be $1,600 ($20,000 × .10 × .80 = $1,600).

Source: Reprinted by permission of the publisher, from *Compensation and Benefits Review,* May/June 1988,

top managers might be eligible to earn up to 50 percent more than their salary, middle managers 25 percent, and lower-level employees 10 percent.

Bonuses not only help the employer control costs, but appear to improve employee satisfaction. A company that gives a raise to an employee is making a permanent change that improves his or her pay now, in the future, and also in retirement, through a pension. This is a more costly commitment than a one-time bonus payment. Because bonuses arrive in one lump sum, they may feel to the employees like more money than a comparable sized raise. Suppose an employee earning $20,000 is given a $1,000 bonus. The sizable bonus check is equal to 5 percent of the salary. If a raise of the same size were given, the $1,000 would be distributed across 52 weeks, and the employee would see only about $20 more per week in his or her paycheck. Bonus plans are easy to maintain because they do not require much documentation and are quite flexible.[17] A major advantage of a bonus plan is that it is based partly on organizational performance; in a bad year, when corporate performance is down and resources are strained, bonuses will be much smaller or even nonexistent.

Skill-based Pay

Skill-based pay (or **pay for knowledge**) is a reward system that pays employees on the basis of the work-related skills they possess rather than associating rewards with performance levels or seniority.[18] Under a typical skill-based pay plan, an employee is hired and receives initial training on one job. He or she then joins a work group at the entry-level rate of pay and has the opportunity to learn new job-related skills through on-the-job experience and further training. As the employee demonstrates mastery of different jobs performed by other group members, his or her pay is increased.[19] Typically, a minimum of four to five years is required for employees to top out—that is, master all the skills.[20] Skill-based pay is frequently used in conjunction with autonomous work groups or other job enrichment programs.[21]

There are several models used to design skill-based pay plans. The *stair-step model* is applicable when the learning progression is fairly logical. Successive skill levels are defined, and pay is increased as the learning of additional skills is verified. The *job-point accrual model* is used when there is a wide variety of jobs. The varied jobs are given a relative point rating based on value added or learning difficulty, and the points for each job mastered then determine the employee's pay grade. The *cross-department model* places a premium (in terms of rewards) on employees who learn the skills required to fill in at another department as needed.[22]

Skill-based pay is thought to improve productivity by creating a more competent and flexible work force. Tying pay increases to skill acquisition creates an incentive for learning, self-improvement, and performance.[23] The success of such plans depends on the needs of the organization and the employee. Skill-based pay should be implemented only if the organization has a commitment to employee training and development and has something to gain from increased flexibility.[24]

This system also rests on the assumption that employees want to grow and to improve their job skills. Although no formal studies have yet tested the cost-benefit utility of pay-for-knowledge systems, they appear to be gaining in popularity. It is estimated that between one-third and one-half of all new plants built in the last ten years either use skill-based pay or plan to do so in the near future.[25]

Merit Pay

Merit pay, because it is the standard procedure for attempting to tie pay increases to individual performance, is a major motivational device for employees at all levels—managerial, professional, and hourly.[26] **Merit pay** is an annual increment tied to the employee's performance during the previous year. For example, top performers may receive a 10 percent increase, whereas average performers receive 5 percent.

Even though merit pay continues to be widely used, in the last few years it has come under major criticism.[27] Merit raises represent a permanent commitment to an increased salary (pay is virtually never reduced if performance falls), thereby creating an annuity that can be an expensive fixed cost to an organization during economic downturns.

In practice, the size of merit raises usually depends on both performance and the employee's current position in the salary range established for that job. If all top performers were given large raises, within a few years outstanding employees might be making more than the allowable maximum for their jobs—more than the jobs are worth, no matter how well they are performed. Thus, merit increases guidelines, like those shown in Table 13.5, are often used. Among employees in the same part of the pay range, better performers receive a larger percentage increase. However, an excellent performer near the maximum of the range allowed for the job will receive a smaller percentage increase than an excellent performer earning below the midpoint of the range.

There are several important difficulties in using merit increases to link pay to performance. First, merit increases are almost always based on the supervisor's subjective evaluation, so employees may perceive a weak link between performance and pay. Many employees like the idea of a merit system, but feel that the

TABLE 13.5 Merit Increase Guidelines

	Performance Level			
Current Position in Range	*Excellent*	*Good*	*Average*	*Poor*
Top Quarter	5%	3%	1%	0
Third Quarter	6%	4%	2%	0
Second Quarter	7%	5%	3%	0
Lowest Quarter	8%	6%	4%	0

system in their organization is not implemented in a completely fair, unbiased manner. Recall from Chapter 11 that supervisors can make a number of intentional and unintentional errors in judging performance. These errors may lead to perceived inequities in the way merit money is distributed. Second, merit increases are usually awarded annually, so they do not immediately follow the specific instances of good performance that the organization wishes to reinforce. Third, variations in the size of merit raises are generally not large enough to be highly motivating. For example, using the guidelines illustrated in Table 13.5, an excellent performer would receive a 5 to 8 percent raise whereas a poor performer would receive nothing. Yet the excellent performer certainly makes more than an 8 percent difference, possibly even a 100 percent difference, in terms of contribution to the organization. Fourth, the size of the total merit budget may vary substantially from year to year, so that the same performance level does not always earn the same reward.

The bottom line with respect to merit pay was aptly stated by Edward E. Lawler:

> The combined effect of year-to-year differences in salary-increase budgets and the annuity feature of merit raises almost always creates a situation in which the total compensation of individuals is unrelated to their performance at any point in time.[28]

According to Lawler, the best paid individuals are likely to be those employees who are among the most senior and who have performed adequately.

Despite the problems with merit pay, it is likely to remain as a staple of compensation systems. At the same time, it is likely that in the future merit programs will be supplemented with other types of individual or group incentives. Organizations will rely on merit pay for the broad range of adjustments but will reward top performers with individual bonuses or all employees with a group incentive based on company performance.[29]

GROUP INCENTIVES

Group incentives are designed to accomplish the same objectives as individual incentives—that is, to link rewards to performance. The difference is that performance is measured on the level of an organizational unit and is viewed as resulting from the combined efforts of a group rather than from individual effort.

A group incentive system was developed and evaluated by the Navy Personnel Research and Development Center for the Pearl Harbor Naval Shipyard.[30] Shipyard production workers typically work together in gangs of ten to twenty employees. Thus, it seemed reasonable that the work gang be the basis for assessing productivity. Work gangs were studied to develop a baseline measure of person-hours needed to complete various assignments. Performance efficiency was then calculated by dividing the hours expected by the actual hours needed. The shipyard paid out half of the cost savings associated with performance efficiency to gang members as incentive awards. In addition to performance improvement and cost savings, the project produced other positive benefits, including more sophisticated labor cost accounting and improved allocation of people. Surveys of participants revealed that 80 percent of the workers had a favorable opinion of the system.

In another study, production workers on a series of tightly interconnected assembly lines in a unionized iron foundry participated in a group incentive program.[31] Productivity standards were established for each assembly line, and credit was given for output above the established standard. The researchers found a sustained trend of increasing productivity over several years following implementation of the incentive system. Sharp early increases in output were due to increased effort, whereas continued small increases over the years were attributed to employee innovations. The presence of the incentive encouraged employees continuously to develop new and more efficient ways to complete their group tasks.

Group incentives, like those for individuals, have possible negative aspects. If the group is too large, employees may feel that their efforts will have little effect on total performance. Group members may also become concerned about overproduction and thus restrict output.

Gain Sharing Plans

Gain sharing is a type of group incentive in which a portion of the *gains* the organization realizes from group effort is *shared* with the group. The concept also implies an organizational philosophy that engenders the kind of cooperativeness and trust needed to facilitate group efforts.

As Figure 13.2 shows, many organization are seeking productivity and quality improvement through gain sharing plans. Other important reasons for adopting gain sharing plans have to do with employee relations, labor costs, and a desire to link pay to performance.

Scanlon Plan One very popular and widely used form of gain sharing is the **Scanlon Plan,** which was first implemented in the late 1920s. Its developer, Joseph Scanlon, was a union leader who was trained in cost accounting and had a strong concern for management-labor cooperation. Scanlon believed that the average worker was a great reservoir of untapped information concerning labor-saving methods. Workers needed a mechanism permitting them to "work smarter, not harder."[32]

The Scanlon Plan involves employee participation in reducing labor costs. The two main features are a system of departmental and plantwide screening committees to evaluate and implement employee cost-saving suggestions and the sharing of labor cost savings with employees as an incentive. Savings are determined as the ratio of payroll to sales value of production and are usually calculated monthly and compared with baseline months to determine the bonus to be shared.[33] A typical distribution of savings would be 50 percent to employees, 25 percent to the employer, and 25 percent retained for an emergency fund to reimburse the company for any months when the actual wage bill is larger than the

FIGURE 13.2 Reasons for Adopting Gain Sharing

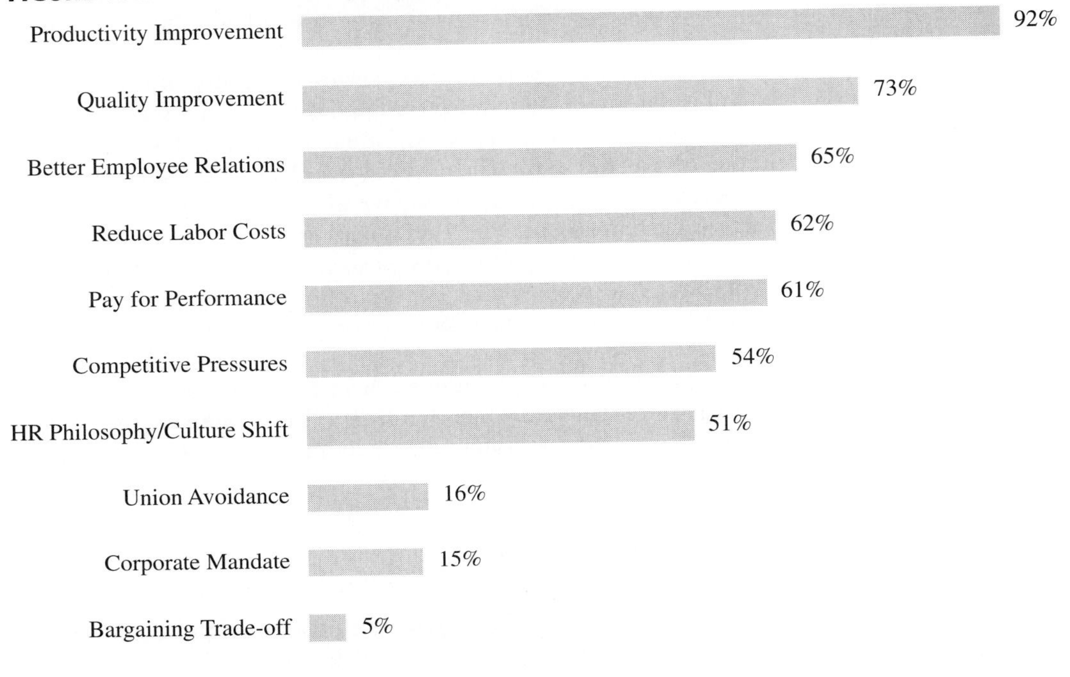

Based on a 5-point scale:
1 = not important at all *2 = not very important* *3 = moderately important* *4 = important* *5= very important*

Source: People, Performance, and Pay, American Productivity & Quality Center, 1987. Reprinted by permission.

baseline. Remaining emergency funds are distributed to workers at the end of each year.

Improshare Another noteworthy approach to gain sharing is the **Improshare** (*Im*proved *Pro*ductivity Through *Shar*ing) Plan developed by Mitchell Fein and first used in 1974.[34] Improshare is similar to the previously discussed plan at the navy shipyard, but at an organization level. A standard of the number of person-hours required to produce an expected level of output is developed. This standard could be determined from a base period (as with the Scanlon Plan) or through time and motion studies. For example, the base may be established as 5,000 hours of labor (direct and indirect) to produce 1,000 units each week, or 5 hours per unit. If in a given week 5,000 hours are used to produce 1,300 units, 1,500 hours have been saved (300 units at 5 hours per unit). The company splits the gains fifty-fifty with its employees, giving a bonus for 750 hours. Since the 750 hours represent 15 percent of the 5,000 hours worked (750/5,000), employees receive a 15 percent bonus for the week.

Rucker Plan The **Rucker Plan** is similar to the Scanlon Plan, but the bonus formula includes the dollar value of all materials, supplies, and services that are used to make the product. The resulting formula is

$$\frac{\$ \text{ value of personnel costs}}{\$ \text{ value of production} - \$ \text{ value of materials, etc.}}$$

The resulting bonus formula is the value added to a product per labor dollar. The Rucker Plan provides an incentive to save on all inputs, both human and material.

Summary At first glance, the three gain sharing plans seem much the same. All base the bonus paid on the savings resulting from productivity improvement. However, as shown in Table 13.6 there are differences. For example, with the

TABLE 13.6 Principal Features of Three Gain Sharing Programs and Profit Sharing

	Scanlon	*Rucker*	*Improshare*	*Profit Sharing*
Management Practices	Participative system highly stressed	Participative system recommended	Reduction in conflict between labor and management recommended	Better education and communications recommended
Employee Participation	Suggestion committees or work teams	Rucker committees	Good ideas used when they occur	None specified
Productivity Target	Reduction in cost and/or labor	Cost reduction with emphasis on labor	Reduction in labor time, direct and indirect	Improved profit
Bonus Basis	Ratio of costs to sales value of production	Labor: percentage of value added	Hours saved compared to standard	Share of profit
Bonus Frequency	Monthly to quarterly	Monthly to quarterly	Weekly	Annually—usually deferred
Participants	All employees	Hourly employees—others optional	Hourly employees only	All employees

Source: Reprinted, with permission of publisher from, *Gainsharing and Productivity: A Guide to Planning, Implementation, and Development,* by Robert Doyle, © 1983 AMACOM, a division of American Management Association.

Scanlon Plan, the sales value of production (i.e., the amount received for the produced products) is part of the bonus calculation. With the Improshare Plan, the standard is the number of hours required to produce an expected level of output. Thus, with the Scanlon Plan, it is possible that productivity improvements will be overshadowed by sales or price fluctuations. This will not be the case with the Improshare Plan.

All three gain sharing plans work best with smaller firms or units (e.g., divisions or plants) that have fairly stable production processes, good labor-management relations, and a culture emphasizing employee participation.[35] In smaller firms or units there is a "line of sight" from individual performance to firm or unit improvement. Individual employees can see that their efforts make a difference. A stable production process is necessary because any cost savings plan that involves comparisons with a base period will be misleading if technology is continually changing or if production varies for reasons beyond the employees' control.

Profit Sharing

Profit sharing is an incentive system in which designated employees share the business profits. Profit sharing plans differ from gain sharing in two respects:

1. They are often implemented corporationwide rather than by unit.
2. They do not use a formula that measures only increases in productivity improvement.

The usual profit sharing program establishes a base-level profit target. After this target is achieved, a percentage of additional profits is set aside in a bonus pool to be distributed to participants. Sometimes the bonus pool is distributed in equal dollar shares to all employees. At other times the distribution is a function of organizational level or salary/wages.

There are three broad types of profit sharing plans:

1. *Current distribution plans* (or cash plans), which pay a share of the company's profits in cash or company shares.
2. *Deferred payout plans,* in which an employee's share of the company's profits is placed in a trust fund to be distributed at a later date. These payoffs are usually distributed upon retirement, disability, death, or termination.
3. *Combination plans,* which provide both cash payments and deferred payments.[36]

Some features of profit sharing plans are very attractive. First, when there are no profits, the company bears no costs from this type of reward system. These plans also make employees more aware of the organization's competitive position in its industry and facilitate a cooperative atmosphere. Although profit sharing may be best suited for smaller companies, where the line of sight from individual performance to corporate profits is more evident, such plans are easy to administer in larger companies as well. The profit sharing deferment plan allows employees to postpone taxation and therefore increase rewards.

One disadvantage of profit sharing plans is the fact that when companies have a bad year even good employees may go unrewarded. Low profits may be due to things beyond the employees' control, such as economic conditions. Another drawback is that deferred payout plans may have less incentive value because of the long time lapse between the good performance and the eventual payment. Also, employees' shares of the profits are seldom tied to individual performance. Most commonly, all employees share in the profits, either equally or in proportion to their base pay. Thus, there is virtually no line of sight between how hard individuals work and the size of their profit sharing payoffs, especially if the organization is large. For all these reasons, the link between pay and performance is very weak.

Both gain sharing and profit sharing plans are summarized in Table 13.6. Differences in management practices, employee participation, the productivity target, and the basis for the bonus across the four plans are shown.

Employee Stock Ownership Plans (ESOPs)

In many companies, employees at all levels own stock in the organization for which they work. Changes in the federal tax laws since the late 1970s have made **employee stock ownership plans (ESOPs)** a common vehicle for profit sharing and the funding of pension plans. ESOPs have also been used by employees to buy out firms that might otherwise have been sold or closed.

Typically, a public company borrows money to buy its own stock, either from the company treasury or on the market, and places the shares in its ESOP. As the loan is paid down, a trustee allocates stock to individual employees, usually in the form of a deferred pension benefit.[37] According to the ESOP Association, as of 1989 there were more than 10,000 ESOPs in force covering 11.5 million employees, with the recent growth being among publicly held companies, such as Avis, Procter & Gamble, and J. C. Penney.[38]

The recent popularity of ESOPs has less to do with employee participation than with tax breaks, restructuring, and pension paring. The more stock a company's ESOP holds, the better the company can fend off a raider, proceed with a leveraged buyout, or undertake other forms of reorganization. Some companies use an ESOP to reduce or replace benefits, such as pension benefits, thus leading to considerable savings.

There is some evidence that employee ownership may increase employee commitment, loyalty, and motivation, but such benefits are by no means preordained.[39] The key to gaining the benefits is to combine ownership with the line of sight link between individual and organizational performance.[40] Avis is an example of a company that is 100 percent employee-owned that used this ownership to engender the type of employee participation that led to improvements and gains in stock price.[41] However, as was seen with profit sharing, especially deferred profits, the link between employee effort and company results is generally weak.

With ESOPs, this relationship is further diminished since success is not only a function of profits, but also of the whims of Wall Street with respect to the valuation the financial markets put on companies—a factor employees find difficult to control. Burlington Industries, the textile giant, is an example of an ESOP gone wrong as employees watched the price of the stock go from $38 at the time of the employee buyout to $15, thus greatly devaluing retirement nest eggs for individual employees.[42]

BARRIERS TO PAY-FOR-PERFORMANCE SUCCESS

There is tremendous disparity between theory and reality when organizations try to use pay to motivate performance. The anticipated benefits of pay-for-performance systems, in terms of motivation and satisfaction, are extremely elusive. Success may be made difficult by the nature of the task, performance measurement, the amount of payout, and the failure to achieve a credible link between pay and performance.

Nature of the Task

The design of a pay-for-performance system requires consideration of the employee's task. If the purpose is to engender motivation, the employee needs to feel that he or she can influence results—that is, control the performance that is being measured.[43] This simple principle can be a major stumbling block in practice. For example, imagine twenty-five data-entry specialists, each working at a terminal and paid on the basis of the number of characters entered per hour (piece rate). Is some of the data entry more challenging than others, for example from handwritten data sheets versus printed material? Are the twenty-five terminals equivalent—the same make and model? Do some of the terminals work better than others? Are some areas of the work location better than others in terms of lighting, ventilation, and freedom from glare or distractions? Are there variations in the comfort of the work-stations? The point is that whereas data entry is a good example of a job where effort is tied to results (performance), there still exists some level of opportunity bias—unevenness in opportunity of the data-entry operators to produce at their respective maximum levels as a result of situational differences.

Very few employees have total control over their own performance. Direct pay-for-performance incentives should be adopted only when employee skill and effort have a substantial impact on output. Skill-based pay and bonus or profit sharing approaches are more appropriate if employees are less able to control performance.

Performance Measurement

Any pay-for-performance system presumes accurate and fair measurement of performance. Subjective measures of performance are notorious for their lack of validity. As a result, individuals are likely to feel that their rewards are not related to their effort but instead are a function of the judgments of their particular supervisor. Objective measures are not always better, as suggested by the example of the data-entry specialists. Almost any individual whose pay is a function of "objective" performance, such as sales, can point to numerous inequities or contaminants in the measurement procedures.

Amount of Payout

To be effective, the incentive reward for successful performance needs to be significant. The appropriate size is a subjective judgment, but this issue is frequently a barrier to the successful linkage of pay and performance. For example, recent merit pay increases have about equaled the rate of inflation, between 4 and 5 percent during the past few years. A company fortunate enough to be able to offer 7 percent average increases during this period, almost a best-case scenario, would typically have 75 percent of its employees receive increases between 3 and 10 percent. How many employees will go all out all year long for a 10 percent increase when they could receive 3 or 4 percent for minimal effort? If top performers received four times what below-average performers received, 16 versus 4 percent, motivational value would be greater.

Frailty of the Linkage

Pay-for-performance systems tend to focus attention on monetary rewards to the exclusion of other potential rewards. In fact, managers have the opportunity to influence employees in more ways than they may realize. Depending on the position and organization, the manager may be able to manipulate a large number of job elements to link tangible and intangible rewards with performance. There may be twenty-five to thirty "rewards" or job features at stake, each of which can make an employee's life easier and more enjoyable, or, alternately, more difficult. Table 13.7 lists the job elements that a university department head might use to influence or motivate a faculty member. A similar list could be developed for other types of organizations, and most supervisors would be surprised at the length of the list.

To have the maximum motivational impact, both money and these other rewards should be closely tied to performance. Unfortunately, managers who do not understand all of the rewards they control may unintentionally send mixed signals to their subordinates. Thus, an employee who is evaluated as a below-average performer and is given a low merit increase may later be granted a request to attend a prestigious conference. The manager believes the low annual merit increase has successfully linked performance to rewards. Understandably, the employee is not so sure.

The situation is no different for top-performing employees. A good employee who is given an undesirable office, the poorest secretary, or the greatest number of extraneous assignments may well wonder about the value of his or her contribution, whatever the size of the annual merit increase. The manager is then

TABLE 13.7 Rewards for University Faculty

1. Base salary/salary increases
2. Number of courses assigned to teach
3. Types of courses assigned to teach
4. Schedule of courses assigned to teach
5. Location of courses assigned to teach
6. Amount of secretarial support
7. Technical capability of secretarial support
8. Amount of student assistant support
9. Level of qualification of student assistant support
10. Office location/size
11. Furniture for office
12. Permission to travel
13. Resources to travel (professional conventions, etc.)
14. Consulting referrals
15. Permission to consult
16. Funds to use mainframe computer
17. Supplies
18. Telephone access (including long distance)
19. Photocopy access
20. Access to equipment
21. Funds to attend workshops
22. Parking location
23. Availability of department head and dean for meetings
24. Committee assignments within department and college
25. Contact with distinguished visitors to department
26. Invitations to social events
27. Nominations for awards/honors
28. Support for promotion
29. Involvement in activities of department
30. Praise

shocked to find that the employee who received the top merit increase has decided to quit and join a competitor. These situations are all too typical. Most of the week-to-week activities of the manager convey to the employee the absence of a link between performance and rewards.

Summary

Pay-for-performance systems are problematic. In some organizations, the forces tending to weaken and negate the links outweigh the factors that enhance and strengthen the relationship between pay and performance. The typical pay-for-performance system, whether individual incentive or organizationwide bonus, is perceived positively as long as payouts are forthcoming. When individual and/or organizational performance decreases and payouts are reduced or eliminated, employee commitment and trust in the system are lost. At this point, the motivational capacity of the pay-for-performance link is greatly diminished. Although one study of an incentive system in a unionized foundry found positive and long-lasting results, as described above, this pattern of results is not always obtained.[44]

Despite the problems, the idea of pay for performance remains popular in the United States. For most organizations, the attempt to link pay and performance represents an important competitive quest, an effort to attract, motivate, and retain talented individuals in the work force.

EXECUTIVE COMPENSATION

Until very recently, few were overly concerned with executive pay. For over forty years, a spring issue of *Business Week* reported on executive pay at more than

350 publicly held companies. Performance of these companies was also rated for the most recent three years, and the generally tenuous links between company performance and chief executive officer (CEO) pay was noted. Until the recent past, people were interested and even envious, but most understood that these executives represented a special resource to most organizations because of their potential to influence results, and hence deserved quite high pay.

All of that has changed. It is hard to imagine a more highly charged HR topic than executive compensation has been during 1991 and 1992. The reason for the intense interest can be summed up in two words, *equity* and *excess*, as evidenced by these statistics:[45]

- CEO pay increased 212 percent in the decade of the 1980s while worker pay increased 53 percent (less than the rate of inflation) and corporate profits increased 78 percent.
- In 1980, CEO pay was 42 times the pay of the ordinary factory worker; by 1991, this ratio increased to 104. (The relationship between CEO and factory worker pay is illustrated in Figure 13.3).
- CEO pay has increased while company performance has decreased; in 1990, profits slid 7 percent while the CEOs' average total pay climbed by an equal amount, 7 percent, to just under $2 million. (Interestingly, in 1991, for the first time in the past forty-two years, CEO salary and bonus fell 7

FIGURE 13.3 Change in Average CEO Pay Relative to the Change in Average Pay of Hourly Production Workers, 1979–1988

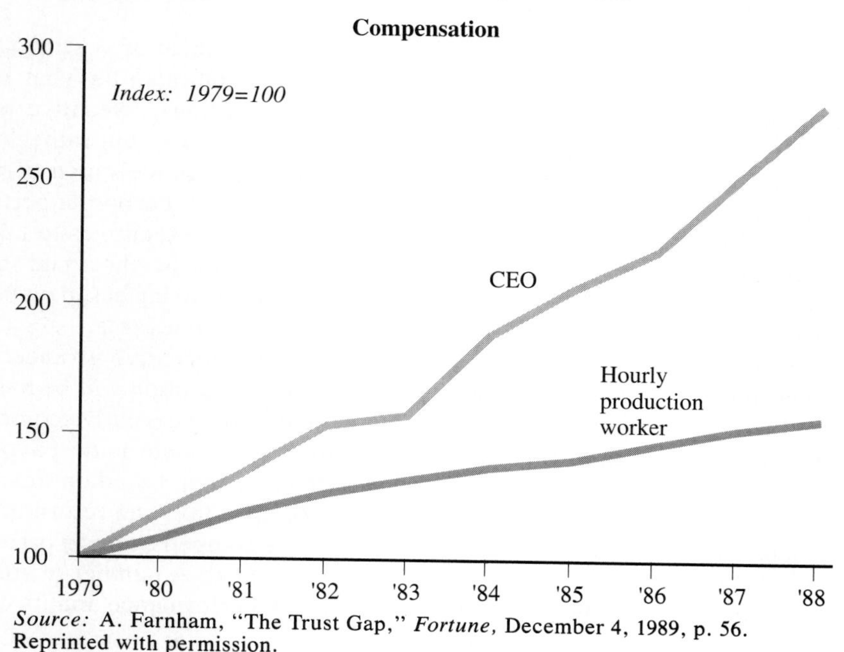

Source: A. Farnham, "The Trust Gap," *Fortune*, December 4, 1989, p. 56. Reprinted with permission.

percent, although total pay, including stock options and other long-term incentives, jumped 26 percent. Much of the increase was the result of unusually large long-term incentives by a few CEOs; six out of ten CEOs saw their total compensation fall from 1990 levels.)

- The ten top-paid CEOs for 1991 headed companies that were among the bottom 7 percent in terms of CEO pay versus shareholder return (as compared to industry peers) and bottom 15 percent in pay versus corporate profits.
- Robert Stempel, CEO of General Motors Corp., earned $5.6 million in 1991, at the same time that GM was losing $4.9 billion—or $2,700 per hour while GM was losing $2,356,000 in that same hour.
- CEO pay has continued at high levels while many of the same companies underwent major reductions in force.
- The highest paid CEO made $75 million in 1991 (Anthony O'Reilly, CEO of H. J. Heinz), while the average pay of CEOs of the nation's 363 largest corporations was $2.4 million.

National attention was focused on some of these disparities early in 1992 when President George Bush took American automotive CEOs to Japan to meet their lower-paid but more successful counterparts. Extremely high executive compensation compared to the wages being earned by lower-level participants in the organization led to perceptions of unfairness and low distributive justice.

Goals of Executive Compensation

The theory of compensating the top people in an organization is straightforward: what is in the best interest of the shareholders should also be what brings the greatest reward to the executives. In most organizations, executive pay is not supposed to be based on individual performance measures but rather on unit or organizational performance. The reason is that an executive's own performance is assumed to be directly reflected in measures of unit or corporate performance. Of course, situations differ, but shareholders want the executives to take the organization forward, that is, to improve things, both in the short and in the long term. This wish translates into executive compensation being based on both short-term incentives (e.g., annual bonuses) and long-term ones (e.g., stock options). Consideration must be given to the structure of the incentive arrangements and the performance measures on which incentive compensation will be based.

In practice, incentives are important in determining executive compensation. Although various performance measures are used to determine payouts, most management incentive plans are "formula-driven" plans, based on financial measures such as return on equity, profit before or after tax, and return on invested capital. However, these attempts to tie executive compensation to organizational performance have not proved as effective as intended. A number of studies have found no correlation between a company's stock performance and its compensation of executives.[46] The sense of inequity described previously is related to the fact that executive compensation continues to increase while company performance languishes.

Several special considerations complicate the process of determining executive compensation. For example, because executives generally enjoy a high base salary, compensation arrangements seek to minimize their income tax liability. Attention to tax considerations can make a large difference in the after-tax income of an executive. Another consideration has to do with nonfinancial incentives—the perquisites associated with the executive position.

Executive Bonus Plans

Bonuses play an important role in today's competitive executive payment programs. One study found that 92 percent of manufacturing companies in the United States have annual incentive bonus plans for their managers and executives (varying from an average 57 percent of salary for CEOs to about 20 to 25 percent for lower-level executives).[47] This type of incentive is usually a short-term one (annual) and is based on performance. Consequently, the definition of performance is especially critical.

There are almost as many bonus systems as there are companies using this form of executive compensation. In some systems, the annual bonus is tied by formulas to objective measures, such as gross or net profits, earnings, share price, or return on investment. Other executive bonus plans are based on the subjective judgment of the board of directors and CEO. More complex systems establish certain targets—for example a 10 percent increase in corporate earnings from the previous year—and generate a bonus pool after the target is attained. The bonus is then distributed, either in accordance with a preset formula or on the basis of subjective judgments.

Long-Term Incentives

Publicly held organizations in the United States have been criticized for their focus on the short term. To encourage a longer perspective, many boards of directors are adopting programs of long-term incentives for executives. In the six years from 1985 to 1991, the proportion of executive pay related to long-term incentives increased fourfold, from 8 to 31 percent of total compensation.[48] The most popular approach is to give stock or stock options to executives. The options are valuable as long as the price of the stock keeps increasing. However, the stock purchased (or the right to buy stock) can decrease in value and even become worthless if the company goes bankrupt. Executives of many large companies have suffered this fate in recent years.

Stock options are also attractive to shareholders. First, an option is not a bonus. Executives must use their own resources to exercise their right to purchase the stock. Second, the executives are assuming the same risk as all other shareholders, namely that the price could move in either direction. Options are a form of profit sharing that links the executive's financial success to that of the shareholders. Finally, stock options are one of the few ways to offer large rewards to executives without the embarrassment of "millions of dollars of obvious money changing hands."[49] Nevertheless, the risk factor in this type of incentive may be too great for it to be attractive to executives.

Perquisites

Perquisites, better known as **"perks,"** are the extras that frequently go with executive status. Used to supplement the basic benefit package, perks range from such amenities as special parking and plush offices to pay for vacation travel, auto expenses, and company-paid memberships in clubs. More personal perks, such as low-cost loans and personal use of company facilities (e.g., airplanes), have been slowly disappearing over the last ten years as various tax and regulatory agencies have ruled that their value must be included in the executive's taxable income. However, the list of perks offered is long and will remain an expected feature of the upper levels of the executive ladder.

Determining Executive Compensation

Who determines the pay of the top people in a publicly held organization? Obviously, it would be a conflict of interest to have the CEO determine the reward structure for the top executives, including himself or herself. Most publicly held companies in the United States have a compensation committee composed of members of the board of directors who are not officers of the firm. The compensation committee makes recommendations to the board on overall organizational pay policies, including salaries, incentives, and perquisites for top officers. Frequently, the compensation committee seeks advice from consultants who specialize in salary and rewards for executives.

Reforming Executive Compensation

Having a committee of shareholders develop a plan that combines salary, annual bonus for short-term performance, and longer-term stock options sounds like a good way to align executive interests with those of critical constituencies, including shareholders, the investment community, and employees. In the recent past, there have been several reasons that this approach has not worked as envisioned.

Frequently, the members of the board of directors, including those serving on the compensation committee, are not independent. This lack of independence can have several causes. For instance, members of the board may be appointed by the chairman and CEO. Or the members of the board may be attorneys or investment bankers who receive fees from the company. It is not unusual for a CEO to have the CEO of another company on the board and, in turn, serve on the other CEO's board. All of this leads to potential conflicts of interest.[50] As a confirmation, a recent study showed that the longer the tenure of the CEO, the less of a link there is between compensation and company performance—a result of the CEO's ability to build influence within the board and use this influence to weaken incentive alignment mechanisms.[51]

Incentives are frequently not what they seem. Whereas shareholders have something at risk, namely their investment in purchasing the shares, many of the forms of long-term incentives and options offered to executives have only upside potential. For example, stock appreciation rights and restricted stock require no investment or risk.[52] In other cases, boards have been known to reprice stock options to allow executives to reap benefits even though performance targets were not realized. For example, options are issued to an executive when the stock is $50, but then it falls to $30. Instead of allowing the executive to be out of the money, as should be the case, the board may cancel the $50 options and issue new ones at $30.

In its 1992 annual issue on executive compensation, *Business Week* offered a number of suggestions for reforming executive compensation. The first is to simplify plans by providing a salary, bonus, and straightforward stock options rather than other types of perks, golden parachutes, huge pensions, and other gimmicks. Second, limit CEO salaries to $1 million per year, no matter how large the company. Any payment beyond this amount must be earned by achieving tough performance standards. Third, board members should keep a closer eye on compensation and utilize the opinions of independent experts when designing executive compensation systems. Finally, all aspects of executive compensation should be clearly disclosed.[53] It is worth noting that many companies are adopting the procedures outlined.[54] Several organizations hold the CEO's base salary to a multiple of the average worker salary. (For instance, CEO salary and bonus at Herman Miller is limited to twenty times the average paycheck.)[55] Besides, the Securities and Exchange Commission has moved to require disclosure of executive pay and trends in executive pay in proxy statements and to allow shareholders a nonbinding vote on corporate pay policies.[56]

All the signs point to heightened sensitivity to executive pay on the part of executives, members of the board, and shareholders. In fact, evidence exists to show that visible and concrete steps are already being taken to address the issue of executive pay—the problems of both equity and excess discussed earlier.[57]

THE ROLE OF BENEFITS IN REWARD SYSTEMS

Once a largely neglected issue, the topic of benefits has become front-page news in the past decade. Child care, health care costs and coverage, flexible benefits, and changes in pension benefits are among the most dynamic compensation topics today. Whereas the issue of executive compensation will recede from the front page in time, issues related to benefits will remain.

A major reason for the increased attention to benefits is costs.[58] Fifty years ago, indirect compensation cost less than 5 percent of the direct compensation offered to most employees. In 1990, benefits equaled just under 40 percent of the cost of direct compensation.[59] Most of the increase does not reflect new benefits rather the higher costs of legally required payments (e.g., the employer's share of Social Security) and of optional benefits (especially health insurance); the costs for both doubled over a twenty-year period.

Because benefits are contingent on membership in the organization, they help a company attract and retain employees. Benefit programs do not directly motivate increased employee performance, for the link between performance level and benefit level is virtually zero. All employees receive similar benefit coverage, regardless of their performance levels.

Benefit plans have positive valence to employees. Employees gain several advantages by receiving part of their compensation in this indirect form. For example, even though employees may contribute to or even pay the entire cost of benefits such as insurance, the cost associated with the group coverage of all employees is likely to be considerably lower than equivalent insurance purchased individually. In addition, some benefits are given favorable tax treatment: the employee need not pay tax on the value of health insurance, for example. The following sections review many of the common benefit plans currently in use and discuss related issues, such as cost containment and legal considerations.

TYPES OF BENEFITS

The major categories of benefits include mandatory protection programs, pay for time not worked, optional protection programs, private retirement plans, and a wide variety of other services.

Mandatory Protection Programs

Several benefits are provided to employees because they are legislatively mandated, by either the federal or the state government. The most notable required protection program is specified by the Federal Insurance Contribution Act (FICA) of 1935, better known as the Social Security Act. Social Security is designed to protect employees and their dependents by providing retirement income, disability income, health care (Medicare), and survivor benefits. Other mandated protection programs include workers' compensation and unemployment compensation.

Social Security For many employers and employees, Social Security is the most expensive benefit purchased. Two-thirds of the workers in the United States pay more toward Social Security than they pay in income tax.

In 1991, both employee and employer contributed 7.65 percent—15.3 percent in all—of earnings up to a maximum of $53,400, for a combined total of as much as $8,170. A total of 6.2 percent of the tax rate is for Social Security; 1.45 percent is for Medicare. For employees who have annual wages in excess of $53,400, the Medicare tax of 1.45 percent continues up to $125,000. This is more than double the contribution of just ten years ago. In 1980, the maximum combined contribution was $3,175.34.

Social Security is not funded on an actuarial basis, as are most pension or insurance programs. In other words, the contributions are not invested in such a way as to grow and thereby cover the promised pension. Instead, money collected from currently employed individuals is used to meet the program's monthly obligations to those who are now retired or disabled. In the late 1970s, it was realized that changing demographics (a rapid increase in the elderly population) would mean too few workers to support those entitled to payments. Accordingly, Social Security has undergone major changes in the last several years, the most significant being the 1983 amendments to the Social Security Act. These changes increased both the percentage of earnings contributed and the maximum earnings base. At the same time, some benefits were eliminated and future benefits were scaled back. For example, an earnings test was added. In 1992, Social Security beneficiaries aged sixty-five to seventy could earn $10,200 a year without penalty; benefits are then cut $1 for every $3 earned above that amount.

The future of Social Security is not without controversy. Some of the issues are as follows:

- *Income redistribution.* Baby boomers and young people are paying much more than they are getting. A typical twenty-year-old will contribute $65,000 to Social Security over his or her lifetime but receive only $12,000 in benefits (in today's dollars).
- *Retirement age.* Currently, those retiring at the age of sixty-five qualify for full Social Security benefits. In the future, that age will shift upward, to sixty-seven years in 2027.
- *Earnings test.* The test penalizes retirees who must work but does not affect the wealthy who may have income of many thousands each month from private pensions, investments, and other nonwage sources.
- *Safety of the Social Security trust fund.* The system is now solvent and gradually building up an enormous reserve at the rate of $150 million a day, estimated to peak at $8 trillion by 2027. This reserve is part of the resources of the U.S. Treasury. Can the government (legislators) keep its hands off a multitrillion dollar fund for the next forty years?
- *Means testing.* At present, many well-off retirees receive more benefits than they need while many poor ones receive fewer benefits than they require.[60]

According to one expert, a better system would be one in which people buy their retirement-income coverage privately and tax subsidies are used exclusively to boost the retirement incomes of low-income people. This could be achieved through a two-tiered system, where the first tier provides a flat or means-tested benefit for the elderly and the second tier involves something like a mandated

Income Retirement Account (IRA).[61] One thing is certain: the Social Security system will continue to be debated and analyzed.

Unemployment Compensation The Social Security Act of 1935 also established a system of **unemployment compensation insurance (UCI)** in the United States. UCI provides benefits, at the rate of 50 to 80 percent of normal pay, to out-of-work employees who have been laid off and who are actively looking for work. Those seeking benefits must be registered with the state employment office in their area and are expected to accept work commensurate with their skills. The benefit period is a function of the length of prior employment, up to a maximum of twenty-six weeks of benefits. Workers who are fired for misconduct, quit voluntarily, or do not actively seek employment are generally not eligible for UCI benefits.

Unlike Social Security, which is managed by the federal government, UCI is handled by the states in accordance with federal guidelines. As a result, the exact details of employer contributions, employee eligibility for coverage, and amount of benefits vary considerably. In most states, employers finance this benefit by paying a small tax on the first $7,000 of an employee's wages. The size of the employer's contribution varies on the basis of past claims against that employer, thus providing an incentive to employers to avoid frequent layoffs. The experience-based tax rate also provides an inducement for employers to keep careful records of the reasons that employees leave and to document all discharges due to misconduct.

In periods of an extended economic downturn, it is not unusual for the twenty-six week limit on benefits to be extended. In 1992, Congress passed legislation extending benefits, and this legislation was signed into law by President Bush.

Workers' Compensation As the United States became increasingly industrialized in the late 1800s and early 1900s, disabling worker injuries and worker deaths became more common. Most workers had no avenue of redress and no employee benefits if they were injured on the job. Injured workers and their families simply went without compensation, and employers were not accountable for workplace hazards, which were often very great.

The first **workers' compensation,** a type of no-fault insurance for occupational disabilities and death, was initiated in the early 1900s, and most states have had such a program since 1920. Currently, all states have some form of workers' compensation, which offers reasonable and prompt benefits when workers are injured or killed on the job, regardless of fault. Workers do not need to bear the expense of time-consuming court action against their employers.

As with most insurance, the cost to employers is based on injury experience. The costs of medical treatment, rehabilitation programs, and disability income can be high, especially in cases of serious injuries. As a result, employers have an incentive to encourage employee safety. Unlike other mandated protection programs, workers' compensation is handled entirely by the state, with no federal standards or involvement. Consequently, the specific benefit provisions vary from state to state.

Compensation for Time Not Worked

Almost all employers provide full-time employees with some payments for time not worked. Figure 13.4 illustrates a wide range of such benefits.

Holidays Virtually all employers pay employees for major national holidays. Some employers have additional holidays, such as Presidents' Day (February), Columbus Day (October), or Veterans Day (November), whereas others observe religious holidays like Good Friday and Rosh Hashanah. Employers that must operate on holidays (for example, hospitals or police departments) generally provide overtime pay to employees who work on holidays.

Vacation Most employers offer paid vacations to their permanent employees, the amount depending on length of service. A majority of employers stagger vacation schedules to remain well staffed throughout the year, whereas some schedule a plant shutdown and have all employees take vacation at that time.

FIGURE 13.4 Payment for Time Not Worked

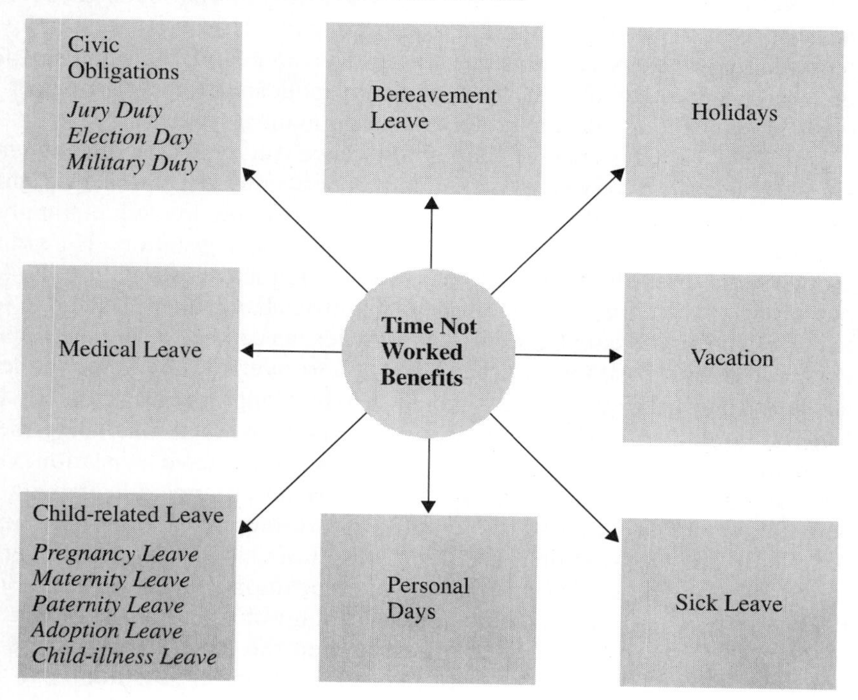

Sick Leave A usual pay-for-time-not-worked benefit is sick leave. Many employees accrue sick leave in proportion to days worked. For instance, one half-day of paid sick leave may be given for each fifteen days worked. Some firms allow unused sick leave to accumulate over the years, to be used in case of extended illness. Another popular alternative is to pay employees for unused sick leave as an incentive to come to work regularly and to use sick leave only when it is really needed.

Personal Days Some employers offer one or two personal holidays each year. Employees can decide when to use these days off—for instance, to celebrate a birthday. Personal days off are sometimes called *mental health days*—for the occasional times one has to get away from work or "go crazy."

Child-related Leave Many organizations are offering leaves in conjunction with the last weeks of pregnancy (pregnancy leave) and the initial weeks following the birth of a child (maternity leave). Realizing the importance of having both parents care for a newborn, some organizations allow the father to take time off following the birth of a child (paternity leave).[62] Employees adopting a young child may also be offered maternity or paternity leave. Sometimes, too, leave is provided to employees with gravely ill children.

The Pregnancy Discrimination Act of 1978 requires that pregnancy and childbirth be treated like any other medical condition that would require a leave. Thus, an employer cannot provide a medical leave for an employee recovering from heart surgery but refuse to grant a maternity leave. However, the employer is not required to give a woman her same job, or even a job with the same pay, following maternity leave. Again, whatever company policies exist with respect to other medical leaves must be applied to women on maternity leave.

In 1990, Congress passed the Family Leave Act, which would have mandated unpaid leave of up to twelve weeks, with benefits and reinstatement rights, in the event of the birth or adoption of a child or illness in the immediate family, including parents. However, President Bush vetoed the legislation. He argued that, though he favored the family leave concept, such leaves should not be legislated but left up to the employers. (European countries have taken the lead in providing maternity and child care benefits to employees, as can be seen in the International Perspective box.) Although Congress failed to override the veto, the legislation has been reintroduced and was again passed by Congress and vetoed by President Bush in the fall of 1992. In the meantime, nineteen states (including the District of Columbia) have enacted various versions of family leave legislation. Generally, the state laws allow employers to offset the required unpaid leave with any paid leave provided. In many states, employers are required to continue health care benefits to an employee on leave. Most state laws also require employers to reinstate the employee in the same or equivalent position. Finally, in early September 1992, a consortium of 137 companies and nonprofit groups, including 11 major corporations, announced that they had formed the American Business Collaboration for Quality Dependent Care. The goal of the consortium is to raise $25

INTERNATIONAL PERSPECTIVE

European Nations Far Surpass the United States in Maternity and Child Care Benefits

The United States is now the only industrialized nation without a federal law guaranteeing female employees a reasonable length of leave for childbirth and reinstatement into a comparable job at the conclusion of the leave. In fact, most industrialized nations and even many developing countries provide for *paid* maternity leaves.

In Europe, the average length of paid maternity leaves is six months. Sweden provides the most comprehensive benefits, allowing nine months of leave at 90 percent of regular pay, plus an additional three months at a lower rate and job reinstatement rights for one and one-half years after the child is born. Paid leave may be taken by either parent and may be collected over more than a one-year period if the employee returns to work part-time. In addition, parents may opt to work six-hour days (at a proportionately reduced salary) until their child reaches eight years of age.

European countries have also taken the lead in providing child care for working parents. In these countries, one author observes, children have long been regarded as "a major societal resource," and there is a sense that "the whole society should share in the costs of rearing them" (Kamerman, 1980, p. 23). Moreover, a sharp decline in the birthrate to below replacement levels has spurred European governments to increase services, subsidies, and incentives for working women who choose to have children. Services often include free public day care. In France, Belgium, Germany, Italy, and most Eastern European countries, more than 75 percent of three- to six-year-olds attend public preschools.

However, some fear that advances in child care made in Eastern Europe will soon be rolled back. Increasing unemployment and empty government coffers are generating pressure for women to stay out of the paid labor force and care for their children at home.

Sources: Kenneth A. Kovach, "Creeping Socialism or Good Public Policy: The Proposed Parental and Medical Leave Act," *Labor Law Journal,* July 1987, pp. 427–432; Sheila B. Kamerman, "Maternity, Paternity, and Parenting Policies: How Does the United States Compare?" in *Family and Work: Bridging the Gap,* ed. Sylvia Ann Hewlett, Alice S. Ilchman, and John J. Sweeney (Cambridge, Mass.: Ballinger, 1986), pp. 53–65; Sheila B. Kamerman, "Child Care and Family Benefits: Policies of Six Industrialized Countries," *Monthly Labor Review,* November 1980, pp. 23–28; Chantal Paoli, "Women Workers and Maternity: Some Examples from Western Europe," *International Labour Review,* January–February 1982, pp. 1–16.

million to fund a variety of child- and elder-care projects across the United States.[63]

Other Leaves As indicated in Figure 13.4, additional benefits include medical, civic, and bereavement leave. Medical leave allows employees extended time off for major medical reasons. Frequently, such leave is unpaid and takes effect when all sick leave days have been exhausted. Leave for civic obligations includes time off for jury duty, part (or all) of the day off to vote in national elections, and leave for military duty, such as National Guard or reserve military service. Bereavement leave allows the employee time off for a death in the immediate family.

Optional Protection Programs—Health Insurance

Optional protection programs are not mandated by law but are offered to make the employer more competitive in the labor market and to improve employee satisfaction and quality of life. Medical or health insurance is a major optional protection benefit offered by most employers. The goal of health insurance is to provide partial or complete coverage of medical expenses incurred by the employee and the employee's family. In practice, this means either paying directly or reimbursing the employee for hospital charges, surgery, and other personal or family medical expenses. Many plans also pay for dental care.

Health plans vary in their comprehensiveness of coverage and specifics of funding, but rapidly rising costs have made health insurance a major concern in most organizations. As shown in Figure 13.5, over the last eleven years, health care expenditures have grown at more than triple the rate of the consumer price index. The problem of health care costs is illustrated by the fact that General Motors spent more on medical coverage—$3.2 billion in 1990 for 1.9 million employees, dependents and retirees—than it spent on steel.[64] The simple fact is that most organizations cannot afford to provide as much coverage as they have done in the past. Cost containment strategies have included the redesign of medical plans, a search for funding alternatives, and other approaches aimed at slowing the increase in health care costs.

Health Plan Redesign In the past, health care insurance was typically regarded as a total package shielding employees from all health care costs. Increasingly, however, the goal is shifting to protection of employees against major and catastrophic costs. Instead of reimbursing employees for all medical bills, many employers have begun using deductibles, copayments, and coordinated coverage as ways of containing costs.

Many medical plans have a **deductible** of $100 to $400 or more for each family member each year. Only expenses over this amount will be reimbursed by the insurance fund. Thus, a person in good health, who makes only one or two medical or dental visits in a year, may receive no reimbursement.

Coinsurance means that expenses beyond the deductible are shared, usually in a ratio of 80:20 or 90:10. Thus, an employee submitting a bill of $500 for simple surgery in the doctor's office would receive reimbursement for $400, assuming an 80:20 split and no deductible. To take care of catastrophic expenses, costs beyond a maximum of several thousand dollars are then reimbursed 100 percent under most coinsurance plans. For example, an individual with bills of $75,000 for heart surgery might pay 20 percent of the first $5,000 (or $1,000), with insurance covering the remaining $74,000. Copayment plans have the advantage of making employees more aware of health care costs. Also, because the employee pays some of each expense, copayments tend to discourage unnecessary use of health insurance benefits.

Another common alternative is to require employees to contribute some of the costs of health insurance. The strikes against several telephone companies in

FIGURE 13.5 Growth in Health Care Expenditures Relative to Consumer Price Index

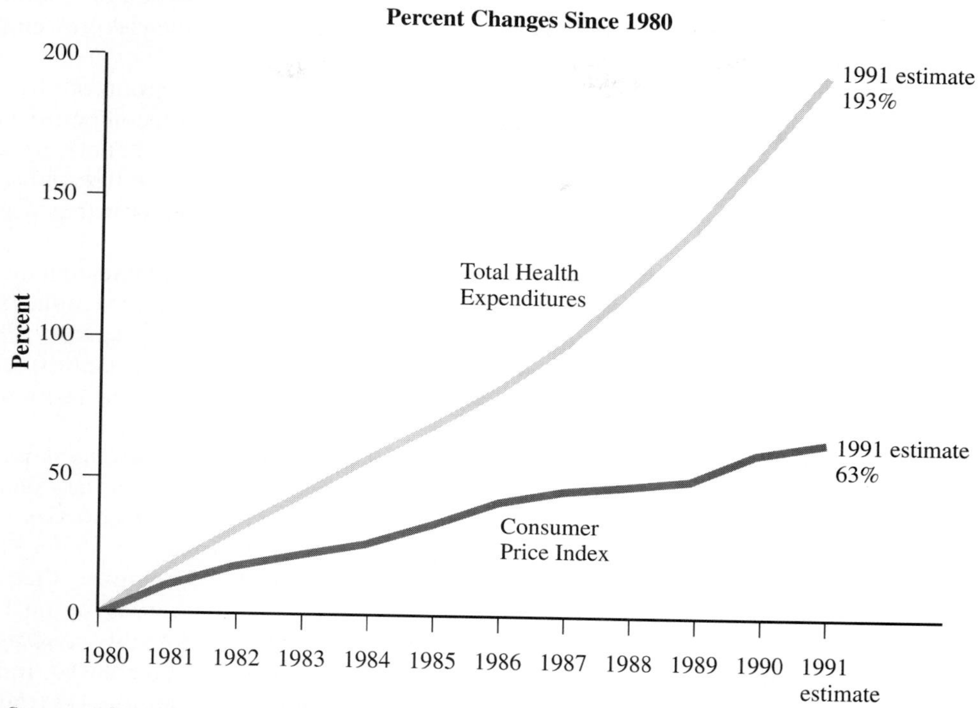

Source: "Condition Critical," *Time,* November 25, 1991, pp. 34–35.

the summer of 1989 were triggered by employer demands that employees share in the costs of health insurance. Thus, employers must be very careful if they switch from noncontributory, no-deductible, full-coverage plans to systems in which employees become responsible for a share of health costs. Employees tend to regard existing benefits as rights rather than privileges and strongly resent any reductions in benefit levels. It may help to appoint a benefits-cost task force, including employees from various organizational levels, to study the problem and to communicate the reasons for a cost-reduction move.

Employees are increasingly concerned with **coordinating benefits** as a way of containing costs. The objective is to prevent duplicate payment for the same health care service. For instance, an employee may be covered both by his or her employer's plan and by a working spouse's benefits. Careful checking is necessary to ensure that reinbursement is made only once.

Health Funding Alternatives Another approach to cost containment has been to seek funding alternatives. Instead of relying on insurance companies such as Blue Cross/Blue Shield, some employers have begun to self-insure or to use preferred provider organizations or health maintenance organizations. By self-insuring, an employer sets aside funds to pay health claims in lieu of insurance coverage. If the base of employees is large enough to spread the risk, the employer can achieve significant savings.[65]

A **preferred provider organization (PPO)** is a limited group of physicians and hospitals that agree to provide services in accordance with competitive fee schedules negotiated in advance. The physicians and hospitals benefit from knowing that they have a guaranteed customer base. Employees are free to use any physician or hospital that is part of the PPO or another provider if they are willing to pay any difference.

A **health maintenance organization (HMO)** provides complete medical care for employees and their families at a fixed annual fee. Supplemental policies typically cover hospitalization for those HMOs not associated with hospitals. Since doctor visits are not charged on a per visit basis, individuals are more likely to seek preventive care, thus reducing the incidence and costs of more serious illness.

Legal Requirements for Health Care Health benefits programs have been relatively free from government regulation, though this situation may change in the near future. Health insurance for the working poor was a major issue in the 1992 presidential campaign.

The Health Maintenance Organization Act of 1973 requires that companies with at least twenty-five employees living in an area served by an HMO offer HMO membership as an alternative to regular group health coverage. Consequently, the number of HMOs and their participants has increased dramatically.

In 1985, the Consolidated Omnibus Budget Reconciliation Act (COBRA) was passed to prevent gaps in health care coverage. It requires employers with twenty or more employees to provide extended health care coverage for up to eighteen months to employees who are terminated and up to thirty-six months for widowed or divorced spouses and dependent children of former or current employees. The employer may pass along the full cost of the premium to the employee or employee's family, along with a 2 percent administrative fee.

Health Benefits for Retirees Companies that provide health coverage for employees typically provide continuing coverage for retirees. Such continuing coverage is coordinated with Medicare, which provides certain benefits beginning at age sixty-five. Companies try to cover the costs—and there are many—not paid by Medicare.

In an effort to clarify the potential costs of retiree medical coverage, the Financial Accounting Standards Board (FASB) adopted Financial Accounting Standard 106, which requires organizations to subtract a portion of their obligations from their annual earnings reports, starting in 1993. Organizations must (1) set up a huge "catch-up" reserve for current and retired employees and (2) accrue, or set aside, a reserve each year for postretirement medical benefits of employees who are currently working. As Table 13.8 shows, the cost will be staggering for many organizations. For example, General Motors will have a one-time charge of

TABLE 13.8 How New Medical Benefits Accounting Rule Will Impact Profits

Company	*One-Time Charge (In Millions of Dollars)*	*Charge as Percent of Equity*	*Annual Continuing Charge (In Millions of Dollars)*	*Percentage Reduction in Pretax Profits*
Companies That Have Already Adopted Rule				
Bell Atlantic	$1,550	17%	$183	0%*
Equifax	49	13	10	6
General Electric	1,799	8	279	0*
General Mills	70	11	12	1
Georgia-Pacific	119	4	23	3
IBM	2,263	5	394	8
International Paper	215	4	37	3
Pennzoil	49	4	12	8
Philip Morris	921	8	216	2
Woolworth	115	5	14	1
Companies That Have Disclosed Rule's Impact But Not Adopted It				
Alcoa	1,200	24	150	11
American Brands	175	4	35	2
American Express	120–180	2	42–76	4–9
AT&T	5,500–7,500	34–46	558–725	0–4*
Chrysler	2,400–6,000	35–88	358	41
Deere	1,200–1,700	42–60	178	64
Du Pont	3,000–4,000	18–24	500–750	6–12
Ford Motor	5,000–9,000	22–39	915	22
General Motors	16,000–24,000	59–88	2,023–2,356	22–33
Sears, Roebuck	1,750–2,500	14–19	250–415	9–28
USX	1,200–1,800	20–31	317–483	14–27

*Zero means earnings are unaffected because company was already "pre-funding" to cover retirees' future medical costs.

Note: Figures are estimates, based on recent financial results.

Source: "New Medical-Benefits Accounting Rule Seen Wounding Profits, Hurting Shares," *The Wall Street Journal,* April 22, 1992, p. C1. Reprinted by permission of The Wall Street Journal.

$16 billion to $24 billion, an amount equal to between 60 and 88 percent of GM's equity or total value. In addition, GM will have a continuing charge of $2 billion to $2.3 billion—a 22 to 33 percent reduction in pretax profits.[66] The impact is not as large for other companies, and some organizations have "prefunded" retiree medical costs. But for most organizations, the one-time and continuing charges can be measured in millions of dollars, with double-digit reductions in pretax profits being common.

Retiree medical benefits have gone from a long-accepted and little noticed element of a benefit package to a front-burner issue in terms of impact on profits.

The strategic, legal, accounting, and financial constraints will be weighed against general HR practices of doing nice things for retirees as organizations re-evaluate the level of medical benefits they will provide for retired workers.

Health Benefits for Non–Family Members Given the general trend to control and cut back on the expense of health care, why would organizations offer to extend coverage to other people besides employees and their legal dependents? Lotus Development Corp., with more than 3,000 employees, is offering to provide the same benefits for the long-term partners of homosexual employees as it does for the spouses of heterosexual employees.[67] The company's offer is limited to homosexual couples, and to qualify, such couples must sign an affidavit stating that they live together, intend to stay together, and are responsible for one another. Several other companies, the municipal governments of Seattle, and several California cities provide similar benefits.

The rationale at Lotus was simple: studies showed that committed homosexual couples are at no greater risk of illness, including the catastrophic illness of AIDS, than are married heterosexual pairs. On a cost-benefit basis, Lotus figures that the benefits in terms of attracting and retaining employees outweigh the cost of the coverage.

Optional Protection Programs—Life and Disability Insurance

Many companies offer life insurance as a benefit, providing support for the employee's family in the case of the death of the wage earner. By purchasing a group package, the employer can obtain coverage at far lower rates than would be available to individuals. Coverage is generally based on annual earnings, and for many employees coverage is offered for twice annual earnings. Some organizations allow employees to purchase additional life insurance at the group rate.

Many employers provide long-term disability insurance to guarantee income for employees who become disabled and are unable to work—an event far more likely than the death of the wage earner.[68] Disabled employees and their families are entitled to payments from Social Security, but most need additional income to approach replacement of prior earnings. Long-term disability payments typically do not begin until the employee has been unable to work for a specified period, usually three to six months.

Private Retirement/Pension Plans

A very important benefit to most employees is a private pension plan. In some cases, pensions are funded entirely by employer contributions, but most involve both employer and employee contributions. A **pension** is essentially an investment to which contributions are added at regular intervals. Invested funds, along with interest, dividends, and/or capital gains, grow and accumulate to provide income during retirement. Under some plans, an account identified as belonging to the employee is established. With other pensions, funds are pooled, with a known share reserved for the employee upon retirement. Pensions are subject to intricate financial, legal, and tax rules and considerations.

Virtually all pensions are "qualified"—that is, they conform to stringent Internal Revenue Service requirements. Both employer and individual contributions to qualified plans are exempt from income tax, and interest, dividends, and gains are allowed to accumulate tax free. Retired employees must pay income tax on the pension payments they receive, but often their tax rate is lower than when they were working and had a larger income. Thus, employee contributions are a valuable means of deferring tax on income. In this context, pensions are deferred wages: rewards for long service. However, if an employer wishes to implement a pension plan for a select group of employees, such as key executives, the plan must be nonqualified. This approach is frequently used to provide supplemental retirement benefits for executives.

Retirement plans are expensive, costing the employer an estimated 8 to 10 percent of payroll.[69] The amount that the employee will receive on retirement is usually based on length of service with the company and salary level. Benefits average between 20 and 30 percent of preretirement salary for most plans. (Remember that the retired employee will also qualify for Social Security.) The pension plans in use today can be categorized into three broad types: defined benefit plans, defined contribution plans, and capital accumulation plans.[70]

Defined Benefit Plans The **defined benefit plan** is the most prevalent type, comprising 91 percent of all plans in American industry.[71] Under a defined benefit plan, retirement benefits depend on a formula that includes length of service and average earnings in the final years of employment. Such plans have the advantage that employees know the amount of their retirement benefits ahead of time. Employer and employee contributions are determined by actuarial calculations.

Defined Contribution Plans A less expensive—and less widely used—type of pension is the **defined contribution plan,** also termed a **money purchase plan.** Contributions are made at a fixed rate to an account established for the employee. Benefits are a function of contributions plus gains (or losses) as a result of interest, dividends, or capital gains. Profit sharing plans and employee stock ownership plans (ESOPs) fall in this category. Defined contribution plans offer less security and predictability of retirement benefits because the employee, not the company, assumes the risk of investment performance.

Capital Accumulation Plans Through **capital accumulation plans,** employees have the opportunity to establish individual retirement accounts. The principal capital accumulation vehicles are thrift plans and 401(k) plans. Employees may make tax-deferred contributions, which, under thrift plans, may be matched by the organization. A common matching rate would be $1 of employer contribution for each $2 contributed by the employee.

Thrift plans were popular in some industries for many years and then became the basis for 401(k) plans as a part of the Internal Revenue Act of 1978.[72] Although they involve no employer match, 401(k) plans allow employees to set aside salary and participate in tax-deferred earnings. In 1988, employee contributions to 401(k) plans were limited to 20 percent of salary, up to a maximum of $7,313 a year, a figure that is adjusted annually for inflation.

Regulations Governing Retirement Plans

Private employer retirement plans were subject to little government regulation before 1974. Employers had great latitude in establishing and administering pension plans for their employees. As it turned out, many of the pension plans were not sound, because of either poor actuarial planning or company economic reversals. Thus, many employees believed that they were accruing pension rights when in fact they were not. In response to those problems, during the last twenty years a wide array of legislation has been enacted and IRS regulations formulated with respect to pensions.

ERISA The initial legislation setting standards in pensions was the Employee Retirement Income Security Act of 1974 (ERISA), which established reporting requirements and fiduciary standards, along with rules regarding plan participation, vesting, funding, and pension plan termination. Favorable tax treatment of employer contributions is available only for plans that meet ERISA guidelines. (Note that employers are not required to offer private pensions.)

In terms of participation, ERISA requires that employees who are twenty-one years old and have completed one year with the company be eligible to participate in the pension plan. Another important concept is **vesting,** the right to receive pension benefits contributed on the employee's behalf by the company even if the employee leaves the company before retirement. ERISA established complex alternate rules regarding vesting but basically ensured that any employee would have rights to at least 50 percent of the employer's contributions after ten years of service and would be 100 percent vested after fifteen years. Thus, employees can be assured of certain pension levels if they have worked a minimum number of years, even if they leave the company before retirement. Vesting rules also prevent company abuses, such as firing long-service employees shortly before retirement in order to avoid paying them a pension. Vesting applies only to employer contributions. Employees retain rights to any contributions they make and can withdraw them or roll them over into another private pension plan if they leave the company.

Before ERISA, many private pension plans were not protected if the company went bankrupt. To protect employees and retired employees, ERISA created a system of **pension plan termination insurance** and a government agency, the Pension Benefit Guaranty Corporation, to administer the program. The insurance is funded through premiums paid by employers.

The long-range goals of ERISA are to make private pensions equitable and to put them on a firm financial footing. The burden imposed on employers or pension trustees is substantial. As a result, in the initial years of ERISA, many employers terminated their pension plans rather than comply with the law.

Tax-Reform Act of 1986 Certain provisions of the Tax Reform Act (TRA) of 1986 were intended to eliminate discrimination in benefits that favor highly paid employees. A very complicated set of nondiscrimination rules—the now infamous Section 89 of the Internal Revenue Code—was scheduled to take effect in late 1989. More than 160 pages of clarifying rules were issued by the Treasury Department in March of that year, but before they could take effect, they were repealed by Congress at the end of 1989.

Although the provisions for controlling discrimination in favor of highly compensated employees were set aside in 1989, they will no doubt reappear at some time in the future.[73] This is especially likely given the scrutiny that compensation and benefits granted to highly paid executives have recently received.

Single-Sex Pension Benefits A final legal issue concerning pensions involves sex bias. Before 1978, it was common to use actuarial tables in planning pension contributions and payouts. Women as a group live longer than men and as a result, under most pension plans, were required to make greater contributions to receive retirement benefits equal to those of men. Alternately, women were forced to accept lower monthly benefits after retirement than men, again because they can statistically expect to collect benefits for more years.

In 1978, the U.S. Supreme Court found this practice illegal.[74] This concept was extended by the Court in 1983, forcing pension plan administrators to eliminate sex distinctions in mortality tables used to determine pension benefits.[75] The Retirement Equity Act of 1984 was passed to bring legislation in line with these court decisions. As a result, there is now no distinction in the benefits received by men and women.

Other Benefits

Many organizations offer additional benefits, some of which provide innovative opportunities for employees. Included are such benefits as vision care, prescription drugs, legal counseling, and financial counseling. Many organizations have established employee assistance programs (EAPs), offering short-term counseling for employees under stress as a result of work or nonwork problems.[76] EAPs are discussed in more detail in Chapter 14. Other important benefits include those described in the sections that follow.

Wellness Programs In an effort to stimulate wellness, many employers provide exercise or recreational facilities for employees or reimburse employees for health club membership. Other companies provide incentives in the form of monthly stipends or similar payments for employees to participate in exercise programs, quit smoking, lower blood pressure or cholesterol, and take similar steps toward good health.[77] Such programs are discussed in Chapter 14.

Educational Assistance Another important benefit is educational assistance. Typically, employees are reimbursed for tuition and possibly for books or other associated costs. In general, educational assistance is limited to courses or degree programs that are job related.

Child Care Assistance It is likely that every major company will soon consider offering child care assistance as an employee benefit. Such assistance can take the form of on-site child care, financial assistance, or information and referral. The number of women in the labor market has increased dramatically, and today more than 4,000 organizations with 100 or more employees provides some type of child care benefit; some 1,000 of these organizations have on-site centers.[78] Further, satisfaction with child care arrangements has been found related to less work/family conflict, and lower levels of absenteeism.[79]

Because child care needs and preferences are extremely diverse, multifaceted, and changing, employers are advised to undertake a systematic needs assessment of employees before developing specific programs.[80] Many employers find that the best method of assisting a diverse work force is through referral services. Such services allow employees to more readily find the type of child care best suited to their needs.

Of the 4,000 companies with some type of child care benefit, approximately half provide financial assistance, typically through a dependent care option in a flexible benefits plan. Organizations can help employees pay for dependent care through pretax salary deductions. The Internal Revenue Code specifies that up to $5,000 of employee payments for dependent care expenses may be excluded from an employee's annual taxable income. For example, if the proper administrative arrangements are established, an employee needing dependent care could agree to have the employer reduce his or her salary by $300 per month ($3,600 per year), with this amount then being directed to an account to pay for dependent care. Although there are administrative costs, there is no direct cost to the employer, and the employee is, in effect, paying for dependent care with pretax dollars. Without this type of plan, $3,600 worth of dependent care would cost a family earning $40,000 a total of $5,000—$3,600 for care and about $1,400 for federal income tax. Thus, the savings involved can be significant. The only drawback is that any balance in a dependent care account cannot be directly refunded or carried forward at the end of the plan year. Also, to take advantage of the tax savings, care providers need to have a Social Security number or an employer identification number. Thus, the dependent care provided by the student wife from Spain cannot be paid for with before-tax contributions to a dependent care account.

Note that such plans can be used for any qualified dependents, not just children. Many families need to arrange day care for elderly parents. Elder care is clearly one of the new benefits issues of the 1990s, and its importance is expected to increase in the twenty-first century as the population ages.[81]

Finally, a recent study sought to derive a quantitative index of a family-friendly company.[82] The index considers seven HR policy areas, the most important of which is dependent care services (maximum of 155 points). The family-friendly policies, along with associated point maximums and top scoring companies, are shown in Table 13.9.

7

TABLE 13.9 The Family-friendly Index and Top Scoring Companies

Family-friendly index

Policy	*Maximum Score*
Flexible Work Arrangements: Variable starting and quitting times, part-time work.	105
Leaves: Length of parental leaves, who's eligible, job guarantees.	40
Financial Assistance: Flexible benefits, long-term-care insurance, child-care discounts.	80
Corporate Giving/Community Service: Funding for community or national work/family initiatives.	60
Dependent Care Services: Child care and elder care referral, on-site centers, sick-child programs.	155
Management Change: Work/family training for managers, work/family coordinators.	90
Work-Family Stress Management: Wellness programs, relocation services, work/family seminars.	80
Total Possible: Because all policies may not fit every company, the ideal score is probably below the maximum.	610

Top Scoring Companies

Company	*Score*
Johnson & Johnson	245
IBM	223
Aetna	195
Corning	190
AT&T	178
John Hancock	175
Warner-Lambert	175
U.S. West	165
Du Pont	163
Travelers	158

Sources: Ellen Galinsky, Dana Friedman, and Carol Hernandez, *The Corporate Reference Guide to Work-Family Programs* (New York: Families and Work Institute, 1991); "Corporate America is Still No Place for Kids," *Business Week*, November 25, 1991, pp. 234–238.

ISSUES IN INDIRECT COMPENSATION

Cost Containment

Because of the rapidly increasing costs of health care, pensions, and other benefits, employers must focus on strategic cost containment if they are to survive. As mentioned previously, benefit packages can add up to 40 percent above the cost of direct compensation. A tradeoff analysis can help in evaluating benefit possibilities. In one case, a firm with 5,000 employees had high productivity, but profits were being eroded by rising health insurance costs.[83] Premiums had increased 75 percent in 1985, and a 20 percent increase—to $8.5 million—was projected for 1986. The executives were determined to reduce costs by 10 percent while identifying potential improvements in the system.

After the initial analysis, a decision was made to limit tradeoffs to health benefits. Employee satisfaction with alternative tradeoffs was solicited by inviting a 15 percent sample from all levels to participate in half-hour discussion meetings. Employees rated how much less satisfied they would be with their benefits if each alternative were implemented. The "satisfaction loss" (expressed as a percentage) for each of the potential reductions is shown in Table 13.10. Similarly, satisfaction gains were identified for suggested improvements to the plan. The satisfaction losses and gains were then divided by the percentage of premium saved (or spent) for each change. The resulting column "satisfaction loss per dollar saved" of Table 13.10 provided guidance as to changes in medical coverage that could yield the needed savings with minimal dissatisfaction from employees. As can be seen, the first choice was to add the requirement of precertification prior to hospitalization as a means of eliminating unneeded hospital days. As far as the deductible for hospitalization, the satisfaction loss doubled in going from $100 to $200, but the loss per dollar saved was equivalent for these two alternatives. The organization decided to select the $200 deductible. The clear preference, both in terms of satisfaction loss and loss per dollar saved, was for a $150 major medical deductible. The same was true with dependent coverage options: a charge of $10 had the least satisfaction loss per dollar saved. The result was a 13.3 percent reduction in cost, with 1.4 percent then being allocated to three new plan improvements with high satisfaction gain per dollar spent. The net result was four plan reductions with a projected 1986 savings of just over $1 million, along with added premium of $119,000 for plan improvements for total savings of 10.9 percent in benefit costs. The tradeoff analysis guided the effort in selecting health plan changes that would produce the savings with minimal employee dissatisfaction.

Two methods of reducing costs of benefits are through copayments and self-insurance. Both alternatives have already been discussed as funding alternatives for health insurance, but they apply more broadly. Plans with copayment require that the employee contribute to the benefit costs. This technique is cost effective and also an indirect way of communicating the high cost of benefit packages to employees. When copayment makes employees aware of the costs of medical care, a reduction of unnecessary or abusive uses of the available benefits may result. There is some evidence that employees view benefits as part of their em-

TABLE 13.10 Example of Tradeoff Analysis to Evaluate Potential Health Care Savings

Plan Reductions

Benefit	*Change (From/To)*	*Satisfaction Loss*	*Employer Savings (% of Prem.)*	*Satisfaction Loss per Dollar Saved*	*Cumulative Savings (% of Prem.)*
Pre-certification	Not. Req./Req.	11.4%	4%	2.85	4.0%
Hospital Deductible	None/$100	5.7%	1.7%	3.35	7.4%
	None/$200	11.4%	3.4%	3.35	
Major Medical Deductible	$100/$150	11.4%	2.5%	4.56	9.9%
	$100/$200	32.9%	5.0%	6.58	
Dependent Coverage	$5/$10	14.3%	2.4%	5.96	12.3%
	$6/$15	31.4%	4.7%	6.68	
Hospital Coinsurance	100%/95%	18.6%	3.0%	6.20	
	100%/90%	41.4%	6.0%	6.90	
Surgical Coinsurance	100%/90%	27.1%	1.0%	27.10	
	100%/80%	50.0%	2.0%	25.00	

Source: "Benefits: Profiting from Trade-Off Analysis," by Jesse A. Sherman and Michael Carter reprinted with permission from *Personnel Journal*, Costa Mesa, California. Copyright August, 1987. All rights reserved.

ployment rather than as a privilege. For this reason, care must be taken when switching over to a copayment plan to ensure that employees do not see this as a reduction in the compensation package.

Larger organizations can establish a fund to cover some benefit costs and thus avoid the premium expenses. In addition to the potential savings, self-insurance allows organizations to become familiar with the benefit program through in-depth knowledge of day-to-day claims and other issues related to use. In this way, still further areas of potential saving may be discovered.

Flexible Benefit Options

One way to increase employee satisfaction without increasing the cost of the compensation package is by offering a **flexible benefit package,** also termed a **cafeteria-style benefit plan.** Under this plan, employees are automatically given a core plan with minimum coverage in medical insurance and retirement benefits. In addition, they receive benefit credits each year, which they can "spend" on additional benefits of their choice (e.g., more vacation time, more life insurance, more dental insurance, and so on).[84]

Flexible benefit plans are very effective and popular because they recognize that employees of different ages and life situations have differing personal needs.

Flexible benefits allow individual employees to choose the benefits that they want. Most companies provide a request form annually, allowing employees to modify their package.

A flexible benefit program involves several additional costs. First, communication of benefit options is more difficult. As many organizations can attest, it is extremely difficult to get the word out on a single benefit package. When there are multiple packages, as with flexible benefits, the communication problem is far more difficult. Administrative costs also increase with the number of options.

For companies willing to invest the extra effort to ensure that flexible benefit programs will work, the advantages outweigh the disadvantages. Flexible benefit programs enhance an organization's reputation for progressive treatment of its employees.

Communicating About Benefits

The main goal of both direct and indirect compensation should be to achieve company goals by providing rewards that are valued by employees. Employers must weigh both the costs of implementing benefit packages and the employee reaction to such plans, which may include behaviors such as turnover. Communication is critical for the successful administration of benefits. Organizations that do not invest effort in communicating a specific benefit might be better off not offering the benefit in the first place.

If the employer's intention is to attract entry-level employees, marketing immediate benefits such as a longer vacation or educational incentives may be more effective than advertising the pension plan, a benefit that will be more likely to reduce midcareer turnover. Also, if employees are to be satisfied with their benefit package, they must first be able to appreciate what goes into it. Although benefits may equal 40 percent or more of direct compensation, employees often grossly underestimate their cost and value.[85]

Organizations have at least two ways to correct the undervaluing of benefits. The first is to explain clearly to employees the objective costs of these benefits, pointing out why particular benefits may be of greater value than direct payment (e.g., because of tax considerations and favorable group insurance rates). Second, one study reported that employees know the value of their specific benefits almost to the penny when they make contributions to the fund.[86] Thus, contributing and copayment systems not only reduce the organization's costs, but have communication and educational advantages as well.

Communicating about benefits is not an easy task. Plans and options can be quite complex, and employees tend to have little interest in benefits until they need to use them. There are several ways to improve communication about benefits. First, written communication should be in plain language, not insurance jargon. Second, communication should be frequent and timed to occur when employees are likely to listen. Describing benefits when employees first begin work is unlikely to be effective, as new employees have many more pressing issues to attend to in the first few weeks on the job. Finally, communication should be directed not just to the employee, but also to other consumers of the benefit—most commonly, the spouse.

SUMMARY OF KEY POINTS

Performance-based rewards are an attempt to link compensation to performance. The two major reasons for seeking such a linkage are employee preference and the motivational aspects of tying pay to performance. Linking pay to performance has other advantages as well. It provides an increased incentive for top performers to remain with the organization, a means of reinforcing organizational objectives, and a method of keeping labor costs in line with productivity.

Pay can be linked to performance at the individual, group, or organizational levels. Individual plans can only be used where individual performance is measurable. Group systems are important where worker cooperation and coordination are necessary.

Individual plans include piecework, commission, individual bonus, and merit salary increases. In addition, an increasing number of organizations are basing pay on the number of different skills or jobs mastered, as a way of motivating continued learning and flexibility.

Group incentives may be piece rates based on group output, gain sharing plans, or profit sharing plans. Gain sharing plans include the Scanlon Plan, Improshare, and the Rucker Plan, all of which seek employee suggestions to cut costs and then share the savings with the employees. These plans work best in small- to medium-sized organizations. Profit sharing is an incentive system in which designated employees share the business profits.

Though linking pay to performance has its advantages, a number of factors may hinder its successful implementation. First, linking pay to performance is not going to work if employees have only limited control over performance, as is often the case. Second, performance is frequently difficult to measure. Third, many incentive rewards are not large enough to be motivational. Finally, many managers think incentive systems alone will provide the necessary linkage between pay and performance, and they may ignore many other aspects of the work or work-related environment that can reinforce the association between performance and rewards.

Executives are especially important to organizations and thus usually operate with a somewhat different system of compensation and incentives. Frequently, executive reward packages include bonus plans based on organizational performance and long-term incentives in the form of stock options. Executives may have perks such as company-paid automobiles, club memberships, and other considerations associated with their role. Executive pay has been criticized as being excessive in amount and inequitable when compared with organizational performance. Furthermore, executive pay has increased much faster than the pay of the average worker or than inflation.

Issues related to employee benefits have become a major topic, not only in most organizations, but also at the national level. Greater interest in benefits stems from the overall cost, averaging just under forty cents for every dollar in payroll; the rapid increases in the expense of some programs; the effectiveness of various programs; and an increase in legislation associated with benefit programs. Employee benefits include mandatory protection programs, compensation for time not worked, optional protection programs, and private retirement (pension) plans.

Mandatory protection programs include Social Security, unemployment compensation, and workers' compensation. Unemployment compensation provides benefits to out-of-work employees who are actively looking for work. Workers' compensation is a type of no-fault insurance for occupational injuries, disabilities, and death. Both unemployment compensation and workers' compensation systems are operated by the states, whereas Social Security is a federal government program.

Many employees receive pay for holidays and vacations. Pay for time not worked may also include sick leave, personal days, and leaves for maternity and infant care. Other protection programs include health insurance, life insurance, and disability insurance. As a result of the skyrocketing costs of health care, employers have been forced to redesign plans by increasing deductibles, splitting some costs with employees (coinsurance), and exploring alternatives such as preferred provider and health maintenance organizations.

Pension plans are funds established by employers to provide income to employees after retirement. Some plans require contributions by employees in addition to those of employers. Plans vary, with most providing defined benefits. Others define contributions, with benefits being a function of investment growth. In addition, many employers provide other types of capital accumulation plans, such as thrift plans or 401(k) plans that allow employees to invest pretax dollars toward retirement.

In the last twenty years, there have been a variety of federal laws and regulations regarding benefits. ERISA specified vesting and fiduciary standards to which private plans must adhere. COBRA requires the extension of group medical benefits to terminated employees, at the employees' expense.

Benefits raise several important issues, including cost containment and flexible-benefit options. As benefit costs have increased more rapidly than inflation, employers have had to resort to innovative ways of containing costs, such as copayments. Some companies have resorted to self-insurance by establishing funds to cover benefit costs and thus eliminating the segment of premiums that go to insurance companies. Flexible benefits provide an important means of tailoring benefits to employee needs. Such programs have additional administrative costs and are difficult to communicate to employees, but if used effectively they can enhance the organization's reputation as a progressive, employee-oriented firm.

Questions for Discussion

1. In what ways can the expectancy theory of motivation be used to improve compensation systems?
2. What are the advantages of linking pay to performance? The disadvantages?
3. What are some of the reasons employees tend to resist piece-rate pay systems?
4. What are the five major individual incentives described? How would each be best matched with the following groups of employees: (a) production workers, (b) sales employees, (c) professional employees, (d) electronics assembly workers, (e) managers, (f) scientists/engineers?
5. What are some of the considerations involved in using individual versus group incentives?
6. Describe the advantages and disadvantages of the various gain sharing plans.
7. What are the major barriers to successfully linking pay to performance? Which barriers are most associated with each type of incentive?
8. What recent issues have arisen in compensation for executives? What changes seem likely?
9. What are some of the reasons that employee benefits as a proportion of total labor costs have increased substantially in the past several years?
10. What is the federal government's role in regulating benefits?
11. What are the differences between unemployment compensation and workers' compensation, both as to the purpose of the programs and as to how they are administered?
12. Define each of the following medical insurance terms:
    a. Deductible
    b. Coinsurance
    c. Coordinated benefits
    d. Self-insurance
    e. PPO
    f. HMO
13. What is the difference between defined benefit and defined contribution pension plans?
14. What is a 401(k) and what advantages does it offer?
15. What is ERISA and what impact does it have on private pension plans?
16. What are the advantages and disadvantages of flexible benefits over standard benefit packages?
17. What are the key elements of communicating benefits to employees? Why is communication so important?

CASE 13.1

The Gyro Chemical Corporation

The Gyro Chemical Corporation produces and sells a broad line of more than 400 high-quality industrial cleaning and custodial products to companies throughout the United States. Sales are made through a network of 1,500 sales representatives. The sales representatives are compensated entirely by commission.

An effective sales force is the key factor in Gyro's profitability. It is important that each of the sales territories be fully staffed with trained, effective sales representatives. A number of sales representatives are extremely successful and earn between $100,000 and $300,000 each year in commissions. At the same time, the firm has recruited, hired, and trained many others (at a cost of $10,000 each), only to find that they are not suited to commission sales.

About 100 sales managers, each assigned to a district, are responsible for recruiting, hiring, supervising, and field-training approximately 15 sales representatives each. Initial training of sales representatives is through a 10-day program at Gyro headquarters. The sales managers find that they spend so much time recruiting and hiring that the daily supervision and field training of current salespeople are neglected.

In an effort to remedy this situation, Gyro's top management has decided to hire twelve professional recruiters, one for each of the sales regions. The recruiters will be responsible for finding job candidates, performing initial screening, and proposing final candidates to sales managers. Hiring decisions will continue to be the responsibility of the sales managers.

The commission system that underlies the compensation of sales representatives provides the impetus for various incentive plans that pervade all levels of the organization. Even though the recruiters have a limited role, they represent an important component in assisting the sales managers. Naturally, Gyro wants the compensation of the recruiters to have an incentive component of some type.

1. What are the individual incentive alternatives for compensating the recruiters, along with the advantages and disadvantages of each? Pay particular attention to possible dysfunctional aspects of each alternative.
2. Should incentive payments to recruiters be based on (1) the number of candidates interviewed, (2) the number of candidates recommended to sales managers, (3) candidates recommended and hired, or (4) candidates hired and successful? What are the advantages and disadvantages of each possibility?
3. What compensation arrangement, including combination of base and incentive pay, would you recommend for the recruiters?
4. How might sales managers be compensated in order to motivate them to choose and nurture highly effective salespeople?

CASE 13.2

An Incentive System for Greenland Manufacturing

Greenland Manufacturing of Houston, Texas, makes a high-technology catalytic component used in the refining of oil and in other petro-chemical processes. The catalytic components, like those manufactured by Greenland, are an important aspect of every refinery and petro-chemical facility on a worldwide basis. Even though the company is based in the United States, it has been successful in marketing and selling catalytic components worldwide. Greenland Manufacturing is the largest supplier with between 15 and 18 percent of the market in a very competitive business.

Greenland is the subsidiary of Consolidated Industries, a very tranditional organization with headquarters in St. Louis. Over the years, Consolidated and its subsidiaries have followed established compensation practices of hourly pay for nonexempt personnel and salary for professionals and managers. However, the new CEO, John Delary, has indicated his willingness to give more autonomy to the subsidiaries, including the opportunity to experiment with incentive compensation.

This news was welcomed by Stu Youngman, president of Greenland Manufacturing. Over the past months, a number of Greenland personnel have expressed interest in some type of incentive pay. Youngman has hired you as a compensation consultant to recommend an incentive plan.

During your initial meeting with Youngman, you learn that Greenland Manufacturing has sixty employees who are organized into three production lines, along with twenty additional personnel in the areas of maintenance, shipping, administrative (including clerical), and engineering (production and R&D). Most of these eighty individuals have been long-time employees of Greeland.

The first production line is responsible for the main product, the catalytic component used worldwide as part of the equipment to refine oil. This segment is by far the most profitable one of Greenland. The second production line makes customized versions of the main product for special orders. This line is extremely profitable on a per unit basis because of the tailor made nature of the products, but its volume is much lower. The third line manufactures a second product, but sales and profits for this item have been extremely low for the past twelve months. The future of this related product is not clear.

1. What additional information, if any, would you need before making any recommendations? Indicate the questions you would need to ask at this initial meeting with Youngman, along with possible answers. Specifically:
   a. What do you need to know about the past and future history of Greenland Manufacturing and its employees?
   b. What do you need to know about the production process?
   c. If you were to interview employees (hourly and salaried), what would you want to ask them?
2. Given the facts, what recommendations would you offer? What incentive compensation system would you recommend for Greenland and why? How might the recommendation change as a result of answers to your questions from the initial meeting and discussions with employees?

EXERCISE 13.1

Controlling Medical Benefit Costs

A company finds that the cost of its medical benefits has increased far beyond what was expected, and further increases are projected.

1. List the alternatives available to bring medical costs under control.
2. Compare and contrast the advantages and disadvantages of each alternative for controlling costs.
3. What input, if any, should employees have in evaluating various alternatives to contain health care costs?
4. How can employee input best be solicited? How can decisions, once reached, best be communicated to employees?

EXERCISE 13.2

*Flexible Benefit Decisions**

You have just been hired by Pico Electronics. In addition to salary or wages, Pico Electronics has a flexible benefit arrangement for each employee. Employees have a benefit account and can draw from this account to fund various benefits.

Your salary and position entitle you to $1,000 per month in benefit dollars to allocate among the various choices. If your total benefit cost is less than $1,000 per month, you will keep half the difference as a monthly cash bonus. If your total is over $1,000 per month, the difference is deducted from your salary. Under normal circumstances, benefit options, once selected, cannot be altered for five years.

Go through the benefit choices listed below and indicate how much of your $1,000 in monthly benefit dollars you will allocate to each benefit. Place a -0- for benefits you do not wish to purchase. Then total the allocated amounts and place the total in the last row.

Amount Allocated	*Benefit*	*Cost*
________	Pension Plan	Up to $500/mo., matched 50:50 by Pico
________	Paid Vacations	$50/mo. for 2 weeks/yr.
________	Paid Holidays	$50/mo. for 10 days/yr.
________	Paid Sick Leave	$50/mo. for 10 days/yr.
________	Guaranteed Maternity or Paternity Leave	$50/mo.

*Reprinted with permission of Merrill, an imprint of Macmillan Publishing Company from *Personnel: Human Resource Management*, Third Edition by Michael R. Carrell, Frank E. Kuzmis and Norbert F. Elbert. Copyright © 1989 by Merrill Publishing Company.

Amount Allocated	*Benefit*	*Cost*
___________	Medical Insurance	$250/employee, $350/family/mo.
___________	Health Maintenance Organization Health Care	$200/employee, $250/family/mo.
___________	Legal Insurance	$50/mo. for $100% legal needs
___________	Vision Care	$50/mo.
___________	Subsidized Child Care	$60/mo. per child for on-site care
___________	Credit Union	$25/mo.
___________	Subsidized Company Cafeteria	$50/mo. for free lunches
___________	Tuition Reimbursement	$50/mo. for 100% of tuition
___________	Funeral Leave	$50/mo. for 3 days/year
___________	Life Insurance	$50/mo. for $100,000
___________	Disability Insurance	$75/mo. to cover salary if disabled
___________	Dental Insurance	$50/mo. for all check-ups and required care
___________	Parking	$50/mo. (local lots charge $75/mo.)
___________	Total	

1. What assumptions did you make about your situation, now and for the immediate future? (For example: Married? Children? Further education?) How were these assumptions reflected in your choices?
2. Was your goal to use all of the $1,000 (and possibly more) to purchase options needed and desired or to maximize the amount left over each month?
3. What three benefit options are worth the most to you? Why?
4. What three benefit options are worth the least to you? Why?
5. Do you perceive any of the options as "too good to pass up?" Why or why not?

Notes and References

1. "How American Industry Stacks Up," *Fortune,* March 9, 1992, pp. 30–46; Alan S. Blinder, "Pay, Participation, and Productivity," *The Brookings Review,* Winter 1989/90, pp. 33–38.
2. "The Workers of the Future," *Fortune,* Vol. 123, Spring/Summer 1991, pp. 68–72.
3. Bureau of National Affairs, "Non-Traditional Incentive Pay Programs," *Personnel Policies Forum Survey No. 148* (Washington, D.C.: The Bureau of National Affairs, May, 1991).
4. Hewitt Associates, *Total Compensation DataBase CompBook 1989–1990* (Lincolnshire, Illinois: Hewitt Associates, 1990).
5. "Paying Workers to Meet Goals Spreads, But Gauging Performance Proves Tough," *The Wall Street Journal,* September 10, 1991, p. B1.
6. L. Dyer, D. P. Schwab, and R. D. Theriault, "Managerial Perceptions Regarding Salary Increase Criteria," *Personnel Psychology,* Vol. 29, 1976, pp. 233–242.

7. George Graen, "Instrumentality Theory of Work Motivation," *Journal of Applied Psychology,* Vol. 53, 1965, pp. 1–25; R. D. Prichard, D. W. Leonard, C. W. Von Bergen, Jr., and R. J. Kirk, "The Effects of Varying Schedules of Reinforcement on Human Task Performance," *Organizational Behavior and Human Performance,* Vol. 16, 1976, pp. 205–230.
8. Carla O'Dell, with Jerry McAdams, *People, Performance, and Pay: A Full Report on the American Productivity and Quality Center,* American Compensation Association, National Survey on Non-Traditional Reward and Human Resource Practices (Houston, Texas: American Productivity Center, 1987).
9. Deborah A. Mohr, James A. Riedel, and Kent S. Crawford, "A Group Wage Incentive System Can Boost Performance and Cut Costs," *Defense Management Journal,* 1986, 2nd Qtr., pp. 13–17; B. S. Georgopolous, G. M. Mahoney and M. W. Jones, "A Path Goal Approach to Productivity," *Journal of Applied Psychology,* Vol. 41, 1957, pp. 345–353; D. P. Schwab and L. Dyer, "The Motivational Impact of a Compensation System on Employee Performance," *Organizational Behavior and Human Performance,* Vol. 9, 1973, pp. 215–225.
10. V. H. Vroom, *Work Motivation* (New York: Wiley and Sons, 1964).
11. T. R. Mitchell, Mabmoub A. Wabba, and Robert J. House, "Expectancy Theory in Work Motivation: Some Logical and Methodological Issues," *Human Relations,* Vol. 27, No. 2, 1974, pp. 121–147.
12. Donald P. Schwab, "Impact of Alternative Compensation Systems on Pay Valence and Instrumentality Perceptions," *Journal of Applied Psychology,* Vol. 58, No. 3, 1973, pp. 308–312.
13. N. L. Kerr and S. E. Bruun, "Dispensability of Member Effort and Group Motivation Losses: Free-Rider Effects," *Journal of Personality and Social Psychology,* Vol. 44, No. 1, 1983, pp. 78–94.
14. B. Latane, K. Williams, and S. Harkins, "Many Hands Make Light the Work: The Causes and Consequences of Social Loafing," *Journal of Personality and Social Psychology,* Vol. 37, No. 6, 1979, pp. 822–833.
15. Edward E. Lawler, *Pay and Organizational Effectiveness.* (New York: McGraw-Hill, 1971).
16. Amy Dunkin and Kathleen Kerwin, "Now Salespeople Really Must Sell for Their Supper," *Business Week,* July 31, 1989, pp. 50, 52.
17. Daniel C. Rowland, "Incentive Pay: Productivity's Own Reward," *Personnel Journal,* March 1987, pp. 48–57.
18. Dale Feuer, "Paying for Knowledge," *Training,* May 1987, pp. 57–66; Richard L. Bunning, "Skill-Based Pay: Restoring Incentives to the Workplace," *Personnel Administrator,* June 1989, pp. 65–70.
19. Edward E. Lawler and Gerald E. Ledford, Jr., "Skill-Based Pay: A Concept That's Catching On," *Compensation and Benefits Review,* January-February 1986, pp. 54–61.
20. Gerald E. Ledford, Jr., "Three Case Studies on Skill-Based Pay: An Overview," *Compensation and Benefits Review,* March/April 1991, pp. 11–22.
21. N. Gupta, G. D. Jenkins, Jr., and W. P. Curington, "Paying for Knowledge: Myths and Realities," *National Productivity Review,* Spring 1986, pp. 107–123.
22. Richard L. Bunning, "Models for Skill-Based Pay Plans," *HRMagazine,* February 1992, pp. 62–64.
23. Edward E. Lawler, "The New Plant Revolution Revisited," *Organizational Dynamics,* Autumn 1990, pp. 4–14; Edward E. Lawler, "The New Plant Approach: A Second Generation Approach," *Organizational Dynamics,* Summer 1991, pp. 4–14.
24. Gupta, Jenkins, and Curington, "Paying for Knowledge," pp. 107–123.
25. Bureau of National Affairs, "Non-Traditional Incentive Pay Programs."
26. Edward E. Lawler, G. E. Ledford, and S. A. Mohrman, *Employee Involvement in America.* (Houston, Texas: American Productivity and Quality Center, 1989).
27. Edward E. Lawler, *Strategic Pay* (San Francisco: Jossey-Bass, 1990) pp. 71–85.
28. Ibid., p. 73.
29. John F. Sullivan, "The Future of Merit Pay Programs," *Compensation and Benefits Review,* Vol. 20, May/June, 1988, pp. 22–30.
30. Mohr, Riedel, and Crawford, "A Group Wage Incentive System." pp. 13–17.

31. John A. Wagner III, Paul A. Rubin, and Thomas J. Callahan, "Incentive Payment and Nonmanagerial Productivity: An Interrupted Time Series Analysis of Magnitude and Trend," *Organizational Behavior and Human Decision Processes,* Vol. 42, 1988, pp. 47–74.
32. Brian E. Graham-Moore and Timothy L. Ross, *Productivity Gainsharing* (Englewood Cliffs, N.J.: Prentice-Hall, 1983).
33. A. J. Geare, "Productivity from Scanlon Type Plans," *Academy of Management Review,* Vol. 1, No. 3, 1976, pp. 99–108.
34. W. C. Freund and E. Epstein, *People and Productivity* (Homewood, Ill.: Dow Jones-Irwin, 1984).
35. Charles R. Gowen and Sandra Jennings, "The Effects of Changes in Participation and Group Size on Gainsharing Success: A Case Study," *Journal of Organizational Behavior and Management,* Vol. 11, 1990, pp. 147–169.
36. Don Nightingale, "Profit Sharing: New Nectar for the Worker Bees," *Canadian Business Review,* Spring 1984, pp. 11–14.
37. "ESOPs: Are They Good for You?" *Business Week,* May 15, 1989, pp. 116–123.
38. "ESOP Survey 1989" (Washington, D.C.: The ESOP Association, 1989).
39. "ESOPs Broaden Employee Stock Ownership," *The Wall Street Journal,* January 7, 1987, p. 1; J. L. French, "Employee Perspectives on Stock Ownership: Financial Investment or Mechanism of Control?" *Academy of Management Review,* July 1987, pp. 427–435.
40. See Lawler, *Strategic Pay,* p. 26–27.
41. "ESOPs: Are They Good for You?"
42. "This Is Some Way to Build Employee Loyalty," *Business Week,* March 2, 1992, p. 84.
43. Gene Milbourne, Jr., "The Relationship of Money and Motivation," *Compensation Review,* 1980, 2nd Qtr., pp. 33–44.
44. Ledford, "Three Case Studies," pp. 11–12.
45. "The Flap Over Executive Pay," *Business Week,* May 6, 1991; A. Farnham, "The Trust Gap," *Fortune,* December 4, 1989; "What, Me Overpaid? CEOs Fight Back," *Business Week,* May 4, 1992, pp. 142–148; "Executive Compensation Scoreboard," *Business Week,* May 4, 1992, pp. 149–162.
46. Jeffery Kerr and Richard A. Bettis, "Boards of Directors, Top Management Compensation and Shareholder Returns," *Academy of Management Review,* December, 1987, pp. 645–664; C. J. Loomis, "The Madness of Executive Compensation," *Fortune,* Vol. 106, No. 1, 1982, pp. 42–52; M. Haire, E. E. Ghiselli, and M. E. Gordon, "A Psychological Study of Pay," *Journal of Applied Psychology Monograph,* Vol. 51, 1967, whole No. 636; John L. Pearce, William B. Stevenson, and James L. Perry, "Managerial Compensation Based on Organizational Performance: A Time Series Analysis of the Effects of Merit Pay," *Academy of Management Journal,* Vol. 28, 1985, pp. 261–278.
47. Charles Tharp, "Linking Annual Incentives and Individual Performance," *Personnel Administrator,* January 1986, pp. 85–90.
48. Geoffrey Colvin, "How to Pay the CEO Right," *Fortune,* April 6, 1992, pp. 60–69.
49. Jane Bryant Quinn, "Slow Profits, Slow Pay," *Newsweek,* December 22, 1986, p. 52.
50. "Comp Committees, or Back-Scratchers-in-Waiting?" *Business Week,* May 4, 1992, pp. 146–147.
51. Charles W. L. Hill and Phillip Phan, "CEO Tenure as a Determinant of CEO Pay," *Academy of Management Journal,* Vol. 34, 1991, pp. 707–717.
52. Graef S. Crystal, "Incentive Pay That Doesn't Work, *Fortune,* August 28, 1989, pp. 101, 104.
53. "Executive Pay," *Business Week,* March 30, 1992, pp. 52–58.
54. Calvin, "How to Pay the CEO Right," pp. 60–69.
55. "Herman Miller Links Worker-CEO Pay," *The Wall Street Journal,* May 7, 1992, pp. B1, B8.
56. "SEC Unveils New Rules on Disclosures of Corporate Executives' Pay Packages," *The Wall Street Journal,* February 14, 1992.
57. "Executive Pay: The Shareholders Strike Back," *Time,* May 4, 1992, pp. 46–48.
58. Robert J. Greene and Russel G. Roberts, "Strategic Integration of Compensation and Benefits," *Personnel Administrator,* May 1983, pp. 79–81.
59. Chamber of Commerce of the United States,

Employee Benefits 1990 (Washington, D.C.: U.S. Chamber of Commerce, 1990).

60. "Social Security: Invaluable or Outmoded?" Modern Maturity, Vol. 35, April/May 1992, pp. 34–46, 84–85.

61. Ibid.

62. "Taking Baby Steps Toward a Daddy Track," *Business Week,* April 15, 1991, pp. 90–92.

63. "Family Care: Tips for Companies That Are Trying to Help," *Business Week,* September 28, 1992, p. 36.

64. "Condition: Critical," *Time,* November 25, 1991, pp. 34–42.

65. Ronald Bryan, "A Primer on Self-Funding Health Care Benefits," *Personnel Administrator,* April 1983, pp. 61–64.

66. New Medical-Benefits Accounting Rule Seen Wounding Profits, Hurting Shares," *The Wall Street Journal,* April 22, 1992, pp. C1–C2.

67. "Gay in Corporate America," *Fortune,* December 16, 1991, pp. 42–56.

68. Jerry S. Rosenbloom and G. Victor Hallman, *Employee Benefit Planning,* 2nd ed. (Englewood Cliffs, N.J.: Prentice-Hall, 1986).

69. Harry E. Allen, "Recent Developments in Private Pensions," *Management Review,* January 1987, pp. 54–55.

70. Allen Stiteler, "Finally, Pension Plans Defined," *Personnel Journal,* February 1987, pp. 44–53.

71. Ibid.

72. Barbara Rudolph, "Shelter from April Showers," *Time,* February 22, 1988, p. 51.

73. Thomas H. Paine, "Employee Benefits in 1995," Address delivered before the Council on Employee Benefits, October 9, 1987.

74. *Los Angeles* v. *Manhart,* 435 U.S. 702 (1978).

75. *Arizona Governing Committee* v. *Norris,* 103 U.S. 3492 (1983).

76. *"Employee Assistance Programs: Drug, Alcohol, and Other Problems"* (Chicago: Commerce Clearing House, 1986).

77. "Paying Workers for Good Health Habits Catches On as a Way to Cut Medical Costs," *The Wall Street Journal,* November, 26, 1991, p. B1.

78. The Conference Board, "Special Report: Work-Family Issues," *Human Resources* (New York: The Conference Board, 1989).

79. Stephen J. Goff, Michael K. Mount, and Rosemary L. Jamison, "Employer Supported Child Care, Work/Family Conflict, and Absenteeism: A Field Study," *Personnel Psychology,* Vol. 43, 1990, pp. 793–809.

80. Ellen Ernst Kossek, "Diversity in Child Care Assistance Needs: Employee Problems, Preferences, and Work-Related Outcomes," *Personnel Psychology,* Vol. 43, 1990, pp. 769–791.

81. "The Baby Boomers' Triple Whammy," *Business Week,* May 4, 1992, pp. 178–179; Neville Tompkins, "Child Care and Elder Care Assistance," *HR Horizons,* (Winter 1991), pp. 53–55.

82. Ellen Galinsky, Dana Friedman, and Carol Hernandez, *The Corporate Reference Guide to Work-Family Programs* (New York: Families and Work Institute, 1991); "Corporate America is Still No Place for Kids," *Business Week,* November 25, 1991, pp. 234–238.

83. Jesse A. Sherman and Michael Carter, "Benefits: Profiting from Trade-off Analysis," *Personnel Journal,* August 1987, pp. 120–122.

84. *"Flexible Benefits: Will They Work For You?"* (Chicago: Commerce Clearing House, 1984).

85. Marie Wilson, George B. Northcraft, and Margaret A. Neale, "The Perceived Value of Fringe Benefits," *Personnel Psychology,* Vol. 38, 1985, pp. 209–320.

86. Ibid.

PART SIX

Maintaining Human Resources

External Environment
Economy Government Labor Markets Competitors Demographics

Human Resource Functions

Planning for Organizations, Jobs, and People
Strategic HRM (2)
Human Resource Planning (3)
Job Analysis (4)

Acquiring Human Resources
EEO (5)
Recruiting (6)
Selection (7, 8)

Building Performance
Human Resource Development (9)
Productivity and Quality (10)

Rewarding Employees
Performance Appraisal (11)
Compensation and Benefits (12, 13)

Maintaining Human Resources
Safety and Health (14)
Labor Relations (15)
Exit (16)

Managing Multinational HRM (17)

Organizational Environment
Management's Goals and Values
Corporate Culture
Strategy
Technology
Structure
Size

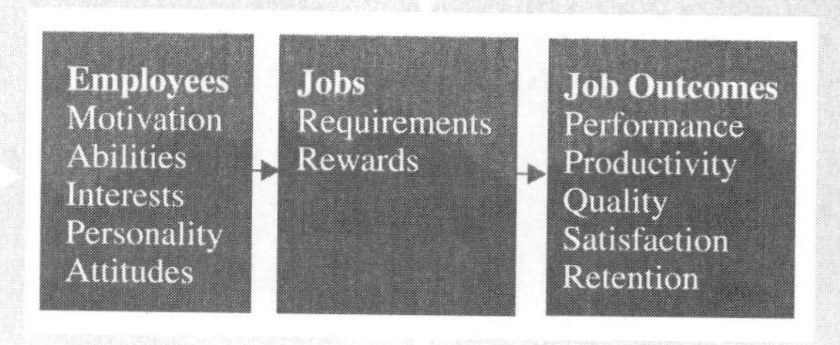

Organizational Outcomes
Survival
Competitiveness
Growth
Profitability

14

Safety and Health: A Proactive Approach

Most organizations are very much concerned about providing a safe and healthy workplace. Part of this concern is simple humanitarianism. Few firms would knowingly send unprotected employees into a dangerous situation. Aside from altruism, there are two other reasons for corporate concern about the work environment. First, there are definite bottom-line consequences of mental and physical health. Second, state and federal laws require that reasonable levels of safety be maintained in the work environment.

In the United States, 10,500 employees died from work-related injuries in 1990, down by 200 from 1989. Injuries that caused the loss of at least one day of work were suffered by 1,800,000 employees. Of these, 60,000 were permanently impaired. (See the International Perspective box for an international comparison of job-related deaths and injuries.) The National Safety Council estimates that work-related deaths and injuries cost the economy $63.8 billion in 1990 alone. In addition to the above figures, there were 280,000 new cases of occupational disease diagnosed in 1989 (the last year for which data are available). On average, 37.1 people per every 10,000 full-time employed workers suffered from occupational disease in 1989.[1] Furthermore, in the mid-1980s, an estimated 40 million Americans were suffering from high-blood pressure; work-related stress is thought to be one factor causing and sustaining this illness.[2] Stress can also lead to alcohol and drug abuse. Research indicates that problem drinkers are 2.5 times more likely to take extended leaves of absence than nonabusers, and they file five times more workers' compensation claims and use three times more accident benefits than nonabusers.[3] As long ago as 1982, Rockwell International Corporation estimated that alcoholism and drug abuse cost the company $250 million annually, and the U.S. Postal Service estimated losses of $168 million annually.[4]

Several organizations have reported significant savings from actively promoting the health of their work forces. In 1986, *Business Week* estimated that adopting a strict no-smoking policy would save a company up to $5,000 a year per employee. The gains result from less work time devoted to smoking "rituals," lower absenteeism, reduced cleaning costs, and discounts on life, disability, fire, and accident insurance.[5] Earlier in that decade, the city government of Phoenix, Arizona, estimated that it was saving $2.5 million annually through its psychological, physical, and financial counseling programs, while New York Telephone reported saving $2.7 million per year by conducting stress management programs.[6]

In addition to bottom-line reasons, the other major incentive for companies to be concerned with employee safety is to avoid the penalties for violating occupational safety laws.[7] Before 1970, a company that was a dangerous place to work might have had higher insurance rates. Since then, however, the penalties have become more severe. Fines are common, and top managers can be sent to prison for criminal negligence when unsafe conditions cause the death of a worker.[8]

Chapter 14 describes occupational health and safety legislation and explains the role of HR managers in an effective workplace safety program. Stress at work is considered, with a focus on causes, consequences, and prevention. The last two sections discuss employee assistance and fitness programs.

FEDERAL SAFETY AND HEALTH LEGISLATION

Worker health and safety have been the subject of much federal legislation. Some of these laws designate various federal agencies to oversee specific issues. The Department of Transportation is charged with regulating workplace safety in the trucking industry; the Federal Aviation Administration, in airlines; and the Federal Railroad Administration, in the railroad industry. After several fatal accidents

INTERNATIONAL PERSPECTIVE

Job Safety: An International Comparison

Comparing rates of occupational accidents and injuries across countries is quite difficult. Nations follow different reporting standards regarding what constitutes an injury and whether it must be reported. Even for workplace fatalities, which should be less ambiguously reported than injuries, variation in methods makes cross-national comparisons difficult. For instance, some countries include deaths that occur when a person is traveling to or from work, whereas others exclude deaths from occupational disease.

In the United States, occupational fatalities are reported in relation to the number of person-hours worked. In 1987, the rate was .027 deaths per million person-hours. Japan uses the same method and reports fatality rate of .010.

Most other countries report fatalities per 1,000 people employed per year. Data for a sample of these countries in 1987 are shown below. (Remember that these figures are not directly comparable to the rates given above.)

Austria	.097
Canada	.075
Cuba	.112
Denmark	.030
Egypt	.160
France	.075
Greece	.058
Hong Kong	.075
New Zealand	.072
Norway	.040
Poland	.107
Spain	.120
United Kingdom	.017

Rates vary widely for a number of reasons, including the mix of industries present in each country. Some industries are inherently more dangerous than others. For instance, the mining and quarrying industries tend to have the highest fatality rate in most countries, while construction, transportation, utilities, and agriculture have moderately high rates. The retail trade, banking, and social service industries generally have many fewer fatalities.

A country's occupational safety and health laws and enforcement procedures may also influence fatality rates. A comparative 1986 study of five European countries and the United States concluded that the United States is the weakest in terms of law and enforcement mechanisms. Sweden, the former East Germany, and Finland were the highest ranked, followed by the former West Germany and the United Kingdom. The study concluded that a strong national union movement facilitated the passage and active implementation of effective health and safety measures. In Sweden, union-run safety committees may order production stopped if they believe that a hazard exists, and keep it stopped until the hazard is remedied. These committees also have a great deal of control over the hiring and firing of industrial physicians and safety engineers.

In general, unions and the philosophy of industrial democracy are stronger in Europe than in the United States. In recent years, these factors have led to the passage of laws giving European employees or their elected worker representatives a stronger role in monitoring and enforcing workplace safety. Legally mandated works councils or workers' safety committees in the Netherlands, Luxembourg, France, Belgium, and Denmark give workers substantially more control over occupational safety than U.S. workers have.

The European Economic Community has adopted a common framework for occupational health and safety. Pursuant to the framework, member nations are modifying their workplace safety laws to achieve harmonized standards throughout the community. The intent is to retain the high safety standards set in the more progressive countries, while minimizing the competitive advantage that might otherwise flow to nations with less stringent standards.

At the opposite end of the spectrum, the state of occupational safety remains deplorable in developing countries. Most developing countries have rudimentary occupational safety laws and few funds for enforcing such laws. Furthermore, efforts to attract foreign investment are likely to be more successful if the country offers a business environment relatively free from government regulation. Unions are weak or are preoccupied with more basic issues such as politics, wages, and fair treatment, so they provide little impetus toward improved workplace safety. Labor-intensive industries, dated equipment, pressure for production, and lack of safety training also contribute to the poor safety record in many developing nations.

Source: The above information comes from the 49th issue of the *Yearbook of Labour Statistics* (Geneva: International Labour Organization, 1989–1990, pp. 982–995; Ray H. Elling, *The Struggle for Workers' Health: A Study of Six Industrialized Countries* (Farmingdale, N.Y.: Baywood Publishing, 1986), pp. 427–450; J. K. M. Gevers, "Worker Participation in Health and Safety in the EEC: The Role of Representative Institutions," *International Labour Review,* July–August 1983, pp. 411–428; David C. E. Chew, "Effective Occupational Safety Activities: Findings in Three Asian Developing Countries," *International Labour Review,* 1988, pp. 111–124; Michael B. Bixby. "Emerging Occupational Safety Issues in the United States, Europe, and Japan," *Proceedings of the Third Conference on International Personnel and Human Management,* Vol. 1. Berkhamsted, England, July 1992.

in coal mines, the U.S. Bureau of Mines was created to develop and enforce safety regulations for all mining companies. Even the U.S. Coast Guard has been granted authority to enforce safety conditions in maritime matters. However, the dominant piece of legislation is the Occupational Safety and Health Act of 1970. The purpose of this act is to centralize the regulation of workplace safety and to expand coverage to include all organizations in the United States. In passing the act, Congress declared its purpose to be "to assure so far as possible every working man and woman in the nation safe and healthful working conditions and to preserve our human resources."[9]

History of the Occupational Safety and Health Act

It took more than 100 years for the federal government to respond to the public's desire for a comprehensive workplace safety bill. There had been several federal and state actions prior to the Occupational Safety and Health Act, but they were contradictory, ineffective, or noncomprehensive. The history of government intervention in workplace safety and health is a fascinating study of politics, good intentions, and frustrations.[10]

The public first became aware of the need for workplace safety legislation in the 1870s. The Industrial Revolution had created factories that were a collection of machines and tools with no real safety devices or protective guards. Consequently, serious injuries were commonplace. And there was no compensation or financial protection for employees who were injured or killed on the job.

Between 1911 and 1948, each state passed a workers' compensation law requiring businesses to compensate employees injured on the job, and all states still have such laws in effect. Compensation includes some replacement of lost income while injured, medical and rehabilitation expenses, payments (lump sums) for certain permanent disabilities, and death benefits for survivors. Most employers participate in an insurance plan to cover these expenses. Because premiums go up if there are many injury claims, workers' compensation laws provide some incentive for employers to maintain a safe work environment. However, workers' compensation laws also limit employers' liability for injuries and deaths to the amounts specified by state law. Employees who accept workers' compensation benefits give up their right to sue the employer. Thus, employers actually save money by avoiding costly litigation and large settlements. In this sense, workers' compensation laws somewhat reduce organizations' need to be concerned with workplace safety. This fact provided part of the impetus to pass a comprehensive federal workplace safety law.[11]

Figure 14.1 traces the development of the Occupational Safety and Health Act. The drive for the bill was initiated and gained momentum as inadequacies of previous laws were painfully revealed by ever-increasing accidents and some major workplace catastrophes. Passing the final legislation required public awareness and the right political climate in terms of constituency support and concerned political leaders. Figure 14.1 also shows the three new agencies created by the bill, along with each agency's actions and how they interrelate.

The Occupational Safety and Health Act set out to improve two types of problems: on-the-job-injuries and occupational diseases.

On-the-Job Injuries

Figure 14.2 shows the most common parts of the body injured in workplace accidents. Back injuries are by far the most common and most costly, accounting for 22 percent of the cases and 32 percent of the compensation. This is followed by injuries to legs, arms and fingers. The most common causes of injury are overexertion (31.3 percent), such as hyperextending a limb or picking up a heavy object, being struck by or struck against an object (24 percent), and falling (17.1 percent).[12]

According to the Occupational Safety and Health Act, it is the responsibility of each employer to make the workplace free from recognized hazards that could cause physical harm. Most employers actively work to accomplish this task. Yet accidents and injuries still occur. Although there are various causes for these accidents, an estimated 88 percent of them result directly from employees performing unsafe acts, often in direct violation of company policies.[13] A well-publicized example is the refusal of longshoremen to wear hard hats. Company policy, federal regulations, and simple common sense mandate head protection on this job, where cargo is constantly being loaded and unloaded. Nevertheless, many workers refuse to wear their hats, usually because they say the hats are uncomfortable.[14] Regardless of whether an employee violates a safety regulation knowingly or unknowingly, if an accident occurs, it is the responsibility of the employer.

Figure 14.3 shows factors that have been statistically related to work-site accidents. Aside from employee disregard for safety regulations, accidents are related to several other employee factors. New workers show a higher incidence

FIGURE 14.1 Development of the Occupational Safety and Health Act

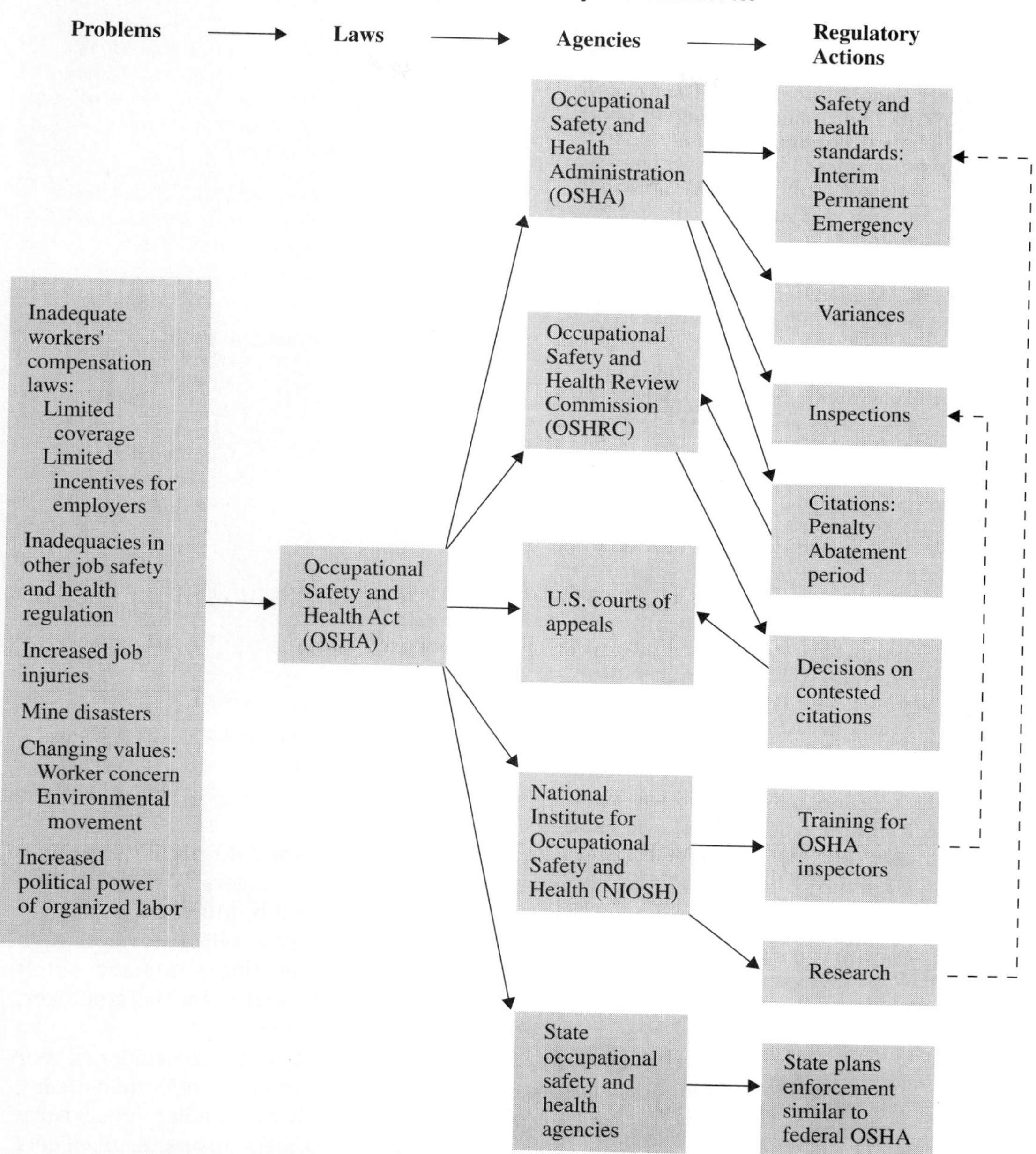

Source: James Ledvinka and Vida G. Scarpello, *Federal Regulation of Personnel and Human Resource Management* 2/e (Boston: PWS-Kent Publishing Company, 1991), p. 211.

FIGURE 14.2 Part of Body Injured in Work Accidents

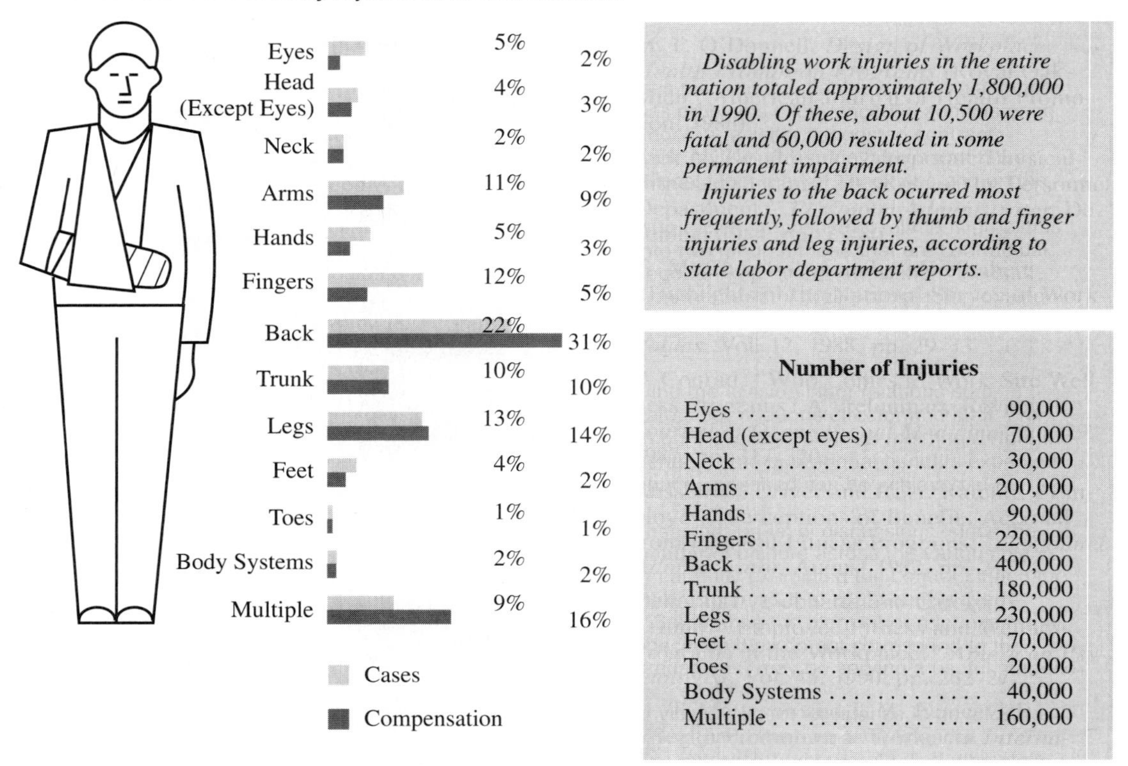

Source: Accident Facts, 1991 Edition, National Safety Council, p. 38. Data from State Labor Departments, 1989–1990; cases—23 states, compensation—10 states. Reprinted by permission.

of accidents than senior employees, perhaps because they do not have enough training or experience to fully comprehend workplace dangers. Workers under severe stress also appear to have more accidents on the job. More dangerous yet are practices in which employees either remove or by-pass safety devices, such as taping back the guards on saw blades or disconnecting automatic cutoff switches. All these factors can be controlled to some degree by the employer, through increased awareness and proper employee training.

Task-related factors also appear to contribute to workplace accidents. For example, there is a much higher incidence of accidents on night shifts than on day shifts. This discrepancy may be attributable to the typically smaller supervisory staff on night shifts, as well as employee drowsiness and inattentiveness. Accidents also tend to occur early in the shifts, rather than after breaks or toward the end of shifts. Also, employees on rotating shifts have more accidents.[15]

The size of the firm is an organizational factor that is related to on-the-job accidents. Moderate-sized organizations—with 50 to 100 employees—have higher

FIGURE 14.3 Factors Related to Accidents at the Worksite

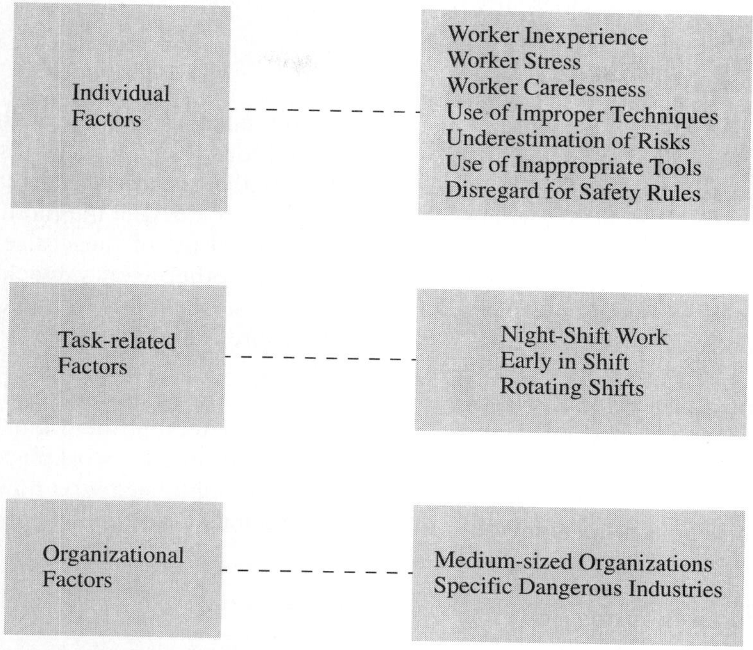

Source: Robin C. Ballau and Roy M. Buchen, "Study Shows That Gender Is Not a Major Factor in Accident Etiology," *Occupational Health and Safety,* September, 1978, pp. 54–58.

accident rates than do smaller or larger companies. This statistic may reflect the fact that smaller companies supervise their employees closely and personally and that larger organizations can afford comparatively elaborate safety programs.

Finally, because of their work processes, certain industries experience more risks than others. For example, banks and insurance companies are usually safer than construction sites or industrial plants. The tools used, the environments in which they are operated, and the tasks that need to be performed contribute to this difference.

The Occupational Safety and Health Administration (OSHA) has developed a list of "target" industries with the highest rates of job-related accidents. These industries are roofing and sheet-metal work, meat and meat processing, lumber and wood-products processing and utilization, manufacturing of recreational vehicles, and stevedoring.

Although a company may be in a dangerous industry, it does not have to be a dangerous place to work. Du Pont, through massive safety programs, has an accident record that is many times lower than its industry's average. Thus, a corporate commitment to safety—through training, increasing safety awareness, and developing safe practices for employees—may go a long way toward reducing accidents, even in an inherently dangerous industry.

Occupational Diseases

The prevention of occupational diseases is the second dimension of the regulations concerning safe and healthful working conditions. Occupational diseases are long-term health problems caused by substances that are absorbed through the skin, inhaled from the atmosphere, or taken internally through the mouth, or that affect one of the five senses.[16] Table 14.1 is a partial list of these diseases. Examples include lung cancer caused by asbestos and other agents; black lung disease caused by the long-term inhalation of coal dust; leukemia from exposure to radiation; and hearing loss from prolonged exposure to loud noise.

Detecting Occupational Disease The major problem with reducing the occurrence of occupational diseases is the difficulty of detecting them and then pinpointing their cause. Typically, the disease is linked to the workplace through statistics. Researchers compare the percentage of employees who have the disease with the percentage of people in the general population who have the disease.

TABLE 14.1 Some Occupational Diseases and Their Causes

Disease	*Causes*
Lung Cancer	Arsenic Asbestos Bichloronethylether Coke Oven Emissions Passive Cigarette Smoke
White Lung Disease	Asbestos
Black Lung Disease	Coal Dust
Brown Lung Disease	Cotton Dust
Leukemia	Benzene Radiation
Cancer of Other Organs	Asbestos Coke Oven Emissions Radiation Vinyl Chloride
Sterility/Reproductive Problems	Radiation
Deteriorating Eyesight	Chemical Fumes Office Technology
Hearing Loss	High Noise Levels

Source: Adapted in part from Abigail Trafford, "Is Your Job Dangerous to Your Health?" *U.S. News and World Report,* February 1979, pp. 39–42.

If the percentage is significantly greater for the employees than for the general population, researchers suggest that something at the workplace may have caused the disease.

Such detective work is not always simple. The disease may surface only after many years of exposure or years after the employee is exposed. Thus, the organization and the workers may be ignorant that a problem exists since the causal agent has not been around long enough for people to show symptoms of the disease. Sometimes symptoms do not appear until long after a worker's retirement. Another difficulty is that most individuals work in different jobs at several organizations throughout their careers. Thus, to determine which organization and which job caused the disease, researchers must perform analyses that consider all the jobs and all the employees who have held the jobs in the previous years.

Even if an organization is able to determine that its employees are suffering from an illness related to their occupation, the difficulties are not over. Next, the company must determine exactly what aspect of the work environment and/or the job caused the illness. Statistics and medical research help in this process. But the detective work may have to be done up to forty years after the exposure.

Of course, the detection of occupational diseases is not always difficult. Medical science aids the process through studies of the impact of various environmental factors on health; and sometimes the cause is apparent, as in the case of hearing loss from sustained exposure to loud noises. When an illness is determined to be caused by something in the work environment, the organization is just as responsible in cases where the cause is not readily apparent as it is in more obvious cases.

Smoking in the Workplace A workplace contaminant that has been receiving much attention in the last several years is secondhand tobacco smoke. The 1986 report of the U.S. Surgeon General concluded that secondhand smoke causes 2,400 to 4,000 lung cancer deaths annually among nonsmokers.[17] Besides the health of nonsmokers, employers must consider that the employee who smokes can cost an employer up to $5,000 per year more than the nonsmoker in health insurance claims, absenteeism, maintenance, productivity, and other related costs.[18]

As a result of this evidence that secondhand smoke poses a hazard to nonsmokers, more and more employers are moving to limit or abolish smoking in the workplace; their number has risen from 16 percent in 1980 to 84 percent in 1990.[19] In 1991, the Bureau of National Affairs developed a model policy for smoking in the workplace. The policy has as its purpose the health and accommodation of all employees and provides nine guidelines. These guidelines specify smoking areas, locations where smoking is prohibited, departmental options to formulate smoking policies, and procedures for resolving disputes.[20] The model program also offers employees free smoking-cessation programs and provides a one-time $50 bonus for any employee who successfully quits smoking for one year. Clearly, workplace smoking is becoming a thing of the past for more and more employers.[21]

Cumulative Trauma Disorder Another type of problem that is officially categorized as an occupational disease is called **cumulative trauma disorder (CTD)** or **repetitive strain injury.** Of the 280,000 cases of occupational illness recognized or diagnosed in 1989, disorders associated with repeated trauma were the most common, accounting for 146,900 (52 percent) of the cases.[22]

CTD seems to be caused by repeating the same movement many times without a break. Butchers in meat-packing plants are the most frequently afflicted group, and word processing and data entry personnel are reporting the problem more and more often. Automation seems to be a culprit—it simplifies the motions needed and removes the chance to take breaks. For instance, word processor operators type constantly for hours on end. In past years, these employees would have alternated their activities by inserting paper into a typewriter, manually erasing errors, and returning the typewriter carriage. Carpal tunnel syndrome is the CTD that occurs most commonly in people working with computer keyboards. It results in pain and loss of grip strength in the hands and arms due to swelling of tissues and subsequent pressure on nerves that run through the carpal bones of the wrist.[23]

CTD reached epidemic proportions in Australia in the mid-1980s with 10 to 50 percent of keyboarding workers complaining of wrist pain in some organizations. Strangely, other organizations remain virtually unaffected. Although carpal tunnel syndrome is a genuine physiological problem, there is speculation that the epidemic in Australia was exacerbated by other factors, such as job dissatisfaction, resistance to technological change, extensive publicity about CTD, and the adoption of this threat as a cause by militant labor unions and feminist groups.[24]

OSHA has recognized CTD as a legitimate problem, and levied fines of $5.7 million against IBP, the nation's largest meat packer. The fines were subsequently reduced because IBP implemented a $1-million to $2-million program to research and correct the problem. In the mid-1980s, U.S. West Communications spent about $1 million on redesigned work-stations for telephone operators after a large number of CTD claims were filed.[25] Besides redesigning work-stations, some employers are rotating workers among jobs or incorporating active rest periods so that workers have a chance to engage in other movements with the affected tendons and muscles.[26] CTD seems likely to remain an important and expensive workplace health issue in the 1990s.

Other Workplace Health Issues Other issues of health and safety in the workplace include video display terminals (VDTs), acquired immune deficiency syndrome (AIDS), fetal protection policies, and drugs.

Aside from issues of CTD, the increased use of computers and VDTs has generated intense debate over possible hazards, specifically visual difficulties and radiation hazards. Many employees fear that a possible radiation hazard from VDTs can cause reproductive problems, including miscarriages and birth defects. Although many fears about VDTs have been shown to be unfounded, complaints and concerns continue.[27]

In the past decade, employers have had to learn to deal with issues of AIDS in the workplace. As was noted in Chapter 5, AIDS is a handicap covered by legal statutes. Employees who have AIDS or who test positive for the virus that causes AIDS must be considered handicapped and must be accommodated.[28] Despite the legal statutes and the fact that there is no evidence that AIDS can be spread through casual contact in the workplace, people greatly fear the disease. For this reason, employers are put in the role of educating their employees about AIDS, its transmission, and the treatment of coworkers with AIDS.

In the past, some companies excluded women of childbearing age from jobs in which exposure to chemicals or radiation could pose a health hazard to their reproductive systems. In a landmark 1991 decision (*UAW* v. *Johnson Controls, Inc.*), the Supreme Court ruled that fetal protection policies are a form of illegal sex discrimination prohibited by Title VII.[29] Among other things, Johnson Controls manufactures automotive batteries, which contain lead, a known danger to a developing fetus. In an effort to protect employees from this danger and to avoid potential liability, Johnson Controls excluded women employees capable of bearing children from jobs—many of which were highly paid—involving lead exposure. The Court ruled that risk and childbearing decisions are best left to employees, but this ruling has resulted in companies being caught between Title VII of the Civil Rights Act and OSHA requirements to provide a workplace free from recognized hazards. Companies must provide information to female employees about fetal health risk and allow them to make their own decisions.

More and more employers are concerned about drugs in the workplace and the potential for serious accidents connected with drugs. Under the 1988 Federal Drug-free Workplace Act, federal contractors must certify that they will maintain a drug-free workplace.[30] Among other things, this certification includes a drug-free policy, awareness programs, and making absence of substance abuse a condition of employment.

Many employers are testing applicants or current employees for drug abuse. The American Management Association found that the number of employers testing for drug use more than doubled, to almost half of those surveyed, between 1986 and 1988.[31] It is important that organizations have appropriate policies for testing either applicants or current employees. Such policies need to involve (a) informed consent, (b) scheduling, (c) assurance of test validity, and (d) confidentiality. Such screening is likely to increase as drug use continues to be a problem for the larger society, and the liability associated with having an employee under the influence of drugs is a cost companies are expected to bear.

Three Agencies Created by the Occupational Safety and Health Act

The Occupational Safety and Health Act created three autonomous but related agencies to ensure occupational safety and health. These three agencies are the Occupational Safety and Health Review Commission, the National Institute for

Occupational Safety and Health, and, as already noted, the Occupational Safety and Health Administration.

The **Occupational Safety and Health Review Commission (OSHRC)** is based in the Department of Labor. This commission plays a judicial role in administering workplace safety and health. Organizations can appeal a safety or health citation by requesting a review by OSHRC. If dissatisfied with an OSHRC ruling, an employer may appeal through the federal court system.

The **National Institute for Occupational Safety and Health (NIOSH)** has primary responsibility for conducting and coordinating research on workplace safety and health. This research could be to determine safe levels of particular chemicals in the atmosphere or what decibel level of machine noise requires ear protection to prevent injury. NIOSH's research provides the basis for making recommendations to OSHA concerning possible regulations. In addition, employers can use NIOSH findings in creating a safe and healthy work environment without OSHA's intervention.

The **Occupational Safety and Health Administration (OSHA)** was established as a branch of the Department of Labor. It is by far the most visible of the three agencies because it is responsible for formulating and enforcing the regulations for on-the-job safety and health.[32] OSHA has also become one of the most controversial federal agencies with which HR managers must deal. The early antagonism of business toward OSHA has been reduced by changes in procedures that the Supreme Court has forced on the agency.

OSHA's Primary Tasks

OSHA's first task was to develop health and safety standards and regulations. Initially, these regulations were formulated under a policy of creating a no-risk environment. That is, OSHA's standards held employers responsible for eliminating any possible threat in the workplace, regardless of the costs involved, even if the risk to workers was very slight. The no-risk policy reflected OSHA's very strict interpretation of its mission and a lack of knowledge as to what constituted a "safe" level of various workplace contaminants.

OSHA's vinyl chloride standard illustrates the overzealousness of its early approach to regulation. Medical studies indicated that exposure to the chemical vinyl chloride could cause cancer of the liver. The maximum exposure found in any U.S. workplace was determined to be 500 parts per million (ppm) in the atmosphere. Experimental studies showed that a level of 50 ppm caused cancer among lab animals. Studies done on humans indicated that they experienced no risk at 50 ppm. Even with this evidence, OSHA established an acceptable standard of 1 ppm. OSHA kept this standard even after a study that it commissioned found that the 1 ppm level was technologically impossible to attain.[33]

Many industries objected to the no-risk standards.[34] Employers were willing to make changes, but the extreme costs of the OSHA requirements were generally considered to be wasteful. The Supreme Court made several judgments against OSHA.[35] The court replaced the no-risk standard with significant-risk regulations, which recognized that the law requires safety but not necessarily a risk-free environment. Instead, an unsafe workplace was redefined as one that threatens workers with significant risks of harm.[36] OSHA regulations and standards were changed to ensure protection from foreseeable health and safety hazards.

Enforcing the health and safety regulations is the second responsibility of OSHA. The agency conducts workplace inspections for this purpose. Originally OSHA was allowed to inspect any work area at any "reasonable" time. Once again, business objected to OSHA's liberal interpretation of the legislation, and the Supreme Court ruled to curb OSHA's freedom. A 1978 decision established that employers could require OSHA to obtain a search warrant before conducting an inspection.[37]

An **OSHA inspection** is a very complete examination of the workplace. The inspector looks for unsafe conditions and violations of OSHA standards. Typically, the inspector is accompanied by representatives of both management and labor. If a violation is discovered, the OSHA inspector will issue a citation, identifying the specific violation and stating a time by which the employer must correct the situation.[38] The types of citations issued are shown in Table 14.2. If a violation is not corrected in the allotted time, OSHA will levy a fine against the employer. Even when the violation involves an employee's disregard for company policies, only the employer is penalized.

Given the millions of workplaces in the United States, it is impossible for one government agency to inspect all employers. OSHA first followed a policy of random inspections (inspecting workplaces without a set pattern or plan) but later

TABLE 14.2 Types of OSHA Violations

1. Willful—violations determined to be willful which cause an employee's death may result in a criminal violation with a fine of up to $10,000 and a prison term of up to six months. "Willfulness" is established by a conscious, intentional, deliberate decision and also may be characterized by a careless disregard of the requirements of the Act or an indifference to employee safety.
2. Repeated violations—a prior violation of the same standard constitutes a "repeated violation." Penalties for repeated violations may range up to $10,000.
3. Serious—a violation where there is a substantial likelihood that serious physical harm or death could result. Proposed penalties of up to $1,000 are mandatory.
4. Nonserious—a violation which has an immediate relationship to job safety, but which probably would not cause serious physical harm or death. The 1981 Labor-HEW Appropriations Act prohibited the assessment of penalties for nonserious violations unless ten or more nonserious violations are cited, with the maximum penalty being $1,000.
5. De Minimus—a violation which has no immediate relationship to job safety. A notice is issued, but citations and proposed penalties are not.

Source: Adapted from David P. Twomey, *A Concise Guide to Employment Law* (Dallas, TX: South-Western Publishing Company, 1986), p. 131. Reprinted by permission.

TABLE 14.3 OSHA Inspection Priorities

1. Imminent danger situations
2. Catastrophes and fatal accident sites
3. Valid employee complaints
4. Target industries
5. Random inspections
6. Reinspections

developed a priority system for its inspections.[39] Under this system, which is illustrated in Table 14.3, OSHA's highest priorities are imminent danger situations, actual accident sites, and organizations about which there have been valid employee complaints. Next in priority are target industries, which have especially high rates of accidents. OSHA has been known to exempt a company from inspections if it creates a worker-management safety committee to seek out and respond to employee complaints and conduct monthly safety inspections.[40]

OSHA also requires employers to keep records of all occupational injuries and illnesses that result in a lost workday, medical treatment beyond first aid, transfer to light duty, loss of consciousness, or death. These and other health and safety records kept by management must be available to OSHA inspectors and to employees and their representatives on demand.[41]

Company Strategies for a Good Safety and Health Program

All employers have safety rules, but many organizations also establish more proactive safety programs. OSHA has identified seven elements of a good company-sponsored safety and health program.

1. Top management should assume the leadership role. If top management pays only lip service to safety, the workers will follow its lead and disregard the policies as unimportant.
2. Responsibility for plant safety and health programs should be clearly assigned, to ensure that the activities will be accomplished. One survey found that this responsibility is assigned to or shared with the HRM department in 68 percent of companies.[42]
3. All causes of accidents should be identified and either eliminated or controlled in order to prevent a recurrence of the accident.
4. An essential part of any safety program is a good training program to instruct employees on proper safety procedures.
5. Employers should use their accident record system to identify patterns of accidents or health problems that could otherwise be overlooked.
6. All employers should have emergency medical and first aid systems in place to treat accident victims quickly.

7. Companies should continually encourage on-the-job awareness and acceptance of safety responsibility on the part of the employees.

Perhaps the most common and effective strategy for maintaining a healthy and safe work environment is the use of company safety committees consisting of management and nonmanagement employees.[43] These committees identify safety hazards through self-inspections, statistical analyses, and employee input. Typically, they also attempt to find solutions to identified hazards or suggest that experts be hired to resolve the problem. In addition, safety committees arrange for training seminars and other activities to increase employee awareness of safety.

Safety training is often successful in teaching employees how to behave safely. Most employees know how to use safety devices and protective equipment properly. The problem is motivating employees to follow the safety rules on a daily basis. Doing things in a less safe way may be faster and require less effort; so safety practices tend to be ignored, even though employees know how to be safe. Two studies provided strong evidence that safe behavior can be elicited and maintained at a high rate by the use of frequent safety feedback after training. In both a food manufacturing plant and vehicle repair facility, posting and updating a chart on the percentage of behaviors performed safely each week was effective in raising safe behaviors from preintervention levels of 30 to 60 percent to a 90 percent level.[44]

Some organizations have adopted emergency medical services (EMS) systems. Steelcase, a major manufacturer of office furnishings, has developed a program considered to be the model for EMS systems.[45] First, the company developed its own on-site medical center, staffed by physicians and nurses. Company security guards were then replaced with protection services officers, who, in addition to their typical security duties, were also responsible for administering first aid to accident victims. All the officers had college training in emergency medical assistance, including the use of advanced technological devices such as defibrillators. A telephone hotline was also created to serve as an in-house 911 emergency number.

In addition to this system, the Steelcase medical center installed an automatic telephone link with a local ambulance service. The entire system is computerized so that information on the location and nature of any incident can be obtained instantly by both the medical staff and the ambulance service. Having trained its employees on how to use the service, Steelcase can respond quickly to workplace accidents and has saved lives through fast, efficient treatment.

STATE HEALTH AND SAFETY LEGISLATION

State Health and Safety Enforcement

OSHA allows a state to take over responsibility for inspections and enforcement of workplace safety if its laws are at least as stringent as the federal standards. Twenty-one states have their own OSHA programs that cover private and public-sector worksites.[46] Two states have programs that cover only public-sector worksites. States may wish to take responsibility for occupational safety and health for two reasons. First, state programs can consult with employers before inspection, advising them how to reduce potential problems. OSHA has no provision for such voluntary advising, and a company that asks for help may invite a stringent inspection and accompanying citations and fines. Second, a state may have an advantage in attracting industry if it can free employers from the need to deal with OSHA, which some managers regard as an unreasonable adversary.[47]

North Carolina is one of the states with its own OSHA program. However, as a result of the workplace fire that killed twenty-five workers at a chicken-processing plant in Hamlet, North Carolina, in September 1991, efforts are under way to have the state program decertified. Fire exits at the plant were found to be locked or blocked, and the plant's fire-safety procedures were said to have been inadequate.[48] More to the point, it was found that state inspectors had never inspected the Hamlet plant or others with similar problems, despite notification of problems in some cases—hence OSHA's desire to reassume responsibility for occupational safety and health in North Carolina.

State Right-to-Know Laws

State regulations may go beyond federal regulations, and this is what has taken place with respect to **right-to-know laws.** Such laws, adopted in many states, require that employees be informed and educated about any possibly hazardous substance that they may encounter in the workplace. Some laws also give physicians, fire departments, public health officials, and area residents a right to information about toxic substances in nearby workplaces.[49] Table 14.4 gives further details on the provisions of right-to-know laws.

TABLE 14.4 Common Features in State Right-to-Know Laws

1. Employers have an obligation to post on bulletin boards in the work area that employees have a right to request information about toxic substances in the work area. And these notices commonly require the employer to state that no reprisals will be taken against employees who exercise their right to request information.
2. Employers have an obligation in some states to inform prospective and current employees of reproductive hazards, including whether radioactive materials are used in the workplace.
3. Employers have an obligation to label containers of toxic substances.
4. In some states employers must conduct training programs for employees, which inform employees of the properties of the toxic substances in the workplace, train employees concerning the safe handling of the substances, and instruct employees on emergency treatment for overexposure to the substances.

Source: David P. Twomey, *A Concise Guide to Employment Law* (Dallas, TX: South-Western Publishing Company, 1986), p. 133. Reprinted by permission.

Led by state efforts, OSHA published the federal worker right-to-know regulations in 1988. The rules apply to over half a million hazardous chemicals and affect more than 300,000 businesses employing 32 million workers.[50]

MENTAL HEALTH AND THE WORKPLACE

The employer's responsibility for the psychological well-being of employees has been addressed to a limited extent by case law. Employers are sometimes held responsible for mental and psychological distress that is work related, just as they are for on-the-job physical injury.[51] One company was sued for $6 million by the widow of an executive who committed suicide. Constantly overworked, he had been persuaded not to take early retirement and promised additional assistants to relieve some of his stress. The additional help was never allocated, however, and the executive suffered from severe anxiety, which led to his suicide. The widow claimed that the company was negligent, because of its "callous and conscious disregard" for its employees' mental health.[52]

A less drastic example of psychological trauma is the strain that may result from evening and graveyard shift work. Working on these odd shifts may cause tensions in an employee's home life. These tensions can be especially harmful because a normal social life outside work helps offset work-related stress.[53]

The courts have established four categories of on-the-job stress for which individuals may be allowed to file for workers' compensation.[54] These are listed in Figure 14.4. The first category involves mental stimuli from the job that result in a physical illness—for example, when consistent stress causes a heart attack.

FIGURE 14.4 Court-established Psychological Traumas Eligible for Workers' Compensation—Possible Causes and Effects

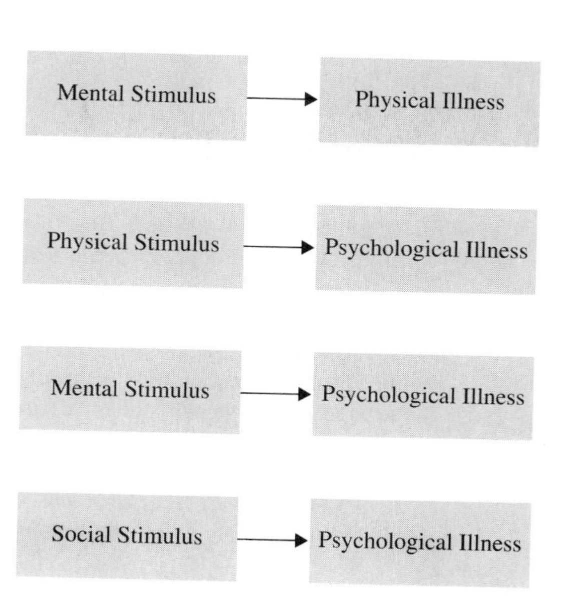

The second category consists of physical stimuli on the job that result in a psychological illness—for example, a work accident that causes anxiety so severe that the employee cannot go back to work. The third category covers situations in which a mental stimulus on the job causes a psychological illness. One example would be a person who suffers from depression and loss of self-esteem because of on-the-job stress and consequently is unable to perform his or her job.

The final category relates to a slightly different pattern of circumstances. The courts have maintained that individuals may obtain damage awards when they experience distress due to intentional or reckless acts of the employer that degrade or humiliate the employee. This principle may cover a wide range of possible actions, including sexual harassment.[55]

To provide conditions of work that are not mentally unhealthy and to avoid the performance problems associated with poor physical and mental health, organizations are adopting three strategies: stress management, employee assistance plans, and employee fitness programs.

STRESS MANAGEMENT

Stress is one of the most talked about and most misunderstood topics in organizations. **Stress** is commonly defined as any response, either physiological or psychological, to a stressor. A **stressor** is any event that requires an action from an individual.[56] Thus, stress is not always a detrimental phenomenon. In fact, some stress is essential in getting people to perform.

The relationship between performance and stress is illustrated in Figure 14.5. This relationship has been compared to tuning a violin. If there is not enough tension on the strings, there will be no music; but if there is too much tension, the strings will break. The optimum level of tension will result in maximum performance.

Consequences of Stress

It is not easy to determine the optimum level of stress for employees, and this optimum may vary as a function of other things going on in the employee's life, along with demographic characteristics (race, sex, age) and occupational status.[57] Consequently, many employees and organizations suffer from the effects of experiencing too much stress. Generally, the consequences of overstress are grouped into four categories: psychological, physiological, behavioral, and organizational.[58] Individuals subjected to excess stress probably will not experience consequences in all four categories, since reactions depend on the individual, the type of stressor, and the amount of stress being experienced.

Psychological Consequences Psychological effects of being overstressed include high levels of irritability, frustration, anxiety, aggression, and nervousness.

FIGURE 14.5 The Relationship Between Stress and Performance

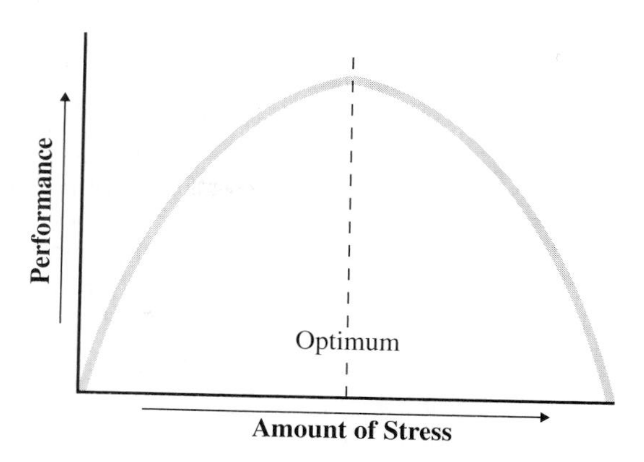

In some individuals, however, too much stress leads to a very different pattern of apathy, boredom, depression, moodiness, and loss of self-esteem.

Physiological Consequences An individual subjected to too much stress may experience hormonal changes, high blood pressure, increased heart rate, difficulties in breathing, and numbness of the limbs. These problems can lead to even more serious health problems, such as ulcers and heart disease.[59]

Behavioral Consequences Related to the physiological and psychological effects are possible changes in how well employees can perform their jobs. Workers experiencing too much stress may find themselves less able to make decisions. Excess stress may also lead to forgetfulness, hypersensitivity, and passiveness. Finally, the employee may attempt to reduce the effects of stress through alcohol and drug abuse.

Organizational Consequences Usually, when employees experience serious problems, the organization also suffers. Companies whose employees consistently experience too much stress are likely to experience high levels of absenteeism and turnover. Accident rates may also tend to rise. Finally, employee satisfaction with the job and with the organization, industrial relations, and productivity can suffer from excessive stress.

Causes of Employee Stress

Organizations can and should manage the stress experienced by their employees. Although no method can be guaranteed to reduce stress, because of its highly individual nature, certain strategies can help to manage stress. But first the causes of employee stress must be identified. There are several possible sources of employee stress, both outside and within the organization.

Extraorganizational sources The stress that an employee experiences on the job may be caused by something outside his or her immediate work life. Such extraorganizational sources of stress could include family problems, marital problems, financial troubles, or conflicts in extracurricular activities. A self-administered survey has been developed for individuals to monitor these outside stressors. As shown in Table 14.5, a certain number of stress points are associated with each stress event. The higher one's total life-change score, the greater the stress and the greater the likelihood of suffering a major stress-related health problem.

Individual-Level Stressors Within the organization, there are three levels of possible stressors: individual, group, and organizational. The individual level involves sources of stress that are found at the person-job interface. The most common of these problems is known as role overload, which occurs when an employee simply has too much work to do or is under extreme time pressure.

Another common individual source of stress is role conflict, which occurs when the employee's various on-the-job responsibilities conflict with each other. For example, if two supervisors assign tasks to an employee, performing either one of the jobs may make it impossible to accomplish the other. Conflict may also arise if employees are required to do things that go against their personal values or morals.

A third common source of individual-level stress is role ambiguity, which occurs when the job itself is not clearly defined. Because employees are unable to determine exactly what the organization requires from them, they worry constantly about whether their performance is adequate. Managers often suffer from role ambiguity.

Some people may experience stress from being given responsibility, especially for other people. An individual's career itself could become a stressor. If employees believe that their career progress has been too slow, too fast, or in an unwanted direction, they could experience high levels of stress.

Work schedule, too, can cause stress. Figure 14.6 shows how shift work can cause stress both directly, through physiological processes, and indirectly, through its effect on family life. Rotating shifts are especially stressful, as the constantly changing schedule makes both social and physiological adjustment nearly impossible.[60]

Finally, another source of stress has to do with work-family conflicts. For example, a startling 70 percent of BellSouth's unmarried employees support at least one child.[61] A total of 53 percent of children under five and 66 percent of children aged six to seventeen have working mothers. Many employees, both married and unmarried, have child or elder care responsibilities (or both) that contribute to the level of individual stress.

Group-Level Stressors Stressors at the group level generally involve social pressures. The first such stressor is felt when the individual is a member of an incohesive work unit. Disagreements and divisions among the employee's peers can be distracting and emotionally fatiguing. A lack of group support can also add to

TABLE 14.5 Life Events, Ranked from Most to Least Stressful

Stress Points	*Events*
100	Death of a spouse
73	Divorce
65	Marital separation
63	Death of a close family member
63	Jail term
53	Personal injury or illness
50	Marriage
47	Fired at work
45	Retirement
45	Marital reconciliation
44	Change in health of a family member
40	Pregnancy
39	Sexual difficulties
39	Gain of a new family member
39	Business readjustments
38	Change in financial state
37	Death of a close friend
36	Change to a different line of work
35	Change in number of arguments with spouse
31	Sizable mortgage
30	Foreclosure of mortgage or loan
29	Change in responsibilities at work
29	Son or daughter leaving home
29	Trouble with in-laws
28	Outstanding personal achievement
26	Wife begins or stops work
26	Begin or end school
25	Change in living condition
24	Revision of personal habits
23	Trouble with boss
20	Changes in work hours or conditions
20	Change in schools
20	Change in residence
19	Change in recreation
19	Change in church activities
18	Change in social activities
17	Smaller mortgage or loan
15	Change in number of family get-togethers
15	Change in sleeping habits
15	Change in eating habits
13	Vacation
12	Christmas
11	Minor violations of the law

Source: T. H. Holmes and R. H. Rahe, "The Social Adjustment Rating Scale," *Journal of Psychosomatic Research*, 1967, pp. 213–218. Reprinted by permission.

FIGURE 14.6 Shift Work, Family Roles, and Physiological Stress

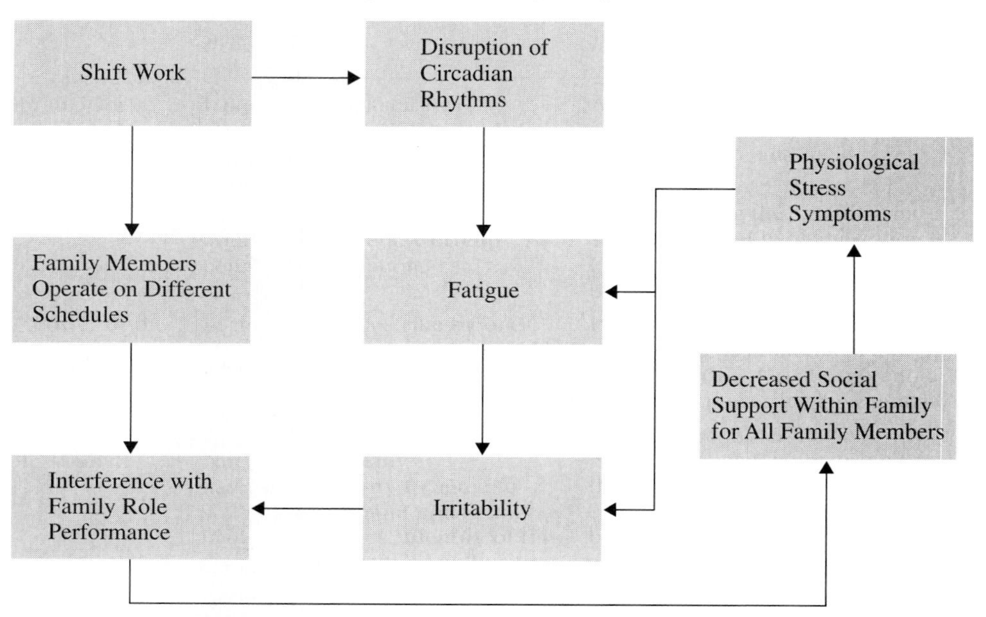

Note: This model is theoretical only and not fully tested by Hood and Milazzo's data.

Source: J. C. Hood and N. Milazzo, "Shift Work, Stress, and Well-Being," *Personnel Administrator,* December 1984, p. 96. Reprinted by permission.

the overall level of stress. Finally, conflicts between groups or departments can be a stressor because such conflicts create additional work and worry for individuals.

Organizational-Level Stressors Stressors at the organizational level involve variables in the climate and structure of the company: rules and regulations, extent of centralization, distribution of power, management style, and the openness of communications. The design of the individual's work space can also heighten or relieve stress. Working in a crowded or unpleasant area could create more stress. Conversely, having a separate, roomy area of one's own may serve as a buffer against some forms of stress.

A final organizational stressor may be technology, the machines and processes used to perform a job. Although designed to make a job simpler, a machine can also be a stressor. Sometimes, for example, employees may view machines as potential threats to their health or safety. Or changes in machines or processes may be threatening because they require employees to acquire new skills or because they signal worker obsolescence and possible dismissal. When perceived in these ways, technology can be a definite source of stress. Such is the case of the video screens for computers and word processors. Although fears of radiation are unwarranted, some individuals find working at the screens very uncomfortable, especially if the screens have not been correctly installed.[62]

Stress Reduction

Recently, a model of worksite stress, including a framework for intervention, was developed; it is shown in Figure 14.7. This model illustrates the intervention targets, types of interventions, and outcomes. As indicated, stress can be a function of the individual, the organization, or the individual/organization interface. Stress is sensed or appraised by the individual experiencing the stress, or by others. Once the sources of stress have been identified, the organization or individual can act to correct the problem. Coping strategies include physiological and psychological responses and changes in worksite behavior.[63]

Organizational Strategies for Managing Stress For managers, the key to managing stress successfully is to be alert for cues that subordinates are experiencing

FIGURE 14.7 Framework for Examining Worksite Stress

Targets of Stress Management Interventions		Types of Interventions		Outcomes
Situational Stressors *Individual* *Organizational* *Individual/ Organizational* Appraisal of Stressors *Self* *Others* Coping Strategies *Physiological* *Psychological* *Worksite Behavior*	→	Individual *Meditation* *Excercise* *Relaxation Techniques* *Cognitive Approaches* *Goal-Setting* *Time Management* Organizational *Organizational Structure* *Job Design* *Selection and Placement Programs* *Working Conditions* *Training and Development* Individual Organizational Interface *Job Demands-Person Style Fit* *Participation Preferences-Practices* *Autonomy Preferences-Practices* *Coworker Relationships*	→	Individual *Blood Pressure, Heart Rate, Catecholamines* *Quality of Life* *Anxiety, Depression, Etc.* *Psychosomatic Complaints* Organizational *Productivity Quantity and Quality* *Turnover* *Absenteeism* *Health Care Costs* *Accidents* Individual Organizational Interface *Job Performance* *Job Satisfaction* *Burnout* *Health Care Utilization*

Source: Adapted from John M. Ivancevich, Michael T. Matteson, Sara M. Freedman, and James S. Phillips, "Worksite Stress Management Interventions," *American Psychologist,* Vol. 45, February 1990, p. 254.

too much stress. These cues will indicate when to initiate stress-reduction programs and whether such programs are working.[64] There is little a company can do directly to reduce stressors that are located outside the organization. However, employee assistance programs, which will be discussed later in this chapter, could help individuals to overcome some personal problems.

Some companies have used ergonomics to reduce stress and discomfort in the workplace. **Ergonomics** is the science of designing work-related machines and equipment to fit the requirements of the human body. This science combines industrial engineering with the physiological and psychological requirements and limitations of the individuals who will use the equipment. Innovative chair designs allow workers to sit for extended periods of time with less lower-back distress, colored video screens make it easier to work with a computer monitor, and proper positioning of the keyboard can reduce carpal tunnel syndrome.

One highly effective organizational strategy for managing stress is to carry out a careful role analysis and clarification.[65] Such an undertaking is similar to a job analysis, but it also considers how employees perceive their jobs and their supervisors and where conflicts, overloads, and ambiguities may develop. This information helps the organization correct the problems and communicate better with employees.

In addition, an organization may be able to reduce stress by altering its climate and structure. It may be helpful, for instance, to develop employee participation in decision making, reduce bureaucratic procedures, and alter the leadership styles of managers.[66]

Finally, as described in Chapter 13, organizations are becoming more family-friendly and thus are assisting employees with stress resulting from family conflicts. For example, some corporations offer employees subsidized child care. Companies can do a great deal to reduce stress through smaller gestures, such as making a telephone available to workers who would not otherwise have access to a phone so they can check on their children, or letting workers slip out for a parent-teacher conference.

Individual Strategies for Managing Stress There are many ways for individuals to manage their own stress. However the individual chooses to manage stress, five guidelines seem essential for success. First, a person must make an explicit decision to manage stress. Second, faddish methods should be avoided, for they are often ineffective and may actually prove harmful in the long run. Third, patience is essential. Lifestyle changes seldom take effect very quickly. Fourth, stress management should be regarded as a lifelong process, and not something that can be done once for all time. Finally, the best rule is not to fight a battle you cannot win. If there is no way to resolve the stress from the job or the organization, then it may be best for the employee to leave the company.

Table 14.6 presents some additional stress management techniques, including proper nutrition, exercise, and certain psychological approaches. These techniques do not attempt to reduce stress directly but instead represent methods of coping with the physiological and psychological effects of stress.

TABLE 14.6 Self-Management Techniques

Good Nutritional Habits

1. Balanced diet
   - Sufficient vitamins, minerals, protein, complex carbohydrates, and fiber
   - Minimized consumption of sugar, salt, saturated fats, refined white flour, and chemical additives
2. Regular meals
3. Maintenance of recommended weight
4. Moderate use of alcohol and caffeine
5. No smoking

Good Exercise Habits

1. Regular aerobic exercise to improve cardiovascular fitness
2. Regular recreational exercise for tension reduction and diversion

Self-Awareness

1. Understanding of personal needs, preferences and idiosyncracies
2. Assertive behavior and role negotiation

Letting Go Techniques

1. Regular relaxation habits (e.g., meditation, prayer, healing visualization)
2. Seeking closure on tasks and interpersonal situations—finishing unfinished business

Personal Planning

1. Effective time management day to day
2. Life and career planning for the long term

Source: Reprinted with permission from the June 1979 issue of *Personnel Administrator,* copyright 1979, The Society for Human Resource Management, Alexandria, VA.

EMPLOYEE ASSISTANCE PROGRAMS

Concern for workplace health and safety is critical in creating a productive work environment. There is more to an employee's life, however, than the job. Organizations are beginning to realize that the quality of employees' nonwork lives can have a dramatic effect on their job performance. Problems outside the organization can interfere with a worker's concentration, endurance, and motivation.

Definition of Employee Assistance Programs

Many employers have been offering **employee assistance programs (EAPs)** in an attempt to improve performance and retention by helping employees solve their personal problems.[67] In 1980, about 12 percent of American workers had access to EAPs. In 1991 that figure exceeded 36 percent.[68] More than three-fourths of all

TABLE 14.7 A Sample of Possible Employee Assistance Programs

Purpose	*Program*
Physical Assistance	Stress Management Weight Control Blood Pressure Control Smoking Cessation
Psychological Assistance	Stress Management Marital Counseling Family Counseling Psychological Treatment Alcoholism Treatment Drug Abuse Counseling
Other Assistance	Financial Counseling Legal Advice

Fortune 500 companies and about 12,000 smaller companies have EAPs. Amoco, for example, offers counseling and referral for stress, marital and family problems, drug and alcohol dependence, and similar problems. Some types of employee assistance programs that employers can offer are listed in Table 14.7. Carol Irons, EAP coordinator at Amoco's General Office in Chicago, points out that EAP usage is increasing as the declining economy and threat of retrenchment magnify other problems employees were already experiencing.[69]

Establishing Employee Assistance Programs

To set up an EAP, a company should follow a four-stage process of problem identification, program development, implementation, and evaluation.[70]

Problem Identification The first step is to determine what problems are afflicting employees. Experience to date has shown marital and family relationship problems tend to be the most common problems employees bring to EAPs, accounting for 40 to 50 percent of EAP referrals.[71] Substance abuse ranks high on the list of job performance referrals and generally costs more to treat. Interestingly, demographics and geography play a role in determining the type of EAP a company adopts. Companies near Atlantic City, New Jersey, home of many gambling casinos, tend to see problems related to such activities. The EAP for the Association of Flight Attendants, an EAP that represents 30,000 flight attendants from 19 airlines, has an unusual number of people seeking help for weight loss.

Two important considerations at this stage are whether the problem is significantly affecting employee performance and whether enough employees suffer from the problem to make an EAP cost effective. Even if productivity improvement is not a major motivation for the program, it is important to determine how widespread the problem is in the work force. A relatively isolated problem may be best handled by referring affected employees to private counseling, paid for through insurance.

Program Development The second stage in offering an EAP is to develop specific appropriate programs. The employer must decide whether to conduct the program on the premises or at an outside agency. An in-house program could be more expensive and might raise questions about confidentiality but would offer some major advantages too.[72] A workplace location illustrates management's commitment and also gives the employer full control over the program and the philosophy of the treatment.

Management must also decide whether the counseling will be conducted during regular hours or after work. Employers prefer not to disrupt work, but employees may be more likely to attend the therapy if it is offered on company time. Decisions about publicizing the EAP must also be made. Emphasizing the success of the program and the personal benefits gained through participation will help to ensure employee commitment.[73]

Program development also includes communication to employees about the EAP. One study found that the willingness of employees to use an EAP was related to familiarity with the program, perceptions of its trustworthiness, and opportunities for personal attention.[74] For this reason, it is important that employees understand the EAP, how it works, and the benefits that might accrue.

Implementation The third stage is the delivery of the various programs. Most often it is the employer who initiates treatment. After realizing that an employee has a problem that is affecting job performance, a supervisor recommends the employee for treatment. (The problems typically covered in EAPs need much more than homespun advice; managers should let professionals handle the problem once it is detected.) Thus, it is essential that supervisors be trained how to recognize various problem symptoms and how to approach a troubled employee.[75] For example, Table 14.8 shows some of the symptoms that supervisors should notice as warnings of possible alcohol abuse in a subordinate.

Evaluation The final stage in an EAP program is evaluation. One approach is simply to count the number of employees who make use of the program and ascertain their reactions to it. Additionally, a utility approach can be used to assess the dollar benefits realized (the effects of improved employee performance and tenure minus the costs of offering the program).

A simple utility approach was developed by the city of Phoenix to estimate the value of its EAP. Using this procedure, a company would first determine its average annual wage costs, then multiply this figure by the estimated percentage of troubled employees (17 percent at the time the utility study was done). Twenty-five percent of the resulting figure represents the company's losses due to employees' problems, if it is assumed that personal problems degrade performance by one quarter. EAP intervention can be expected to recover 50 percent of those losses, reflecting the fact that 100 percent rehabilitation is not possible in all cases.

TABLE 14.8 Workplace Symptoms of Alcohol Abuse

- Excessive absenteeism, especially on Mondays and Fridays
- Unexcused and frequent absences
- Tardiness and early departures
- Altercations with fellow employees
- Causing other employees injuries through negligence
- Poor judgment and bad decisions
- Unusual on-the-job accidents
- Deteriorating personal appearance

Source: Reprinted with permission from the August 1982 issue of *Personnel Administrator,* copyright 1982 The Society for Human Resource Management, Alexandria, VA.

To determine the net benefit of the program, its costs are subtracted from the estimated savings.[76] Using this method, the city of Phoenix calculated that it saved $2.5 million by adopting an EAP.

Other studies have shown similar results. McDonnell Douglas Corp. tracked 25,000 employees over a four-year period and showed that the company's EAP saved $4 in health claims and absence for every dollar spent. In another study, General Motors was able to attribute an annual saving of $37 million to its EAP, which serves 10,000 employees.[77] Of course, not all EAP benefits can be measured in dollar terms. Just knowing that the company provides the resources for employees to resolve problems whether they be work related, as with a coworker or supervisor, or a family matter, is important to individuals.

Types of Employee Assistance Programs

Alcoholism and Drug Counseling Drug and alcohol abuse is a major employee problem in many organizations and is increasing in severity. According to the American Council for Drug Education, drug and alcohol abuse costs U.S. business more than $98 billion each year in lost productivity. Drug and alcohol users are five times as likely to file workers compensation claims and use three times the average level of sick benefits.[78]

Most counseling programs follow the Alcoholics Anonymous format of frequent group meetings with peer support teams. Others send the employee through a hospital-administered program on either an in-patient or outpatient basis. A few programs include family therapy to help other members of the household deal with anxieties caused by the addiction and assist in the treatment of the employee.

Compared with other programs for treating alcohol and drug abuse, employer-sponsored efforts have a higher success rate, as they carry with them "the clout of the job." Employees know that if they fail to control the problem, they are likely to lose their jobs. Such an incentive can be critical to success. EAP treatment for alcoholism is almost always cost effective. Employer-offered programs tend to be more effective than other programs for drug-abuse counseling but typically are only marginally cost effective for this problem.[79]

Marital and Family Counseling As indicated previously, marital and family problems tend to be the most common reasons for employees to seek assistance from the EAP. EAPs for marital and family problems typically resemble traditional family counseling. The couple or family meet with a trained professional and attempt to talk out their problems and discover solutions. Some EAPs will also refer to the employee for legal assistance if the problems cannot be resolved.

Financial Assistance Many employees find themselves financially overextended, especially younger employees who are experiencing financial responsibility for the first time. Financial troubles can be a major distraction for employees. Some may be harassed by creditors while they are at work, which further disrupts job performance. Consequently, some employers offer financial services for the troubled employee, such as counseling on budgeting and legal assistance for resolving indebtedness. Some EAPs will contact the employee's creditors and work out extended payment plans. These programs tend to be very successful. The employee regains lost self-esteem and peace of mind; the company finds performance improved and avoids being put in the uncomfortable position of garnisheeing the employee's wages.

EMPLOYEE FITNESS PROGRAMS

Fitness programs involve employees in some form of controlled exercise or recreation activities. Included are wellness programs that promote employee health by encouraging lifestyle changes designed to reduce the risk of illness. Such programs have resulted from employer awareness of the direct and indirect benefits of healthy workers, including increased productivity and reduced insurance costs. Many large corporations, such as Xerox Corp., Johnson & Johnson, and IBM, now sponsor fitness and wellness programs.

Types of Fitness Programs

The wide range of fitness programs that companies offer can be grouped into three categories, based on the costs and commitment of the company in both time and money.[80] At the most basic level, companies organize awareness programs that include newsletters, health fairs, screening sessions, posters, flyers, and educational classes.[81] Also included are programs consisting of corporate sponsorship of outside programs, for example, the employer may pay for employee membership at private fitness clubs. Typically, however, relatively few employees take advantage of the program, and so health improvements are minimal.

The second category of fitness programs involves company-organized and company-sponsored activities that use outside facilities. The firm may sponsor athletic teams or rent a gym for employees to use for daily exercise programs. Expenses are higher than for outside programs, and someone must be assigned to administer the activity. Because of their social nature, these activities are likely to be fairly popular among the employees and will enhance the group's esprit de corps.

The final category consists of fitness programs organized and sponsored by the company and carried out in a company-owned facility, typically including exercise rooms, running course, showers, and lockers. Most of these programs were started after 1974 but expanded quickly. Kimberly-Clark Corporation, for example, constructed a $2.5 million fitness center and staffed it with fifteen full-time professional employees. By the mid-1980s, Xerox had seven facilities, one of which cost $3.5 million and included putting greens, soccer fields, a swimming pool, two gyms, tennis and racquetball courts, a weight room, and 2,300 acres of wooded land with running trails.[82]

Programs like these are typically staffed with three to five specialists and administered by a director with a master's degree in physical education. Well-planned programs include pretesting, instruction, monitoring, and feedback to the employee. Despite the expense, many organizations are developing their own facilities in an effort to provide the greatest opportunity for maximum employee participation and enable the company to integrate the fitness programs with other activities, such as stress management, wellness programs, and other forms of employee assistance.

Results of Fitness Programs

A 1988 survey of worksite programs conducted by the U.S. Public Health Service found that 66 percent of the worksites with more than fifty employees offered at least one health promotion activity, with 22 percent offering fitness programs.[83] Although this seems to indicate extensive availability, participation in worksite fitness programs in the 1980s has usually ranged from 15 to 30 percent for white-collar workers and 3 to 5 percent for blue-collar employees.[84]

Organizations can benefit in several ways from sponsoring employee fitness programs. The more elaborate the programs, the greater the potential benefits. One of the basic gains is in employee morale. Employees view the activities as fun, and they feel better about themselves. The employees may also be healthier, and so insurance rates may decrease. There is some evidence that employee job satisfaction can increase. Besides enhancing group spirit and corporate identification, fitness programs can help the organization attract high-quality job applicants.

Employers may receive some direct benefits from having healthier employees. Absenteeism due to illness may decrease, for example, and employee productivity may increase. Finally, employee fitness programs have a positive effect on the corporate image and visibility in the community and the industry.[85]

A recent review of the evaluative studies of fitness programs concluded that the benefits in reduced absenteeism, injuries, and health care costs have been satisfactorily demonstrated.[86] At the same time, these benefits have been realized far more by white-collar than by blue-collar employees.

One author pointed out a potential drawback of fitness plans that may become visible in years to come. If employees live longer after retirement because of company-sponsored wellness and fitness programs during the working years, companies' pension liabilities may increase significantly.[87]

SUMMARY OF KEY POINTS

There are three reasons why organizations try to create a safe and healthy work environment for their employees. The first reason is altruism; that is, the organization genuinely cares for its members. The second is the financial and nonfinancial benefits for the company: lower absenteeism and turnover, higher productivity, reduced insurance rates, improved employee morale, and enhanced appeal to job applicants. The third reason is compliance with federal, state, and local regulations. Violations of health and safety laws can mean large fines, bad publicity, and even jail sentences for top managers.

Safe and healthy work environments can be achieved through many different types of programs. The Occupational Safety and Health Act mandates that organizations be proactive and pay close attention to removing possible health and safety hazards from the workplace. Efforts must be made to reduce on-the-job accidents and occupational diseases.

Most worksite accidents are caused by employee errors, but the organization remains responsible nevertheless. Employee factors that contribute to accidents include lack of experience, high stress, and poor judgment. Shift work, organizational size, and industry are organizational factors that have been found to be related to accidents. Occupational diseases are health problems caused by long-term exposure to something at the worksite, such as chemicals that cause cancer or loud noises that may lead to hearing loss.

A century of social awareness preceded passage of a comprehensive workplace health and safety bill. The Occupational Safety and Health Act of 1970 created three separate federal agencies for administering the law. The Occupational Safety and Health Administration (OSHA) is responsible for developing and enforcing regulations. OSHA enforces its regulations by inspecting workplaces and issuing citations for violations. The Occupational Safety and Health Review Commission (OSHRC) holds hearings on employers' appeals of citations and penalties. The third agency, the National Institute of Occupational Safety and Health (NIOSH), conducts research on workplace safety and health.

Managing stress is another aspect of providing a good work environment. Too much stress can produce psychological, behavioral, physiological, and organizational consequences. Organizations that want to manage stress adopt a two-stage process. First, they determine the cause of the stress: pressures outside work, individual factors such as role overload, group factors involving social pressures, and organizational factors such as structure and climate. Second, they make a conscious effort to manage stress through ergonomics, role analysis and clarification, and changes in organizational climate and structure. Individuals also may take several kinds of steps to reduce or cope with excessive stress.

Some organizations offer employee assistance programs to help workers overcome personal problems that affect job performance. Employee fitness programs represent another attempt at improving employee well-being.

Questions for Discussion

1. Why should organizations be concerned about health and safety in the workplace?
2. What is workers' compensation?
3. Explain the difference between an injury and an occupational disease.
4. What factors tend to cause on-the-job injuries?
5. Think of a job you have held, and list the specific aspects of that job and work setting that could contribute to injuries. What actions, if any, did the employer take to minimize the risk of accidents and injuries?
6. Explain why it may be difficult to determine whether a disease is caused by exposure to substances in the workplace.
7. What are the purposes of OSHRC and NIOSH?
8. How does OSHA enforce workplace safety?
9. Describe an ideal company-sponsored safety program.
10. What role do states play in assuring a safe work environment?
11. Under what circumstances might an employer be found liable for the mental health problems of an employee?
12. What kinds of factors can cause employees to experience stress at work? What are possible consequences of stress?
13. What methods have employers used to lower or manage the level of stress among employees?
14. What is an EAP, why do some organization have them, and what are the steps in developing such a program?
15. Why do some organizations offer employee fitness programs?

CASE 14.1

Refusing to Work in "Unsafe" Conditions

The Occupational Safety and Health Act states that employers have a specific duty to comply with safety regulations and standards promulgated under the act, as well as a "general duty" to provide a workplace free of recognized hazards that are likely to harm employees. The act further prohibits employers from discriminating against employees who exercise their rights under the law. Rights include notifying OSHA of unsafe conditions and talking with inspectors. An additional regulation issued by the secretary of labor states that an employee may refuse to perform a task that he or she reasonably believes would pose a serious threat to safety or life, if he or she is unable to notify OSHA of the problem immediately. Of course, under the general duty clause, an employer should not ask any employee to perform a highly dangerous task. However, people may differ in their perceptions of whether a task is dangerous, and employers do have a right to assign work and discipline employees for insubordination.

Discuss the following two situations. In each case, do you think the employee has the right to refuse the work, or is the employer justified in imposing discipline? Why?

Situation 1 Bambi Clark had been a word processor operator for Central States Manufacturing for six months. One morning she appeared at work in a very agitated state. She told her office manager, Diane Holmes, that she and her husband were trying to start a family, and that she had just read in the *National Inquirer* that prolonged exposure to video display terminals causes mutations and birth defects. Clark was quite upset, worried that she might already have conceived a monster. She flatly refused to turn on her word processor and begin work. Holmes called the chief safety engineer, who assured Clark that the terminals did not give off harmful radiation. In his professional opinion, there was absolutely no danger to her or to her potential offspring in working with a video screen. Clark still refused to operate the word processor, or even to perform other duties in the office where the word processor operators worked. Holmes gave her one last chance to change her mind, then suspended her without pay for the rest of the day.

Situation 2 An overhead conveyor belt delivered materials throughout a manufacturing plant. A wire mesh screen had been installed just below the conveyor belt to catch items that rolled off the belt. The screen was about 20 feet above the floor. Every week employees would climb up and stand on the iron braces supporting the screen while removing items from the screen. It was sometimes necessary to step out on to the wire mesh itself to recover an object. Several employees had fallen part way through the screen when they stepped on it, and in June an employee had stepped on the old mesh and fallen to his death. The company recognized this safety hazard and was in the process of replacing the old mesh with stronger mesh. In the meantime, employees were told to step only on the iron braces, not on the mesh.

On July 9, two employees complained to the plant safety director about the screen, and requested the phone number of the regional OSHA office so that they could report what they saw as a serious problem. The next night the same two employees were ordered to service an older section of the screen. They refused, stating that there seemed to be a very real probability of injury or death associated with working on the screen. The employees were suspended without pay and later received written reprimands for failing to obey orders. (Abstracted from *Whirlpool Corporation* v. *Marshall,* Supreme Court of the United States, 445 U.S. 1 1980.)

EXERCISE 14.1

Job Stress

Think of a job you have held, and answer the questions below about sources of stress on that job.

yes ___ no___ *1.* Did you have too much work to do for the amount of time allowed?

yes ___ no___ *2.* Did you have to do things that conflicted with your personal values?

yes ___ no___ *3.* Did you receive conflicting orders or instructions?

yes ___ no___ *4.* Did you have heavy responsibility for other people?

yes ___ no___ *5.* Did you work late or rotating shifts?

yes ___ no___ *6.* Was there political turmoil and infighting in the organization?

yes ___ no___ *7.* Did you worry about your job security?

yes ___ no___ *8.* Was the job extremely monotonous and meaningless?

yes ___ no___ *9.* Did you have few or no friends at work?

yes ___ no___ *10.* Were you vague about what was expected of you?

yes ___ no___ *11.* Were you uncertain about what your boss thought of your performance?

yes ___ no___ *12.* Did you work in uncomfortable, crowded, or unsafe conditions?

Add up the number of items you answered "yes." In a group, have the two people with the lowest stress scores describe their jobs. Did any other group members perform a similar job but perceive it as more stressful? Why? Have the two people with the highest stress scores describe their jobs. Pick one of these jobs and discuss what could be done to reduce or manage the stress level in this job.

EXERCISE 14.2

Safety and Health Programs

The class should be divided into eight groups and each group asked to investigate and report on one of the following programs within the college or university where this course is being taken. Specifically, what is your college or university doing in each of the following areas?

1. *Smoking in the Workplace.* Does your college or university have a formal policy? When was it developed? What problems or issues led to the development of the policy? Are there plans to review or alter the current policy? How do employees feel about the policy?
2. *Workplace Injuries.* What does your college or university do to prevent workplace injuries? Is there a safety specialist? What is this individual's training? What responsibilities does this individual have?

3. *AIDS in the Workplace*. Does your college or university have a formal policy concerning employees or students with AIDS? When was the policy developed? What problems led to its development? How has it worked?
4. *Right to Know*. Do right-to-know laws apply to your college or university? Where do they apply? What is done to meet right-to-know requirements?
5. *Employee Fitness Programs*. Does your college or university have an employee fitness program? What level of commitment by the institution is involved? What is the level of participation?
6. *Employee Assistance Programs*. Does your college or university have an EAP? What types of problems is it designed to address? Is the program offered on campus or given off-campus by community professionals (or some combination of the two)? How do employees know of the program? What is the level of participation? Has the effectiveness of the program been evaluated relative to its costs?
7. *Occupational Disease*. Have there been instances of repetitive strain injuries among employees at your college or university? What has been done to reduce problems associated with repetitive strain? Have there been concerns with any other occupational diseases?
8. *Stress Management*. Does your college or university have any programs to deal with stress among employees or students? What types of programs are offered?

Notes and References

1. *Accident Facts 1991 Edition* (Chicago: National Safety Council, 1991).
2. Dennis L. Breo, "Living with Stress," *Chicago,* March 1986, pp. 121–127.
3. J. F. Madonia, "Managerial Responses to Alcohol and Drug Abuse Among Employees," *Personnel Administrator,* June 1984, pp. 134–139.
4. S. H. Appelbaum, "A Human Resources Counseling Model: The Alcoholic Employee," *Personnel Administrator,* August 1982, pp. 35–44.
5. Lois Therrien, "Warning: In More and More Places Smoking Causes Fines," *Business Week,* December 29, 1986, p. 40.
6. William G. Wagner, "Assisting Employees with Personal Problems," *Personnel Administrator,* November 1982, pp. 59–64; S. W. Hartman and J. Cozzetto, "Wellness in the Workplace," *Personnel Administrator,* August 1984, pp. 108–117.
7. Based in part on D. S. Thelan, D. Ledgerwood, and C. F. Walters, "Health and Safety in the Workplace: A New Challenge for Business Schools," *Personnel Administrator,* October 1985, pp. 37–46.
8. Jonathan Tusini, "A Death at Work Can Put the Boss in Jail," *Business Week,* March 2, 1987, pp. 37–38; "Company, Supervisor Assessed Criminal Fines," *Occupational Hazards,* August Vol. 53, 1991, p. 9.
9. Occupational Safety and Health Act of 1970, Public Law 91–596, 91st Congress, S.2193, December 29, 1970.
10. For a lengthy discussion of the history of workplace safety, see Judson MacLaury, "The Job Safety Law of 1970: Its Passage Was Perilous," *Monthly Labor Review,* January 1981, pp. 18–24.
11. James Ledvinka and Vida Gulbinas Scarpello, *Federal Regulation of Personnel and Human Resource Management* (Boston: PWS-Kent, 1991).
12. *Accident Facts 1991 Edition,* p. 36.
13. Albert Opdyke and Jan Thayer, "The Work Environment: A Social and Technical Re-

sponse to Injury and Illness Losses," *Personnel Journal,* February 1987, pp. 37–42.

14. Roger A. Jacobs, "Employer Resistance to OSHA Standards: Toward a More Reasonable Approach," *Labor Law Journal,* April 1977, pp. 219–230.

15. "Rotating Shift Work Causes Many Problems," *Occupational Health and Safety,* September 1978, p. 21; Fred K. Foulkes, "Learning to Live with OSHA," *Harvard Business Review,* November–December 1973, pp. 58–69.

16. N. A. Ashford, "The Nature and Dimension of Occupational Health and Safety Problems," *Personnel Administrator,* August 1977, p. 45.

17. Report of the U.S. Surgeon General (Washington, D.C.; Office of the U.S. Surgeon General, 1986).

18. Philip R. Voluck, "Burning Legal Issues of Smoking in the Work-place," *Personnel Journal,* Vol. 66, June 1987, pp. 140–143; Therrien, "Warning."

19. J. Carroll Swart, "An Overlooked Cost of Employee Smoking," *Personnel,* Vol. 67, August 1990, p. 54.

20. The Bureau of National Affairs, *Employment Guide* (Washington, D.C.: The Bureau of National Affairs, 1991).

21. Jim Collison, "Workplace Smoking Policies: 16 Questions and Answers," *Personnel Journal,* April 1988, pp. 80–82; Sherry C. Hammond, David A. Decenzo, and Mollie H. Bowers, "How One Company Went Smokeless," *Harvard Business Review,* November–December 1987, pp. 44–45.

22. *Accident Facts 1991 Edition,* p. 50.

23. Maria Mallory and Hazel Bradford, "An Invisible Workplace Hazard Gets Harder to Ignore," *Business Week,* January 30, 1987, pp. 92–93.

24. Sara Kiesler and Tom Finholt, "The Mystery of RSI," *American Psychologist,* Vol. 43, December 1988, pp. 1004–1015.

25. Mallory and Bradford, "An Invisible Workplace Hazard," pp. 92–93.

26. Peter A. Stori, "Getting a Grasp on Carpal Tunnel Syndrome," *Risk Management,* Vol. 37, March 1990, pp. 40–48; Larry Reynolds, "OSHA Asks Can You Repeat That? *Personnel,* Vol. 68, No. 2, February 1991, p. 19; Michelle Neely Martinez and Joe Lamoglia, "Hands-on Answers to Hidden Health Costs," *HRMagazine,* March 1992, pp. 48–53.

27. Yvette Debow, "Just How Dangerous Are VDTs?" *Management Review,* Vol. 77, August 1988, pp. 44–46.

28. Linda C. Kramer, "Legal and Ethical Issues Affecting Conduct Toward AIDS Sufferers," *Occupational Health and Safety,* Vol. 59, January 1990, pp. 49–50, 57.

29. "Justices Bar 'Fetal Protection' Policies," *The Wall Street Journal,* March 21, 1991, pp. B1, B8; *United Automobile Workers* v. *Johnson Controls, Inc.,* U.S. Sup. Ct., No. 89-1215 (March 20, 1991).

30. Janet Deming, "Drug-free Workplace is Good Business," *HRMagazine,* Vol. 35, April 1990, pp. 61–62.

31. Michael R. Carrell and Christina Heavrin, "Before You Drug Test . . .," *HRMagazine,* Vol. 35, June 1990, pp. 64–68.

32. Foulkes, "Learning to Live with OSHA," pp. 58–69.

33. Ledvinka and Scarpello, *Federal Regulations.*

34. "The Cost of Safety," *The Wall Street Journal,* July 10, 1980, p. 18.

35. Industrial Union Dept., *AFL-CIO* v. *American Petroleum Institute,* 448 U.S. 607 (1980); *American Textile Institute* v. *Donovan,* 452 U.S. 490 (1981).

36. Ledvinka and Scarpello, *Federal Regulation.*

37. *Marshall* v. *Barlow's, Inc.,* 436 U.S. 307 (1978).

38. U.S. Department of Labor, *OSHA Inspections* (Programs and Policy Series, OSHA, June 1975).

39. Ibid.

40. M. Corn, "An Inside View of OSHA Compliance," *Personnel Administrator,* November 1979, pp. 39–44.

41. David P. Twomey, *A Concise Guide to Employment Law* (Dallas: South-Western, 1986).

42. Maryellen Lo Bosco, "Safety Programs in the Work Place," *Personnel,* May 1986, pp. 59–67.

43. For a complete discussion of company

safety committees, see G. R. Carnehan, "Using Safety Committees Effectively," *Personnel Administrator,* 1974, pp. 46–49.

44. Judi Komaki, Kenneth D. Barwick, and Lawrence R. Scott, "A Behavioral Approach to Occupational Safety: Pinpointing and Reinforcing Safe Performance in a Food Manufacturing Plant," *Journal of Applied Psychology,* Vol. 63, August 1978, pp. 434–445; Judi Komaki, Arlene T. Meinzmann, and Loralie Lawson, "Effect of Training and Feedback: Component Analysis of a Behavioral Safety Program," *Journal of Applied Psychology,* Vol. 65, June 1980, pp. 261–270.
45. Sharon Nelton, "Planning That Saves Lives," *Nation's Business,* May 1986, pp. 41–42.
46. Mark A. Hofmann, "Diverse State Plans Share Common Goal," *Business Insurance,* October 7, 1991, pp. 94–95.
47. Ledvinka and Scarpello, *Federal Regulation.*
48. David Warner, "Protecting OSHA from 'Reform,'" *Nation's Business,* February 1992, pp. 16–21.
49. "Justices Bar 'Fetal Protection' Policies," pp. B1, B8; James O. Castagnera, "Right-to-Know Issues at State and Local Levels," *Personnel,* May 1986, pp. 9–12.
50. *Chemical Hazard Communication* (Washington, D.C.: U.S. Department of Labor, OSHA #3084, 1988).
51. M. S. Novit, "Mental Distress: Possible Implications for the Future," *Personnel Administrator,* August 1982, pp. 47–53.
52. B. Berkeley Rice, "Can Companies Kill?" *Psychology Today,* June 1981, pp. 78–85.
53. Jane Hood and Nancy Milazzo, "Shift Work, Stress, and Well-Being," *Personnel Administrator,* December 1984, pp. 95–105.
54. "The Cost of Safety," p. 18.
55. For a complete discussion of sexual harassment on the job, see R. H. Faley, "Sexual Harassment: A Critical Review of Legal Cases with General Principles and Practice Measures," *Personnel Psychology,* December 1982, pp. 583–600.
56. John M. Ivancevich and Michael T. Matteson, *Stress and Work: A Managerial Perspective* (Glenview, Ill.: Scott Foresman, 1980).
57. Marianne Frankenhaeuser, Ulf Lundberg, Mats Fredrikson, Bob Melin, Martii Tuomisto, Anna-Lisa Myrsten, Monica Hedman, Bodil Bergman-Losman, and Leif Wallin, "Stress On and Off the Job as Related to Sex and Occupational Status in White-Collar Workers," *Journal of Organizational Behavior,* Vol. 10, 1989, pp. 321–346.
58. Ivancevich and Matteson, *Stress and Work.*
59. Daniel C. Ganster and John Schaubroeck, "Work Stress and Employee Health," *Journal of Management,* Vol. 17, 1991, pp. 235–271.
60. John Zalusky, "Shiftwork—A Complex of Problems," *AFL-CIO American Federationist,* May 1978, pp. 1–6.
61. "Can Your Career Hurt Your Kids?" *Fortune,* May 20, 1991, pp. 38–56.
62. Vico Henriques and Charlotte LeGates, "Facts About Visual Display Safety," *Personnel Administrator,* September 1984, pp. 64–68.
63. Philip J. Dewe, "Examining the Nature of Work Stress: Individual Evaluations of Stressful Experiences and Coping," *Human Relations,* Vol. 42, 1989, pp. 993–1013.
64. Terry A. Beehr, "Management of Work-Related Stress," in *Current Issues in Personnel Management,* ed. Kendrith M. Rowland and Gerald R. Ferris, 3rd ed. (Boston: Allyn and Bacon, 1986), pp. 305–311.
65. John M. Ivancevich and Michael T. Matteson, "Optimizing Human Resources: A Case for Preventive Health and Stress Management," *Organizational Dynamics,* Autumn 1980, pp. 4–25.
66. For a discussion of changing organizational culture to manage stress, see R. Weigel and S. Pinsky, "Managing Stress: A Model for the Human Resource Staff," *Personnel Administrator,* February 1982, pp. 56–60.
67. Robert W. Hollman, "Beyond Contemporary Employee Assistance Programs," *Personnel Administrator,* September 1981, pp. 37–41.
68. Stuart Feldman, "Today's EAPs Make the Grade," *Personnel,* Vol. 68, February 1991, p. 3.
69. Jim Spangler, "Assistance Available for

Those Under Stress," *Amoco Torch,* June 29, 1992, pp. 1–2.

70. Andrew J. Brennan, "Worksite Health Promotion Can Be Cost-Effective," *Personnel Administrator,* April 1983, pp. 39–42.

71. Feldman, "Today's EAPs Make the Grade," p. 3.

72. Art Durity, "Can You Keep A Secret?" *Personnel,* Vol. 68, February 1991, p. 1.

73. William G. Wagner, "Assisting Employees with Personal Problems," *Personnel Administrator,* November 1982, pp. 59–64.

74. Michael M. Harris and Mary L. Fennell, "Perceptions of an Employee Assistance Program and Employees' Willingness to Participate," *The Journal of Applied Behavioral Science,* Vol. 24, 1988, pp. 423–438.

75. "Companies Train Supervisors to be EAP Savvy," *Personnel,* Vol. 68, February 1991, p. 5.

76. Mary F. Davis, "Worksite Health Promotion," *Personnel Administrator,* December 1984, pp. 45–50.

77. Feldman, "Today's EAPs Make the Grade," p. 3.

78. Jerry Beilinson, "Are EAPs the Answer?" *Personnel,* Vol. 68, January 1991, pp. 3–4.

79. Madonia, "Managerial Responses," pp. 134–139; Dale Masi, "Company Responses to Drug Abuse from AMA's Nationwide Survey," *Personnel,* March 1987, pp. 40–47.

80. J. J. Hoffman and C. J. Hobson, "Physical Fitness and Employee Effectiveness," *Personnel Administrator,* April 1984, pp. 101–114.

81. M. P. O'Donnell, *Design of Workplace Health Promotion Programs* (Royal Oak, Mich.: American Journal of Health Promotion, 1986).

82. Jack N. Kondrasuk, "Corporate Physical Fitness Programs: The Role of the Personnel Department," *Personnel Administrator,* December 1984, pp. 75–80.

83. G. M. Christenson and A. Kiefhaber, "Highlights of the National Survey of Worksite Health Promotion Activities," *Health Values,* Vol. 12, 1988, pp. 29–33.

84. P. Conrad, "Who Comes to Work-Site Wellness Programs? A Preliminary Review," *Journal of Occupational Medicine,* Vol. 29, 1987, pp. 317–320.

85. Russell W. Driver and R. A. Ratcliff, "Employers' Perceptions of Benefits Accrued from Physical Fitness Programs," *Personnel Administrator,* August 1982, pp. 21–24.

86. Deborah L. Gebhardt and Carolyn E. Crump, "Employee Fitness and Wellness Programs in the Workplace," *American Psychologist,* Vol. 45, 1990, pp. 262–272.

87. M. T. Matteson and J. M. Ivancevich, "Health Promotion at Work," in *International Review of Industrial and Organizational Psychology,* ed. C. L. Cooper and I. R. Robertson (New York: Wiley, 1988), pp. 279–306.

15

Labor Relations and Collective Bargaining

Many employers must deal with formal organizations of their employees. Under various laws, employees have the right to form unions for the purpose of improving working conditions, such as wages, hours, and benefits. Contemporary unions pursue such goals primarily through a process called collective bargaining. Without unions, employers typically set employment terms and conditions unilaterally (that is, without consulting employees), within constraints imposed by market conditions and the Fair Labor Standards Act. Collective bargaining imposes an additional set of constraints on employers, allowing employees to participate in setting important terms and conditions of employment through representatives of their own choosing.

Because they want to participate in setting important employment conditions, unions provoke controversy and opposition. The history of their development in the United States has had many ups and downs. Today, unions as a whole face some serious challenges. Union membership is declining, and employers are more aggressively resisting the unionization of their employees and demanding concessions from unions at the bargaining table. On the other hand, unionization among public sector employees has increased considerably in the past twenty-five years, in part because of the growth of a special type of union, the professional bargaining association. Originally formed as nonbargaining professional organizations, these associations later began to engage in the primary activity of contemporary unions, namely collective bargaining. The National Education Association is perhaps the best-known example of the type.

Chapter 15 discusses the history of unionization in the United States and the legal system that evolved to regulate and ultimately protect certain union activities. Employees' reasons for joining or not joining a union are discussed, and the process of forming a new union is described. Once a recognized union is in place, HR managers must participate in collective bargaining with the aim of agreeing on a contract covering the terms and conditions of employment. The last topics in Chapter 15 describe additional means of reaching and enforcing a contract, various dispute resolution procedures, and the grievance system.

A BRIEF HISTORY OF LABOR UNIONS IN THE UNITED STATES

Figure 15.1 depicts the major developments that have shaped the labor relations environment in the United States. Developments that occurred to and within organized labor are closely related to changes in the political, social, and economic environments. Organized labor has been affected by developments in the society at large and at the same time it has influenced society.

The First Unions

The formal organization of employees for the purpose of improving working conditions, including pay, can be traced to the early days of our national history. The expansion of markets that resulted from the development of rail and water transportation exacerbated competitive forces in both the labor and product markets. The first unions were formed primarily as a response to attempts by employers to reduce costs by cutting wages. These unions focused on three goals: first, controlling the apprenticeship process and thus the supply of skilled labor; second, demanding a specific pay scale; and finally, controlling output.[1]

One of the first enduring unions emerged among shoemakers in Philadelphia in 1792. Other skilled workers, including carpenters, followed suit in the late eighteenth and early nineteenth centuries. Concentrated in the major cities, these groups were geographically decentralized, and generally short-lived. Most collapsed during the depression that followed the War of 1812.[2]

Organizations of skilled workers reappeared during the subsequent decades as part of a broader movement to improve the social conditions of ordinary people. Again, the emphasis was on reducing working hours and raising wages. This period also witnessed the emergence of the world's first workingmen's political parties, as workers sought changes through politics as well as through negotiations with employers. (At this time, political rights for workers were far better established than bargaining rights; the field of labor-management relations was still essentially unregulated, at least in terms of statutory law.) The workingmen's parties sought, among other things, free public education, banking reforms, and the abolition of debtors' imprisonment. Like their earlier counterparts, most of these organizations were geographically decentralized. The first *national* labor organization, the National Trades Union, was formed in 1834 and numbered 300,000 members at its peak. Along with many other labor unions, it disintegrated in the depression of the 1830s.[3]

The first major set of longer-lived unions emerged in the 1850s and 1860s, a by-product of the early phases of the industrial revolution. Formed along occupational or craft lines, these unions furthered the practice of collective bargaining, although they remained unprotected by any labor relations statute. Major inroads were made in the railroad and printing industries. In fact, the typographers' union, formed in 1852, has become the longest-lived labor organization in the United States. Many of the midcentury unions organized on a broader geographical basis than had their organizational ancestors. About thirty national unions were in existence in the early 1870s. A quasi-federation of unions, called the National Labor Union, was also formed but existed only briefly.

The Knights of Labor and the American Federation of Labor

Formed in Philadelphia in 1869, the Knights of Labor was initially a reformist secret society. Within two decades it had become a nationwide coalition of local assemblies, including 700,000 occupationally diverse members. The Knights emphasized a variety of tactics to achieve its principal goals, which included political action, producer and consumer cooperatives, education, and arbitration rather

FIGURE 15.1 United States Labor History Timeline

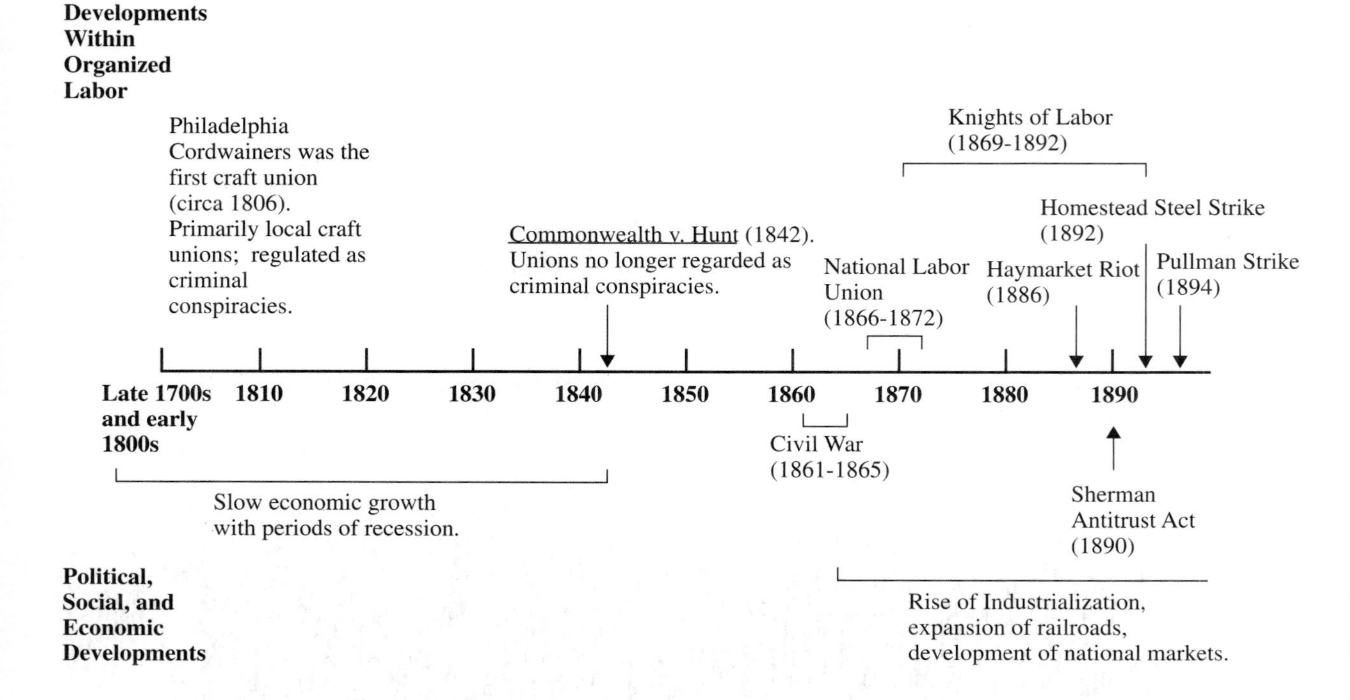

Source: Reprinted with the permission of Macmillan Publishing Company from *Collective Bargaining and Labor Relations* by Terry L. Leap. Copyright © 1991 by Macmillan Publishing Company.

than strikes. The organization's rapid growth and heterogeneous membership, however, produced internal schisms, which contributed to its decline in the 1880s and 1890s. Nevertheless, the Knights showed the value of a national federation of labor organizations, as well as the difficulty of maintaining national alliances that departed from bread-and-butter issues common to all working people.[4]

The American Federation of Labor (AFL) was formally established in 1886 by a group of craft unions. Under the leadership of cigar maker Samuel Gompers,

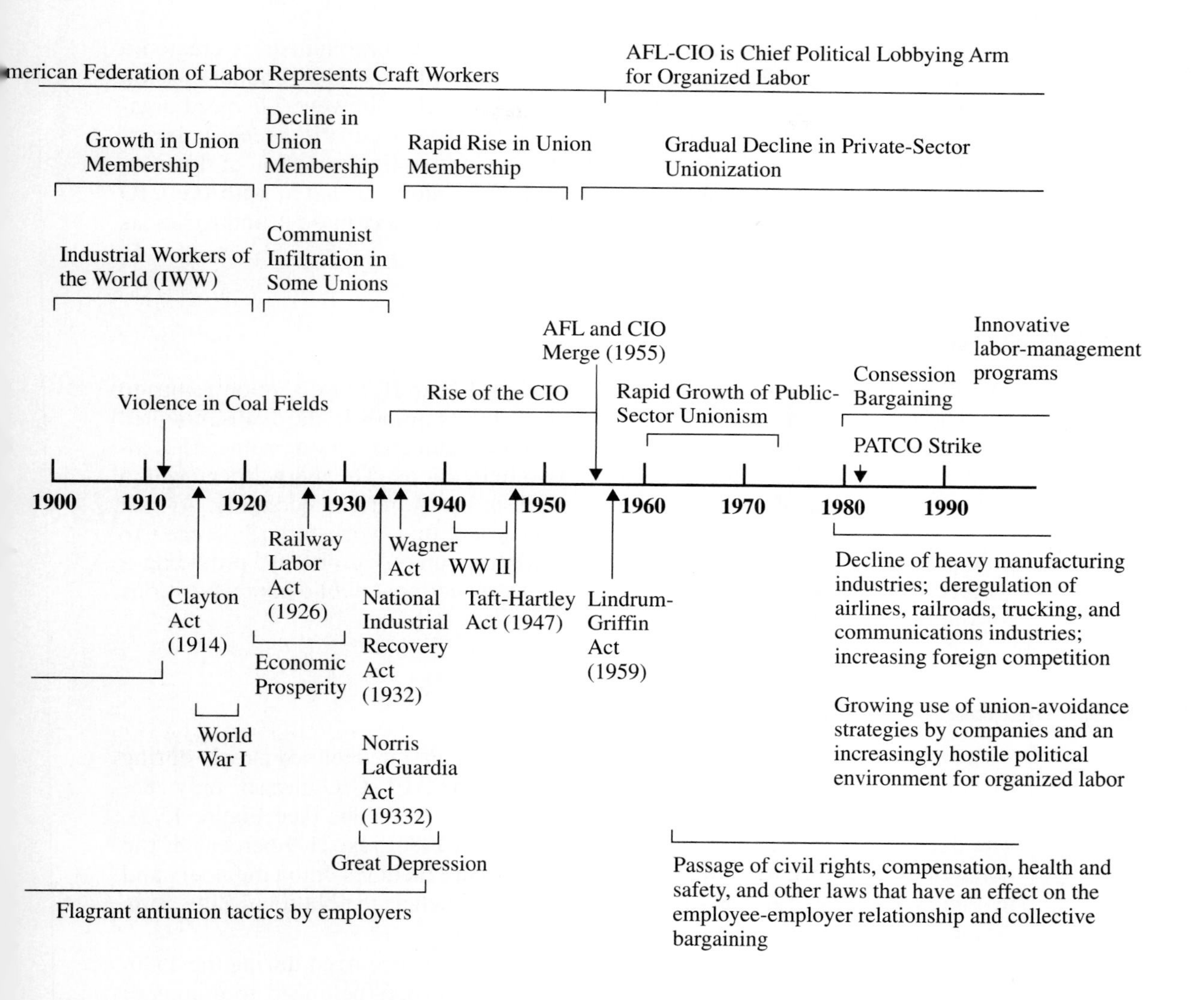

the AFL set the stage for contemporary unionism. It emphasized the organization of skilled workers into unions separated along craft lines. In contrast to the Knights, the AFL emphasized collective bargaining rather than political action as a means of improving working conditions for skilled workers. Although a federation, it granted considerable organizational autonomy to its member unions. With these objectives, the AFL grew from about 250,000 members in 1897 to more than 2 million in 1914.[5]

The Industrial Unions

The rapid expansion of mass production facilities in several industries created a growing class of unskilled workers essentially beyond the organizational mission of the AFL craft unions. Several unions within the AFL, however, favored organizing these workers on an industry-wide rather than occupation-specific basis. In the 1930s, the AFL rebuffed these efforts, prompting the formation of the Congress of Industrial Organizations (CIO) in 1938. Unions affiliated with the CIO proceeded to organize workers on an industry-wide basis in such industries as textiles, rubber, steel, and auto manufacturing.[6]

The AFL-CIO Merger

The economic expansion associated with World War II caused union ranks to swell. The combined successes of the AFL and CIO unions in the 1940s, coupled with the decline in the pure craft philosophy of organizing among some AFL affiliates, provided a basis for merging the two federations. The merger occurred in 1955, at the height of modern union strength in the American economy. At that time, roughly one-third of the nation's nonagricultural work force belonged to unions. The AFL-CIO continued the tradition of union autonomy, providing a variety of services to individual unions and taking national public policy positions for the bulk of organized labor.[7]

Union Membership Trends

As a percentage of the total work force, union membership declined slowly during the late 1950s and 1960s. In 1965, ten years after the AFL-CIO merger, only 28.4 percent of the nonagricultural work force belonged to unions (see Figure 15.2). The decline accelerated in the 1970s and 1980s. In 1980, just 21.9 percent of the nonagricultural work force was unionized (this figure includes union members and members of the emerging bargaining associations, such as the National Education Association).[8] By 1990, the figure was 16.1 percent.

A substantively important shift in union emphasis occurred during the 1970s and 1980s. Before the early 1960s, few public employees belonged to unions or bargaining associations. In 1953, for example, only 11.6 percent of government employees belonged to unions. In 1980, however, the figure was 35 percent, and it has remained fairly stable during the last decade, with 36.5 percent of public workers being unionized in 1990.[9] (See Table 15.1.) The National Education Association, the American Federation of State, County, and Municipal Employees, and the American Federation of Teachers represent some of the largest and most powerful employee organizations in the country.

Union membership rates vary significantly across industries (see Table 15.1). Membership is relatively high in the transportation, communications, and public

FIGURE 15.2 Union Membership as a Percentage of the Nonagricultural Labor Force, 1930–1990

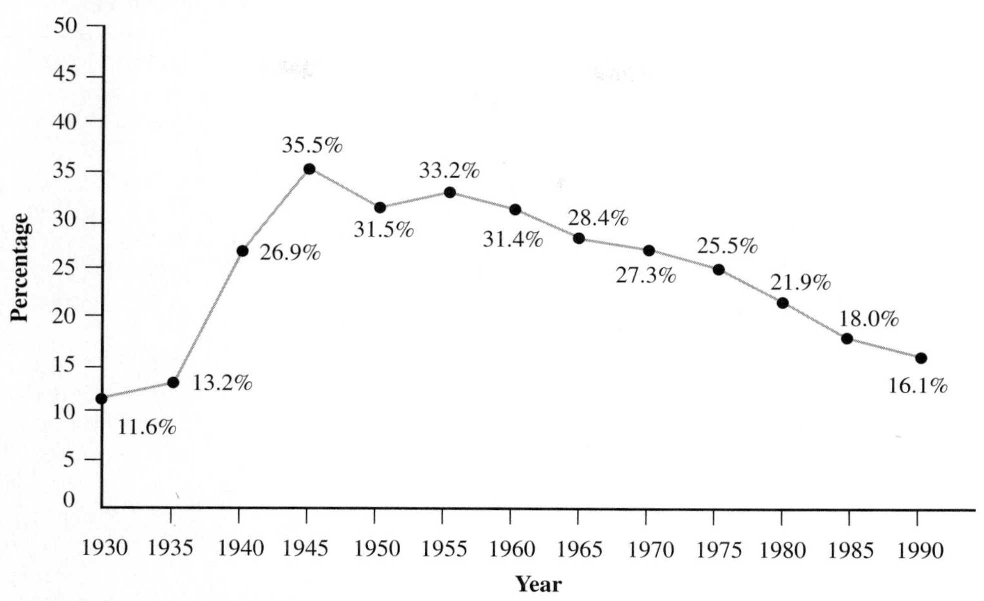

Note: The 1985 and 1990 figures are the percentage of employed wage and salary workers in all industries, private and public, who were union members. In 1980, this figure was 23.0 percent.

Source: Harry C. Katz and Thomas A. Kochan, *An Introduction to Collective Bargaining and Industrial Relations*. Copyright © 1992 (New York: McGraw-Hill Book Company), p. 144. Reprinted with permission of McGraw-Hill, Inc.

utilities industries, as well as in the public sector. It is quite low in the services, finance, insurance, and real estate industries.

Table 15.1 also illustrates several interesting characteristics of union membership. First, union membership varies across occupations, with blue-collar workers showing larger unionization rates than any other group. Second, unionization rates among blacks appear to be higher than those among whites and Hispanics, and unionization rates for women are consistently lower than those for men.

Although unions now constitute less than 20 percent of the nonagricultural work force, their impact is not confined to their organizational perimeters. Many wholly or partially nonunionized employers copy the practices of unionized firms with regard to wages and benefits, in order to discourage the further unionization of their work forces. In addition, wage increases won by unions affect the price of production and hence the price of goods. They also affect the number of jobs employers are willing or able to provide, as well as the profitability of firms.[10]

TABLE 15.1 Demographics of Union Membership

	Percentage of Work Force Unionized				
	1983	*1985*	*1987*	*1989*	*1990*
Total Work Force	20.1	18.0	17.0	16.4	16.1
Industry					
Manufacturing	27.8	24.8	23.2	21.6	20.6
Mining	20.7	17.3	18.3	17.5	18.0
Construction	27.5	22.3	21.0	21.5	21.0
Transportation, communication, and utilities	42.4	37.0	33.5	31.6	31.6
Trade	8.7	7.2	7.1	6.3	6.3
Finance, insurance, and real estate	2.9	2.9	2.3	2.3	2.5
Government	36.7	35.8	36.0	36.7	36.5
Other Characteristics					
Race					
Black	27.2	24.3	22.6	22.2	21.1
Hispanic	21.1	18.9	17.1	15.2	14.8
White	24.0	17.3	16.3	15.7	15.5
Sex					
Female	14.6	13.2	12.6	12.6	12.6
Male	24.7	22.1	20.9	19.7	19.3
Occupation					
Blue-collar	35.4	31.8	29.3	27.4	26.4
Clerical	15.0	13.5	13.1	13.0	13.6
Service	15.3	14.4	14.1	13.5	13.8
Managerial professional specialty	24.0	15.2	15.0	14.7	14.3
Sales, technical and related support	12.1	10.8	10.3	10.1	10.4

Source: U.S. Department of Labor, Bureau of Labor Statistics, *Employment and Earnings*, various years.

THE LEGAL ENVIRONMENT

Union-management relations in the United States are governed by a highly regulated, legalistic system, with the federal government playing a very active part. This section considers the role of the federal government, especially Congress, in establishing rules of conduct for unions and employers. The executive branch, through such agencies as the National Labor Relations Board and the Department of Labor, and the judicial branch, through the federal courts, have played significant roles as well. Some states and municipalities have also enacted legislation affecting labor relations issues.

This highly regulated framework has not always been in place. For much of our history, unions and employers were much less constrained by law, especially statutory law. Yet the courts often imposed constraints, particularly on employees, before Congress set the tone in this century. The gradual increase in congressional involvement in private sector labor-management relations can be divided into three stages: the common law, the business law, and the statutory law periods. Explicit labor relations law emerges only in the last period. We first discuss the evolution of labor relations regulation in the private sector and then address the collective bargaining rights of public sector employees.

The Common Law Period

The common law period corresponds to the appearance of the first local and national unions. Employers saw the attempts by labor organizations to affect the level of wages and the conditions of employment as an invasion of the employer's right to control the workplace. Lacking enough leverage to confront these labor organizations at the workplace because of the relative shortage of skilled labor, employers turned to the courts for relief.

The common law period extended from the early nineteenth century to 1890, when the Sherman Antitrust Act was passed. During this period, judge-made law was applied to particular situations involving employees attempting to improve their working conditions or to restrict their employer's hiring to unionized labor. The first major court case, which occurred in 1806, involved a group of Philadelphia shoemakers who had gone on strike for the purpose of maintaining their wages. The strikers were arrested and tried for violating the common law doctrine of criminal conspiracy. The doctrine held that concerted activities that had the effect of harming third parties were unlawful, even though similar activities engaged in individually would not be unlawful. For example, it was permissible for an individual to attempt to use market power to raise a wage, but individuals could not combine for such a purpose. Combinations of workers engaged in activities aimed at improving their economic conditions thus automatically became illegal conspiracies. Between 1806 and 1842, the conspiracy doctrine was applied to combinations of workers in seventeen trials. Shoemakers, as one of the first groups of workers to unionize, were involved in nine of these cases.[11]

In 1842, Chief Justice Shaw of the Supreme Judicial Court of Massachusetts decided a case involving a similar set of circumstances. A group of shoemakers had struck in response to the hiring of a nonunion shoemaker at a lower wage. In his opinion, Shaw rejected the argument that the concerted strike rendered the combination of workers an illegal conspiracy per se. He argued that unions were inherently capable of good things, as well as evil, and that the conspiracy doctrine did not apply unless illegal objectives were involved. Withholding labor so as to prevent the hiring of nonunion workers was not necessarily an illegal conspiracy. This case (*Commonwealth* v. *Hunt*),[12] however, did not prevent the future invocation of the conspiracy doctrine.[13] There were actually more so-called conspiracy trials during the latter half of the nineteenth century than during the first half.

The Business Law Period

The business law era emerged after the enactment of the Sherman Antitrust Act in 1890. Intended to restrict the formation of business monopolies, the Sherman Act specifically forbade combinations or conspiracies aimed at restraining "trade or commerce among the several states." This language turned out to provide a powerful tool for squashing union power.

The 1908 *Danbury Hatters* case illustrates this use of the Sherman Act. The United Hatters of America had initiated a boycott against Loewe & Company, a hat manufacturer located in Danbury, Connecticut. The union was attempting to unionize all hat manufacturers in the United States, partly so as to remove wages from competition. Having successfully organized seventy-two of eighty hat-manufacturing plants, it was attempting to unionize the one at Danbury. The employer rebuffed the union's request for recognition and collective bargaining. The United Hatters then called a strike, which was unsuccessful. However, the union expanded its efforts to force the employer to bargain by calling for a boycott of hats manufactured by Loewe & Company. The employer argued that the nationwide boycott constituted an illegal restraint on interstate trade in violation of the Sherman Antitrust Act. The U.S. Supreme Court concurred, holding that the union boycott violated the prohibition on "any combination whatever to secure action which essentially obstructs the free flow of commerce between the States, or restricts in this regard, the liberty of a trader to engage in business."[14]

The unions reacted angrily to this interpretation of the Sherman Act. Seeking legislation to prevent a recurrence of this situation, the AFL supported the Clayton Act of 1914. Hailed by Gompers as organized labor's Magna Carta, the act declared that unions were not illegal conspiracies and that labor was not a "commodity or article of commerce." This apparent victory, however, was hollow. Faced with a set of facts remarkably similar to those found in the *Danbury Hatters* case, the Supreme Court, in the 1921 *Duplex Printing Press* case,[15] ruled that union boycotts that restrained interstate trade were illegal violations of the Sherman Act, notwithstanding the Clayton Act.

Such applications of the Sherman Antitrust Act severely limited the weapons unions could use to impel a recalcitrant employer to bargain collectively. The act not only forbade restraining combinations but imposed punitive damages on violators, including the union and union members themselves, who could ill afford to pay. Furthermore, there were few limits on the employers' ability to penalize employees for expressing union sentiments. Employers sought injunctions against union agitators and sympathizers; fired such workers; required the signing of "yellow-dog" contracts, which forbade an employee to join a union during his or her employment with the firm; and formed company-dominated unions to create the illusion of employee participation.[16] All of these tactics were legal. In contrast, unions were not protected in their efforts to gain a foothold in the workplace. No major statute extended the right to organize and to bargain collectively; other concerted activities also went unprotected. Unions were not illegal conspiracies, but neither were they protected entities. Table 15.2 summarizes the crucial cases and laws from the common law and business law periods.

The Statutory Law Period

The legal environment changed dramatically in the 1920s and 1930s with the enactment of laws designed specifically to regulate labor relations. Part of the motivation was to preserve the uninterrupted flow of goods and services in key industries, such as rail transportation. Another reason was the recognition that the existing balance of power between employee and employer was monumentally

TABLE 15.2 Major Events of the Common Law and Business Law Periods

	Date	*Event*	*Description*
Common law period	1806	*Cordwainers' case*	A combination of workers seeking a wage increase is a criminal conspiracy.
	1842	*Commonwealth* v. *Hunt*	Unions are lawful. Combinations of workers are allowed as long as lawful means are used to gain lawful ends. Courts still hostile to unions.
Business law period	1890	Sherman Antitrust Act	"Every combination . . . or conspiracy in restraint of trade or commerce among the several states . . . is hereby declared to be illegal." Used by employers seeking injunctions for union activity.
	1894	*Debs* case	A famous use of the injunction. Eugene Debs jailed for refusing to obey a court back-to-work order in the American Railway Union strike.
	1908	*Danbury Hatters* case	Union boycott of goods in violation of the Sherman Act. Union is assessed triple damages.
	1914	Clayton Act	"Labor is not a commodity," but courts continue to find union acts illegal.

Source: Thomas A. Kochan and Harry C. Katz, *Collective Bargaining and Industrial Relations* (Homewood, Ill.: Irwin, 1988), p. 74. Reprinted by permission.

lopsided. A third reason was the economic disaster wrought by the Great Depression, and the New Deal efforts to engineer a recovery.

Three major pieces of labor legislation enacted during the 1920s and 1930s have withstood constitutional challenge: the Railway Labor Act of 1926, the Norris-LaGuardia Act of 1932, and the National Labor Relations Act of 1935. (See Table 15.3 for significant events in the statutory law period.) The Railway Labor Act, as amended, gave railroad and airline employees the right to form unions, bargain collectively, and strike. The Norris-LaGuardia Act established severe limitations on the judicial issuance of injunctions to halt labor activity; it also outlawed the yellow-dog contract. The National Labor Relations Act (NLRA), known as the Wagner Act, gave nonagricultural (and nonrail and nonair) employees the right to form unions, to bargain collectively, and to strike, among other things.[17]

The Wagner Act The Wagner Act has been the bedrock of American labor relations public policy. Its first section is a declaration of policy to the effect that the

TABLE 15.3 Major Labor Laws

1926	Railway Labor Act	Railway workers are allowed to organize and bargain collectively.
1932	Norris-LaGuardia Act	Federal courts are severely restricted in issuing injunctions against unions; yellow-dog contracts "shall not be enforceable."
1935	NLRA (Wagner Act)	Establishes organizing rights, unfair (employer) labor practices, and the National Labor Relations Board.
1947	Taft-Hartley Act	Amends the NLRA. Adds unfair union labor practices, Sec. 8(b).
1959	Landrum-Griffin Act	Establishes a bill of rights for union members. Requires financial disclosing by unions. Lists guidelines for trusteeships and elections.
1962	Executive Order 10988	Encourages public sector bargaining. Requires maintenance of management rights. Orders added by Kennedy in 1963, Nixon in 1969 (Executive Order 11491). Followed by passage of state laws giving employees of local and state governments the right to bargain.
1978	Civil Service Reform Act	Sets up the current system for federal employee unionization, bargaining, and impasse resolution.

Source: Adapted from Thomas A. Kochan and Harry C. Katz, *Collective Bargaining and Industrial Relations* (Homewood, Ill.: Irwin, 1988), pp. 74–75. Reprinted by permission.

"protection by law of the right of employees to organize and bargain collectively safeguards commerce." Other major provisions of the act include the following:

- Section 2 defines various terms, such as *employers* and *employees*. The law covers employees who work for employers engaged in interstate commerce who are not covered by the Railway Labor Act and who do not work for the federal government, states, or localities, or in the agricultural sector. Managerial and supervisory employees are excluded.
- Section 3 establishes the National Labor Relations Board (NLRB) to administer the act. The board is a five-person independent agency whose members are appointed by the president, with the advice and consent of the Senate, for five-year terms.
- Section 7 gives employees the "right to self-organization, to form, join, or assist labor organizations, to bargain collectively through representatives of their own choosing, or to engage in other concerted activities for the purpose of collective bargaining."
- Section 8 establishes a set of unfair labor practices by management. These are shown in the left side of Table 15.4.
- Section 9 provides for the election of representatives of employees as bargaining agents and holds that "representatives designated or selected for the purpose of collective bargaining by the majority of the employees in a unit appropriate for such purposes, shall be the exclusive representatives of all the employees in such unit for the purpose of collective bargaining in respect to rates of pay, wages, hours of employment, or other conditions of employment."

The Taft-Hartley Act After the adoption of the Wagner Act, union activity rose sharply. In 1946, a peak year for strikes, some 4,985 strikes caused the loss of 116 million person-days of productivity. This disruption set the stage for the passage of the Labor Management Relations Act in 1947. Known as the Taft-Hartley Act, this legislation shifted the balance of power between unions and management. Many politicians, employers, and even some unions had felt that the Wagner Act went too far in regulating and limiting management while leaving union actions unconstrained. In response, Taft-Hartley specified several unfair labor practices of unions, created the Federal Mediation and Conciliation Service to aid in the resolution of disputes, and provided a mechanism for handling strikes that create a national emergency.[18] Unfair labor practices of unions appear on the right side of Table 15.4.

Public Sector Unionization

Although there had been isolated instances of public sector unionization since the 1800s, most public sector employees did not receive the right to bargain collectively with their employers until the 1960s. Public sector employees were explic-

TABLE 15.4 Unfair Labor Practices

By Management (Wagner Act)	*By Union (Taft-Hartley Act)*
• Interfere with, restrain, or coerce employees in the exercise of their rights to organize, bargain collectively, and engage in other concerted activities for their mutual aid or protection. • Dominate or interfere with the formation or administration of any labor organization or contribute financial or other support to it. • Encourage or discourage membership in any labor organization by discrimination with regard to hiring or tenure or conditions of employment, subject to an exception for valid union-security agreements. • Discharge or otherwise discriminate against an employee because he [or she] has filed charges or given testimony under the Act. • Refuse to bargain collectively with the majority representative of his [or her] employees.	• Restrain or coerce employees in the exercise of their rights under the Act. • Restrain or coerce an employer in the selection of his [or her] bargaining or grievance representative. • Cause or attempt to cause an employer to discriminate against an employee on account of his membership or non-membership in a labor organization, subject to an exception for valid union-shop agreements. • Refuse to bargain collectively (in good faith) with an employer if the union has been designated as bargaining agent by a majority of the employees. • Induce or encourage employees to stop work for an object of forcing an employer or self-employed person to join a union or of forcing an employer or other person to stop doing business with any other person (secondary boycott). • Induce or encourage employees to stop work for an object of forcing an employer to recognize and bargain with the union where another union has been certified as bargaining agent (strike against a certification). • Induce or encourage employees to stop work for an object of forcing an employer to assign particular work to members of the union instead of to members of another union (jurisdictional strike). • Charge an excessive or discriminatory fee as a condition to becoming a member of the union. • Cause or attempt to cause an employer to pay for services that are not performed or not to be performed (featherbedding).

Source: Adapted with permission from *Primer of Labor Relations*, 24th Edition, by John J. Kenny and Linda G. Kahn, pages 1–3. Copyright 1989 by The Bureau of National Affairs, Inc., Washington, D.C.

itly excluded from coverage under the Wagner Act, for two reasons. First, the doctrine of sovereignty stated that public employee unions would interfere to an unacceptable degree with the sovereign power inherent in a legitimate government. Second, the "special status" concept suggested that public employees already enjoyed better benefits and more job security than private sector workers, and hence they had no need for union protection.[19]

In the 1960s and 1970s, public employment grew rapidly, and some financially hard-pressed cities laid off public employees, a virtually unprecedented occurrence. Thus, the perceived need and desire for union protection of public employees increased. A series of executive orders by Presidents Kennedy, Nixon, and Ford expanded the rights of federal employees to organize and bargain on a limited range of topics. The Civil Service Reform Act of 1978 replaced the executive orders, making the Federal Labor Relations Authority (FLRA) responsible for overseeing certification elections and investigating unfair labor practice charges in the federal sector. Unions may bargain on a variety of issues, but not on wages, retirement, life and health insurance, and discipline for national security reasons. Strikes by federal employees are illegal, and negotiation impasses are resolved with the aid of the Federal Mediation and Conciliation Service, by arbitration, or by the Federal Impasse Panel.

All employees of state and local governments have the right to form unions, but only thirty-one states require employers to bargain with such unions. Thirty-nine states forbid strikes by public employee unions, whereas most other states limit the right to strike to nonessential employees. A number of problems in nonfederal public employee labor relations remain unresolved. For instance, some localities deny the right to strike but do not provide effective dispute resolution alternatives, and some legislatures fail to allocate the funds needed to fulfill the terms of properly negotiated contracts with public employee unions.

Table 15.5 presents the major differences between private and public sector collective bargaining. A major difference relates to the nature of the bargaining process. Unlike the private sector, in which collective bargaining is bilateral in nature, bargaining in the public sector is typically multilateral, with many groups other than the union and the employer exerting pressures on the bargaining process. Another significant difference relates to the fact that in the public sector collective bargaining is critically intertwined with other governmental functions, such as budgeting, which involves several other parties and interests not found in the private sector.

WHY PEOPLE JOIN UNIONS

Why do some people belong to unions and others do not? Some people never have the chance to make the choice. Others have the opportunity to join and must decide whether or not to do so. The first situation pertains to the supply (or lack) of union services. The second involves a direct calculation of the costs and benefits of unionization.

TABLE 15.5 Differences Between Public and Private Sector Collective Bargaining

	Private Sector	*Public Sector*
Statutory Framework	Uniform federal statutes (National Labor Relations Act, Railway Labor Act).	A federal statute for federal government employees plus numerous state and local statutes.
Unionization Trends	Gradually declining number of organized workers. Currently 16 percent unionization.	Growth during the 1960s to mid-1970s, followed by stabilization. Currently over 40 percent unionization.
Bargaining Power of the Employees	In the event of a strike by one firm, other firms can continue providing services. Less potential bargaining power for private-sector employees.	Public services may be unavailable or in limited supply during a strike. Greater potential bargaining power for government employees.
Negotiations Climate	Negotiators usually have full authority to agree to settlements without consulting higher authorities. Identity of the employer having final authority is well defined.	Negotiators may be restricted in their ability to make bargaining concessions. Concessions may be dependent on legislative approval. The identity of the employer having final authority is not well defined.
Third-Party Interests	Because alternative goods and services are available, consumers and other constituents are less concerned about the prospects of a work stoppage. Little pressure is placed on negotiators by "outside" parties.	Constituents are generally interested in the outcome of a strike because alternative services are not readily available. As a result, more pressure may be exerted by taxpayers and special-interest groups to quickly and, perhaps, prematurely resolve an impasse. Diverse political interests often affect bargaining.
Bargaining Structure	Ranging from highly centralized (employer associations) to highly decentralized (local negotiations).	Generally highly decentralized. Almost all bargaining is done on a single-employer basis.
Scope of Bargaining	Broad scope of mandatory bargaining topics.	A narrow scope of bargaining topics in many instances.
Right to Strike	Broad right to engage in economic strikes and other types of work stoppages.	Limited or no right to engage in work stoppages.
Impasse Resolution Procedures	Primarily mediation.	Mediation, fact-finding, interest arbitration (in which the arbitrator determines the final provisions of the collective bargaining agreement if the parties are unable to reach an agreement).

TABLE 15.5 Differences Between Public and Private Sector Collective Bargaining (*cont.*)

	Private Sector	*Public Sector*
Contract Provisions	Relatively few legal restrictions on contract provisions. Contracts are of several years duration.	Contracts are often pre-empted by civil service statutes and regulations. Contracts are of shorter duration.
Contract Administration	Influenced primarily by the terms of the collective bargaining agreement.	Influenced by the collective bargaining agreement as well as civil service regulations.

Source: Reprinted with the permission of Macmillan Publishing Company from *Collective Bargaining and Labor Relations* by Terry L. Leap. Copyright © 1991 by Macmillan Publishing Company.

In the simplest sense, workers who have a choice will weigh the expected costs and benefits of joining a union. They will join when the expected benefits outweigh the expected costs.

Benefits of Union Membership

A union may provide material, social, and political benefits.[20] The first category is undoubtedly the most important. That is, unions offer job security (and hence the protection of income), higher wages, greater benefits (e.g., better retirement and health insurance), and better occupational safety and health protection. These are the benefits that unions emphasize during their campaigns to gain members.[21]

Social benefits may be derived from belonging to an organization of fellow workers. Some individuals value the opportunity to join and interact with others on an informal and formal basis in pursuit of common goals. In the political category, union membership offers the opportunity to participate in establishing important terms and conditions of employment, to gain sufficient power to ensure fair treatment by management, to influence lawmaking bodies to adopt prolabor legislation, or even to advance within the governing structure of the union itself.

Costs of Union Membership

The principal costs associated with unions are economic: unions collect dues from their members to cover the costs of their activities. A typical union member's dues might amount to the equivalent of two hours' pay per month. Unions may also charge initiation fees or special assessments.[22] In the late 1980s, the United Steelworkers' dues were raised to an average of $28 per month. Some unions, however, charge much less. The American Federation of Government Employees charged a maximum of $8.35 per month in 1986.[23] Other costs of union membership that might be considered include the potential loss in income because of a strike.

Motivation to Join

The expectancy theory of motivation can shed light on why individuals do or do not join a union. As shown in Figure 15.3, individuals first consider the likelihood that organizing efforts will result in the actual formation of a union with representation rights in their workplace. This is called expectancy. Second, they consider the likelihood that having a union will lead to certain benefits and costs. Benefits and costs vary in terms of their valence, or desirability to individuals.[24]

The concept of **union instrumentality** has proved to be very powerful in differentiating union joiners from nonjoiners. That is, employees appear much more likely to join a union if they perceive it as being instrumental in attaining desired goals. Typically, these goals have to do with workplace issues, such as wages, hours, and benefits, potentially obtainable through collective bargaining. As one author put it, to distinguish between people who would and would not support unionization, "we must first identify the job-related concerns of workers, and their views of the instrumentality of unionization as a strategy for improving their

FIGURE 15.3 The Decision to Support or Oppose a Union: An Expectancy Theory Model

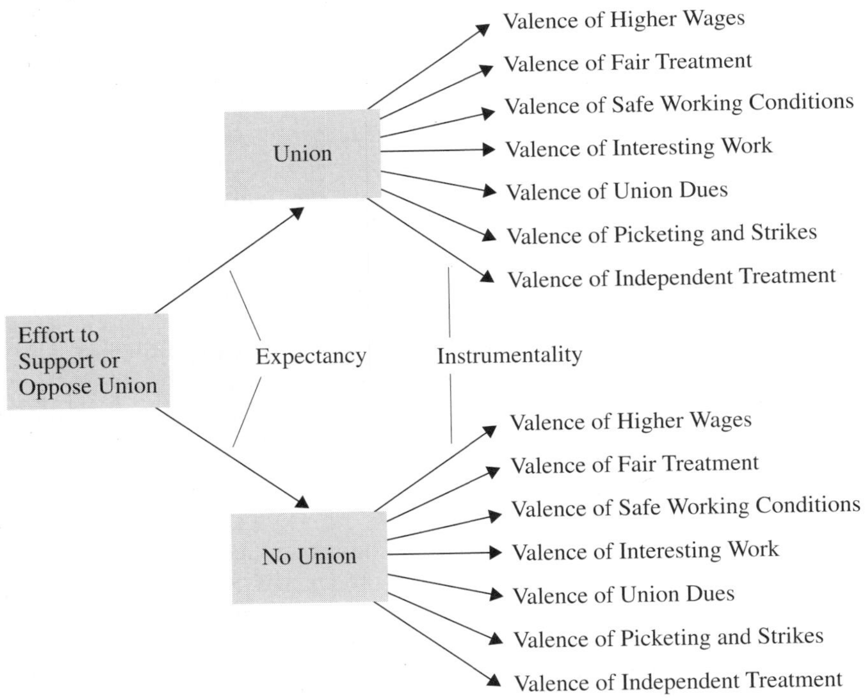

Effort to Support or Oppose Union
Union
No Union
Expectancy
Instrumentality
Valence of Higher Wages
Valence of Fair Treatment
Valence of Safe Working Conditions
Valence of Interesting Work
Valence of Union Dues
Valence of Picketing and Strikes
Valence of Independent Treatment
Valence of Higher Wages
Valence of Fair Treatment
Valence of Safe Working Conditions
Valence of Interesting Work
Valence of Union Dues
Valence of Picketing and Strikes
Valence of Independent Treatment

Source: Adapted from R. Allen/T. Keaveny, *Contemporary Labor Relations*, © 1988 by Addison Wesley Publishing Company, Inc. Reprinted with permission of the publisher.

well-being versus the perceived costs or negative consequences of unionization."[25] One study found a strong correlation between workers' perceptions of the "work place instrumentality" of unions and pro-union voting.[26] Employees are also more likely to vote for a union if their wages are relatively low, they are dissatisfied with the financial rewards from their job, and they believe management's administrative procedures are unfair.[27]

In short, employees may join or refuse to join a union for many reasons. In particular, the more instrumental unions are perceived to be in attaining desired objectives, through either collective bargaining or political action, the more likely individuals are to support them.

THE CERTIFICATION PROCESS

The amended National Labor Relations Act establishes procedures by which employees may secure representation through an exclusive **bargaining representative** (union). The procedures involve the formal recognition of the representative.

The process starts when either a union representative contacts a potential target group of employees or the employees themselves contact the union and inquire about the possibility of organizing their workplace. At this point the union has to analyze the target plant, assess the possibility of success in organizing the workers, and, if it decides to proceed, start the initial advances to reach the employees.

Authorization cards are then signed. These cards serve as evidence of the desire of employees to form a union. Under the NLRA at least 30 percent of the employees must sign the cards for the National Labor Relations Board to consider a petition for an election. However, most union organizers do not petition for an election unless they have managed to obtain signatures from more than 50 percent of employees during the authorization card campaign. The union's rationale is that during the election campaign it is likely to face employer opposition, which could convince some workers not to support the union. Thus, if the union receives less than 50 percent of employee support, it may drop the current organizing effort or start a new authorization card campaign.

If support for the union during the authorization card campaign exceeds 50 percent, the union typically seeks recognition through the process of **certification,** which usually involves the election of the representing union by employees within a proposed bargaining unit. In the simplest case, a proposed representative of employees can approach management and request to be recognized as the exclusive bargaining agent, claiming that it represents a majority of members in a proposed bargaining unit. If management grants such recognition, it will be legally required to bargain in good faith over the terms and conditions of employment. But if management rebuffs the request, then the process of certifying the representative through an election will begin.[28] This process may be broken down into several stages, described below and also shown in Figure 15.4.

FIGURE 15.4 The Certification Process

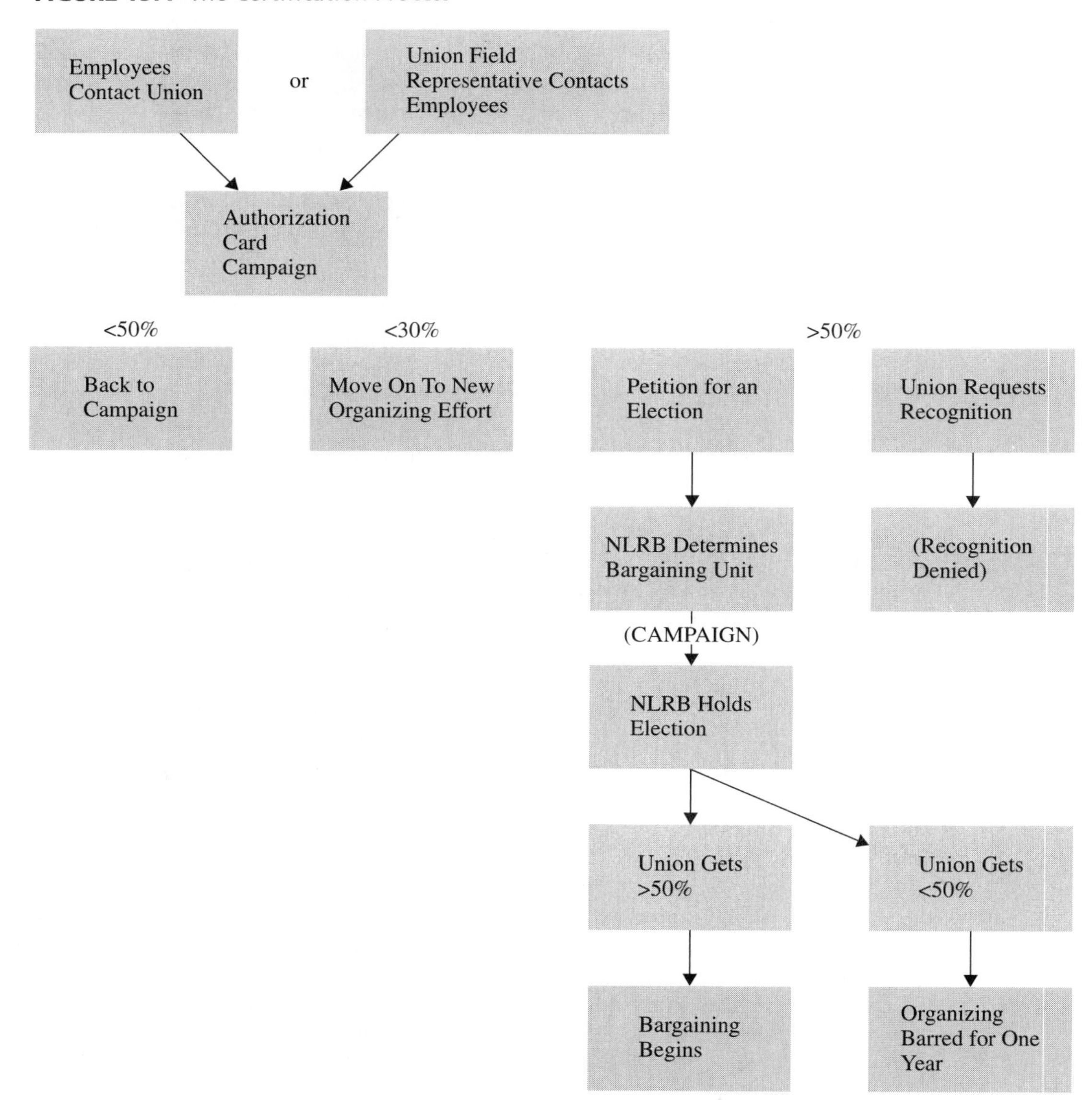

Petitions

Employees first petition the National Labor Relations Board requesting recognition of a bargaining representative, which may be a new or pre-existing union of employees. Typically, groups of employees or unions make the formal petition. Employers are also permitted to petition for a recognition election if they are confronted with competing representational claims (that is, if two or more competing unions are being proposed for the same group of employees).[29]

NLRB Determinations

The National Labor Relations Board must make several determinations before it will hold a recognition election. When it receives a petition, its first step is to determine whether it has jurisdiction over the matter (i.e., whether the employees and employer are covered by the National Labor Relations Act). Second, the NLRB will investigate the degree of interest in the election among the employees in the proposed bargaining unit. Its rule is that at least 30 percent of the employees in the unit must have expressed interest in having the union recognized for bargaining purposes. Note that they must have stated a preference for a specific union as an exclusive representative, not just asked for a representation election in general. Such interest is manifested through the signing of authorization cards. An employee who signs such a card authorizes the proposed representative to be his or her exclusive bargaining representative.

Perhaps the most difficult set of determinations involves the appropriateness of a proposed bargaining unit. The bargaining unit is made up of all employees who will be eligible to join the union and who will be covered by the union contract. The National Labor Relations Act requires that the NLRB give employees "the fullest freedom in exercising the rights guaranteed" in deciding representation cases, but it also restricts eligibility to certain types of employees. The law prohibits managers and supervisors from belonging to a bargaining unit. It also prohibits plant guards from being in the same unit with other employees, and it gives professional employees the right to remove themselves from a bargaining unit consisting of other employees.[30]

These are not the only considerations. The NLRB also looks for a "community of interests" among employees in a proposed unit with respect to wages, hours, skills, and working conditions. Furthermore, it may take into account the history of past bargaining representation, the interaction and degree of interdependence among departments, and the arrangement of labor relations functions within a firm (i.e., whether they are decentralized or centralized).

Some recent developments in the health care sector illustrate the importance of the issue of bargaining unit determination. In a 1991 case, *American Hospital Association* v. *NLRB,* the U.S. Supreme Court upheld the NLRB's use of its rule-making powers to define appropriate bargaining units for workers in the nation's private acute care hospitals.[31] The eight generic bargaining units are (1) registered nurses, (2) physicians, (3) professionals other than registered nurses and physicians; (4) technical employees, (5) skilled maintenance employees, (6) business office clerical employees, (7) guards, and (8) nonprofessional employees except technical employees, skilled maintenance employees, business office clerical employees, and guards.

The significance of the American Hospital Association's decision is twofold. First, the decision endorsed the agency's power to set a priori rules governing appropriate bargaining units within particular industries. Following this decision, the board can set predetermined bargaining units in certain industries, instead of determining bargaining units on a case-by-case basis. Second, the decision should have a positive effect on unions' organizing efforts. When the appropriate bargaining units are defined in advance, the organizing efforts will not be delayed by questions as to the bargaining unit determination. Since, in general, legal delays work to the employer's advantage, unions should benefit from this ruling.

Elections

If the NLRB's preliminary investigations reveal that a recognition election is warranted, it will approach the parties (the proposed union and employer) and seek an informal agreement as to the conditions under which an election will be held. If the parties agree on the time, places, and eligible voters, then an informal election occurs. It is informal in the sense that the parties have agreed not to ask the NLRB to conduct a potentially protracted formal hearing to investigate questions that might be in dispute (such as whether there is real interest in a union or whether the proposed unit is appropriate). The parties may agree to either of two types of informal agreements. In a **consent election,** they agree to accept the NLRB's regional director's certification of the election results. In other words, they will not appeal to the NLRB itself to review the director's decision. In a **stipulated election,** the parties do not relinquish their right to appeal the director's decision to the NLRB.[32]

If the parties cannot agree to hold an informal election, then the NLRB will conduct a formal investigation to determine if an election is warranted. After a hearing, the board may order that a formal, **directed election** take place.

The vast majority of elections are informal ones, particularly of the stipulated type. Comparatively few are directed. This means that most elections are held without a formal hearing and the long delays that result from a formal procedure.[33]

Election Outcomes

Recognition elections are conducted by secret ballot. The choice may be between a proposed representative and no representative, or between more than one representative and no representative. The option that receives a majority of the votes cast wins the election. If there are more than two options (that is, the choice is between more than one proposed representative and no representative) and no one receives a majority, then a runoff election is held between the two highest

TABLE 15.6 Results of Representation Elections, 1973–1988

Year	*Total Elections*	*Union Victories*	*Percent Union Victories*
1973	9,389	4,786	51.1%
1974	8,958	4,425	50.0%
1975	8,577	4,138	49.2%
1976	8,638	4,159	48.1%
1977	9,484	4,363	46.0%
1978	8,240	3,791	46.0%
1979	8,043	3,623	45.0%
1980	8,198	3,744	45.7%
1981	7,512	3,234	43.1%
1982	5,116	2,064	40.3%
1983	4,405	1,895	43.0%
1984	4,436	1,861	42.0%
1985	4,614	1,956	42.4%
1986	4,520	1,951	43.2%
1987	4,069	1,788	43.9%
1988	4,153	1,921	46.3%

Source: Adapted from the *Fifty-Third Annual Report of the National Labor Relations Board for the Fiscal Year Ended September 30, 1988* (Washington, D.C.: Government Printing Office, 1988).

vote getters. Table 15.6 shows the percentage of union victories in certification elections.

Conduct During an Organizing Campaign

As previously noted, it is considered an unfair labor practice for either unions or employers to violate Section 7 of the National Labor Relations Act (as amended), which gives employees the right to form unions and to engage in collective activities or to refrain from doing so. In numerous decisions, the National Labor Relations Board and federal courts have interpreted the meaning of these provisions, thereby regulating various aspects of the parties' conduct. With respect to the certification process itself, the NLRB and the courts have made decisions relevant to how all parties conduct themselves during an organizing campaign.

To what extent does someone arguing for unionization have the right to obtain access to employees in order to deliver that message? The answer turns substantially on the employment status of the messenger. The Supreme Court has ruled that employers have the right to severely restrict nonemployees' access to employees. In other words, employers may bar nonemployees (such as professional union organizers) from their premises, provided two conditions are met. First, nonemployees must have reasonable access to the employees through some other means, such as print or electronic media or social functions away from the workplace. In addition, the employer must enforce a general ban on nonemployee solicitation of employees at the worksite, a ban that is not selectively applied to unions. For instance, a company that permits nonemployees into the workplace to solicit for charities or political causes would have a hard time denying union organizers similar access to employees. Pro-union employees, however, have much more extensive rights to approach their peers at work. They may carry the union message to employees during nonworking periods in nonworking areas—for instance, during lunch time in the cafeteria.[34]

To what extent are employees and employers free to express their views regarding unionization during the course of a campaign to unionize? Section 8(c) of the amended National Labor Relations Act establishes a general principle that "the expressing of views, argument, or opinion, or the dissemination thereof, whether in written, printed, graphic, or visual form, shall not constitute or be evidence of an unfair labor practice . . . if such expression contains no threat of reprisal or force or promise of benefit." For example, during the campaign, an employer may not promise to raise wages if employees reject a union; nor may he or she threaten to reduce wages if the union wins the recognition election. Nor may the employer grant certain benefits otherwise unplanned that are timed in such a way as to influence the campaign.[35]

A related issue has to do with false claims or charges. The NLRB has changed its position several times. It first held that it would overturn elections "where there has been misrepresentation or other similar campaign trickery, which involves a substantial departure from the truth, at a time which prevents the other party or parties from making an effective reply, so that the misrepresentation, whether deliberate or not, may reasonably be expected to have a significant impact on the election."[36] After several flip-flops, in 1982, in the *Midland National Life Insurance* case, the NLRB reversed its original position.[37] The parties now have considerable latitude in terms of what they can say during a recognition campaign as long as threats or promises of benefits are not involved. Table 15.7 shows the issues that management and labor raise most frequently in their appeals to employees before a certification election.

The pre-election campaigns conducted by the union and management can be very important. One study found that the average union representation election was decided by a margin of eight or fewer votes.[38] Thus, successfully and legally influencing just a few voters can make a significant difference in the election. However, extensive unfair labor practices by either party during the campaign can cause the NLRB regional director to overturn the election.

Decertification

The amended National Labor Relations Act provides for the decertification of union representatives. Employees who are dissatisfied with their union may pe-

TABLE 15.7 Issues in Pre-Election Campaigns

Management Issues	*Percent of Campaigns*	*Union Issues*	*Percent of Campaigns*
Improvements not dependent on unionization	85	Union will prevent unfairness, set up grievance procedure/seniority system	82
Wages good, equal to/better than under union contract	82	Union will improve unsatisfactory wages	79
Financial costs of union dues outweigh gains	79	Union strength will provide employees with voice in wages, working conditions	79
Union is outsider	79	Union, not outsider, bargains for what employees want	73
Get facts before deciding, employer will provide facts and accept employee decision	76	Union has obtained gains elsewhere	70
If union wins, strike may follow	70	Union will improve unsatisfactory sick leave/insurance	64
Loss of benefits may follow union win	67	Dues/initiation fees are reasonable	64
Strikers will lose wages, lose more than gain	67	Union will improve unsatisfactory vacations/holidays/pensions	61
Unions not concerned with employee welfare	67	Employer promises/good treatment may not be continued without union	61
Strike may lead to loss of jobs	64	Employees choose union leaders	55
Employer has treated employees fairly/well	60	Employer will seek to persuade/frighten employees to vote against union	55
Employees should be certain to vote	54	No strike without vote by members	55
		Union will improve unsatisfactory working conditions	52
		Employees have legal right to engage in union activity	52

Source: From *Labor Relations: Development, Structure and Process,* Fifth Edition by John A. Fossum. Copyright © 1992 by Richard D. Irwin, Inc., Homewood, IL.

tition the NLRB to hold a **decertification election.** Since the 1950s, the number of decertification elections held annually has increased substantially; in 1990, for example, a total of 558 decertification elections were held, and unions lost in 73.8 percent of them.[39]

Labor-Management Joint Committees: An Unfair Labor Practice?

An issue that is of particular importance to those in human resource management concerns the status of labor-management joint committees established by an employer in a nonunionized workplace. Are those committees a violation of Section 8(a)(2) of the NLRA, which makes it illegal for an employer to "dominate or interfere with the formation or administration of any labor organization or contribute financial or other support to it"? The problem is particularly acute when a union attempting to organize a given facility argues that the employer has violated Section 8(a)(2) by establishing the joint committee. Employee committees have been established all over the United States to deal with a variety of issues, such as productivity, health and safety, and quality of work life.

Under Section 2(5) of the NLRA, a labor organization is defined as "any organization of any kind, or any agency or employee representation committee or plan, in which employees participate and which exists for the purpose, in whole or in part, of dealing with employees concerning grievances, labor disputes, wages, rates of pay, hours of employment, or conditions of work." A broad reading of this section will appear to include most kinds of employee involvement programs, such as joint employee/employer committees and quality circles. A more restrictive reading will probably outlaw only those programs that amount to clear domination by the employer of the employees' organization, which has the effect of limiting the employees' ability to freely choose union representation.

In deciding on the legality of employee participation programs, two questions must be resolved. First, are joint committees labor organizations as defined under Section 2(5), and second, are these "labor organizations" employer-dominated organizations as prohibited by Section 8(a)(2)?

As to the first question, several court and NLRB decisions have given a broad reading to Section 2(5). The main thrust of these decisions is that committees formed for the purpose of discussing problems of mutual interests, including grievances and other employee problems, could be considered labor organizations.[40]

In a few recent cases, however, several courts have recognized that employee involvement programs can be legitimate avenues of communication between the employer and the employees, and thus not necessarily a violation of the NLRA. Participation programs intended to identify problem areas and to discuss resolutions to these problems might not necessarily be considered labor organizations.[41]

As to the issue of whether employee participation programs constitute an employer-dominated labor organization, the question turns on whether there must be a showing of actual domination or whether a showing of potential domination is enough to make the employee involvement program illegal. Traditionally, the fact that the employer has created the program, set up the program agenda, and decided who is to participate in the program makes the program an employer-dominated one, regardless of whether domination actually occurred.

Some courts, however, have required an actual showing of employer domination for a violation of Section 8(a)(2) to occur. In the view of these courts, for an employee participation program to be considered a violation of the NLRA, the employer must have actually used the program as a way to thwart union organizing efforts or otherwise coerce the employees on their free choice of union representation.[42]

In short, supporters of the position that joint committees in nonunionized settings constitute employer-dominated labor organizations argue that they fear employers will use the committees as a means of thwarting unions' organizing efforts. Opponents argue that in a new era of labor-management cooperation employers value joint committees not as an anti-union tool but as part of their business strategy to survive in an increasingly competitive business environment.[43]

PREPARING FOR NEGOTIATIONS

Once a union has been certified as a bargaining representative, it has the right to approach management for the purpose of negotiating a contract for members of the bargaining unit with respect to "rates of pay, wages, hours of employment, or other conditions of employment."[44] (See the International Perspective box for information on how unions influence the terms and conditions of employment under Australia's labor relations system.) Employers and unions have a mutual obligation to bargain in good faith toward the settlement of a collective-bargaining contract. Before negotiations or the renegotiation of a contract about to expire, both parties have an opportunity to plan. This section reviews the types of planning the parties might contemplate and the elements of basic planning involved in preparing for negotiations.

Types of Planning

The first type of planning that may be associated with negotiating a contract is *strategic* in nature.[45] It may be defined as the process of setting long-term (e.g., five- or ten-year) goals for the organization and determining how to set collective bargaining objectives so as to support those broader goals. For instance, a firm facing global competition might set the goal of reducing labor costs by 10 percent during the next five years. Accordingly, it might define negotiating objectives not only for the upcoming contract, but for the next round as well, in order to make this broader goal realizable.

Tactical planning involves developing short-range tactics aimed at achieving longer-term objectives. For instance, if a firm with a history of labor relations strife has set itself a long-term goal of avoiding strikes, it might work toward this objective by proposing that negotiations continue even after the contract has expired if the parties cannot reach an agreement sooner. This tactic attempts to break a pattern of strike activity, at least in the short run, in the hope that the parties will become used to a less confrontational approach to resolving differences.

Administrative planning concerns such matters as the assignment of negotiating roles and responsibilities—that is, dividing the tasks among the members of a bargaining team. These are nontrivial decisions, as the negotiating skills and substantive expertise of the participants can affect the outcome of negotiations.

Elements of Planning

Planning for upcoming negotiations may include four major elements: setting goals, analyzing the issues, setting priorities among bargaining issues, and getting

INTERNATIONAL PERSPECTIVE

Industrial Relations in Australia: The Award System

Australia has developed a unique industrial relations system which is quite different from the system used in the United States. The Australian system is much more centralized. Few agreements are negotiated at the enterprise level, between a single company and the union representing its employees. Instead, nationwide agreements, called *awards*, are established or approved by the Industrial Relations Commission. This government body considers the demands of a national union and the response of the relevant employer association, and then imposes an arbitrated settlement that applies to all employees in that industry or occupation. A single employer may be covered by one award or by several. For instance, an automobile plant may be covered by metal worker, painter, drafter, mechanical fitter, security guard, cleaner, and clerical awards, among others.

Awards contain a remarkable amount of detail considering that they are national in scope and apply to hundreds of worksites with differing needs. They also seem quite generous compared with typical U.S. conditions. For instance, awards often cover hours of work (a maximum of forty hours per week, which for day shift workers must occur between 7:00 and 5:30), sick leave accrual and use procedures (five days in the first year, increasing thereafter), vacation entitlements (commonly four weeks, with vacation pay at 117.5 percent of the regular rate, on the assumption that it costs more to vacation than to live in a regular fashion), long-service leave (thirteen weeks after fifteen years of service), tool or uniform allowances, rest breaks, bereavement leave, shift premiums (usually 15 percent), weekend premiums (often time and a half for the first two hours on Saturday, then double time; double time on Sunday; and double time and a half on public holidays, regardless of hours already worked during the week), time off with pay to donate blood to the Red Cross, and special rates for having to work in very hot or cold conditions.

About 90 percent of Australian employees are covered by awards. Awards are generally in force for three years but in fact are renegotiated more frequently. The dispute is always considered to be legally open, and either party can propose changes at any time. In some years, there is a "National Wage Case," which may provide automatic raises for a large number of awards.

Under this centralized system, direct negotiations between unions and management need not occur but may in some cases. For instance, unions and specific employers can negotiate regarding over-award payments. There is presently a move toward enterprise level agreements rather than national awards, but it is in its infancy. There is also increasing emphasis on tying pay raises to documented changes in productivity, widening craft lines, and multiskilling (cross-training), as Australia tries to become more competitive in the world market.

One of the major differences between the Australian system and the U.S. system is the pervasiveness and power of trade unions, regardless of employee wishes. An example is provided by SPC Ltd., a fruit canning company. In late 1990, the union stewards and employees of this financially troubled firm overwhelmingly approved a temporary wage cut to below award rates in order to save their jobs and help their employer survive. National labor leaders went to the Industrial Relations Commission against the wishes of the employees, in an attempt to prohibit the employees from accepting less than award conditions. The national union felt that this precedent would undermine gains won for employees nationwide. Ultimately, both sides won: the company saved nearly $2,000,000 in labor costs by dropping a number of over-award provisions, but the national union officials succeeded in preventing minimum award conditions from being violated. The SPC case is considered a landmark in modern Australian industrial relations because it generated great public sympathy for the company and its embattled employees and brought the issue of enterprise bargaining into the news in a positive light.

Sources: Richard B. Sappy and Maryanne Winter, *Australian Industrial Relations Practice* (Melbourne: Longman Cheshire Pty. 1992), Raymond J. Stone, *Human Resource Management* (Brisbane: Wiley, 1991; John A. Mathews, "Theoretical Perspectives on Enterprise and Award Restructuring in Australia," *Asia Pacific Human Resource Management,* November 1990, pp. 30–39; "Industrial Strategy Bears Fruit at SPC," *Australian Financial Review,* October 28, 1991, p. 14.

to know the bargaining opponent. Setting goals should not be confused with developing a wish list. The process should be more exact and realistic. The goals set for upcoming negotiations, however, may vary in specificity, and they may be tied to other organizational objectives. Often they will involve ranges of acceptable solutions. Upper and lower limits can be defined by both the management and the union. These limits will depend on the parties' bargaining objectives, expectations, and resources. For example, profitability and growth issues are critical factors in management's selection of an upper limit.[46] Similarly, concerns about employment levels and the ability to endure a strike figure high for the union when it sets its bargaining ranges. Figure 15.5 illustrates bargaining ranges for a few bargaining issues. Note the area where the management's and the union's ranges overlap. Resolution of these issues through negotiation is likely. Proposals that fall outside the area where the management's and the union's ranges overlap will presumably be rejected. These ranges, however, may change as negotiations proceed, particularly if unexpected concessions are given or received on other issues.

Analyzing the issues includes identifying the extent to which particular issues are likely to cause problems in negotiations and the reasons that they are particularly troublesome. Other aspects of issue analysis include examining the parties' prior experience with respect to specific issues, collecting and studying information on the costs and benefits of various proposals, and examining recent precedents and trends in contract settlements at other firms in similar situations.

Setting priorities involves crucial decisions on which there may be considerable disagreement within the employer's or the union's negotiating team. Which issues are most important? Which items will not be negotiated away at the bargaining table? Priorities can be set in many ways: by having team members simply rank the issues in order of importance, by holding group meetings in which differences and intensities of opinion are aired, or by polling individuals as to their preferences.[47] Priority setting is particularly important for the union, since any agreement it negotiates must be ratified in some way—often by a vote of the full

FIGURE 15.5 Settlement Ranges of Management and Union

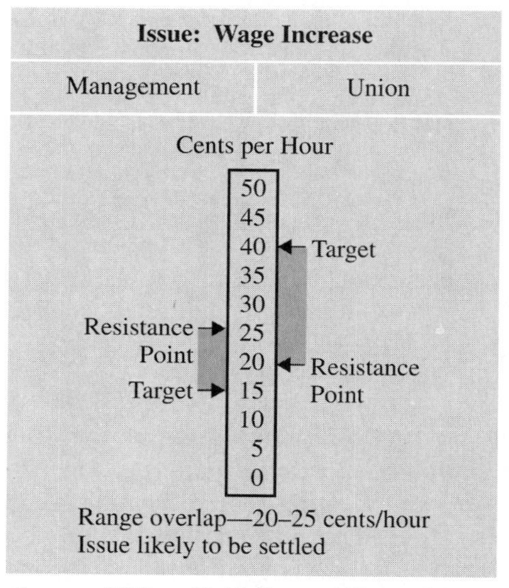

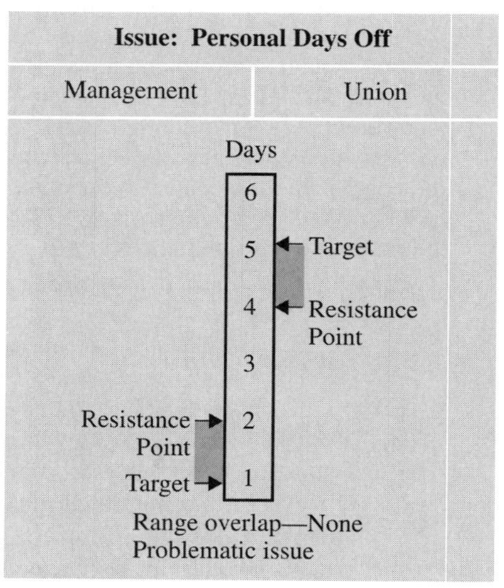

Source: William H. Holley and Kenneth M. Jennings, *The Labor Relations Process*, 4th ed., 1991. Chicago: The Dryden Press, p. 175.

membership. Union negotiators who neglect the preferences of members covered by the contract may weaken the chances of ratification.

The fourth element of planning is to understand the negotiating opponents. What are their organizational, occupational, and demographic characteristics? Is their negotiating style confrontational or accommodative? What are their likely settlement ranges? What are their needs and internal political tensions? What kind of decision-making authority does the negotiating team have?

Figure 15.6 illustrates some of the issues that a multi-plant organization has to consider during the planning states of the collective bargaining process.

COLLECTIVE BARGAINING

Collective bargaining in the United States is a comparatively decentralized phenomenon. Thousands of agreements are in place. With so many different employers and unions involved across the country, bargaining relationships are understandably highly varied. There are, however, some distinctive structures and types of bargaining that help to provide a frame of reference for ordering these diverse relationships. This section discusses the basic types of bargaining structures, the characteristics of the negotiation process, the types of issues of bargaining that arise between and within parties, and the types of issues over which the parties typically negotiate.

Structure of Bargaining

The structure of bargaining refers to the range of persons covered or affected by a current or planned collective bargaining agreement. The formal structure consists of those employers and employees who are legally tied to the contract under negotiation. The informal structure includes those who may be materially affected by the negotiations. Often a settlement between two parties sets a pattern for subsequent settlements among many of the employers and unions in that industry.[48] For instance, such so-called **pattern bargaining** occurs in the automobile manufacturing industry. The United Auto Workers typically focuses on negotiating a settlement with one of the big domestic manufacturers, calling a strike against the target company if necessary. After a settlement is reached, quite similar agreements are quickly concluded with the other large automakers.

Another aspect of bargaining structure has to do with centralization within and among employers. A decentralized structure of bargaining is typified by a single-employer–single-plant arrangement, in which an employer negotiates with a union on a plant-by-plant basis. In a more centralized approach, an employer may negotiate on a multiplant basis, bargaining with the same union for employees in multiple plants. A higher level of centralization occurs when employers combine to negotiate a common agreement with a union. This is **multiemployer bargaining.**

Multiemployer bargaining is often conducted in a geographically defined region or a single labor market. For instance, most of the builders in a metropolitan area might form an employer association to negotiate master agreements with the unions representing carpenters, electricians, plumbers, and bricklayers. However, some multiemployer bargaining covers an entire industry. For example, a number of interstate trucking companies have formed an association to negotiate the National Master Freight Agreement with the Teamsters Union. Similarly, many coal producers belong to the Bituminous Coal Operators Association, which negotiates on their behalf with the United Mine Workers. Often the major economic (wage and benefit) issues are decided in the organization-wide multiplant contract or industry-wide master contract. Further bargaining on noneconomical local issues, such as work rules, is conducted at the plant level.[49]

The Negotiations

The actual negotiation process has been described as "(1) a poker game, with the largest pots going to those who combine deception, bluff, and luck, or the ability to come up with a strong hand on the occasions on which they are challenged or 'seen' by the other side; (2) an exercise in power politics, with the relative strengths of the parties being decisive; and (3) a debating society, marked by both rhetoric and name calling."[50] This description emphasizes the fact that in addition to the substance of the issues discussed during negotiations, behavior, attitudes, and procedure all play significant roles in the outcomes of negotiations.

FIGURE 15.6 Management's Preparations for Negotiations: A Typical Firm

Input from the Plants

The first step in the process of preparing for negotiations takes place at the plant level. The plant labor relations staff holds meetings with plant supervisors to discuss problems experienced in administering the existing contract. From these discussions the staff puts together a list of suggested contract changes. At the same time, the staff also conducts a systematic review of the grievances that have arisen under the current contract and collects information on local labor market conditions and on the wages in other firms in the community.

The staff then holds a meeting with the plant manager who raises the industrial relations problems confronted in the plant. The plant's concerns are classified into two groups: those that are contractual problems, and those that should be addressed outside the negotiating process. In addition, the staff asks the plant manager to rank suggested contract changes on the basis of their potential for making a significant improvement in plant operations.

Input from Higher Levels of the Firm

Next a series of meetings are held at the division level involving the division labor relations staff, operations management at the division level, and the corporate labor relations director and staff. From time to time outside industrial relations consultants also sit in on these division-level meetings. Here the concerns of the various plants are evaluated against two criteria: (1) the operational benefits expected from proposed contract changes, and (2) the likelihood the changes desired can be achieved in the negotiations process.

The corporate labor relations staff plays a vital role in these division-level discussions, since the expected benefits of different contractual changes can be a matter of dispute across the various plants. In addition, the division labor relations staff is responsible for carefully examining the contract language that exists in the various local agreements for inconsistencies or problems that could be removed by clauses that reflect corporate labor relations preferences. Sometimes the plant labor relations representatives object to changes suggested at the division level because they do not correspond to the priorities of the plant officials and because the existing "discrepancies" may be serving a useful purpose in the plant.

The corporate labor relations staff works closely with the vice president for finance to develop the wage targets. Information on plant labor costs, corporate earnings, and the long-term financial prospects of the company and the industry are built into the wage target the corporate staff ultimately recommends.

Input from Research

A *research subgroup* within the labor relations staff of the company also carries out background research that is used in management's preparations for negotiations. At least a year and a half before the opening of formal negotiations the research staff begins to prepare the background information necessary for developing the company's proposals.

The researchers use a data base on employee demographic characteristics and analyze personnel statistics such as turnover, absentee, and grievance rates. They also monitor internal union developments, specifically, union convention resolutions, union publications, and union leader's statements about the upcoming negotiations. In addition, they survey plant managers for their views on their relations with the union and on the problems they would like to see addressed in the negotiations. The staff also consults plant labor relations staff members to obtain their suggestions. Note, this firm probably invests more resources and assigns more authority for bargaining preparation to its research staff than do most other corporations.

The research staff is ultimately responsible for putting together a summary report that goes to the vice president of industrial relations and the corporate director of compensation. These executives then work with the manager of the research and planning department to develop targets for bargaining.

The Final Steps in Management's Preparations

The final step in management's preparation for negotiations is a meeting involving the corporate labor relations staff, the chief executive officer, and the board of directors. At this meeting the corporate labor relations director presents for board approval the proposed wage targets and other proposed contract changes and the reasons for seeking the proposed changes. Sometimes this meeting does not take place until after the first negotiations session with the union. The industrial relations director might prefer waiting until then because it may be useful to hear from the union before making his recommendation to top management. This helps him identify both the relative importance the union is likely to place on pay issues and the intensity of the union's concern about other areas of the contract.

The industrial relations director described to us how he presents his recommendation to top management in this way: "I always number my proposed target settlements as proposed settlement target number 1. Someone once asked me what that meant. I said that this is what I think it will take to get a settlement but I number it because I may have to come back to you at some point with my proposed settlement number 2 or even my proposed settlement number 3, et cetera."

In the early stages of bargaining, an important issue to be decided is the agenda and the ground rules for the remainder of the session. How the proposals are to be presented, whether new demands can be introduced at any time during the negotiations, and the sequence of bargaining issues are all important considerations. Decisions concerning these issues could set the atmosphere for the whole bargaining session. For example, negotiating easy-to-resolve issues at the beginning of the session could create an atmosphere of trust and build good rapport between the parties, leading to a smoother resolution of difficult issues later on.[51] Initial demands also have a strategic dimension. A seemingly unreasonable demand could provide future room for negotiation or serve as a tradeoff in return for concessions on other issues.

After the initial demands are presented, more reasonable demands are expected to follow. Proposals and counterproposals are exchanged. Soon thereafter, if the negotiations are progressing properly, concessions are likely to follow. Concessions should be carefully timed. A hastily offered concession could convey a message of weakness or unpreparedness to the other side. More significant, however, is the possibility of having failed to consider all the ramifications of a concession. This mistake could have serious economic consequences for the conceding party. In this regard, costs estimates must be made on every proposal to fully appreciate the impact of the concession in all possible dimensions.

As the negotiation approaches the contract expiration date, the parties should address several important matters: what is the likelihood of reaching a settlement and how to reach this settlement; whether third-party intervention (a mediator) is needed in order to avoid a work stoppage; how to implement the strike if it is imminent; and other postnegotiation issues.[52]

Types of Bargaining

Labor-management relations in the United States are commonly perceived as being marked by a great deal of conflict. Press coverage of unions focuses attention on strikes, which are an obvious manifestation of conflict. More recently, however, there has been an emphasis on labor-management cooperation, especially in industries that have suffered massive unemployment caused by strong international competition. In practice, the negotiating parties can take a position anywhere along a broad spectrum of conflict to cooperation. Distributive bargaining and integrative bargaining differ with respect to the degree of conflict exhibited. A third type of bargaining is intraorganizational bargaining.[53]

Distributive bargaining, the most common type, has been defined as "the complex system of activities instrumental to the attainment of one party's goals when they are in basic conflict with those of another party."[54] This is zero-sum negotiation, in which one party's gain is the other party's loss. Wage issues typify distributive bargaining—every additional dollar paid to employees means a dollar less in profit for management.

Integrative bargaining, on the other hand, refers to activities "instrumental to the attainment of objectives which are not in fundamental conflict with those of the other party. Such objectives are said to define an area of common concern, a problem."[55] In this situation, one party's gain need not translate into another party's loss. Integrative bargaining can result in collaborative problem solving in which both parties come out ahead. Examples include joint labor-management programs to improve the quality of work life, provide retraining for employees with obsolete skills, or improve plant safety.

Both the distributive and the integrative types of bargaining involve negotiations between two parties that presumably have different interests. **Intraorganizational bargaining,** on the other hand, is the process of resolving differences or finding areas of common agreement among members of the same party. Participants on each side have to make a number of decisions among themselves before and during bargaining. Union negotiators, for instance, must decide on their priorities and secure the ratification of a tentatively negotiated agreement (this may involve a referendum among the rank and file). Hence, they might have to "sell" the settlement to their own constituents. In this regard, it is a potentially serious mistake to assume that all union members, or even all union negotiators, have the same preferences and priorities. Significant differences can and do emerge.

Scope of Bargaining

As noted earlier, Section 9 of the amended National Labor Relations Act provides that exclusively recognized representatives of employees within a bargaining unit have the right to engage in "collective bargaining in respect to rates of pay, wages, hours of employment, or other conditions of employment." That is, the law defines the **scope of bargaining**: the range of items over which the parties are required or permitted to negotiate. Over time, three distinct types of bargaining items have emerged—mandatory, permissive, and illegal—giving more precise meaning to the scope of bargaining.[56] These distinctions are not trivial, for they affect the rights of the parties in other areas, such as strikes.

Types of Bargaining Items Both parties have an obligation to negotiate **mandatory items** in good faith if either party insists on negotiation. However, the parties are not required to reach an agreement. For items to be mandatory, they must be material and significant to the employment relationship. Wages, hours, and most

TABLE 15.8 Bargaining Items with Examples

Mandatory Items	*Permissive Items*	*Illegal Items*
Wages	Changes in Benefits for Retired Employees	Featherbedding
Hours of Work	Union Input into Prices of the Company's Products	Discrimination in Hiring
Incentive Pay	Contract Ratification Process of Union	Closed Shop Agreements
Overtime	Performance Bonds for Union or Management	
Layoff and Recall Procedures		
Union Security Clauses		
Management Rights Clauses		
Grievance Procedures		
Seniority		
Safety		

Source: Adapted from R. Allen/T. Keaveny, *Contemporary Labor Relations,* © 1988 by Addison-Wesley Publishing Company, Inc. Reprinted with permission of the publisher.

benefits fall into this category, which is described in more detail in Table 15.8. **Permissive items** are matters over which the parties may negotiate if they both agree to, but neither is required to do so. For example, they might discuss extending the provisions of a proposed bargaining agreement to employees who are not covered by the National Labor Relations Act or changing the internal governance arrangements of a union. (See Table 15.8 for more examples.) Neither party may pursue a permissive item in negotiations to the point of impasse.

Finally, neither party can legitimately bring **illegal items** to the bargaining table. Examples include a proposal to discriminate against members of a bargaining unit on the basis of race, sex, or religion.

The next few pages offer a closer look at some of the specific issues that might appear in a typical bargaining session and the resulting contract. For convenience, these issues have been divided into economic and noneconomic categories; in the main, they are mandatory bargaining items. It should be emphasized, however, that the so-called noneconomic items may have considerable economic impact.

Economic Issues The economic matters commonly discussed in negotiations may be divided into two subgroups: wages and benefits. Several aspects of the wage system may be discussed. First, unions seek to raise the average wage level within the establishment in order to improve the standard of living among bargaining unit members. Pay ranges for particular jobs may also be negotiated. Unions generally prefer to standardize pay treatment by limiting management's discretion to assign different pay to persons performing the same jobs.[57] Unions typically favor seniority as the basis for pay differences among persons doing the same work, rather than more subjective, management-controlled criteria, such as performance appraisal ratings. A third type of wage issue concerns the relationship between wage adjustments and inflation. Many contracts specify a cost-of-living allowance, which provides for pay raises during the life of a contract, based on changes in some index of inflation. These inflation-connected adjustments can be made in several ways.[58] The basic purpose, however, is to preserve whatever real wage gains the union secured in the original settlement.

In more specific terms, firms and unions may negotiate over these matters:

- The use of hourly pay rates, perhaps with increments based on seniority, or incentive-based systems, such as piece rates, which tie pay to level of production.
- The deferment of wage increases over the life of a contract. Contracts may include a front-end loading provision, so that a large proportion of the negotiated wage increase takes place early in the contract period; a back-loaded contract, in contrast, delays much of the pay raise until later in the contract.
- The introduction of cost-of-living adjustments, which may be made annually. These adjustments may be capped, or limited to a certain percentage per year.
- The introduction of profit-sharing or bonus plans.
- The kinds of benefits to be offered. Included in the benefits area are pension plans, supplemental unemployment benefits, severance pay, death and disability insurance, health insurance, legal aid, wellness programs, employee assistance programs, paid holidays, paid vacations, and sick days. Benefits have become an increasingly significant aspect of total labor costs in both the unionized and nonunionized sectors.

Noneconomic Issues A number of issues may arise in the noneconomic area, including work rules, job security, quality of work life, management rights, and union security. The term *work rules* covers a great deal of ground, from crew size and the types of work that can and cannot be performed by members of various crafts to rest periods and dress codes. Job security refers to the protections from discharge or layoff afforded to employees. Unions typically attempt to negotiate **just cause provisions,** which limit an employer's right to discharge employees to situations where there is just cause for such an action (for instance, incompetence, excessive absenteeism, or insubordination). Other provisions to enhance job security may specify that layoffs will be based on seniority and regulate the conditions under which more senior employees whose jobs are ending may "bump" less senior employees out of their positions. Finally, unions usually negotiate a grievance procedure through which employees can protest managerial decisions involving contract administration. The quality of work life (QWL) area includes a host of issues ranging from occupational safety and health, job training or retrain-

TABLE 15.9 Examples of Management Rights Clauses

The Company retains the exclusive right to manage the business and direct the work force. In the exercise of its rights, the Company shall obey the provisions of this Agreement.
The right to hire, promote, discipline or discharge for cause, transfer, and layoff due to lack of work remain the sole responsibility of the Company. The Company also has the exclusive right to control the products to be manufactured, the subcontracting of work, plant locations and plant closings, and the introduction of new technology.

ing, and educational opportunities, to social and recreational facilities and child care.[59]

In negotiating a contract, both parties are understandably mindful of their institutional position and needs. In this context, management typically seeks a **management rights clause,** which explicitly reserves to management certain decision-making prerogatives. For instance, these clauses may give management alone the right to decide on the types of products to produce or services to deliver, to supervise employees, to control production processes, and to control the introduction of new technologies into the production process.[60] Table 15.9 shows two sample management rights clauses. The top one reserves to management all rights not specifically shared with the union in other provisions of the contract. The second clause enumerates the rights kept by management.

Unions also have an institutional status to protect. As recognized exclusive representatives, they have the obligation to negotiate for *all* members of the bargaining unit, whether or not they have joined the union. Thus, nonmembers who work in the bargaining unit will benefit from union representation as much as union members, even though they do not have to bear any costs, such as dues. To prevent employees in these units from "free-riding," unions negotiate **union security clauses** of various kinds. These arrangements ensure that nonunion members of bargaining units will assume at least part of the cost of union representation. The union shop and the agency shop are two common union-security arrangements. The **union shop** requires nonmembers to join the union within a certain time period (such as sixty days after hire) as a condition of continued employment. The **agency shop** requires that nonmembers in represented bargaining units pay a representational fee (usually equal to the dues paid by members) as a condition of continued employment. Both union and agency shop provisions are legal under the amended National Labor Relations Act. However, the act allows states to pass "right-to-work" laws that disallow these union security arrangements. Approximately twenty states have enacted such laws.

A third and milder form of union security clause is the **maintenance of membership clause.** It requires individuals who are already members of the union to remain members in good standing (that is, to pay their dues on time) for the life of the contract. However, still another form of union security clause is not permitted under the NLRA: the act prohibits the **closed shop,** in which union membership is a precondition for hiring rather than a condition for continued employment among those already employed.[61]

A noneconomic issue that has become increasingly significant in the last few years concerns the ability of the firm to subcontract union work. Subcontracting refers to the employer's decision to reassign bargaining unit work to outside firms or to employees that work outside of the bargaining unit. Restraints on subcontracting are sought by the union as a means of protecting members' job security. Employers, on the other hand, prefer as few restrictions as possible on their ability to contract out bargaining unit jobs.[62]

Over half of the collective bargaining agreements surveyed by the Bureau of National Affairs in 1989 contained provisions relating to subcontracting.[63] The nature of the provisions varies significantly, but some common trends can be identified. A majority of the contracts contain a clause requiring the employer to notify or discuss with the union the decision to contract out bargaining unit jobs. One-fourth of the contracts prohibit subcontracting if there are employees on layoff status or if the subcontracting would create layoffs.[64] Under current labor law, subcontracting is considered a mandatory issue for collective bargaining.[65] A duty to bargain over subcontracting arises when the managerial decision to subcontract is based on labor costs.[66]

IMPASSES AND STRIKES

Bargaining Impasses

Under the amended National Labor Relations Act, if a union and employer are covered by a collective bargaining agreement, the parties must notify each other sixty days before the contract expires if they wish to renegotiate particular provisions or terminate the contract. The party or parties seeking change must offer to meet to attempt to negotiate a new contract. Within thirty days of this notice, the party or parties must notify the Federal Mediation and Conciliation Service if they have not settled their differences. Neither party may be forced to make any particular concession, and reaching an agreement is not mandatory. However, both parties are required to confer and make a good faith effort to resolve differences.[67]

If satisfactory progress is being made in the negotiations when the existing contract expires, both sides may agree to extend the old contract on a day-to-day basis until a new settlement is reached. However, if the parties are unable to settle their differences or to move forward in negotiations, they have reached an impasse. After the contract expires, a strike may be called to put pressure on management. A strike is hard on employees as well because they stop receiving a paycheck. Thus, strikes are a test of economic strength and ideological stamina for both sides.

A newly established bargaining unit presents a somewhat special situation. Obviously, unions seek recognition in order to secure the right to bargain collectively with a particular employer. However, there is no legal requirement that the bargaining result in an agreement. Management might conceivably adopt an especially difficult posture during the initial negotiations with a new union in order to avoid operating under a contract. Thus, recognition may not always result in a viable union that succeeds in negotiating the critical first contract. One study found that negotiations failed to result in agreements in about 22 percent of the cases of newly recognized unions.[68]

Contract Ratification

Negotiated contracts are tentative until they are ratified by employees according to procedures established by the union's constitution and bylaws. Ratification may be either direct or indirect. In a direct referendum, members of a bargaining unit vote specifically to approve or disapprove the proposed contract. The United Auto Workers and the United Mine Workers, for instance, require that bargaining unit members vote for or against the tentative settlement in a direct referendum. Alternatively, local leaders or specially designated officials may approve the negotiated accords. The Teamsters provide for this indirect method of ratification. Until recently, the United Steelworkers also used an indirect method of membership ratification, referring negotiated settlements to a bargaining committee of local union presidents, called the Basic Steel Industry Conference.[69]

Statistics compiled by the Federal Mediation and Conciliation Service reveal that roughly 11 percent of tentative agreements are rejected.[70] A proposed contract is more likely to be rejected if it compares unfavorably with negotiated settlements in the nearby vicinity or among similarly situated employees in the industry. In other cases, tentative agreements are rejected because negotiators misgauged the preferences of the rank and file or neglected to identify their preferences before bargaining. Yet another reason for rejection is simple dissatisfaction with the union leaders who were responsible for negotiating the contract.

Theory of Strikes

Given that strikes impose costs on both the employer and the union, why do strikes occur? Should not the costs be an incentive for parties to avoid a strike? Several theories of strike activity have been advanced in the industrial relations literature. Two of them are examined here: the Hicks model and the political model.[71]

A simple but intuitively rich model of strike activity was introduced by John Hicks. The **Hicks model** is a cost-benefit analysis that explains how the union's wage demands and the employer's wage offers change as the length of a strike increases. The strike begins because the wage demand presented by the union exceeds the wage offer made by the employer. The strike, however, is costly to both the employer and the union. The employer's costs are manifested in a loss of customers and consequently a loss of market share. The strike is also costly for the union members. Aside from causing a loss of income for the members because they are out of work, the strike depletes unions funds and exacts a physical and emotional price. As a result, both the union and the employer change their behavior as the strike progresses. The employer's wage offer is expected to increase, and the union's wage demand is expected to decrease, in order to minimize losses.

The Hicks model points out several important aspects of strikes. Most significantly, it shows that "any strike reflects a conflict of interests between the two parties to collective bargaining."[72] Strong union militancy will result in a strike only if accompanied by steep employer resistance. The model also provides insights into the different strategies that both the union and the employer can undertake to reduce the costs associated with a strike—for example, the use of strike insurance and the availability of unemployment insurance for strikers.

A second theory of strikes, the **political model,** looks at the internal structure of unions as an explanation for the occurrence of strikes. This model takes into account the fact that union leaders and union members might have different objectives and that this dichotomy of interests might help explain the occurrence of a strike. Union members are mainly concerned with maximizing their monetary and nonmonetary conditions of employment. Union leaders, on the other hand, are also concerned about the long-term survival of the union and about their own political survival, and the issue for them is how to maximize these objectives.

For example, if a union leader is convinced that management's absolute best offer is smaller than what the union members have asked for, she has two options. First, she can try to convince the members about the actual situation and recommend acceptance of management's last offer. Yet by doing so, she runs the risk that the members will reject her proposal, accuse her of selling out to management, and vote her out of office in the next election. The second option is for the union leader to recommend a strike. Such a recommendation will make her look strong and militant. After the strike, the settlement will probably be the same as in the first option, but the leader will not be accused of selling out and will probably retain her office. Thus, union leaders are likely to follow the second strategy since it maximizes their objectives.

Level of Strike Activity

Thousands of contract negotiations take place each year, although the precise number is unknown. Historically, most contract negotiations have resulted in a settlement without a strike. The estimate is that strikes occur in less than 2 or 3 percent of negotiations.[73] Strikes are more likely to occur in larger bargaining units. One study of negotiations involving units of 1,000 or more employees in the manufacturing sector between 1971 and 1980 found that nearly 14 percent of the negotiations resulted in a strike.[74]

Table 15.10 summarizes strike activity in the United States since 1970. Several points can be made from an inspection of these data. Both the absolute number of strikes and the number of workers involved have declined in the 1980s compared with the 1970s. The total percentage of work time lost to strikes has

TABLE 15.10 Strike Activity, 1970–1991[a]

Year	*Number of Work Stoppages*	*Number of Workers Involved*[b]	*Days Idle*[b]	*Percentage of Work Time Lost*
1970	381	2,466	52,761	.29
1971	298	2,516	35,538	.19
1972	250	975	16,764	.09
1973	317	1,400	16,260	.08
1974	424	1,796	31,809	.16
1975	235	965	17,563	.09
1976	231	1,519	23,962	.12
1977	298	1,212	21,258	.10
1978	219	1,006	23,774	.11
1979	235	1,021	20,409	.09
1980	187	795	20,844	.09
1981	145	729	16,906	.07
1982	96	656	9,061	.04
1983	81	909	17,461	.08
1984	62	376	8,499	.04
1985	54	324	7,079	.03
1986	69	533	11,861	.05
1987	46	174	4,456	.02
1988	40	118	4,381	.02
1989	51	452	16,996	.07
1990	44	185	5,926	.01
1991[c]	29	369	3,496	n/a

[a]Data are only for strikes involving 1,000 or more workers.

[b]In thousands.

[c]Through September 1991.

Source: Data for 1970–1984, *Monthly Labor Review,* December 1985, p. 74. Data for 1985–1991, various issues of Monthly Labor Review, 1986–1991.

never been particularly large. However, these figures do not capture the full cost of many large strikes that have occurred in recent decades. Many strikes have taken a considerable toll on particular firms and industries, as well as on the union members involved.

Types of Strikes and Rights of Strikers

There are fundamentally different types of strikes, and the rights of strikers and employers depend on the type. Four types are discussed here: the economic strike, the unfair labor practice strike, the wildcat strike, and the illegal strike. In each case, we examine the right of employers to replace strikers and the right of employees to return to their jobs after the strike.

Economic Strikes As mentioned earlier, employers and unions have a duty to negotiate in good faith. Good faith may be breached by such actions as refusing to respond to a party's request to bargain; refusing to send bargaining representatives with sufficient authority to the negotiations; continually shifting bargaining positions in a clearly obstructionist manner; delaying and hampering negotiations; campaigning to undermine bargaining representatives; and refusing to make any counterproposals at all. If the parties have negotiated in good faith but fail to reach an agreement, a strike that follows contract expiration is called an **economic strike.**[75]

An economic strike is a protected activity under the amended NLRA if it occurs as a result of impasses relating to mandatory bargaining items. However, management also has the right to continue operating during a strike. If firms had no right to keep operating, unions would have enormous power over them in the bargaining process, and a strike threat could easily force employers into submission. A struck firm may continue operating by using management personnel, any nonstriking employees who are willing to cross picket lines to come to work, or temporary or permanent replacement workers who are hired after the strike begins. At the same time, economic strikers cannot be terminated for engaging in protected collective activity. Thus, they retain a right to return to their jobs after the strike, so long as the jobs still exist and the employer has not hired permanent replacements.[76]

Recent legislation to protect economic strikers has resurfaced recently at both the federal and state levels. At the federal level, legislation has been introduced to prohibit the use of permanent replacements, make it illegal to offer incentives to strikers who cross picket lines, and forbid discrimination against strikers when the dispute has ended.[77] Unions argue that such legislation is necessary to restore balance in labor relations. Employers, on the other hand, argue that without the ability to operate during a strike by hiring permanent replacements the employer would be forced to accept unreasonable union demands or in the alternate to endure lengthy strikes.[78]

Several studies indicate that the use of permanent replacements is fairly common in U.S. labor relations. According to a study published by the Bureau of National Affairs in 1989, replacement workers were hired in 78 (or 18 percent) of the 444 work stoppages included in the sample; in 1990, permanent replacements were hired in 59 (or 14 percent) of the 425 work stoppages.[79]

Unfair Labor Practice Strikes If a strike is provoked or prolonged by an employer's unfair labor practice, the law has been interpreted as disallowing the permanent replacement of the strikers. (The reasoning is that such conduct on the part of employers should not be rewarded.) Employers found guilty of causing an **unfair**

labor practice strike have a legal obligation to reinstate the strikers, even if they have hired permanent replacements in the interim.[80]

Wildcat Strikes **Wildcat strikes** occur in violation of a collective bargaining agreement, usually without the official approval of union leaders. Contracts almost always contain no-strike clauses, through which the union pledges not to strike during the life of the contract but instead to use the grievance procedure to resolve any disagreements about the way the contract is applied. Employees who strike in defiance of such a clause are said to be on a wildcat strike. In June 1989, more than 43,000 coal miners in ten states staged wildcat strikes in support of a two-month-old economic strike by 1,900 mine workers against the Pittston Coal Group. United Mine Workers of America members felt that the Pittston strike involved important issues and would set a precedent for all miners, so they engaged in a wildcat sympathy strike.[81] Generally, wildcat strikers have no protection. They may be discharged and have no automatic "right" to return to their jobs. In practice, however, few employers find it feasible to terminate and replace their entire work force because of an unprotected strike.

Illegal Strikes Because federal employees do not have the right to strike, any strike by these workers is illegal, and strikers have no rights to return to their jobs. One of the best-known examples of an **illegal strike** by federal employees was the Professional Air Traffic Controllers Organization (PATCO) strike in 1981. The Federal Labor Relations Authority ordered the decertification of PATCO, and, much to PATCO's surprise, President Reagan fired all the striking controllers and permanently replaced them.[82]

Preventing Strikes

In a disagreement between labor and management, several methods can increase the probability that a settlement will be reached without a strike. These methods include mediation, conventional interest arbitration, final offer arbitration, mediation-arbitration, and fact finding.

Mediation A **mediator** is a third party who has no binding authority but who assists union and management in reaching agreement. Mediators help by scheduling meetings, keeping the parties engaged in negotiations, carrying messages between the parties, and making suggestions. Mediators can be obtained from the Federal Mediation and Conciliation Service.

Interest Arbitration **Interest arbitration** is permitted under the NLRA as a means of resolving impasses, although it is rarely used in the private sector. **Arbitrators** are third-party neutrals authorized to make binding decisions to resolve disputes between management and labor. The parties abstain from an economic contest (a strike) and allow the arbitrator to settle outstanding differences.

In **conventional arbitration,** the arbitrator receives the final offers of the parties, hears the evidence from each side, and renders a decision. The arbitrator can impose any compromise between the two final offers made by the parties. Conventional arbitration has been criticized on several grounds. First, it relinquishes authority to an unaccountable party—the arbitrator does not have to live within the bounds of the contract for three years. Second, it produces a "chilling effect" on bargaining; that is, it discourages good faith efforts to reach a settlement because the parties know that they can ultimately turn the problem over to someone else to solve. Third, arbitration can produce a "narcotic effect": the parties become addicted to arbitration and unable to handle conflicts on their own. Finally, some charge that this approach encourages a rather thoughtless "splitting the difference" phenomenon. Arbitrators tend to choose a middle point between the management and union positions. This tendency also reduces the chance of meaningful concessions by either side during negotiation.[83]

Final offer arbitration is intended to reduce some of the problems associated with the conventional approach. Specifically, it raises the risks to parties that fail to reach an agreement on their own. In this approach, the arbitrator must choose one or the other party's final offer. There is no opportunity to split the difference. Final offer arbitration takes two forms: final offer by package, in which the arbitrator accepts one of the parties' entire package of final offers on all items, and final offer by issue, in which the arbitrator accepts one or the other final offer on each item remaining to be resolved. An agreement to use final offer arbitration encourages the parties to move toward reasonable final offers that will be attractive to the arbitrator; as a result, they may reach a settlement without resorting to arbitration at all.[84]

Other Dispute Resolution Procedures **Mediation-arbitration** combines the two processes just described. When an impasse exists, a mediator-arbitrator first attempts to mediate the disputes. After an agreed-upon period of time, the mediator assumes the role of arbitrator and unilaterally resolves any remaining issues. One of the most widely publicized incidents of mediation-arbitration occurred during the postal negotiations in 1978.[85]

Fact finding lies somewhere between mediation and arbitration. In fact finding, a neutral third party gathers facts about the bargaining situation and offers made. The facts are then organized and reported publicly in such a way as to generate external pressure to produce a settlement.[86]

National Emergency Dispute Procedures

The Taft-Hartley Act provides a set of procedures to help resolve strikes that constitute a national emergency because they threaten the health or safety of the general public. The act allows the president of the United States to seek an injunction to prohibit the strike for eighty days. During this so-called cooling-off period, the parties continue to bargain with the aid of the Federal Mediation and Conciliation Service. Meanwhile, fact finding and the force of public opinion are brought to bear on the parties. If no settlement is reached within the cooling-off period, the union is free to resume the strike. Since the late 1940s, these procedures have been invoked nearly forty times, most frequently in the coal mining, atomic energy, maritime, and longshoring occupations.[87]

THE GRIEVANCE PROCEDURE

Disputes may arise during the life of a contract. Although both parties have agreed to live by the provisions of the contract, there is still room for disagreement about interpretations and enforcement in specific cases. An employee who believes that his or her rights under the contract have been violated may file a **grievance.** (See the Ethical perspective box for a different view of employee rights.) Virtually all contracts provide a grievance procedure for resolving disagreements about contract administration.[88]

Steps in the Grievance Procedure

A typical grievance procedure clause is shown in Table 15.11. The procedure starts when an employee believes that he or she has been treated unfairly with respect to some item of the contract. For instance, the contract may specify that the "most senior qualified employee" be chosen for promotion. If someone else is promoted, the most senior employee may then file a grievance claiming that he or she was qualified and should have been selected. In the first step of a typical grievance procedure, the employee and/or his or her shop steward presents the complaint, usually orally, to the grievant's immediate superior. The superior must respond within a fixed time period, either agreeing that the employee has a valid point and suggesting a remedy or denying that the grievance has merit. If the answer received does not satisfy the grievant, the union puts the grievance in writing and appeals to the next level of management—perhaps to the foreman or a representative of the human resource management department. If the decision received at this level is not satisfactory, the grievance may be appealed yet again, to upper management. At this point, a representative from the national union may be present to help represent the grievant.

Most grievances are settled through the early steps, but when no mutually acceptable resolution is reached during the in-company stages, 96 percent of contracts specify binding arbitration as the final step.[89] Some contracts specify a particular person as the permanent arbitrator for the life of the contract. More commonly, however, the contract states how an arbitrator will be selected for each case. Usually a list of qualified arbitrators (labor law or labor relations professors, semiretired labor relations experts, etc.) is obtained from the Federal Mediation and Conciliation Service or the American Arbitration Association, and the parties alternately strike off names until they arrive at a choice acceptable to both sides. Union and management typically share the costs of hiring an arbitrator.

ETHICAL PERSPECTIVE

Employee Rights

What rights, if any, do employees have in the workplace? The legal framework provides for certain rights, for instance, the right to fair and impartial treatment regardless of race, sex, religion, age, and handicap, to minimum wages and benefits, and to a reasonably safe workplace. It also provides for the right to organize and bargain collectively. Where employees have chosen to unionize, the union provides another layer of rights, both by assuring employees of a voice in their employment conditions and by including specific rights in the contract, such as the right to due process in discipline and discharge situations.

However, some authors have speculated about the general lack of civil liberties in the employer-employee relationship. These are liberties we take for granted in everyday life, such as the right to free speech, privacy, and association. For instance, what happens to an employee who publicly disagrees with his or her employer or dates a manager from a competitor organization or works for an American automobile company but buys a foreign car? What happens to a worker who refuses to contribute to the office charity drive or moonlights in a related business area? What consequences do employees face if they get into a minor scrap with the law or commit some other indiscretion outside of working hours?

In many cases, courts or arbitrators have reinstated employees who were discharged for actions such as these. On the other hand, an off-duty act that reflects very directly and badly on the employer's reputation or on the employee's ability to perform the job may be acceptable grounds for dismissal. Examples include a hotel security guard found guilty of selling a stolen weapon and a school drug counselor who allowed her home to be used for the sale of drugs by her husband.

David W. Ewing has proposed the following Employee Bill of Rights to guarantee civil liberties inside the organization:

1. No organization or manager shall discharge, demote, or in other ways discriminate against any employee who criticizes, in speech or press, the ethics, legality, or social responsibility of management actions.
2. No employee shall be penalized for engaging in outside activities of his or her choice after working hours, whether political, economic, civic, or cultural, nor for buying products and services of his or her choice for personal use, nor for expressing or encouraging views contrary to top management's on political, economic, and social issues.
3. No organization or manager shall penalize an employee for refusing to carry out a directive that violates common norms of morality.
4. No organization shall allow audio or visual recording of an employee's conversations or actions to be made without his or her prior knowledge and consent. Nor may an organization require an employee or applicant to take personality tests, polygraph examinations, or other tests that constitute, in his opinion, an invasion of privacy.
5. No employee's desk, files, or locker may be examined in his or her absence by anyone but a senior manager who has sound reason to believe that the files contain information needed for a management decision that must be made in the employee's absence.
6. No employer organization may collect and keep on file information about an employee that is not relevant and necessary for efficient management. Every employee shall have the right to inspect his or her personnel file and challenge the accuracy, relevance, or necessity of data in the file. Access to an employee's file by outside individuals and organizations shall be

limited to inquiries about the essential facts of employment.

7. No manager may communicate to prospective employers of an employee who is about to be or has been discharged gratuitous opinions that might hamper the individual in obtaining a new position.

8. An employee who is discharged, demoted, or transferred to a less desirable job is entitled to a written statement from management of its reasons for the penalty.

9. Every employee who feels that he or she has been penalized for asserting any right described in this bill shall be entitled to a fair hearing before an impartial official, board, or arbitrator.

Some scholars feel that these rules go too far in limiting the organization's legitimate interest in certain types of relevant employee behavior, whether on or off the job. What do you think?

Sources: David W. Ewing, "A Proposed Bill of Rights," in *Ethical Issues in Business,* ed. Thomas Donaldson and Patricia H. Werhane (Englewood Cliffs, N.J.: Prentice-Hall, 1988), pp. 305–310 (the nine rules are direct quotations); William Shaw and Vincent Barry, *Moral Issues in Business,* (Belmont, Calif.: Wadsworth, 1989), pp. 244–246; Max Ways, "The Myth of the Oppressive Corporation," in *Ethical Issues in Business,* pp. 310–312; Terry L. Leap, "When Can You Fire for Off-duty Conduct?" *Harvard Business Review,* January–February 1988, pp. 28–36.

Nearly all contracts limit the arbitrator to interpreting the existing contract. The arbitrator is not allowed to change or amend the contract in any way but merely to clarify and apply its provisions. Within this context, the arbitrator will hold a hearing in which both sides present their cases. The arbitrator will then provide a written decision and impose a solution that both sides must follow.[90]

The Legal Status of Grievance Arbitration

Grievance arbitration is regarded by the courts as a very positive development in industrial relations. Since 1957, the Supreme Court has protected the institution of grievance arbitration in at least four issues.[91]

1. *The enforceability of arbitration clauses.* What would happen if the employer should refuse to submit a case to arbitration, even if the collective bargaining agreement provides for arbitration of that dispute? Can the union ask the court to force the employer to submit a dispute to arbitration? In *Textile Workers* v. *Lincoln Mills,* the Supreme Court held that when a collective bargaining agreement contains an arbitration clause and the employer refuses to proceed to arbitration the union may compel arbitration by obtaining an injunction in a federal court.[92]

2. *The relationship between the courts and arbitration.* Having resolved the issue of the enforceability of the arbitration clause, the next issue for the courts to decide was what kind of review power the courts had over the arbitrator's decision. Would the courts have the power to overturn the arbitration award in all cases (i.e., anytime the court disagreed with the award) or only under limited circumstances (i.e., when the arbitrator had committed a legal error)?

TABLE 15.11 A Grievance Procedure Clause

Step 1	The employee and the department steward, if the employee desires, shall take the matter up with his [or her] foreman. If no settlement is reached in Step 1 within two working days, the grievance shall be reduced to writing on the form provided for that purpose.
Step 2	The written grievance shall be presented to the foreman or the general foreman and a copy sent to the production personnel office. Within two working days after receipt of the grievance, the general foreman shall hold a meeting, unless mutually agreed otherwise, with the foreman, the employee, and the departmental steward and the chief steward.
Step 3	If no settlement is reached in Step 2, the written grievance shall be presented to the departmental superintendent, who shall hold a meeting within five working days of the original receipt of the grievance in Step 2 unless mutually agreed otherwise. Those in attendance shall normally be the departmental superintendent, the general foreman, the foreman, the employee, the chief steward, departmental steward, a member of the production personnel department, the president of the UNION or his representative and the divisional committeeman.
Step 4	If no settlement is reached in Step 3, the UNION COMMITTEE and an international representative of the UNION shall meet with the MANAGEMENT COMMITTEE for the purpose of settling the matter.
Step 5	If no settlement is reached in Step 4, the matter shall be referred to an arbitrator. A representative of the UNION shall meet within five working days with a representative of the COMPANY for the purpose of selecting an arbitrator. If an arbitrator cannot be agreed upon within five working days after Step 4, a request for a list of arbitrators shall be sent to the Federal Mediation & Conciliation Service. Upon obtaining the list, an arbitrator shall be selected within five working days. Prior to arbitration, a representative of the UNION shall meet with a representative of the COMPANY to reduce to writing wherever possible the actual issue to be arbitrated. The decision of the arbitrator shall be final and binding on all parties. The salary, if any, of the arbitrator and any necessary expense incident to the arbitration shall be paid jointly by the COMPANY and the UNION.

Source: From *Labor Relations: Development, Structure and Process,* Fifth Edition by John A. Fossum. Copyright © 1992 by Richard D. Irwin, Homewood, IL.

or only under limited circumstances (i.e., when the arbitrator had committed a legal error)?

In the *Steelworkers Trilogy,* the Court granted arbitrators a broad scope of power.[93] In *American Manufacturing Company,* the issue was whether the courts could refuse to force the employer into arbitration on the argument that the court disagreed with the merits of the grievance.[94] The Supreme Court held that the courts were to decide the arbitrability of the dispute (whether the issue is covered by the contract) but should not decide the merits of a case. That is, once a court decides that the issue is subject to arbitration under the collective bargaining agreement, it cannot refuse to require arbitration on the grounds that it disagrees with the merits of the dispute.

In *Warrior Gulf,* the issue was what disputes are subject to arbitration. The Court held that disputes over contract terms are assumed to be arbitrable unless they are specifically excluded from arbitration in the collective bargaining agreement.[95]

Finally, in *Enterprise Wheel,* the Court held that, as long as the arbitrator's decision "draws its essence" from the collective bargaining agreement, the arbitrator's award is enforceable in court, even if a court disagrees with the arbitrator's award. Only in cases of fraud, clear violation of public policy, or mistake of law, would the court be allowed to reverse the arbitrator's award.[96]

These cases have granted arbitrators the power to evaluate the merits of a grievance and render a final and binding decision that the courts cannot reverse except under unusual circumstances.

3. The relationship between the NLRB and arbitration. The issue involved here is what would happen if a dispute that gives rise to an arbitration award also involves an unfair labor practice charge? Is arbitration pre-empted by the NLRA? In general, federal law takes precedence over contractual terms. The NLRB has decided to defer to arbitration as long as the arbitrator's decision is not inconsistent with the objectives of the NLRA. The NLRB recognizes the advantages of arbitration over other dispute resolution methods and tries to encourage it.[97]

4. Arbitration and individual employees' rights. Two issues arise here. First, what deference should be given to the arbitrator's award when the dispute involves racial discrimination under Title VII? Because of the importance of individual rights involved in cases claiming racial discrimination, the Court held that such an award can be reversed by the courts and that the employee can pursue additional legal remedies through federal agencies, with no weight given to the arbitrator's award.[98] Second, what weight should be given to an award that resulted from inadequate representation by the union of the employee? In *Hines* v. *Anchor Motor,* the Court held that an arbitration award should not be sustained by the court when the union has violated its duty to represent the grievant fairly.[99]

THE FUTURE OF U.S. LABOR RELATIONS

What challenges lie ahead for unions and employers within the next several years?[100] In the last two decades—just as in the 1930s, a major turning point in American labor relations—the United States has experienced major structural change. The increased competition in the domestic markets, resulting from the globalization of markets, and the policy of economic deregulation, pursued in the United States since the 1970s, require that the nature of labor relations be reassessed.

Harry C. Katz and Thomas A. Kochan identify three possible strategic directions for U.S. labor relations to follow.[101] The first is reliance on deregulation and the market. Further reducing government intervention in markets would increase competition and might result in a more efficient allocation of labor, as well as a decrease in government-imposed inefficiencies. Proponents of this alternative strategy argue for even less intervention by government in the regulation of labor relations. Such a reduction in government intervention could be accomplished either through the repeal of current labor law or through a weakening in the enforcement practices of regulations currently on the books.

A second strategic option involves the promotion of traditional collective bargaining. With minor changes to current labor laws, the argument goes, union and employer will be left alone to resolve substantive issues. The government would set only procedural rules and impose only broad limits on the parties' behavior.

Finally, Katz and Kochan suggest the option of a new industrial relations system. This new system would require a more integrative approach to industrial relations by both employers and unions, as well as significant changes at multiple levels of the labor relations process. At the strategic level, the new system would call for information sharing between management and workers, worker participation and representation, and integration of industrial relations with business strategies. "The new system would break with the principle that it is management's job to manage the enterprise and the union's solely to negotiate over the effects of management actions."[102] At the collective bargaining level, a commitment to employment continuity, employment security, and training and development would be necessary. The focus would be to make wages responsive to economic conditions without eroding the workers' standard of living. In addition, at the workplace level, there would need to be more employee participation in workplace decisions, a more flexible organization of work, and extensive informal communication. "The goal," according to Katz and Kochan, "is to develop trust and avoid the conflict often found in traditional collective bargaining relationships."[103]

This new industrial relations system will require some changes in the behavior of its main participants. Federal and state policymakers, argue Katz and Kochan, will need to play a more active and supportive role in industrial relations. Their approach could include substantially reforming the NLRA to prevent its use as an anti-union device, facilitating employees' decisions to choose union representation without undue delays; eliminate the restrictions on the ability of supervisors and middle managers to unionize; and get rid of the "mandatory"/"permissive" distinction with respect to collective bargaining issues. This more active government role in industrial relations must be accompanied, say Katz and Kochan, by the development of national policies concerning employment, training, education, and economic expansion.

Besides the new role for government, there must also be changes in the attitudes and strategies of both management and labor. The changes needed for this new system to succeed are summarized by the statement of principles of the 1988

Collective Bargaining Forum (an organization of national union leaders and corporate chief executives).

- Acceptance in practice by American management both of the legitimacy of unions and a broader role for worker and union participation.
- Acceptance in practice by American unions of their responsibility to work with management to improve the economic performance of their enterprises, in ways that serve the interests of workers, consumers, stockholders, and society.
- Encouragement of a public policy which assures choice, free from any coercion, in determining whether to be represented by a union and which is conducive to labor-management relations based on mutual respect and trust at all levels.
- Acceptance by American corporations of employment security, the continuity of employment for its work force, as a major policy objective that will figure as importantly in the planning process as product development, marketing, and capital requirements.[104]

SUMMARY OF KEY POINTS

Unions have had a long and uneven history in the United States. Craft unions were formed first, and later workers began to organize by industry. Union membership as a percentage of the work force peaked in the late 1940s and has been declining since the late 1950s, despite a rise in unionization among public sector employees.

In the beginning, unions were considered illegal conspiracies, which had no right to exist at all. Later, unions were considered illegal if they engaged in any action that restrained interstate trade. In 1935, the Wagner Act opened the door to widespread unionization by establishing election procedures for unions to become certified bargaining agents for groups of employees, requiring management to bargain in good faith with a properly certified representative of their employees, and preventing discrimination against employees regarding their right to unionize. In 1947, the Taft-Hartley Act placed some limits on union behavior, making the balance of power with management more equal. In the 1960s and 1970s, federal, state, and local governments began to extend limited collective bargaining rights to public sector employees.

Once a union has been certified as representing a group of employees, it can begin negotiations with management in an attempt to secure a contract. Both parties must plan carefully for negotiations. Bargaining can be conducted in several different structural arrangements: informal pattern; single employer–single plant; single employer–multiplant; or multiemployer. Mandatory bargaining issues include wages, hours, and conditions of employment. Permissive items may be discussed, but neither party may insist upon them to the point of impasse, and illegal items may not be bargained over.

If an impasse is reached, private sector employees may choose to strike. Economic strikers have some right to return to their jobs after a strike, whereas unfair labor practice strikers have unconditional rights and wildcat or illegal strikers have no rights. As an alternative to strikes, mediation or various forms of arbitration may be used. To settle disagreements over contract administration during the life of a contract, the grievance system is used.

Questions for Discussion

1. Describe the evolution of labor unions in the United States from the beginning to the merger of the AFL with the CIO.
2. How were unions viewed during the common law and business law periods?
3. What are the major provisions of the Wagner Act? The Taft-Hartley Act?
4. How are public sector labor relations different from private sector labor relations?
5. List some of the demographic characteristics of union membership in the United States.
6. What factors explain the high unionization rate among public sector workers as compared with that of workers in the private sector?
7. What factors do individuals consider in choosing whether or not to support a union? What arguments does management commonly use in trying to persuade employees not to support a union?
8. Describe the certification process by which a union can become recognized as the sole bargaining agent for a group of employees. What are some of the things that management *must not do* during an organizing campaign?
9. What is a bargaining unit? Does the collective bargaining contract apply to employees in the bargaining unit who have chosen not to join the union?
10. On what basis could labor-management joint committees be considered illegal?
11. Describe how management might go about planning and preparing for negotiations. In what ways is planning by the union similar to that conducted by management? How is it different?
12. How can procedural issues during negotiations be strategically used by the parties?
13. What is meant by the term *bargaining structure?* What might be the advantages and disadvantages to management of becoming part of a multiemployer association for the purpose of negotiating a master agreement?
14. How is integrative bargaining different from distributive bargaining?
15. Explain three types of legal union security clauses.
16. Suppose the union wants a cost-of-living adjustment in the pensions being paid to current retirees. May the union press this issue to the point of impasse and then strike because of it? Why or why not?
17. Discuss the implications of the Hicks model and the political model of strike activity.
18. Distinguish between four types of strikes, and describe the rights (if any) that strikers have to return to their jobs after each type of strike.

19. What are the ways of resolving impasses without a strike?
20. Explain how the grievance procedure is used to enforce a contract.
21. Discuss the legal status of grievance arbitration.

CASE 15.1

Employer Formation of a President's Advisory Council

The company manufactures and services recreational vehicles in three plants in Jackson Center, Ohio. The union filed a certification petition with the National Labor Relations Board on January 21, 1985, to represent the production and maintenance employees at the three plants. In late February 1985, the company president announced the formation of the President's Advisory Council (PAC), which formalized an arrangement that had existed within the company for the last four years. This arrangement included monthly "rap sessions" with employees on a rotating basis. The sessions were attended by the company president, and employees could ask any questions and make any suggestions they wished.

On March 1, each department was asked to vote for three representatives to sit on the PAC. At the first meeting of the PAC a few days before the union election, the president discussed the comparative merits of an attendance bonus program favored by management versus a personal sick day program favored by employees. He agreed to review the attendance/sick leave policy but said no changes could be made until after the union election. On March 15, the election was held, and the union lost by a vote of 106 to 181.

A week later after the election, a second meeting of the PAC was held, and the president announced the reinstatement of the personal sick day program preferred by employees. At the third meeting of the PAC, the job bidding system was discussed and, again, changes were made in accordance with the suggestions of employee representatives of the meetings.

The union filed charges of unfair labor practices with the National Labor Relations Board and claimed that the PAC was an employer-dominated labor organization intended to undermine support for the union. In addition, the union charged that the company had unlawfully interfered with the election by holding meetings with the PAC members and discussing terms and other conditions of employment.

The company responded that it had only formalized an arrangement that had lasted for four years and it was careful not to discuss matters that would have been discussed with the union if it had won the election. Likewise, the company was careful not to take any action as a result of discussions with the PAC members until after the union election. Furthermore, since the union lost the election, the company practiced good management by continuing the PAC meetings and responding affirmatively to employee suggestions and recommendations.

Source: William H. Holley and Kenneth M. Jennings, *The Labor Relations Process*, 4th ed. (Chicago, Ill.: Dryden Press, 1991), p. 160.

1. Is the PAC a labor organization? Why or why not?
2. Have the company actions violated the National Labor Relations Act?
3. Should the company be directed to recognize the union since it has already begun to hold meetings with employee representatives and to discuss and act on proposals on terms and conditions of employment?
4. How should the National Labor Relations Board decide this case? Justify your answer.

CASE 15.2

The Arbitration Process

Kim and Janice are employees at the Missouri Composites Co., which manufactures and assembles plastic parts used in toys. Kim and Janice work together on the assembly line. They have been friends for several years. One day Kim and Janice left work for lunch and went to a nearby pizza parlor. Kim had two glasses of beer with her pizza. When they returned to work on the assembly line, Shari (who also works on the assembly line) noticed they were whispering back and forth, laughing all the time. Their behavior was very distracting. Shari motioned for the supervisor to come over and told the supervisor about their behavior.

The supervisor pulled them off the line and asked them to come with her. As she walked with them to the conference room, she could smell traces of alcohol on Kim's breath. She asked them to submit to a blood/alcohol test, which was the routine practice in such cases. Both Kim and Janice refused. The supervisor then suspended them for two weeks, per Section XIII of their contract, which reads as follows:

XIII: Any employee may be required to submit to a blood/alcohol test if just cause exists to believe the employee has been consuming alcohol during work hours. Refusal to submit to the test (on the first occurrence) will result in an immediate suspension of 2 weeks. Refusal to submit to the test on the second occurrence will result in dismissal.

Immediately after their suspension, Kim and Janice filed a grievance according to the grievance procedure established under the current collective bargaining agreement. The grievance was upheld through the grievance process and is now before an arbitrator.

1. As the union (or management) representative, how would you prepare the case to be presented in the arbitration hearing? What issues would you focus on? What evidence (witnesses, records, etc.) would you like to introduce to support your case?

Source: Reprinted with the permission of Macmillan Publishing Company from *Collective Bargaining and Labor Relations: Practice, Cases and Law,* Third Edition by Michael R. Carrell and Christina Heavrin.

2. If you were the arbitrator, how would you decide this case? What is (are) the major issues to be decided? Write a short decision explaining your award.
3. How would you rewrite Section XIII of the current contract to prevent disputes in the future?

CASE 15.3

To Spy or Not to Spy

Buck Callahan is beginning his final semester at College of the Badlands in Medina, North Dakota. He is pursuing a business degree with a specialization in human resource management. While attending school, Callahan has been supporting himself by working as a tanner at the Leather Unlimited saddle plant just east of town. Leather Unlimited is the only large employer in the area, with several local plants producing a variety of leather goods. Callahan has applied to move into an entry level professional position in the human resource department at Leather Unlimited. He strongly desires to stay in Medina after graduation, and Leather Unlimited is by far his best job opportunity in the human resource management field.

Shortly after submitting his application to the human resource department, Callahan is called into the office of the vice president for human resources, Joe-Bob Harley. Harley tells Callahan that he is impressed with Callahan's grades and course work and that Callahan would be an asset to any company's human resource department. He then tells Callahan that the Leather Unlimited boot factory west of town will be short a tanner for the next three months while one of their workers is out on maternity leave. He asks Callahan if he would be willing to transfer to the boot factory until he graduates and "moves to a professional position somewhere." Callahan is eager to impress Harley and readily agrees to the transfer.

One week after moving to the boot factory, Callahan is again called in by Harley. After some preliminary chat about Callahan's role in the company bowling team's recent victories, Harley asks if Callahan has heard anything about a union organizing campaign at the boot plant. Harley says that he has been hearing some rumors to that effect for the last few weeks and would like to know what is going on. In particular, he would like to know exactly which employees are speaking out in favor of the union and what degree of support the unionization campaign seems to have. He points out that Callahan is (still) an hourly employee and as such has every right to talk to his peers about the union and attend any organizational meetings that might be called. Harley suggests that this is an opportunity for Callahan to demonstrate that he has some of the skills needed for a career in human resource management—the ability to communicate with both rank-and-file employees and with management. He closes the meeting by mentioning that Leather Unlimited will soon be adding another position in its human resource department and asking Callahan to get back to him as soon as he has any information about the union.

1. What are Callahan's options in this situation?
2. Is Harley's request legal? Is it ethical? What are the pros and cons of each?
3. What would you recommend that Callahan do?

Notes and References

1. John R. Commons and Associates, *History of Labour in the United States,* 2 vols. (New York: Macmillan, 1918).
2. Henry Pelling, *American Labor* (Chicago: University of Chicago Press, 1960), chap. 2.
3. Foster Rhea Dulles and Melvyn Dubofsky, *Labor in America: A History* (Arlington Heights, Ill.: Harlan Davidson, 1984), chap. 3.
4. Ibid., chap. 8.
5. Ibid., chap. 9.
6. Ibid., chap. 16.
7. Ibid., chap. 19.
8. E. Edward Herman, Joshua Schwarz, and Alfred Kuhn, *Collective Bargaining and Labor Relations* (Englewood Cliffs, N.J.: Prentice-Hall, 1992), chap. 2.
9. Ibid., chap. 15.
10. Richard Freeman and James Medoff, *What Do Unions Do?* (New York: Basic Books, 1985).
11. Benjamin J. Taylor and Fred Witney, *Labor Relations Law* (Englewood Cliffs, N.J.: Prentice-Hall, 1987), chap. 2.
12. *Commonwealth* v. *Hunt,* 45 Mass. (4 Metc.) 111 (Sup. Jud. Ct., 1842).
13. Ibid.
14. Ibid., p. 46; quote is from the Supreme Court decision in *Loewe* v. *Lawlor* (Danbury Hatters) 208 U.S. 274 (1908).
15. *Duplex Printing Press* v. *Deering*, 254 U.S. 445.
16. Taylor and Witney, *Labor Relations Law,* chap. 4.
17. Ibid., chap. 8.
18. Ibid., chap. 10.
19. The section on public employee unionization is based on Taylor and Witney, *Labor Relations Law,* chap. 21.
20. John A. Fossum, *Labor Relations: Development, Structure, and Process* (Homewood, Ill.: Irwin, 1985), chaps. 8 and 9.
21. Julius G. Getman, Stephen B. Goldberg, and Jeanne B. Herman, *Union Representation Elections: Law and Reality* (New York: Russell Sage Foundation, 1976), chap. 4.
22. Arthur A. Sloane and Fred Witney, *Labor Relations* (Englewood Cliffs, N.J.: Prentice-Hall, 1988), pp. 190–193.
23. Information obtained from the union's LM–2 annual financial disclosure form filed under Title VII of the Civil Service Reform Act.
24. Robert E. Allen and Timothy J. Keaveny, *Contemporary Labor Relations* (Reading, Mass.: Addison-Wesley, 1983), pp. 162–170.
25. Thomas A. Kochan, "How American Workers View Labor Unions," *Monthly Labor Review,* Vol. 102, April 1979, pp. 23–31.
26. Jack Fiorito, "Political Instrumentality Perceptions and Desire for Union Representation," *Journal of Labor Research,* Summer 1987, pp. 271–290.
27. Stephen L. Premack and John E. Hunter, "Individual Unionization Decisions," *Psychological Bulletin,* Vol. 103, March 1988, pp. 223–234.
28. Fossum, *Labor Relations,* chap. 6.
29. Ibid.
30. Bureau of National Affairs, *Primer of Labor Relations,* 24th ed. (Washington, D.C.: Bureau of National Affairs, 1989), chap. 4.
31. *American Hospital Ass'n.* v. *NLRB,* 111 S.Ct. 1539 (1991).
32. Allen and Keaveny, *Contemporary Labor Relations,* chap. 7.
33. *Forty-eighth Annual Report of the National Labor Relations Board for the Fiscal Year Ended September 30, 1983* (Washington, D.C.: Government Printing Office, 1986).
34. Fossum, *Labor Relations,* chap. 6.
35. Bureau of National Affairs, *Primer of Labor Relations,* chap. 4.
36. Taylor and Witney, *Labor Relations Law,* p. 290; quote is from the ruling in *Hollywood Ceramics,* 140 NLRB 221 (1962).
37. *Midland National Life Insurance*, 263 NLRB 24(1982).
38. M. Roomkin and R. N. Block, "Case Processing Time and the Outcome of Representation Elections: Some Empirical Evidence," *University of Illinois Law Review,* 1981, pp. 75–97.
39. *Labor Relations Week,* Vol. 5, No. 18, 1991.
40. See, for example, *NLRB* v. *Cabot Carbon Co.,* 360 U.S. 203 (1959); *Perry Norvell Co.,* 80 NLRB 225(1948); and *NLRB* v. *Kennametal Inc.,* 182 F2d 817 (CA 3 1950).

41. See, for example, *NLRB* v. *Scott and Fetzer Co.,* 691 F2d 288 (CA 6 1982); *Airstream Inc.,* v. *NLRB,* 877 F2d 1291 (CA 6 1989).

42. See, for example, *NLRB* v. *Northeastern University,* 601 F2d 1208 (CA 1 1979).

43. *Labor Relations Week,* Vol. 5, No. 3, 1991, pp. 753–754.

44. Section 9 of the amended National Labor Relations Act.

45. Roy J. Lewicki and Joseph A. Litterer, *Negotiation* (Homewood, Ill.: Irwin, 1985).

46. William H. Holley and Kenneth M. Jennings, *The Labor Relations Process,* 4th ed. (Chicago, Ill.: Dryden Press, 1991), p. 174.

47. Thomas A. Kochan and Harry C. Katz, *Collective Bargaining and Industrial Relations* (Homewood, Ill.: Irwin, 1988), chap. 5; see also Fossum, *Labor Relations,* chap. 10.

48. Kochan and Katz, *Collective Bargaining,* pp. 136–140.

49. Fossum, *Labor Relations,* chap. 7.

50. John T. Dunlop and James J. Healy, *Collective Bargaining,* rev. ed. (Homewood, Ill.: Irwin, 1955), p. 53.

51. Terry L. Leap, *Collective Bargaining and Labor Relations* (New York: Macmillan, 1991), p. 303.

52. Ibid., pp. 313–316.

53. Richard E. Walton and Robert B. McKersie, *A Behavioral Theory of Labor Negotiations* (New York: McGraw-Hill, 1965).

54. Ibid., p. 4.

55. Ibid., p. 5; see also Edward Cohen-Rosenthal and Cynthia E. Burton, *Mutual Gains: A Guide to Union-Management Cooperation* (New York: Praeger, 1987).

56. Allen and Keaveny, chap. 8.

57. Freeman and Medoff, *What Do Unions Do?*

58. Fossum, *Labor Relations,* chap. 8.

59. Ibid., chap. 9.

60. Commerce Clearing House, *Labor Law Course,* 26th ed. (Chicago: Commerce Clearing House, 1987), p. 3351.

61. Bureau of National Affairs, *Primer of Labor Relations,* chap. 6.

62. Leap, *Collective Bargaining,* p. 238.

63. Bureau of National Affairs, *Collective Bargaining Negotiations and Contracts* (Washington, D.C.: Bureau of National Affairs, 1989), pp. 65.1–65.7.

64. Leap, *Collective Bargaining,* p. 569.

65. *Fibreboard Paper Products Corp.* v. *NLRB,* 379 U.S. 203 (1964).

66. *Otis Elevator Company,* 269 NLRB No. 62 (1984).

67. Kochan and Katz, *Collective Bargaining,* chap. 8.

68. William N. Cooke, *Union Organizing and Public Policy: Failure to Secure First Contracts* (Kalamazoo, Mich.: Upjohn Institute for Employment Research, 1985).

69. James Dworkin, Sidney P. Feldman, James M. Brown, and Charles J. Hobson, "Workers' Preferences in Concession Bargaining," *Industrial Relations,* Winter 1988, pp. 7–20.

70. Kochan and Katz, *Collective Bargaining,* chap. 8.

71. The section on the theory of strikes is based on Robert F. Flanagan, Lawrence M. Kahn, Robert S. Smith and Ronald G. Ehrenberg, *Economics of the Employment Relationship* (Glenview, Ill.: Scott, Foresman, 1989) pp. 468–474.

72. Ibid., p. 469.

73. Kochan and Katz, *Collective Bargaining,* chap. 8.

74. Cynthia L. Gramm, "The Determinants of Strike Incidence and Severity," *Industrial and Labor Relations Review,* April 1986, pp. 361–376.

75. Taylor and Witney, *Labor Relations Law,* pp. 396–399.

76. Bureau of National Affairs, *Primer of Labor Relations,* chap. 7.

77. *Replacement Workers: Evidence from the Popular and Labor Press, 1989 and 1990* (Washington, D.C.: Bureau of National Affairs, 1991). The House version of the bill was passed on July 17, 1991. The Senate, however, failed by three votes to overcome a filibuster led by Republican Senate leaders that prevented the bill from being brought to the floor for a vote. Labor and business leaders predict that similar legislative initiatives are unlikely to be reconsidered again by Congress as long as a Republican administration is in office. *Labor Relations Week,* vol. 6, No. 25, 1992, p. 587.

78. *Labor Relations Week,* Vol. 5. No. 21, 1991, pp. 482, 483.

79. *Replacement Workers: Evidence from the Popular and Labor Press, 1989 and 1990* (Washington, D.C.: Bureau of National Affairs, 1991).

80. Taylor and Witney, *Labor Relations Law,* pp. 467–470.

81. John H. Gormley, Jr., "Solidarity in the Coal Fields," *Baltimore Sun,* June 25, 1989, pp. 1E and 4E.

82. Kochan and Katz, *Collective Bargaining,* chap. 2.

83. Ibid., chap. 9; Fossum, *Labor Relations,* chap. 15.

84. Ibid.

85. John T. Tierney, *The U.S. Postal Service: Status and Prospects of a Public Enterprise* (Dover, Mass.: Auburn House, 1988).

86. Fossum, *Labor Relations,* chap. 15.

87. Taylor and Witney, *Labor Relations Law,* chap. 19.

88. *Collective Bargaining Negotiations and Contracts* (Washington, D.C.: Bureau of National Affairs, 1989), pp. 51.5–51.8.

89. Ibid., p. 51.6.

90. Maurice S. Trotta, *Handling Grievances: A Guide for Management and Labor* (Washington, D.C.: Bureau of National Affairs, 1976).

91. The section of the legal status of arbitration is based on Leap, *Collective Bargaining,* pp. 402–408.

92. *Textile Workers* v. *Lincoln Mills,* 353 U.S. 448 (1957).

93. *Steelworkers Trilogy*: *Steelworkers* v. *American Manufacturing Co.*, 363 U.S. 564(1960); *Steelworkers* v. *Warrior Gulf and Navigation Co.*, 363 U.S. 574(1960); *Steelworkers* v. *Enterprise Wheel and Car Corp.*, 363 U.S. 593(1960).

94. *Steelworkers* v. *American Manufacturing Co.*

95. *Steelworkers* v. *Warrior Gulf.*

96. *Steelworkers* v. *Enterprise Wheel.*

97. See, for example, *Collyer Insulated Wire,* 192 NLRB 837 (1971); *Olin Corporation,* 268 NLRB No. 86 (1984); and *United Technologies,* 268 NLRB No. 83 (1984).

98. *Alexander* v. *Gardner-Denver,* 415 U.S. 36 (1974).

99. *Hines* v. *Anchor Motor* 424 U.S. 554 (1976).

100. The section on the future of labor relations in the United States is based on Harry C. Katz and Thomas A. Kochan, *An Introduction to Collective Bargaining and Industrial Relations* (New York: McGraw-Hill, 1992), pp. 431–440.

101. Richard N. Block, "The Public Stake in Labor-Management Cooperation: Some Policy Implications" in Ameritech Distinguished Speaker Series, School of Labor and Industrial Relations, Michigan State University (1991), pp. 49–55.

102. Katz and Kochan, *An Introduction to Collective Bargaining,* p. 435.

103. Ibid.

104. *Labor-Management Commitment: A Compact for Change, Views from the Collective Bargaining Forum* (Washington, D.C.: United States Department of Labor, Bureau of Labor Management Relations and Cooperative Programs, Report No. 141, 1991).

16

Organizational Exit

A great deal of human resource literature has accumulated over the years on the selection, training, appraisal, and compensation of employees. Until recently, however, HR managers paid little attention to the final stage in a person's organizational life—organizational exit. In the past, retirement was the predominant form of exit. Today rapid technological change, economic recession, and the need to become more competitive relative to international rivals have led many organizations to reduce their work force. In addition, employees are now more likely to move from one organization to another because of desires for career progress or an increased emphasis on high pay. Voluntarily or involuntarily, employees are moving into and out of organizations more often. Consequently, it has become important for companies to manage the exit process in a strategic manner.

Exit can be divided into two major categories, depending on whether the organization or the employee initiates the move. In the first category, some employees are terminated for cause, owing to poor performance, excessive absenteeism, or other problems. Organizations also initiate reductions in force, laying off employees because of poor economic conditions, improvements in efficiency, or changes in the organization's strategic plan. Employee-initiated exit includes voluntary turnover and retirement.

Distinctions between different types of employee exits may have important implications. A common concern is the issue of when an employee is eligible for unemployment compensation. When an employee voluntarily leaves a job or is fired for some good reason, he or she is not eligible to receive unemployment benefits. Only when employees lose their jobs through no fault of their own (as in a reduction in work force) are they entitled to unemployment compensation in most states.[1]

This chapter first examines the process of terminating an employee when there is an adequate reason for doing so—a just cause. The second section of the chapter looks at the concept of employment-at-will—that is, whether or not an employer needs *any* cause to justify terminating an employee. The chapter then examines the process involved in laying off significant portions of an organization's work force—a reduction in force. Outplacement programs, which sometimes accompany reductions in force, are also discussed. The chapter then turns to the issues associated with voluntary employee turnover. Finally, Chapter 16 looks at the issue of retirement, a form of organizational exit that will become increasingly important to U.S. firms as the population ages.

TERMINATION FOR CAUSE

Termination occurs when an organization decides not to employ an individual any longer. In this section, we assume that termination is undertaken for a good reason—that is, for some "just cause." Later in the chapter, legal and other implications of terminating an employee without just cause are discussed.

Difficulty of Termination for Cause

Terminating an employee, even when his or her job behavior is unacceptable, may be the most difficult type of organizational exit to manage, for several reasons.

Termination for cause is personal. The decision cannot be blamed on the nation's economy, technological change, or foreign competitors. Supervisors are typically reluctant to tell employees that their job performance is inadequate and may fear a hostile employee reaction to the news of termination. As recent mass shootings of work colleagues by disgruntled former employees show, the results of an employee termination can sometimes be extremely severe. Terminating a subordinate may also damage the supervisor's image with the remaining employees.[2] Furthermore, supervisors involved in hiring the employee may be reluctant to admit that they made a mistake. Terminating an employee may seem to be an admission that the supervisor failed to select, train, or motivate the employee properly. Finally, a supervisor may feel that the responsibility for a termination rests with the organization, which allowed a situation to deteriorate until termination was the only solution.

Managing Termination for Cause

A combination of strategies can make terminations easier on everyone. First, organizations should develop performance appraisal and feedback systems that incorporate procedures for dealing with low-performance employees. Training supervisors in how to prevent or, when necessary, handle termination is also important. Finally, organizations can develop personal counseling programs for problem employees. Like appraisal and feedback systems, these programs give the employee additional opportunities to correct behavior that will otherwise lead to termination.

Performance Appraisal and Feedback Chapter 11 stresses the importance of feedback for maintaining and improving employee performance. Good appraisal systems catch problems early and give employees a chance to improve and so avoid termination. When terminations do occur, a good appraisal system makes the reasons clear. The so-called DAP, MAP, RAP system represents one approach to helping employees avoid termination (see Table 16.1). For high-performing employees who have potential for further improvement, the **developmental action plan (DAP)** involves setting of performance goals, clarifying performance standards, and determining what training is needed to help the employee prepare for advancement. The **maintenance action plan (MAP)** is used for employees who are performing adequately but have little potential for further improvement. Meetings between the supervisor and employee are less frequent than in the DAP, and the supervisor provides considerable direction about what goals are to be accomplished and how.

The **remedial action plan (RAP)** is used for problem employees. Clear feedback about the nature of behavior problems is given to the employee, and a highly specific program to correct deficiencies is imposed. Monthly review sessions are conducted, and the supervisor and employee may meet more often if the employee's behavior continues to deteriorate. If performance improves, meetings can be less frequent. An escalating series of punishments is applied if performance does not improve. These sanctions, along with the timetable for their application, are

TABLE 16.1 The DAP, MAP, RAP Appraisal System

Evaluation of Past Performance	*Plan of Action*
Good	*Developmental Action Plan (DAP)* For high-performing employee with potential for advancement Frequent setting of participative challenging goals Determining development needed for future positions Focus on future
Neutral, O.K.	*Maintenance Action Plan (MAP)* For adequate performance with little potential for improvement Annual meetings between the supervisor and employee Supervisor provides direction about what to accomplish and how Focus on current job
Poor	*Remedial Action Plan (RAP)* For problem employees Clear feedback about performance problems Highly specific, short-term goals to correct performance deficits Monthly review sessions
If performance does not improve	*Escalating series of punishments is applied*
Still no improvement	*Terminate*

Source: Adapted from L. L. Cummings and Donald P. Schwab, *Performance in Organizations: Determinants and Appraisal* (Glenview, Ill.: Scott, Foresman, 1973), p. 120. Reprinted by permission of the authors.

clearly described to the employee at the outset. For example, if behavior does not improve to a certain level within two months, the employee may receive an official letter of reprimand in his or her personnel file. After two more months without improvement, the employee may be suspended from work without pay for a week. One month after that, if no improvement is apparent, the employee will be fired.

Whenever this type of process is used, it is essential to keep accurate, *written* documents that detail the levels of performance involved and the nature of the sanctions used. Warnings issued to an employee should be in written form and should be placed in his or her permanent file.

Training Supervisors How to Terminate Supervisors and line managers need to be well trained to handle terminations. Even the best-designed remedial action plan will be ineffective if supervisors are not trained in its use. Supervisors should also be kept aware of the training and development programs offered by the organization so that they can direct a poorly performing employee to the appropriate training program.

Sometimes, however, a termination is unavoidable. The trauma associated with the event can be lessened if the supervisor has been adequately trained in how to conduct the **termination interview.** The purpose of this meeting is to inform the employee of the decision to terminate his or her employment and to explain why. Given the emotionally charged nature of the encounter, the supervisor must carefully plan for it. He or she must know all the important facts of the case and must be able to explain the reasons for the termination and give specific examples of the employee's inappropriate behavior. These examples help justify the termination decision and make it easier for the supervisor to respond to a challenge from a defensive or hostile employee. If an effective and systematic feedback system has been used, nothing in the termination interview should come as a surprise to the terminated employee. The supervisor should also evaluate his or her own attitudes and prejudices toward the employee before the meeting. A termination interview is not the place to air them. Finally, the supervisor should use the meeting to learn what went wrong and how the organization can help keep another employee from arriving at the same point.

Employee Assistance Programs Another way in which organizations can reduce the incidence of termination is to institute some type of employee assistance program. These programs help employees with personal problems that affect performance, such as drug or alcohol abuse. (Chapter 14 discusses such employee assistance programs in detail.) These programs may help keep an employee from being fired.[3] Even if termination does occur, employees may feel less hostile if they recognize that the organization has done its best to help them stay employed. Supervisors may also feel less troubled about firing employees who have been given ample opportunity to correct their behavior.

EMPLOYMENT-AT-WILL

So far our discussion has assumed that the organization has some reason for terminating a person's employment. But what if the employee disagrees or if there truly is no just cause for an employee's firing? Is this termination legal? What are the rights of employers and employees in this type of situation? In recent years, this issue—commonly referred to as the question of **employment-at-will**—has generated considerable debate. This section presents a definition and brief history of the concept of employment-at-will and discusses the factors that limit an employer's ability to terminate employees at will. Finally, some suggestions for how management should deal with the employment-at-will controversy are given.

What Is Employment-at-Will?

The employment-at-will doctrine stems from a nineteenth-century view that an employment contract is a private matter between free agents, with which government should not interfere. A person is hired for an indefinite duration, and either the employer or the employee may end the employment relationship for any reason and at any time. In 1884, this doctrine found support in the case of *Payne* v. *Western and Atlantic RA Co.*, when the court confirmed the right of an employer to hire or fire any individual for good cause, bad cause, or no cause at all.[4] Discussion of the employment-at-will issue has generally centered on the employer's right to fire a worker rather than on the employee's right to leave a job. With the Wagner Act of 1935, unions were able, through the collective bargaining process, to introduce into employment contracts the idea that employees should be fired only for just cause. Many public employees have also received statutory protection from arbitrary termination. The tenure system among university teachers, for example, protects teachers from arbitrary firing. More recently, managerial and professional employees have, in some instances, been able to negotiate employment contracts that protect them from at-will termination. However, between 70 and 75 percent of employees in the United States have no such explicit protection.[5] Nevertheless, an employer's right to fire employees at will is limited by several factors, including civil rights legislation, union contracts, and employees' limited right to sue on the grounds of wrongful discharge.

Civil Rights Legislation

Federal civil rights legislation has provided protection against employment discrimination for minority group members, women, handicapped persons, older workers, and other protected groups. Organizations have learned to be careful about the fairness of their selection systems but frequently neglect to apply the same safeguards to their exit procedures. The dismissal without cause of employees who are members of protected classes can be a dangerous affair, even when termination is part of a legitimate company-wide layoff. A worker who is discharged for *any* reason might claim that age, sex, or race was the *real* cause of the termination. If prima facie evidence of discrimination is found, the organization must spend considerable time, effort, and money to defend itself against the charge, or it must make a settlement with the plaintiff (possibly including back pay or reinstatement of the employee). Charges of discrimination also damage the organization's public image.

In the past few years, the issues of employment-at-will and employment discrimination have become closely linked in the matter of firing older employees. Chapter 5 describes the Age Discrimination in Employment Act, passed by Congress in 1967 and amended in 1978, which prohibits employers from using age as a basis for hiring or firing people aged forty or above. Age discrimination suits are an increasingly common type of workplace bias charge. The typical age-bias litigant is a white male supervisory or professional employee between the ages of fifty and fifty-nine, discharged in a corporate reduction in force. Such employees have no unions to represent them but are sufficiently aware of the law to challenge their dismissal on their own. As is evidenced in *Murphy* v. *American Home Products Corporation,* age discrimination can be used to successfully challenge at-will terminations when other, more traditional, means of challenge are unsuccessful.[6]

Union Contracts

Collective bargaining agreements also limit an organization's application of the employment-at-will doctrine. Typically, these agreements between unions and management specify the reasons for which an employee may be discharged and the procedures that should be followed in such a discharge. Unions often negotiate seniority provisions that determine who is discharged in the event of a company-wide layoff. However, if an organization takes care to follow the terms of the contract and appropriately documents all cases of termination for cause or layoffs, the constraints imposed by unionization should not be a major difficulty.

If proper discharge processes are not followed, a grievance may be filed by the employee. A formal grievance procedure then begins. The complaint is discussed at a series of meetings between representatives of the union and management at successively higher levels if agreement cannot be reached at lower levels. If the grievance procedure does not resolve the complaint, arbitration may follow. Arbitration avoids the expense and delay involved in an external judicial solution to an employee's claim, and arbitration judgments are almost always considered to be legally binding on both parties involved in the labor contract.[7]

The Concept of Wrongful Discharge

Relatively few employees can rely on federal legislation, labor contracts, or individually negotiated contracts in dealing with employment discharge situations. For most U.S. workers, a lawsuit charging **wrongful discharge** is the only protection against wholesale application of the employment-at-will doctrine.[8] (The situation is quite different in Europe—see the International Perspective box on page 732.) Court decisions associated with the wrongful discharge concept have delineated four types of situations under which the employment-at-will doctrine does not apply: (1) the employee was discharged for reasons that contradict a fundamental principle of public policy; (2) there is an express or implied guarantee of continued employment; (3) the employer's conduct violates the concepts of "good faith and fair dealing"; and (4) other tortious conduct by the employer.[9] These exceptions are summarized in Table 16.2.

INTERNATIONAL PERSPECTIVE

Unfair Dismissal Protection in Europe

Most U.S. employees are not protected from unjust dismissal by law. This is not the case for employees in Great Britain, France, Germany, or Italy. In Britain, for example, the Employment Protection Consolidation Act of 1978 and the Redundancy Payments Act of 1965 provide specific rights to employees who are fired. The 1978 law requires that employers give workers up to twelve weeks' notice of dismissal depending upon the length of service of the employee. The Redundancy Act requires employers to give lump-sum payments to workers with two years' service or more who are dismissed as part of reductions in force. In Britain, workers may complain to industrial tribunals if they believe they have been unjustly dismissed. Employers may be asked to provide written reasons for the dismissals.

In France, a law passed in 1973 states that an "employer may dismiss employees at any time" but only for a "genuine and serious cause and by following a specified procedure." Genuine and serious causes must relate directly to the ability of the employee to perform his or her job. These causes might include incompetence, loss of physical ability to do the job, offensive behavior, repeated unexcused absences or lateness, and so on. The dismissal procedure involves a variety of steps, some of which must be carried out within a specific time period after the precipitating incident. These include summoning the employee by registered mail to a hearing, informing the employee of the reasons for dismissal, and providing an opportunity for reconciliation. If no reconciliation occurs, the employer must inform the employee by registered mail that he or she will be dismissed. The employee may ask for a written explanation of the reasons for dismissal and may sue for wrongful dismissal. If the employee wins, he or she may be reinstated or receive not less than six months' pay.

In Germany, the Civil Code, Act on Protection Against Unfair Dismissals (APAUD), and the Work Council Act protect employees from arbitrary firing. The Civil Code and APAUD require that notice be given prior to dismissal, with the amount of notice varying according to length of service. These laws also define circumstances under which dismissal is justifiable, such as disability, misconduct, and economic reasons. The Work Council Act established worker councils to represent employees in organizations. These councils must review dismissal cases before firing can occur. Labor courts handle disputes concerning unjust dismissals.

In Italy, the Civil Code requires that notice or payment of an equivalent amount of wages must be given prior to dismissal. The Code also requires that dismissed workers receive a special dismissal payment based on seniority. Laws that require written explanations for dismissal and define justifiable reasons for dismissal were passed in 1966 and 1970.

Source: B. A. Hepple, "Unfair Dismissals Legislation in Great Britain," in *Protecting Unorganized Employees Against Unjust Discharge* ed. Jack Stieber and John Blackburn (East Lansing, Michigan: School of Labor and Industrial Relations, Michigan State University, 1983), pp. 135–146; Jacques Rojot, "Protection Against Unfair Dismissals In France" in *Protecting Unorganized Employees Against Unjust Discharge*, ed. Jack Stieber and John Blackburn (East Lansing, Michigan: School of Labor and Industrial Relations, Michigan State University, 1983); Manfred Weiss, "Protection Against Unfair Dismissals in West Germany," in *Protecting Unorganized Employees Against Unjust Discharge*, ed. Jack Stieber and John Blackburn (East Lansing, Michigan: School of Labor and Industrial Relations, Michigan State University, 1983), pp. 147–152; Tiziano Treu, "Protection Against Unfair Discharge in Italy," *Protecting Unorganized Employees Against Unjust Discharge*, ed. Jack Stieber and John Blackburn (East Lansing, Michigan: School of Labor and Industrial Relations, Michigan State University, 1983), pp. 159–165; R. Blanpain (ed.) "Restructuring Labour in the Enterprise; Law and Practice in France, F. R. of Germany, Italy, Sweden, and the United Kingdom," *Bulletin of Comparative Labour Relations* 15 (1986).

TABLE 16.2 Exceptions to Employment-at-Will

Exception	*Example*	*Important Cases/Laws*
Employment Discrimination	Termination based on sex or age	Title VII, Civil Rights Act Age Discrimination in Employment Act
Union Contracts	Seniority based terminations	Wagner Act
Public Policy Violations	Whistle blowers	*Palmateer* v. *International Harvester* *Sheets* v. *Teddy's Frosted Foods*
Express or Implied Guarantee of Employment	Verbal contracts Written policies in employee manuals	*Touissant* v. *Blue Cross & Blue Shield*
Good Faith and Fair Dealing	Firing to prevent receiving benefits	*Fortune* v. *National Cash Register Co.*
Tortious Conduct	Interfere with legitimate contract	*Monge* v. *Beebe Rubber Co.*

Violations of Public Policy Employees may not be fired for exercising rights protected by law—for instance, for filing workers' compensation claims or refusing to commit perjury or taking time off to serve on a jury. Various forms of whistle blowing are also protected (see the Ethical Perspectives Box on page 734). For example, in *Palmateer* v. *International Harvester,* an employee was subject to wrongful discharge after he had reported coworkers who were involved in criminal activity. In *Sheets* v. *Teddy's Frosted Foods,* an employee who insisted that the company comply with the Food, Drugs, and Cosmetics Act was found to have been wrongfully discharged.[10] Although most states have accepted the concept of wrongful discharge as a result of violations of public policy, the situation is usually defined very narrowly. The critical issue is not whether the employee's behavior is of *benefit* to the public, but whether a *clear and legal mandate* of public policy is involved.

Express or Implied Guarantee of Continued Employment While violation of public policy is the most recognized exception to the employment-at-will doctrine, courts in some states have recognized that an express or implied contract between the employer and the employee may limit arbitrary firing. Implied contracts are created in several ways. In one case—*Touissant* v. *Blue Cross and Blue Shield of Michigan*—employees had been fired for no apparent reason, even though there had been statements by the employer to the effect that "you can have your job as long as you do your job." These statements were deemed to form a contract between employee and employer.[11] In the same case, there were also written personnel policies stating that good cause was required before any

ETHICAL PERSPECTIVE

Whistleblowing in Organizations

What should an employee do when he or she learns of ethically questionable behavior on the part of peers, superiors, or other groups in the organization? Until recently, many organizations took the view that the employee should either exhibit loyalty to the superior and the organization by doing nothing, or quietly leave the organization and find another job. These options conform to two of Hirschmann's classical categories of responses to dissatisfaction: loyalty and exit. The other response he suggests is "voice,"—speaking up in an effort to get the situation remedied.

Voice in the context of suspected organizational wrong-doing is called **whistleblowing.** Internal whistleblowing is making one's suspicions known to a responsible person in the organization in the hope that the problem will be corrected. External whistleblowing is making the wrong-doing known to someone outside the organization, such as the press, law enforcement agency, or regulatory agency. Both internal and external whistleblowing can be done anonymously or openly.

Whistleblowing is a relatively rare behavior in many organizations for this reason: Before taking such action, an employee must (1) become aware of unethical behavior in the organization, and have sufficient evidence to support his or her suspicions, (2) see the behavior as morally serious and/or having serious consequences for others, (3) feel personally responsible for doing something about the situation, and (4) perceive that an effective course of action is possible. Even under these conditions, individuals often fear the consequences of speaking up. Gene G. James notes that whistleblowers quite often face retaliation. Forms of retaliation can range from ostracism by one's coworkers to loss of professional reputation, demotion, discharge, blacklisting, and in some cases even physical assault and murder.

As ethical issues in business have become more salient over the past decade, many organizations have changed their view of whistleblowing. Instead of seeing it as disloyalty or boat-rocking, they are now trying to harness it as an early warning that problems are occurring that need to be addressed. By making internal whistleblowing easier and more effective, these firms hope to discover and correct potential wrongdoing before public damage is done. This is especially important if the employee is incorrect in his or her suspicions, but could do substantial harm to the organization's reputation by going to an external party with allegations of misconduct. In one recent survey, 70 percent of responding organizations said that they had a formal procedure for employees to bring legal and ethical concerns to the attention of management.

An effective whistleblowing policy should:

- Be written.
- Be well communicated to employees.
- Allow employees to go to someone other than their immediate supervisor with complaints (because the supervisor is often the one committing or condoning the problematic act).
- Allow for anonymous reporting.
- Specify a formal investigation procedure, with feedback to the employee on the outcome of the investigation.
- Forbid any form of retaliation against whistleblowers.
- Provide an appeal process if the employee is still not satisfied.

HR managers are often involved in whistleblowing cases. In the survey mentioned above, 77 percent of formal policies specified the HR department as one outlet for employees who wish to make a complaint. HR managers may also be involved in educating supervisors about the policy and in assuring that whistle-blowers are not penalized by unfair personnel actions such as distorted performance apprais-als, zero raises, demotions, forced transfers, or unjust discharge.

Sources: Timothy R. Barnett and Daniel S. Coch-ran, "Making Room for the Whistleblower," *HRMagazine*, January 1991, pp. 58–61; Richard P. Nielsen, "Changing Unethical Organizational Behavior," *Academy of Management Executive*, May 1989, pp. 123–130; Jill W. Graham, "Princi-pled Organizational Dissent: A Theoretical Es-say," *Research in Organizational Behavior*, 1986, Vol. 9, pp. 1–52; Gene G. James, "In Defense of Whistle Blowing," in *Moral Issues in Business*, William Shaw and Vincent Barry (Eds.) Belmont, CA: Wadsworth, 1989, pp. 337–346.

nonprobationary employee would be fired and that employees could be fired only after receiving a series of warnings and a disciplinary hearing. The employees had been fired without benefit of these procedures. They filed suit against the company and won the case. The availability of this form of protection against at-will termination varies from state to state. Some states have rejected this type of implied contract argument, while other states have taken no clear stance on the issue.

Good Faith and Fair Dealing Judicial tradition also holds that a contract contains an implied promise of good faith and fair dealing. Any violation of good faith on the employer's part may provide the basis for a suit claiming an exception to the employment-at-will doctrine. In *Fortune* v. *National Cash Register Co.*, Fortune, a salesman, had worked for the company for twenty-five years under a contract that specifically stated that he had been hired on an at-will basis.[12] He was fired after having made a large sale—because, he charged, the company wanted to avoid paying him the commission it owed him. Although his contract included an at-will clause, the court ruled that National Cash Register had not acted in good faith and thus had violated the employment contract.

Tortious Conduct Some discharged employees have argued successfully that they were victims of tortious conduct. In law, a tort is the violation of a duty owed another person (aside from breach of specific contracts). An employer who acts with malicious intent in terminating employees, intentionally inflicting emotional distress on them or defaming their character, can be found guilty of wrongful discharge.[13] In addition, an organization can be found guilty of tortious conduct if it interferes with an employment contract between other parties, resulting in an employee's discharge. For example, in a 1985 Minnesota case, a bus terminal company was found guilty of wrongful interference in an employment contract. The terminal had told a bus company that unless it "got rid of" a certain employee, it could no longer use the terminal.[14]

Management's Response

Organizations may approach the issue of employment-at-will in several ways. Some companies have taken actions such as including explicit at-will statements on job application forms; or statements in their personnel manuals indicating that there are no assurances of continued employment; and/or statements in policy manuals that clearly indicate that termination can occur without just cause.[15] Some organizations have even asked employees to sign notarized releases waiving age-bias claims.[16] However, such actions often convey a rather negative view of the company to prospective and current employees. Who would want to work for a company that obviously has no sense of loyalty and fair play when dealing with employee terminations?

Another approach has been to encourage unionization and specific labor contracts.[17] Discharge cases are then handled within the framework of a collectively bargained grievance and arbitration procedure rather than in the courts. Given management's traditional desire to avoid unionization, this seems a radical solution to the problem.

Organizations may also voluntarily adopt policies guaranteeing discharge only for just cause and specifying the procedures that must be used before an employee is fired. If carefully developed, these policies can help increase (rather than decrease) an organization's ability to discharge poorly performing employees.[18]

A highly proactive and relatively little used approach is to take measures to reduce the need for discharges.[19] Management can improve employee selection procedures and, during the selection process, avoid making promises that it does not intend or cannot keep. Companies can provide realistic orientation programs, where employees both learn what level of performance is expected and receive the training that can help them achieve this level. Management may also develop an accurate performance appraisal system, in which escalating sanctions for poor performance are clearly specified (as in the RAP system described earlier) and a paper trail of performance is maintained. Performance feedback provided by the system may help employees avoid termination. If termination is necessary, everyone understands why. The lack of a comprehensive and accurate paper trail documenting an employee's poor performance may prove disastrous for the organization if it is sued for wrongful discharge. In one case, a company argued that workers laid off because of a reduction in force were the least productive employees. The plaintiffs' lawyer produced personnel files showing that the employees had been given excellent performance appraisal ratings over the years. The jury found the company guilty of willful discrimination and awarded the employees substantial damages.[20]

REDUCTIONS IN FORCE

In recent years, many American businesses have found it necessary to cut costs by reducing their work forces. A survey by the American Management Association (AMA) found that of the 1219 firms responding to the survey 43 percent had downsized, with reductions in force averaging 10.7 percent. *Time* reported that 375,000 jobs had been lost in the United States between June 1991 and June 1992.[21] Although **reductions in force** (also called **layoffs** or **downsizing**) are not a new idea, they have historically been confined to the lowest levels of the corporate hierarchy. The recent wave of layoffs, in contrast, has been felt throughout the hierarchy in an unprecedented number of organizations. According to the AMA survey, 43 percent of the positions eliminated in the downsizing firms were managerial. Another survey indicates that 85 percent of the Fortune 1000 firms downsized white-collar employees between 1987 and 1991, while 50 percent of these firms downsized in 1990 alone. Even some well-known firms downsized very substantially. For example, ITT Corp. reduced its white-collar employees by 40 percent, K mart Corp. by 20 percent, and both AT&T and Sears, Roebuck and Co. by 10 percent. In 1990 almost 1 million managers with salaries above $40,000 a year lost their jobs. Between 1 million and 2 million managers have been laid off during each of the last three years.[22] Although politicians indicate that the economic recovery is "just around the corner," the issue of handling reductions in force is likely to remain an important one. Even after the world economy recovers, the need for firms to become leaner, more efficient, and more productive in order to meet the challenge of international competition will keep reductions in force a critical management concern. Therefore, managers must learn ways to effectively plan for and manage the layoff process.

The Importance of Planning

Planning is a crucial element in effectively managing layoffs. It is critical that the organization develop plans for coping with a labor oversupply situation *before* the need arises. Decisions made hastily under economic pressure may be poor ones. Yet a 1988 survey found that 50 percent of HR managers responding indicated that their firms were unprepared for reducing their work force.[23] General policies and procedures for handling layoffs should include (1) viable methods of reducing the work force; (2) procedures for identifying candidates for layoffs and for dealing with them at the time of layoff; and (3) procedures for managing people who remain with the organization. Many reductions in force suffer from a lack of planning. Often, for example, each major company function is dealt with as a relatively isolated, independent unit. Furthermore, cutting labor costs by layoffs may be chosen as a quick fix, but management may fail to solve the underlying problems that made a cost-reduction program necessary, and soon further cost-cutting strategies may be necessary.[24]

Methods of Work Force Reduction

Management should seriously consider options that do not include outright dismissal.[25] In another AMA survey, organizations reported using various work force reduction tactics (See Table 16.3). Offering early retirement incentives was the

TABLE 16.3 Tactics for Reducing Work Force Size

Attrition
The organization implements a "no hiring" policy, then allows the natural processes of terminations, retirements, voluntary turnover, etc., to reduce the work force. This approach is possible only when the organization has sufficient time before work force reductions are necessary.

Early Retirement Incentives
Offering bonuses or additional retirement benefits to employees who volunteer to retire early.

Job Redeployment and Retraining Opportunities
In-house relocation of employees to different jobs with training provided in the new job skills.

Job Sharing
Two employees work part-time at a job that would require only a single full-time employee.

Part-Time Employment
Cutting back full-time positions to part-time.

Voluntary Lack-of-Work Programs
Employees voluntarily take "no work, no pay" days while being paid for days they do work.

Across-the-Board Salary Reductions
Reduces the wage demands on the organization so that labor costs are reduced without laying off workers. In unionized organizations, such reductions generally require renegotiation of union contracts.

Source: Eric R. Greenberg, "Downsizing: Results of a Survey by the American Management Association." Reprinted, by permission of publisher, from *Personnel,* October 1987, © 1987. American Management Association, New York. All rights reserved.

most popular approach, whereas actions requiring the renegotiation of union contracts were least popular. In deciding how to reduce its work force, management should take into account the length of time that the reduction is likely to be needed, that is, how much time might elapse before the company can grow in work force size again. In addition, the labor market associated with various job groups where layoffs will occur should also be considered. If the need for a reduction in force is expected to be relatively short term and the availability in the labor market of employees with particular job skills is restricted, then management may have to consider more innovative ways to reduce labor costs without completely losing the attachment of the employee to the organization. For example, job sharing, part-time employment, reduced work hours, or across-the-board pay cuts all reduce labor costs while retaining employees in the organization. Once economic conditions allow for work force growth, the organization will not be forced to recruit in the open labor market for new employees but can simply increase the reduced workload of current employee to normal levels. Such an approach represents a far more strategic way of dealing with an oversupply of labor, and the organization can avoid the cost of recruiting, orienting, and training new employees.

Those Who Are Laid Off

Deciding which employees are to be laid off is often a difficult matter. In some cases, union contracts specify a "last hired, first fired" approach. When such contractual procedures do not exist, management must decide on some fair and appropriate way of selecting those who will be laid off. In a few cases, where attractive early retirement or enhanced severance pay is offered, there may be enough volunteers to preclude the need for nonvoluntary layoffs. In most situations, however, employees may be eliminated based upon the functions they perform as a result of their individual level of performance in those functions.[26] From the organization's point of view, keeping the best-performing employees is essential. These "survivors" are often asked to take on additional tasks, which were formerly carried out by other employees. Good performers are more likely able to manage the extra workload. But in order to base layoffs on performance, the organization must have an appropriate performance evaluation system in operation.

Regardless of how individuals are selected, there are some actions that management should take. When the organization has decided to implement a work force reduction, affected personnel should be informed as quickly as possible. Face-to-face, individual discussions between the employees and their immediate supervisors are best. The supervisor should tell the employee why the layoffs are being made and should discuss the severance package in detail. When possible, it is a good idea to offer extended benefits to laid off employees—for example, to increase severance pay somewhat or to pay for the employee to remain on the firm's health insurance plan for some time after the layoff. The employee should sign a detailed agreement that includes a description of the severance pay that he or she will receive, along with any noncash benefits and outplacement services that the organization may provide. (Outplacement services are discussed in detail later in this chapter.) In the case of employees who possess knowledge of the company's trade secrets, the severance agreement may also prohibit disclosure of proprietary information to the organization's competitors. In all cases, laid-off workers should be treated in as fair and courteous a manner as possible.[27]

Managing the Survivors

Often those who remain after a reduction in force are considered the lucky ones and are often ignored by management. However, research has shown that survivors of a reduction in force suffer significant problems, which may have a dramatic impact on the organization. Survivors frequently show decreased productivity and satisfaction. They lose their motivation to work and worry about the future of their own jobs, wondering if they will be the next ones laid off. After a reduction in force, many survivors seek new jobs.[28]

Dealing effectively with survivors may be more important for the long-term health of the organization than dealing effectively with those laid off. Practitioners and researchers have suggested several ways to minimize the negative effects of layoffs on survivors. Survivors should be told why the terminations are occurring and who will be affected. It is critical that the same information be given to survivors as to the employees being laid off. Any discrepancies will be discovered as employees compare notes, reducing the organization's ability to inspire confidence and commitment in its remaining employees. It is also important to inform survivors when layoff goals have been met, to relieve their anxiety that they might be next in line for termination. When organizations provide generous outplacement and severance benefits, survivors feel more positive toward the firm, more comfortable and less stressed by the layoffs.[29] Increased training for survivors may also be essential. Survivors may be asked to add new tasks to their job duties—tasks that they may not have done before.[30] Without adequate training, survivors may not only feel guilty about those laid off, but also experience a sense of inadequacy and even failure in their newly defined jobs.

A layoff, if it is handled properly, may actually have a positive effect on survivors. The equity theory of motivation suggests that people who survive a layoff compare themselves with laid-off employees and feel guilty about not losing their jobs. Consequently, they may work harder in order to relieve their sense of inequity and guilt.[31] One study found support for this notion, but only under certain conditions. It appears to make a difference whether employees are selected for termination on the basis of merit (lower-performing employees are terminated whereas higher-performing workers are not) or through a more random selection process. The laboratory study showed that when layoffs were due to random selection, survivors felt guilty and worked harder in order to assuage their guilt. Their *quantity* of task performance increased significantly, although *quality* of performance declined. In the merit layoff situation, no effects on performance were found.[32] It may be that when layoffs are based on merit, survivors have a rationale to explain their continued employment with the company. There is then no need to feel guilty and no need to improve performance to reduce guilt.

Other Issues in Effectively Managing a Reduction in Force

A recent study of white-collar reductions in force has identified firms that seem to have handled layoff situations well. These firms were able to deal effectively with a number of contradictions that arose during the process. Some of these contradictions are listed in Table 16.4. In the firms that handled the layoffs well, top management took an aggressive, strong, visible, and hands-on approach to the problem. At the same time, much of the analysis of job redundancies and workplace inefficiencies was done by teams of employees knowledgeable about those activities in the firm. Across-the-board layoffs were made to get everyone's atten-

TABLE 16.4 Managing Contradictions During a Reduction in Force

Contradictions	*What it Means*
1. Top-Down Management	Aggressive, strong, visible, hands-on leadership
Bottom-up Management	Employees involved in finding inefficiencies
2. Across-the-Board Layoffs	Get everyone's attention, energize the firm
Selective Layoffs	Change the organization's structure, effect culture change
3. Laid Off Employees	Outplacement, counseling, sponsorship, covering relocation costs
Survivors	Increased communication, training
4. Within the Organization	Target inefficiencies within the firm
Outside the Organization	Cut back external network where possible
5. Centralize	Look for economies of scale
Decentralize	Move decisions to point closest to the action
6. An End in Itself	Layoffs are needed to survive now
A Means to an End	Layoffs are part of a program to make the organization more competitive in the long term

Source: Adapted with permission from K. Cameron, S. J. Freeman and A. K. Mishra, "Best Practices in White-Collar Downsizing: Managing Contradictions," *Academy of Management Executive,* Vol. 5, No. 3, 1991, pp. 57–73.

tion as to the seriousness of the problems faced. Other, more targeted layoffs were used as part of a longer-term approach to organizational restructuring and culture change. Effective firms developed programs for both those laid off and the survivors. Cutbacks were made not only within the organization, but also among external suppliers and subcontractors. Effective firms centralized the functions that allowed them to gain economies of scale, while at the same time pushing the decision-making process downward in the organization when appropriate. Finally, effective firms treated the reduction in force as both an end in itself and as a means to a longer term goal of increasing overall efficiency and competitiveness.[33]

Legal Constraints on Reductions in Force

In planning a work force reduction, organizations must consider legal constraints, as well as their own needs and those of employees. The current trend is for the courts to support management decisions in which seniority is used as the basis for layoffs. In a 1984 case, *Firefighters Local Union 1784* v. *Stotts*, the Supreme Court ruled it was illegal to lay off white employees with greater seniority to protect black workers who had less seniority but had been hired as part of an affirmative action plan.[34] Another Supreme Court ruling underscores the need to consider state regulations on layoffs. The court ruled that a Maine law requiring workers laid off in a plant closing to be given one week of severance pay for each year of employment did not conflict with federal law on employee benefits.[35]

The Worker Adjustment and Retraining Notification Act (WARN), commonly known as the Plant Closing Bill, requires employers covered by the law to give affected employees sixty days' written notice of anticipated plant closings or other mass layoffs.[36] WARN, which went into effect in 1989, covers employers that have 100 or more full-time employees or have 100 or more employees who, together, work at least 4,000 hours per week, excluding overtime. WARN covers nonprofit organizations but not federal, state, or local government.

WARN defines **affected employees** as all workers, including managerial and supervisory personnel, who may suffer some employment loss as the result of a plant closing or mass layoff. Individuals who work less than twenty hours per week or who have been employed for less than six out of the twelve months immediately preceding the layoff are not covered. An **employment loss** means a layoff exceeding six months or a reduction in work hours of 50 percent or more for a period of six months.

According to WARN, a **plant closing** is any temporary or permanent shutdown of an entire facility or significant part of a facility if the closing results in employment loss during a thirty-day period for fifty or more employees. A **mass layoff** occurs when a facility is not closed, but there is a reduction in force affecting at least fifty employees in a thirty-day period if these fifty employees constitute at least one-third of the work force. A mass layoff may also occur if, cumulatively, at least one-third of the work force is laid off over a ninety-day period, unless the employer can show that layoffs within a series of layoffs were due to different causes.

Employers violating the law may be required to provide back pay and benefits for up to sixty days to workers laid off without proper notification. In some cases, employers may be required to pay fines of $500 per day, up to $30,000.

There are some exceptions to WARN. A "faltering company" is exempt if it was actively seeking capital to prevent the plant closing or layoff and reasonably believed that giving notice to employees would have prevented the company from receiving the financing. An "unforeseeable business circumstance" may also exempt a company, as when employees at a major supplier suddenly and unexpectedly go on strike and the company cannot operate without the supplies. Closings due to natural disasters such as floods and earthquakes likewise exempt a company from the sixty-day notice requirement. A final exemption covers closings of plants that were originally established as "temporary facilities" if employees were hired with the understanding that their employment was not permanent.

Organizations must ensure that any plans for work force reductions take into account the provisions of WARN. More generally, employees should keep abreast of federal and state legislative activities and update their plans for a reduction in force accordingly.

OUTPLACEMENT

With the trend toward downsizing during the 1980s and 1990s, many organizations have developed comprehensive approaches to dealing with employees who face termination. These so-called **outplacement** procedures help laid-off employees find other jobs. This section discusses the functions that outplacement serves, the ways to provide outplacement services, the kinds of activities that may be included, and the effectiveness of such programs.

Functions of Outplacement Programs

Outplacement serves several functions. First, if an organization helps discharged employees find new jobs, reductions in force are likely to be less stressful and traumatic. Second, knowing that an organization is willing to look after its departing employees enhances the morale of those who remain behind. It is crucial to maintain the good will and motivation of surviving employees, especially if the layoffs are due to problems in the organization. Third, outplacement seems to help employees find new jobs faster than would otherwise be possible. Over the long run, helping people become re-employed reduces the organization's unemployment insurance benefit costs. Fourth, some experts feel that outplacement tends to reduce the threat of litigation about the discharge.[37] As Chuck Albrecht, an executive vice president of Drake Beam Morin, America's largest outplacement firm, said, "If people are talking to an outplacement counselor, they're not talking to a lawyer."[38] Finally, more and more business organizations are simply recognizing that they have a moral and ethical responsibility toward their employees.

Who Provides Outplacement?

Outplacement can be provided by an organization's own human resource staff or by an external consultant. An in-house approach is less expensive, as outplacement consultants themselves agree, but the organization's human resource staff may not be credible to employees and may not have the resources needed to assist laid-off employees in their career transitions. Some organizations choose external outplacement consultants in the belief that employees will be more open to suggestions from, and willing to work with, a third party.[39] The extent of demand for outplacement services should also be considered. If a company is facing large-scale layoffs at all organizational levels, external outplacement or a mix of external and internal services might be appropriate. Small-scale terminations or layoffs of primarily lower-level employees might be better served by in-house sources.

Outplacement Activities

Outplacement activities include (1) counseling to provide psychological and emotional support; (2) helping to develop job search skills; and (3) helping to ensure that the employee will continue the job search even after the outplacement service ends.[40]

The function of counseling is twofold. First, it helps employees work through their feelings of anger, resentment, grief, and shock at losing their jobs and begin to accept the situation. Several researchers have drawn a parallel between the emotions experienced by people who have lost their jobs and those who are terminally ill. Not all these emotional stages may be experienced, but one purpose of outplacement counseling is to help an individual reach the acceptance stage. At that point, energy can be directed into job search activities, rather than into experiencing emotional stress.

After helping an employee resolve negative feelings about termination and begin seeking re-employment, outplacement counseling continues to serve a useful support function. As Figure 16.1 indicates, a person may go through four stages of unemployment after dealing with the shock of the layoff decision. Training in job search skills may be the most important goal during the first two stages, but if the person remains unemployed, outplacement personnel need to be prepared to provide supportive, motivational types of counseling that will build self-esteem.

Training in job search skills is a central outplacement activity. It generally involves helping the employee set goals for the job search, as well as develop a personal marketing strategy and good interview skills.[41] Employees who are laid off after working for many years in the same organization will have had little recent experience in looking for jobs. Psychological research has made a connection between confidence in job search skills and reemployment rates. A study of thirty-five laid-off hospital employees showed that those who found new jobs had been more confident about their job search skills than were the people who remained unemployed. The confident, reemployed persons had also engaged in more job search behaviors.[42] Outplacement services can build people's confidence by training them in relevant skills. Laid-off employees of Control Data Corporation, for example, can participate in a three-day seminar in which they learn to assess their career goals and their skills and abilities. They are also offered workshops in writing résumés and job application letters.[43] Stroh Brewery provided individualized skills testing and assessment for employees when it closed its Detroit brewing facility. Stroh also established a library of information about potential employers to help employees research companies before interviewing with them.[44] Although small firms may be unable to offer such extensive outplacement

FIGURE 16.1 Emotional Stages of Job Loss and the Stages of Unemployment

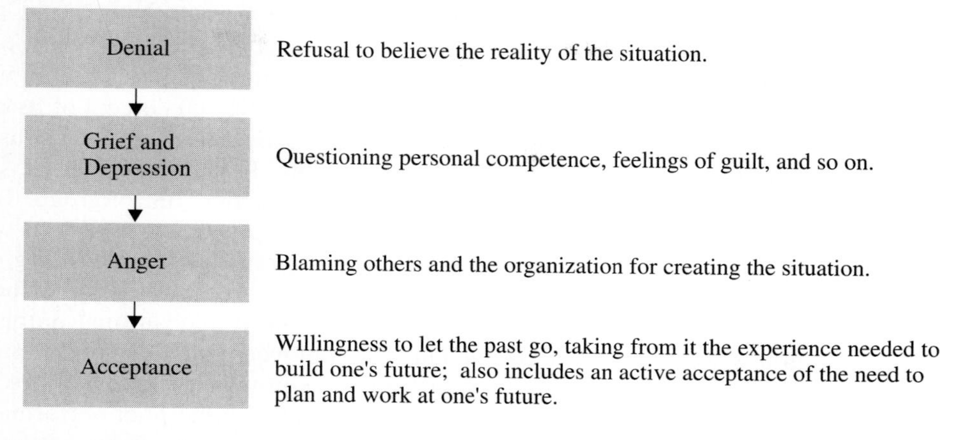

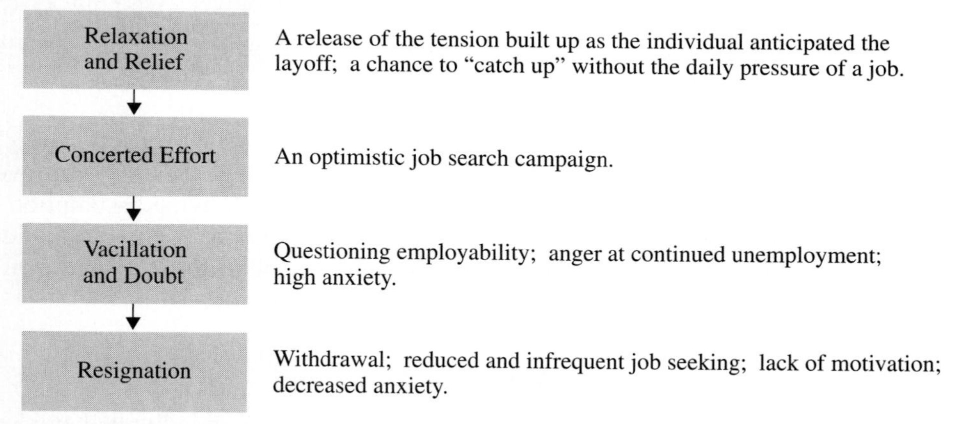

Source: Adapted from Janina C. Latack and Janelle B. Dozier, "After the Ax Falls: Job Loss as a Career Transition," *Academy of Management Review,* Vol. 11, 1986, pp. 375–392. Reprinted by permission.

services, they can provide significant aid to their laid-off workers. Small firms can provide on-site services to help with job search, such as telephones (with long-distance capability), an office, postage, good stationery, photocopiers, and some career counseling.[45] For example, after a recent retrenchment of administrative staff, Bond University in Queensland, Australia, allowed many of those retrenched to use personal computers and laser printers at the university to aid them in sending out professional-looking résumés.[46]

Does Outplacement Really Help?

Professionals contend that outplacement is very successful in helping people find jobs, and several studies support this view. Figure 16.2 illustrates the results of two such studies. The first study compared two groups of sixty persons each, matched in age, work experience, and education level. One group was given outplacement assistance. At the end of three months, 90 percent of its members had found new jobs. The other group, which received no assistance, was only 55 percent reemployed at the end of three months. In addition, average salary was 36 percent higher for the assisted group than for the control group. In the second study, conducted by the U.S. Department of Labor, 1,000 persons were assigned to one of several job search assistance programs or to a control group. The job search assistance groups were almost twice as successful as the control group.[47] The results of these two studies would seem to indicate that outplacement programs are effective in helping laid-off employees find new jobs.

So far, we have focused on situations in which employees are involuntarily discharged by their organization as the result of either poor performance (or other just cause) or a general reduction in force. The rest of this chapter focuses on voluntary organizational exits—that is, on employees who quit or retire.

TURNOVER

For decades, management scholars have studied voluntary turnover in order to understand why people quit their jobs. The underlying assumption has generally been that turnover is dysfunctional and should be reduced to the lowest possible levels. However, some researchers suggest that an organization's optimal turnover rate is well above the minimum possible rate.

Research on the Causes of Voluntary Turnover

A number of external factors influence whether an individual employee perceives that moving from one job to another will be easy (see Table 16.5), and perceived ease of movement influences the likelihood of turnover.[48] Turnover is higher when unemployment in the general labor market is low, so that alternative employment appears readily available to job leavers. However, studies indicate that the impact of general labor market conditions on turnover may be overstated. The availability of alternate jobs in the employee's *specific* labor market (i.e., the market most relevant to the person's skills and job experience) is more critical in determining turnover than the state of the general labor market. Furthermore, this research suggests that, even when the general labor market is very unfavorable for job movement, if an employee considering turnover receives a job offer, this may overcome any influence of the level of unemployment in the broader labor market.[49]

FIGURE 16.2 Success Rates of Outplacement Programs

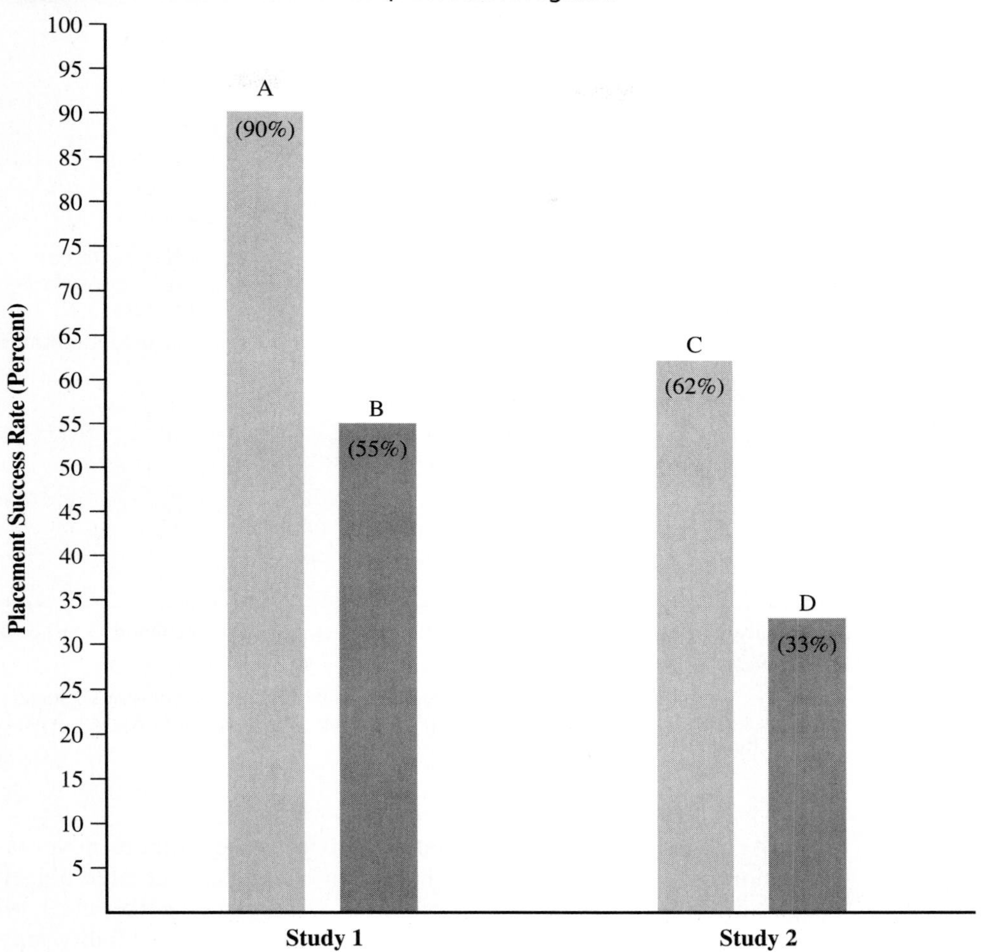

Study 1 *A = Job Search Program (60 people);*
B = Control Group (60 people);
Study 2 *C = Job Search Program (U.S. Dept. of Labor);*
D = Control Group (U.S. Dept. of Labor).
In the U.S. Dept. of Labor study, 1000 people were assigned randomly to either the control group or one of the five job search programs.

Source: Adapted from Lawrence J. Stybel, "How Managers React to Their Own Dismissal: Implications for Intervention Theory and Practice" (paper presented at the Academy of Management Conference, August 1981, San Diego, Calif.); and R. Wegmann, "Job Search Assistance: A Review," *Journal of Employment Counselling,* Vol. 12, 1979, pp. 197–225.

TABLE 16.5 Factors Correlated with Turnover

External Factors	
Perceived availability of alternative employment (+)	
Unemployment rate (−)	
Union presence (−)	
Work-related Factors	
Pay (−)	Satisfaction (with pay, work itself, supervision, coworkers, promotion opportunities) (−)
Job performance (?)	Organization commitment (−)
Role clarity (−)	
Task repetitiveness (+)	
Overall job satisfaction (−)	
Personal Factors	
Age (−)	Tenure (−)
Education (+)	Being married (−)
Number of dependents (−)	
Met expectations (−)	

+ Indicates a positive relationship between the factor and the likelihood of turnover.

− Indicates a negative relationship.

Source: Adapted from John L. Cotton and Jeffrey M. Tuttle, "Employee Turnover: A Meta-Analysis with Implications for Research," *Academy of Management Review,* Vol. 11, 1986, p. 57. Reprinted by permission.

Analyses at the organizational and job level show that turnover is often lower in unionized settings. It may be that union efforts have created objectively *better* jobs (in terms of pay, working condition, work place justice, etc.), which people are less likely to leave. On the other hand, this greater stability may reflect the advantages associated with longer tenure in the seniority systems usually established in unionized companies. A few studies have found that turnover is lower in organizations that give employees a "voice mechanism," such as an open door policy, union grievance procedure, or ombudsman. These mechanisms offer employees a constructive way to try to change a work situation perceived as unfair or dissatisfying. Without such an opportunity, dissatisfied employees often choose to vote with their feet.[50]

At the individual level, job satisfaction is negatively related to turnover. Employees who are more satisfied with their job as a whole—with pay, supervision, the nature of the work itself, and/or opportunities for advancement—are less likely to quit. Turnover is also less likely if the job meets the employee's initial expectations, held at the time of hiring. Individuals lured into accepting a job by false or inflated promises are quick to leave when they become disillusioned.[51]

Job involvement and organizational commitment also seem to influence turnover rates. Some research indicates that these two factors interact to influence turnover. In a 1987 article, Gary J. Blau and Kimberly B. Boal suggested that Institutional Stars (employees high in both job involvement and organizational commitment) are the least likely to quit, whereas Apathetics (low involvement and commitment) are the most likely to leave. Corporate Citizens (high commitment, low involvement are less likely than Lone Wolves (high involvement, low commitment) to leave. Later research has supported their ideas.[52]

Turnover is also more likely among people who experience greater stress in their jobs. Commonly mentioned job stressors include role conflict, role ambiguity, and role overload. Turnover is also more frequent among employees with higher levels of education, probably because their employment alternatives are better, they may be more loyal to their own careers or profession than to a particular organization, and they desire the rapid advancement that may be achieved by changing employers. Personal characteristics associated with lower turnover include having longer current tenure, being married, having more dependents, and being older.[53]

Models of Employee Turnover

In addition to identifying predictors of turnover, a number of researchers have investigated the *process* of deciding to quit a job. Two distinct types of models have emerged from this research. The first type treats the decision to quit as a logical choice that is reached in incremental stages. For instance, a model developed by William Mobley suggests that individuals begin by evaluating their current job and level of satisfaction or dissatisfaction.[54] If they are dissatisfied, they may begin to think of quitting, then assess the costs of quitting and the costs and likely success of searching for an alternative job. After some thought, they may begin to conduct a search for alternatives, weigh them against the present job, develop intentions to quit, and finally quit. A somewhat abbreviated version of the Mobley turnover model is presented in Figure 16.3.

A different approach uses a "catastrophe model" of the decision to quit.[55] This view of turnover suggests that sudden shifts in employee behavior (from staying to quitting) may be brought about by relatively minor changes in job satisfaction or stress. Catastrophe models describe the process leading up to the proverbial straw that breaks the camel's back. An employee who shows no signs of distress and is not seriously considering quitting may still have a cumulatively dissatisfying experience in the organization. At some point, even a single small extra problem or an unpleasant job experience may push that person over the edge.

There is research support for both of these models, but it is not possible to predict when each type of quitting will occur, or exactly who will or will not quit. The two models have somewhat different implications for the prevention of turnover. If the decision to quit is a relatively continuous and rational process, the employer probably has time to notice that the employee is gradually losing interest

FIGURE 16.3 Abbreviated Mobley Turnover Model

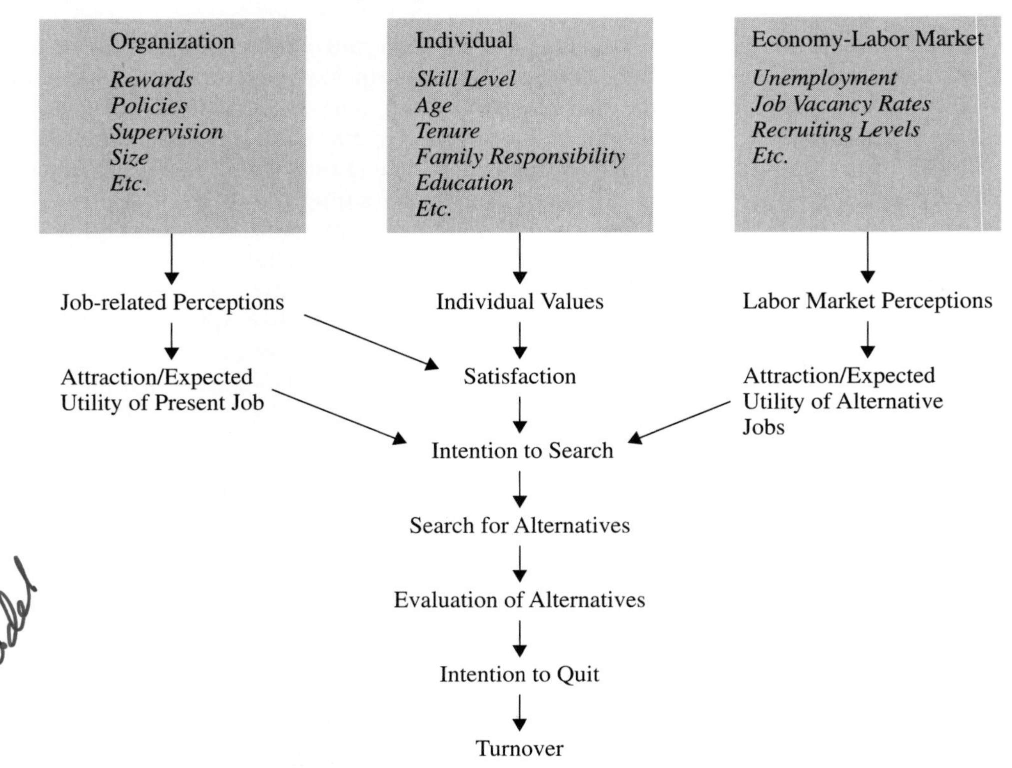

Source: Adapted from William H. Mobley, *Employee Turnover: Causes, Consequences, and Control,* © 1982 by Addison-Wesley Publishing Company, Inc. Reprinted with permission of the publisher.

and starting to consider employment alternatives. Managers may be able to take remedial action to retain a valued employee. On the other hand, if an employee's decision to leave approximates a catastrophe process, he or she may give little warning of impending turnover, and the triggering event may be trivial yet irrevocable. The first model suggests that an employer can wait to intervene until the employee begins the long process of rationally deciding to quit; the second suggests that constant efforts to increase satisfaction and reduce workplace stressors will be necessary.

Costs and Benefits of Turnover

As mentioned earlier, management scholars have often assumed that turnover is dysfunctional and should be reduced to the lowest possible level. But turnover has benefits, as well as its highly visible costs.

Costs of Turnover The disadvantages of turnover include the costs of recruiting, selecting, and training a replacement; lost production until the newcomer becomes as skilled as the worker who quit; supervisory time and attention required to break in a new hire; and disruption or demoralization of the work group. High rates of turnover may also damage the organization's reputation as an employer or render it unable to exploit growth opportunities because of insufficient staff.[56]

Benefits of Turnover More recently, scholars have suggested that a moderate rate of turnover can have positive effects on organizations, including opportunities to replace departing employees with better performers, individuals with more current training, or entry-level workers who can be paid at a lower rate. Replacement hiring can be an excellent means of introducing innovation and diffusing new technologies across organizations. At the CEO level, turnover is often considered a necessary and beneficial phenomenon in troubled organizations, with the appointment of an outsider seen as most likely to result in a successful turnaround. Turnover also opens up opportunities to promote remaining employees. A reasonable rate of turnover above the entry level may motivate current employees to develop themselves for future jobs and to stay with the organization in anticipation of internal advancement. Finally, if the employees who leave were vocal malcontents who caused conflict and contributed to a hostile work atmosphere, their departure may be a welcome relief for those left behind.[57]

If the aggregate turnover rate is very low, the organization does not have a chance to reap such benefits. Two industries that have been notorious for their inefficiency—railroads and the postal service—have historically had the longest average employee tenure and lowest turnover of all industries studied. While the causes remain uncertain, these data do suggest that turnover rates can be too low, as well as too high.

The Strategic Management of Turnover

Current thinking suggests that organizations should seek an optimal rate of turnover, rather than try to reduce it to the lowest possible level. One article suggests that the optimal rate occurs where the curve of turnover costs crosses the curve of retention costs, as shown in Figure 16.4. As the turnover rate increases, so do the costs of replacement and lost productivity. The organization can reduce turnover, but only by incurring retention costs, such as higher wages, better benefits, quality of work life programs, and so on. The point at which these two curves cross represents the lowest total cost, and thus the optimal turnover rate for the organization. This type of analysis suggests that a relatively high turnover rate may sometimes be less costly than a lower one. Consider the case of fast-food preparation employees. Turnover tends to be high, and wages are quite low. If wages were doubled or tripled, turnover would surely drop, but this strategy would not be cost-effective since replacing fast food workers is fairly inexpensive.

FIGURE 16.4 Optimal Organizational Turnover

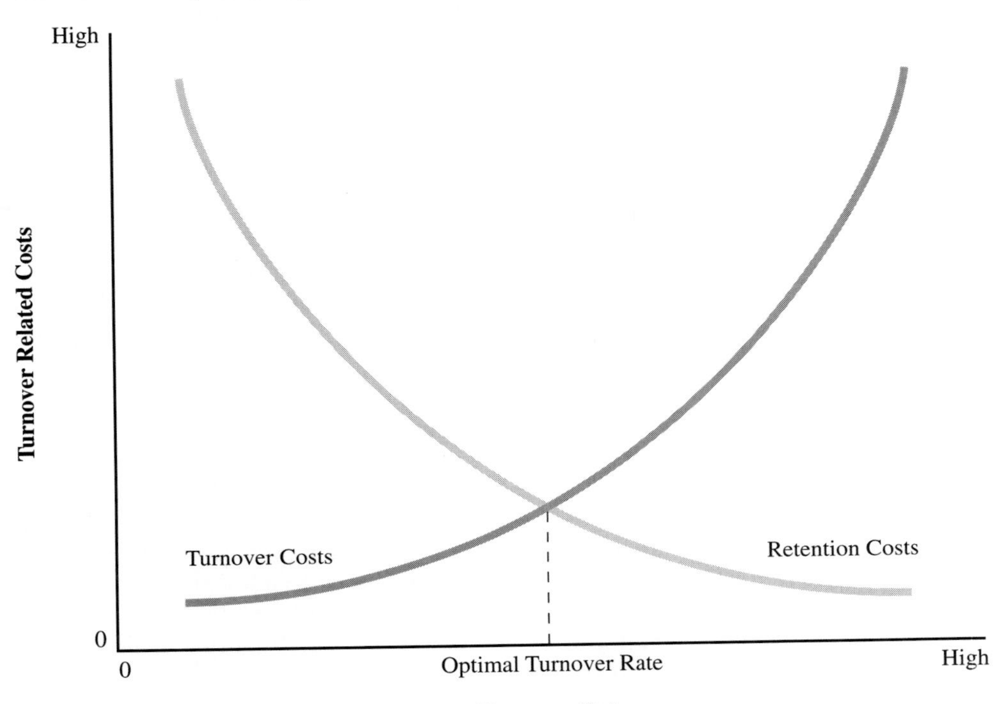

Source: Adapted from Michael A. Abelson and Barry D. Baysinger, "Optimal and Dysfunctional Turnover: Toward an Organizational Level Model," *Academy of Management Review*, Vol. 9, 1984, p. 333. Reprinted by permission.

Looking at the overall turnover rate may be misleading. It is important to consider what types of employees are choosing to leave. Whether a given turnover event hurts or helps the organization depends in part on the performance of the person leaving: is he or she someone the organization would prefer to retain? Several studies have examined whether good or bad performers are more likely to leave.[58] While the results have been mixed, on the whole, poorer performers seem to be somewhat more likely to quit than good performers, but this may not be true for all organizations or at the extremes of the performance continuum. For instance, the worst performers may not leave voluntarily, because they have few alternatives elsewhere. High performers may be lured away by other organizations if their performance is readily visible to the other firm and the firm is able to offer rewards significantly higher than those currently being received.[59] Thus, it is not safe to assume that the organization is better off without the people who choose to leave.

A more sophisticated model for evaluating turnover functionality is shown in Figure 16.5. This model suggests that it is necessary to distinguish among turnover

FIGURE 16.5 Performance Replaceability Strategy Matrix

		Replaceability
Performance	Difficult	Easy
High	A Highly Dysfunctional Turnover *Retain/Develop Employee* *Prepare Replacement Backup*	B Dysfunctional Turnover *Retain/Develop Employee*
Average	C Dysfunctional Turnover *Retain/Prepare Backup*	D Functionality Depends On Cost *Retain*
Low	E Short-Run Dysfunctional *Prepare Backup, Increase Performance, or Terminate*	F Functional *Increase Performance or Terminate*

Source: D.C. Martin and K.M. Bartol, "Managing Turnover Strategically." Reprinted with permission from the November 1985 issue of *Personnel Administrator,* copyright 1985, The American Society for Personnel Administration, Alexandria, VA.

events in terms of both employee performance level (high, acceptable, and low) and replaceability (easy, difficult). To maximize benefits to the organization, quite different techniques should be applied in each cell of the matrix in Figure 16.5 to discourage or encourage turnover.

In cell A, turnover is highly dysfunctional because incumbents are excellent performers who are difficult to replace, for the position requires either a skill that is in short supply in the labor market, or a great deal of organization-specific knowledge and experience. Employers should make every effort to retain employees in this cell, such as paying at least a competitive base salary, providing development and advancement opportunities, and recognizing outstanding performance with both tangible and symbolic rewards. In addition, it is wise for employers to identify and develop potential successors for these hard-to-replace personnel.

Cell B is populated by high performers who are easier to replace. Turnover in this cell is dysfunctional but not disastrous. Efforts to retain these employees should be made, but extremely costly retention strategies are probably inappropriate. Sophisticated succession planning systems will also be unnecessary in this cell.

Cell C contains acceptable performers who are hard to replace. Because of the disruption caused by their departure, turnover in this cell is considered dysfunctional. Efforts should be made to retain these employees and plan for replacements in case turnover occurs. Furthermore, organizations should attempt to move cell C employees to higher levels of performance through training and development, goal setting, and performance-contingent rewards.

Cell D consists of acceptable performers who are easy to replace. Whether turnover in this cell is functional depends on the cost of finding and training a replacement, and on the probability that the replacement will perform better than the current incumbent. If the skill level of the labor market is declining (as seems to be the case with literacy and numeracy), so that replacements are unlikely to outperform incumbents, then retention should be encouraged. If replacements are inexpensive and likely to possess better or more current skills than present employees, then special efforts to retain cell D employees will not be needed. However, any acceptable performers with potential should be trained, coached, and given incentives to improve their performance.

The final two cells contain poor performers. The organization's appraisal and reward system should encourage these employees to improve their performance to acceptable levels. If this effort fails, then turnover probably will be functional. Individuals in cell F, who are easily replaced, should be discharged or encouraged to leave by progressive discipline, accurate appraisals, and minimal rewards under merit or bonus systems. Hard-to-replace employees (cell E) whose performance does not improve to acceptable levels should be retained only until replacements can be located or developed, and then encouraged to seek more suitable employment elsewhere.

In a study of bank tellers, a worrisome 32 percent annual turnover rate became less alarming when broken down by performance and replaceability.[60] Some of those who left had been poor performers; the turnover rate among good and acceptable tellers was only 18 percent. When supervisory ratings of the ease of replacement were considered, the rate of truly harmful turnover (departure of hard-to-replace acceptable and good performers) dropped to 9 percent. Similarly, a study of department store clerks found that more than half of the 13.4 percent turnover rate was due to functional departures.[61] Thus, the organization's goal should not necessarily be to reduce the overall rate of turnover but to reduce dysfunctional turnover. In some cases, if poor performers are neither improving nor leaving, an increase in the rate of functional turnover would be recommended.

Making reward systems contingent on performance and performance appraisal accurate should facilitate both goals. Positive feedback and rewards based on good performance should encourage high performers to stay, while negative feedback and zero raises should have the opposite effect on poor performers. Systematic training and development, together with a bias toward promotion from within, should help to retain high performers and motivate acceptable performers to improve. Other interventions, such as participative management, supervisory training, general pay raises, and quality of work life programs may increase job satisfaction and commitment and thus reduce turnover. However, these techniques will tend to reduce turnover in *all* employee groups, including low performers, whom the organization does not wish to retain.

No organization can expect to control all voluntary turnover.[62] Many employees leave for reasons unrelated to the organization, such as family demands, relocation of a spouse, ill health, or a return to school. If a large share of departures falls into these categories, then expensive turnover management strategies will be ineffective and wasteful. Thus, before undertaking any steps to address a supposed "turnover problem," an organization should

1. Calculate the total annual turnover rate.
2. Break this rate down by the performance level of the leavers—acceptable and high versus low performers.
3. Assess the difficulty of replacing individuals who leave.
4. Determine, looking just at turnover incidents among acceptable and high performers, how many left for reasons beyond the organization's control.
5. Compare—in the case of acceptable and high performers who left for reasons the organization might be able to control (e.g., salary, development opportunities, or conflict with a supervisor)—the cost and difficulty of replacement with the cost and likely effectiveness of a turnover reduction program.

Exit Interviews

Any approach to managing turnover should include the systematic use of **exit interviews.** When an employee is leaving the organization voluntarily, it is important to collect information about the reasons for his or her departure. The exit interview is generally conducted by a human resource professional, not by the employee's supervisor. Several major topic areas should be discussed (see Table 16.6). The interview should follow a relatively standardized format, which begins with a discussion of administrative matters associated with the employee's departure, followed by a fact-finding session, in which the interviewer obtains information that may be used for retaining other employees. Exit interviews should be taken seriously. Carefully analyzed, they can help to identify and correct organizational problems.

RETIREMENT

Traditionally, older employees have represented a relatively small proportion of the work force, and the issue of retirement has had low priority in management thinking. With mandatory retirement prohibited by law, and the Baby Boom demographic bulge inexorably moving toward old age, older employees make up an

TABLE 16.6 Useful Exit Interview Questions

Resources, Job Information, and Training

How adequate was the help and equipment to get the job done?

How clearly were job responsibilities defined?

How adequate and timely was job information?

How helpful and competent was supervision and management?

What suggestions could you provide relative to resources and job information?

How well trained were you for the job? Suggestions?

Job Challenge and Opportunity for Advancement

How would you rate your job in terms of interesting work?

How adequate was your authority to do the job?

How much of an opportunity did you have to develop your special abilities?

How much freedom did you have to do your work?

What was most difficult to learn on your job?

How do you feel about advancement opportunities here?

Relations with Supervisors, Coworkers, and Other Departments

How well did you get along with your supervisor?

How would you evaluate the way your supervisor handled his or her employees? made work assignments? acted on complaints?

How well did you get along with your coworkers? friendly? helpful?

What is your evaluation of how well the various departments work together?

Comfort and Working Conditions

How did you feel about the physical surroundings?

How did you feel about the level of job stress?

How did you feel about the work load?

How much flexibility was there in working hours?

How convenient was travel to and from work?

Financial

How did you feel about your salary?

How about job security?

How about the fringe benefits?

Company Policies

What comments can you make about our company policies? Are there any changes you would suggest?

Overall Questions

What do you think were some of the good features of your job?

What do you think were some of the good features of this organization?

TABLE 16.6 Useful Exit Interview Questions (*cont.*)

What were some of the less desirable features of your job?
What were some of the less desirable features of working for this organization?
What overall improvements could you suggest?
What was the main factor in your decision to leave?

Source: Reprinted with permission of Science Research Associates, an imprint of Macmillan Publishing Company from *Interviewing: Key to Effective Management* by Joseph P. Zima. Copyright © 1983 by Science Research Associates.

increasing share of the work force.[63] The importance of retirement has greatly increased. Four basic issues concerning retirement are significant from a human resource perspective: (1) what exactly is retirement? (2) what factors determine when an employee will decide to retire? (3) how does retirement affect the individual and the organization? and (4) what actions should an organization take to manage the retirement process?

Types of Retirement

Instead of regarding retirement as a homogeneous phenomenon, it is useful to recognize differences in voluntariness, completeness, and timing. Research has shown that the factors that influence an individual's decision to retire depend on the type of retirement involved.[64] First, while the Age Discrimination in Employment Act has essentially eliminated mandatory retirement, other forms of involuntary retirement exist, as when health problems force an employee to stop working. Second, retirement may or may not take place at the age considered "normal" for most employees in an organization. Finally, retirement may be either complete (the individual withdraws from all forms of employment) or partial (he or she continues to work part-time).

It is important for HR managers to understand how employees usually retire. As the population ages, organizations are confronted with two problems. On the one hand, a greater percentage of their work force is nearing the typical retirement age. Thus, helping these employees' transition into retirement is important. On the other hand, demographic trends may mean that capable, younger workers are less available to replace those who are retiring. If most employees retire voluntarily, completely, and on time, it is easier to develop plans to replace them and structure programs to help them make the transition to retirement than if some employees take early, partial retirement, others late complete retirement, and so on.

Factors That Influence the Decision to Retire

In many ways, retirement resembles turnover. One model of the retirement decision process, shown in Figure 16.6, is very similar to the Mobley model of turn-

FIGURE 16.6 Factors Proposed to Influence the Process of Retirement

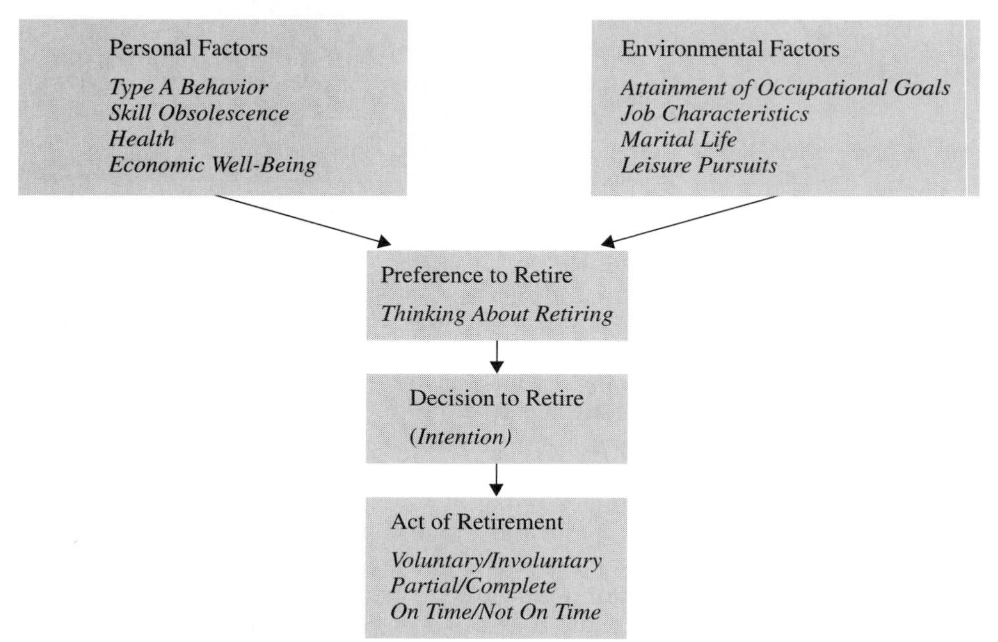

Source: Adapted from Terry A. Beehr, "The Process of Retirement: A Review and Recommendations for Future Investigation," *Personnel Psychology,* Vol. 39, 1986, p. 46. Reprinted by permission.

over described earlier. The factors affecting the decision to retire are divided into personal and environmental categories. Individuals who have Type A behavior styles (hard-driving workaholics) are thought to be less likely to retire. Individuals whose skills have become obsolete, who have health problems, or who are economically secure are more likely to decide to retire. The same is true of employees who have attained their lifetime work goals and of those who work in jobs with undesirable characteristics (e.g., stress, danger, long hours). Family and marital situations may also affect the retirement decision. For example, if workers see their job as a means of escaping an unpleasant home life, they may be reluctant to quit. An older worker still paying tuition for children in college will be less willing to retire. Finally, the availability and nature of leisure activities may help determine when an employee retires. These personal and environmental factors influence the extent to which an employee begins thinking about retirement. If conditions are favorable, a decision to retire is made and finally acted upon.

The Impact of Retirement

Much of the research on retirement has been done by gerontologists or other specialists on aging and has focused on its effect on individuals. However, employee retirement also has an impact on organizations.

Impact on Individuals An employee's job provides a sense of personal identity, a place in society, and opportunities for power, prestige, and the fulfillment of self-esteem and other ego needs. The job also provides a major source of friends and other important social interactions.[65] Research has focused on the extent to which retirement affects the physical health, level of activity, and attitudes and mental health of retirees. In the 1970s, retirement was deemed a stressful event that damaged the physical and mental health of individuals and caused them to withdraw from activities that they had pursued earlier.[66] But by the early 1980s, research indicated that retirement is not as psychologically stressful as first thought and that the frequency and severity of illness actually drops after retirement. Unless they suffer from health problems, retirees tend to maintain their preretirement level of activity.[67] With adequate planning and financial resources, it appears, retirement is likely to be a positive experience for individuals.

Impact on the Organization From the organization's perspective, retirement can be a very positive process. It allows new employees with up-to-date skills to enter the organization and replace older workers whose skills may have become obsolete. This process encourages innovation and new thinking in the organization. Retirement also motivates employees, since older workers tend to be higher in the organizational hierarchy and their departure provides opportunities for promotion. New employees also typically cost less than older workers because their salaries are lower.

Not all effects of retirement are positive, however. If the process is handled inappropriately and retirees are simply "given a gold watch and told to go," morale within the organization may suffer. The loss of older workers also may increase the level of environmental uncertainty with which the organization must contend. In an increasing number of cases, well-qualified replacements for retiring workers are extremely difficult to find. When older workers leave, they take with them a wealth of knowledge about the organization's environment; the contacts and influence they have built up in dealing with the environment are also lost. The climate within the organization may become more unstable, since older workers are often a main source of internal knowledge about "who's who" and how to get things done, as well as about the organization's norms and traditions.

Managing the Retirement Process

It is increasingly important to manage the retirement process effectively. Many companies have instituted retirement planning programs for their employees. In one survey, 38 percent of 386 companies indicated that they had retirement planning programs.[68]

There are many varieties of preretirement assistance programs. For instance, employees may be offered tuition rebates for any courses taken within three years of retirement, on the assumption that learning new skills will help them adjust to and be productive in their postretirement lives.[69] Another approach, the phased retirement program lets employees gradually reduce the number of hours they work, over an extended period of time. While helping individuals wean themselves away from their work life, these programs also allow the organization to adjust to losing their employees' knowledge and problem-solving skills. In addition, organizations are developing programs to bring former employees back to the company as part-time consultants. They lend their skill and knowledge to solving specific organizational problems, and then return to retired life until called again. Such programs benefit the organization by providing additional skilled labor and give retirees a chance to augment their income and to use valued skills and abilities. As the U.S. work force grows older, such programs will almost certainly continue to increase and develop.

SUMMARY OF KEY POINTS

Much attention as been given to selecting, training, and motivating employees. Until recently, however, little effort has been focused on the circumstances under which employees leave an organization. Effectively managing organizational exit is important. When terminating an individual's employment for cause, organizations must work within the limitations placed on them by employment discrimination laws and union contracts. In dealing with poor performers, it is important to use performance appraisal and corrective feedback, accompanied by an escalating series of punishments for employees who are unable or unwilling to improve their behavior. Some state legislation and court decisions have restricted the right of organizations to terminate employees at will. Workers may challenge their firing using legal arguments based on the concepts of violation of public policy, implied contracts, or tortious acts. Organizations must have proper written documentation that supports their reasons for terminating an employee.

Organizations may also need to carry out company-wide reductions in force. Companies should be particularly careful when laying off older workers. Thorough advance planning for reductions in force is critical. Organizations must communicate early and often with employees about the reasons for the reductions and their exact nature. Many companies offer outplacement programs that help laid-off workers find new jobs. These programs often include counseling sessions that help employees deal with the psychological shock of being laid off and sessions to teach job search skills. It is equally important for the organization to manage the survivors of a company-wide layoff. Proper counseling for survivors can help ensure a motivated and stable postlayoff work force.

Turnover is another important form of organizational exit. Traditional wisdom held that turnover was always bad and should be reduced to a minimum. However, research has shown that some turnover has positive effects on the organization. Functional turnover gives the organization a chance to rid itself of poorly performing employees. Better workers can then be hired and promotion opportunities offered to current employees. Dysfunctional turnover occurs when good performers leave and the company must spend considerable time and money to recruit and train replacements. It is essential for organizations to analyze turnover in terms of both its functional and dysfunctional effects. Rather than attempt to minimize all turnover, organizations should seek to reduce dysfunctional turnover but tolerate a level of functional turnover.

Retirement has become an important organizational issue as the population grows older. Retirement can take many forms, and the factors that affect an individual's decision to retire may depend on the type of retirement involved. Some individuals may partially retire at an earlier than normal age, while others may retire on time or late but leave the labor market completely. Retirement can be either voluntary or involuntary, and it may have positive and negative effects on both the organization and individual. Many organizations are developing retirement planning programs to help manage the retirement of employees.

Questions for Discussion

1. Why is a performance appraisal and feedback system important when an organization is terminating an employee for cause?

2. What are the DAP, MAP, RAP methods of appraisal and feedback? How do they compare with the methods used in organizations with which you are familiar?

3. What is employment-at-will? How does civil rights legislation restrict a company's ability to terminate employees at will?

4. Describe the difference between wrongful discharge as the result of an implied contract and as the result of a tortious act.

5. Why is the Worker Adjustment and Retraining Act important for organizations planning a reduction in force? Who is covered by the law, and what does it require organizations to do?

6. What are some of the ways by which an organization might reduce labor costs? Discuss some of the advantages and disadvantages associated with each method.

7. Managing the survivors of a reduction in force is important. How would you help survivors deal with *not* having been laid off?

8. Defend or refute the following statement: "Organizations should routinely provide outplacement programs for workers laid off in a reduction in force."

9. Describe some of the advantages and disadvantages associated with employee turnover. What is the optimal turnover level in an organization?

10. What are exit interviews, and what can the organization learn from them?

11. Why should an organization be interested in helping employees retire successfully?

EXERCISE 16.1

Conducting an Exit Interview

Step. 1. In class, identify all students who have held full-time or part-time jobs and have quit those jobs for one reason or another.

Step 2. Depending on the number of students identified in Step 1, divide the class into groups that each include one student who has quit a job.

Step 3 (20 mins.). Use some of the questions in Table 16.6 and your own original questions to develop an exit interview for the job leaver.

Step 4. Conduct the exit interview. What kind of turnover do you think occurred: functional or dysfunctional? Did the organization have any real control over this turnover? Are there issues that the organization might need to deal with in order to retain productive employees in the future?

EXERCISE 16.2

Whom Would You Lay Off?

The class should divide into groups of three to five. Each group member should read the following scenario, then discuss his or her individual recommendations with the other group members. Each group may also present its suggestions to the class as a whole following this part of the exercise.

The Scenario* Because of severe economic conditions, your company is undergoing a major reduction in force. You have recently been assigned to the "execution committee," which must decide who will be laid off and who will be retained. So far the committee's decisions have been made without the benefit of any set policy for determining layoffs. The company is not unionized. The committee's decisions have resulted in the following distribution of layoffs among age groups of employees:

Ages	*Work Force Percentage Before Layoffs*	*Percentage of Persons Terminated in Group*
<40	50	5
40–44	10	5
45–49	10	7
50–54	10	9
55–59	10	12
60–64	10	25

The committee must decide whether to lay off Sam or Fred. Some information about these two employees is provided in the following table. What would you do? What thoughts do you have about the decisions of the committee so far?

*Adapted from Barbara L. Schlie and Paul Grossman, *Employment Discrimination Law,* 2nd ed., pp. 530–531, Bureau of National Affairs, Washington, D.C., Copyright 1983 American Bar Association. Reprinted with permission.

	Sam	Fred
Age	45	59
Children	Still in college	On their own
House	Large mortgage	Owns home, clear
Retirement benefits	Not vested	Vested
Hobbies	Workaholic	Golf
Results if terminated	Try to find job (difficult)	Retire
Past performance	Very good	Very good

Notes and References

1. Marc J. Wallace, Jr., and Charles H. Fay, *Compensation Theory and Practice,* 2nd ed. (Boston, Mass.: PWS-Kent, 1988), pp. 140–142.
2. Beth Tognetti, "How to Fire Someone Without Destroying Your Self-Esteem," *Supervision,* August 1987, p. 6.
3. D. W. Myers, *Employee Assistance Programs* (Chicago: Commerce Clearing House, 1986).
4. *Payne* v. *Western and Atlantic RA Co.,* 82 Tenn 507, 1884.
5. D. P. Twomey, *Equal Employment Opportunity,* 2nd ed. (Cincinnati: Southwestern, 1990), p. 132.
6. *Murphy* v. *American Home Products Corporation* (461 N.Y. 2d 232 N.Y. State Ct. of Appeals, 1983).
7. Robert Coulson, *Labor Arbitration: What You Need to Know* (New York: American Arbitration Association, 1981).
8. Daniel J. Koys, Steven Briggs, and Jay Grenig, "State Court Disparity on Employment-At-Will," *Personnel Psychology,* Vol. 40, 1987, pp. 565–576.
9. Twomey, *Equal Employment Opportunity,* pp. 133–134.
10. *Palmateer* v. *International Harvester* (85 Ill. 2d 124, 421 NE 2d 876, 1981); *Sheets* v. *Teddy's Frosted Foods, Inc.* (Supreme Ct. of Conn., 179 Conn. 471, 427 A.2d 385, 1980).
11. *Touissant* v. *Blue Cross and Blue Shield of Michigan* (408 Mich. 579, 292 N.W. 2d. 880, 1980).
12. *Fortune* v. *National Cash Register Co.* (373 Mass. 96, 36 N.E. 2d 1251, 1977).
13. This exception to the employment-at-will doctrine is sometimes referred to as "abusive discharge." The court case most closely linked to this concept is *Monge* v. *Beebe Rubber Co.* (114 N.H. 130, 316 A.2d 549, 1974), in which a female employee was fired for not agreeing to date her supervisor. This was deemed abusive discharge. A case like *Monge* v. *Beebe Rubber* would, today, most likely be handled as a case of sex discrimination. However, other instances of abusive discharge may occur that would be considered a tortious act.
14. Koys, Briggs, and Grenig, "State Court Disparity," p. 573.
15. Twomey, *Equal Employment Opportunity,* pp. 133–134.
16. Sydney P. Freedberg, "Forced Exits? Companies Confront Wave of Age Discrimination Suits," *The Wall Street Journal,* November 13, 1987.
17. Walt Baer, "Most U.S. Workers Still May Be Fired Under the Employment-at-Will Doctrine," *Supervision,* December 1987, p. 6.
18. Twomey, *Equal Employment Opportunity,* p. 134.
19. W. E. Fulmer and A. W. Casey, "Employment At Will: Options for Managers," *Academy of Management Executive,* Vol. 4, No. 2, 1990, pp. 102–107.
20. Freedberg, "Forced Exits?"
21. Eric R. Greenberg, "Downsizing: AMA Survey Results," *Compensation and Benefits Review,* Vol. 23, No. 4, 1991, pp. 33–38; John Greenwald, "The Great American Layoffs," *Time,* July 20, 1992, pp. 64–65.

22. K. Cameron, S. J. Freeman, and A. K. Mishra, "Best Practices in White-Collar Downsizing: Managing Contradictions," *Academy of Management Executive,* Vol. 5, No. 3, 1991, pp. 57–73.

23. Reported in Richard R. Bunning, "The Dynamics of Downsizing," *Personnel Journal,* Vol. 69, No. 9, 1990, pp. 68–75.

24. John L. Neuman, "OVA: Avoid Slash-and-Burn Overhead Reduction," *Management Review,* January 1987, p. 34.

25. Linda Laarman, "Cut Compensation Costs to Avoid Layoffs," *Employment Relations Today,* Vol. 18, No. 2, 1991, pp. 137–142; Gloria M. Portela and Rory K. Zaks, "Reductions in Force: A Practical Approach," *Employment Relations Today,* Vol. 16, No. 3, 1989, pp. 219–225.

26. Xiong Xiaoge, "How to Minimize the Trauma of Downsizing," *Electronic Business,* Vol. 17, No. 7, 1991, pp. 51–54.

27. Daniel C. Feldman and Carrie R. Leana, "Managing Layoffs: Experiences at the Challenger Disaster Site and the Pittsburgh Steel Mills," *Organizational Dynamics,* Summer 1989, pp. 52–64.

28. Joel Brockner, "Layoffs, Self-Esteem and Survivor Guilt: Motivational, Affective, and Attitudinal Consequences," *Organizational Behavior and Human Decision Processes,* Vol. 36, June, 1985, pp. 229–244; Joel Brockner, Steven L. Grover, and Mauritz D. Blonder, "Predictors of Survivor's Job Involvement Following Layoffs: A Field Study," *Journal of Applied Psychology,* Vol. 73, No. 3, 1988, pp. 436–442.

29. William A. Nowlin, "Work Force Downsizing: Impact on Survivors," *Supervision,* January 1988, p. 16; Joel Brockner, "The Effects of Work Layoffs on Survivors: Research, Theory, and Practice," *Research in Organizational Behavior,* Vol. 10, 1988, pp. 213–255; Frank R. Strasbourg, "Corporate Outplacement," *Business and Economic Review,* Vol. 38, No. 1, 1991, pp. 11–13.

30. Cameron, Freeman, and Mishra, "Best Practices in White-Collar Downsizing," pp. 57–73.

31. J. F. Adams, "Inequity in Social Exchange," in *Advances in Experimental Social Psychology,* ed. L. Berkowitz (New York: Academic Press, 1965), pp. 267–299.

32. Joel Brockner, Jeff Greenberg, Audrey Brockner, Jenny Bortz, Jeannette Davy, and Carolyn Carter, "Layoff, Equity Theory, and Work Performance: Further Evidence of the Impact of Survivor Guilt," *Academy of Management Journal,* Vol. 29, 1986, pp. 373–384.

33. Cameron, Freeman, and Mishra, "Best Practices in White-Collar Downsizing," pp. 57–73.

34. *Firefighters Local Union 1784* v. *Stotts* (U.S. Sup. Ct, 34 FEP 1702, 1984).

35. Stephan Wermiel, "High Court Rules States May Require Companies to Pay Severance in Layoffs," *The Wall Street Journal,* June 2, 1987, p. 10.

36. Larry M. Wolf and Meryl B. Davis, "Plant Closures: The New Law and Its Effect on Plant Closure, Relocation, and Layoffs," presented as part of the 1989 Employment Law Update conducted by Whiteford, Taylor, & Preston Law Offices, Baltimore, May 24, 1989.

37. Robert J. Nobile, "Outplacement Counselling: Minimizing Legal Liability," *Personnel,* Vol. 68, No. 10, 1991, p. 5.

38. Quoted in Chris Lee, "Outplacement: Throwing Them Life Preservers," *Training,* July 1987, p. 43.

39. Ibid.

40. Jeanne C. Hill and William R. Fannin, "Developing an Effective Outplacement Program," *Business Forum,* Vol. 16, No. 1, 1991, pp. 14–17.

41. Strasbourg, "Corporate Outplacement."

42. Ruth Kanfer and Charles L. Hulin, "Individual Differences in Successful Job Searches Following Lay-Off," *Personnel Psychology,* Vol. 30, 1985, pp. 835–847.

43. Lee, "Outplacement."

44. Joseph Jannotta, "Stroh's Outplacement Success," *Management Review,* January 1987, pp. 52–53.

45. Jeanne C. Hill and Earl R. Thomas, "Outplacement: Considerations for the Small Firm," *SAM Advanced Management Journal,* Vol. 56, No. 2, 1991, pp. 10–15.

46. Both the first and third authors of this textbook worked at Bond University during this period and were aware of layoff policies.

47. Douglas T. Hall and James G. Goodale, *Hu-*

man Resource Management: Strategy, Design and Implementation (Glenview, Ill.: Scott, Foresman, 1986), p. 460.

48. J. L. Cotton and J. M. Tuttle, "Employee Turnover: A Meta-Analysis and Review with Implications for Research," *Academy of Management Review,* Vol. 11, 1986, pp. 55–70.

49. Robert Steel and Rodger W. Griffeth, "The Elusive Relationship Between Perceived Employment Opportunity and Turnover Behavior: A Methodological and Conceptual Artifact?" *Journal of Applied Psychology,* Vol. 74, No. 6, 1989, pp. 846–854; Barry Gerhart, "Voluntary Turnover and Alternate Job Opportunities," Journal of Applied Psychology, Vol. 75, No. 5, 1990, pp. 467–476.

50. Cotton and Tuttle, "Employee Turnover."

51. Ibid.

52. Gary J. Blau and Kimberley B. Boal, "Conceptualizing How Job Involvement and Organizational Commitment Affect Absenteeism and Turnover," *Academy of Management Review,* Vol. 12, No. 2, 1987, pp. 288–300; Gary J. Blau and Kimberley B. Boal, "Using Job Involvement and Organizational Commitment Interactively to Predict Turnover," *Journal of Management,* Vol. 15, 1989, pp. 115-127; J. E. Mathieu and S. S. Kohler, "A Test of the Interactive Effects of Organizational Commitment and Job Involvement on Various Types of Absence," *Journal of Vocational Behavior,* Vol. 36, 1990, pp. 33–44.

53. Cotton and Tuttle, "Employee Turnover."

54. William H. Mobley, *Employee Turnover: Causes, Consequences, and Control* (Reading, Mass.: Addison-Wesley, 1982).

55. John E. Sheridan, "A Catastrophe Model of Employee Withdrawal Leading to Low Job Performance, High Absenteeism, and Job Turnover During the First Year of Employment," *Academy of Management Journal,* Vol. 28, 1985, pp. 88–109.

56. D. C. Martin and K. M. Bartol, "Managing Turnover Strategically," *Personnel Administrator,* November 1985, pp. 63–73; Barry M. Staw, "The Consequences of Turnover," *Journal of Occupational Behavior,* Vol. 1, 1980, pp. 253–273.

57. Daniel R. Dalton and William D. Todor, "Turnover Turned Over: An Expanded and Positive Perspective," *Academy of Management Review,* Vol. 4, 1979, pp. 225–235; Martin and Bartol, "Managing Turnover Strategically," pp. 63–73.

58. Glenn M. McEvoy and Wayne F. Cascio, "Do Good or Poor Performers Leave? A Meta-Analysis of the Relationship Between Performance and Turnover," *Academy of Management Journal,* Vol. 30, 1987, pp. 744–762; T. N. Martin, J. L. Price, and C. W. Mueller, "Job Performance and Turnover," *Journal of Applied Psychology,* Vol. 66, 1981, pp. 57–75; Donald P. Schwab, "Contextual Variables in Employee Performance-Turnover Relationships," *Academy of Management Journal,* Vol. 24, No. 4, 1991, pp. 966–975.

59. Schwab, "Contextual Variables in Employee Performance-Turnover Relationships," pp. 966–975.

60. Dan R. Dalton, David M. Krackhardt, and Lyman W. Porter, "Functional Turnover: An Empirical Assessment," *Journal of Applied Psychology,* Vol. 66, 1981, pp. 716–721.

61. John R. Hollenbeck and Charles R. Williams, "Turnover Functionality Versus Turnover Frequency: A Note on Work Attitudes and Organizational Effectiveness," *Journal of Applied Psychology,* Vol. 71, 1986, pp. 606–611.

62. Michael A. Abelson, "Examination of Avoidable and Unavoidable Turnover," *Journal of Applied Psychology,* Vol. 72, 1987, pp. 382–386.

63. G. R. Horton and Saied Y. Eidgahy, "Retirement Should Be Obsolete," *HRMagazine,* Vol. 35, No. 12, 1990, pp. 61–62; Martin N. Greller and David M. Nee, *From Baby Boom to Baby Bust: How Business Can Meet the Demographic Challenge* (Reading, Mass.: Addison-Wesley, 1990).

64. E. B. Palmore, L. K. George, and G. G. Fillenbaum, "Predictors of Retirement," *Journal of Gerontology,* Vol. 37, 1982, pp. 733–742.

65. James B. Shaw and Lisa L. Grubbs, "The Process of Retiring: Organizational Entry in Reverse," *Academy of Management Review,* Vol. 6, 1981, pp. 41–48.

66. R. C. Atchley, *The Social Forces in Later Life* (Belmont, Calif.: Wadsworth, 1977);

B. D. Bell, "Life Satisfaction and Occupational Retirement Beyond the Impact Year," *International Journal of Aging and Human Development,* Vol. 9, 1978–79, pp. 44–54.

67. S. V. Kasl, "The Impact of Retirement," in *Current Concerns in Occupational Stress,* ed. C. L. Cooper and R. Payne (Chichester, England: Wiley, 1980), pp. 137–186; M. Minkler, "Research on the Health Effects of Retirement: An Uncertain Legacy," *Journal of Health and Social Behavior,* Vol. 22, 1981, pp. 117–130.

68. Donna Brown, "Pre-retirement Planning and the Bottom Line," *Personnel,* Vol. 68, No. 6, 1991, pp. 3–4.

69. Jeffrey Sonnenfeld, "Dealing with the Aging Work Force," *Harvard Business Review,* November–December 1978, pp. 81–92.

Computers in Human Resource Management

Applications and Future Directions

The earlier insert on human resource information systems (HRISs) on pages 348–361 introduced the concept of a relational database and information system to manage HR applications. The number of organizations using HRISs is continuing to grow, as is the number of applications being used.[1] Computers are used in human resource management both in connection with an HRIS and for a number of freestanding purposes. The area of HR development provides examples of both kinds of uses. The HRIS may include modules for keeping track of the training history of each employee and for training expenditure accounting. Separate, non-HRIS programs may be used to deliver computer-based training to employees throughout the organization. In this section, examples of computer applications in human resource management are explored for most of the functional areas discussed earlier in the text. Finally, some newly emerging uses and potential future applications are described.

STRATEGIC HRM AND HR PLANNING

One of the primary reasons for the existence of an organizational HRIS is to improve organizational and human resource planning and decision making. The often vast amount of data on employees and jobs in the organization provides the opportunity for management to use this information in many new ways in making plans for the organization. An HRIS can be used to analyze hiring, transfer, and exit trends. Projections of future HR needs can be created and used to develop recruiting plans, to restructure promotion paths, or to assist in planning organi-

This section is modified and updated from a similar section written by Dr. Jon Beard of the University of Richmond (Virginia) for the first edition of this book.

zational restructuring, mergers, and acquisitions. Complex simulation models can be used to forecast outcomes under a number of alternate scenarios or HR policies.

HR planning is essential if an organization is to balance the multiple demands of the changing organizational environment. Employees are constantly leaving the organization, entering the organization, and being moved around within the organization. The planning process, therefore, has an impact on employee selection and placement. A human resource information system, with its data on jobs and employees in the organization, can provide management with the information it needs to plan for short-, medium-, and long-term operations.

JOB ANALYSIS

Another area in which HRISs can be used is job analysis (discussed in Chapter 4). Job data can be collected using structured questionnaires such as the Position Analysis Questionnaire (PAQ) or a task inventory. Statistical programs for cluster analysis can be used to identify common characteristics of jobs and to create job descriptions and job families. Inconsistencies in the work activities of employees in the same job title can also be identified. Once common characteristics have been determined, the information can be used in developing or redefining job titles, the salary structure, and promotion paths.[2]

HRISs can also assist in maintaining current job analysis information. Once a job analysis is completed, the information can be placed in the HRIS. As the job undergoes incremental changes, the ability requirements and task descriptions can be easily updated. Some systems print out the most recent job description for each employee, along with a notice that a performance appraisal on this employee is due. Part of the performance feedback discussion includes superior/subordinate negotiation about job duties and a revision of the job description if needed.

EQUAL EMPLOYMENT OPPORTUNITY AND AFFIRMATIVE ACTION REPORTING

Equal employment opportunity (EEO) and affirmative action (AA) reporting has been one of the driving factors in the rapid growth of HRISs. Requirements to monitor and report the proportion of the work force of a given age, race, and sex have led to the creation of large databases. As people enter and leave the organization, these proportions change. Monitoring this data is necessary to identify any apparent adverse impacts on protected groups. The early identification of adverse impact may also allow the organization to consider corrective action before a problem develops. The characteristics of job applicants who are rejected must also be monitored to ensure compliance with EEO legislation. Tracking and reporting this information without an HRIS is very difficult and time consuming.

TABLE 1. Time Savings from an HRIS

Task	*Time Savings*
Salary Planning	5%
Business Unit Compensation Standing	50%
Equal Employment Opportunity Status Report	98%
Retirement Forecast	94%
Pension Inquiry	64%
Headcount Report	94%
Demographic Report	94%
Attrition Analysis	94%
Compensation Summary	94%
Salary Range Penetration Report	94%

Source: Adapted from B. G. Clayton, "A Helping Hand Named HuRBIE," *Human Resource Planning,* Vol. 13, No. 3, 1990, p. 184.

As EEO/AA legislation changes, the type and amount of information to be reported may also change. It may be very difficult with separate systems for several types of reports to keep all the reporting systems consistent with current legislation. With an integrated HRIS, all the changes can be made at once with a minimum amount of variance among the affected applications.[3] Computerizing EEO reporting produced enormous savings for Westinghouse Electric Corp. Before the advent of a centralized, integrated HRIS, preparing a monthly EEO status report for the organization took twenty-five hours. With the system, it takes twenty-five minutes.[4] Table 1 shows the time saved in producing several types of routine reports related to human resources.

RECRUITMENT

Recruitment is discussed in Chapter 6. Clearly, an organization's HRIS would be very useful for internal recruiting. Some HRIS modules control the internal job posting and bidding process, generate the posting notices, and then match internal applicant qualifications with job specifications. For jobs that are not posted, the automated skills inventory component of an HRIS can be used to generate a list of qualified internal candidates. This capability is especially useful in large organizations with multiple locations, where the identification of internal job candidates across sites is sometimes very difficult.

External recruiting is also made easier by various computer applications. One example of computerized recruiting is a system called ProNet. Developed at Stanford University, ProNet allows subscribing companies to search through a database of information on Stanford alumni who have consented to being listed. Profiles in the database contain job-relevant information on the alumni. Companies are provided with profiles of people who match their job requirements. No information on the candidates' names, sex, or age is provided to the companies until a good match is identified and the potential candidate indicates an interest in pursuing the matter further.[5]

An additional function is applicant tracking and correspondence. An accurate system is needed to record applicant source, EEO category, and hiring decisions and to generate routine correspondence related to recruiting. Often the computerized applicant tracking system is not part of the HRIS per se, as a very large number of applicants are handled and only a small number of them eventually wind up being hired. After hire, the records of these individuals would be transferred to the employee database in the HRIS.[6]

SELECTION

Decision-making issues and the devices used in selection are described in Chapters 7 and 8. Computers can assist in employee selection in several ways. For instance, the administration and scoring of ability tests can be handled by computer. The system can evaluate test performance and provide management with recommendations about the qualifications of the applicant. Adaptive testing can also be used. This type of testing varies the length of the test and the content of the questions based on the responses of the job candidate.

Computer-aided interviewing can assist in the selection process by providing a structured interview directly with the applicant, even when a human interviewer is not present. These interviews often involve specific questions about the applicant's background, education, experience, skills, interests, and general knowledge. After initial screening of unqualified candidates, the computerized interview would be followed by the more familiar personal interview to clarify answers and seek information on other questions. Computer-aided interviewing has been applied successfully in a number of different settings.[7] A second use of computers in interviewing is to prompt human interviewers to ask the most appropriate questions given the job specification and applicant answers to previous questions.

Once information on candidates has been acquired, the HRIS can match it with available jobs within the organization. This matching process could look for candidates who meet minimal requirements for several different job characteristics, or it could identify the candidate who has the "best fit" along a number of criteria.

Finally, an HRIS may prove invaluable in conducting validation studies. For instance, one large organization familiar to the authors recently planned a concurrent validation study of a personality test for telemarketing supervisors. The HR researcher needed to identify a sample of good and poor performers to participate in the study. To make sure that no one felt threatened or worried about being tested, the researcher wanted to exclude individuals and work units from the study if reductions in force or other adverse HR actions were planned for their group in the near future. A well-designed HRIS would be a tremendous aid in identifying a sample of employees with the desired characteristics.

HUMAN RESOURCE DEVELOPMENT AND CAREER PLANNING

HRIS modules are used to register employees for courses, track who has been trained in what areas, monitor training costs, and even schedule trainers and classrooms. Additional uses of computers include actual delivery of training content. Chapter 9 describes computer-based training, interactive-videodisc training, and computerized management simulation games as areas with great potential for future growth. Computers are playing still another role in some executive development programs. Extensive computer-administered self-assessment questionnaires relating to management style and executive skills are being used to assist managers in diagnosing their own developmental needs. When similar ratings are collected from the people with whom the manager works, feeding back the data on how others perceive the manager is very useful in "unfreezing" the manager and generating useful discussion in training sessions.[8]

Computers are also being used increasingly for career and managerial succession planning. As Stephen E. Forrer and Zandy B. Leibowitz pointed out, career planning is ideally suited for computer applications. This is because the steps in career planning include a thorough self-assessment of skills, preferences, and values and an exploration of a large number of alternative jobs and career paths relative to one's own pattern of strengths and preferences. Confidentiality is also desired to improve the chances of honest and useful responses. Computers have the capability to administer and score a number of standardized ability tests and interest inventories and can readily compare results with stored information on a wide variety of jobs within an organization. They can also allow individual employees to undertake the assessment and exploration process at their own time and pace, and in complete privacy.[9] The main menu of a system developed by Forrer and Leibowitz called CareerPoint is shown in Figure 1.

Other computerized career planning or succession systems are designed more for HR professionals' and top managers' use than for target employees' use. For instance, AT&T's Leadership Continuity Program Tracking System keeps data on the leadership abilities of 3,000 high-potential managers and professionals from among its 275,000 person work force in forty-one countries. This system feeds the succession planning system, which covers 130 top jobs.[10]

PERFORMANCE APPRAISAL

Performance appraisal is discussed in Chapter 11. One of the areas of potential trouble in performance evaluation is inaccurate appraisal due to rater bias. This bias can be either positive (leniency error) or negative (severity error). An HRIS

FIGURE 1. CareerPoint Main Menu

```
                    CareerPoint Main Menu

* A.  How do I use the system?
* B.  What should I know about the organization?
- C.  What are my values, interests, and preferences?
  D.  What are my skills?
- E.  How do I identify job opportunities?
  F.  What are my goals for attaining a position?
- G.  What is my development plan for reaching my goals?
  H.  What skills should I have for job searching?
  I.  How do I create a résumé?
  J.  What is my CareerPoint summary?
  K.  Final hints
  L.  System evaluation
  ()  Exit the system

- section started    * section completed

Use ↑ and ↓ cursor keys to highlight desired section,
       then press <Enter>

<F2> for Express Menu             <F6> for CareerPoint
                                       familiarization
<F9> for more completion data     <F8> for job database
```

Source: Forrer, Stephen E. and Leibowitz, Zandy B. *Using Computers in Human Resources: How to Select and Make the Best Use of Automated HR Systems*. p. 89. Copyright © 1991 by Stephen E. Forrer, Zandy B. Leibowitz and Jossey-Bass Inc., Publishers.

can evaluate the rating distribution of each rater to look for trends suggesting one of these errors.

Several commercial modules are available to assist with performance appraisal. One program is called Performance Trak. Introduced in 1990, it provides for assessment in fifteen performance areas (such as problem analysis) and contains rating scales for several critical skills and abilities under each performance area (such as "skill at identifying alternative solutions to problems"). The organization can use the scales as provided or drop, customize, or differentially weight various skills or performance areas. After the superior has rated an employee using the appropriate scales, a profile of scores in each performance area is displayed. Also available are comparisons across employees and work groups or between supervisor appraisals and self-, peer, or subordinate appraisals on the same dimensions. In addition, raters can be asked to indicate their degree of confidence in the accuracy of each rating they have made. This may remind supervisors to remain open to employee input during the performance discussion that follows appraisal.[11]

There has also been a limited amount of experimentation with the use of expert systems (discussed later in this insert) to assist in the appraisal and feedback process. Although such systems cannot perform the evaluation itself, they can guide those doing the appraisal by helping them focus on the most important aspects of performance.[12]

COMPENSATION AND BENEFITS

Compensation systems, performance-based pay, and employee benefits are considered in Chapters 12 and 13. There are numerous ways in which an HRIS can facilitate the administration of compensation and benefits. One of the earliest uses of automation in human resources was in monitoring work attendance and time worked. Computerized systems can be invaluable in maintaining the records needed to comply with the Fair Labor Standards Act, ensuring that overtime is paid when it is due, and making appropriate payroll deductions. Specialized modules are also available for tracking executive compensation such as stock options, bonuses, and other forms of deferred compensation. Finally, being largely quantitative activities, job evaluation, building wage structures, and tying wage structures to the results of market wage surveys are tasks ideally suited to computerized assistance.

Many organizations try to link pay to performance. Clearly, a flexible automated payroll system would be needed to most effectively implement a gain sharing or individual incentive pay system. Computers can even be useful in making merit raise decisions. For instance, one system can use performance requirements and appraisal ratings to recommend equitable compensation adjustments.[13] An experimental computer simulation has been developed at Lockheed Missiles and Space Company to maximize the productive use of merit funds. The pool of funds set aside for merit is often not fully utilized by the end of the year, as some employees who have received increases leave the organization. Others are transferred or promoted to different positions and paid the going rate for that position, not the rate plus merit adjustment. The work force flow model is able to accurately forecast these dynamics and allow otherwise unused merit funds to be injected into the system at midyear.[14]

Employee benefits can also be maintained and monitored by an HRIS. Without a computerized system, a cafeteria-style set of benefit options would be extremely difficulty to administer. An additional advantage of computerization is that the organization can easily monitor the extent of use of various benefit options in order to fine-tune its benefit packages. Some organizations are also freeing up HR specialists' time by giving employees terminal access to benefit system information. For instance, an employee who wishes to inquire about pension entitlements or to file a medical insurance claim can be assisted by a computer rather than a person.[15]

HEALTH AND SAFETY

At General Dynamics, one module of the HRIS is called the Healthnet System. It keeps records of occupational diseases and injuries, provides reports for the Occupational Safety and Health Administration, and tracks hazardous materials. Other functions performed by similar systems might include recording who has received which type of safety training, printing and distributing required "right to know" documents for employees who may be exposed to hazardous chemicals at work, and preparing documents related to workers' compensation claims. Other uses for computers in health maintenance include self-administered programs for health risk assessment, life-style modification, stress management, or diet planning.[16] Some organizations offer access to these programs through their wellness or employee assistance programs.

LABOR RELATIONS

Computers have a role to play in labor relations, from the point of view of both management and unions. For instance, management's HRIS can be used to track disciplinary actions and grievances, as well as to spot trends in union membership across locations and job types. It is increasingly common for both management and union negotiators to bring a personal computer to the bargaining table with them. This allows for proposals and counter proposals to be costed very quickly by the use of spreadsheet programs. If the PCs are connected to an on-line information search and retrieval system, such as the Human Resource Information Network, or to labor law information networks, either side may be able to quickly assess the legality or prevalence of any contract clause proposed by the other side or to find precedents for its own position. On-line access to information from the Bureau of Labor Statistics and financial information databases may allow negotiators to produce persuasive graphs documenting company performance relative to that of other organizations. Furthermore, word processing programs allow proposed contract wording to be modified, printed out, and distributed on the spot, saving time and greatly enhancing understanding of exactly what each side is suggesting.[17]

ORGANIZATIONAL EXIT

Organizational exit is discussed in Chapter 16. HRIS data can be used to monitor and assess the causes of voluntary turnover or to examine the impact of the likely retirement patterns of employees under various augmented retirement programs. Some organizations have automated exit interview procedures, whereas others have computerized the process of sending layoff and recall notices to employees. A complex computer model to help in determining the appropriate degree and pattern of reductions in force in a shipyard is described in Chapter 3, and the first

HRIS insert (pages 348–361) describes a module for accurately dealing with COBRA requirements for health insurance for departing employees.

NEW AND FUTURE APPLICATIONS

In the future, HR professionals can expect to see more widespread adoption and greater power in the types of applications described above. In addition, many new applications may become available.

One innovative use of computers that has been adopted at IBM is an on-line employee opinion survey. Like many large progressive organizations, IBM has long had a regular opinion survey program in place. Surveying is done continuously, and every single employee is surveyed at least once every two years. The survey focuses on topics such as satisfaction with various aspects of the job and perceptions of corporate values. The task of surveying 383,000 employees worldwide is daunting, but computerized survey administration has greatly streamlined the process. Each employee can access the survey with his or her own personal computer and respond to the questions in complete privacy and anonymity. If the individual is called away, the program saves the responses to date and allows the employee to continue where he or she left off. Most questions are close ended (offering choices on numerical scales such as 1 = strongly disagree to 5 = strongly agree), but there is also an open-ended section, in which employees are invited to express their opinions in their own words. The advantages of the system are greater employee participation and acceptance, greater flexibility to add questions when employee opinions on "hot" topics are suddenly desired, and much faster coding and analysis. The system helps managers listen to employees more effectively and provides early warning when problems requiring further attention arise.

Another wave of the future is the use of expert systems technology in human resource applications. Computers are good at working with quantitative information; expert systems allow them to work with qualitative information in the same way that humans do. An **expert system** is a computer program that applies inference rules to facts in order to duplicate the reasoning process of a human expert. In the case of selection decision making, facts might include an applicant's grade point average, interview ratings, extent of past experience, specific university and degree, and details of technical positions expected to be open in the company in the next three months. An experienced HR specialist might be able to subjectively weight these facts into hiring and placement decisions, following such unwritten rules as (1) grade point average is a pretty good predictor of success in chemical engineering positions but not in technical sales positions; (2) Midwestern University produces particularly well qualified chemical engineers; (3) new graduates with co-op work experience seem to settle into the organization more easily; and (4) supervisor A is better at socializing new employees than supervisor B. If the human expert's decision scheme can be captured and inputted into an expert system, then the computer will be able to duplicate reliably the process that it took the expert years of experience to learn.

Some expert systems are already available for HR applications, such as the one referred to earlier for performance appraisal. Others in use include systems for authorizing compassionate leave fairly and consistently and for advising supervisors on unfair dismissal cases. Many more seem likely to be developed in the near future.[18]

A final trend seems to be toward even greater use of HRIS data and functions by non-HR specialists. As systems become more user-friendly and managers more computer-literate, an increasing number of managers will be able to generate their own HR reports, forecasts, and what-if scenarios to facilitate day-to-day management and future planning. The development of truly integrated HRIS, in which all applications share the same internal structure, look, feel, and basic commands, will greatly facilitate this increase in users.[19]

EXERCISE 1

Compensation at WCE

The following table of information concerns twenty-nine electronic assemblers employed by the Western Consolidated Electronics Company (WCE). Each employee is identified by an employee number. Additional columns give the employee's sex, years of service with WCE, most recent performance appraisal rating on a 1–9 point scale, current hourly pay rate, and past year's attendance figure as a percentage of scheduled work time.

In your new role as a compensation and benefits assistant, it is your job to perform certain calculations related to wage increases for employees in the coming year. These calculations can be easily completed using any spreadsheet program, such as LOTUS 1–2–3 or Microsoft Excel, on virtually any type of personal computer.

Your first task is to *calculate the new hourly rate* that should be paid to each employee following the next round of raises. There are three components to each employee's new rate:

1. A merit increase of 6.3 percent for employees whose performance rating is 8 or 9; 5.5 percent for ratings of 6 or 7; 4.4 percent for ratings of 5; 3 percent for ratings of 4; and no increase for those below 4
2. A long-service raise of 1 percent for employees with more than five years of current service
3. A raise of 1 percent for employees whose attendance was 98 percent or higher

Your next task is to *calculate the total annual wage cost* to the organization of these new wages. The average number of regular work hours paid per employee per year at WCE is 2080 (forty hours per week times fifty-two weeks, including paid vacation, paid sick leave, and paid public holidays).

Employee Number	*Sex*	*Years of Service*	*Performance Rating*	*Present Pay*	*Attendance %*
1	F	1	5	$8.00	90
2	F	1	4	$8.00	91
3	F	1	6	$8.20	91
4	F	2	3	$8.50	98
5	F	2	7	$8.50	96
6	F	3	2	$9.00	95
7	F	3	8	$9.00	98
8	F	4	5	$9.40	100
9	F	5	5	$9.40	100
10	M	1	3	$8.00	100
11	M	1	8	$8.00	100
12	M	1	5	$8.30	100
13	M	2	4	$8.55	98
14	M	2	6	$8.50	98
15	M	4	5	$9.50	98
16	M	3	2	$9.00	97
17	M	3	9	$9.10	95
18	M	3	2	$9.00	95
19	M	3	9	$9.30	90
20	M	2	3	$8.50	85
21	M	1	7	$8.50	100
22	M	6	4	$10.70	100
23	M	6	6	$10.00	98
24	M	9	5	$11.50	98
25	M	5	5	$9.70	97
26	M	7	5	$10.20	94
27	M	2	7	$8.30	92
28	M	6	3	$10.00	100
29	M	8	2	$11.20	98

If a recently submitted bid is won by WCE, production will have to be increased, and all electronic assemblers will be asked to work about four hours per week of overtime for the first six months of the coming year. *If the new business materializes, what will the total wage cost be for the next year?*

Finally, the compensation manager has asked you to check on whether there are any *differences in the average pay of males versus females* in this job. You are aware that the Equal Pay Act mandates equal pay for men and women doing the same job, unless the basis for the unequal pay is due to any factor other than sex. Do you find any differences either in current pay or next year's pay? If so, how would you explain them to your boss? Does WCE have anything to worry about under the Equal Pay Act? Why or why not?

Prepare a report on your findings that includes both tables and narration.

Notes and References

1. M. E. Grossman and M. Magnus, "The Growing Dependence on HRIS," *Personnel Journal,* September 1988, pp. 53–59.
2. L. F. Schoenfeldt and J. L. Mendoza, "The Use of the Computer in the Practice of Industrial and Organizational Psychology," in *The Computer as Adjunct in the Decision-Making Process,* ed. T. B. Gutkin and S. Wise (Hillsdale, N.J.: Lawrence Erlbaum Assoc., 1988).
3. J. Egbert, "Legislative Tracking," *Personnel Administrator,* October 1988, pp. 21–27; "Record-Keeping and Reporting Requirements," *Personnel Administrator,* December 1985, pp. 84–98.
4. B. G. Clayton, "A Helping Hand Named HuRBIE," *Human Resource Planning,* Vol. 13, No. 3, 1990, pp. 179–187.
5. N. R. Fritz, "In Focus: Computer Recruiter," *Personnel,* February 1988, pp. 4–5.
6. Sandra E. O'Connell, "Automate the Entire Employment Function," *HRMagazine,* June 1991, pp. 36–37.
7. D. D. Rodgers, "Computer-Aided Interviewing Overcomes First Impressions," *Personnel Journal,* April 1987, pp. 148–150.
8. Stephen E. Forrer and Zandy B. Leibowitz, *Using Computers in Human Resources,* (San Francisco: Jossey-Bass, 1991).
9. Ibid.
10. Jerry Rocco, "Computers Track High-potential Managers," *HRMagazine,* August 1991, pp. 66–68.
11. Paul Slattery, "A New Way to Appraise," *HRMagazine,* October 1991, pp. 27–31.
12. T. O. Peterson, "The Acquisition of Managerial Performance Feedback Skills Through the Use of a Knowledge-Based Expert System: An Empirical Evaluation," Ph.D. dissertation, Texas A & M University, 1988.
13. J. D. Finch, "Computers Help Link Performance to Pay," *Personnel Journal,* October 1988, pp. 120–126.
14. Michael O. Quigley and Terrance J. Henshaw, "A Model to Simulate the Effects of Work Force Dynamics on Compensation Policy," in *Strategic Human Resource Planning Applications,* ed. Richard J. Neihaus (New York: Plenum Press, 1987), pp. 185–194.
15. Gary Meyer, "Hard-working Micros Aid Managers," *HRMagazine,* August 1990, pp. 54–60.
16. Forrer and Leibowitz, *Using Computers in Human Resources.*
17. Deborah Cohen, "Increase Your Research Staff," *HRMagazine,* December 1991, pp. 31–34; Deborah O. Cantrell, "Computers Come to the Bargaining Table," *Personnel Journal,* September 1984, pp. 27–30.
18. Pai-Cheng Chu, "Developing Expert Systems for Human Resource Planning and Management," *Human Resource Planning,* No. 3, 1990, pp. 159–178.
19. Sandra E. O'Connell, "Expert Tells How to Have the Best of Both Worlds," *HRMagazine,* February 1992, pp. 29–30.

PART SEVEN

Multinational Human Resource Management

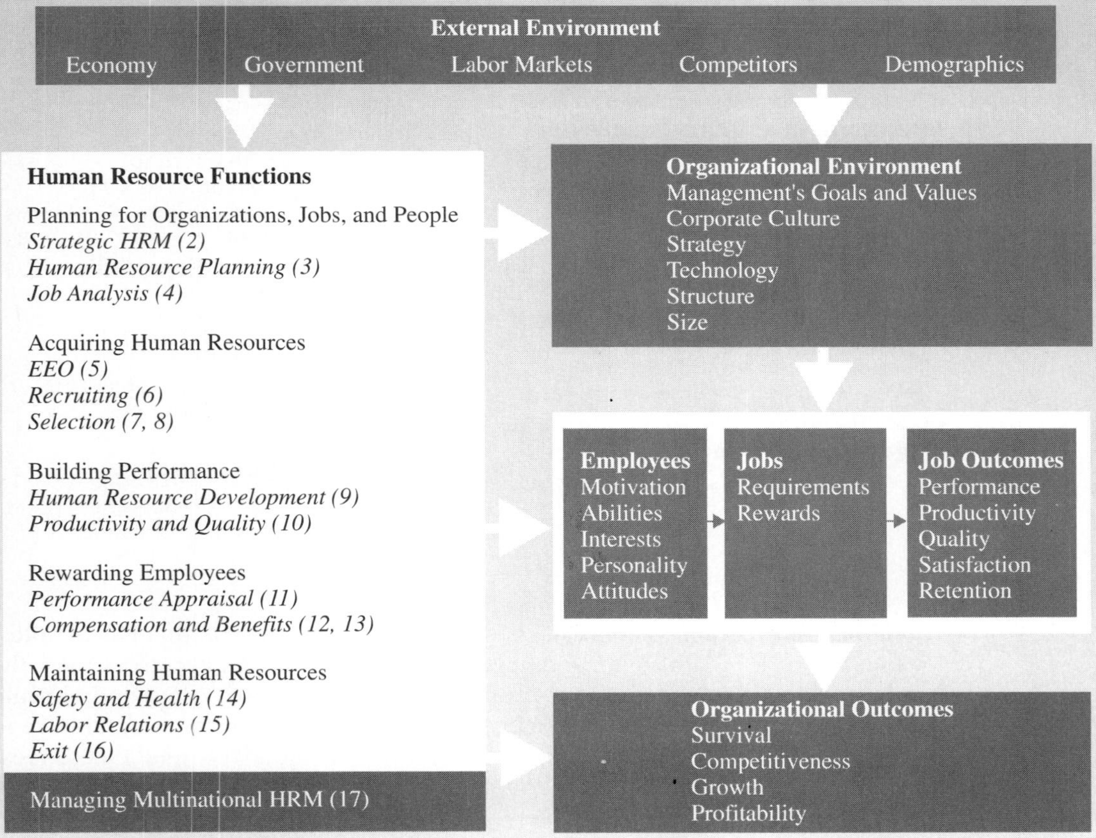

External Environment
Economy | Government | Labor Markets | Competitors | Demographics

Human Resource Functions

Planning for Organizations, Jobs, and People
Strategic HRM (2)
Human Resource Planning (3)
Job Analysis (4)

Acquiring Human Resources
EEO (5)
Recruiting (6)
Selection (7, 8)

Building Performance
Human Resource Development (9)
Productivity and Quality (10)

Rewarding Employees
Performance Appraisal (11)
Compensation and Benefits (12, 13)

Maintaining Human Resources
Safety and Health (14)
Labor Relations (15)
Exit (16)

Managing Multinational HRM (17)

Organizational Environment
Management's Goals and Values
Corporate Culture
Strategy
Technology
Structure
Size

Employees
Motivation
Abilities
Interests
Personality
Attitudes

Jobs
Requirements
Rewards

Job Outcomes
Performance
Productivity
Quality
Satisfaction
Retention

Organizational Outcomes
Survival
Competitiveness
Growth
Profitability

17

Managing Human Resources in Multinational Organizations

A **multinational corporation** (**MNC**) is defined as "an enterprise that has an interlocking network of subsidiaries in several countries, whose executives view the whole world as its theater of operations, and who therefore obtain and allocate financial, material, technical, and managerial resources in a manner conducive to the achievement of total enterprise objectives."[1] In the 1950s and 1960s, most large multinational companies operating in the world were American.[2] They operated in a world economy relatively safe from competition from firms of other nationalities. In the 1970s and particularly in the 1980s, the environment in which American multinationals operated became far more complex and competitive. This competition took place not only in markets outside the United States, but also struck deep at the U.S. domestic market. Sony Corp., Samsung, and Toyota Motor Corp. are a few of the foreign multinational firms whose names have become household words to most Americans. In many cases, the loss of the American competitive edge has been quite dramatic. For example, Xerox Corp. introduced the first fax machine in 1964 but in 1989 held only 7 percent of the fax market, while Japanese firms controlled 67 percent. In the 1980s, American automobile manufacturers closed thirteen major assembly plants, and the Japanese opened eleven.[3] American problems are not limited to trade with Japan. American firms have lost competitive advantage relative to firms from Canada and many European nations.[4]

The question, of course, is how do American MNCs confront this competitive challenge? In her 1988 book *The New Expatriates: Managing Human Resources Abroad,* Rosalie L. Tung states that "human resource planning is pivotal to the successful operation of a multinational corporation (MNC) because technology, capital, and know-how cannot be effectively and efficiently utilized nor transferred from corporate headquarters without using human power."[5] Although many other factors contribute to or detract from American international competitiveness, the efficient use of human resources is certainly an important one.

This chapter examines issues involved in managing human resources in multinational corporations. The process is referred to as international human resource management. We begin with a discussion of the differences between human resource management in domestic and international environments and then look at the approaches to international human resource management that MNCs can take and the factors that affect the choice of approach. In the rest of the chapter, we consider specific HR functions within an MNC, such as staffing, training, performance appraisal, and compensation, examining them from two perspectives. The first perspective is that of the HR manager operating within a foreign subsidiary, and the second, that of an HR manager based in the MNC's headquarters.

WHAT IS IHRM?

It is not easy to provide a precise definition of international human resource management. What an HR manager does in a multinational corporation varies from firm to firm. It also depends on whether the manager is located in the MNC's headquarters or on site in a foreign subsidiary.

A Definition

Broadly defined, **international human resource management (IHRM)** is the process of procuring, allocating, and effectively utilizing human resources in a multinational corporation. Although some argue that IHRM is not unlike HRM in domestic settings, others point out that there are significant differences. Specifically, IHRM requires a much broader perspective, encompasses a greater scope of activities, and is subject to much greater risks than is domestic HRM.[6]

When compared with domestic human resource management, IHRM requires a much broader perspective on even the most common HR activities. This is particularly so for HR managers operating from the MNC's headquarters (HQ) location. For example, when dealing with pay issues, the HQ-based HR manager must coordinate pay systems in different countries with different currencies that may change in relative value to one another over time. An American expatriate in Tokyo who receives a salary of $100,000 (U.S.) may suddenly find the buying power of that salary dramatically diminished if the Japanese yen strengthens in value relative to the U.S. dollar. A U.S. dollar purchased 248 yen in 1985 but only 128 yen in 1992. In the case of fringe benefits provided to host country employees, some very interesting complications might arise. For example, it is common in the United States for companies to provide health insurance benefits to the employee and the employee's family, which usually means spouse and children. In some countries, however, the term "family" may encompass a more extended group of relatives—multiple spouses, aunts, uncles, grandparents, nephews and nieces. How does the firm's benefit plan deal with these different definitions of family?[7] Although such issues are important for the HQ-based manager, they are also relevant to the HR manager located in a subsidiary. This manager must develop systems that are not only acceptable in the host country, but also compatible with the company-wide systems being developed by his or her HQ-based counterpart.

In general, the scope of IHRM activities is much larger than the scope of domestic HRM activities. For HQ-based managers, the most obvious contrast is that they must coordinate the procurement, allocation, and use of employees in more than one country. For on-site managers, there are many complications that arise from this greater scope. It is not unusual for subsidiary HR managers to be involved in arranging housing, health care, transportation, education, and recreational activities for expatriate and local staff. For example, an RCA manufacturing facility in Taiwan provides dormitory housing for local assembly workers; this housing is managed by the HR staff at the plant. Furthermore, expatriates often find themselves in a situation in which both home and host countries claim the right to tax their income. Procedures must be designed to deal with this problem of dual taxation—something that does not occur in domestic HRM.

In general, IHRM activities are influenced by a greater number of external forces than are domestic HRM activities. The HQ-based manager may have to set equal employment opportunities (EEO) policies that meet the legal requirements of both the home country and a number of host countries. Because of the visibility that MNCs tend to have in foreign countries (especially Third World developing countries), the subsidiary HR managers may find themselves dealing with government ministers, other political figures, and a greater variety of social and economic interest groups that would normally be encountered in purely domestic HRM. A final aspect of the broader scope of IHRM is that HQ-based and subsidiary HR managers deal with employee groups that have very different cultural backgrounds. The HQ manager must coordinate policies and procedures to manage expatriates from the firm's home country, as well as third-country nationals (e.g., a French manager working for an American MNC in the firm's Nigerian subsidiary) in subsidiaries around the world. Even within a specific subsidiary, the HR manager may be dealing with a mixture of host, home, and third-country nationals working together in the subsidiary.

There are certainly major risks associated with HRM in domestic situations. Unfair hiring practices may result in a firm being charged with violation of EEO laws and subjected to financial penalties. The failure to establish constructive relationships with domestic unions can lead to strikes and other forms of labor actions. However, international HR managers face these same risks, as well as some additional ones that are unique and more threatening. Depending on the countries where the MNC operates, HQ and subsidiary HR managers may have to worry about the physical safety of employees. A colleague of the authors related his experience during a coup attempt in a South American country. As HR manager for the local subsidiary of a foreign firm, he found himself arranging transport of his expatriate employees and their families to the safety of the subsidiary's manufacturing plant. The process involved death threats, wild rides through the jungle, and standoffs at gunpoint. This is not the sort of problem usually confronted by domestic HR managers. In all too many countries, kidnapping and terrorism are of concern to international HR managers.

Besides these risks, it has been estimated that an average expatriate manager, with family, costs an MNC nearly $250,000 (U.S.) per year to maintain overseas.[8] If these managers do not perform well and must be recalled to the home country, this failure represents a huge financial loss for the firm. The risks associated with poor selection decisions are great.

A final risk is that of expropriation or seizure of the MNC's assets in a foreign country. If HR policies antagonize host country unions or important political groups, the MNC may be asked to leave the country, have its assets seized, or find the local government taking majority control of its operation. Again, this is not the sort of risk that most domestic HR managers face.

Approaches to IHRM

MNCs can approach the management of international human resources in a number of ways. Four of them are presented in Table 17.1. In the **ethnocentric approach,** the MNC simply transfers HR practices and policies used in the home country to subsidiaries in foreign locations. Expatriates from the MNC's home country manage the foreign subsidiaries, and the MNC's headquarters maintains tight control over the subsidiaries' policies. In the **polycentric approach,** the subsidiaries are basically independent from headquarters. HR policies are developed to meet the circumstances in each foreign location. Local managers in the foreign sites are hired to manage HRM activities. The **regiocentric approach** represents a regional grouping of subsidiaries. HR policies are coordinated within the region

TABLE 17.1 Four Approaches to IHRM

Aspect of the Enterprise	***Orientation*** *Ethnocentric*	*Polycentric*	*Regiocentric*	*Geocentric*
Standard Setting, Evaluation, and Control	By home country headquarters	By local subsidiary management	Coordination across countries in the region	Global as well as local standards and control
Communication and Coordination	From HQ to local subsidiary	Little among subsidiaries, little between subsidiary and HQ	Little between subsidiary and HQ, medium to high among subsidiaries in region	Totally connected network of subsidiaries and subsidiaries with headquarters
Staffing	Home country managers	Host country managers	Managers may come from nations within region	Best people where they can be best used

Source: Adapted from D. A. Heenan and H. V. Perlmutter, *Multinational Organizational Development*, © 1979 by Addison-Wesley Publishing Company, Inc. Reprinted with permission of the publisher.

to as much an extent as possible. Subsidiaries may be staffed by managers from any of the countries within the region. Coordination and communication within the region are high, but quite limited between the region and the MNC's headquarters. In the **geocentric approach,** HR policies are developed to meet the goals of the global network of home country locations and foreign subsidiaries. This may include policies that are applied across all subsidiaries, as well as policies adapted to the needs of individual locations—depending on what is best to maximize global results. The firm is viewed as a single international business entity rather than a collection of individual home country and foreign business units. HRM and other activities throughout the MNC are managed by individuals who are most appropriate for the job regardless of their nationality.[9] Thus, you might find a British manager handling HRM activities in the New York office of a Dutch MNC.

Factors Affecting the Approach to IHRM

A number of factors may influence the IHRM approach taken by an MNC. Included among these are political policies and legal regulations within the host countries; the state of managerial, educational, and technological development in the host countries; the technology and nature of the product or products of the MNC; the life cycle of the organization; and cultural differences.[10]

Political Policies and Legal Regulations Firms that take an ethnocentric approach to IHRM and would prefer to use many expatriates to manage and staff their subsidiaries may find themselves restricted by government policies and legal regulations in the host country.[11] Policies limiting expatriates and requiring extensive employment of host country nationals are put into place to encourage MNCs to hire, train, and develop local employees, particularly managerial and technical staff. This is especially likely in developing countries, where management and technical training within the host country's education system is rudimentary and the local government views the presence of MNCs in the country as a means of developing local expertise.

Managerial, Educational, and Technological Development in the Host Country An MNC opening subsidiaries in Europe faces a much different IHRM challenge than one opening subsidiaries in a country in western Africa. In Europe, the available work force is likely to be well educated and have considerable technical and management experience (see the International Perspective box on page 786). Therefore, the opportunity to develop polycentric, regiocentric or geocentric IHRM strategies is available. In western Africa countries, management and technical education is likely to be limited, and the bulk of the work force may lack basic skills needed to deal with modern production processes or service activities. A more centralized IHRM strategy is necessary, with careful on-site monitoring by host country personnel.

Technology and the Nature of the Product This factor interacts with the two factors mentioned above. For technologically sophisticated products or services, the need to maintain specific production standards and quality control necessitates a greater degree of centralization of IHRM functions at the MNC's headquarters location and the use of home country managers and technical personnel to monitor these standards. This is the case particularly when the subsidiaries involved are located in host countries with low levels of technological and managerial expertise. On the other hand, some products must be adapted to host country tastes in order to succeed in the local market. For example, some food items that are highly popular in the United States would be viewed as quite repulsive in other countries. In this case, the reliance on local talent to adapt the product to suit the host country market may require a very different approach to managing the subsidiary's recruiting activities.

Organizational Life Cycle Some researchers argue that the appropriate IHRM approach will depend on the life cycle of the organization and the life cycle of the firm's products within various international markets.[12] Four stages of an organization's life cycle have been proposed (see Table 17.2). During the initiation stage, the organization is concentrating on getting itself started and establishing itself within domestic and limited foreign markets. International involvement may be restricted to exporting or very limited international sales operations. During this phase, the organization tends toward an ethnocentric approach to IHRM. In the second stage, the organization is established and experiencing reasonable growth. International operations become a significant part of this growth, with foreign product divisions established within the firm. At this time, the firm views foreign

HRM in Europe: Some Environmental Contrasts

European HRM scholars have pointed out that somewhat different assumptions and environments surround the practice of human resource management in Europe compared to the United States, and that not all American HR ideals and practices are transferable. Although there are large country-by-country variations in Europe, some common threads seem to characterize a number of these countries and differentiate them from the United States. David E. Guest (1990) suggests that U.S. HRM is rooted in the American Dream, based on individualism, self-achievement, minimal assistance from the government, and a frontier mentality. In contrast, European HRM is more characterized by concerns for social democracy and heavier governmental involvement.

One study found that U.S. HRM texts are full of references to strategy and the strategic role that must be played by the modern HR manager, whereas European texts seldom mention this topic. Chris Brewster of the Cranfield School of Management in England suggests that European HR managers may place less emphasis on a strategic role because managers in general have less control and autonomy than is assumed in American models. However, European managers also enjoy a greater level of government support for the labor market, and in some ways this gives them more choices in the HRM arena.

The following environmental factors differentiate the European HRM context from that in America:

1. More collectivist national cultures, on average, than the United States.

2. More government regulation of the employment relationship, both at the national level and at the European Community (EC) level. At the EC level, a social charter pertaining to a number of employee rights has been adopted, and more detailed programs for assuring these rights in the member nations are being developed.

3. More concentrated patterns of ownership, with greater governmental ownership in many industries, and ownership of public firms tending to be concentrated in fewer hands, often those of powerful banks. The banks realize that businesses are in business to stay in business rather than just to turn a profit in the next quarter. This longer-term perspective means that takeovers and mass retrenchments are less common responses to temporarily flagging performance.

4. Greater unionization and much greater recognition of unions as legitimate and necessary partners in the process of running a business.

5. Mandated employee involvement in some European countries. Employers may be required to consult both the employees and the union before making some kinds of decisions.

6. More centralized bargaining and wage setting. More so than in the United States, wage rates in European countries are set by law or by multi-employer or industry-level bargaining rather than by organizational-level talks with a local union.

7. More government involvement in the labor market. Governments spend much more in some European nations on vocational and apprenticeship training and retraining than is the case in the United States. There is also greater government support for employees who are temporarily or partially unemployed. The highly qualified labor force gives employers in Europe greater freedom to recruit either internally or externally, and the support for the unemployed makes part-time and contract labor more feasible and popular.

Sources: David E. Guest, "Human Resource Management and the American Dream," *Journal of Management Studies*, July 1990, pp. 377–397; Chris Brewster, "European Human Resource Management: Reflection of, or Challenge to, the American Concept?" Invited paper presented at the Third Conference on International Personnel and Human Resource Management, Berkhamsted, England, July 1992; Martyn Wright, "Is There a European Theory of HRM? An Empirical Comparison of European and American Texts," Proceedings of the Third Conference on International Personnel and Human Resource Management, Berkhamsted, England, July 1992.

TABLE 17.2 Stages of an Organization's Life Cycle

Stage	*Defining Characteristics*	*IHRM Approach*
Initiation	Start-up, entrepreneurship, limited markets and products, research and development, informal management, limited overseas involvement	Ethnocentric
Functional Growth	Growth, technical specialization, expanding markets and products, more formal management and structure, establishing significant overseas operations	Polycentric
Controlled Growth	Focus on productivity and costs due to scarce resources and competition, diversified products, focus on integration of organizational structure, substantial overseas operations	Regiocentric
Strategic Integration	"Global" integration of activities to meet domestic and overseas competition, new forms of organizational structure, global alliances/joint ventures, strategic management	Geocentric

Sources: Based on information from L. Baird and I. Meshoulam, "Managing Two Fits of Strategic Human Resource Management," *Academy of Management Review,* Vol. 13, No. 1, 1988, pp. 116–128; and John F. Milliman and Mary Ann Von Glinow, "A Life Cycle Approach to Strategic International Human Resource Management in MNCs," in *Research in Personnel and Human Resource Management: Supplement 2,* ed. James B. Shaw, John E. Beck, Gerald R. Ferris, and Kendrith M. Rowland (Greenwich, Conn.: JAI Press, 1990), pp. 21–36.

operations as "add-ons" to its organizational growth but not necessarily integral parts of its overall strategic development. A polycentric approach to IHRM is likely to evolve, with the firm's headquarters relying on local management to run each foreign location.[13] In the third stage, the firm begins to seek ways to increase productivity and control costs. Ways are examined to find economies of scale and functional integration across major overseas and domestic units. This pattern extends to HRM activities. As a result, a more regiocentric approach to IHRM may evolve, and trends toward a geocentric approach may develop. In the final stage of the firm's life cycle, domestic and international competition forces the firm to view its operations as a truly global unit. Global networks, alliances, and joint ventures are formed. Functional areas within the organization (both domestic and international) must be integrated to maximize competitive advantage. As a result, a global, geocentric approach to IHRM is needed to match the integration of research and development, marketing, production, and distribution worldwide.

Cultural Differences Culture also plays a role in determining what approach an MNC takes to IHRM. Since the approach taken is determined at the MNC's headquarters location, the impact of culture at the headquarters level is the significant issue here. It seems that culture may affect HQ decisions in at least two ways.

First, some cultures are simply more comfortable than others in taking an ethnocentric approach to management. For example, data indicate that Japanese MNCs more frequently staff management positions in their foreign subsidiaries with home country managers than do American or European MNCs. There are, of course, regional exceptions, but worldwide this tendency toward ethnocentric staffing is greater in Japanese MNCs than in American or European firms.[14]

Second, the mix of cultures in the subsidiaries of an MNC and the level of cultural difference among the subsidiaries will restrict the IHRM approach taken. As the number and level of cultural differences among subsidiaries increase, it becomes much more difficult for HR staff at the MNC's headquarters to formulate and implement consistent HR practices worldwide. Thus, even though an MNC might prefer an ethnocentric approach to managing human resources, the policies and practices formulated at HQ may be totally inappropriate and unacceptable in particular subsidiary locations. A more polycentric or regiocentric approach may be necessary.

MANAGING HUMAN RESOURCES IN A FOREIGN SUBSIDIARY

Culture not only influences an MNC's overall approach to IHRM, but also plays a critical role in determining the activities of HR managers within foreign subsidiaries. In fact, culture has a potential impact on every HR function.

Culture and HR Functions Within a Foreign Subsidiary

The role of a subsidiary HR manager is to develop HR practices that are (1) acceptable within the local culture and (2) acceptable to management at the MNC's headquarters. The balancing of these two requirements is a particularly difficult task for a home or third-country HR manager working within a foreign subsidiary. These managers bring their own "cultural baggage," which may affect their ability to accommodate cultural differences in the host work force. The same may be said of host country HR managers whose cultural background makes it difficult for them to understand the HR policy needs of headquarters. As mentioned earlier in this chapter, employees in a subsidiary may consist of a mixture of home, host, and third-country nationals—all with their own distinct cultural backgrounds and preferences. The host country HR manager must help home and third-country nationals adapt to the HR practices operating in the subsidiary, even though these practices may be derived from very different cultures. (See the Ethical Perspective box on page 790 for more on this issue.)

Numerous studies indicate that cultural differences do affect how managers manage and how subordinates react to different management styles.[15] In order to relate differences in culture to differences in IHRM practices, it is first necessary to identify the aspects, or dimensions, of culture that vary from one culture to another. In 1961, F. Kluckhohn and F. L. Strodtbeck suggested that cultures vary from one another in how they view some very basic issues; these dimensions and a brief definition of each are presented in Table 17.3. In addition, any discussion of the effect of culture on organizations would be incomplete without mentioning the work of Gerte Hofstede and his four dimensions of culture. These dimensions, along with their definitions, are presented in Table 17.4.

Differences in culture based on Kluckhohn and Strodtbeck's or Hofstede's dimensions may significantly affect HR practices. The following sections on subsidiary HR planning, staffing and training, performance appraisal, and compensation describe the difficulties faced by the subsidiary HR manager in developing effective HR systems. Many of these difficulties stem from cultural differences. They are discussed along with other problems facing the HR manager that are not exclusively cultural in nature.

HR Planning

The importance of HR planning has received considerable attention of late. Particularly in MNCs with strategic global objectives, planning for the efficient use of human resources is essential if the MNCs are to meet their goals.[16] However, the implementation of HR planning procedures may be more difficult in some subsidiaries than in others. In cultures where people are viewed as basically subjugated to nature, there is very little need for HR planning. After all, why plan when people are unable to determine what happens? The implementation of extensive HR planning systems in such cultures would be met with bemusement at best and significant resistance at worst. Likewise, cultures that are oriented toward the present would not view long-term planning as valuable. In cultures oriented toward the past, planning would tend to focus on purely historical data and the use of these data in predicting future HR needs. Such an approach might be appropriate for firms that operate in relatively stable environments but would not work well for firms operating in highly variable environments, where the past has little to do with the future.

Staffing in the Subsidiary

A subsidiary HR manager ought to use a hiring process that fits the local labor market. For example, an MNC may need the services of a local personnel selection agency to identify the sources of skilled employees. Local employment laws must be adhered to, and premium salaries may have to be offered to lure highly qualified individuals away from local firms. In Japan, the collective nature of Japanese society has made it difficult for foreign companies to hire qualified Japanese employees. These individuals tend to "stay in the family" and work for Japanese, not foreign, employers. Once employees have worked for a foreign firm, Japanese companies are extremely unlikely to employ them. Although this attitude has become less prevalent in recent years, it still remains a problem.

In some countries hiring may require using a government-controlled labor bureau. This may be particularly prevalent in hierarchical cultures with high power distance (see Table 17.4). In the People's Republic of China, for example,

ETHICAL PERSPECTIVE

Ethical Relativity Versus Ethical Absolutism: HR Decision-Making in Overseas Operations

What should an international human resource manager do when an employment practice that is illegal and morally repugnant in the home country is commonplace and legal in the host country? Examples might include blatant sex or race discrimination in hiring, job assignment, or compensation; use of child labor; or providing unsafe working conditions.

Ethicists discuss two opposite approaches to questions of this type. One approach is ethical relativism, which suggests that what is good is what a society defines as good. If a society says that virgins shall be sacrificed at every full moon or that women shall not be paid the same as men for the same work, those rules are right for that society at that point in time. There can be no external frame of reference for judging that one society's set of rules is better than another's. IHR managers who try to impose their values on human resource practices in the host country are guilty of ethical imperialism. Under the doctrine of ethical relativism, it is entirely appropriate to follow local practices regarding the treatment of employees. Though appearing on the surface to be a liberal, open-minded approach, this view may result in actions that most home country constituencies would find entirely unacceptable, such as child labor or gross inequality.

The opposite position is called ethical absolutism. This is the view that there is a single set of universal ethical principles, which apply at all times and to all cultures. This approach would be very useful, as it would suggest which local practices—though different from those of the home country—are morally acceptable because they do not violate universal principles and which are not morally acceptable and must not be followed. The problem with this view is specifying what the universal principles are and developing a logical case for why these, and only these, principles are truly universal. In adopting the values of a single culture or religion as universal one again runs the risk of ethical imperialism.

Ethicists can marshal impressive arguments against both these views. So where does an expatriate decision maker turn for guidance? Thomas Donaldson has attempted to provide a framework for multinational decision making involving an ethical dimension. He states that the task is to "tolerate cultural diversity while drawing the line at moral recklessness" (Donaldson, 1989, p. 103). In some ways, his approach is absolutist because it relies on a statement of ten fundamental international rights: freedom of physical movement, ownership of property, freedom from torture, right to a fair trial, nondiscriminatory treatment, physical security, freedom of speech and association, right to minimal education, political participation, and subsistence. Organizations need to avoid depriving individuals of these rights, wherever they may do business.

However, these rights alone are not a sufficient guideline. When IRH managers are trying to decide if their corporation can follow a practice that is legal and morally acceptable in the host country but not in the home country, Donaldson suggests that they ask themselves a series of questions. First, ask *why* the practice is acceptable in the host country but not at home. Answers to this question fall into two categories: (a) because of the host country's relative level of economic development or (b) for reasons unrelated to economic development. If the answer is (a), the next question is whether the home country would have accepted the practice when (or if) it was at the same level of economic development. If it would have, the practice is permissible. An example would be building a fertilizer plant that provides a product absolutely crucial to feeding the starving population of a nation, despite the fact that there is some slight risk of occupational disease for individuals working in the plant. If the home country were itself starving, it would accept the risk to workers in the service of the larger good.

The second answer, that the difference is not based on economic considerations, requires a more complicated decision process. The manager must ask two additional questions: Is it possible to conduct business successfully in the host country without undertaking the practice? and Is the practice a clear violation of a fundamental international right? (Donaldson, 1989, p. 104). The practice is permissible *only if* the answer to both questions is no. That is, the practice is acceptable if it is critical to doing business in the country *and* it does not violate a fundamental right. Otherwise, the organization should refuse to follow the local practice.

In Singapore, it is common to see help-wanted ads for "Chinese women, age 21–28." This type of advertisement violates U.S. laws and mores regarding age, sex, and ethnic discrimination. Would it be permissible for a U.S. subsidiary in Singapore to run an ad like this? According to Donaldson, the answer is no because the discrimination is not tied to level of economic development, is not necessary for doing business in Singapore, and violates the fundamental international right to nondiscriminatory treatment.

Sources: Walter T. Stace, "Ethical Relativity and Ethical Absolutism," in *Ethical Issues in Business*, ed. Thomas Donaldson and Patricia H. Werhane (Englewood Cliffs, N.J.: Prentice-Hall 1988), pp. 27–34; William Shaw and Vincent Barry, *Moral Issues in Business* (Belmont, Calif.: Wadsworth, 1989), pp. 11–13; Thomas Donaldson, *The Ethics of International Business* (New York: Oxford University Press, 1989).

local labor bureaus must be notified of hiring needs and grant permission to recruit. In some cases, these labor bureaus simply assign employees to work for the MNC; in other instances, the MNC is allowed to recruit only in certain locations and for certain types of workers.[17] Sometimes the local bureaus may supply a foreign subsidiary with employees who are not adequately skilled for the job, and it may be difficult for the subsidiary to refuse employment. Important staffing issues may have to be approved by officials very high in the government hierarchy.

The development of an adequate selection system may be complicated by the fact that selection tests used in the home country of the MNC may be culturally biased and inappropriate elsewhere. For example, many personality tests were developed using Western samples. The personality profiles provided by such tests, and certainly their normative data, would be meaningless in trying to understand the behavior of Japanese or Thai job applicants. Assertive individuals who take initiative and stand out from the crowd may appear well adjusted according to the norms of Western personality tests. However, a Japanese job applicant with a similar score might be a disaster if hired to work in the MNC's subsidiary in Tokyo since "standing out" as an individual is inconsistent with the more collectivist Japanese culture. Even if the concepts measured by the tests are

TABLE 17.3 Kluckhohn and Strodtbeck's Dimensions of Culture

Dimension	*Orientation*	*Definition*
Basic Nature of Human Beings	Good	Left to their own devices, people are basically good and will act in a reasonable and responsible manner.
	Evil	People are basically evil and cannot be trusted.
	Mixed	People are a mixture of good and evil.
Relationships Among People	Individualistic	The primary responsibility of an individual is to him/herself. Individual characteristics and abilities are of most concern.
	Group	Responsibility to family and group is most important. Ability to fit into the group rather than individual ability is paramount.
	Hierarchical	Basically the same orientation as for group, with the addition that distinct differences in status are expected and respected.
Activity Orientation	Being	The point of life is to live and understand. Activity, in and of itself, is not important.
	Doing	The point of life is to do things, be involved in activities, and accomplish objective goals.
Relation to Nature	Subjugation	Human activities are determined by nature and the environment.
	Harmony	Humans should live in harmony with their environment.
	Domination	Humans can control their destiny and can exert domination over their environment.
Time Orientation	Past	History is important in determining our present actions.
	Present	Our actions should focus on the present, and the current situation should determine what we do.
	Future	Our actions should focus on the future and the attainment of future goals.

Source: F. Kluckhohn and F. L. Strodtbeck, Variations in Value Orientations (Evanston, Ill.: Row, Peterson, 1961).

applicable, there are difficulties in getting many tests adequately translated into the host country language.

Issues of racial, age, sex discrimination can cause considerable difficulties for the subsidiary HR manager. In Singapore, a fairly hierarchical and masculine culture, it is acceptable and legal to place job advertisements that specifically state the race, age range, and sex of employees being sought. This would blatantly violate American EEO laws. An American working as HR manager in a Singapore

TABLE 17.4 Hofstede's Dimensions of Culture

Dimension	*Definition*
Power Distance	The degree to which power is unequally distributed in a society or organization.
Uncertainty Avoidance	The degree to which a society considers itself threatened by uncertain events and ambiguous situations, and tends to avoid these types of situations or tries to control them through formal means.
Individualism-Collectivism	The extent to which society emphasizes the importance of the individual versus the group.
Masculinity-Femininity	The extent to which society values masculine characteristics of aggressiveness, assertiveness, and not caring for others. Also, the extent to which male and female roles are clearly defined.

Source: Gerte Hofstede, *Culture's Consequences: International Differences in Work Related Values* (Beverly Hills, Calif.: Sage Publications, 1980).

subsidiary could experience a considerable moral dilemma in following practices that are in line with local laws and culture but conflict with home country laws and home country organizational culture.

There can also be unexpected disadvantages associated with hiring particular types of local employees. For example, in a multicultural society, the use of an employee from one ethnic group in a managerial position may not be acceptable to members of other ethnic groups. In India, the caste system, which has historically played a prominent role in Indian society, would make it inappropriate to hire someone from a lower caste to supervise employees of a higher caste. In some countries (Japan for example), it may be inappropriate to hire a younger person for a job that has supervisory responsibilities over older employees.

Training in the Subsidiary

One of the major problems associated with hiring in less developed countries is that the skill level of individuals may be less than desired. In such circumstances, it is important to invest considerable time and effort in the selection process and to provide increased training to local employees when they arrive on the job.[18] However, much like the problem of transferring HQ-based selection procedures to subsidiaries, training programs designed in the home country to teach employees the skills needed to perform their jobs may be inappropriate for use in other cultures. The problem of translating materials and a number of subtle problems further complicate training.

How people learn and the methods of training with which they are comfortable vary across cultures. For example, the Chinese, whose culture is very hierarchical, are taught respect and deference for teachers. As a result, Chinese students see themselves as the "receivers" and the teachers as the "givers" of knowledge.[19] Chinese students rarely ask questions or challenge a teacher's statements. To do so would be disrespectful. Consequently, Chinese students take a passive role in learning, and the very active, high-participation methods often used in Western training programs would be inappropriate. An HR manager must develop culturally appropriate methods for use in a subsidiary.

Appraising Performance of Subsidiary Staff

Culture helps determine what aspects of performance should be appraised and how that appraisal should be conducted. Hofstede's four dimensions of culture are widely cited in the cross-cultural management literature (see Table 17.4), and so make a useful framework for how culture influences the appropriateness of performance appraisal systems.[20]

Organizations use a variety of methods to assess employee performance. Management by objectives (MBO) or other forms of goal setting are widely accepted in managing and appraising performance. In MBO, subordinates and supervisors agree on moderately difficult and challenging goals that the subordinates must achieve. In high power distance cultures, this goal-setting process may prove difficult because subordinates may hesitate to get involved in it. After all, their supervisor has higher status and power, and it is the supervisor's job to tell subordinates what to do. In India, for example, employees expect their supervisors to make these kinds of decisions, and supervisors who try to share decision-making roles with subordinates are viewed as "not doing their job."[21] By requiring subordinates to set moderately difficult and challenging goals, users of MBO may face considerable difficulties in countries high on uncertainty avoidance (see Table 17.4). Employees from such cultures are typically not risk takers, and it is hard to obtain from them a public commitment to challenging, somewhat risky goals.

Many of the performance appraisal methods discussed earlier in this text focus on the assessment of individual performance (e.g., behaviorally anchored rating scales, behavioral observation scales). Most of these procedures were developed in the United States, a very individualistic society. Attempts to transfer these methods to more collective cultures like Japan or China may be unsuccessful. There group performance is critical, and singling out individuals for praise or criticism is highly threatening. Employees in collective cultures gain much of their sense of identity from membership in work groups. Individually oriented appraisals serve to separate individuals from those sources of identity.

A culture's standing on individualism-collectivism also determines how "good performance" is defined (see Table 17.4). In Japan, for example, behaviors directed toward maintaining group harmony and cohesiveness (e.g., helping resolve conflicts among group members) may be valued as much, if not more, than behaviors focused on more objective performance activities (e.g., producing more widgets). Task performance at the expense of group harmony would certainly be viewed as inappropriate. A similar situation may exist in feminine cultures, in which maintenance of good personal relationships is valued. Managers who maintain good personal networks and develop warm, trusting relationships with their subordinates may be viewed as better managers than those with higher levels of objective task performance.

Culture may also influence whether performance appraisal of *any* type will be accepted or resisted. During the 1980s, the Singapore government encouraged local organizations to develop performance appraisal systems. The government hoped that individual appraisal, combined with performance-based merit pay systems, would increase productivity and efficiency in Singapore. Initially, the development of appraisal systems met with resistance. Singapore's population is predominantly Chinese, and the culture is relatively high on power distance, influenced by the Confucian tenets of respect for hierarchy and age. Pay and promotion had historically been based on age and tenure. Appraisal systems that might reward young employees more than their older colleagues were viewed with concern.[22]

Subsidiary Compensation Systems

The task facing the international compensation manager is pictured in Figure 17.1. Compensation policies within each subsidiary must be consistent with the local wage market, wage legislation and regulations (e.g., minimum wage), union influences, other legal restrictions (e.g., prohibitions against sex-based wage discrimination), and cultural preferences. At the same time, the subsidiary's compensation system must provide an adequate level of strategic consistency within the MNC's overall business strategy. Besides dealing with a pay system developed for host country employees, the subsidiary HR manager must also deal with a separate system applicable to home country expatriates and third-country nationals working for the subsidiary. Expatriate pay systems, which are discussed later in this chapter, are often very different from those used for host country employees within a subsidiary. In some cases, expatriate employees make more money than host country nationals who have jobs of equal or greater importance and complexity. These differences can often result in host country employees feeling that they are being treated unfairly.

Factors Affecting Compensation Systems

It is beyond the limits of this chapter to discuss the intricacies of wage markets, wage and other legislation, and union influences on compensation practices around the world. Suffice it to say that the subsidiary HR manager must know or have access to information about these issues. Regulations concerning pensions, social security, medical insurance, and other benefits are critically important and vary greatly. In some countries, benefits such as housing, transportation, and year-end bonuses are common; in others they are not.

Issues relating to sex-based or racially based wage differentials are of particular concern for subsidiaries of U.S. firms. Even though such differentials may

FIGURE 17.1 Multinational Compensation Systems

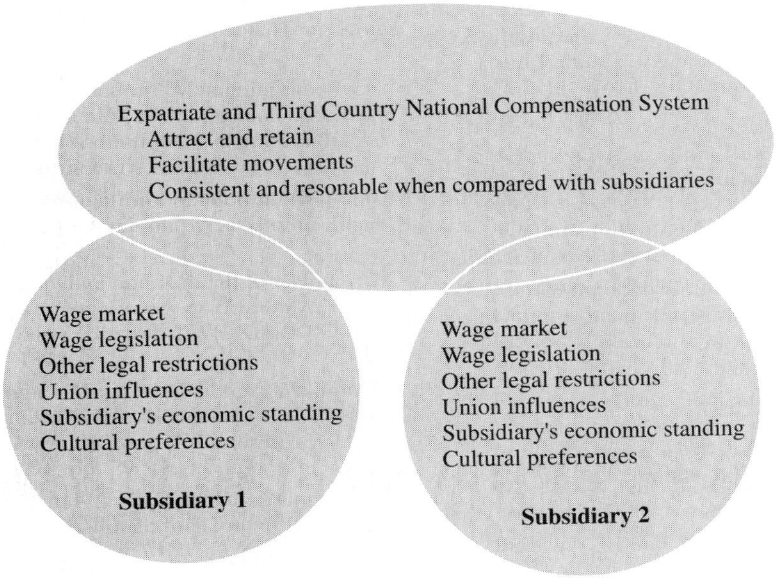

Expatriate and Third Country National Compensation System
Attract and retain
Facilitate movements
Consistent and resonable when compared with subsidiaries

Wage market
Wage legislation
Other legal restrictions
Union influences
Subsidiary's economic standing
Cultural preferences

Subsidiary 1

Wage market
Wage legislation
Other legal restrictions
Union influences
Subsidiary's economic standing
Cultural preferences

Subsidiary 2

be acceptable in countries where American MNCs operate, they are certainly not consistent with U.S. HR philosophies. An American HR manager in a foreign subsidiary must make decisions as to whether it is ethical to have discrimination in one part of the MNC organization but not in another.

Union influences may play an important role in determining wage policies in some countries but not in others. For example, Australia has had for some years now a national wage-setting system in which the government and unions negotiate pay rates for workers that apply countrywide. In Hong Kong, by contrast, labor unions are extremely weak, and wage rates are determined by the free market.

One aspect of compensation that varies from country to country and has important implications for both subsidiary HR managers and HQ-based managers is the issue of what happens if their MNC decides to leave a foreign country. When such a decision is made, termination liabilities may result in significant payouts to employees.[23] By tradition, law, or union contract, MNCs may be required to pay up to two years' salary to employees who are involuntarily terminated. In some countries, firms intending to close down operations may be required to develop a systematic plan to deal with severance payments, relocation expenses, retraining, and other services for employees who are laid off.

As with performance appraisal systems, cultural preferences may influence the type of compensation system that is appropriate. In high power distance cultures, compensation systems should reflect hierarchical divisions within the firm. Pay should reflect job and status differences with large differences in the pay levels of the highest- and lowest-level workers. In contrast, compensation systems in low power distance cultures should be more egalitarian, with relatively small differences between the top and bottom earners. In individualistic cultures, compensation systems should reward individual achievement, and in collective cultures pay should be group based or seniority based.[24]

The job of the HR manager in a foreign subsidiary is a difficult one. The procedures and policies developed must be consistent with the host country's legal requirements and cultural traditions. Overlaying this HR system are the policies and procedures of the home country MNC. If the overall HR approach of the MNC is polycentric, then the HR manager's job is much simpler since subsidiaries are given substantial autonomy in developing their own HR policies. Where the MNC takes a more ethnocentric approach, inevitable conflict occurs as the subsidiary HR manager attempts to work within HQ's guidelines while providing procedures that are acceptable to the host country's work force. With regiocentric or geocentric IHRM approaches, the subsidiary HR manager's job becomes a delicate balancing act of local adaptation and strategic consistency to ensure that HR policies and procedures result in efficient use of subsidiary human resources to the maximum benefit of both the subsidiary and global MNC.

IHRM: THE VIEW FROM HEADQUARTERS

MNCs are increasingly faced with the problem of how to allocate limited resources among multiple subsidiaries around the world. The development of global markets and the existence of global competitors have made it necessary for MNCs to exert centralized, strategic control over their worldwide operations. At the same time, intensified competition in local markets, specific cultural conditions, and unique regulatory systems put pressure on MNCs to be locally responsive. To be competitive, an MNC cannot afford to sacrifice global competitiveness for local subsidiary performance. Neither can it keep sacrificing local performance and expect to survive globally. An MNC and its subsidiaries must, therefore, carefully balance the demands of strategic global control and local adaptability. The international HR manager located at an MNC's home country headquarters can play a key role in this balancing act.[25]

Many forms of control can be used to limit and coordinate the activities of subsidiaries. **Bureaucratic control** relies primarily on a set of explicit rules and regulations that specify the expected output and required behaviors of subsidiaries. **Resource control** manipulates the objective resources that are available to subsidiaries, such as capital, access to markets, financial data, or technological information. The use of HR activities to control subsidiaries and integrate them into the broader strategic goals of the MNC has been referred to as **cultural control** or **control of organizational context.** Several HR activities can be used to exert this cultural control. These include selection, training and development, transfer policies, performance appraisal, and reward systems.[26] The goal of these strategic HR control practices is to develop employees at both headquarters and subsidiary locations who are sensitive to local conditions *and* loyal to the goals of the parent multinational corporation.[27]

Much of what has been written about IHRM has focused on the problems of selecting and training home country managers for international assignments. More recently, there has been considerable discussion about the problem MNCs face in successfully repatriating expatriate managers when their foreign tours of duty end. The remaining sections of this chapter examine the important aspects of dealing with expatriate managers.

SELECTING EXPATRIATES

A model of the life cycle of an expatriate assignment is given in Figure 17.2. It involves a process of determining the need for an expatriate assignment, identifying and then selecting likely candidates, preassignment training, departure, postarrival orientation and training, crisis and adjustment or crisis and failure, reassignment abroad and/or repatriation and adjustment. The failure of an expatriate (particularly one in a managerial position) can have disastrous results. There are substantial monetary costs associated with sending expatriates abroad, bringing them back to the home country, and finding replacements. One estimate is that U.S. companies lose $2,000,000,000 a year as a result of expatriate failure.[28] Furthermore, the poor performance of an expatriate may damage the firm's image in the host country. There are also the personal tragedies of employees who fail

FIGURE 17.2 The Expatriate Assignment Life Cycle

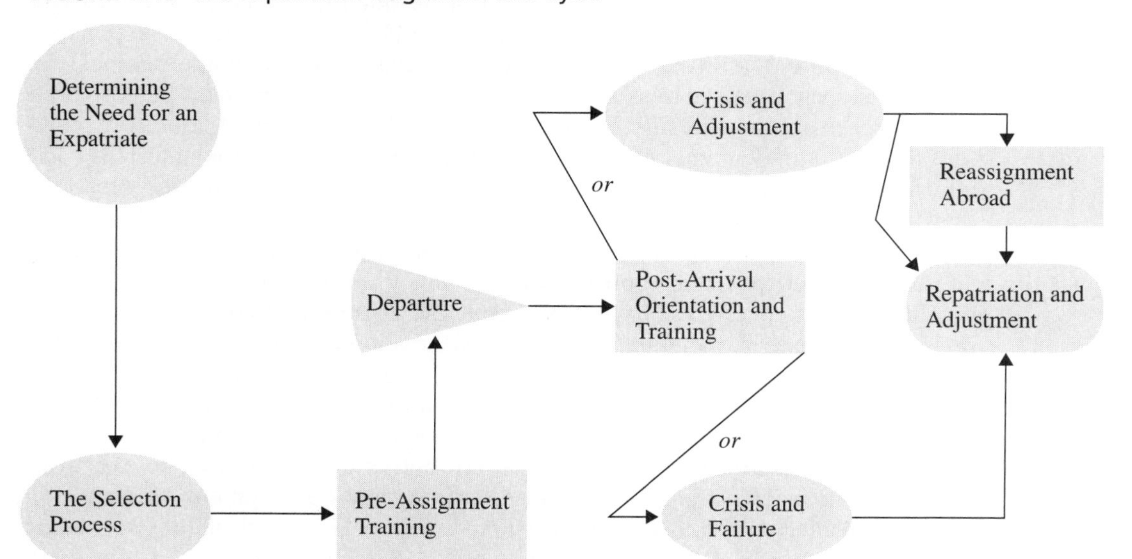

even though they had been viewed as competent managers within the domestic organization. These individuals may have sold their homes, left jobs they liked, and uprooted their families to take a foreign assignment—only to find themselves back in the home country branded as failures. Thus, managing the expatriate life cycle is a very important function of the international HR manager.

Determining the Need for an Expatriate

As already noted, the decision as to whether a particular foreign assignment is filled with a home country national, host country national, or third-country national may derive partly from the overall IHRM approach taken by the MNC—an approach that is influenced by the factors described in previous sections of this chapter. However, other factors must also be taken into account.

The level of the position in the foreign subsidiary is one such factor. One survey of U.S., European, and Japanese MNCs has indicated that expatriates are more likely to be found at the senior management level than at the middle or lower management level.[29] On the average, home country expatriates filled 56 percent of senior management positions but less than 30 percent of lower management positions.

The degree of interaction between host country nationals and the person in the position is also an important issue in deciding whether an expatriate should be used. If the position requires a high level of interaction, which in turn requires a high level of knowledge about the local culture, then it may be best to use a host country national. Such individuals often have political connections and influence networks that are of great value to the firm, and these connections and networks would be very difficult for an expatriate to develop.

The similarity of the home and host cultures must be considered as well. If those cultures are very different, it may be difficult to identify an expatriate able to adapt and perform well in the foreign subsidiary. The MNC must then weigh any advantages associated with using an expatriate against the increased probability of the expatriate failing to adjust and perform well in the assignment. The cost of the training needed to prepare the expatriate for the assignment in a very different culture must also be taken into account in this cost-benefit analysis.

Political factors, too, may determine whether an expatriate should be used to fill a foreign position. As noted earlier, there may be policies or regulations limiting the number of expatriates that can be used to fill positions in a foreign subsidiary. In situations where no such policies exist, it still may be good public relations to fill a large number of positions in a subsidiary with host country nationals. In other cases, local people may have political or social disadvantages that would warrant the use of an expatriate. For example, in a country with many ethnic groups, giving a local person a prominent position in the subsidiary may alienate local employees from other ethnic groups. The perceived neutrality of an expatriate might be extremely important in such instances.

Another factor in deciding whether an expatriate is used is the organization's overall strategic view of foreign assignments. Some MNCs view foreign assignments as a means of developing international expertise among their cadre of managers and professional staff. The Montedison Group in Italy, which gains approximately 50 percent of its sales from foreign operations, views foreign assignments as part of the overall internationalization of the firm.[30] Thus, even though local nationals could do the job, some positions may be filled by expatriates because the positions give home country managers the opportunity to develop skills in international dealings.

Finally, cost factors can play a part in determining whether an expatriate fills a foreign position. In most cases, host country nationals are considerably less expensive to employ than expatriates.[31] As mentioned earlier, an expatriate with family may cost more than $250,000 (U.S.) per year to maintain abroad.

The Selection Process

In a recent survey, sixty managers in MNCs from thirteen different countries were asked to rank the importance of ten characteristics used to select individuals for international assignments.[32] The results indicate that managers recognize the importance of such factors as personal adaptability and the adaptability of the spouse and family and know that these factors should be considered in selecting expatriates. However, other evidence indicates that, particularly in U.S. firms, expatriates are often chosen for international assignments primarily on the basis of their technical competence.[33]

Factors Associated with International Success For many years, much of our knowledge about selecting expatriate managers was based on anecdotal data. MNC managers were asked to report factors that they used in selecting expatriates and factors that seemed to contribute to the failure of expatriates in their international assignments.[34] More recently, several studies have identified in a more rigorous way the underlying factors that contribute to expatriate success and, thus, the types of factors that should be used in selecting individuals for international assignments.

One of the most interesting and informative of these studies was published in 1985 by Mark Mendenhall and Gary Oddou.[35] From an extensive review of the literature, Mendenhall and Oddou identified four major dimensions of expatriate acculturation—that is, factors that influenced whether an expatriate could successfully adapt to a foreign assignment.

The first, **self-oriented dimension,** concerns activities that contribute to the expatriate's self-esteem and self-confidence. There are three subfactors in this dimension: (1) *reinforcement substitution,* (2) *stress reduction,* and (3) *technical competence*. Expatriates who are high on the reinforcement substitution factor are able to readily substitute activities in the new culture for those that they liked to do in their home culture. For example, an American manager in Australia would find it difficult to attend American football games. Instead, the manager might develop an interest in rugby, thus substituting a local sport for one that he or she enjoyed in the United States. Expatriate managers also tend to acculturate more readily if they engage in activities that help them reduce stress. To say that an expatriate's job is stressful is an understatement. Expatriates must adapt to a foreign environment and in most instances, adjust to having greater responsibility than they did in their home country. Yet they are expected to perform at a higher level almost immediately upon arriving in the new assignment. Individuals who can reduce stress by reading, jogging, sailing, watching television, meditating, or whatever tend to acculturate more readily than those without such means of relief. Technical competence also has a strong bearing on the acculturation process. Expatriates who are technically competent and feel confident in their ability to handle their international assignments acculturate more easily than those who are less qualified.

The second major dimension of acculturation, the *others-oriented dimension,* consists of two subfactors: (1) *relationship development* and (2) *willingness to communicate*. Expatriates who are able to develop lasting friendships and close relationships with people different from themselves acculturate more easily in overseas assignments. Additionally, individuals who are willing to communicate in the host country's language also adapt more readily. It is interesting to note that this second subfactor suggests that simply being able to speak a host country's language is unimportant unless one is willing to do so. A person who is less proficient in the host language but willing to use it even at the risk of making mistakes and looking foolish, may adapt more easily than someone with excellent knowledge of the language but a reluctance to try it out in daily conversation.

The third dimension of acculturation, the **perceptual dimension,** concerns the ability of expatriates to understand *why* foreign nationals behave the way they do. Expatriates who do not jump to conclusions about the causes of a local employee's behavior have an easier time of adjusting than those who make judgments more quickly. There is a large body of research in social psychology indicating that people are motivated to attribute causes to other people's behavior. Thus, if an employee is performing poorly or acts in a dour, uncommunicative manner, the typical manager will attribute some cause to those actions—the employee is lazy or stupid or has a sullen personality. Social psychological research indicates that we are not very good at accurately assessing the causes of the behavior of people from our *own* culture. Imagine how poorly we do in explaining the behavior of persons from cultures very different from our own. Mendenhall and Oddou suggest that expatriates who are able to reserve judgment and gather more facts before assigning causes to behavior are able to adjust more readily to foreign assignments.

The final dimension discussed by Mendenhall and Oddou characterizes situations rather than people and is called **cultural toughness.** Some foreign assignments are tougher than others. American expatriates sent to a small village of yak herders in Mongolia would have a much harder time adjusting than if they had been assigned to Sydney, Australia—a modern city, with friendly people and the same basic language.

Rosalie Tung has also studied the factors that contribute to expatriate success or failure, identifying eighteen variables that affect success. She groups them into the four general categories: job competence; personality traits and relational abilities; environmental variables; and family variables.[36] Tung's categories are similar to those of Mendenhall and Oddou except that she also highlights the importance of family considerations in acculturation. More recent research points to five major categories of expatriate characteristics that influence assignment success. These are presented in Table 17.5.

Taken collectively, these studies indicate that persons selected for an international assignment must meet six criteria: (1) they must be willing and motivated to go overseas, (2) they must be technically able to do the job, (3) they must be adaptable, (4) they must have good interpersonal skills and be able to form relationships, (5) they must have good communication ability, and (6) they must have a supportive family situation. The importance of each of these criteria becomes greater as the cultural toughness of the foreign assignment increases. These factors in expatriate selection are summarized in Figure 17.3.

Procedures for Selecting Expatriates Since there is a good deal of knowledge about the factors linked to the success or failure of individuals in foreign assignments and since expatriate failures are expensive, one might assume that MNCs spend considerable time and effort in screening employees and their families before sending them abroad. In reality, the sophistication of selection procedures

TABLE 17.5 Attributes Contributing to the Success or Failure of Expatriates

General Factor	*Specific Attributes*
Job Factors	Technical skills Knowledge of HQ and host country operations General managerial skills Administrative competence
Relational Traits	Ability to tolerate ambiguity Behavioral flexibility Ability to be nonjudgmental Level of cultural empathy and ethnocentrism Interpersonal skills
Motivational State	Belief in the mission Congruence of assignment with career path Interest in overseas experience Interest in the host country culture Willingness to acquire new behavior patterns and attitudes
Family Situation	Willingness of the spouse to live overseas Adaptibility and supportiveness of spouse Stability of the marriage
Language Skills	Host country language ability Ability in nonverbal communication

Source: From "Training the International Assignee," by Simcha Ronen from *Training and Development in Organizations,* Goldstein and Associates, eds. Copyright © 1991 by Jossey-Bass Inc., Publishers.

FIGURE 17.3 A Model for Selecting Expatriates

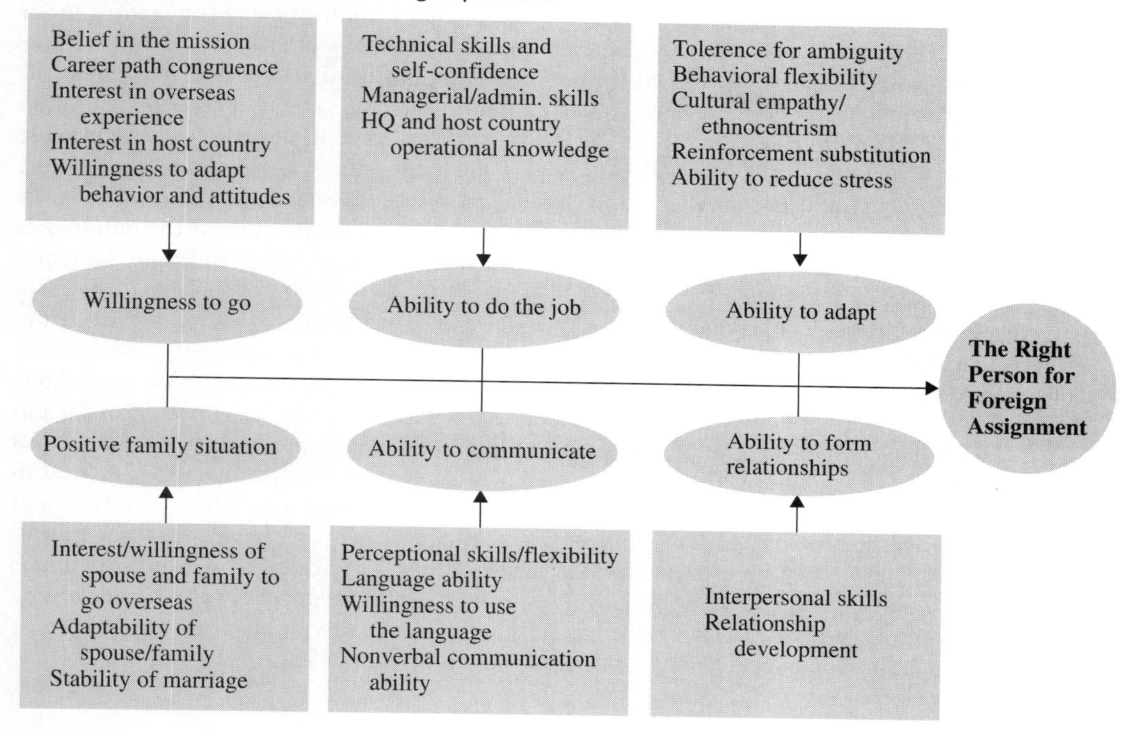

varies widely from MNC to MNC and from nationality to nationality. Tung notes that, when asked if tests are used to assess the candidate's technical competence, only 3 percent, 5 percent and 14 percent, respectively, of the U.S., Japanese, and Western European firms in her study said yes. As for testing a candidate's "relational abilities," 5 percent of the U.S. firms, 21 percent of the Western European ones, and none of the Japanese answered in the affirmative. A somewhat more encouraging picture emerged when these companies were asked if they conducted interviews with the candidate and his or her spouse before selection for an international position. Of the U.S. firms, 52 percent indicated that they conducted interviews with both the candidate and spouse; 47 percent, that they interviewed only the candidate; and 1 percent, that they had no interviews when the position was managerial. When a technical position was involved, the figures for U.S. firms were 40 percent, 59 percent and 1 percent, respectively. For Western European firms, the figures were 41 percent, 59 percent, and 0 percent when the job was managerial, and 38 percent, 62 percent, and 0 percent when the job was technical. None of the Japanese firms conducted interviews with the spouse, regardless of the job. In the case of managerial positions, 71 percent of the Japanese firms indicated that they interviewed prospective candidates, but only 62 percent of the firms did such interviewing for technical positions.[37]

The fact that many firms do not use sophisticated procedures to measure such attributes as relational skills and adaptability does not mean that they lack interest in the issues. Rather, they often assess such characteristics using less formal methods. The British firm Imperial Chemical Industries (ICI) assesses the spouse's suitability for foreign assignments "through social interactions, rather than in an interview." The British bank NatWest annually assesses its employees on a variety of characteristics such as knowledge, drive, ability to communicate, judgment, and personality. Since most of those sent abroad have been with the firm for some time, NatWest believes that the appraisal profiles of the employees (including their family situation) are sufficient for judging their ability to deal with a foreign assignment.[38]

Although NatWest's approach may seem reasonable, it is important to develop selection procedures specifically for international assignments and not rely on selection methods used for domestic hiring or on information about candidates that was collected with purely domestic purposes in mind. It is possible, for example, that an individual who is an excellent manager in a domestic situation does not have the ability to take on the additional responsibilities usually attached to international assignments. An American manager who is considered an excellent communicator by his U.S. colleagues because of his direct, face-to-face, to-the-point style may be a total disaster when required to communicate with Chinese or Japanese subordinates who value subtle, indirect forms of communication. Examples of methods that might be used to identify individuals with the important attributes for international success are given in Table 17.6.

The Special Issue of Female Expatriates

In a survey more than 600 U.S. and Canadian firms, only 3 percent of 13,338 expatriates identified were women. In another survey of 60 U.S. firms, 54 percent indicated a reluctance to place women in expatriate positions. The reason for this reluctance was the firms' belief that many foreigners were prejudiced against female managers and that international assignments for women often cause problems for dual-career marriages.[39] This attitude is disturbing, particularly given the fact that many highly qualified women are interested in international careers. In a survey of 1129 graduating M.B.A. students from seven management schools in the United States, Canada, and Europe, 84 percent of the students wanted an international assignment sometime in their careers. There were no differences between male and female M.B.A.'s in their interest in international positions.[40] These potential female international managers represent a significant source of expertise and ability that, at least at present, MNCs seem to be underutilizing. As noted in Chapter 5, on equal employment opportunity, the discrimination against U.S. women in international assignments may violate the sex discrimination clauses in Title VII of the Civil Rights Act of 1964.

An important question is whether female expatriates have a more difficult time handling international assignments. After all, some Middle Eastern countries

TABLE 17.6 Some Methods for Selecting Successful Expatriates

Willingness to Go

- Interview questions to assess the person's understanding of the mission and why the person thinks that he or she has the characteristics that will help accomplish that mission.
- Discussions of the career implications of the foreign assignment. What skills and experiences, in the individual's view, will the foreign position provide for advancement in the chosen career path? What position would the individual expect to receive upon return from the foreign assignment?
- Biodata that might indicate the level of the individual's interest in and knowledge of the host country—for example, history of holiday trips overseas, family connections to the country, and so forth.

Ability to Do the Job

- For individuals who may have made short-term (one to two weeks) troubleshooting trips overseas, assessments of their performance during those assignments collected from individuals with whom they worked.
- Technical knowledge tests related to particularly important or unusual aspects of the job that will occur in the foreign assignment, e.g., technical standards required by the host country, knowledge of labor relations laws relevant to operation in the host country. Obviously, what is tested is determined by the exact nature of the foreign job assignment and what can be readily learned on the job.
- Assessment by domestic colleagues of the individual's managerial and administrative abilities. Current performance appraisals.
- Situational exercises, role-plays, or simulations in which the individual must deal with situations likely to arise in the foreign location. For example, the candidate might have to explain a relatively complicated technical procedure to a host country national and might also be asked to role-play a performance feedback session with the person.

Ability to Adapt

- Situational exercises characterized by high levels of ambiguity and time pressure to examine how well the candidate performs under such conditions.
- Behavior description interviews focused on previous examples of behavioral flexibility.
- Biodata concerning nature and breadth of hobbies and other leisure activities and a check of the availability of those activities in the foreign location. For example, an individual whose sole hobby is horse jumping may have a difficult time finding an adequate substitute for that hobby in a country where practically no one has ever seen a horse and the few horses that do exist are used for food or as pack animals.

Ability to Form Relationships

- Psychological tests of traits typically associated with relationship development.
- Assessment of how the individual typically deals with conflict and how that compares with the conflict management norms in the host country.
- Situational exercises where the individual must meet, greet, and establish initial positive social interactions with people from different cultures.
- Biodata relating to the person's ability to establish friendships with people from other cultures.

(continues)

TABLE 17.6 Some Methods for Selecting Successful Expatriates (*cont.*)

Ability to Communicate

- Traditional written and oral tests of language ability.
- Situational exercises in which the language ability must be used, e.g., explaining a technical procedure to individuals from the host culture using the host language.
- Videos of host country nationals in which the candidate is asked to interpret the nonverbal communication taking place in the situation on the video.
- "Diplomacy exercises"—asking that the candidate, without saying the phrase "your performance is lousy and I am going to have to fire you if you do not improve," to express this same sentiment tactfully to a Japanese subordinate.

Family Situation

- Interviews with spouse and family members to determine interest and willingness to go overseas.
- Family biodata to identify possible predictors of adjustment, e.g., previous experiences abroad.
- In addition, most of the above selection procedures also may be used to assess the spouse's ability to adapt and communicate in a foreign environment.

will not provide work permits for female employees, even if they are appointed to the foreign assignments by their firms.[41] In one study, fifty-two female expatriates were were interviewed during their assignments in Asia or shortly after their return from an Asian assignment. Ninety-seven percent of these women described their assignments as successful, and many of the women suggested that the most difficult part of their assignment had been getting their firm to send them abroad. Others suggested that they were discriminated against more by Western expatriates than by local Asian businessmen.[42] Many of these women cited their sex as an advantage. Their distinctiveness caused their clients and associates to remember them more readily—an asset in any sales position. Many of their male clients found it easier to talk with a woman, particularly in cultures where the aggressive American male approach is overly threatening. Throughout these interviews, a common theme appeared: female expatriates were regarded, first and foremost, as foreigners (*Gaijin* in the words of the Japanese), and the normal rules associated with the behavior of local females were not applied to them. Just because a society discriminates against its own women does not mean that it will not accept female expatriates.

To summarize, MNCs that have discriminatory policies concerning the assignment of women to international positions may be losing out on a considerable human resource. Even in very masculine societies like Japan and Korea, female expatriates may provide important skills and competitive advantages to their international operation. In selecting individuals for foreign positions, it seems most rational to look for the kinds of attributes associated with success in foreign assignments, regardless of the sex of the candidate.

TRAINING EXPATRIATES

The goal of good expatriate selection procedures is to identify individuals who will have the skills necessary to adjust and perform well in an international assignment. However, J. Stewart Black, Mark Mendenhall, and Gary Oddou point out that selection is only one of many factors that determine adjustments to an international assignment.[43] Among the other important factors affecting adjustment is the degree of training, both predeparture and postarrival, that the expatriate receives. Nearly 70 percent of American expatriates are sent on foreign assignments with little, if any, predeparture training.[44] The following example is not uncommon.

> A young, "high-flier" financial expert who worked for a large American multinational bank was selected to take up a prominent position in a British subsidiary. The individual was selected, given a couple of weeks' notice of the assignment, and then, as he was boarding the plane, his manager handed him some brochures on the best places to shop in London. The entire predeparture cross-cultural training for this individual consisted of those shopping brochures.[45]

Is Training Effective?

The lack of adequate predeparture training for individuals assigned abroad is unfortunate, given the evidence that training enhances cross-cultural skills, subsequent adjustment to the assignment, and performance.[46] Research on cross-cultural training has shown that it increases the perceived competence and self-confidence of individuals faced with cross-cultural interactions. Other research indicated that supervisors who had undergone cross-cultural training used more culture-appropriate leadership behaviors when interacting with foreign subordinates. Another study found that, when asked to explain the reasons for the behavior of a foreign national, persons who had received cross-cultural training made attributions more similar to those of foreign nationals (i.e., people of the same nationality as the person being observed) than did untrained persons.[47] As noted earlier, this sort of perceptual skill is an important factor in acculturation.

In addition, a study of managers assigned to expatriate positions in South Korea found that managers who had received predeparture training adjusted more readily than those without such training. The same study also indicated that training had a positive effect on performance in the assignment. Managers who had been trained perceived their assignment as less difficult to adjust to and reported higher levels of performance than those who had received no training.[48] Given the benefits of predeparture training, it is vital to examine some of the methods available for use in such training and to consider when the various types of training are most appropriate.

Training Approaches

Two convenient ways of categorizing the varied approaches to training expatriates are by the content of the program and by the specific technique used. Within the content category, some programs focus primarily on the job or organization, whereas others concentrate on aspects of the culture in the foreign location. Job training may stress the new operational or supervisory skills that will be needed in the foreign assignment. Another form of job training can be referred to as "strategic training": expatriates are given the "big picture" of the global business strategy of the MNC, with emphasis placed both on the global strategy and on how the particular subsidiary to which the expatriate will be assigned fits into that strategy. Strategic training might also include the enhancement of strategic skills, such as the development and use of global information management systems or interpersonal communication skills that could aid in the transmission of critical information to and from headquarters and units around the world. One sort of cultural training may offer basic information such as geography, cost of living, and general customs. Other types of cultural training may aim at increasing the expatriate's attributional and perceptual skills—that is, helping the expatriate accurately perceive and understand the behavior of persons from a foreign culture.

Cultural and job training can be accomplished through a variety of techniques. Lectures, briefings, and assigned readings can convey factual information to trainees. Involving the trainees in role-playing, case analyses, and simulations is a more active learning method. In cultural assimilator training, the employee must consider 75 to 100 cultural incidents selected by a panel of experts as representative of situations that the person may confront in the host culture. The trainee has to analyze what is happening in the situation and why it is happening; then the trainee receives feedback on the correctness of the analysis.[49] Trainees may undergo field experiences as well, by visiting either the host country or enclaves of the host culture within the home country (e.g., they may visit a predominantly Chinese part of a city within the home country).

Training programs may also be differentiated according to how long and vigorous they are, for they range from very short briefings on the superficial aspects of the foreign assignment and culture to sessions lasting several days and dealing with both the assignment and the culture at some depth. Using these concepts of content, technique, rigor, and duration, J. Stewart Black and Mark Mendenhall have divided training programs into eight basic "scenarios." These categories are presented in Table 17.7.

A Contingency Approach to Expatriate Training

The international HR manager faces a difficult task in deciding which of the various approaches to training should be used. Obviously, some are more expensive

TABLE 17.7 Black and Mendenhall's Eight Training Scenarios

Scenario	*Rigor*	*Duration*	*Techniques*	*Content*
A	High	60–180 hours	Lecture, factual briefing, books, culture assimilator, role plays, cases, field experiences, simulations	Equal emphasis on job and culture—job demands, constraints, choices, country economics, history, religion
B	Moderate	20–60 hours	Lecture, books, culture assimilator, cases	Equal emphasis on job and culture
C	Moderate	20–60 hours	Lecture, film, books, cases, role-plays, simulations	Emphasis on job demands, constraints, choices; less emphasis on culture
D	Low–Mod	20–40 hours	Lecture, factual briefing, cases	Strong job emphasis with very little on culture
E	Moderate	40–80 hours	Lecture, film, books, cases, culture assimilator, role-plays, simulations	Little emphasis on job; much emphasis on culture, country economics, politics, history, religion
F	Low–Mod	20–60 hours	Lecture, films, books, cases	Little emphasis on job; more on culture
G	Low–Mod	30–60 hours	Lecture, films, books, cases, role-plays	Little emphasis on job; more on culture
H	Low	4–8 hours	Lecture, film, books	Little treatment of either culture or job

Source: "A Practical but Theory-Based Framework for Selecting Cross-Cultural Training Methods," from *Human Resource Management*, Vol. 28(4), 1989 by J. Stewart Black and Mark Mendenhall. Copyright © 1989 by John Wiley & Sons, Inc. Reprinted by permission of John Wiley & Sons, Inc.

to conduct than others. To maximize efficiency, the international HR manager should select and develop training programs that best fit the particular assignment and individual. Recently, a number of authors have identified factors that can be used in making these decisions.[50]

Five factors are important in selecting the type of training program needed: (1) business strategy, (2) level of headquarters control, (3) novelty of the new job, (4) novelty of the host country, and (5) amount of required interaction between the expatriate and local nationals. The first two factors are important only for training expatriate managers, but the remaining three apply to the training for any type of expatriate position.

Business Strategy and Control Business strategy and level of control interact with one another to determine whether global strategy training is needed. The international involvement of some MNCs is limited primarily to a group of international sales offices or subsidiaries in various countries. There is no integrated strategy for the international units, and they are treated as independent parts of the home organization. Foreign profits and activities are simply "add-ons" to the activities and profits of the domestic organization. The manager of these overseas units may be given a great amount of discretion as to how the units operate. In such cases, the expatriate manager may need only a very basic understanding of overall business strategy. The primary focus would be on operational aspects of the subsidiary and the expectations that the domestic organization has of this particular foreign business unit. In other situations, the MNC may not have an integrated strategy for its overseas units but may retain more central control over the activities within each unit because of product quality standards, legal requirements, or whatever. In these cases, the expatriate manager moving to an international assignment needs even less knowledge of the overall strategic plan of the organization.

In contrast to these first two scenarios, some MNCs are truly global businesses that have developed a worldwide business strategy. Their markets are global. Their competitors are global. To be competitive, the MNC must maximize efficiency through careful coordination of its worldwide resources. In this scenario, each foreign unit of the MNC is considered an integral part of the overall business strategy of the firm. Each unit's activities and profits (or losses) have implications for other units around the world. As a result, strategic training becomes an essential preparation for the expatriate. However, as in MNCs without a global strategy, the level of central control maintained over individual foreign business units may temper the need for strategic training. For example, McDonald's is an MNC with a highly integrated global strategy. In this corporation, standard procedures related to product quality are strictly maintained by the headquarters organization. This limits the discretion of foreign subsidiary managers and thus reduces their need for extensive strategic training.

Novelty of the New Job Job novelty simply refers to whether the job in the foreign location is similar to other jobs that the expatriate has held. Although the basic functions of the domestic and foreign jobs may seem alike, often the scope and responsibility levels associated with the expatriate position are considerably greater.[51] For example, an individual may be transferred to a foreign assignment from a managerial position in the domestic organization that involved supervising fifty employees. In that position, when equal employment opportunity issues arose, the manager had a legal staff within the organization to call on for advice. If governmental regulations became important, there were specialists within the firm who dealt with governmental affairs. Union-management issues were handled by the labor relations department. In the foreign assignment, the manager may once again be supervising fifty employees carrying out the same basic task as in the domestic situation—for example, selling insurance to local businesses.

However, in the foreign location the managers may have to deal with *all* the issues that other departmental specialists took care of at the home office.

To the extent that the foreign assignment requires new and different job skills compared with the domestic position, job content training becomes more critical as a component of predeparture training. As noted in the section on expatriate selection, MNCs tend to choose individuals for foreign assignments on the basis of their competence in a domestic position. This approach often means that a person who has been an effective performer is assumed to have all the skills needed in the new assignment. The failure of many expatriates may stem from this assumption. Good international HR managers do not make such assumptions but instead carefully evaluate the novelty of the foreign position relative to the person's job history.

Cultural Novelty and Degree of Interaction The novelty of the host culture and the degree of interaction with local nationals required of the expatriate combine to determine the importance of cross-cultural training. As stressed earlier in this chapter, cultures vary from one another on a number of dimensions. Expatriates may find themselves transferred from a domestic culture that is high on individualism, low on power distance, and moderately feminine to a foreign culture that is highly collective, has high power distance, and is extremely masculine. The values, attitudes, and behaviors in these two cultures would be quite different. In such a situation—for instance, in moving from the United States to China—cross-cultural training to help the expatriate understand the attitudes and values of the new culture and to learn appropriate behavior patterns becomes more important. When the home and host country cultures are relatively similar (e.g., the United States and Australia) the need for cross-cultural training decreases.

Besides the issue of cultural novelty, the degree of interaction with local nationals must also be considered in deciding the necessary level of cross-cultural training. To determine the level and importance of the interaction, at least four key questions should be asked.

1. How familiar are the norms and pattern of interactions in the host culture? Most Americans know that when greeting one another the Japanese bow, but most Americans would have little idea of greeting behavior in Azerbaijan.

2. How frequently will the expatriate have to interact with local workers, managers, neighbors, and so forth?

3. Will interaction be primarily one-way or two-way communication? That is, will the expatriate be mostly just giving orders or be engaged in problem solving, negotiation, or similar two-way communication activities?

4. How important are the interactions with local nationals? This question deals with the issue of what happens if the expatriate does something culturally stupid. It may be that in some situations culturally inappropriate behavior may cost the MNC lots of money, whereas in others, the worst effect will be some embarrassment for the expatriate.[52]

Determining the level and importance of interaction is critical. Even though the home and host cultures are quite different, if the expatriate is *not* expected to interact with local nationals to any great extent or if the interactions are of little importance, then limited cross-cultural training in the form of general cultural information might suffice. For example, some American expatriates in Jakarta, Indonesia, hold positions that require them to interact mainly with other expatriates from MNCs in the region—not local Indonesians. These Americans live in expensive expatriate neighborhoods outside the city. Houses are surrounded by high walls, protected by security personnel, and represent little replicas of Western society in an Asian land. Interaction with local nationals is confined to a few key Indonesian government officials and businessmen (who may have been educated in the West, possibly in the United States) and servants hired to clean, cook, wash, take care of the children, and drive the expatriates to work.

In other circumstances, even though the cultures are relatively similar, if extensive interaction with local nationals is required, cross-cultural training becomes vital. An American sent to Australia to set up a new subsidiary would have to interact with many different types of local Australians: union leaders, managers, government officials, and so on. Even though Australia and the United States are relatively alike in culture, there are differences. The American expatriate who arrives to establish a new business in Australia and exhibits inappropriate behavior and attitudes would probably return home a failure since establishing the new business would require the American to gain acceptance by local Aussies. Some moderate level of cross-cultural training in this situation would be warranted.

J. Stewart Black and Mark Mendenhall have developed a model that can aid the international human resource manager in deciding what level of job content and cross-cultural training is necessary.[53] Their eight training scenarios (see Table 17.7) differ from each other in the level of rigor, duration, specific training techniques used, and content. The scenarios range from a relatively superficial level of cross-cultural training to very intensive and extensive training. To determine which of the scenarios is most appropriate, Black and Mendenhall use a decision tree based on the answers to three questions. The decision tree is presented in Figure 17.4.

Postarrival Training and Training for the Expatriate Family

The training of expatriates involves two additional issues: (1) postarrival training and support and (2) training for the expatriate family. In a sense, the term *postarrival training* is somewhat inappropriate. What it actually refers to is the initial socialization of the expatriate into the work setting and practical assistance in getting settled into a new home and environment.

Postarrival Training and Support While predeparture training may have accomplished what has been called "anticipatory adjustment," the shock of arriving at the foreign assignment may warrant additional fine-tuning of cross-cultural or job

FIGURE 17.4 Decision Tree for Selecting Appropriate Training Scenario

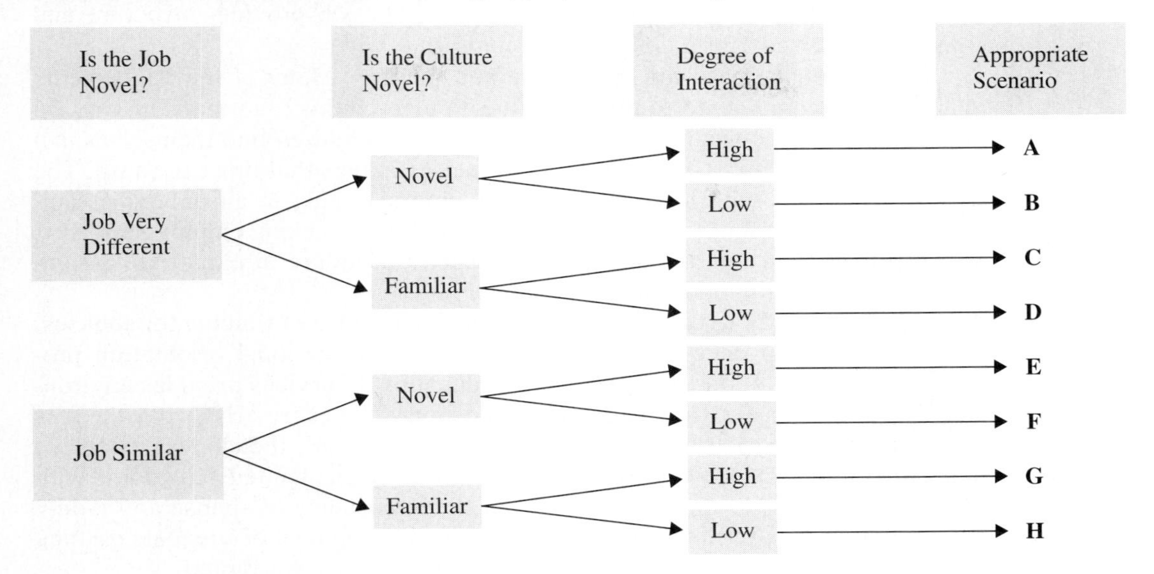

Source: M. Mendenhall and J. S. Black, "Selecting Effective Training Systems for Global Managers: A Contingency Approach," unpublished manuscript, School of Business, University of Tennessee at Chattanooga.

skills.[54] As with any training program, the problem of transferring the training from the training site to the job is always present. Thus, resources need to be available to help expatriates use in the actual foreign situation what they learned before departure. For example, if knowing the host country's language is important in the expatriate's position, additional language training once the individual has arrived in the foreign location would be helpful.[55] Providing a more experienced expatriate mentor or a reliable local contact is also a good idea. For instance, in every country of operation, Unilever assigns a manager who is a local expert to meet all expatriates as they arrive in the country.[56] Large MNCs with significant numbers of expatriates in any one location also have informal networks of expatriates who help new arrivals adjust and learn the lay of the land. Support from others is especially crucial during the first few months of adjustment when everything is unfamiliar and many questions need answers.

Training for the Spouse and Family In many ways, the adjustment of the spouse and family to an expatriate assignment may be more difficult than that of the expatriate. After all, the expatriate arrives at the foreign assignment with an already structured environment (the job) that has many similarities to the old environment. The expatriate is still working for the same company and using many of the same work procedures and practices. The expatriate's work helps insulate him or her from the foreign world outside the office, and there is a readily available source of friends and colleagues at work. The job provides structure and consistency—a sense of familiarity and comfort.

This is not the case for the spouse and family.[57] Many of the adjustments required to accommodate to daily life in a foreign country fall more heavily on the children and spouse than on the expatriate. The children find themselves in a strange school and must cope with all the social traumas that this can cause. The spouse must cope with local tradespersons and shopping in an unfamiliar language, make new friends, and may be prohibited from seeking employment. It is not surprising then that one of the major causes of failure of expatriate assignments is the inability of the family to adjust.[58]

Japanese MNCs have come to realize the importance of training for spouses, and many of them encourage spouses to attend international orientation programs. For example, the Japan Overseas Educational Services provides environmental briefings on a variety of countries, and many Japanese MNCs pay the fees required for their expatriates' spouses to attend. A similar, though less extensive (one-day), program, Living Overseas, is offered in the United Kingdom, with many British MNCs supporting it.[59] Given the importance of spouse and family adjustment for long-term expatriate success, the development of adequate training and support, both predeparture and postarrival, is clearly warranted.

APPRAISING THE PERFORMANCE OF EXPATRIATES

Along with the problems common to the development of any appraisal method, there are significant environmental and task factors that affect how MNCs appraise expatriate performance in foreign subsidiaries.[60] The physical distance that usually separates expatriate managers and their HQ superiors makes it difficult for HQ-based personnel to adequately observe and record expatriates' behavior. Environmental conditions vary considerably across different countries. Political upheavals may reduce the capacity of expatriates to perform. The conditions in some countries may be very difficult so that expatriates and third-country nationals may spend considerable effort simply adapting to daily living. This expenditure of effort would affect job performance. The education and skill level of the local work force may also affect performance. Managers of relatively unskilled employees may spend much of their time training workers and supervising the most basic activities within their subsidiary. Objective indicators of subsidiary performance may be low, even though the manager is doing a great job given what he or she has to work with.

The nature of an expatriate's specific task affects the performance dimensions that are appropriate for use in appraisal. Expatriate managers, for example, may be sent to work in a subsidiary as trouble-shooters, "structure reproducers," "operators," or chief executive officers.[61] Trouble-shooters, who are sent to fix specific problems within the subsidiary, and operators, sent as technical operations specialists, may be most appropriately appraised on short-term performance. Structure reproducers are expatriates sent to a subsidiary in order to reorganize its basic organizational structure. These individuals, along with expatriates sent to serve as CEOs, would most appropriately be judged on longer-term results.

What further complicates matters is that MNCs must appraise an expatriate CEO's performance in terms of both the operational performance of the subsidiary and its strategic performance level.[62] Operational performance is the performance of a subsidiary as a single business unit within the MNC. Strategic performance refers to how the performance of the subsidiary fits into the overall strategic objectives of the MNC. A subsidiary may perform well at an operational level, yet not contribute significantly to strategic performance. For example, a subsidiary may have done well because of a large infusion of capital from the MNC parent organization. However, this capital might have contributed more to the overall strategic objectives of the MNC if it had been used in another subsidiary. A number of factors must be considered in developing operational and strategic measures of subsidiary performance; they are summarized in Table 17.8.

The development of performance appraisal systems for use with expatriates requires extreme care. Physical distance, task differences, and a variety of factors in the international environment may make it impossible to apply to managers on foreign assignment the same procedures that are used successfully in the domestic organization. The task of effectively developing and managing a compensation system in an MNC is equally complex.

PAYING EXPATRIATES

Most expatriate compensation plans are designed to achieve three major objectives: (1) attract employees who are qualified and interested in international assignments; (2) facilitate the movement of expatriates from one subsidiary to another, from home to subsidiaries, and from subsidiaries back home; and (3) provide a consistent and reasonable relationship between the pay levels of employees at headquarters, domestic affiliates, and foreign subsidiaries.[63]

Although specific policies vary across companies, most MNC expatriate compensation systems try to equalize the balance sheet between living at home and living abroad. Four categories of expenses are commonly included in this balance sheet: housing; goods and services such as food, clothing, transportation, recreation, and medical care; income taxes; and reserve (that is savings and investments).[64] The typical expatriate compensation package contains a variety of allowances and other benefits in order to equalize the costs of living at home and living abroad. Table 17.9 summarizes these components.

When expatriates move abroad, they usually receive the equivalent of their domestic salary or the going-rate salary in the host country, if that is higher. In addition, there are usually a number of premiums paid to encourage and reward employees for going abroad and to compensate them for any hardships that may exist in the new assignment. These premiums may be paid in several ways. In

TABLE 17.8 Factors Affecting Operational and Strategic Appraisal

Factor	*Implication*
Currency Conversions	A 10% profit of a subsidiary may be wiped out if the local currency is suddenly devalued relative to the home country's currency. This lack of results is not under the control of the subsidiary management.
Accounting Methods	Different countries have different accounting practices, which makes it difficult to compare results across subsidiaries.
Ethical and Legal Issues	Many MNCs assess performance using results-oriented measures. It may be important, however, to assess how the subsidiary management is achieving the results. For example, the Foreign Corrupt Practices Act makes it illegal for U.S. managers operating overseas to use bribes and payoffs to achieve business advantages.
Strategic Role	A subsidiary may be opened in a market primarily to counter a competitor that has a dominant position in that market. Subsidiary performance may be limited, but the existence of the subsidiary has a strategic benefit.
Time and Distance	Time and distance make it difficult for headquarters to understand the problems and situation of subsidiaries. Higher-level managers may have little real opportunity to observe the performance of subsidiary managers unless considerable time, effort and money is expended in traveling to visit at subsidiary locations.
International Volatility	Economic, social and political changes may occur very rapidly in the world. These changes may directly affect subsidiary performance yet are often very difficult to monitor and predict.
HQ-Subsidiary Interdependence	How the subsidiary performs depends, to some extent, on how well the MNC as a whole performs.
Market Maturity	Some markets are simply less well developed than others. Subsidiaries in these markets may perform much less well in terms of sales volume than subsidiaries in more established markets. This makes any purely bottom-line assessment of performance inappropriate.

Source: Based on information from Peter J. Dowling and Randall S. Schuler, *International Dimensions of Human Resource Management* (Boston, Mass.: PWS-Kent, 1990), pp. 83–88.

TABLE 17.9 Components of an Expatriate Compensation Package

Salary	*Taxation*	*Benefits*	*Allowances*
Salary equivalent to home or typical host salary (whichever is higher) paid in either home dollars or host country currency or mixture of both	Tax protection by structuring payments in such a way as to minimize exposure to host country taxation	Transportable benefits from the home country, e.g., medical insurance, pension benefits	Cost-of-living allowances for countries with higher cost of living
Lump sum "hardship" payment to cover cost associated with moving to a particularly difficult geographic location	Tax equalization so that the expatriate will pay no more taxes than would normally be paid in the home country	Additional benefits that are typical in the host country but not at home, e.g., extended paid holidays	Housing allowance so that employee can live in house comparable to that in home country even if housing is more expensive in host country
Bonus for accepting overseas assignment	Repayment of any salary paid into host country long-term social security systems where the employee will be unlikely to receive the benefits of the social security system		Education allowances for children
Currency protection to cover income loss due to currency fluctuations			Relocation allowances to cover costs associated with setting up new home in foreign location, e.g., purchase of appliance
			Shipping and storage costs of moving goods to foreign location and storing home country goods if necessary
			Home leave—usually fares for family to have one visit home per year

some cases, a one-time payment of 10 to 20 percent of salary is made to encourage the employee to move abroad. In other cases, a constant premium is paid each year while the employee is on a foreign assignment. A final variation is a "phase-out" method: a premium is paid in decreasing amounts until it is phased out after a certain number of years. Continuous premiums encourage the expatriate to remain abroad whereas phased-out payments tend to encourage the person to return home or move to another foreign location, where the premiums will start again.

When an employee takes an assignment in an undesirable location, a hardship premium is often paid, with the amount varying according to the level of hardship. Determining this level is not easy. ICI, a British MNC, uses the services of Employment Conditions Abroad (ECA) to determine the amount of hardship pay to be given. ECA assesses countries on 10 hardship dimensions: (1) distance from Britain, (2) ease of travel to and from Britain, (3) ease or difficulty of learning the local language, (4) climate, (5) health considerations (e.g., the types of diseases that are prevalent), (6) the quality of local health care facilities, (7) availability of English language schools, (8) quality of education, (9) availability of goods, services, and recreational facilities, and (10) risks to expatriates and their families such as terrorism or crime. Hardship premiums may be given in the form of direct cash payments or in more innovative forms. For example, ICI provides expatriates in a certain African location with trips to a seaside resort every six to eight weeks and with two annual trips home (rather than the usual one) to help compensate for the hardships of living in this locality.[65]

Tax protection or equalization are also common aspects of an expatriate's pay package. There are many ways in which companies may cover the expenses of expatriates so that the employees do not incur a tax liability (or, at least are taxed at a low rate) in foreign countries. A perquisite, such as the use of a company car might not be taxable, whereas an increase in salary sufficient for buying or leasing a car would be. Companies usually deduct income taxes from the employee's pay at the rate that would be paid in the home country. The company then pays any additional tax owed because of higher tax rates in the foreign location. For U.S. expatriates, the taxation problems are particularly troublesome, for they are taxed by both the foreign country where they earn their salary and by the U.S. government. U.S. expatriates can shelter from U.S. taxes up to $70,000 (U.S.) of their salary earned abroad. Income above that level is taxed at applicable U.S. rates.

Finally, there is a group of allowances provided to cover differences in the cost of living between the home and foreign countries and to cover the additional expenses associated with setting up home in a new location. Since public schools in the foreign location are often not suitable for the children of expatriates, companies often provide funds to allow expatriates to send their children to private English-language schools. Shipping and storage costs are paid by the firm, and there is usually some allowance for home visits by all members of the expatriate's family at least once a year.[66]

Clearly, then, developing and monitoring an expatriate pay system is a complex task. Expatriates may work in a number of different countries, each with a pay system based on its own cultural preferences, traditions, and legal precedents. Expatriate compensation systems must be flexible enough to take into account this variability and not create unacceptable levels of perceived inequity on the part of local employees when they compare their wages and benefits to those of their expatriate colleagues.

EXPATRIATE RE-ENTRY

One aspect of the HQ-based HR manager's job that often gets overlooked is the task of effectively repatriating employees after their foreign assignments. The problems associated with re-entry are often not anticipated by the employee, the family, or the organization. All assume that returning home will be an easy, natural process. However, the evidence suggests that this is not the case and that significant problems can arise.

The Problems and Impact of Re-entry

Twenty percent of expatriates leave their firm within a year after they return home, and many returnees suggest that returning home results in a greater "culture shock" than moving abroad. Upon returning, expatriates and their families often feel an initial sense of elation and joy, which lasts less than a month. This joy is usually followed by a period of relative dissatisfaction and disappointment lasting two to three months, followed by an acceptance stage, when returnees report feeling "average" about their return home.[67] In general, it seems that U.S. organizations do not do a particularly good job at helping expatriates through this readjustment process, even though the costs of readjustment problems may be significant—just as they are when an expatriate begins a foreign assignment.[68] The problems associated with re-entry adjustment can be divided into those related to general cultural readjustment and those specifically dealing with readjustment to the job.

General Cultural Readjustment There is often a cultural and social loss associated with re-entry into the home culture. The international assignment may have been an exciting, interesting, and fulfilling experience. The lifestyles of many expatriates may have been of a considerably higher standard (servants to take care of the cooking, cleaning, and children) abroad than it can be upon return to the home culture. Long days spent playing tennis at the American Club or traveling to interesting cultural sites and festivals may have been the routine. All that is lost upon return to the "real world" of home.

Children may have a difficult time readjusting to school. Children in the last year or two of high school may find that they are restricted in the types of extracurricular activities in which they can participate. How can they be members of the football team or band when they have missed the first two years of training in high school? Marital problems may develop as each spouse faces the problems of returning to the domestic lifestyle.[69] There may be increased and unexpected financial pressures as salaries revert to domestic levels and allowances disappear.[70]

Job Readjustment The nature of foreign assignments often creates difficulties when the expatriate returns home.[71] Because of the physical distance of expatriates from the home office, individuals often find that the home office has forgotten about them and has done little or no planning for their return. Poor communication often leaves expatriates unaware of and isolated from many of the problems and changes that may have occurred in the home office during their assignment abroad.

Expatriates who have been abroad for a relatively long period of time may be technologically obsolete when they return home. Technology levels used in foreign subsidiaries may be less advanced than those in the home country. As a result, returnees may find themselves asked to deal with technological systems with which they are unfamiliar. It may take a considerable amount of time for an expatriate to get "up to speed" on the new technology.

Many expatriates find themselves passed over for promotion opportunities that occur in the home office while they are abroad. This is partly due to the out-of-sight, out-of-mind phenomenon, but it is also a function of the unclear career paths that many MNCs have for their expatriates. Often, when expatriates take foreign assignments, neither they nor their superiors know how that international experience will fit into the individual's career progression within the domestic organization.[72] Consequently, the expatriate is often placed in a holding pattern and must wait until an appropriate position becomes available.

Another significant problem arises when an expatriate re-enters the domestic organization in a job with a level of responsibility and authority much lower than that in the foreign assignment. Expatriates often have considerable autonomy and decision-making power abroad, but much of that disappears once they are back in the home office. This transition is very difficult to make.

What further complicates the adjustment is that other organizations often seem more aware and more appreciative of the returning expatriates' skills and experience than their own company. The expatriate may receive attractive job offers that have many of the positive aspects—such as responsibility and authority—of the foreign position. While these offers are to the advantage of the expatriate who may be experiencing financial difficulties on returning home, they may represent a significant (if sometimes unrealized) loss to the home organization. Even if the expatriate does not leave the company, such head hunting may make it more difficult for the individual to accept and adjust to the home situation.

Enhancing the Likelihood of Re-entry Adjustment

In a 1991 paper, Daniel C. Feldman outlines six criteria that should be met before re-entry can be considered as successful. According to Feldman, the returning expatriates should

- perform at a level and quality expected by supervisors.
- exhibit a reasonable level of job satisfaction with the new position.
- be able to use the skills developed during the foreign assignment.
- be able to maintain a career progression that is comparable to cohorts who did not go abroad.
- remain or at least intend to remain with the employer for a reasonable period of time after returning.
- experience a level of stress during re-entry that is not dysfunctional.[73]

Feldman also hypothesizes that some factors would make successful re-entry more or less difficult. These are (1) the type of the international versus domestic work assignment, (2) the extent to which environmental changes have taken place in the home organization, (3) individual and personality differences among expatriates, (4) the support available to and coping strategies used by returning expatriates, and (5) the career-planning system provided by the organization. Table 17.10 describes each of these factors, summarizes their effect on re-entry adjustment, and suggests some measures that the individual and the organization can take to enhance re-entry adjustment.

TABLE 17.10 Factors Affecting the Ease of Re-entry Adjustment

Factor	*Impact*	*Implications*
Work Assignment (Foreign vs. Domestic) • Skill similarity • Performance criteria used to appraise performance • Level of autonomy • Work culture similarity	The more similar the foreign and domestic job assignments are in terms of skills used, criteria against which performance is evaluated, level of autonomy, and work culture, the easier the re-entry adjustment.	Individuals—during overseas stay, should seek information about performance relative to standards applied at home office; should maintain contact with colleagues at home to find out what is happening in home office. Organization—should place returnees in position where they can use skills acquired overseas; should also provide regular communication with expatriate and systematic review of expatriate's overseas performance.
Environmenal Changes in the Firm • Corporate structure • Economic successes/failures • Technological change • Length of time overseas	The more changes that have occurred in corporate structure, the economic standing of the firm, and technology, the more difficult re-entry adjustment. The longer the employee has been overseas, the more difficult the re-entry.	Individuals—should maintain network of colleagues to provide updates on structural or technological changes at home and how the firm is doing financially; should visit home office occasionally for updates. Organization—should establish formal communication channels to provide information about changes at home; if overseas assignment will be lengthy, should provide regular visits by expatriate to home office for updates, retraining.

(*continued*)

TABLE 17.10 Factors Affecting the Ease of Re-entry Adjustment (*cont.*)

Factor	*Impact*	*Implications*
Individual Differences • Age • Career stage • Hierarchical level • Self-efficacy and hardiness • Number of overseas assignments	Middle-aged, midcareer middle managers have more difficulty returning to home office than either younger or more senior managers. Hardy individuals with a sense of self-efficacy will readjust more easily than those low in these characteristics. The more overseas assignments, the easier the re-entry.	Individuals—should engage in prereturn planning, take control of their return, seek information. Organization—should provide multiple overseas experiences, even if relatively short in length, to improve "returning skills"; select expatriates carefully on factors other than simply technical competence; and provide additional support of all types to midlevel, middle-aged midcareer expatriates.
Support and Coping • Social support available • Problem-focused vs. symptom-focused coping	The more social support available upon return, the easier the re-entry. Returnees who engage in behaviors focused on taking advantage of opportunities and avoiding threats in the new situation will adjust more easily to re-entry than those who use primarily emotional coping behaviors, such as drinking, smoking, sleeping.	Individuals—should seek out support for their return before they arrive and let colleagues know that they will want their help after they return; talk with former expatriates who have successfully made the transition back home; identify likely problems that will arise; and examine options for dealing with these problems.
Career Planning System • Definite assignment upon return • Relationship of new job to career • Availability of mentors • Amount of retraining and reorientation • Compensation/housing assistance	A career-planning system that provides definite job assignments consistent with an overall career plan, as well as mentors, retraining, reorientation, and compensation/housing assistance, makes re-entry adjustment easier.	Individuals—should prepare before departure by seeking out mentors, setting up formal communication channels, and discussing the career implications of the overseas assignment with those in charge. Organization—should set up formal re-entry reorientation and assistance program, with particular focus on career issues associated with overseas moves; and work to develop an organizational norm about what to do with expatriates back home.

Sources: From information found in Daniel C. Feldman, "Repatriate Moves as Career Transitions," *Human Resource Management Review*, Vol. 1, No. 3, 1991, pp. 166–175; Michael C. Harvey, "The Other Side of Foreign Assignments: Dealing with the Repatriation Dilemma," *Columbia Journal of World Business*, Vol. 17, 1982, p. 55.

The HQ-based HR managers may have successfully handled the myriad problems associated with selecting, training, appraising, and paying expatriates. But unless they take care to ensure a successful re-entry for the expatriates into the domestic organization, the company may lose the skills and experience that these employees have gained during their foreign assignment.

SUMMARY OF KEY POINTS

International human resource management is distinct from domestic human resource management because of its broader perspective, the greater scope of activities included in IHRM, and the higher level of risk associated with IHRM activities. Multinational corporations may take any one of a number of different approaches to HRM, and the choice of approach depends on political policies and legal regulations, the level of managerial, educational, and technological development in the host country, technology and the nature of the product, the stage of the organization's life cycle, and differences between the home and host cultures.

HR managers located in an MNC's foreign subsidiaries have many tasks. Often they must deal with labor markets that lack the level of skill needed for technical and managerial positions in their subsidiaries. Selection, training, and appraisal systems used in the headquarters location of the MNC may be inappropriate for local use. Pay systems must conform to local laws and customs while fitting into global MNC policies.

The HQ-based manager must coordinate IHRM operations in a variety of countries, each with its own local cultural, legal, and traditional influences. Headquarters policies must be flexible enough to allow for these local variations. However, policies must also be developed to help achieve the overall strategic global objectives of the MNC.

One important IHRM activity is the selection of expatriate managers. MNCs often base their choice of expatriates on technical competence, although research shows that many other factors are important in determining expatriate success. The ability of an expatriate's spouse and family to adapt to the new location is a significant determinant of expatriate success or failure. The expatriate's ability to establish personal relationships and understand the behavior of people from a foreign culture is a critical factor. Training, both before and after the foreign assignment begins, plays a crucial role in determining how expatriates perform. Extensive training is required when the job and culture to which the individual is being sent are very different from the person's current job and cultural background.

MNCs often underestimate the desirability of sending female employees to foreign assignments. They believe that women will not be accepted by businesspeople in many cultures. However, research contradicts this view and indicates that female expatriates can perform extremely well.

Care must be taken in developing performance appraisal systems for expatriates. Physical distance, the nature of the expatriate's task, and a variety of environmental factors make accurate assessment of expatriate performance very difficult. The development and coordination of compensation systems for expatriates is also a complex task. Expatriate pay systems that attempt to balance the living costs of home and foreign assignments must also be integrated into the overall MNC compensation system. Besides managing expatriates while they are abroad, the company must also design programs to effectively reintegrate the expatriates upon their return so that it can make maximum use of the skills and experience that these employees have gained in their international assignments.

Questions for Discussion

1. What are the differences between international and domestic human resource management?
2. What are some of the different approaches that MNCs take to managing human resources? What factors determine which approach an MNC is likely to take?
3. How can culture affect HR planning, staffing, training, and performance appraisal in a subsidiary?
4. What is cultural control? Give some examples of how IHRM can serve as a form of cultural control in an MNC.
5. Several researchers have identified the factors that seem to make it easier or more difficult for expatriates to adjust to foreign assignments. What are these factors, and which of them do you think are the most important?
6. Defend or refute this statement: "It is not a good idea to send female managers to countries that are very masculine in nature."
7. What methods of cross-cultural training would you use to prepare an American manager for foreign assignment in China? Why?
8. What are the components of an expatriate compensation system? What purposes do these components serve?
9. What is the difference between operational and strategic performance appraisal?
10. Suppose that you were an expatriate about to complete a foreign assignment in France. What steps would you take to get ready to return to a position in your home country? What would you have done before you left for the French assignment?

EXERCISE 17.1

Culinary Clues to Culture

The class should be divided into groups of three or four students. If there are foreign students in the class, particularly if they have a common culture, they should be placed in groups of their own.

The students in each group should be asked to compile a list of the foods that are most popular in their home culture and to answer the following questions:

1. What are these foods?
2. Who eats them?

3. When are they eaten?
4. How are they eaten?
5. Under what conditions are they usually eaten?

The group should then note the important cultural characteristics that these foods represent and that an expatriate should be aware of when being assigned to the culture. For example, Americans like to eat hot dogs. They are eaten with the hands and are generally eaten at sports event. Hot dogs represent two important American cultural characteristics: informality and love of sports. An expatriate manager coming to the United States should probably expect his colleagues to be fairly informal. One way to win the hearts of important customers would be to invite them to the big football game at the local university.

CASE 17.1

The Office Equipment Company

In 1992, the Office Equipment Company (OEC) had to replace its manager in San Salvador, El Salvador, because the present managing director (a U.S. national) announced suddenly that he would leave within one month. OEC manufactured a wide variety of small office equipment (such as copying machines, recording machines, mail scales, paper shredders) in eight different countries that was distributed and sold worldwide.

OEC had no manufacturing facilities in El Salvador, but had been selling and servicing there since the early 1970s. OEC had first tried selling in El Salvador through independent importers but quickly became convinced that it needed to have its own staff there to make sufficient sales. Despite political turmoil, which over the last few years had bordered on being a full-scale civil war, OEC's operation in El Salvador (with about 100 employees) had enjoyed good and improving sales and profitability.

OEC was in the process of constructing a factory in El Salvador that would begin operations in early 1993. This factory would import components for personal computer printers and assemble them locally. The government would allow up to 10 percent of the output to be sold locally, provided at least 90 percent was exported. The assembly operation would employ approximately 150 people. El Salvador offered an abundant supply of cheap labor. Furthermore, by assembling and exporting, OEC expected to be able to ward off any import restrictions on the finished goods it sold within El Salvador. The construction of this plant was being supervised by a U.S. technical team, and a U.S. expatriate would be assigned to direct the production. This expatriate director would report directly to the United States on all production and quality control matters but would report to the managing director in El Salvador for all other matters, such as accounting, finance, and labor relations.

The option of filling the managing director position with someone from outside the firm was alien to OEC's policy. Otherwise, the options were fairly open. OEC used a combination of home-country, host-country, and third-country nationals in top positions in foreign countries. It was not uncommon for managers to rotate among

Source: John D. Daniels and Lee H. Radebaugh, *International Business:*

foreign and U.S. domestic locations. In fact, it was increasingly evident that international experience was an important factor in deciding who would be appointed to top corporate positions. The sales and service facility in El Salvador reported through a Latin American regional office located in Coral Gables, Florida. A committee at the regional office quickly narrowed its choice to the following five candidates.

Tom Zimmerman. Zimmerman had joined the firm thirty years before and was well versed in all the technical and sales aspects required in the job. He had never worked abroad for OEC but had visited various of the company's foreign facilities as part of sales teams during his career. He was considered competent in the management of the duties he had performed during the years and would retire in about four and a half years. Neither he nor his wife spoke Spanish; their children were grown and living with their own children in the United States. Zimmerman was currently in charge of an operation about the size that the one in El Salvador would be after the factory began operating. However, that operation was being merged with another, so his present office would become redundant.

Brett Harrison. At age forty, Harrison had spent fifteen years with OEC. He was considered highly competent and capable of moving into upper-level management within the next few years. He had never been based abroad but had worked for the last three years in the Latin American regional office, and he frequently traveled to Latin America. Both he and his wife spoke Spanish adequately. Their two children, ages fourteen and fifteen, were just beginning to study Spanish. His wife was a professional as well, holding a responsible marketing position with a pharmaceutical company.

Carolyn Moyer. Moyer had joined OEC after getting her MBA from a prestigious university twelve years earlier. At age 37 she had already moved between staff and line positions of growing responsibility. For two years she was second-in-command of a product group about the size of the expanded one in El Salvador. Her performance in that post was considered excellent. Currently she worked as a member of a planning staff team. When she joined OEC, she had indicated her eventual interest in international responsibilities because of her undergraduate major in international affairs. She had expressed a recent interest in international duties because of a belief that it would help her advancement. She spoke Spanish well and was not married.

Francisco Cabrera. Cabrera was currently one of the assistant managing directors in the larger Mexican operation, which produced and sold for the Mexican market. He was a Mexican citizen who had worked for OEC in Mexico for all his twelve years with the company. He held an MBA from a Mexican university and was considered to be one of the likely candidates to head the Mexican operation when the present managing director retired in seven years. He was 35, married with four children (ages two to seven). He spoke English adequately; his wife did not work outside the home and spoke no English.

Juan Moreno. At 27 he was assistant to the present managing director in El Salvador, a position he had assumed when he joined OEC after completing his undergraduate studies in the United States four years before. He was considered competent, especially in employee relations, but lacking in experience. He had been successful in increasing OEC's sales, an advantage being that he was well connected with the local families who could afford to buy new office equipment for their businesses. He was not married.

1. Whom should the committee choose for the assignment and why?
2. What problems might each individual encounter in the position?

3. How might OEC go about minimizing the problems that the chosen person would have in managing the El Salvador operations?

Notes and References

1. Arvind V. Phatak, *Managing Multinational Corporations* (New York: Praeger 1978), pp. 21–22.
2. Lawrence G. Franko, "Multinational: The End of U.S. Dominance," *Harvard Business Review,* Vol. 56, No. 2, 1978, pp. 95–96.
3. Michael A. Hitt, Robert E. Hoskisson, and Jeffrey S. Harrison, "Strategic Competitiveness in the 1990s: Challenges and Opportunities for U.S. Executives," *Academy of Management Executive,* Vol. 5, No. 2, 1991, pp. 7–22.
4. "Analysis of U.S. Competitiveness Problems," in *America's Competitive Crisis: Confronting the New Reality,* a report by the Council on Competitiveness, April 1987, pp. 121–126.
5. Rosalie L. Tung, *The New Expatriates: Managing Human Resources Abroad* (Cambridge, Mass.: Ballinger, 1988), p. 1.
6. Patrick V. Morgan, "International HRM: Fact or Fiction," *Personnel Administrator,* Vol. 31, No. 9, 1986, pp. 43–47; Peter Dowling and Denise E. Welch, "The Strategic Adaptation Process in International Human Resource Management: A Case Study," *Human Resource Planning,* Vol. 14, No. 1, 1991, pp. 61–69.
7. Morgan, "International HRM," pp. 43–47.
8. Ibid.
9. D. Heenan and H. V. Perlmutter, *Multinational Organization Development* (Reading, Mass.: Addison-Wesley, 1979).
10. Eduard Gaugler, "HR Management: An International Comparison," *Personnel,* August 1988, pp. 24–30; John F. Milliman and Mary Ann Von Glinow, "A Life Cycle Approach to Strategic International Human Resource Management in MNCs," in *Research in Personnel and Human Resource Management: Supplement 2,* ed. James B. Shaw, John E. Beck, Gerald R. Ferris, and Kendrith M. Rowland (Greenwich, Conn.: JAI Press, 1990), pp. 21–36; André Laurent, "The Cross-Cultural Puzzle of International Human Resource Management," *Human Resource Management,* Vol. 25, No. 1, 1986, pp. 91–102.
11. C. M. Korth, *International Business: Environment And Management* (Englewood Cliffs, N.J.: Prentice-Hall, 1985).
12. Milliman and Von Glinow "A Life Cycle Approach"; N. Adler and F. Ghadar, "Globalization and Human Resource Management," in *Research in Global Strategic Management: A Canadian Perspective,* ed. A. Rugman (Greenwich, Conn.: JAI Press, 1990), pp. 179–205; L. Baird and I. Meshoulam, "Managing Two Fits of Strategic Human Resource Management," *Academy of Management Review,* Vol. 13, No. 1, 1988, pp. 116–128.
13. Adler and Ghadar, "Globalization."
14. Tung, *The New Expatriates.*
15. For example, see Laurent, "The Cross-Cultural Puzzle," p. 93.
16. Tung, *The New Expatriates*; Wayne F. Cascio, *Human Resource Planning, Employment & Placement* (Washington, D.C.: BNA Books, 1989).
17. Wang Dezhong, "Some Issues in Human Resource Management in China's Joint Ventures," in *Research in Personnel and Human Resource Management: Supplement 2,* pp. 279–292.
18. R. L. Desatnick and M. L. Bennet, *Human Resource Management in the Multinational Company* (New York: Nichols, 1978).
19. Paul S. Kirkbride, S. F. Y. Tang, and W. C. Shae, "The Transferability of Management Training and Development: The Case of Hong Kong," *Asia Pacific Human Resource Management,* Vol. 27, No. 1, 1989, pp. 7–20; M. Boiset and M. Fiol, "Chinese Boxes and Learning Cubes: Action Learning in a Cross-Cultural Context," *Journal of Management Development,* Vol. 6, No. 2, 1987, pp. 8–18.
20. Some of the following discussion on the impact of culture on performance appraisal is based on information from Manuel Mendonca and Rabindra N. Kanungo, "Designing Performance Management for Develop-

ing Countries," paper presented at the 2nd International Conference on Personnel & Human Resource Management, Hong Kong, 1989.

21. Example provided in "Managing the Overseas Assignment," a film produced by Copeland Griggs Productions, 411 Fifteenth Avenue, San Francisco, Calif.

22. Personal information obtained by first and third authors during one year stay in Singapore in 1986–87.

23. Peter J. Dowling and Randall S. Schuler, *International Dimensions of Human Resource Management* (Boston: PWS-Kent, 1990), pp. 131–134.

24. Luis Gomez-Mejia and Theresa Wellbourne, "Compensation Strategies in a Global Context," *Human Resource Planning,* Vol. 14, No. 1, 1991, pp. 29–41.

25. Yves Doz and C. K. Prahalad, "Controlled Variety: A Challenge for Human Resource Management in the MNC," *Human Resource Management,* Vol. 25, No. 1, 1986, pp. 55–71.

26. Vladimir Pucik and Jan H. Katz, "Information, Control, and Human Resource Management In Multinational Firms," *Human Resource Management,* Vol. 25, No. 1, 1986, pp. 121–132; C. K. Prahalad and Yves Doz, "An Approach to Strategic Control in MNCs," *Sloan Management Review,* Summer 1981, pp. 5–13; Collette A. Frayne and J. Michael Geringer, "The Strategic Use of Human Resource Management Practices as Control Mechanisms in International Joint Ventures," in *Research In Personnel and Human Resource Management: Supplement 2,* pp. 37–52.

27. Stephen J. Kobrin, "Expatriate Reduction and Strategic Control in American Multinational Corporations," *Human Resource Management,* Vol. 27, No. 1, 1988, pp. 63–75.

28. L. Copeland and L. Griggs, *Going International: How to Make Friends and Deal Effectively in the Global Marketplace* (New York: Random House, 1985), pp. 82–86.

29. Tung, *The New Expatriates.*

30. Ibid., pp. 106–110.

31. M. C. Harvey, "The Multinational Corporation's Expatriate Problem: Application of Murphy's Law," *Business Horizons,* Vol. 26, No. 1, 1983, pp. 71–78.

32. Raymond J. Stone, "Expatriate Selection and Failure," *Human Resource Planning,* Vol. 14, No. 1, 1991, pp. 9–18.

33. Tung, *The New Expatriates,* p. 20.

34. Jerry Newman, Bhal Bhatt, and Thomas Gutteridge, "Determinants of Expatriate Effectiveness: A Theoretical and Empirical Vacuum," *Academy of Management Review,* Vol. 3, No. 3, 1978, pp. 655–661.

35. Mark Mendenhall and Gary Oddou, "The Dimensions of Expatriate Acculturation: A Review," *Academy of Management Review,* Vol. 10, No. 1, 1985, pp. 39–47.

36. Rosalie L. Tung, "Selection and Training of Personnel for Overseas Assignments," *Columbia Journal of World Business,* Vol. 16, No. 1, 1981, pp. 68–78.

37. Tung, *The New Expatriates,* pp. 10–12.

38. Ibid., pp. 71 and 53.

39. Nancy J. Adler, "Women in International Management: Where Are They?" *California Management Review,* Vol. 26, No. 4, 1984, pp. 78–89; Nancy J. Adler, "Expecting International Success: Female Managers Overseas," *Columbia Journal of World Business,* Vol. 19, No. 3, 1984, pp. 79–85.

40. Nancy J. Adler, "Do MBAs Want International Careers?" *International Journal of Intercultural Relations,* Vol. 10, No. 3, 1986, pp. 277–300; also see N. J. Adler, "Women Do Not Want International Careers and Other Myths About International Management," *Organizational Dynamics,* Vol. 13, No. 2, 1984, pp. 66–79.

41. See Dowling and Schuler, *International Dimensions of Human Resource Management,* p. 64.

42. Mariann Jelinek and Nancy J. Adler, "Women: World-Class Managers for Global Competition," *Academy of Management Executive,* Vol. 2, No. 1, 1988, pp. 11–19; Nancy J. Adler, "Pacific-Basin Managers: A Gaijin, Not a Woman," *Human Resource Management,* Vol. 26, No. 2, 1987, pp. 169–192.

43. J. Stewart Black, Mark Mendenhall, and Gary Oddou, "Toward a Comprehensive Model of International Adjustment: An Inte-

gration of Multiple Theoretical Perspectives," *Academy of Management Review,* Vol. 16, No. 2, 1991, pp. 291–317.

44. J. C. Baker and J. M. Ivancevich, "The Assignment of American Executives Abroad: Systematic, Haphazard, or Chaotic," *California Management Review,* Vol. 13, 1971, pp. 39–44; Tung, "Selection and Training of Personnel," and *The New Expatriates.*
45. Personal story related to the third author of this text by a guest speaker in his undergraduate international management course.
46. J. Stewart Black and Mark Mendenhall, "Cross-Cultural Training Effectiveness: A Review and Theoretical Framework for Future Research," *Academy of Management Review,* Vol. 15, No. 1, 1990, pp. 113–136.
47. G. J. Neimeyer, M. A. Fukuyama, R. P. Bingham, L. E. Hall, and M. Mussenden, "Training Cross-Cultural Counsellors: Comparison of the Pro-Counsellor and Anti-Counsellor Training Models," *Journal of Counselling and Development,* Vol. 64, 1986, 437–439; M. M. Chemers, "Cross-Cultural Training as a Means of Improving Situational Favorableness," *Human Relations,* Vol. 22, 1969, pp. 531–546; D. E. Weldon, D. E. Carlston, A. K. Rissman, A. K. Slobodin, and H. C. Triandis, "A Laboratory Test of Effects of Culture Assimilator Training," *Journal of Personality and Social Psychology,* Vol. 32, 1975, pp. 300–310.
48. P. Christopher Early, "Intercultural Training for Managers: A Comparison of Documentary and Interpersonal Methods," *Academy of Management Journal,* Vol. 30, No. 4, 1987, pp. 684–698.
49. Tung, *The New Expatriates,* p. 12.
50. The following discussion is based on information on contingency training models described in Dowling and Schuler, *International Dimensions of Human Resource Management*; J. Stewart Black and Mark Mendenhall, "A Practical but Theory-Based Framework for Selecting Cross-Cultural Training Methods," *Human Resource Management,* Vol. 28, No. 4, 1989, pp. 511–539, and an earlier unpublished version of the *HRM* article; and Tung, *The New Expatriates,* p. 25.
51. See A. Rahim, "A Model for Developing Key Expatriate Executives," *Personnel Journal,* 1983, p. 313, for a model of the increased number of "relations" with which an expatriate manager may have to cope.
52. Black and Mendenhall, "A Practical but Theory-Based Framework."
53. Ibid.
54. Ibid.
55. A. Lanier, "Selecting and Preparing Personnel for Overseas Transfers," *Personnel Journal,* March 1979, pp. 160–163.
56. Tung, *The New Expatriates,* p. 158.
57. Ibid., p. 44.
58. Rosalie L. Tung, "Selection and Training Procedures of U.S., European, and Japanese Multinationals," *California Managment Review,* Vol. 25, No. 1, 1982, pp. 57–71.
59. Tung, *The New Expatriates,* p. 46.
60. Dowling and Schuler, *International Dimensions of Human Resource Management,* pp. 80–82.
61. Richard Hays, "Expatriate Selection: Insuring Success and Avoiding Failures," *Journal of International Business Studies,* Vol. 5, No. 1, 1974, pp. 25–37.
62. Dowling and Schuler, *International Dimensions of Human Resource Management.*
63. Morgan, *"International HRM."*
64. C. Reynolds, "Compensation of Overseas Personnel," cited in Dowling and Schuler, *International Dimensions,* pp. 118–119.
65. Tung, *The New Expatriates.*
66. Dowling and Schuler, *International Dimensions of Human Resource Management,* pp. 118–130.
67. Nancy J. Adler, *International Dimensions of Organizational Behavior* (Boston: PWS-Kent, 1991), pp. 233–235.
68. "Workers Sent Overseas Have Adjustment Problems, A New Study Shows," *The Wall Street Journal,* June 19, 1984, p. 1; J. E. Harris, "Moving Managers Internationally: The Care and Feeding of Expatriates," *Human Resource Planning,* Vol. 12, No. 1, 1989, pp. 49–53; Tung, *The New Expatriates*; Adler, *International Dimensions.*
69. Michael C. Harvey, "Repatriation of Corporate Executives: An Empirical Study," *Journal of International Business Studies,* Vol. 20, 1989, pp. 131–144.

70. Ibid; D. W. Kendall, "Repatriation: An Ending and a Beginning," *Business Horizons,* Vol. 24, No. 6, 1981.

71. Kendall, "Repatriation," Michael C. Harvey, "The Other Side of Foreign Assignments: Dealing with the Repatriation Dilemma," *Columbia Journal of World Business,* Vol. 17, 1982, pp. 53–59; Adler, *International Dimensions.*

72. Cecil G. Howard, "Integrating Returning Expatriates Into the Domestic Organization," *The Personnel Administrator,* January 1979, pp. 62–65; Nancy Napier and Richard B. Patterson, "Expatriate Re-entry: What Do Repatriates Have to Say," *Human Resource Planning,* Vol. 14, No. 1, 1991, pp. 19–28.

73. Daniel C. Feldman, "Repatriate Moves as Career Transitions," *Human Resource Management Review,* Vol. 1, No. 3, 1991, pp. 163–178.

Author Index

Subject Index